Models in Archaeology

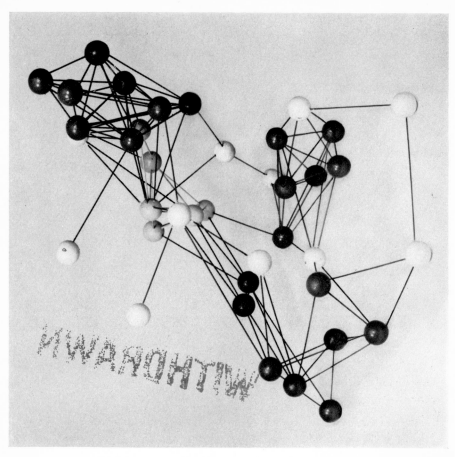

An indirect artificial hardware model. A model of the correlation values between attributes within the artefact type population of British beaker pottery *c.* 2000–1500 B.C. The current weakness of this and comparable cluster analysis models of archaeological data is that no *a priori* models have yet been developed with which to compare these *a posteriori* models for goodness of fit and evaluation.

Models in Archaeology

EDITED BY

DAVID L. CLARKE

METHUEN & CO LTD

11 NEW FETTER LANE LONDON EC4

First published 1972
by Methuen & Co Ltd
11 New Fetter Lane London EC4
© 1972 Methuen & Co Ltd
Printed in Great Britain by
William Clowes & Sons, Limited
London, Beccles and Colchester

SBN 416 16540 0

Distributed in the USA by
HARPER & ROW PUBLISHERS INC.
BARNES & NOBLE IMPORT DIVISION

TO A MODEL BABY — ANDREW DAVID CLARKE

Contents

List of Figures   xi

List of Plates   xxi

Acknowledgements   xxiii

1   Models and paradigms in contemporary archaeology   I
    D. L. CLARKE

2   The methodological debate in contemporary archaeology: a model   61
    J. N. HILL

3   Contemporary model building: paradigms and the current state of Palaeolithic research   109
    L. R. BINFORD

4   Early phases of human behaviour: models in Lower Palaeolithic archaeology   167
    G. LL. ISAAC

5   Research design models   201
    S. G. H. DANIELS

6   A model for classification and typology   231
    J. N. HILL AND R. K. EVANS

7   What mean these stones? Ethno-taxonomic models and archaeological interpretations in the New Guinea Highlands   275
    J. P. WHITE AND D. H. THOMAS

8   Introduction to imaginary models for archaeological scaling and clustering   309
    LEROY JOHNSON, JR

9   Models, methods and techniques for seriation   381
    G. L. COWGILL

10   Computer models as tools for archaeological hypothesis formation   425
    J. E. DORAN

Contents

11 Initial model formulation *in terra incognita* 453
C. F. W. HIGHAM

12 Socio-economic and demographic models for the Neolithic and
Bronze Ages of Europe 477
A. G. SHERRATT

13 Ecosystem models and demographic hypotheses: predation and
prehistory in North America 543
P. F. WILKINSON

14 Energy and ecology: thermodynamic models in archaeology 577
W. SHAWCROSS

15 Ethno-historic and ecological settings for economic and social
models of an Iron Age society: Valldalen, Norway 623
K. ODNER

16 Ethno-archaeological models and subsistence behaviour in Arnhem
Land 653
C. SCHRIRE

17 A computer simulation model of Great Basin Shoshonean subsistence and settlement patterns 671
D. H. THOMAS

18 A territorial model for archaeology: a behavioural and geographical
approach 705
M. R. JARMAN

19 Set theory models: an approach to taxonomic and locational relationships 735
J. LITVAK KING AND R. GARCÍA MOLL

20 Locational models and the site of Lubaantún: a Classic Maya
centre 757
N. D. C. HAMMOND

21 A provisional model of an Iron Age society and its settlement
system 801
D. L. CLARKE

22 Locational models of Transvaal Iron Age settlements 871
R. J. MASON

23 Locational models and the study of Romano-British settlement 887
I. R. HODDER

24 Settlement and land use in the prehistory and early history of southern England: a study based on locational models 911

A. ELLISON AND J. HARRISS

25 Models in medieval studies 963

E. M. JOPE

26 Scientific inquiry and models of socio-cultural data patterning: an epilogue 991

R. P. CHANEY

Index 1033

S. I. CLARKE

Figures

1.1   A model of the archaeologist at work   6

1.2   A schematic map of the world of archaeological operational models   12

1.3   Distribution densities, regularities and map projections   16

1.4   Comparison between theoretical and actual map patterns by way of map transformations   17

1.5   Iconic, deterministic mathematical, and statistical models of the relationship between date and the mean bore diameter of clay tobacco pipes from Europe and North America   18

1.6   Random walk changes   21

1.7   A fragmentary palimpsest distribution of some 500 years of Körös Neolithic settlement along the river Tisza   25

1.8   The overriding consequences of variability introduced by sampling effects and the consequent dangers of 'type fossil' nomenclature – a model of the interdigitation problem   27

1.9   A system model for a category of Iron Age hill fort in Cornwall   31

1.10   A developed system model for a Danish medieval parish   32

1.11   The flow of energy in a hunting society   33

1.12   The flow of energy in a slash-and-burn agricultural society   34

1.13   Black Box system process and response models for complex unknown systems   35

1.14   A simplified algorithm model for the classification of British beaker pottery   36

1.15   A schematic model of the cumulative consequences of fluctuating food resources   38–9

1.16   The 'New Archaeology' defined as a bundle of newly focused paradigms and new methods within a new ideology   44

1.17   Some elementary architectural models for the analysis of within-site structures and activity patterns   48

1.18 Gravity model to simulate interaction between activities within sites, or between sites within systems   50

1.19 A study of the site categories, site systems, base camps and satellite painted sites of prehistoric hunter-fisher-gatherers in eastern Lesotho   51

3.1 Distribution of cases on percentage scales for Factors I and IV   148

3.2 Distribution clusters   150

3.3 Factor I distribution clusters   154

4.1 Diagrammatic illustration of physical, economic and cultural factors influencing the morphology of a stone artefact   177

4.2 Diagrammatic representation of possible time and space relations between pairs (or sets) of varying archaeological occurrences   179

4.3 A diagrammatic representation of archaeological sample densities in relation to space and time. An enlargement of part of the east African sample series   181

4.4 A graphic representation of analysis of variation in the percentages of major categories of artefacts   182

4.5 Graphic representation of analysis of variation in the numerical measures of biface morphology   183

4.6 Diagrammatic representation of differing systems of interaction between human groups.   187

4.7 Differences in biface form numerically defined by three ratios between linear measurements   190–1

5.1 A model of the causation of data from a single settlement site   203

5.2 A flow chart showing the application of quality control techniques to a process in archaeological research   212

5.3 Impressionistic flow charts showing the elements of design as machines which can modify or intensify the extent to which various error sources distort the data   213

7.1 Daily production of single tool types plotted in relation to components 1 and 2   295

7.2 Daily production of single tool types plotted in relation to components 1 and 3   296

7.3 Daily production of single tool types plotted in relation to components 2 and 3   297

7.4 Daily tool production plotted in relation to components 1 and 2 to show individual variation   300–1

7.5	Daily tool production plotted in relation to components 1 and 3 to show individual variation	302–3
8.1	Scaling models	311
8.2	Matrices of hypothetical similarity scores	313
8.3	Areas of agreement and disagreement for a Robinson index of agreement between two hypothetical assemblages	327
8.4	Data matrix with Robinson indexes of agreement for eleven Late Tertiary vertebrate collections	330
8.5	Seriated and coded matrix of similarity scores for eleven Late Tertiary vertebrate collections	332
8.6	First matrix of similarity scores with three basic pairs, Late Tertiary vertebrate collections	336
8.7	Second matrix with two basic pairs. Third matrix with one basic pair	337
8.8	Fourth matrix with one basic pair. Fifth matrix with one basic pair	338
8.9	Sixth matrix with one basic pair. Seventh matrix with one basic pair	338
8.10	Dendrogram for Late Tertiary vertebrate collections	339
8.11	Dendrogram with lots placed in seriated array	341
8.12	Ogives for lots 2, 3, 4, 5, 9 and 10	343
8.13	Sequence of Upper Palaeolithic culture types with lot assignments	347
8.14	Seriated and coded matrix of similarity scores for twenty-six Upper Palaeolithic artefact collections	349
8.15	Frequency distribution of similarity scores for twenty-six Upper Palaeolithic artefact collections	351
8.16	Dendrogram of twenty-six Upper Palaeolithic artefact collections	353
8.17	Ogives for Cluster A, Lots 3 through 6	356
8.18	Ogives for Cluster B, Lots 8, 9, 11, 12, 13	358
8.19	Ogives for Cluster C, Lots 19 through 24	360
8.20	MDSCAL with Palaeolithic lots: stress *v.* No. of dimensions	369
8.21	Three-dimensional plotting	373
9.1	Model for a pair of types whose occurrences are consecutive and whose ranges of occurrence overlap	401
9.2	Model for pairs of types whose occurrences are consecutive and whose ranges of occurrence do not overlap	401

9.3	Model for a pair of types whose occurrences are consecutive, where the range of occurrence for one type completely includes that of the other	401
9.4	Occurrence matrix for invented ideal data in 'true' sequence of units	407
9.5	MDSCAL configuration for the ten types of Fig. 9.4	408
9.6	Main axis and perpendiculars fitted to the configuration of Fig. 9.5, as a basis for scaling predicted occurrence midpoints.	408
9.7	Predicted occurrence midpoints derived from Fig. 9.6, plotted against true midpoints derived from Fig. 9.4	409
9.8	Randomized rearrangement of the sequence of units in the occurrence matrix of Fig. 9.4 and result obtained from reordering the input sequence according to the predicted midpoints from Fig. 9.6	415
9.9	Occurrence matrix for invented non-ideal data in 'true' sequence of units	416
9.10	Predicted occurrence midpoints, derived from MDSCAL results for the data of Fig. 9.9, plotted against true mean points derived from Fig. 9.9	417
9.11	Randomized rearrangement of the sequence of units in the occurrence matrix of Fig. 9.9, and result obtained from reordering the input sequence according to the predicted midpoints	418
9.12	MDSCAL configuration for data from the Hualfín valley, Argentina	419
9.13	Main axis and perpendiculars fitted to the configuration of Fig. 9.12, as a basis for scaling predicted occurrence midpoints	419
9.14	Occurrence matrix model for the Hualfín data in random order of units	421
9.15	Results obtained from reordering the sequence of Fig. 9.14, according to the predicted midpoints derived from Fig. 9.13	421
10.1	Flow chart of the computer program HEURISTIC DENDRAL	436
10.2	Flow chart of a computer program which simulates the formation of cemeteries	441
10.3	Flow chart for a computer program to interpret the cemetery excavation records generated by the simulation program of Fig. 10.2	443
11.1	Northern and north-eastern Thailand	457
11.2	The Phu Wiang area	459
11.3	The Roi Et area	469

11.4	Basic structure of two alternative models for the prehistory of northern and north-eastern Thailand	472
12.1	Model for fertility and mortality levels with increasing density of population	485
12.2	Model for output with increasing density of population, with inelastic resources and a single pattern of exploitation	486
12.3	Model of the reaction of population to a fluctuating environment	487
12.4	Hypothesized relationship between population density, habitat and utilization of resources among hunter-gatherer groups	488
12.5	Linear programming solution to the problem of finding the optimum allocation of land and labour	496
12.6	Relationships between the two elements of a north European type of farming system	498
12.7	Relationships between the elements of a 'Mediterranean' type of farming system	498
12.8	Population and sex-ratio in two vegetational regions of Ghana	501
12.9	Growth of population to a ceiling and transition to next state or stabilization at optimum for first state	503
12.10	Normal surplus – model for the fluctuating yearly excess over subsistence requirements	503
12.11	Standard surplus – model for regularly achieved production for exchange requiring additional labour input	504
12.12	Socio-economic transactions in the primitive economy within a centralized political authority system	512
12.13	Schematic map of structure of south-east Europe	521
12.14	Generalized geological features of two areas of Fig. 12.13	524
12.15	Landscape types and characteristic patterns of early settlement	526–7
12.16	South-east Europe showing routes used in transhumance	528
12.17	Schematic representation of major concentrations of population in south-east Europe in Neolithic times	529
12.18	Fission model for the genesis of a new culture during the colonization of a new area	530
12.19	The growth of settlement in part of the south-western Peloponnese during the Bronze Age	537
14.1	The Mount Camel site, Houhora area, New Zealand	604
14.2	Comparison between the weights of prehistoric and modern fish populations	610
14.3	The work value of the meat weight at Mount Camel	613

15.1	The Ullshelleren site, Valldalen area, Norway	624
15.2	Decisions for the simultaneous exploitation of several resources	630
15.3	Model of the capacity of a single resource	631
15.4	The yearly cycle of work	635
15.5	Two alternative models for the Ullsheller annual cycle	636
15.6	Genealogy from Egil Skallagrimsson's Saga	641
16.1	Map of Arnhem Land, Northern Territory	654
16.2	Position of the aboriginal 'bush camp' at Camburinga in relation to the chief environmental zones. Diagrammatic cross section at Caledon Bay showing some of the habitats traversed by foragers in a typical day in the dry season	656
17.1	Cross section of the Reese river valley	673
17.2	Flow chart of the scientific cycle	673
17.3	System flow chart for Shoshonean economic cycle	679
17.4	Key to FORTRAN symbols used in Fig. 17.3	680
17.5	200 year simulation of piñon nut productivity	687
17.6	Löschian model of homogeneous piñon groves in central Nevada	688
17.7	Radius of foraging plotted against logarithm of number of potential areas available and probability of successful harvest	688
17.8	Histogram of April–June rainfall in Austin, Nevada, 1924–1969	693
17.9	Probability density function for successful procurement of Indian ricegrass seeds and pronghorn antelope	694
17.10	Histogram comparing expected with observed frequencies for primary procurement systems of BASIN I	695
17.11	Simulated point distributions within a grid system	699
18.1	Topographical transformation showing chronological and topographic distance between Birmingham and three other cities	711
18.2	Exploitation territory of Grotta Romanelli	717
18.3	Exploitation territory of Monte Aquilone	722
18.4	Exploitation territory of Grotta Sant'Angelo	724
18.5	Exploitation territories of some Romanellian sites	727
18.6	Tavoliere and Gargano, showing Monte Aquilone	728
18.7	Plains of Sibari and Serra Dolcedorme, showing Grotta Sant'Angelo and modern access route	731
19.1	Venn diagrams	736
19.2	Representation of tropical agriculture as a series of sets of traits	738

19.3	A theoretical example of how set theory can assist in the definition of subregions and in explaining historical processes	739
19.4	Diagrams and formulae describing the intersection of traits in Tlatilco figurines	741
19.5	Diagrams for the distribution of vessel support types in a site in the La Villita region	742
19.6	Formulae describing general results for site distribution of traits and strata distribution of traits	743
19.7	Diagrams for total finds per site, by stratum, in six sites	746
19.8	Tridimensional models for total finds per site, by stratum, in six sites	747
19.9	Diagram and tridimensional representation of total finds by stratum, for six sites	748
19.10	Diagram for site results for the La Villita region	749
19.11	Base map of protoclassic sites in the Xochicalco valley	750
19.12	Set theory used to define site identity in the Xochicalco valley	751
20.1	The operational Chinese Box model	758
20.2	Relationship of the constituent parts of the operational model on the G-scale	758
20.3	The operational model fitted to a map of the Maya area	760
20.4	Restored plan of the final phase of the Lubaantún ceremonial centre	761
20.5	Differentiation of structure functions by graphic means and visual discrimination	763
20.6	Concentric zone model of the ceremonial centre of Lubaantún	765
20.7	Layout and functions of plazas in the ceremonial centre	766
20.8	Relative sizes of plazas in the ceremonial centre	766
20.9	Planar graph of connections between plazas	767
20.10	Relative centrality of plazas	767
20.11	Relative accessibility of plazas	767
20.12	Central accessibility of plazas	767
20.13	Variation in central accessibility of plazas	769
20.14	Distance in one-step units from the most centrally accessible plaza	769
20.15	Trend from high central accessibility to high seclusion within the core of the site	769
20.16	Block diagram based on Fig. 20.15	769
20.17	Residential units in the sample area mapped around the ceremonial centre	771

20.18 Concentric zone model of Fig. 20.6 with settlement area added 773

20.19 Network of Dirichlet regions based on Fig. 20.17 775

20.20 Concentric zone model of Fig. 20.18 with exploitation territory added 777

20.21 Postulated form of settlement area under environmental constraints 778

20.22 Relationship of the concentric zone model to the present distribution of land used for *milpa* agriculture 779

20.23 The concentric zone model and distortions induced by environmental factors 780

20.24 A sector of the concentric zone model. 783

20.25 Distribution of major ceremonial centres around the Maya mountains and in south-east Petén 784

20.26 The network of Fig. 20.25 785

20.27 Postulated boundaries of the realm of Lubaantún 786

20.28 Major landforms and site distribution within the realm of Lubaantún 787

20.29 Environmental zones within the realm of Lubaantún 787

20.30 Major routes within the realm of Lubaantún 789

20.31 Possible factors governing settlement location 790

20.32 The realm of Lubaantún in the Maya area 792

20.33 External contacts of the realm of Lubaantún 793

20.34 A model for redistributive exchange and a possible correlation of social and site hierarchies 796

21.1 The social and architectural building block of which the settlement is a multiple – the modular unit 815

21.2 The site – Phase I 831

21.3 The site – Phase II 832

21.4 The site – Phase III 833

21.5 The site – Phase IV 834

21.6 The site – Phase IV: a tentative social model of the structural pattern of the site 835

21.7 The territory – Box 1 841

21.8 The area – Box 2 842

21.9 The region – Box 3 844

21.10 A hypothetical economic cycle model for the Glastonbury settlement 856

21.11 The parish of Cadbury: territory and settlement hierarchy, and an idealized model of the system 862

21.12	Schematic model of a late, fully developed, Celtic settlement hierarchy	864
22.1	Distribution map of Iron Age sites	876
22.2	Plan views of Iron Age settlement classes	877
22.3	Settlement profiles	879
22.4	Distribution map for Fig. 22.3	881
23.1	Two patterns of spatial organization according to Christaller	890
23.2	The pattern of Romano-British settlement in diagrammatic form according to the transport principle of Christaller	894
23.3	The application of elements of Fig. 23.2 to the real distribution of Romano-British walled towns	895
23.4	An alternative pattern of spatial organization	898
23.5	Service areas of higher order and lower order settlement centres in south-western Wisconsin	898
23.6	Thiessen polygons constructed around the Romano-British walled centres	899
23.7	Service areas predicted for the Romano-British walled centres	901
23.8	The distribution of stamped tiles in the Gloucestershire–Wiltshire area	902
23.9	The distribution of certain types of mosaic pavements and stamped tiles	903
23.10	The idealized pattern of settlement according to the transport principle	904
24.1	Southern England, showing the areas studied	912
24.2	The nature of the evidence used	913
24.3	Wiltshire – zones of land use potential	920
24.4	South-central Sussex – zones of land use potential	921
24.5	Idealized catchment areas of sites in Wiltshire and south-central Sussex	924
24.6	Histograms showing Iron Age and Roman site catchment areas and land use categories in Wiltshire	925
24.7	Locations of pre-Roman Iron Age sites of Wiltshire	926
24.8	Locations of the 'native settlements' of Roman Wiltshire	928
24.9	Locations of the villas of Roman Wiltshire	928
24.10	Diagram illustrating the combination of land use types from the Iron Age to Saxon periods in Wiltshire	930
24.11	Histograms for Bronze Age to Saxon site catchment areas in south-central Sussex	934
24.12	The Romano-British settlement pattern of the Brighton district	935

24.13 The distances of native settlements in Fig. 24.12 from the junction of good all-purpose farmland and Downland soils 935

24.14 Model of Romano-British land use in the Brighton district 935

24.15 The Chippenham area of Wiltshire 943

24.16 Models of settlement expansion: Model I 944

24.17 The Chichester area of Sussex 945

24.18 Models of settlement expansion: Model II 946

24.19 The Worthing area of Sussex 948

24.20 Models of settlement expansion: Model IIIA 949

24.21 Parish boundaries of around Poling, Sussex 949

24.22 The Cannings area of Wiltshire 950

24.23 Models of settlement expansion: Model IIIB 951

24.24 The Henfield area of Sussex 953

24.25 Models of settlement expansion: intermediate case 954

24.26 The parish of Upper Beeding, Sussex, showing probably early Saxon boundaries marked by continuous hedge lines 955

24.27 Models of settlement expansion: summary diagram 958

25.1 An iconic representation of the growth of an Oxford manor 967

25.2 A representation of the development from a twelfth-century longhouse to a thirteenth-century farm 967

25.3 A model of the rising popularity in Britain of shaped gables 970

25.4 A model of the penetration of an innovation, the shaped gable 972

25.5 A map showing the extent to which craftsmen came from a distance to work on major structures 973

25.6 A model of the different origins and developments of English Saxon 'towns' 976

25.7 Towns and markets in the Oxford region of the eleventh century 977

25.8 The distinctive artefact as an indicator of market service areas 978

25.9 Town and markets in the Oxford region of thirteenth- and fourteenth-century England 980

25.10 Towns and markets in the Devonshire region of post-medieval England 981

25.11 Towns and markets in the Lincolnshire region of post-medieval England 982

26.1 Extra-local jurisdictional hierarchy and subsistence types mapped for 839 societies 1022–3

26.2 Residence and descent types, mapped for 855 societies 1024–5

Plates

An indirect artificial hardware model   *Frontispiece*

facing page

7.1 Flaked stone tool (*aré*) used for carving designs on an arrow
     linkshaft   284
7.2 *Aré kou* being used to drill a hole in a piece of shell   285
7.3 Man from Aluni flaking *aré*   285
21.1 Glastonbury site: the excavation plan reassembled *between* 816, 817
25.1 A scale model of Houchin's Farm, Feering, Essex   965

Acknowledgements

The editor and publishers wish to thank the following for permission to reproduce the figures listed below:

The Witwatersrand University Press, Johannesburg, for Fig. 22.1 from R. J. Mason, 'Transvaal and Natal Iron Age settlement revealed by aerial photography and excavation', *African Studies*, 27 (1968); The Society of Antiquaries of London for Fig. 25.1 from E. M. Jope, 'The 12th-century castle at Ascot Doilly', *Antiquaries Journal*, 39 (1959); The Royal Archaeological Institute for Fig. 25.6 from J. M. Hassall and D. Hill, 'Pont de l'Arche: Frankish influence on the west Saxon burh', *Archaeological Journal*, 127 (1970); Dr Marcial Echenique for Figs. 1.17 and 1.18 from 'A model of the urban spatial structure', *Architectural Design*, 41 (1971); CWK Gleerup Publishers, Sweden, for Fig. 1.4 from W. Bunge, *Theoretical Geography* (1966); Edward Arnold (Publishers) Ltd for Fig. 19.1 from P. Haggett, *Locational Analysis in Human Geography* (1965); The Cornwall Archaeological Society and the author for Fig. 1.9 from R. M. Newcomb, 'Geographical location analysis and Iron Age settlement in West Penwyth', *Cornish Archaeology*, 7 (1968); The University of Chicago Press for Fig. 12.12 from G. Dalton, 'Economic anthropology', *Current Anthropology* (1969); Edinburgh University Press for Fig. 10.1 from B. Buchanan, G. Sutherland and E. A. Feigenbaum, 'Heuristic Dendral: a program for generating explanatory hypotheses in organic chemistry', in B. Meltzer and D. Michie (eds.) *Machine Intelligence*, 4 (1969); Faber & Faber Ltd for Fig. 21.11 from G. Hoskins, *Fieldwork in Local History* (1967); the Geographical Institute, Aarhus University, for Fig. 1.10 from R. M. Newcomb, 'A model of a mystery: the medieval parish as a spatial system', *Skrifter fra Geografisk Institut Ved Aarhus Universitet*, 28 (1970); The Longman Group Ltd and the author for Figs. 12.6 and 12.7 from C. T. Smith, *An Historical Geography of Western Europe* (1967); The Longman Group Ltd and Geographical Publications Ltd for Figs. 25.10 and 25.11 from L. D. Stamp, *The Land of Britain: Its Use and Misuse* (1950); The Salisbury and South Wiltshire Museum for Fig. 25.2 from D. M. Wilson and D. G. Hurst, 'Gomeldon, Wiltshire: medieval Britain in 1965', *Medieval Archaeology*, 10 (1966); Norwegian Universities

Press for Figs. 15.2, 15.4 and 15.5 from K. Odner, *Ullshelleren I Valldalen, Roldal*, Aarbok for Universitetet I Bergen, Humanistik Serie, 1 (1969); The Hamlyn Publishing Group Ltd for Figs. 25.3 and 25.5 from E. M. Jope, *Studies in Building History* (1961); The Clarendon Press, Oxford, for Figs. 25.7 and 25.9 from E. M. Jope, 'The medieval period', in A. F. Martin and R. W. Steel (eds.) *The Oxford Region* (1954); Routledge & Kegan Paul Ltd for Fig 25.8 from E. M. Jope, 'The regional cultures of medieval Britain', in I. L. Foster and L. Alcock (eds.) *Culture and Environment* (1963); the Science Museum, London, for Plate 25.1 (Crown Copyright); Scientific American Inc. for Fig. 1.11 from W. B. Kemp, 'The flow of energy in a hunting society' and Fig. 1.12 from R. A. Rappaport, 'The flow of energy in an agricultural society', both in *Scientific American*, 224 (Copyright © 1971), all rights reserved.

1
Models and paradigms in contemporary archaeology

D. L. CLARKE
University of Cambridge, England

Introduction

Models are undeniably fashionable and especially so in the primitive disciplines that range between the Arts and the Sciences – geology, geography, archaeology, anthropology, sociology, economics, psychology and aspects of biology. Indeed, in some quarters this vogue and this setting are, in themselves, taken as sufficient reason to dismiss the significance of the model-using approach. This repudiation only requires the additional evidence of the dangerous errors that have arisen from the mistaken use of bad models, an outline of their clear limitations and the assertion that scholars have in any event long known and tacitly used these procedures, and the case is complete.

The question is, however, not whether models are fashionable and dangerous toys of long standing, but *why* models are so fashionable in disciplines of this primitive kind, *why* are some models inadequate, and *why* do models generate such strong feelings if they are part of immemorial usage? If we have an old and dangerous component performing an important variety of tasks in a number of disciplinary machines, should we then ignore it because it is fashionable – or learn about it, improve upon it and explicitly develop its potential? Beach's (1957, p. 9) remark that 'the history of economics could be thought of to a very large extent as a history of misapplied models' might be generalized for all academic disciplines but could also hardly be improved upon as a sufficient justification for a more explicit appreciation of models, their variety, their uses, abuses, capacities and limitations – fashionable or unfashionable (Harvey, 1969, p. 142).

What is a model? Models are pieces of machinery that relate observations to theoretical ideas, they may be used for many different purposes and they vary widely in the form of machinery they employ, the class of observations they focus upon and the manner in which they relate the observations to the theory or hypothesis. It is therefore more appropriate to describe models than to attempt a hopelessly broad or a pointlessly narrow definition for them. Models are often partial representations, which simplify the complex observations by the selective elimination of detail incidental to the purpose of the model. The model may thus isolate the essential factors and interrelationships which together largely account for the variability of interest in the observations; in this way the model may even share a similarity in formal structure with the observations.

If explanation in general, and explanation in archaeology in particular, is viewed merely as a form of redescription which allows predictions to be made, then models as predictive forms of redescription are essential parts of archaeological explanation. However, here we enter the domain of the Philosophy of Disciplines, more commonly miscast as the Philosophy of Science, and since this introductory chapter will make no extensive attempt to consider the essential background of patterns of explanation, the role of hypotheses, theories and laws, or the problems of causality and indeterminism, the reader is recommended to consult sources noted in references throughout this volume.

The relation between the model and the observations modelled may in general be said to be one of analogy, or in the case of logical and mathematical models more usually one of isomorphism (Clarke, 1968, pp. 59–60). The analogy implies similarity between the analogues in some respects and dissimilarity in others, since otherwise the analogy would amount to identity. The set of shared similar characteristics is conveniently called the positive analogy, the dissimilar characteristics the negative analogy, and characteristics about which it is not yet known whether they are similar or dissimilar, the neutral analogy (Hesse, 1963). In general, models serve as heuristic devices for manipulating observations and hypotheses; they may also act as visualizing devices, comparative devices, organizational devices, explanatory devices or devices for the construction and development of theory (Harvey, 1969, p. 141). Models are usually idealized representations of observations, they are structured, they are selective, they simplify, they specify a field of interest and they offer a partially accurate predictive framework. In this way a map will schematically present an idealized representation of a selected item and its distribution on a simplified projection of a map surface, or a classification system may provide a crudely predictive algorithm based upon the identification of selected key attributes, or a mathematical equation may symbolically express the interdependence of systems of selected variables from within an archaeological situation.

2

Why need the archaeologist concern himself with models? There are five main reasons, which may be briefly outlined:

(1) Whether we appreciate it or not our personal archaeological opinions, approach, aims and selection of projects are *controlled* by largely subconscious mind models which we accumulate through time. We should realize that we are thus controlled.

(2) Whether we appreciate it or not we always *operate* conceptual models in the interpretation of observations. We all resemble the Molière character who was delighted to find that all his life, unknowingly, he had been speaking prose. We should make these operational models explicit and testable.

(3) The construction, testing, verification or refutation and modification of explicit models is the essence of the empirical and scientific approaches – providing the progressive cycle by means of which fresh information and insight are gained and theory is accumulated. Observations, hypothesis, experiment, conclusions, fresh hypothesis, fresh observations . . .

(4) The existence of a model presupposes the existence of an underlying theory, since a model is but one simplified, formalized and skeletal expression of a theory – be it tacit or explicit – developed for a particular situation. A careful study of groups of models apparently expressing a common underlying theory for different situations may therefore help us to expose, and articulate latent theory in a palpable and widely powerful form (Harvey, 1969, pp. 146–7). Model definition is a route to the explicit theory which essentially defines a vigorous discipline.

(5) Finally:

> Hypotheses are generated from the model expression of a theory.
> Explanation comes from tested hypotheses.
> Hypotheses are tested by using relevant analyses on meaningful categories of data.

Thus models are a vital element in all archaeological attempts at hypothesis, theory, explanation, experiment, and classification.

Model building is important in archaeology, therefore:

> Because it is inevitably the procedure used.
> Because it is economical, allowing us to pass on and exchange generalized information in a highly compressed form.
> Because it leads to the discovery of fresh information and stimulates the development and articulation of general theory of more than parochial importance. (Haggett, 1965, p. 23)

3

However, we must be clear about the peculiarities and weaknesses of models. It is particularly important to realize that since models mirror only selected aspects of the observations then it is both possible, permissible and desirable to have more than one model of different aspects of a single situation – an economic model, perhaps, and a sociological model of the same set of assemblages, where a trivial observation under one model may become a central factor under another. Under this pluralist viewpoint there are many competing models for each archaeological situation, where none may be finally picked out as uniquely and comprehensively 'true'. The interaction between archaeologists and their material thus reflects a continuous flowering of models whose criteria are both internally and externally adapted to the contemporary climate of thought, and often between which no rational choice is possible. Let a million models grow (Hesse, 1963).

Very well, we may have more than one model at a time, all 'true', and the devising of a new model does not necessarily mean that all others are wrong. However, this permissible pluralism only holds for models selecting different bases for analogy. Clearly there are good models and bad models, powerful models and restricted models. Bad models are most frequently misused models whose function has not been clearly specified and controlled, or where the model has been over-identified or unidentified with theory, or that display a lack of clarity about which are the positive, negative and neutral characteristics of the model analogy (Harvey, 1969, p. 160). Although some models simply present pluralist alternatives based on the varying selectivity of the analogy, others will offer successive approximations of greater power and in that sense may be ranked relative to one another for a given function upon a chosen field, and a choice may be made between rival models in such a way that successively more powerful models are employed. Even the exercise of this choice between models on the basis of relative power is complicated by the many dimensions of model power which combine comprehensive, predictive, efficiency and accuracy elements.

Comprehensiveness = the size of the set of situations to which the model is applicable.

Predictiveness = the number of bits of information that the model can predict about individual situations in that set.

Efficiency = the parsimonious capacity of the model to make the most predictions using the fewest statements and the most elegant structure.

Accuracy = the quality of goodness of fit of the model predictions to the observations.

Controlling models

Amongst the reasons offered as justification for an archaeological concern with models it was implied that the archaeologist is the victim of a set of *controlling models* which affect his behaviour, including the discriminatory selection of the *operational models* which he chooses to deploy against archaeological observations. The nature of these cognitive or controlling mind models is both complex and composite. Through exposure to life in general, to educational processes and to the changing contemporary systems of belief we acquire a general philosophy and an archaeological philosophy in particular – a partly conscious and partly subconscious system of beliefs, concepts, values and principles, both realistic and metaphysical. These beliefs are then more consciously related to certain aims or goals by the mediating effects of our archaeological philosophy and its values, upon a series of alternative paradigms and methodologies. Thus, Kuhn (1970), in his fundamental work on the structure of changes in intellectual disciplines, has described the paradigm class of supermodel as implicit in the behavioural conventions held by a group of practitioners which delineate, focus upon and recognize a limited subset of data and experimental achievements, within their much wider disciplinary field, which for a time emphasizes the significant problems and exemplary solutions for that community of scholars.

The overall model of an archaeologist at work, therefore, may be represented as a set of controlling models which are embodied in the archaeologist's philosophy, the paradigms he chooses to align himself with, the methodologies that he finds most congenial and the aims that this system constrains. The controlling models encapsulate the archaeologist and his chosen operational models, although there is feedback between all these changing elements. In effect the archaeologist is operating in a plastic sack and from within it seeks to push selected operational models against the complex archaeological reality, constantly seeking for goodness of fit, but the constraints of the controlling models always remain to obscure his perception of the reality (Fig. 1.1).

Archaeologists, like most other practitioners, have the greatest difficulty in believing that their own perceptions are controlled to this degree – they may always apply to other archaeologists, of course. But the history of archaeology and science is full of examples. Archaeology has witnessed the successive difficulties engendered by controlling models that could not accommodate the acceptance of the human manufacture of stone tools, an antiquity of man before 4000 B.C., a Palaeolithic origin for cave paintings, or tool-using apes 2 000 000 years ago. Medieval man, with his theocentric and geocentric con-

5

trolling model of the universe, similarly resisted the scientific and heliocentric model of Copernicus and Galileo even in the face of evidence that the old model did not fit the new observations. In the eighteenth century, observed eccentricities in the orbit of Mercury were accounted for, using Newton's model of the universe, by the presence of an unknown planet, which was promptly named Vulcan and sighted and described several times. The eccentricities are now accounted for in terms of other phenomena and the planet Vulcan has never been seen since. Even the direct photography of Mars has failed to convince observers who have spent a lifetime mapping the canals from low-power telescopes that the canals are not there. We observe what we believe and then believe in that which we have observed (see p. 219).

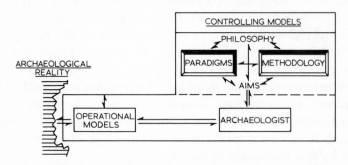

FIG. I.I. A model of the archaeologist at work – the archaeologist enmeshed within a complex set of controlling models which constrain his conscious selection of operational models and interfere with his interpretation of archaeological reality. Contemporary changes in paradigms and methodology are the main stimuli that lead the archaeologist to adapt his views.

Since an archaeologist's philosophy changes, as a rule, very slowly and by infinitesimal steps, it is mainly the more rapidly fluctuating rival paradigm fashions and innovations in methodology that alter his aims, leading him to reject some as trivial and others as unattainable in the light of the new evidence. Paradigm literally means 'example' and at any one time the prevailing paradigms within a discipline are best represented by those 'exemplary' groups of experiments which are commonly held to enshrine the most progressive patterns of archaeological activity – the leading sectors of an expanding discipline. In this way, the contemporary archaeological scene might be roughly construed in terms of the emergence of four 'new' paradigms:

(1) Morphological paradigm – the detailed study of artefact and assemblage systems, especially in terms of the widely general regularities involving their

6

intrinsic structures and relationships, mainly using computer techniques. Intimately involved with the numerical, statistical and taxonomic approaches (Clarke, 1968; Gardin, 1970; Hodson, 1970; Kolchina and Shera, 1970).

(2) Anthropological paradigm – the study and identification of patterning and variability in archaeological data and its relationship to patterning and variability in the social structures with which it once formed an integral system; intimately linked with ethnological control experiments (Deetz, 1965; Longacre, 1970; Meggers, 1968; Whallon, 1968; Hill, 1970; McPherron, 1967).

(3) Ecological paradigm – the detailed study of archaeological sites as an integral part of the mutually adjusting environmental and ecological systems in which they were once adaptively networked. Linked to ethology, economics and demography, and more deeply involved with faunal and floral contextual evidence, rather than with the artefacts (Coe and Flannery, 1964, 1967; Higgs, 1972; Higham, 1968; MacNeish, 1961, 1962).

(4) Geographical paradigm – the study of sites as patterned systems of features and structures within systems of sites territorially distributed over landscapes in a mutually adjusted way. At the micro-level linked to architectural theory and settlement archaeology, at the macro-level with locational theory and spatial relationships; principally focused on sites and the spatial manifestations of activity patterns (Chang, 1968; Trigger, 1966; Ucko, Dimbleby and Tringham, 1971; March and Echenique, 1971).

It is particularly diagnostic of the current state of archaeology as a developing discipline that we suddenly have a number of new, competing paradigms, that they are international, and that some individual archaeologists simultaneously embrace several of them or move uncertainly from one to another in the course of their work. In order to understand this contemporary state of flux it is necessary to look at the overall direction and pattern of development of archaeology.

The early history of the discipline of archaeology is a history first of individuals then of regional schools. Finding no established and common body of archaeological philosophy each archaeologist has felt forced to build his discipline anew from its foundations (Kuhn, 1970, p. 13). These individual philosophies then emerged as pre-paradigm regional schools based on the inevitable involvement of localized groups of men confronting the same regionally peculiar range of archaeological phenomena within a common regional, national, linguistic and educational environment; increasingly separating themselves from other groups of archaeologists confronting the same

7

range of phenomena but not in the same particular form or national context. Archaeology became a series of divergent regional schools with cumulatively self-reinforcing archaeological education systems and with regionally esteemed bodies of archaeological theory and preferred forms of description, interpretation and explanation.

The various archaeological schools have since become increasingly aware that they hold most of their problems in common and that these problems have been more effectively solved in some schools of archaeology than in others. Although national, linguistic and educational structures still support regionally focused schools of archaeology, horizons have been considerably widened by the emergence of internationally shared cross-school *approaches*, or proto-paradigms, and by the fruitful exchange of research students. These cross-cutting approaches now appear to be rapidly blossoming into the transient but full paradigms already noted and the convergence of the schools upon a common disciplinary code with regional variations now appears distantly perceivable (Clarke, 1970b).

The history of archaeology, then, is the history of its embryonic paradigms and their successive displacement – a history of 'paradigms lost'. However, paradigms are rarely lost altogether; instead they die very slowly as their substance is reincorporated in fresh patterns of research – new paradigms. Paradigms are thus successively augmented as the range of problems raised by them is solved and replaced by newer ones, and in this sense it is evident that some archaeologists are still content to work in terms of nineteenth-century paradigms where only the inevitable freshness of new material prevents them from actually writing nineteenth-century textbooks. There can be little harm in this activity but it can hardly be said to be a central contribution to the strength and widening powers of the discipline.

Kuhn (1970) has described the way in which paradigm changes are marked by periods of professional insecurity with the competitive emergence of a number of alternative paradigms, by practitioners oscillating between them, and by uncertainty about valid objectives and the most useful procedures. We are currently in the middle of just such an upheaval in archaeology as the result of the piecemeal integration of a large number of important new methodologies and approaches introduced over the last decade. This uncertainty is particularly apparent in the partisan competition between the paradigms and the differential importance they attach to faunal, floral, territorial and site evidence, as opposed to 'implement-focused' traditionalist archaeology. The debate also extends to controversies about the appropriate or inappropriate nature of quantitative, numerical, statistical and nomothetic approaches to data traditionally handled on an ideographic and historically oriented basis (Trigger, 1968). These debates and arguments are widely shared by disciplines comparable to archaeology in their primitive development and ambivalent raw material, and comparable too in a renewed interest in the fundamental topics of theory, explanation and interpretation and their articulation within a disciplined approach (Harvey, 1969).

Once a comprehensive paradigm is fully established, the debate languishes through general acceptance and effort is concentrated upon squeezing the old lemon in the new way. Instead, research concentrates upon the determination of significant facts within the new paradigm frame, the testing of models appropriate to this new frame against those facts, and the consequent modification, extension and articulation of models within new theory. The ingredients for such a comprehensive new paradigm are (Chorley and Haggett 1967, pp. 37–8):

(1) It must be able to solve some of the problems that brought the existing paradigms into a patently unsatisfactory position.

(2) It must be more general, powerful, parsimonious or accurate than the displaced paradigms.

(3) It must contain more potential for development and provide an expanding rather than a contracting disciplinary field.

In summary, we can at least see that our archaeological philosophies are related to certain aims or goals by a series of fashionable or archaic paradigms and methodologies which together control what we select to study, how we choose to analyse it, and how and whether we test and reapply it. The types of study and model that are regarded as satisfactory at any given time are, then, a function of the individual's controlling models and the prevailing paradigms. There follows an unavoidably powerful chain of interdependence between the paradigm held, the aims of a particular study, the nature of the appropriate sample, the models and analyses suitable to these, the scale used, the patterns detectable given the scale and the methods of analysis, and the processes relevant for explanations at that scale (Nagel, 1961, p. 144; Harvey, 1969, pp. 382–4). Thus the paradigm is both a benefactor and a tyrant. The scrutiny of new categories and taxonomies brought into existence by paradigm shifts will define freshly relevant parameters, variables, attributes, relationships and entities, leading to the articulation of new theory. But surrender to a paradigm is the deliberate relinquishment of certain freedoms and an inevitable narrowing of intellectual focus. It often happens, paradoxically, that the paradigm-free research of lone, independent workers may provide the roots of future

9

paradigms. The archaeologist must therefore learn not to surrender this free-dom without careful thought; like the scientist, if he is completely a scientist, he must be unique among the users of models in that he should not become addicted to a particular way of perceiving (Rapoport, 1953, p. 306). Blind addiction to unspecified models of a limiting kind can only be avoided by a comprehensive knowledge and explicit understanding of their roles and weak-nesses.

Operational models

For the purposes of discussion we have separated the class of operational models, which the archaeologist consciously and deliberately deploys, from the obscure set of controlling models, which subtly constrain his every move. This separation is, of course, an artificial one and many authorities would not extend the use of the term model to the controlling sets of philosophical con-straints. However, there appears to be some value to be gained from noting the way in which archaeological controlling concepts influence the selection of particular operational models and that, conversely, the habitual use of particular operational models itself modifies our controlling concepts (feed-back arrows, Fig. 1.1). The importance of this 'inward' relationship of operational and controlling models is hardly less significant than the important 'outward' constraint that the selected form of operational model imposes upon the kinds of information that can then be recovered. Not only does the decision to employ a particular operational model, technique or apparatus in a particu-lar way carry with it an assumption that only certain sorts of circumstances prevail in the observations, but even in the results of the use of such a model the ideas of the operational procedure are inevitably absorbed into the state-ments of the experimental observations; nowhere more so perhaps than in excavation procedure in the field (Fig. 5.1) (Nagel, 1961, p. 83; Kuhn, 1970, p. 59).

Operational models, then, are the experimental analogues or the hypotheses produced from them, which the archaeologist pushes against a sample of archaeological reality to test the goodness of fit between the two. If the model hypotheses fit the archaeological sample accurately then we can speculate that the sample fulfils the preconditions assumed in the model – we may have recovered more information about the sample. If the archaeological sample deviates from the model prediction then this deviation is highlighted and provides a focus for further attention – this in turn reveals more information about the sample. By the repetition of this process in a continuous cycle of model building, testing, modification and retesting we can gain a continuously expanding set of information about the archaeological sample.

There are many schemes for the classification of operational models according to which of their many qualities one wishes to emphasize – classification in terms of their philosophical standing (*a posteriori, a priori*), by the stuff from which they are made (hardware, abstract, natural, artificial), the operating machinery that they employ (electrical, mechanical, mathematical, statistical), the field in which they operate (morphological, anthropological, ecological, geographic, demographic, economic) or the purpose for which they were designed (classification, simulation, reconstruction) and the dimensional qualities of the sample under investigation (static, dynamic, synchronic, diachronic). These and many other possible criteria allow a variety of classificatory arrangements for models in various multidimensional continua where model category overlaps and grades into model category in an 'infinite' series of potentially useful schemes. It is this universe of interlinked concepts that makes model methodology both infinitely stimulating and fruitful but at the same time exceedingly dangerous (for the problems of model use, see Harvey, 1969, p. 158).

In practice, an archaeological segment of the real world is usually most fruitfully modelled by building up or building down groups of interlinked partial models, so harnessed together as to produce an output which begins to approach the real complexity of the data. These composite models hold the greatest potential for archaeology and many are illustrated in the chapters that follow. The pure metamodel classifications for models are therefore mainly of interest as simplified charts of archaeological activity using schematic map projections (Fig. 1.2).

The elementary map that we will take as our guide around the world of archaeological operational models is related to the analogous map of geomorphological models devised by Chorley (Chorley and Haggett, 1967, p. 59). In this particular portrayal a line is drawn between artificial models fabricated by the operator and natural real-life models extracted from physical, historical or ethnographic parallels; within each sector both material hardware analogues and abstract theoretical analogues are employed (Fig. 1.2). In fact the map may be conceptualized as a continuous surface with the hardware analogues from real-life to the east of the map merging into the artificial hardware analogues to the west. The spherical or cylindrical projection then has a longitudinal pole of model complexity, where artificial theoretical system analogues converge upon real-life system analogues abstracted from historic-

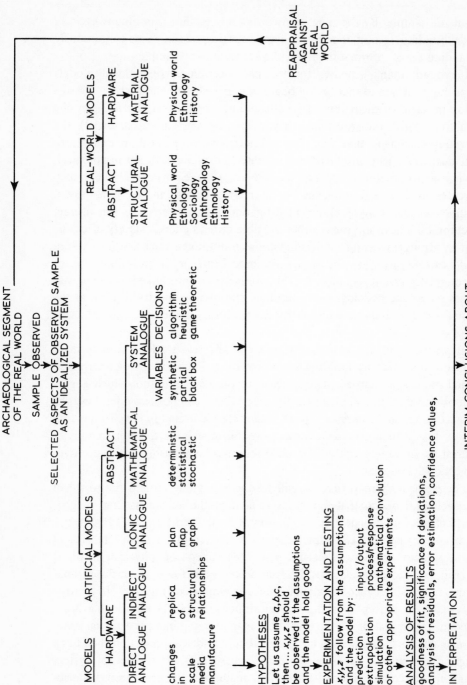

FIG. I.2. A schematic map of the world of archaeological operational models – one of many alternative projections.

12

ethnographic situations, opposite a corresponding pole of simplicity where the simple hardware parallels and replicas meet.

In the simple region of artificial hardware models we encounter direct models of archaeological artefacts and sites with elementary predictive capacities – museum demonstration models, reconstruction models of buildings and structures, or direct replicas of artefacts. Of all operational models these are the best known to archaeologists at large – flint tools and projectile points have been copied and used, woodland has been cleared with stone, bronze and iron axes, ploughed with replica ards then planted and reaped with flint, bronze and iron sickles, facsimile houses have been built, burned and excavated, earthworks have been erected, storage pits tested, iron and copper smelted, pottery fired, all carefully reproducing archaeological prototypes (Ascher, 1961; Coles, 1966). These replicas are often full-size scale models, and even complete 'prehistoric' farmsteads with fields, crops and domestic animals have been set up on the 30 ha site at Lejre in Denmark and at Butser Hill experimental farm, Hampshire, England, whilst a comparable scheme exists at Adesina Oja, Nigeria (see Daniels, Chapter 5 of this volume).

It is usually, but not always, the case that the artificial hardware model either changes the scale, modifies the medium of manufacture, or deviates from the technology used to produce the original and it is these distortions that must be carefully noted and controlled. However, selected distortions deliberately and carefully thought out enable us to compress the passage of time by reducing some factors and scaling up others, or to gain useful results without attempting total replication – for example the use of a $1/12$ scale model has provided acceptable information on the erection of stones at Stonehenge (Stone, 1924). Nevertheless, such distortion in scale and production often leads to the formidable complications that arise from the differential consequences experienced by different variables – some will change together linearly with scale or material, others non-linearly and independently, and others even exponentially. It is at this point that the results from studying artificial hardware models produced by the workshop are often run against and compared with appropriately selected real-life ethnographic hardware parallels to control these aspects – a modern copy of an Iron Age smelting furnace against a comparable Sudanese furnace, for example (Coles, 1966, p. 5).

These hardware models enable us to learn by imitation, to estimate the original cost in time and labour and the efficiency and life-expectancy of the item – primitive steps in quantification which may also be matched from comparable ethnographic data. The models also allow predictive hypotheses to be formed relating the similarity of behaviour – or its artefact consequences – observed in the present to that preserved from the past. These hypotheses, or the models themselves, may then be tested by experiment and simulation and the results analysed and interpreted. A recent experiment illustrates this procedure. A full-scale earthwork was constructed at Overton Down, Wiltshire, in 1960 with various materials and artefacts embedded within it at exactly measured locations. This model then allows two different aspects to be simultaneously investigated, first of all providing an estimate of the labour time and methods required to build a massive bank and ditch with replicas of prehistoric artefacts, second to record the complex micro-geomorphological post-depositional processes of decay and collapse by sampling the earthwork, at appropriately estimated intervals of time, by excavation. The observations from this experiment are only just beginning but they have already contributed new information of great importance in modifying the traditional, erroneous and purely intuitive opinions previously held about silting and erosion processes on chalk soils (Jewell, 1963, 1966).

Here is an interesting example of an artificial hardware simulation model with a dynamic capacity. The drawback of having to wait 5, 10, 20, 50 and 100 years before being able to take the appropriate readings is a problem that might have been overcome by miniaturization in scale accompanied by changes in media and the simulation of erosional processes, but in this case the distortional consequences of such a procedure would probably have outweighed any convenience. An alternative might be the excavation of sections of a chosen series of historic earthworks of known date – perhaps ranging from Roman banks, through Medieval park boundaries to Recent railway embankments – but here again a degree of control on comparable media and erosional processes is lost; perhaps a composite procedure involving all three approaches and yet other possibilities might represent a solution.

In contrast with the direct artificial hardware models we may also distinguish an interesting category of indirect artificial hardware models, transitional between the imitative replicas and their consequences on one hand and the more powerful class of abstract, iconic or symbolic models on the other. The indirect hardware analogue imitates in concrete form not the direct external appearance of an archaeological artefact or site but instead provides a tangible replica of certain relationships noted and abstracted at a derivative and secondary level from primary and direct observations and analyses. The output of complex correlation analyses and cluster analysis studies may be expressed in this model form and it may be possible to consider to what extent aspects of the model thus visualized may be generalized to aspects of comparable situations (see Frontispiece).

A simple but effective example of an indirect artificial hardware model can be used, for example, to illustrate the dangers that follow from naive comparisons of distribution densities plotted on flat map projections. Take a flat disc of silver foil and let it represent a large flat alluvial plain and mark upon it a dozen archaeological sites of a given period. Take an exact copy of this disc and the distribution over an identical area of silver foil, crush it into a ball and unroll it over an eggbox to give the effect of a mountainous terrain overriding complex small scale relief; then compare the 'flat' map projections of the two distributions of the dozen sites on the plain and the same sites, distributed in the same way, over an identical surface area (Fig. 1.3). It will be found that in practice the distribution of finds appears to be three to seven times more dense in the projection of the mountainous terrain than in the flat plain – although the density of sites per unit area is in fact the same in both cases. Now take the sparse distribution of Mesolithic sites in the Hungarian plain and compare it with the dense distribution in the map projection of the Alpine region, add in a multiplying factor for the differential loss of sites under considerable aggradation in the flat alluvial plain, and perhaps the degree of difference becomes less significant?

In any event this model reminds us that all archaeological distributions, artificially portrayed on flat map projections, were once distributed over complex surfaces – topographic, demographic, ecological surfaces, etc. – and what may appear to be a counter-locational analysis case of irregular distribution on one surface may provide a perfect case of evenly and regularly adjusted site distribution when mapped on another surface under a different transformation for the same area and material (Figs. 1.4, 18.1, 21.9) (Harvey, 1969, ch. 14).

The class of indirect hardware models takes us some way from the elementary domain of simple artificial *hardware* analogues towards the complex realm of artificial *theoretical* models with its iconic, mathematical and system analogues. Iconic models merely represent observed properties as iconic symbols using a selective, distorted, simplified code distributed over an equally simplified field space of few dimensions – an elementary representational and demonstrative device but yet with some limited predictive and experimental capacities. Beyond these lie the symbolic mathematical and system models where properties and relationships in the archaeological sample are again represented by symbols, but which unlike the iconic codes are now explicitly integrated in a specified calculus of relationships or system of equa-

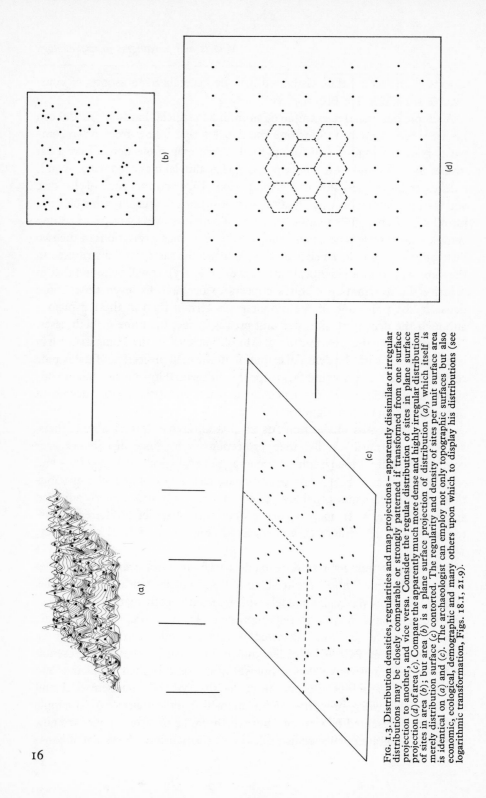

Fig. 1.3. Distribution densities, regularities and map projections – apparently dissimilar or irregular distributions may be closely comparable or strongly patterned if transformed from one surface projection to another, and vice versa. Consider the regular distribution of sites in plane surface projection (d) of area (c). Compare the apparently much more dense and highly irregular distribution of sites in area (b); but area (b) is a plane surface projection of distribution (a), which itself is merely distribution surface (c) contorted. The regularity and density of sites per unit surface area is identical on (a) and (c). The archaeologist can employ not only topographic surfaces but also economic, ecological, demographic and many others upon which to display his distributions (see logarithmic transformation, Figs. 18.1, 21.9).

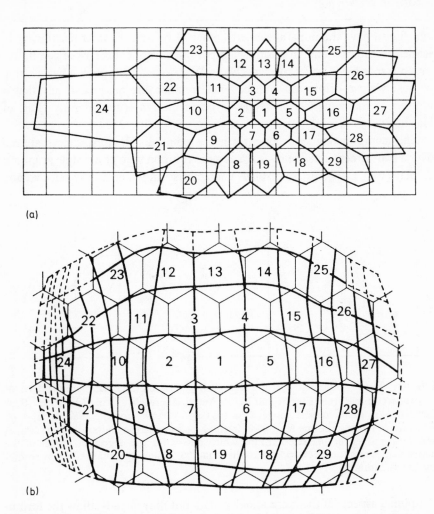

(a)

(b)

FIG. 1.4. Comparison between theoretical and actual map patterns by way of map transformations. (a) An approximation to Christaller's theoretical model in an area of disuniform rural population density. (b) A transformed map to produce even population densities and the superimposition of the theoretical Christaller solution (from Harvey, 1969).

tions. Here we have an emerging capacity to cope with dynamic and diachronic developments, variables varying together and separately over large but nevertheless constrained ranges, with due allowance for stochastic elements and the complex sampling effects inherent in the archaeological data. Here we also meet the infinite variety of symbolic mathematical, numerical, algebraic, geometrical and statistical languages, amongst which we may choose, and which also have the unparalleled advantage of being both interdisciplinary in scope and international in meaning; important additional means of communication across fields and between schools. We must not suppose, however, that because we can display an archaeological relationship mathematically that it is itself of mathematical character – representation is not identity (Earl of Halsbury, 1968).

The iconic analogues frequently use a point distribution code scattered over a two-dimensional field – such as a distribution map or a simple graphical display (Fig. 1.5A). These displays characteristically model only selected and

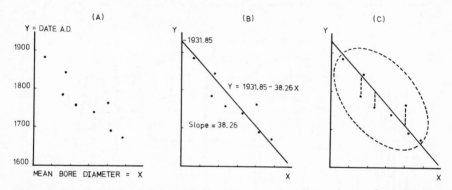

FIG. 1.5. (A) An iconic model of the relationship between the mean bore diameter of clay tobacco pipes from Europe and North America between *c.* A.D. 1600–1900. (B) A deterministic mathematical model ($Y = 1931 \cdot 85 - 38 \cdot 26X$) for the relationships derived from the straight line regression formula best fitting the scatter of values. (C) A statistical model for the relationships which allows for the degree of scatter of the actual values and their deviation from the ideal line model (schematized from studies by Lewis Binford).

simplified aspects of the archaeological data but they already allow the formulation of simple hypotheses about probabilities and expectations from analysis or extrapolation and thus provide a frame for testing such predictions. The statistical properties of the dispersion and the relationship between the points and the field space lead almost inevitably to the conversion of such iconic displays into statistical models which more succinctly account for the display pattern. In this way the iconic model demonstrating how the mean bore diameter of seventeenth–nineteenth century clay tobacco pipes varied with their date and technology of manufacture (Fig. 1.5B) may be crudely but adequately expressed in a mathematical deterministic model derived from the straight line regression formula for the scatter of values – allowing the prediction of a date with a fair degree of accuracy, given a few hundred stem frag-

18

ments such as are frequently found on European and Colonial sites (Walker, 1967):

let x = the mean bore diameter of pipe stem fragment
y = the date of its manufacture

then analysis shows that

$y = 1931 \cdot 85 - 38 \cdot 26x$ for north European and American pipes.

Such deterministic mathematical models are rare in archaeology since they assume that all the operating factors are known and are capable of exact expression. However, Carneiro (1960) offers a deterministic model relating shifting cultivation factors and length of settlement tenure for slash-and-burn agriculturalists under tropical forest conditions. Cook and Heizer (1968) have developed an allometric (loglog) model relating living floor area and population in aboriginal Californian settlements, where this approach might usefully be compared with another deterministic model for population estimates based on cemetery size and the age distribution of the skeletons therein (Birabon, 1971). All deterministic mathematical models, it may be noted, are only strictly applicable to a very limited field of data, although they may be very powerful over that range and at least suggest potential relationships beyond it.

Statistical models differ from deterministic models by including a capacity to cope with random effects, which may arise either from inherent fluctuations, from the effect that no two repetitions of an experimental test give identical results (C14 dating), or from variability within a sampled category. Statistical models can be derived from deterministic models by including an additional random component – thus the deterministic regression line model for clay pipes (Fig. 1.5B) could be modified to allow for the real cigar-shape scatter of points by estimating an appropriate error component (E):

$$y = 1931 \cdot 85 - 38 \cdot 26x + E \quad \text{(Fig. 1.5C)}$$

A precisely comparable random component is included in statistical models for analysing three-dimensional trend surfaces in order to distinguish significant residuals from localized small-scale fluctuations – an important technique for scrutinizing distribution maps of archaeological data for regional trends, and a reminder that the egalitarian dots on archaeological maps have differing quantifiable values (Clarke, 1968, p. 481).

Stochastic models differ from the ordinary statistical model in incorporating, in addition to the preceding considerations, a specific random process which replicates a sequence of changes on a probability basis; reproducing net effects of myriads of differently directed infinitesimal factors – individually unspecifiable but jointly predictable. Stochastic models are thus especially suitable for simulating processes of change, developmental sequences, and the consequences of randomly impinging effects at a very small scale when compared to the level of the study of the phenomenon as a whole. The particular process involved may be described in terms of successive chains of probabilities – chains that may be classified as random walk, Monte Carlo, or Markov chains, etc., according to the precise pattern of the transition probabilities. Archaeologists are currently discovering that the general theory of stochastic processes provides a whole series of model formulations in probabilistic languages very appropriate for certain archaeological situations (Harvey, 1969, p. 266).

Thus random walk models describe processes in which the path or sequence traced by an element moves or changes in steps, each step or change being determined by chance in regard to direction, magnitude, or both. The cases most frequently considered are those in which the element moves on a lattice of points in one or more dimensions and at each step is equally likely to move to any of the nearest neighbouring points. The fluctuation and aimless wandering of the time trajectories of the majority of non-functional artefact and assemblage attributes, meandering within the range of their stable configurations, has been compared with random walk models, and much of the stylistic variation in Acheulean assemblages has been accounted for under such a model (Fig. 1.6) (Clarke, 1968, pp. 448–9, 471, 575; Isaac, 1969, p. 19). In this volume a random walk model has also been used to represent the wanderings of discarded artefacts on the abandonment of a site (p. 806).

However, the mention of random walk movements in conjunction with nearest neighbour points reminds us of their geographical implications and its potential significance for modelling the colonization, movement or diffusion of archaeological artefacts and sites. For example, if we wish to simulate the successive settlement site movements of Danubian I slash-and-burn agriculturalists in fifth millennium B.C. Europe, then a random walk model provides many interesting possibilities. Within a relatively homogeneous loess zone there will be an infinite number of acceptable settlement locations stretching in all directions to the limits of the loess band. So, when a settlement is to be resited from time to time it will move on a lattice of points in two dimensions and is equally likely at each transition to move to any of the nearest neighbouring acceptable location points in any direction. Such a movement typically arises in situations where the moves are affected by a great many independently variable factors (Fig. 1.6).

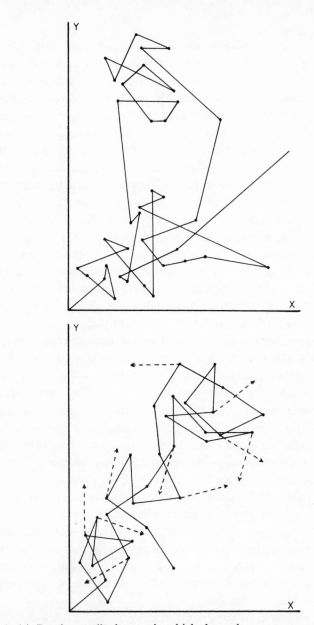

FIG. 1.6. (a) Random walk changes in which the path or sequence traced changes in steps, each step or change being determined by chance in regard to direction and magnitude. X and Y might be a pair of variables in an artefact study or geographical axes when the graph becomes a map. (b) Random walk changes in which the magnitude of each step remains the same, and which at every third move generates another element, also executing a comparable random walk pattern. This random walk and birth process may be applicable to settlement or population movements and fissioning and is related to the important general class of Yule Process models.

The general properties of random walk processes predict that the direction of movement of the settlement will be unbiased between north and south, east or west – other things being equal. Equally, because the Brownian motion or random walk is recurrent, the settlement path is almost sure to return infinitely many times to a small neighbourhood of former settlement locations, although the longer the settlement drifts the likelier it is to wander far from its starting point. However, this process will be intensified because every two or three moves each Danubian village will have generated enough surplus population both to continue itself and give rise to an additional new village unit by a kind of social binary fission (see p. 843). The result of this compounding multiplication will endorse even more firmly the probability that some derivative settlements of any given ancestral village will remain in the general vicinity of the ancestral sites, although the multiplication of settlement units and their constant mutual readjustment will also ensure that over a long period of time the many derivative village units will become widely dispersed in an expanding mass of hunt-and-seek settlement pathways.

Now, this random walk model for Danubian I settlement expansion matches the archaeological observations in a far more satisfactory way than the east–west linear movement model customarily employed, and more significantly offers new explanations for some unique aspects of the Danubian I phenomenon – the characteristics that, despite continuous development through 600 years, and despite a dispersed distribution covering more than a 1500 km of forested terrain, the Danubian I ceramic tradition remained remarkably conservative, relatively homogeneous in motif vocabulary, and everywhere passed through broadly comparable stylistic changes, from Romania to the Rhine. In the ensuing Danubian II phase these unique characteristics were dispersed in a mosaic of regionally diverse ceramic traditions, perhaps stimulated by the introduction of less mobile and more intensive agrarian and settlement systems, possibly including the development of plough agriculture. Many factors will have interacted to produce and maintain the ceramic uniformity of Danubian I, but it is probable that the pattern of settlement movements and relationships was one key factor.

The random walk model shows how settlement expansion into distant areas may be accomplished without loss of contact across the mass of mutually interacting settlement territories, constantly in motion, constantly colliding in fresh random associations with a constant interchange of inhabitants and artefacts updating every unit's behaviour patterns. Yet the same model reconciles this constant movement with the continuous occupation of regions by some descendants of villages that were formerly in that area hundreds of years previously. It also shows that at this scale the movement is only directional in so far as it is channelled within the loess bands and across the network of river and stream systems. When the universe under scrutiny is Europe as a whole and the scale half a millennium, then the Danubian I phenomenon may indeed be adequately represented by a linear movement model with a directed expansion along the loess 'railway lines' from eastern to western Europe. If the boundaries of the loess represent the universe and the scale is the lifetime of a given village then a random walk model is more appropriate – once again reminding us that the scale of the study determines the level of model appropriate for its representation and the process appropriate for its explanation.

Above all else, the random walk model suggests one factor and one mechanism which would maximize the *opportunity* for the maintenance of common ceramic features changing in step across a vast distribution of widely dispersed communities. However, *opportunity* for such a homogeneity does not explain *why* this opportunity was in this case taken up, neither does it explain the conservatism of the tradition. Here we must consider other factors and perhaps suggest a mixed model upon the following lines:

(1) Random walk of settlement communities, like the movement of gas particles, maximizes 'collisions' and offers maximum opportunity for community interaction and homogeneous diffusion across a large area.

(2) Ethno-economic models suggest that a characteristic social concomitant of shifting agricultural communities is the considerable inter-village mobility of families. This amounts to a random walk of family units between the random walking settlement communities – the family feuding with this group, moving to another, fissioning to a third and so on. This kind of social mobility would put the *opportunity* for interlinked parallel development into *practice*.

(3) There is probably some additional factor needed to maximize ceramic homogeneity and conservatism in what still could have been a commonly held but rapidly changing ceramic tradition. This might probably involve social considerations of the kind modelled by Deetz (1965) and Longacre (1970):

Matrilocality would favour ceramic conservatism but only bring males into the village.
Patrilocality would exchange women between villages maintaining ceramic homogeneity but not necessarily conservatism.
Village endogamy would favour ceramic conservatism but also between-site divergence.
Village exogamy would assist homogeneity but not conservatism.

The kinship solution with maximum within and between village *homogeneity and conservatism* would probably be some form of bilocal residence with 50% village endogamy and 50% exogamy, such as we see for example amongst the analogous Iban (Freeman, 1955). This speculation might be tested by comparing the variability of male-produced artefacts with associated female artefact variability, making certain assumptions.

(4) Finally, one factor cited in the linear movement model remains significant in setting up an initial level of homogeneity over a large area – the comparative rapidity of the expansion, which will have been largely a consequence of demographic, ecological and swidden regime economic factors.

This thumbnail sketch may serve to illustrate this class of stochastic model at the macro-level of settlement movements whilst the similar model for discarded artefact movements serves a similar purpose at the micro-level (see Clarke, Chapter 21 of this volume). In a wider context the sketch illustrates the building up of composite models, the role of the model as a fountain of hypotheses for testing, the model as an explanatory device, the potential use of ethnographic data as a control on pure, theoretical models, and the importance of scale in the modelling and analysis of archaeological material.

Monte Carlo, Markov chain, Queueing Theory and Ergodic Theory represent other kinds of stochastic process models which are emerging or may emerge in archaeological contexts. The Monte Carlo technique suggests solutions to stochastic problems by employing sampling experiments upon a simulated model of the process under investigation (Fig. 17.10) (Haggett, 1965, pp. 58–60, 97–8). For example, the study of the surviving distribution of Körös Neolithic settlement sites along the river Tisza has produced a fragmentary but remarkably regularly adjusted lattice of settlement locations (Fig. 1.7); and yet how could locational analysis infer a regular inter-site adjustment of 2 km when we know the distribution to be a very fragmentary palimpsest of more than 500 years of occupation in this area? A simulation model was developed which assumed a random walk settlement movement within the suitable dry loess terraces close to running water but with the assumed constraint that two factors would lead to movement in the first instance to new locations about 2 km from the old:

(1) An appropriate agricultural surface to support villages of this size on this terrain under the given technology would be a *c.* 1 km radius territory. Therefore, invoking the Law of Least Effort, the minimal move would be 2 km.

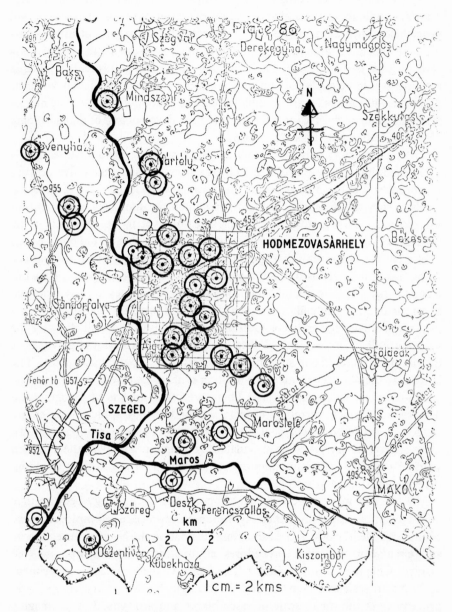

FIG. 1.7. A fragmentary palimpsest distribution of some 500 years of Körös Neolithic settlement along the river Tisza; the sites date between *c.* 5000–4500 B.C. radiocarbon. Sites within the amplitude of the river will in the main have been destroyed by its meanderings. (Based on original research by Dr John Nandris.)

25

(2) However, disregarding the above considerations, a former village territory, although about to be abandoned on the grounds of soil exhaustion, will nevertheless include many residual resources and the results of much communally expended labour – cleared and drained areas, accessible water, pasture, residual tree crops, etc. Therefore, the old territory represents a valuable resource still to be exploited and thus requiring a move immediately adjacent to it yet ensuring fresh arable radius – therefore a move of 2 km. At the micro-level this same model accounts for the 'lily pad' development of floors in some classes of settlement (Figs. 21.1–21.6).

These two factors may give a contemporary series of site adjustments on a 2 km modulus but how could this emerge from a fragmentary five century palimpsest ? Well, a series of Monte Carlo samples taken at 2%, 10% and 50% levels of survival of detectable Körös sites upon the simulated model output for 500 years showed that, for complex reasons yet to be analysed, if the modulus of adjustment remained of the same order for that period of time then a false pattern enshrining that modulus is likely to be preserved, the pattern being 'false' in so far as it is not a pattern of actually contemporary sites but a sample in a spatial-temporal cube. This example illustrates the way that such experiments may gradually develop a special and probably statistically complex set of theory for archaeological locational analysis that will allow for the special problems of the archaeological sample and the crucial way in which its distributions differ from superficially comparable geographical cases. The latter may then be seen as merely a limiting synchronic case of a more general spatio-temporal locational theory. There are other aspects of Geographical Theory, too, which current archaeological and ethnographic enquiries are suggesting may merely represent a partial theory of modern limiting cases in a more general theory yet to be articulated by taking into account the 2 million years of adaptively changing hominid settlement patterns and their changing determinants (see p. 51).

Monte Carlo models are especially important in archaeology because they offer a technique capable of reflecting the sampling procedures employed in excavation and field work, at the same time elucidating the hidden consequences and circularity that such procedures all too frequently incorporate (see Daniels, Chapter 5 of this volume). The Körös village simulation experiment at the macro-scale may be paralleled, for example, by elementary Monte Carlo procedures at the micro-scale of assemblages and artefacts. Let us imagine that we have a multiple-layered site at which the repeated visits of the same group employed an identical assemblage in every layer of the site. Then let us suppose that a varying 60% sample was itself accidentally left for selective sampling by sondage excavation (Fig. 1.8). It will at once be perceived that, although the successive assemblages were in fact identical, the sampling effects are such as to make uncommon artefact types seem to appear and disappear in successive levels (this experiment is best simulated by successively drawing

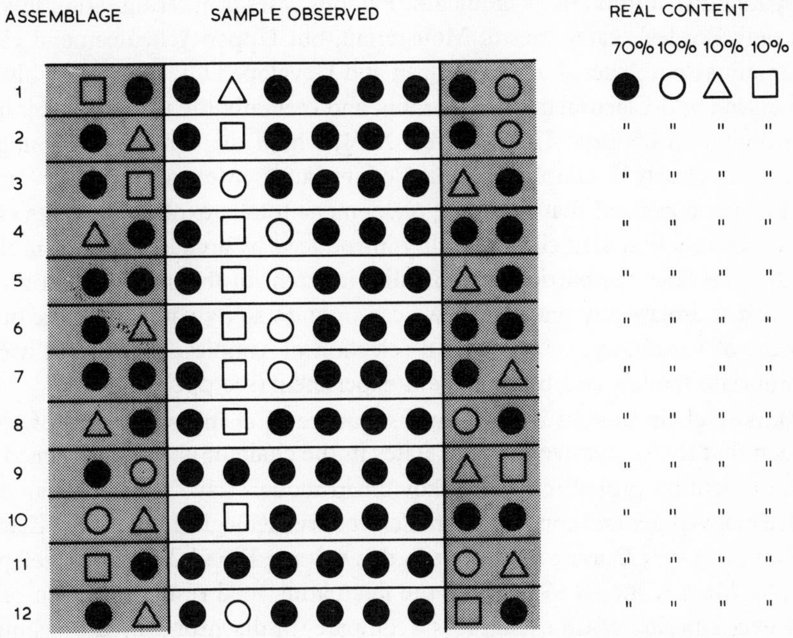

FIG. 1.8. The overriding consequences of variability introduced by sampling effects and the consequent dangers of 'type fossil' nomenclature – a model of the interdigitation problem. The figure can be conceived as a stratified site at which the same artefact assemblage was repeatedly used (see 'real content' of each horizontal assemblage). Sondage excavation or other sampling vagaries recover for classification and comparison only 60% of each assemblage – the selection in the vertical unshaded section ('sample observed'). If the triangle, square and unfilled circle are rare (infrequent) nominating type fossils, the column falsely appears to contain different assemblages coming and going in an irregular manner (interdigitation). If the triangles are hand-axes, the squares scrapers, the open circles denticulates, and the filled circles 'Typical Mousterian', then this model provides a crude simulation of the kind of interdigitation observed at Combe Grenal and other Mousterian sites.

In a more general setting the assemblage samples (1–12) could represent any set of incomplete assemblages from unstratified single sites widely distributed in space.

from a bag of coloured marbles, the assemblage in the bag remaining identical whilst the 60% of marbles successively grabbed varies). Now it is a well-known archaeological vice to nominate and classify assemblages by the presence or absence of rare 'type fossils' – thus, imagine that the most abundant artefacts in our model assemblage represent Typical Mousterian, that each of the rare types represent, say, scrapers, handaxes or denticulates, then our model has at least partially simulated the phenomenon of 'interdigitation', where assemblage categories appear and reappear in a random way in a stratigraphic column or spatial distribution of assemblages. Famous cases of interdigitation involve not only Bordes's categories of Mousterian, but Upper Acheulean and Hope Fountain assemblages, Late Acheulean and Developed Oldowan, possibly the Acheulean and Clactonian phenomenon, and certainly the Ceramic/Aceramic interdigitation of Çatal Hüyük levels X–V, where the coming and going of pottery is clearly a sampling artefact of its rarity (Mellaart, 1966, p. 170).

It is not suggested that sampling phenomena totally explain the cases cited above, merely that artificial variability introduced by archaeological sampling always overrides the particular variability inherent in the material and that if we wish to isolate any one source we can only do so by controlling the other sources of variability, by the skilful selection of samples, the careful use of appropriate models and by intelligent experiment (see pp. 119–63).

Markov chain models imply that a sequence of changes or series of steps is such that the successive series of states in the chain or chains are related by given transition probabilities. Markov chain models have so far appeared in archaeology as general conceptual models for archaeological processes (Clarke, 1968, pp. 63–77; Doran, 1970), but in this volume David Thomas develops a specific Markov model to simulate the fluctuating food resource output of an area over a period of time (Fig. 17.5) (compare the diachronic model of similar situation, Fig. 1.15). Queueing Theory appears in a number of anthropological papers relating to individual mobility and probabilities of promotion to varying grades and statuses within various patterns of social hierarchies and these may yet have archaeological manifestations (Harvey, 1969, pp. 246, 266).

Ergodic models make the assumption that the statistical properties of a set of observations in a time series are essentially the same as the statistical properties of a set of observations of the same phenomenon taken over a synchronic spatial ensemble (Harvey, 1969, pp. 128–9, 269–70). Models incorporating this special type of stationary stochastic process may have something to contribute to the modelling of spatio-temporal distributions like that sketched above for Körös villages. Curry (1967) has already applied such a model to central place systems with the implication that the statistical properties of activity patterns over *time* can be taken as implicit in the statistical properties of the *spatial* pattern of site locations. It is interesting to note that an implicit ergodic model must also underlie the frequent practice of using ethnographic-historic data from one area and period to model an archaeological situation in a 'comparable stage of development' (stadial models), or when data from many such areas and periods are used to model some general historical process (Harvey, 1969, p. 129). Even the statistical properties of attributes, artefacts and assemblages may be modelled in ergodic terms on the assumption that the affinity between any such items in space is comparable to identical affinity between such items in time (Clarke, 1968, pp. 262–5). Thus two artefacts sharing a 75% affinity with a reference artefact may fall into this same category because they were both contemporary but made from a chain of copies effectively equidistant from the reference, or because they were both made equitemporally from the reference, or because one was phenetically as far removed in space as the other was in time from the reference.

Thrown back by the glimpses of these mathematical mountains and dangerous precipices, our schematic map shows the archaeological explorer that beyond the diversity of stochastic process models lies a broad area of models with a comparable capacity to simulate complex processes – system models (Fig. 1.2). We are still within the realm of artificial theoretical models, but are beginning to approach the frontier with system models abstracted from real-life ethnographic, historical or physical situations.

System models are preoccupied with the flow of consequences between ensembles of interlinked components rather than with the detailed mathematical symbolism of particular elements. The particular components linked within the system are selected by the operator as his guess at the set which interacts to account for most of the variability of interest to him, in the frame of his particular study. The guess may be a bad one and it is therefore important to bear this in mind when first examining an impressive flow chart. Putting components in boxes in a system does not necessarily explain a process or even model it accurately; it depends what is in the boxes that are included and what is not in those boxes. All too often we may be presented with a flow chart that crisply formulates the obvious and only succeeds in modelling the satisfaction of the operator.

However, it has been repeatedly pointed out that these are universal criticisms of bad models and nobody is defending a case for bad models. The study of the interaction of components in systems is unavoidable because all situations may be conceived as systems of components and this is one of the ways in which dynamic processes may be modelled. The expression of such a system as a flow-interaction chart is both an explicit and potentially testable expression of a set of assumptions and hypotheses, and a vital step in setting up a computer simulation – this in itself accounts for the current popularity of the flow chart in some quarters and its vilification in others (Garvin, 1965).

System models may represent the flow of consequences between ensembles of interlinked variables or the flow of consequences between networks of decisions. The former class of system, systems of variables, is defined by sets of components such that changes in the values or states of some of these components can be shown to affect or alter with the value or state of some of their neighbours (Clarke, 1968, pp. 43–82). The overall state of the system therefore changes with the changing values, states, compositions and organizations of the components, and with the flow of correlation, energy, mass, commodity or information changes, according to the nature of the system being modelled. In general, such systems exhibit very common categories of 'behaviour' brought about by their structural similarities and it is these general system properties that enable the operator to compare systems which may share elements of deep structure although quite dissimilar in surface structure. Thus two superficially very different systems are said to have 'equivalence' when they transform the same inputs into identical outputs, opening up new realms of classificatory possibilities. Other common system properties may include – constraints, critical thresholds, stochastic oscillation, adaptive regulation and control by positive or negative feedback, convergence upon equilibrium states, replication and related concepts (Clarke, 1968, pp. 43–82; Chorley and Haggett, 1967, pp. 76–89).

System models have emerged at a range of levels of power and specificity in contemporary archaeological debate. At the lowest level the system approach has proved an extremely useful way of reconceptualizing archaeological problems ranging from general theory (Clarke, 1968) to models for food-collecting and food-production regimes in Mesoamerica 8000–200 B.C. (Flannery, 1968), and the Neolithic 'revolution' in the Near East 10 000–5000 B.C. (Binford, 1968). By restricting the scope of the modelling, a more specific predictive or simulation power develops with the addition of qualitative information about the links and components in the system – the flow of consequences is specified and directions indicated, positive and negative feedback is identified and the nature of the inputs and outputs related. Finally, with an even more tightly defined frame of reference and still more information, it is possible to quantify the components and the input and output of the system and thus move towards quantified, measurable and testable predictions. These three levels of utility and capacity are aptly illustrated by Newcomb's models for Iron Age settlements in Cornwall (Fig. 1.9), the more powerful systems models of various forms (Figs. 1.10–1.12), and Thomas's semi-quantified model of the Shoshone economic cycle (Fig. 17.3). Many detailed verbal descriptions and quantitative estimations represent primitive archaeological movements to-

30

wards the goal of an explicit, quantified, system display of the step-by-step logic of a problem which might then be susceptible to a powerful, testable computer simulation (Doran, 1970).

A particularly attractive feature of system models is their capacity to cope with very complex and unknown aspects of archaeological situations. Because of system closure, for example, models with infinite numbers of variables are in fact sometimes more tractable than models with a finite but large number of variables (Tobler, 1969). Similarly, where the details of the system components are known, it still remains possible to relate given system outputs (like demographic structure, perhaps) to preceding system inputs such as the

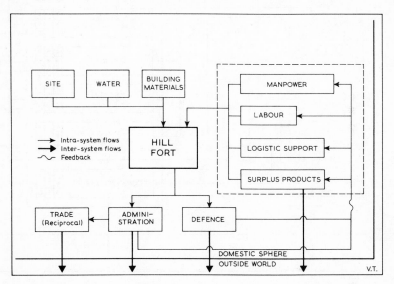

FIG. 1.9. A simple system model for a category of Iron Age hill fort in Cornwall (from Newcomb, 1968).

population in the immediately preceding time period. Given the inputs and outputs, or estimates of them, it is possible to calculate the characteristics of the unknown system in the Black Box and thus infer the process (Fig. 1.13) (Clarke, 1968, pp. 59–62).

Black Box systems are the last of the three categories of models for systems of variables distinguished by Chorley (Chorley and Haggett, 1967, p. 85). The unknown subsystems of Black Box process-response models grade into the Grey Box of incompletely specified partial system models and the White Box of the completely specified but arbitrarily selected variables of synthetic models. Synthetic system models begin with the selective identification of key elements in a given archaeological complex, together with the adoption of some views about their interrelationship. A detailed study of the changing correlation patterns of these selected elements then allows the 'variable system' to be mapped under successive conditions and its correlation structure examined by regression or cluster analysis for indications of yoked changes in

A SYSTEMS MODEL OF THE MEDIEVAL PARISH

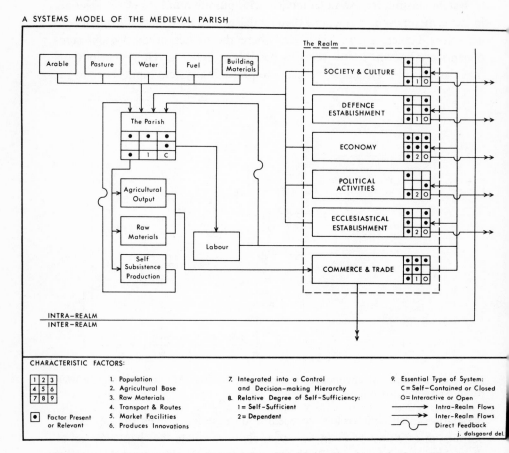

FIG. 1.10. A developed system model for a Danish medieval parish (from Newcomb, 1970).

groups of variables and scrutinized for cause and effect. When the variables are numerous and acting with composite effects it is useful to collapse the data matrix by factor analysis into a small number of idealized variables, which account for most of the observed variability of the data (Figs. 3.1–3.3) (see Binford, Chapter 3 of this volume). Synthetic system models have already proved especially valuable for the analysis of correlation patterns in attributes within artefact systems and artefact categories within assemblage systems (Binford and Binford, 1966; Clarke, 1968, pp. 541–2; Glover, 1969). However, synthetic system studies of trends in the values or states of mapped distributions, considered as 'response surfaces', offer far wider applications of

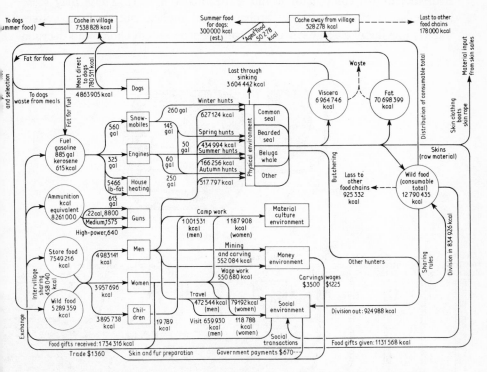

FIG. I.II. The flow of energy in a hunting society; the system is outlined for two Eskimo households from direct observations over thirteen months. The input of imported energy in the form of fuel and ammunition, along with the input of native game and imported foodstuffs (far left), enabled the four hunters and their kin to heat their dwellings and power their machines, and also join in many seasonal activities that utilized various parts of the environment in the manner indicated (right). The end results of these combined inputs of energy are shown as a series of yields and losses from waste and other causes (far right). The net yields then feed back through various channels to reach the starting point again as inputs. All figures are in kilocalories (from Kemp, 1971).

process-response models linking artefact or site distributions and ecological, environmental or demographic variability (see Clarke, Chapter 21, p. 847).

However, the primitive flow-interaction chart which may model the flow of consequences between systems of variables may also model the flow of consequences between systems of decisions – the realm of operational research and control and decision theory (Fig. 5.2) (see Daniels, Chapter 5). Decision systems and their models match the capacity of mathematical models in their range from the deterministic to the probabilistic, from algorithm models to heuristic, linear, combinatorial and game theory models. These may seem remote areas of the world of archaeological models but decision system models inevitably emerge wherever complex processes of choice and decision

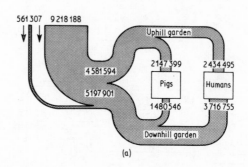

(a)

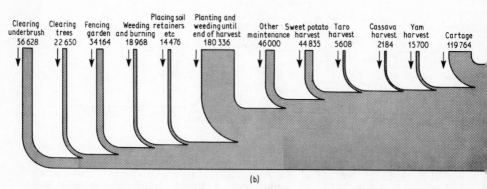

(b)

FIG. 1.12. The flow of energy in a slash-and-burn agricultural society; the system is outlined for 204 Tsembaga tribesmen from direct observations in New Guinea (from Rappaport, 1971).

(a) The biomass of the crop yield in yams, cassavas, sweet potatoes and pigs, etc., measured in kcal. If this yield is compared with the major energy input (b), it gives more than a sixteen to one return on the human energy investment, although this static model would fluctuate over a run of good and bad years.

(b) The twelve major inputs of energy required in Tsembaga agriculture. The flow diagram shows the inputs in terms of the kcal per acre required to prepare and harvest a pair of gardens. Weeding, a continual process after the garden is planted, demands the most energy; bringing in the harvest (right) ranks next.

are studied or simulated – whether simulating the complex routing of restricted manpower and materials in a plan for a large excavation, or simulating and optimizing the economic schedule of the Shoshone or !Kung (Fig. 17.3).

Algorithm models present a precise set of instructions for solving a well-defined problem, whether the solution itself is imprecise or not. Many archaeological algorithm models are therefore key steps in computer studies like Gardin's reconstruction of early Assyrian trade networks (Gardin, 1965, fig. 3). In practice no scheme of archaeological classification is really acceptable unless it is accompanied by an algorithm which will both instruct the novice how to employ the classification on real material and highlight the key attributes in the material (Fig. 1.14) (Lewis and Woolfenden, 1969).

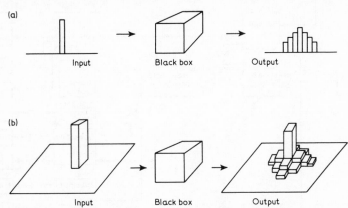

FIG. 1.13. Black Box system process and response models for complex unknown systems (after Tobler, 1969).

Heuristic models, by comparison, involve successive approximations, often made on a probabilistic basis, sometimes adaptively changing with changing circumstances. These models can be used either where there is no algorithm available – playing chess, for example – or where the available algorithm is hopelessly uneconomic in use. Heuristics are rough formulations of systems of hypotheses; they have the advantage that they are flexible, especially suited to complex adaptive situations within changing circumstances, and they can cope with situations that cannot be quantified; they are therefore closely associated with probability theory, management information systems and heuristic non-numerical computer programming (George, 1970). Doran's use of a 'HEURISTIC DENDRAL' technique to generate explanatory hypotheses within a simulation model for an Iron Age cemetery illustrates many of these qualities at work (Figs. 10.1–10.3) (see Doran, Chapter 10).

35

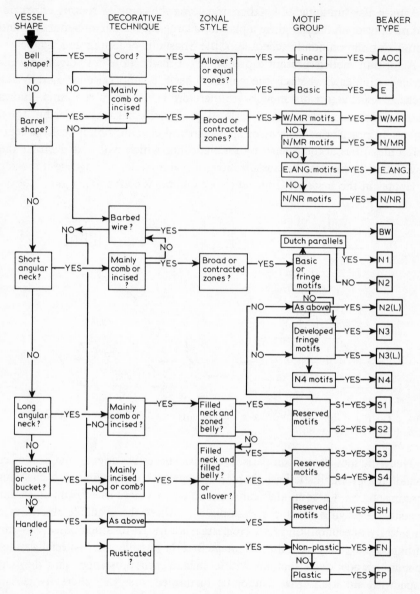

FIG. 1.14. A simplified algorithm model for the classification of British beaker pottery (Clarke, 1970a). Particular vessels are scrutinized and classified in terms of the covariation of their shape, decorative technique, zonal style and motif vocabulary. The partitioning of these sets of attributes produces twenty subsets or categories of vessel. A full algorithm would allow rapid and automatic computer classification of archaeological data.

36

Linear programming and combinatorial models develop further aspects of decision systems. Linear programme models have been devised to solve and simulate situations that require the allocation of available resources to meet varying demands, indicating the optimal utilization of available resources in given circumstances (Vajda, 1960). The archaeological techniques of catchment area analysis and site system studies already produce data on utilization patterns and resource distribution especially suited to simulation in linear programme or game theory models (see Jarman Chapter 18), and Thomas has taken his model of the Shoshone economic system some way in this direction (see Thomas, Chapter 17).

Game theory models further develop these possibilities by realistically introducing the uncontrollable but ever present counter-optimal moves of the environing system or of competitor systems; thus many solutions that appear optimal under static and synchronic conditions turn out to be positively dangerous under dynamic and diachronic competition (Fig. 1.15). Decisions must often be taken where the chances of success rely not only upon the action of uncontrollable factors but also upon the interaction of moves made by other persons, entities or systems. It is for circumstances such as these that the theory of games has been developed. The theory demonstrates to each player the strategy he should choose to maximize his advantage and thus introduces the concepts of strategies, high risk and low risk moves, alternative outcomes, and minimax and other prudential solutions.

The application of the theory in archaeology and anthropology is usually based on the assumption that over long periods of trial and error cultural systems and subsystems adaptively shake down within a schedule of satisfactory if not optimal moves – resembling a player who may have to make his moves without precise foreknowledge of how his opponent will move but with a body of past experience which assists him to make a decision in such a way that, had he known his opponent's move, he would still have reached the same decision. The theory and its models are therefore potentially very well suited to simulating changes in economic systems operating within a changing environment and it may well prove possible to 'game' the optimal or least-risk schedule of resource exploitation within the annual routine of a hunter-fisher-gatherer band or its adaptive 'best moves' through a series of environmental changes – thus producing predictive models that could be tested by excavation and analysis in a specific context. Some elementary game theory models have already been used to simulate economic transactions and at the general level of archaeological theory (Clarke, 1968, pp. 94–6; Gould, 1969).

The richness and complexity of decision system and variable system models

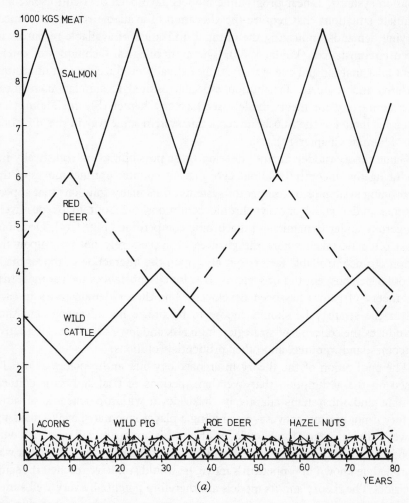

FIG. 1.15. A schematic model of the cumulative consequences of fluctuating food resources. The model has been devised for a population hunting-fishing-gathering a small inland territory of several kilometres radius, with a salmon river: perhaps a Mesolithic group in Britain or northern France after the oak/hazel maximum *c.* 5500–3000 B.C. The value of the oscillating resources has been taken from recorded preindustrial annual game returns, assuming a culling factor which will allow the survival of the stock at a constant level. (*a*) gives the demographic and natural order of fluctuation of the key resources. (*b*) gives the summation of these fluctuating resources over eighty years and illustrates one reason why the demographic optimum capacity for

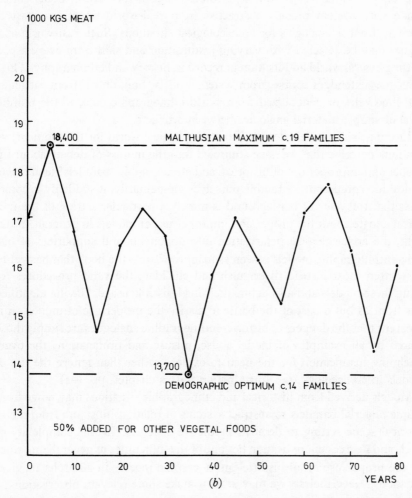

1000 KGS MEAT

18,400 — MALTHUSIAN MAXIMUM c.19 FAMILIES

13,700 — DEMOGRAPHIC OPTIMUM c.14 FAMILIES

50% ADDED FOR OTHER VEGETAL FOODS

(b)

YEARS

such an area is considerably lower than its hypothetical carrying capacity – the dynamic, diachronic model explains what a static synchronic study would find inexplicable.

The importance of resource oscillations and cycles as a source of population control and as an economic governor operates at three levels: (i) the annual cycle with a season of minimal resources; (ii) the successive annual oscillations with inevitable periodic 'bad years' when cycles in major and primary resources randomly coincide (as in this figure); (iii) occasional disastrous years or runs of years in which the factors above are accidentally exacerbated by bad weather or disease at crucial periods.

may be elaborated by building mixed models harnessing chains of decisions to networks of variables. At this level these artificial theoretical models intergrade with system models abstracted from real-world situations, past or present, used as analogies for archaeological situations. Such real-world analogues may be selected with varying justification and skill from every aspect of the physical world and its human record in history and ethnography. These analogues extend, of course, from system models 'built down' from particular real-life cycles or generalized from world ethnographic data, to the humble level of simple material analogies between artefacts.

Leaving aside models derived from the physical world for the moment, we can now perceive that we have stumbled into the morass of debate about the proper and improper use of historical and ethnographic 'parallels' in archaeological interpretation. Extracting ourselves momentarily, it suddenly becomes clear that this ancient battleground is merely a particular setting of the universal debate about the proper and improper use of models in general. In this light, the archaeological polarization into opponents and supporters of historic-enthnographic models is seen as inappropriate – the book that has yet to be written must instead distinguish and elucidate the valid procedures for using these models and also define their inadmissible usage. Having identified this front as but a part of the battle to clarify the proper use of models, it is apparent that the dangers of historic-enthnographic analogues are simply those shared by all examples of model abuse, misuse and profanation; the overwhelming justification for the need to explore rather than ignore the use of models in archaeology (see Introduction to this chapter, pp. 1–4).

Models derived from historical and ethnographic situations may range from simple material parallels to abstract systems of relationships, and from metaphorical scene-setting to detailed predictive schemes. In this complexity of levels and degrees of application lies one of the difficulties of generalizing rules for the proper use of all historic-enthnographic models in all archaeological situations. Nevertheless, we may at least make some relevant observations:

(1) We have learned that it is a general property of models that many different models will fit a given situation (see pp. 1–4). There are always many different historic-ethnographic models that could be found to fit an archaeological situation; it is no solution to stop looking after sighting the first. Therefore, goodness of fit is not sufficient justification for selecting one particular analogy – detailed if limited comparability must be established in terms of explicit criteria, which comparative ethnology must then confirm as functionally related to some constants shared by the archaeological case and

the ethnographic set (e.g. shellfish-gathering communities with a primitive technology, say) (Levine, 1969).

(2) Historic-ethnographic analogies generate potential models for isomorphic archaeological observations – history and ethnology provide alternative models, only archaeology can test their applicability in a given archaeological context. Otherwise we perpetrate the circularity of using the same ethnographic data to derive *and* to support an interpretation, often tacitly on the first leg and then explicitly on the second leg of the argument (Clarke, 1968, pp. 59–60, 442–3, 646–8; Levine, 1969; Hill in Longacre, 1970, p. 51).

(3) The exclusive use of historic-ethnographic models in archaeological interpretation must follow a tacit assumption that there has been no greater range of hominid behavioural and artefact variability over 2 million years than has been recorded in the miniscule sample of recent written histories and ethnographies – when surely we not only admit that the recorded variability is itself a tiny sample but that it is also the product of continuous adaptation from the infinitely greater set of fossil, now extinct, behaviour patterns that we wish to identify in order to trace and explain the disappearance of some and the survival of others. It would not only be poor science but it would be a scientific tragedy if we forced the social and economic life of *Australopithecus* into the recent pattern of either so-called modern 'Primitives' or the highly evolved pattern of the modern apes. Uniformitarianism has proved a principle applicable at only the crudest level in interpreting the past, whether in geology or archaeology; certainly the patterns and processes of past hominid behaviour are related to those still observable to this day but the survivors are transformed relations, with many new additions and lacking many forms once existing (Binford, 1968).

Whether it is a bone with a hole in it from the Upper Palaeolithic and an Eskimo analogue, or the social pattern of the Arikara and Murdock's social structures extracted from the files of the Cross-Cultural Survey of 250 recent societies, goodness of fit is not enough. It must be supplemented by a case for comparability and must be tested against the archaeological record; even then, the historic-ethnographic model is no more than a powerful supplementary means of generating hypotheses to be added to the *a priori* models and hypotheses imagined, deduced or dreamed by the archaeologist from the direct scrutiny of the archaeological evidence. Only the latter procedure could possibly reveal to us that in Neanderthal society, say, the women did the hunting, clustered in bands of up to 300, each served by only a handful of males.

The great majority of real-world models employed in archaeology arise from historical or ethnographic contexts and their records and artefacts (see Chapters 15 and 16). However, no source is excluded as a means of generating models and hypotheses to be tested in archaeological settings – the analogy may come from the movements of molecules in a gas, the mutual adjustments of magnets floating in a bath, or the boundary patterns of bubbles in a soap film. Models derived from the physical world, in its broadest sense, may be as homomorphic with an archaeological situation as any 'parallel' derived from ethnography or anthropology. Indeed, such a model is likely to be considerably more general and powerful than the latter class of analogy. The model derived from the physical world and the archaeological situation being modelled, upon closer investigation, may usually be shown to share latent structural similarities of a mathematical nature – the model from the physical world is but a particular representation, easily perceived, of a previously unnoticed and more general mathematical model. In this way, the molecular movements in a gas may model a situation in archaeological diffusion, but beneath both may lie the theory of probability and random interaction (see earlier sketch of Danubian I random walk settlement model). The polygonal territories of the floating magnets and the hexagonal patterns of bubbles in a soap film may illustrate the locational and territorial structures of archaeological settlement systems (Figs. 23.1–23.10) and geographical theory, but beneath both stretches the formal concepts of packing theory and optimized networks (Chorley and Haggett, 1967, plates 17.8–17.13).

Physical hardware and theoretical models derived from the real-world therefore take their place with artefact and structural models extracted from ethology, ethnology, sociology and anthropology. In their hardware forms these models approach the 'pole' of simple material analogues to the far east of the chart (Fig. 1.2) in a meridian shared by the artificial hardware models on the far west and we have now completed our cursory glance at the model map. This chart of operational models is not an original one, it is badly copied from the work of a distinguished early cartographer (Chorley in Chorley and Haggett, 1967, fig. 3.1). Neither is it the only possible map – other projections with different categorizations are both useful and desirable for plotting special courses. At least some of the monsters painted as lying in wait for the intrepid explorer may now be seen to be either avoidable or mythical and it may be admitted that a greater knowledge of model lands is preferable to navigation in ignorance. The fashionable nature of model cartography is then revealed not as a contemporary parlour game but rather as an important early elucidatory phase shared by primitive disciplines exploring their domains.

Discussion and speculation

Archaeological interpretation changes generation by generation, and we are accustomed to interpret this succession as 'progress'. But is it? There is an uncomfortable suspicion that much of this change is directionless and that the changes we may wish to see as cumulative progress towards more exact knowledge are little more than a succession of contemporary mythologies. If there is some justice in this view, then the cause is clear – only the explicit construction and testing of archaeological models can provide the progressive cycle by means of which fresh information is gained, theory is accumulated and the cumulative knowledge within the discipline expanded. The development of powerful and explicit archaeological operational models, however, itself depends on the careful consideration of the cognitive models that frame *their* development, the controlling models generated by the system of philosophy, paradigms, methodology and aims of archaeologists and archaeology (Fig. 1.1).

Following Kuhn's philosophy of disciplines we have noted that contemporary archaeology exhibits all the characteristics of diverse and rapid change on an almost international front. After perhaps half a century of relatively steady change within a compartmented but broadly universal artefact-based, particularizing, qualitative, culture historical paradigm expressed in literary narrative clichés, we now have at least four newly formulated competing approaches, which we have crudely designated the morphological, anthropological, ecological and geographical paradigms. These new paradigms are clearly themselves transient phenomena, although that may mean a generation or more of independent existence; they share a wider philosophy than artefact classification, and a generalizing, quantitative, experimental attitude expressed in literary and symbolic jargon. They are also cross-cut by a number of new methodologies, which may change independently of the paradigms that share them (Fig. 1.16). This broad common basis to the group of currently rather partisan paradigms suggests at least the possibility that they will in due course merge within a new conformity. Nevertheless, at the moment each paradigm is intent on asserting its reasonable claims to existence and discarding the shackles that formerly bound it within the 'traditionalist' paradigm. Since we have argued that the proper use of our operational models will be controlled by our preferred paradigm, let us take a brief look at the positions of these freshly polarized positions (Clarke, 1969, 1970b).

The position of the *morphological paradigm* embraces the expanding nucleus of studies whose main objectives are the cross-cultural definition of widely

43

NEW ARCHAEOLOGY	NEW PARADIGMS			
NEW METHODOLOGY	*Morphological Paradigm*	*Anthropological Paradigm*	*Ecological Paradigm*	*Geographical Paradigm*
New Field Methodology	Problem focused excavation, Area study and site system approach, Sampling considerations and methods, Pre-excavation and post-depositional model studies, Full use of scientific aids for location, processing and analysis of sites and deposits, including fine sieving, flotation and centrifuging, etc.			
Model Methodology	Explicit development, borrowing and modification of appropriate models; thus Fig. 1.2: Observations, Models, Hypotheses, Experimentation and testing, Analysis of results, Interim conclusions and theory, Reappraisal of observations: repeat cycle.			
System Theory Methodology	Cybernetic models for the pattern of system variables and their relationships, correlations, etc., or decisions and the flow of energy, mass, commodities, and information changes.			
Quantitative Methodology	Counting and measuring *significant* variables and parameters to give values to the system models.			
Mathematical Methodology	Natural languages and machinery for the expression of generalizations, especially quantifiable ones, Mathematical notation and expression, Statistical notation and analyses, Numerical taxonomic expression and measurements, Probability theory and methods, Error and confidence estimates, etc.			
Computer Methodology	Analog and digital techniques for experimentation, simulation, analysis, visual display and graphics.			

FIG. 1.16. An earlier diagram suggested that changes in contemporary paradigms and methodology are the main stimuli that lead to new archaeological views (Fig. 1.1). This figure defines the 'New Archaeology' as a bundle of such newly focused paradigms (pp. 6–7), bound by a related ideology and cross-cut by new developments in methodology. In reality, the discrete orthogonally intersecting categories must be conceived as irregular, blurred and mutually intersecting complex sets.

general regularities in the structural morphology of archaeological entities, as defined in terms of their components, the integration of these entities in yet higher organizations, and the exposition of the grammar of their developmental transformations (Clarke, 1968, fig. 40; Deetz, 1967, fig. 17). The studies within this nucleus are much concerned with the basic common particles of 'implement-focused' archaeology – attributes, artefacts, types, assemblages, cultures, culture groups and other complexes of material artefacts – together with their static and dynamic configurations. The basis upon which this approach is founded seems to be an explicit modern reformulation of the Montelian Principle that every artefact entity is related to every other artefact entity, but near entities are more related than distant entities, where 'nearness' is a three-dimensional measure of nearness in space and time distribution, nearness in associations, and nearness in taxonomic affinity (see Chapters 8 and 9, and contrary view, pp. 156–63).

The advocates of this approach are perhaps more intimately concerned with the mathematical, statistical and computing machinery of the 'new methodology' than any other group, but not exclusively so. This concern obviously follows the attempt to quantify and measure 'nearness' in the relationships observed in the data and may perhaps lead to some kind of 'taxonometrics'.

The critics of this developing polarization suggest that it is too much concerned with crude, generalized regularities and that it is merely an abstract and sterile revival of the old typological and classificatory approaches of the last century, decked out in borrowed finery. These accusations imply an unduly atomistic approach with a tendency to treat complex entities as billiard balls, without sufficient regard for the social and ecological environments of the once living contexts. The partisans would dismiss these charges as romantic misrepresentations of the initial treatment of empirical data – claiming that the individual sources of variability sought by the other paradigms may *only* be recovered and identified when separated from the despised general regularities shared by structurally comparable entities. They would further point out that archaeological classification has remained a contentious and intuitive skill because its purposes and procedures have never been subjected to explicit discussion, measurement and quantitative tests. Indeed, the morphologists have succeeded in establishing that behind the seeming first-order information on the presence–absence and dimensions of attributes, once thought to have been the prime factors in archaeological classification, lies a second order in which every attribute itself has attributes of space and time distribution, association patterns, and affinity with other attributes. Thus the gap between taxonomic classification and intuitive classification is not fundamentally altered by differing purposes, but only separated by the difficulty of putting into explicit practice procedures that may be furtively half-accomplished in the brain (Clarke, 1970a, chs. 3 and 4).

The *anthropological paradigm* reflects the interesting nucleus of studies that focus on the relationships between patterning and variability in archaeological data and patterning and variability in the social structures behind that data. The philosophy involved seeks a probabilistic mean path between the usual archaeological positions, which either assert that nothing can be deduced about the social attributes of archaeological entities, or tacitly assumes a naively simple equivalence at the other extreme. The partisans point out that social conventions and organizations, although weird and wonderful arrays of strange stochastic elements, nevertheless represent important and successful adaptive mechanisms. Where they are adaptively useful they will arise again and again and we then note them as an anthropological regularity or pattern. Where they are or become adaptively neutral they remain idiosyncratic, unlikely to be repeated and therefore not a recurrent pattern; where a social structure becomes disadvantageous and non-adaptive it dies out. Thus social conventions and organizations such as kinship and taboo systems possess important adaptive qualities, they vary with environment and as such are an interesting source of archaeological variability (see Chapters 2, 6 and 7).

However, the anthropological approach goes further than a restricted interest in social structure. The proper use of anthropological and ethnological evidence and models in archaeological interpretation is a central concern. Here, too, there are clear emergent attempts to introduce quantification and measurement from anthropological analogues, if only to produce archaeological discussions in terms of appropriate orders of magnitude – the sizes of social units, crop yields under various conditions, the numbers of pots a household smashes in a year, the number of axes a man uses in a lifetime – crude improvizations in 'ethnometrics'.

The critics of this paradigm find its practitioners anthropologically under-equipped and over-naive (Allen and Richardson, 1971). The machinery for expressing the relationships between archaeological and social entities are thought to be inadequate, and doubt is expressed about the possibility of separately distinguishing the archaeological variability arising from social sources and variability arising from other sources. The partisans react by pointing out control cases where variability in social structure is indubitably correlated with variability in material artefacts. Then, it is argued, although your specialist material may not appear to preserve this category of variability – in stone artefacts, perhaps – at least it is a potential source of variability which must be sought for and allowed for.

The practitioners within the *ecological paradigm* follow a contrasting theme, which may be epitomized by the comment of Reed (1963, p. 205): 'who – except possibly archaeologists – would dig for artefacts when there are bones to be salvaged', where seeds, pollen and other floral, faunal and environmental evidence might be substituted for 'bones'. They would see their sphere as the study of the relationships between configurations of archaeological material and the environmental context in which it was once set, the mutual relations between such systems and their local ecology, together with the temporal and regional adaptive changes of these systems. This bold band talks of habitats, demes, clines, niches, trophic levels, biomes and ecosystems, and would see archaeology as a biological science connecting hominid behaviour with the variety in the environment of the globe in terms of energy exchange systems.

The cultural ecologists point with disdain to the infinitesimal pedantry of the archaeological taxonomist and to the contradictory conclusions of decades of dusty categorization more akin to philately than to the study of the unique 2-million-year-deep record of hominid behaviour patterns. They would contrast this with their increasingly quantified catchment analysis studies and the potentially fundamental measurements of energy flow and activity efficiency in energetics and thermodynamics (see Chapters 13, 14, 15, 16, 17 and 18 of this volume).

Unabashed by these gibes, the critics of the ecological paradigm claim that the study has simply elevated the bathwater to a greater level of importance than the baby. The approach is improperly equipped to formulate biological statements, it is currently naive in its understanding of the samples that constitute its own raw material and anachronistically determinist in making insufficient allowance for the idiosyncratic degrees of freedom permitted to human activities in even the most constrained conditions. At its worst, the ecological paradigm merely substitutes the differential minutiae of bone or seed measurements for those of typology and transfers doubtful behavioural generalities from medieval peasants and song birds to prehistoric hominids, whilst its reports often regress to the level of the nineteenth century, simply illustrating a few archaeological 'belles pièces'.

The *geographical paradigm* concentrates instead on the evidence relating within-site and between-site activity patterns with spatial patterning in artefact, feature, structure and site distributions; the study of archaeological sites as systems within systems of sites territorially distributed over landscapes. Starting with the within-site approach of architectural locational theory, sites are seen as encapsulating complex sets of man–man relationships in a spatial system in which activity patterns demand a building stock infrastructure, which, once built, itself restricts the further location of activities (Fig. 1.17) (March and Echenique, 1971). This model may then be extended to the scale

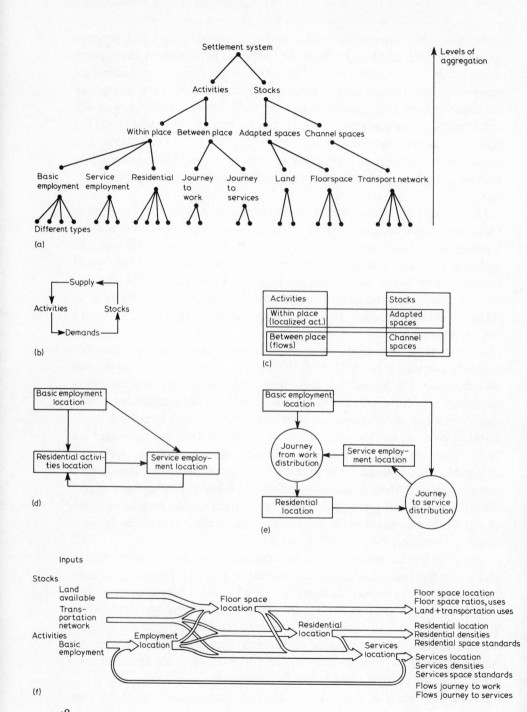

of between-site relationships within settlement systems or hierarchies. Space and surface then become relativistic notions so that camp sites, farmsteads, villages, hill forts, oppida, and other extinct and contemporary settlement forms, influence the properties of the space around them; varying patterns of human activity thus form fields of influence which distort the properties of space (Harvey, 1969, p. 209). The relationships of a site system or artefact distribution become relative to some surface – it may be a two-dimensional map, a three-dimensional topography, or a demographic, environmental, economic iso-cost surface; regularities and patterning may appear if an appropriate surface is mapped and necessary transformations employed (Fig. 1.4) (Harvey, 1969, pp. 219–29).

Archaeologists working in this area can make use of the great body of locational theory and the well-established methods of measuring spatial relationships or quantifying site utilities (Cole and King, 1969). Thus Zipf's principle that the volume of activity over distance declines as a function of the distance from the reference site provides a frame for archaeological catchment area analysis and the Chinese Box territorial models (Figs. 18.2, 20.1, 21.9) (see Chapters 18–24). Even gravity models may be employed to simulate interaction between activities within sites, or between sites within systems (Fig. 1.18). These techniques have already been used with great success to model and predict the relative locations of thirty-three pre-Hittite towns in Bronze Age Anatolia, for example (Tobler and Wineburg, 1971). These and many other theories and measures are fundamentally relevant to the spatial information enshrined in archaeological observations.

The critics of this approach are vociferous (Taylor, 1970). They rightly criticize the unthinking transference of geographical models derived from perfect information and modern world situations to fragmentary time-palimpsest archaeological samples, imperfectly known and in prehistoric contexts. However, the partisans observe that this is simply a criticism of the improper use of models, and claim that it is nevertheless possible to adapt and adopt

FIG. 1.17. Some elementary architectural models for the analysis of within-site structures and activity patterns (Echenique, 1971). (*a*) Levels of resolution of settlement models. (*b*) Relationship at the first level of disaggregation, by which activities demand stock of infrastructure; once built it restricts the further location of activities. (*c*) Relationships between the elements at the second level of disaggregation. (*d*) The structure of the Lowry within-place location model. (*e*) The Garin-Lowry activity location model in which the interactions of within-place activities are expressed as flows (between-place activities). (*f*) The simple static model contains the interaction of all the elements of the settlement spatial structure at the third level of disaggregation (stocks and activities).

49

geographical models, after carefully rethinking them from the base upwards. In their more excited moments the partisans suggest that the locational theory of the geographers is a post-industrial, recent limiting case of an as yet latent and more general locational theory. Thus geographers regard settlement location, and therefore the central place theory describing it, as an economic process to which non-economic processes contribute a 'noise' or error-term

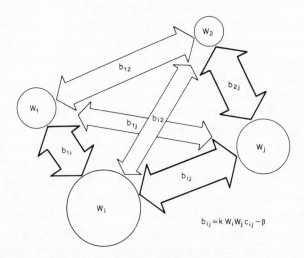

$$b_{ij} = k\, W_i W_j\, c_{ij}^{-\beta}$$

FIG. 1.18. Gravity model to simulate interaction between activities within sites, or between sites within systems (Echenique, 1971). The interaction (b_{ij}) between two within-place activities $(W_i$ and $W_j)$ is directly proportional to the product of the within-place activities and inversely proportional to some power of the cost of travel $(c_{ij} - \beta)$ separating them.

$$b_{ij} = k\,\frac{W_i W_j}{c_{ij}\beta}$$

where
b_{ij} = traffic between zone i and j
k = constant of proportionality
W_i = within-place activity (e.g. residents) at zone i
W_j = within-place activity (e.g. residents) at zone j
c_{ij} = cost of travel between zones i and j
β = parameter

element (Harvey, 1969, pp. 118–120, 128, 139). However, archaeological and ethnographic data rather suggest that central place theory is the limiting case – observed for modern, Western communities in which the economic factor has been deliberately and especially intensified – of a more general locational theory in which site location is a multifactor process, which in different contexts may have differently weighted and selected variables.

Thus aspects of central place theory appear to work where they ought not to work, in contexts where optimalization, rationalized planning, even towns and villages are not found, in systems of base camps, cemeteries, communal tombs, and hill forts (Figs. 1.7, 1.19) (Clarke, 1968, figs. 113–15; Carter, 1970, fig. V). The more general theory seems to stem from the complex operation of

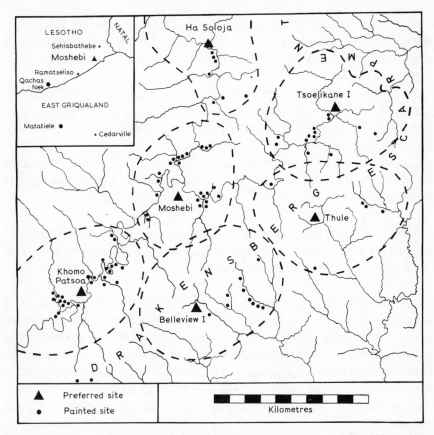

FIG. 1.19. A study of the site categories, site systems, base camps and satellite painted sites of prehistoric hunter-fisher-gatherers in eastern Lesotho (from Carter, 1970).

packing theory upon mutually adjusted populations and their material insignia, in which a certain range of proximity of certain elements, sites or resources is essential for the system's functioning. In this view, long-term adaptive human behavioural, demographic, social and environmental processes dominate the satisfaction of mere economic requirements. If there is any truth in these partisan thoughts, and they at least make stimulating speculation, then the 2 million years record of archaeology and recent ethnology must have a major role to play in the elucidation of this important general behavioural and locational theory.

At the minimal level, the geographical paradigm in archaeology would rest its case on three salient points:

(1) Even if it may not be possible to recover the contemporary elements in an archaeological site system, at least it must be admitted that different kinds of site existed in systems of relationships over landscapes and must be so hypothesized.

(2) It should be possible to postulate an 'idealized site system' from the integration of the fragmentary evidence of neighbouring regions; like an 'ideal gas' this model then becomes predictive and allows itself to be tested and refined against evidence and experiment.

(3) Indeed, inter-site adjustment across landscape *is* observed in complex archaeological data and *must* be explained; although the explanations may in many cases discover the distribution to be a sampling artefact.

Now, if we make the vain attempt to detach ourselves from the tyranny of the particular paradigms, some interesting common elements emerge from this explosion of anti-traditionalist views:

(1) The new paradigms mark the full recognition that the domain of archaeology is greater than the realm of material implements. They show that there is a wider information pool than simply observations on material culture, and even material culture is seen to contain more and different kinds of information than previously assumed. The material equipment must be put in perspective as only *one* category of the artefacts of hominid behaviour – all of which preserve for us some overlapping information on the activities of our ancestors.

(2) The new paradigms individually represent the exploitation of particular new spheres of information – morphological, social, environmental and spatial. They are preoccupied with the patterning and variability of their own limited information pool; indeed one would have a greater confidence in the claimed identifications of particular sources of variability if each researcher had taken into account the variability sources sought by the others, and other than the one he was determined to find. Most archaeological data embrace many sources of variability in a cumulative but non-additive pattern, including very gross sampling sources of imposed variability (Figs. 5.1–5.3).

(3) The preoccupation with single aspects of variability in the archaeological record is carefully justified in some cases, in others it is the accident of the exclusive interest of the observer – a victim of his own controlling models and the dimensions of variability peculiar to the material that he knows well and extrapolates to the rest of archaeology. In the Palaeolithic we have stone plus a little bone and a few sites; in the Neolithic we have stone plus pottery and more sites; in the Metal Age we have stone, pots, metals, many sites of many categories, and many house and settlement plans. It is not surprising that each paradigm pursues its source of information in restricted archaeological contexts where temporal scale and observations are of a special kind.

(4) Finally, we may note that each paradigm is struggling to produce a scheme of measurement and quantification in relation to its own dimensions – taxonometrics, ethnometrics, energetics, measures of utility, relative distance and interaction. Contrary to common opinion archaeology is made difficult by the very variety of potentially measurable elements and the choice which this presents.

Do these developments represent a 'New Archaeology'? If so, how does it relate to 'Traditionalist Archaeology'? Well, of course, it depends on the point of view of the observer. When viewed at a fine level all the strands of the 'new' developments go back into the last century and beyond. When viewed at a coarse level what emerge are new configurations of old elements within a rather different philosophy, with different modes of expression and a different approach to those that preceded it and distinguished from them by a spasm of greatly increased rate of change and innovation, when compared with the preceding phase of development. Precariously trying to preserve our balance, these 'new' developments would appear to be different but not necessarily better than their traditional antecedents, which continue in a flourishing form. They would, however, appear to have rapidly expanded into hitherto little-explored areas of the archaeological domain and to have infiltrated freshly available niches with a vigorous capacity to make fresh contributions to the discipline as a whole.

It is hardly surprising that when questioned some archaeologists would say that a 'New Archaeology' does not exist – it does not exist for them; others would claim that it does exist but then differ about what it is, depending upon which of the new paradigms they espouse. It is clear, at least, that the term 'New Archaeology' has been directly borrowed from the infant 'New Geography'. That prodigy seems to have been named by analogy with the Renaissance and in memory of Galileo's fundamental treatise on physics and mechanics, 'Two New Sciences' (1610), and Bacon's 'The New System' (*Novum Organum*, 1620). In terms of these analogies it is quite clear what 'New' means – it implies a new philosophical position, an experimental, generalizing, theory-developing approach, with an empirical emphasis upon the formulation and testing of hypotheses, and following Bacon in his glorification of mathematics as 'the Queen of the Sciences' and Galileo's dictum that 'the book of Nature is written in a Mathematical language; without its help it is impossible to comprehend a single work therein'.

Under this view there is a case for extending the nomenclature to the 'New Archaeology', which may be represented by the bundle of newly focused paradigms bound by their new ideology and cross-cut by the new methodology, of which explicit model-using is a fundamental part (Fig. 1.16). It is then possible to set up a contrasting impression of the 'New' and 'Traditionalist'

	Traditionalist archaeology	*New archaeology*
Philosophy	Historical	Experimental
Approach	Qualitative	Quantitative
	Particularizing	Generalizing
Modes of expression	Literary	Symbolic
	Narrative	Jargon
Attitude	Isolationist and authoritarian	Condisciplinary and anarchic

archaeology, which antagonists are quick to see as a new versus old confrontation. However, as we shall argue, both approaches have their vices and virtues, the new will become old and the old will continue and give rise to yet newer paradigms; their roles are complementary and mutually useful. For example, the mathematical and model symbolism of the 'New Archaeology' communicates to a wider audience of scientists and mathematicians, whereas the style of 'Traditionalist' literature is more acceptable to the non-scientist. In other words, together they will draw upon a greatly enlarged pool of informants and information, and the artificial confrontation may be avoided by combining the elements from each column in many different ways for many different purposes.

New Archaeology

(1) *Experimental.* Let us assume (or if we assume) *a*, *b*, *c*, then *d*, *e*, *f* should follow. Question – do we observe *d*, *e*, *f* Experiment – Answer. The development of a model with explicit assumptions– formation of hypotheses from the

model – test the hypotheses experimentally, or test between the consequences thereof.

(2) *Quantitative.* Counting and measuring reduce vagueness, increase specificity, upgrade standards of argument, allow error estimates, numerical manipulation and explicit *testing* of model hypotheses.

(3) *Generalizing.* It is necessary to generalize in order to make probabilistic predictions about some class of items; we must generalize in order that we may particularize more powerfully. The inevitable use of classes of items requires appropriate classifications. In archaeology some information is more important than other information for certain purposes; therefore what is classificatory information depends upon the purpose.

(4) *Symbolic.* The use of mathematical, statistical and numerical languages in addition to prose. Symbolic languages are the natural mode of expression for generalizations; in addition they are interdisciplinary and international means of communication over and above ordinary language, a series of *lingua franca.* Conveniently, mathematics solves puzzles even before a real-world example of the puzzle has been identified.

(5) *Jargon.* The use of condensed special-purpose code to express complex analogies; ugly and deplorable from the point of view of prose but aesthetics are not the prime criteria of communication within specialized disciplines; in any event, yesterday's jargon is tomorrow's prose (Clarke, 1970, p. 26).

(6) *Overall attitude.* Out-turned, across archaeological specializations and between disciplines, over paradigms, through regional schools and linguistic blocs (Kolchina and Shera, 1970); hence the role of interconnecting jargon, symbolic languages and the interdisciplinary exchange of isomorphic models (Clarke, 1968, p. 646). Although fraught with dangers this attitude allows the possibility that archaeology can make outward contributions to other disciplines, an essential feature if the discipline is to survive; this outward contribution has already begun on a small scale towards branches of mathematics, computer studies and classification, and to the social and behavioural sciences. Within the discipline a fresh freedom is allowed to choose alternative space scales, different mapping surfaces, varied geometries; we can use diverse process time scales, alternative mathematical notations and variform symbolic languages; we can select different frames of reference, different sample spaces, classifications, entities, attributes, relationships and parameters. What may appear irregular under one view may emerge as a patterned and powerful regularity under another transformation.

Conclusion

It has already been suggested that the contemporary flowering of rival archaeological paradigms is a transient phenomenon and that these may, in due course, recombine within a new conformity founded on the broad common basis in methodology and ideology. However, this integration cannot take the form of a simple physical merging of views, or the tying together of a bundle of unrelated approaches with decorative ribbon, which so frequently stands for an integrated interdisciplinary approach. We have seen that preoccupation with a single paradigm leads to a dangerous preoccupation with a single set of sources of variability, leading only to an unbalanced interpretation and a new sectarianism. Instead we must turn to our advantage the many sources of archaeological variability and the many disciplinary domains that specially describe them. This can be achieved by using models from other disciplines to generate hypotheses about a particular archaeological situation and then using the archaeological evidence to test those hypotheses; similarly, archaeological models describing different sources of variability can be used to control and test one another. Thus non-artefactual data should be used to try and test hypotheses derived from other classes of data, and vice versa. In all this, the testing of models and hypotheses will be much enhanced by the embryonic developments in quantification, which we have already noted within all the separate paradigms.

In so far as there might be said to be a New Archaeology with a New Methodology and a New Ideology, we can see that it is a composite but convergent development of much older ideas – it is only new in terms of the particular patterning and integration of older elements, and in its quite proper attempt to explore the boundary possibilities of archaeology and to open up new ground. It does not replace Old Archaeology but rather augments it, as we learn from the theory of the cumulative development of paradigms. However, neither may these new developments simply be dismissed on the basis of their fashionable vogue and contemporary jargon; these are part of its outward connections. The New Archaeology has already begun to yield new kinds of information, to offer new solutions to some old problems and to show that other old problems were caused by attempting the impossible with the implausible. In addition, the strong theoretical content of the New Archaeology offers the beginnings for a strong and international body of explicit archaeological theory and methodology – where it should be remembered that a healthy discipline is defined not only by its particular body of observations but by the vigorous network of theory and methodology reticulating its parts.

56

Indeed, it is the corpus of theory and methodology of greater than regional and sectarian importance that is the vital element that serves to coagulate those parts within the whole of one discipline – the theory that makes explicit how we do what we already do intuitively, and more, providing the basic tenets of the discipline in a form as appropriate in Peru as Persia, Australia as Alaska, Sweden as Scotland, on material from the twentieth millennium B.C. to the second millennium A.D.

It is clearly going to be very important to avoid needless and wasteful conflict of all kinds, between partisans of the various paradigms, or between the generations over the New Archaeology, much of which is unsound (intermediate imperfect), and Traditionalist Archaeology, much of which is equally unsound but which is nevertheless the foundation of much that is useful (complementary not rival elements in the same mosaic). Statistical, taxonomic and computer archaeology are here to stay, together with the morphological, anthropological, ecological and geographical approaches. But they will very rapidly fade into perspective as means towards ends, intellectual machinery, which, as always, may be employed usefully or stupidly. The shock and novelty of these innovations will surely be as incomprehensible to future archaeologists as the terror caused by the early motor cars is now incomprehensible to us. Non-numerical 'old archaeologists' will be delighted to find that their potential is in no way diminished and that there will always remain scope for an infinite amount of valuable narrative synthesis, and high-level intuitive speculation – except that *now* their research students will test their professors' dicta and not simply accept them.

References

ALLEN, W. L. and RICHARDSON, J. B. (1971) The reconstruction of kinship from archaeological data: the concepts, the methods and the feasibility. *American Antiquity*, **36** (1), 41–53.

ASCHER, R. (1961) Experimental archaeology. *American Anthropologist*, **63** (4), 793–816.

BEACH, E. F. (1957) *Economic Models*. New York: Wiley.

BINFORD, L. R. (1968) Post-Pleistocene adaptations. In BINFORD, S. R. and BINFORD, L. R. (eds.) *New Perspectives in Archeology*, 313–41. Chicago: Aldine.

BINFORD, L. R. and BINFORD, S. R. (1966) A preliminary analysis of functional variability in the Mousterian of Levallois facies. *American Anthropologist*, **68**, 2 (2), 238–95.

BIRABON, J. N. (1971) Les méthodes de la démographie préhistorique. *International Population Conference, London 1969*, **4**, 2315–20. Liège.

CARNEIRO, R. L. (1960) Slash-and-burn agriculture: a closer look at its implication for settlement patterns. In WALLACE, A. F. C. (ed.) *Men and Cultures*. Philadelphia: University of Pennsylvania Press.

CARTER, P. L. (1970) Moshebi's shelter: excavation and exploitation in eastern Lesotho. *Lesotho,* 1.

CHANG, K. C. (ed.) (1968) *Settlement Archaeology*. Palo Alto, Calif.: National Press.

CHORLEY, R. J. and HAGGETT, P. (eds.) (1967) *Models in Geography*. London: Methuen.

CLARKE, D. L. (1968) *Analytical Archaeology*. London: Methuen.

CLARKE, D. L. (1969) Towards analytical archaeology: new directions in the interpretative thinking of British archaeologists. In EHRICH, R. W. (ed.) *Flagstaff Symposium* (in press).

CLARKE, D. L. (1970a) *Beaker Pottery of Great Britain and Ireland*. Cambridge: Cambridge University Press.

CLARKE, D. L. (1970b) Analytical archaeology: epilogue. *Norwegian Archaeological Review,* 3, 25–33.

COE, M. D. and FLANNERY, K. V. (1964) Microenvironments and Mesoamerican prehistory. *Science,* 143 (3607), 650–4.

COE, M. D. and FLANNERY, K. V. (1967) *Early Cultures and Human Ecology in South Coastal Guatemala*. Washington: Smithsonian Press.

COLE, J. P. and KING, C. A. M. (1969) *Quantitative Geography: Techniques and Theories in Geography*. London: Wiley.

COLES, J. M. (1966) Experimental archaeology. *Proceedings of the Society of Antiquaries of Scotland,* 99, 1–20.

COOK, S. F. and HEIZER, R. F. (1969) Relationships among houses, settlement areas and population in aboriginal California. In CHANG, K. C. (ed.) *Settlement Archaeology,* 79–116. Palo Alto, Calif.: National Press.

CURRY, L. (1967) Central places in the random spatial economy. *Journal of Regional Science,* 7 (2), supp., 217–38. Philadelphia.

DEETZ, J. D. F. (1965) *The Dynamics of Stylistic Change in Arikara Ceramics*. Illinois Studies in Anthropology No. 4. Urbana: University of Illinois Press.

DEETZ, J. D. F. (1967) *Invitation to Archaeology*. New York: Natural History Press.

DORAN, J. (1970) Systems theory, computer simulations and archaeology. *World Archaeology,* 1 (3), 289–98.

ECHENIQUE, M. (1971) A model of the urban spatial structure. *Architectural Design,* 41, 278–9.

FLANNERY, K. V. (1968) Archaeological systems theory and early Mesopotamia. In MEGGERS, B. J. (ed.) *Anthropological Archaeology in the Americas*. Washington: Anthropological Society.

FREEMAN, J. D. (1955) *Iban Agriculture*. Colonial Research Studies No. 18. London: H.M.S.O.

GARDIN, J. C. (1965) Reconstructing an economic network in the ancient Near East with the aid of a computer. In HYMES, D. (ed.) *The Use of Computers in Anthropology*. The Hague: Mouton.

GARDIN, J. C. (ed.) (1970) *Archéologie et Calculateurs*. Paris: Centre National de la Recherche Scientifique.

GARVIN, P. L. (1965) Computer processing and cultural data: problems of method. In HYMES, D. (ed.) *The Use of Computers in Anthropology*. The Hague: Mouton.

GEORGE, F. H. (1970) Heuristics: short cuts to better use of computers. *The Times*, 26 June 1970, 25.

GLOVER, I. C. (1969) The use of factor analysis for the discovery of artefact types. *Mankind*, 7 (1), 36–51.

GOULD, P. R. (1969) Man against his environment: a game theoretic framework. In VAYDA, A. P. (ed.) *Environment and Cultural Behaviour*. New York: Natural History Press.

HAGGETT, P. (1965) *Locational Analysis in Human Geography*. London: Arnold.

HALSBURY, EARL OF (1968) 'Time's Arrow': an informational theory treatment. *The Human Agent*, edited for the Royal Institute of Philosophy Lectures, vol. 1, 1966–7, London: Macmillan.

HARVEY, D. (1969) *Explanation in Geography*. London: Arnold.

HESSE, M. B. (1963) *Models and Analogies in Science*. London: Sheed & Ward.

HIGGS, E. (ed.) (1972) *Cambridge Papers in the Early History of Agriculture*. Cambridge: Cambridge University Press.

HIGHAM, C. F. W. (1968) Patterns of prehistoric economic exploitation on the Alpine foreland. *Vierteljahrsschrift der Naturforschenden Gesellschaft in Zürich*, **113** (1), 41–92.

HILL, J. N. (1970) *Broken K Pueblo: Prehistoric Social Organization in the American Southwest*. Anthropological Papers of the University of Arizona No. 18.

HODSON, F. R. (1970) Cluster analysis and archaeology: some new developments and applications. *World Archaeology*, **1** (3), 299–320.

ISAAC, G. LL. (1969) Studies of early culture in east Africa. *World Archaeology*, **1** (1), 1–28.

JEWELL, P. A. (ed.) (1963) *The Experimental Earthwork on Overton Down, Wiltshire, 1960*. London: British Association for the Advancement of Science.

JEWELL, P. A. and DIMBLEBY, G. W. (1966) The experimental earthwork on Overton Down, Wiltshire, England: the first four years. *Proceedings of the Prehistoric Society*, **32**, 313–42.

KEMP, W. R. (1971) The flow of energy in a hunting society. *Scientific American*, **224** (3), 105–15.

KOLCHINA, B. A. and SHERA, Y. A. (eds.) (1970) *Statistiko-kombinatornye metody v arkheologii*. Moscow: Akad. Nauk SSSR, Inst. Arkheologii.

KUHN, T. S. (1970) *The Structure of Scientific Revolutions*. 2nd ed. Chicago: University of Chicago Press.

LEVINE, M. H. (1969) Interpreting Palaeolithic art: some methodological considerations. In EHRICH, R. W. (ed.) *Flagstaff Symposium* (in press).

LEWIS, B. N. and WOOLFENDEN, P. J. (1969) *Algorithms and Logical Trees: A Self-Instructional Course*. Cambridge: Cambridge Algorithms Press.

LONGACRE, W. A. (ed.) (1970) *Reconstructing Prehistoric Pueblo Societies*. Albuquerque: University of New Mexico Press.

MACNEISH, R. S. (1961) *First Annual Report of the Tehuacan Archaeological–Botanical Project*. Andover, Mass.: Phillips Academy.

MACNEISH, R. S. (1962) *Second Annual Report of the Tehuacan Archaeological–Botanical Project*. Andover, Mass.: Phillips Academy.

MCPHERRON, A. (1967) *Jutunen Site*. Anthropological Papers No. 30. Ann Arbor: University of Michigan Press.

MARCH, L., ECHENIQUE, M. *et al.* (1971) Models of environment. *Architectural Design*, **41**, 275–320.

MEGGERS, B. J. (ed.) (1968) *Anthropological Archaeology in the Americas*. Washington Anthropological Society.

MELLAART, J. (1966) Excavations at Çatal Hüyük. *Anatolian Studies*, **16**, 26.

NAGEL, E. (1961) *The Structure of Science*. New York: Harcourt, Brace & World.

NEWCOMB, R. M. (1968) Geographical location analysis and Iron Age settlement in West Penwith. *Cornish Archaeology*, **7**, 5–14.

NEWCOMB, R. M. (1970) A model of a mystery: the medieval parish as a spatial system. *Skrifter fra Geografisk Institut ved Aarhus Universitet*, **28**.

RAPOPORT, A. (1953) *Operational Philosophy*. New York: Wiley.

RAPPAPORT, R. A. (1971) The flow of energy in an agricultural society. *Scientific American*, **224** (3), 117–32.

REED, C. A. (1963) Osteo-archaeology. In BROTHWELL, D. and HIGGS, E. (eds.) *Science in Archaeology*, 204–16. London: Thames & Hudson.

STONE, E. H. (1924) *The Stones of Stonehenge*. London: Robert Scott.

TAYLOR, C. C. (1971) The study of settlement patterns in pre-Saxon Britain. In UCKO, P., DIMBLEBY, G. W. and TRINGHAM, R. (eds.) *Settlement Patterns and Urbanisation*. London: Duckworth.

TOBLER, W. R. (1969) A computer movie simulating urban growth in the Detroit region. *International Geographical Union Commission on Quantitative Geography*.

TOBLER, W. R. and WINEBURG, S. (1971) A Cappadocian speculation. *Nature*, **231**, 39–41.

TRIGGER, B. C. (1966) Settlement archaeology: its goals and promises. *American Antiquity*, **32**, 149–60.

TRIGGER, B. C. (1968) *Beyond History: The Methods of Prehistory*. New York: Holt, Rinehart & Winston.

UCKO, P., DIMBLEBY, G. W. and TRINGHAM, R. (eds.) (1971) *Settlement Patterns and Urbanisation*. London: Duckworth.

VAJDA, S. (1960) *Introduction to Linear Programming and the Theory of Games*. London: Methuen.

WALKER, I. C. (1967) Statistical models for dating clay pipe fragments. *Post-Medieval Archaeology*, **1**, 90–101.

WHALLON, R. (1968) Investigations of late prehistorical social organization in New York. In BINFORD, S. R. and BINFORD, L. R. (eds.) *New Perspectives in Archeology*. Chicago: Aldine.

2

The methodological debate in contemporary archaeology: a model

J. N. HILL
University of California, Los Angeles, U.S.A.

The discipline of archaeology is no longer as disciplined as it was ten or fifteen years ago.[1] It is currently in a state of flux, particularly with respect to theory, goals and methods. The reason for this is that traditional theories and methods have failed to solve many of the problems for which they were intended – namely those involving the adequate description of prehistoric behaviour, and explanation of variability and change in this behaviour.

This intellectual dissatisfaction is not new, of course (see esp. Tallgren, 1937; Steward and Setzler, 1938; Taylor, 1948; Sears, 1961; Binford, 1962, 1964, 1965, 1967, 1968a; Adams, 1968). Taylor's book, *A Study of Archeology* (1948), was a monumental attempt both to point out our failures and to construct some new theory and method. In the years since his presentation of the 'conjunctive approach' there have been other 'approaches' to claim our attention – notably the 'interdisciplinary approach', the 'ecological approach', the 'settlement approach' and the 'systems approach' (cf. Adams, 1968). All these developments have been productive, but they are by no means panaceas. What is most evident is that the 1960s has been a period of intradisciplinary controversy, with defenders of various views in healthy debate.

This kind of intellectual ferment is known to occur in any science immediately preceding and during what Thomas Kuhn (1962) has called a 'Scientific Revolution'. In his book, *The Structure of Scientific Revolutions*, Kuhn points out that the growth of a science can be described in terms of relatively long periods of great stability ('normal science'), punctuated by rather abrupt changes, which revolutionize the entire framework of the science. Such a revolution is marked primarily by a change in *theory* (or 'paradigm', in Kuhn's terms), and it results from the fact that the traditional paradigm has not satisfactorily served to explain the kinds of observations it was designed to explain (Kuhn, 1962, pp. 52–65). The change is characterized as follows:

The transition from a paradigm in crisis to a new one from which a new tradition of normal science can emerge is far from a cumulative process, one achieved by an articulation or extension of the old paradigm. Rather it is a reconstruction of the field from new fundamentals, a reconstruction that changes some of the field's most elementary theoretical generalizations as well as many of its paradigm methods and applications. (Kuhn, 1962, p. 84)

My own feeling is that such a paradigm change is now taking shape, in the form of the 'New Archaeology' or 'Systems Archaeology' (cf. esp. Binford, 1962, 1964, 1965, 1967, 1968a; Binford and Binford, 1968). The basic change being proposed is not one of either general or specific method, but rather one of theory. It is a change in archaeological 'world view' – in the ways in which we understand the nature and operation of culture, and the way we explain cultural variability and change.[2] While this paradigm is not yet well formalized, it has already provoked some heated argument (see Chang, 1967a; Flannery, 1967; Sabloff and Willey, 1967; Adams, 1968; Binford, 1968a, 1968c; Taylor, 1969, p. 383).

The degree to which these changes represent a 'Revolution' cannot yet be decided, of course, and I will not argue it here; this is a methodological paper. The point I am making is simply that there is an intimate relationship between theory and method, and it is likely that the general and specific methods employed by 'New Archaeologists' cannot be fully appreciated without first understanding the underlying theory (cf. Section 3 of this chapter). A change in theory, as Kuhn points out, is always accompanied by 'a decisive difference in the modes of solution' (1962, p. 84; see also Nagel, 1967, p. 3).

In any event, the current controversy has brought our methods as well as our theories into question, and my purpose in this paper is to examine the crux of the methodological debate – the question of whether our research should proceed in a primarily *inductive* manner, or whether we should emphasize a *deductive* procedure. Strictly speaking, this is a false dichotomy, since no research is entirely inductive or entirely deductive (Creighton, 1945, p. 574; Hanson, 1965). Nonetheless, the matter of where the emphasis is laid at particular points in research procedure is important, and we are faced with a very real choice (Fritz, 1968, pp. 19–20, 40).

The argument involves a number of questions, including these: Can we collect 'all the data' and then interpret them? Should we be 'problem-oriented', and collect our data on the basis of their relevance to problems and hypotheses? Will not a problem-oriented deductive approach bias data collection? If we cannot collect all the data, then what data should be collected?

62

How do we decide? For that matter, what *are* data? What is the primary unit of data? How do we use data to solve problems? What are the limits, if any, to what we can infer about the past? And finally, how do we know that our inferences are correct? Can they be tested, or must we rest with the citation of ethnographic analogy?

I will explore answers to these questions, and will attempt to support the deductive side of the argument. The question, as I see it, is not one of whether one or the other research emphasis is inherently good or bad, correct or incorrect; rather it is whether one is more efficient in terms of getting answers to questions. I attempt to demonstrate, through both argument and example, that the hypothetico-deductive approach (Braithwaite, 1960; Hempel, 1966) is not only more efficient, but is critical to the advancement of archaeology as a science.

Specifically, the points I make in each of the succeeding numbered sections of the paper are as follows:

(1) The two methods are different, both with regard to reasoning and procedure, and they provide us with real alternatives.

(2) The 'inductive' emphasis in research is, however, impractical and inefficient; it is based on the false premise that one can go into the field with an open, unbiased mind and collect a large body of 'basic data' suitable for a wide variety of subsequent analyses. In fact, there is an infinite amount of potential data, and choices of what to observe must be (and always are) made in the light of *a priori* ideas.

(3) One of these *a priori* biases is *theory*. All archaeologists subscribe (often implicitly) to theory-like premises, which guide the selection of research problems and the nature of the data to be collected – they also guide the interpretation of data. Thus, a thoroughgoing inductive method is impossible. Since all researchers are biased with regard to theories and problems, they might as well make these biases explicit and useful.

(4) It is particularly important that our *problems* be clearly defined prior to data collection, since we will not otherwise know what data to collect.

(5) In addition to having specific problems, we cannot collect data efficiently without *hypotheses*. Hypotheses are bridges between problems and data, and provide explicit frameworks for interpretation (as well as an objective means of evaluating research results).

(6) In the hypothetico-deductive method, the terms 'data' and 'analysis' take on different meanings than they have in the traditional method.

63

I follow these considerations with a concrete example of the usefulness of hypothesis formulation in guiding data collection and analysis; and the concluding section is an attempt to meet some of the frequently heard objections to the hypothetico-deductive method.

The first step, then (No. 1 above), is to show that the two approaches imply fundamentally different views about the nature of data, and how we gain knowledge in archaeology. These metaphysical and epistemological issues have not been made explicit (except by Fritz, 1968). Most of the useful ideas in this section of the paper are drawn from Fritz's unpublished manuscript (cf. Note 1). My statements are excerpts from his more extensive and truly elegant work, but my emphases are occasionally somewhat different from his.

1 The epistemic foundations

In spite of the fact that during periods of normal science the epistemic foundations of research are implicit and taken for granted, there is one excellent published examination of the current (traditional) inductive emphasis in archaeological research (cf. Thompson, 1958).[3] Others, while less useful and dwelling more on the practical implications of this method, include Swartz (1967) and Rouse (1953) (see also Hawkes 1954, pp. 161–2; Willey and Phillips, 1958, p. 4; Ascher, 1961; Chang, 1967b; Taylor, 1967, pp. 35, 94, 112, 144, 183, 192, 150–1).

The epistemology of any science is based in a particular *metaphysic*, and this metaphysic may itself change during periods of revolution (Kuhn, 1962, p. 41 and elsewhere). Current archaeological research method is based in the empiricist school of philosophy (e.g. Hume, Mill and Bacon), and subscribes implicitly to the metaphysical notion that every object existing in nature has a meaning or significance inherent within it – if we can but discover it. Each item contains within it (or is a manifestation of) a single truth or bit of knowledge. It is reasoned that because the item is itself real, it must have some particular reality or meaning; there is a single best way to understand or interpret it.

The implication of this view for archaeology is that artefacts and features (and even artefact associations) are regarded as discrete, independent entities, each having a single primary meaning to be discovered (cf. Taylor, 1967, pp. 122, 143; Deetz, 1968). It is our task to perceive this inherent meaning. In a sense, then, our inferences about the data are contained in the artefacts and features themselves. If we are well trained, experienced and perceptive we should, it is said, be able to recognize the inferential possibilities ('indicators') that the artefacts and associations of artefacts have (Thompson, 1958, pp. 1–5): 'Indication is that quality of the evidence which describes its inferential possibilities. It is this indicative quality of data which makes inference possible. An indication suggests a conclusion.' (Thompson, 1958, p. 3)

If this is true, it follows that items and clusters of items found in archaeological sites are themselves basic data. If scientific knowledge is found *in* the data, then we are clearly restricted in the inferences we can make by the nature of the data themselves (and we are aware of how few data are preserved for the archaeologist). The implication is that our knowledge of the past must not only be based on the items recovered, but our inferences must be *about* the items themselves (Fritz, 1968, pp. 26–31)! This means that both our problems and their solutions are contained in and governed by the specific nature of the items recovered (Rouse, 1965, p. 1), and that 'It is advisable . . . to select only those objectives which are best suited to the nature of the available data . . .' (Rouse, 1962, pp. 100–1). Fritz (1968, p. 44) characterizes this narrow inductive view as follows: '. . . hypotheses are statements of the qualities in the data that an archaeologist thinks he perceives. These statements must be limited to the qualities that the data possess and therefore that may potentially be perceived. . . . It follows that the nature of the phenomena [data] must determine the content of the hypotheses made about them.'

The limitations this view imposes on archaeological inference are overwhelming. In subscribing to it, we are admitting, in agreement with Hume, that the only things we can know with certainty are those things that can be directly observed (Black, 1967, p. 199).[4] Since prehistoric peoples are extinct, we are not able to observe their activities directly and hence cannot safely make and test inferences about their behaviour. While there are certain things that can legitimately be inferred, especially with regard to the technology of manufacture and use of particular material items, we are on unsafe ground in attempting to infer anything about social organization or culture processes (Smith, 1955; Thompson, 1958, p. 4). Such inferences constitute conjecture or going 'beyond the data', and when an archaeologist does this he is said not to have 'due respect for his material' (cf. Smith, 1955).

It follows from this view that our research task is to excavate sites, examine the recovered artefacts and associations for 'indicators' of the information they each supposedly contain,[5] and then add up these discrete pieces of information – the sum of which is taken to be the extent of our knowledge about a particular 'culture'. What we can know about a prehistoric society is in direct proportion to the numbers of different kinds of artefacts (discrete bits of information) we dig up![6] Fritz (1968, pp. 99–100) succinctly summarizes the traditional metaphysic and epistemology as follows:

> ... knowledge is inherent and to be discovered in empirical phenomena. A corollary to this view is that because phenomena are discrete, knowledge of them must also be discrete. ... Another corollary is that certain knowledge is only that which is gained by direct perception; all other knowledge is suspect. Science is inductive in procedure because it must start with data; it is inductive in logic because reasoning proceeds from data to the potential knowledge gained from it. This knowledge must always be uncertain.

Thus if we find a ceramic vessel with a burned bottom in an archaeological site, we might learn (from its indications) something about the technology used in its manufacture, as well as the fact that it was used in cooking. But we would *not*, according to this view, be able to establish with any degree of certainty that the pot was made and used by a particular residence unit, and that it was used in ritual cooking performed by a high status female! While we might suspect such to be the case, based on ethnographic information, we could never approach certainty.

Carl Hempel (1966, p. 11) calls this epistemological view the 'Narrow Inductivist conception of scientific inquiry', and he maintains that it is an 'untenable' way of going about scientific research. He sets forth the basic research procedures (in order of accomplishment) that its proponents advocate:

(1) Observation and recording of all facts.
(2) Analysis and classification of these facts.
(3) Inductive derivation of generalizations from the facts.
(4) Further testing of the generalizations.

The first two steps are assumed not to make use of any guesses or hypotheses with regard to the ways in which the facts might be connected to one another (usually in the belief that this will reduce 'bias', i.e. increase objectivity). The view holds that in terms of procedure (and logically) research begins with particulars, attempts to discover what the particulars mean, and then generalizes from these particulars.

Most of the textbooks and overtly methodological publications in archaeology reveal that this is exactly the procedure many archaeologists advocate and teach their students. In archaeological terms, research is said to proceed as follows:

(1) Excavation
(2) Classification and dating
(3) Analysis
(4) Interpretation

These are usually regarded as separate steps, with the idea that one should go from one to the next in orderly fashion. The clearest statement of it is found in Swartz (1967), but similar versions are ubiquitous in the literature (e.g. Hawkes, 1954; MacWhite, 1956; Willey and Phillips, 1958, pp. 1–7; Rouse, 1962; Taylor, 1967, ch. 6).[7]

One of the major effects of this narrow inductive emphasis is that it permits (and even encourages) researchers to go into the field without specific problems or hypotheses in mind; there is little guidance in terms of selecting *relevant* data. This is not a drawback, according to this view, however, since *all* items of data are deemed relevant. The frequent result is a rather blind and indiscriminate collection of 'data', aimed at recovering 'all the data', or as much of it as possible (Rouse, 1962, p. 86; Adams, 1968, p. 1192). This vacuum cleaner approach makes sense, of course – given the metaphysic and epistemology described above; indeed, it follows from it (cf. Harris, 1968, pp. 314–15, also 250–318).

The implicit assumption is that if we simply collect enough data, the mass of 'data' will in a sense speak to us; we will somehow be presented with both the important problems and their solutions. This doesn't happen, however. Even if we could wait until all or most of the data were in (cf. Rouse, 1939, p. 143), a careful examination of them would not lead us to the solutions of questions involving the description of prehistoric societies or the processes of their operation and change (Harris, 1964, p. 16, 1968, p. 288; Binford, 1968a, p. 26).

Any metaphysic and epistemology that requires that our inferences be *about* the data themselves, will effectively prevent us from making and testing inferences about the so-called 'intangibles'.[8] This approach restricts us to describing artefacts and features, dating them, and comparing their forms in time and space; analysis becomes description, taxonomy, and the pigeon-holing of assemblages into time charts – the essential complaint made by Walter Taylor (1948). This is natural history in the nineteenth-century sense, and while it is a pursuit that is internally consistent and logically valid, it is relatively uninteresting.

A further implication of the inductive emphasis in research should also be mentioned. Namely, that since data can be collected prior to and separate from problem or hypothesis formulation, it is also reasonable that field work can be adequately carried out by a man who has no interest in theory, problems and so forth – i.e. field work can be for the most part separate from analytical or interpretative concerns (cf. Swartz, 1967, p. 488; Taylor, 1967, p. 42). Unfortunately, this has been found unworkable, since the data that are collected by the field man are not always applicable to the problems of the theorist. That this is the case should become clear as the discussion proceeds (cf. esp. pp. 86–9).

So much for the empiricist (or primarily inductive) epistemology and its effects on research. The deductive (positivist) programme for gaining knowledge is quite different; it can be handled briefly here, since much of the remainder of the paper concerns its practical operation (see also Binford, 1965, 1967, 1968a; Hill, 1968, 1970a; Fritz, 1968).

In the deductive emphasis, the metaphysic is that artefacts, features and so forth do *not* have inherent meanings that we must try to discover (e.g. norms, templates, preferences, functions, etc.). It is our own perception of them that gives them meaning. An axe or a ceramic vessel, for example, has no meaning as a thing in itself; it has only the meaning(s) that our minds confer upon it. If we view a pot as a cooking vessel, this is because some of its attributes fit our preconception of what a cooking vessel must be like. If we did not already know what characteristics to expect (ahead of time), we would not recognize it as a cooking vessel; it would have no meaning in that regard.

For example, upon unearthing such a vessel, we might consider it as a cooking pot, a storage jar or a food-serving vessel (and there might be other possible interpretations). While the vessel cannot 'tell' us which interpretation is most likely correct, we already have in our minds an understanding of the kinds of attributes that we would *expect* to find if one or another interpretation was the case. For example, we might interpret it as a cooking pot if it had the following expected attributes: unpainted, burned bottom, technical characteristics that would permit the withstanding of heat without cracking, location near a hearth . . . etc. If the vessel did not fit any of these prior ideas, we would not interpret it as a cooking vessel; we would search our minds for other possible interpretations and test *them* against the characteristics observed, in the same manner. Thus all of our inferences are made in the mind, and checked against the data for goodness of fit. Even the inference that an object *is* a pot is a matter of determining whether or not it has the characteristics we would expect of a pot – however unconsciously this test is performed by the investigator (cf. Coombs, 1964; Hanson, 1965; Fritz, 1968, pp. 31–4).

And further, every material item (or cluster of items) has an infinite number

68

of attributes, and thus an infinite number of possible meanings or ways in which it can be interpreted. The attributes we actually observe depend on what we are looking for, and this in turn depends on prior concepts and ideas (e.g. problems and hypotheses) (Binford, 1965; Hanson, 1967; Hole and Heizer, 1969, p. 177). For example, a pottery vessel has attributes ranging from physical and chemical attributes to those resulting from where it was made, who made it, how it was used, and how it was disposed of – not to mention the infinite number of measurements that could be made on it. If we are interested in a vessel's characteristics for containing liquids, then we look for those attributes we believe will be useful for that purpose. If, on the other hand, our interest lies in identifying the vessel as having been made by a single individual or member of a particular residence unit, we would look for those characteristics of motor-habit or detailed design-style that might be relevant to the problem – and so on to practical infinity. The idea that an item is best interpreted in only one way (e.g. as a reflection of what was 'in the minds of the people') is absurd (cf. Binford, 1965). Similarly, a cooking vessel need not be interpreted solely as a cooking vessel; it may also be interpreted as a status symbol, a product of a specialist, an indication of the size of the group using it, and so forth.

The major effects of this deductive epistemology on research should be obvious. Since meaning is supplied by the mind rather than by material items themselves, the primarily deductive researcher *begins* his research with an idea or hypothesis about how to interpret or explain his data; he then deduces from the hypothesis (or set of them) the kinds of evidence he would *expect* to find in his materials if his hypothesis is correct (or not correct). Then, by gathering and examining the *relevant* data, he is able to evaluate the degree to which the facts actually conform to what he expected if his proposition were correct (i.e. goodness of fit).

This does not mean that the practitioner of the deductive emphasis will either ignore or fail to see obvious things in the field that he is not preprogrammed to see, nor that he should not modify his hypotheses (and generate new ones) when faced with new or unexpected kinds of observations (cf. pp. 94–5). There should certainly be a process of continuous feedback between data and hypotheses, with each being modified as necessary (Creighton, 1945, p. 574; Nagel, 1961; Hanson, 1965; Hempel, 1966; Rudner, 1966, p. 66).

The important point to emphasize, however, is that in the hypothetico-deductive method we do not have to wait for a collection of mute data to somehow provide us with inferences. We may invent our own inferences, and the sources of inspiration for them are irrelevant (Binford, 1967; Hill, 1968). They may be *about* virtually anything – e.g. relationships among artefacts, their contexts in activities, the location and nature of residence units, changes in the scope of social integration, and so on. Even more importantly, we may generate both descriptions and explanations of culture processes, which obviously cannot be regularly induced (or abduced)[9] by examining a body of archaeological data. Any such inferences must of course be tested against data.

At this point, the significant differences in epistemology between the two general research methods should be clear; and it should also be clear that they provide us with a definite choice with regard to both reasoning and research procedure. I now attempt to demonstrate that the inductive (empiricist) approach is really not a practical choice to make, since two of its most basic assumptions are not valid – i.e.

(1) That it is possible to make a thorough data collection that will be widely useful to others in later interpretation.

(2) That data collection can proceed in the absence of prior ideas that influence it.

2 Unstructured data collection

While some archaeologists seem occasionally to realize that prior ideas govern observation and data collection, and that thorough unbiased collections are not possible to make, there are still many who avidly hold these views (cf. Rouse, 1962, pp. 86–7; Swartz, 1967; Taylor, 1967, pp. 152–4, 180, 189; Hole and Heizer, 1969, pp. 124–6, 162, 206). Some even maintain that the 'universally useful' data collection is not only possible but morally obligatory (Mayer-Oakes, 1966, p. 10).

One reason that this goal is unattainable is that there is an *infinite* amount of potential data in a single archaeological site, as well as an infinite number of potential problems to be solved. The data that most of us collect are data that lie ready at hand – they are more or less obvious things to collect – and they will not include the large amounts of more recondite data that many problems require. An infinite amount of potential data is simply too much to warrant even paying lip-service to collecting a large portion of it! 'Even the first phase [of research] could never be carried out, for a collection of *all* the facts would have to await the end of the world, so to speak; and even all the facts *up to now* cannot be collected, since there are an infinite number and variety of them.' (Hempel, 1966, pp. 11–12). Are we to analyse the humic content of post-holes? Must we take pH, pollen, flotation, column samples? How and from exactly what locations should samples be taken? Which chemical analyses are appropriate? Should we excavate in 10 cm levels, with quarter inch screens? How many measurements should we record, and how accurately? Must we take detailed measurements of each stone in a masonry wall? Again, we simply cannot collect everything that might be relevant to something (Sellitz *et al.*, 1959, p. 207).

There are even occasions during field work when one must make a choice between one kind of data and another, since the collection of one destroys the other. As a single example, consider the investigator whose problem dictates that he locate *all* house structures on a given archaeological site (say, in order to plot spatial distributions and test a hypothesis about residence units). This requirement may force the investigator to locate the houses with heavy equipment, thus destroying certain other data that would also be useful. A listing of further examples could continue indefinitely.

There are also numerous occasions when the necessity of collecting certain kinds of information in great *detail* prohibits the adequate collection of other kinds of data. Conversely, 'complete' excavation of a site may necessitate the slighting of certain detailed information needed for the solution of a specific problem. The question of what are 'representative' data is unanswerable – until at least one problem is at hand.

Further, nobody would even *try* to collect 'all the data' from a site – much less a region – since limitations of time and money preclude it. And even when large amounts of data are collected, much of it never gets reported (cf. Hole and Heizer, 1969, pp. 97, 390).

The futility of trying to make a generally useful data collection should be clear to those who have tried to use the field reports of others. Much of the necessary data, even for current problems, is not there – even though the authors of the reports may have tried very hard to live up to the goal of making a reasonably 'complete' collection. Most reports (and field notes) do not even provide information suitable for describing activity areas within sites, much less for describing aspects of prehistoric social organization, warfare, seasonality, storage techniques, and so on – not to mention data for solving complex explanatory problems. Walter Taylor devoted all of chapter 3 of *A Study of Archeology* (1948, 1967) to a brilliant and well-documented study of this fact.

But aside from the fact that it is a physical impossibility to observe, collect and record more than a fraction of the potential data, there is another reason that objective data collection is impossible; that is, our preconceived ideas literally prevent us from seeing most of what is potentially available to observe. We are all guided in our choices of data by theories, problems or interests of one sort or another – no matter how vague or implicit they may be. Everything that *is* observed is observed only because it fits into some conceptual framework (see controlling models, p. 5, Fig. 1.1).

> ... to observe X is to observe X as something or other. (Hanson, 1967, p. 91)

> ... any significant gathering of facts ... is *controlled* by assumptions of various kinds which must be supplied by the inquiring scientist and not by the subject of his research. In particular, since facts do not proclaim themselves to be relevant or irrelevant for a given problem, the scientist must adopt at least some preliminary hypothesis as to what sorts of facts are pertinent to his problems ... (Nagel, 1967, p. 10)

> That is, all archaeologists make explicit and implicit, conscious or unconscious decisions about what data to collect and what to leave behind. Moreover, data are interpreted in the light of principles which are held *a priori*. (Fritz, 1968, p. 34)

In further support of this view, see Kuhn (1962, pp. 4–5), Kaplan (1964, p. 255), Hempel (1966, pp. 11–12), Harris (1968, p. 290) and Hole and Heizer (1969, pp. 389–90).

The basic point I am making here is that, since we are faced with a potentially infinite amount of data, we are *forced* to make choices as to what to collect; these choices are determined by ideas held *a priori* – i.e. theories, problems, and so forth. The inductivist program of making thorough, unbiased data collections is not possible.

Further, since no research is free of bias, I argue that it is both profitable and necessary to make our biases explicit. If they are not made explicit, we will not know why we are emphasizing certain kinds of data, slighting others, and ignoring all the other potential data. The mere fact that there *are* virtually an infinite number of potential data makes it mandatory that we know why we are selecting as important the few data we do! In fact, as the discussion proceeds, I will be arguing that we need *more* (and more specific) biases in our research rather than fewer of them.

First, however, I must present more convincing argument in support of assertion that biases are in fact unavoidable; and I must show some of the ways in which they actually affect research in archaeology today. The argument should make it apparent that at least a vague deductive approach in archaeology cannot be avoided, and our only choice is to either refine our biases (premises) and take advantage of them, or simply leave them ill defined and uncontrolled.

As I indicated earlier (p. 63), the most important of the *a priori* ideas guiding research is *theory*, and I consider it next.

3 The influence of theory

While archaeologists may not have any real theory, in the strict sense, they do have vague premises or 'theoretical orientations' that affect research. These theory-like premises may be almost unconscious at times, but they exert an indirect influence in the problems we are interested in, the hypotheses we generate, and the data we collect (Fig. 1.1).

> Theory . . . functions throughout inquiry, and does not come into its own only when inquiry is successfully completed. It has a greater responsibility than that of an accessory after the fact: it guides the search for data, and for laws encompassing them. (Kaplan, 1964, p. 302)

> Every theory serves, in part, as a research directive; theory guides the collection of data and their subsequent analysis, by showing us beforehand where the data are to be fitted, and what we are to make of them when we get them. (Kaplan, 1964, p. 268)

Most philosophers of science agree with these ideas, as does at least one archaeologist (Willey, 1962, p. 170). For more thorough discussions, see Kuhn (1962, pp. 32–3, 42, 55–7, and elsewhere) and Kaplan (1964, pp. 57–60).

To illustrate these effects of theory, I turn first to what I would call 'traditional' archaeological theory (cf. Rouse, 1939; MacWhite, 1956; Willey and Phillips, 1958; Hole and Heizer, 1965, 1969, pp. 300, 312, 328–30). This traditional set of basic premises has guided our research for the last thirty years or so, and has served as the underpinnings of current 'normal science' in archaeology.

As I see it, there are two basic tenets to consider. The first one is that 'cultures' can be viewed as trait-lists (Rouse, 1939; Willey, 1966; Hole and Heizer, 1969, pp. 328–30). This is a logical result or concomitant of the empiricist-inductive school of research discussed earlier. Each trait is discrete and has its own inherent meaning, and we are led to a pursuit of problems involving the description and comparison of assemblages of traits. While it is likely that most archaeologists no longer consciously espouse this 'theory', they still often collect, manipulate and interpret data as if they did – regardless of whether the traits are individual artefacts, features or settlement patterns (cf. Chang, 1968; Hill, 1969).

The second tenet is that culture traits represent ideas, beliefs, preferences, mental templates or norms of the people who made them. In fact, many archaeologists would hold that material remains are not 'real' culture at all; culture is a collection of ideas and norms that are held in people's minds (Taylor, 1948, 1967, pp. 95–100, esp. chs. 4 and 6; Rouse, 1965; Deetz, 1968; Hole and Heizer, 1969, pp. 300, 312, 328–9). This is what Binford (1965, 1968a) refers to as the 'univariate' view of culture (see also Harris, 1968, pp. 1–7, 39). The view holds that culture is just one thing – norms. The primary meaning of each artefact is thus presumed to be its indication of ideas, preferences, and so forth.

A related tenet of this theory is that cultural variability and change are *explained* in terms of variability and change in cultural norms! Since cultures *are* norms, it follows that they change as a result of new ideas or norms that are introduced, usually by means of 'influence' or 'diffusion' from other cultures (though sometimes by independent innovation).

The effects of these premises on both problem and data selection should almost be obvious. The primary research problem that results is that of describing prehistoric cultures as lists of traits, and the inferring of cultural norms from these traits (cf. Rouse, 1939; Ford, 1954). The next step then is to compare trait assemblages and explain their similarities and differences in terms of differential diffusion or influence of ideas from other peoples. The problem of finding the origins or 'donors' of the ideas represented by culture traits is a paramount one, and while crude ecological explanations of variability and change are sometimes invoked, they are far from common.

The effects of traditional theory and problem-orientation on data collection are direct and understandable. Since the implicit goal of research is to describe, compare and trace the spatial and temporal distributions of materials representing cultural norms, it follows that the investigator should devote most of his attention to observing and collecting the materials that are most representative of these norms – i.e. most 'diagnostic' of the cultures being studied. His biases thus lead him to emphasize the observation and collection of those things that have demonstrable usefulness in identifying and comparing different cultures, or 'peoples', in Rouse's terms (Rouse, 1965). He will frequently ignore (either in the field or later) many of the small, commonly occurring cultural materials because they are neither diagnostic of cultures nor of time periods (e.g. lithic waste, small bone fragments, etc.).[10]

These biases are clearly the reason for the fact that more emphasis has been given to the observation of gross *stylistic* variability in material remains than to functional or adaptational variability. Stylistic variability in such things as projectile points, pottery, architecture, the orientation of burials, and so forth, is understandably most important if the purpose of research is to describe the flow of norms or ideas in time and space, since styles are considered (intuitively) to be the best possible manifestations of norms and mental templates. There is really no need, given this theory, to collect materials or information relevant to dealing with the description and explanation of functional variability within and among sites, or the nature of prehistoric residence patterns – and so on; these data are either not emphasized or they are ignored completely.

This is not the end of it, however. Trait-list-normative theory affects not only the data collected by the archaeologist, but also the *techniques* he uses in the field and laboratory. A single example that comes immediately to mind is the effect on sampling techniques. Since the theory assumes that sites and local regions are relatively homogeneous culturally (i.e. normatively), it is not logically necessary to collect large samples or get even coverage when sampling sites; a few pits or trenches should be sufficient to gather enough artefacts to infer norms. The spatial distributions of materials within a site or region are relatively unimportant (except stratigraphically), since the description of spatial variability within a single contemporaneous culture unit is not prerequisite to cultural description and comparison. Traditionally the archaeologist is much more interested in making inter-component and inter-phase comparisons than in describing intra-component or intra-cultural variability.

It should be clear, without further examples, that traditional theory does in fact lead (even if indirectly) to the kinds of problems and observations of data that most archaeologists emphasize. The 'New Archaeology', on the other hand, has a different set of theory-like premises, and while they affect research problems and data collection just as heavily as traditional theory does, the results are quite different. This theory has been called 'systems theory' or 'ecological' systems theory (cf. Binford, 1962, 1964, 1965, 1968a; Flannery, 1967; Miller, 1965; Odum, 1959, and others). Although I cannot adequately deal with it here, I can present some of its major tenets and their influence on research.

The ecological systems view is that cultures are neither summations of material traits nor bodies of norms or mental templates. Instead, they are viewed as complex behavioural systems made up of subsystems and components (such as residence units, task units, sodalities and statuses). A cultural system can be described by describing its subsystems and components, together with the matter-energy-information exchanges that occur between and among these subunits of the system, and between components of the system and its environment (see esp. Miller, 1965; Hole and Heizer, 1969, pp.364–85).

Changes in cultural systems are not explained by appealing to contacts with the ideas of other cultural systems. The systems theorist views culture change as resulting from systemic responses to empirical, measurable environmental variables. As inputs of matter and energy into the system change in kind and quantity, the system must alter to some degree to compensate for these variations. In short, the system modifies itself as a means of adapting to an altered environmental situation (Miller, 1965; Hole and Heizer, 1969, pp. 344–7, 364–85). Inputs of information (e.g. ideas, etc.) into a cultural system are not ignored by this theory; they are simply regarded as insufficient in themselves to explain change.

The indirect effects that this theory has on problem formulation and data collection are already evident in the literature (cf. esp. Binford and Binford, 1968). First of all, problems of description involve attempts to describe variability *within* cultural systems as well as variability between and among such systems. Put simply, we are now making consistent efforts to describe the ways in which societies are organized – their task organization, political organization, etc. We also want to find out how these components of societal organization articulate with their environments in either maintaining or failing to maintain a semblance of equilibrium with the environment.

We are thus not only trying to *describe* cultural systems as organizations of institutions and materials, but we are also trying to discover the specific ecological variables (especially inputs) that promote variability and change in aspects of societal operation. This involves a search for a great many more possible causal variables than simply information inputs (diffusion). Such variables as population growth, decreasing food or fuel, locations of critical resources, warfare, and so on, may be found to explain variability and change.

Given research problems of this nature, it is predictable that the 'systems' archaeologist will want to recover and use large quantities of data that others will neither observe nor have any use for. For example, the problems of the systems researcher may require him to plot the horizontal spatial distributions of artefacts in order to describe activity areas. He may require measures of the degree of randomness of a distribution, as well as measures of differential density of cultural remains. It may be important that he measures the volumes and orifice sizes of pots if he is trying to discover the kinds of activities that took place within or among prehistoric sites. Or he might need to record rather precise measurements of the shapes of fire pits (Hill, 1966, 1970b) or minute style differences in ceramic designs (Longacre, 1964; Deetz, 1965; Hill, 1966,

1970b; Whallon, 1968). It is also likely that his sampling designs will be different from that of the trait-list or normative theorist (cf. Binford, 1964; Hill, 1966, 1967, 1970b).

Such examples could be multiplied, but there is little advantage in doing so. The point of this oversimplified discussion of theory is simply that we are all 'biased' by the theory-like premises we hold. Differences in theory lead not only to differences in the research problems we tend to favour, but to differences in the data we collect and the techniques of collection. Our theories even affect the results we get, since they are by definition answers themselves. They are general explanations of phenomena, and by subscribing to one kind of theory or another, we are favouring (*a priori*) particular kinds of explanations of what we observe.

Because these premises are so important to the everyday practical affairs of scientific research, it is vital that we make ourselves fully aware of them.

4 The importance of problems

The intimate relationships that exist among theory, problems and data collection should now be clear enough to warrant little further comment. Data collection is dependent on both theory and problems, however vague they may be (cf. pp. 71–2). It is further evident that we cannot go into the field with our basic premises alone; it is important that our biases be further refined. Any significant gathering of facts requires the prior formulation of at least one problem (Nagel, 1967, p. 10). As Hole and Heizer (1969, p. 144) point out:

> The clever use of advanced techniques for excavation and analysis is wasted if it is not directed toward, and designed for, the solution of a particular problem. The suitability of approaches and the scope of the dig should develop naturally out of an archaeologist's intention. As R. J. C. Atkinson says . . . 'It is no longer considered sufficient, or even justifiable, to excavate a site in a repetitive manner, merely waiting, like Mr Micawber, for something to turn up. On the contrary, every excavation and every part of one must be planned to answer a limited number of quite definite questions'.

This relationship between problems and data is not only upheld by philosophers of science (cf. Cohen and Nagel, 1934; Nagel, 1961), but has also been espoused by many archaeologists (cf. Rouse, 1939, p. 138, 1962, pp. 100–1; Binford, 1964, p. 441; Taylor, 1967, pp. 67, 87, 152, 192; Hole and Heizer, 1969, pp. 144, 407 and ch. 17).

But how do problems lead us to data? There is a difficulty here. The planning of field work to solve problems has been difficult for most archaeologists to operationalize – and this is even true of many avowedly problem-oriented investigators. While problems may be formulated, and data gathered, many of our problems are never solved. Somehow, the data rarely get articulated with the problems such that a solution is evident (except in the case of rather simple problems). The truth of this is seen in many of our reports: problems may be posed and data are presented, but the brief section on 'Conclusions' simply presents inferences that are left unsupported by data. There is little demonstration, or even argument, to show precisely *how* the data relate to and support the conclusions.

There are several reasons for this. The first is that many of our problems are not well defined and specific enough to be solved (Hole and Heizer, 1969, p. 404). While on the one hand we ask certain very simple or specific questions, we also tend to ask the broad unanswerable variety – there is rarely a middle ground. The specific problems we generate include such questions as 'How old is it? ', 'What does it look like ?', 'How is it distributed in space and time ?' (i.e. 'What is the regional sequence, or area of contact ?'). Most archaeologists spend most of their time answering such specific questions (Hole and Heizer, 1969, pp. 390, 407), partly because they are relatively easy to answer. Having done this, however, we then leap directly to the big 'important' problems, such as 'the origins of cultures', or 'the effects of Mexican contact on the American Southwest'. It has even been suggested that our primary problem is the study of 'culture' (Swartz, 1967, p. 494)! While many such broad questions may be worth answering, they will first have to be made specific enough that they can be solved with empirical, measurable data.

Another difficulty that often occurs with problems is that they are not really problems at all; they are simply topics or general 'approaches'. The investigator may embark on a 'study of culture-change', or 'Illinois Hopewell', or the 'Southern Cult' – or he may wish to employ the 'Settlement Approach', the 'Ecological Approach', or some other such generality. Such topics suffer not only from their lack of specificity, but also from the fact that they are not even questions! It is no wonder, then, that solutions or answers are not found. In addition to the accusation that they are non-intellectual and hence have no place in an inquiring, scientific mind, they simply cannot guide us in the collection of relevant data.[11]

While most archaeologists go into the field with *general* problems, the difficulty is that: 'Problems and objectives too often are formulated as armchair generalizations, rather than as sharply focused hypotheses to which

78

definite answers must be sought...' (Adams, 1968, p. 1192). Those who subscribe to the inductive emphasis in archaeology have a strong tendency to do this – indeed, as Fritz (1968) has shown, their metaphysic and epistemology dictate that they operate in this way. The procedure is inefficient, at best.

> The selection of a topic for research does not immediately put the investigator in a position to start considering what data he will collect, by what methods.... Before he takes these steps, he needs to formulate a specific problem which can be investigated by scientific procedures. Unfortunately, it happens not infrequently that an investigator attempts to jump immediately from the selection of a topic to the collection of observations. At best, this means that he will be faced with the task of formulating a problem after the data collection; at worst, that he will not produce a scientific inquiry at all. (Sellitz *et al.*, 1959, p. 30)

In summary, it is not only important to have problems in mind prior to collecting data, but also important that they be specific and phrased in terms of ideas and concepts that are actually measurable (Sellitz *et al.*, 1959, p. 4). This means, of course, that such concepts as 'diffusion', 'migration', 'preference', 'adaptation', 'contact', and so forth, must usually either be left out of a problem statement or defined such that they can be operationalized.

5 The necessity for hypotheses

A problem alone, however, is not enough – regardless of how well defined it is. We cannot collect data efficiently unless we refine our *a priori* ideas to the point of generating specific hypotheses or other testable propositions.[12] Nagel (1967, p. 11) goes so far as to say that 'Without ... hypotheses, inquiry is aimless and blind.' While this is a strong statement, its validity is supported by experience in all fields of science, including the social sciences.

There are at least two major reasons for the fact that hypotheses are necessary to research:

(1) Hypotheses provide a necessary link between problems and data. Without them, we will not know what data are important to collect, and we will miss much of the relevant data.
(2) Hypothesis testing provides the only efficient means for evaluating the correctness of our inferences.

While hypotheses are important for other reasons as well, these are the reasons most important to this paper, and I consider them both in turn.

First of all, then, the mere statement of a problem (without hypotheses) usually does not permit efficient choices of what data to observe and collect (Wilson, 1952, p. 23). This difficulty can be illustrated with an analogy. The problem of what causes cancer, for example, is a relatively specific problem, yet it does not tell us what data to examine. We know that one obvious general body of data to look at includes people who have the disease, but we might examine such people for decades without ever discovering either the causes or the data that might 'indicate' the causes. If the problem itself were enough to indicate the relevant data, we would have discovered the causes of cancer long ago (Hempel, 1966, p. 14)!

The same situation holds in archaeology. Consider the problem of whether or not sites were seasonally occupied, or the problem of what caused the widespread abandonments in the eleventh through fourteenth centuries in the American Southwest. Neither problem leads us to the collection of specific kinds of data, and we could excavate sites for hundreds of years without ever knowing what data were necessary to collect in order to solve the problems. It matters little whether the general body of data being examined is artefacts from archaeological sites or symptoms of cancer patients; there is no way of knowing what data are really relevant to problem solution unless we first provide *tentative solutions* or answers to the problems prior to data collection (Hempel, 1966, p. 12).

The 'solutions' or 'answers' I refer to are, of course, hypotheses. Once such a tentative answer or solution is presented, it becomes possible to enumerate the specific kinds of data that would either support or refute it. 'When a hypothesis has been devised to fit the observed facts, it becomes possible to apply the rules of formal logic and deduce various consequences [to be looked for in the data]. Logic does not enter science until this stage is reached.' (Wilson, 1952, p. 27)

The problem of what caused the Southwestern abandonments is a good illustration. Once the hypotheses are suggested that the adandonments may have been promoted by invaders, or by a shift in the physical environment resulting in diminishing agricultural productivity (or something else), we can deduce a series of very specific *expectations* of data that should occur in the archaeological record if either proposition is correct – and also the kinds of evidence that might show that one or the other proposition is *not* correct. These expectations are the deductive consequences or 'test implications' of the hypotheses (Hempel, 1966); they constitute the data necessary to test each proposition.

I cannot present a long list of the many test implications that could be generated for each of these propositions, but a few of the more obvious ones can be given (cf. Hill, 1965, 1970b):

I. *Warfare (invaders) proposition:*
   (A) Evidence of the invading peoples – villages, camps, burial grounds, etc.
   (B) Burned *pueblo* villages (*pueblo* rooms should be found to have been burned indiscriminately; i.e. large blocks of rooms should have burned, not just one or two types of rooms in each *pueblo*).
   (C) Many *pueblo* villages should have defensive works and be found in locations that would have been easy to defend.
   (D) Other evidence of violence should be found (e.g. mass or group burials).
   (E) There should be evidence of a higher mortality rate among young adult males than among young adult females.

II. *Environmental–agricultural proposition:*
   (A) Evidence of an environmental shift (pollen, tree ring and physiographic data, especially).
   (B) Evidence that the abandoned areas were unsuited to growing food crops, and that later sites are found in 'favourable' areas in this respect (there should probably be a general relocation of villages from tributary streams to the floodplains of major drainage ways, and around springs).
   (C) Immediately prior to abandonment, there should be evidence of subsistence difficulties – for example:
      (1) Decrease in domestic crops.
      (2) Increase in wild food crops.
      (3) Increased hunting and gathering of specific kinds of animals and plants expected to occur in the area, given the conditions postulated.
      (4) Changes in kinds and relative frequencies of tools used in exploitive tasks (e.g. more hunting tools and gathering implements).
      (5) Changes in kinds and relative frequencies of food processing and preparation facilities.
      (6) An increase in storage space.
      (7) An increase in the sizes of villages (and sub-village residence units).
      (8) Decrease in *numbers* of villages.

81

(9) Alterations in the nature of ritual activities, as different food resources become important.

There are not only many additional test implications that can be generated, but it is also important to note that each of the above can be greatly refined. Each expectation implies a large number of subimplications (or test implications for the test implications!).

The point is simply that a list of test implications such as this provides the investigator with specific kinds of data to be observed, collected and analysed – and all of these data will clearly be found relevant.

A corollary to this, of course, is that without the guidance of hypotheses, much of the data necessary to solve any given problem will *not* be collected; they will be missed. An example of this is the measurement of changing storage volume in the illustration above. There would be no cause to observe storage capacity at all in the absence of this hypothesis – yet it is clearly data. Further, one might ordinarily fail to look for evidence of increasing dependence on wild food crops, changes in the relative frequencies of food processing facilities, and so on. The mere description of within-village residence units requires a long list of test implications to itself (cf. Longacre, 1964; Hill, 1965, 1966, 1970b), perhaps including a wide range of information on the spatial distributions of minute style elements in artefacts, architecture, plant usage, and so on. Much of this information would come from features and house structures, and would have to be recorded in the field rather than in the laboratory after the field work was completed. Most of such data would be regarded as irrelevant exotica in the absence of a hypothesis determining their relevance.

As a matter of fact, even when items are already collected and in the laboratory, most of the virtually infinite numbers of attributes they possess that might be relevant to something are never observed. For example, unless one has a hypothesis that directs him to examine the lengths and fracture characteristics of fragments of burned bone, such observations will probably not be made – they are not relevant, and hence will go unnoticed.

But in addition to the fact that hypotheses guide us in observing and collecting relevant data, they are also necessary because they provide the best possible framework for evaluating how well the data support our inferences (p. 79, No. 2). While I cannot go into detail with respect to the rules and procedures of hypothesis testing here, it is important to describe briefly what is meant by the term 'test'[13] (for detailed requirements, see Hempel, 1966; Binford, 1967; Fritz, 1968, pp. 68–84; Fritz and Plog, 1968; Hill, 1968, 1970a; Lazarsfeld, 1968).

82

In the first place, any given research question will usually have more than one possible answer (or hypothesis), as was seen to be the case in the South-western abandonment question. If there were only one possible hypothesis available, there would be little need to conduct a test; we would probably accept the hypothesis, at least until a viable competitor is presented. When there are two or more hypotheses available, however, it is important that they all be tested (Platt, 1964; Chamberlin, 1965). Only in this way can we compare test results and evaluate the degree to which each hypothesis is supported by data.

After each competing hypothesis has been formulated as an empirically testable statement, and its test implications listed, the investigator will proceed to the data (in the field or elsewhere) in an effort to determine which hypothesis is best supported by the evidence. A tabulation of the numbers (and weights) of the test implications that are confirmed in the data for each hypothesis will permit him to compare the test results of each, and evaluate the degree to which each is supported. It may even be possible to devise 'crucial tests' – i.e. generate test implications which, if found in the data, would definitely exclude one or more of the hypotheses as being correct (Hempel, 1966, pp. 25–8).[14]

In evaluating the support that is given each hypothesis, one must consider (among other things) not only the *numbers* of test implications in the data, but also their *variety* (Hempel, 1966, pp. 33–46). Thus, if a hypothesis is supported by a large number of very diverse test implications (relative to alternative hypotheses), we are in a good position to believe that the hypothesis is in fact correct. The reasoning involved here is that since a variety of otherwise disparate observations are *predicted* from the hypothesis, the actual discovery of many of them in the data would be very improbable if the hypothesis was not actually correct.

This does not mean, of course, that a hypothesis can be proven correct simply by showing that most of its test implications are found in the data. Since there is rarely 'proof' in science, we must usually evaluate test results in terms of non-statistical probabilities (cf. Hempel, 1966, pp. 8, 28; Nagel, 1967, p. 7). We simply observe that one or another hypothesis receives more support from the data than others, and hence must be favoured – for the moment at least.

In the same vein, it would be unreasonable to insist that in order for a hypothesis to gain credibility we must find *all* of its test implications supported in the data; in fact this rarely happens. The reason for this is that these implications can themselves be incorrect. While they are presumed to be likely consequences of a given hypothesis, they do not follow *of necessity* from it. They are not deduced from a hypothesis in the sense that there is a strict formal logical connection between the hypothesis and its test implications.[15]

This difficulty can be obviated to some degree by presenting what Binford calls 'arguments of relevance', and Fritz calls 'bridging hypotheses' (cf. Binford, 1968a; Fritz, 1968, pp. 63–70; Hempel, 1966, pp. 22–5). These arguments provide the necessary logical linkage between a hypothesis and its test implications. They are simply presentations of the investigator's own arguments or chain of reasoning for *why* each implication ought to be expected in the data if his hypothesis is correct. The mere stating of such arguments often leads us to the conclusion that certain test implications are not good ones (i.e. not actually to be expected under the hypothesis), and should be discarded; the arguments also frequently lead to the development of new and different test implications. At the very least, they force the investigator to think clearly about the relevance of his data – and, more importantly, they provide the only real satisfaction that the discovery of the test implications in the data *would* in fact be relevant to supporting the proposed hypothesis.

For example, in the 'environmental-agricultural' proposition I gave earlier (pp. 80–2), one of the test implications was the expectation that storage volume should be found to increase as a consequence of the proposed subsistence stress. But why should this follow? My argument of relevance is that under such stress conditions, crops would have been less dependable than previously, and people would then have had to wait longer periods between good crops; they would thus need to store larger quantities of seed, as well as crops for consumption, in order to carry themselves from one good harvest to the next. This would require an increase in storage space.

Although this argument may be wrong, it is important for at least the following reasons:

(1) It forces a re-evaluation of the hypothesis; it requires us to specify more precisely what kind of environmental shift might be referred to, and how it would be expected to affect agricultural productivity.

(2) It provides us with some confidence that if storage space *is* found to have increased, this increase really does lend support to the hypothesis (because of its deductive linkage with the hypothesis).

(3) If the test implication is found in the data, we have increased confidence in the entire argument of relevance – i.e. the actual *processes* through which the environmental shift affected storage capacity.

(4) It provides us with ideas for additional test implications. For example,

84

what would be the other expectations in the data if a people had to go two or three years without a good crop? What are the other kinds of adaptations that might be made to a situation involving undependable crops? What kinds of evidence would be expected in the agricultural fields?

(5) If the test implication is not borne out in the data, we are often able to discover that something is wrong with the argument of relevance; perhaps the implied processes did not take place – and we must revise the initial hypothesis.

Thus the importance of arguments of relevance is indeed great. If we can get our colleagues to agree that our test implications and arguments of relevance are for the most part reasonable ones (given a particular hypothesis), we have reason to believe that their confirmation in the data will lend substantive support to the hypothesis – and that failure to confirm them will provide reason to reject the hypothesis.

At this point, enough has been said to make it clear that the hypothesis testing method is indeed necessary to research – both because hypotheses lead us to specific data to observe (i.e. test implications), and because the method permits us to evaluate the data and actually *test* our inferences.

Both of these points are amply supported by both scientists and philosophers of science. As Carl Hempel (1966, p. 13) says,

... the maxim that data should be gathered without guidance by antecedent hypotheses about the connections among facts under study is self-defeating, and it is certainly not followed in scientific inquiry. On the contrary, tentative hypotheses are needed to give direction to a scientific investigation. Such hypotheses determine, among other things, what data should be collected at a given point in a scientific investigation.

And further, 'Scientific knowledge ... is not arrived at by applying some inductive inference procedure to antecedently collected data, but rather by what is called "the method of hypothesis", i.e. by inventing hypotheses as tentative answers to a problem under study, and then subjecting these to empirical test. ...' (Hempel, 1966, pp. 17–18)

Without hypotheses, we cannot hope to do more than collect vast quantities of raw information, most of which will never be used in the solution of significant problems. 'We speak piously of taking measurements and making small studies that will "add another brick to the temple of science". Most such bricks just lie around the brickyard' (Platt, 1964, p. 351). The narrow inductivist approach is, as Platt (1964, p. 351) states, '. . . a substitute for thinking, a sad waste of intelligence . . . and a mistraining whose crippling effects may last a lifetime.' No less a notable than Charles Darwin would agree: 'How odd it is that anyone should not see that all observation must be for or against some view, if it is to be of any service' (In Sellitz *et al.*, 1959, p. 200).

I am not arguing here that archaeologists should never carry out 'exploratory' studies prior to formulating hypotheses. There are certainly occasions when such relatively blind data collection is justifiable (Wilson, 1952, p. 2). Nonetheless, the excuse that one does not know enough about the subject matter to formulate hypotheses is usually not valid, and it is an excuse that is far overworked.

6 Data and analysis

Given the major point that hypotheses provide a necessary link between problems and data, the reader may already be aware of an important and intimately related point – namely, that the hypothesis testing method imposes on us a non-traditional view of what 'data' are, and a greatly altered view of what constitutes the 'analysis' of data.

First of all, in traditional usage the term 'data' refers to any and all bodies of material and observations gathered by an investigator for purposes of 'analysis'. A site may be excavated, for example, and everything recovered from it is considered to be data. Since the investigator is not gathering data to test previously formulated propositions, he will have a tendency to view everything as relevant; and the view is reasonable, given the more or less inductive epistemology previously discussed.

In the hypothetico-deductive method, however, the term 'data' usually does not refer to a large corpus of miscellaneous items and observations that might *potentially* be useful to some analysis or other; it refers primarily (if not exclusively) to those bits of information that are actually *known* to be useful to a given analysis. In this sense, data constitute those things that are known to be relevant to either confirming or rejecting some hypothesis or proposition. If they are not useful in this way, then they are by definition irrelevant to analysis, and hence should not be called 'data'. Kaplan (1964) expresses this view clearly:

The word 'data', it cannot too often be emphasized, is an incomplete term, like 'later than'; there are only data *for* some hypothesis or other. (1964, p. 268)

. . . we do not observe 'everything that there is to be seen'. An observation is *made*; it is the product of an active choice, not of a passive exposure. Observing is a goal-directed behaviour; an observational report is significant on the basis of a presumed relation to the goal. . . . Data are always *data for* some hypothesis or other. . . . In his *Theory of Data* Clyde Coombs proposes that the term 'data' be used for observations already interpreted in some particular way. I am saying that there are no other sorts of observations, though often the interpretation at work is far from explicit and clear. (1964, p. 133)[16]

A major implication of this view, of course, is that there is no such thing as 'basic data' – i.e. there is no single corpus of items and observations that are basic to all or most analyses that we might wish to perform. The question of what are data can only be answered *after* an investigator has at least one specific proposition in mind; the test implications of the proposition then become 'data'. Every time we have a new problem or ask a new question, the alternative hypotheses generated from it will also be different from those that have gone before; and the data necessary to test them will obviously be different. In most cases newly required data will be *very* different, not just a little different.

The idea that one can collect a body of 'basic data' has merit only to the degree that a large number of our colleagues share the same problems and are testing the same hypotheses. Such a situation occurred during archaeology's recent long period of 'normal science', when everyone intuitively *knew* what problems were important, and what data were necessary to collect. It is no longer so true today (although I would not deny that there are some problems and hypotheses shared by many archaeologists).

The second point I want to make is that our understanding of 'analysis' in archaeology is changing. I previously pointed to the fact that in the primarily inductive research emphasis, one of the first steps in research is the gathering of 'data'; these data are then brought into the laboratory for 'analysis'. The term 'analysis' refers in this case to examining the data in various ways in an effort to induce or abduce inferences (cf. Note 9). Problems are solved by examining the data for 'indicators' of their solutions (pp. 64–5). There is no systematic or efficient way to relate the data to the problems, however (pp. 77–8).

In the hypothetico-deductive method, this common predicament is obviated. Hypotheses provide an already existing framework for interpreting the data. Since hypotheses are tentative solutions to problems, and since data are the bits of information used to test hypotheses (i.e. test implications), it is evident that we know ahead of time precisely how the data are to be interpreted. In this situation, 'analysis' refers primarily to the act of organizing and manipulating the data in such a way that the investigator can see the degree to which the test implications of his various hypothesis are confirmed. The actual evaluation of test results would also be termed 'analysis' (or perhaps interpretation).

This is not simply a matter of definition. I am saying that the *processes* of analysis are different from those carried out in the more inductive research emphasis. We are no longer frequently faced with a vast body of potential data that may or may not be useful in interpretation; and the process of analysing the data is no longer a haphazard procedure depending primarily on the ability of the investigator to 'juice out' the significant information. There is not only a loose deductive linkage among problems, hypotheses, and the data to be collected – there is also a built-in linkage in the other direction: data→ hypothesis→problem!

This advantage of the hypothetico-deductive method cannot be over-emphasized; the difficulty of getting from a problem to data, and back again, is virtually insurmountable without this method. In the absence of hypotheses or other testable propositions, we can formulate problems and collect data forever without knowing specifically which data are applicable to the problems, or precisely how the applicable data are to be usable in solving them. As Sellitz *et al.* (1959, p. 36) say, 'Regardless of the source of a hypothesis, it performs an important function within a study: It serves as a guide to (1) the kind of data that must be collected in order to answer the research question and (2) *the way in which they can be organized most efficiently in the analysis*' [italics mine].

An important implication of this intimate relationship among hypotheses, data collection and interpretation is that it is inappropriate to advocate separate, discrete 'stages' in the research process (cf. pp. 64–8). Observation and interpretation are so inextricably intertwined that they cannot efficiently be separated: '. . . scientific observation and scientific interpretation need neither be joined nor separated. They are never apart, so they need not be joined. They cannot, even in principle, be separated, and it is conceptually idle to make the attempt' (Hanson, 1967, p. 99). This means, of course, that there is really no such thing as the 'good field man' who can gather data in expert fashion without understanding how the data are to be analysed (i.e. without testable propositions in mind).

The most efficient way to proceed in research is to carry on what Binford (1964, pp. 438–40) calls a 'running analysis' or 'phase excavation' (see also Hole and Heizer, 1969, p. 111). This involves a continuous process of generating hypotheses, testing them, modifying them, and gathering more data for further testing and modification. In this kind of situation the field man must clearly be an analyst or interpreter as well as a technician (cf. Sellitz *et al.*, 1959, pp. 8–9).

In conclusion, it is clear to me that the hypothetico-deductive method is crucial to the advancement of archaeology as a science. If we are really seriously interested in getting answers to research questions, we must employ hypotheses to bridge the gap between our problems and the relevant data to observe. If we want more or less objective evaluations of the correctness of our inferences, we must *test* these tentative answers against the data. As Fritz (1968, p. 42) indicates, '[Testing] is at the core of any science because it is through testing that its knowledge is verified. Moreover, it is more basic to science than any particular hypothesis since it is a method that cross-cuts all sciences. Archaeology can do without a particular idea, but it cannot do without testing.'

7 An example

In the course of discussing the advantages of the hypothesis testing method, I have already presented a limited example of its efficiency. There are a number of examples in the literature, as well (cf. esp. Longacre, 1964; Deetz, 1965; Hill, 1965, 1966, 1967, 1970b; Binford and Binford, 1966; Binford, 1968b; Whallon, 1968; Chartkoff, 1969; Plog, 1969; also Hole and Heizer, 1969, p. 79). Nonetheless, it will be useful to provide a more detailed substantive example of my own here.

In the spring of 1966, I began an extended research project in the Santa Monica mountains region of southern California. One of several of my research questions was as follows: Why do people locate their villages (and other sites) where they do? I asked this question with the then vague understanding that an acceptable answer to it would constitute a scientific law (cf. Hempel, 1966; Fritz and Plog, 1968). My intention was to generate several tentative law-like answers to this question, and then test them against data from the Santa Monica mountains.

My problem stemmed, at least loosely, from systems-ecological theory.

Given my preconception of what a cultural system is, it was evident that I could not answer my question by excavating a single site. People carry out their activities at more than one site, and any settlement system involves more than one kind of site (however temporarily some of them may be used). This meant that I would have to test my hypotheses against data from several kinds of sites, and against information concerning how these sites functioned with respect to one another in a settlement system. The first step, then, was to describe a settlement system; and I decided to restrict my research to Late Horizon systems (cf. Wallace, 1955).

The description of a settlement system is, in itself, a big order, and I have by no means completed it. I decided, however, that since there was already a small amount of published data from two presumably different kinds of sites from this period (large villages and rock shelters), I should focus my initial attention on kinds of sites not yet well reported. I also decided that, as an initial step, I should try to distinguish 'main village sites' (essentially those occupied by men, women and children, for relatively long periods of time) from 'limited use sites' (i.e. sites occupied by a small segment of a community, for brief periods, and for the purpose of exploiting specific resources).

These considerations, among others, led me to choose to excavate a small, presumably late, site about 24 km inland from the Pacific Ocean, near Thousand Oaks, California (Ven-39). It was neither a rock shelter nor a large village site, and it appeared to be a limited use site used in some specific set of exploitive tasks.

The proposition that this was a limited use site was generated on the basis of the fact that the site was relatively small and shallow; there were very few artefacts on the surface; the site was isolated from apparent major travel routes; and finally, it was located in an oak grove (which suggested that it might have been an acorn collecting and processing station).

The test implications deduced from the proposition are given below, together with brief versions of the arguments of relevance. While it would consume too much space to present the test implications for the alternative hypothesis (i.e. that the site was a main village site), it will be recognized that most of the implications for it are opposite to those suggested for limited use sites.

1. The site would be expected to have no house structures or ceremonial structures (or very few, and they would not be of permanent construction). This would be expected because the site would not have been involved in residence activities of a large, stable group of people.

2. There should be few or no burials, since people usually bury their dead in or near their primary villages.

3. There should be little evidence of women and children on the site, since adult or adolescent males usually perform exploitive tasks that are carried out some distance from a main village.

(*a*) There should be few or no female or child burials.

(*b*) The clusters of material items found on the site should be *male*-associated items, with few or no female-associated items (using only items upon which sex association might be generally agreed upon).

4. Few or no storage pits or other storage facilities would be expected, since this would presumably be an exploitive (and perhaps processing) site only. (The test implications for storage facilities alone is a long list, and cannot be presented here.)

5. There should be fewer hearths or fireplaces on the site than on other sites (unless these were used in processing a specific resource), since ordinarily these are more frequently associated with residence activities.

6. There ought to be a much smaller *variety* of classes of artefacts on the site than would be expected on a main village site, since very few different kinds of activities would be expected in a nearly functionally specific site (variability can be compared by a coefficient of variability; cf. Whallon, 1968).

7. There should be a smaller variety of different kinds of features (pits, rock clusters, etc.) than on a main village site, since fewer kinds of activities would be performed.

8. One would expect fewer manufacturing tools than on other sites (e.g. tools to make other tools and facilities), since fewer kinds of activities would be performed.

9. There should be less debris or waste material from the manufacture of tools on the site than on other types of sites, since few manufacturing activities would be expected (other than those associated with the primary use of the site).

10. Fewer ornaments or items that might be construed as decorative or ceremonial would be expected, since neither public display nor ritual activity is expected to be common at exploitive sites.

11. There would probably be less patterning or non-randomness of the layout of the features on the site, since exploitive sites usually would not require careful, systematic planning in terms of the locations of features, etc.

12. Fewer varieties of harvested vegetal foods and animal foods should be found in the remains of the site (compared to a main village site), since the site would usually be occupied for only a short duration, and people would

tend to have a more restricted diet (perhaps even relying solely on local crops near the site).

13. There should be no evidence of year-round occupation, since the site would presumably be used only once or twice each year.

(*a*) Botanical and zoological remains should show that foods were being harvested during a single short segment of the year (analysis of the seasons at which molluscs were harvested should be useful here).

(*b*) While this evidence should indicate seasons in which the site was occupied, it will not establish the fact that it was *not* occupied in other seasons or periods. However, I would expect to find *no* evidence that the common food resources that one would expect to be harvested during the *remainder* of the year were being exploited on the site.

14. One would *not* expect the site itself to be located in an ecological-edge situation (ecotone), but rather nearer the centre of the distribution of the particular resource being exploited. There would be no need for it to be located between biotic zones, since the efficiency of exploiting several resources at one time would not be an important factor.

15. One would not expect the site to be located strategically with respect to certain of the critical resources of existence (e.g. water, fuel, chert, game), since temporary occupation of the site would presumably not require having these resources near at hand (except perhaps water).

16. The site would probably not be located on a major drainage way or other potential major communication or travel route, since such a location is not requisite to exploitive activities.

While I have not defined all of my terms adequately here – either in the test implications or in the hypothesis itself – enough has been given to illustrate some of the kinds of data that had to be collected in order to carry out the test.

Although the analysis of the data is not yet completed, it appears likely that the proposition will be confirmed. Whether it is or not is of little importance; *one* of the two propositions will surely receive more support than the other, and I will have learned a great deal that would not otherwise have been learned. I suspect that this proposition (and its alternative) will have to be refined, and perhaps even drastically modified. And further, it will be necessary to test such propositions against data from other sites in the area, since many of the above test implications are measured in terms that are *relative* to other sites. It is most important to note, however, that these propositions were generated *before* going into the field. They, and innumerable others, can clearly be formulated without first excavating a site and examining the materials it contains.

Furthermore, while a large portion of the data needed for testing these propositions might have been collected without a hypothesis, an equally large amount would have been overlooked. The sampling procedure used, for example, was predicated on the fact that it was necessary to sample all portions of the site evenly and thoroughly; only in this way could I be assured of obtaining accurate measurements of the spatial distributions of features (and subclasses within them), as well as other artefacts and debris. Such detailed distributional information was required by the propositions (cf. pp. 90–2), and I do not think it could have been obtained by most normal sampling procedures.

It is perhaps even more important, however, to note that *each one* of the above test implications has a further list of test implications that had to be looked for in the field, and they required the collection of many other kinds of information. As an example, consider the kinds of evidence needed to establish not only the differences among features on the site, but also their uses. Ethnographic data provided me with some of the test expectations that should be found in association with features that served different kinds of uses, and this information had to be looked for. It was important, for instance, to exert a great deal of effort in determining whether or not each feature contained evidence of burning, and whether each had been a surface feature, or had been situated in a pit of some kind. It was also necessary to record the sizes of the rocks in the features, to an accuracy of plus or minus one centimetre. Pollen samples had to be taken not only from the 'floors' of features, but from areas outside their boundaries. And various sampling and excavation techniques had to be devised simply to *locate* the boundaries of features.

The fact that most of this information would not have been recorded in the absence of the propositions is attested by the fact that such kinds of data have not been adequately gathered (or reported) in connection with other excavated sites in the area – and hence it is difficult for me to test my propositions with data from these sites (while these data *are* being used, the test results will simply not be as good as I had hoped).

This situation underscores the difficulty of generating and testing hypotheses *after* excavation has been completed. Many of the esoteric data needed are simply not collected. While this by no means suggests that we cannot use the reports of others for certain purposes, it *does* indicate that on many occasions this will be difficult or impossible.

This example, while it is as yet incomplete, serves not only to illustrate the point that we would miss important data without hypotheses, but also the point that when the relevant data *are* collected there is little question concerning how to interpret them. There can be no doubt that I will end up with a test of the two competing propositions, and will be able to evaluate the respective validity of each.[17] Even if I cannot demonstrate that one is precisely correct, I will gain enough knowledge to be able to revise the propositions so that I or others can continue the testing process in the future. Thus, the hypothetico-deductive method is not only efficient with regard to data collection and analysis – it also ensures us that new knowledge will be gained. A primarily inductive method offers no such assurances, since in that method there is no systematic way to evaluate competing ideas or inferences, nor to find out what is *wrong* with them, so that adjustments can be made.

8 Objections

In concluding this paper, it is important to consider some of the major objections that have been raised with regard to using the hypothetico-deductive method. While I have already tried to answer some of these objections, there are a few points worthy of brief comment here.

The first, and probably most important, objection is that the method tends to outlaw the use of inductively or abductively drawn inferences – that is, inferences made while the investigator is confronted by data. The common view is that the subscriber to the hypothetico-deductive method *imposes* his *a priori* ideas (hypotheses) on the data without regard to the fact that he might learn something by looking closely at the data themselves. It is almost as though the researcher might generate hypotheses that are completely out of line with the available data, and then proceed to accept the hypotheses as fact (without having 'due respect' for what the data actually 'say').

This is a serious misunderstanding. In the first place, it assumes that once hypotheses are generated they are unalterable in the face of data – which is not the case. Hypotheses can be altered, should be altered, and nearly always *are* altered in the face of data. Binford (1964), in his plea for 'phase excavation' or running analysis, clearly indicates this. Hypotheses are generated, and they are tested against data. In the process of doing this, there is an abductive feedback in which we pair our hypotheses and other ideas with the characteristics of the data, and change the hypotheses when there is a lack of fit with the data. This leads to further data observation and further testing, until eventually our gain in knowledge has reached the point that we can reject some hypotheses and accept others. Even when hypotheses are disconfirmed, we learn a great deal that would not be learned without this method (cf. Hill, 1968, 1970a).

Nothing is ever 'imposed' that violates the nature of the data – unless, of course, a hypothesis is proposed but not *tested*! That kind of behaviour, however, is rarely found among practitioners of the hypothetico-deductive method, while its occurrence is commonplace among most other social science researchers (Wilson, 1952, pp. 26–7).

Thus there is no argument here that inferences cannot be inspired by looking at data. As a matter of fact many of our initial working hypotheses are provoked by data, in one form or another. We may be inspired by archaeological data, ethnographic data (cf. Binford, 1967; Hill, 1968), zoological data, or anything else in our range of experience (Wilson, 1952, p. 26; Sellitz *et al.*, 1959, p. 36; Hempel, 1966, pp. 14–15) (see diagram on p. 873).

Nonetheless, no matter how any given proposition is generated (i.e. whatever its source), it can only be *tested* by deducing test implications and checking them against the data. It is at this point in research that deduction becomes of primary importance. Carl Hempel (1966) likes to think of the hypothesis generating step as the 'context of discovery', and the testing step as the 'context of validation'. In any event, the two procedures should be kept separate. While there are no particular 'rules' with regard to the sources of inspiration for a hypothesis, there *are* commonly accepted rules for testing once a hypothesis has been generated (Hempel, 1966) (see Fig. 17.2).

But given the fact that both deductive and inductive reasoning and procedure are necessary to research, there may still be those who object to employing the hypothetico-deductive method. Many feel that collecting data to test hypotheses will so severely bias what is observed that the investigator will tend to collect only the information that would tend to confirm his hypotheses, and ignore the things that might refute them – thus employing a built-in mechanism that might promote the confirmation of hypotheses which in fact should *not* be confirmed.

This can happen, of course, although there are at least two important safeguards built into the method that can prevent it. In the first place, when the method is properly used, an investigator will not test only *one* hypothesis or answer to a problem; he will test two or more competing hypotheses. If multiple working hypotheses are employed, there is little possibility of uncritically accepting a single 'ruling' hypothesis (Chamberlin, 1965). The investigator will consciously gather data to test even those hypotheses he does not favour. And further, he will make a concerted effort to find the data that will *refute* each of his hypotheses. Platt (1964) refers to this method as 'strong inference', and makes a very good case for its use.

It is also worth pointing out that most investigators have more than one problem, and hence more than one set of hypotheses in mind when carrying out their research. This, in itself, should help ensure that a wide range of different kinds of data is collected.

And further, the problem of biasing data collection is offset by the fact that even the most strongly hypothesis-oriented researchers do not frequently disregard data they know their colleagues will want. Most such data are fairly obvious and ready at hand, and most of them are generally found to be useful in testing one or another hypothesis. In any event, I am not aware that hypothesis testing has prevented any investigator from gathering traditionally important categories of data. What has usually happened is that many *more* data are required when hypotheses are being tested – not fewer! At the same time, of course, I would not deny that there may be occasions when one must sacrifice certain kinds of information solely for reasons of efficiency and financial responsibility.

I have previously made the point that it is not just hypotheses that bias data collection – we are always biased in one way or another and cannot avoid it (pp. 70–7). And the biases are just as great, regardless of the general methods we subscribe to. Hypothesis testing has the distinct advantage of making our biases conscious, so that we can control for them. If we know what the biases are, then our results can be more objectively evaluated than would otherwise be the case.

Hypothesis testing, then, is not a restrictive method; it is not something that limits the numbers of inferences we make, or something that requires us to collect only the data that might support our *a priori* ideas. On the contrary, the hypothetico-deductive method is an *expansive* one. It encourages more different kinds of research questions to be asked, more inferences to be made, and more kinds of data to be collected. An investigator is not restricted to simply examining his data and coming up with a few more or less untestable and unalterable inferences (as is the case in the more inductive emphasis). He may invent any number of hypotheses, then test them, modify them, invent new hypotheses inspired by previous results, and so forth. There is, in this method, no known limit to the kinds of inferences we can make – the only requirement is that they be tested. In this way, our knowledge of the past can expand virtually without limit. The major limiting factor would seem to be the number of different kinds of useful hypotheses we are capable of inventing.

This means, of course, that we can invent hypotheses about the so-called 'intangibles' of the past just as readily as about anything else. The data required by the test implications of such hypotheses will be every bit as tangible as any data for any hypothesis. The data will either be found in the record or they will not. There is no way to know whether they will be there or not until we look – and it is hypotheses that guide us in the looking! The idea that the hypothesis testing method goes 'beyond the data' is a flagrant misunderstanding of the method. It is true, to be sure, that not all of our hypotheses will be supported by the data (many will be refuted) – but this is the beauty of the method! We will have a reasonably objective means of knowing whether our inferences are correct or not, and we will reduce the possibility of accepting false hypotheses as fact.

Even the old objection that poor preservation will limit our inferences is vastly overdone (cf. Hole and Heizer, 1969, pp. 82, 270, 343, 363, 186–7). First of all, since hypotheses are formulated in the mind, it is not possible for any condition of the data to limit them *a priori*; it is only in attempting to test them that we may find the data unavailable. And secondly, it is likely that *some* data will be available to test most (or a large number) of the hypotheses we might be interested in. The reason for this is that the data needed to test any given hypothesis usually consist of many and diverse kinds of observations, and at least a few of these test implications are likely to be observable, even in conditions of poor preservation. This is not always true, but it will frequently be the case if the investigator has done a conscientious job of generating test implications. Most of the 'intangibles' of the past leave a great many kinds of evidence of their former existence. This should be evident from the examples I have already given (see also Hill, 1966, 1968, 1970a).

A further complaint that is sometimes made is that the method advocated here obviates archaeological expertise. There seems to be a fear that hypothesis testing is a mechanical, impersonal method that can somehow provide us with answers without involving the skill, imagination or other human characteristics of the investigator. It should by now be clear that this is not the case; if anything, *more* expertise is required to formulate and test hypotheses. One must not only be methodologically sophisticated, but one must also have a great deal of knowledge of other things as well. The better one's educational background and experience, the better able he will be to know what problems are in need of solution, and what hypotheses have been (and can be) suggested as solutions to them. In fact, many ideas for both problems and hypotheses may come from fields outside of anthropology – from systems theory, ecology, geography, botany, zoology, and so forth. A wide acquaintance with other fields, as well as anthropology, is thus desirable (p. 55).

One can rarely even generate test implications for hypotheses without knowing a great deal about the phenomena implied by the hypotheses. For example, it would be difficult to develop test implications for matrilocal residence without knowing a great deal about what matrilocal residence is and how it works. And similarly, it would be difficult to generate test implications for prehistoric warfare without knowing a great deal about the kinds of warfare that exist in the world. In short, good ideas are usually an outgrowth of expertise and experience. Some archaeologists are clearly more 'expert' than others in generating problems, thinking up hypotheses, and carrying out other aspects of research. Expertise and intuition are the most important assets we have!

I *do* want to make the point, however, that expertise is not a *testing* device. We cannot judge the worth of an inference by the educational background or competence of the investigator (see Thompson, 1956). Inferences must be tested against empirical data, and their worth is measured by evaluating the degree to which the data support one hypothesis as opposed to others (cf. Sellitz *et al.*, 1959, pp. 389–90; Hempel, 1966, p. 15).

An additional point sometimes raised is that hypothesis testing is peculiarly inappropriate in archaeology, because archaeologists cannot know what is in a prehistoric site *before* they have excavated it. Thus, we might generate hypotheses, and then find later that the site does not contain the expected data for testing. While this can presumably happen, the idea suggests an additional misunderstanding of the method. In the first place, I have already pointed out that there is no requirement that *all* hypotheses be generated prior to data collection. And secondly, it is evident that a great many hypotheses *can* be generated before going into the field (cf. esp. Longacre, 1964; Hill, 1965, 1966). We can test propositions concerning such things as seasonality, residence patterns, uses of artefacts, status differentials, and so forth, at many sites within almost any region of the world. Most hypotheses do not depend on knowing precisely what is in a site ahead of time. But at the same time I must point out that we almost always *do* have a great deal of knowledge about the general kinds of things a site might contain. In fact, we are wasting this information if we do not make use of it in the formulation of problems and hypotheses prior to excavation.

Another objection occasionally brought up is that hypothesis testing will not work in archaeology the way it does in other sciences because we are not experimental scientists who can manipulate and control our data in the laboratory. In short, it is said that every archaeological site is unique, and once it is dug up, we must take what we find and recognize that the 'experiment' can never be repeated. While we might be able to test hypotheses against data from a particular site, we could not test the same hypotheses elsewhere in the world, at other sites, where the 'data' are different (Rouse, 1962, pp. 100–1).

This argument, also, is invalid. There is no clear-cut distinction between laboratory experimentation and field observation (Wilson, 1952, p. 28). While strictly speaking no two events or observations are the same (even in the laboratory), it is exceedingly impractical not to recognize the fact that there are regularities, or approximate repetitions of our specified variables and conditions (Wilson, 1952, p. 24). As an example, consider the general hypothesis that changes in degree of stylistic variability are primarily related to changes in the rate of interaction between people (cf. Whallon, 1968, p. 228). This has not only been tested by Whallon using eastern North American data, but indirectly also by Cronin (1962), Deetz (1965), Longacre (1964) and Hill (1965, 1966, 1970b). While most hypotheses may not be testable everywhere, they are testable in a large number of places – otherwise we would have to discard the idea of ever getting cross-cultural generalizations.

While many of the specific characteristics of the physical data may vary from place to place, cross-cultural hypotheses (law-like statements) do not depend on finding precisely similar physical data in each location. They depend, rather, on our being able to observe generally similar kinds of variables. The presumption is, for example, that if we want to explain such a phenomenon as 'increasing political centralization', we can test our hypotheses concerning it anywhere in the world where political centralization has occurred or is occurring. This presumption of regularity is, of course, the basic premise of social science (and all other sciences).

Another difficulty with the hypothetico-deductive method is, it is said, that hypothesis testing is usually *post hoc* – i.e. we do not really do research that way, but rather simply recast our results after the fact to make it *look* as if we had tested hypotheses. This is the distinction Kaplan (1964, pp. 3–11) makes between 'logic in use' and 'reconstructed logic'. The idea, in essence, is that we actually gather the data first, and *then* generate and test hypotheses.

I would argue, in the first place, that this is by no means always true; there are several extant examples of hypothesis testing that are in no sense *post hoc* (see esp. Longacre, 1964; Hill, 1966, 1970b). I would argue, however, that it really makes no difference whether a hypothesis is tested after the data have been collected or not – even whether we recast a piece of research in a form other than what it was when originally carried out (e.g. Hill, 1968). The only matter of real concern should be how well a given hypothesis is supported by empirical data. If the data appear to support (or refute) a hypothesis, then it seems irrelevant to be worried about the processes of logic and procedure used by the investigator in achieving this end product. While this view differs from my earlier understanding (Hill, 1968), I am convinced that it is more reasonable.

A further drawback to the method that is sometimes brought forth is that hypothesis testing cannot be carried out adequately unless we first acquire a solid spatial-temporal framework (Hole and Heizer, 1969, p. 102). A good, dated 'culture' sequence is especially mandatory if we are to begin testing ideas about such things as social organization and culture process. In rebuttal, I can only state again what should by now be obvious – after a question is asked, and hypotheses formulated, *then* we can determine what data are required for testing. Chronology may well be of great importance, and usually is, but dating is not something inherently primary to all other considerations. In some cases, of course, dating may have to be more refined than is as yet possible to achieve. The point, again, is that there are really no kinds of data that can be considered inherently 'basic' – not even dates or standard pottery types!

I think that at this point I have briefly answered most of the major objections that are commonly advanced against the hypothetico-deductive method. The only other objection I have frequently heard is not really a charge against the usefulness of the method at all – it is simply the unwillingness to believe that hypothesis testing is anything *new* in archaeology. The charge is that those of us who advocate hypothesis testing do not have a very good grasp of the history of anthropology – in which, it is said, there are innumerable examples of hypothesis testing extending back many years.

This is really a moot argument. There have, to be sure, been some examples of hypothesis testing by archaeologists in the past (either formal or informal testing); there has also been a great deal of lip service paid to testing. At the same time, my experience with archaeological text books, syntheses, field reports and research proposals leads me to the conclusion that testing has in fact not been a common occurrence; even now it is not. Testing is talked about, but rarely put into practice. Data collection is still most commonly guided only by vague problems, and interpretation involves the presenting of untested inferences.

It is unfortunate that there is still a common feeling that one method is as good as another in archaeology, and that one will do equally well in subscribing to either the hypothetico-deductive method or the more inductive one (or an unsystematic combination of the two). Actually the choice is an important one; it is real, and it has significant practical effects on our results. The eclectic approach to choice of general research method ignores the fact that there are more and less efficient ways of getting and evaluating answers to our problems. As Marvin Harris (1968, p. 6) recently said, 'One might argue that the choice of a particular . . . research strategy does not prevent others from making a different set of choices. But the limitations on deployable time and manpower oblige us to consider carefully the relative contributions of alternative research options and strategies to the development of nomothetic theory.'

Whether we admit it or not, most archaeologists are trying to describe and explain various aspects of prehistoric human behaviour; the literature amply supports this assertion (cf. Hole and Heizer, 1969, pp. 46–8 and ch. 17). The difficulty is that our commonly accepted methods have not been conducive to achieving our goals.

Given the increasing acceptance of systems and ecological theory as a set of basic premises, and the shift in problem emphasis that has resulted, it is not surprising that the hypothetico-deductive method is gaining ground proportionally. The research questions being asked are increasingly those involving the description and explanation of the 'intangibles' (e.g. process). These things cannot usually be induced or abduced from the archaeological record, and it has been necessary to begin shifting from a heavily empiricist method to a more positivistic one.

As in manufacture so in science – retooling is an extravagance to be reserved for the occasion that demands it. The significance of crises is the indication they provide that an occasion for retooling has arrived. (Kuhn, 1962, p. 76)

Notes

1. The ideas of several people have been incorporated into this paper. I am especially grateful to John M. Fritz (University of California, Santa Cruz), who not only offered extensive criticism of the paper, but also permitted me to draw heavily on his unpublished manuscript, *Archaeological Epistemology: Two Views* (Masters Paper, University of Chicago). Contributions were also made by Michael A. Glassow (University of California, Santa Barbara) and Fred. T. Plog (University of California, Los Angeles). I am also grateful to Stephen Williams and the enthusiastic students in his graduate seminar on 'The Discipline of Archaeology' (Harvard University, Anthropology 275, Spring 1969).

2. Walter Taylor (1948) presented a new paradigm that did not get all the attention it deserved. His 'conjunctive approach' argued that trait-list theory was not very useful, and that archaeologists should study prehistoric behaviour systems (through studying associations among prehistoric remains). It is currently being argued, by Taylor

(1969, p. 383) and others, that the New Archaeology offers little beyond this twenty-four year old statement. It is clear that the New Archaeologists are indebted to Taylor (and others) for stating some of the tenets of the modern systemic approach. At the same time current systemic archaeological theory represents some major departures from Taylor's theory – notably in the realm of explanation. Taylor held strongly to the traditional normative-ideational view of culture and culture change (cf. 1967, pp. 95–100, 141, 144–5, 161, 164, 180, and all of ch. 4). He also resorted to trait-list theory when discussing cultural comparisons (extra-community comparisons) (cf. 1967, pp. 166–7). His theory is probably most accurately characterized as 'eclectic' (Harris, 1968, pp. 1–7).

3. I do not intend to imply that Thompson subscribes wholly or in part to this inductive methodology today. His statement of it is, however, unsurpassed.

4. Boas and his followers subscribed to this view (cf. Harris, 1968, pp. 268–9), and it is likely that the epistemic predicament of archaeology today can be ascribed to the earlier pervasive influence of Boasian anthropology.

5. The tentative inferences derived from the 'indicators' are then 'tested' against 'probative' data (ethno-historical analogues) (Thompson, 1958; Chang, 1967a). This is not an adequate test procedure, however (cf. Binford, 1967; Hill, 1968, 1970a).

6. Rouse (1939, pp. 7–35) establishes the idea that information can be derived from parts or attributes of artefacts as well (modes). Taylor (1948, 1967) and others have suggested that information can also be derived from *associations* among artefacts. I do not mean to imply that attributes and associations are not observed by empiricist researchers, nor that inferences about them are not made. Even though they are sometimes observed, however, they are regarded as discrete entities having some internal meaning or 'indicator' to be discovered – in the same way that individual 'artefacts' are viewed. It is considered possible to induce inferences *from* them.

7. Hole and Heizer's *An Introduction to Prehistoric Archaeology* (1965) tended to support this empiricist reasoning and procedure. The second edition (1969), however, is equivocal in this regard.

8. A related reason for the fact that we have not been very successful at studying process is that we (and other anthropologists as well) lack *theory* from which to generate problems and hypotheses about process. While anthropology has considerable theory concerning the structure of societies, it has little to account for the dynamic workings of these structures or structural change (John M. Fritz, personnal communication).

9. Fritz (1968), following Hanson (1965), employs the term 'abduction' to refer to the reasoning and research procedure I am calling 'induction'. Abduction is a more specific term, which takes account of the fact that pure induction is impossible; there is always interplay between data and prior ideas held by an investigator. Abduction, then, refers to the situation in which an investigator generates an inference while confronted with data; it recognizes that both induction and deduction are involved.

10. The decision as to what is 'diagnostic' is often based on the importance of an artefact type in dating and measuring culture 'contact'. It is more likely to be diagnostic if it is a good 'fossile directeur'.

11. I find that the major difficulty students have with research papers is the failure to have real, solvable *problems* – i.e. to ask real questions. This results in an almost aimless perusal of a certain segment of the literature in the hope that a problem may later be defined. This is frequently unsuccessful.

12. The term 'hypothesis' usually denotes a testable *explanatory* statement, rather than a descriptive one (cf. Braithwaite, 1960; Hempel, 1966). A descriptive statement such as 'This room was a ceremonial room', or 'That site was occupied during the winter', is not a hypothesis in this sense. I reserve the term 'proposition' to refer to testable descriptive statements of this kind.

13. It is notable that while Walter Taylor (1948, 1967) presented theoretical ideas that in some respects approximate modern 'systems theory' in archaeology, he presented no well-formulated method for testing inferences. A 'test' was considered to involve at least one of three things: (1) the gathering of additional data, (2) appeal to ethnographic analogy, or (3) appeal to the expertise of the investigator (see esp. Taylor, 1967, pp. 90, 109, 113, 117, 120–1, 123, 129, 143, 155, 169, 188).

14. Popper (1959, p. 41) and Platt (1964, pp. 350–2) argue convincingly that since there is no real proof in science, and since it is usually easier to disconfirm a hypothesis than to confirm it, we should spend most of our efforts trying to *disconfirm* our hypotheses – beginning always with the ones most easy to disconfirm. We may eventually be left with a single hypothesis.

15. At some stage in the development of a science, it should be possible to derive test implications from hypotheses (and hypotheses from theory) via strict formal deductive logic; but this requires a degree of mathematical formalization that will not be seen in anthropology for many years. We should try to approach this goal, however.

16. For further discussion of this view, see Hanson (1965), Putnam (1959) and Coombs (1964).

17. I am also attempting to test these propositions against surface survey data from the Santa Monica mountains region. This attempt, while useful, is suffering from the fact that the standard survey records do not provide for recording many of the kinds of data required by the hypotheses.

References

ADAMS, R. MCC. (1968) Archaeological research strategies: past and present. *Science*, **160** (3833), 1187–92.

ASCHER, R. (1961) Analogy in archaeological interpretation. *Southwestern Journal of Anthropology*, **17**, 317–25.

BINFORD, L. R. (1962) Archaeology as anthropology. *American Antiquity*, **28** (2), 217–25.

BINFORD, L. R. (1964) A consideration of archaeological research design. *American Antiquity*, **29** (4), 425–41.

BINFORD, L. R. (1965) Archaeological systematics and the study of culture process. *American Antiquity*, **31**, (1) (2), 203–10.

BINFORD, L. R. (1967) Smudge pits and hide smoking: the use of analogy in archaeological reasoning. *American Antiquity*, **32** (1), 1–12.

BINFORD, L. R. (1968a) Archaeological perspectives. In BINFORD, S. R. and BINFORD, L. R. (eds.) *New Perspectives in Archeology*, 5–32. Chicago: Aldine.

BINFORD, L. R. (1968b) Post-Pleistocene adaptations. In BINFORD, S. R. and BINFORD, L. R. (eds.) *New Perspectives in Archeology*, 313–41. Chicago: Aldine.

BINFORD, L. R. (1968c) Some comments on historical versus processual archaeology. *Southwestern Journal of Anthropology*, **24** (3), 267–75.

BINFORD, L. R. and BINFORD, S. R. (1966) A preliminary analysis of functional variability in the Mousterian of Levallois facies. *American Anthropologist*, **68**, 2 (2), 238–95.

BINFORD, S. R. and BINFORD, L. R. (eds.) (1968) *New Perspectives in Archeology*. Chicago: Aldine.

BLACK, M. (1967) The justification of induction. In MORGENBESSER, S. (ed.) *Philosophy of Science Today*, 190–200. New York: Basic Books.

BRAITHWAITE, R. B. (1960) *Scientific Explanation*. New York: Harper.

CHAMBERLIN, T. C. (1965) The method of multiple working hypotheses. *Science*, **148**, 754–59. Reprinted from *Science*, 7 February 1890.

CHANG, K. C. (1967a) *Rethinking Archaeology*. New York: Random House.

CHANG, K. C. (1967b) Major aspects of the interrelationship of archaeology and ethnology. *Current Anthropology*, **8** (3), 227–34.

CHANG, K. C. (ed.) (1968) *Settlement Archaeology*. Palo Alto: National Press.

CHARTKOFF, J. L. (1969) *The Change from Food Collection to Food Production in the Prehistoric Near East: Some Tests of Possible Causes*. MS., Masters Paper, Dept of Anthropology, University of California, Los Angeles.

COHEN, M. R. and NAGEL, E. (1934) *An Introduction to Logic and Scientific Method*. New York: Harcourt.

COOMBS, C. H. (1964) *A Theory of Data*. New York: Wiley.

CREIGHTON, J. E. (1945) Deduction. *Encyclopedia Americana*, **8**, 574.

CRONIN, C. (1962) An analysis of pottery design elements indicating possible relationships between three decorated types. In 'Chapters in the Prehistory of Eastern Arizona, I' by MARTIN, P. S., RINALDO, J. B. et al., *Fieldiana: Anthropology*, **53**, 105–14. Chicago: Field Museum of Natural History.

DEETZ, J. (1965) *The Dynamics of Stylistic Change in Arikara Ceramics*. Illinois Studies in Anthropology No. 4. Urbana: University of Illinois Press.

DEETZ, J. (1968) Cultural patterning of behaviour as reflected by archaeological materials. In CHANG, K. C. (ed.) *Settlement Archaeology*, 31–42. Palo Alto: National Press.

FLANNERY, K. V. (1967) Culture history v. cultural process: a debate in American archaeology. *Scientific American*, **217**, 119–22.

FORD, J. A. (1954) The type concept revisited. *American Anthropologist*, **56** (1), 42–54.

FRITZ, J. M. (1968) *Archaeological Epistemology: Two Views*. MS., Unpublished Masters Paper, University of Chicago.

FRITZ, J. M. and PLOG, F. T. (1968) *The Nature of Archaeological Explanation*. MS., presented at 33rd Annual Meetings of the Society for American Archaeology, Santa Fé, New Mexico, May 1968 (presented as two separate papers).

HANSON, N. R. (1965) *Patterns of Discovery: An Inquiry into the Conceptual Foundations of Science*. Cambridge: Cambridge University Press.

HANSON, N. R. (1967) Observation and interpretation. In MORGENBESSER, S. (ed.) *Philosophy of Science Today*, 89–99. New York: Basic Books.

HARRIS, M. (1964) *The Nature of Cultural Things*. New York: Random House.

HARRIS, M. (1968) *The Rise of Anthropological Theory*. New York: Crowell.

HAWKES, C. (1954) Archaeological theory and method: some suggestions from the Old World. *American Anthropologist*, **56** (2), 155–67.

HEMPEL, C. G. (1966) *Philosophy of Natural Science*. Englewood Cliffs: Prentice-Hall.

HILL, J. N. (1965) *Broken K: A Prehistoric Community in Eastern Arizona*. MS., Doctoral Dissertation, University of Chicago.

HILL, J. N. (1966) A prehistoric community in eastern Arizona. *Southwestern Journal of Anthropology*, **22** (1), 9–30.

HILL, J. N. (1967) Structure, function and change at Broken K Pueblo. In 'Chapters in the Prehistory of Eastern Arizona, III' by MARTIN, P. S. *et al.*, *Fieldiana: Anthropology*, **57**, 158–67. Chicago: Field Museum of Natural History.

HILL, J. N. (1968) Broken K Pueblo: patterns of form and function. In BINFORD, S. R. and BINFORD, L. R. (eds.) *New Perspectives in Archeology*, 103–42. Chicago: Aldine.

HILL, J. N. (1969) The reconstructing of prehistoric societies. Review of *Settlement Archaeology* by K. C. Chang (ed.). *Science*, **166** (3903), 367–8.

HILL, J. N. (1970a) Prehistoric social organization in the American Southwest: theory and method. In LONGUERE, W. A. (ed.) *Reconstructing Prehistoric Pueblo Societies*. Albuquerque: University of New Mexico Press.

HILL, J. N. (1970b) *Broken K Pueblo: Prehistoric Social Organization in the American Southwest*. Anthropological Papers of the University of Arizona No. 18 Tucson: University of Arizona Press.

HOLE, F. and HEIZER, R. F. (1965) *An Introduction to Prehistoric Archaeology*. New York: Holt, Rinehart & Winston.

HOLE, F. and HEIZER, R. F. (1969) *An Introduction to Prehistoric Archaeology*. 2nd ed. New York: Holt, Rinehart & Winston.

KAPLAN, A. (1964) *The Conduct of Inquiry*. San Francisco: Chandler.

KUHN, T. S. (1962) *The Structure of Scientific Revolutions*. Chicago: University of Chicago Press.

LAZARSFELD, P. F. (1968) Evidence and inference in social research. In BRODBECK, M. (ed.) *Readings in the Philosophy of the Social Sciences*, 608–34. New York: Macmillan.

LONGACRE, W. A. (1964) Archaeology as anthropology: a case study. *Science*, **144** (3625), 1454–5.

MACWHITE, E. (1956) On the interpretation of archaeological evidence in historical and sociological terms. *American Anthropologist*, **58**, 3–25.

MAYER-OAKES, W. J. (1966) *Toward a Theoretical Framework for Doing Archaeology*. MS., University of Manitoba.

MILLER, J. G. (1965) Living systems: basic concepts. *Behavioral Science*, **10** (3), 193–237. Living systems: structure and process, Living systems: cross-level hypotheses, both in *Behavioral Science*, **10** (4), 337–411.

NAGEL, E. (1961) *The Structure of Science: Problems in the Logic of Scientific Explanation.* New York: Harcourt, Brace & World.

NAGEL, E. (1967) The nature and aim of science. In MORGENBESSER, S. (ed.) *Philosophy of Science Today,* 3–13. New York: Basic Books.

ODUM, E. P. and ODUM, H. T. (1959) *Fundamentals of Ecology.* 2nd ed. Philadelphia: Saunders.

PLATT, J. R. (1964) Strong inference. *Science,* **146** (3642), 347–53.

PLOG, F. T. (1969) *An Approach to the Study of Prehistoric Change.* MS., Doctoral Dissertation, University of Chicago.

POPPER, K. R. (1959) *The Logic of Scientific Discovery.* New York: Basic Books.

PUTNAM, H. (1959) Review of *Patterns of Discovery* by N. R. Hanson. *Science,* **129,** 1666–7.

ROUSE, I. (1939) *Prehistory in Haiti: a Study in Method.* Yale University Publications in Anthropology No. 21. New Haven: Yale University Press.

ROUSE, I. (1953) The strategy of culture history. In KROEBER, A. L. (ed.) *Anthropology Today,* 57–76. Chicago: University of Chicago Press.

ROUSE, I. (1962) The strategy of culture history. In TAX, S. (ed.) *Anthropology Today: Selections,* 84–103. Chicago: University of Chicago Press.

ROUSE, I. (1965) The place of 'peoples' in prehistoric research. *Journal of the Royal Anthropological Institute,* **95** (1), 1–15.

RUDNER, R. S. (1966) *Philosophy of Social Science.* Englewood Cliffs: Prentice-Hall.

SABLOFF, J. A. and WILLEY, G. R. (1967) The collapse of Maya civilization in the southern lowlands: a consideration of history and process. *Southwestern Journal of Anthropology,* **23** (4), 311–36.

SEARS, W. H. (1961) The study of social and religious systems in North American archaeology. *Current Anthropology,* **2** (3), 223–31.

SELLITZ, C., JAHODA, M., DEUTSCH, M. and COOK, S. W. (1959) *Research Methods in Social Relations.* Rev. ed. 1 vol. New York: Holt, Rinehart & Winston.

SMITH, M. A. (1955) The limitations of inference in archaeology. *The Archaeological Newsletter,* **6** (1), 1–7.

STEWARD, J. H. and SETZLER, F. M. (1938) Function and configuration in archaeology. *American Antiquity,* **4** (1), 4–10.

SWARTZ, B. K., JR (1967) A logical sequence of archaeological objectives. *American Antiquity,* **32** (4), 487–97.

TALLGREN, A. M. (1937) The method of prehistoric archaeology. *Antiquity,* **11** (42), 152–61.

TAYLOR, W. W. (1948) A study of archeology. American Anthropological Association Memoir No. 69. *American Anthropologist,* **50** (2) (3).

TAYLOR, W. W. (1967) *A Study of Archeology.* Carbondale; Southern Illinois University Press.

TAYLOR, W. W. (1969) Review of *New Perspectives in Archeology* by S. R. Binford and L. R. Binford (eds.), *Science,* **165** (3891), 382–3.

THOMPSON, R. H. (1956) The subjective element in archaeological inference. *Southwestern Journal of Anthropology,* **12** (3), 327–32.

THOMPSON, R. H. (1958) Modern Yucatecan Maya pottery making. Memoirs of the Society for American Archaeology No. 15. *American Antiquity,* **23,** 2 (4).

WALLACE, W. J. (1955) A suggested chronology for southern California archaeology. *Southwestern Journal of Anthropology*, 11 (3), 214–30.

WHALLON, R., JR (1968) Investigations of late prehistoric social organization in New York State. In BINFORD, S. R. and BINFORD, L. R. (eds.) *New Perspectives in Archeology*, 223–44. Chicago: Aldine.

WILLEY, G. R. (1962) Archeological theories and interpretations: New World. In TAX, S. (ed.) *Anthropology Today: Selections*, 170–94. Chicago: University of Chicago Press.

WILLEY, G. R. (1966) *An Introduction to American Archaeology. Vol. I: North and Middle America*. Englewood Cliffs: Prentice Hall.

WILLEY, G. R. and PHILLIPS, P. (1958) *Method and Theory in American Archaeology*. Chicago: University of Chicago Press.

WILSON, E. B. JR (1952) *An Introduction to Scientific Research*. New York: McGraw-Hill.

3
Contemporary model building: paradigms and the current state of Palaeolithic research

L. R. BINFORD
University of New Mexico, Albuquerque, U.S.A.

In recent years there has been an increasing use of the term 'model' in the writings of archaeologists. There have been explicit calls for more model building and these have frequently been coupled with calls for a greater use of scientific method. The purpose of this discussion is to examine the current state of theory and model building in the field of palaeolithic archaeology.

> . . . the relevant facts of nature do not of their own accord separate themselves from all the others, nor do they come with all their significant characteristics duly labelled for us. Which of the infinite variety of nature's circumstances we would turn to as relevant to or bearing upon any specific problem depends upon our general ideas as to how that which is sought for can possibly be related to what we already know. Without such guiding ideas or hypotheses as to possible connections we have nothing to look for. (Cohen, 1964, p. 77).

We always bring to our observations some expectations in the form of 'models' of nature. These are our particular cognitive maps of what nature is like and what we can expect from it. It has been argued that the 'desire' for an explanation originates from a reaction of surprise to some experience. 'This surprise . . . is generated by a conflict between our expectations in a given situation and our actual experience of it' (Harvey, 1969, p. 11). One might argue that all persons whether scientists or not generally approach nature in this manner. They have a series of 'models' of nature, a series of cognitive expectations, and it is when these expectations are not met that an 'explanation' is demanded or sought. Kuhn (1962, p. x), in his fascinating review of patterning in the history of intellectual activity, has argued convincingly that

109

in science as well as intellectual life in general there are accepted 'models' of nature, which are shared among a community of scholars. He calls these 'models' a paradigm. The dynamic relations between the paradigm shared among a community of scholars, the activities of the scholars, and the problems selected for solution, are well described by Kuhn (1962, p. 37) as follows:

> ...a scientific community acquires with a paradigm...a criterion for choosing problems that, while the paradigm is taken for granted, can be assumed to have solutions. To a great extent these are the only problems that the community will admit as scientific or encourage its members to undertake. Other problems, including many that had previously been standard, are rejected as metaphysical, as the concern of another discipline, or some times as just too problematic to be worth the time. A paradigm can, for that matter, even insulate the community from those socially important problems that are not reducible to the puzzle form, because they cannot be stated in terms of the conceptual and instrumental tools the paradigm supplies.

Archaeology appears to me to provide an interesting case of the traditional use of a paradigm, a model of what the archaeological record is like, what we can expect from it, and its significance. Many archaeologists will object, maintaining that they are empiricists, collecting the facts and arranging them according to the order inherent in them. Let us examine the empiricists' argument.

Archaeology is the science concerned with the description and explanation of differences and similarities observed in the archaeological record. The archaeologist may carry out three major kinds of activities in the context of his role as an archaeologist. These might be summarized as exploration, explication, and explanation.

(1) *Exploration.* Much of the work of the past, and of that continuing today, is justified on the basis that we simply do not know what the archaeological record is like in a given region or for a given time period. We may engage in exploratory work solely for the purposes of correcting recognized lacks in our observations on the record. During the course of our investigations, whether prompted by exploratory considerations, or by problems posed by the record as known, the archaeologist makes discoveries. Most of the time these are not considered surprising and the archaeologist treats them as mundane, referring to them as 'data'.

Sometimes, however, discoveries are surprising: observations that do not conform to our expectations, or our 'model' of what the archaeological record is like. Discoveries of the latter class may be of two general types: curiosities, and new information regarding the character of the archaeological record. Much of the public appeal of archaeology comes from the announcement of archaeological discoveries, which attract attention because of their 'surprise' nature. Curiosities may consist of items or extraordinary conditions that we would not expect to be preserved in the archaeological record. Such things as the recently reported frozen body of a man preserved since approximately 20 000 years ago, complete with clothing, or the 'ghost' of a body preserved for an even greater length of time in a Spanish deposit, are examples. These 'surprise' us because of our expectations regarding the nature of the archaeological record. We demand explanations as to how they were preserved. Rarely do such curiosities add appreciably to our understanding of the past or our knowledge of the dynamics of cultural processes.

Another type of discovery is one that challenges our expectations about the past itself. Discoveries of this type were the major challenges to the 'Biblical' paradigm regarding the history of man, his antiquity, and early condition. Every student is familiar with the discoveries of men like Frere and Boucher De Perthes, who discovered materials that should not have existed if the old paradigm was correct. Discoveries of this type are generally falsifying discoveries, in Popper's (1959) sense of the term. Their importance derives from the fact that they clearly imply an inadequacy in the prevailing theory, or controlling model of nature.

There is a third type of discovery that one may make. This is the anticipated 'surprise'. Not anticipated in the particular incidence of its discovery, but anticipated by the model of nature that the investigator works within. I will discuss this again under the rubric of 'explanation'.

It should be clear that even at the exploratory level of investigation we bring certain expectations to our work. These are derived from our paradigm or model of either the archaeological record itself, or of the past. Problems are defined and new questions asked as a result of the interaction between our observations and our expectations derived from a paradigm. The empiricists' position seems difficult to defend even at the exploratory level of research.

(2) *Explication.* Explication generally refers to some systematic description of observations. In this the archaeologist faces the task of breaking down a whole into parts, generally with the aim of elucidating its componential make-up, and the interrelationships among its components. Analysis presupposes an

aim or goal in research. We may justifiably ask, analysis for what? Leaving aside for the moment this important question, a discussion of the character of the archaeological record is in order.

The archaeological record exhibits only two kinds of variability: organizational and distributional. Organizational variability refers to all the associations and correlations that in the context of repetition permit the recognition of an entity, or association of entities or characteristics having definable structural properties. Distributional variability refers to the patterning manifest when recognized units or characteristics are plotted spatially, or across populations isolated independently of the unit or characteristic being studied. One of the most common procedures is to plot the distribution of recognized components of the archaeological record across populations isolated with respect to the inferred dimension of time. Thus, heuristically, we may speak of the distributional study of variability with respect to the temporal dimension (see Spaulding, 1960).

Taking an empiricist's position the archaeologist may be concerned with assessing something of the character of observed organizational and distributional variability, uninformed as to its significance, or meaning, in terms of the past. An empiricist would suggest that this may be accomplished by the development of a taxonomy for classifying observations and materials. A crucial point to be emphasized is that as a scientific tool taxonomies are instruments for measurement. A taxonomy developed in the context of an inductivist's philosophy can be said to be an instrument for measuring 'recognized' differences and similarities. Classifications of data in terms of such taxonomies cannot be said to inform in any direct way on the significance of the differences or similarities measured. In spite of this limitation there are criteria that will allow us to evaluate the adequacy of a taxonomy. A taxonomy can be judged adequate if all the 'recognized' variability is accommodated and the criteria for inclusion in the various categories are unambiguous. The adequacy of a taxonomy is, however, no measure of its reliability for measuring variability of specified significance. Similarly the inadequacy of a taxonomy in the above terms provides no necessary argument against its reliability for measuring characteristics of specified significance. Significance and adequacy are very different characteristics of taxonomies.

Errors with regard to the above are common in archaeological debate. For instance, it has frequently been asserted that the quantity of differences as measured by some taxonomic evaluation among assemblages is a measure of ethnic affinity between the groups responsible for the archaeological remains. Our ability to measure quantitatively differences and similarities between assemblages and to synthesize our results into such taxonomic units as 'phases' or 'traditions' is in no way a test of the validity of the proposition that measured differences are indicative of degrees of ethnic affinity. This is a point that many archaeologists have failed to recognize.

> I suggest that we are justified in proceeding on the hypothesis that similarity of style and content of assemblages is an indicator of common cultural tradition. (Collins, 1969, p. 270)

> If culture tradition theory were entirely wrong, I feel sure that the archaeological data would not pattern as neatly as it does into traditions and stages. (Collins, 1969, p. 268)

This fallacy is frequently defended on the basis that an independent body of data is utilized, namely the results of distributional studies. This position is equally indefensible. The most common framework for distributional studies is a time-space matrix. Time is the conventional referent for evaluating the dynamics of transformations occurring within or among organizations. Space is the normal referent for evaluating the disposition of systemic processes and functions. Time and space, however, cannot be considered components of a system, or variables which act on the system. To argue that time acts causally in activating systemic change or to cite changes in time or space as independent determinants of the phenomena being studied is inconceivable. Time and space are reference dimensions which we use for monitoring the operation of system dynamics. The demonstration of clustering along either of these dimensions only informs us that some systemic processes were at work. Such a demonstration does not inform us as to the nature of those processes. The citation of differential distributional patterning as supporting evidence for a particular attribution of significance to the phenomena so patterned is not conclusive. All such a demonstration ensures is (*a*) that an organizational difference has been isolated, and (*b*) that the dynamics of organizational process were existentially independent. It in no way supports directly the validity of the particular characterization of the process proposed by the archaeologist.

Similarly, the argument that the particular method used for giving taxonomic recognition affects the validity of the arguments advanced to account for organizational variability isolated is difficult to defend. For instance David Clarke has recently advocated a rigid inductivist's approach to taxonomy following the procedures outlined by Sokal and Sneath (1963) as

Numerical Taxonomy. Clarke has criticized other procedures and attempts to solve questions posed by their application in the following way:

> The importance of developing an adequate definition for the artefact types and then applying the definition with all possible rigour cannot be over-estimated. Many contemporary studies, particularly in the palaeolithic field, make great play about variations from artefact assemblage to assemblage of the relative percentages of given artefact types. . . . However, hardly any of these studies define their unit artefact types on other than an intuitive and arbitrary basis . . . and one which is certainly not sufficiently comprehensive in application or accurately defined in terms of attributes. The consequent danger is that an alternative or conflicting definition of the artefact types within such assemblages would radically alter the much discussed relative percentages and correspondingly alter their meaningful interpretation. (Clarke, 1968, p. 188)

This appears as a strange statement coming from a man who in many ways exhibits a sophistication not shared with many of his colleagues. Surely Clarke knows that this statement would be true regardless of the methods used in establishing the typology, including his numerical methods. A classification system depends upon a selection by the investigator of criteria considered 'significant' for use in classifying data. Selection of different criteria may result in a 'conflicting definition of the artefact-types' even if both classifications were being generated by inductive means using numerical taxonomic procedures. If an investigator specifies the criteria to be used and applies them consistently, then differences or similarities noted are 'real' and demand explanation. Simply because another investigator selects another set of criteria and generates a different taxonomy by whatever consistent method is no basis for an argument against the 'validity' of the first evaluation of differences and similarities. The latter argument can only be claimed if the competing investigators are in disagreement over the relevance of different sets of criteria as adequate measures of a specified variable. This does not appear to enter into Clarke's criticism. Seeking an explanation for differentiations made by whatever method is a valid pursuit. The explanation may take the form of recognitions that the taxonomy is not measuring what it is alleged to measure, that the differentiations are spurious because of the methods used, or that the specified organizational properties of the archaeological record are understandable in terms of a developed argument about the past.

At the level of explication there are clearly several problems: (1) the selection of analytical criteria, (2) the selection of analytical techniques, and (3) the ascription of significance to the organizational or distributional patterning made explicit through the analytical procedures. In the absence of a paradigm or set of expectations as to relevance, no selection could be made from the infinity of characteristics potentially present in the body of empirical material being studied. In the absence of a paradigm no criteria of judgement could be made explicit for evaluating procedures since they must be offered in terms of specifiable sets of research goals. Similarly, it is through the paradigm that arguments of significance are generated for the results of analysis. The empiricists' argument appears hard to defend.

(3) *Explanation*. As previously mentioned, the desire for an explanation originates from a reaction of surprise to some experience. This surprise 'is generated by a conflict between our expectations in a given situation and our actual experience of it' (Harvey, 1969, p. 11). The expectations have been supplied to traditional archaeologists by a minimal set of theoretical propositions, a bridging argument, a model of cultural dynamics, and a set of conventions to be used in 'interpreting' surprises. In short, the traditionalists' paradigm anticipates surprises and supplies the archaeologist with a set of conventions for bringing his surprise observations back into line with his expectations. It is through the use of these conventions that the archaeologist reconstructs 'culture history'.

Archaeological theory has been a mentalist theory. The concept of culture is a central theoretical concept and for archaeologists it has been explicated by reference to other primitive concepts such as ideas, values, mental templates, etc. These are theoretical concepts also and as such are not capable of direct sensing, or observation. How does the archaeologist 'operationalize' his theory? The following operational definition or bridging argument is traditionally offered: 'Culture is patterned. . . . (Therefore) the patterning which the archaeologist perceives in his material is a reflection of the patterning of the culture which produced it' (Deetz, 1967, p. 7).

The bridging argument allows the archaeologist to argue that the organizational characteristics of the archaeological record informs him directly on the character of culture. Such patterning may be recognized at several levels. At the level of the artefact the archaeologist seeks to identify patterning,

> identifying distinct patterns of behaviour . . . which can be acquired by one human being from another . . . serve as the tools for the retracing of cultural development and interactions. . . . It is therefore the task of the analyst . . . to recover . . . the mental patterns which lay behind these manifold works. (Krieger, 1944, p. 272)

> Artefacts are man-made objects; they are also fossilized ideas. In every clay pot, stone axe, wooden doll, or bone needle, we see preserved what someone once thought pots, axes, dolls or needles should look like. In every culture, there are conventions which dictate the form of artefacts. (Deetz, 1957, p. 45)

If the single artefact reflects patterning at the individual level, redundancy observed among numerous cases of artefacts is a measure of the degree that 'ideas' are shared among individuals. Artefact typology is the instrument for measurement in this case.

The other basic observational content unit with which the archaeologist works is the assemblage. The totality of materials recovered from an archaeological site is believed to represent a restricted segment of the history of the people represented. Redundancy noted between a number of assemblages is taken as a measure of the shared 'ideas' among the social units represented. Archaeological systematics generally proceed as a progressive grouping of assemblages into broader and broader units said to be a measure of different degrees of culture sharing. The differential distribution of such groupings, both temporally and spatially, is said to reflect the history of culture transmitted among social segments of the human reproductive continuum.

As previously mentioned, the archaeological record is capable of yielding two major kinds of information: organizational and distributional. The traditional archaeologist searches the archaeological record for patterning on both organizational (artefact types, assemblage types) and distributional (traditions, phases, etc.) dimensions.

By an operational definition, the archaeologist has 'translated' a set of theoretical concepts into observational experience. In so doing he has assigned meaning, or significance, to his observations. He has transformed his taxonomic endeavours from an exploratory function to a measurement function. His classifications of organizational differences and similarities become an instrument for measuring degrees of shared 'culture' among the human populations represented. His classifications of different units of observation, since they are generated by the recognition of patterning, all become instruments for measuring a single 'variable' culture.

The archaeologist's expectations as to the character of patterning to be anticipated in the archaeological record derive from a 'model' of the dynamics of culture. This model provides the archaeologists with a frame of reference for the recognition of problems as well as their solution.

Most archaeologists have not given much explicit thought to the analogue model of cultural dynamics which they employ, others have been very explicit. One of the clearest statements has been given by the late James Ford (1962):

> Fortunately the mechanics of change are simple, at least in principle. There are only three ways in which innovations can occur; invention, discovery, and borrowing. . . . (Ford, 1962, p. 7)

> Culture change is remarkable in that it is the only perfect example of the democratic process. If individuals do not 'vote' for customs, the cultural feature does not drift in that particular direction. The student of cultural processes therefore finds himself faced with the necessity of 'tallying' . . . in effect the archaeologist must conduct a prehistoric opinion poll. (Ford, 1962, p. 9)

> We have examined some of the facets of evolving cultures, fluid streams of ideas that passed from human brain to human brain. These were ideas regarding the proper and best ways men should adapt themselves to their environment or modify that environment to meet their needs and desires. (Ford, 1962, p. 11)

Although not presented in point by point fashion, I believe Ford to have expressed the major components of *the model* of cultural dynamics accepted by most traditional archaeologists.

This model as I understand it may be summarized into several basic statements:

(1) *Culture is localized in individual human beings* – this derives from the fact that only humans are considered to have the biological capacities for cultural cognition.

(2) *Culture is transmitted among human beings* – through learning individuals assimilate culture from other persons.

(3) *Culture is shared* – sharing results from the cumulative effects of common learning experiences, in short the degrees of association of interaction occurring among human beings.

(4) *Culture derives from humans* – it may be generated only by human acts of invention.

(5) *Culture is cumulative* – inventions once made add to the alternatives

among which choices may be made and serve as the basis for recombination into new inventions.

(6) *Culture is a continuum* – it is a continuum because the succession of individuals in generational succession is a continuum. Since culture (e.g. ideas, information, etc.) is transmitted across generations, it also is a continuum.

(7) *Culture is continuously changing* – this derives from the fact that culture bearers are continuously being replaced, thereby ensuring that the cumulative effects of individual choices at any two points in time vary as the composition of individuals in the population varies. This also derives from the expectation that individuals are continuously being presented with new alternatives through acts of invention.

(8) *Culture changes gradually* – this is expected because individuals are replaced gradually in human populations resulting in minute shifts in relative popularity among varying alternatives.

Converting these components of the traditionalist's model into expectations regarding the character of the archaeological record is relatively easy. As an example I will specify some of the traditionalists' expectations for a relatively well-investigated region:

(1) We expect a continuous sequence of variability, patterning as gradual directional changes in the relative frequencies of recognized artefact taxa. These expectations are explicated by Deetz (1967, pp. 26–37), Clarke (1968, pp. 187–227) and many others.

(2) A gradual increase in the numbers of artefact taxa recognizable if the isolated part of the archaeological record spans a 'sufficient' period of time.

(3) Transformational sequences showing a 'development' of artefact forms from antecedent forms (see Clarke, 1968, pp. 131–85).

The archaeologists' model serves to provide him with his expectations as to the character of the patterning in the archaeological record. It provides him with a set of 'justified' meanings to be assigned when the expected forms of patterning are observed. In addition it provides him with a set of interpretative principles to be used when his expectations are not met. For instance, since our model assumes that culture changes gradually, we expect to observe gradual replacive patterning in an archaeological sequence. If such is not observed and we are 'surprised', then we appeal to our model for an interpretative principle. We find that since culture is localized in individuals and is derived from humans, then breaks in continuity of cultural patterning must derive from breaks in the continuity of human populations in the area. Population replacement, migration, becomes the necessary explanation.

I will examine some of the cases where expectations have not been met and evaluate how archaeologists have dealt with such 'surprises'. The expectations under review are that contemporary assemblages should be roughly alike, and inter-assemblage variability should therefore exhibit some directional patterning temporally. Several good examples of the archaeological record presenting some surprises are well documented.

The big surprise – the nonconformity

A nonconformity is an observed situation where the expectation of gradual change is not met. Instead abrupt changes, and major differences characterize assemblages in contiguous temporal positions.

THE MOUSTERIAN PROBLEM (see pp. 27–8, Fig. 1.8)
Early researchers investigating the character of Mousterian remains recognized some inter-assemblage variability and interpreted it to meet their expectations. One form of assemblage was considered to succeed another in a temporal succession of gradual changes. Early textbooks will show that three 'phases' of the Mousterian 'tradition' were recognized. Early industries were characterized by the presence of handaxes and a blending of the new with the older traits of the Acheulean. This was called Mousterian of Acheulean tradition. Following this were industries showing less traits in common with the earlier Acheulean and characterized by a wide variety of flake forms of tools. This was called Typical Mousterian. Finally there was a kind of Mousterian characterized by many steeply retouched scrapers, frequently found in association with fauna indicative of cold climates. This was called cold Mousterian, or Quina Type. This synthesis produced no surprises and our expectations were met. Later detailed stratigraphic work (Peyrony, 1930), and an increased sophistication in taxonomic evaluation of assemblage variability largely accomplished by François Bordes, resulted in the recognition that the older syntheses were inaccurate. Bordes demonstrated that the character of the archaeological record was very surprising, it did not conform to our expectations and therefore demanded explanation. He found that there were

at least four major types of assemblage, two of which could be further broken down into subtypes or facies. These were termed Denticulate Mousterian, Typical Mousterian, Mousterian of Acheulean tradition (broken into two facies, A and B) and Charentian Mousterian (broken into two subtypes, Quina and Ferrassie). Comparative stratigraphic studies showed that these various forms did not succeed each other through temporal sequence in any regular manner. On the contrary, an interdigitation of types of assemblage was characteristic in stratigraphic sequences. Comparative stratigraphic studies showed the different forms to frequently be roughly contemporary at locations very close to one another. This situation clearly demands explanation. Bordes (1961) 'explains' these surprises as resulting from the presence of four distinct ethnic groups or 'tribes' living in the area of south-western Europe during the Middle Palaeolithic. These distinct groups moved relatively frequently leaving their distinctive assemblages interstratified at single locations. Once again we see the use of our model, since patterning in the form of archaeological assemblages is a direct measure of cultural patterning in the ideas and values held by people; differences in the composition of assemblages *must* mean differences in the ethnic composition of the groups represented. Having recognized four distinct and parallel cultural traditions, the culture historian must now seek to rearrange his phylogenetic tree of culture history. Seeking the 'origins' of these four traditions, Bordes has tentatively related these traditions to variability known during the Rissian times but unfortunately not as systematically studied as the Mousterian (Bordes, 1968, pp. 98–105). This case provides us with two kinds of 'surprise': (1) ungraded variability among contemporary assemblages, and (2) lack of directional patterning in the observed temporal variability. The latter surprise is accounted for by painting a picture of conservatism and isolation:

An objection to the existence of these four Mousterian lines has also been raised on the score of a lack of geographical isolation. Contacts, it is said, must have been numerous, and must have led to a blending of cultures. . . . If a woman from the Quina-type Mousterian was carried off by an Acheulean-tradition Mousterian man, she may perhaps have continued to make her tribal type of thick scraper . . . but after her death probably no one went on making them. And finally, it must always be remembered that the Palaeolithic world was an empty world. . . . A man must often have lived and died without meeting anyone of another culture, although he knew 'that there are men living beyond the river who make handaxes'. (Bordes, 1968, p. 145)

Many examples could be collected, but I hope that this one is sufficient to demonstrate the strategy of archaeological 'reconstructions of history'. We have a series of expectations of the archaeological record based on a model of culture. When these expectations are not met, we explain our observations by appealing to the belief which has been stated clearly by Ford: 'information will always show that these local "non-conformities" result from the replacement of one population by another, with concomitant replacement of cultural baggage' (Ford, 1962, p. 8).

I would like to paraphrase this belief into a generalization: 'investigation will always show that these local "nonconformities" will be interpreted by traditional archaeologists as the replacement of one population by another, with concomitant replacement of cultural baggage'.

'Little surprises' or 'big surprises' a problem?

The previous problem was a situation in which some 'break' in continuity, or lack of directional change characterized the archaeological record as a whole. 'Little surprises' are cases where there is a demonstrable continuity in many features, but where 'new' features of the archaeological record exhibit little or no demonstrable 'continuity' with the archaeological record as known previously. This is the classic problem of 'diffusion' or 'independent development'.

THE PROBLEM OF THE OLDOWAN–ACHEULEAN TRANSITION

In 1951 L. S. B. Leakey published the results of his earlier investigations at the impressive site of Olduvai Gorge. Based largely on survey data he argued that there was a clear and gradual transition from the crude pebble tools from the lower beds at Olduvai to the more sophisticated 'handaxe' cultures of the upper beds. He argued that the archaeological record at Olduvai conformed to his expectations for a situation of *in situ* change, invention and 'evolution'. Based on this argument archaeological texts summarized 'culture history' this way:

It has been found that whereas in the basal or Oldowan stage pebbles were made into cutting instruments by the removal of a few flakes in two directions at one end or along one side, as time went on it became the custom to chip them more extensively. The pebbles were flaked all around the edges first in one direction and then in the other, so that they became two-faced lumps (bifaces), roughly oval or pear-shaped in outline, with a sinuous or zigzag margin formed by the intersection of deep-biting flake-scars. These tools represent the dawn of handaxe culture, the first stages of which are called Early Chellean, or Abbevillian.

The available evidence suggests that this culture developed in central Africa . . . it spread over the greater part of the continent, and has extended northwards into western Europe on the one hand, and less certainly into southern Asia on the other. (Oakley, 1956, pp. 40–1)

After the war intensive work was started in Olduvai Gorge and detailed attention was given to chronology, geological stratification, etc., resulting in a much more detailed knowledge of the nature of the archaeological record. This knowledge failed to accord with the previous 'interpretation'; the archaeological record contained a 'surprise'. The situation is summarized by Mary Leakey (1967, pp. 431–2) as follows:

Nine sites have been excavated in the Middle and Upper Bed II, all of which have proved exceedingly rich in cultural material. They have revealed an unexpected cultural development, more complex and quite unlike the simple succession originally thought to have existed. The occurrence of Oldowan tools in Middle and Upper Bed II has always been recognized, but there now appears to be no progressive evolution from the Oldowan through the 'Chellean' to the Acheulean. On the contrary, the handaxes earliest known represent an early Acheulean stage of development. Some primitive specimens of the 'Chellean' type are also present but they are in unquestionable association with more evolved forms. The Acheulean, how-ever, does not occur in all living sites at this level. At other sites, which are broadly contemporaneous, the culture is a developed form of the Oldowan. At a third group of sites, Acheulean handaxes occur in association with the developed Oldowan culture. It would seem therefore that there were two distinct but co-existent cultural elements, during Middle and Upper Bed II, which at times made some degree of contact with one another.

This is a classic example of a 'surprise'. There is a lack of gradual, minute change resulting in a continuous transformational sequence from pebble tools to handaxes. In addition, roughly contemporary sites do not look alike, some have handaxes, some Oldowan diagnostics, and some have both. How is this situation 'explained'? The argument offered is completely consistent with the operational definition of culture previously discussed: e.g. comparisons between populations of artefacts and assemblages are considered to be a measure of the amount of shared 'culture' or 'ideas' between the human populations represented. Therefore, inter-assemblage variability is interpreted as evidence for the presence and interaction between two distinct ethnic populations. The possibility that these two populations might also represent biologically distinct populations is entertained but left in abeyance due to an absence of associated fossil material with the Acheulean (Leakey 1967, pp. 441–2). I think we can look forward to a revision of the 'culture history' of early man and much exchange of opinion; for instance, in response to Mary Leakey's summary of the data, Balout comments (Leakey, 1967, p. 442): 'questions of a general nature arise. . . . The problem of the relationship between the Oldowan and the Acheulean; elsewhere, we have reached a different conclusion, that the Acheulean develops out of the "Pebble Culture".' In reply to this comment Mary Leakey (1967, p. 442) says: 'I do not think that the Oldowan developed into the Lower Acheulean, locally, at Olduvai, though presumably it did somewhere else.'

These examples of 'explanation' should be sufficient to demonstrate the general character of the role of the traditionalists' paradigm in archaeological thinking. Most of the controversy occurring among adherents to this paradigm arises over the evaluation of the particular character of a given surprise. That is over which alternative convention is to be used in 'explaining' the surprise. I have tried to spell out in detail what these conventions are (Binford, 1971). Many of these involve the use of distributional information. Let us examine briefly the logical basis for this appeal.

As previously mentioned, time and space are reference dimensions serving as reference frameworks for monitoring systemic processes. Propositions set forth about the disposition of particular cultural referents in time or space can never serve other than descriptive functions. Such facts only become relevant in the context of hypothetical arguments dealing with the dynamics of processual functioning or change. Unfortunately in contemporary archaeology such arguments are rare.

A common form of archaeological argument might be developed as follows:

(1) A sequence of archaeological materials is known from two nearby but non-contiguous regions (Area I and Area II).

(*a*) In both areas up until point A in time each was distinct.

(*b*) At point A in time a trait previously unique to Area I appears in the archaeological record of Area II, lacking any evidence of 'crude' or experimental beginnings.

(2) This dispositional change is cited as indicative of some alteration in the prior state of the cultural processes documented archaeologically. Several alternative steps are then open to the traditional archaeologist.

(*a*) The archaeologist may cite the appearance of the exotic trait in Area II as an 'influence' from Area I. This is of course a categorical statement and as such can only be questioned conceptually or in terms of the degree that the term 'influence' is accurately used categorically. Empirical testing is out of the question in this case.

(*b*) The archaeologist may cite the appearance of the exotic trait in Area II as evidence for the operation of a 'process' termed diffusion (the trans-mission of cultural content among independent socio-cultural units in the absence of population movement or exchange). This too is a categorical statement, which can only be tested as to its situational applicability. Nevertheless, many archaeologists might predict that in an area inter-mediate between the two relevant areas the trait would be found dating to the period just prior to time A when the trait appeared in Area II. If future research in the intermediate area should reveal the presence of the trait at time $A-x$, to what degree could one argue that a hypothesis has been tested? One could not. The new distributional referent simply betrays the operation of cultural processes, something already known from the initial observation! It in no way adds to the ability of the investigator to justify the observation as covered by the diffusion concept, since the new obser-vation in no way eliminates the alternative of population movement or exchange – a necessary criteria for the categorical equation of diffusion with the observations.

Other possibilities are certain to occur to those familiar with archaeologi-cal interpretation: the new trait may be cited as evidence for a migration (lots of shared 'culture' translated spatially), or a case of 'independent invention' (very rare in archaeological interpretation). Regardless of the particular decisions reached by the archaeologist as to the appropriate 'concept' to be applied, he has in no way tested a hypothesis. He may make certain predic-tions, which if confirmed would tend to justify his opinion as to the proper concept to be used; such predictions would be about empirical information which would satisfy categorical criteria not previously met. The accuracy of the prediction would then serve to justify the prior opinion as to the ap-propriateness of the term applied in the absence of complete information. The stating of a proposition about future distributional observations in the context of traditionalists' arguments does nothing more than allow the archaeologist to establish the categorical relevance of a descriptive term applied to his observation.

I have stressed this point because to many archaeologists diffusion, migration and independent invention are the 'processes' of culture history (Trigger, 1968, pp. 26–31). Accurate decisions as to which of these concepts applies in any given empirical situation allow the 'accurate' reconstruction of culture history. We know we have accurately applied these terms when our 'expectations' are met as to the observed features of distribution and association. Our expectations derive from our paradigm, or model, of the way culture as a mentalist phenomenon works.

The traditionalists' paradigm consists of a few primitive theoretical concepts, operationalized empirically by a single bridging argument regarding patterning. An analogue model is built treating the dynamics of culture change. This model provides the archaeologist with his expectations regarding the archaeological record. When 'surprises' are met there is a series of 'conventions' used to interpret these surprises in historical terms. The degree that each case meets the criteria for categorical inclusion under three major classes – migration, invention and diffusion – determines the character of the 'historical' systematics generated.

Challenges to the traditionalist paradigm

The traditionalists' paradigm, which sees culture as a mental phenomenon manifest in behaviour and its conceptual and material expressions, is operationalized as we have shown by the bridging argument of patterning. What does the archaeologist do when he observes uncorrelated patterning?

THE LEVALLOIS PROBLEM: A FORESHADOWING OF THINGS TO COME

Early researches, primarily by Breuil (Breuil and Koslowski, 1931), resulted in the recognition of assemblages distinguished by the presence of flakes struck from prepared cores, generally called 'tortoise cores'. Using the name of the 'type site' near Paris, assemblages characterized by the use of the prepared core technique became known as the Levalloisian. This was postulated to represent a separate tradition derived from the 'Clactonian' and contemporary with the Acheulean. Careful work by Bordes and Bourgon (1951) and Bordes (1956) has shown that most of the materials discussed by Breuil were later than he had thought, most being contemporary with known Mousterian assemblages of the Würm. Bordes has further argued, quite convincingly, that what was taken as evidence for a separate tradition by Breuil represents

125

only an alternative method of working flint. It may or may not occur in assemblages that in terms of tool frequency composition is otherwise similar (Bordes, 1956). The presence of the technique prior to the Würm is well established and assemblages clearly recognizable as Acheulean are known both with and without evidence of Levallois technique (Waechter, 1968). This is a case of patterning in one characteristic which varies independently of patterning in other characteristics. Immediately the archaeologist is presented with the problem of which kind of patterning is informing him about 'culture history'. Is sharing of culture, and hence 'ideas' about how to make tools, more or less important for charting the 'streams' of transmitted 'culture' than the ideas or 'mental templates' about the forms of the tools manufactured? The tendency has been to give preference to the latter and to consider the former only when it supports the 'conclusions' of the latter. There have been suggestions as to what might be the context conditioning the use of the Levallois technique; the character of the raw material (Bowler-Kelley, 1937, p. 15; Tester, 1958; Collins, 1969, p. 290) is a frequently cited argument. The implications of such a suggestion as well as the validity of the argument have not been followed out by the archaeologists. If an example of patterning, well documented in the archaeological record, can be shown to vary significantly with some contingency variable, such as character of the raw material, then behaviour cannot be taken as an adequate and sufficient measure of the 'reservoir of ideas' present in the population carrying out the behaviour. If this is the case, the patterning in behaviourally manifest 'culture' is not a reliable measure of the 'culture' present. Measures of similarity and differences among archaeologically recovered materials would at best be a measure of behavioural similarity. The degree that such similarity would exhibit 'expected' spatial and temporal patterning should be more a function of the stability and distribution of the conditioning contingencies than a measure of the distribution and stability of the populations possessing the knowledge of the behaviour, or a 'mental template' as to how to behave if those contingencies were present.

The paradigm of archaeologists is essentially an 'irrationalist's' position in which human behaviour was seen as determined by the enculturative milieu of individuals. This has been well stated by Collins (1969, p. 312): 'People X made handaxes (and other Acheulean traits) because their ancestors made them.' Man is viewed as an uninventive, essentially an automaton, behaving like his ancestors did unless there were interruptions or changes in communicative links between generations or among contemporary populations.

The Levallois case provides a 'rationalist' challenge. Man behaved like his ancestors did *in certain situations*. In short, transmitted knowledge and belief are viewed as a reservoir of accumulated knowledge *to be used differentially when appropriate*. Thus, similarities and differences in the archaeological record are no longer sufficient measures of the degree that two population segments share a common culture. They may equally be seen as two population segments sharing or not sharing common situations of appropriateness in the context of a common culture, or differing culture! Patterning in the archaeological record results from behavioural patterning; the degree that behavioural patterning is a direct and sufficient measure of shared 'ideas' is something that is not quite clear.

The response of most archaeologists was not to view this as a direct challenge to the traditionalists' paradigm. Instead this case as well as others was seen as the justification for shifting from comparative studies of specific traits as the basis for historical reconstruction to the comparative study of assemblages. It was argued that particular traits may have individual histories and that only by the comparative study of assemblages as populations could accurate reconstructions be made. This shift in emphasis with regard to the units appropriate for comparison was pioneered by Bordes (1950). It has been widely applied to materials from both the earlier and later ranges of time in western Europe and has been adopted at the appropriate strategy by many Africanists. There has been a strong reaction against the use of the 'fossil' approaches (see Sackett, 1968, pp. 66–9, for a good discussion of this history). Given a shift in emphasis in the units considered appropriate to the task of reconstructing culture history, there has been a general equation of the assemblage as an adequate sample of the shared 'culture' present in a community:

> The concept of an assemblage of stone artefacts, rarely stressed 25 years ago, has been increasingly emphasized in recent years. I see it to mean all the available artefacts from a restricted locality, and where levels have been noted, from a specific stratigraphic horizon. . . . These restrictions increase the likelihood that such an aggregate has been left by a single community over a limited time. (Collins, 1969, p. 267)

The equation of assemblages with communities, and assemblage types with communities sharing a body of culture has greatly modified much of the systematics of Old World archaeology. Not nearly as marked effects have been seen in New World studies, where 'historical' sequences are still generally based on comparative studies of ceramics, or projectile points, and total assemblages are rarely even summarized, much less used as the basic units for comparison.

The response of most archaeologists to this potential challenge has been to argue strongly for a shift in the units considered appropriate to comparative analysis for purposes of historical reconstruction. The accuracy of the paradigm has gone relatively unchallenged in spite of the behavioural implications. Archaeologists have generally continued in the traditionalists' manner: 'Archaeologist X makes culture history the way he does because his intellectual ancestors made it that way.'

The conscious challenge – the so called functional 'model'

THE HOPE FOUNTAIN – ACHEULEAN CASE

In 1929 N. Jones described the materials recovered from a site in the Maramba quarries near Hope Fountain, Rhodesia. The distinctiveness of the assemblage was recognized, and in traditional fashion this distinctiveness was cited as evidence for a different 'tradition'. A later summary of the assemblage characteristics was given as follows:

> The culture represents all the attributes of a pure flake and chopper culture. The only primary technique employed is block-on-block ... it would appear that the flakes were removed by resting the core on an anvil and striking it with a hammer-stone rather than by striking the core itself against the anvil. The secondary working is almost always of an irregular, resolved nature and is usually very steep. The industry as a whole presents a very crude and primitive appearance. . . . (Clark, 1950, p. 83)

Leakey writing about the cultural sequences of Africa states:

> The Hope Fountain Culture of Africa . . . is . . . a very crude culture with certain superficial resemblances to the Clactonian in tool types which occurs both in East Africa and in Northern and Southern Rhodesia.
>
> At Olorgesailie in Kenya, this culture which is in process of being studied and has not yet been described in detail, occurs in the same geological deposits as Stage 4 of the Acheulean phase of the Chelles–Acheul culture. . . . (Leakey, 1960, p. 86)

The conclusion drawn from the later analysis of Olorgesailie by Leakey is summarized by Sonia Cole (1954, p. 142) as follows:

An industry which may be related to the Hope Fountain culture of Rho-desia, in which the implements are made by the block-on-block techniques, is found unrolled on land surface 2 and rolled on land surface 6. . . . Pos-sibly the presence of the Hope Fountain industry at Olorgesailie may denote the arrival of a different band of people, who either turned out the former inhabitants for a time or influenced them in the making of their implements.

Up until this point the developments are completely predictable knowing the traditionalists' paradigm. A distinctive assemblage is recognized, it is equated with a distinct cultural 'tradition'. Later it is found at other locations and its presence is taken as evidence for the movement of people or their 'ideas' from one place to another.

In 1953 J. D. Clark published a short note in *Antiquity* in which he ques-tioned the validity of Hope Fountain as representative of a distinct cultural line, pointing out that Hope Fountain forms were demonstrably associated with recognized cultural phases all the way from what we would now call Oldowan through the Sangoan. Clark (1959b) writes:

There are also certain unspecialized groups of flake and chopper industries which do not fit into the normal pattern and so have been grouped under the term Hope Fountain . . . though it is now doubtful whether these repre-sent anything more than a special occupational phase of culture. (p. 40) On the Rhodesian plateau an Acheulean living floor at Broken Hill . . . has demonstrated the intimate association of handaxes, cleavers and polyhedral stones with small unspecialized flake tools. Small flake tools of the same type and the core choppers from which they were made, have sometimes been found unassociated with any other tools and this gave rise to the suggestion that they may represent the work of an entirely separate flake culture people. Recent work has, however, shown that there is little to support this view and that these assemblages (Hope Fountain industries) most probably represent a special phase of Handaxe Culture such as might have resulted at some 'special purposes' camp. (p. 128)

Later Clark (1959a, p. 221) remarks that the people of the Late Acheulean 'followed a regular seasonal progression over their hunting areas' and 'their temporary camping places . . . might . . . be expected to reflect in the stone industry the different occupational activities of its makers'.

In this argument Desmond Clark is offering a direct and conscious chal-lenge to the traditionalists' paradigm. He is suggesting that variability in the archaeological record arises from behaviour contingent on the operation of variables other than 'culture'. This means that all variability cannot be accepted as a direct measure of the 'amount' of shared culture. He seeks to understand the behavioural significance of variability rather than assuming its significance as a measure of cultural 'distance'. It should be pointed out, however, that these 'data' do not speak for themselves. A traditionalist would view the co-occurrence of 'Hope Fountain' forms with 'Acheulean' or some other recognized 'culture' as evidence for a 'mixed culture', a hybrid resulting from the contact of distinct peoples. Clark's challenge derives from a shift in perspective in which he quite clearly views archaeological remains as the by-products of behaviour conditioned in its variability by many factors, regardless of the character of the cultural repertoire brought to the life situations by the people.

Subsequently, work by Howell and Clark (1963) and Kleindienst (1961a, 1961b) strikingly demonstrates the wide range of variability in tool frequencies characteristic of Acheulean assemblages. More important, however, is the demonstration by Kleindienst that variability as measured by tool 'type' frequencies varies independently of variability as measured by morphological characteristics within a single class or type of tool (compare land surfaces 8 and 9 from Olorgesailie with J12 from Isimila (Howell and Clark, 1963, pp. 503, 505, 508). This demonstration of independent variability is clear evidence that independent sets of determinants are at work. It should be pointed out that it is variability *within* a general class of tools that has served as the common demonstration that the traditionalists' model is accurate.

The demonstration that differences between assemblages in the frequencies of similar tool types vary independently of variability as measured by variant forms of a single class of tools is conclusive evidence that both are not measuring the same phenomenon. Continuing work on the problems of variability in the African Acheulean, particularly by Isaac (1968), has led him to summarize the situation as follows:

> ... preliminary reports on Olorgesailie, Isimila and Kalambo Falls strongly suggest that in Africa assumptions of regularity should not lightly be made. ... It emerges that pene-contemporaneous samples do not behave as normal deviants about a norm either for 'type list' percentage composition or for measurable aspects of the morphology of major artefact categories such as bifaces, scrapers or flakes. For instance, one Olorgesailie set of eight site samples was recovered from a single silt member three feet thick. The percentage of bifaces varied from 0 to 95%; and the mean length

of handaxes ranged from 150 mm to 215 mm! Stable long-term trends within the Eastern African Acheulean have proved hard to identify. It is not yet possible to interpret the apparently irregular pattern of variation in detail. Activity differences are probably one contributory factor, but there seem to be other components, including unstable local idiosyncrasy of craft norms. It seems possible that in some areas during the Middle Pleistocene random walk variation was more conspicuous than stability and regular directional change. (Isaac, 1968, p. 306)

These materials seem to me to provide a critical case, a case in which the traditionalists must ignore one form of variability in assemblages in favour of the other if they insist in the construction of unidimensional 'dendrograms' of 'culture history'. In ignoring one form of variability they must seriously consider the implications of using the same form in other cases where comparable studies of both forms have not been conducted, such as the 'Clactonian–Acheulean problem' or the 'Mousterian problem'. In short, traditionalists can no longer defend their position that measured variability among assemblages is a measure of 'shared culture' pure and simple; they must consider the problem of 'what they are measuring' and face the problem of 'what it means' in terms of the past.

In spite of the critical character of this example and the striking failure of the expectations deriving from the paradigm to be met, the approach to comparison followed by the researchers has been a summarizing approach treating all tools as having additive properties. That it is an assemblage is expressed numerically as a summation of the frequencies of its components generally expressed as percentages. Evaluations are then made as to similarity and difference in the basis of comparisons of percentage graphs or more rarely in terms of some 'distance' measure. This results in the recognition of 'assemblage types', such as proposed by Kleindienst and summarized by Howell and Clark (1963, pp. 502–7). This procedure pioneered by F. Bordes on Mousterian assemblages, although a great improvement over earlier methods of assemblage comparison, assumes a unidimensional set of determinants and a corresponding unidimensional set of manifestations.

The multidimensional argument

Under the traditionalists' approaches the composition of an assemblage is measured by relative frequencies of recognized classes of artefacts. Redundancy is accepted as 'patterning' and hence a manifestation of the 'culture norms' of behaviour transmitted and shared among the people represented. The assemblage is equated with the community. The expectations are that, as long as we are dealing with the remains of an identical or related group of people, the composition of the assemblage should remain relatively similar since they share a common body of culture.

The behavioural model recognizes that behaviour is the dynamics of adaptation. People draw upon a repertoire of cultural background and experience to meet changing or variable conditions in their environment, both social and physical. Our expectations then are for variability in the archaeological record to reflect a variety of different kinds of coping situations. Activities will vary with the particular adaptive situation of the group and the character of tasks being performed. We would therefore expect variability in the archaeological record to reflect these different situations.

Assemblages may be therefore expected to exhibit variability concomitant with the various 'structural poses' (Gearing, 1962) of a community through its annual adaptive cycle. In addition, many assemblages may be expected to vary directly with the degree the community may be partitioned into specific kinds of task groupings for performing work at different locations. In short, assemblage variability may be expected to reflect a variety of segments of community life and cannot always be expected to exhibit similarities as a direct reflection of the continuities among the persons performing the acts. Similarities may equally reflect continuities in the character of the acts performed. Differences may arise when the organization of activities varies temporally and/or spatially, resulting in a variety of assemblage types characteristic of the life of a given community. Thus far, this is a restatement of the behaviourists' argument, which questions the validity of the equation of the assemblage with the community.

Many years ago I began exploring the implications of a multidimensional model of assemblage variability. This model, rather than assuming and treating assemblages as if they were statistical clusterings of examples along a continuous scale of unidimensional variability, as is the case with a colour spectrum, asks 'What if assemblages were compounds of many independent spectra of variability?' Clearly such a suggestion can be supported by observations on the character of human behaviour. For instance, the major subsistence activities of hunters and gatherers are sets of event sequences generally broken down into a number of different steps. All such steps are rarely performed at the same location. Add to this condition the frequent characteristic of environments – namely, that the critical resources in the forms of foods, water, appropriate life space and raw materials of technological importance are rarely aggregated and clustered in such a way as to make possible the procurement of all of these things in exactly the same spot. This ensures that each human adaptation will be characterized by a logistics system in which mobility, optimal positioning so as to reduce the mobility required, and the partitioning of activities into sets, components of which will be conducted at different locations, will in general characterize the adaptive strategy. This is a particularly human strategy based on a culturally partitioned social aggregate minimally partitioned into reproductive units capable of maintaining themselves as separate self-sustaining units at least for part of a seasonal cycle. Cross-cutting these units are dimensional characteristics (minimally, sex and age), which serve as the basis for the formation of work or task groups performing different types of jobs, which contribute to the maintenance of the group as a whole. Since tools are the technical aids used in the performance of work, in the literal sense of the word, we should expect that, other things being equal, the composition of tool assemblages would vary directly in accordance with the tasks performed. The differential distribution of assemblages in space should exhibit compositional differences in direct relation to the character of the logistic strategies carried out. Inter-assemblage variability in composition should increase in direct relation to the degree of mobility characteristic of the adaptive strategy and the degree that mobility was differentially exercised by task group segments of the larger social unit. It should vary inversely with the degree that tools were multifunctional, and/or curated in anticipation of future tasks.

Let us further complicate this picture by introducing the expectation that among culturally organized social units many forms would exhibit characteristics unrelated directly to their functional or specific contexts of use. Similarly we can expect different patterns of association to frequently correspond to different forms of organization, both of which might be shown to vary with the identity or social distinctiveness of the persons responsible.

The analytical task presenting itself to the archaeologist given these expectations is far greater than the task facing the traditional archaeologist. For a number of years I experimented with analytical methods that might permit us to analyse assemblages into the components of meaning approaching as near as possible the behavioural contexts that in life contributed to the accumulation of an assemblage (see Binford and Binford, 1966, p. 293, footnote 1). Some preliminary results of this work have been reported (Binford and Binford, 1966, 1969).

As a by-product of this research I began to recognize certain variations in the structural properties of variability among populations of assemblages.

133

These observations suggested that invalidation of the traditionalists' paradigm was quite possible. I have chosen to argue for such a disproving demonstration with the following materials.

This demonstration is presented as a basis for the analytic recognition of certain properties of assemblage variability. The traditionalists' expectations regarding variability may be seen as dependent upon several assumptions. A most important expectation is that associations between things, the coincidence of recognized classes of tools at sites, will exhibit directional patterns of gradual replacement and drift in their relative proportions when plotted accurately either temporally or spatially. For this expectation to be met, all classes of items in the assemblages compared must exhibit some patterns of mutual covariation. That is, as class (*a*) increases, class (*b*) decreases; or as classes (*x* and *y*) increase, classes (*w* and *v*) also increase. Recurrent associations of tool classes at locations is accepted as a form of patterning. Given the traditionalists' expectations, the recognition of patterning in the associations among tool classes permits us to identify assemblage types, which, depending upon their degrees of similarity, are accepted as measures of cultural differences between the human populations represented. The expectations that the recognition of different forms of assemblage based on a comparative analysis of associational patterns should result in directional patterning when assemblage types are plotted temporally is dependent upon an implicit assumption that associations also are patterned in a covariant fashion. Things found together should also tend to covary among themselves. When replacive patterning is not observed, a nonconformity is encountered. Nonconformities are recognized by the failure of assemblage types to adequately cluster either temporally or spatially; assemblage types are defined on the basis of associational patterning. Continuity is expected because assemblages are assumed to express in their content a set of integrated norms, values, ideas, etc., common to a culturally distinct social unit. Culture change is assumed to proceed as a gradual shifting of popularity or drift among forms related to one another as 'alternatives'. We therefore expect in situations of change, a patterned 'trajectory' to be expressed in the archaeological record characterized by covariant relationships between forms that are shifting in popularity. For the traditionalist, a nonconformity must therefore indicate cultural replacement rather than change. Migrations, diffusion, etc., are then postulated as an explanation.

I propose to examine the character of relationships among artefact classes in a sample of assemblages. If the assumption that associational relationships are also covariant relationships can be demonstrated as unjustified, then

I will have successfully disproved the traditionalists' paradigm by striking down as invalid one of the basic assumptions serving to permit the deduction of expectations about the archaeological record.

THE SAMPLE

The materials used in this analysis represent thirty-two assemblages from seven locations in east Africa. These are the primary locations which have served as the basis for the behavioural challenge to the traditionalists' paradigm.

Nine assemblages are used from the site of Olorgesailie located some 64 km south of Nairobi, Kenya. This site was originally excavated by the Leakeys (1952) and later worked by Posnansky (1959). More recently Glynn Isaac (1966, 1967, 1968) has been conducting research at this location. This site is characterized by numerous stratigraphically distinct beds, which have been grouped into three major units. Levels 1–5 represent one unit, separated by thick layers of fine sediments from the succeeding levels 6 through 9. Levels 10 through 13 are the third group, presenting more problems in their delineation (Isaac, 1966). It is the opinion of several authorities that each land surface yielding artefacts may represent more than one occupation, possibly occupations of short duration repeated numerous times (Isaac, 1966, pp. 141–2).

Nine assemblages were excavated in primary archaeological context from the Isimila location in southern Tanzania. Work was conducted at this site beginning in 1954 by F. C. Howell and continued through 1958, when he was assisted by Glen Cole and Maxine Kleindienst (Howell, 1961; Howell, Cole and Kleindienst, 1962). Further work is currently under way at this location by Keller.

Nine samples are available from the important sites excavated by J. D. Clark at Kalambo Falls, Tanzania. These represent samples reported in 1964 by Clark.

One sample each is taken from Lochard (Howell and Clark, 1963), Kariandusi (Howell and Clark, 1963) and Broken Hill (Kleindienst, 1961b; Clark, 1959a).

These are all Acheulean assemblages provisionally accepted as representing broadly contemporary materials of the 'Late' Acheulean period of east African prehistory.

THE VARIABLES

The artefact categories developed and applied by Maxine Kleindienst are used as the variables in the analysis. Several modifications have been made, however, in order to eliminate bias as well as obtain comparability between all the assemblages. (1) The category 'broken handaxes/cleavers/knives' has been deleted, since one of our interests is the degree that these different forms

TABLE 3.1. *Percentages of implement and artefact classes of Late Acheulean assemblages at Olorgesailie (Kleindienst, 1961b)*

	Land surfaces								
	I	2	3	6	7	8	9	10	11
SHAPED TOOLS									
Handaxes (Ha)	1·5	7·5	10·7	23·5	30·0	47·2	34·1	16·2	6·9
Cleavers (Clv)	1·5	1·9	2·4	2·9	29·0	13·6	27·4	10·3	1·7
Knives (Knv)	0·0	0·0	0·0	5·8	7·0	8·8	23·1	7·3	1·7
Flake scrapers (S)	0·0	0·0	0·0	1·5	3·0	4·8	3·3	2·2	0·0
Discoids (D)	0·0	0·0	0·0	1·5	1·0	0·0	0·0	1·5	0·0
Core scrapers (CS)	1·5	4·7	0·0	0·7	1·0	0·0	0·0	2·2	0·0
Picks (P)	0·0	0·0	2·4	0·7	0·0	0·0	0·0	0·0	0·0
Choppers (Ch)	1·5	5·7	3·7	2·9	5·0	4·8	2·2	2·2	3·5
Spheroids (Sph)	0·0	9·4	3·7	5·8	14·0	3·2	3·3	5·9	3·5
Other large tools (O)	0·0	0·9	1·2	0·0	1·0	2·4	0·0	0·0	0·0
Small scrapers (SS)	52·0	44·3	36·9	29·9	5·0	4·8	2·2	19·8	31·0
Other small tools (OST)	42·0	25·5	39·3	24·8	4·0	10·4	4·4	32·4	51·6
TOTAL NUMBER	69	106	84	137	102	125	91	137	58
ASSEMBLAGE									
Tools	25·5	35·7	38·5	34·1	59·5	41·3	59·1	32·2	29·9
Shaped	16·4	23·5	18·7	20·3	54·6	30·5	46·1	16·7	13·6
Modified[a]	1·4	2·7	8·6	1·4	—	—	—	—	—
Utilized[b]	7·7	9·5	11·2	12·4	4·9	10·8	13·0	15·2	16·1
Waste	74·5	64·3	61·5	65·9	40·5	58·7	40·9	68·2	70·0
Cores	2·3	11·9	12·0	7·2	14·1	3·7	3·7	7·5	7·1
Large flakes (10 mm)	0·9	0·7	0·0	2·8	6·3	3·6	9·3	3·9	3·5
Small flakes	64·7	50·2	47·5	44·5	17·6	48·3	27·4	54·4	59·0
Chips and chunks	6·5	1·3	1·9	11·5	2·4	3·6	0·5	2·2	0·2
TOTAL NUMBER	428	451	465	740	205	443	215	890	434

(*a*) The few on land surfaces 7, 8, 9, 10 and 11 were not segregated from the utilized flakes.

(*b*) Includes hammerstones (1 on land surface 3; 2 on surface 7; 1 on surface 9; 7 on surface 10; 1 on surface 1).

are mutually dependent; this grouped class could add nothing in this regard. (2) Desmond Clark does not report a category of 'discoids' from Kalambo Falls; for this reason the average percentage frequency occurring in other

TABLE 3.2. *Percentages of implement and artefact classes of Late Acheulean assemblages at Isimila (Kleindienst, 1961b)*

| | Isimila occupation areas | | | | | | | | |
| | Sandstone 3 | | Sst. 2 | | Sandstone 1b | | | Sandstone 1a | |
	K19	K18 Tr. 2	L. H15	J12	K6	L. J6 -7	K14	H9 -J8	U. J6 -7
SHAPED TOOLS									
Handaxes	6·8	6·4	9·8	46·0	63·6	21·6	13·7	41·4	35·1
Cleavers	50·0	9·8	14·6	18·9	11·6	18·2	40·3	27·6	35·1
Knives	5·7	4·3	0·0	18·9	4·0	2·3	1·6	2·3	1·1
Flake scrapers	5·7	0·0	7·3	5·4	5·8	1·1	0·0	3·4	4·3
Discoids	0·0	2·2	0·0	0·0	0·0	1·1	1·6	1·2	0·0
Core scrapers	1·2	5·4	14·6	0·0	4·0	5·7	0·8	2·3	3·2
Picks	0·0	0·0	12·2	2·7	4·6	0·0	1·6	0·0	0·0
Choppers	6·8	14·1	19·5	0·0	0·0	5·7	9·7	9·2	10·5
Spheroids	0·0	0·0	0·0	0·0	1·2	2·3	7·3	4·6	0·0
Other large tools	0·0	2·2	9·8	0·0	2·3	0·0	1·6	2·3	1·1
Small scrapers	17·0	29·0	12·2	5·4	0·0	25·2	13·7	5·7	5·3
Other small tools	6·8	25·9	0·0	2·7	2·9	15·8	8·1	0·0	4·3
TOTAL NUMBER	88	93	41	37	173	88	124	83	94
ASSEMBLAGE									
Tools	28·4	15·2	22·6	31·8	63·6	23·9	39·4	58·1	57·3
Shaped	17·0	6·0	12·6	27·0	58·0	9·4	28·8	51·1	40·1
Modified	4·2	5·0	6·1	2·7	0·6	8·8	6·9	4·8	14·1
Utilized[a]	7·2	4·2	3·9	2·0	4·9	5·7	3·7	2·2	2·1
Waste	71·6	84·8	77·4	68·2	36·4	76·1	60·6	41·9	42·7
Cores	0·9	1·3	2·4	2·7	5·2	1·4	4·6	3·2	0·9
Large flakes	0·3	0·1	4·3	6·1	1·1	0·6	1·6	7·0	0·0
Small flakes	30·8	20·6	42·1	36·5	30·0[b]	21·5	20·3	25·8	18·7
Chips and chunks	39·1	62·8	28·6	22·9	—	52·6	34·1	5·9	23·9
TOTAL NUMBER	528	1546	328	148	305	932	434	186	233

(a) Includes anvils (3 on K18 Tr. 2; 3 on Lower 815; 1 on J12; 1 on Lower J6–J7) and hammerstones (1 on K14; 2 on H9–J8).

(b) Chips and chunks not separated from small waste flakes.

sites has been used as the best estimate for the Kalambo data. Percentages were then adjusted for the Kalambo samples. The basic data used in the analysis is presented in Tables 3.1–3.4.

THE DEFINITION OF PATTERNS OF COVARIATION

Covariation refers to the degree that one variable varies in value in a related and predictable manner with another variable. Independence between variables indicated when frequency or value variation in one variable exhibits

TABLE 3.3. *Percentages of implement and artefact classes of Late Acheulean assemblages at Kalambo Falls (calculated from Clark, 1964)*

				Occupation floors				
	A1/56/4	A1/56/V A1/56/ Va	A1/56/ 58	5	6A	6B	7	8
SHAPED TOOLS								
Handaxes	19·1	13·5	17·2	30·0	31·1	20·6	7·8	15·2
Cleavers	11·9	29·8	14·0	18·6	34·5	8·4	31·4	22·2
Knives	0·0	5·8	1·5	4·0	6·9	4·7	3·9	8·1
Flake scrapers	7·1	15·4	4·7	7·0	6·9	4·7	5·8	5·0
Discoids	0·6	0·6	0·6	0·6	0·6	0·6	0·6	0·6
Core scrapers	16·7	8·6	20·4	7·3	3·4	14·9	11·8	11·1
Picks	4·8	0·0	6·3	1·4	1·7	0·0	0·0	0·0
Choppers	9·5	3·8	9·4	4·6	5·2	8·4	5·8	2·0
Spheroids	2·4	1·0	1·5	0·2	0·0	0·9	0·0	0·0
Other large tools	0·0	1·0	0·0	2·0	0·0	0·0	0·0	0·0
Small scrapers	21·4	19·2	20·4	20·5	8·6	33·7	33·4	36·4
Other small tools	7·1	1·9	3·1	4·4	1·7	3·7	0·0	0·0
TOTAL NUMBER	42	104	64	816	58	107	51	99
ASSEMBLAGE								
Tools	19·5	32·0	29·6	16·4	42·2	12·4	12·0	8·5
Shaped	12·2	23·6	24·0	12·2	31·0	7·4	7·3	4·3
Modified	nc	nc	nc	nc	nc	nc	nc	nc
Utilized	7·3	8·4	5·6	4·2	11·2	5·0	4·7	4·2
Waste[a]	*80·5*	*68·0*	*70·4*	*83·6*	*57·8*	*87·6*	*88·0*	*91·5*
TOTAL NUMBER	343	440	267	6696	187	1456	686	2308

(a) This category was not broken down in Clark's analysis.
nc = No count was given.

138

only random and non-directional relationships with respect to other variables. When a series of variables are studied we may be interested in the definition of sets of variables which exhibit similar patterns of mutual covariation and independence as a set with regard to other sets of individual variables. In

TABLE 3.4. *Percentages of implement and artefact classes of Late Acheulean assemblages at Lochard, Kariandusi, Broken Hill and Nsongezi (Cole, 1967; Howell and Clark, 1963; Kleindienst, 1961b)*

				Nsongezi		
	Lochard	Kari-andusi	Broken Hill	C17 M-N	C13 M-N	C1 M-N
SHAPED TOOLS						
Handaxes	24·1	39·4	1·1	10·9	8·2	5·7
Cleavers	7·1	16·7	8·5	12·7	18·4	3·5
Knives	1·6	13·9	1·1	0·0	0·0	2·3
Flake scrapers	1·1	6·9	1·1	7·3	6·1	2·3
Discoids	6·6	0·9	0·0	0·0	0·0	1·1
Core scrapers	0·5	1·6	1·1	12·7	12·2	17·3
Picks	0·0	2·2	0·0	0·0	2·0	0·0
Choppers	16·9	1·9	4·2	1·8	8·2	16·1
Spheroids	1·6	1·6	26·6	0·0	0·0	0·0
Other large tools	4·3	2·4	0·0	0·0	4·1	9·2
Small scrapers	24·6	5·1	37·2	12·7	4·1	9·2
Other small tools	11·5	7·3	19·1	41·9	36·7	33·3
TOTAL NUMBER	187	336	93	55	49	87
ASSEMBLAGE						
Tools	24·3	60·1	64·6	7·4	40·6	21·6
Shaped	14·9	47·3	57·3	2·6	13·2	8·3
Modified	7·2	3·3	3·0	1·7	9·1	5·8
Utilized	2·2	9·5	4·3	3·1[a]	18·3[a]	7·5[a]
Waste	75·7	39·0	35·4	92·6	59·3	78·4
Cores	2·9	3·1	17·7	2·1	8·2	nc
Large flakes	0·0	17·6	0·0	0·9	1·4	nc
Small flakes	52·9	18·8	17·7[b]	55·5	47·0	nc
Chips and chunks	19·9	0·5	—	34·1	2·7	nc
TOTAL NUMBER	1265	717	164	1280	219	615

(a) Cole (1967) classifies these as 'trimmed flakes', since he does not agree with Kleindienst that they are artefacts.

(b) Chips and chunks were not separated from small waste flakes.

order to explore the character of covariant relationships among the variables in this study a factor analysis was performed.

Using a factor analytic programme (Bio-Med × 72) originally developed at the University of California, Los Angeles, a varimax rotation was performed on the matrix of linear correlation coefficients (R) derived from the matrix in which the twelve tool 'types' of Kleindienst were the variables and the thirty-two assemblages were the cases. The data entered in the original matrix were the percentages of tool types within each assemblage as presented in Tables 3.1–3.4. A cut-off point for the suggestion of factors was established by specifying an eigenvalue of 0·95. This was elected because it represented a clear break in the distribution of eigenvalues, the next lower value being 0·72. The programme generated a correlation matrix which did not alter the diagonal elements. A varimax rotation was then performed. A five factor solution was obtained in which 80·32% of the total variance in the matrix was accounted for as common variance. Table 3.5 presents the commonalities and factor loadings for the solution obtained on these data. Commonalities are the percentage of variance for each variable demonstrated to exhibit variance in common with other variables.

TABLE 3.5

Proportion of total variance   26·60% 49·84% 62·94% 72·33% 80·32%

Variable	Factor I	Factor II	Factor III	Factor IV	Factor V	Commonality
1 Handaxes	(−0·884)	0·024	−0·037	−0·183	−0·045	0·818
2 Knives	(−0·701)	0·366	−0·041	−0·183	−0·085	0·669
3 Cleavers	−0·116	0·159	0·040	(−0·882)	−0·028	0·819
4 Flake scrapers	−0·123	−0·098	−0·402	(−0·553)	(−0·519)	0·762
5 Picks	−0·093	(−0·753)	−0·419	−0·059	−0·072	0·759
6 Core scrapers	(−0·462)	(−0·474)	−0·281	−0·133	(−0·505)	0·790
7 Other large tools	−0·098	(−0·859)	0·185	0·136	−0·123	0·815
8 Choppers	0·284	(−0·771)	0·481	−0·127	−0·059	0·926
9 Discoids	−0·002	−0·138	(−0·898)	0·010	−0·018	0·825
10 Spheroids	0·117	0·081	−0·081	0·007	(0·927)	0·886
11 Small scrapers	(0·722)	0·303	0·053	0·355	0·135	0·761
12 Other small tools	0·312	0·154	0·009	(0·828)	0·014	0·807

As one can see, about 20% of the variance exhibited by the variables among the thirty-two samples appears as unique variability, with knives exhibiting the lowest amount of common variance of any of the variables.

This solution provides us with considerable information of some fascination. There are two clear 'bipolar' factors, I and IV; two specific factors exhibiting bipolar characteristics, III and V; and one grouped factor. A bipolar factor has the property of significant factor loadings occuring as both positive and negative values. Relationships among the variables so represented are of an oppositional type. An example given by Harmann (1962, p. 10) is as follows: 'A bipolar factor . . . is one for which several of the variables have significant negative projections.' Such variables may be regarded as measuring the negative aspect of the usual type of factor. Thus, if a number of variables identified with 'fear' are represented by the positive projection, variables with negative projections might be interpreted as measuring 'courage'. These are inversely related phenomena. In our case the best predictor of the low frequency of handaxes is the high frequency of small scrapers. A specific factor is one that is primarily defined by a single variable. Factors III and V are specific factors; however, both exhibit bipolar characteristics in that both have fairly high negative loadings on two variables each. Factor II is a normal group factor. This overall pattern of factor results is unique in my experience with archaeological materials and must express certain unique features of these data.

Factor I
Diagnostic tools grouped under Factor I are handaxes, with knives as negative projections and small scrapers as an equally strong positive projection. Here we see a clear covariant dichotomy between 'heavy duty tools' and 'small tools'. The significance of this dichotomy may well have been partially isolated by Desmond Clark in a most provocative comparative study of locations where fauna were preserved sufficiently for evaluation. He notes that four general types of site are recognizable on which tool associations occur. He notes that on sites where a single or only a few animals have been butchered, articulated parts are numerous and small tools dominate the assemblage. On sites where many animals are represented, disarticulation is common and bones are broken up, large tools are more common and the character of the assemblage is more complex. He also notes that large tools may occur on sites where little fauna is represented, and that which occurs is broken and dismembered. He states 'the evidence suggests that Palaeolithic butchering and meat processing equipment consisted predominantly of small numbers of light duty tools, cutting flakes and small scraping tools with only a few of the large elements' (Clark and Haynes, 1970, p. 409). The correlations noted by Clark between fauna, evidence of butchering and small tools (particularly

small scrapers and utilized flakes, a class not included in this study) is strongly indicative of their use. Our results demonstrating a dependent but mutually exclusive association between handaxes and large knives on the one hand and small scrapers on the other are completely compatible with Clark's observations of small scrapers in the absence of handaxes with butchered animals and handaxes with few flake tools occurring on sites with little or no fauna. I suggest that handaxes and large knives were used in a context unrelated to the butchering and processing of meat and that the conditions obtaining when they were used were such that the probability of obtaining meat was very remote. The implications of such a suggestion are enormous. If true, the common occurrence of handaxes during the Lower Palaeolithic may well betray greater dependence upon non-animal foods than was previously considered. Collins observes that Acheulean assemblages tend to indicate a 'preference for grassland and open terrain, mainly but not always in warm latitudes. . . . Unlike the Acheulean, the distribution of the Clactonian and comparable groups does not yet extend into a zone warmer than the temperate zone, or more especially into the Savannah' (1969, p. 289). Quite clearly the further north one goes the greater the dependence upon animal foods would be expected (Lee, 1968), and, according to the results of this analysis, the greater the dominance of assemblages by small flake cutting tools would be expected. This condition is clearly met in material Collins discusses as the 'Clactonian tradition'.

Another provocative feature of the European material noted by Bordes is a major change in the character of Acheulean assemblages during the early phases of the Riss glaciation. 'It would seem that there is a turning point in this Acheulean culture, when from this point onwards flake tools become more numerous than the bifacial implements' (Bordes, 1968, p. 58). This turning point may well betray a shift in subsistence strategies in favour of greater dependence upon animal foods.

Factor II
This is a normally grouped factor exhibiting strong factor loadings on three variables: picks, other large tools and choppers. The most obvious characteristic of this factor is the inclusion of variables frequently considered diagnostic of the Sangoan materials of east Africa. Also loaded on this factor are core scrapers, a variable that exhibits significant loadings on two other factors, indicating 'general purpose' tools being used in a number of contexts or a variable that is inadequately broken down at the typological level of analysis. The recognition in this analysis of a normally grouped factor

exhibiting diagnostics of the Sangoan industry is not surprising in light of the recognition of these tools as frequently occurring in the late Acheulean of east Africa:

> The Isimila late Acheulean assemblage is of interest in that it contains certain artefact types reminiscent of types common and characteristic of the later Sangoan industrial complexes. These include various forms of picks, push-planes, core-scrapers, chisel-ended tools, discoids and the like. . . . This manifestation appears then to be a general characteristic of the later Acheulean industries in the central and eastern African areas, a fact of considerable importance in understanding the origins of the later Sangoan industrial complexes. (Howell, Cole and Kleindienst, 1962, p. 75)

Of interest in this regard is the fact that the tools exhibiting low and opposite (positive) factor loading to this group are handaxes, knives, cleavers, spheroids, small scrapers and other small tools – all classes that have been traditionally considered diagnostic of the Acheulean if we included the small tool variant. The significance of these findings for understanding the 'transition' to the Sangoan is left here to the experts in the field.

Factor III
This is a specific factor exhibiting some bipolar characteristics. Part of its weak development may be due to a mistaken assumption made at the time the original data matrix was compiled. In viewing the failure to mention discoids at Kalambo Falls and the problems of equating Clark's and Kleindienst's typological categories, I made the mistaken assumption that Clark's failure to mention discoids resulted from differences in the typologies used. I therefore added to the Kalambo frequencies as the best estimate of occurrence the average percentage for discoids in the other assemblages. I now know that this was a mistake, and discoids were in fact absent at Kalambo Falls (Howell, Cole and Kleindienst, 1962, p. 76). My guess is that if the discoids were deleted from the Kalambo samples, we would have derived a well-defined bipolar factor for III. As it is, discoids are heavily loaded positively and picks and flake scrapers moderately loaded negatively. Discoids have been mentioned as a 'diagnostic' of Sangoan industries; however, our analysis shows them to vary quite independently of other diagnostics, indicating that the determinants of their frequencies are quite different from the determinants of the frequencies for Factor II.

Factor IV

This is a classic bipolar factor with the highest loading shown negatively on cleavers and the next highest negative loading on flake scrapers; however, this variable is loaded on several factors, demonstrating that it is a 'general purpose' tool, or that greater typological breakdown may be warranted. The highly dependent but inversely related variable expressed positively is 'other small tools'. This class included such classes as proto-burins, burins, points and borers of various forms, tools that are frequently considered to be 'tools to make tools'.

Cleavers are generally cited as tools diagnostic of the Acheulean in Africa. This factor, as in the case of Factor I, clearly demonstrates that the 'small tools' traditionally considered to be an independent tradition are strongly a part of the Acheulean, exhibiting strong inverse relationships to cleavers. As in the case of Factor I, the conditions under which cleavers were used and discarded was such that as their use increased the probability of conditions favouring the use of other small tools decreased directly.

The recognition that cleavers vary independently of handaxes in Africa makes even more provocative their general absence from Acheulean assemblages over much of Europe. What were the conditions in Africa favouring the use of these tools? Were such conditions absent in the more northern latitudes?

Factor V

This factor exhibits many of the characteristics of Factor III in that it is a specific factor with a weakly developed bipolar quality. Spheroids are the variable most definitive of this factor, with flake scrapers and core scrapers showing significantly high negative loadings. These are both variables that do not exhibit any exclusive association with any one factor. They both show fairly high loadings on several factors. It is tempting to see this factor as a 'stylistic variant' of Factor III, which, as we have mentioned, is sometimes seen in its positive manifestation as a diagnostic of the Sangoan. In any event both of these factors III and V have in common a negative projection of flake scrapers.

GENERAL DISCUSSION

These five factors can be seen as definitive of the character of covariant relationships occurring in this sample of Later Acheulean assemblages from east Africa. Each factor isolates tools which, with the exception of flake scrapers, tend to exhibit exclusive patterns of covariation among those diagnostic of each factor and independence between the variables grouped into the five sets. Accepting the traditionalists' paradigm we would expect these five sets of variables to represent five traditions, since a relationship of independence obtains between them. Further, we would expect these bipolar factors to betray some patterned distribution temporarily or spatially, since inverse relationships should betray 'replacive' kinds of variation.

THE CHARACTER OF ASSOCIATIONAL PATTERNING IN THE SAMPLE

Associational patterning has been the form used as the basis for the recognition of assemblage types and hence has served as the basis for comparisons between locations and for temporal studies. Associational patterning simply refers to the recurrent association between two things, although the frequencies of these things may or may not vary in a related fashion. Association says that *A* tends to co-occur with *B*, but it does not imply that the frequency of *A* varies in a related fashion with the frequency of *B*.

Maxine Kleindienst (1961b) conducted a comparative analysis of Late Acheulean assemblages from Olorgesailie, Isimila and Broken Hill. Her work resulted in the recognition of two major patterns of assemblage variability, with two minor variants. These are as follows:

(A) Assemblages with a high percentage of handaxes, cleavers and knives, low percentages of other large tools and low percentages of small implements.

(B) Assemblages with high percentages of small tools and low percentages of handaxes, cleavers, knives and other types of large tools.

(A–B, intermediate) Assemblages with approximately equal percentages of handaxes, cleavers, knives and small implements, with lower percentages of other large tool types.

(C) Assemblages with a high percentage of core scrapers, picks and choppers compared to other assemblages, plus some handaxes, cleavers, knives and small implements.

These generalizations summarize something of the character of associational patterning observable among our samples. I will further explore these relationships making use of a number of kinds of data informed in terms of the results of factor analysis. I will initially discuss variability in terms of percentage frequencies of tool classes discretely isolated as exhibiting covariant relationships. I have chosen to use percentages for the analysis of Factor I and IV variables, since most readers are familiar with their use, and, as will be shown, when informed by factor analysis percentages may be quite informative.

In this analysis we will be concerned with two kinds of variability. The first has to do with the degree to which particular values for a specified relationship are evenly distributed or alternatively exhibit clusters of redundant values for a number of cases in the sample. The second kind of analysis seeks to discover the degree to which there are redundant associations between the measured value of one specified relationship and another independent relationship. The latter is a description of associational patterning between phenomena known not to vary in a covariant fashion.

Since we know that handaxes and knives vary inversely with small scrapers we may ask if the distribution of relative frequencies of these related classes of tools is normally distributed. If not, the distribution will exhibit clustering indicative of repetitive patterning in the content of sites. A value was calculated by summing the percentage values for all three classes of tools and then dividing this sum into the summed frequencies for handaxes and knives. The result is the percentage of Factor I diagnostics represented by handaxes and knives.

TABLE 3.6. *Percentage of summed percentages for handaxes, knives and small scrapers represented by handaxes and knives*

Isimila	J12	92·3	Olorgesailie	11	22·3
Isimila	K6	100·0	Kalambo	8	39·0
Olorgesailie	9	96·1	Kalambo	A1/56/4	47·1
Kariandusi		91·3	Kalambo	A1/56/5B	47·9
Olorgesailie	8	92·1	Kalambo	7	24·6
Isimila	H9–J8	88·4	Broken Hill		5·5
Olorgesailie	7	88·1	Kalambo	6B	42·9
Kalambo	6A	84·9	Kalambo	A1/56/V	50·1
Olorgesailie	6	49·4	Isimila	K19	42·3
Olorgesailie	10	54·4	Isimila	K14	52·8
Nsongezi	C–1	46·5	Isimila	U.J6–7	87·2
Olorgesailie	3	22·5	Lochard		51·1
Isimila	K18	26·9	Kalambo	5	64·2
Nsongezi	C–17	46·1	Isimila	H15	44·5
Olorgesailie	2	14·4	Isimila	L.J6–7	48·6
Olorgesailie	1	2·8	Nsongezi	C–13	66·6

Plotting of the values in Table 3.6 reveals that they are not continuously distributed nor are they normally distributed. Two major clusters and three minor clusters are clearly recognizable (see Fig. 3.1).

Class A: Cases where less than 27% of the diagnostics of Factor I are handaxes and knives (seven cases).

Class B: Cases between 35% and 55% of the diagnostics of Factor I are represented by handaxes and knives (fourteen cases).

Class C: Cases where between 63% and 67% of the diagnostics of Factor I are represented by handaxes and knives (two cases).

Class D: Cases where between 81% and 100% of the diagnostics of Factor I are represented by handaxes and knives.

Factor IV

Using the same approach we may now ask a similar set of questions with regard to relative contributions from opposing diagnostics of Factor IV. The percentages of cleavers and other small tools were summed and this sum was divided into the percentage of cleavers present. The result is the per cent of the diagnostics for Factor IV represented by cleavers. Table 3.7 presents the values obtained.

TABLE 3.7

Isimila	J12	87·4	Olorgesailie	11	3·2
Isimila	K6	80·0	Kalambo	8	100·0
Olorgesailie	9	86·1	Kalambo	A1/56/4	62·6
Kariandusi		69·5	Kalambo	A1/56/5B	81·3
Olorgesailie	8	56·6	Kalambo	7	100·0
Isimila	H9–J8	100·0	Broken Hill		30·8
Olorgesailie	7	87·9	Kalambo	6B	69·4
Kalambo	6A	95·8	Kalambo	A1/56/V	94·0
Olorgesailie	6	10·6	Isimila	K19	88·0
Olorgesailie	10	24·1	Isimila	K14	83·2
Nsongezi	C–1	9·5	Isimila	U.J6–7	89·0
Olorgesailie	3	5·7	Lochard		38·1
Isimila	K18	24·8	Kalambo	5	80·8
Nsongezi	C–17	23·2	Isimila	H–15	100·0
Olorgesailie	2	6·9	Isimila	L.J6–7	53·5
Olorgesailie	1	3·5	Nsongezi	C–13	33·4

Plotting the values in the Table 3.7 demonstrates a very different pattern than was observed for Factor I (see Fig. 3.1).

There are clearly four clusters of values indicating sites in which the relationships between the two ends of the bipolar determinant are balanced in a roughly identical fashion.

Class I: Cases where only between 0% and 10% of the diagnostics of Factor IV are cleavers.

Class II: Cases where between 20% and 40% of the diagnostics of Factor
IV are cleavers.

Class III: Cases where between 50% and 70% of the diagnostics of Factor
IV are cleavers.

Class IV: Cases where between 80% and 100% of the diagnostics of
Factor IV are cleavers.

A comparison of the two distributions shows a very different pattern of
clustering (see Fig. 3.1). Cases tend to cluster at the two ends of the scale for

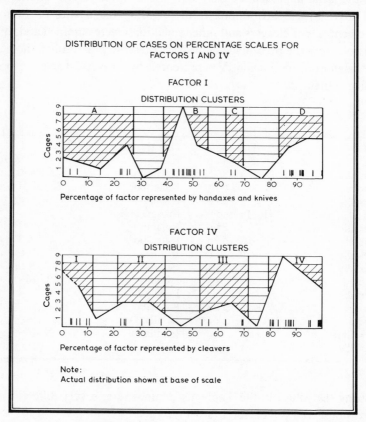

Fig. 3.1. Distribution of cases on percentage scales for Factors I and IV.

Factor IV – that is, where the percentage of cleavers is less than 20% or over
80%. Cases falling near the 50/50 point are fewest. I suspect that if we had a
larger sample, which included those so-called 'Hope Fountain' assemblages,
we would obtain a bipolar distribution of values for the proportions of other

small tools to cleavers. This means that not only are the tasks represented by the two tool classes inversely related, but they also strongly tend to occur at *spatially independent locations*. In contrast the graph for percentage values of handaxes and knives to small scrapers exhibits a clustering at the upper end of the scale, a marked peak in the centre indicating approximately half handaxes and cleavers and half small scrapers, and then a low curve of cases dispersed along the low half of the scale. As in the discussion above, I suspect that if we had a truly representative sample of late Acheulean materials, we would obtain either a trimodal distribution with the majority of cases falling in the centre of the case, or a bimodal distribution with the central cluster exhibiting a marked skew to the left. In any event the curve of cases as known from this sample demonstrates several things: (*a*) cases at the high end of the scale tend to be tightly clustered above the 80% level; and (*b*) cases at the low end of the scale are not nearly so tightly clustered, indicating much greater variability in the incidence of handaxes on sites where the percentage is less than 30% than we note between sites where the percentage is greater than 70%.

We are now in a position to construct a matrix, in terms of which we may observe the degree that there are patterned associations of cases when the distributional clusterings characteristic of the two dimensions are considered together. Fig. 3.2 quite clearly shows that there is clustering. All those sites having greater than 50% of the diagnostics for Factor IV represented by cleavers cluster in classes C and D with regard to the handaxe-scraper distribution. Conversely, all those sites where less than 50% of the diagnostics for Factor IV are cleavers cluster in classes A and B of the handaxe-scraper distribution. The only overlap is seen in the B class for handaxe-scraper values – that is, where between 35% and 55% of the diagnostics for Factor I are handaxes. Three exceptions mar this almost perfect separation: Kalambo 7 and 5 and Nsongezi C–13.

The important point to be made at this juncture is that these materials provide the most graphic demonstration of the structural properties of variability in these archaeological assemblages. First, I have demonstrated that two independent dimensions of covariate relationships dominate the quantitative relationships between four classes of tools in *all the samples*. Small scrapers vary inversely with handaxes and cleavers; similarly cleavers vary inversely with other small tools. These relationships characterize late Acheulean assemblages regardless of variability in the associations noted between the clustered forms of their expression. Since the assemblages are clustered distributions of artefacts in space (e.g. sites), we observe that there are consistent patterns in the *associations* at sites of patterned expressions of the relationships manifest by the two independent sets of covariant phenomena. These recurrent patterns of association form the basis for the recognition of assemblage types. Based on Fig. 3.2 we may recognize an assemblage

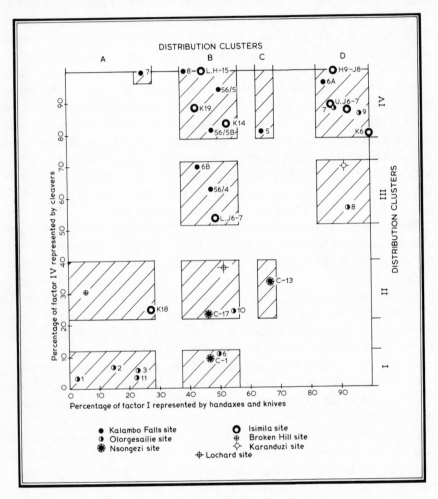

FIG. 3.2. Distribution clusters.

type characterized by over 80% handaxes and knives and less than 20% small scrapers, and over 80% cleavers and less than 20% other small tools (Class IV–D in the table and Type A of the Kleindienst typology). Similarly, we may recognize another assemblage type characterized by over 70% small scrapers and less than 30% handaxes, and over 70% other small tools and less

150

than 30% cleavers (Classes IA, IIA, in Fig. 3.2 and Type B of the Kleindienst typology). Clearly these are very different and represent patterned recurrent associations at different sites. The difference is of such a magnitude that the traditional archaeologist would most certainly recognize these as expressions of different cultures. In fact in their extreme form this has been done: Acheulean–Hope Fountain; the analogous situation outside of Africa, Acheulean–Clactonian; and a more tenuous analogy for earlier African material, the Developed Oldowan–Acheulean dichotomy. Our analysis has shown, however, that these seemingly different forms are simply reverse images of an identical set of relationships! In both, scrapers will covary with handaxes and knives, and other small tools will covary with cleavers. Each set will vary independently of the others. The assemblage types represent identical behavioural responses to a common set of determinants. The only difference between them is in the expression of dichotomous determinants. This is a highly patterned association between non-covariant forms. We would therefore expect that assemblage types defined on the basis of these associations would not exhibit directional patterning through time or across space. *The traditionalists' assumption that associational patterning is also covariant patterning is not met.*

The reader will realize that I have not exhausted the information derived from the factor analysis. There were three additional factors isolated. What complications arise when this information is added to that already discussed? In order to explicate these relationships, I must shift to a slightly different approach, since the other three factors isolated were all characterized by classes of tools that exhibited multiple high factor loadings on more than one factor. Using the actual percentages of tool classes as I have done above is therefore not possible without a great deal of involved effort. Instead I will use the factor scores as a means of measuring the distribution of the isolated relationships among the assemblages in the sample. Factor scores are a means of expressing the amount of information contributed by each case to the definition of the isolated factors. Table 3.8 presents the factor scores for all thirty-two assemblages for all factors.

By using the factor scores we may recognize that Factor II, the 'Sangoan Factor', is only significantly indicated at Isimila L.H.–15, Nsongezi C–1, Kalambo A1/56/4, Kalambo A1/56/5B and Nsongezi C–13.

Comparison of the factor scores for Factors III and V, both specific factors with weakly developed bipolar characteristics, allows us to recognize classes of association between the two sets of determinants in the same way as such associations were uncovered by studying the percentages of diagnostics for

TABLE 3.8

Site	I	II	III	IV	V
			Factors		
Isimila					
K14	0·346	−0·262	1·013	−1·208	1·437
H9–J8	−0·739	−0·341	0·779	−0·819	0·623
U.J6–7	−0·270	−0·049	0·333	−1·076	−0·026
L.J6–7	0·307	0·492	0·478	0·086	0·030
K6	−2·122	−0·644	−1·204	0·459	−0·026
J12	−2·204	−0·664	−0·692	−0·093	−0·372
H15	0·156	−3·991	−1·163	−0·272	0·066
K18	0·587	−0·164	1·665	0·681	−0·376
K19	0·689	0·886	0·217	−1·819	−0·143
Kalambo					
A1/56/4	0·843	−0·764	−0·881	−0·464	−0·484
A1/56/5	0·650	0·672	−0·556	−1·654	−1·318
A1/56/5B	0·855	−1·012	−0·988	−0·505	−0·464
5	−0·171	0·035	−0·245	−0·332	−0·622
6A	−0·481	0·395	−0·048	−1·168	−0·372
6B	0·803	0·283	−0·048	−0·178	−0·820
7	1·334	0·731	0·047	−1·324	−0·736
8	0·696	0·993	−0·165	−0·653	−0·824
Olorgesailie					
11	0·379	0·766	−0·264	1·976	0·172
10	−0·247	0·750	−0·300	0·874	0·239
9	−1·919	1·016	−0·103	−0·362	0·107
8	−1·667	0·034	−0·171	0·361	0·146
7	−0·649	0·045	0·166	−1·001	1·924
6	−0·301	0·588	0·291	1·089	0·449
3	0·371	0·172	−0·514	1·716	0·516
2	1·068	0·266	−0·355	0·951	1·135
1	1·126	1·144	−0·268	1·827	−0·330
Nsongezi					
C–1	0·298	−1·886	0·863	1·243	−0·973
C–13	0·373	−0·786	−0·558	0·477	−0·872
C–17	0·657	0·606	−0·914	0·709	−1·333
Lochard	−0·207	−0·829	4·144	0·311	−0·171
Broken Hill	1·199	0·094	−0·936	−0·138	3·784
Kariandusi	−1·760	0·096	−0·223	−0·119	−0·367

Factors I and IV. Associations of significant factor scores are shown in Table 3.9.

We may recognize several associations between Factors III and V:

Group I. Associations are all those combinations where positive loadings are characteristic, indicating discoids and/or spheroids.

TABLE 3.9
Factor V   + = spheroids,   − = flake sc. and core sc.

Factor III	Positive			Negative		
	high	moderate	insig.	insig.	moderate	high
Positive						
high				Lochard		
moderate		K14				
		H9–J8		K18	C–1	
insig.	o–7				Kalambo 7	
Negative						
insig.		o–3			6B, Kal 8	
		o–2			A1/56/V	
moderate			Isimila	A1/56/4	C–13	
			LH–15	A1/56/5B	C–17	
				K6		
high						

Set A. These are assemblages in which both Factors III and V are positively loaded. Discoids and spheroids co-occur (Isimila levels K14 and H9–J8).

Set B. These are assemblages in which Factor V is positively loaded with Factor III insignificantly represented (Olorgesailie levels 7, 3 and 2).

Set C. These are assemblages in which Factor III is positively loaded with Factor V insignificantly represented (Lochard and Isimila K18).

Group II. A single case is recorded in which Factor III is positively represented and Factor V is negatively represented. This occurred in Nsongezi C–1.

Group III. Associations are all assemblages in which negative loadings on Factors III and V are characteristic.

Set A. These are assemblages in which Factor III is negatively represented and Factor V has insignificant loadings (Isimila L.H.–15, Kalambo A1/56/4, Kalambo A1/56/5B and Isimila K6).

Set B. These are assemblages in which Factor V is negatively represented with Factor III showing insignificant loadings (Kalambo 7, Kalambo 6B, Kalambo 8 and Kalambo A1/56/V).

Set C. This assemblage has both factors represented by significant negative loadings (Nsongezi C–13, and Nsongezi C–17).

Assemblages exhibiting properties isolated as Factors III and V as well as the Sangoan Factor II are indicated on Fig. 3.3. Quite clearly there is a clustering of associations in which both Class III associations for Factors III and V as

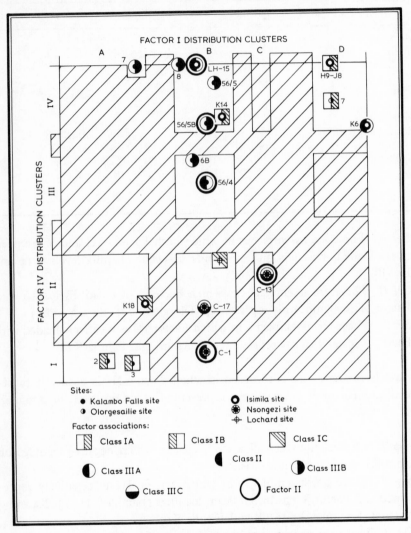

FIG. 3.3. Factor I distribution clusters.

well as the Sangoan Factor II are clustered with assemblages exhibiting between 35% and 55% handaxes and knives of Factor I diagnostics (Class B). Conversely, assemblages with significant positive loadings on Factors III and

V are almost exclusively distributed among those falling either at the low or high ends of the distribution for handaxes and knives versus small scrapers. Discoids, spheroids and (to some extent) choppers tend to associate with assemblages exhibiting over 80% handaxes or over 70% small scrapers. Conversely, flake scrapers and/or picks, other large tools and the majority of choppers associate with sites exhibiting between 35% and 55% handaxes. These associations further complicate the picture, since the two classes of assemblages least alike in terms of associations for Factors I and IV variables are those with over 80% handaxes, knives and cleavers, versus sites where over 70% are small scrapers, and where other small tools share spheroids and/or discoids to the general exclusion of flake scrapers, core scrapers and picks. Those assemblages least alike in terms of associations between forms of expression for similar covariant relationships along two independent dimensions (Factors I and IV) turn out to be most alike in their associations with respect to two additional independent dimensions of variability (Factors III and V)! Clearly associational relationships are not covariant relationships in these assemblages. This demonstrates two independent dimensions of patterning: (*a*) mutual patterns of covariation among classes of tools; and (*b*) patterned associations at locations of classes of tools among which there is not demonstrable mutual covariation.

These findings show a structure of variability among archaeological assemblages which cannot be accommodated by the traditionalists' paradigm. That paradigm assumes that patterns of association are also covariant in character. When an interruption in covariant patterning is observed it is assumed that an independent organization of patterning measured in terms of associations is intrusive. The intrusive unit is expected to exhibit covariant patterning with other units sharing the same pattern of associations some-where else. We have demonstrated that those sets of tools most regularly associated are those among which no covariant relationships obtain. The fact that the two dimensions of patterning – associational and covariant – may vary independently of one another clearly demonstrates the potential complexity of assemblage composition. It further demonstrates a number of points: if covariant patterning is the expected form when assemblage composition is viewed against a temporal or spatial dimension, then patterns of covariation should correlate with associations between tool classes if the assemblage is to be the unit of comparison. That is, if the traditionalists are right and tool forms gradually replace one another in 'popularity' through time and across space, then we would expect them to exhibit patterns of mutual covariation. Yet we observed in this case patterns of covariation between classes of tools that are generally not associated with each other in large numbers, e.g. other small tools and cleavers, etc. Clearly this means that transformational patterning will not be demonstrable among assemblages arranged against a temporal dimension or a spatial dimension. This is clearly what we observe in the stratified locations (see Howell and Clark, 1963), an alternation of assemblage types such that those closest in time may be most different in the character of assemblage composition, while those separated in time may exhibit greater compositional similarities. It is only when assemblages are exclusively composed of tool classes among which varying degrees of mutual covariation are demonstrable that it is possible for total assemblage composition to exhibit directional patterning when arrayed against a time or space dimension. The greater the degree of covariant independence between associated forms, the less directionality that will be demonstrable when assemblages are compared. I have demonstrated that a 'nonconformity', as demonstrated by the comparison of assemblage types defined on the basis of associational patterning, does not indicate any lack of continuity in covariant patterning. If a lack of continuity in covariant patterning is the basis for the definition of a nonconformity, why do we view alternations of assemblage types as nonconformities? Because the traditionalists' paradigm assumes an equation between association and covariation!

I submit that the degree to which associational patterning is also characterized by covariant relationships among the associated forms is a variable phenomenon. My expectations are that the degree of directionality demonstrable in frequency variations among components of assemblages through time or across space will vary directly with the degree that associated classes of items are also related in a covariant fashion. I further suggest that this relationship will vary inversely with the degree of mobility characteristic of the adaptation represented. It will vary directly with the degree that tools are curated and transported in anticipation of future tasks, and will vary directly with the level of behavioural integration achieved within the adaptive system under study.

Clearly within the Late Acheulean the independence between association and covariation is almost complete. As expected, we observe an alternation of assemblage types. This same characteristic is a marked feature of assemblage variability for the Mousterian and, it is suspected, for the earlier ranges of time in general. It is my impression that it is not until the Upper Palaeolithic that sequences of assemblage types begin clearly to pattern temporally or to exhibit directional change through a time sequence. This contrasts with the growing number of sequences characterized by alternating assemblage types clustering in the earlier time ranges. This has a number of implications for both archaeological theory and for our understanding of the past.

First, it is commensurate with the adoption of the behavioural view of assemblage variability in which similarities are seen as a result of a similar constellation of behaviour having been enacted at a given location. We may therefore ask what are the determinants of behavioural similarities. If we accept covariant relationships as a measure of regular and similar behavioural responses, how are we to understand patterned associations between variables not covariantly related. These must be seen as associations deriving from the patterned coincidental occurrences of stimuli which elicit different behavioural responses. The consistent association of high frequencies of small scrapers and other small tools that do not exhibit mutual patterns of covariation must be seen as the result of the common association in the environment of stimuli which independently elicit different behaviour manifest by the two classes of tools. In short, assemblages are compounds of independently stimulated behavioural responses. The degree to which assemblages exhibit associations that do not also have covariant properties should be a direct measure of the degree of integration or organization of the behavioural regime expressed. For instance, in the case of the chimpanzee's manufacture of termiting sticks, it would appear that the number of sticks manufactured does not vary with the number of termites consumed; instead it appears to vary directly with the number of distractions experienced by the chimpanzee during his stay at the termite nest. In this case, although termite nests and termiting sticks would be expected to be strongly associated, we would not expect a covariant relationship between the numbers of sticks and the size of the termite nests. On the other hand, in a highly integrated behavioural regime we might expect the sticks to be discarded directly as a function of their loss of rigidity resulting from repeated licking. The number of sticks manufactured at any one location would then vary directly with the number of termites present, given some vagaries in the degree of hunger experienced by different animals.

The character of assemblage variability documented for the Late Acheulean and implied for the Mousterian by a temporal pattern of assemblage type alternation, and suspected for the earlier time periods in general, may well be informing us about a very different organization of adaptive behaviour than we customarily assume for modern man. The traditionalists' paradigm when applied to these materials distorts the character of the variability and denies to us any chance of gaining knowledge of the behaviour of our biological ancestors.

The traditionalists' paradigm is rooted in the main on casual or 'obvious' features of the contemporary human experience, 'Frenchmen have different things from Japanese, etc.' Aside from the assumptions previously discussed regarding the covariant character of relationships between associated materials, the paradigm assumes that the human species is partitioned into culturally maintained distinctive populations. The very notion of ethnic groups implies this assumption.

Although rarely stated, the traditionalists' paradigm assumes that this ethnic distinctiveness is 'natural' to cultural man and arises in the context of 'drift' or minor shifts in the 'popularity' of alternative cultural forms. Social groups interacting at the local level, but independently distributed geographically, should experience different 'drift' histories, making it possible for the archaeologist to recognize different 'traditions'. Given this view, the number of traditions should vary directly with the number of geographically localized subpopulations and inversely with the amount of inter-group interaction, there being a greater tendency toward convergence as rates of interaction increased and its attendant effect in 'diffusing' cultural characteristics among the 'traditions'. On the other hand the rates of drift, or change in the content of traditions, should vary directly with the numbers of people participating, since the source of variability is believed to be individual variability. We would then expect rates of change and the magnitude of variability both to increase as the numbers of individual participants increased.

If the traditionalists' paradigm is correct we would expect a number of features to characterize the archaeological record for the early periods of the Pleistocene.

Between the beginning of the Pleistocene until the beginning of the Würm, man radiated over much of the Old World. There must have been a major increase in the number of localized human populations. Nevertheless, we do not have documented any major increase in the number of traditions, three being all that most would admit by the end of this vast span of time! Contrast this with the span of time currently said to represent the history of human occupation in the New World (few would admit more than 30 000 years). At the end of this relatively short span of time there must be a thousand or more 'traditions' recognized by archaeologists!

The evidence for institutionalized between-group interaction between early Pleistocene populations is meagre, if even present. Evidence of trade and between-group social ritual is completely lacking. Clearly such evidence is well established for the later periods of human occupation in the New World. This should mean that we would expect a greater convergence between traditions in the New World and greater independence, and hence greater numbers of unambiguously defined traditions, during the early parts of the Pleistocene. We observe just the reverse!

The lack of variability and almost incredible stability characteristic of the earlier phases of the Pleistocene is even more striking if we adopt the generally accepted notion that human populations were sparse and thinly distributed. These conditions should promote more recognizable and distinct traditions, yet they seem to have had the reverse effect during man's early history!

Another expectation regarding the character of the archaeological record, if the traditionalists' paradigm is correct, has reference to rates of change and within-tradition variability. As previously mentioned, the rates of change in the content of traditions should vary directly with the numbers of people participating. Clearly, there is an increase in the rates of culture change during the later phases of the Pleistocene, with a parallel increase in human population; nevertheless during the earlier phases of the Pleistocene defined traditions covered enormous spans of time and tremendous geographical areas. The actual number of participants must have in many cases equalled or possibly surpassed the numbers participating in many later traditions. Why was there so little change and so little variability?

Since the early years of the twentieth century, anthropologists have expended tremendous energy in attempting to evaluate the degree to which variations in the biological characteristics of modern geographical races affect the general form and level of complexity of the cultures borne by such diverse forms of men.

The results of these researches have overwhelmingly pointed to the conclusion that variations in culture among modern populations cannot be attributed to biological differences in 'capacities for culture'. This recognition has lead to the assumption as expressed by White (1959) that for purposes of explaining cultural variability we may 'consider the organism a constant'. I feel that archaeologists, although generally not expressing their views, have tended to think of the archaeological remains of the Lower and Middle Palaeolithic as if they too could 'consider the organism a constant'. Certainly, the demonstrable anatomical contrasts between the men of the earlier time ranges when compared with those of modern man are warning of a potential fallacy.

One of the more fascinating and absorbing aspects of prehistoric research is the realization that one may work with the products of men anatomically different from ourselves. On reflection this becomes a major challenge, for it becomes incumbent upon the prehistorian to provide what knowledge we may acquire concerning the psychological, social and cultural capabilities and capacities of our pre-modern ancestors. The recognition that man of the Lower and Middle Pleistocene was in all probability a very different kind of creature from modern man has stimulated much of the basic research on the social and psychological capacities of non-human primates. Such information is provocative and suggestive, yet the only direct evidence we have concerning the behaviour of our ancient forebears rests in their archaeological remains. To what degree is the archaeologist doing his job when he *assumes* he knows the significance of his archaeological observations, and *assumes* further that paradigms built from analogue models from modern behaviour are directly applicable to the products of early man?

The application of the traditionalists' paradigm to the interpretation of the products of early man makes several assumptions. One basic tenet of the traditionalists' approach is that man passed a threshold, a 'cultural Rubicon', before which his behaviour was 'non-human', after which his behaviour was 'human' and therefore cultural in the sense of modern man. This proposition is no longer acceptable. In a number of recent papers the assumption of a 'cultural Rubicon' has been strongly questioned (Geertz, 1969; Hallowell, 1959). Did all the aspects of culture as observed in *Homo sapiens* come into being together at an early hominid stage? White has pointed out the importance of the capacity to symbol as a criterion for cultural behaviour as we know it. Hallowell has expanded and elaborated in psychological terms what is implied by symboling, namely a self-conscious actor. Hallowell suggests that symboling capacity makes possible a creature capable of conceptualizing himself and analysing his environmental matrix using as a point of reference the self-image.

Anthropologists have generally accepted the presence of manufactured tools, 'man the toolmaker', as evidence of such capabilities, and hence a marker for the passing of the 'cultural Rubicon'. Recently, new data and new approaches to the study of man cast strong doubt on this rule of thumb. Goodall has demonstrated that chimpanzees in the wild manufacture tools. Hallowell has questioned on other grounds whether tool manufacture does require the cultural and psychological matrix within which modern man exists. I have already mentioned that a basic assumption standing behind the traditionalists' paradigm is that the human species is partitioned into culturally maintained distinctive populations, or ethnic groups. I am convinced that much of the variability noted between the material products of distinct socio-cultural units known ethnographically results not from unconscious 'drift' but from a conscious response to selective advantages accruing to the maintenance and explicit recognition at the cognitive level of group identities and individual identities. I suggest that many of the patterns of variability that are directly referable to groups recognized by others, and self-cognizant of their distinctiveness, are products of a particular context of selection and the attendant context of socio-cultural development. I suggest that much of the 'conservativeness' notable among many ethnic groups, as well as their obvious distinctiveness, may well be a response to the operation of a particular set of selective pressures arising in the context of a relatively complex social geography. Such conditions may not have existed during most of the Pleistocene. When did man exercise his human prerogative and assign meaning to the various segments into which the species was partitioned geographically? Were local human groups culturally bounded during much of the Pleistocene? Instead of assuming answers to these questions and viewing inter-assemblage variability as a measure of 'cultural' distance or 'ethnic' distinctiveness, we might more profitably concern ourselves with establishing when we can demonstrate variability in the archaeological record referable to ethnic differentiations among human groups. My impression is that little if any of the variability thus far demonstrated in the archaeological record prior to the Upper Palaeolithic is referable to 'ethnic' units of hominid populations that were 'culturally' bounded.

The Palaeolithic archaeologist is faced with a dual problem and a real challenge: (1) change in the character of the organism may well have modified considerably the capacities of man for engaging in cultural behaviour; and (2) changes in the ecological adjustments of man to man and man to nature would have modified the selective contexts favouring the exercise of these changing capacities in differing and expanding domains of the hominids' experience. As I have argued, the traditionalists' paradigm denies us the chance of studying these problems. In spite of my demonstration that the basic assumptions standing behind traditional interpretation of archaeological remains are not met in the empirical world of Palaeolithic remains, I predict that traditionalists will continue to defend the old 'secure' paradigm.

Karl R. Popper (1959) has argued quite convincingly that theories cannot be proven – only by their invalidation or inadequacy can we evaluate our lack of understanding or knowledge of the way the natural world works. He has further argued that during periods in which theories are being doubted, either on the basis of claims of their having been disproved, or on an intuitive 'uneasiness' with their efficacy, there will appear a defensive strategy on the part of apologists for the traditional paradigm, which he has called 'conventionalism'

(Popper, 1959, p. 78). 'According to this conventionalists' point of view, laws of nature are not falsifiable by observation, for they are needed to determine what an observation, and more especially, what a scientific measurement is' (Popper, 1959, p. 80). This prediction has almost a frightening accuracy when viewed against several recent statements made by traditionalists:

> His view that detailed stylistic similarities between assemblages must be due to a community of cultural tradition cannot be challenged. As he clearly points out, the functional approach to accounting for differences is not applicable, since we simply do not possess a single shred of reliable evidence bearing on the possible function(s) of the various categories of tools found in Lower and Middle Palaeolithic assemblages. Therefore, the problem of use becomes a sheer game of hypotheses with no established limits, in which everyone's guess has just as much potential validity as the next person's. In the final analysis, the basic assumption of continuity of cultural tradition is abundantly supported by the manner in which patterns emerge when distributions of traditions and stages of common cultural entities are plotted in time and space. (Movius, 1969, p. 307)

> In contrast to the single-community . . . [view], the hypothesis of continuity of culture tradition is not opposed by an important indication either from archaeological data or from ethnographic analogy. . . . It does not conflict with the view that assemblage types sometimes represent different activities, for it is in their activities as much as in their culture 'traits' that societies are distinguished from one another. A crude example would be the proposition that the cultures of France and that of the Australian aborigines are different only because they indulge in different activities. . . . It is indeed fortunate that the study of culture traditions does not necessarily involve knowing the functions of artefacts, since we can rarely do more than guess at these. I suggest that we are justified in proceeding on the hypothesis that close similarity of style and content in assemblages is an indicator of common cultural tradition. We may also conclude that we have no good evidence for two or more assemblage-types belonging to a single community in Pleistocene Europe. (Collins, 1969, pp. 269–70)

I have tried to document that a mentalistic cultural theory, its model, and a single operational definition, serve to identify for the traditionalist what relevant observation is and more importantly what it measures.

I have tried to demonstrate that the basic assumptions about the nature of the archaeological record are not met empirically, and further that there are serious reasons for doubting those that have not been subjected to empirical testing.

In such times of crisis this conflict over the aims of science will become acute. We, and those who share our attitude, will hope to make new discoveries; and we shall hope to be helped in this by a newly erected scientific system. Thus, we shall take the greatest interest in the falsifying experiment. We shall hail it as a success, for it has opened up new vistas into a world of new experience. And we shall hail it even if these new experiences should furnish us with new arguments against our own most recent theories. But the newly rising structure, the boldness of which we admire, is seen by the conventionalist as a monument to the total collapse of science. . . . In the eyes of the conventionalist one principle only can help us to select a system as the chosen one from among all other possible systems; it is the principle of selecting the simplest system – the simplest system of implicit definition; which of course means in practice the 'classical' system of the day. (Popper, 1959, pp. 80–1)

References

BINFORD, L. R. (1971) *Mortuary Practices, their Study and their Potential.* Memoirs of the Society for American Archaeology No. 25.

BINFORD, L. R. and BINFORD, S. R. (1966) A preliminary analysis of functional variability in the Mousterian of Levallois facies. *American Anthropologist*, **68**, 2 (2), 238–95.

BINFORD, S. R. and BINFORD, L. R. (1969) Stone tools and human behavior. *Scientific American*, **220** (4), 70–84.

BORDES, F. H. (1950) Principes d'une méthode d'étude des techniques de débitage et de la typologie du Paléolithique ancien et moyen. *L'Anthropologie*, **54** (1–2), 19–34.

BORDES, F. H. (1956) Some observations on the Pleistocene succession in the Somme valley. *Proceedings of the Prehistoric Society*, **22**, 1–5.

BORDES, F. H. (1961) Mousterian cultures in France. *Science*, **134**, 803–10.

BORDES, F. H. (1968) *The Old Stone Age.* London: Weidenfeld & Nicolson.

BORDES, F. H. and BOURGON, M. (1951) Le complexe Mousterian. *L'Anthropologie*, **55**, 1–23.

BOWLER-KELLEY, A. (1937) *Lower and Middle Paleolithic Facies in Europe and Africa.* Philadelphia: Lippincott.

BREUIL, H. and KOSLOWSKI, L. (1931) Études de stratigraphie paléolithique dans le Nord de la France. *L'Anthropologie*, **41**, 450–88.

CLARK, J. D. (1940) *The Stone Age Cultures of Northern Rhodesia.* Capetown: South African Archaeological Society.

CLARK, J. D. (1953) New light on early man in Africa. *Antiquity*, **108**, 242–3.

CLARK, J. D. (1959a) Further excavations at Broken Hill, Northern Rhodesia. *Journal of the Royal Anthropological Institute*, **89**, 201–32.

CLARK, J. D. (1959b) *The Prehistory of Southern Africa*. Harmondsworth: Penguin Books.

CLARK, J. D. (1964) The influence of environment in inducing culture change at the Kalambo Falls prehistoric site. *South African Archaeological Bulletin*, **19** (76), 93–101.

CLARK, J. D. and HAYNES, C. V. (1970) An elephant butchery site at Mwanganda's Village, Karonga, Malawi, and its relevance for Palaeolithic archaeology. *World Archaeology*, **1** (3), 390–411.

CLARKE, D. L. (1968) *Analytical Archaeology*. London: Methuen.

COHEN, M. R. (1964) *Reason and Nature, the Meaning of Scientific Method*. London: Collier-Macmillan.

COLE, G. H. (1967) The Later Acheulian and Sangoan of southern Uganda. In BISHOP, W. W. and CLARK, J. D. (eds.) *Background to Evolution in Africa*, 481–528. Chicago: University of Chicago Press.

COLE, S. (1954) *The Prehistory of Southern Africa*. Harmondsworth: Penguin Books.

COLLINS, D. (1969) Culture traditions and environment of early man. *Current Anthropology*, **10** (4), 267–316.

DEETZ, J. (1967) *Invitation to Archaeology*. New York: Natural History Press.

FORD, J. A. (1962) A quantitative method for deriving cultural chronology. *Technical Manual, Pan American Union No. 1*. Washington.

GEARING, F. (1962) *Priests and Warriors*. American Anthropological Association Memoir No. 93.

GEERTZ, C. (1969) The transition to humanity. In TAX, S. (ed.) *Horizons of Anthropology*, 37–48. Chicago: Aldine.

HALLOWELL, A. I. (1959) Behavioral evolution and the emergence of the self. *Evolution and Anthropology*. Washington: The Anthropological Society of Washington/ Smithsonian Institution.

HALLOWELL, A. I. (1960) Self, society and culture in phylogenetic perspective. In TAX, S. (ed.) *Evolution After Darwin*, vol. 3, 309–71. Chicago: University of Chicago Press.

HARMANN, H. H. (1962) *Modern Factor Analysis*. Chicago: University of Chicago Press.

HARVEY, D. (1969) *Explanation in Geography*. London: Arnold.

HOWELL, F. C. (1961) Isimila: a Paleolithic site in Africa. *Scientific American*, **205**, 118–29.

HOWELL, F. C. and CLARK, J. D. (1963) Acheulian hunter-gatherers of the sub-Saharan Africa. In HOWELL, F. C. and BOURLIÈRE, R. (eds.) *African Ecology and Human Evolution*, 458–533. Chicago: Aldine.

HOWELL, F. C., COLE, G. H. and KLEINDIENST, M. R. (1962) Isimila: an Acheulian occupation site in the Iringa Highlands, Southern Highlands Province, Tanganyika. In MORTELMANS, G. and NENQUIN, J. (eds.) *Actes du IVe Congrès Panafricain de Préhistoire* (Tervuren, Belgium), 43–80.

ISAAC, G. LL. (1966) New evidence from Olorgesailie relating to the character of Acheulian occupation sites. In DIEGO CUSCOY, L. (ed.) *Actes du Ve Congrès Panafricain de Préhistoire* (Canary Islands), 135–45.

ISAAC, G. LL. (1967) Some experiments in quantitative methods for characterizing assemblages of Acheulian artifacts. In HUGOT, H. (ed.) *Actes du VIe Congrès Panafricain de Préhistoire* (Dakar).

ISAAC, G. LL. (1968) Traces of Pleistocene hunters: an east African example. In LEE, R. B. and DEVORE, I. (eds.) *Man The Hunter*, 253–61. Chicago: Aldine.

JONES, N. (1929). Hope Fountain. *South African Journal of Science*, **26**, 631–47.

KLEINDIENST, M. R. (1961a) Components of the east African Acheulian assemblage: an analytic approach. In MORTELMANS, G. and NENQUIN, J. (eds.) *Actes du IVe Congrès Panafricain de Préhistoire* (Tervuren, Belgium), 81–111.

KLEINDIENST, M. R. (1961b) Variability within the Late Acheulian assemblage in eastern Africa. *South African Archaeological Bulletin*, **16**, 35–52.

KRIEGER, A. D. (1944) The typological concept. *American Antiquity*, **9**, 271–88.

KUHN, T. S. (1962). *The Structure of Scientific Revolutions*. Chicago: University of Chicago Press.

LEAKEY, L. S. B. (1952) The Olorgesailie prehistoric site. In LEAKEY, L. S. B. and COLE, S. (eds.) *Proceedings of the Ist Panafrican Congress of Prehistory* (Oxford), 209.

LEAKEY, L. S. B. (1960) *Adam's Ancestors*. New York: Harper & Row.

LEAKEY, M. D. (1967) Preliminary survey of the cultural material from Beds I and II, Olduvai Gorge, Tanzania. In BISHOP, W. W. and CLARK, J. D. (eds.) *Background to Evolution in Africa*, 417–46. Chicago: University of Chicago Press.

LEE, R. B. (1968) What hunters do for a living, or, how to make out on scarce resources. In LEE, R. B. and DEVORE, I. (eds.) *Man The Hunter*, 30–48. Chicago: Aldine.

MOVIUS, H. L. (1969) Comments. *Current Anthropology*, **10** (4), 307–8.

OAKLEY, K. P. (1956) *Man The Tool-Maker*. London: British Museum of Natural History.

PEYRONY, D. (1930) Le Moustier: ses gisements, ses industries. *Revue Anthropologique*, Nos. 1–3, 4–6.

POPPER, K. R. (1959) *The Logic of Scientific Discovery*. New York: Basic Books.

POSNANSKY, M. (1959) A Hope Fountain site at Olorgesailie, Kenya Colony. *South African Archaeological Bulletin*, **14**, 83–9.

SACKETT, J. R. (1968) Method and theory of Upper Palaeolithic archaeology in south-western France. In BINFORD, S. R. and BINFORD, L. R. (eds.) *New Perspectives in Archaeology*, 61–83. Chicago: Aldine.

SOKAL, R. R. and SNEATH, P. H. A. (1963) *Numerical Taxonomy*. San Francisco: Freeman.

SPAULDING, A. C. (1960) The dimensions of archaeology. In DOLE, G. E. and CARNEIRO, R. L. (eds.) *Essays in the Science of Culture: In Honor of Leslie A. White*, 437–56. New York: Crowell.

TESTER, P. (1958) The age of the Bakers Hole industry. *Archaeological Newsletter*, **6**, 123–5.

TRIGGER, B. G. (1968) *Beyond History: The Methods of Prehistory*. New York: Holt, Rinehart & Winston.

WAECHTER, J. (1968) The evidence of the Levallois technique in the British Acheulian and the question of the Acheulio-Levallois. In PIVETEAU, J. (ed.) *La Préhistoire: Problèmes et Tendances*, 491–7. Paris.

WHITE, L. A. (1959) *The Evolution of Culture*. New York: McGraw-Hill.

4

Early phases of human behaviour: models in Lower Palaeolithic archaeology

G. LL. ISAAC

University of California, Berkeley, U.S.A.

This essay is about experiments with various lines of interpretation in that vast segment of prehistory that is commonly termed 'Lower Palaeolithic'. It is convenient to make use of the models metaphor, which archaeology borrows from other sciences, because the word has qualities of flexibility and vague but stimulating suggestiveness (cf. Piggott, 1959; Renfrew, 1968, 1969; Trigger, 1969, 1970; Clarke, 1968).[1] In Palaeolithic archaeology as in other sciences it is now recognized that 'facts' are never reported without some frame of reference, some notion of how things work. This essay is concerned with these frames of reference, whatever they may be called.

Although Lower Palaeolithic studies share many interpretational problems with the archaeology of other periods, there are highly distinctive features that arise, in particular from the following circumstances:

(1) The fact that profound changes occurred not only in the cultural systems but in the neurophysiological system, especially the brain, which supported them.
(2) The vast span of time that is involved.
(3) The very low density in space and time of sites providing useful information.

A major challenge facing Lower Palaeolithic archaeology is the delineation of stages and processes in the evolution of the human capacity for culture. Realistic organization of theoretical concepts and research strategy depends in large measure on recognizing that available evidence amounts to a very sparse scatter of samples. As in all archaeology the pattern perceived from a single Palaeolithic occurrence relates only to a sample portion of the total culture of the former occupants, while in turn the total culture of the occupants is a

167

sample only of the total space-time segment concerning which inferences are to be made. For example, the material recovered from the Olorgesailie Acheulean sites is comprised of stone artefacts and utensils, together with bone food refuse. Each of these probably represents only a small fraction of equipment and diet respectively, while material culture and subsistence arrangements in turn were only components of the total behavioural system formerly in operation at the particular sites. Within the activity range of the hominids using the Olorgesailie lake basin the sites represent only those patterns appropriate to the valley floor (Isaac, 1968a). The behaviour of the Olorgesailie Acheuleans was probably not identical with those at nearby Olduvai, let alone with those at more distant sites such as Torralba. Thus we have to recognize that even in comparatively favourable cases such as the Olorgesailie sites, we are dealing with a highly biased subsample of something that was already only a small sample of Middle Pleistocene culture. When, as in Lower Palaeolithic studies, material culture is comparatively simple, preservation is often indifferent, and the space-time sample densities are very low, these problems become acute. Theoretical considerations taken on their own might tempt us to abandon the whole pursuit, were they not tempered by the empirical demonstration that good Lower Palaeolithic sites have high intrinsic interest and that some regularities in technology and economy do emerge and do seem worth more careful investigation.

In designing research, the density of samples is usually adjusted in relation to variability in the properties about which inferences are to be made. However, in a situation where overall sample density is irrevocably low, the choice of variables to be stressed must be adjusted instead.

There is at present some sense of crisis with regard to models in Palaeolithic archaeology (cf. Bordes and Bordes, 1970; Binford, 1968; Sackett, 1968; Mellars, 1970; Isaac, 1971a). This stems in large measure from dissatisfaction with historical (i.e. ideographic) approaches and from growing unease over assumptions of regularity in the transmission and expression of material culture traditions. Various workers are experimenting with alternative lines of interpretation, sometimes involving the allegation of morphological regularities induced by functional determinants – such as the specific exigencies of butchery. Most new studies are more concerned with process than narrative.

The development of attitudes and theory

Palaeolithic archaeology could have no suitable status as a legitimate research field until the antiquity of man was recognized. Pre-Darwinian European thought patterns prevented even perceptive men who had observed stratified Lower Palaeolithic tools from making any real sense out of their finds. John Frere had reported that his discovery of handaxes deeply buried, and in association with fossil bone, tempted him 'to refer them to a very remote period indeed; even beyond that of the present world. . . .'[2] Frere did not pursue his find, but a little later the eccentric Boucher De Perthes made a succession of similar discoveries and, though he himself lacked a coherent scheme into which his results could be fitted, he insisted in effect that his facts should not be disregarded just because they could not be accommodated in current 'models' (Daniel, 1950, p. 59; Heizer, 1969, pp. 96–109). However, before the issues had received wide attention the enunciation of the theory of evolution by descent with modification through natural selection (Darwin, 1858, 1859; Wallace, 1858) effectively circumvented the antiquarians' dispute by making it an integral part of a much larger one. The theory of evolution established as one corollary hypothesis the proposition that the ethnographic and historic complexity of culture must have grown from a state of effectively zero material culture. Not only could the new paradigm tolerate the discovery of very ancient artefacts: it demanded them ! The challenge met with a ready response and a wealth of artefactual evidence for man's antiquity came flooding in (Gaudry, 1859; Lyell, 1863; Lubbock, 1865; Evans, 1872). Within a few decades the belief arose that the features of stone tools could be used to demarcate stages in the evolution of culture – or at least technology (de Mortillet, 1883; Sollas, 1911). Those concerned with Lower Palaeolithic archaeology during the nineteenth century were preoccupied with considerations of artefact morphology and stratigraphy. Although there was little or no explicit discussion of the mechanisms of cultural development, it appears from nineteenth-century writings and from the legacy they left to twentieth-century scholarship that subconscious models were adopted, which were closely allied to the evolutionary principles of contemporary biology. The implicit rules of interpretation can be reconstructed as follows:

(1) Each phase, or culture, is demarcated by a distinctive stone tool kit, and conversely each distinctive stone tool assemblage must derive from a significantly different phase, or culture.

(2) Specific resemblances between assemblages from successive stratigraphic zones must result from a continuous chain in the transmission of craft tradition. That is to say that alleged patterns of similarity linking assemblages of different ages must be due to the former existence of 'phyla' of culture.

The rules were applied to impressions of the morphology of artefact assemblages in a way closely analagous to the operations of a palaeontologist engaged in recognizing taxonomic identity, affinity and phylogeny from the morphology of fossils. Indeed as Sackett (1968, p. 67) has remarked, many writers report on their material as though the models really involved the notion that the stone tools formed sexually active, breeding populations with a phylogeny of their own! These assumptions of stability and of regularity in lineages of change were a reasonable part of the first approximations of Lower Palaeolithic prehistory; but now that the magnitude of Pleistocene time is better understood and great variability has been observed, uncritical retention of them constitutes an escape from the realities of having to deal with very low sample density. They are attractive because they enable what might otherwise appear as a bewildering scatter of instances to be transformed to a hypothetical culture history; but the details and processes of such histories have proved to be illusory.

Now although few modern prehistorians are as naive as might be implied by this caricature, these principles of interpretation have only very recently been formally challenged and the great bulk of Palaeolithic research continues to appear as though it rests on these unverified assumptions. Of course, in confronting these tacit rules of interpretation, we are not dealing with neat true or false propositions. Common sense and the experience of ethnography all combine to show that resemblances between items of material culture are often correlated with degrees of interconnectedness, and the converse. However, all resemblances or differences need not be so determined, and the dangers are particularly acute when tool forms are simple and the space-time sample density is very low.

Initially, and in conformity with the organic model of material culture evolution, there was an expectation that the stages would be universal. Further, technological progress was treated as though it was an intrinsic and inexorable tendency in human evolution. Results accruing from research into areas outoutside western Europe gradually persuaded scholars to abandon this model in favour of one involving more complex mechanisms such as regional differentiation and migration.

The recognition of regional differentiation in Palaeolithic archaeology helped to give its development as a discipline the historical orientation it has retained until very recently. The first objective in study became the taxonomy of tools and assemblages, which was avowedly undertaken in order to establish 'culture histories', or ideographic narratives, of changing artefact design through space and time. Through most of this century work has tended to be descriptive and there was little attempt to establish processual models which would facilitate explanation of the detail that began to be compiled. Rather dramatic particularistic explanations were offered for a few allegedly gross differences in artefact sets. These sometimes involved racial or specific differentiation of the hominids – as in the case of the replacement of Neanderthal makers of Mousterian industries by the 'Neanthropic' men of the Upper Palaeolithic (e.g. Burkitt, 1933; Leakey, 1934; McBurney, 1960; Howell, 1965). In other cases, distinctions between ecogeographic zones were offered as partial explanations, as in the case of Clacton and Acheulean industries (e.g. McBurney, 1950; Collins, 1969). Neither the racial nor the geographic models and the theories based on them are held up for mockery, but it must be pointed out that little has been done to bridge the gulf between the descriptive nature of reports on the material evidence and the sociological, ecological or behavioural implications of the models.[3]

In summary, during its first 100 years Lower Palaeolithic archaeology developed unconsciously into a historical pursuit without any well-defined concern with economics, sociology, or the processes underlying the details of culture change. Stone artefacts were important at the outset because of their ubiquity and their usefulness in demonstrating the antiquity of man. Abundance and fascination have kept them as the prime focus of research, but a reaction against excessive reliance on them is now apparent. Beginning some twenty years ago and intensifying over the past decade, there has been a growing awareness that 'occupation sites' rather than stone artefacts might constitute the most informative evidence to survive from Lower Palaeolithic times.

Concern with occupation sites

'Occupation site' is here used as a loosely defined term, which denotes archaeological situations in which artefacts occur in spatially patterned sets, which may be indicative of activities other than stonecraft and which are sometimes associated with food refuse and other organic traces. There are isolated instances of the study of the contextual implications of such occurrences prior to 1940 (e.g. Worthington-Smith, 1894; Commont, 1908; Cerralbo, 1913), but in general the modern research drive can be said to have begun with M. D. and L. S. B. Leakey's excavations at Olorgesailie in 1943. The 'floors' then exposed were visited by delegates to the Pan African Congress on Prehistory in 1947, and subsequently similar work on an expanded scale followed elsewhere in Africa: for example, Kalambo (J. D. Clark, 1954, 1969), Olduvai (L. S. B. Leakey, 1963; M. D. Leakey, 1967, 1971), Isimila

(Howell *et al.*, 1962). Later comparable work has been done also in Eurasia: for example, Torralba-Ambrona (Howell, 1966), Latamne (Clark, 1966), Vertesszöllös (Kretzoi and Vértes, 1965), 'Ubeidiya (Stekelis, 1966), Terra Amata (de Lumley, 1969), and High Lodge. There is a growing number of such field studies. This reorientation of research effort has stemmed from the belief that the rare, well-preserved sites provide far more useful information than a myriad of distorted artefact assemblages which lack significant contextual evidence. The first two decades of this movement have been exploratory. At the outset no one had any very clear idea of what might turn up on a series of Lower Palaeolithic occupation floors. Though a general sense of optimism about the utility of such investigations prevailed, the questions that were to be answered by the data recovered were by no means clearly formulated.

Palaeolithic archaeology is not alone in having diversified itself by turning from preoccupation with typology and assemblage taxonomy to consider also settlement patterns, economic systems and subtle traces of social arrangements. Studies of the post-Pleistocene prehistory of Europe took a very early lead in this direction (J. G. D. Clark, 1954; C. Fox, 1948; Childe, 1935). Palaeolithic archaeology has also participated in the recent resort to quantitative methods. Some of the consequences of quantitative experiments are discussed below in the section dealing with models for the interpretation of artefacts.

Models inspired by comparative studies of behaviour

Prehistory derives research problems in part from observation of features in existing archaeological data, but questions also arise as a result of concern with the development of behaviour. Particularly, the growth of field studies of animal behaviour has resulted in fresh interest in aspects of early hominid activity and organization (e.g. DeVore and Washburn, 1963; Morris, 1967; Tiger, 1969). Many authors have been especially concerned with possible evolutionary consequences of hunting as a means of subsistence. This is a matter that can be investigated by archaeological means (Isaac, 1971a).

Ethnography is widely regarded as being of crucial importance as an aid to interpreting the Palaeolithic (c.f. Clark, 1968; Isaac, 1968a), but what is borrowed is usually a specific analogy. In the scale of concepts discussed in the introduction this is usually a hypothesis or a theory rather than a model. The use of such parallels implies a vague sense of equivalence in the processes of culture regardless of time differences. As Binford (1968, p. 17) has pointed out, this is both useful and dangerous. Carried to an extreme it would limit our exploration of prehistory to the terms of ethnography, whereas presumably we practice archaeology in part out of the conviction that it will give information on different, antecedent cultural conditions. This caveat is especially important for the formative phases comprising the Lower Paleolithic, since they must surely have included intermediate conditions of a kind that no longer exist among either men or primates. Ethnographic analogy has been extensively discussed in recent years and is not pursued here (e.g. various essays in *Man The Hunter*, edited by Lee and DeVore, 1968).

Field studies have demonstrated that animal behaviour is made up of a highly complex set of components interrelated as an integrated *system*, which mediates between physiology, ecology and society. The most promising models for interpreting the evolution of human behaviour are thus systems models. These enable us to consider how selection pressure would act on genetic and cultural innovations to bring about far-reaching biological and sociological changes. Given appreciation of the high degree of integration commonly exhibited by behavioural systems, we can recognize that changes in one component necessitate or facilitate changes in others. Analogy with the cybernetic phenomenon of 'feedback' now appears to be an indispensable means of discussing the interrelations of aspects of evolving behaviour.

Versions of hominid evolutionary processes have often rested implicitly on additive models involving seriatim accumulation of components by chain reaction. For example, a version envisaged in the writings of Elliot-Smith (1927) can be summarized as follows:

(1) Development of enlarged brain
(2) Tool manufacture
(3) Bipedal stance
(4) Cultural elaboration

The discovery of the Piltdown hoax, the recognition of the Australopithecines and the archaeological evidence from Bed I at Olduvai Gorge have all combined to render this specific hypothesis untenable, but revised formulations involving comparatively simple additive models remain current. For example, several authors including Campbell (1966) and Pfeiffer (1969) appear to have envisaged something like the following chain of developments:

(1) Shift to open country habitat
(2) Bipedalism and tool use

(3) Tool manufacture
(4) Small game hunting
(5) Cooperative big game hunting
(6) Division of labour and the bonding of family units
(7) Enlargement of the brain
(8) Language and cultural elaboration

This is in some ways an unfair caricature of what was a very useful first approximation of a complex transformation process. However, the discovery that several of these behaviour patterns are present at least in incipient degrees in the repertoire of wild chimpanzees necessitates revision of the models (Goodall, 1964; Lancaster, 1968). Integrated growth is a better analogue than chain reaction. Thus I would favour models involving concurrent development with mutual reinforcement of adaptive advantages by matching changes in all components, and from this stance I would argue that hunting, food sharing, division of labour, pair bonding, and operation from a home base or camp, form a functional complex, the components of which are more likely to have developed in concert than in succession (Isaac, 1971b). It is easy to see that tools, language and social cooperation would fit into the functional complex as well, and very likely had equally long developmental histories within the overall system.

The findings of comparative studies of mammal behaviour have become a source of inspiration for palaeo-anthropological reconstructions. Generalizations about arboreal behaviour, savannah behaviour, carnivore behaviour or seed eating behaviour can function as components of models, which in turn generate theories explaining the transformation of ancestral anthropoid organization into hominid systems (e.g. Washburn and Lancaster, 1968; Reynolds, 1966; Fox, 1967; Morris, 1967; Schaller and Lowther, 1969; Jolly, 1970). Of particular value in developing such models are observations on the same species under differing ecological conditions (e.g. Crook and Gartlan, 1966; Gartlan and Brain, 1968).

Theories based on the results of comparative studies have an interest and intellectual validity of their own, but ultimately they must remain speculative if they are not tested for consistency with palaeontological and archaeological facts. Since the hypotheses involve retrodictions of the distribution and nature of potentially discernible traces of various kinds of behaviour, they can be tested against the archaeological record.

In practice the nature of surviving traces places restraints on the components which can presently be included in models designed for testing by palaeo-anthropological research. In Table 4.1 I have attempted to summarize inferences currently feasible on the basis of Lower Palaeolithic archaeological evidence without intending to define limits as to what will eventually be possible. It is already established that each of these lines of behavioural reconstruction is possible, when conditions of preservation are suitable. However, many classes of evidence are in fact only very rarely available. No site or site complex is yet known where all of these kinds of inference have simultaneously been possible, and it is apparent that studies must proceed in the hope that interpretable regularities will be found in an opportunistically accumulated patchwork of information.

TABLE 4.1

Archaeologically observable phenomena	Possible interpretations
Location and density of sites and relicts	Aspects of demographic arrangement, land use and ecology
Site sizes and internal structure	Estimates of community size and aspects of organization
Seasonality and duration of occupation	Patterns of movement and aspects of economic strategy
Food refuse and faeces	Aspects of diet and subsistence practices
Introduced materials	Range of movement or contact
Artefact forms	Aspects of role in economy/society Level of complexity of material culture rule systems (in part) Propagation patterns of material culture traditions (historical, geographic and sociological implications)

The interpretation of artefact sets

Stone artefacts constitute by far the most abundant trace of Pleistocene hominid activity. In varying versions of prehistory, aspects of their characteristics are used as indices of technological elaboration, as markers of culture-historic connections, as indicators of diverse economic activities and as clues to the nature of socio-cultural systems. Now it is probable that the importance of stone artefacts relative to other kinds of evidence has been exaggerated, but it is also clear that they constitute a source of evidence rich enough to demand the development of refined analytical systems. 'Models' are involved in the description and analysis of artefacts as well as in interpretation (Neustupný,

1971). Concepts and assumptions with regard to 'typological' and morphological treatment of artefacts are discussed in Sackett (1966), Clarke (1968), Isaac (in press) and elsewhere. The attention of this essay is focused on models that facilitate the interpretation of the results of comparative operations.

Distinctive features that appear to be emerging from comparative studies of Lower Palaeolithic stonecraft can be summarized as:

(1) 'Conservatism' in the sense of prolonged failure of tool kits to transcend certain limits of technology, typological composition and morphology.
(2) Great variability in the specific permutations of attributes within the conservative limits.

The conservatism is widely seen to be explicable in terms of neurophysiological limitations of early hominids and/or supposed resistance of primitive culture to change, but variability has met with a wider range of interpretational responses. On logical grounds it would appear that the morphology of a stone tool is governed by the interaction of (1) the *physical properties* of the stone being employed, and (2) the *'intentions'* (design concepts) and the *motor habits* of the craftsman. The design concepts themselves are presumably related in turn to two kinds of determining influences: firstly, the *functional requirements* of the tool will place limits on the range of forms that would be effective; secondly, systems of *transmission of traditions* provide a craftsman with a set of technical and morphological patterns that are functionally adequate and socially acceptable. The traditional tool patterns may be few in number, and embody only simple rules with wide tolerances – as is apparently the case among stone tool using aborigines of the Western Australian deserts (Gould, 1968). In contrast, some late prehistoric stone tool kits give the impression of involving fairly numerous distinct 'patterns', each with comparatively low variability. The archaeological record probably documents a gradual oscillating rise in the maximum level of design complexity through time, but methods of measuring this have not yet been devised (Isaac, 1971b).

Fig. 4.1 summarizes diagrammatically the supposed system of determinants affecting artefacts. Differential emphasis on the importance of two of the above listed determinants of stone tool morphology has given rise to distinct schools of thought in the interpretation of the results of comparative study. Each school stresses one factor in the models it uses to 'explain' variations (differences) among stone artefact assemblages.

(1) *Traditional or 'phylogenetic' models* assume tremendous inertia in craft transmission systems so that successive generations of craftsmen are tightly bound to particular patterns. Where instances of marked diversity among contemporary assemblages are detected, variants are liable to be explained as the products of distinct 'phyla' of culture, i.e. separate, coexistent systems of cultural transmission. This is the conventional approach to Palaeolithic archaeology, which has already been discussed (cf, Warren, 1926; Breuil, 1932; Leakey, 1934; Bordes, 1950, 1953, 1961; Collins, 1969, 1970).

(2) *'Activity variant models'* differ from traditional models by assuming that functional requirements exert an influence on assemblage character, which creates variety and which commonly transcends differences in the degree of culture-historic interconnectedness. It is further supposed that distinctive tool kits for specific tasks must have existed, and that variety among stone artefact assemblages can often be explained as the result of differing intermixtures of the 'tool kits'. Extensive concern with this kind of model is fairly recent (cf. Clark, 1959; Kleindienst, 1961; Binford and Binford, 1966, 1969).

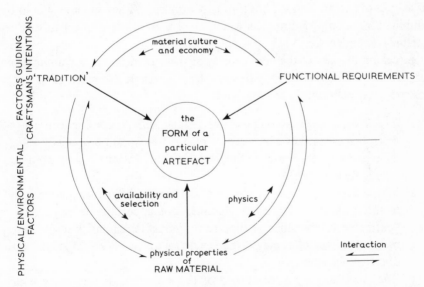

FIG. 4.1. Diagrammatic illustration of physical, economic and cultural factors influencing the morphology of a particular stone artefact. The factors interact.

The two schools advocating these models are engaged in 'competition' generally involving attempts to attack the credibility of interpretations based on the models of their 'opponents' (e.g. Bordes and Bordes, 1970; Binford and Binford, 1966, 1969; Collins, 1969; Mellars, 1970). Logically there is a niche for a third school, which advocates the physical properties of raw material as the primary determinant of variation. However, although all parties recognize the influence of this factor, there has been little formal attempt to use it as a major basis of explanation.

Both of these contending 'schools' make assumptions of regularity: 'tradition' is seen as providing tight constraints and long-term constancy; in the other case 'function' is seen as a binding determinant which gave rise to prolonged constancy of complex, patterned variation. However, there are possible solutions to the problem of variation that do not assume constancy and regularity. For instance, if we accept that there may be wide tolerances for the morphology of tools with equivalent functions, and that 'tradition' itself may be subject to change through time and space, then it becomes apparent that *stochastic models* may provide an important alternative to phylogenetic or activity difference models (Binford, 1963; Isaac, 1969, p. 19). A stochastic model allows for 'random walk'[4] drift of 'craft norms' within the constraints of functional and technological limits. It should be apparent that these lines of explanation are not mutually exclusive. They can and should be combined into composite models which involve all of these 'mechanisms' as variable components.

In seeking to explore the applicability of these models for explaining artefact variation it is useful to partition the observable diversity of samples (assemblages) between three categories:

(1) *The first category* is composed of regular differences between sets of assemblages, each of which can be related to *time* and/or *space* divisions. These sets are the entities of orthodox culture history or archaeological taxonomy (Fig. 4.2).

(2) *The second category* is composed of consistent differences between definable sets of assemblages which do not appear to be restricted to specifiable subdivisions of time or to definable regions, but are legitimately believed on some positive evidence to have been associated with different activities.

(3) *The third category* is composed of the residuum of variability which *cannot* be associated with time, space or activity factors on the basis of existing evidence.

Each of these three categories of variance is fairly directly associable with one of the three aforementioned models.

178

Now for the Lower Palaeolithic this division of variability is a difficult procedure to follow because for many regions, such as Europe, the sites yielding evidence of variation are geographically scattered and the precision of chronological control is low. It simply is not feasible to isolate many assemblage sets

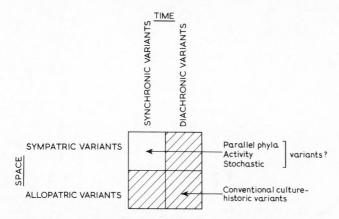

FIG. 4.2. Diagrammatic representation of possible time and space relations between pairs (or sets) of varying archaeological occurrences. Conventional entities of archaeological taxonomy involve the recognition of more or less consistent differences between assemblage variants, which are either separated in time (diachronic) or in geography (allopatric) or both. Debate concerning the relative applicability of parallel phyla, activity difference and stochastic models arises in cases of synchronic and sympatric assemblage variants.

from segments of space and time which have anything like the same order of magnitude as the space-time coordinates of Late Pleistocene or Holocene cultures. The overall situation in east Africa is worse, since we have fewer samples from a larger area and a longer time span. However, during my work in east Africa I became aware that the subcontinent offered opportunities of an almost experimental nature for clarifying the nature of variation among at least some Middle Pleistocene occurrences.

The overall space-time density of excavated Middle Pleistocene assemblages from east Africa is appallingly low – less than one sample per 10 000 years per 1 000 000 km^2; but local sample densities in the 'lake basins' for which the region has become archaeologically famous, are much higher (Fig. 4.3). Site complexes like those at Olorgesailie, Olduvai, Isimila and Kalambo provide situations where assemblage variation can be studied in relation to very restricted spatial limits and reasonably well-controlled time spans. The pattern and magnitude of variation in each of these microcosmic experimental situations can then be compared with the overall variation in the whole

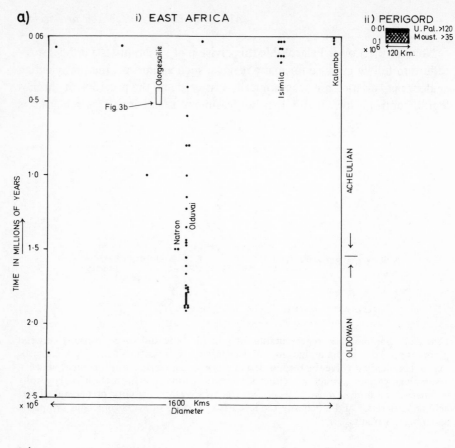

a)

i) EAST AFRICA

ii) PERIGORD

0·01 ▨ U. Pal.>120
0·1 ▨ Moust.>35
×10⁶ ◄──────► 120 Km.

Olorgesailie

Fig.3b →

Isimila

Kalambo

ACHEULIAN

Natron

Olduvai

OLDOWAN

TIME IN MILLIONS OF YEARS

0·06
0·5
1·0
1·5
2·0
2·5
×10⁶

◄────── 1600 Kms ──────►
Diameter

b)

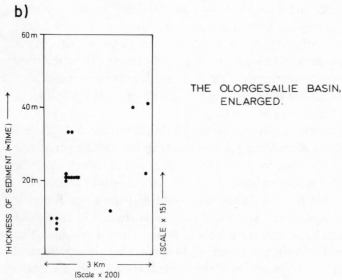

THE OLORGESAILIE BASIN,
ENLARGED.

THICKNESS OF SEDIMENT (∝TIME)

60 m
40 m
20 m

(SCALE × 15)

◄── 3 Km ──►
(Scale × 200)

Acheulean series from the subcontinent – that is, from the one million year long, 1·75 million km^2 macrocosm.

If the range of variation of each of the several microcosms proved to be much smaller and more tightly clustered than the total range, then one might conclude that a succession of distinctive localized and time-restricted 'cultures' had existed within the region – even though the available sample densities were inadequate for one to resolve the culture history in full. However, comparative operations employing either percentage frequency of categories or averages for the size and shape indices of tool forms indicate that, for many variables, the localized 'short-term' sets are almost as varied as the whole series (see Figs. 4.4 and 4.5 for examples). These experiments thus run counter to expectations implicit in traditional culture-historic or culture-evolutionary thinking. What do numbered stage divisions such as those formerly employed in the Somme, Morocco or Olduvai mean if a penecontemporaneous set shows almost as much diversity as a markedly diachronic series? Whatever models we employ in seeking to account for variation in east Africa, it is clear that they must be able to cope with behavioural systems which involved the abandonment of markedly different stone artefact sets at sites within a single valley during a time span that is at least very short by comparison with the whole Middle Pleistocene.

The conventional culture-taxonomic entities of archaeology show allopatric and/or diachronic relations with each other (Fig. 4.2). Very few of the observed patterns in these experiments can be meaningfully partitioned into such culture-historic entities, but a choice between a variety of other models remains. Parallel phyla models can be applied, if they are used to generate theories involving prolonged territorial interdigitation by differing cultures all over east Africa. This line of interpretation would be rendered particularly credible by evidence that each of the allegedly stable non-blending cultural lineages was associated with a genetically isolated species of hominid, and such

FIG. 4.3. (*a*) A diagrammatic representation of archaeological sample densities in relation to space and time. Data for the Lower Palaeolithic of east Africa are contrasted with those for the Middle and Upper Palaeolithic of the Perigord, France. Each dot represents a significant, excavated occurrence. Space is represented by the horizontal dimension of each rectangle, which is drawn proportional to the diameter of the region. Time is represented by the vertical dimension (modified after Isaac, 1971b). (*b*) An enlargement of part of the east African sample series – the occurrences within the 'microcosm' of the Olorgesailie lake basin. The scales are enlarged by factors of 10 (time) and 375 (space). Low density and unequal spacing remain apparent. Of the greatest value for studies of variation is the set of seven spatially clustered and penecontemporaneous sites.

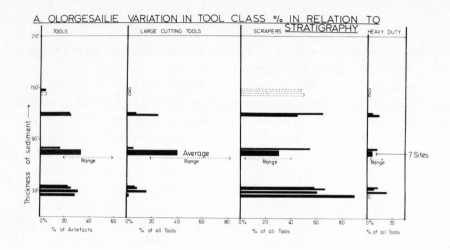

A. OLORGESAILIE VARIATION IN TOOL CLASS % IN RELATION TO STRATIGRAPHY

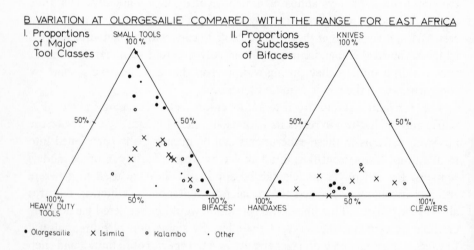

B VARIATION AT OLORGESAILIE COMPARED WITH THE RANGE FOR EAST AFRICA

I. Proportions of Major Tool Classes

II. Proportions of Subclasses of Bifaces

• Olorgesailie   × Isimila   ∘ Kalambo   · Other

FIG. 4.4. A graphic representation of analysis of variation in the percentages of major categories of artefacts. 'A' shows variation among the Olorgesailie occurrences in relation to thicknesses of accumulated sediment (∝ time). 'B' uses ternary diagrams to compare variation in the Olorgesailie 'microcosm' with the range observable in a wider series of east African occurrences (after Isaac, 1968b).

FIG. 4.5. Graphic representation of analysis of variation in the numerical measures of biface morphology. 'A' shows variation in relation to sedimentation. Weak time trends with 'oscillations' are reflected in relative thickness (Th/B) and in the number of trimming scars (ξ Scar) but length and relative elongation (B/L) appear to vary erratically in the series (see Isaac, 1969). 'B' provides graphic representation of the extent of variation in the Olorgesailie 'microcosm', compared with a wider range of east African occurrences.

182

A. OLORGESAILIE - VARIATIONS IN SIZE, FORM - INDICES ETC. IN RELATION TO STRATIGRAPHY.

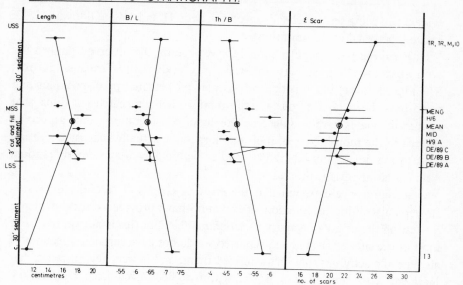

B. VARIATION AT OLORGESAILIE COMPARED WITH THE RANGE FOR EAST AFRICA.

MEAN LENGTH ———→

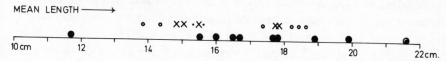

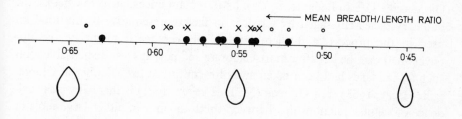

MEAN THICKNESS / BREADTH RATIO ———→
Other sites ——→
Olorgesailie ——→

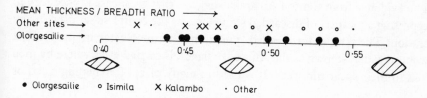

• Olorgesailie   ○ Isimila   X Kalambo   · Other

evidence is being tentatively advanced for Beds II and IV at Olduvai (M. D. Leakey, personal communication).

Hitherto the most popular model for explaining the observed pattern has been that involving activity differences (Clark, 1959; Posnansky, 1959; Kleindienst, 1961) but this depends in part on personal predispositions and there have been no rigorous tests. Among other alternatives I think that stochastic models have also become worthy of consideration: some aspects of pattern in the morphology of tools at Olorgesailie actually suggested cultural drift to me during my laboratory studies before I had considered 'random walk' as an important process.[5]

One might have expected that the growing corpus of carefully excavated Lower Palaeolithic 'occupation sites' would have provided critical evidence for testing the utility of activity variation models, but this is not yet true. For most of the sites excavated and reported we do not have certain indications of any specific activities that characterized them, and in very few instances has localization of subsidiary tool kits within a floor even been claimed (cf. Freeman and Butzer, 1966).

The only activity for which evidence external to tool morphology is fairly widely distributed is butchery – and, by extension, hunting. Desmond Clark has put together comparative data which indicate that instances of impoverished tool kits dominated by smallish, rather informal tools, including scrapers and denticulates, have been found associated with butchery sites of all ages from Oldowan to Later Stone Age (Clark and Haynes, 1970). However, some sites at which carcasses were undoubtedly cut up do show wider ranges of forms, which include large bifaces – e.g. Torralba, Ambrona (Howell, 1966; Freeman and Butzer, 1966), Terra Amata (de Lumley, 1969), Olorgesailie DE/89 B (Isaac, 1968a). I still remain uncertain as to whether the butchery facies envisaged by Clark is in fact representative of the total kit used in the process of dismemberment, or whether it might be the impoverished residue left after more elaborate and perhaps less dispensable tools such as handaxes had been taken away for continued use. Neither at Olorgesailie (Isaac, 1968a) nor Olduvai (M. D. Leakey, 1971) is there any clear evidence of regular relationships between the frequency of either large tools or small tools and the density or species composition of bone refuse.

The evidence from Central Australia suggests that great care is necessary in interpreting a local set of discarded stone tools as the complete set used in any operation. The scraper form called 'purpunpa' by the Ngatatjara people, but now more widely known as the 'tula adze flake', is carried everywhere by men hafted to their spear throwers. It is used in many places for shaping wood or cutting things. In many of these places other *ad hoc* stone forms may be made (or selected) and immediately discarded. However, worn-out 'eloura adzes' would be discarded only in places where fire, mastic and stone were available to permit its leisurely replacement. The activity documented would be spear thrower repair, not eloura flake usage (cf. Thomson, 1964; Gould, 1968).

The extent of variation between assemblages from the floors of the sedimentary basins containing the east African site complexes makes it clear that if activity patterns determined the variation then the activities represented were not specific to gross ecological divisions of the terrain such as uplands, woodlands or plains. A variety of kits were abandoned within the range of micro-environments pertaining to lake or riverside floodplains. Recognition of this restriction on appropriate activity theories does not preclude differing seasonal pursuits, the division of labour by sex and age, the exploitation of differing localized resources, etc., from having been determinants of diversity in the tool kits. However, as yet we lack specific evidence for any of these – and, given the evidence for 'stylistic' variability in the morphology of sets of artefacts which seem very likely to have been functionally equivalent, I am very inclined to think the activity variation model may hitherto have enjoyed undue appeal. Schemes that have been put forward sometimes smack rather of a Rand Corporation 'Design for Palaeolithic Living'. While it may be flattering to envisage our ancestors as having been equipped with a tool for every need, it is disquieting to learn what a broad range of basic functions can be accomplished with poorly differentiated stone tools of the simple kinds reported for the Bindibu and Ngatatjara of Central Australia (Thomson, 1964; Gould, 1968).

While the testing of various activity difference hypotheses should continue with vigour, it seems to me that we should seriously consider that an appreciable proportion of the variation not yet accounted for by time, space and activity differences may be a residuum generated by stochastic change. That is to say the result of local band-specific 'drifts' in craft norms, both with regard to 'style' in standardized forms such as handaxes, and with regard to assemblage composition. As envisaged here such drift might accumulate over several, even many generations and lead to quite widely divergent craft manifestations. However, the micro-traditions involved would be unstable and would lose their identity in new short-term directions of drift. This is an equilibrium basin model (Clarke, 1968, p. 51) of the processes underlying assemblage patterning in the East African Middle Pleistocene and it has the attraction that it helps account for the conservatism shown with regard to gross technological and typological features, while also accommodating variation and permutation among the components. A simple mechanical analogy for the pattern would be the trajectory of a ball-bearing in a bowl being tilted or vibrated in a random fashion.

Stochastic or 'random walk' change is of course in some sense a non-explanation: it is a residue of variation which defies attempts to see persistent patterns or trends. As such it should be treated as a null hypothesis: never proven and persistently re-examined as fresh data accrue.

Stochastic models of the kind I envisage may also have implications with regard to the socio-cultural systems that underlie drifting craft idiosyncrasy. Binford (1963), Owen (1965) and Deetz (1965) have all pointed out that demographic arrangements, residence and marriage exchange systems affect craft and cultural transmission. I have argued elsewhere (Isaac 1968b, unpublished, 1971b) that the persistence of the basic features of Acheulean stone tool assemblages over large parts of three continents during approximately a million years may be connected with features of the cultural transmission systems as well as with neurophysiological limitations on the craftsmen's 'inventiveness'. The model treats relations between bands or communities as a communications system. It is conceivable that a widespread low density network lacking in mechanisms for preventing the equalization of information content between neighbouring nodes would have great inertia to fundamental changes (cf. Owen, 1965), while a more tightly knit network involving culturally determined differentials in the rate of information exchange might engender localized partial isolates, which, on occasions, might be more prone to the acceptance and exploitation of innovations (Fig. 4.6). This process may have the same kind of importance for cultural change as isolating mechanisms have in genetic evolution.

Now the Lower Palaeolithic might legitimately be characterized as a situation involving a low density network of population (bands) with considerable variability in the permutations of a very restricted number of artefact traits, while the Late Pleistocene and Holocene are perhaps characterized by higher population densities, greatly increased numbers of traits and increasingly diverse regional combinations of these traits. It is tempting to suggest that the contrast arose from changes in the communications network of the kind schematically formulated in Fig. 4.6. In addition to possible changes in population densities this model accommodates the development of cultural arrangements conducive to differential rates of communication. Paradoxically, fully developed, effective language may, by virtue of the complexity of its rule systems and the arbitrariness of its vocabulary, have led to the establishment of intelligibility barriers. This model is speculative at present, but can be applied and

186

tested against archaeological data. It gives comparative study of patterns of cultural drift some positive interest, whereas otherwise it would have only the negative value of raising objections to traditional culture-historic lines of interpretation.

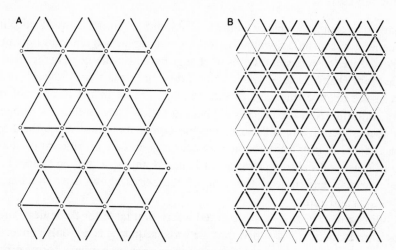

FIG. 4.6. Diagrammatic representation of differing systems of interaction between human groups. Line thickness denotes increasing frequency of exchanges. 'A' depicts a low density arrangement in which linguistic and cultural factors do not create differentials in the extent of interaction and in which there is a constant tendency toward equalization between nodes. 'B' represents a hypothetical situation of higher density in which linguistic and other cultural factors affect interaction frequency. Short-term 'partial cultural isolates' result.

In suggesting that the development of linguistic barriers may have had an important influence on the rate and characteristics of cultural change and diversification, I do not wish it to appear that another kind of parallel phylum theory is advanced. Linguistic and cultural isolates were, to judge from history and ethnography, almost certainly not stable over any great length of time. Inasmuch as they were segments of culture involving at least several generations of relatively numerous closely interacting humans, they may have constituted a mechanism for readier development and establishment of innovations, which might have been lost or rejected in a more diffuse situation.

The data presented by Smith (1966) and by Wendorf and co-workers (1968) on the late Pleistocene artefact assemblages of the Nile valley constitute a possible example of correlation between demographic pressures and an allegedly complex pattern of contemporaneous and successive cultural differentiation. Comparative studies and further internal research on the Nile evidence will be necessary to check this.

Time series

Progressive change was long a universal assumption for all Lower Palaeolithic sequences, but instances where both the stratigraphic sequence and quantitative evidence for persistent trends of change have been adequately reported are in fact remarkably rare. At Olorgesailie I detected weak trends towards reduction in the relative thickness of bifaces and increase in the number of flake scars resulting from the process of shaping them. These trends are known to have been operative in differentiating the Upper Acheulean from the Lower (Isaac, 1969, p. 18), but there is room for a great deal of random oscillation within a general drift of change which lasted almost a million years (Isaac, 1969, 1971b), and indeed the Olorgesailie series shows such fluctuations (Figs. 4.4a and 4.4b).

Collins (1969, p. 274) has presented a seriation table for Acheulean industries from Britain. It is claimed that the serial sequence is not only concordant for various apparently independent variables such as handaxe form, proportion of Levallois flakes, and numbers of scrapers, but it is in accord with stratigraphic evidence documenting a span from Late Holstein to Mid-Riss. The stratigraphic evidence is not defended in detail and we have no secure means of assessing the length of time involved in the alleged series, or its duration in relation, say, to the time span represented by individual site complexes in Africa such as Isimila and Olorgesailie. This does seem to be an example of persistent regional trends through a segment of Lower Palaeolithic time. Other examples have emerged from M. D. Leakey's study of the Olduvai sequence (M. D. Leakey, 1971).

Derek Roe (1968) has compiled an unprecedented body of metrical data relevant to morphological patterns in handaxe assemblages in Britain. The series is believed to span a time range from 'Mindel' to 'Early Würm', but unfortunately very few of the sites are dated with any security. Roe did not attempt seriation with his numerical data. Because he became convinced that at least two parallel phyla were represented ('pointed tradition' and 'ovate tradition'), he chose to use his numerical data for setting boundaries on classificatory classes. Fig. 4.7A shows mean values computed by Roe, arranged on three-dimensional graphs. A rather striking pattern emerges, and consideration of those sites that are dated may suggest that a time trend in changing forms does run through the series. If so, it is a complex recurved trend. Further work on the dating of sites is necessary to check this. Fig. 4.7C shows a similar graphic representation of the Olorgesailie sites and such other East African Acheulean sites as have been measured. It can be seen that the range of variation in handaxe form at Olorgesailie is much less than the total for British Lower Palaeolithic sites, although the scatter is larger than might be expected on traditional grounds for a penecontemporaneous set.

Statistical findings and methodology

Detailed treatment of either statistics or other aspects of methodology lie beyond the scope and ambitions of this essay. However, it should be pointed out that very close, though not necessarily very clearly recognized relations exist between paradigms, models and research procedures.

It seems to me that the 'statistical' movement, which began to be felt in Palaeolithic archaeology about twenty years ago and which has intensified over the past decade, started with the vague assumption that quantitative data would help bring into sharp focus some of the features of prehistory that were rendered fuzzy by differences between individual intuitive perceptions. Research proceeded as though it was expected that percentage inventory tables would group into statistically homogeneous sets, while measures and attribute counts would cluster around statistical norms which could be used to characterize segments of culture.

In many areas of research, such as French Palaeolithic studies, the formal use of statistics other than the computation of percentages and indices has been avoided by reversion to a 'second-order' typology involving arbitrarily ordered graphic representations of the percentage values. This may have been a wise act of restraint since conventional statistical testing where applied has produced what are initially bewildering rather than clarificatory results.

In my own experiments on the Olorgesailie site complex, both per cent frequency values and many metrical attributes of individual samples from a highly restricted space-time segment failed to behave as random deviants varying about a common norm such as is implied in traditional views of cultural taxonomy (Isaac, 1968b, 1969). Analogous departures from expectations were demonstrated by Sackett (1966) when he tested the clustering of scraper attributes in relation to a current system of typological classification.

It now seems very likely to me that the numerical parameters of distinct archaeological occurrences will commonly fail to group into sets which behave as random sample deviants with respect to an inferable norm. This means that conventional statistical tests of significance have a minimal role in

Fig. 4.7. Differences in biface form have been numerically defined by three ratios between linear measurements (Roe, 1968):

B/L   relative elongation
B^1/B^2 degree of 'pointedness'
T/B   relative thickness

If the mean values of these form defining ratios for each assemblage are plotted against the axes of a three-dimensional Cartesian graph, then an array of points in space reflects variations in 'mean form'. Because of the difficulties of drawing and examining three-dimensional graphs, the effect has been achieved by plotting the points on the faces of an imaginary cube containing the three-dimensional array. Isometric projection drawings of these cubes are shown opposite. On each face there is a bivariate scatter, but the combination of these enables the overall array to be visualized.

'A' shows the total array for the thirty-eight British Acheulean sites measured and reported by Roe (1968). Sites for which stratigraphic data permit a tentative age classification (largely based on Roe) are shown with distinctive symbols.

In 'B' the tentatively dated assemblages only are shown, with rings drawn around the allegedly time-related sets. Arrows show shifts in mean form which are indicated if one accepts that the time sets are valid and representative – which is highly uncertain. The trace represented in the graph shows zigzag oscillations in degree of pointedness (B^1/B^2) and an erratic drift in the direction of reduced relative thickness (T/B) and reduced relative elongation (B/L).

Roe gives warning that time/stratigraphic relations among the sites are poorly known and this graph should therefore be treated with the utmost caution. It is presented here for its methodological interest rather than as a securely established instance of long-term trend and oscillation in artefact morphology. A more detailed explanation and discussion of the graphic method and its results is in preparation for publication elsewhere.

'C' shows variations in the same indices for the samples from the microcosm of the Olorgesailie basin. The dotted encircling line indicates, for comparison, the overall range of variation in the British series.

KEY
1 (L) Possibly pre 'Hoxnian interglacial' occurrences (Lowestoft)
2 (H) Full 'Hoxnian' occurrences
3 Possible late 'Hoxnian'/early 'Gipping' occurrences
4 (G) Post 'Hoxnian' but pre 'Würm' occurrences
5 (W) Probable 'Würm' occurrences (Mousterian of Acheulean tradition)

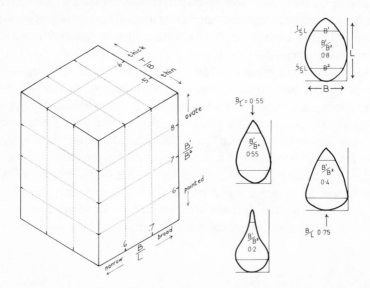

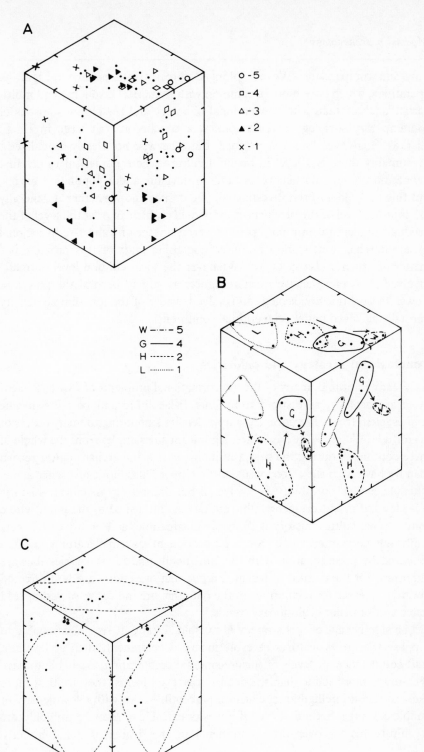

inter-site comparisons. We are plunged directly into pattern recognition operations, which have more in common with numerical taxonomy and multi-variate analysis than with conventional biometry and the classic statistics of contemporary sociology and economics, a conclusion writ large in D. L. Clarke's *Analytical Archaeology* (1968) but otherwise not clearly articulated.[6] Presumably there is a level in material culture where numerical values that define morphology do behave as random deviants about population norms, but this has seldom been investigated. We do not know whether it generally exists at the level of the products of individual craftsmen, or at the level of the products of a craft community such as a craft lineage or a short-term regional social interchange network. Careful ethnographic study of this problem is a matter of urgency (Isaac, 1971c). Whatever the socio-cultural level normally involved, it is one that we must recognize as largely beyond the power of Lower Palaeolithic archaeology to resolve because of the low sample density normally achieved under even optimal conditions.

Conclusions: strategy and priorities

As already indicated, many of the interpretational problems of Lower Palaeo-lithic archaeology, as distinct from Late Palaeolithic and post-Pleistocene studies, stem from differences in sample density amounting to many orders of magnitude. We probably have fewer significant site samples from the whole of three continents during the first 2 million years of the archaeological record than we have from the 20 000 years of the Upper Palaeolithic of France alone. This means that our ability to resolve all but the most gross culture-historic episodes and/or culture-geographic entities is diminished to the point where conventional culture history is probably not feasible, and in any case is cer-tainly not very informative. Since perception of systemic features is often obscured by preoccupation with the ephemeral local idiosyncrasies that are important for the culture historian, I argue that our efforts are best directed toward the search for regularities in the data that are indicative of widespread states and of major evolutionary trends.

The significance of this strategy is twofold. Firstly, it seems reasonable to suppose that gross features of evolutionary development, such as levels of craft competance, or levels of socio-economic organization, are liable to have been much more stable than the details of artefact forms: they are thus more likely to reveal intelligible regularities, perceptible even with a low density of sample coverage. Secondly, even if it was practicable to record 2 million years of culture history over three continents in the degree of detail hitherto achieved in cases such as the Upper Palaeolithic of France, summary narrative records alone would fill several libraries – and would be incredibly boring.

It is in the nature of science (Kuhn, 1962) that proponents of the various possible models must compete in order to establish the relative utility and acceptability of their ideas. This process is certainly evident in present-day Palaeolithic studies.

There is widespread dissatisfaction with the conventional assumption of regularity and stability in the transmission of the details of craft tradition. As a consequence elaborate attempts at culture taxonomy and culture history appear futile. However, the alternative that has been most vigorously espoused has involved the assertion that long-term regularity exists in the functional determinants of stone industries (e.g. Binford and Binford, 1966, p. 291). This view has been advocated largely on the basis of complex 'multivariate' patterning in the covariation of type categories. There exists as yet very little empirical, contextual evidence showing that particular tool kits were really discrete entities associated with specific activities. It seems to me that the assumption of regularity in functional determinism is just as dangerous as the assumption of regularity in culture history. In both instances regularities have to be recognized and demonstrated by reference to a given body of data.

In conclusion I will restate my conviction that there is good reason to believe that stone tool morphology has in part been erratically determined, and that the study of occupation sites and their contents seems more promising than preoccupation merely with artefact assemblages. While comparisons of aretfact sets remain important, it seems likely that there will be a shift towards emphasis on behavioural system models, which facilitate the interpretation of site locations, food refuse, site size and site character as well as artefact morphology.

Notes

1. It appears from the growing volume of abstract literature that controlling ideas with very broad applicability may be termed paradigms, while more specific lines of interpretation may be styled as models (Chorley and Haggett, 1967, pp. 26–7, 35, based on Kuhn, 1962). Models as used in this essay relate to ideas about processes rather than to specific accounts of particular situations or transformations. Thus 'activity differentiation' is a possible label for various related models (interpretative principles), whereas, for example, the actual explanation of a distinctive stone industry at Broken Hill (Clark, 1959) is not a model but a hypothesis, which involves the conjunction of a model and a specified situation.

The term 'models' is a piece of jargon, albeit useful jargon. It should be appreciated that some authors who do not use the term are writing about thought categories that are closely allied to those being called 'models'; for instance, Binford (1968) in a cogent essay, 'Archaeological perspectives', uses the labels 'interpretative principles' and 'explanatory propositions' to convey concepts that Clarke (1968) would probably have classified as models.

2. J. Frere (1800), quoted from Daniel (1950, p. 27).

3. In his doctoral thesis on *The Tools of Neanderthal Man* (Cambridge University, 1948) McBurney did report systematic quantitative tests, but these have never been published.

4. The concept of 'random walk' change is probably implicit in much of the ideographic or narrative treatment of post-Pleistocene prehistoric material culture; what may be new is explicit, or nomothetic, concern with stochastic change as an important process (cf. Clarke, 1968, p. 448).

5. A comment by Dr L. S. B. Leakey at the Fourth Pan African Congress on Prehistory shows that his perception of the same phenomenon entirely preceded the statistical work that demonstrated its reality. I quote: 'I am quite sure that from Acheulean times onward and probably even earlier, the assemblage at any given living site was very considerably influenced by the tool makers of that particular home and their skill. I am perfectly certain you can find, in places like Olorgesailie, on exactly the same horizon, from the same year, with an accumulation of tools made by one family, another by another family; because X was more clever than Y or because X had rather different ideas as to what he wanted than Y, the two things are completely contemporary of the same culture, of the same sub-culture. Yet statistically they are completely different to look at.' (Mortelmans and Nenquin, 1962, p. 127).

6. In a series of as yet unpublished experiments C. B. M. McBurney has found that a harmonic system of internal correlations may characterize a series of related assemblages even when many individual parameters fluctuate in an erratic fashion (personal communication).

Acknowledgements

The development of many of the ideas expressed here has stemmed from discussions with former mentors such as the late A. J. H. Goodwin and C. B. M. McBurney – as well as from exchanges with such present colleagues as J. D. Clark, F. C. Howell, M. D. Leakey, R. J. Rodden, D. A. Roe, J. R. Sackett, S. J. Washburn and my wife. Between completion of the first draft and the final typescript I read L. R. Binford's contribution to the volume, and also attended a seminar on the east African Acheulian organized by C. M. Keller in Urbana, Illinois. Both of these encouraged some sharpening of emphasis but no changes in content were undertaken.

My wife has helped with the preparation of the essay and has drawn the diagrams. Tom Lengyel has clarified the text by thoughtful editorial work.

References

BINFORD, L. R. (1963) 'Red ocher' caches from the Michigan area: a possible case of cultural drift. *Southwestern Journal of Anthropology*, **19**, 89–108.

BINFORD, L. R. (1968) Archaeological perspectives. In BINFORD, S. R. and BINFORD, L. R. (eds.) *New Perspectives in Archeology*, 5–32. Chicago: Aldine.

BINFORD, L. R. and BINFORD, S. R. (1966) A preliminary analysis of functional variability in the Mousterian of Levallois facies. *American Anthropologist*, **68**, 2 (2), 238–95.

BINFORD, S. R. and BINFORD, L. R. (1969) Stone tools and human behaviour. *Scientific American*, **220** (4), 70–84.

BORDES, F. (1950) L'évolution buissonnante des industries en Europe occidentale. Considérations théoriques sur le Paléolithique ancien et moyen. *L'Anthropologie*, **54**, 393–420.

BORDES, F. (1953) Essai de classification des industries 'Moustériennes'. *Bulletin de la Société Préhistorique Française*, **50**, 226–35.

BORDES, F. (1961) Mousterian cultures in France. *Science*, **134**, 803–10.

BORDES, F. and SONNEVILLE-BORDES, D. DE (1970) The significance of variability in Palaeolithic assemblages. *World Archaeology*, **2**, (1), 61–73.

BREUIL, H. (1932) Les industries à éclats du Paléolithique ancien. *Préhistoire*, **1** (2), 125–90.

BURKITT, M. C. (1933) *The Old Stone Age: A Study of Palaeolithic Times*. Cambridge: Cambridge University Press.

CAMPBELL, B. G. (1966) *Human Evolution: An Introduction to Man's Adaptations*. Chicago: Aldine.

CERRALBO, MARQUIS DE (1913) Torralba, la plus ancienne station humaine de l'Europe? *Congrès International d'Anthropologie et d'Archéologie Préhistorique*, Comptes Rendus, XIV session (277–90). Génève.

CHILDE, V. G. (1935) Changing methods and aims in prehistory. *Proceedings of the Prehistoric Society*, n.s. **1**, 1–15.

CHORLEY, R. H. and HAGGETT, P. (1967) *Models in Geography*. London: Methuen.

CLARK, J. D. (1954) An early Upper Pleistocene site on the Northern Rhodesia–Tanganyika border. *South African Archaeological Bulletin*, **9**, 51–6.

CLARK, J. D. (1959) Further excavations at Broken Hill, Northern Rhodesia. *Journal of the Royal Anthropological Institute*, **89**, 201–32.

CLARK, J. D. (1966) Acheulian occupation sites in the Middle East and Africa: a study in cultural variability. *American Anthropologist*, **68**, 2 (2), 202–29.

CLARK, J. D. (1968) Studies of hunter-gatherers as an aid to the interpretation of prehistoric societies. In LEE, R. B. and DEVORE, I. (eds.) *Man The Hunter*. Chicago: Aldine.

CLARK, J. D. (1969) *Kalambo Falls Prehistoric Site, Vol. I: The Geology, Palaeoecology, and Detailed Stratigraphy of the Excavations*. Cambridge: Cambridge University Press.

CLARK, J. D. and HAYNES, C. V. (1970) An elephant butchery site at Mwanganda's Village, Karonga, Malawi, and its relevance for Palaeolithic archaeology. *World Archaeology*, **1**, (3), 390–411.

CLARK, J. G. D. (1954) *Excavations at Star Carr: An Early Mesolithic Site at Seamer, near Scarborough, Yorkshire.* Cambridge: Cambridge University Press.

CLARKE, D. L. (1968) *Analytical Archaeology.* London: Methuen.

COLLINS, D. (1969) Culture traditions and environment of early man. *Current Anthropology,* **10,** 267–316.

COLLINS, D. (1970) Stone artefact analysis and the recognition of culture traditions. *World Archaeology,* **2,** 17–27.

COMMONT, V. (1908) Les industries de l'ancien Saint-Acheul. *L'Anthropologie,* **19,** 527–72.

CROOK, J. H. and GARTLAN, J. S. (1966) The evolution of primate societies. *Nature,* **210,** 1200–3.

DANIEL, G. E. (1950) *A Hundred Years of Archaeology.* London: Duckworth.

DARWIN, C. (1858) Extract from an unpublished work on species. *Journal of the Linnean Society,* Zoology, III (9), 45–62.

DARWIN, C. (1859) *The Origin of Species by Means of Natural Selection or the Preservation of Favoured Races in the Struggle for Life.* London.

DEETZ, J. (1965) *The Dynamics of Stylistic Change in Arikara Ceramics.* Illinois Studies in Anthropology No. 4. Urbana: University of Illinois Press.

DEVORE, I. and WASHBURN, S. L. (1963) Baboon ecology and human evolution. In HOWELL, F. C. and BOURLÈIRE, F. (eds.) *African Ecology and Human Evolution.* Chicago: Aldine.

ELLIOT-SMITH, G. (1927) *The Evolution of Man.* 2nd ed. London: Oxford University Press.

EVANS, J. (1872) *The Ancient Stone Implements, Weapons and Ornaments of Great Britain.* New York.

FOX, C. (1948) *The Archaeology of the Cambridge Region.* Cambridge: Cambridge University Press.

FOX, R. (1967) In the beginning: aspects of hominid behavioural evolution. *Man,* **2,** 415–33.

FREEMAN, L. G., JR, and BUTZER, K. W. (1966) The Acheulian station of Torralba (Spain): a progress report. *Quaternia,* **8,** 9–21.

FRERE, J. (1800) Account of flint weapons discovered at Hoxne in Suffolk. *Archaeologia,* **13,** 204–5 (quoted from Daniel, 1950, p. 27).

GARTLAN, J. S. and BRAIN, C. T. (1968) Ecology and social variability in *Cercopithecus aethiops* and *C. mitis.* In JAY, P. C. (ed.) *Primates: Studies in Adaptation and Variability,* 253–92. New York: Holt, Rinehart & Winston.

GAUDRY, A. (1859) Haches trouvées dans le diluvium, près d'Amiens. *Bulletin de la Société Géologique de France,* **2** (17), 17–19.

GOODALL, J. M. (1964) Tool-using and aimed throwing in a community of free-living chimpanzees. *Nature,* **201,** 1264–6.

GOULD, R. A. (1968) Chipping stones in the outback. *Natural History,* **77,** (2), 42–9.

HEIZER, R. (1969) *Man's Discovery of His Past.* Englewood Cliffs, N.J.: Prentice-Hall.

HOWELL, F. C. (1965) *Early Man.* New York: Time-Life.

HOWELL, F. C. (1966) Observations on the earlier phases of the European Lower Palaeolithic. *American Anthropologist*, **68**, 2 (2), 88–201.

HOWELL, F. C., COLE, G. H. and KLEINDIENST, M. R. (1962) Isimila, and Acheulian occupation site in the Iringa Highlands, Southern Highlands Province, Tanganyika. In MORTELMANS, G. and NENQUIN, J. (eds.) *Actes du IVe Congrès Panafricain de Préhistoire* (Tervuren, Belgium), 43–80.

ISAAC, G. LL. (1968a) Traces of Pleistocene hunters: an east African example. In LEE, R. B. and DEVORE, I. (eds.) *Man The Hunter*, 253–61. Chicago: Aldine.

ISAAC, G. LL. (1968b) *The Acheulian Site Complex at Olorgesailie, Kenya: A Contribution to the Interpretation of Middle Pleistocene Culture in East Africa*. Doctoral Thesis, University of Cambridge.

ISAAC, G. LL. (1969) Studies of early culture in east Africa. *World Archaeology*, **1**, 1–28.

ISAAC, G. LL. (1971a) The diet of early man: aspects of archaeological evidence from Lower and Middle Pleistocene sites in Africa. *World Archaeology*, **2** (3), 278–99.

ISAAC, G. LL. (1971b) Chronology and the tempo of cultural change during the Pleistocene. In BISHOP, W. W. and MILLER, J. A. (eds.) *The Calibration of Hominoid Evolution*. Edinburgh.

ISAAC, G. LL. (1971c) Whither Archaeology? *Antiquity*, **45**.

ISAAC, G. LL. (in press) Some experiments in quantitative methods for characterizing assemblages of Acheulian artefacts. In HUGOT, H. (ed.) *Actes du VIe Congrès Panafricain de Préhistoire* (Dakar, 1967).

JOLLY, C. (1970) The seed-eaters: a new model of hominid differentiation based on a baboon analogy. *Man*, n.s. **5** (1), 5–26.

KLEINDIENST, M. R. (1961) Variability within the late Acheulian assemblages in eastern Africa. *South African Archaeological Bulletin*, **16**, 35–52.

KRETZOI, M. and VÉRTES, L. (1965) Upper Biharian (Inter Mindel) pebble industry occupation site in western Hungary. *Current Anthropology*, **6**, 74–87.

KUHN, T. S. (1962) *The Structure of Scientific Revolutions*. Chicago: University of Chicago Press.

LANCASTER, J. B. (1968) On the evolution of tool-using behaviour. *American Anthropologist*, **70**, 56–66.

LEAKEY, L. S. B. (1934) *Adam's Ancestors*. 1st ed. London.

LEAKEY, L. S. B. (1963) Very early east African hominidae and their ecological setting. In HOWELL, F. C. and BOURLIÈRE, F. (eds.) *African Ecology and Human Evolution*, 448–57. Chicago: Aldine.

LEAKEY, M. D. (1967) Preliminary summary of the cultural material from Beds I and II, Olduvai Gorge, Tanzania. In BISHOP, W. W. and CLARK, J. D. (eds.) *Background to Evolution in Africa*, 417–46. Chicago: University of Chicago Press.

LEAKEY, M. D. (1971) *Olduvai Gorge, Vol. 3: Excavations in Beds I and II, 1960–1963*. Cambridge: Cambridge University Press.

LEE, R. B. and DEVORE, I. (eds.) (1968) *Man The Hunter*. Chicago: Aldine.

LUBBOCK, J. (1865) *Prehistoric Times*. London.

LUMLEY, H. DE (1969) A Paleolithic camp at Nice. *Scientific American*, **220** (5), 42–50.

LYELL, C. (1863) *The Antiquity of Man*. London.

MCBURNEY, C. B. M. (1950) The geographic study of the older Palaeolithic stages in Europe. *Proceedings of the Prehistoric Society*, **16**, 163–83.

MCBURNEY, C. B. M. (1960) *The Stone Age of North Africa*. Harmondsworth: Penguin Books.

MELLARS, P. (1970) Some comments of the notion of 'functional variability' in stone tool assemblages. *World Archaeology*, **2** (1), 74–89.

MORRIS, D. (1967) *The Naked Ape*. London: Cape.

MORTELMANS, G. and NENQUIN, J. (eds.) (1962) *Actes du IVe Congrès Panafricain de Préhistoire* (Tervuren, Belgium).

MORTILLET, G. DE (1883) *Le préhistorique: antiquité de l'homme*. Paris.

NEUSTUPNÝ, E. (1971) Whither archaeology? *Antiquity*, **45**, 34–9.

OWEN, R. C. (1965) The patrilocal band: a linguistically and culturally hybrid social unit. *American Anthropologist*, **67**, 675–90.

PFEIFFER, J. E. (1969) *The Emergence of Man*. New York: Harper & Row.

PIGGOTT, S. (1959) *Approach to Archaeology*. London: Black.

POSNANSKY, M. (1959) The Hope Fountain site at Olorgesailie, Kenya Colony. *South African Archaeological Bulletin*, **16**, 83–9.

RENFREW, A. C. (1968) Models in prehistory. *Antiquity*, **42**, 132–4.

RENFREW, A. C. (1969) More on models. *Antiquity*, **43**, 61–2.

REYNOLDS, V. (1966) Open groups in hominid evolution. *Man*, **1**, 441–52.

ROE, D. A. (1968) British Lower and Middle Palaeolithic handaxe groups. *Proceedings of the Prehistoric Society*, **34**, 1–82.

SACKETT, J. R. (1966) Quantitative analysis of Upper Palaeolithic stone tools. *American Anthropologist*, **68**, 2 (2), 356–94.

SACKETT, J. R. (1968) Method and theory of Upper Palaeolithic archaeology in south-western France. In BINFORD, L. R. and BINFORD, S. R. (eds.) *New Perspectives in Archaeology*, 61–83. Chicago: Aldine.

SCHALLER, G. B. and LOWTHER, G. R. (1969) The relevance of carnivore behaviour to the study of early hominids. *Southwestern Journal of Anthropology*, **25** (4), 307–41.

SMITH, P. L. (1966) The late Palaeolithic of northeast Africa in the light of recent research. *American Anthropologist*, **68**, 2 (2), 326–55.

SOLLAS, W. J. (1911) *Ancient Hunters: And Their Modern Representatives*. London: Macmillan.

STEKELIS, M. (1966) *Archaeological Excavations at 'Ubeidiya 1960–1963*. Jerusalem.

THOMSON, D. F. (1964) Some wood and stone implements of the Bindibu tribe of central Western Australia. *Proceedings of the Prehistoric Society*, **30**, 400–22.

TIGER, L. (1969) *Men in Groups*. London: Nelson.

TRIGGER, B. W. (1969) More on models. *Antiquity*, **43**, 59–61.

TRIGGER, B. W. (1970) Aims in prehistoric archaeology. *Antiquity*, **44**, 26–37.

WALLACE, A. R. (1858) On the tendency of varieties to depart indefinitely from the original type. *Journal of the Linnean Society*, Zoology, III (9), 45–62.

WARREN, S. H. (1926) The classification of the Lower Palaeolithic with special reference to Essex. *Transactions of the South-Eastern Union of Scientific Societies*, 38–51.

WASHBURN, S. L. and LANCASTER, C. S. (1968) The evolution of hunting. In LEE, R. B. and DEVORE, I. (eds.) *Man The Hunter*, 293–303. Chicago.

WENDORF, F. (ed.) (1968) *The Prehistory of Nubia*. Dallas, Texas: Southern Methodist University Press.

WORTHINGTON-SMITH, G. (1894) *Man the Primeval Savage: His Haunts and Relics from the Hilltops of Bedfordshire to Blackwall*. London.

5
Research design models

S. G. H. DANIELS
University of Ibadan, Nigeria

Introduction

The growing body of quantitative and statistical methods in archaeology has, for the most part, not been developed within the framework of archaeology as a discipline, but has been borrowed piecemeal and with varying degrees of success from other disciplines. As a result a number of unsatisfactory practices have been imported through false analogy between, for example, archaeological and biological data, and through the use of tests which are proper only to random samples when the samples concerned are manifestly non-random. However, the successful use of quantitative methods depends in general on the one field where borrowing has been minimal – the field of experimental design. Archaeology, of course, is not an experimental science and the true experiment, in which factors other than those under study are strictly controlled, is not possible in the study of the past. Nevertheless the general principles of design, that the effects of unwanted factors should be controlled or nullified, are applicable.

Stress has long been placed on the need for archaeological research to be undertaken in order to answer specific questions, and the importance of methodical and standardized practices has been emphasized by writers from Pitt Rivers (1887) to Wheeler (1954) and Alexander (1970). But it is perhaps significant that the 304 pages of Alexander's book on *The Directing of Archaeological Excavations* contain no reference to the design of research in the sense used above.

It is the essence of good design that it must be related to the questions asked in individual cases. In this article, therefore, I have not attempted a comprehensive treatment of the field, but have tried to erect a general model of the way in which research information originates, to outline broad principles of good design, and to highlight some areas of practice in which it seems most important and most profitable.

A model of the origin of archaeological information

The most useful model for the origination of data seems to be one based on the same assumptions as the multifactorial methods of analysis developed in the observational sciences. In this model, phenomena, which in this case may be taken as the published data from a research project, result from the effects of a large number of causal factors. Thus a numerical measure, such as the percentage frequency of a tool type, may be thought of as having had some original value, which has been increased by some factors and decreased by others to produce the final result on the printed page. These factors may usefully be grouped under three headings:

(i) *Historical factors.* These comprise all the causal factors stemming from the way of life of the makers and users of the artefacts, their environment and their reactions to it. As complex and entangled as any set of data and causes in social sciences, these are the proper field of study of the archaeologist.

(ii) *Post-depositional factors.* Included in this group are all causal agencies that alter the state or position of artefacts after they have been abandoned and before the archaeologist begins to study them. They are unwanted factors which serve only to mask those with which we are concerned, but, since they are by definition completed when research begins, they cannot be controlled. The most that can be done is to estimate their effects and attempt in some way to allow for them.

(iii) *Research factors.* Factors stemming from the archaeologist's own work begin to operate when an excavation is located and continue until publication is complete. Their effects can produce gross distortion of the data and have the added disadvantage of being almost undetectable, but they can for the most part, and for particular purposes, be controlled. It is primarily with these factors that research design is concerned.

A simple version of the causation of data from a single settlement site is shown diagrammatically in Fig. 5.1. It is intended to relate only to portable artefacts but could with slight modification be extended to cover structures and environmental evidence. Different causative factors are shown in rectangular boxes to the right and left of the figure. The central column of circles shows what may be thought of as bodies of information which are successively modified by the effects of the factors. The two broken circles at the bottom of the figure are information in the usual sense that they are encoded records of reality. The four solid circles above them are actual bodies

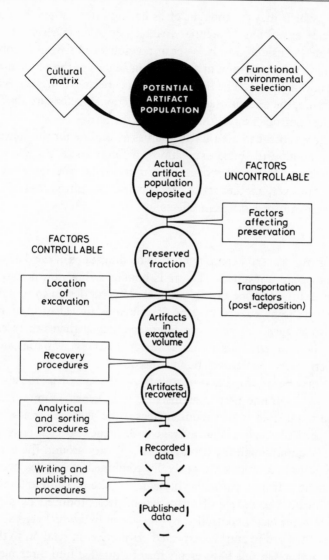

FIG. 5.1. A model of the causation of data from a single settlement site. The broken rings represent bodies of information, the solid rings bodies of artefacts, and the solid black circle a hypothetical population. Each body is derived from the one above it by the operation of causative factors, represented by rectangles to left and right of the figure.

of artefacts, which may be thought of as having information content in the more specific sense. The 'Potential Artefact Population' has no objective existence but is considered to be a set of possible events whose probabilities are determined by the cultural matrix: it is analogous to the set of all possible deals in a game of Bridge. The historical factors are shown in diamonds at the top of the figure, the uncontrollable post-depositional factors are shown at the right and the controllable research factors at the left.

It will be convenient to use this diagram as an outline for the consideration of design in relation to single excavations, before considering the more important aspects of historical reconstruction and palaeosociology on a wider scale. First, however, another set of concepts must be introduced: the various kinds of error and their different effects.

ERROR

The term 'Error' is used here to refer to all modifications of the data produced by factors that are unwanted. 'To err is human' – but not, in this context, necessarily sinful. It is one of the essentials of good design to recognize that error is never absent, indeed may be described as prevalent in archaeology. However, some forms of error are more deleterious than others and these may often be converted into comparatively harmless varieties, while less damaging error may sometimes be measured.

All error may be regarded as probabilistic, in the sense that the effect of any one error source in one particular instance is in general unpredictable, but that as the number of observations increases the average error effect tends towards a particular value. This average is then the expected error effect for single instances, although the actual effect will vary around the expectation. Archaeological observations are generally combined in groups, such as 'the stone assemblage from a particular horizon' or 'the megalithic tombs from a particular area'. The degree of distortion of data produced by a particular error source is primarily controlled by the size of individual errors in relation to the size of the group and the expected error effect in relation to the definition of the group. On this basis errors may be divided into three main kinds:

(i) *Random noise.* This is a term borrowed from information theory. It may be used here to refer to any error effect for which the expected value is zero, but in which some degree of error is generally present in individual observations, the amount, whether positive or negative, being distributed at random. The chief characteristic of random noise is that while it will disturb and blur the outlines of patterning in the data, it is not expected to create spurious patterns. In the same way reception of a radio program may be made difficult or even impossible by static, but the static does not pattern itself to give the impression of a completely different program.

(ii) *Gross error*. This describes errors that are rare, but have large effects when they do occur. In other words the usual effect from such an error source is zero, but when a positive or negative effect does occur it may be much greater than the variation between groups which are being studied. Examples of gross error are such misfortunes as the incorrect labelling of bags of excavated material, or the misprinting of a figure in published numerical data. In this case it matters little whether the expected error effect is zero or not, since the size of the group being observed is seldom large enough in relation to the degree of error for the observed error effect to approach the expected value.

(iii) *Bias*. Bias occurs when the expected error effect is not zero. It cannot be eliminated or lessened by increasing the number of observations, but provided that it is consistent over all the field under study it will not disturb the pattern of interrelationships any more than random noise. In some cases, where it occurs consistently in certain identifiable circumstances but not in others, it may be detected and allowance made for it. However, most commonly, the bias will not be consistent over the field, but will be in part dependent on the group observed or on the value of some variable under study. This correlated bias is the most destructive kind of error and it is this that experimental design has been chiefly concerned with controlling. Where, as is the case with much archaeological classification, a considerable element of subjectivity is involved, controlling this type of error has necessitated such precautions as the 'double-blind trial' in medical research. By contrast, a number of accepted archaeological procedures might almost have been designed to maximize, rather than eliminate, the effects of correlated bias. It is particularly dangerous in a subject such as archaeology, since, unlike random noise, it can create spurious patterns in the data where none were previously present; these patterns may then creep into the body of 'accepted historical fact', and in the nature of the discipline cannot be checked by rigorous prediction and experiment. Having drawn a distinction between these three types of error, we may return to the effects of the various unwanted factors in the single site model.

POST-DEPOSITIONAL FACTORS

These factors are by definition beyond the control of the archaeologist and cover the circumstances of deposition, the differential rate of decay of objects in the deposit, and the effects of vertical and horizontal transport of material within the deposit. Although they are by definition uncontrollable, it is still possible to make some allowance for them. The factor in question may be identified and a generalized non-quantitative allowance made when drawing inferences. For example, where abraded stone implements are found in a river gravel, which has been transported and sorted selectively according to size, no inference is drawn concerning artefacts which would lie outside the general size range of the gravel. Similarly, no inference concerning organic remains can be drawn when the nature of the deposit is hostile to their preservation, though there has been at least one recent instance of a reputable archaeologist apparently attempting to infer from the absence of organic remains just what they would have been if they had been preserved.

However, the effects of differential preservation may be more subtle than this and remain undetected. At the Iron Age site of Igbo Ukwu, in eastern Nigeria (Shaw, 1970, p. 233) there were three single period features containing, among other material, large quantities of beads. In the filling of one of these features the frequency of a particular type of yellow glass bead appeared to be related to the depth in the deposit, forming a higher percentage of all beads in the upper levels. Had the deposit been formed gradually over a period of time, this trend might have been put down to a time-related change in the material culture, whereas it seems to have resulted from the greater susceptibility of the yellow beads to processes of decay which were more active at lower levels.

In order to cope successfully with such effects as this it is necessary to have more sound information on what really does happen in the deposit, both in terms of preservation and in terms of transport. This entails true experimentation, which can be designed with appropriate rigour. The need for experimental projects of this nature is well recognized and has been carried into practice at such places as Overton Down (Jewell and Dimbleby, 1966) in Wiltshire, and the recently started project at Adesina Oja, near Ibadan (Shaw, 1966). Much, however, remains to be done, particularly on the disturbing question of transport within the deposit.

Hole and Shaw (1967) put the problem succinctly: 'At best there are only rare exceptions to the general rule that there is always mixing of artefacts in sites that were occupied for more than one discernible period.' Myers (1958) observed the vertical distribution of broken sherds from the same pot at the site of 'Abka, in the Sudan, and reported that 'sherds in stratified levels show a distribution curve vertically through different strata, even when the latter are well defined'.

The mechanisms giving rise to vertical transport must be many and varied ranging from the easily detected ravages of rabbits or aardvarks, through the scuffing of human feet on a continuously inhabited and accumulating deposit, to the action of worms and termites in an apparently 'undisturbed' deposit. The nature of the deposit, climatic regime and micro-climate, level and location of biological activity, and relative size of objects involved, may all be expected to influence the effect.

An alternative approach to the problem of 'allowing for' uncontrollable factors may be illustrated with respect to this problem. We may set up an entirely theoretical probabilistic model in which it is assumed that, for a limited area and a limited depth of roughly homogeneous deposit, all these various causative agencies can be represented by a single random variable. Thus if N objects are lying on the surface of a deposit, and there is a probability, p, of any one object descending through a unit depth in a given time, then the expected number of objects in the ith unit of depth after the given time has elapsed is:

$$Np^{i-1}(1-p).$$

For any particular case p is unknown and is estimated from the data as:

$$p = \mu^{-1}(\mu - 1),$$

where μ is the mean depth of the objects. A predicted vertical distribution of objects can be calculated and compared with the actual distribution.

This model was suggested by the distribution of sherds at the Late Stone Age rock shelter site of Iwo Eleru in the forest zone of Nigeria (Shaw, 1966). The greater part of the deposit contained a Late Stone Age industry and yielded radiocarbon dates ranging from the tenth to the second millennium B.C. The latest stages of this industry were expected to contain some pottery, but in the very top of the deposit was a considerable quantity of comparatively recent Iron Age pottery. Sherds of this pottery were also found, in decreasing numbers, to a considerable depth where they were incompatible with the stone industry and the carbon dates. It was therefore considered whether a process such as that described above could have been operating. The site was divided into areas, each composed of a number of excavated grid squares, on the basis of topography and deposit, and the observed distribution of sherds in each area compared with the model. The results for four selected areas are shown in Table 5.1, together with the results of Kolmogorov-Smirnov tests for goodness of fit. The data of Areas F and E do not depart significantly from the model. Those of Area G do depart significantly but show the same overall pattern as the model in the rate of decrease and the level at which sherd counts are expected to be near zero. Area A departs radically from the model in both the above respects, and this departure accords well with the presence there of later elements of the stone industry together with a substantial proportion of sherds which, on typological grounds, might be associated with a late phase of the Late Stone Age occupation.

TABLE 5.1. *Sherd counts at Iwo Eleru with numbers predicted from a probabilistic model of in situ vertical transport*

Area	Level	1	2	3	4	5	6	7	8 or below	μ
F	Observed	192	76	40	7	5	2	0	0	1·64
F	Predicted	196	77	30	12	5	2	1	0	1·64
E	Observed	582	43	10	1	0	0			1·10
E	Predicted	576	54	5	1	0	0			1·10
G	Observed	641	355	65	25	8	3	0		1·55
G	Predicted	706	252	90	32	11	4	2		1·55
A	Observed	112	77	130	4	4	0	0	0	2·12
A	Predicted	154	82	43	23	12	6	3	4	2·12

Probability of observed data occurring by chance on the basis
of the model

Area	Probability
F	Greater than 0·2
E	Greater than 0·2
G	Less than 0·01
A	Less than 0·01

A further important point concerning design is also involved in this example. The data shown in Table 5.1 do not constitute a valid set of data for strict application of the Kolmogorov-Smirnov test, since the excavation was not designed with such tests in mind. Specifically, a prior surface collection of sherds was made, thus systematically impoverishing the uppermost level, and no control was applied to the effects of more vigorous workmen breaking pieces of pottery and thus creating more sherds during excavation. Further reference will be made later to the cardinal point that the analysis of data is inextricably bound up with the design of the research that produced those data.

We have seen how the uncontrollable depositional factors can to some extent be allowed for through the application of general experience, through the results of experimental archaeology or through the erection of theoretical models. All these approaches involve the use of assumptions concerning processes that may have been operating and the manner of their operation. It is only when we turn to the research factors that we can so design operations as to control the error effects whether or not the factors are operating.

CONTROL OF ERROR PRODUCING FACTORS

Before considering how particular error factors in the research process can be dealt with, we may take a general look at the mechanisms available for this control. Some of these are well tried and accepted in archaeology: others, though commonplace in many other fields, have received little attention from the archaeologist.

(i) *Procedural rigour.* This, in the sense of proceeding with practical work as methodically and accurately as possible, is fundamental to good archaeological practice and I would not wish to underrate its importance. It is essential for suppressing noise and cutting down on the possibility of gross errors: unfortunately it has no effect on bias, and bias becomes more and more dangerous as subjectivity increases. Thus in the study of an African Late Stone Age industry made on indifferent quartzite, subjectivity plays a large part in the classification of artefacts. Under such conditions gross distortions due to noise and bias may survive the most rigorous procedure.

(ii) *Use of redundancy.* Redundancy is a term proper to, and strictly defined in information theory. It may be roughly translated here as the degree to which the elements of a message can be altered or lost without changing or losing the meaning of the message. Thus the message 'four hundred and thirty five' has a much higher degree of redundancy than the message '435', since the former is still recognizable as 'four hunderd and thrity fve' while the latter is completely changed if it appears as '235'. The use of redundancy to control gross error in archaeological research is well established in such practices as duplicate labelling of bags of finds. Any good recording system will contain a fairly high degree of redundancy. However, depending on the way in which it has been designed it may allow for the detection and correction of gross error or only for its detection and rejection. In the latter case rejection is imperative since it is generally better to have a complete absence of information in a particular part of the project than to include information which is known to have fallen victim to a gross error and reflects this fact rather than any historical reality.

(iii) *Randomization.* Randomization is fundamental to all experimental

209

procedures where unwanted factors with significant effects cannot be directly and physically controlled. The basic principle is that identifiable error sources should be prevented from becoming correlated with groupings and expected patterns in the data, and should instead be so arranged in relation to these groupings and patterns that the error effects can be handled in the light of probability theory. This generally implies that error sources and observations should be paired at random. An example may be useful.

Suppose we have two assemblages (*X* and *Y*) of stone waste flakes, to be measured by two different observers (*A* and *B*). The simplest way to organize this operation would be to give assemblage *X* to observer *A* and assemblage *Y* to observer *B*. However, it may be that on the day the measurements are made observer *A* has a tendency to estimate incorrectly to the nearest millimetre above, while observer *B* has a similar tendency to estimate to the nearest millimetre below. When we come to compare the mean size of the two assemblages, we shall also be comparing the different tendencies of the observers, and there will be no way of disentangling the wanted from the unwanted effect. A step towards solving this problem might be taken by assigning half of each assemblage to each observer on a systematic basis. But this will not provide a complete solution. Observer *A* may have a tendency to measure high before the lunch break and low after it, while observer *B* has a reverse tendency. In the words of Fisher (1960), 'it would be impossible to present an exhaustive list of such possible differences appropriate to any one kind of experiment, because the uncontrolled causes which may influence the result are always strictly innumerable.' In this particular case the observers are the error sources and accordingly the only satisfactory solution is to assign the flakes, regardless of which assemblage they come from, at random to the two observers. In this way each flake in the two assemblages has an equal chance of being measured by either observer and at any point in the sorting order. As a result the error effects are randomized, the bias from these particular error sources converted to random noise, and the demands of probability theory satisfied. Appropriate techniques may then be used to test whether the difference between the two assemblages is likely to have been unacceptably altered by the different tendencies of the observers. The actual mechanics of randomization and the use of appropriate tests will be discussed later in the section devoted to particular research factors.

(iv) *Quality control.* Quality control is the system used in industry for ensuring that an acceptably small proportion of goods produced or purchased is defective, while making an acceptably small expenditure on the inspection process. For this purpose small samples of batches of products or components are taken and inspected or tested. From these samples an estimate can be made of the probability that the batch concerned contains an unacceptably large proportion of items that do not meet the specifications. For a particular process an appropriate inspection scheme can be devised in which the decision to reject or accept is dependent simply on the number of defective items, or the degree to which items depart from the ideal specifications.

Two important points may be noted. In industry the specifications are fixed in advance, so that the concern is with departure of observed values from a particular known value. Secondly, the decision as to what proportion of defectives is acceptable, and the probability of accepting a batch with too high a proportion of defectives, are both arbitrarily decided in the light of the realistic needs of producer or purchaser. This second point is equally true of the use of any form of quality control in archaeological research, where the decision must be determined by the nature of the project, the resources available and the degree of accuracy required for historical reconstruction. However, the research process will not normally produce items with known specifications, but observations with an unknown true value and a certain degree of observational error. Our concern will be with the reproducibility of results produced by a single observer, and with the agreement of results produced by different observers. Depending on the nature of the research involved the degree to which two sets of observations should agree with each other may be fixed and a scheme devised for ensuring that the probability of observations with an unacceptable error finding their way into the body of accepted data is suitably low.

Fig. 5.2 shows a generalized flow chart for a process in archaeological research. It may be applied either to an observational process such as the classification of stone tools within an assemblage, or to processes such as recording, where errors are likely to be gross error rather than noise. For the purpose of control, the material is divided into batches so that an estimate of the error within each batch can be obtained. A small sample is drawn from the batch, and the error assessed, by repeating or duplicating observations, or by comparing independent duplicate records. If the error is unacceptably high, the whole batch may be processed again, if possible: if the process is not repeatable, then the data from the whole batch are to be regarded as unacceptable and discarded, although in some cases it may be possible to proceed to total inspection of the batch and to discard only those items affected by gross error. If the error is within acceptable limits, the data for the batch can be accepted and, at the same time an estimate obtained of how great the error is.

(v) *Combining control mechanisms.* The various mechanisms for controlling, transforming and monitoring the effects of error can be suitably combined for use in any stage of a research project. An attempt has been made in Fig. 5.3 to illustrate the effect on the recorded data of a traditional design for a research project compared with one in which the various mechanisms are deployed so as to minimize the effects of error. The illustration is not intended to be an exact analogue of the information flow: for example, the three error sources shown will normally operate together to distort the data resulting from a single process, rather than affecting different processes as shown. In both designs the recorded data are shown as distorted versions of the 'true data', the information content inherent in the material under study before it is

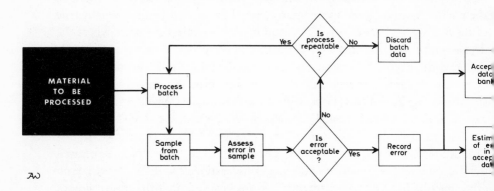

FIG. 5.2. A flow chart showing the application of quality control techniques to a process in archaeological research.

disturbed and interpreted by the process of study. Three types of error source (bias, noise and gross error) each contribute towards the distortion of the output. Control mechanisms common to both designs are procedural rigour, which may be regarded as cutting down the potential noise level or as suppressing some noise at source, and the specific planned use of redundancy to reduce the number of gross errors affecting the output. In their remaining features the two designs have very important differences.

In the 'traditional' design, bias is allowed to affect the results to a degree that cannot be measured. Not only is it frequently correlated with the groupings under study, as in the common practice of sorting potsherds one layer at a time: the effect of bias is actually intensified by adherence to the principle that classification of objects should be carried out in the light of their stratigraphic origin. There is no suggestion here that there is conscious falsification of the results, but that the element of subjectivity is generally high in

212

archaeological classification, that bias is an inbuilt defect of the human observer, and that the instances where classes are so clear cut that bias will have no effect, are special and delightful cases. In the modified design, the intensifying effect of prior knowledge is omitted: indeed classification takes place without a knowledge of the stratigraphic origin. Furthermore, by the appropriate use of randomization the effect of bias on the results is converted to random noise.

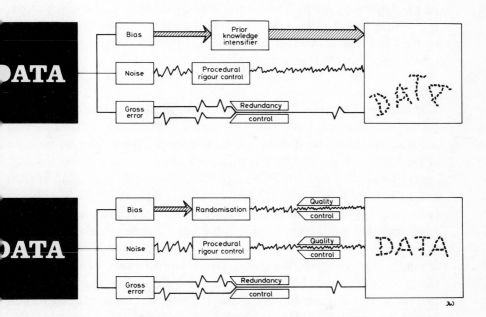

FIG. 5.3. Impressionistic flow charts showing the elements of design as machines which can modify or intensify the extent to which various error sources distort the data. Above: a 'traditional' design. Below: a design recommended for reducing the amount of distortion. For detailed explanation see text.

The extent to which the recorded data are distorted in the 'traditional' design is unknown. Rigorous procedure, while cutting down the level of noise at the outset, will not remove it entirely, and the only measure of the remaining noise must be in terms of general confidence in the correctness of the observer. The application, at appropriate points, of quality control techniques, as shown in the modified design, not only serves to reduce the noise level still further, but provides an estimate of the remaining noise.

SPECIFIC APPLICATIONS

The two designs shown in Fig. 5.3 are generalized and only broadly representational. The extent to which the modified design can be implemented must depend on the aim, circumstances and resources of particular research projects, and the stage of research that is involved. We may now consider some specific applications under the headings of *location of excavation, recovery procedures, sorting and analytical procedures* and *writing and publishing procedures*. These may serve as examples of the application of the general principles to particular instances, and also to amplify the brief outline given above. In each case we shall be considering only single excavations, the design of projects including a number of excavations being a more complex matter which will be touched on later.

Location of excavation

The location of trenches within a site will, in general, profoundly affect the nature of the material recovered. This is clearly recognized in the excavation of urban and related sites, where it is frequently possible to infer the function of the feature or area in which material is located. It is sometimes less well appreciated in the study of Stone Age sites. The spatial patterning of such industries as the Gravettian of Dolní Vestoniče (Klima, 1963), the Mousterian of Molodova I (Klein, 1969) and the Middle Stone Age of Orangia I (Sampson, 1968) underline the extent to which Stone Age industries should be regarded as generally heterogeneous with regard to areal distribution. The location of trenches in part only of a living site will therefore not produce a representative sample of the total industry at the site, and the degree and direction of bias so introduced cannot be assessed where the functional distinction cannot be inferred, either because of the absence of recognizable features or because of the lack of knowledge of the original living pattern. Nevertheless stone and pottery assemblages from partial excavations are frequently treated as representative of the entire industry. If the main aim of an excavation were to recover a representative sample of an industry whose stratigraphic position was already known, this difficulty could be simply solved by siting small square trenches at random over the area and thus acquiring a random sample of the industry. However, this would seldom be realistic since most excavations must serve other ends as well. A clue to the treatment of the problem may be gained by considering a site with three separated artefactual layers. The industries from these layers are classified into typological categories and percentage figures prepared for each layer. The question may then be asked, 'Do the differences between the percentages in these three assemblages reflect differences in the three industries from which they were drawn? Or are the differences explained by the fact that some functional areas are more heavily represented in some layers than in the others?' The latter possibility may be discounted if the variability between the artefacts found at different functional areas is less than the differences between the layers. Where the functional areas are themselves unidentifiable, this comes down to an assessment of the differences between the layers in the light of the observed variability between different areas of the same layer. Such assessments can be made by the use of standard statistical techniques such as analysis of variance (see for example Yamane, 1967) and partitioning of chi-square tests (summarized in Maxwell, 1961). Discussion of these techniques would be out of place here: the important point is that an excavation needs to be so designed that quantitative changes in the artefact content in the vertical or time dimension can be viewed in the light of variability in the horizontal or contemporary dimension. If, for example, a Stone Age open site is to be partially excavated, experience would suggest that a long narrow trench would provide a better estimate of horizontal variability than a square trench of equivalent area, though this must be weighed against the desirability of a square trench for recovering details of living floors. Similarly, in the excavation of occupation mounds, the common practice of considering the entire contents of a level or layer together, without areal subdivision, results in a loss of the estimates of contemporary variability.

Recovery procedures
During excavation, whether an artefact is recovered *in situ*, found on the spoil heap, or lost completely, depends on fallible and variable human beings. Even skilled and experienced workers cannot, in general, recover every piece of artefactual material: the problem is greatly exacerbated when labour is unskilled. The concern here is not so much with the loss of a single object, regrettable though this may be, but with the overall distortion of the data. When a ground stone axe is found on the spoil heap, two consequences must be faced. In the first place we have a ground stone axe without a definite stratigraphic context. In the second place there is some one stratigraphic unit within the site for which the data have been distorted since one ground stone axe has been subtracted from the artefacts contained there. The second consequence is likely to be the more serious one for quantitative work.

Some workers are more competent than others and unskilled workers become more competent as an excavation proceeds. These differences must in some way be prevented from becoming correlated with differences between successive levels or between different contemporary areas. Ideally we should arrange that workers are assigned to stratigraphic units either at random or in accordance with a systematic factorial design in which each worker contributes the same error effect to each level and to each square. In practice this cannot be achieved for a number of reasons. The necessity of excavating upper levels before lower ones, lack of knowledge of the depth and extent of deposit, and the shifting membership of an excavation crew, all militate against it. We can, however, reduce the likelihood of correlation between workers' bias and the real distribution of artefacts by attempting to apply an appropriate scheme. Table 5.2 shows, schematically, a trench eight squares long and four levels deep, together with four schemes for assigning workers to stratigraphic units. All the schemes meet the requirements that adjacent squares are not dug at the same time and that one level is completed before proceeding to the next. Scheme 1 may produce spurious areal differences. Scheme 2, in which workers A and B are replaced after Level 2 by workers C and D, may produce spurious differences between the upper and lower halves of the deposit. In Scheme 3 there is a possibility of correlation with real differences related to undetected sloping stratification. Only Scheme 4 is satisfactory, in that the distribution of workers is not correlated with levels or squares, no worker digs two adjacent units, and 'diagonal patterning' has also been reduced. A subsequent estimate of the variability of workers could be obtained by analysis of variance techniques, showing what proportion of the total between-unit variance was contributed by between-level, between-square and between-worker variance. What is true of the workers who dig the deposit is also true of those who may operate sieves, and a similar scheme for reducing correlated bias is necessary here.

The reliability of information cannot be achieved without cost, and in this case the cost will lie in greater delays while faster workers are waiting for slower ones and in the necessity for increased vigilance to prevent mixing or mislabelling of material at the sieves. A particular problem is raised by the treatment of special areas, such as the deposit immediately surrounding a human skeleton. If special attention is paid to recovery of artefacts from such an area, the work perhaps being done by supervisory staff rather than by labourers or assistants, a strong element of bias may be introduced since a greater proportion of artefacts may be recovered. There may well be compelling reasons for special treatment, but it is well to remember that material from such an area cannot be properly compared with that from areas that received standard treatment.

One of the chief differences between workers will often lie in the size

TABLE 5.2. *Four schemes for assigning four workers (ABCD) to excavate stratigraphic units within a single trench*

SCHEME 1

	Squares							
	1	*2*	*3*	*4*	*5*	*6*	*7*	*8*
Levels								
1	A	A	B	B	C	C	D	D
2	A	A	B	B	C	C	D	D
3	A	A	B	B	C	C	D	D
4	A	A	B	B	C	C	D	D

SCHEME 2

	Squares							
	1	*2*	*3*	*4*	*5*	*6*	*7*	*8*
Levels								
1	A	A	B	B	A	A	B	B
2	B	B	A	A	B	B	A	A
3	C	C	D	D	C	C	D	D
4	D	D	C	C	D	D	C	C

SCHEME 3

	Squares							
	1	*2*	*3*	*4*	*5*	*6*	*7*	*8*
Levels								
1	A	A	B	B	C	C	D	D
2	D	A	A	B	B	C	C	D
3	D	D	A	A	B	B	C	C
4	C	D	D	A	A	B	B	C

SCHEME 4

	Squares							
	1	*2*	*3*	*4*	*5*	*6*	*7*	*8*
Levels								
1	A	C	B	D	C	A	D	B
2	C	A	D	B	A	C	B	D
3	D	B	A	C	B	D	C	A
4	B	D	C	A	D	B	A	C

In each level the odd-numbered squares are dug before the even-numbered ones. Schemes 1, 2 and 3 are all likely to produce strong correlation between worker's bias and true distribution of artefacts. Scheme 4 is systematically designed to reduce this.

range of objects recovered, smaller objects only being recovered by the more diligent. This can seriously affect quantitative data on a site such as a stone chipping floor, where, depending on the nature of the raw material, the percentage of waste material recovered from a unit may be almost entirely dependent on the amount of time spent searching through the loosened deposit. In situations such as this a considerable improvement in the data can be obtained by using a *threshold system*. This requires strict application and can more easily be done in the workroom than during excavation. A specific threshold, defined in terms of size, weight, length or similar criterion, is laid down, and all specimens that fall below this threshold are discarded. If an object that falls below the threshold is of interest, it may be retained but must be rigorously excluded from any quantitative analysis. The ideal value for a threshold is one for which an object with a higher value is certain to be recovered, and an object with a lower value is certain to be of no importance. This situation will never obtain in practice and a value must be chosen as a compromise between the two requirements based on the nature of the objects under study. An estimate of the size range of objects that are frequently not recovered may be obtained by systematic spot checking of loads of deposit after excavation or after sieving, and this estimate may be used to help fix the threshold value. A threshold system may be particularly useful in the analysis of microlithic industries where waste material grades down to the microscopic, or large quantities of pottery, particularly where the latter are to be used for any kind of analysis based on association of decorative features (see for example Daniels, 1965).

Sorting and analytical procedures

It is in the analysis and sorting of artefactual material that good design is at once most important and most widely applicable. This is because it is during this phase that the greatest subjectivity and bias is injected into the data, and also because there is a greater flexibility of procedure than in excavation. The chief difficulty lies less with measurement, as in the example already given, than in sorting artefacts into categories or types. Two apparently separate questions arise, in both of which the answers are likely to be biased. In the first place we ask 'Is this artefact a specimen of Type A?', but lying behind this is the more problematical question 'What constitutes a Type A artefact?' The latter question may be easy to answer in the case of coins or factory-made pottery, but becomes much more difficult for stone implements and hand-made pottery produced by many independent potters. I have given

218

elsewhere (Daniels, 1967, 1968) my reasons for regarding types as generated by the assemblage that is being analysed and for stating that 'It is therefore fundamentally improper to classify an assemblage of artefacts from one site on the basis of the type sets contained in the assemblage of another site'.

Thus, in general, and in the absence of further assumptions about the nature of the material being studied, the first stage in the analysis of an assemblage must be the establishment of categories into which it is to be sorted. Ideally these categories must be so defined that two observers sorting the same material would assign the same artefacts to the same categories, and that the same observer will always assign the same artefact to the same category. It may be instructive here to bear in mind the results obtained by two successive teams of American radiologists in attempts to define reproducible classificatory terms for the description of pulmonary shadows in tuberculosis (Yerushalmy, 1969). Amongst the experiments carried out by the first group was an investigation into the agreement between pairs of observers in the classificatory use of twelve descriptive terms. Out of these twelve terms, only two showed agreements of over 60% and in only four cases did agreements occur more than twice as often as would be expected by chance. The second group, classifying pairs of films taken on the same patient into the categories 'better', 'no change' and 'worse', found that two observers disagreed with each other in about one third of the cases and the same observer, on repeating the observation, disagreed with himself in about one fifth of the cases. It is difficult to accept that skilled observers, having previously reached agreement on the criteria to be applied, can have such a high degree of disagreement in actual classification. Any expert challenged on this score in his own particular field may well feel that his own hard-won expertise is being called in question and that any disagreement between himself and another observer is due to the lesser competence of the other observer. It is salutary here to read the words of a member of the second group of radiologists: 'The members of the Committee confess that when they were on the sidelines, viewing the attempts of the first group, their results appeared incredible. At least two members of the second group had felt that *they* knew whether a lesion was homogeneous or not, whether it was fuzzy or sharply defined, and what its shape was, but experience awakened them' (Garland, 1949). Admittedly the results quoted concern X-ray films and not archaeological material, but the present writer is convinced, after bitter experience, that the situation with artefacts, though perhaps different in degree, is not different in kind. It is with this in mind that stress is laid on the rigorous use of design in the process of classification.

219

The goals to be aimed at during analysis and sorting in the workroom may be summarized as follows:

(i) Each subset of the data should, as far as possible, be subjected to the same treatment.

(ii) Where treatments cannot be kept constant, their application should be randomized so that there is no correlation between varying treatment and different data subsets.

(iii) Categories into which material is to be sorted should arise from and be defined for the total data set under study, so that subsets can be validly compared.

(iv) The decision as to which category an object should be assigned must not be affected by knowledge of the data subset to which it belongs.

A scheme for analysing large quantities of material along these lines was given in Daniels (1966) and essentially the same outline is given here, though more generally and with greater flexibility. The discussion is concerned throughout with processing of material in the workroom rather than in the field, since there are added difficulties in designing a sorting operation to take place at the same time as the excavation. Despite the value of a preliminary evaluation of material as it is recovered, only when excavation is completed can the assemblage be treated as a whole, and measures taken to prevent correlation between the order of sorting and the age of artefacts.

Before actual sorting begins a set of categories to which artefacts are to be assigned must be established. Ideally this should result from an examination of the total assemblage and determination of modal tendencies within it. Categories are then defined by suitable placing of boundaries between the various modes. This process may be achieved by somewhat lengthy statistical means or intuitively following close study of the material. In either case, though the modal tendency is of cultural interest, it is the boundaries between modes that must be clearly defined, since these are the criteria that will decide whether an artefact should be placed in one category or another. Where the assemblage is at all large, examination of the whole assemblage in order to define categories is out of the question. In this case a valid estimate of the modal tendencies in the assemblage can be obtained by sampling. Again, ideally this should be so arranged that each object in the assemblage has an equal and independent chance of being included in what may be called the *type series sample*. Since this requires the counting and individual labelling of every object in the assemblage it will usually be impracticable, and a compromise may be obtained by arranging that the material from each stratigraphic unit (S.U.) should have an equal chance of selection (an S.U. is the smallest unit volume of deposit from which the finds are treated as a single assemblage). Since suspected cultural units will have been broken down into a number of S.U.s in order to provide estimates of within-level or within-period variation, the type series sample should then contain a small proportion of the material from each culturally or functionally distinguishable part of the deposit. The total size of the type series sample will be arbitrarily determined but should be large enough to give reasonable representation to culturally distinct subsets of the data and to give an acceptable chance of detecting genuine modal tendencies.

Clearly, in a large number of cases the theoretically desirable determination of types arising simply from the assemblage under study will be impracticable and modified in practice by the use of categories that have been established for some other body of material. If this is done it is well to remember the assumptions entailed. Any artefacts or group of artefacts so classified must be assumed to be a sample drawn from the same field as that for which the category was originally defined (Daniels, 1968).

When the categories have been determined, the question of controlling bias during the sorting process must be faced. If an observer is aware of the stratigraphical origin of material that he is classifying, his decisions on the categories to which objects should be assigned must in part be influenced by his expectations. These include not only specific expectations such as the greater likelihood of finding ground stone axes towards the later part of a West African Late Stone Age sequence, but also more general ones such as the likelihood of finding some form of consistent time-related change among the proportions of artefacts assigned to different categories. One way of partially eliminating this bias is to assign to each S.U. a different code number, chosen at random, and to replace the normal labels showing stratigraphic origin by labels showing only the code number, before sorting takes place. Data are then recorded under the code number and subsequently reinstated in their stratigraphic context when the analysis is complete. Such a process needs extreme care to avoid the introduction of gross errors but is perfectly practical with a small amount of methodical assistance from some worker other than the observer actually doing the classification. Indeed it represents a compromise between what is practically possible and the theoretical requirement that each piece, not each S.U., should come anonymously before the observer.

We have already seen, when discussing excavation, the dangers of giving special treatment to a particular subset of the data, and this should also be avoided as far as possible during analysis and sorting. Thus the consolidation of poorly fired sherds generally changes their appearance. If this consolidation is carried out selectively before sorting, it may, where all the sherds are also badly weathered, seriously distort subsequent classification into fabrics if this is done without chemical or physical analyses. Working conditions are a variable which can usually be controlled and which may seriously influence results. From work performed at the University of Ibadan it would seem that extremes of temperature and humidity make for generally unreliable work by the observer, and, perhaps more importantly, that changes in the lighting conditions may lead to considerable changes in classifications obtained. It is therefore regarded as essential that sorting should be done under constant adequate lighting, and in the tropics in air-conditioned rooms. However, the most important way in which treatment may vary is by altering the identity of the observer. Ideally the whole operation should be performed by one observer, but for large assemblages this may not be possible, and if more than one observer is involved a system must be devised for assigning S.U.s to observers at random.

One important way in which the treatment of the material can change is through progressive change in the real criteria used by observers. However closely the criteria for assigning objects to categories are defined, the real criteria used by any one observer at a particular time will be only an approximation to the definition. These real criteria will, particularly with unfamiliar material and during long analyses, tend to change, either continuously in one direction, or by drifting back and forth. If the material is sorted in stratigraphic and presumably chronological order, the changes in criteria will be correlated with the time-related changes that are being studied. It is for this reason that any irreversible sorting process carried out at the same time as excavation may be dangerous, since the sorting order is determined by the order of excavation and this in turn to a large extent by the order of deposition. Accordingly, even when observers are ignorant of the stratigraphic origin of material, it is also essential to randomize the order in which material from the various S.U.s is sorted. Since each S.U. has already been randomly labelled with a unique code number, sorting can proceed in the order of the code numbers. The effect of this is shown in Table 5.3, which gives, in uncoded form, the beginning of a randomized sorting schedule for four observers sorting material from ten squares each with ten levels. If there was also material from particular stratigraphic features these too would have been assigned code numbers and included in the randomization of the sorting order. The actual schedule presented to the observers would of course show the code numbers not the stratigraphic origin.

The reliability and consistency of the sorting process can be assessed by repeat sorting of selected S.U.s by the same observer or by different observers. If the inconsistency is so large as to obscure the differences that are being studied, some form of remedial sorting of particular categories of material may be undertaken. While this can never make the results as reliable as consistent sorting of the total assemblage, it may nevertheless be valuable when resources of time, money and manpower are short. If such sorting is

TABLE 5.3. *Beginning of a sorting schedule for four observers sorting material from ten squares, each with ten levels*

Observer A			Observer B	
1. Square 10	Level	9	Square 4	Level 10
2. Square 7	Level	9	Square 7	Level 4
3. Square 9	Level	2	Square 8	Level 1
4. Square 3	Level	8	Square 3	Level 9
5. Square 1	Level	2	Square 8	Level 2
etc.			etc.	

Observer C		Observer D	
1. Square 5	Level 7	Square 5	Level 1
2. Square 9	Level 9	Square 5	Level 5
3. Square 1	Level 1	Square 6	Level 6
4. Square 1	Level 5	Square 1	Level 10
5. Square 2	Level 2	Square 4	Level 5
etc.		etc.	

The order in which material from S.U.s is sorted, and the observer to which each is assigned, have both been randomized. The observers will sort the material under code numbers, in ignorance of the stratigraphic position.

undertaken, considerable care must be exercised not to reintroduce the bias that the original sorting procedure was designed to combat. The safest procedure is to re-examine every artefact assigned to a particular category, again without reference to its stratigraphic origin, a condition that requires that specimens should be labelled with the code number of their S.U., not with their stratigraphic origin. Re-examination of material in this way is not a substitute for proper design of the original sorting procedure since the original classification will doubtless influence the decisions made during the remedial sorting.

Measurements are in general less vulnerable to correlated bias than classification procedures, and it may be sufficient to impose some form of quality control to keep errors within an acceptable margin and to provide an estimate of the error which is included in the measurements. For example, one of the measurements made on the pottery from Iwo Eleru (Shaw, 1969) was the maximum thickness of sherds measured to the nearest millimetre. This is liable to error not only in the reading of a scale but also in estimating the position of the thickest part of the sherd. Four groups of potsherds, with mean maximum thicknesses between 6·0 and 7·0 mm, were selected at random for remeasurement without reference to the original figures. For each sherd, the best estimate of the true maximum thickness was taken to be

TABLE 5.4. *Estimates of error in measuring maximum thickness of potsherds*

Group	I	2	3	4	Total
Number of sherds	16	17	6	16	55
Mean error (mm)	−0·13	0·21	0·33	−0·13	0·03
$\sigma(e)$ (mm)	0·61	0·37	0·50	0·43	0·48

Four randomly selected groups of sherds from Iwo Eleru were remeasured. The error is defined as the difference between the first measurement and the best estimate, while $\sigma(e)$ is the standard deviation of the errors.

the mean of the two independent observations, and the estimated error on the first measurement was therefore the deviation of the first measurement from the mean of the two measurements. The standard deviation of errors (denoted by $\sigma(e)$) for each group and for the total sample was then calculated. The results are shown in Table 5.4, from which it becomes clear that some two thirds of the individual measurements may be expected to deviate from the best estimate by an amount between +0·5 and −0·5 mm, a deviation no larger than that entailed by measuring to the nearest millimetre. This appeared to be acceptable for the purposes for which the measurements were required, but a value of $\sigma(e)$ as high as 1·0 mm for any one group would have suggested the necessity of taking some steps towards making the measuring procedure more precise.

Writing and publishing procedures
It would be out of place here, and beyond the author's competence, to consider this field in any detail. It is, however, important to recognize that errors,

usually gross, arising during this stage can affect the final output of the research process, just as they can during the earlier stages. This is particularly true of quantitative data, where redundancy is so much lower than in verbal description. Quite apart from the occurrence of misprints in the published text, the process of copying figures from one data listing to another and the modification or inversion of data formats to provide the best form for publication afford numerous opportunities for gross errors. It is frequently desirable to build in a degree of redundancy where none is inherent in the figures being copied. One useful method is to enter row and column totals on the original listing, even where, as in Table 5.4 of this chapter, they would have no real meaning. These totals are copied on to the new listing, and if recalculation of the totals from the new listing produces no discrepancies, the totals are then discarded.

BALANCING INFORMATION AND RESOURCES

The procedures considered so far have been aimed at eliminating the effects of bias and obtaining generally greater precision in the data. This can only be obtained at the cost of a greater expenditure of resources, largely in terms of time, though the extra expenditure involved varies from one part of the research process to another, and is nowhere as formidable a time-consumer as it may seem at first sight. One of the aims has been to obtain a great increase in the reliability of information while making a small increase in expenditure of resources. The converse approach may also be used to advantage, by attempting to make a considerable reduction in expenditure while incurring only a small reduction in the amount and reliability of information obtained. This might be termed a policy of *planned information loss*, and is, in effect, employed by every excavator who only partially excavates a site, discards undecorated sherds or in any way elects to refrain from making a particular set of observations. The manner and degree to which such a policy should be followed must depend both on the historical or palaeosociological questions being asked and on the specific numerical or statistical analyses to which quantitative data will be submitted. The demands of a rescue excavation differ from those of the detailed recovery of the living pattern from an Upper Palaeolithic open camp site. Investigation of the history of a single medieval town will require a different balance from a project to provide a broad framework for 2000 years of Iron Age history in a little-studied area of Africa. Whatever balance we are trying to strike, one cardinal principle remains constant. While we may accept an increased amount of random noise in our data, or even the total loss of some of them, the planning must prevent the introduction of the very bias the foregoing procedures were designed to eliminate.

The clearest way in which information may safely and economically be lost is through sampling instead of studying whole populations. If an excavation produces a large body of artefacts, there is no particular virtue in classifying every single artefact. Even the total assemblage recovered is itself only a sample, biased by depositional factors, from the population we would like to be able to study. The selection of a sample from the assemblage must fulfil two simple requirements. It must be representative of the assemblage from which it is drawn, and it must be large enough to allow comparisons of samples to be made with the reasonable confidence that comparisons of the assemblages would yield similar conclusions. Thus during sorting and analysis it may be possible to decide, from estimates of the frequency of different categories of artefact, on a sample size large enough to give an acceptably reliable characterization of the assemblage from which it is drawn. Then if any S.U. contains more than the desired sample size it need not be sorted *in toto*, but can instead be sampled. In practice it will only be economical to sample if the number of artefacts in an S.U. considerably exceeds the desired sample size. Thus if a sample of 2000 pieces from a stone industry is considered satisfactory, it might be advisable to sort *in toto* S.U.s containing up to 3000 pieces and to take samples of approximately 2000 pieces from any S.U. containing more than 3000. As already stated, true random sampling requires the enumeration and unique labelling of each object in the assemblage, and a systematic pseudo-random sample will usually represent the best compromise. This is easily obtained by 'sowing' the objects, one at a time, into the squares of a numbered sampling board marked with a rectangular grid. The sample is obtained by collecting all the objects from a set of regularly spaced columns, the spacing being determined by the required sample size and the total number of pieces in the S.U.

There would also seem to be room for the application of sampling theory in improving the expenditure/information balance of some types of excavation. Where the purpose of the excavation is simply to provide information about the frequency, morphological characteristics and age range of certain predetermined classes of artefacts, a small test excavation might yield sufficiently good estimates of the frequency of these artefacts in the deposit to determine an optimum size for the main excavation. Another approach might be made through the use of sequential methods in which data are accumulated as they are obtained, without previously fixing the sample size (see for example Wetherill, 1966), though subsequent sorting would also be necessary in order to eliminate bias.

THE LARGER VIEW

So far we have considered an archaeological research project as consisting of a single excavation and the subsequent procedures leading up to final publication. In fact hardly any project can be as isolated as this and even a single excavation report requires historical reconstruction based on comparison with other sites and other artefacts. At the other end of the scale are projects in which excavation is not involved at all and artefacts of a limited class or classes and from many different contexts are compared with each other.

When we come to consider comparisons between the results of different excavations, the error sources we have considered become even more important. Within a single excavation a certain degree of uniformity in excavation and analytical procedure is to be expected: between two different excavations conducted by different archaeologists a much lower degree of uniformity must be assumed, even when both are following good archaeological procedure. This lack of uniformity may be such as to make quantitative comparison of published data almost impossible. A case in point is that of three archaeologists who worked in fairly close contact and reasonable agreement with one another on the Iron Age of southern Zambia. In classifying decorative techniques on pottery, Fagan (1967) distinguishes between 'channelling', 'grooving' and 'incision'. Daniels (1965) distinguishes between 'channelling' and 'grooving or incision', while Phillipson (1968) distinguishes between 'grooving' and 'incision' and regards the distinction between 'channelling' and 'grooving' as tenuous. Since one or more of these techniques occur with high frequency in many southern Zambian Iron Age sites, meaningful quantitative comparisons of frequencies at different sites become extremely difficult. This is a case in which the difference in procedure has been made relatively explicit: in many cases similar differences must exist without being made explicit, so that apparently useful quantitative comparisons are in fact comparing something other than the original material.

Thus, in the larger view, problems of differences in procedure and terminology are added, while the original problems of bias and noise are in no way reduced. The answer must lie in a similar application of design to reduce or eliminate the error sources, and this implies that a strictly valid comparison can only be made between sites that have been subjected to the same overall procedures, whose artefacts have passed through the same classificatory or

227

observational net, and, above all, the elements of which have been *jointly* treated by the same controls and randomization techniques. In other words, the safeguards necessary for the valid comparison of two sites are no different from those required for the valid comparison of different levels at the same site.

The only framework within which this appears to be possible is that of the unified project with specific boundaries in time and space and carried out under the same overall direction. Within this framework procedures could satisfactorily be standardized, and a proper design formulated which would take account of the biases of different excavators and analysts. The artefactual material from such a project would then be treated initially, for the establishment of categories and randomization of the sorting order, as a single assemblage like that from a single site.

Within such a unified time/area project, designed as a single 'experiment', quantitative methods could be applied with precision and with confidence that historical reality was being reflected in the results. In the absence of some such design, there is a grave danger of these methods reflecting not historical reality, but the procedural differences and bias of particular archaeologists at a particular time.

References

ALEXANDER, J. (1970) *The Directing of Archaeological Excavations*. London: Baker.

DANIELS, S. G. H. (1965) Statistical determination of pottery types from the recently excavated site at Dambwa, near Livingstone, Northern Rhodesia. In SNOWBALL, G. J. (ed.) *Science and Medicine in Central Africa*. Oxford: Pergamon.

DANIELS, S. G. H. (1966) An operational scheme for the analysis of large assemblages of archaeological material. *Archaeometry*, **9**, 151–4.

DANIELS, S. G. H. (1967) Comments on the terminology and typology recommendations of the Burg-Wartenstein Conference (1965). *West African Archaeological Newsletter*, **7**, 15–22.

DANIELS, S. G. H. (1968) The genesis of types: a logical model. *West African Archaeological Newsletter*, **10**, 43–7.

FAGAN, B. M. (1967) *Iron Age Cultures in Zambia*, vol. I. London: Chatto.

FISHER, R. A. (1960) *The Design of Experiments*. 7th ed. London: Oliver & Boyd.

GARLAND, L. H. (1949) On the scientific evaluation of diagnostic procedures. *Radiology*, **52**, 309.

HOLE, F. and SHAW, M. (1967) Computer analysis of chronological seriation. *Rice University Studies*, **53** (3), 1–166.

JEWELL, P. A. and DIMBLEBY, G. W. (1966) The experimental earthwork on Overton Down, Wiltshire, England: the first four years. *Proceedings of the Prehistoric Society*, **32**, 313–42.

KLEIN, R. G. (1969) The Mousterian of European Russia. *Proceedings of the Prehistoric Society*, **35**, 77–111.

KLIMA, B. (1963) *Dolní Vestoniče*. Prague.

MAXWELL, A. E. (1961) *Analysing Qualitative Data*. London: Methuen.

MYERS, O. H. (1958) 'Abka re-excavated. *Kush*, **6**, 131–43.

PHILLIPSON, D. W. (1968) The Early Iron Age in Zambia – regional variants and some tentative conclusions. *Journal of African History*, **9**, (2), 191–211.

PITT RIVERS, J. A. (1887) *Excavations in Cranborne Chase*, vol. I.

SAMPSON, C. G. (1968) *The Middle Stone Age Industries of the Orange River Scheme Area*. Memoir of the National Museum, Bloemfontein, No. 4.

SHAW, T. (1966) Experimental archaeology. *West African Archaeological Newsletter*, **4**, 38–9.

SHAW, T. (1969) Archaeology in Nigeria. *Antiquity*, **43**, 187–99.

SHAW, T. (1970) *Igbo-Ukwu*, vol. I. London: Faber.

WETHERILL, G. B. (1966) *Sequential Methods in Statistics*. London: Methuen.

WHEELER, R. M. (1954) *Archaeology from the Earth*. London: Oxford University Press.

YAMANE, T. (1967) *Statistics: An Introductory Analysis*. 2nd ed. New York: Harper & Row.

YERUSHALMY, J. (1969) The statistical assessment of the variability in observer perception and description of roentgenographic pulmonary shadows. *Radiologic Clinics of North America*, **7**, 381–92.

6

A model for classification and typology[1]

J. N. HILL and R. K. EVANS

University of California, Los Angeles, U.S.A.

The 'typological debate' in archaeology, especially in American archaeology, has been conducted for several decades now, and the already voluminous literature continues to accumulate (e.g. Clarke, 1968, pp. 187–91; Sabloff and Smith, 1969; Rouse, 1970a, 1970b; Dunnell, 1971; Whallon, 1971). In the meantime, archaeologists continue to carry out fieldwork and continue to sort their materials into types. Some of these classifications are found to be useful and are used in analytical studies, while others, it seems, are not necessarily designed to be useful and are viewed as ends in themselves (Clark, 1952, p. 1).

Much of the literature dealing with archaeological classification (especially the programmatic statements) is confused, and must be confusing to the reader. Major issues have been confused with minor issues and neither have been clearly communicated. As a result, there has been (and still is) argument over a number of questions regarding the nature and significance of types. We are all familiar, for example, with the following important and highly related (if often imprecisely stated) issues:

(1) Are types 'real' or are they 'invented' by the archaeologist to suit his own purposes?

(2) Is there a continuum of variability among artefacts (and other things), or are there non-random clusters of attributes to be discovered?

(3) Is there a single, 'best' type division or classification of a given body of materials, or can there be many equally 'good' divisions?

(4) Can we formulate standardized types?

(5) Do types in some sense represent 'basic data'?

(6) Do we need more or fewer types?

(7) What should our types mean? Should they represent ideas, preferences, customs, or mental templates (i.e. something in the mind of the maker), function, chronology, something else, or all of these?

231

We do not expect to answer all these questions to the satisfaction of every-one, but we do hope to provide a general model[2] that will be useful in thinking about the nature and significance of types. As a part of this we also hope to stimulate thinking about *why* we classify in the first place. This is a question that is seldom raised and has received little attention in the literature, but we believe that it is of primary importance. Unless we fully understand the rationale underlying our class or type divisions, we are not likely to create classifications that will be very useful to us or to others.

In fact, the point of our discussion is that useful classifications depend on antecedent research problems and hypotheses, and that classification should not be divorced from this context. We think that when this point is fully understood the answers to most of the above questions will become obvious and the 'typological debate' will be a thing of the past.

While much of our discussion concerns the classification of ceramics and other artefacts, we consider that it is applicable to the formulation of types or classes of *any* sort, whether they be types of settlement systems, types of economy, types of residence patterns, or even types of processes. The ideas apply as much to the divisions of the world made by ethnologists and other social scientists (in fact all scientists) as they do to the typological divisions of the archaeologist.

Some definitions

Before proceeding with our discussion of classification, it is necessary to discuss briefly the process of classification and to define the terms 'class' and 'type'. Classification is simply an extension of the recognition of differences and similarities among phenomena. Those materials, events or processes that are more similar than different, according to the classifier, are placed together into classes. This process involves the classifier's assessment of the degree of 'sameness' among the phenomena (Harris, 1964). '*Classification* is the process of putting objects, events, and so forth, into classes by virtue of properties which they possess in common' (Benjamin, 1965, p. 62).

As numerous authors have pointed out, classification is a tool of analysis. It is carried out for the purpose of bringing order to a set of observations. This process occurs at all times and at various levels of consciousness, from the everyday ordering of items or events, to the scientific ordering of phenomena. Phenomena may be ordered by a person's mental processes, with little or no conscious realization of why they are so ordered; or, at the other end of the scale, they may be ordered according to specific properties which have been consciously selected by scientific deductive method (Oliver, 1951; Harris, 1964; Haggett, 1966). The advantages of the latter method are discussed below.

The meanings of the terms 'class' and 'type' must be made clear at the outset. The term 'class' is a generic term referring to *any* division of materials or events into groupings based on similarities and differences. Any such group is called a 'class'. The term 'type', however, has a more special meaning. It refers to the division of an assemblage of materials or events into groupings based on the conscious recognition of dimensions of formal variation possessed by these phenomena. A 'type', then, is a group that has been formed on the basis of a consistent patterning of attributes of the materials or events, and it is distinguished from other types, which are different patterns of attributes (Krieger, 1944, 1960, p. 143; Spaulding, 1953; Sackett, 1966).

Thus, a 'type' is a specific 'class' of phenomena, which is characterized by a non-random cluster of attributes.[3] Groupings based on a sorting of a single attribute dimension are not types. For example, a sorting of pottery vessels on the single attribute dimension of surface colour (e.g. black, white, red) would not produce different types of pots. If, however, the pottery vessels were simultaneously sorted for the attribute dimension of surface colour and some other attribute dimension (such as technique of decoration or capacity), the resulting groups could be considered as types (see Spaulding, 1953, and Sackett, 1966, for a complete discussion).

A traditional model

In order to fully appreciate the general model for classification we are proposing, it is important to look first at the most common traditional archaeological model – what we will call the 'empiricist' model. We think that the 'typological debate' stems, at least to some degree, from fundamental epistemological differences between this and the 'positivist' model. We present the empiricist model first in its most extreme form, and then make our qualifications later.

The empiricist view subscribes, at least implicitly, to the general empiricist school of philosophy (e.g. Hume, Mill and Bacon; cf. Fritz, 1968). This school holds to the metaphysical notion that all phenomena (including artefacts) have meanings or significance inherent in some sense within themselves. Each item has a single meaning, or very few meanings at most; and in archaeology it is the task of the archaeologist to discover these meanings. Each item that is excavated or observed is treated as a discrete unit carrying its own meaning

233

(cf. Thompson, 1958, pp. 1–5; Taylor, 1948, 1967, pp. 122, 143; Deetz, 1967). And usually these 'inherent' meanings are considered to be one of three things: ideas, customs or mental templates; functional meaning; or 'historical-index' meaning (cf. Taylor, 1948, 1967, pp. 95–100, esp. chs. 4 and 6; Steward, 1954; Ford, 1954b; Rouse, 1960, p. 317, 1965; Deetz, 1967; Hole and Heizer, 1969, pp. 300, 312, 328–9). It follows from this that the more items we recover, the more bits of knowledge we will have in hand, and the better our inferences about prehistoric societies will be (cf. Hill, Chapter 2 of this volume, and Fritz, 1968).

It further follows, in this view, that since our information or inferences are derived *from* the data (Thompson, 1958), we ought to gather our data *before* we make our inferences. This view has become almost a truism. It is said that we begin with data collection, then proceed to classification, and then to analysis and interpretation (see esp. Swartz, 1967, but also Hawkes, 1954; MacWhite, 1956; Willey and Phillips, 1958, pp. 1–7; Rouse, 1962, pp. 86–7; Taylor, 1948, 1967, ch. 6; Hole and Heizer, 1969, pp. 124–6, 162, 206). By now the reader is familiar with the pros and cons of this general argument (cf. Adams, 1968).

What is important to note here is that, in this general methodological paradigm, classification comes most properly *before* analysis and interpretation. The reason should be obvious – we cannot analyse and interpret until we know what bits of information we have to work with! Since the items we recover are direct representations of knowledge (i.e. they 'contain' the inferences we will discover), it stands to reason that they should first be grouped or ordered in such a way as to make the information they contain more obvious. For example:

> Classification – which for the most part means identifying and naming artefacts – and a description of all data are basic to archaeological analysis. (Hole and Heizer, 1969, p. 167)

> The recognition and naming of types serve many purposes. First, as we have said, they are a means of introducing order or system into a varied assortment of objects. The array of archaeological materials recovered thus becomes capable of being understood and handled in a meaningful way. (Hole and Heizer, 1969, p. 168)

> If the behavioural regularities of societies are documented by means of ceramic and other schemes of classification, some of the laws of human behaviour which may exist will become apparent. (Gifford, 1960, p. 342)

Associated with this idea, of course, is the view that it would not be quite legitimate to make inferences before classifying the materials. It is frequently feared that such an approach would bias analysis and interpretation, and it might lead to unsubstantiated conclusions.

But given this view, what is the best way to order the materials? By what criteria can we establish an order, if not on the basis of preconceived ideas or tentative inferences? If we were to actually find an archaeologist who consciously subscribed to this extreme inductive research paradigm (and there are a few), he would probably argue that one simply classifies like with like – i.e. that one should consider all of the major characteristics of his artefacts, and place them into types accordingly (sometimes with the use of statistics) (cf. Rouse, 1970a, p. 10).

In short, he would look for the 'best' classificatory divisions possible, given the nature of the materials. And the 'best' usually turns out to be the most *obvious* classification. One would usually not, for example, group red pots possessing wide necks with white pots having narrow necks, any more than he would group dogs with giraffes! The categorizations here would be obvious. This attempt to find the best type divisions based on the most obvious characteristics is what Rouse calls 'taxonomic' classification (1960, p. 313), and it leads to what he calls 'analytical' types (1970a, p. 7), and to what Steward (1954) calls 'morphological' types, and Bakka (1968) calls 'empirical' types (in Rouse, 1970a, p. 10).

This approach to typology works, of course. It works because there are indeed differences among phenomena. As Spaulding (1953, 1954) eloquently pointed out, these differences are often intuitively obvious because the phenomena involved possess different distinct clusters of attributes, which can be demonstrated to be statistically highly non-random. And good attribute clusters can often even be generated when attribute clustering is not intuitively obvious. So in this sense, the attribute clusters the empiricist archaeologist (or any archaeologist) discovers in his data are indeed 'real' – we will not pursue that particular old issue further (see esp. Brew, 1946, pp. 48–9; Ford, 1954a, b, c; Spaulding, 1953, 1954).

The point is simply that the empiricist metaphysic and epistemology considered above often leads the archaeologist into viewing his types as *the* types – as if there were no other equally good types or class divisions he could make with his materials. His types become phenomenological or existential types, and they become canonized in the literature as 'truth'; and once canonized, they serve as frameworks into which new data are pigeon-holed:

Once types have been established . . . they may be used to identify new

235

artefacts without the necessity of actually grouping the artefacts into classes. One need only determine that the new artefacts have the modes comprising a certain type and then apply the name of that type ... to identify an unknown artefact, one need only trace it down through the key by means of its modes. (Rouse, 1960, p. 317; cf. also Colton and Hargrave, 1937, pp. 36–41; Colton, 1952, 1955a)

Many archaeologists seem, in fact, to have a propensity for wanting to develop single, all-purpose taxonomic systems, and then wanting to stick to them (Brew, 1946, p. 64).

Within such a taxonomic system each such type presumably contains (or is a manifestation of) one or more bits of information; and this information should, it is hoped, become apparent to the archaeologist once he divides his material into types and examines or analyses the results. It seems clear to us that if one subscribes to the empiricist metaphysic he *must* not only regard data collection as the starting point for research, but he must also regard the types he generates as somehow fixed, fundamental units of observation, upon which he can subsequently build his inferential structure. J. O. Brew pointed this out twenty-five years ago: 'The force of the [type] scheme itself produces a new type of archaeological conservatism, the conservatism of false reality. ... These schemes often lead us into what A. N. Whitehead calls the fallacy of misplaced concreteness' (Brew, 1946, p. 61). The types thus become, in essence, 'basic data', which do not often need to be questioned; the types are primary data, and only the inferences made from them (and subsequent to classification) are open to serious critique.

This entire discussion is, of course, somewhat of an overstatement. Even though there are archaeologists who subscribe to it in their programmatic statements (e.g. Swartz, 1967), we know of no archaeologist who really conforms in practice to the tenets of the empiricist model in its pure form. We think, in fact, that nearly all archaeologists devise their typologies with at least vague problems or tentative inferences in mind ahead of time; and we think these past and current typologies have, as a result, been useful (see for example Ford and Willey, 1949, p. 40). But we also believe that the research problems governing the criteria for classificatory divisions have often been so vague as to be virtually unconscious; and this has permitted the empiricist model for classification to achieve credence, both as an idea and to some extent in practice.

Some examples

It is important that we select a few examples to illustrate our primary points. We will thus set the stage for the argument that we should not pursue all-purpose, standardized typologies; if our types are to be maximally useful, they must vary with the specific problems and hypotheses we are interested in. We will argue that archaeological materials can be typed in many different ways, and have many different kinds of meanings. Before arguing this in detail, however, we must show that archaeologists actually *do* think of typologies as 'ideal', all-purpose or phenomenological, and that they *do* severely restrict the meanings they attach to their materials; in fact, they often do this quite unconsciously.

An examination of both the programmatic and empirical literature clearly supports our contention. Most authors do seem to assume that there is a 'best' typology inherent in their materials if they can but discover it. A relatively early example of this view is found in the American Southwest. The first Pecos Conference in 1927 developed a taxonomic scheme for pottery, which was modelled after the Linnaean system of biological taxonomy. Each discovered pottery type was to be given a binomial label, 'the first name to be indicative of the locality of highest development, the second a technically descriptive term . . .' (Kidder, 1927, p. 470). The 1930 Pecos Conference went even further and adopted the following scheme: 'Kingdom: artefacts; Phylum: ceramics; Class: pottery; Order: basic combination of paste and temper; Ware: basic surface colour after firing; Genus: surface treatment; Type or Subtype . . .' (Hargrave, 1932, p. 8). A 'key' was to be constructed, and sherds were to be identified as biologists identify plants and animals.

Each standard ceramic type in this and other Southwestern ceramic schemes was viewed as a cluster of *all* of the attributes that made it different from all other ceramics: '[A type] . . . has been defined by usage as the totality of characteristics which make a given ceramic group different from all others' (Kidder, 1931, pp. 21–2; cf. also Roberts, 1935, p. 24). And each such phenomenological type was to be reified with a standardized name – for example, Deadman's Black-on-white, Flagstaff Red, Jeddito Plain, etc. (cf. Kidder, 1927; Hargrave, 1935; Colton and Hargrave, 1937).

Thus types were viewed as so real and immutable that they did in fact become canonized; and they have, with minor modifications, persisted as the 'standard' types to this day (cf. Hargrave, 1932, 1935; Colton and Hargrave, 1937; Colton, 1942, 1952, 1955a, 1955b; Breternitz, 1968; McGregor, 1965). It has even been suggested that these 'natural types' have genetic relationships and actually evolve in a sense similar to evolution in animal species (cf. Krieger, 1944, p. 273).

Another early contribution to typology was made by Alex Krieger (1944), who presented what he called 'the typological method' (pp. 277, 283). He recognized the fact that artefacts possess non-random clusters of attributes, and are not simply a result of arbitrary divisions made by the archaeologist. On the other hand, it is clear that he regarded types resulting from his method as *the* best types – the 'true typological method' is one in which 'types are taken to be specific groupings of structural features [attributes] which have proved historical significance' (p. 273). And he argued that these were the kinds of types we all ought to discover, since they are the ones we can most profitably use in identifying cultures and tracing their 'histories' in space and time. He was thus saying that while one *can* create a number of different kinds of types with a given body of materials, there is really only one correct result (for any given specific region or culture).

Perhaps the best known and most widely used typological scheme that can serve as an example here is the 'type-variety' system of classification, which developed somewhat later (Wheat, Gifford and Wasley, 1958; Phillips, 1958; Gifford, 1960; Smith, Willey and Gifford, 1960; Sears, 1960). Like Krieger's work, this too was inspired by developments in the American Southwest; in fact, the initial intent of the type-variety system was to extend and modify the basic descriptive system of ceramic taxonomy that had already been developed in the Southwest. But it was also intended to apply to other areas of the world as well (Wheat, Gifford and Wasley, 1958, p. 34). This scheme originated primarily because a bewildering array of ceramics was being found in the Southwest, and it was observed that many of the types were so similar to one another that they were better considered as subtypes or varieties of the established types than as types in their own right. Wheat, Gifford and Wasley's scheme was based simply on the idea that each established type should (potentially) include a series of named 'varieties'. They coined the term 'type cluster' to refer to the 'type' and all of its varieties, and the term 'ceramic system' to refer to a group of type clusters. There were, in fact, four hierarchical levels of classification in the scheme: variety, type, type cluster, and ceramic system.

Even a casual reading of the type-variety literature will indicate the presumed and implied phenomenological nature of these categorizations. The scheme was implied to be the best (or at least most economical) scheme to use in ordering cultural reality; it was even suggested that ceramic classification be standardized with the scheme: 'Our concept of established types, each with

238

its own constellation of varieties, is outlined here to provide a standard method for identification and designation of varieties' (Wheat, Gifford and Wasley, 1958, p. 38).

This scheme has indeed been influential, as is indicated by the extremely widespread usage of it (in one form or another). One of the most recent examples of its application is seen in Sabloff and Smith (1969), in which the authors describe some of the benefits of using a combination of both typological analysis and modal analysis (taxonomic and analytic classifications) in ceramic analyses (cf. also Culbert (1965), Wallrath (1967) and Parsons (1967) for recent examples of the type-variety system in use).

Sabloff and Smith, using Mayan data as examples, present a modified type-variety scheme that they think is *best* for describing Mayan pottery; and they imply that it will be found useful elsewhere too: 'It is our belief that the type-variety system of ceramic analysis is *the best* classificatory method available today in southern Mesoamerica and perhaps in other areas as well' (1969, p. 283; italics ours). And they go on to say that the type-mode description they advocate should make it possible to present such useful ceramic descriptions that they will be found useful for nearly all kinds of analyses that might be proposed.[4]

> The presentation format just described makes it possible to use the ceramic material from Mayapan to develop *any sort of investigation* because it employs *all attributes* and has complete numerical counts and separations of counts into numerous *fundamental* categories. (Sabloff and Smith, 1969, p. 282; italics ours)
>
> ... one of the major aims of the method of presentation should be to provide the readers with sufficient data ... *for any approaches,* be they ones of intersite comparison or *total reanalysis* of the ceramic data, that they may care to take in future studies. (Sabloff and Smith, 1969, p. 280; italics ours)

Their scheme is also hierarchical, as has always been the case in the type variety system. And it is implied that each level of categorization is a natural or inherent kind of division which can be objectively distinguished (discovered) by the investigator – and each is reified with the assignment of a name (p. 281). The implication is that these types represent *the* types, and they are considered to represent 'basic data'.

It is probably fair to say that the type-variety system has pervaded almost all of American archaeology; while it has been refined on occasion, it is still regarded as the best way to describe ceramics (and perhaps other things as well).

As a further example, we turn away from classification schemes designed for ceramics or other artefacts, in order to illustrate our contention that the phenomenological view of typology extends even to the classification of 'cultures'. We have chosen to consider Willey and Phillips's 'historical-developmental' scheme, which they presented in two articles in *American Anthropologist* (Phillips and Willey, 1953; Willey and Phillips, 1955), and in their influential book, *Method and Theory in American Archaeology* (1958). We do this simply because the Willey and Phillips scheme is well known; we could equally well use their 'culture-historical integration' scheme, or single out almost any of the phase or stage schemes that have been devised before or since 1958.

The Willey and Phillips scheme was an attempt to synthesize American archaeology in terms of general stages of complexity, with a view to at least setting the stage for a future 'explanatory level' of analysis (which they had hoped to be able to reach; Willey and Phillips, 1958, pp. 1–7, 61). Without providing any details, it is sufficient to point out that an examination of New World data, together with some *a priori* problem interests, led them to construct a typology of New World cultural developments, in terms of the following stages: Lithic, Archaic, Formative, Classic, and Post Classic. They presented the scheme, and proceeded to place most New World prehistoric societies into one or another of these slots (or as close thereto as possible).

While Willey and Phillips did not intend this typology of societies to represent the *best* one to be had, many archaeologists since that time have viewed it as such, implicitly. In fact, many have organized their books and university courses in terms of this typology, or something else similar to it, with the implied idea that it is the best current way to 'synthesize' a broad and diverse range of data.

The same statement can be made with regard to Service's (1958) classificatory division of societies based on complexity. Service's 'Bands', 'Tribes', 'Chiefdoms', 'Primitive States' and 'Archaic Civilizations' were clearly considered to represent the 'best' typology of societies. This is indicated when he points out that his book was intended to present 'a sample of *the* major types of non-Western cultures' (1958, p. x; italics ours). In his preface, he asks the following rhetorical questions: 'What are the major types [of societies]? What are the most striking ways in which cultures differ?' (p. x). He then proceeds to present the types, which were regarded as stages in cultural evolution. He felt that the evolutionary changes represented by the classification were 'readily apparent, and make the best criteria for evolutionary status' (p. xviii). While he did not regard this as the *only* typology of societies, he clearly saw it as the *best* one, assuming that one is interested in cultural evolution.

We can make the same kind of criticism of any of the so-called culture classifications. It also applies to the Pecos Classification (Kidder, 1927; McGregor, 1965, pp. 63–73) and the McKern system (McKern, 1939), and to all of our areal or spatial classifications. It applies to Murdock's (1949) classification of residence and descent, to Sonneville-Bordes's (1960) classificatory divisions of the Upper Palaeolithic, and to the classification of culture-contact situations (Willey, 1956), as well as other processes; also, of course, it applies to the classification of the non-ceramic artefacts, features and settlement patterns recovered by the archaeologist. In all of these cases (and most others), types tend to be viewed as immutable realities constituting the best types; and these types are regarded as basic data, the building blocks for inference. For some reason, this seems to be true even in those cases in which investigators or theoreticians explicitly deny that such is intended.

Types tend to be viewed not only as basic, all-purpose data, but as advancements in knowledge, in themselves (since they somehow represent cultural reality). It seems to be implied that the more 'correct' our standard types are, the more knowledge we will have gained about cultures – and it is further implied that classification is itself a primary method for gaining knowledge. If this were true, of course, it would be easy for us to understand the continuing desire of many archaeologists to develop standard, all-purpose typological schemes, as suggested by Hole and Heizer (1969, p. 179): 'In spite of archaeologists' traditional preoccupation with classification, a universally accepted system has never been devised. Until one is developed, archaeology will continue to be plagued by descriptions that are not comparable with one another.'

We think, at this point, that we have adequately demonstrated that types are often regarded phenomenologically. But it is also important to briefly document the fact that they are usually assigned severely restricted meaning – almost as if these meanings were actually inherent in the materials, or assumed without question.

Of course, some typologies are consciously assigned no meaning at all – they are simply 'morphological', 'taxonomic' or 'descriptive' types (cf. Krieger 1944, p. 275; Rouse, 1970b, p. 9), designed largely to bring some order to the data. Rouse (1970b, p. 9) suggests that such types are 'the most elementary kind, since . . . [they are] based solely on form'. Their meanings are rarely discussed in the scientific reporting (cf. Sabloff and Smith, 1969, p. 283).

But most types are assigned at least implicit meaning, and the most common assumed meaning is 'mental template' meaning. Rouse (1939) was one of the earliest to raise the issue of whether or not we are ultimately seeking types that represent ideas and concepts in the minds of the makers of archaeological materials; and he concluded in the affirmative: 'Types are stylistic patterns, to which the artisan tries to make his completed artefacts conform. Modes are community-wide standards which influence the behaviour of the artisan as he makes the artefacts' (Rouse, 1939, p. 15). Others certainly shared this view (e.g., Byers and Johnson, 1940, p. 33; Krieger, 1944, p. 278, 1960):

> Each type should approximate as closely as possible that combination of mechanical and aesthetic executions which formed a definite structural pattern in the minds of a number of workers, who attained this pattern with varying degrees of success and interpretation. (Krieger, 1944, p. 278)

> It is therefore the task of the analyst . . . to recover, if possible, the mental patterns which lay behind these manifold works, the changes in patterns which occurred . . . and the source of such changes. (Krieger, 1944, p. 272)

An even more forceful presentation of this view was given by Ford (1954a, 1954b). To him, types were a *result* of culture, not culture itself; types were reflections of mental templates, and in fact this was the *only* meaning they had to him: 'These arrangements of wood, bamboo and grass are of interest to the ethnologist [and archaeologist] solely because they illustrate the aborigine's ideas as to the proper way to construct dwellings' (1954b, p. 47). Types were thus considered to inform us about the 'shared ideas' of the people in question (Ford, 1954a, 1954b).

The type-variety literature also emphasizes this view, although the view is often implicit (cf. Wheat, Gifford, and Wasley, 1958). Gifford (1960) explicitly said that types reflect norms; 'varieties' were regarded as individual or small group deviations from the norms, while the 'type' reflected the norms themselves. 'In this regard, the scheme of classification discussed approaches a definition of ceramic value system which pertains to any given archaeological culture. In other words, when recognizing and defining types, the analyst is describing the material manifestations "of preferred paths of behaviour that take their direction from varying concepts of the desirable (Kluckhohn, 1958, p. 473)"' (Gifford, 1960, p. 343).

While this normative view is not explicitly espoused in Sabloff and Smith's recent article (1969), the authors do subscribe to both a 'typological' and

242

'modal' analysis; and it seems likely that they agree with Rouse's views as to the normative meaning of modes (Rouse, 1939, 1960, 1970a, 1970b). But, in any event, it is clear that most theoreticians and users of the type variety system (and others as well) have at least implicitly shared the normative view. Rouse restated the view, again explicitly, in 1960 and 1970:

> By the term 'mode' is meant any standard, concept, or custom which governs the behaviour of the artisans of a community which they hand down from generation to generation, and which may spread from community to community over considerable distance. (Rouse, 1939)
>
> Such modes will be reflected in the artefacts as attributes which conform to a community's standards, which express its concepts, or which reveal its customary ways of manufacturing and using artefacts. Analytic classification focuses on these attributes and, through them, attempts to get at the standards, concepts, and customs themselves. (Rouse, 1960, p. 313)

> In effect . . . each type represents the artisans' and users' conception of a kind of artefact, while each mode represents their conception of a kind of feature. (Rouse, 1970a, p. 9)

These quotations represent only a small fraction of those that can be found in the literature, of course. Other relatively recent and notable statements that forcefully espouse the view include Smith (1962), Deetz (1967), Clarke (1968, pp. 135, 227) and Hole and Heizer (1969, pp. 172, 328).

Another primary meaning commonly attached to 'types' is time-space or historical-index meaning. Ordinarily, in fact, both the normative meaning and the historical-index meaning go hand in hand in the most frequent understanding of types. The basic idea is that types have normative or ideational meaning, and thus can be used in *identifying* prehistoric ethnic groups – or 'peoples', as Rouse (1965) calls them. They can also be used, then, in tracing spatial and temporal distributions of peoples, including their migrations and origins. And at the same time, since types have this cultural 'reality', they are useful in establishing chronologies.

> Ware characteristics are thus fundamental and can be traced in time and space as peoples moved from one region to another. Type characters are less stable and reflect strongly minor time and space differences so that the time of certain movements of peoples may be determined when the life of a type can be told in years. (Hargrave and Colton, 1935, p. 50)

> [A type represents] . . . a unit of cultural practice equivalent to the 'culture trait' of ethnography . . . [because] both concepts may serve the same

243

purpose, namely, that of identifying distinct patterns of behaviour or technology which can be acquired by one human being from another, and thus serve as tools for the retracing of cultural developments and interactions. (Krieger, 1944, p. 272)

Thus *the* purpose of a type in archaeology must be to provide an organizational tool which will enable the investigator to group specimens into bodies which have *demonstrable historical meaning in terms of behaviour patterns.* (Krieger, 1944, p. 272; first italics ours)

This view of Krieger's, to the effect that types really are not types at all unless they have chronological and 'historical' meaning, has always been a dominant view in archaeology – in both theory and practice. In 1949, for example, Ford and Willey said that their types 'were created for one purpose: to serve as a measure of time and space' (1949, p. 40). The same view is implicit in Wheat, Gifford and Wasley (1958), and in Rouse (1960, pp. 319–21). Rouse's 'historical' types are to be used simply in distinguishing 'peoples and periods' (1970a, p. 10). And Sabloff and Smith (1969, p. 279) explicitly point out that their types are designed for intersite comparison and space-time ordering: 'Through the combined use of the ware, type, variety, and group categories, the establishment of ceramic complexes and a ceramic sequence is made possible, and the chronological development, of pottery in time and space is brought to light.' Hole and Heizer (1969) put it this way: 'In order to bring system and order to a chaotic assemblage of data, the archaeologist must put all items into convenient categories. . . . Archaeological classifications are *intended to simplify making comparisons among artefacts from several sites so that chronological relations can be readily established*' (p. 167; italics ours). And, 'Most archaeological effort has been directed toward refining classifications and in working out the detailed chronological sequences and interrelations of cultures within areas' (p. 407).

There are, of course, other views of what types mean. There are an ample number of statements in the literature suggesting, for example, that types can have functional (use) meaning (cf. Brew 1946, pp. 46, 64; Steward, 1954; Rouse, 1960, 1970a, 1970b; Hole and Heizer, 1965, p. 120, 1969, p. 169; Whallon, 1971, p. 32; and others). And several authors have suggested that types (and modes) can have a diversity of other meanings as well (e.g. Brew, 1946; Rouse, 1960, 1970a, 1970b). Nonetheless, it is evident that such ideas have not frequently been recognized in empirical studies. It is still the case that most of us think of types as having normative and space-time-comparison meaning, and little more. Types are regarded as *the* 'all-purpose' types, and their meanings are at least implicitly considered to be *the* meanings. This seems particularly true when we consider what many archaeologists *do* rather than what they *say* they do! Even those who espouse 'functional' types (or something else) seem at least implicitly to subscribe to this kind of phenomenological view.

We must, however, emphasize the fact that by no means all archaeologists explicitly or implicitly subscribe to this empiricist view of classification and typology. Some archaeologists seem to recognize, at least partially, the fact that any given body of archaeological materials can be classified or typed in a great diversity of ways, with a great diversity of 'meanings' (depending on research problems). Krieger (1944) is a good example: '[In generating types] . . . it becomes necessary to give preference to some criteria over others; that is, to choose those that are "basic" for the main divisions. This choice may be guided by several considerations . . .' (p. 276). '[The criteria) . . . must be adjusted to the material and problems in given areas, with a maximum of flexibility' (p. 284). He was thus *almost* suggesting that there is nearly an infinite number of attributes to be observed in a given collection of archaeological materials, and that the type clusters one ends up with are heavily dependent on those attributes the investigator chooses to be concerned with. Unfortunately, as we said earlier, he went on to say that while archaeologists select their attributes, they *should* select primarily those attributes reflecting the 'true' types (i.e. those useful in making 'historical' or space-time inferences). Thus the gist of his argument was that there is indeed a 'best' typology to be discovered.

J. O. Brew contributed by arguing against the use of standardized classificatory schemes, pointing out that classification is merely a tool to be used in the solution of problems:

At present, it seems to me that the 'ideal complete-classification' is an impractical concept because of the impossibility of arriving at standardized criteria which can meet the needs of actual study of the material with a view to solving particular problems. (1946, p. 51)

. . . there is no ideal system of classification in which all objects or groups of objects have a place because of their natural characteristics. This is a very important consideration, for in recent years much time and energy has been spent in attempting to 'find' or devise such schemes and in forcing objects into them. The attempts cover a great range of material, from fragments of artefacts, that is potsherds, to large assemblages of traits called

245

by various names such as 'cultures', 'periods', 'phases', 'aspects', etc. (1946, p. 50)

A group of objects to be studied must be classified in a number of different ways depending upon the information the student wishes to obtain, and generally the classes will not coincide. (1946, p. 46)

And then, of course, there is Brew's famous statement:

We must classify our material in all ways that will produce for us useful information. . . . We need more rather than fewer classifications, different classifications, always new classifications, to meet new needs. We must not be satisfied with a single classification of a group of artefacts or of a cultural development, for that way lies dogma and defeat. . . . Even in simple things, no single analysis will bring out all that evidence. (1946, p. 65)

The difficulty with Brew's argument, however, was that he then went on to state forcefully the view that the clusters of attributes we call types have no reality! To him, they were not discovered, but rather imposed by the archaeologist on his collection (1946, p. 46). Spaulding (1953, 1954) is correct in criticizing this view. Simply because an investigator selects the attributes he is interested in does not at all mean that the attribute clusters he gets are not real, or non-random (nor that the makers of the items did not recognize this fact). Non-random clusters of attributes certainly have some meaning other than what is in the mind of the archaeologist (Brew, 1946, p. 57); otherwise, non-random clusters would not occur at all (Spaulding, 1953, 1954). It can thus be seen that, while Brew was in part correct, his major misunderstanding has served to create a measure of confusion since that time.

Following Brew, in time, Ford (1954a, 1954b) took a somewhat similar view, but even more forcefully argued for the complete arbitrariness of types. While he rightly argued that the investigator has a great deal of choice in defining his types, he confused the issue by saying that types were in no other sense real.

In a 'Reply to Ford' (1954), Spaulding made this point clear, and in fact pointed out that there are no inherent, all purpose types such as the sort commonly used for chronology and historical reconstruction. He correctly pointed out that some attributes are useful in functional analyses, and some are useful in studying other things – but that this does *not* mean that attribute clusters are not real and discoverable.

In 1954, Julian Steward also almost made our point when he suggested that there are several different kinds of types that one can make use of: 'I am concerned here with four meanings of "type" – there are, of course, many other meanings – which I shall designate as "morphological", "historical-index", "functional", and "cultural"' (1954, p. 54). And Gordon Willey (1962, p. 172) also stated that we can construct different types for different problems: 'It is, of course, conceivable that a quite different typological breakdown of the same material could be set up for the study of problems of use or function of pottery.'

It seems likely that many of the statements like this in the literature were inspired by the major contribution made by Irving Rouse in 1939. Rouse made the point that 'types' were composed of what he called 'modes' (which were 'attributes' to him at that time: 1939).[5] Types were composed of modes, yet he recognized that modes could and did cross-cut type divisions. While 'types' were basic descriptive, morphological categorizations based on differences in all the major attributes or modes, the modes themselves were attributes of technique or appearance, 'which seem to be historically significant' (1939, p. 12). His major contribution was in showing that different parts or attributes of items may inform us about different things, and thus should be considered *independently* of the 'basic' morphological types themselves (since they distribute independently). That is, any given mode can be found on several different 'types'. He also showed that modes have historical meaning, and are often more useful than 'types' *per se* in studying culture history.

In 1960, and since, Rouse has refined his views and made a number of terminological distinctions (1960, 1970a, 1970b). He now recognizes that within any given collection there are both different kinds of types and different kinds of modes that can be discovered – and each is most useful for gaining particular kinds of information desired by the investigator (1960, pp. 319–21; 1970a, 1970b): 'Classification, like statistics, is not an end in itself but a technique by means of which to attain specified objectives, and so it must be varied with the objective. The main opportunity for variation comes in selecting the criteria which are to be considered diagnostic of one's classes' (Rouse, 1960, p. 313).

It would appear, then, that Rouse is not what he would call a 'narrow classifier' (personal communication, May 1970), nor what we would call an empiricist or phenomenological classifier (cf. also Rouse, 1970a, p. 12). Nonetheless, some of his statements seem inconsistent with this conclusion. In 1960, for example, he stated that while there are several ways to arrive at 'types', the end product is the same – 'In all cases the end result is the same: a single series of classes or subclasses' (1960, p. 316).

With regard to the *meanings* of types and modes, Rouse's statements also

247

seem equivocal. While he frequently suggests that such entities may have various meanings (including function), he also seems to be insisting that they have normative meaning primarily. While we may be wrong, it seems to us that Rouse does regard normative or ideational meaning as primary, because even when he discusses 'functional' types (and his other types and modes as well), he seems usually to imply that these entities are reflections of the ideas and preferences of the people. In the case of his functional entities, for example, he implies that they are the result of functional cultural templates of some sort, and that this template is really what we are making inferences about (at least usually, and most importantly).

We do not cast blame on Rouse or any of the others we have used as examples here; all have made notable contributions. We are concerned simply to point out that the phenomenological view of classification is having a slow and difficult death. While on the one hand there are innumerable statements in the literature like the ones we presented above, and like the following, 'Classification is a tool that can be made to work for many purposes. Theoretically, there is an almost infinite number of typologies for any body of material' (Hole and Heizer, 1969, p. 167), it is nonetheless evident that in both program and practice, types tend to be regarded and used as if they were *the* types, each having a single primary meaning. There are exceptions, of course; and we cite here Dunnell (1971) and Whallon (1971).

This concludes our examples of the empiricist view of classification and typology. While our documentation is somewhat more anecdotal than quantitative, we hope nonetheless that our point is clear – namely, that archaeologists frequently do not seem to realize that there can be a multiplicity of types constructed for any given set of materials, and that these types may be assigned a diversity of meanings.

It is fair to point out here that this phenomenological view of types is probably *not* something that could easily have been avoided in the development of archaeology as a discipline. This seems evident, not because archaeologists often tend to be philosophical empiricists by nature, but rather because the *purposes* for their types have been rather restricted in scope. These purposes in no sense required the development of a view emphasizing the necessity of a multiplicity of types and a multiplicity of meanings.

The reason for this is that archaeology has for years been in a 'discovery' stage of development, in which it has been necessary to describe new finds, and find out where and when they occurred. It was thus quite natural that types, and discussions of typology, would be oriented toward these necessary goals. Given the goal of 'culture history' in this sense, it stands to reason that our types should have been developed in such a way as to aid in this pursuit; and it is clear that they have been:

... when American archaeologists describe projectile points, they go to great lengths to discern differences that may help define geographical and chronological versions of cultures. (Hole and Heizer, 1965, pp. 121–2)

In answering this pair of questions [where and when], the archaeologist must use a form of classification that will bring out the chronological implications of his remains. In other words, his classification must be designed to produce patterns of attributes that are indicative of areas and periods. (Rouse, 1970b, p. 12)

The usual practice is to formulate historical-index types only for pottery, projectile points, and other stylistically significant artefacts, and to formulate functional types only for tools, implements and other functionally significant artefacts. The remainder of one's collection is treated analytically. (Rouse, 1970a, p. 10)

Rouse's concept of 'mode' was also designed for culture-historical use, since modes were presumed to be informative with regard to identifying 'peoples' (i.e. preferences, customs, etc.) in space and time (cf. Rouse, 1939, 1960, 1970a, 1970b).

That the types and modes archaeologists have discovered and used are real and useful cannot be denied. And they will continue to be refined and used – not simply because they are already standardized and canonized, but because it will continue to be necessary to establish space-time frameworks in carrying on other kinds of archaeological research.

It is important to recognize, however, that the standard types are not *the* types in any fundamental sense, and should not be viewed as such, even unconsciously. The recent development in archaeology of a multiplicity of different kinds of research problems has made it necessary to begin emphasizing the idea that types can also be 'multiple', and can be constructed to be useful in solving a multiplicity of research problems. We feel that the reason this has not been more fully and consciously emphasized (and operationalized) is that our problems have until recently been restricted (usually) to the space-time systematics, or to 'culture-history'.

A difficulty

There is at least one major difficulty with the traditional empiricist approach to typology, which must be made clear. This difficulty makes the pheno-

249

menological view of types unworkable for the long-run development of archaeology.

The reader will recall that in pursuing *the* natural and universally useful types the investigator tends to feel that he must be cognizant of *all* (or most of) the attributes of the materials with which he is working. After examining all the attributes, he then sorts into types on the basis of as many similarities and differences as he can. This stands to reason in the empiricist view because if the types are to be widely useful, both for the investigator and for other archaeologists, they must consist of non-random clusters of as many attributes as might now or later be of interest. While this view is usually held implicitly, it has sometimes been stated explicitly:

> If one proceeded in an ideally inductive manner, he would identify and record all recognizable attributes of a collection of artefacts. . . . The next step would be the sorting of artefacts into classes and then the relating of attributes to these classes for type descriptions. . . . To avoid processing the collection a second time, it can be initially sorted into classes, which can then be described for class range and attribute identification simultaneously. (Swartz, 1967, p. 490)

It is true, of course, that one can generate types in this intuitive manner. They would be what we have called the 'obvious' types. We can presume that such types would involve non-random clusters of attributes, and would thus have 'meaning' in some sense or other – although we might not know precisely what meanings to assign. The difficulty, however, is with the basic premise that one can identify all or most of the possibly significant attributes. There is virtually an infinite number of attributes connected with any item, and it is physically impossible to take account of them all, or even more than a small percentage of them.

In the case of ceramics, for example, are we to consider the curvature of the lip of the rim, the unevenness of the bottom, the width of the brush strokes, and the ratio of wall thickness to volume? And, if so, to what degree of accuracy of measurement? Most of our standard types today take account of very few attributes, and usually only two or three of them are of primary importance in type definition (cf. Whallon, 1971). To insist that we be aware of all or most attributes is untenable, for whatever the attributes described, each of them can be further divided into a nearly infinite number of additional attributes. 'Every artefact, indeed every material object, contains an infinity of attributes or variables and therefore of possible systems networking these attributes' (Ross Ashby, 1965, p. 39, in Clarke, 1968, p. 136).

250

The futility of trying to take account of all attributes, or even most of the potentially important ones, is evident when one tries to make use of the types that other investigators have defined. For example, consider the standard Southwestern painted pottery types again. The attributes given emphasis in these types are generally those of colour and decorative design (and only certain attributes of those). One cannot construct 'functional' types with these because such important attributes as volume, orifice size, presence or absence of burned bottom, and so forth, are usually not measured or reported.

The point is, no matter who is constructing a typology, and no matter how thorough and careful he hopes to be, *choices* must be made with regard to which attributes are to be emphasized.

To say that *all* 'attributes' are used is just as profitless as it is nonsensical. . . . If one stops to consider the matter, choices are made in creating or defining modes, then further choices are made when some are selected as criteria for classes. The question then becomes: Upon what basis are the choices made? (Dunnell, 1971, p. 117)

It is . . . necessary to select the particular attributes and the particular system that we wish to study – which attributes are relevant to the frame of our problem. (Clarke, 1968, p. 137)

Most of the other attributes are what Clarke (1968, p. 137) calls 'inessential'. They simply are not seen as relevant to anything at the moment. To record all of them would be a hopeless task. Thus, we cannot construct a general, universally useful typology of anything. 'The diagnostics of classificatory groups are too closely associated with the immediate problem in hand to permit a general classification which can be generally applied to a heterogeneous mass of problems' (Brew, 1946, p. 51). The fact that we must make choices is inherent, and the question that remains is: how and by what criteria is the selection of attributes to be made?

It should be evident from our previous discussion that *all* of our standard typologies (in fact all typologies) represent choices that were made by the investigators. In the case of the Southwestern pottery types, and most other pottery types, the selection of attributes has been heavily influenced by the general problems that the investigators have had. Since the primary interest was in establishing chronologies and tracing spatial distributions and cultural 'influences', the attributes selected and emphasized were those aspects of style (colour and decorative design) that were shown to be useful in such pursuits. And, these attributes have indeed been useful!

We argue in fact that useful data observation and recording (whether it be of attributes of artefacts, artefacts themselves, or whatever) is guided by *a priori* problems or interests of the investigators involved (cf. Hanson, 1967; Hole and Heizer, 1969, p. 177; Hill, Chapter 2 of this volume). The observations that are irrelevant to these concerns are usually, though not always, not made. We cannot be objective and select observations or attributes in an unbiased manner. We are all biased, especially by our problems and the general theoretical paradigms to which we subscribe. And since we would be fooling ourselves to think we can escape bias in selecting attributes for our typological analyses, we argue that it is important to recognize precisely what our biases are. In short, we should be aware of precisely what our types are to be used for, and we should select attributes accordingly. And, further, we will argue below that having a vague or general research problem in mind is not sufficient to guide attribute selection; we need specific hypotheses as well.

A different model

Before considering the importance of hypotheses, and the details of the 'positivist' model for classification, it is important to show how it differs philosophically from the empiricist view. The positivist view is fundamentally different.

The positivist view is that phenomena do *not* have inherent or primary meanings to be discovered. Rather, any phenomenon, or set of phenomena, is assigned meaning by the human mind, and it may be assigned as many different meanings as the investigator chooses to give it. The positivist holds that there is no single or best natural typology of materials and other phenomena. For the archaeologist this means that there is no inherent meaning (e.g. norms, templates, preferences, functions, etc.) to be discovered in an assemblage of artefacts. In fact, he can choose to make many different typologies, each with its own meaning. The meanings he chooses to impose depend on *a priori* problems, hypotheses, or other interests.

To take an example, consider the tools we call screwdrivers and pliers. They are obviously different, and the empiricist classifier would place them into different types without hesitation. The division would be based on the understanding that these tools are not only morphologically different, but their 'meanings' are different as well – one is used for screwing, the other for squeezing. This functional typology is correct of course – as far as it goes.

But is this *the* best type division? The positivist would say no, not necessarily. He would point out that there are other type divisions that could equally well be made, depending on one's interests.

Let us suppose, for example, that one is interested in segregating those tools that one would expect might be used by an electrician. We might propose that such tools ought to have rubber handles (to protect against shock), and they would be long and thin (for use in getting into the deep recesses of electrical boxes, etc.). In examining a collection of screwdrivers and pliers, then, the positivist would group into *one type* all those tools having the attribute cluster 'long', 'thin' and 'rubber handled'. This type would thus be composed of *both* screwdrivers *and* pliers. We would be placing both tools in the same type, since they meet the attribute requirements in which we are interested.

Kaplan (1964, p. 51) points out this principle in discussing the classification of books. While one might feel that the best, or most natural, classification of books would be on the basis of differences in content, this is certainly not fundamental. One might desire to type them in terms of size and weight. 'A classification of books by size and weight is not as "natural", we feel, as one based on their content. But the printer and freight agent have claims as legitimate as the librarian's' (1964, p. 51). And further, if one is a printer he might be interested in a number of other attributes. He might sort on the basis of the type of print, distance between letters, thickness of the page, quality of the paper, and so forth. One of his types might include those books having a non-random clustering of large print, relatively long distance between letters, thick pages, and inexpensive paper. Another type might have a different cluster of attributes. These types would be as real as any other type division, and they would meet the requirements Spaulding has set forth as necessary for the existence of types.

What we are suggesting is that the positivist *begins* his work with his problems, tentative inferences or hypotheses about the materials he is observing or has observed, and then proceeds to select the kinds of attributes he feels will lead to typologies that will be useful to his particular analysis. For example, if an archaeologist wants to test the proposition that certain pottery vessels were used for cooking, while others were used for water storage, he must emphasize those attributes that he thinks represent those functions. Water storage vessels might be expected to be relatively larger than cooking vessels; they should have narrow necks and small orifices; and they might be expected to have painted designs on their exteriors. Cooking vessels, on the other hand, ought to be smaller, with wide orifices, and burned bottoms (*inter alia*). The archaeologist might find that his attributes do indeed cluster in this way, and he will have established *types* which are directly relevant to his question.

And further, these types will certainly be expected to cross-cut other pottery vessel type divisions of the same assemblage. For example, one might develop types on the basis of attributes believed to reflect economic status differences in the society. And each of *these* types might include both water storage and cooking vessels. The point is that within any collection of vessels (or anything else) a large number of different and cross-cutting types can be generated.

Lewis Binford made this clear in one of his theoretical discussions, entitled 'Archaeological systematics and the study of culture process' (1965). The importance of this article to typological considerations is evident in its title, yet it apparently has not been fully recognized as a paper on typology (as well as culture theory). The reason for this may be that much of what Binford had to say was not specifically directed toward the old 'typological debate'. His focus was rather on attacking what he called the 'normative' or 'univariate' view of culture. He emphasized the idea that types are not manifestations of just one thing (i.e. shared 'culture'). On the contrary, types can be generated which will inform us about the *variability* within and among cultures. 'Formal variation in artefacts need not, and in most cases probably does not have a single meaning in the context of the functioning cultural system' (1965, p. 206). He used pottery as an example, and pointed specifically to the fact that within any given collection of items (or other things) there is a tremendous amount of variability, and each kind of variable can be significant in terms of information we might gain about different aspects of cultural behaviour.

For example, he pointed out that in pottery there are technological attributes of both form and decorative design, and there are stylistic design morphology attributes of form and decoration. Some of these attributes are indicative of the 'primary functions' of the vessels – that is, the uses for which the vessels were intended. Other attributes are indicative of 'secondary functions' – that is, the contexts of production and use of the vessels. For example, the temper or orifice size of a pot may be meaningful in the context of cooking, while certain variations in technique or design may reflect motor-habit differences among manufacturers, or represent status or ownership symbols, and so forth.

This is similar to our argument here, except that we are not concerned primarily with demolishing the 'normative view' of culture, nor even with considering culture theory directly. Rather, our emphasis is in pointing out

254

that regardless of theoretical leanings, it must be recognized that materials can be typed in a multiplicity of ways, depending on the specific problems and hypotheses of the investigator. The attributes one chooses to emphasize in generating types will (and should be) dependent on the precise interests of the investigator. Carl Hempel sums this up well: 'if a particular way of analysing and classifying empirical findings is to lead to an explanation of the phenomena concerned, then it must be based on hypotheses about how those phenomena are connected; without such hypotheses, analysis and classification are blind' (1966, p. 13).

It follows from this discussion, of course, that if all archaeologists had the same interests and the same hypotheses, we would all be examining the same kinds of attributes in our materials, and we would come up with very similar kinds of types – in fact, we could standardize them. But, due to the diversity of our interests, we cannot do this. There are too many different problems and hypotheses to consider, both those already formulated and those yet to be developed.

It is even conceivable to us that some investigators might want to generate types composed of clusters of attributes informative of mental templates or social psychology (although we doubt the fruitfulness of this for archaeological studies). In this event, one would try to deal with the kinds of attributes presumed to be useful in this regard. Attributes useful in discovering function, chronology, or other things, would profitably be ignored. But, if someone is investigating something else, he should choose his attributes accordingly.

Perhaps the best way to illustrate the usefulness of the positivist approach to typology is to present some detailed examples. By doing this we think we can further demonstrate the fact that universally useful, 'natural' types cannot exist. Also, we can demonstrate our contention that archaeological materials should not be assigned any single, primary meaning.

Examples

Our first example is drawn from the work of Longacre (1964, 1970) and Hill (1966, 1970).[6] About 1962, Longacre proposed that matrilocal residence had existed in the American Southwest by at least A.D. 1100, and he decided to gather evidence to test this proposition. Looking at historic and contemporary *pueblo* ethnography, he hypothesized that if his proposition were correct, he would expect to find localized clusters of pottery design elements in his prehistoric *pueblo*. These would identify the specific room-blocks in which each residence unit had lived. The reason for arguing this was that if females had been making the pottery in the context of separate, localized residence units (as among the historic western *pueblos*), each residence unit would have made stylistically slightly different pottery than the other units. Thus, different areas of the *pueblo* should have pottery design peculiarities, which characterize each area.

Without providing further justification for the study, it is sufficient to say that Longacre found the expected, non-random distribution of pottery design elements. He concluded that he had indeed discovered prehistoric matrilocal residence. In fact, he could interpret his results in no other reasonable way.

Hill's study (1966, 1970) was an attempt to 'test' Longacre's findings by conducting a similar study with a much larger *pueblo* in the same area (cf. Martin, Longacre and Hill, 1967). This study employed not only the distribution of minute pottery design elements, but additional stylistic data as well. The results appear to corroborate Longacre's findings.

What is notable for our purpose here is that the standard Southwestern pottery types found at the two sites in question were not useful in isolating residence units. Since the residence unit proposition called for studying the spatial distributions of minute design style differences, it was necessary to 'type' the sherds into categories (types) differing in terms of extremely fine style attributes. In short, the attributes used in generating sherd typologies for this analysis were actually attributes of design elements, and the investigators developed types of design elements, and the sherd types themselves were based on these. Had the investigators used whole vessels, the vessels would have been typed on the basis of non-random clusters of these elements, and *not* on the usual criteria for pottery classification in the Southwest (e.g. colour and gross design).

In fact, the types derived for this study cross-cut the standard types. That is, it is not necessarily the case that any given design element is peculiar to a specific 'standard' pottery type. Rather, a given element can occur on a number of standard types. Thus, when grouping vessels (or sherds) on the basis of design element types, each type may contain vessels belonging to more than one of the standard types. And, conversely of course, any given standard pottery type may possess style elements peculiar to *several* of the types based on style elements. Nonetheless, both kinds of typologies seem equally valid, and they are correctly referred to as types in the Spaulding (1953) sense.

It is also clear that Longacre's and Hill's sherd typologies may *not* represent types that were in any way recognized by the prehistoric inhabitants of the sites involved. Although the individual manufacturers of the pottery undoubtedly had things in mind, and knew what they were trying to paint on the vessels, they were not necessarily aware of the minute attribute differences taken into consideration in these studies. They might have recognized quite different design elements in their own folk taxonomies of the pottery.

We should also point out, by the way, that had the investigators not had their residence unit proposition in mind, they would almost certainly not have thought of examining their sherds with regard to minute style differences. There would have been no reason to do so, and these style attributes would have gone unnoticed. This clearly illustrates how unlikely it is that any investigator can be aware of *all* of the potentially useful attributes his material contains. All investigators must make choices on the basis of *a priori* ideas.

We would further argue that even having a general research problem in mind is not sufficient to provide the guidance necessary in forming useful typologies. In this example, for instance, the investigators had to state more than an interest in discovering the locations of residence units, since this interest itself would not require looking at ceramic design elements in such detail. Before the necessity of doing this could become obvious, it was necessary to formulate the specific proposition that matrilocal residence should be characterized by non-random clusters of design elements.

Thus, by having hypotheses in mind *prior* to type formation, the investigator will not only have the best chance of selecting the relevant attributes, but he will also be assured that the types that result are relevant – and he will know ahead of time precisely *how* they are relevant. In the example above, they were relevant to testing a descriptive proposition about the occurrences and location of matrilocal residence units. Different attributes and types would necessarily have to have been developed for testing a hypothesis about vessel function, trade, technology, etc.

All of the points just made are even better illustrated in a piece of research currently being conducted by one of the authors (Hill). The goal of the study is to attempt to identify the work of individual potters in collections of both historic and prehistoric *pueblo* pottery. The purpose of the work is to develop a tool for measuring prehistoric craft specialization and distribution networks.

It seems evident that individual potters possess fine motor-habit peculiarities that should permit us to identify the pottery they manufactured. Each potter would presumably use his hands, paint brushes, and so forth, differently from any other potter. He might have slightly wider lines than another potter, or greater distances between his lines, or a different slant to his lines, different characteristics of brush stroke, and so forth. Such motor-habit differences among individuals have long been known in the case of handwriting and painting, and it seems likely that pottery will be no exception.

If this study yields the expected results, Hill will have generated vessel types based on clusters of attributes that reflect motor-habits. These types are expected to cross-cut 'standard' pottery type categories, since presumably each individual potter would manufacture more than one of the standard Southwestern types. The types will also cross-cut functional types, since again, each manufacturer can be expected to make several functionally different vessel forms (all of which should exhibit his peculiar cluster of motor-habit variables).

If such non-random clustering of motor-habit characteristics can be discovered, the resulting types will be valid in Spaulding's sense. Although they will not represent types that were recognized by the prehistoric peoples involved, they will be useful in measuring craft specializaton and distribution networks. Thus, we agree with Watson, LeBlanc and Redman (1970, pp. 27–8): 'Statistically verified types reflect patterned behaviour, which may or may not correspond to mental templates. This patterned behaviour can result from motor habits, idiosyncratic behaviour, or behaviour defined as appropriate by the culture in question. Hence, there is certainly no necessary correspondence between type and mental template.'

And further, it is evident that motor-habit attributes would not be examined unless an investigator had a quite specific reason for doing so. Otherwise, who would bother making these variables part of a type description?

It is important to emphasize the idea that there is a great deal of stylistic variability (and other variability) on pottery and other artefacts that would not normally be recognized without a specific hypothesis in mind. If we consider *only* painted design elements, for example, it is evident that different aspects of these elements can be used in discovering types that are useful for quite different kinds of analyses. Some style element characteristics might be informative with regard to status differences, some may represent ownership, others may represent sodality affiliation, and so forth. It may one day be possible to demonstrate what specific *kinds* of style variability are most reflective of these sorts of determinants.

We will rest our case with one further example. We consider again the so-called 'culture classifications', such as those of Willey and Phillips (1958) and Service (1958). We have already demonstrated that such classifications tend to be regarded phenomenologically, as *the* types. But it remains to be shown that there is nothing inherently 'best' about such classifications, and that societies can equally well be typed in other ways.

Consider, for example, the general proposition that as human populations approach carrying capacity, land and other resources become increasingly scarce, and it becomes necessary for the societies in question to introduce organizational means for ensuring orderly transference or inheritance of these resources (Meggitt, 1965). If this proposition is correct, one would expect to be able to demonstrate it by showing the following (at the very least):

(1) In cases (and time periods) in which populations are well below carrying capacity, and land and other resources are plentiful, there should be no organizations designed to safeguard transmission of land, etc. Such property should be communally regulated and available for use by anybody who needs it. Such societies should exhibit little or no evidence of competition over land or other non-movable resources, and thus there should be no evidence that resources are in fact scarce and in need of regulatory organization.

(2) In cases (and time periods) in which populations are approaching carrying capacity, there should be evidence that land, etc., is becoming scarce, and there should be evidence of competition for it. Thus, there would be a need for regulatory organization, and such organization should be found to occur. In fact, it should be demonstrated that without such regulatory organization, property distribution and inheritance would soon create serious imbalances within the society, which would lead to its change or collapse.

There are probably other kinds of data that would be needed to test this simple idea. The point, however, is that in order to test the hypothesis the investigator might want to categorize societies into at least two *types*: (1) those societies having population densities approaching carrying capacity, with evidence of scarcity of land and other resources, and (2) those societies having low population densities and no scarcity of land, and so forth. There would, of course, be a number of specific attributes that one would want to employ in generating these two types – i.e. attributes believed to measure population density, carrying capacity, critical resources, scarcity of resources, and so on.

The investigator might also wish to classify his societies in terms of those having property regulation mechanisms and those without them – or those having frequent warfare and those without it. In any event, one would expect that there might indeed be two types based on at least the following clusters of attributes:

Type 1
(1) Regulatory organization absent
(2) Low population density

259

(3) Little competition
(4) Little or no warfare

Type 2
(1) Regulatory organization present
(2) High population density
(3) Much competition
(4) Much warfare

It is conceivable that no such types would be discovered, of course – especially types in the sense of representing truly non-random clusters of attributes. Nevertheless, one might properly attempt to classify societies in this way, given the kind of hypothesis considered. And, if these types were discovered, they would be quite different from those presented by most of the authors who have attempted to provide culture classifications. In fact, these types would, at least to some degree, cross-cut most such culture types.

For example, one might expect to find some of Willey and Phillips's Lithic, Archaic and Formative types falling into our Type 1 societies, others would be in our Type 2 societies, while, in Service's classification, we might expect to find that some of his Bands and Tribes would fall into our Types 1 or 2. But the point is, there might indeed be no correlation at all between our types and those of either Willey and Phillips or Service. They are simply different kinds of types, based on different kinds of attributes, and resulting from different kinds of problems.

Discussion

At the beginning of this paper we listed some of the key issues that have arisen in discussions of classification and typology, and suggested that the ways in which these issues have been argued have often been far from intelligible. We hope that this paper will not simply add to the confusion, but rather will be of some use to those who are thinking about these issues. While we realize that we may not have resolved them to everyone's satisfaction, we have at least offered our understanding of the basic philosophical differences that seem to underly the arguments.

There is, of course, more to understanding these issues than is implied in our discussion of the 'empiricist' and 'positivist' philosophies of typology. If one really hopes to understand why some archaeologists seem to emphasize all-purpose, natural or phenomenological classifications, while others emphasize the 'multiplicity of types' idea, it is equally important to consider differences in theoretical background among these archaeologists. We have not done this, primarily because Lewis Binford (1965) has already done it most elegantly. But we think that our argument, taken in conjunction with his, should provide a good basis for understanding the foundations of these different 'models' for classification.

At this point it will be useful to summarize our discussion in the context of resolving our initial list of issues (p. 231):

The first issue was: 'Are types "real", or are they "invented" by the archaeologist to suit his own purposes?' It should be clear by now that this is a badly stated issue. Types are indeed real, and we agree with Spaulding (1953) on this point. There *are* non-random clusters of attributes that can be discovered and called 'types'. To believe otherwise is to take a position contrary to fact. Thus, we have not dealt with this issue in detail. Even most of those typologies that have been developed intuitively rather than statistically probably represent non-random clusters of attributes (if not in Spaulding's sense, then at least in the sense discussed by Whallon, 1971).

Thus, types are not 'invented' in the sense that Ford (1954a, 1954b; 1961) and Brew (1946) were viewing them. They are not completely arbitrary, resulting solely from the interests of the archaeologist. The so-called 'arbitrariness' comes into the picture only at a particular stage in the discovery of types – namely, at the point when the investigator selects (chooses) the particular attributes with which he is going to be concerned. We have shown that such choices must be made, since not all attributes can conceivably be considered. Thus, the investigator must either select his attributes to suit his specific problems, or decide simply to select those attributes that most of his colleagues have considered important. Either way, he is in fact making his attribute selection in terms of at least some vague *a priori* interests. But, on the other hand, this fact does not imply that the attributes he selects are not real, nor that the cluster of attributes he discovered are not real. They are indeed real, and can presumably be demonstrated statistically. Spaulding has stated this relationship between the archaeologist and his materials nicely:

Once the selection of variables whose inter-relationships are to be studied is made, the properties of the archaeologist drop out of the picture, and so does the concept 'arbitrary'. The result of the study is determined by the properties of the collection and the nature of the analytical techniques applied to it. Any number of archaeologists employing the same analytical techniques on the same variables in the same collection should come up with the same results. (Personal communication, May 1970)

And Watson, LeBlanc and Redman (1971, p. 27) put it this way: 'The attributes one chooses to work with should reflect one's problems, whereas the types defined by those attributes should reflect the real world.'

Thus, it can be seen that there *are* empirical properties in a collection of archaeological materials, and quite often non-random clusters can be demonstrated to exist. Yet, at the same time, it is the archaeologist who selects the variables or attributes he wants to consider as important in the clustering process (whether it be an intuitive or a statistical process).

It can be seen, too, that our second question has already been answered – 'Is there a continuum of variability among artefacts (and other things), or are there non-random clusters of attributes to be discovered?' The answer is clearly a matter for empirical demonstration, not a matter for *a priori* judgement. Given any corpus of materials, one might indeed discover that there is a continuum of variability, but it may be (and often is) discovered that there are in fact boundaries between or among things (non-random clusters). There are also empirical cases of something in between – i.e. non-random clusters with fuzzy boundaries (there can even be different degrees of fuzziness). But only empirical investigation will determine whether, for a particular set of materials (or observations), we have a continuum, non-random clusters, or something in between.

Our third question was: 'Is there a single, "best" type division or classification of a given body of materials, or can there be many equally "good" divisions?' This question has been given the greatest emphasis in this paper, and our answer is clear: there is no such thing as a 'best' typology. However, we would like to qualify this statement, since it appears that under certain strictly specified conditions such a typology can exist.

Our argument is, in essence, that once an investigator has selected his problems or hypotheses, and has a specific collection of materials to work with, *and* has already selected the attributes that are relevant to his concerns, there is indeed a 'best' typology of the materials. Spaulding puts it this way:

> Returning directly to your question of whether or not there is a *single* or *best* division into types that we should discover, the answer is yes *if* the question means (*a*) best with respect to a given body of materials, and (*b*) with respect to a given set of attributes, and (*c*) if the notion of type has 'characteristic pattern' as its central feature, and (*d*) if the body of materials does in fact exhibit sharp association of attributes. Given the body of materials and the attributes and the purpose of investigating the associations of those attributes, then there is a 'best' answer, although the answer

is not necessarily a sharp division into types defined by the associations; the nature of the answer is contingent on the empirical data, and it may be a clear set of associations defining types neatly, or it may be a clear demonstration of no association, or it may be something in between. (Personal communication, May 1970)

We fully agree with this. In the absence of these conditions, of course, there is no inherently 'best' typology of anything. In short, the world is not made up of 'best' or 'natural' types that we are obligated to discover in a given body of data.

The fourth issue we raised was the question: 'Can we formulate standardized types?' We have indicated our belief that the answer is no – yet we have qualified this also. We maintain that to the extent that we all share similar problems and hypotheses, and thus can agree on the attributes we wish to consider, then standardized types might be possible. However, it does not seem likely that archaeologists will agree on any small number of common problems. Our problems and hypotheses are becoming increasingly multitudinous and divergent.

Spaulding points out that we can conceive of such ultimate standardized typologies, but implies that they are not likely:

We can in principle conceive of an ultimate typology of a set of artefacts constructed from *every* culturally patterned physico-chemical variable (this is a concept akin to the perfect sphere or the frictionless machine). The typology so constructed would be relevant to all possible archaeological hypotheses to which the collection itself is relevant; and so would be in one sense a 'best' typology. (Personal communication, May 1970)

But, of course, such a typology cannot really be developed.

Nevertheless, both Spaulding and Fred T. Plog (University of California at Los Angeles) have argued with us the idea that we ought not give up the idea of at least standardizing our types to some extent. They suggest that archaeological objectives *are* in fact somewhat limited, and thus there must be some specific set of attributes we can record (in a standardized way) for any given kind of archaeological material. These attributes would at least meet the needs of *most* of our problems, now and in the near future. Those who want to go beyond such standard types could, it is argued, go ahead and deal with those additional attributes they are interested in.

Clearly there are a great many (infinite ?) ways to divide a collection, any one of which may make sense in connection with some sensible hypothesis. But one general purpose way of dividing the collection is into types, here defined as sets of artefacts exhibiting pronounced associations of attributes. The type concept may have some sort of *strategical* (as opposed to logical) priority in terms of archaeological objectives. By strategical priority, I mean highly useful for many hypotheses. (Spaulding, personal communication, May 1970)

Thus, Spaulding clings to the idea that there should be some kind of 'substratum' typology of standard types, which we may depart from on specific occasions where they are found to be inadequate. George Cowgill (Brandeis University) argues in the same vein:

... that in principle there may be an unlimited number of classifications suitable for different purposes. What next needs to be done is to look at some of the most common and important problems we want to tackle, and spell out what kinds of classifications ... make most sense (or offer most promise) for each of these problems or objectives. Very likely there are less than half a dozen kinds of problems which are most important most of the time in most archaeological projects, and less than half a dozen kinds of classifications (or families of closely related classifications) that would be most useful. (Personal communication, June, 1970)

We go along with this idea, but only part way. Certainly if we are ever to store our attribute data on tape for the retrieval and mutual use of others, *some* standardization will have to be done. We think that it may be possible to agree on recording certain kinds of attributes in a standardized way, much as Ericson and Stickel (1971) have done with regard to pottery vessel form classification. We could agree, for example, on a standard set of functional attributes to be recorded, a standard set of historical-index attributes, stylistic attributes, and so forth.

This would be useful, but at the same time it would have to be recognized as a short-term solution. Even the *common* problems are changing rapidly, and the number of new hypotheses being generated is many times as great, and will continue to grow rapidly. Such a standardized list of attributes would have to be amplified every year or two, and even then we doubt that it would actually meet most of our requirements in research. We predict that within five years the list of attributes would be so long that it would be impossible to get archaeologists to take the time to record them all! And, if they had to try to do it for many different kinds of materials (including settlement patterns, etc.), they simply would not do it.

Still, such a standardized system would be useful for those who are working on the old problems and hypotheses – which, of course, will continue to be of interest. This does not mean that we support the idea of standardized typologies. Rather, we support, with caution, the idea that standardized sets of attributes might be profitably recorded.

If it were in fact true that there exist basic, indivisible and fundamental attributes in our materials, we would have to support this idea even more wholeheartedly. Some archaeologists have suggested that such basic units do exist:

> . . . modes are inherent in one's collection. If two archaeologists analyse the same collection and do an equally good job of it, they should produce the same modes. (Taylor, 1948, pp. 129–30)

> The mode, therefore, is a natural unit of cultural study, whereas the type is an arbitrary one. (Rouse, 1960, p. 318)

> An archaeological attribute is a fundamental element, a logically irreducible lowest common denominator of artefacts and the result of a piece of premeditated and deliberate hominid behaviour. (Clarke, 1968, p. 138)

We do not agree. No matter how small and minute the attributes are that we wish to consider, they are still further divisible – i.e. each has its own attributes. Presumably, even atoms have attributes, and thus are not indivisible or immutable natural units of observation.

How, then, do we answer our fifth basic issue: 'Do types in some sense represent "basic data"?' Our answer is that they do not. If types were basic data, it would clearly make sense to discover our types first, prior to analysis, and we have shown why this approach is unworkable: 'there is no such thing as "basic data" – i.e. there is no single corpus of items and observations [including attributes] that are basic to all or most analyses that we might wish to perform. The question of what are data can only be answered *after* an investigator has at least one specific proposition in mind' (Hill, Chapter 2 of this volume, p. 70). Cowgill (personal communication, June 1970) sums it up nicely: 'The point which seems to me essential is to get away from the idea that one does *the* classification, then applies the results to whatever problems may be of interest. Rather, I think it's better to start with a set of problems (or tasks or objectives) and go through some sort of reasoning process to derive the kinds of classifications . . . that make sense in terms of solving the problems.' We have argued that the 'reasoning process' Cowgill refers to ought to be the generation of a specific hypothesis and the specific kinds of observations needed to test it.

The answer to our sixth question – 'Do we need more or fewer types?' – is by now obvious. There will always be more, not fewer types, whether we agree that there should be or not. The reason, of course, is that we will continue to have more and different problems and hypotheses.

Our last issue – 'What should our types mean?' – however, requires some further comment. Spaulding is correct in pointing out that *any* non-random cluster of attributes must mean something, otherwise it would not be non-random. Thus, one could indiscriminantly select a series of attributes in a collection of materials (e.g. projectile points or pots, etc.) and he might very well discover clustering. The clustering would represent types, and would have 'meaning' in some sense (although we might not know what the best way to interpret the clustering might be). We argue that if one selects his types on the basis of specific problems and hypotheses, the meaning of his types will be automatically apparent.

For example, if one is interested in the functions or uses of a set of pots, and if he can reasonably argue that the attributes he selects are relevant to discovering function, then the clustering he gets can at least tentatively be viewed as representing a functional typology. If he is interested in mental templates, and chooses attributes which he can argue represent these, then his types might tentatively be viewed as mental template types – and so forth.

We have argued, most emphatically, that one cannot assume that all types, modes, and so forth, represent a single thing ultimately (such as norms, templates, or preferences). Thus, we cannot agree that the following statements are necessarily correct:

> . . . classification into types is a process of discovery of combinations of attributes *favoured by the makers of the artefacts.* (Spaulding, 1953, p. 305; italics ours)

> Each attribute thus is equivalent to a piece of *premeditated and deliberate* hominid behaviour. (Clarke, 1968, p. 138; italics ours)

We have already shown that types may be composed of clusters of attributes that have nothing at all to do with conscious human goals or preferences (e.g. types of motor-habit attributes). We argue that, while one might conceivably wish to select attributes that might be regarded as measuring social norms or preferences, we feel that this is in no sense the most fundamentally important pursuit. One may well be interested in measuring what people actually do, rather than what they think (the latter being difficult at best).[7]

Before closing, we would like to raise an important caution with regard to the generation and use of typologies in anthropology. It seems to us that both archaeologists and ethnologists have a strong tendency to want to categorize or 'type' their observations, even when it is not appropriate to do so. In short, types are proclaimed without the investigator first making sure that such types do *in fact* represent non-random associations of attributes, and then these types take on a life of their own. This is particularly true of our phase and stage classifications, and includes all or most of the so-called culture classifications (e.g. Willey and Phillips, 1958; Service, 1958). Spaulding and others have pointed out that it is our task to *find out* whether or not non-random associations exist, *not* simply to proclaim them on the basis of intuition. Are there really non-random associations of attributes that clearly distinguish 'Tribes' from 'Chiefdoms', 'Lithic' from 'Archaic', 'Mogollon' from 'Anasazi'. 'proto-neolithic' from 'neolithic', 'Sesklo' from 'Starčevo', etc. ? The point is, we must *measure* the variability we observe, and objectively determine where, if at all, the 'breaks' occur in the real world. We might find that there is actually a continuum of variability in a given case; or we might find varying degrees of clustering into more or less discrete groupings of attributes. To presume that clustering occurs *a priori* is 'misplaced concreteness' of the most damaging sort. 'During the past thirty years archaeologists have warned against the mixing of levels and inaccurate partitioning of archaeological deposits; the warning here is against . . . the partitioning of our observational universe into irrelevant analytical units' (Binford, 1968, p. 25).

This leads us to suggest another caution. There are many instances in anthropology in which the generation of types is inappropriate. In fact, we think that as anthropologists become more and more concerned with specific problems, and in describing and explaining processes of variability and change in cultural systems, the establishment of discrete types will seem increasingly less useful. Instead of dividing our observational universes into discrete, reasonably tightly bounded categories, we will more frequently find it necessary to measure variability on a *continuous* or interval scale of measurement.

We can illustrate this by reference to Service's culture classification, using his 'Tribe' and 'Chiefdom' categories. It seems generally inappropriate to use such a typology, not only because it may not represent reality accurately, but because it is also inappropriate to ask a question like: 'Why do societies sometimes evolve from Tribes to Chiefdoms?' or 'Why are Tribes and Chiefdoms different?' Even in considering specific empirical examples, this kind of question is not the kind of question we will be increasingly concerned to ask, *if* we want to study processes.

There are two reasons for this. In the first place, such concepts as 'Tribe' and 'Chiefdom' include so many variables of human behaviour that we cannot hope to measure variability among them in a quantitative way. They are simply too complicated, multivariate and ill defined. And, secondly, the process-oriented anthropologists are not interested in asking why a tribe differs from a chiefdom, or evolves into one. What they are interested in is how and why measurable aspects of what we call tribes and chiefdoms vary. For example, we will be increasingly interested in such questions as 'What causes increases in the centralization of power?' or 'Why do we get increases in the degree of administrative specialization?' And 'Why is there variability in the rates at which such things occur?' We are interested in why people behave in the ways they do, and we must ask specific questions if we want specific and meaningful answers.

The questions we have just asked can be operationalized into measurable variables. We can measure variability and change in such things as 'degree of centralization of power' and 'increasing administrative specialization', and we can do so on a continuous scale such that *degrees* and *rates* of variability can be measured. And we will then be able to explain variability and change by reference to variables which also are measured on continuous scales (e.g. rates of population increase, population density, decreasing availability of arable land, and so forth).

In pursuing process, then, we may not need to develop as many discrete categorizations as we have in the past. We may be able to think in terms of variables rather than types, at least for many studies.

We hope that this paper may not only be useful in stimulating thought about the nature and significance of classification and typology, but also that it will generate increasing concern for evaluating the necessity for types in the first place. Thus, when are types appropriate, and when are they not? 'What are we measuring when we apply various scales to the archaeological record: either nominal scales (typologies) or ordinal scales (stage classifications)?' (Binford, 1968, p. 25). In considering this, we must also ask ourselves whether the questions we are asking are the ones we really want to ask?

Notes

1. This is a revised version of a paper entitled, 'The nature and significance of types', presented by the authors at the Thirty-fifth Annual Meeting of the Society for American Archaeology, Mexico City, May 1970. While we may not have taken full advantage of all of the constructive criticism of that paper, we are most grateful

to Albert C. Spaulding, Irving Rouse, Fred T. Plog, Watson Smith, J. O. Brew and George L. Cowgill in that regard.

2. The term 'model' refers here to a general paradigm or viewpoint for understanding the nature and significance of types; it should not be confused with more technical definitions.

3. It should be noted that Robert Whallon, Jr, of the University of Michigan has devised an approach to typology which views types as *hierarchies* of attributes rather than as tight clusters of attributes in the sense discussed by Krieger (1944) and Spaulding (1953). Using collections of sherds previously collected and 'typed' by William Ritchie and R. S. MacNeish in New York State, Whallon found that he could not replicate the defined types using such clustering procedures as those suggested by Spaulding (1953); in fact, he got no good clustering at all. But using his hierarchical model he was able to statistically replicate the defined types. He concludes that it is likely that many of our standard typologies probably do not represent tight attribute clusters, but rather are hierarchies of attributes ordered in tree-type fashion in terms of the relative *importance* of the attributes in type definition. In this approach, the criteria for definition of types can *shift* from one type to the next ' . . . depending upon where one is in the process of subdividing along the hierarchy of attributes' (Whallon, 1971, p. 7). Whallon's discovery does not affect the basic points being made in our paper, however; nor does it demonstrate that tight statistical clustering of attributes cannot often be discovered. What he has shown is that in his sherd collections such clustering was not evident, and that Ritchie and MacNeish had actually defined types through an intuitive process that weighted their attributes in terms of a hierarchy of recognized importance.

4. Sabloff has disclaimed the intention of conveying the idea that the Sabloff-Smith scheme represents the best way to classify ceramics in his area, and that it is good for all or most research purposes (personal communication). Nonetheless, the published statement (1969) clearly argues to the contrary.

5. Rouse's latest definition of 'mode' is clear in the following: 'In an effort to avoid confusing types of artefacts with types of features, the custom has developed in the United States of limiting the term *type* to the pattern of attributes which is diagnostic of a class of artefacts and to substitute the term *mode* for the pattern of attributes that is diagnostic of a class of features' (Rouse, 1960). A type, then, is the end product of the procedure of classifying artefacts and a mode, the end product of the procedure of classifying individual features of artefacts (Rouse, 1970b, p. 11).

6. For somewhat similar studies, see Deetz (1965) and Whallon (1968).

7. It is true, of course, that the prehistoric peoples who made our artefacts were consciously aware, and striving to make the things they made; but it is insufficient to regard their 'templates' as *explanations* of these things. They would be descriptions that would themselves be in need of explanation – assuming that such descriptions of templates could be made at all.

References

ADAMS, R. MCC. (1968) Archaeological research strategies: past and present. *Science*, **160**, (3833), 1187–92.

BAKKA, E. (1968) Reply. *Norwegian Archaeological Review*, **1**, 45–50.

BENJAMIN, A. C. (1965) *Science, Technology and Human Values*. Columbia: University of Missouri Press.

BINFORD, L. R. (1965) Archaeological systematics and the study of culture process. *American Antiquity*, **31**, (2), 203–10.

BINFORD, L. R. (1968) Archeological perspectives. In BINFORD, S. R. and BINFORD, L. R. (eds.) *New Perspectives in Archeology*, 5–32. Chicago: Aldine.

BRETERNITZ, D. A. (1968) *An Appraisal of Tree-Ring Dated Pottery in the Southwest.* Anthropological Papers of the University of Arizona No. 10. Tucson: University of Arizona Press.

BREW, J. O. (1946) The use and abuse of taxonomy. In *Archaeology of Alkali Ridge, Southeastern Utah.* Papers of the Peabody Museum of American Archaeology and Ethnology, Harvard University, No. 21, 44–66. Cambridge, Mass.: Harvard University Press.

BYERS, D. S. and JOHNSON, F. (1940) Two Sites on Martha's Vineyard. *Papers of the R. S. Peabody Foundation for Archaeology*, Vol. I. Andover, Mass.

CLARK, G. (1952) *Prehistoric Europe: The Economic Basis.* London: Methuen.

CLARKE, D. L. (1968) *Analytical Archaeology.* London: Methuen.

COLTON, H. S. (1942) Types and Wares. *Clearing House for Southwestern Museums Newsletter*, No. 49.

COLTON, H. S. (1952) *Pottery Types of the Arizona Strip and Adjacent Areas in Utah and Nevada.* Museum of Northern Arizona Ceramic Series No. 1.

COLTON, H. S. (1955a) *Check List of Southwestern Pottery Types.* Museum of Northern Arizona Ceramic Series No. 2.

COLTON, H. S. (1955b) *Pottery Types of the Southwest.* Museum of Northern Arizona Ceramic Series No. 3.

COLTON, H. S. and HARGRAVE L. L. (1937) *Handbook of Northern Arizona Pottery Wares.* Museum of Northern Arizona Bulletin No. 11.

CULBERT, P. T. (1965) *The Ceramic History of the Central Highlands of Chiapas, Mexico.* Papers of the New World Archaeological Foundation, Publication 14, No. 19.

DEETZ, J. D. F. (1965) *The Dynamics of Stylistic Change in Arikara Ceramics.* Illinois Studies in Anthropology No. 4. Urbana: University of Illinois Press.

DEETZ, J. D. F. (1967) *Invitation to Archaeology.* New York: Natural History Press.

DUNNELL, R. C. (1971) Sabloff and Smith's 'The importance of both analytic and taxonomic classification in the type-variety system' (*American Antiquity*, **34**, 278–86, 1969). *American Antiquity*, **36**, (1), 115–18.

ERICSON, J. E. and STICKEL, E. G. (1971) *A Proposed Classification System for Ceramics.* MS., unpublished, University of California, Los Angeles.

FORD, J. A. (1954a) Comment on A. C. Spaulding, 'Statistical techniques for the discovery of artefact types'. *American Antiquity*, **19**, 390–1.

FORD, J. A. (1954b) The type concept revisited. *American Anthropologist*, **56**, (1), 42–54.

FORD, J. A. (1954c) Spaulding's review of Ford. *American Anthropologist*, **56**, 109–114.

FORD, J. A. (1961) In favor of simple typology. *American Antiquity*, **27**, 113–14.

FORD, J. A. and WILLEY, G. R. (1949) *Surface Survey of the Viru Valley, Peru*. Anthropological Papers of the American Museum of Natural History, 43 (1).

FRITZ, J. M. (1968) *Archaeological Epistemology: Two Views*. MS., unpublished Masters Paper, University of Chicago.

GIFFORD, J. C. (1960) The type-variety method of ceramic classification as an indicator of cultural phenomena. *American Antiquity*, **25**, (3), 341–7.

HAGGETT, P. (1966) *Locational Analysis in Human Geography*. New York: St Martin's Press.

HANSON, N. R. (1967) Observation and interpretation. In MORGENBESSER, S. (ed.) *Philosophy of Science Today*, 89–99. New York: Basic Books.

HARGRAVE, L. L. (1932) Guide to forty pottery types from the Hopi country and the San Francisco Mountains, Arizona. *Museum of Northern Arizona Bulletin*, No. 1.

HARGRAVE, L. L. (1935) Concerning the names of southwestern pottery types. *Southwestern Lore*, **1**, (3), 17–23.

HARGRAVE, L. L. and COLTON, H. S. (1935) What do potsherds tell us? *Museum of Northern Arizona Museum Notes*, 7 (12).

HARRIS, M. (1964) *The Nature of Cultural Things*. New York: Random House.

HAWKES, C. (1954) Archaeological theory and method: some suggestions from the Old World. *American Anthropologist*, **56**, (2), 155–67.

HEMPEL, C. G. (1966) *Philosophy of Natural Science*. Englewood Cliffs: Prentice-Hall.

HILL, J. N. (1966) A prehistoric community in eastern Arizona. *Southwestern Journal of Anthropology*, **22**, (1), 9–30.

HILL, J. N. (1970) *Broken K Pueblo: Prehistoric Social Organization in the American Southwest*. Anthropological Papers of the University of Arizona No. 18. Tucson: University of Arizona Press.

HOLE, F. and HEIZER, R. F. (1965) *An Introduction to Prehistoric Archeology*. New York: Holt, Rinehart & Winston.

HOLE, F. and HEIZER, R. F. (1969) *An introduction to Prehistoric Archeology*. 2nd ed. New York: Holt, Rinehart & Winston.

KAPLAN, A. (1964) *The Conduct of Inquiry: Methodology for Behavioral Science*. San Francisco: Chandler.

KIDDER, A. V. (1927) Southwestern Archaeological Conference. *Science*, **66** (1716), 489–91.

KIDDER, A. V. (1931) *The Pottery of the Pecos*. Vol. I. Andover, Mass.; Phillips Academy.

KLUCKHOHN, C. (1958) The scientific study of values and contemporary civilization. *Proceedings of the American Philosophical Society*, **102** (5), 469–76.

KRIEGER, A. D. (1944) The typological concept. *American Antiquity*, **9**, 271–88.

KRIEGER, A. D. (1960) Archaeological typology in theory and practice. In *Selected Papers of the Fifth International Congress of Anthropology and Ethnological Sciences, Philadelphia*, 141–51.

LONGACRE, W. A. (1964) Archeology as anthropology: a case study. *Science*, 144, 1454–5.

LONGACRE, W. A. (1970) *Archaeology as Anthropology: A Case Study*. Anthropological Papers of the University of Arizona No. 17. Tucson: University of Arizona Press.

MCGREGOR, J. C. (1965) *Southwestern Archaeology*. 2nd ed. Urbana: University of Illinois Press.

MCKERN, W. C. (1939) The Midwestern taxonomic method as an aid to archaeological culture study. *American Antiquity*, 4, 301–13.

MACWHITE, E. (1956) On the interpretation of archeological evidence in historical and sociological terms. *American Anthropologist*, 58, 3–25.

MARTIN, P. S., LONGACRE, W. A. and HILL, J. N. (1967) Chapters in the prehistory of eastern Arizona, III. *Fieldiana: Anthropology*, 57. Chicago: Field Museum of Natural History.

MEGGITT, M. J. (1965) *The Lineage System of the Mae-Enga of New Guinea*. London: Oliver & Boyd.

MURDOCK, G. P. (1949) *Social Structure*. New York: Macmillan.

OLIVER, W. D. (1951) *Theory of Order*. Yellow Springs: Antioch Press.

PARSONS, L. A. (1967) Bilbao, Guatemala: an archaeological study of the Pacific coast Cotzumalhuapa region. *Milwaukee Public Museum, Publications in Anthropology*, No. 11, Vol. I.

PHILLIPS, P. (1958) Application of the Wheat–Gifford–Wasley taxonomy to eastern ceramics. *American Antiquity*, 24, (2), 117–25.

PHILLIPS, P. and WILLEY, G. R. (1953) Method and theory in American archaeology: an operatonal basis for culture-historical integration. *American Anthropologist*, 55, 615–33.

ROBERTS, F. H. H., JR (1935) A survey of Southwestern archaeology. *American Anthropologist*, n.s. 37 (1), 1–35.

ROUSE, I. (1939) *Prehistory in Haiti: A Study in Method*. Yale University Publications in Anthropology No. 21. New Haven.

ROUSE, I. (1960) The classification of artifacts in archaeology. *American Antiquity*, 25, (3), 313–23.

ROUSE, I. (1962) The strategy of culture history. In TAX, S. (ed.) *Anthropology Today: Selections*, 84–103. Chicago: University of Chicago Press.

ROUSE, I. (1965) The place of 'peoples' in prehistoric research. *Journal of the Royal Anthropological Institute*, 95, 1–15.

ROUSE, I. (1970a) Classification for what? Comments on *Analytical Archaeology* by D. L. Clarke, 1968. *Norwegian Archaeological Review*, 3, 4–12.

ROUSE, I. (1970b) *Classification in American Prehistoric Archaeology*. MS., prepared for the International Symposium on Archaeological Method and Theory, Flagstaff, Arizona, 1969.

SABLOFF, J. A. and SMITH, R. E. (1969) The importance of both analytic and taxonomic classification in the type-variety system. *American Antiquity*, 34 (3), 278–85.

SACKETT, J. R. (1966) Quantitative analysis of Upper Paleolithic stone tools. *American Anthropologist*, 68, 2, (2), 356–94.

SEARS, W. H. (1960) Ceramic systems and eastern archaeology. *American Antiquity*, 25, (3), 324–9.

SERVICE, E. R. (1958) *Profiles in Ethnology.* New York: Harper & Row.

SMITH, R. E., WILLEY, G. R. and GIFFORD, J. C. (1960) The type-variety concept as a basis for the analysis of Maya pottery. *American Antiquity,* **25**, (3), 330–40.

SMITH, W. (1962) Schools, pots and potters. *American Anthropologist,* **64** (6), 1165–78.

SONNEVILLE-BORDES, D. DE (1960) *Le Paléolithique Supérieur en Périgord.* 2 vols. Bordeaux: Delmas.

SPAULDING, A. C. (1953) Statistical techniques for the discovery of artifact types. *American Antiquity,* **18**, (4), 305–13.

SPAULDING, A. C. (1954) Reply to Ford. *American Antiquity,* **19**, (4), 391–3.

STEWARD, J. H. (1954) Types of types. *American Anthropologist,* **56** (1), 54–7.

SWARTZ, B. K. (1967) A logical sequence of archaeological objectives. *American Antiquity,* **32** (4), 487–97.

TAYLOR, W. W. (1948) *A Study of Archaeology.* American Anthropological Association Memoir No. 69.

TAYLOR, W. W. (1967) *A Study of Archaeology.* Carbondale: Southern Illinois University Press.

THOMPSON, R. H. (1958) Modern Yucatecan Maya pottery making. Memoirs of the Society for American Archaeology No. 15. *American Antiquity,* **23**, 2 (4).

WALLRATH, M. (1967) Excavations in the Tehuantepec region, Mexico. *Transactions of the American Philosophical Society,* **57** (2).

WATSON, P. J., LeBLANC, S. A. and REDMAN, C. L. (1970) *Explanation in Archeology.* New York: Columbia University Press (in press).

WHALLON, R., JR (1968) Investigations of late prehistoric social organization in New York State. In BINFORD, S. R. and BINFORD, L. R. (eds.) *New Perspectives in Archeology,* 223–44. Chicago: Aldine.

WHALLON, R., JR (1971) A new approach to pottery typology. *American Antiquity* (in press).

WHEAT, J. B., GIFFORD, J. C. and WASLEY, W. (1958) Ceramic varity, type cluster and ceramic system in Southwestern pottery analysis. *American Antiquity,* **24**, (1), 34–47.

WILLEY, G. R. (1956) *An Archaeological Classification of Culture Contact Situations.* Society for American Archaeology Memoir No. 11, 1–30.

WILLEY, G. R. (1962) Archaeological theories and interpretation: New World. In TAX, S. (ed.) *Anthropology Today: Selections,* 170–94. Chicago: University of Chicago Press.

WILLEY, G. R. and PHILLIPS, P. (1955) Method and theory in American archaeology, II: historical-developmental interpretation. *American Anthropologist,* **57**, 723–819.

WILLEY, G. R. and PHILLIPS, P. (1958) *Method and Theory in American Archaeology.* Chicago: University of Chicago Press.

7

What mean these stones? Ethno-taxonomic models and archaeological interpretations in the New Guinea Highlands[1]

J. P. WHITE
University of Sydney, Australia

D. H. THOMAS
American Museum of Natural History, New York, U.S.A.

Although ethnographic data have been used as a basis for interpretive analogies throughout the history of archaeological research, the collection of this data by archaeologists, who have specific problems of prehistory in mind, is a relatively new venture. This new ethnography focuses primarily on the nature of the in-the-ground data produced by the technical, economic and social behaviour patterns of societies still living in traditional, pre-Industrial Revolution ways. For example, it is not the marriage rules of a society that are of interest *per se* but the way these are expressed in such features as bridewealth payments (stone axes and pottery are preferred!) and the relocation of persons and houses within and between settlements.

This new ethnography may be divided into two kinds, in a manner similar to that proposed by Ascher (1961). The first, and much scarcer kind, is that collected directly to interpret a specific problem, usually in a situation where there is a clear cultural continuity between prehistoric and present situations. A prime example of this type is Stanislawski's continuing study of the transmission of pottery styles among the Hopi-Tewa in order to test some recent generalizations about social patterning in Southwestern United States sites within the last millennium (Stanislawski, 1969). We would also cite N. David's study of Fulani residence compounds, which tests various posited relationships between settlement size and pattern, and population numbers in prehistoric situations (David, 1971), as well as R. Gould's use of Indian informants both to set up projectile point classifications and to interpret residence patterns at Point St George site, California (Gould, 1966).

The second kind of data is usually collected without a specific and tightly defined problem in mind, but with the aim – or hope – that they will be analogically applicable to some prehistoric problem. These data range from dietary and residence studies of hunter-gatherers (Lee and DeVore, 1968; Hiatt, 1967–8) and the distribution of various pottery types and their breakage rates within a village (Foster, 1960) to the spatial and numerical distribution of women's grinding stones in Arnhem Land (Peterson, 1968) and the long-term study of the modification and decay of a settlement after abandonment (Ascher, 1968). The actual use of this material by archaeologists is infrequent and limited in its scope. Usually, we suspect, these data do no more than generally enhance our understanding of how societies and their various components articulate. Occasionally, they provide the basis for an interpretive analogy.

This chapter discusses an example of each kind of data from the point of view of one restricted system – flaked stone taxonomy in the Central Highlands of Papua-New Guinea. The first section examines a particularistic problem – namely, the use of ethnographic data to set up a classification of prehistoric artefacts. The second section describes an ethnographic experiment, which should be of some general interest to archaeologists working with flaked stone tools. We will now set each problem in context.

There is, we are well aware, a continuing and acrimonious debate as to whether the taxa used by an archaeologist to describe artefacts can and/or should reflect the maker's taxa. This debate is generally futile, since operational tests of the relationship between the two taxonomic systems can rarely be designed. The test of an archaeologist's taxonomy lies in its suitability for solving his 'puzzles' (cf. Kuhn, 1970, pp. 36–40) rather than its possible similarities to a prehistoric folk classification. This is not to say that ethnographic taxonomies can always be ignored by the archaeologist, even if they may often fail to describe an order which is visible in the material and useful in comparative and cross-cultural studies (Vayda and Rappaport, 1968, p. 491). Ethnographic taxonomies may well suggest new classificatory systems to the archaeologist who has been forcing objects into a Procrustean system, convinced that it is the only one available for solving his particular problems. It is with the aim of providing a further contribution to the range of useful taxonomic systems that we present here an ethnographic classification of stone artefacts applied to some archaeological materials. In this system the functional edge of the artefact is used as the basic unit of analysis and each stone tool is treated simply as the record of a series of unrelated uses. When applied to culturally related prehistoric assemblages, albeit in an initial and limited fashion, it does appear to be more useful in the study of culture history and process than does a classical 'typology'. Further, it seems likely that a similar taxonomic system is applicable to stone tool assemblages from other areas of south-east Asia and Australasia, in which case it is probable that, in a broader sense, this classificatory system is in fact related to taxonomic concepts held by the makers of these artefacts.

In the second part of this paper we take up another problem, that of individual variability within a taxonomic system. We are concerned to show how an ethnographically recognized 'type' will vary in its form between individuals within a small, socially conscious group of people. We will show that the 'mental templates' that seem to exist, around which a group constructs its technology, are in fact subject to the same kinds of individual variability as has been observed in other aspects of culture (Harris, 1968, pp. 584 f.; Bulmer and Tyler, 1969; Sanday, 1968). Our observations suggest that the extent to which artefacts can differ while remaining within the same taxon is considerable (cf. Deetz, 1967, pp. 45–51), and we will metrically demonstrate the variation within two stone tool 'types' made by two small communities within a single language group. We suggest that these data may be of relevance to archaeologists who find tightly defined 'types' restricting their investigations but lack ethnographic support for a looser system.

I

The Central Highlands region of Papua-New Guinea is bounded on the west by the Strickland Gorge, on the east by the Ramu-Markham Fall, and by towering ranges such as the Bismarcks to the north and the Kubors to the south. Within these boundaries today live numerous groups of people all of whom speak non-Austronesian languages of the same (micro-)phylum (Wurm, 1964), share a basically similar technology and pattern of land use, are primarily dependent on sweet potato, and raise pigs for protein and prestige (Brookfield, 1964). Similarities also abound in their social and religious life (Watson, 1964). Within this culture area two subregions may be distinguished in terms of languages, settlement patterns, material culture and prehistory (Read, 1954; Wurm, 1961; White, 1967b). These subregions lie east and west of the Mai-Asaro watershed, with the majority of the present population living in the latter area. Our study will discuss ethnographic materials from both subregions, but archaeological specimens from the eastern one only have been subjected to detailed study. Inspection of material excavated in the western subregion suggests that our conclusions are applicable to the region as a whole.

When Europeans first entered the Highlands in the early 1930s they found people using two main kinds of stone implements – polished axes or adzes and simple unretouched flake tools. Throughout the Highlands, flake tools are made by percussion, using either a hand-held core or a hammer and anvil technique. The occurrence of these methods seems to vary to some extent within the Highlands, and the widest range has been observed in the most westerly part of the region, among the Duna-speaking people of Lake Kopiago. The most complex technique among the Duna is a bipolar one, with the core being wrapped in bark before flaking. This method seems to result in relatively longer, thinner and smaller flakes, which are kept neatly together by the bark wrapping and are not scattered around by the flaking process. The worked-out bipolar cores often resemble *outils écaillés* in all significant respects (White, 1968b). Stone hammers are universally used and consist of any fist-sized stone to hand. No preparation or trimming of cores has ever been observed. Raw materials are normally chert of various kinds, but a true flint is used by some Duna.

Flakes without any secondary retouch are used as tools, and they constitute the only category of flake tools: no secondary retouch with the aim of shaping flake tools has ever been observed among the New Guinea highlanders. In all societies so far studied[2] all flakes used as tools, as well as those not regarded as suitable for use, are classified within a single taxon to which a general name is given.

Flakes and cores – the distinction is irrelevant to highlanders – are selected for tasks if they have features suitable for the work in hand. The two most important features – namely, edge type and size – are functionally determined. Thus, if a knife is required to cut arrow barbs, then a small flake with an acute angled edge is chosen; if a bow stave or axe handle needs to be smoothed, then a piece with a more obtuse edge is selected (White, 1968a). Functional limitations, however, set only broad formal limits, and tools of very varying sizes are used for any particular task. A correlate of this attitude is that any piece of stone may be applied to different tasks, provided it has an edge and is of a size suitable for the work. A lump of chert, for example, can serve successively as a hammer, core, scraper, plane and knife. Modern highlanders, then, do not regard their flaked stone tools as a series of formal or single-functional types, but as pieces of stone, parts of which may be used to perform certain activities.

Flake tools are used for a variety of tasks such as scraping, cutting, gouging and drilling wood, bone and shell, shredding fibre, and sawing out stone axes. They are particularly important for these activities, but may be used casually in many other ways – cleaning off encrustations, peeling vegetables, shaving ochres into powder for paint, and so on (see Strathern, 1969, p. 318). It should be noted that most activities involving flake tools are carried on by males; women are rarely seen using tools and almost never make them. Bamboo knives would appear to be the most common traditional woman's tool.

Two modifications to flakes used as tools have been observed in the ethnographic present. Occasionally, if a sharp edge interferes with a comfortable grip on the stone, then the edge will be blunted by striking it with a hammer or on an anvil (White, 1968a, p. 513). The other modification occurs when small flakes are roughly hafted by inserting them into the split end of a pitpit (cane grass), bamboo or cane stem and bound with fibre. These flakes are used for drilling, in which case pointed ones are selected, or for teasing and shredding fibres, in which case they tend to be blunt-ended and have at least one straight, sharp, working edge aligned parallel to the handle. Hafted flakes have been recorded only from the western and southern areas of the Highlands, although a similar artefact used as an arrow for ceremonial incision is known from the eastern subregion. Hafted flaked tools are taxonomically distinguished by at least one group of people – the Duna of the Western Highlands – although they do not class the stones themselves, prior to hafting, as a separate group. It should be stressed that, although some highlanders have said that flakes are resharpened after use has blunted them, and that this implies that secondary retouch is practised, this has never been observed in the field. Further, what appear to be retouched edges on prehistoric flake tools were 'conspicuously ignored' by Mount Hageners asked to demonstrate flake tool use (Strathern, 1969, p. 316, and pers. comm.).

The fact that this standardized pattern of flake tool classification and use is found among approximately 1 million highlanders would be of little interest were it not that these people appear to be the descendants of long-term residents of the area. This allows us to suggest that their current technological patterns may be used legitimately to assist in the interpretation of prehistoric artefacts from the Highlands. We will now, therefore, briefly document the fact of long-term residence. More detailed accounts are given in Bulmer and Bulmer (1964), Bulmer (1966), White (1967b, 1971).

The earliest settlement of the island of New Guinea is currently dated to around 25 000 years B.P. (White, Crook and Ruxton, 1970), although rather older dates may be expected on the basis of the Australian evidence (Bowler

et al., 1970). Within the Central Highlands, dates of *c.* 11 000 B.P. for industries containing ground stone axe-adzes, stone waisted blades and flake tools
are probably associated with hunting and gathering communities. Similar
assemblages, though without waisted blades in more recent times, are found
in cave sites throughout the prehistoric record (i.e. until A.D. 1930), although
root crop horticulture and animal husbandry became the economic norm by at
least 2500 B.P. and probably a good deal earlier. Too little work has been
undertaken in the Highlands – or anywhere else in New Guinea – for estimates
to be made of prehistoric population sizes, economic structures or community
patterning, while even the occurrence of subregional variation between east
and west Highlands is only vaguely indicated. However, although data from
only four dated sites are available, the picture given by the flaked stone tools is
more comprehensive than most others because of the number of specimens.
Throughout Central Highlands prehistory the bulk of the industry is composed of flake tools with step-flaking retouch and unretouched, utilized flakes.
The retouched tools are small and chunky and exhibit no consistent formal
patterning. The retouch is nearly always unifacial, its incidence varies widely
on closely adjacent parts of the same edge and it is often found in more than
one plane of the tool. It is, therefore, most logically interpreted as resharpening
retouch, and this is confirmed to some extent by the presence of trimming or
resharpening flakes, which carry heavy but truncated step-flaking on their
dorsal surfaces (cf. Clark, 1954, p. 100). While the ratio of these flakes to
secondarily retouched pieces varies between sites, there is some consistency
in the pattern of occurrence within sites (Table 7.1). Although retouched tools
are found in all Highlands sites, there is evidence from two sites to suggest
that within the last thousand years they were becoming much less important,
and that simple utilized flakes began to form an ever-increasing part of the
stone tool assemblage (Table 7.1). The reasons for this change have not been
satisfactorily explained, but the fact remains that there is a record of the start
of a process which could lead to a total absence of retouched tools in the
ethnographic record. It should be noted that fine-grained diachronic evidence
for the last millennium is not yet available. Overall, however, there do not
appear to be any sudden or major changes in the technological record.

Synchronic data also suggests that the current population of the Highlands
has been in the area for thousands of years. Languages of the Highlands all
belong to one stock (Wurm, 1964), while the present pattern of blood groups
is seen by Simmons *et al.* as 'the result of differentiation developing from a
small, reasonably homogeneous population' (1961, p. 662). Various social
aspects of ethnography such as male–female relationships (Meggitt, 1964) and

TABLE 7.1. *Flaked stone tools from archaeological sites (Nos.)*

Site	Horizon	Secondarily re-touched tools	Utilized pieces No.	Utilized pieces %	Trimming flakes No.	Trimming flakes Ratio to sec. ret. tools	C14 (approx.) years, B.P.
	1	42	36	46	28	0·7	
	2	37	33	47	62	0·6	
							4 500
Kafiavana	3	151	35	19	85	0·6	
(White, 1967b)	4	174	33	16	59	0·3	
	5	212	40	16	84	0·4	
	6	118	26	18	66	0·6	
	7	119	22	16	37	0·3	
							9 000
							10 000
	8–9	183	42	19	49	0·3	
	1	136	59	30	10	0·07	
							750
Aibura	2	198	31	14	56	0·3	
(White, 1967b)	3	103	7	6	19	0·2	
							4 000
							850
	1	115	22	16	52	0·5	
Batari	2	123	23	16	72	0·6	
(White, 1967b)	3	168	20	11	101	0·6	
	4	115	29	20	78	0·7	
							8 000
Niobe	1	404	73	15	301	0·7	none
(White, 1967b)	2	392	52	12	217	0·5	
	2	108	35	24	n/a		
	3	27	8	22			3 000
	4	43	17	28			
	5	26	6	19			
Kiowa	6	25	9	26			4 100
(Bulmer, 1966)	7	49	16	25			
	8	54	34	39			
	9	19	13	41			
	10	9	20	69			7 500
	11	5	2	29			
	12	9	6	40			8 400

social structure (de Lepervanche, 1967–8) also exhibit pan-Highlands similarities. It is the historical continuity demonstrated by both diachronic and synchronic evidence which, to us, justifies the idea that the classificatory system used by Highlanders for their stone tools may have been that used by the prehistoric inhabitants of the areas. The fact that it is a classificatory method unlike that normally used by archaeologists also suggests that it may be helpful in looking at this formally amorphous material.

The methods used to apply the Highlands ethnographic classification to the archaeological materials from the same area have been published in detail elsewhere (White, 1969). They are based on making the altered (i.e. used or retouched) edge on an artefact the prime unit of analysis, and treating each piece of stone as the record of a series of discrete processes acting on it, rather than as a functional whole in the normal archaeological sense. Thus the final shape and size of the stone is simply that considered an adequate 'handle' by the final user of an edge. Three groups of observations are made. The first consists of the nature of the raw material and the number of planes and edges that were used. The second group of observations relates to each edge – whether the implement is whole in relation to that edge, whether the edge is made on a core or flake and the size of this stone, whether the edge is whole, its size, angle, retouch and curvature. The third group of observations is made in relation to macroscopic use-wear – its nature, size, shape and angle. These observations were made on some 3000 tools from three sites in the eastern subregion. The varying occurrence of individual attributes was charted, and correlations have been attempted only between pairs of attributes. The results of this simple analysis, which we hope eventually to make more comprehensive, suggest that there is a very high degree of similarity between all assemblages studied and that edge attributes do divide, broadly speaking, into two presumptively functional classes, a feature already observed, although using somewhat different criteria, in the ethnographic present (White, 1967b, 1968a). Each of the three sites, however, exhibits a slightly different patterning of attributes that characterize each of the two classes, and there appears to be more consistency within sites through long periods of time than there is between levels dated to the same period at different sites. Furthermore, there seem to be greater similarities between two sites in the same valley system than between either of these two and a third site some 60 km away.

Similar results to those described above were not obtained when a more morphologically formal classification was used. In this case the most 'satisfactory' typology was derived by dividing the tools according to the position of the retouch in relation to the long axis, so that a series of end, side, end and

282

side, etc., tools were distinguished. The occurrence of these classes, however, exhibited no consistent patterning, except that tools with the least amount of retouch were the most common and vice versa. Also, tools with retouch on more than one plane increased in number in the same more recent levels as did the unretouched flakes, so that the observed technological change was confirmed. The only other completed study of these industries uses a similar classification without obtaining more consistent results (Bulmer, 1966), and we see this as further supporting the validity of the 'edge analysis'.

In relation to the results of the edge analysis, it is interesting to speculate on the social implications of the long-term continuation of intra-site patterns in artefacts that we have reason to believe were made and used by men. It might, for example, lend some weight to the idea that the extreme 'looseness' of current Highland residential patterns (e.g. Langness, 1964) may be a development of more recent times. Alternatively, it may be more appropriate to suggest that even if male movement occurred it was never on a sufficient scale or from a sufficient distance to change the long-term trends in artefact manufacture. Testing these hypotheses, however, can only be done with considerably more fine-grained data than is now available.

At a less speculative level, it is theoretically fairly simple to test the primary model we have used. Microscopic use-wear studies on both ethnographic and prehistoric artefacts should suggest that patterns of tool use have not changed, and should also show that prehistoric retouched tools were used for the same functions as are unretouched tools at the present time. Unfortunately, attempts to study micro-wear on Highlands tools have not so far proved particularly successful, the main difficulty being that of detecting use-wear on a sufficiently large sample.

The classification system we have used on Highlands material may well have a wider application. In 1954, Movius recognized that it was difficult to distinguish formal types in many south-east Asian industries dating from Pleistocene times. Faced with this problem, Gorman (1971) has also drawn attention to the fact that the formal typologies of Hoabinhian materials have been quite unsuccessful, and reports that he can discern some patterns in the Spirit Cave material, using an analysis based on similar technological and edge damage attributes to the ones reported here. In discussing a pre-microlithic industry in Australia, Mulvaney and Joyce (1965) recognized that the application of a purely formal typology was not appropriate, and described such attributes of the artefacts as percentage of edge retouched and implement thickness, though without attempting to formulate classes. W. Shawcross, however, makes the most explicit statement, when, discussing the New

Zealand flake stone industries, he says (1964, p. 17): 'it would seem better to ... assume that the needs of prehistoric New Zealanders for edge tools could often be met by utilitarian selection or slight modification of a suitably angled piece of stone, rather than by preparing an object to some preconceived notion of ideal shape.' Similar situations may also be found from time to time in other parts of the world, although we would hesitate to predict their appearance. We would like to simply note here that Mellars, discussing the Greek Mousterian (1964), makes comparable observations to ours, as does Wendorf in relation to some Nubian material (1968, p. 992). We would suggest, then, that (especially east of the Movius line) the normal patterns of formal typology may often be missing, and that the ethnographic taxonomy observed in the New Guinea Highlands can provide a more useful model with which to approach some prehistoric industries.

II

The ethnographic experiment described in this section is designed to illustrate some of the parameters inherent in the flaked stone artefact taxonomy of one New Guinea Highlands group. We will discuss three aspects of variance:

(i) The variations in the definition of an artefact class that artisans will allow from day to day.

(ii) The variations that occur between the classifications made by different members of a socially conscious, face-to-face group, within the space of two weeks.

(iii) The variations that exist between artefacts which are similarly classified by two face-to-face groups who speak the same language.

We describe first the location and design of the research programme, then the results obtained.

The men who participated in this experiment all speak Duna, a language spoken by some 14 000 people in the Lake Kopiago area of the Western Highlands District. Like other highlanders, the Duna are subsistence farmers growing primarily sweet potato and raising pigs. Their socio-political organization is acephalous, with the largest of their socially recognized and geographically distinguished groups being the parish, named after an eponymous ancestor and containing from 25 to 550 people. The Duna have had regular, if limited, access to European technology only since about 1960, and all men now living grew to adulthood in a society where stone tools were in everyday

PLATE 7.1 Flaked stone tool (*aré*) used for carving designs on an arrow linkshaft. Baranda parish.

PLATE 7.2 *Aré kou* being used to drill a hole in a piece of shell. Man from Hareke.

PLATE 7.3 Man from Aluni flaking *aré*. His piles of *aré kou* and *aré* are in the foreground.

use. Even today stone tools may, from time to time, be used in place of steel (cf. White, 1967b, p. 109), although most men own a steel knife or axe.

Hareke and Aluni, the two parishes involved in this study, are some 25 air kilometres (at least five hours walk) apart and their members speak slightly different, but mutually intelligible, dialects of the Duna language. The population of each parish, according to the 1966–7 census of the Department of District Administration was:

	Men	Women	Children	Total
Hareke	123	113	140	376
Aluni	57	44	58	159

These figures should be taken as approximate only.

Work in the area was carried out by White from August to November 1967. At each parish, an initial approach was made by asking some senior men (i.e. those who appeared to be older than about 30 years) to make bows, arrows, string, shell ornaments and other traditional items of material culture using only traditional tools (Plates 7.1, 7.2). The manufacture and use of these tools was discussed at length through a Duna–Neo-Melanesian (pidgin) interpreter.[3] After a week or more of work and discussion, several men were asked to come each day to make some flaked stone tools and to classify these, indicating how they would be used and what criteria were being used for their selection (Plate 7.3).

The Duna, like other highlanders, use only unretouched flakes as tools and these are selected for use according to the appropriateness of their edge type and size to the work in hand. Within both parishes all flakes and chunks used as tools, together with the waste pieces and the nodules of stone from which flakes are produced, are called *aré*. Where a distinction must be made, flaked tools are referred to as *aré ne kana* (sharp *aré* stone; literally, *aré* tooth stone), or *aré kone* (real or true *aré*). No distinction is made between flakes and cores – all are *aré* and all may be used as tools. Among the *aré kone*, however, some are selected for setting into a small cane haft so that they can be used for shredding fibres or drilling or gouging holes. Flakes thus hafted tend to be small, and most Duna regard any small blade-like flakes they produce as being especially suitable for hafting. Hafted flakes are called *aré kou* (bound or hafted *aré*); this classification refers to the tool as a whole and not simply to the flake, since many *aré* may be either hafted or

285

used in the hand. The smallest *aré*, which are too small to hold comfortably in the hand and therefore can only be used in a haft, are not separately classified by the Duna. Nor is a distinction made between *aré kou* used as drills, where the haft is essential to the mechanics of drilling (Plate 7.2) and those used for fibre shredding, where the haft is desirable but not essential. However, some differences are visible in these flakes, since drills must have a point, while shredders need only a sharp edge parallel to the haft (cf. Strathern, 1969).

The Duna, then, designate only one class of flaked stone artefacts (*aré* (*kone*)) from which some are selected to form a subclass (*aré kou*). All men participating in the experiment were asked to divide their artefacts into these two groups (along with waste). Their basis for sorting appeared to be primarily size, with shape entering as a secondary consideration. This is, of course, predictable, since nearly all small sharp edged stones can be *aré kou* and would therefore be selected out from the overall range of stones first, with only chunky pieces, difficult to haft, being candidates for inclusion among the *aré* rather than the *aré kou*. Edge angle appeared to enter the classification only marginally – apparently all except very obtuse edges may be used for shredding fibres, etc. Thus the *aré kou* collected in this experiment comprise a full range of the implements that are so classified in each Duna parish, while the *aré* we describe are a residual category of tools remaining after the *aré kou* have been removed. If further work is attempted, a more sophisticated design would distinguish artefacts which artisans consider can only be used in a haft from those which can be used either this way or in the hand.

Some field tests of the consistency of these classifications were made. Several men were asked to re-sort material classified by other people, and in each case some of the samples were minimally affected while others were drastically reorganized. Each man so tested was able to approximately repeat his classifications of both his own and other people's material. Regrettably, inadequate records of these tests were kept so that they cannot be documented here.

We would like to point out that it is difficult to conduct a tightly controlled experiment in a New Guinea society. As well as language problems and the predictable complexity of another culture's taxonomic system, not only is the whole idea of 'an experiment' foreign, but colonial conditioning has also to some extent trained New Guineans to give a 'pleasing' response to any white man. Therefore, this study avoided as far as possible any verbal or financial pressure on the men either to produce a certain number of artefacts each day or to return to work each day, while a continuing discussion and employment of stone tools hopefully served to suggest that the observer was interested in and possessed some knowledge of stone technology, probably a prerequisite for collecting good data about it (cf. Bulmer, 1969).

Nearly 9000 *aré* were collected at Hareke and Aluni. As will be seen in Table 7.2, ten men at Hareke and eight men at Aluni made tools, but much of the material came from only a few men, especially at Hareke. Each type of tool made by each man on each day was kept separately and taken to Sydney for description. All artefacts collected are now deposited in The Australian Museum, Sydney (reference E 64421–Z).

TABLE 7.2. *Aré made at Hareke and Aluni, divided according to person and day of manufacture (Nos.)*

Note: Samples in italics were excluded from the study (see p. 289). Code numbers are those used Figs. 7.1–7.5 and are allocated sequentially by date within each person's output.

	Individuals										
	1	2	3	4	5	6	7	8	9	10	Total
Hareke											
aré kou											
Date											
21/9	—	*18*	—	—	—	—	—	—	—	—	
22/9	—	*9*	—	—	—	*8*	—	—	—	—	
28/9	*18*	*8*	27	19	28	*13*	—	—	—	—	
29/9	38	24	52	33	28	*19*	29	22	—	—	
30/9	38	—	91	33	36	41	27	26	*56*	—	
1/10	—	—	74	59	32	—	73	55	—	—	
2/10	90	—	96	50	72	39	—	—	*85*	—	
10/10	—	—	—	—	—	46	—	—	—	29	
11/10	56	66	69	—	—	44	—	—	—	*40*	
12/10	140	69	88	—	—	—	—	—	—	—	
13/10	82	49	—	—	88	—	—	—	—	—	
Totals	462	243	497	194	284	210	129	103	141	69	2332
Code nos.	1–6	7–10	11–17	18–21	22–7	28–31	32–4	35–7	—	—	
Hareke											
aré											
Date											
21/9	—	39	—	—	—	—	—	—	—	—	
22/9	—	*18*	—	—	—	7	14	—	—	—	
28/9	47	31	32	39	42	*18*	18	—	—	—	
29/9	47	41	*24*	31	35	*13*	—	3	—	—	
30/9	65	—	31	43	41	26	20	24	21	—	
1/10	—	—	—	—	—	—	—	—	—	—	
2/10	—	—	—	—	—	—	—	—	—	—	
10/10	23	—	—	—	—	16	—	—	—	19	
11/10	36	—	37	—	—	—	—	—	—	37	
12/10	16	*14*	51	—	—	—	—	—	—	—	
13/10	24	*19*	—	—	—	—	—	—	—	—	
Totals	258	162	175	113	118	80	52	27	21	56	1062
Code nos.	38–43	44–6	47–50	51–3	54–5	56	57	58	—	—	

TABLE 7.2—*continued*

Individuals

	1	2	3	4	5	6	7	8	Tot
Aluni aré kou									
Date									
1/11	27	89	77	38	31	55	36	65	
2/11	37	78	46	12	35	57	45	53	
3/11	62	110	111	45	57	93	60	49	
4/11	—	90	87	43	68	—	—	88	
5/11	—	76	126	—	43	—	70	71	
6/11	58	125	130	101	70	—	41	50	
7/11	86	110	105	104	67	121	58	60	
8/11	80	81	—	95	77	81	—	59	
Totals	350	759	682	438	448	407	310	495	388
Code nos.	59–64	65–72	73–9	80–5	86–93	94–8	99–104	105–12	
Aluni aré									
Date									
1/11	35	14	62	14	10	60	18	32	
2/11	10	35	19	10	9	25	14	23	
3/11	27	38	26	22	12	26	6	47	
4/11	—	—	26	34	9	—	—	29	
5/11	—	29	20	—	15	—	11	31	
6/11	36	46	45	128	55	—	14	34	
7/11	35	39	60	41	6	14	15	34	
8/11	56	35	—	35	25	23	—	34	
Totals	199	236	258	284	141	148	78	264	160
Code nos.	113–17	118–23	124–9	130–4	135–6	137–40	—	141–8	

Grand total: 889

Total used: 805

Six attributes were selected to describe the parameters of each tool 'type'. These are not, as will be seen, logically independent variables, a feature normally required of attributes selected for use in taxonomic systems (Sokal and Sneath, 1963; Sackett, 1969). However, in this case we are primarily concerned with the attributes as independent entities and are not attempting to integrate them into a classification. The fact that some attributes covary will mean only that we are, to some extent, repeating our illustration of classificatory variance.

The attributes were chosen partly in the light of the Duna classification and partly by default, since there are very few attributes of simple unretouched flakes made by simple percussion that can be used profitably in taxonomic discussions. The attributes are:

(1) Length (cm). This is the maximum dimension of the stone in any plane. Normally it will measure the main axis of a flake.

(2) Width (cm). The maximum dimension of the stone measured at right angles to its long axis but in the same plane.

(3) Thickness (cm). The maximum dimension of the stone taken in the plane at 90° to that in which length and breadth measurements were taken.

(4) Angle of the working edge(s). This was measured with a goniometer to the nearest 5°. The working edge was that indicated as such by the maker of the artefact. The angle is often the same for most of the length of the edge, but where necessary several measurements were taken and averaged. Each stone may have up to three working edges and the angle of each of these was recorded separately.

(5) Weight (g). Measured in grammes to the nearest 0·1 g.

(6) Length/width ratio. This expresses the blade-like qualities of a piece of stone and is one of the criteria used by the Duna to designate a piece of stone which will make a 'good' *aré kou*.

One of the problems with the current experiment was to distinguish between the sources of artefact variation. Three such sources may have affected the final result – technical competence, differences in raw material, and cognitive variability. In this experiment the first of these is irrelevant since the crude flaking technique, absence of secondary retouch, and practice of selecting implements from the general pile of debris produced by flaking, preclude the existence of technical as opposed to referential discrimination. The same raw material is used by all workers within each parish, but the two parishes have access to different material sources. All men at Hareke flaked nodules of blackish flint with a weathered white cortex, while Aluni men used a weathered chert of a translucent yellow-brown to dark brown colour. The material from Aluni contains more impurities and, being more weathered, is more inclined to shatter during flaking. We therefore hypothesize that the implements from Aluni will be both smaller and more variable than those from Hareke, representing an adjustment by Aluni men to the poorer qualities of their material. Variations within each parish, however, will be explicable in terms of the factor of cognitive variability, since the same raw material is being used by all workers. We will show below how the two sources of variation affect our results.

The material used in this analysis was made by eight individuals in each parish. An artisan's output was included only if he had made at least twenty of one class of artefacts a day for two days or more, since the possibility of distortion arising from the use of smaller samples would seem to be very high. Some 800 artefacts (samples *underlined* in Table 7.2) were excluded from the total collection, either because the samples were too small or the field records were unclear, leaving a sample of 8053 specimens.

Histograms of the six variables were plotted, using the Burroughs Advanced Statistical Inquiry System (BASIS) computer package. All distributions except edge angle showed a marked skewness to the right. Since most bivariate and multivariate statistical tests require normal distributions, the skewed distributions had to be transformed. Empirical curve fitting indicated that the common log (base 10) transformed length, width and thickness to approximately normal form. Weight and length–breath ratio were transformed by a square root routine.

We were interested, initially, in differences between subpopulations of the sample, especially differences between the two tool types and the two parishes Sets of *t*-tests were applied to each division. At the 0·001 level, all variables except edge angle showed consistent differences between both parishes and tool types. We will discuss each of these differences in turn.

Table 7.3 shows that, as predicted, the artefacts from Hareke are significantly larger than those from Aluni. It does not indicate, however, that the Aluni artefacts show a greater range of variation than those from Hareke. We must therefore consider that the appreciation of variation is not significantly altered by differences in the material, although gross size is changed. It is also noticeable that edge angles of Aluni artefacts are larger than those made at Hareke, but that the difference is significant only at the 0·02 level. We suggest that this difference may result from cognitive variation. It is difficult to see how, even if raw material caused significant variation in the range of angles produced at each place, which seems somewhat unlikely, the artisan's selection of artefacts from among the flakes produced would fail to take account of this. It might be the case, of course, that Aluni men tend to select flakes with a rather thicker working edge, which breaks and blunts less frequently, thus compensating for the more fragile raw material. On the other hand, availability of raw material is not a problem and it is therefore difficult to see why thicker edges should be selected rather than that more flakes be used. Thus, while we would consider that if raw material were the only factor operating to produce between-parish difference the result should not encompass significant variance, it is clear that we cannot state that there is an unambiguous cognitive difference between the two parishes in terms of edge angle. Using individual attributes, then, our research design does not adequately allow us to control the possible variables involved in variation.

Within each parish, Table 7.3 shows that the two types of artefacts are significantly different (at the 0·02 level or less) in terms of each variable with one exception – edge angles at Hareke. These differences follow the parameters that would be expected on the basis of the ethnographic classification and therefore validate it. As expected, *aré kou* are smaller than *aré*, they are more blade-like, but have a low or insignificant difference in edge angles.

TABLE 7.3. *Artefact measurements and tests of similarity*

(A) means and standard deviations (cm)

	Hareke				Aluni			
	aré kou		*aré*		*aré kou*		*aré*	
	mean	*s. dev.*	*mean*	*s. dev.*	*mean*	*s. dev.*	*mean*	*s. dev.*
Length	32·75	2·94	39·17	5·12	25·01	2·35	33·34	4·50
Width	14·69	1·51	29·48	3·22	12·41	1·29	20·34	2·61
Thickness	6·85	0·77	11·32	1·97	5·61	0·67	9·19	1·67
Edge angle	51·26	4·94	53·66	7·65	54·50	5·54	57·65	5·09
Weight	2·60	0·69	9·71	3·85	1·35	0·32	5·25	2·22
Length-breadth ratio	2·41	0·29	1·59	0·09	2·17	0·25	1·69	0·17

(B) *t*-tests between types from each parish and between parishes within each type: values of p

	Hareke	Aluni	*aré kou*	*aré*
Length	0·001	0·001	0·001	0·001
Width	0·001	0·001	0·001	0·001
Thickness	0·001	0·001	0·001	0·001
Edge angle	0·1	0·01	0·01	0·02
Weight	n/a	0·001	0·001	0·001
Length-breadth ratio	0·001	0·001	0·001	0·01

We next wished to examine the data in multivariate fashion, in order to study those aspects of variation described above (p. 284). Given the sets of tools made by each individual, we wanted to know if there were notable patterns within and between individuals, considering all variables simultaneously. We chose the technique of Principal Components Analysis (PCA), which attempts to render the most parsimonious summarization of a mass of observations (Seale, 1964, p. 113). The basic unit employed in this analysis is the type–man–day (TMD). A TMD is comprised of all the artefacts of a particular type produced by one man on a single day. We will also use the abbreviation TM to refer to all artefacts of one type produced by one man. A total of 148 TMDs were used in this experiment, the number of artefacts in any one ranging from 20 to 140 (Table 7.2).

The analysis begins with a $p \times p$ correlation matrix, where p is the number of variables involved. Point representations – the data *per se* – are plotted in a p-dimensional space, usually forming ellipsoidal swarms of points. The principal components analysis involves the rotations of the coordinate axes in the variable space. The result describes the p original variables in terms of p new principal components. All components are *orthogonal* to each other, i.e. they are statistically independent. In addition, each component accounts for a maximum amount of variance of the variables. The first component accounts for the most variance, the second component is independent and at right angles to the first. The second component is responsible for the second largest amount of variance, and so on. The sum of the variance of the p components must equal the total variance of the original p variables. For this reason, it is desirable that the p variables be measured in the same units to eliminate bias because of disparity between scales of measurement. When different measurements have been used, the scores must be standardized into comparable units. Output from PCA consists of the $p \times p$ correlation matrix, the per cent of total contribution of variance of each principal component, and the importance of each of the original variables in the new orthogonal component. The most important components can then be used as coordinate axes to determine the placement of point values in the new, reduced-dimensional variable space. This is the purpose of principal component analysis as applied here.

Although a general discussion of multivariate analytical methods would be inappropriate here, we wish to distinguish between *principal components analysis*, as discussed above, and the more ubiquitous *factor analysis*. The model for PCA is simply (Harman, 1967, p. 15):

$$z_j = a_{j1}F_1 + a_{j2}F_2 + \cdots + a_{jp}F_p$$

where each of the p original variables is described in terms of p new orthogonal components, $F_1, F_2, \ldots, F_p$. The objective of PCA is to render the most concise summary of the initial data. For this reason, PCA has been termed the 'maximum variance approach'. By way of contrast, Harman (1967, p. 15) presents the model of *classic factor analysis* as:

$$z_j = a_{j1}F_1 + a_{j2}F_2 + \cdots + a_{jm}F_m + d_jU_j$$

where the p original variables are described in terms of m ($m < p$) *common factors* and a *unique factor*, d_jU_j. The unique factor accounts for the residual error of each variable. This second model is designed to maximally reproduce the correlations themselves. The common axes in a factor analysis can be rotated to new orthogonal or oblique axes to conform with the theoretical ideas underlying the formulation of the model (Seale, 1964, p. 153). While the results of PCA and factor analysis may appear rather similar, especially when one ignores the last few of the p components, the conceptual models and computational procedures are quite different. Since we require only the efficient summarization of multivariate data, rather than an estimation of underlying structure, we have chosen the simpler method of principal components. The reader is referred to Haggett (1966, pp. 223–4) and King (1969, pp. 175–6) for examples of PCA in geography and to Seale (1964, p. 122) and Boyce (1969) for applications in the biological sciences.

In our analysis, we adapted the principal components FORTRAN IV program of Wahlstedt and Davis (1968) to a Burroughs 5500 computer at the University of California, Davis. The transformed data were standardized according to the formula

$$z_{ij} = \frac{X_{ij} - \bar{X}_j}{s_j}$$

where the standardized score z_{ij} is computed by subtracting the attribute mean $\bar{X}_j$ from the raw score X_{ij}, and then dividing by the attribute standard deviation, s_j (see Sokal and Sneath, 1963, p. 295). The result is that each attribute is distributed with a mean value of one and a standard deviation of zero. In this fashion, the edge angle and weight measurements can be properly compared with linear values such as length, width and so on. The correlation matrix was computed on these transformed variables in the first step of the PCA.

Table 7.4 shows that three components contribute 98·4% of the total variance of the implements. The first component, which contributes two thirds of the total variance, includes the highly intercorrelated variables of length, width, thickness and weight, and is thus interpreted as size. This accords well with the ethnographic data, which suggests that size is a major factor in distinguishing *aré* from *aré kou*. Component 2 is primarily loaded on the width variable. This was not predicted to be an important variable and it was not one to which any Duna drew attention. Our interpretation is that this variable may be functionally important. Since *aré kou* must be hafted in cane grass or similar wood, there is a great deal more limitation on the width of artefacts than on their length. The same is true, to a much lesser extent, of *aré* which have to be held in the hand. However, if our suggestion is valid, we would also expect thickness to be relevant here, whereas the only associated variable in this component is edge angle, and that to a very minor extent. Edge angle forms the major part of Component 3, suggesting that it is not of primary importance in discriminating between *aré* and *aré kou*, but that it is a feature recognized by the Duna, since its correlation with other variables is low.

TABLE 7.4. *Eigenvectors and components (transformed and standardized data)*

	Components					
	1	2	3	4	5	6
% of total contribution per eigenvalue:	68·7047	16·6199	13·1691	0·792631	0·661099	·525538E-01
log length	0·4220	−0·0490	−0·5624	0·5088	−0·1285	−0·4774
log width	0·4814	0·1777	0·0716	0·3910	−0·0675	0·7577
log thickness	0·4793	−0·1174	−0·0884	−0·6424	−0·5795	0·0112
edge angle	0·1383	−0·9129	0·3345	0·1828	0·0457	0·0044
sqrt weight	0·4831	0·0092	−0·0926	−0·3478	0·7965	−0·0499
sqrt lb ratio	−0·3285	−0·3445	−0·7419	−0·1455	0·0812	0·4419

It is interesting that length–breadth ratio contributes only about 0·5% of the total variance, which implies that it is neither important nor associated with any other variable. This result is an acute expression of a discontinuity between technology and preference. All Duna artisans regard blade-like flakes as being of superior quality and more 'appropriate' for *aré kou* than normal flakes. Nonetheless, they appear to be unwilling to restrict their selection to these flakes or to employ a technology that would produce blade-like flakes with greater frequency (cf. also Strathern, 1969, plates XVI–XVII).

The main results of the principal components analysis are set out in Figs. 7.1–7.5. Figs. 7.1–7.3 are maps of the position of each TMD plotted in relation to each of the three pairs of important components (1–2, 1–3, 2–3). Figs. 7.4–7.5 give the two TMs of each of the sixteen men involved in the experiment plotted in relation to component pairs 1–2 and 1–3. The numbers used on each diagram are the code numbers of the TMDs, given in Table 7.2.

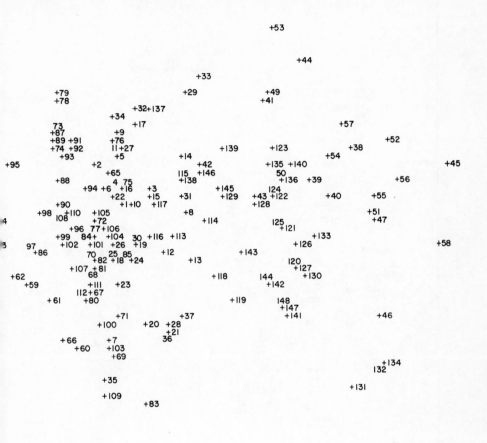

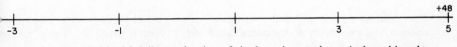

FIG. 7.1. All individuals' daily production of single tool types (TMDs) plotted in relation to components 1 (horizontal axis) and 2 (vertical axis). See Table 7.2 to identify particular TMDs.

Taking the overall picture first, it is clear that size is the best single discriminator between types, but that a combination of size and edge angle also allows us to discriminate, with very few exceptions, between the *aré kou* from

295

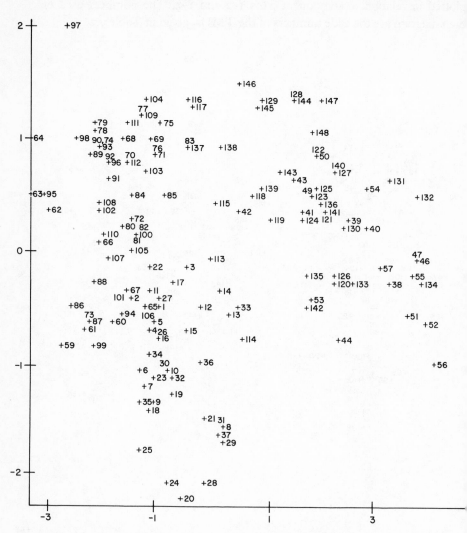

F IG. 7.2. All individuals' daily production of single tool types (T MD s) plotted in relation to components 1 (horizontal axis) and 3 (vertical axis). See Table 7.2 to identify particular T MD s.

Hareke and those from Aluni. Thus, *aré kou* with small edge angles from Aluni are, with one exception (TMD 2), smaller in size than *aré kou* with comparable edge angles from Hareke. This clear distinction may, as we pointed out earlier, be the result of raw material differences, but we are in-

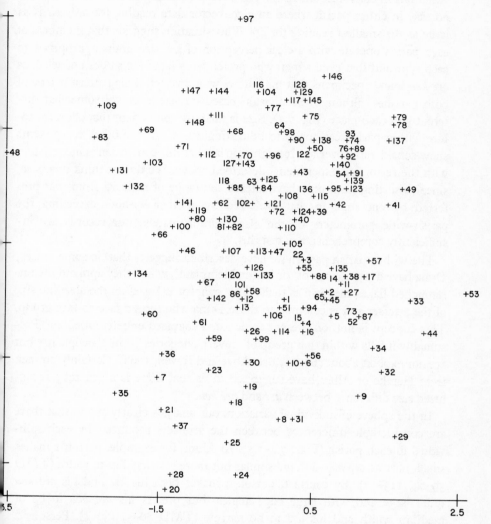

FIG. 7.3. All individuals' daily production of single tool types (TMDs) plotted in relation to components 2 (horizontal axis) and 3 (vertical axis). See Table 7.2 to identify particular TMDs.

clined to think that the variation is so large that a classificatory difference must also be involved.

Looking at the pattern within each parish, the size component alone discriminates absolutely between *aré* and *aré kou*, irrespective of any individual variations in classification. In the eigenvectors relating to each TMD there is no case in either parish where an eigenvector data reading for *aré kou* is as large as the smallest reading for *aré*. This situation suggests that members of each parish operate with a clear perception of the size limits appropriate to each type and that even a man who prefers very large tools does not select as *aré kou* many specimens that his fellows would reject. This pattern is true of both parishes, although the division based on size is drawn somewhat differently in each place (Fig. 7.1). Size is the only component that allows absolute within parish categories to be distinguished, for the other components show considerable overlap. It might appear that this conclusion is inconsistent with the re-sorting experiments described above. We do not think this is so, since re-sorting need only have altered the range of material from that preferred by one man to that preferred by another without exceeding the parish-wide parameters of the class. Unfortunately, our records are insufficiently comprehensive to test this.

The within-parish pattern we have described suggests that, in some senses, Duna have a 'type concept' or 'mental template', which they apply to the unretouched flakes they use as tools. This concept is based on the absolute size of the artefact and is common to those Duna who form a face-to-face group. This concept is not, on present evidence, a cognized or referential one. Presumably it falls within that group of 'covert categories', which people use but are not explicit about (Berlin, Breedlove and Raven, 1968). Certainly no men from Hareke or Aluni have suggested to us that there is a generally recognized size difference between *aré* and *aré kou*.

In the sphere of individual variation, our analysis clearly shows that there are considerable differences between the artefacts produced by each individual in each parish (Figs. 7.4–7.5). At Aluni, for example, person 1 makes small, narrow *aré kou*, and *aré* similar but more restricted as to width (TMD 59–64, 113–17). By contrast, person 4 makes both his *aré* and his *aré kou* quite large and with large edge angles, but prefers his *aré kou* to be of medium width and his *aré* to be narrow (TMD 80–5, 130–4). Persons 2 (TMD 65–72, 118–23) and 5 (TMD 86–93, 135–6) are very restrictive as to the sizes of both their tool types, but allow a considerable range of angles and widths. Person 3 (TMD 73–9, 124–9) tends to select his *aré kou* to have very large edge angles, while person 8 (TMD 105–12, 141–8) prefers smaller ones.

Similar differences may be seen at Hareke. Person 5 (TMD 22–7, 54–5) prefers medium-sized tools and is quite restrictive in this respect about *aré kou*, while he allows a wider range of edge angles and widths. Person 6 (TMD 28–31, 56) displays an approximately similar pattern. Person 7 (TMD 32–4,

57) prefers very wide tools, and person 8 (TMD 35–7, 58) rather narrow ones. Person 1 (TMD 1–6, 38–43) is restrictive in all three components as regards *aré kou*, but his *aré* are quite variable as to size.

We would also like to draw attention to the fact that each man exhibits parallelisms in his classifications. Thus, in general, people make large or small tools of both types, or they have a preference for tools of particular widths or edge angles and this is expressed in all their work. However, the overall range of variability allowed in the *aré* is rather wider than that of the *aré kou*, as would be expected given the wider range of tasks for which these tools are used, the fact that *aré* are hand-held, and that, in this experiment, they form a residual category.

Some very interesting results emerge when we take account of the sequence of manufacturing dates. It is clear that in Aluni there is a general shift in edge angles of *aré kou* from more acute to more obtuse in the period studied (Figs. 7.4, 7.5). This is most marked in persons 1, 6 and 7, but is generally true of all other men in the group. The same phenomenon is observable, though to a much lesser extent, in the *aré*, especially in person 1, and to a smaller degree in 3, 5 and 7. It is difficult to account for this shift as anything other than a change in perception of the artefacts, since all other variables would appear to be being held constant. This drift, moreover, occurs in men who worked on most days (5, 8) as well as those who took a break (1, 6 and 7). It is difficult to think either that this change is an intentional one or that these results are simply random. Nor is it likely that the presence of an experimental situation is the cause, since one would expect in this case to see a drift in *aré kou* edge angles towards those of *aré*. Further, since edge angle is not a critical factor in distinguishing the two types it is surprising that it is this variable that exhibits consistent patterning over time. We would expect such patterning to be most obvious in the size variable. We also draw attention to the fact that the 'drift' we document could not have proceeded indefinitely, since angles would soon have become too obtuse to be serviceable. Indeed the data from persons 2 and 4 suggest that there may in fact be a cyclical 'drift' in classifications, which, over a longer period of time than has been observed, would exhibit steady fluctuation about a norm. We cannot explain, however, why the pattern should be so regular with respect to this one variable. Other shifts in TM variables that do occur are not so consistent between persons, although they are so within individuals – for example, *aré* made by persons 1 and 4 at Hareke and person 6 at Aluni and *aré kou* made by person 8 at Hareke and person 4 at Aluni (Figs. 7.4, 7.5).

The archaeological correlates of the patterns described here may provide an

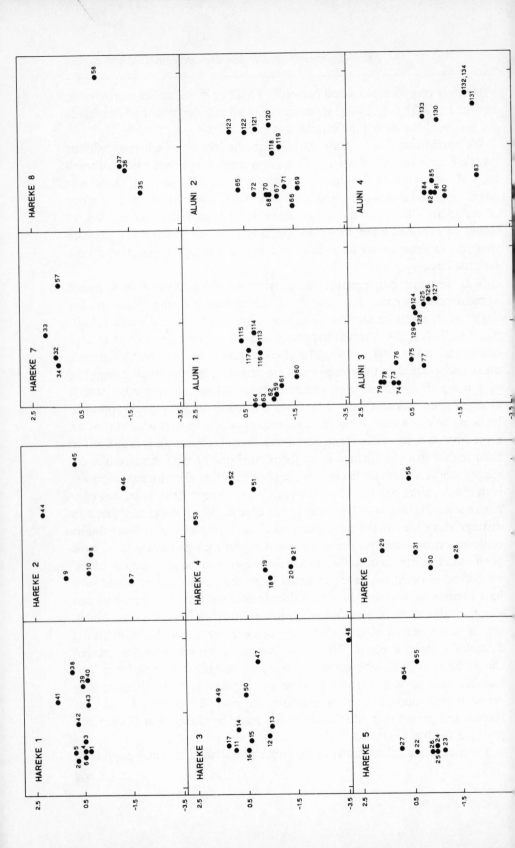

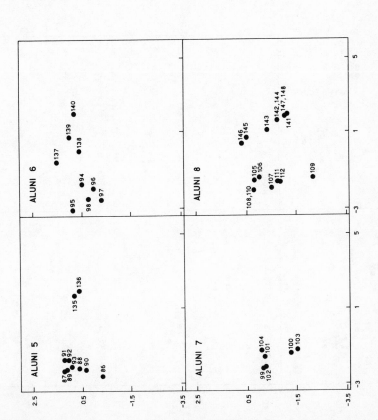

FIG. 7.4. Daily tool production of individuals plotted in relation to components 1 (horizontal axis) and 2 (vertical axis) to show individual variation. Refer to Table 7.2 to identify types and chronological sequences.

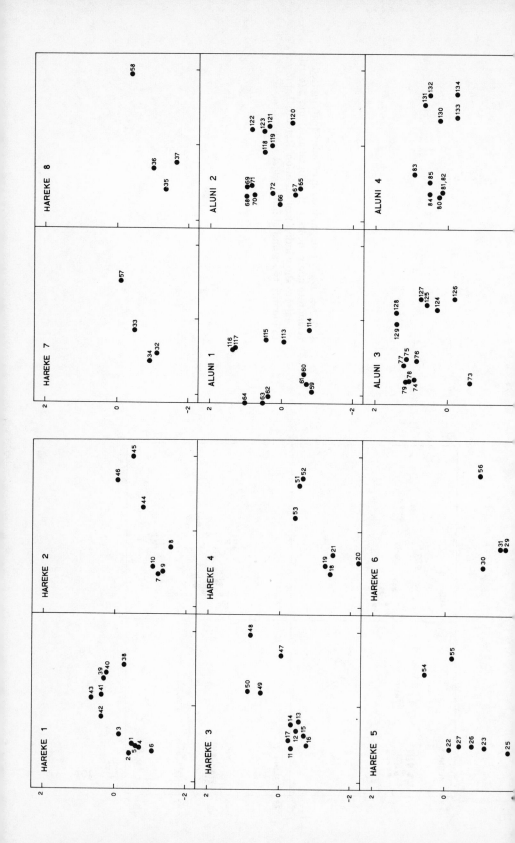

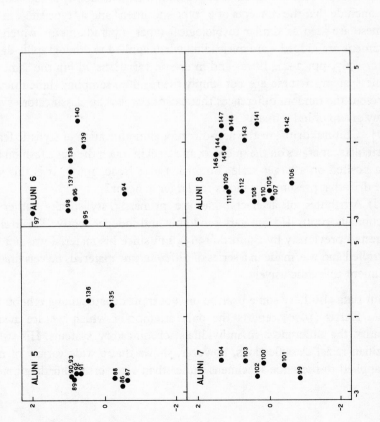

FIG. 7.5. Daily tool production of individuals plotted in relation to components I (horizontal axis) and 3 (vertical axis) to show individual variation. Refer to Table 7.2. to identify types and chronological sequence.

ethnographic basis for some hitherto undocumented archaeological beliefs. We make no claim, however, for their universal validity and to some they will appear to prove the obvious. We suggest that our experiment allows the following conclusions:

(i) Raw material can play a major role in determining the metrical attributes of artefacts even where similar classificatory, technological and functional criteria are involved.

(ii) Covert 'type' categories with metrically defined limits can exist within small face-to-face groups and these categories are applied by members of that group irrespective of their own idiosyncrasies.

(iii) Individuals vary sufficiently in their classifications to cause measurable differences between their artefacts, suggesting that some intra- and inter-site variability should be regarded in this light.

(iv) Each individual's classifications vary both in their short-term stability and in the features in which variability is allowed to occur. Within a group of people there are not only more and less 'variable' classifiers, but also differences in the selection of attributes within which variability is allowed. Thus we conclude that the concepts of a 'type specimen' and a 'type site', in so far as these are seen as similar to biological types – paradigms by which other specimens are judged – are misleading when applied to ethnographic data (cf. Isaac, 1967, pp. 3–4). Intra- and inter-site variations within the same technomic system, if these are not simply the result of sampling difficulties, may represent the random differences that exist between the classificatory systems of any group of individuals.

(v) 'Cultural drift', or the non-directional modification of stylistic features of artefacts, operates on the microcosmic level in much the same fashion as has been posited on a larger scale (Binford, 1963; Isaac, 1967). It is this small-scale drift that presumably allows the larger to occur.

(vi) Attributes of artefacts that are primarily stylistically rather than functionally controlled can vary randomly and independently. This has been suggested previously by Binford (1963), but since his material was not time-controlled and was made in a series of different raw materials he was unable to document this conclusively.

Our data also have some bearing on a current debate among ethnotaxonomists. Harris (1970) reports the only attempt of which we are aware to quantify the differences in individuals' classificatory systems. His study of Brazilian racial classifications, however, shows that a wide variety of names are applied to the same specimens rather than vice versa. Our data point toward the view that, even among speakers of the same language, there are clear differences in the range of objects for which people employ the same terminology and that these are not necessarily the result of differences in 'competence'. There is also some suggestion that the differences are more marked between small face-to-face groups than within them. These conclusions would tend to support some of Harris's views about current difficulties with ethnotaxonomic research. For archaeologists, our conclusions would appear to complicate whatever procedures may exist for arriving at 'the idea behind the Indian behind the artefact'.

This preliminary and rather incomplete experiment was designed to illustrate some of those aspects of a group's behaviour likely to provide archaeologists with analogies to their own data. We are less interested in the rules by which a society thinks it organizes its existence than in the material expression of these rules. Although the rules and their expression are unlikely to be completely at odds, the articulation between them is often very complex. Only if we have evidence about a wide range of relevant behaviour is there even the possibility of working from it to the rules that its originators held. We think that the possibility is rather remote, but as we comprehend more fully the relationships between social rules and individual behaviour, the hypotheses we can formulate about the past will become more meaningful.

Notes

1. White is primarily responsible for the ethnographic and archaeological data in this paper, Thomas for the analysis in Section II. However, we are jointly responsible for the context and conclusions. White's field work in New Guinea was carried out under the auspices of the Australian National University in 1963–5 and The Australian Museum, Sydney, in 1967. Field work among the Duna was analysed and written up in 1970 while on leave from The Australian Museum and during the tenure of a Harkness Fellowship held at the University of California, Berkeley. White wishes to thank these institutions, the Commonwealth Fund of New York, and especially Professor Jack Golson, Dr Frank Talbot and Professor J. Desmond Clark. Dr Glyn Isaac, Mrs Jan Smith, Miss Marilyn Little and Mr Charles Modjeska were more than ordinarily helpful and must take some credit, without responsibility, for the result. The computer time was generously provided by the Computer Center, University of California, Davis. The authors wish to thank Mrs E. Kemnitzer for the illustrations.

2. Detailed observations have been made among the Tairora (White, 1967b) and Yagaria (White, 1967a, 1967b, 1968a) in the eastern subregion and Mount Hageners (Strathern, 1969), Wiru (Strathern, 1969) and Duna (White, 1968b) in the western subregion. Very similar patterns seem to occur in some other parts of New Guinea,

such as the Telefomin area (B. Craig, pers. comm.), Lake Kutubu (Williams, 1941) and the Grand Valley of the Balim river (Heider, 1970, p. 279).

3. In 1967 almost no Duna people spoke Neo-Melanesian. White spoke no Duna and relied on his interpreter, Mr Poke Kama. In 1969–70 Mr Charles Modjeska of the Australian National University worked in the area and, gaining some knowledge of the Duna language, confirmed with only very minor modifications the ethnographic data pertinent to stone technology collected by White.

References

ASCHER, R. (1961) Analogy in archaeological interpretation. *Southwestern Journal of Anthropology*, **17**, 317–25.

ASCHER, R. (1968) Time's arrow and the archaeology of a contemporary community. In CHANG, K. C. (ed.) *Settlement Archaeology*, 43–52. Palo Alto, Calif.: National Press.

BERLIN, B., BREEDLOVE, D. E. and RAVEN, P. H. (1968) Covert categories and folk taxonomies. *American Anthropologist*, **70**, 290–9.

BINFORD, L. R. (1963) 'Red ocher' caches from the Michigan area: a possible case of cultural drift. *Southwestern Journal of Anthropology*, **19**, 89–108.

BOWLER, J. M., JONES, R., ALLEN, H. and THORNE, A. G. (1970) Pleistocene human remains from Australia: a living site and human cremation from Lake Mungo, western New South Wales. *World Archaeology*, **2**, 39–60.

BOYCE, A. J. (1969) Mapping diversity: a comparative study of some numerical methods. In COLE, A. J. (ed.) *Numerical Taxonomy*, 1–31. New York: Academic Press.

BROOKFIELD, H. C. (1964) The ecology of Highland settlement: some suggestions. *American Anthropologist*, **66**, No. 4, Pt 2, 20–38.

BULMER, R. N. H. (1969) *Field Methods in Ethno-zoology with Special Reference to the New Guinea Highlands*. Mimeo.

BULMER, R. N. H. and TYLER, M. J. (1969) Karam classification of frogs. *Journal of the Polynesian Society*, **77**, 333–85.

BULMER, S. (1966) *The Prehistory of the Australian New Guinea Highlands*. Unpublished M.A. thesis, University of Auckland.

BULMER, S. and BULMER, R. (1964) The prehistory of the Australian New Guinea Highlands. *American Anthropologist*, **66**, No. 4, Pt 2, 39–76.

CLARK, J. D. G. (1954) *Excavations at Star Carr*. Cambridge: Cambridge University Press.

DAVID, N. (1971) The Fulani Compound and the Archaeologist. *World Archaeology*, **3**, 111–31.

DEETZ, J. (1967) *Invitation to Archaeology*. New York: Natural History Press.

FOSTER, G. M. (1960) Life-expectancy of utilitarian pottery in Tzintzuntzan, Mexico. *American Antiquity*, **25**, 606–9.

GORMAN, C. F. (1971) The Hoabinhian and after: subsistence patterns in southeast Asia during the late Pleistocene and early Recent periods. *World Archaeology*, **2**, 300–20.

GOULD, R. A. (1966) *The Archaeology of the Point St George site and Tolowa Prehistory.* University of California Publications in Anthropology No. 4.

HAGGETT, P. (1966) *Locational Analysis in Human Geography.* New York: St Martin's Press.

HARMAN, H. H. (1967) *Modern Factor Analysis.* 2nd ed. Chicago: University of Chicago Press.

HARRIS, M. (1968) *The Rise of Anthropological Theory.* New York: Crowell.

HARRIS, M. (1970) Referential ambiguity in the calculus of Brazilian racial identity. *Southwestern Journal of Anthropology,* **26**, 1–14.

HEIDER, K. G. (1970) *The Dugum Dani.* Chicago: Aldine.

HIATT, B. (1967–8) The food quest and the economy of the Tasmanian aborigines. *Oceania,* **38**, 99–133, 190–219.

ISAAC, G. LL. (1967) Identification of cultural entities in the Middle Pleistocene. In HUGOT, H. (ed.) *Actes du VIe Congrès Panafricain de Préhistoire* (Dakar).

KING, L. J. (1969) *Statistical Analysis in Geography.* Englewood Cliffs, N.J.: Prentice-Hall.

KUHN, T. S. (1970) *The Structure of Scientific Revolutions.* 2nd ed. Chicago: University of Chicago Press.

LANGNESS, L. L. (1964) Some problems in the conceptualization of Highlands social structures. *American Anthropologist,* **66**, No. 4, Pt 2, 162–82.

LEE, R. B. and DEVORE, I. (eds.) (1968) *Man The Hunter.* Chicago: Aldine.

LEPERVANCHE, M. DE (1967–8) Descent, residence and leadership in the New Guinea Highlands. *Oceania,* **38**, 134–58, 163–89.

MEGGITT, M. J. (1964) Male–female relationships in the Highlands of Australian New Guinea. *American Anthropologist,* **66**, No. 4, Pt 2, 204–24.

MELLARS, P. A. (1964) The Middle Palaeolithic surface artefacts. In DAKARIS, S. I., HIGGS, E. S. and HEY, R. W. The climate, environment and industries of Stone Age Greece, Part I. *Proceedings of the Prehistoric Society,* n.s. **30**, 229–44.

MOVIUS, H. L., JR (1954) Palaeolithic archaeology in southern and eastern Asia, exclusive of India. *Cahiers d'Histoire Mondiale,* **2**, 257–82, 520–53.

MULVANEY, D. J. and JOYCE, E. B. (1965) Archaeological and geomorphological investigations on Mt Moffatt Station, Queensland, Australia. *Proceedings of the Prehistoric Society,* n.s. **31**, 147–212.

PETERSON, N. (1968) The pestle and mortar: an ethnographic analogy for archaeology in Arnhem Land. *Mankind,* **6**, 567–70.

READ, K. E. (1954) Cultures of the Central Highlands, New Guinea. *Southwestern Journal of Anthropology,* **10**, 1–43.

SACKETT, J. R. (1969) Factor analysis and artifact typology. *American Anthropologist,* **71**, 1125–30.

SANDAY, P. R. (1968) The 'psychological reality' of American–English kinship terms: an information-processing approach. *American Anthropologist,* **70**, 508–23.

SEALE, H. (1964) *Multivariate Statistical Analysis for Biologists.* London: Methuen.

SHAWCROSS, W. (1964) Stone flake industries in New Zealand. *Journal of the Polynesian Society,* **73**, 7–25.

SIMMONS, R. T., GRAYDON, J. J., ZIGAS, V., BAKER, L. L. and GAJDUSKEK, O. C. (1961) Studies on Kuru, V. A blood group genetical survey of the Kuru region and other parts of Papua-New Guinea. *American Journal of Tropical Medicine and Hygiene*, **10**, 639–64.

SOKAL, R. R. and SNEATH, P. H. A. (1963) *Principles of Numerical Taxonomy*. San Francisco: Freeman.

STANISLAWSKI, M. B. (1969) *Hopi-Tewa Pottery Making: Styles of Learning*. Paper presented to the 34th Annual Meeting of the Society for American Archaeology.

STRATHERN, M. (1969) Stone tools and flake tools: evaluations from New Guinea. *Proceedings of the Prehistoric Society*, n.s. **35**, 311–29.

VAYDA, A. P. and RAPPAPORT, R. A. (1968) Ecology, cultural and noncultural. In CLIFTON, J. A. (ed.) *Introduction to Cultural Anthropology*, 477–97. Boston, Mass.: Houghton Mifflin.

WAHLSTEDT, W. J. and DAVIS, J. C. (1968) *FORTRAN IV Program for Computation and Display of Principal Components*. Kansas State Geological Survey Computer Contribution 21.

WATSON, J. B. (1964) Anthropology in the New Guinea Highlands. *American Anthropologist*, **66**, No. 4, Pt 2, 1–19.

WENDORF, F. (1968) Site 117: a Nubian Final Paleolithic graveyard near Jebel Sahaba, Sudan. In WENDORF, F. (ed.) *The Prehistory of Nubia*, Vol. 2, 954–95. Dallas: Southern Methodist University Press.

WHITE, J. P. (1967a) Ethno-archaeology in New Guinea: two examples. *Mankind*, **6**, 409–14.

WHITE, J. P. (1967b) *Taim Bilong Bipo*. Unpublished Ph.D. thesis, Australian National University.

WHITE, J. P. (1968a) Ston naip bilong tumbuna: the living Stone Age in New Guinea. In SONNEVILLE-BORDES, D. DE (ed.) *La Préhistoire: problèmes et tendances*, 511–16. Paris: Centre National de la Recherche Scientifique.

WHITE, J. P. (1968b) Fabricators, outils écaillés, or scalar cores ? *Mankind*, **6**, 658–66.

WHITE, J. P. (1969) Typologies for some prehistoric flaked stone artefacts in the Australian New Guinea Highlands. *Archaeology and Physical Anthropology in Oceania*, **4**, 18–46.

WHITE, J. P. (1971) New Guinea: the first phase in Oceanic settlement. In GREEN, R. and KELLY, M. (eds.) *Studies in Oceanic Culture History*, Vol. 2, 45–52. Pacific Anthropological Records No. 12, Hawaii.

WHITE, J. P., CROOK, K. A. W. and RUXTON, B. P. (1970) Kosipe: a Late Pleistocene site in the Papuan Highlands. *Proceedings of the Prehistoric Society*, n.s. **36**, 152–70.

WILLIAMS, F. E. (1941) *Natives of Lake Kutubu, Papua*. Oceania Monographs No. 6.

WURM, S. A. (1961) New Guinea languages. *Current Anthropology*, **2**, 114–16.

WURM, S. A. (1964) Australian New Guinea Highlands languages and the distribution of their typological features. *American Anthropologist*, **66**, No. 4, Pt 2, 77–97.

8
Introduction to imaginary models for archaeological scaling and clustering

LeROY JOHNSON, Jr.
Research Consultant, Eugene, Oregon, U.S.A.

INTRODUCTION

I like to use Peter Achinstein's (1968) typology of models. According to him, when a person proposes a *theoretical* model of X, he wants to approximate to what X actually is by making assumptions about it. In an *analogue* model of X he wants to construct or describe some different item Y that bears certain analogies to X. In an *imaginary* model of X he wants to consider what X could be if it were to satisfy conditions he specifies (p. 222). In this last type, some system or structure of data relations usually makes up the main part of the model, and of course it is an imaginary one.

When an archaeologist engages in scale analysis, cluster analysis, or another similar study, in effect he determines some kind of agreement or fit between his data and an imaginary, structured system of data relations such as a one-dimensional similarity scale. In certain cases, as when making tree diagrams from similarity scores, there is no question of determining 'degree of fit' between the data and the imaginary model, since the structure of the model is entirely flexible and accommodating. At any rate, our borrowing, constructing or use of imaginary models of a graphic and/or numerical sort helps us to understand archaeological data because it helps simplify and synthesize them. Productive interpretation can follow easily upon sound descriptive (synthetic) analysis.

The present paper will review, in Part I, some elementary models of scaling and clustering and will do this from the standpoint of the familiar topic of archaeological seriation. Seriation is clearly a reasonable point at which students and research workers may be introduced to the useful techniques of scale analysis and cluster analysis, since it is already somewhat familiar. The exposition is addressed, then, to people having a minimum acquain-

309

tance with these topics. Part II will deal with slightly more complex models of data relations.

Two previously published data sets will be used as illustrative examples: one is palaeontological, the other archaeological. The former is simple and its item relations can easily be appreciated. As an illustration, therefore, it gives the reader a chance to appreciate and check, intuitively if you will, the results of the analyses. The second data set is larger and more complex. It is given to illustrate the usefulness of imaginary models for generating patterns of data relations which cannot be readily seen.

PART I SIMPLE MODELS OF SCALING AND CLUSTERING

Seriation has long been used as a simple technique for scaling items according to their similarities, and as a preliminary analytical step in grouping items into homogeneous units or clusters. From the 1890s onward, it has been applied sporadically and largely unsystematically. Nevertheless, the use of item seriation as a research tool has been slowly and constantly refined, especially in anthropological classification and in archaeological dating.

Not a few publications have appeared recently which treat explicitly some of the problems involved in seriation, and they will be mentioned below. Several things need to be set straight, however. There is confusion in the literature about what seriation is and how it should be performed. Problems of interpretation are confused with problems of description and analysis. And the archaeological mania for estimating temporal relations between artefact assemblages has overrated the potential of item seriation for relative dating.

The following discussion will treat seriation from several standpoints, notably (1) its basic nature, (2) its history and treatment in the literature, (3) its problems for computer processing, and (4) its proper use, particularly in conjunction with other aids, in generating overviews for bodies of numerical data.

Item seriation: its definition

In general, the term *seriation* means the placing of items in a series so that the position of each best reflects the degree of similarity between that item and all other items in the data set. Thus seriation is one form of scale analysis. It

310

arranges items by position alone, and does not use variation in metric distance between item positions as an expression of degree of similarity. As such it is simpler than the scaling procedures of Shepard (1962a, 1962b) and Kruskal (1964a, 1964b), which use the distance between item points to show the magnitude of the similarity between the items.

Fig. 8.1 illustrates three kinds of scaling models with ten hypothetical items. Type A has points located in multidimensional space, where the distances between the points indicate corresponding similarities. Type B is a

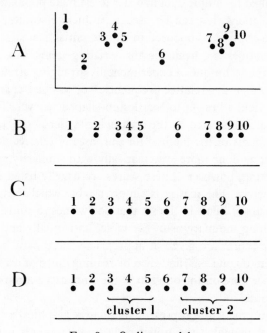

FIG. 8.1. Scaling models.

one-dimensional scaling of items where both position and distances between points are used as measures of similarity. Type C presents a scale identical to B with the exception that metric distance between points is disregarded and position alone expresses the similarities between the items.

The use of the term *seriation* in this paper will be restricted to C-type series. This type may initially appear to be considerably more limited in potential than either A or B. Once they are properly seriated, however, items of C-type series may further be tested for clustering to produce clumps of closely similar items, as illustrated in Fig. 8.1D. C-type scaling is a simple sort, but if used in conjunction with clumping tests like those discussed later in this paper it can give information about item clustering similar to that produced by A- and B-type studies.

The *items* that are seriated in any study are a set of *individuals* scored on a set of *characters*. Seriation involves the so-called *Q*-technique when it considers the similarities between pairs of individuals (collections, assemblages, etc.) present in a population in terms of their characters (species, types, etc.), and is considered an *R*-technique study when it treats the similarities between pairs of characters present in a population (Stephenson, 1953). Since seriation is applied to sample data in order to estimate population parameters, it gives data relations that can be used in inductive studies, although *sensu stricto* it is a descriptive, as opposed to an inferential, statistic.

Several techniques are available for seriating items. An old standby in archaeology is the technique of experimentally arranging artefact assemblages in such a way that the relative frequencies of various characters (usually artefact types) yield a best fit to 'battleship-shaped' curves. The method has been restated and illustrated by the archaeologist Ford (1962), who is one of the main proponents of the method for purposes of relative dating.

Seriation can be done more systematically with similarity scores than with visual curve fitting, however. These scores are usually listed in a correlation or similarity matrix. The matrix is simply a table which contains numerical scores for all pairs of items in the set that one wishes to study. The items are listed in line along the margins of the table, horizontally and vertically, and their respective scores are given at appropriate coordinates in the table. By locating any item on one axis, and then by reading down or across to the cell in line with another item on the other axis, the similarity score between the two items can be found.

It is common practice to represent the matrix graphically in its double or symmetric form in which the upper right and lower left halves are mirror images separated by the primary diagonal of identity scores. Each half of the matrix, however, includes all the different similarity scores. If we let n represent the number of items, there are $n(n-1)/2$ different similarity scores for the $\binom{n}{2}$ pairs of items, excluding the identity scores. Fig. 8.2 (*a*) illustrates a double matrix of hypothetical scores, while Fig. 8.2 (*b*) gives the same matrix in its single form.

The actual seriation process consists of shifting the positions of the items until an arrangement is found which causes the similarity scores to fit as nearly as possible some criterion specifying score patterning in the matrix (more will be said about the problem of shifting items through their permutations later on). This trial manipulation of similarity scores, by shifting item positions, can be thought of as the ordering process necessary to seriate the item set properly.

The difficult thing about seriation has proved to be the definition of criteria about score patterning. Most descriptions of the model seriated matrix state either that its scores should form clusters of similar values, or that the scores

Items	A	B	C	D	E
A		27	25	21	8
B	27		31	24	11
C	25	31		25	12
D	21	24	25		14
E	8	11	12	14	

(*a*)

Items	A	B	C	D	E
A		27	25	21	8
B			31	24	11
C				25	12
D					14
E					

(*b*)

FIG. 8.2. Matrices of hypothetical similarity scores. (*a*) Symmetric or double matrix. (*b*) Asymmetric or single matrix.

should decrease gradually or continuously away from the diagonal in both directions. For example,

... the resultant pattern of agreement indexes will show a definite structure, in that as any row is read from left to right *in a double matrix* the indexes will progressively decline from that point on. ... In other words ... the resulting table of agreement indexes will show high values clustering about the diagonal, with decreasing values as one goes away from the diagonal either vertically or horizontally. (Robinson, 1951, pp. 294–5)

... the highest values, representing closest similarity, *should* occur nearest the diagonal axis of identity, and the remaining values decrease consistently toward the corners of the matrix opposite the diagonal. (Kuzara *et al.*, 1966, p. 1443)

Neither of these statements is precise enough to provide a usable seriation model. For example, following the above criteria, can a score two positions away from the primary diagonal be equal to a score one position away from the primary diagonal without doing violence to the model? And just how much uniformity may there be in the horizontal and vertical decrease of values as one moves away from the primary diagonal? What if the rate of decrease is marked near the diagonal but only slight or entirely non-existent farther away from the primary diagonal? In these cases have the criteria for the model been met?

Such questions could not be answered until the nature of the seriation model itself was stated in exact terms. W. B. Craytor recently did just this. His definition of seriation is the following: 'Seriation arranges, as well as possible, a number of items into a vector array such that each item pair (except the outermost) is surrounded by less similar or equally similar item pairs' (Craytor and Johnson, 1968, pp. 1, 2).

The use of Craytor's simple explanation of seriation makes it possible to define the accurately seriated item set as one whose scores satisfy a number of inequalities specified within the matrix. If we let S_{ij} represent the similarity score between items i and j, and S_{kl} the score between items k and l (where the subscripts denote the position of the items in the vector array), the inequalities requisite for the perfect seriation of any group of n items are

$$S_{ij} \geqslant S_{kl} \qquad \begin{aligned} j &= 2, 3, \ldots, n \\ i &= 1, 2, \ldots, j-1 \\ k &= 1, 2, \ldots, i \\ l &= j, j+1, \ldots, n. \end{aligned}$$

The number of these inequalities, excluding the identity scores for items with themselves, is $(n^4 + 2n^3 - 13n^2 + 10n)/24$ (for the derivation of this quantity see Craytor and Johnson, 1968, p. 7).

It is apparent that a large number of inequalities must be satisfied by a perfectly seriated item set. Yet not all inequalities can necessarily be satisfied in given sets of empirical data. Seriation simply involves arranging the items so that their similarity scores will satisfy, *as closely as possible*, all the specified inequalities.

A brief history of seriation

There are two distinct lines of development for item seriation, and the two are apparently independent of one another. The earlier of the two is the application of tabular item ordering in ethnography, linguistics, physical anthropology, archaeology and, later, in biology, mainly for item cluster classification. The other line is represented by the development of item seriation to solve problems of chronology in archaeology.

This sketch will place most of its emphasis on the early applications of seriation in order to furnish the interested reader a background and perspective for the later seriation studies which have been reviewed adequately elsewhere. This will especially be the case in the review of works on cluster classification. Interestingly, the latter are not always recognized as examples of seriation. Since classification *via* clustering is the goal of these studies, the fact that item seriation was a preliminary step in such classification sometimes tends to be overlooked.

ITEM CLASSIFICATION BY CLUSTERING

In the year 1895, the Berliner Gesellschaft für Anthropologie, Ethnologie und Urgeschichte published an article by Franz Boas titled *Indianische Sagen von der Nord-Pacifischen Küste Amerikas*. To my knowledge, this is the first use by an anthropologist of a matrix of similarity values as an aid in organizing and analysing data. It is remarkable that Boas should have the distinction of having introduced the method since he later renounced the use of statistics in anthropology.

In this paper, Boas presented matrix tables containing the number of shared *Sagenelemente* (folktale motifs) for all pairs of fifteen American ethnic groups, twelve of which belonged to the Northwest coast culture area and three of which were located elsewhere. In compiling and organizing the tables (Boas, 1895, pp. 341–2), it appears that Boas shifted the item positions about so as to produce loose clusters of high-frequency cells along the matrix primary diagonal, thus in effect seriating the items by inspection. Among other things, Boas's interest was in comparing relationships between neighbouring ethnic groups to determine, if possible, which ones were dissimilar to their neighbours and hence, by inference, recent arrivals in their area of occurrence. The Tsimshian were isolated as one such group of newcomers. This early attempt at Q-technique item seriation is historically important in spite of Boas's crude treatment of his frequency data – he failed to standardize his element counts correctly – and his unsystematic use of the matrix itself.

In 1908, S. A. Barrett used a tabular matrix to organize linguistic data for purposes of language classification, grouping Pomo (a California Indian language) dialects into several different kinds of speech, and showing the nearness of the dialects to each other. Eleven years later, Dixon and Kroeber's 'Linguistic families of California' (1919) combined dialects into languages within a matrix by employing the number of shared cognates as similarity scores. Similar linguistic studies followed these leads.

In 1911, J. Czekanowski published his important paper, 'Objective Kriterien in der Ethnologie'. In this study he used data from Ankermann's African work to compile culture traits for forty-seven African ethnic groups. He calculated coefficients for a Q-type comparison between tribes and ordered the tribes in a double matrix to produce two areal groupings. Czekanowski considered the clusters that were discernible after seriation as particularly valuable in historical reconstruction, on the assumption that high association had historical cause. Czekanowski's technique was later used extensively in Oceanic and American studies by members of the Polish–German school of historical anthropology, and provided an impetus for similar studies by American scholars. The more recent efforts of this genre are summarized in brief but excellent form by Driver (1965, pp. 323–8).

In the field of physical anthropology, Czekanowski early used item seriation with a tabular matrix to analyse anthropometric and other physical data. Since the accomplishments of the Polish school of physical anthropology have recently been reviewed by Czekanowski himself (1962), these studies will not be mentioned here other than to call to the reader's attention the fact that item seriation as a technique initial to clustering is still commonly used by Polish physical anthropologists (for a fairly recent example see Kóčka, 1953).

In archaeology, analyses much like Czekanowski's 1911 ethnographic study have been made to define and describe archaeological units. Kroeber (1940) tested archaeological units already reported in Tennessee (the Norris Basin complex) and in Ohio and Kentucky (the Fort Ancient aspect). To cite a more recent example, Lewis and Kneberg (1959) similarly compared a number of Archaic lithic collections from the south-eastern United States.

However, the principles of seriation had already been applied to archaeological assemblages in the pioneer work of Flinders Petrie in 1899 (*J. Anthrop. Inst.* (N.S.) 29, 1899, 295–301). Petrie was confronted with some 900 predynastic Egyptian graves containing representatives of about 800 ceramic types. More recently, attempts have been made to define artefact type populations with seriated matrices of similarity scores (Tugby, 1958, 1965; Clarke, 1962, 1963).

The foregoing illustrations are quite noticeably mainly anthropological, although similar matrix analyses were once common in the behavioural sciences generally. It is directly through the anthropological line, however, that the technique evolved to the point, represented by Craytor's work cited earlier, where seriation can be used as a systematic research method.

In biology, seriation has been treated in connection with numerical taxonomy. Interestingly, Sokal and Sneath (1963, pp. 176–80) clearly recognize the basic oneness of the processes used in matrix cluster analysis and in archaeological seriation for dating purposes. The taxonomist's interest, however, is in seriation for cluster-classification: 'One can . . . visualize the search for group structure as a rearranging of the rows or columns of this matrix in such a way as to obtain the optimum structure in the system. Such a procedure has been suggested by Robinson (1951)' (Sokal and Sneath, 1963, p. 178).

A more popular and, in some ways, more detailed account of taxonomic seriation appears in a *Scientific American* article by Sokal (1966). An unseriated data matrix and a symmetric, seriated similarity matrix (Sokal, 1966, p. 110) show the degree of similarity between pairs of twenty-seven individuals from seven species of nematode worms. Sokal illustrates how seriation and dendrogrammatic analysis can be used jointly to provide more information than yielded by either technique singly.

CHRONOLOGY AND ITEM SERIATION

It was pointed out earlier that seriation by means of curve-fitting procedures has been part of the archaeologist's analytical tool kit for quite a while. In 1951, W. S. Robinson, a sociologist, and G. Brainerd, an archaeologist, published a matrix seriation technique which could be used to arrange artefact collections into temporal sequences. This is a kind of relative dating which allows one to say that a particular archaeological collection is earlier or later than certain other collections in the data set. The basic tenet involved is that collections that are close together in time will show similar frequencies of their respective artefact types. To measure percentage distributions, a coefficient or index of agreement was devised by Robinson (1951) to be used in the matrix as a similarity score between item pairs. This index will be discussed shortly.

Several applications of the so-called Robinson technique – seriation with *Robinson Indexes of Agreement* for relative dating – have been made with apparently good results. Belous (1953) temporally seriated a collection of archaeological sites from central California, and Dixon (1956) re-examined the Snaketown, Arizona, sequence using this method. Dixon was unable to seriate the archaeological material in terms of the chronological model, but did demonstrate the clustering tendencies of the archaeological 'phases' at Snaketown.

In 1957, R. C. Troike chronologically seriated a large ceramic collection from the famous site of La Venta, Tabasco State, Mexico, with passable results, and Flanders (1960) applied the Robinson technique to a group of ceramics from Iowa. More recently, Hole and Shaw (1967) seriated west Iranian collections from the regions of Deh Luran, Khuzistan, and Khorramabad, Luristan.

The chronological seriation technique of Dempsey and Baumhoff (1963) is an outgrowth of the Robinson technique, but treats only the presence and absence of types or traits. Their method will not be described here, other than to state that there are special provisions for selecting the most desirable artefact types for chronological seriation, and for excluding other, less desirable, types. A process is provided whereby certain types can be weighted more strongly than others, to count most heavily those that are sensitive for dating purposes.

An attempt by non-archaeologists to use seriation for evolutionary or causal analyses is the study by Driver (1956; Driver and Massey, 1957, pp. 425–34) which deals with kinship terms, descent, land tenure, residence and division of labour in American Indian societies. A possible causal sequence of forms was obtained and interpreted.

Problems of item ordering and computerization

Two stubborn problems face the analyst who wishes to do a seriation study. First, there is the matter of defining suitable criteria to recognize a successful seriation among several trial orderings of an item set and, second, there is the enormous amount of time necessary to rearrange the item positions by trial and error to find the best seriation of items. The two problems are not easily separated.

ORDERING CRITERIA

If different permutations of an item set are tried experimentally, it is necessary to be able to judge between them and pick out the best seriation for the set. A criterion for judgement is necessary, and several have been suggested and used.

Robinson (1951) suggests three criteria to be used in sequential stages of the seriation procedure. First, each time the item positions are rearranged along the matrix margins, the effect of the change can be measured by determining the magnitude and direction of the difference between adjacent similarity scores. This is done either in rows or columns, moving away from the diagonal in both directions (Robinson always works with the double matrix). A negatively signed difference occurs when, of two adjacent scores, the one farther from the primary diagonal is larger than the one nearer the diagonal, and hence out of place. All signs would be positive if the similarity scores showed exactly the desired pattern.

The foregoing can produce a measure of seriation if the number of negatively signed differences is divided by the total number of differences, both positive and negative. As the proportion of negative differences decreases in trial orderings of the same data set, the better seriated the items become. This criterion, slightly modified, has been called Coefficient A by Kuzara *et al.* (1966, p. 1448). Whereas Robinson divides the number of negatively signed differences by the total differences, Kuzara *et al.* divide by the number of similarity scores.

Another criterion of Robinson's is the patterning of the column totals of the matrix of similarity scores. 'Beginning at either end of the . . . ordered series, the totals will rise progressively to a maximum, and then will decrease progressively to a minimum at the other end of the series' (Robinson, 1951, p. 298). The effects of item rearrangement can be seen in this pattern, and the best seriated permutation can be recognized.

A third criterion is the sum of the squares of the negatively signed differences divided by the sum of the squares of all differences, positive and negative. Using the squares of all differences in this calculation gives relatively greater importance to larger score differences. Kuzara *et al.* (1966, p. 1448) have titled this Matrix Coefficient B.

Other criteria have also been used, e.g. Driver and Massey's (1957, pp. 432–4) use of the mean of each diagonal set of scores parallel to the primary diagonal of identity. Beginning at the end farthest from the primary diagonal, the averages should rise progressively toward the diagonal which contains the identity scores. Rearrangement of item positions should eventually produce a good approximation to this pattern. Hole and Shaw (1967, p. 14) simply use the sum of the errors (the differences that are negative as one moves away from the diagonal) which occur in the matrix. This criterion decreases as the trial orderings improve, zero indicating perfect seriation in terms of the ideal model.

These criteria are all biased measures of seriation and will not be considered further. They are limited either by hazy definitions of the ideal seriation model or by the fact that only relationships between adjacent similarity scores are considered. W. B. Craytor has given the most suitable definition of seriation and the most suitable ordering criterion to date (Craytor and Johnson, 1968). His PROGRAM SERIATE,[1] which incorporates this criterion, will be used to analyse the two data sets used as illustrations later in the paper.

Craytor's statement about the inequalities that should be met in any matrix of similarity scores make it possible to define a useful and logically consistent criterion for evaluating different orderings of the same data. This is called Coefficient H (Craytor and Johnson, 1968, p. 3), and is the sum of all the score differences, that is

$$H = \sum_{j=2}^{n} \sum_{i=1}^{j-1} \sum_{k=1}^{i} \sum_{l=j}^{n} S_j^i - S_l^k.$$

Let n represent the number of items to be seriated in a given data set, S_j^i represent the similarity score between the item in row i and the item in column j in the similarity matrix, and S_l^k represent the similarity score between the item in row k and the item in column l. In the process of seriating an item group, Coefficient H would be maximized. *Note that H takes account of the magnitude of the similarity score differences and considers inequalities other than those between adjacent scores.* The degree to which inequalities are satisfied is important, since similarity scores are often imprecise. Small differences between them are commonly insignificant and may be due to sampling error.

At this point it is important to mention a major difference between Craytor's treatment of the similarity matrix and the treatment employed by most other published seriation procedures. Craytor never uses the identity scores in calculating score differences to be used in Coefficient H and Matrix Coefficient C (defined below). It was empirically demonstrated that for many data sets the major score differences were those between the identity scores and the scores adjacent to the primary diagonal. Including the identity differences tends to mask the important score differences located away from the diagonal of identity. Also, there is simply no theoretical justification for their consideration.

Craytor has also invented a seriation criterion for comparing the degree of seriation between different sets of items, a job for which Coefficient H is ineffective. H is standardized into a general seriation coefficient, called Matrix Coefficient C (Craytor and Johnson, 1968, p. 3). It is calculated by dividing Coefficient H by the number of inequalities tested, that is by $(n^4 + 2n^3 - 13n^2 + 10n)/24$, to get the average inequality difference, and then dividing by the standard deviation of the $n(n-1)/2$ similarity scores.

Matrix Coefficient C has an approximate value of zero for a randomly arranged set of items, but in general the value of C becomes larger as the matrix is more perfectly seriated. It has been empirically determined that a C-value of approximately 2 is indicative of excellent seriation; that is to say, 2 is approached as the requisite inequalities are satisfied. Both H and C will be used with the data sets analysed later in this paper.

ITEM MANIPULATION

The experimental rearranging or manipulating of items is the second major problem in the seriation technique. This is not as simple as it may sound. Every time the position of a row is changed, the position of the corresponding column has to be changed. Such a process becomes unwieldy and time-consuming when many items make up the item set. Computerization of the procedure solves the unwieldiness problem, but not the time problem.

There are $n!/2$ essentially different permutations for an item set, where n is the number of items (of the $n!$ permutations, those that are the reverse of the others represent the same sequence, since the direction of the permutation is unimportant). Table 8.1 gives the number of essentially different permutations for the values of n below 21. Quite clearly, a prohibitive amount of time would be necessary to try all these permutations except when working with very small n's.

Even when the analyst uses a digital computer to seriate an item set, it is feasible to try all positions of n with only, say, sets of five items or less. At least four computer programs for seriation have been written and used by American archaeologists: Ascher and Ascher (1963), Kuzara *et al.* (1966), Hole and Shaw (1967) and Craytor and Johnson (1968).

If one uses Craytor's PROGRAM SERIATE and his estimations of run time (Craytor and Johnson, 1968, p. 14), twenty items would demand a minimum of 600 billion years of computer time to try all one quintillion, two-hundred and twenty quadrillion essentially different permutations! It does seem that some kind of short cut has to be adopted to choose certain of the possible $n!/2$ permutations for trial orderings. It has already been decided that these tries will be compared by Craytor's Coefficient H and Matrix Coefficient C to select the best one. We can review, briefly, the short cut procedures that have been proposed and explain the one that will be used here, the one incorporated in PROGRAM SERIATE.

The Aschers' basic procedure (1963, pp. 1047–8) instructs the computer to insert, one at a time, each row column of the item array (1, 2, 3, ..., n), beginning with 1 and preceeding through n, until the full matrix for the data

TABLE 8.1. *No. of essentially different item permutations for values of n below 21*

n	$n!/2$
2	1
3	3
4	12
5	60
6	360
7	2 520
8	20 160
9	181 440
10	$1 \cdot 82 \times 10^6$
11	$2 \cdot 00 \times 10^7$
12	$2 \cdot 40 \times 10^8$
13	$3 \cdot 12 \times 10^9$
14	$4 \cdot 36 \times 10^{10}$
15	$0 \cdot 66 \times 10^{12}$
16	$1 \cdot 04 \times 10^{13}$
17	$1 \cdot 78 \times 10^{14}$
18	$3 \cdot 20 \times 10^{15}$
19	$0 \cdot 61 \times 10^{17}$
20	$1 \cdot 22 \times 10^{18}$

set is complete. Each placement decision is based on the assumption that the items already ordered are in correct position, although there is no justification for this assumption. The number of negatively signed differences between scores is used as an ordering criterion. Understandably, the Aschers note that the order of the input array can influence the final seriation markedly.

The procedure used by Kuzara *et al.* (1966, pp. 1445–6) is different from the above in its basic conception. It involves three stages. Stage I consists of moving row-column 1 into position 2, so that the original row-column 2 then occupies position 1; next, the original row-column 1, which is now in position 2, is moved down to position 3. The procedure is continued until row-column 1 is tried in all positions of the item array. Matrix Coefficient A or Matrix Coefficient B is used to compare the different permutations, and the permutation producing the best ordering coefficient is held in storage. This permutation is then used as a new starting matrix, and row-column 2 is tried in the same fashion as row-column 1 in all positions. If a particular shift in the position of row-column 2 yields a better ordering coefficient, the corresponding item permutation is held in memory. Using this permutation as a starting matrix, row-column 3 is shifted through all positions, continuing the process through the n items.

Stage II starts with the item permutation having the best ordering coefficient that was found in Stage I, and the whole process is repeated again. This is continued until the best ordering obtained by trying every row-column in every successive position is identical to the previous best ordering. Stage III, the last stage, repeats Stage I and II procedures, but randomizes the input array at the beginning of each Stage I action, since input order introduces a bias in this type of seriation, and the employment of different input orders helps reduce this bias.

Hole and Shaw's program (1967, pp. 16–17) specifies two short-cut techniques for trying items in different positions, which they call search patterns. The first they call pairwise interchange. First, the items that occupy the first and second positions are interchanged, and the resultant matrix evaluated by an ordering criterion (the sum of the errors, the negatively signed differences). Next, the second trial ordering interchanges the first and third positions of the matrix item array, and so on until all possible pairwise interchanges have been made and evaluated. The second technique is called successive rotation, and is apparently identical to the item manipulation process of Kuzara *et al.* (1966).

Craytor's PROGRAM SERIATE uses the item manipulation technique of Kuzara *et al.* (1966), but Craytor's decision to use it cannot be readily grasped until another matter is discussed. It is necessary to consider the relations between the ordering coefficients and their successive permutations. If a group of item permutations is plotted against the respective ordering coefficients of the items (as illustrated in Craytor and Johnson, 1968, fig. 3), where the permutations are ordered along the horizontal axis on the basis of similarity of successive arrays to all others, several local modes or maxima may result, one of which is the best. It is normally this best maximum that the analyst desires in seriating a data set.

The ideal procedure is to generate a random sequence of items and then change their positions in the item series until the permutation corresponding to the highest local maximum is found. But necessary to such a procedure is the use of some criterion to determine if a permutation corresponds to a local maximum. The item manipulation technique of Kuzara provides the needed criterion, which is therefore called *Kuzara's Criterion* (Kuzara *et al.*, 1966, p. 4). It works as follows.

An item permutation whose Coefficient H is in the close vicinity of a local maximum possesses an H-value greater than, or equal to, any other Coefficient H corresponding to the permutations that might be formed by shifting any item, but only *one item at a time*, through the positions of the item permutation being considered. Thus Kuzara's manipulation technique provides an excellent method of shifting item positions *one at a time* until good seriation is achieved, as indicated by H-values that must be in the vicinity of maxima of the type defined above. If the ordering procedure is repeated many times, it should be possible to approximate the absolute maximum (if, indeed, more than one maximum exists) corresponding to the best seriated permutation of the item group. Kuzara's Criterion for reaching the vicinity of the highest local degree of seriation is fulfilled by repeating the ordering attempts until the ordering coefficient for the item permutation produced by one ordering is equal to the ordering coefficient for the item permutation produced by the pass previous to it.

Each seriation of a randomly generated item sequence may be referred to as an ordering. Whether or not there is more than one local maximum for an item group can usually be determined in one ordering. If an ordering produces a nearly perfectly seriated item permutation (as would be indicated by a value of approximately 2 for Matrix Coefficient C), then there is very little chance of getting different or dissimilar permutations from more orderings. But a poorly seriated item permutation indicates an inherent instability within the item set, which is to say, the presence of complex and multidimensional relationships between the items. In such cases several local maxima may occur for the degrees of seriation of the different permutations.

Similarity scores

The number of different similarity scores that could conceivably be used for item seriation is large. Some kinds of scores are much better suited for item seriation than others, and their suitability needs to be considered from two standpoints. The first has to do with the nature of score relations in the seriation matrix; the second has to do with the problem of emphasis and reliability of the raw data whence the similarity scores are derived.

The most suitable similarity scores (1) are normatized (standardized) and (2) state similarity in terms of an equal-unit scale. The prime reason for normatizing item similarity scores is to make samples of different sizes comparable for the study. The simplest way to normatize is to equate each sample n with 100% and then calculate similarity scores from the resultant percentages. Normatizing is, of course, necessary when the availability samples are unequal, not when equal samples can be drawn during data collection. Availability samples, however, are commonly used in anthropological, archaeological and natural-historical analyses.

It was said above that suitable similarity scores must state similarity in terms of an equal-unit scale. In concrete terms, a given difference in score size between two high-value scores must mean the same thing as the same size difference between two low-value scores. This is a necessary assumption underlying the summation of inequalities used in Craytor's Coefficient H and in Matrix Coefficient C. All the inequalities must have the same unit meaning; e.g. an inequality of 8 must have twice the magnitude, in meaning, as an inequality of 4.

Most coefficients of association and correlation do not behave according to this criterion, especially measures like *phi* which are based on Pearson's product-moment coefficient r. Values of r falling between zero and ± 1 are not easy to interpret intuitively. If one were not forewarned, he might think that an r of 0·80 was twice as good or twice as strong as an r of 0·40. But it is easily demonstrated that $100 \times r^2$ % of the variation of one variable is explained by differences in the other variable.[2] If $r = 0·80$, then 64% of the variation of one variable is accounted for by the variation in the other. When $r = 0·40$, only 16% of this type variance is accounted for. Thus an r of 0·80 is four times as strong as an r of 0·40, not twice as strong. Correlation coefficients, to be used in a matrix for item seriation, can be transformed into percentages, Fisher's z, or to angles that are the arc cosines of the correlation coefficients (for details see Sokal and Sneath, 1963, p. 310).

Another problem is to decide whether to give equal weight to characters in the calculation of a similarity score, as in the case of correlation coefficients, or whether to weight the characters differently, for example in terms of their relative prevalence or dominance. Numerical taxonomists prefer to weight characters equally in order to minimize interpretative bias. In comparing palaeontological and archaeological collections, however, one may wish to allow dominant (abundant) characters to influence similarity scores more strongly than rare characters. This interest in dominant characters usually reflects the kinds of inter-assemblage differences that the palaeontologist or archaeologist deems important in his comparative studies.

A short digression is in order to discuss the suitability of similarity scores for individuals that represent stratigraphic and/or geographic units, since these are my special interest as an archaeologist: that is to say, individuals composed of characters that are found as objects occurring naturally in, or upon, the earth such as palaeontological collections, archaeological assemblages, and the like. The peculiar problem that these data usually pose is that different assemblages often occur near or next to one another, as in superimposed geological strata or depositional zones. Mixture between strata is common or even expected, often difficult to recognize, and needs to be accounted for in calculating similarity scores for the assemblage pairs.

W. Lipe (1964, pp. 103, 104) makes an important observation. He points out that a similarity score that depends on presence and absence counts may not be as useful as the Robinson Index of Agreement, which is based on percentages, in instances where a few specimens from one period or assemblage have been mixed with those of another. In cases where intruded specimens occur, but are not numerous, the Robinson Index of Agreement allows them to influence the similarity score only minimally, since their corresponding percentages will be quite small.

The Robinson (1951) Index of Agreement will be used in the following data analyses for four reasons. First, it is a normalized score. Second, it employs an equal-unit scale. Third, it reduces the effect of moderate interassemblage mixture on the resultant similarity scores. And fourth, it gives strong weight to dominant characters in the assemblages being compared.

The Robinson Index of Agreement is calculated in this way. Each individual assemblage is set equal to 100%. The percentage for each character (type, species, etc.) in each collection is calculated. Each assemblage is compared with all others in respect to the percentages of its characters. Character by character, the smaller percentage (of whichever assemblage) is subtracted from the larger, and the differences for all characters are added to provide the total difference between the assemblages. Next, this figure is subtracted from the figure 200 (100% for each assemblage) to obtain a similarity score between the two assemblages. Fig. 8.3 illustrates this procedure and shows the areas of agreement and disagreement between two hypothetical assemblages, lots A and B.

Although percentage-based scores are very often useful, a danger in their use needs to be underlined. Percentages are frequency data normatized to make possible a comparison of unequal samples. As such, they are interdependent data from the same whole (sample), and may not vary independently of each other. Thus they lend themselves to spurious correlation at times, and can cause biased clusters.

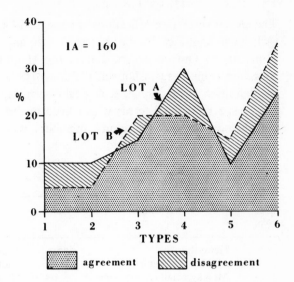

Fig. 8.3. Areas of agreement for a Robinson index of agreement (IA) between two hypothetical assemblages, Lots A and B.

Two example data sets

Two data sets will illustrate item seriation and its use with adjunct comparative techniques. The first set is eleven Late Tertiary vertebrate collections which have been compared and analysed by Shotwell (1955, 1958, 1963). The collections have been classed into community types on the basis of their constituent genera, and therefore make a fine control group for appraising the results of the present comparative approach. The data, further, are not so complex that the reader cannot grasp the major relations between faunas from the raw frequency information.

The second data group is made up of twenty-six Upper Palaeolithic archaeological assemblages from south-western France. Aurignacian, Perigordian and Solutrean lithic collections are represented. D. de Sonneville-Bordes (1960) has interpreted all the assemblages with comparative methods that will be mentioned later, and Smith (1966) has recently re-analysed the Solutrean material. This data set was selected because of its relatively large number of assemblages, because of the large number of characters in the assemblages, and because of the apparent complexity of relations between collections. In other words, this second analysis will be more difficult than that of the vertebrate data, since inter-assemblage relations cannot be discerned so easily. Therefore it is a more demanding test of item seriation.

327

THE LATE TERTIARY FAUNAS

The eleven vertebrate collections are assigned lot numbers in Table 8.2, and each lot is identified by name, sample size and publication source. All are from eastern Oregon except Lot 1, the Hemphill (Coffee Ranch) quarry collection from Texas. Shotwell's (1955, 1958, 1963) analysis had as its goal the definition of functional, ecological community types on the basis of clusters of specific animal forms which lived in the same habitat. The adaptive morphology of the community members was used to infer the habitat characters of each community.

TABLE 8.2. *Key to lot identification, Late Tertiary faunal collections*

Lot No.	Fauna	N	Source
1	Hemphill	3259	Shotwell, 1958, Table 2, p. 274
2	McKay Reservoir	751	Shotwell, 1958, Table 2, p. 274
3	McKay small quarry sample	95	Shotwell, 1958, Table 2, p. 274
4	McKay small float sample	95	Shotwell, 1958, Table 2, p. 274
5	Krebs Ranch 1	91	Shotwell, 1958, Table 3, p. 277
6	Krebs Ranch 2	145	Shotwell, 1958, Table 3, p. 277
7	West End Blowout	549	Shotwell, 1958, Table 3, p. 277
8	Boardman	676	Shotwell, 1963, Table 3, p. 277
9	Black Butte Q11	97	Shotwell, 1963, Table 1, p. 14
10	Black Butte Q3	220	Shotwell, 1963, Table 1, p. 14
11	Otis Basin	66	Shotwell, 1963, Table 2, p. 17

Shotwell used a technique for community typology that involved the concept of a proximal community. Where the number of skeletal elements per individual animal was above average for the data group, Shotwell isolated these genera and species as members of the *in situ* or proximal community. Forms with only a few skeletal elements per individual were segregated and considered as intrusive into the proximal community characterizing a collection. This kind of intrusion is assumed to have occurred during the geological period in which the collection belongs, not as a result of stratigraphic mixture.

Using this method, Shotwell classed the eleven vertebrate collections into the following community types: *pond-bank* (Lots 2, 3, 4, 5 and 9), *grassland* (Lots 1 and 8), *savannah* (Lot 10), *woodland* (Lot 7), *border* – a unique community closely adjacent to several others (Lot 11) and *transitional pond-bank/woodland* (Lot 6). Each type was characterized by specified vertebrate forms (e.g. Shotwell, 1958, p. 282, fig. 13).

The problem now is whether item seriation and adjunct techniques can provide information about community relations that agrees with Shotwell's findings and, if we are fortunate, perhaps provide additional information about these relationships. A Q-technique analysis is planned, one that compares assemblages on the basis of their genera and species. Before doing this, however, it is necessary to combine certain of Shotwell's forms from different geological periods into comparable functional categories, since the emphasis of the study is on functional articulation within community types.

TABLE 8.3. *Key to genus identification*

No.	Form	No.	Form
1	*Scapanus*	26	*Felis*
2	*Hydroscapheus*	27	*Machairodus*
3	Sloth	28	*Hipparion*
4	Chiropterid	29	*Neohipparion*
5	*Hypolagus*	30	*Nannippus*
6	*Ochotona*	31	*Pliohippus Astrohippus*
7	*Liodontia*	32	*Pliohippus*
8	*Mylagaulus*	33	*Aphelops*
9	*Marmota*	34	*Teleoceras*
10	*Citellus* (O)	35	*Prosthennops*
11	*Citellus* (C)	36	*Pediomeryx*
12	*Pliosaccomys*	37	*Procamelus, Pliauchenia*
13	*Perognathus*		and 'small camel'
14	*Leptodontomys*	38	*Paracamelus, Megatylopus*
15	*Dipoides* and *Eucastor*		and 'large camel'
16	*Castor*	39	*Alticamelus*
17	*Prosomys*	40	*Mammut*
18	*Pliozapus*	41	*Capromeryx*
19	*Plesiogulo*	42	*Peromyscus*
20	*Mustela*	43	*Bassariscus*
21	*Pliotaxidea*	44	*Sphenophalos*
22	*Osteoborus*	45	*Hesperosorex*
23	*Canis*	46	*Cupidinomys*
24	*Vulpes*	47	*Hystricops*
25	*Agriotherium*	48	*Ustatochoerus*

Table 8.3 lists the forty-eight vertebrate forms that were decided upon after consultation with Shotwell. Note that the two beavers, *Dipoides* and *Eucastor*, have been combined in Form 15; *Procamelus, Pliauchenia* and 'small camel' in Form 37; and *Paracamelus, Megatylopus* and 'large camel' in Form 38.

Item seriation

The first step in the study is simple scale analysis by item seriation using Craytor's PROGRAM SERIATE, which is similarity scaling as opposed to complexity scaling. Percentages and Robinson Indexes of Agreement were calculated in standard form (Robinson, 1951). These similarity scores were placed into a data matrix (Fig. 8.4) and the items were seriated with the IBM 360-Model 40 computer of the Statistical Laboratory and Computing Center of the University of Oregon.

Lots	1	2	3	4	5	6	7	8	9	10	11
1	200	14	11	9	4	17	27	68	7	51	15
2	14	200	147	163	125	83	65	30	100	7	40
3	11	147	200	157	108	96	81	31	87	6	61
4	9	163	157	200	139	83	73	29	114	4	46
5	4	125	108	139	200	65	38	7	118	0	24
6	17	83	96	83	65	200	104	35	48	11	54
7	27	65	81	73	38	104	200	49	29	43	83
8	68	30	31	29	7	35	49	200	3	78	25
9	7	100	87	114	118	48	29	3	200	2	19
10	51	7	6	4	0	11	43	78	2	200	46
11	15	40	61	46	24	54	83	25	19	46	200

FIG. 8.4. Data matrix with Robinson indexes of agreement for eleven Late Tertiary vertebrate collections.

The best seriation out of ten tries produced a Coefficient H of 33947 and a Matrix Coefficient C of 1·16252. The final item array of lots is (9, 5, 2, 4, 3, 6, 7, 11, 8, 10, 1) (Fig. 8.5). We already know that the position of any lot in the array is a reflection of its degree of similarity to all other lots. The positioning of the items produces an overview of relations according to the C-type scale illustrated earlier in Fig. 8.1.

If Shotwell's community types are listed by the side of each appropriate lot in the seriated array, we obtain the following pattern:

Lot No.	Community type
9	pond-bank
5	pond-bank
2	pond-bank
4	pond-bank
3	pond-bank
6	transitional pond-bank/woodland
7	woodland
11	border
8	grassland
10	savannah
1	grassland

At this point, seriation has produced an interpretable picture according to Shotwell's characterization of the lots in his published studies. Pond-bank communities fall at one end of the series, grassland and savannah communities at the other. The woodland community is in the centre with the transitional and border communities where they would be expected on either side of woodland (Shotwell, personal communication, 1968).

It is now useful to see whether a gradual progression is involved in the array, or else a tendency toward the kind of clumping illustrated in Fig. 8.1D. First, a great deal can be learned from the value of Matrix Coefficient C.

The value of $1 \cdot 16252$ is only slightly more than half the ideal C-value of 2. Taken by itself, this figure indicates an inherent instability within the item set and very strongly suggests the presence of clumps of comparable similarity scores. Once this much has been learned, the clumps can be discovered by additional analyses.

Cluster search

The search for clumps or clusters will consist of a search for *homostats*. A homostat is a group of items that have a degree of similarity to each other above a specified minimum. This is different from a *segregate*, which is a group of items whose in-group similarity is markedly greater than the similarity between the grouped items and items outside the group.

Homostats can be discovered by topographic manipulation of the matrix scores once the items are correctly seriated. Brainerd (1951) suggests contouring the similarity matrix by drawing in contour lines at specified intervals. If homostats exist they will show up as plateaux of uniform scores between groups of ideally adjacent and parallel contour lines which indicate abrupt changes in the distribution of score values.

331

The contoured right half of the matrix in Fig. 8.5, the seriated vertebrate lots, uses a 10-point contour interval with lines representing Robinson Index values of 10, 20, 30, through 170, the last being the interval just above the highest similarity score of 163. Inspection shows a large plateau of high scores

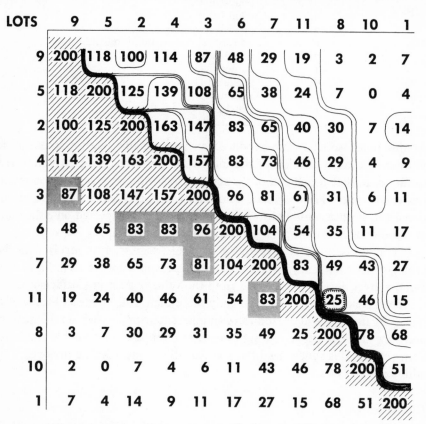

FIG. 8.5. Seriated and coded matrix of similarity scores for eleven Late Tertiary vertebrate collections. Coefficient $H = 33947$, Matrix Coefficient $C = 1 \cdot 16252$.

in the upper corner of the matrix adjacent to the primary diagonal of identity scores. In a contoured symmetrical matrix, rather than the half-matrix contoured in Fig. 8.5, the homostat should show up as a square-shaped cluster split diagonally by the identity scores.

Lots 9, 5, 2, 4 and 3 make up this cluster, which is set off topographically by a series of more or less parallel contour lines separating lots 3 and 6. The similarity scores within the cluster are the highest values found in the matrix.

At this point it should be mentioned that the coding of matrix scores by differential shading used by Czekanowski (1911), Kroeber (1940) and others is a somewhat simpler approach to the same kind of topographic relief work. The left half of the matrix in Fig. 8.5 has been coded this way. After experimenting with different values, three ranges were set: (1) the diagonally striped shading denotes *high* values equal to or greater than 100, the minimum that will be fixed for the homostat; (2) dotted shading denotes *intermediate* values less than 100 and greater than or equal to 80; (3) no shading indicates *low* score values.

In the present instance the inclusion of a single intermediate score (for Lots 9 and 3) in the homostat cluster does not seriously injure its homogeneity. Note, however, that if the coded value ranges were re-set to include Lot 6 in the cluster, the total range of within-cluster scores would be increased enormously and the plateau-like appearance of the cluster would be weakened.

The patterning of similarity scores indicates more, however, than the existence of a single homostat. The presence of numerous intermediate-range values for items located near the centre of the primary diagonal shows that these items are much more similar to the homostatic cluster than to items along the lower right end of the primary diagonal. We note that Lots 9, 5, 2, 4 and 3 are all pond-bank communities, and that the cluster thus has meaning in terms of Shotwell's community assignments. Interestingly, the transitional pond-bank/woodland community (Lot 6) is the non-cluster lot most similar to the pond-bank cluster, as indicated by the patterning of its intermediate-range values. Its transitional nature is thus not only indicated by its position in the item array, but by its coded similarity scores.

At this point the results of the topographic treatment of the matrix can be assessed and new strategies planned to recover further information. Principally, the analysis of the score patterning by contouring and colour coding revealed a single, large, high-value homostat, so that now the item relations can be expressed as follows:

lot array: 9 5 2 4 3 6 7 11 8 10 1
             • • • • • • • • • • •
             ‿‿‿‿‿‿‿‿‿‿
                 cluster

The above homostat represents the strongest similarities within the matrix, and has a mean score of 126 for Robinson's Index of Agreement. It is clear, however, that there are other lot relations in the matrix that ought to be considered, but these cannot be discerned by such an elementary form of cluster analysis.

Dendrograms

A method of analysis, which is independent of item seriation, but which can be used to good advantage with it, is the construction of tree diagrams from similarity scores. Dendrograms, as the tree diagrams are called, show the degree of similarity for all items by branch connections between them, and provide information above and beyond that obtained by defining high-value homostats. Whether such information is often useful is another matter.

Before proceeding to the application of tree diagram analysis to Shotwell's vertebrate data, let us review briefly some of the general aspects of cluster analysis. The most elementary kinds of clusters are (1) single linkage clusters, (2) complete linkage clusters, and (3) average linkage clusters. More sophisticated kinds of dendrogram clusters will be mentioned in Part II.

The single linkage type does not group items that are all similar above a set similarity level. Admission of an item into a cluster is according to the criterion that states that the prospective item addition is similar to any one item in the cluster at a specified level. This form of clustering has no apparent utility in anthropological or archaeological *Q*-type cluster classification, but may be important for solving developmental and evolutionary problems.

Complete linkage clustering states that a given item joining a cluster of other items at a set level must show similarity at or above that level with all items of the cluster. The matrix search for homostats is an example of complete linkage clustering.

Average linkage clustering, proposed by Sokal and Michener (1958), specifies the admission of any item into a cluster on the basis of the average of the similarity scores of that item with the cluster items. As the size of the cluster grows through successive linking, this average similarity necessarily becomes lowered since more remotely similar items are grouped together. The dendrogrammatic technique is of this third type.

Dendrogram analysis was developed in biological taxonomy (Sokal and Sneath, 1963). In it, items in either an *R*- or *Q*-technique study are linked progressively by the criterion that the average similarity between members of the same group is greater than the average similarity between members of different groups. Items are progressively joined, first into pairs, then into larger groups by an iterative process known as the pair-group method, discussed at length by Sokal and Sneath (1963, pp. 181–93, 198–203, 305–17). The recent study on hominid classification by the zoologist A. J. Boyce (1964) is an excellent anthropological example of the use of tree diagrams for clustering purposes.

334

I have decided, then, to continue this study with the pair group, average linkage, method. Further, the decision has been made to use the *unweighted group method*, one of several possible average linkage procedures. It calculates averages from the original scores, whereas the weighted technique calculates averages from other averages, rather than the scores for which they were figured (Sokal and Sneath, 1963, pp. 191–4). The procedural steps of the method were carried out with a desk calculator. There is available, however, an efficient computer program (Bonham-Carter, 1967) for the pair-group method.

The unweighted group method works as follows. An unseriated double matrix of similarity scores for all pairs of items is calculated. Robinson Indexes of Agreement are suitable similarity scores, as are other equal-unit, normatized scores. Correlation coefficients cannot be used unless they are transformed into percentages, Fisher's z, or to arc cosines of the correlation coefficients.

For illustrative purposes Shotwell's vertebrate collections will now be carried through the various steps of the analysis. First, a double matrix of similarity scores is put together (Fig. 8.6) exactly as is done before item seriation. The positions which items occupy along the margins of the table are immaterial. Any item permutation may be used. The first computation cycle is a search for *basic pairs*, pairs of items whose members are more similar to each other than to any other items. This can be done by locating the highest score in each column in the double matrix, which is then underlined or circled. Then, column by column, each 'highest' score is examined to see if it represents a basic pair, i.e. if it is *the* highest score for the two items which it represents.

The highest score of column 1 is 68, for Lots 8 and 1 (Fig. 8.6). The score does not represent a basic pair, however, because one of its items, Lot 8, has a higher similarity score (of 78) with another item (Lot 10). The highest score of column 2 is 163 for Lots 4 and 2. We find that 163 is the highest similarity score for Lot 4 and for Lot 2. Therefore these two lots form a basic pair that can be labelled 2^1. When all columns have been inspected this way, three basic pairs are found: 2^1 (Lots 2 and 4), 6^1 (Lots 6 and 7) and 8^1 (Lots 8 and 10).

The second computation cycle involves constructing a new matrix of similarity scores based on the averages of the basic pairs with each other and with single items that do not belong to the basic pairs. The items along the margin of the new matrix (Fig. 8.7a) are clusters 2^1, 6^1 and 8^1 and Lots 1, 3, 5, 9 and 11. The similarity (S) between lot i and a basic pair composed of

335

lots j and k is calculated as the following mean:

$$\bar{S} = 1/n(S_{ij} + S_{ik} + S_{jk}),$$

where S is the similarity score (Robinson Index of Agreement) and n is the number of original item pair scores being summed. In a like fashion, the similarity between two basic pairs, S_{ij} and S_{kl}, is

$$\bar{S} = \tfrac{1}{6}(S_{ij} + S_{ik} + S_{il} + S_{jk}S_{jl} + S_{kl}).$$

The above computational formulae are not identical to the procedures for calculating averages used by Sokal and Sneath (1963, p. 310). To compute the

Lots	1	2	3	4	5	6	7	8	9	10	11
1		14	11	9	4	17	27	68	7	51	15
2	14		147	163	125	83	65	30	100	7	40
3	11	147		157	108	96	81	31	87	6	61
4	9	163	157		139	83	73	29	114	4	46
5	4	125	108	139		65	38	7	118	0	24
6	17	83	96	83	65		104	35	48	11	54
7	27	65	81	73	38	104		49	29	43	83
8	68	30	31	29	7	35	49		3	78	25
9	7	100	87	114	118	48	29	3		2	19
10	51	7	6	4	0	11	43	78	2		46
11	15	40	61	46	24	54	83	25	19	46	

basic pairs:
2^1 (2 and 4), 6^1 (6 and 7), 8^1 (8 and 10)

FIG. 8.6. First matrix of similarity scores with three basic pairs, Late Tertiary vertebrate collections.

similarity between the basic pairs S_{ij} and S_{kl}, they would perform the operation

$$S_{(ij)(kl)} = \tfrac{1}{4}(S_{ik} + S_{il} + S_{jk} + S_{jl}).$$

It can be seen that similarity scores for the original basic pairs S_{ij} and S_{kl} are omitted. I include them because my interest is in the average value for all possible original item scores of all possible item combinations for the potential grouping.

	2^1	6^1	8^1	1	3	5	9	11
2^1		95	52	62	156	142	126	83
6^2		95	53	49	94	69	60	80
8^1	52	53		66	38	28	28	50
1	62	49	66		11	4	7	15
3	156	94	38	11		108	87	61
5	142	69	28	4	108		118	24
9	126	60	28	7	87	118		19
11	83	80	50	15	61	24	19	

basic pairs:
2^2 (2^1 and 3), 8^2 (8^1 and 1)

(*a*)

	2^2	8^2	6^1	5	9	11
2^2		54	105	140	128	102
8^2	54		48	35	35	47
6^1	105	48		69	90	80
5	140	35	69		118	24
9	128	35	90	118		19
11	102	47	80	24	19	

basic pair: 2^3 (2^2 and 5)

(*b*)

FIG. 8.7. (*a*) Second matrix with two basic pairs. (*b*) Third matrix with one basic pair.

	2^3	8^2	6^1	9	11
2^3		_57_	102	126	101
8^2	57		48	35	47
6^1	102	48		90	80
9	126	35	90		19
11	101	47	80	19	

basic pair: 2^4 (2^3 and 9)

(a)

	2^4	8^2	6^1	11
2^4		_58_	_96·3_	_96_
8^2	58		48	47
6^1	96·3	48		80
11	96	47	80	

basic pair: 2^5 (2^4 and 6^1)

(b)

FIG. 8.8. (a) Fourth matrix with one basic pair. (b) Fifth matrix with one basic pair.

	2^5	8^2	11
2^5		_57_	_84_
8^2	57		47
11	_84_	47	

basic pair: 2^6 (2^5 and 11)

(a)

	2^6	8^2
2^6		54
8^2	54	

basic pair: 2^7 (2^6 and 8^2)

(b)

FIG. 8.9. (a) Sixth matrix with one basic pair. (b) Seventh matrix with one basic pair.

338

A search of the second matrix (Fig. 8.7a) for new basic pairs produces 2^2 (2^1 and 3) and 8^2 (8^1 and 1). The procedure of calculating new, ever smaller matrices and seeking new pairs is continued (Figs. 8.7b, 8.8, 8.9) until finally a minimal two-by-two matrix remains (Fig. 8.9b).

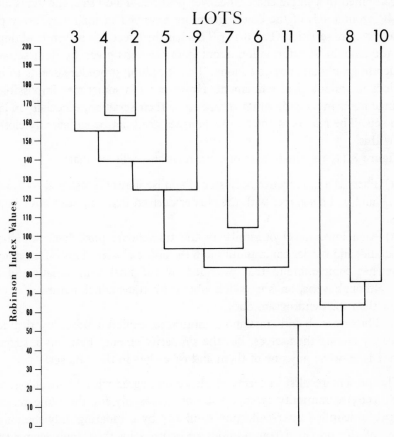

FIG. 8.10. Dendrogram for Late Tertiary vertebrate collections.

At this point all items have been joined at some level, and the dendrogram can be drawn to show the points at which joining has taken place (Fig. 8.10). The vertical scale of Fig. 8.10 gives the average similarity of all the lots joined at any one point on the scale. For instance, Lots 2 and 4, the first basic pair, are joined at 163, the value that represents their similarity score; Lot 3 is joined to Lots 2 and 4 at 156, which is the average ($\bar{S}$) of the three scores S_{23} (147), S_{24} (163), and S_{34} (157).

The horizontal axis of the standard dendrogram is not interpretable. The distances between lots may or may not be equal, as the illustrator wishes. Also, the position of cluster items along this axis is irrelevant.

Something else should be done before the tree diagram is in its final form. It is recommended that the results of item seriation and tree diagram study be combined in a single chart whenever possible. To do this, the items along the horizontal axis of the dendrogram are arranged in their final array produced by item seriation (Fig. 8.11). This has the effect, in one sense, of doubling the amount of information about item relations given by item seriation or dendrogrammatic analysis alone. This graphing procedure seems to be a distinct methodological refinement. However, it is sometimes impossible to arrange items in a dendrogram according to their seriation, especially in large data sets. The results of the two techniques need not be sufficiently close to allow this.

Figure 8.11, the final chart of item relations, tells us that:

(1) There is a homogeneous cluster of similar items represented by Lots 2, 3, 4, 5 and 9. This agrees with the cluster derived from the search for homostats.

(2) At a lower level of similarity the transitional pond-bank/woodland, woodland, and border communities join the above cluster. This information is somewhat comparable to that provided by the final item seriation of the lots, although seriation shows the obviously transitional nature of Lot 6 better than the dendrogram does.

(3) The savannah and grassland communities exhibit a rather low degree of similarity among themselves, but the similarity among these lots is stronger than it is between any one of them and other lots in the data set.

The present results, in terms of clustering, agree with Shotwell's (1955, 1958, 1963) community typing, but not necessarily for the same reasons. Shotwell identified inter-collection similarity by comparing only the animal forms of the proximal communities recognized by their high element per individual ratio. The present study, however, considers the percentages of every form and utilizes the total sample counts. Our basic agreement suggests that the use of percentages, alone, may be just as accurate a way to cluster vertebrate collections as the isolation of proximal community members and their comparison. If this is true, it is so because forms with a high element per individual ratio tend to be dominant in their respective faunal collections. Stating the reverse of this, forms that have a low element per individual ratio tend also to be rare. Happily, the Robinson Index of Agreement is able to minimize the effects of rare, often intruded, forms on a collection whether this mixture results from stratigraphic migration or contemporary intrusions from one or more distal communities.

The present study has perhaps made an additional contribution in that it suggests that Shotwell's community types are not equally homogeneous constructs. There is clearly less variation in the pond-bank community type

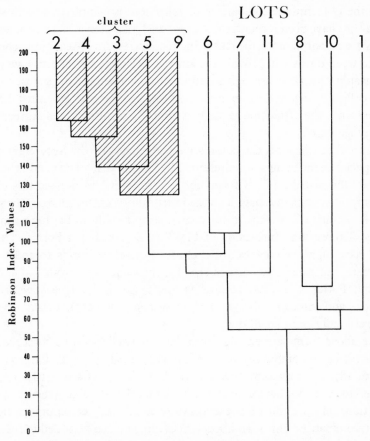

FIG. 8.11. Dendrogram with lots placed in seriated array.

than in the others, and this is reasonable since other types, such as savannah, would be expected to include more varied kinds of habitats than a pond-bank. Unfortunately there are other sources of variation in the data set that make this, at best, only a reasonable hypothesis to be tested with additional data. For instance, several of the pond-bank collections are samples of the same faunal bed. There is less phylogenetic continuity between Lots 1, 8 and 10 than in the forms of cluster Lots 2, 3, 4, 5 and 9. Also, Lot 1 is separated from Lots 8 and 10 by a much greater distance than any of the collections in the pond-bank cluster.

R-technique ogives

Once the Q-technique comparison of collections is completed and clusters of similar lots have been recognized, the next analytical step is to determine which forms are responsible for the clustering tendencies. An R-technique comparison between forms will provide the answer. A simple but effective way to do this graphically is to use ogives, cumulative percentage diagrams, to show inter-collection agreement in item percentages. Percentages must be considered since the Q-technique study with Robinson Indexes of Agreement is percentage based.

Figure 8.12 diagrams the cumulative percentages of the forty-eight genera and species of the homostat represented by Lots 2, 3, 4, 5 and 9, and shows for contrast the distribution of forms for Lot 10, which is outside this cluster. Genera and species that have a marked vertical percentage increase for several lots simultaneously are the forms contributing heavily to the high similarity scores of those lots. Inspection of Fig. 8.12 discloses that Forms 5, 15 and 35 all have high percentages in the cluster lots, while Forms 10 and 23 have moderate, but consistent, percentages for the same lots. From Table 8.3 we see that Forms 5, 15, 35, 10 and 23 are, respectively, *Hypolagus* (rabbit), *Dipoides* and *Eucastor* (beavers), *Prosthennops* (peccary), *Citellus* (ground squirrel), and *Canis* (small dog).

The above forms are among those that Shotwell has used to characterize the pond-bank community type (Shotwell, 1958, p. 282, fig. 13; 1963, pp. 16, 18), but represent only a part of the list of characteristic proximal forms. However, we have determined here that they dominate their respective collections and are most representative of pond-bank communities because of this dominance. This is an important datum and can be added to the extant information about pond-bank vertebrate communities of the Late Tertiary.

Ogives can also be used to simplify the rank ordering of items according to their relative effect on lot clustering. This effect can be determined roughly, and items ranked accordingly, in one of two simple ways. The first involves calculating common influence, the agreement among the percentages for form A, say, in Lots 1, 2 and 3. If A is 35% of Lot 1, 20% of Lot 2, and 30% of Lot 3, its common influence on this lot cluster is 20, the inter-lot agreement

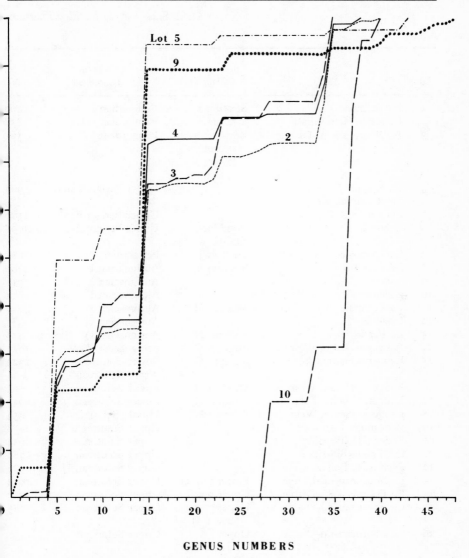

GENUS NUMBERS

Fig. 8.12. Ogives for Lots 2, 3, 4, 5, 9 and 10.

for *A*. Calculating average influence is the second way. The average influence of *A* is $(35 + 20 + 30) = 28$ in the above hypothetical example.

The average influence of the dominant vertebrates of the homostatic cluster can easily be calculated from the ogives of Fig. 8.12. The resulting rank order, with most dominant form first, is 15, 5, 35, 10 and 22: beavers, rabbit, peccary, ground squirrel and small dog, respectively.

TABLE 8.4. *Key to lot identification,*

Lot	Site	Deposit	Cultural Assignment	N
1	La Ferrassie	Stratum E	Perigordian I	1000
2	Laugerie-Haute, East	Stratum B	Perigordian III$_1$	858
3	Le Fourneau-du-Diable	Lower stratum lower terrace	Perigordian IV	561
4	La Roque Saint-Christophe		Upper Perigordian	969
5	Font Robert		Upper Perigordian	1500
6	Labattut	(combined strata)	Upper Perigordian	3096
7	La Ferrassie	Stratum J	Perigordian V$_1$	886
8	La Ferrassie	Stratum F	Aurignacian I	2460
9	Lartet		Aurignacian I	711
10	Castanet		Aurignacian I	1824
11	La Ferrassie	Stratum H	Aurignacian II	4039
12	Castanet		Aurignacian II	1283
13	La Ferrassie	Stratum H"	Aurignacian IV	473
14	Laugerie-Haute, West	Stratum D	Aurignacian V	1621
15	Laugerie-Haute, West	Stratum G	Lower-Solutrean (Proto-Solutrean)	1329
16	Laugerie-Haute, West	Stratum H'	Lower Solutrean	595
17	Laugerie-Haute, East	Stratum H'	Lower Solutrean	933
18	Laugerie-Haute, West	Stratum H"	Middle Solutrean	454
19	Badegoule (Peyrony)		Upper Solutrean	838
20	Badegoule (Peyrille)		Upper Solutrean	654
21	Pech de la Boissière		Upper Solutrean I	760
22	Pech de la Boissière		Upper Solutrean II	976
23	Le Fourneau-du-Diable	Lower terrace	Upper Solutrean	1012
24	Le Fourneau-du-Diable	Upper terrace I	Upper Solutrean	1110
25	Le Fourneau-du-Diable	Upper terrace II	Upper Solutrean	785
26	Le Fourneau-du-Diable	Upper terrace III	Upper Solutrean	1430

Only the one cluster, the homostat, has been examined here to find out which forms are dominant and by inference responsible for clustering. However, new ogival graphs could be computed for any combination of lots from the dendrogrammatic groupings, and the process could be repeated to single out and rank order dominant forms.

Upper Palaeolithic artefact collections

Source

---

de Sonneville-Bordes, 1960, vol. I, Table 19, pp. 256, 257
de Sonneville-Bordes, 1960, vol. I, Table 21, p. 259
de Sonneville-Bordes, 1960, vol. I, Table 30, pp. 272, 273

de Sonneville-Bordes, 1960, vol. I, Table 24, pp. 262, 263

de Sonneville-Bordes, 1960, vol. I, Table 25, pp. 264, 265
de Sonneville-Bordes, 1960, vol. I, Table 29, pp. 270, 271

de Sonneville-Bordes, 1960, vol. I, Table 26, pp. 265, 266
de Sonneville-Bordes, 1960, vol. I, Table 1, pp. 231, 232
de Sonneville-Bordes, 1960, vol. I, Table 5, pp. 236, 237
de Sonneville-Bordes, 1960, vol. I, Table 10, pp. 243, 244
de Sonneville-Bordes, 1960, vol. I, Table 1, pp. 231, 232
de Sonneville-Bordes, 1960, vol. I, Table 10, pp. 243, 244
de Sonneville-Bordes, 1960, vol. I, Table 2, pp. 232, 233
de Sonneville-Bordes, 1960, vol. I, Table 3, pp. 234, 235
de Sonneville-Bordes, 1960, vol. II, Table 32, pp. I, II; Smith, 1966, p. 399

de Sonneville-Bordes, 1960, vol. II, Table 32, pp. I, II; Smith, 1966, pp. 408, 409
de Sonneville-Bordes, 1960, vol. II, Table 32, pp. I, II; Smith, 1966, pp. 409, 410
de Sonneville-Bordes, 1960, vol. II, Table 33, pp. III, IV; Smith, 1966, pp. 408, 409
de Sonneville-Bordes, 1960, vol. II, Table 34, pp. IV, V; Smith, 1966, pp. 410, 411
de Sonneville-Bordes, 1960, vol. II, Table 34, pp. IV, V; Smith, 1966, pp. 410, 411
de Sonneville-Bordes, 1960, vol. II, Table 35, pp. V–VII; Smith, 1966, pp. 412, 413
de Sonneville-Bordes, 1960, vol. II, Table 35, pp. V–VII; Smith, 1966, pp. 412, 413
de Sonneville-Bordes, 1960, vol. II, Table 37, pp. VIII, IX; Smith, 1966, pp. 416, 417
de Sonneville-Bordes, 1960, vol. II, Table 37, pp. VIII, IX; Smith, 1966, pp. 416, 417
de Sonneville-Bordes, 1960, vol. II, Table 37, pp. VIII, IX; Smith, 1966, pp. 416, 417

de Sonneville-Bordes, 1960, vol. II, Table 37, pp. VIII, IX; Smith, 1966, pp. 416, 417

THE FRENCH PALAEOLITHIC

The twenty-six Palaeolithic artefact collections are assigned lot numbers in Table 8.4, and each lot is identified by name, stratigraphic provenance, cultural assignment, sample size and publication source. All the sites are located in the famous valleys of south-western France: along the Dronne,

345

Vézère, Cern and Dordogne rivers. Only lithic specimens will be considered in the comparison that follows.

The artefact collections are Upper Palaeolithic in style and age, and represent three of the four great Upper Palaeolithic cultural traditions – the Perigordian (seven lots), the Aurignacian (seven lots) and the Solutrean (twelve lots). Magdalenian assemblages are omitted to keep the data set within manageable size limits.

The twenty-six collections have been summarized and compared by de Sonneville-Bordes (1960), whence the present data come. The twelve Solutrean collections are also presented in Smith's (1966) excellent synthesis of that cultural tradition. In their comparative studies, de Sonneville-Bordes and Smith use several simple and efficient techniques which are usually considered the hallmark of François Bordes. For the most part they employ cumulative percentage graphs (ogives) for the ninety-two Upper Palaeolithic artefact types (defined in de Sonneville-Bordes, 1960, vol. I, pp. 27, 28), and indexes based on artefact class proportions in the total lithic samples. The indexes, e.g. *I.G.* (Scraper Index) and *I.B.* (Burin Index), are explained in detail elsewhere (de Sonneville-Bordes, 1960, vol. I, pp. 28, 29).

It was necessary to set some arbitrary limit on sample size in selecting from among the many Upper Palaeolithic periodized site collections. Some consist of only a few dozen specimens and are unsuitable for quantitative comparison since there are many artefact types (ninety-two) in the French Upper Palaeolithic. The figure 400 was chosen as a minimum collection size.

It would be ideal in this kind of study to select a large number of collections for each culture type, and then do similarity scaling and cluster studies to find out which resemble each other enough so that they can be classed together. Each culture type would be well represented in the sample. This procedure is impossible to follow because several of the culture types are rare and poorly represented archaeologically. Also, more than one important collection had to be excluded because of its small size.

The twenty-six lots are currently classed by many prehistorians into the culture types given in Fig. 8.13, partly on the basis of diagnostic artefacts called *fossiles directeurs*. The sequence from bottom to top of the figure reflects the known stratigraphic superposition of the culture types at the three key sites of La Ferrassie, Laugerie-Haute and Pataud. Note that the chosen lots fail to represent the Evolved Aurignacian and the Proto-Magdalenian entirely, while other culture types such as the Lower Perigordian and 'Final' Aurignacian are represented by only one collection each. In contrast, eight of the twenty-six lots are Upper Solutrean.

346

The lack of uniformity in the distribution of lots by culture types is unfortunate in some ways but useful in others. As a test case for seriation and cluster classification techniques it is good to have a large number of lots from a single culture type such as the Upper Solutrean. If these lots are classed either separately or together in the following study, something will perhaps have been learned about the 'nature' of the Upper Solutrean. And even with an uneven distribution of lots, there is still the possibility that lots belonging to different culture types may be classed together.

The site of Badegoule provides an interesting test case. Two collections (Peyrony, Peyrille) from the same stratigraphic unit are included as Lots 19 and 20. In effect, one collection is divided in two. As a simple test, seriation

---

latest—Upper Solutrean [lots 19, 20, 21, 22, 23, 24, 25, 26]
    Middle Solutrean [lot 18]
    Lower Solutrean [lots 16, 17]
    Proto-Solutrean [lot 15]
    Proto-Magdalenian
    Aurignacian V [lot 14]
    Perigordian 'III' [lot 2] ⎫ undifferentiated Upper Perigordian
    Perigordian V [lot 7] ⎬ [lots 4, 5, 6]
    Perigordian IV [lot 3] ⎭
    'Final Aurignacian' (IV) [lot 13]
    Evolved Aurignacian (III)
    Middle Aurignacian (II) [lots 11, 12]
    Aurignacian I [lots 8, 9, 10]
earliest—Lower Perigordian (I) [lot 1]

FIG. 8.13. Sequence of Upper Palaeolithic culture types with lot assignments.

---

should be able to show the postulated extreme similarity of the two lots. If it cannot, then the two artefact collections were classified differently, there is extreme sampling error between them, or else we had best look for a new comparative technique!

Item seriation

As in the case of the Late Tertiary vertebrate collections, the first part of the study is simple scale analysis by item seriation with PROGRAM SERIATE. Percentages and Robinson Indexes of Agreement were calculated. Then these similarity scores were placed in a data matrix and seriated with the same data processing equipment used on the first data set.

Since the number of lots is over twice as large as it was for the vertebrate collections, it is likely that lot relations may also be more complex and that a

347

good seriation may be more difficult to find. With this in mind, seventy seriation tries were made with the computer, each with a different lot permutation input to help eliminate input bias. The best seriation produced a Coefficient *H* of 758 660 and a Matrix Coefficient *C* of 1·24139. The corresponding item array of lots appears in Fig. 8.14, providing an overview of relations according to *C*-type similarity scaling (Fig. 8.1).

To begin with, the appropriate culture types can be listed by each lot in the seriated array of Fig. 8.14 as follows:

Lot No.	Culture type
1	Lower Perigordian
7	Perigordian V
2	Perigordian 'III'
16	Lower Solutrean
15	Proto-Solutrean
14	Aurignacian V
6	Upper Perigordian
4	Upper Perigordian
5	Upper Perigordian
3	Perigordian IV
17	Lower Solutrean
11	Middle Aurignacian
9	Aurignacian I
13	'Final' Aurignacian
8	Aurignacian I
12	Middle Aurignacian
21	Upper Solutrean
22	Upper Solutrean
23	Upper Solutrean
19	Upper Solutrean
20	Upper Solutrean
24	Upper Solutrean
10	Aurignacian I
25	Upper Solutrean
26	Upper Solutrean
18	Middle Solutrean

This seriation will, I think, initially appear meaningless to the archaeological reader. For one thing, the archaeologists who normally use seriation have a strong predilection for viewing it only as a dating technique, a method that can be applied more or less automatically to obtain the proper relative ages of items in a given data set. This view is of course nonsense, but it is widespread. Many of the problems which can be seen in the new Hole and Shaw

348

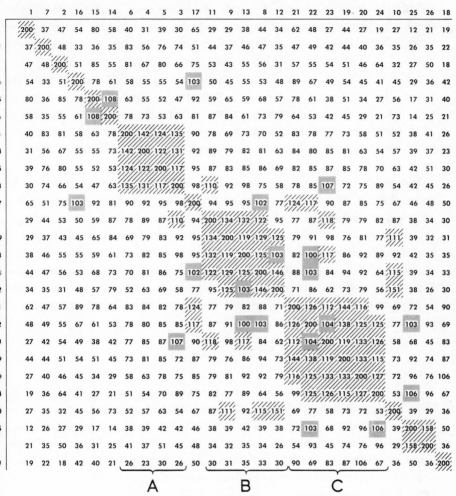

Robinson Indexes of Agreement score values.

░ High   ▓ Intermediate

Absence of shading denotes low score value.

FIG. 8.14. Seriated and coded matrix of similarity scores for twenty-six Upper Palaeolithic artefact collections. Coefficient $H = 758660$, Matrix Coefficient $C = 1.24139$. Homostats A, B and C.

publication (1967) on seriation are due to this kind of misunderstanding. They will be mentioned later.

It is good to emphasize at this point, therefore, that seriation is a descriptive technique and nothing more. It arranges items (collections) unidimensionally so that the position of each item reflects its degree of similarity to all other items, similarity thus being expressed as positional proximity. Whenever one begins discussing relative dating, at that point he is doing interpretation as opposed to description. The latter must always precede the former.

Plainly, the lot sequence of Fig. 8.14 does not agree with the known relative ages of the lots given in Fig. 8.13 as determined by unequivocal stratigraphic superposition. Thus differences between collection positions in the seriated array cannot be explained by gradual artefact type fluctuations and replacements through time, at least not by the regular type of replacement discussed by Robinson (1951) and Brainerd (1951).[3]

Factors other than time must account for the positions of items in the ordered series. If we assume that the French artefact typology is capable of accurately revealing the kind of temporal fluctuation in the frequency of types that is necessary for relative dating purposes, then we can conclude that no such simple evolutionary sequence of culture forms is represented by that segment of the Upper Palaeolithic of south-western France treated here. Historically different traditions must be present among the twenty-six lots. This point will be discussed when interpretations of the French archaeological sequence are dealt with later.

Cluster search

The C-value of 1·24139 for the best seriated item permutation tells us that there is no gradual progression in the final similarity scale from one end of the series to the other. A C-value of approximately 2 would have indicated such patterning. As in the case of the best C-value of 1·16252 for the vertebrate collections, the best Matrix Coefficient C for the Palaeolithic collections very strongly suggests the existence of clumps of comparable similarity scores which need to be sought out.

Homostats were first searched for by contouring the seriated matrix (not illustrated), and by experimenting with shading to find clumps of high scores adjacent to the diagonal of identity (Fig. 8.14). An additional aid was used to set score intervals for the coding process. All the $n(n-1)/2$ similarity scores were plotted in a frequency chart (Fig. 8.15), the purpose being to show natural breaks in score distribution, should they exist, which could serve to set off *high*, *intermediate*, or some such group intervals. Figure 8.15 shows what seems to be an irregular mode of score values above 110. Thus Robinson Indexes of Agreement of this value or greater are coded as *high* scores by using diagonal stripes. Also, an *intermediate* range of 100–109 is set to show score gradation within the matrix, using dots for this range. The absence of shading indicates *low* similarity score values.

Figure 8.14 shows three distinct homostatic clusters labelled *A*, *B* and *C*. Although they are so designated here, clusters *B* and *C* are not perfect homostats; that is to say, not all of their included similarity scores are *high* and fit the set limiting value of 110. But the approximation of these two clusters to homostats is very close, and I see no serious problems in a slight relaxation of definitional criteria when it facilitates pattern recognition.

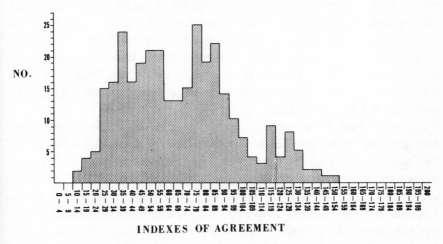

INDEXES OF AGREEMENT

FIG. 8.15. Frequency distribution of similarity scores for twenty-six Upper Palaeolithic artefact collections.

Cluster *A* (Lots 3 through 6) is composed entirely of Upper Perigordian artefact collections from Fourneau-du-Diable, La Roque Saint-Christophe, Font Robert and Labattut. The uniformity within this group of site collections is strong and is interesting from several standpoints. First, the mean similarity score of the homostat is 128, which is quite high when compared to the score distribution of Fig. 8.15. Second, cluster *A* stands apart very distinctly from its nearest neighbouring lots on the primary diagonal (see Fig. 8.14). Lot 14, adjacent to the upper left of cluster *A*, is Aurignacian V and is quite dissimilar to the cluster. Lot 17, situated to the lower right of the cluster, is Lower Solutrean and also quite dissimilar to the cluster lots, but not so markedly so as Lot 14. Third, there is no strong resemblance between the Upper Perigordian lots of cluster *A* and the most ancient Perigordian site collection, Lot 1 (Perigordian I). Fourth, cluster *A* has a brief temporal duration relative to that of the homostat, cluster *B*.

351

Cluster *B* (Lots 8, 9, 11, 12, 13) consists of Aurignacian stratigraphic assemblages from La Ferrassie (three lots), Lartet (one lot) and Castanet (one lot). The mean score for the cluster is 123, only five points less than the average of cluster *A*. However, the cluster merges or blends more gradually with its adjacent collections: Lot 17 (Lower Solutrean) on the upper left, and Lot 21 (Upper Solutrean) on the lower right (Fig. 8.14). Early Aurignacian (I), Middle Aurignacian (II) and later Aurignacian (IV) site collections are represented, giving the cluster a rather considerable temporal range. In comparison with cluster *A*, cluster *B* indicates that 'Aurignacianness' is a more uniform thing (through time) than 'Perigordianness', at least in so far as the two qualities can be measured with Robinson Indexes of Agreement and the extant French artefact typology. This is common knowledge, of course, and is embodied in the nomenclature used largely outside France, in which Perigordian I is called Châtelperronian (*Castelperronien*) and the Upper Perigordian is termed Gravettian.

Cluster *C* (Lots 19 through 24) consists only of Upper Solutrean collections from the sites of Badegoule, Pech de la Boissière and Le Fourneau-du-Diable. In it are all the Upper Solutrean artefact collections included in the present sample of twenty-six lots, except Lots 25 and 26. The average score value is 123. Cluster *C* is like cluster *A* in that it is of brief temporal duration, and like *B* in that it tends to blend or intergrade with its surrounding, non-cluster, lots. The Lower and Middle Solutrean collections do not form part of the cluster, and some of them, such as Lots 15 and 16 (the Lower Solutrean at Laugerie-Haute, West), are located near the opposite end of the seriated array. This means that in terms of dominant lithic artefact types, there are very major differences between the Lower and Upper Solutrean artefact collections that were analysed.

We should note at this point that the two collections, Lots 19 and 20, from the same stratum at Badegoule have been classed similarly. As a test of our seriation and clustering techniques, the two lots pass with flying colours (see p. 347).

Dendrograms

Having finished the complete linkage clustering, we can now try an average linkage analysis of the twenty-six Palaeolithic lots. The unweighted group method of constructing a tree diagram was applied exactly as with the vertebrate data set. The final dendrogram of item relations appears in Fig. 8.16.

The reader will remember that after the search for basic pairs had been

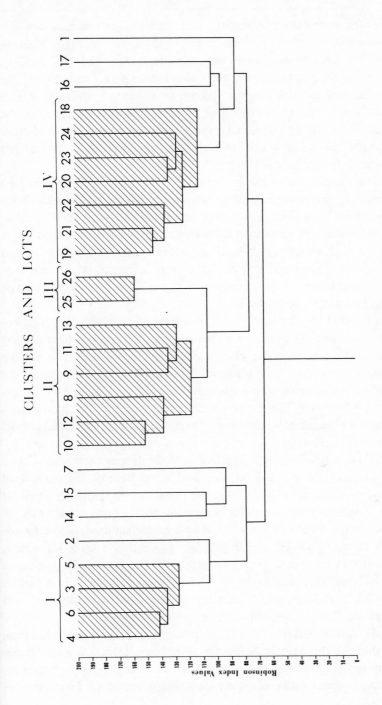

FIG. 8.16. Dendrogram of twenty-six Upper Palaeolithic artefact collections.

353

finished for the vertebrate data, and the basic dendrogram drawn, a new tree diagram was constructed in which the item positions were arranged horizontally across the chart so as to agree with the seriation of the lots (Fig. 8.11). This cannot be done in the case of the Palaeolithic artefact collections. The results of seriation and tree diagram linkage are sufficiently different so that the seriated array cannot be followed in arranging the branches of the dendrogram. Considering that dendrograms are based on average similarities between items, this result is not too surprising in a large and complex data set. Fig. 8.16 will have to stand as it is.

The following information can be obtained from Fig. 8.16. Depending on where one draws cluster limits, several homogeneous groups of similar items can be discerned. If an average similarity score limit of 110 is set (the minimum value for the *high* score interval used in defining the homostats), four clusters result: I (Lots 3 through 6), II (Lots 8 through 13), III (Lots 25 and 26) and IV (Lots 18 through 24). They are average linkage clusters, not homostats. Nevertheless, the content of clusters I, II and IV is very close to that of homostats *A*, *B* and *C*, respectively.

Clusters I and *A* are identical. They contain the Upper Perigordian collections from Fourneau-du-Diable, La Roque Saint-Christophe, Font Robert and Labattut. Cluster II is like cluster *B*, except that it adds Lot 10, the Aurignacian I assemblage from Castanet. This addition does not change the interpretation of cluster *B*, which contains Aurignacian I, II and IV collections from La Ferrassie, Lartet and Castanet. Lot 10, however, strengthens the argument for considerable cluster duration, since it provides an additional early Aurignacian example.

Cluster III is a two-lot (25, 26) grouping of the Upper Solutrean (Upper Terrace II and III) from Le Fourneau-du-Diable. Because the purpose of matrix cluster-classification is to go beyond paired lot similarities, no two-lot groups were defined in the search for homostats. Such a matrix unit would be impossible since it would be represented by a single similarity score, as opposed to a clump of scores. The importance of defining cluster III here is that it shows that clusters of Upper Solutrean collections may be present in the area which are distinct from the Upper Solutrean of cluster *C*. In actuality, however, Lots 25 and 26 illustrate only the similarity of two cultural deposits at the same site. The cluster will not be considered further.

Cluster IV agrees with homostat *C* except that it contains a new collection, Lot 18, which is the Middle Solutrean assemblage from Laugerie-Haute, West. Homostat *C*, it will be remembered, consists only of the Upper Solutrean collections from Badegoule, Pech de la Boissière and Le Fourneau-du-

Diable. The addition of a Middle Solutrean collection to the previous cluster does not alter it much, except to lengthen its temporal range.

It needs to be emphasized that one could reset cluster limits at any average similarity value one wished to choose, and combine appropriate lots into clusters that are different from the foregoing. In the case of the present data set, however, I felt that little would be accomplished. The level of similarity for more inclusive clusters would be so low that interpretation would not be easy. Nevertheless, ogives could be constructed for any grouping to find out what types were responsible for clustering, and this information would perhaps be important in answering questions about broader cultural relations. For instance, one could ask why Lots 7 (Perigordian V), 14 (Aurignacian V) and 15 (Lower Solutrean) join cluster I (Upper Perigordian) at the 79 level, although their typological concordance certainly would not be great.

The interpretation of the total dendrogram will be left to the individual reader with specific questions and problems. The item relations are clear and unambiguous as illustrated in Fig. 8.16. For example, one can easily see that Lot 1 (Perigordian I) is not closely related to any other collections, and comparisons like this can be made for any other lot or lots, as one wishes. The chart shows what the major relations of any specific lot are, given the analytical framework of average linkage analysis with Robinson Indexes.

R-technique ogives

Ogives will be constructed for the three homostats as an example of how the analyst may find out which artefact types are responsible for any cluster grouping of collections that he may establish, either with complete linkage or average linkage techniques. Clearly, clusters I–IV could just as well have been selected here in place of clusters *A–C*.

Figure 8.17 presents cumulative percentage graphs for the four Upper Perigordian lots of cluster *A*. The more abundant artefact types which agree among the four ogives are dichotomized below into *major types*, which will be rank ordered according to their abundance, and *minor types*, which will not be ranked. These determinations are made according to the average influence of each type on the cluster lots. Major types are those whose cluster average is greater than or equal to 5%; minor types have an average less than 5% and greater than 2%. Types whose frequencies are below 2% will be disregarded. These limits could be set differently if one so wished.

355

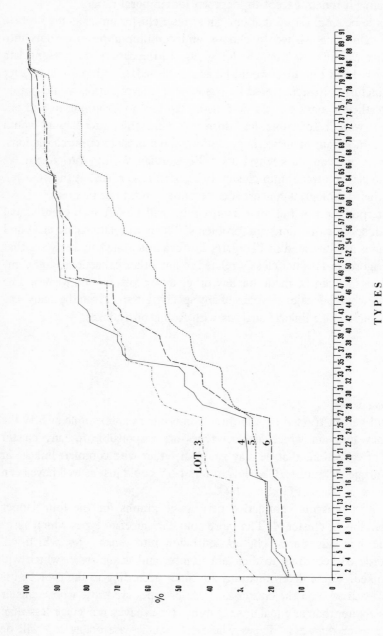

FIG. 8.17. Ogives for Cluster A, Lots 3 through 6.

The six rank ordered major Upper Perigordian artefact types of cluster *A* are, from most to least abundant:

Rank No.	Type No.	Description
1	1	Simple end scraper
2	35	Burin on oblique truncation
3	48	Gravettian projectile point
4	27	Straight dihedral burin
5	28	Lopsided dihedral burin
6	17	Combined scraper-burin

In addition, there are nine unranked minor types:

Type No.	Description
5	Retouched blade scraper
29	Corner dihedral burin
30	Corner burin on break
31	Multiple dihedral burin
40	Multiple burin on truncation
41	'Mixed' multiple burin
65	Blade with continuous retouch on one edge
66	Blade with continuous retouch on two edges

The ogives for the five Aurignacian lots of cluster *B* are superimposed upon one another in Fig. 8.18. The six major artefact types, rank ordered from most common to least common, are

Rank No.	Type No.	Description
1	1	Simple end scraper
2	13	Muzzle-shaped scraper
3	5	Retouched blade scraper
4	65	Blade with continuous retouch on one edge
5	11	Carinate scraper
6	6	Scraper on Aurignacian blade

357

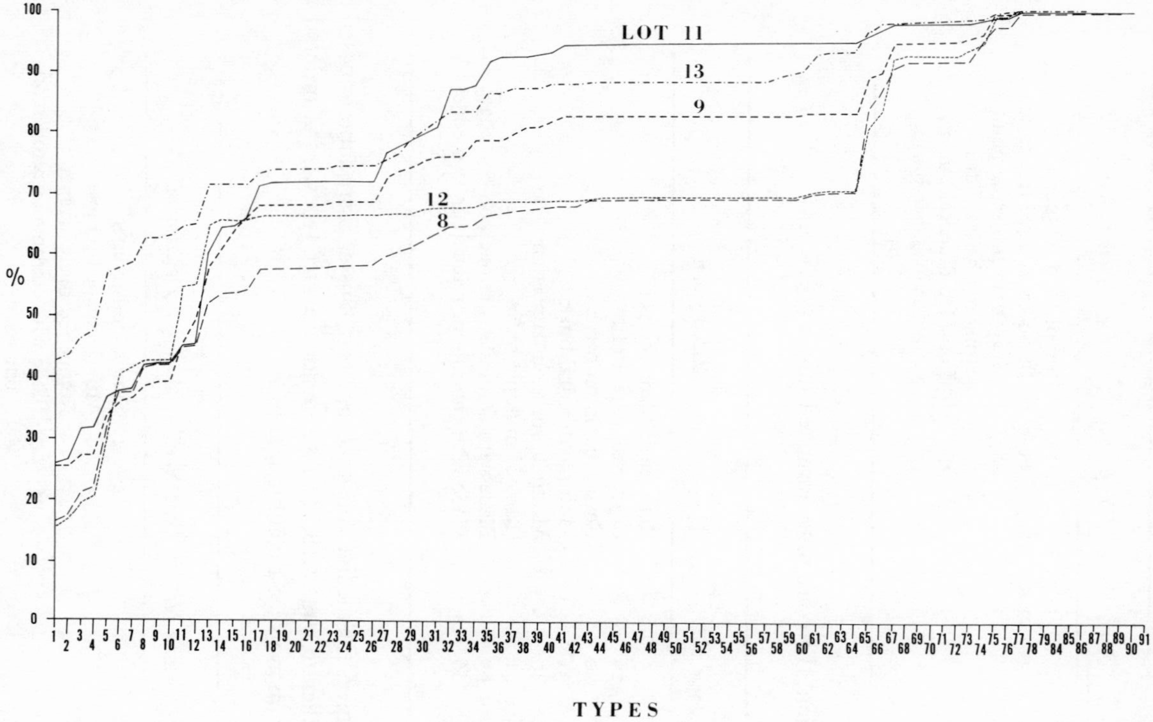

FIG. 8.18. Ogives for Cluster B, Lots 8, 9, 11, 12, 13.

The nine unranked minor types are

Type No.	Description
3	Double scraper
8	Flake scraper
14	Flat muzzle-shaped scraper
17	Combined scraper-burin
27	Straight dihedral burin
30	Corner burin on break
66	Blade with continuous retouch on two edges
67	Aurignacian blade
75	Denticulate tool

Figure 8.19 gives the cumulative percentage graphs for the Upper Solutrean collections of cluster *C*. The four major artefact types, rank ordered in the way described above, are

Rank No.	Type No.	Description
1	1	Simple end scraper
2	70	Laurel leaf projectile point
3	72	Typical Solutrean shouldered projectile point
4	5	Retouched blade scraper

The eleven unranked minor types are

Type No.	Description
3	Double scraper
8	Flake scraper
17	Combined scraper-burin
23	Drill (borer)
27	Straight dihedral burin
35	Burin on oblique truncation
56	Atypical shouldered projectile point
65	Blade with continuous retouch on one edge
71	Willow leaf projectile point
77	Side scraper
85	Backed bladelet

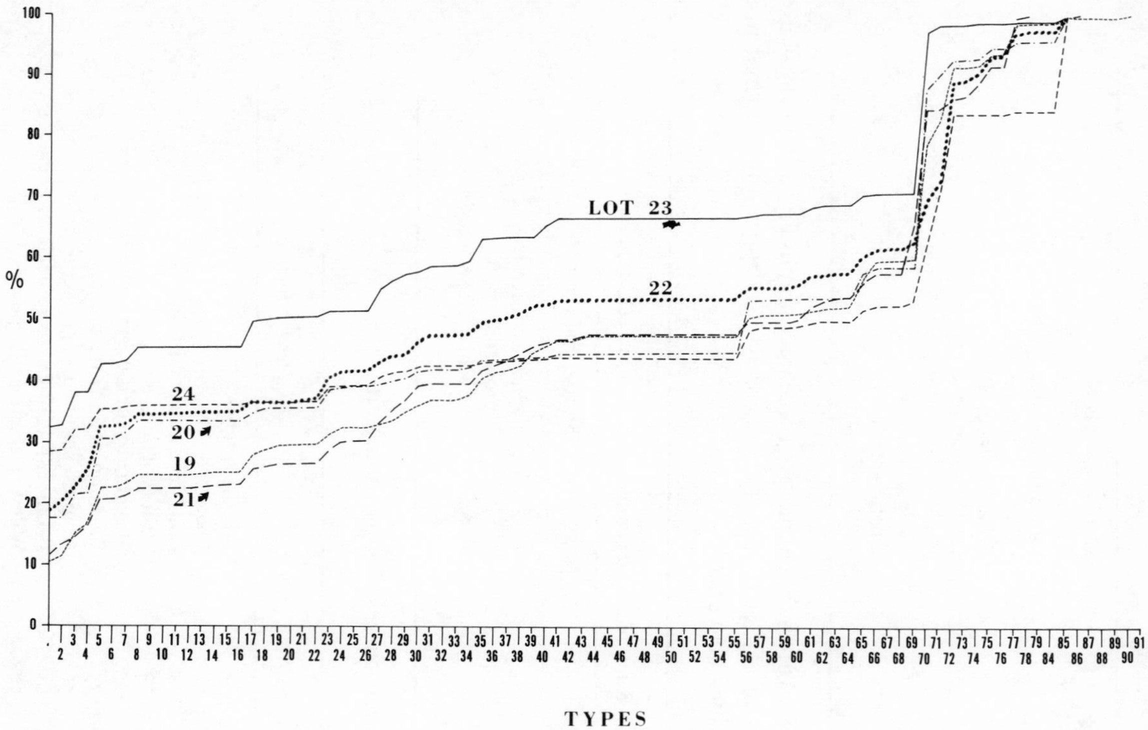

Fig. 8.19. Ogives for Cluster C, Lots 19 through 24.

Archaeological considerations

Before offering a few simple interpretations of the model of the Upper Palaeolithic of south-western France acquired by item seriation and cluster classification, the goal of the study of this data set needs to be stated again. The aim is to select and use appropriate techniques for reducing masses of minutiae to the simplest possible statement of important relations. Appropriate *Q*-technique studies are followed by *R*-technique analyses. There is no implication, no covert intent, to negate the important detailed comparative studies of tool forms, manufacturing traditions, and so forth, which have been and are being carried out on the French artefact collections. Their results are of high value. For example, there is no doubt that the Lower and Upper Perigordian represent a single tool manufacturing tradition, although the present study does not group them together.

My contention is that it is *also* very useful to get simple models of data relations, and to try to determine why patterns of similarities exist at this higher level of abstraction. The use of Robinson Indexes of Agreement in seriation and in clustering studies makes it possible to determine which tool forms are causing inter-collection similarity, where 'similarity' is defined as tool dominance or popularity. François Bordes's and D. de Sonneville-Bordes's use of tool indexes and collection ogives is an attempt to do approximately the same sort of thing.

The interpretation of tool dominance is partly a functional one. That is, the similarity of site collections based on similar dominance of tool types suggests *both functional and historic* (cultural-idiosyncratic) *agreement between them.* Before going further, it will be helpful to set the stage.

The Upper Palaeolithic is clearly a single cultural entity when viewed in terms of the foregoing Mousterian and the succeeding Mesolithic cultural complexes, whatever groupings may occur within it. The distinctions between Upper Palaeolithic cultures are partly stylistic, but also partly functional. But in all the Upper Palaeolithic of south-western France we find an emphasis on bone and horn tools, on small stone artefacts, on the rapid manufacture of tools as opposed to the careful resharpening of old tools, on a general absence of massive choppers and cleavers, and upon the use of many very specialized artefacts, all of this tightly woven into a basic economic fabric of hunting large migratory game animals.

As presently understood, the earliest Upper Palaeolithic, Perigordian I, may possibly have developed locally from a Mousterian base (Pradel, 1966). The origin of the Aurignacian is less clear, but apparently the Perigordian and Aurignacian existed contemporaneously (somewhere!), perhaps as part

361

of an area co-tradition like the Anasazi-Hohokam of the United States South-west (Smith, 1966). However this may be, the Aurignacian and Perigordian (including Perigordian I) seem to be independent of each other, without strong mutual influences (de Sonneville-Bordes, 1960). Also, the clear technical agreement between the Lower and Upper Perigordian would indicate that the Perigordian and Aurignacian evolved separately but at the same time. Some investigators, however, hold that the Aurignacian and Late Perigordian are basically one tradition (Laplace, 1958–61), a thesis hotly denied by others (Bordes, 1963).

The Solutrean is still viewed as a culture whose origins are unclear. It is different from the rest of the Upper Palaeolithic, but represents no real rupture in the cultural sequence as was once thought. It may have developed from earlier French cultures, perhaps from a generalized Aurignacian of the lower Rhône valley, or may even have been introduced from eastern Europe. At any rate, it appears in its most consistent form in the Dordogne area, whence it spread slowly outward to other regions (Smith, 1966).

The following conclusions will be divided into *general* and *specific* inter-pretations. The former have to do with broad questions in general culture history; the latter will concern tool use and inferred economic activities.

General interpretations: (1) The seriation study shows that there is no overall uniform or gradual local development within the twenty-six lots of the type necessary for relative dating with seriation (Robinson, 1951; Brainerd, 1951). If the sample can be considered as an approximately accurate representation of the pre-Magdalenian Upper Palaeolithic of south-western France, this would confound any idea of local (Dordogne) origins for all the cultural units, and of their *in loco* development one from another. Outside areas must be taken into account in any explanation of origins.

Desmond M. Collins's (1965) recent seriation study of some of the collec-tions analysed here yielded rather similar results, and should be consulted by the interested reader. One of his general findings is that collections from a broad area, larger than his Vézère valley example, do not seriate well in terms of their known age. He infers that only a continuity of assemblages of a particular sub-area and ethnic group will chronologically seriate. If so, his data and mine can be used to infer the existence of local ethnic groups with some isolation (segregation) one from another, at least enough to make cross-group chronological seriation difficult.

(2) There is evidence that several lots can be grouped into clusters on the basis of their sharing the same artefact types *in similarly high proportions.*

The three homostats that have been defined are clusters A (Upper Perigordian), B (Aurignacian I, II, IV) and C (Upper Solutrean). The recognition of clusters A and B may be used as evidence against the thesis that the Aurignacian and Upper Perigordian are basically similar (Laplace, 1958–61), although specific technical resemblances can be pointed out. Furthermore, it is important that clusters A and C represent only one historic segment, or period, of the Perigordian and Solutrean, respectively, illustrating a certain strong dissimilarity between their early and late manifestations. On the other hand, the make-up of cluster B means that 'Aurignacianness' is a more uniform thing from one period to another, in so far as uniformity of the kind measured by the Robinson Index of Agreement is concerned. Four average-linkage clusters can also be defined, but their interpretation is not significantly different from that offered for the above homostats.

Specific interpretations: (1) The Upper Perigordian of cluster A is characterized by the following major tools, in order of abundance in their collections: the end scraper, burins on oblique truncation, the Gravettian point, straight and lopsided dihedral burins, and the combination scraper-burin. Minor forms, listed previously, include retouched blade scrapers, various burin types, retouched blades, and backed bladelets. This division of tool forms makes it possible to say something about economic activities and their relative importance in the living sites, in addition to defining the archaeological cluster in useful stylistic terms. The artefacts bespeak, by and large, the killing and processing of large Pleistocene game animals known from associated faunal remains. We would indeed expect to find that projectile points, scrapers, knives and boneworking tools such as burins would be dominant in the site inventories.

It is noteworthy that the knife types (retouched blades and backed bladelets) are not among the major artefact forms. Apparently, many more scrapers than knives were needed for site-linked tasks, such as hide preparation. It is to be expected that major butchering activities – in which knives would be used for skinning, quartering and cutting – took place at the kill sites themselves. The scrapers, on the other hand, are simply made tools that probably dulled quickly, were resharpened several times, finally discarded, and new ones rapidly made. The large numbers of burins, which also were easily and frequently replaced, were used with the groove and splinter method to work bone into effective tools (two parallel cuts were made in horn or bone and a splinter was detached and made into a projectile point, awl or other tool).

363

In brief, we can postulate that the dominant tools indicate that activities at living sites probably involved a great deal of hide defleshing, hide trimming, and the preparation of bone and horn artefacts. The dissecting of carcass parts and carving flesh for food, with knives, did not produce large quantities of these artefacts.

The abundance of Gravettian points is clearly an indicator of hunting, the prime activity which took place away from the rock shelters and caves. An additional suggestion is that, with the exception of the Gravettian points and burins, the major tool types are the forms most likely to be used in women's activities centred in, or near, the caves and rock shelters, while there is perhaps a likelihood that more of the minor tool forms were connected with male-dominated activities away from the living stations (skinning, quartering, etc.) and with tool manufacture (especially with burins) at the living sites.

(2) The Aurignacian of cluster *B* has as its major types the simple end scraper, the muzzle-shaped scraper, the retouched blade scraper, blades with a single retouched edge, the carinate scraper, and the Aurignacian blade scraper. This assemblage is seemingly indicative of local hide preparation (scrapers) and hide trimming as well as flesh carving (retouched blades), all likely women's activities. Although no stone projectile point forms are present in this list, we have to keep in mind the heavy Aurignacian reliance on bone projectile points, which are not considered in this study.

The minor tool forms – especially the two burin types and the two-edged retouched blades – are perhaps more indicative of male activities than female-dominated tasks, both at and away from the living sites, although this is suggested only as a general tendency. Other minor tool types are double scrapers and flake scrapers, combination tools and denticulate artefacts.

(3) The Upper Solutrean, cluster *C*, has only four major tool forms: the simple end scraper, laurel leaf and shouldered projectile points, and the retouched blade scraper. This small number of major types is partly a function of the occurrence of large numbers of specialized Upper Solutrean tool types in the sites. It is interesting that both hunting weapons (projectile points) and simple utilitarian tools (scrapers) constitute the dominant types of artefacts. The minor forms include other scraper and point forms, several burins, the stone borer, one-edged retouched blades, and the backed bladelet.

Activities both distal and proximal to living sites would seem to be indicated in this assemblage. They can be inferred, as in clusters *A* and *B*, to be hunting, meat and hide preparation (including the manufacture of clothing), and the production of bone and antler artefacts.

The above ideas are offered as general 'inference' and analogy from ethnology, and not as concrete cultural reconstructions of behaviours. My purpose is to illustrate what kind of determinations can be made, not to do a detailed study of the twenty-six archaeological collections. It will be easy for the reader with specific questions in mind to use the foregoing graphical and statistical data to come up with further interpretations in response to his own questions. D. de Sonneville-Bordes (1960, vols. I and II) conveniently gives all the percentage data that would be necessary to draw new ogives for lot combinations different from the ones that were made above. The seriated lot array and the tree diagram suggest many more potentially meaningful lot combinations than I have made. I would only say, as a caution, that the reader should consult Part II to see what kind of distortions can be caused by scaling data on one dimension, and to weigh the possible advantages of multidimensional scaling.

Seriation generally

There is such a strong trend among archaeologists and others to view seriation only as a technique for relative dating that the point needs to be made as strongly as possible that seriation is *not* primarily a dating method. Seriation is elementary similarity scaling, nothing else. It places items in positional series, unidimensionally, so that the location of any item relative to the others is a reflection of its degree of similarity to all other items in the data set. Seriation is descriptive analysis.

Data interpretation is a separate matter. Once a data set has been seriated properly, the investigator may then try to determine what would best explain differences in item positions. Shifts through time in the relative dominance of artefact types may be involved in the explanation, but so may other factors. Differences between collections may be due to site specialization: to different economic tasks, with associated tool kits, represented by the artefact assemblages. Or some sites may represent contemporaneous, but different, historic traditions and yet be similarly specialized. The archaeologist has to know a great deal about his area before he can begin making these kinds of interpretations. Seriation is helpful to him, however, because it gives a model of item relations and facilitates the organization of interpretations. When cluster tests are applied to seriated data, patterns emerge which further aid interpretation.

I wish to point out that the general work on seriation by Frank Hole and Mary Shaw (1967) falls directly into the jaws of the 'relative dating fallacy'. There are many fine aspects of their study, however, and I do not wish to criticize it generally. Nevertheless, the emphasis is strictly directed toward a conception of seriation as relative dating, when it is really nothing more than descriptive similarity scaling.

Interestingly, Hole and Shaw attack Kuzara *et al.* (1966) for attempting to find the best ordering inherent in a data set, in accordance with a best-fit seriation model, instead of predetermining the position of collections whose temporal relations may be known beforehand. Hole and Shaw argue that the investigator should first put the items in a preliminary series: for example, a guess at the correct chronological order. This is not so. What must be done is to separate description from interpretation. If Hole and Shaw want to alter positions in an item permutation once the data set has been seriated, that is their option. But they lose the benefits of seriation as a *description of item relations according to a best-fit model* when they fiddle with their data too soon. The general discussion of seriation by Kuzara *et al.* (1966) is much more to the point than that published by Hole and Shaw (1967). From the foregoing it should be plain that item seriation can be considered a dating technique only in certain specific instances, where much is known about inter-lot differences and their explanation.

With the description *v.* interpretation problem in mind, it is instructive to recall the disagreement between A. L. Kroeber and Stanislaw Klimek (a pupil of Czekanowski) having to do with Klimek's (1935) historical interpretation of California ethnographic data. Klimek intercorrelated tribes and clustered them into groups by means of a homostat search within a seriated item matrix. Then he correlated and clustered the traits, too, thus using both *Q*- and *R*-technique approaches. Finally, he correlated clusters of tribes with clusters of traits. Driver (1962) presents the issues of the Kroeber-Klimek debate perfectly, and will be quoted at length. His ending sentence is specially applicable to Hole and Shaw's view of seriation:

Klimek's historical reconstruction . . . differed so much from Kroeber's view that the latter wrote four pages in a preface to Klimek's (1935) work in order to keep the two sets of interpretations separated. This example emphasizes an important point. Two or more researchers, working with correlation methods from the same corpus of data, are likely to show a high degree of agreement in the clusters of tribes or traits they discover, yet may differ considerably in the historical inferences drawn from the clusters. The objective part of the procedure is the taxonomy [*classification*], not the historical inferences derived from it. Therefore, a culture area scheme which claims to be only a taxonomy is likely to be more objective

366

and demonstrable than one which is thought to be historical or genetic. Kroeber's insistence . . . that culture area classification [*or an insistence that archaeological seriation*] must reflect historical factors introduces a subjective element which leaves room for disagreement. (Driver, 1962, p. 17)

PART II MORE COMPLEX METHODS OF SCALING AND CLUSTERING

Multidimensional scaling

The main limit to the usefulness of item seriation is its one-dimensional quality. If data scale well on a single dimension, then there is no problem. But as we know already, the goodness of fit for some data sets can be less than acceptable and their scaling on one dimension can be forced. When, for example, a calculated goodness of fit measure such as Matrix Coefficient C is clearly unsatisfactory, more than one dimension will be necessary for scaling the corresponding data set.

Here we must think of the dimensions or vectors that are generated by the analysis as entities that can be interpreted much as the factors involved in factor analysis. The contribution of items to each scale or dimension can also be figured in something approaching the way that factor loadings for items are figured for individual generated factors. For this reason it is quite important to be concerned with finding the best number of dimensions for explaining covariation in one's data. Although archaeologists have done multidimensional scaling (e.g. Hodson *et al.*, 1966; Hodson, 1970), I know of only one published study (True and Matson, 1970) which attempts to interpret the resultant dimensions individually. Rather, the usual and perhaps myopic tendency is to use the multidimensional scaling solely as a tool for generating interpoint distances between items for cluster analysis.

Both metric (e.g. Torgerson, 1965) and non-metric (e.g. Shepard, 1962a, 1962b; Kruskal, 1964a, 1964b) multidimensional scaling techniques are available and have been computerized. For the same reasons that metric factor analysis is unsatisfactory for the usual nominal and ordinal data of archaeology, metric scaling is likewise inappropriate. Thus I shall describe briefly Kruskal's non-metric MDSCAL (multidimensional scaling) technique and apply it to our French archaeological data set as an example. Because the technique is rather involved and tedious, not all the details of the analytic steps can easily be explained here. I shall try to outline the general procedure instead.

KRUSKAL'S SCALING PROCEDURE

Let us arrange some points, which correspond to items that we wish to analyse, in a space defined by any number of dimensions or coordinates which are free to range from one (where our 'space' becomes linear) to many (where we must deal with very complex hyperspace). We shall arrange the points first in one dimension, then repeat the arranging process in ever increasing numbers of dimensions until we find the best arrangement for each number of dimensions.

For each number of dimensions the points are moved around in space until their configuration has satisfied, in the best way possible, a criterion for goodness of fit described below. This is an iterative procedure a bit like the one used to rearrange a similarity matrix during item seriation. Kruskal uses the algorithm known as 'the method of gradients' or 'the method of steepest descent' (1964b) as a systematic procedure for changing configurations. Usually 15 to 100 steps are necessary to reach the final configuration where no improvement (given a particular input arrangement) is possible – the point at which the best fit has been found. This is called the minimum stress configuration. Different input configurations are used, just as in item seriation, for different iterations since each input can bias the final, ordered configuration in its own way.

If we repeat such an analysis for several different numbers of dimensions, how do we decide exactly how many dimensions to settle upon, to use? We know that as the number of dimensions (t) increases, the minimum stress decreases, but since the purpose of analysis is to simplify a data set by reducing the original number of dimensions (corresponding to individual artefact types, perhaps), we certainly shall want to use the smallest t that will explain or account for the greatest amount of variance in the data set. There are, among others, at least two good guides for choosing a suitable value of t. The first is to plot a curve of stress values by dimensions; if there is an elbow in that curve, it will mark off the number of dimensions that explains the greatest amount of variance. The use of this criterion will be illustrated below. The second criterion is the interpretability of the dimensions or coordinates themselves. There is little profit in using dimensions that cannot be interpreted, except when they may serve to point out a need for more thought about the explanation or cause of data relations.

We have said that the best fitting configuration has a minimum of stress. To find stress, first we rank the $n(n-1)/2$ similarity scores in strictly ascending order. This ranking can become the horizontal scale in a two-axis scatterplot. Next we calculate the distances between all $n(n-1)/2$ pairs of items in

368

the particular configuration we are concerned to evaluate and let them become the vertical axis of the scatterplot, which now gives similarity v. distance (see Kruskal, 1964a, for exact computational procedures). Fit is then measured along the distance axis, where the points themselves are fitted rather than the curve. Raw stress turns out to be the familiar residual sum of squares, which is normalized to give *stress* proper. As said above, the process of minimization is carried out by the method of gradients.

MDSCAL WITH THE FRENCH PALAEOLITHIC

The twenty-six Palaeolithic artefact collections were analysed by a MDSCAL computer program written in FORTRAN, with the calculations being carried

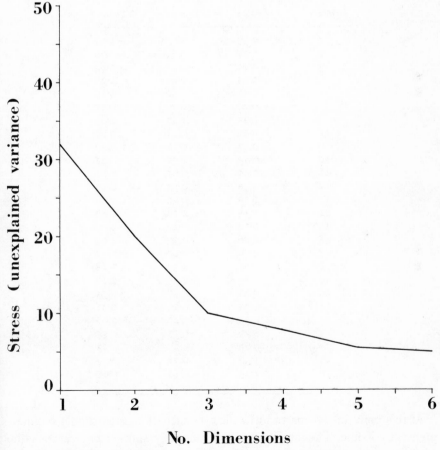

No. Dimensions

FIG. 8.20. MDSCAL with Palaeolithic lots: stress v. No. of dimensions.

out by a Burroughs 5500 computer at the University of California at Davis. A half-matrix of Robinson Indexes of Agreement was used as input. Scalings for one through six dimensions were executed and a best-fitting configuration with a minimum of stress was defined for each number of dimensions. Fig. 8.20, which plots stress against number of dimensions, shows a fairly well-defined elbow in the curve at three dimensions. At this point stress is reduced to 0·10. Thus three dimensions appear initially to be the most appropriate number of vectors with which to represent the relations between the Palaeolithic artefact assemblages.

The selected configuration is defined by the following coordinates on three scales, each of which ranges potentially from −2·00 to +2·00:

Item No.	Scale 1	Scale 2	Scale 3
1	−0·39	−00·25	−1·61
2	0·20	−0·84	−0·70
3	−0·07	−0·57	0·44
4	−0·34	−0·69	0·28
5	0·06	−0·60	0·19
6	−0·20	−0·76	0·11
7	0·23	−1·47	0·09
8	−0·60	0·21	0·21
9	−0·59	0·24	0·47
10	−0·73	0·72	0·22
11	−0·49	−0·01	0·54
12	−0·78	0·54	0·25
13	−0·33	0·10	0·8
14	−1·15	−0·24	−0·42
15	−0·74	−0·10	−0·90
16	−0·06	0·37	−1·03
17	−0·07	−0·00	−0·32
18	0·84	1·32	−0·18
19	0·40	0·35	0·11
20	0·48	0·47	0·35
21	0·23	0·29	−0·21
22	0·33	0·22	−0·00
23	0·29	0·21	0·55
24	0·68	0·29	0·53
25	1·38	0·32	0·39
26	1·43	−0·11	0·05

At this point in the analysis of a data set each dimension should be interpreted if possible. The job is difficult because anything (or any combination of things) that can cause variation in the artefact percentages can, conceivably, represent these vectors: sample size, covariation of artefact types by sites, etc. The magnitude of the problem will hopefully arouse a modicum of sympathy from those who have grappled with the interpretation of factors and factor loadings.

One approach would be to rank the artefact collections by the percentage of each artefact form, yielding thereby a separate site order for each artefact type. Then a rank order correlation coefficient could be calculated between each type-ranking of sites and each of the three scales. Most likely, several artefact types would correlate highly with a particular scale and help explain it. If so, we might quite possibly succeed in isolating tool kits amenable to functional or other interpretation. The results should be valuable. I have not carried out such a study because of problems in developing a suitable computer program which would (1) rank artefact collections by each artefact type, (2) calculate the correlations with each vector, and (3) evaluate the final correlation coefficients for the purpose of selecting the best correlations to explain the vector scalings. The necessary calculations will have to be done at some future time.

Although the three scales cannot now be interpreted individually, the spacial configuration of points itself will be used to refine our previous cluster classifications and to illustrate how MDSCAL may be used in conjunction with cluster analyses.

MORE COMPLEX CLUSTER ANALYSES

Before doing so, I need to point out that cluster analyses are available which are much more complicated, more refined, and even sometimes more productive than the simple kinds we have discussed in Part I or will use in Part II. Here I shall only mention a few. For up-to-date articles the reader should consult Ball's (1965) excellent survey paper as well as the newest issues of *Psychometrika* and *Systematic Zoology*. The recent articles by Rohlf (1970), Hodson (1970) and True and Matson (1970) are helpful.

Dendrogrammatic analysis, as a field, has seen many recent innovations and refinements. Although average linkage cluster analysis is used more commonly than any other type, the employment of double link analysis and the k-means approach is reviewed by Hodson (1970). The latter technique is elegant, works with original data rather than with a similarity matrix, and achieves a segregation of items into k clusters which minimize a measure of dispersion within the clusters. Also, McCammon and Wenninger's (1970) conversion of the one-dimensional dendrogram into a two-dimensional dendrograph reflects both the within-group and the between-group similarities. It appears quite

371

promising for archaeological applications. Wishart's (1969) excellent CLUSTAN program package allows for mode analysis, Lance-Williams's flexible analysis, Ward's error sum technique, and others.

The corpus of recent literature is clearly too large to summarize here. Nevertheless, I will single out one paper because of its excellence. This is Rohlf's 'Adaptive hierarchical clustering schemes' (1970), which gives a detailed comparison of several new methods of clustering, presents a non-linear version of hierarchical clustering capable of defining clusters which are parabolic, ring-shaped, etc., and gives a procedure for measuring the amount of information lost by clustering. Rohlf's is an altogether excellent paper for the archaeologist.

CLUSTERING THE MULTIDIMENSIONALLY SCALED PALAEOLITHIC DATA

Let us return to the multidimensional scaling of the French data, and illustrate how this information may help refine some clustering procedures. Figure 8.21 presents the best item configuration in three dimensions. Scale 2 is the vertical axis, scale 1 the horizontal. The size of the points themselves will represent scale 3. Quite obviously, a plotting of the items by coordinates on three dimensions creates a spatial configuration which may show considerable clustering of items. Various techniques could be used to calculate possible cluster centres (centroids) and thus define the clusters directly from the inter-point distances. But it is also useful, and easy, to combine the results of many sorts of clustering procedures with the multidimensional scatterplot.

To illustrate this procedure, clusters I–IV (Fig. 8.16) are superimposed on the scatterplot. They are average linkage clusters, and show different levels of item juncture or union. Thus basic pairs can be drawn on the scatterplot first by a simple contour line, and other contours can be added to represent the subsequent addition of other items or basic pairs to each cluster. The final arrangement (Fig. 8.21) looks much like a topographic (contour) map and can be interpreted like one. The peaks and slopes of clusters I, II and IV show the strong and weak areas, respectively, of their clusters. In summation, a combination of multidimensional scaling with some form of cluster analysis is a very useful way to present data relations, mainly because of its graphic or visual simplicity. And hopefully we can sometimes avoid thereby some of the distortions that can result from one-dimensional scaling (item seriation), or from cluster analysis done without the benefit of similarity scaling.

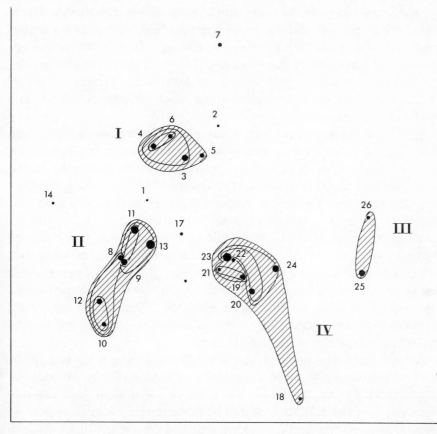

FIG. 8.21. Three-dimensional plotting: multidimensionally scaled Palaeolithic lots with clusters I–IV superimposed.

CONCLUSIONS

The first conclusion I wish to draw is that item seriation is now a precise scaling technique. Measures are available (such as Matrix Coefficient C) to indicate how well a data set has been scaled by this one-dimensional method. Very often, it is sufficient to seriate archaeological data, and then cluster the data by seeking out homostats in the ordered matrix or by defining other kinds of clusters, as by average linkage tree diagrams. A quite useful scaling and clustering of the example palaeontological and archaeological data sets was produced in Part I.

373

An inherent danger in the use of item seriation, however, is that the data in question may not scale well by one dimension. Multidimensional scaling was used in Part II with the Palaeolithic assemblages to illustrate another approach, and it was shown that clustering procedures may fruitfully be combined with multidimensional scaling. Unfortunately, because of purely technical problems the three dimensions on which the data scaled best could not be directly interpreted.

The final conclusion that I wish to make is this: often, simple scaling and clustering procedures are as satisfactory, for the average archaeologist at least, as complex ones. Note that the results we got from scaling the Palaeolithic data on several dimensions, when combined with clustering, were not very different from the results produced by one-dimensional scaling plus clustering. There is a moral here, somewhere. Maybe it has to do with the understanding or control which one should have over one's analytic techniques, especially when one is an archaeologist, or natural historian, or whatever – at least when one is not a sophisticate in statistics. When such a person uses a simple analytic model whose structure and machinations he can understand very well, he is much better off than otherwise. When his analytic model, contrariwise, is too complex for him to understand very well, I question the appropriateness of that model for his study.

Perhaps I need also point out that one very rarely escapes the basic problems or difficulties inherent in an analysis or analytic model by moving from simple techniques to complex models. Some people seem to think that it is invariably best (BEST!) to scale data by multidimensional methods because item seriation is, they think, a mechanically and theoretically weak method, one fraught by many problems. Unfortunately, the grass is only occasionally greener elsewhere. Hodson (1970, p. 305), for example, has said that item seriation is obsolescent, unsatisfactory for most archaeological data, and overly laborious in execution. Also, cluster definition within an ordered matrix is said by him to be uncertain and misguided. He acclaims, rather, dendrogrammatic clustering and multidimensional scaling.

We have already seen that item seriation can be useful. Further, it is not a laborious task for the computer. It is, however, an iterative technique which requires many tries with different input orders since initial order biases the final ordination. Multidimensional scaling *à la* Kruskal, as applied to archaeology by Doran and Hodson (1966) and by Hodson *et al.* (1966), is also an iterative technique needing several different input configurations since the same biases are operative with this scaling technique. One technique is no less laborious nor less susceptible to input bias.

374

Hodson (1970, p. 305) has said that numerical taxonomists do not regard matrix ordering as a practical method preliminary to cluster definition. They choose not to use it, true, but not for this reason. The Biological taxonomists are often interested in hierarchical techniques which relate all items to each other for genetic or phylogenetic considerations; hence their preference for tree diagrams. Interestingly, in most cases where archaeological artefact assemblages or individual artefacts have been clustered into tree diagrams (e.g. Hodson et al., 1966; Johnson, 1968; Hodson, 1969), little interpretation has been made of low-level linkage between clusters; thus only a part of the dendrograms is actually used. This in itself suggests that tree diagrams are not the final solution for the archaeologist's taxonomic and typologic dilemma.

It is useful to consult the recent work on taxonometric maps by Carmichael and Sneath (1969), which points out the following: (1) Dendrograms are best-fit models compressed into one dimension by preserving actual proximities between items only in the closest pairs. Great distortion may occur in lower order linkage. (2) A great shortcoming of some multidimensional models is the feeling of confidence they generate that one has produced a faithful display of the multidimensional relationships. The nearest neighbours, however, in such models need not agree with the original matrix of similarity scores. (3) Tree diagram techniques are not clustering techniques strictly speaking, but are hierarchical splitting or agglomerative models!

I have cited Carmichael and Sneath's remarks to show that there are problems of data distortion and pattern meaning in an analysis done by tree diagrams, and in multidimensional scaling (as well as in most analytic and statistical models) which are as serious as those that exist in homostat definition and item seriation. Let us recognize the abilities and disabilities of each model, and continue to experiment with new ones. At any rate, my hope is that the foregoing discussions have demonstrated or illustrated the service that imaginary models may perform for archaeology.

Notes

1. PROGRAM SERIATE is written in FORTRAN IV for the IBM 360-Model 40 computer. A complete program listing appears in Craytor and Johnson (1968, pp. 15 ff).

2. It should be noted that r^2 and V^2 explain variation if, and only if, the data are linear and homescedastic. ϕ^2 is less instructive because of its low tolerance to marginal variation.

3. It should perhaps be mentioned that seriation within a single functional tool class, such as scrapers or burins, might produce results more in agreement with chronology than seriation based on total lithic assemblages. If this is true, it is because stylistic replacement of one type by another occurs within the limits of a particular functional category or class. Fluctuations in the popularity of burin type X would influence, in such cases, only the percentages of other burin types, not the percentages of non-burin artefact types. Sackett (1966) tried this approach, using end scrapers and burins, with six French Aurignacian sites and produced a seriation of strata which may correspond to true chronological order. However, no such study has been done between deposits of different major traditions, such as the Perigordian with the Solutrean.

Acknowledgements

Responsibility for errors of fact or theory in this paper is strictly my own. However, several people helped both to stimulate my work and to point out fruitful approaches, interpretations, and corrections in this paper or in earlier but related publications.

I extend my special thanks and express my indebtedness to K. A. Bennett, David L. Clarke, Wm Bert Craytor, Everett L. Frost, Joseph G. Jorgensen, Gerald A. King, L. R. Kittleman, R. G. Matson, J. A. Shotwell, D. L. True and Philip D. Young.

References

ACHINSTEIN, P. (1968) *Concepts of Science: A Philosophical Analysis.* Baltimore, Md: Johns Hopkins Press.

ASCHER, M. and ASCHER, R. (1963) Chronological ordering by computer. *American Anthropologist*, **65** (5), 1045–52.

BALL, G. H. (1965) Data analysis in the social sciences: what about the details? *Proceedings: Fall Joint Computer Conference*, **27**, 533–59.

BARRETT, S. A. (1908) *The Ethnogeography of the Pomo and Neighboring Indians.* University of California Publications in American Archaeology and Ethnology No. 6, 1–332.

BELOUS, R. E. (1953) The central California chronological sequence re-examined. *American Antiquity*, **18** (4), 341–53.

BOAS, F. (1895) *Indianische Sagen von der Nord-Pacifischen Küste Amerikas.* Sonder-Abdruck aus den Verhandlungen der Berliner Gesellschaft für Anthropologie Ethnologie und Urgeschichte. Berlin: Asher.

BONHAM-CARTER, G. F. (1967) *FORTRAN IV Program for Q-mode Cluster Analysis of Nonquantitative Data Using IBM 7090/7094 Computers.* Kansas State Geological Survey Computer Contribution No. 17.

BORDES, F. (1963) A propos de la théorie de M. Laplace sur le 'synthétotype aurignaco-gravettien': quelques questions préalables. *L'Anthropologie*, **67**, 347–60.

BOYCE, A. J. (1964) The value of some methods of numerical taxonomy with reference to Hominoid classification. *Phenetic and Phylogenetic Classification*, 47–65. Systematics Association Publication No. 6.

BRAINERD, G. W. (1951) The place of chronological ordering in archaeological analysis. *American Antiquity*, **16** (4), 303–13.

CARMICHAEL, J. W. and SNEATH, P. H. A. (1969) Taxonometric maps. *Systematic Zoology*, **18** (4), 402–15.

CLARKE, D. L. (1962) Matrix analysis and archaeology with particular reference to British beaker pottery. *Proceedings of the Prehistoric Society*, **28**, 371–82.

CLARKE, D. L. (1963) Matrix analysis and archaeology. *Nature*, **199**, 790–2.

COLLINS, D. M. (1965) Seriation of quantitative features in late Pleistocene stone technology. *Nature*, **205**, 931–2.

CRAYTOR, W. B. and JOHNSON, L., JR (1968) *Refinements in Computerized Item Seriation*. Museum of Natural History, University of Oregon, Bulletin No. 10.

CZEKANOWSKI, J. (1911) Objective Kriterien in der Ethnologie. *Korrespondenzblatt der Deutschen Gesellschaft für Anthropologie und Urgeschichte*, **42**, 71–5.

CZEKANOWSKI, J. (1962) The theoretical assumptions of Polish anthropology and the morphological facts. *Current Anthropology*, **3**, 481–94.

DEMPSEY, P. and BAUMHOFF, M. (1963) The statistical use of artefact distribution to establish chronological sequence. *American Antiquity*, **28** (4), 496–509.

DIXON, K. A. (1956) Archaeological objectives and artifact sorting techniques: a re-examination of the Snaketown sequence. *Western Anthropology* No. 3.

DIXON, R. B. and KROEBER, A. L. (1919) *Linguistic Families of California*. University of California Publications in American Archaeology and Ethnology No. 16, 47–118.

DORAN, J. E. and HODSON, F. R. (1966) A digital computer analysis of palaeolithic flint assemblages. *Nature*, **210**, 688–9.

DRIVER, H. E. (1956) *An Integration of Functional, Evolutionary and Historical Theory by Means of Correlations*. International Journal of American Linguistics Memoir 12.

DRIVER, H. E. (1962) *The Contribution of A. L. Kroeber to Culture Area Theory and Practice*. International Journal of American Linguistics Memoir 18.

DRIVER, H. E. (1965) Survey of numerical classification in anthropology. In HYMES, D. (ed.) *The Use of Computers in Anthropology*, 301–44. The Hague: Mouton.

DRIVER, H. E. and MASSEY, W. C. (1957) Comparative studies of North American Indians. *Transactions of the American Philosophy Society*, **47**, 2, 165–456.

FLANDERS, R. E. (1960) A re-examination of Mill Creek ceramics: the Robinson technique. *Journal of the Iowa Archaeological Society*, **10**, 1–35.

FORD, J. A. (1962) *A Quantitative Method for Deriving Cultural Chronology*. Pan American Union Technical Manual No. 1. Washington, D.C.: Organization of American States.

HODSON, F. R. (1969) Searching for structure within multivariate archaeological data. *World Archaeology*, **1** (1), 90–105.

HODSON, F. R. (1970) Cluster analysis and archaeology: some new developments and applications. *World Archaeology*, **1** (3), 299–330.

HODSON, F. R., SNEATH, P. H. A. and DORAN, J. E. (1966) Some experiments in the numerical analysis of archaeological data. *Biometrika*, **53**, 311–24.

HOLE, F. and SHAW, M. (1967) *Computer Analysis of Chronological Seriation*. Rice University Studies (Monographs in Archaeology), **53** (3).

JOHNSON, L., JR (1968) *Item Seriation as an Aid for Elementary Scale and Cluster Analysis.* Museum of Natural History, University of Oregon, Bulletin No. 15.

KLIMEK, S. (1935) *Culture Element Distributions, I: The Structure of California Indian Culture.* University of California Publications in American Archaeology and Ethnology No. 37 (1).

KÓČKA, W. (1953) Wczesnodziejowa antropologia Slowian zachodnich. *Travaux de la Société des Sciences et des Lettres de Wrocaw,* ser. B, No. 17.

KROEBER, A. L. (1940) Statistical classification. *American Antiquity,* 6 (1), 29–44.

KRUSKAL, J. B. (1964a) Multidimensional scaling by optimizing goodness of fit to a nonmetric hypothesis, I. *Psychometrika,* 29, 1–27.

KRUSKAL, J. B. (1964b) Multidimensional scaling by optimizing goodness of fit to a nonmetric hypothesis, II. *Psychometrika,* 29, 115–29.

KUZARA, R. S., MEAD, G. R. and DIXON, K. A. (1966) Seriation of anthropological data: a computer program for matrix ordering. *American Anthropologist,* 68 (6), 1442–55.

LAPLACE, G. (1958–61) Recherches sur l'origine et l'évolution des complexes lepto-lithiques: le problème des Périgordiens I et II et l'hypothèse du synthétotype aurignaco-gravettien: essai de typologie analytique. *Quaternaria,* 5, 153–240.

LEWIS, T. M. N. and KNEBERG, M. (1959) The archaic culture in the middle South. *American Antiquity,* 25 (2), 161–83.

LIPE, W. D. (1964). Comments on Dempsey and Baumhoff's 'The statistical use of artefact distributions to establish chronological sequence'. *American Antiquity,* 30 (1), 103–4.

MCCAMMON, R. B. and WENNINGER, G. (1970) *The Dendrograph.* Kansas State Geological Survey Computer Contribution No. 48.

MATTHEWS, J. (1963) Applications of matrix analysis to archaeological problems. *Nature,* 198, 930–4.

PRADEL, L. (1966) Transition from Mousterian to Perigordian: skeletal and industrial. *Current Anthropology,* 7 (1), 33–6.

ROBINSON, W. S. (1951) A method for chronologically ordering archaeological deposits. *American Antiquity,* 16 (4), 239–301.

ROHLF, F. J. (1970) Adaptive hierarchical clustering schemes. *Systematic Zoology,* 19 (1), 58–82.

SACKETT, J. R. (1966) Quantitative analysis of Upper Paleolithic stone tools. *American Anthropologist,* 68, 2 (2), 356–94.

SHEPARD, R. N. (1962a) The analysis of proximities: multidimensional scaling with an unknown distance function, I. *Psychometrika,* 27, 125–40.

SHEPARD, R. N. (1962b) The analysis of proximities: multidimensional scaling with an unknown distance function, II. *Psychometrika,* 27, 219–46.

SHOTWELL, J. A. (1955) An approach to the paleoecology of mammals. *Ecology,* 36 (2), 327–37.

SHOTWELL, J. A. (1958) Intercommunity relationships in Hemphillian (mid-Pliocene) mammals. *Ecology,* 39 (2), 271–82.

SHOTWELL, J. A. (1963) The Juntura basin: studies in earth history and paleoecology. *Transactions of the American Philosophical Society,* 53 (1).

SMITH, P. E. L. (1966) *Le Solutréen en France.* Publications de l'Institut de Préhistoire de l'Université de Bordeaux, Mémoire No. 5.

SOKAL, R. R. (1966) Numerical taxonomy. *Scientific American*, **215** (6), 106–16.

SOKAL, R. R. and MICHENER, C. D. (1958) A statistical method for evaluating systematic relationships. *University of Kansas Science Bulletin*, **38**, 1409–38.

SOKAL, R. R. and SNEATH, P. H. A. (1963) *Principles of Numerical Taxonomy*. San Francisco: Freeman.

SONNEVILLE-BORDES, D. DE (1960) *Le Paléolithique supérieur en Périgord*. 2 vols. Bordeaux: Delmas.

STEPHENSON, W. (1953) *The Study of Behavior: Q-Technique and its Methodology*. Chicago: University of Chicago Press.

TORGERSON, W. S. (1965) Multidimensional scaling of similarity. *Psychometrika*, **30**, 379–93.

TROIKE, R. (1957) Time and types in archaeological analysis: the Brainerd-Robinson technique. *Bulletin of the Texas Archaeological Society*, **28**, 269–84.

TRUE, D. L. and MATSON, R. G. (1970) Cluster analysis and multidimensional scaling of archaeological sites in northern Chile. *Science*, **169**, 1201–3.

TUGBY, D. J. (1958) A typological analysis of axes and choppers from southeast Australia. *American Antiquity*, **24** (1), 24–33.

TUGBY, D. J. (1965) Archaeological objectives and statistical methods: a frontier in archaeology. *American Antiquity*, **31** (1), 1–16.

WISHART, D. (1969) *FORTRAN II Programs for 8 Methods of Cluster Analysis (CLUSTAN I)*. Kansas State Geological Survey Computer Contribution No. 38.

9
Models, methods and techniques for seriation

G. L. COWGILL
Brandeis University, U.S.A.

The object of this paper is partly to present as clearly as possible my under-standings about the assumptions and models, implicit and explicit, which underly seriation as a method for chronological ordering in archaeology. Also important is a new and highly economical computer technique for seriation.

On the level of method and general assumptions, recent publications of importance include Rowe (1961), Kuzara, Mead and Dixon (1966), Dethlefsen and Deetz (1966), Hole and Shaw (1967), Rouse (1967), Cowgill (1968) and Dunnell (1970). For techniques, important recent work includes Ascher and Ascher (1963), Dempsey and Baumhoff (1963), Johnson (1968), Bordaz and Bordaz (1970) and Renfrew and Sterud (1969). Especially important is recent work by Kendall (1969) and Gelfand (1971).

By seriation as a formal technique, I refer to any technique for arranging a set of entities into a sequence such that, starting from any specific entity, the other entities most similar to it are closest to it in the sequence, and similarity decreases monotonically as one compares entities progressively more distant in the sequence. Monotonic decrease means that as one moves away from the starting point, similarities may stay the same, decrease a little, or decrease sharply, but will in no case increase. A monotonically decreasing function can be graphed by a line which may remain horizontal, drop gradually or steeply, drop a little or a lot, but in no case rises. Sometimes this ideal arrangement of entities can be fully achieved, but for many sets of entities the mutual simi-larities are such that no completely ideal sequence is possible. That is, it may be that whenever the entities are arranged so that the criterion of monotonic decrease in similarity is met with reference to one entity, there is always at least one other entity in the set for which the criterion is not met. For this reason, seriation also includes techniques for obtaining and evaluating the best possible approaches to the ideal sequence.

It is important to notice that one thing *not* included in this definition of seriation as a formal technique is any notion of arranging entities with regard to any assumptions about development or derivation; that is, there is no attempt to consider whether the nature of the similarities are such that one entity is more likely to have developed from or been derived from this or that other entity. This exclusion is not because such approaches are not important or valuable. On the contrary, I think there is great value in further development and testing of such methods both for chronology and for processual understandings of the past (Clarke, 1968, makes some important observations on these matters). I exclude them here simply because they would introduce too much to deal with at one time. Seriation as I have defined it is, as a formal technique, a relatively well-defined and self-contained set of problems, and a considerable amount of work has been done within this general framework. One important and often-mentioned consequence of this limitation to some general concept of overall similarity, without regard for formal features that might suggest that one entity is derived from another, is that all solutions to the seriation problem come in pairs; for any specific sequence of entities, another sequence that is its exact reverse is an equally good seriation.

Considering seriation as a formal technique, there are three broad kinds of problems. Central, of course, is the task of finding, as expeditiously as possible, a sequence which is either ideal or else makes a good case for being as close to ideal as is possible. Second, there is the general topic of deciding between variation 'badness of fit' criteria when no ideal sequence can be found; that is, deciding how to rate various alternative non-ideal sequences. Finally, there is the matter of precisely how similarity is to be measured or evaluated. This itself divides into two topics: decisions about the features of the entities that are to be observed and recorded, and decisions about what mathematical functions of these observations should be used for computing coefficients of similarity.

In the 'graphical' seriation technique of Ford (1962) the solutions adopted for all these problems can remain somewhat vague, ambiguous, intuitive, and possibly inconsistent. Whenever techniques are used that require specific numerical values for similarity coefficients, the answers to all the questions posed above must be made explicit. This is not, perhaps, as inherently damaging a criticism of the graphical technique as one might think; I agree with Dunnell (1970) that there has been a little too much tendency to downgrade it simply because it is more simple-minded than more mathematical techniques. As a technique for seriation, the graphical way is all right if it is not too hard to do, and if different workers can agree (with unimportant differences) on the same 'best' sequence. The troubles with the technique seem to be that too often it does involve a great deal of work and that there can be serious differences of opinion about the best sequence. And where these troubles arise there is surely a need to look for easier techniques and more explicitly defined concepts.

None of the formal problems can be usefully discussed if we continue to think of seriation *only* as a formal technique, without relating it to the problems and objectives of archaeology. Its relationship to models of human behaviour must be made explicit.

For practical purposes, the only archaeological use for seriation is for chronological ordering of units in cases where other techniques (such as stratigraphy, dated inscriptions, firm cross-ties with established sequences, or radiocarbon or other physical or chemical techniques) are inapplicable or inadequate. The units to be seriated are typically either grave lots, caches or hoards; or else archaeological assemblages. In both cases, as Rouse (1967, p. 158) has emphasized, the units of real interest are *events*. In the case of a grave lot, the event would be the bringing together and deposition of grave offerings. For a unit that is an assemblage, the 'event' is the occupation of a site or site segment during the period that saw the creation of the depositional units assigned to one assemblage by the archaeologist. In any case, when I refer to the *duration* of a unit, what I mean is the time span of the event that the unit reflects. The assumption is that differences between units mainly reflect differences in time, and that the seriation sequence is a good approximation to the time sequence of the units. At least two units need to be datable by some other technique, so that the proper time direction of the seriation sequence can be established; additional chronological information of course serves as a test or corroboration of the seriation sequence.

In principle, as Kuzara, Mead and Dixon (1966) especially have pointed out, seriations of archaeological units could arrange them according to many different possible kinds of differences: relative to status, activities, cultural tradition, and so on. In practice, there is little or nothing to recommend seriation as a technique for investigating such differences, because the seriation model only allows for arrangement of units along some single axis or dimension, and this makes sense only if the whole pattern of relationships between all the entities can be tolerably well related to some single 'underlying' variable. Whenever one is looking for contemporaneous variations among units, it generally seems likely from the beginning that several factors may be operating at once, and one should reject a seriation model in favour of explicitly multivariate techniques, such as factor analysis, multidimensional

383

scaling, discriminant functions, or the like. In fact, there is not much to recommend any inherently 'single axis' technique even for chronological ordering, but at least it appears that fairly often one really finds important sets of archaeological units where change over time is far greater than are differences due to other factors. Of course, this is also frequently not true, and, as Dunnell (1970) emphasizes, it always needs to be tested.

A very important feature of the technique described in the latter part of this paper is that it uses a multidimensional scaling in two or more dimensions. This amounts to a test of the 'one axis' hypothesis. The data may or may not fit well into an essentially one-dimensional pattern. If they do, and if chronological data available from other sources are consistent with this one axis being a time axis, then it makes sense to go ahead with a pure seriation technique. Otherwise, one will require some sort of multivariate method which allows for time as one among several axes of change. It should be added that it is hardly necessary to demonstrate that there is *no* source of consistent variation other than time-related change; it is only necessary that such other sources of variation, within the particular set of units being studied, make for differences that are small relative to differences reflecting the smallest time intervals one hopes to reliably distinguish.

Besides the assumption that changes over time are the only important source of differences between units, three other assumptions relating the behaviour of ancient peoples to formal models need discussion. First, there is the view, which I think is a misconception, that seriation models imply relatively gradual and continuous cultural change, a view particularly advocated by James Ford (1962). On the contrary, for seriation to be useful as a basis for chronology, it seems to me that all that is required is that there never, among the set of units being seriated, be a break in the sequence so abrupt and catastrophic that units immediately following the break bear no (or only accidental) resemblance to units before the break. If this were to happen we could still divide all the units into two subsets and do a formally adequate seriation within each subset, but we would not know which end of one sequence to join to which end of the other sequence. If, instead, some units at one end of one sequence show even moderately more resemblance to units at one end of the other sequence than to those at the other end, then it is possible to seriate the whole set of units. In other words, a relatively abrupt and drastic change in material culture is no bar to good seriation, provided that it does not result in total obliteration of earlier forms, and provided that all other conditions required for valid seriation are met.

A second requirement, mentioned by Rouse (1967, p. 162) is that the durations of all units being seriated be roughly comparable. I suggest that this one aspect of a somewhat more general requirement – namely, that for any two units whose chronological positions are claimed to be reliably or usefully distinguished, both have durations that are at least not much greater than their time difference, and preferably durations that are considerably smaller than their time difference. To illustrate, consider a situation where this is not so. This would mean that there is considerable overlap in the durations of the two units. What we mean by saying that one such unit seriates 'earlier' than the other must be that some middle time or time of maximal activity in one unit is earlier than a comparable middle or maximal time in the other unit, but not by very much, relative to the total duration of at least one of the two units. This would mean that much, if not all, of the activity responsible for one unit was actually contemporary with activity responsible for the other unit. Being able to say that 'on the average' the activity in one unit was a little later than activity in the other unit would be of dubious value. Furthermore, in such a situation even the judgement that 'on the average' one unit is a little earlier than the other may depend a good deal on sampling accidents, and may not be very reliable.

In a seriation there is nothing wrong with *some* units having considerable overlap in their duration; to admit such subsets of units is just to admit that there can be ties or near ties in the overall sequence. That is, there can be units whose chronological separation is relatively slight, and little stretches of the overall sequence within which the exact subsequence is not very reliably determined. This is all right as long as it is recognized that what one claims is that units are in the right general position in the total sequence, not that the sequence is exactly right in detail. What *is* important, if the seriation is to be of any practical value, is that there should be a fair proportion of pairs of units for which their time separations *are* large relative to their durations. One consequence is that, even if there may be a number of near ties in the sequence, no unit should have a duration that is any longer than the smallest distinguishable interval to which it is assigned.

The third and most basic requirement is that, in terms of the criteria of similarity used, trends of increasing dissimilarity over time indeed never reverse themselves. In fact it is very easy to develop criteria of similarity that do show reverse trends, so that units toward the beginning and end of some chronologically known sequence rate higher in similarity to one another than to units in the middle of the sequence. Particularly, this can be due to picking too few features to observe, e.g. by using the relative abundance of painted versus plain pottery, where a plain–painted–plain sequence of styles will make

385

earlier units seem like late units, even though they may have little in common except shared absence of painted pottery. But these kinds of reversals are not likely to happen over any substantial time spans if one uses much judgement in selecting the features on which to base indices of similarity. Over short time spans, small-scale reversals may well occur, and this is another reason why one should not put too much faith in the fine details of a seriation chronology.

Commonly the technique for evaluating similarities is begun by sorting pottery or other artefacts into categories ('types'), whose occurrence or relative abundance in each unit is noted; or by noting occurrences or relative abundances of distinctive features ('modes') on objects pertaining to each unit. Typological operations of this general kind are used for many purposes besides seriation and involve a number of methodological issues discussed elsewhere in this volume. For seriation *per se*, I suspect that we have worried too much about these problems. If we really have no other objective than the approximately correct time ordering of a number of units, then we should be able to do this with no more than a tiny fraction of the information potentially available. At least for the sake of argument, I suggest that one needs to use very little of the total richness of the data (much of it of prime importance for other questions) in order to do a good seriation. A principal lesson from the good results often obtained from Meighan's technique of computing percentages of only three well-chosen types (Meighan, 1959; Ascher, 1959; Hole and Shaw, 1967; Cowgill, 1968; Rattray, 1971) is this: often one can throw away most of one's information and still get a good chronological ordering. It is true that much depends on *which* small fraction of the data one retains for seriation purposes, but I suspect that rather than it being a very tricky business to get good types or modes for chronological ordering, it may be difficult to go very far wrong, provided a few general rules are followed.

The general rules for chronological types that I have in mind are: first, that one will look for types that occur in more than a very few but less than half of the total set of units to be seriated; second, one will try to avoid redundant types that nearly always are present or absent in the same units (if presence or absence of one type can be predicted with high success from the presence or absence of some other type, then one adds little information not already provided by the other); and, finally, one will look for types which, on the basis of whatever other chronological information one has, and on the basis of preliminary seriation trials, seem to occur rarely or never before some point in time, then rise fairly monotonically to a single peak frequency of occurrence or peak relative abundance, and then decrease fairly monotonically to the level of few or no occurrences. Of course, it is not necessary that every type exhibit the whole cycle within the set of units being seriated; many types may be 'caught' only on the descending or the ascending segments of their cycles, and the essential thing is that trends up to, or down from, a single peak be fairly monotonic.

Another important point which should be made here is that if an ideal seriation of a data set exists, it is probably easy to find. At any rate, Gelfand (1971) has shown that, for seriations based on relative abundances, if there exists an ideal sequence one can find it simply by beginning with the highest observed similarities, and selecting as nearest neighbours for each unit the other two most similar units, unless one of these is unavailable because it already has two nearest neighbours or unless this would mean linking the head of a chain of units to the tail (thus forming a closed loop). In either of these cases, the most similar units that are not ineligible are picked as nearest neighbours to a given unit. With ideal data, this seems to be a very easy and effective technique. For instance, Kendall (1969) gives a sample set of six units for which he obtained an ideal sequence through multidimensional scaling. He suggests that the reader will find it instructive to try seriating his data set by hand. Indeed it is. Using Gelfand's technique it took me less than two minutes with pencil and paper to obtain the same sequence that Kendall got through multidimensional scaling.

If a set of units cannot be made to fit the seriation ideal perfectly, but something very close to an ideal sequence is possible, Gelfand's technique should enable one to obtain easily a sequence that is at least close to the best possible sequence. On the other hand, if nothing at all close to an ideal sequence is possible, one should not, as I have said before, be trying to do a seriation anyhow. The main justification for techniques more elaborate than Gelfand's seems to be that situations arise, probably rather frequently, where the best possible sequence is far enough from the ideal to require something more than his technique alone, yet not so far from ideal that seriation is inappropriate. In such cases it is still important to look for the best and easiest techniques.

It is to some of these considerations of technique that the rest of this paper is devoted. First, some definitions are in order. Many of these come from Kendall (1969), whose terms I have adopted unless there seemed to be a good reason for change.

It is very useful to think of the data for a seriation as arranged in an array of rows and columns, a *matrix*, in which each row represents a unit and each column pertains to a type (what Kendall calls a variety; I prefer 'type' because it is shorter and perhaps carries fewer confusing connotations of the 'type variety' terminology of some American archaeologists). Such a matrix can be read as a data table, in which units are listed from top to bottom along the left margin, as row headings, and types are listed from left to right across the top, as column headings. It is useful to distinguish two kinds of data matrices. An *occurrence* matrix is one that merely records presence or absence of types in each unit. A '1' in column 5 of row 8, then, indicates that Type 5 is present in unit 8; while a zero in column 3 of row 12 indicates that Type 3 is absent in unit 12. In technical terms, component a_{ij} of an occurrence matrix A is unity if type j occurs in unit i; otherwise it is zero. Components of matrices are conventionally represented by two subscripts, the first of which designates the row and the second the column, so that a_{24} stands for the number in row 2 and column 4 of the array.

Kendall uses the term 'incidence matrix' for what I call an occurrence matrix, a term I find more congenial, which is used by Dunnell (1970).

The other important kind of data matrix also represents types as columns and units as rows; the only difference from an occurrence matrix is that the values shown as per cents or relative proportions of the count for a given type, relative to the total count of all specimens of all types exhibited by a given unit. In such a matrix, B, element b_{ij} is the percentage of type j in unit i, relative to all the relevant material in unit i. For any one row, the percentages must add to 100%. This is the kind of data matrix used as a starting point both for Ford's graphical technique and for Brainerd's (1951) and Robinson's (1951) matrix technique. It is often preferable to an occurrence matrix, especially when the units are sites or site components, where (1) types are commonly represented by numerous examples, (2) many types may occur in at least small amounts in all units, so that an occurrence matrix would be nearly all 1's and very few 0's, and (3) there may be considerable danger of at least slight admixture of earlier material or later material than that pertaining to the unit one hopes to date (a danger discussed by Lipe, 1964). A percentage matrix presents more information than an occurrence matrix, but occurrence matrices are simpler and may be preferable wherever the additional information that a percentage matrix provides does not do much to improve the chronological ordering. Occurrence matrices make most sense when the units are grave lots or other closed finds, where types that occur are rarely represented by more than one example in a given unit, mixture of material that pertains to some other unit is not likely to be unrecognized or unavoidable, and any specific type is absent in a good proportion of all units. Table 9.1 and Figs. 9.4, 9.8, 9.9, 9.11, 9.14 and 9.15 are examples of occurrence matrices – although all the figures are unconventional in replacing zeros by blanks.

388

For an occurrence matrix the formal job of seriation can be phrased as the task of seeking a rearrangement of the rows such that all the 1's in each column are bunched into a consecutive run, uninterrupted by any zeros. If such a sequence is a chronology, it indicates that each type, once it appeared, occurred in every unit until some time of obsolescence, after which it never reappeared. If we define similarity between units as the number of types that occur in both units, so that a unit *u* is most similar to whatever other unit exhibits the largest number of the types that occur in unit *u*, then this definition of seriation is equivalent to the definition given at the beginning of this paper. For percentage matrices, seriation amounts to seeking a sequence such that the percentage for any one type rises monotonically from zero (or some minimum value) to a maximum, then decreases monotonically to zero (or some minimum value). Although they are important, I will make only passing further reference to percentage matrices, and will devote the rest of this paper to occurrence matrices.

Kendall (1969) introduces the term Petrie Matrix (after Flinders Petrie) for an occurrence matrix that is in the ideal pattern, with all the 1's in each column consecutive. He also defines two other matrices that can be formed by matrix multiplication of the occurrence matrix: A and its transpose, A^T. In technical terms, $V = A^T A$ is a matrix whose (i, j)th component is

$$v_{ij} = \sum_{k=1}^{g} a_{ki} a_{kj}$$

where g is the total number of units being studied. What this says is that, for any pair of types i and j, one moves down column i and column j of the occurrence matrix, multiplying the numbers that occur together in the same rows. If either or both the numbers is a zero, the product will be zero, and only for those rows where both numbers are 1's will the product also be unity (this corresponds to the situation where types i and j both occur in the unit represented by this row). The component v_{ij} is the sum of all the 1's thus obtained, summing over all units, and is thus the number of units in which types i and j both occur. The components of the V matrix, as well as a number of fairly simple functions of its components, are coefficients reflecting similarities in the occurrence patterns of pairs of *types*.

As a simple example, Table 9.1 shows an occurrence matrix, A, with four columns (types) and six rows (units).

Table 9.2 shows the V matrix, with four rows and columns, derived from A.

389

If, instead, A and A^T are multiplied in the opposite sequence, we get $G = AA^T$, whose (i, j)th component is

$$g_{ij} = \sum_{k=1}^{v} a_{ik} a_{jk}$$

where v is the total number of types. Here what is done is, for any pair of units i and j, to move across row i and row j, multiplying the numbers that occur

TABLE 9.1. *Sample occurrence matrix*

$$[A =] \begin{pmatrix} 1 & 0 & 1 & 1 \\ 1 & 0 & 0 & 1 \\ 1 & 0 & 1 & 0 \\ 0 & 1 & 0 & 0 \\ 0 & 1 & 1 & 0 \\ 0 & 1 & 0 & 0 \end{pmatrix}$$

together in the same columns. Again, the products will be zero except for those columns where the numbers in both rows are 1's, corresponding to the situation where units i and j both exhibit the type corresponding to that column. The component g_{ij} is the sum of all the 1's thus obtained, summing over all

TABLE 9.2. *Sample V matrix, derived from the A matrix of Table 9.1*

$$[V =] \begin{pmatrix} 3 & 0 & 2 & 2 \\ 0 & 3 & 1 & 0 \\ 2 & 1 & 3 & 1 \\ 2 & 0 & 1 & 2 \end{pmatrix}$$

types, and is thus the number of types that occur in both unit i and unit j. The components of the matrix G, as well as a number of functions of its components, are coefficients reflecting similarities between pairs of *units*. Table 9.3 shows the G matrix derived from the A matrix of Table 9.1.

Both of these new matrices, V and G, are always square and symmetric. That is, unlike the occurrence matrix, they have the same number of rows and columns and in all cases $v_{ij} = v_{ji}$ and $g_{ij} = g_{ji}$ – that is, the component at the intersection of the ith row and jth column is identical to the component at the intersection of the *j*th row and *i*th column. This is, in effect, another way of saying that the similarity of unit (or type) *i* to unit (or type) *j* is the same as the similarity of unit (or type) *j* to unit (or type) *i*, and this is the reason why it is

TABLE 9.3. *Sample G matrix, derived from the A matrix of Table 9.1*

$$[G =] \begin{pmatrix} 3 & 2 & 2 & 0 & 1 & 0 \\ 2 & 2 & 1 & 0 & 0 & 0 \\ 2 & 1 & 2 & 0 & 1 & 0 \\ 0 & 0 & 0 & 1 & 1 & 1 \\ 1 & 0 & 1 & 1 & 2 & 1 \\ 0 & 0 & 0 & 1 & 1 & 1 \end{pmatrix}$$

never clear from a seriation alone which is the early and which is the late end of a sequence. If one were to develop a formal method that made use of notions about what was likely to be derived from what, then the matrix analogous to G would not be symmetrical; in general g_{ij} would not be equal to g_{ji}.

For percentage matrices, the Brainerd–Robinson matrix is analogous to G, and is another example of a square symmetric matrix. In this case, if the components of the initial percentage matrix B are b_{ij}, the (i, j)th component of the Brainerd–Robinson matrix R is

$$r_{ij} = 200 - \sum_{k=1}^{v} |b_{ik} - b_{jk}|$$

That is, for units *i* and *j*, r_{ij} is found by moving across rows *i* and *j* of the percentage matrix, finding for each column (that is, for each type) the difference in percentages of the type for the two units, converting all these differences to positive values, adding the values obtained for all columns, and subtracting the sum from 200 (which is the maximum possible cumulative percentage difference for two units in which *none* of the types that occur in one unit occur in the other; that is, for units that show the greatest possible difference).

I mention the Brainerd–Robinson matrix partly to give readers a feel for what V and G are, and how they compare with R. In the case of V (see Table 9.2) the number of rows and columns is equal to the number of types, and these types are represented in the same sequence from top to bottom for rows, and from left to right for columns. It follows that the intersections of row 1 with column 1, of row 2 with column 2, and so on, along the 'principal diagonal' from the upper left to the lower right corner of the matrix, contain coefficients indicating similarity in occurrence of each type with itself, and these are necessarily maximal values for each row and column. For G or R, the number of rows and columns is equal to the number of units, and the principal diagonal contains values indicating the similarity of each unit to itself, which again are maximal values.

Two important mathematical results have recently been obtained for occurrence matrices. Fulkerson and Gross (1965) have shown that all the information needed to decide whether an occurrence matrix A can be petrified (that is, whether there exists a sequence of the rows such that all the 1's in each column are consecutive; the term was introduced by Kendall) is contained in V, and they give a graph-theoretical algorithm for answering this question. Kendall (1969) has complemented this by showing that if A is indeed petrifiable, then all the information needed to rearrange A into the Petrie form is contained in G. He does this by proving that A will be petrified when the rows are rearranged so that G is in what he calls the *Robinson* form, meaning by this a condition in which all components monotonically decrease as one moves away from the principal diagonal along any row or column.

This point, that a data set is ideally seriated if and only if a certain matrix derived from it is in the Robinson form, is of course just what Robinson (1951) had in mind for his matrix R, derived from a percentage matrix. What is new about Kendall's work is that he proves it also for the different matrix G, derived in a different way from an occurrence matrix.

These results are nice, but, as Kendall recognizes, of somewhat limited use, since (1) for nearly all real archaeological data sets perfect petrification is demonstrably impossible, and (2) even where it is possible, these results do not tell one how to obtain the Petrie sequence. It is here that Gelfand's (1971) work is so valuable, for he shows that if it is possible to put a matrix into the Robinson form at all, it can be done very easily by rearranging rows and columns so that each entity has as its nearest neighbours the other two entities (not already assigned to two nearest neighbours and not already linked through an intermediate chain) with which it shares the highest coefficients. Operating on R, this technique will seriate an ideal percentage matrix and, operating on G, it will seriate an ideal occurrence matrix. For matrices that cannot quite be put into the Robinson form, this technique should provide a very useful preliminary ordering, which one might then try to improve by other means.

Before moving on to the question of what to do when the data are not close enough to the ideal for Gelfand's technique to be sufficient, I would like to add a few comments of my own about some logical properties of petrifiable

392

occurrence matrices. It appears that, if there are v types in such a matrix, then the largest number of distinguishable intervals that could conceivably be recognized is $2v$. It seems that not more than $2v$ different combinations of types could occur, no matter how many units there are. To see this, suppose that the occurrence matrix is in the Petrie form, so that all 1's are in consecutive bunches, and suppose that the beginning and ending point for every type is different from the beginning and ending point of every other type. There can be, then, at most v different beginning points, and v different ending points, or $2v$ altogether. But new combinations of types can occur only when at least one type begins or ends, so it appears that at most $2v$ different combinations can occur in a Petrie matrix.

Since the combinations of types that occur are the same, regardless of the sequence in which the rows of the occurrence matrix happen to be written, an easy partial test of whether or not an occurrence matrix may be petrifiable consists of counting the number of different combinations of types that actually occur. If it is greater than $2v$, it seems clear that the matrix cannot possibly be petrified. Presumably the ratio of the observed number of type combinations to $2v$ will give some useful information about how nearly the data could be made to approximate the ideal Petrie form. On the other hand, if the number of observed type combinations is $2v$ or less, one cannot be certain that the matrix can be petrified. For example, if two or more types happen to have identical end points for their ranges, then there could be fewer than $2v$ distinct type combinations in a petrifiable matrix, or exactly $2v$ or fewer in a non-petrifiable matrix. However, the occurrence of $2v$ or fewer type combinations would strongly suggest that the matrix is probably at least nearly petrifiable.

A different practical implication of this result is that an ideal, petrifiable occurrence matrix is distinctly limited in the amount of chronological information it can provide. If there are more than $2v$ units – that is, if the number of units is more than twice the number of types – all the units in excess of $2v$ must exhibit a combination of types which is identical to those that occur in some other unit, and hence any of these excess units must be tied with one or more other units, and chronologically indistinguishable (unless, of course, information additional to that in the occurrence matrix is used). Actually, the number $2v$ assumes that we include units in which *none* of the types occur. Realistically, we would hardly try to fit any unit into the sequence unless *at least* one of the set of types under consideration occurs in that unit, and this means that at most $2v - 1$ periods can be usefully distinguished if the occurrence matrix is petrifiable.

But if the occurrence matrix is not petrifiable, then the conceivable number of different type combinations that could occur in different units is 2^v (or $2^v - 1$, if we exclude the case where no types occur in a unit). If, for example, we were using twelve types, then a petrifiable occurrence matrix could not usefully distinguish more than twenty-three distinct intervals, but these same twelve types could occur in 4095 combinations, if every combination other than total absence of all twelve types occurred.

This is not to say that an occurrence matrix consisting of 4095 units, each with a different combination of one or more of the twelve types would enable us to distinguish 4095 intervals and arrange them in a convincing sequence; on the contrary, such an occurrence matrix would provide no chronological information at all and would be profoundly unseriatable. But it does seem to be true, paradoxically, that a less than ideal occurrence matrix, with say thirty or forty rather than twenty-three type combinations occurring, would enable one to distinguish (and arrange in a plausible order) more intervals than would an ideal, petrifiable matrix. At any rate, with many more units than types, which is often the case when the units are graves, the only way to avoid having a relatively large number of tied units, in which identical type combinations occur, is by having an occurrence matrix that *cannot* be petrified.

To understand more about this, it is useful to think of the Petrie model in terms of probabilities of occurrences of types. The Petrie model, as formalized by Kendall, assumes that in the ideal case, for any given type, its probability of occurrence during any finite interval is zero before a certain point in time, changes instantaneously and discontinuously to unity at this point, remains unity until a second point in time, and then drops back to zero in a second discontinuous instantaneous step. It is because the probability of occurrence has only two values, and changes value only twice, that, if all types really behaved in this ideal way, any one type's occurrence or non-occurrence in a given unit could only enable one to judge whether the unit belonged to an interval somewhere between the beginning and ending points for that type, or to an interval somewhere outside this range, but would not enable one to make any judgements (based on this one type alone) about *where* within or outside this range the unit belongs.

On the other hand, models of human behaviour that seem more realistic to me will assume that when a type first occurs, it may not be very popular, so that its probability of occurrence rises more or less gradually from zero to some maximum value, then declines more or less gradually to zero again. The implication of this model is that, if we cannot find an arrangement of the occurrence matrix that does not leave some gaps in the occurrences of some

394

types, then an arrangement is to be preferred which puts most of the gaps near the beginning and end of the range of each type (I should add that Kendall also assumes that gaps are most plausibly assigned to intervals near the end points of type ranges, but he does not develop the implications of this alternative model). Here, however, the matter of a 'badness of fit' criterion becomes of some importance, for different specific assumptions about the precise form of the probability function will lead to somewhat different criteria for deciding what is the best seriation – that is, for deciding how best to allocate the unavoidable gaps in occurrences of some types. In short, a non-petrifiable occurrence matrix admits the possibility of more different observed type combinations, and hence the possibility of distinguishing more intervals in the sequence; but, in order to claim that a particular sequence of these intervals has a generally high validity, one has to justify a more complicated assumption about how the probability of occurrence of a type changes over time.

Actually, the only kinds of assumptions that seem reasonable are variations of the monotonic increase from zero to some maximum, followed by monotonic decrease back to zero, but there does remain room for substantial differences within this general family of models. For example, if a type occurs in only 10 out of 100 units, is it more likely that it occurred intermittently over a fairly long time span (its maximum probability of occurrence always remaining well below unity), or that it occurred with high frequency over a very limited span of time? Either case, of course, is quite possible, but the former situation means that the type (whatever its importance for other purposes) is not a very good time indicator. Sporadic occurrence over long time ranges should manifest itself in preliminary work by occurrence of the type together with other types which themselves seem to have little or no association, and types that have this sporadic occurrence pattern should be eliminated or redefined. It seems, then, for formal seriation algorithms, that we should first eliminate types that seem to occur sporadically, and then assume that other relatively infrequent types are infrequent because their occurrence was limited to a relatively brief time span.

Within these limits, different reasonable models of the probabilities of occurrence probably do not differ very much, but it is important to try out and compare different models.

Notice that this general kind of model for non-petrifiable occurrence matrices has some resemblances to the Brainerd–Robinson model for percentage matrices. In the latter case, it is the observed percentage of each type that is expected to show monotonic increase and decrease to and from a single peak; for occurrence matrices it is then *probability* of occurrence that is thought to exhibit this pattern, and the probabilities will be reflected in the matrix itself by a tendency for more or longer gaps in occurrences to appear the nearer one comes to the ends of each type's range. There is the important difference that this assumption provides a unique best sequence for a percentage matrix for which the assumption is true, while it does not, by itself, tell one how to find the best sequence for a non-petrifiable occurrence matrix. For a percentage matrix, putting the Robinson matrix into the Robinson form will yield the ideal sequence, but, for an occurrence matrix, as we have seen, it will be impossible to put the analogous G matrix into the Robinson form if the occurrence matrix is not petrifiable.

How, then, should one proceed for occurrence matrices which are not petrifiable? The brute force method would be to try every possible sequence, but it turns out that this would mean, for eight units, over 40 000 possible sequences; nearly 4 million for ten units; and over 20 million million for sixteen units. Of course, since for every sequence there is another that is its exact reverse and therefore equivalent, only half these need be considered, but it helps little to know one only needs to deal with 10 million million possibilities. The requirements quickly overwhelm computers as well as people.

Computer programs such as that of Hole and Shaw (1967) employ various stratagems to seek for relatively good sequences, then seek improvements in these sequences. But this still involves a good deal of trial and error and a limited sampling of all the possibilities. A much more powerful and attractive approach (and probably less costly in computer time) is the multidimensional scaling technique of Shepard (1962) and Kruskal (1964a, 1964b; Kruskal and Carmone, 1969; Kendall, 1969). In particular, Kruskal's MDSCAL program has been in use, in several versions, for about seven years, and considerable practical experience with it has been gained. I have found it, with a little practice, easy, fast and reliable. Its availability in an already developed state is a major factor in making seriations that use it relatively easy.

Suffice it to say, here, that multidimensional scaling is a way of seeking configurations of points, one point representing one entity, such that the rank order of distances between points is the inverse of the rank order of similarities between the entities represented by the points. That is, if we had four entities, A, B, C and D, of which the most similar pair were A and C, followed by A and D, B and D, C and D, B and C, and A and B, in that order; then the configuration of points sought would be one in which points A and C have the smallest distance, points A and D are next closest to one another, and so on, with points A and B the most distant from one another. Or, if relationships between entities are expressed in terms of differences or dissimilarities, the computer will seek a configuration of points such that the rank order of distances is the same as the rank order of dissimilarities; the points corresponding to the most dissimilar entities being the most distant from one another. In MDSCAL, it is only necessary to inform the machine whether the input is a matrix of similarity or dissimilarity coefficients.

It may be impossible to satisfy the condition sought by this technique unless the points are embedded in a space of nearly as many dimensions as there are entities being compared. In other cases, however, the condition may be met, or nearly met, in a space with much fewer dimensions. In such a case, one is entitled to think that this is because the total pattern of similarities between the entities is mainly due to no more independent factors than the minimum number of dimensions needed. In MDSCAL, the computer finds the best possible configuration in a specified number of dimensions, in terms of the *stress*, a measure of the extent to which the point configuration departs from the ideal of correctly representing *all* rank orders of resemblances between entities. Normally one begins with a space of several dimensions, computes the optimal configuration and the corresponding stress, moves to a space of one fewer dimension and repeats the process, and continues with spaces of progressively fewer dimensions. The least number of dimensions needed can be judged by the point where the stress is judged to be unacceptable, and/or by a sudden rise in the stress. In practice, it is well to repeat the process a few times with different arbitrary starting configurations, since there is a possibility of stopping with a configuration that is the best that can be obtained without some *major* rearrangements of points, but may not be the very best possible. If one repeatedly obtains virtually the same configuration, it is almost surely the best there is (Fig. 8.20).

If the entities are such that their matrix of similarity coefficients can be put into the Robinson form, then multidimensional scaling should lead to a low-stress solution in one dimension. In practice, I strongly agree with Kendall that it is better to seek the best two-dimensional solution. Even if the data fit well into one dimension, there is less danger in two dimensions of getting caught in a 'local minimum'. If the entities do not fit into two dimensions with low stress, or if they do but the configuration is not elongated and essentially one-dimensional (either a nearly straight-line pattern, or at least close to an arc or somewhat sinuous line), then evidently there is more than one major factor underlying variation among the entities, and it is not sensible to attempt a seriation, at least not of the whole set. In this way, multidimensional scaling tests the appropriateness of a seriation model for a given data set.

Another advantage of multidimensional scaling is that, even though it works with ranks rather than metric values, if the number of entities is substantially more than the number of dimensions the result provides a good deal of metric information. Thus, relative distances between points will reflect relative differences. Widely spaced points in the sequence indicate relatively large differences between consecutive units, which could mean either a relatively large time interval, or a period of relatively rapid change. Clusters of points will indicate groups of rather similar units. To some extent, as Hole and Shaw (1967) show, one can get some of this information by looking at the contours of a Robinson matrix, but the spacings provided by a MDSCAL configuration show this more clearly.

The most direct way to use MDSCAL for seriation of an occurrence matrix is to use units as entities, and use the G matrix or some closely related matrix of coefficients of similarities between pairs of units as the input. This is the technique discussed by Kendall (1969). This is excellent, as long as the number of units is not too large. In its present form, MDSCAL cannot handle over about sixty entities, and, while it would certainly be possible to expand this number somewhat, it remains true that the size and expense of the computing job goes up rapidly (from several dollars to several tens of dollars or more) as the number of entities increases. In a symmetric square matrix of similarity coefficients with n rows and n columns there will be n^2 components, but the n components along the principal diagonal need not be considered (since they express similarities of entities to themselves) and of the remaining $(n^2 - n)$ coefficients, the half above and to the right of the principal diagonal merely duplicate the half below and to the left. Therefore MDSCAL need only consider $(n^2 - n)/2$ coefficients in order to do its job. But if n is large, this means that the rate of increase is almost proportional to n^2.

If the number of types is considerably smaller than the number of units, it would be much more economical to use MDSCAL on V, or some other matrix of similarities between pairs of *types*, rather than pairs of *units*. Kendall (1969) quite correctly points out that this is not an equivalent operation. Units are thought of as essentially points in time (or at any rate have durations that do not overlap very much), while on the contrary types have ranges that cover appreciable parts of the whole sequence, and one ought to think of them as represented by lines in one dimension, by disks in two dimensions (and, presumably, by hyper-ellipsoids in k-dimensional spaces), so that their similarities might be expressed by the extent of overlap between the geometric figures corresponding to the different entities. However, no formal method of doing this has yet been developed. Kendall therefore suggests that for seriating

398

more than 50 or at most 100 units the best method would be to break the full set of units up into interpenetrating blocks (presumably on the basis of chronological information available from other methods) 'and to treat each block separately, fitting together the seriations thus obtained in a subsequent operation' (Kendall, 1969, p. 76).

The essential contribution I have to offer here, on the level of technique, is to show a way of overcoming much of the difficulty pointed out by Kendall in using MDSCAL on types rather than units. This means that, where the number of types is more than a little smaller than the number of units, a substantial saving in computer costs can be effected. And, especially, the technique I will describe makes it feasible to seriate several hundred units in a single operation.

As an example of the economies offered, suppose we have 100 units and 20 types. This gives us a choice of dealing with 4950 pairs of units, or 190 pairs of types. Incidentally, if at least one type occurs in all units, and if no two units are identical, this implies that at most there could be a subset of 39 of the 100 units which, by themselves, could be petrified. Each of the other 61 units must, wherever it is fitted in, introduce at least one gap. While I have not made a thorough analysis of this situation, I believe there need not be *more* than one gap for each of these units, for an average of three gaps per type. If one assumes that each type occurs in not less than 10 or more than 50 units, such a less-than-ideal occurrence matrix still seems capable of a quite good seriation, especially since there is no reason why more gaps cannot be allocated to the more often occurring types, and fewer to the less often occurring types.

In seriating types rather than units, the first thing one must do is find a similarity coefficient that will make possible a definite and sensible interpretation of the MDSCAL results if applied to an occurrence matrix which in fact is petrifiable. We should try to get a coefficient that makes sense if the points in the one-dimensional MDSCAL configuration (or, more exactly, the points determined by projecting the points of the two-dimensional MDSCAL result on to the major or main axis of their configuration) are regarded as the *middle* points in the stretches of consecutive 1's in the corresponding column of the occurrence matrix, when it is ideally seriated and in the Petrie form. If we think rather concretely of the occurrence matrix as drawn to a uniform scale, so that each row has the same physical width (distance from top to bottom), then the vertical distance from the level of the middle point of the stretch of consecutive 1's in any column, to the level of the middle point of the stretch of consecutive 1's in any other column, will be some quite specific scalar distance, which could be measured in centimetres or inches. Of course, this does

399

not mean that the petrified occurrence matrix provides a metric time scale, since what we are measuring are distances between *rank* positions of different units. Nevertheless, it gives us a definite idea of a distance which the coefficients of the input matrix for MDSCAL, might represent. Rather than using V as the input for MDSCAL, we should derive a different matrix, whose components are more appropriate coefficients for expressing distances between midpoints of type occurrence stretches.

It is useful, without any loss of precision, to play a little more with our concrete picture of an occurrence matrix, by (1) replacing the zeros by blanks, and (2) drawing each 1 as an unadorned vertical line, stretching from the very bottom to the very top of its row. This means that a bunch of consecutive 1's will simply be represented by an unbroken vertical line, and, in a Petrie matrix, there will be only a single uninterrupted line in each column. Notice also that the total line length in any column is a constant, proportional to the number of units in which the type represented by that column occurs, and is unchanged by any permutation of the rows of the occurrence matrix. In fact, if we make each row of unit width, then the total line length in each column will just equal the number of units in which the given type occurs.

With respect to any two types, i and j, whether the matrix is petrifiable or not, all units must fall into one of four categories: i and j both present, i but not j, j but not i, or neither i nor j. We can denote the number of units where both i and j occur by a; the number with i but not j by b; the number with j but not i by c; and the number with neither i nor j by d. The sum of $a+b+c+d$ must equal g, the total number of units, and is the distance from top to bottom of the occurrence matrix, if all rows have unit width. Notice that a, b, c and d are not changed by permutations of the rows of the occurrence matrix, and can be determined quite easily regardless of the order in which the units are listed.

Now, if the occurrence matrix is petrified, there are three possibilities for the ranges of types i and j. Either they partially overlap one another, as in Fig. 9.1, they do not overlap at all, as in Fig. 9.2, or the range or span of one type completely includes the range of the other type, as in Fig. 9.3. Each of these cases needs to be looked at more closely.

If types i and j overlap and, let us say, i begins earlier than j, as in Fig. 9.1, it means that in some units both types occur, in other units i occurs but not j, and in others j occurs but not i. That is, a, b and c are all greater than zero (d may or may not be greater than zero; its value is not critical). The distance that we want to derive is x, the vertical distance between the midpoints of the ranges of the two types. In this situation, x can be found by reasoning that the

400

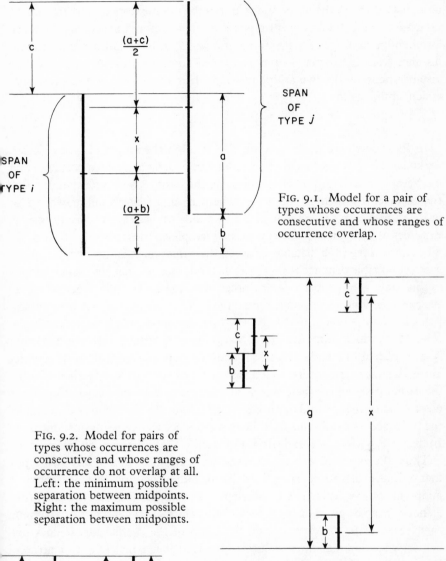

FIG. 9.1. Model for a pair of types whose occurrences are consecutive and whose ranges of occurrence overlap.

FIG. 9.2. Model for pairs of types whose occurrences are consecutive and whose ranges of occurrence do not overlap at all. Left: the minimum possible separation between midpoints. Right: the maximum possible separation between midpoints.

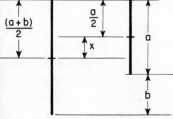

FIG. 9.3. Model for a pair of types whose occurrences are consecutive, where the range of occurrence for one type completely includes that of the other. The situation shown corresponds to the maximum possible separation between midpoints.

total distance from the lower endpoint of type i to the upper endpoint of type j is $a+b+c$. The total range of type i is $a+b$; therefore the distance from the lower endpoint of type i to its midpoint is $(a+b)/2$. By a similar argument, the distance from the upper endpoint of type j to its midpoint is $(a+c)/2$. The distance between the two midpoints, x, is then $a+b+c-(a+b)/2-(a+c)/2$, which simplifies to

$$x = (b+c)/2 \tag{1}$$

In the case where there is no overlap at all in the ranges of types i and j, we know this only because there is no unit in which i and j both occur, so that a is zero. We have no way of knowing, on the basis only of information about the occurrences of these two types, whether i and j barely fail to overlap (as in the example on the left side of Fig. 9.2) or whether they occur at opposite extremes of the total sequence (as in the example on the right side of Fig. 9.2). The shortest possible distance between their midpoints is $(b+c)/2$, while the greatest possible distance is $g-(b+c)/2$. If one reasons that any distance within this range is as probable as any other, then the statistically expected value, the expected long-run average for a large number of cases of non-overlapping pairs, is the midpoint of the range of possible distances, which is $[(b+c)/2+g-(b+c)/2]/2$, which simplifies to $g/2$. Somewhat surprisingly, this expected value is independent of b and c; that is, it does not depend on the number of units in which either type occurs, so long as the types never occur together. Now in the earlier case, where there was some overlap in the type ranges, the largest possible value for x would occur if $a=1$ and $d=0$; that is, if one or the other of the types occurs in all units, but the two types occur together in just one unit. In this case, $b+c=g-1$, and, from Equation 1, the value of x will be $(g-1)/2$.

Thus, the expected average distance between midpoints of *any* two types that do not overlap is greater than the maximum possible distance between midpoints of *any* types that do overlap. This suggests that all type pairs that do not overlap be given distance coefficients which are tied for some maximum value. Since MDSCAL operates on the ranks of the coefficients, it does not matter what this maximum value is, provided it is equal to $g/2$ or greater. However, there is more than one option in MDSCAL for treatment of ties, and it seems best to choose the option that permits the computer to seek a configuration in which distances between points corresponding to tied coefficients have maximum freedom to be unequal, so long as rank order is not violated for any non-tied coefficients. Non-overlapping type pairs are given tied coefficients not because we know distances between midpoints of their ranges are all the same, but because we do not have any information on which to judge that some are greater than others. MDSCAL should not force the computer to seek a configuration in which pairs of points corresponding to types with tied maximal distance coefficients must all show the same distance of separation.

This approach amounts to assuming that *all* non-overlapping types have greater distances between the midpoints of their ranges than do *any* types which ever occur together. On the average this will be true, but there can be specific instances where some types with no overlap have closer midpoints than some types that do overlap. This could occur if the non-overlapping types occur in but a few units while the overlapping types occur in many units. It can be made quite unlikely by choosing types that occur in roughly comparable numbers of units. So our assumption should be true in most cases and nearly true in all cases, if there are not great differences between types in frequency of occurrence. It is very simple, and, importantly, good results have been obtained by using it.

Finally, there is the case where the range of one type is completely included in the range of the other type. Fig. 9.3 illustrates this situation. It can be recognized, independently of the sequence of rows in the occurrence matrix, by the fact that a and b are both greater than zero, but c is zero (if the range of j completely included that of type i, then of course a and c would be greater than zero, and b would be zero). In this case, the maximum possible distance between midpoints of the two types, when the matrix is petrified, is $(a+b)/2 - a/2$, or simply $b/2$. The shortest possible distance is zero. Again assuming that all distances within these limits are equally probable, the statistically expected distance, for the average of such cases, is $b/4$. The condition that $b_{ij}/4$ for types i and j (where i includes the range of j, and where we must now use subscripts to link different variables to the pairs of types to which they pertain) be smaller than the distance x_{mn} between midpoints of the ranges of any overlapping pair of types m and n, is that

$$b_{ij} < 2(b_{mn} + c_{mn}) \tag{2}$$

where b_{mn} and c_{mn} must both be integers greater than or equal to unity. There is no guarantee that this condition will always be met, and perhaps the distance formula $x = (b+c)/4$ should be used whenever b or c is zero. However, my procedure has been the simpler one of setting $x = 0$ in all these cases. That is, whenever one member of a pair of types occurs only in units where the other type also occurs, they are treated as tied with all other such pairs for a distance less than the distances between midpoints of any pairs which overlap

403

(such pairs must have a distance between range midpoints of at least unity). This, again, has given good results.

As a matter of efficient design, in order to get a maximum amount of chronological information for a maximum number of units for a minimum number of types, it would be good to avoid including more than one member of any pair of types for which a is large relative to $b+c$; that is, where the number of units in which both types occur is large relative to the number in which either type occurs without the other, since in such cases the types are relatively redundant. One would also want to avoid using any type that occurs in only a very small proportion of the total set of units since such a scarce type (however significant it might be in marking off those few units as different from others) will not help to seriate many units. Thus, in a well-designed study there should be few or no cases where the range of one type is completely included in the range of another, and also few cases where the condition specified by Equation 2 is not satisfied. Also, in any real data set, almost surely not petrifiable, it is not very likely that any type will never occur except in units where some other type occurs. For all these reasons, the choice between setting $x=0$ or $x=(b+c)/4$ when b or c is zero does not seem to constitute a very important practical problem.

In summary, a distance (or dissimilarity) coefficient has been developed which is very easy to compute, and which expresses distances between midpoints of the ranges of types, for petrified occurrence matrices, and which is untroubled by the fact that the ranges themselves are stretches of finite length, rather than points. It is convenient to standardize the distances by dividing by $g/2$, and, since x/g will always be less than $1/2$ for any overlapping pairs of types, it is also convenient to set the distance equal to unity for non-overlapping type pairs. All the distance coefficients between pairs of types can then be arranged in a square symmetric matrix, W, analogous to V, whose (i,j)th component is

$$w_{ij} = 0 \text{ if either } b_{ij} \text{ or } c_{ij} \text{ is zero} \tag{3a}$$
$$w_{ij} = 1 \text{ if } a_{ij} \text{ is zero} \tag{3b}$$
$$w_{ij} = (b_{ij}+c_{ij})/g \text{ otherwise} \tag{3c}$$

Incidentally, if one works out a_{ij}, b_{ij}, c_{ij} and d_{ij} as functions of v_{ij} (the (i,j)th component of Kendall's V matrix), it turns out that: since $a_{ij}=v_{ij}, b_{ij}=v_{ii}-v_{ij}$, and $c_{ij}=v_{jj}-v_{ij}$, the above three equations could be expressed as

$$w_{ij} = 0 \text{ if either } v_{ii} = v_{ij} \text{ or } v_{jj} = v_{ij}$$
$$w_{ij} = 1 \text{ if } v_{ij} \text{ is zero}$$
$$w_{ij} = (v_{ii}+v_{jj}-2v_{ij})/g \text{ otherwise}$$

Suppose we have an occurrence matrix in the Petrie form, compute the W matrix of distance coefficients according to the formulae given above, and also measure with a ruler the vertical distances between the midpoints of the consecutive bunches of 1's in each column. The computed distance coefficients will have the same rank order as the actually measured distances, subject to the limitations that we *may* have given slightly too low a rank to the distances between midpoints of some of the pairs where one type includes the range of the other; that we *may* have given slightly too high a rank to the distances between midpoints for some of the pairs where there is no overlap at all; and that in either of these cases we have had to treat as ties some distances between which we may be able to observe differences when we actually measure the occurrence matrix.

This means that, with these minor exceptions, the distances measured by our set of coefficients are monotonically related to actual distances measured along a single dimension; namely, up and down, along columns and spanning rows of the occurrence matrix. Therefore a multidimensional scaling of the w_{ij} should result in a low stress configuration in one dimension. Moreover, the measured distance between two points in the MDSCAL output configuration should be directly proportional to the number of rows separating midpoints of the ranges of the corresponding types in the petrified occurrence matrix.

The essential point, of course, is that we do not need to use any particular order of the occurrence matrix in order to compute the w_{ij}; which are uniquely determined by Equations 3a, 3b and 3c, independently of any particular sequence of units. Hence multidimensional scaling of a W matrix which results in a good one-dimensional solution not only tells us that the occurrence matrix A is petrifiable (or nearly so), it also provides a great deal of useful information about the best sequence of rows for A.

One could perfectly well compute the W matrix defined by Equations 3a, 3b and 3c and use it as the input for MDSCAL. Actually, I computed a different matrix, S, whose (i, j)th component, s_{ij}, is $1 - w_{ij}$. The rules for computing s_{ij} are then

$$s_{ij} = 0 \text{ if } a_{ij} \text{ is zero} \tag{4a}$$
$$s_{ij} = 1 \text{ if either } b_{ij} \text{ or } c_{ij} \text{ is zero} \tag{4b}$$
$$s_{ij} = (a_{ij} + d_{ij})/g \text{ otherwise} \tag{4c}$$

It is worth noting that in the general case, where neither a, b nor c is zero – that is, where types i and j partially overlap – the coefficient s_{ij} is just the simple matching coefficient widely used by numerical taxonomists to compare units (not types) (Sokal and Sneath, 1963, p. 133). In all cases, the s_{ij} are similarities, rather than differences, which means only that MDSCAL should attempt to put the pairs with highest s's closest together rather than furthest apart.

I should add that limited experimentation with some other coefficients for which there is a less clear rationale, including what Sokal and Sneath call S_j, the Jaccard coefficient (which counts only positive matches), suggests that they also may give fairly good results. At any rate, with reasonable data sets they seem to yield low stress one-dimensional MDSCAL solutions. Notably bad results have been obtained from Pearson's r, which would be suitable if the probability of occurrence of one type were a linear function of the probability of occurrence of another type. For the seriation models being used here, however, r is highly inappropriate.

Granted that Equations $3a$, $3b$ and $3c$ or $4a$, $4b$ and $4c$ should give good results when the occurrence matrix is in principle petrifiable, the practical question is how it works when the matrix cannot quite be petrified, or when the matrix is rather far from petrifiable. I have not made a formal analysis of the consequences, but have experimented with non-petrifiable sets of test data. The results presented below indicate that if the matrix is near enough to being petrifiable to justify seriation at all, very useful results are still obtained by this technique.

To complete description of the technique, it is necessary to explain how information from the MDSCAL result from the S matrix can be used to seriate A. This is best illustrated by an example. Fig. 9.4 shows a set of invented data consisting of twenty-five units and ten types (1's indicate occurrences; non-occurrences are indicated by blanks), arranged in what by fiat I declare to be their 'true' sequence. As can be seen, this occurrence matrix is petrified. Note that the order in which types appear is not the same as that in which they disappear; some types appear earlier but disappear later than some other types.

The first step is to compute the matrix of similarity coefficients. For types A and B, for example, all units with A also have B, so s_{AB} is unity. Type A occurs in none of the same units as type C, so s_{AC} is zero. Type I and type J occur together in two units and are both absent in sixteen, so s_{IJ} is $(2 + 16)/25$, or 0.72. In all there are forty-five different pairs of types here, and all forty-five coefficients can be computed fairly quickly by hand, though for larger data sets a very simple computer program to do this is convenient. Remember that it does not matter what order the units are listed in; any order leads to the identical S matrix. A change in the order in which *types* are listed would still lead to the same forty-five coefficients, but the arrangement of the rows and columns of the S matrix will be different. If random starting configurations are used for MDSCAL, changes in the rows and columns of S will not matter. The resulting S matrix was used as input for MDSCAL, and the resulting

FIG. 9.4. Occurrence matrix for invented ideal data in 'true' sequence of units. Rows represent twenty-five units; columns A to J represent ten types. Occurrences are consecutive for all types.

best two-dimensional configuration is shown in Fig. 9.5. It is elongated and essentially one-dimensional, and has a very low stress value, 0·022, which indicates an excellent fit.

In order to scale more precisely the predicted midpoint for the range of occurrence for each type, a line was fitted by eye to the longest axis of the MDSCAL configuration, and perpendiculars were drawn to the individual points (Fig. 9.6). A refinement would be to fit this line by least squares, but I doubt if anything worth the trouble would be gained. The distances were read off the central axis in centimetres, and multiplied by a scale factor to convert to numbers of units. The idea here is that since there are two units with type A present and point A (of Fig. 9.6) is supposed to be the midpoint for type A, then point A should be one unit above the lower endpoint of the optimally seriated matrix. Similarly, since there are seven units in which type J occurs, point J should be 3·5 units below the upper endpoint of the optimally seriated matrix. The distance between points A and J, then, should correspond to $25 - (1 + 3·5)$ or 20·5 units. Applying the resulting scale factor to all the midpoints predicted by MDSCAL, the predicted midpoints can be compared with

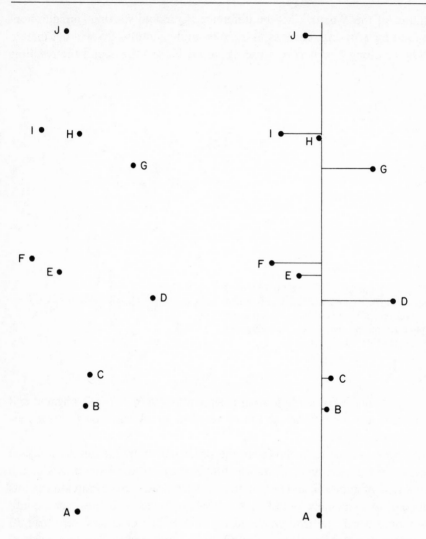

FIG. 9.5. MDSCAL configuration for the ten types of Fig. 9.4.

FIG. 9.6. Main axis and perpendiculars fitted to the configuration of Fig. 9.5, as a basis for scaling predicted occurrence midpoints.

the true midpoints found from measuring Fig. 9.4. The results, given in Fig. 9.7, show a quite good correspondence and perfect rank ordering, except for reversal of the nearly tied types *I* and *H*. Incidentally, this is a good example of how MDSCAL, in spite of working with just rank orders of distances, can

408

recover a good deal of metric information, if there are substantially more points than dimensions.

The most obvious way to use these results about types in order to obtain a seriation of units is to draw every predicted midpoint at the predicted height in a separated column, and draw to scale a vertical line whose length is proportional to the number of units in which the corresponding type occurs. The

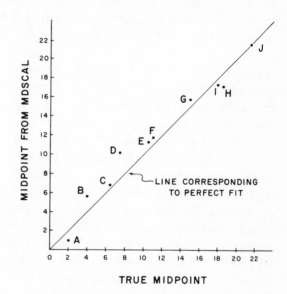

FIG. 9.7. Predicted occurrence midpoints derived from Fig. 9.6, plotted against true midpoints derived from Fig. 9.4.

result looks like Figs. 9.1, 9.2 or 9.3, except that there are lines representing all the types, rather than a single pair. If one then lays a straight edge horizontally across the diagram, it will cross some specific combination of vertical lines, corresponding to some specific combination of types that are predicted to occur together. By keeping the straight edge horizontal and sliding it from the bottom edge of the figure to the top edge, noting in order each different predicted combination of types that appears, one can derive a predicted sequence of occurrence of predicted combinations. This sequence can be compared with the observed combinations, which can now be listed in their predicted sequence. For the ideal data of Fig. 9.4, this method led to perfect recovery of the true sequence, except that the first unit, with only type *B* present, was moved up to join the fourth unit, which also has just type *B*.

It is important to dwell on this little error for a moment, because it has nothing to do with the specific seriation technique used, and would have been an inevitable consequence of *any* attempt to seriate the occurrence matrix of

Fig. 9.4. The point is that, at least in terms of the types being used, units 1 and 4 are identical, and hence no seriation technique could possibly lead to putting them into different intervals of the sequence. Units 1 and 4 are only one example here of tied units; others are units 2 and 3, or units 21–25. Examination of Fig. 9.4 shows that only thirteen different type combinations occur, so that the best any possible seriation technique could do with this occurrence matrix would be to order the twenty-five units in terms of thirteen distinguishable intervals. Furthermore, units 1 and 4 here give an example of identical units which are not actually consecutive (even though in Fig. 9.4 the matrix is petrified), and must necessarily be re-ordered so that they are consecutive by any seriation technique. This should remind one that it is possible to find a seriation sequence, sometimes, which 'improves' on the true sequence, and that, although the results are likely to be correct in their main outlines, one should not put too much trust in the fine details.

A much more serious difficulty is that, with real data, a good many of the type combinations actually exhibited by one or more units will not correspond to any of the predicted combinations. One can use the predicted sequence of combinations as a sort of skeleton matrix (a term I have taken from Bordaz and Bordaz, 1970), and fit the non-predicted but observed combinations in to the places where one judges they look best. I did this by hand in a day or so for the 109 different observed type combinations in the real data set I will discuss below, and obtained a seriation which looked very good in terms of Kendall's 'concentration principle'. That is, there were relatively few zeros interspersed among the 1's in each column of the matrix, and most zeros occurred near the ends of the maximum range of occurrence for each type. The effort was very much less than would have been required without the skeleton matrix derived from the MDSCAL results. Nevertheless, it seemed desirable to do this part of the seriation by computer also.

In order to do this, one must formalize the judgement procedures used for fitting observed type combinations into the predicted sequence. This brings us back to the subject of goodness of fit criteria, for the problem is where best to fit units that do not fit into an idealized sequence. We must invoke some definite (if simple) *model* of cultural change in order to decide how best to handle these units.

A number of models might be tried, but I began with the relatively simple assumption that the probability of occurrence of a given type in a given unit is specified by a normal curve, whose mean is centred on the predicted midpoint of the type's range of occurrence, and whose standard deviation is proportional to the number of units in which this type occurs. A normal curve

410

is one example of a function which monotonically increases to a single maximum, then monotonically decreases. This model does not make the probability of a type's occurrence dependent on the occurrence or non-occurrence of any other types; it may be that contingencies of this kind are sometimes important, but they would lead to far more complex models and, furthermore, would suggest that it was false to assume that change over time was the only major factor accounting for differences between units, and would therefore suggest that seriation as such was an inadequate way for dealing with the occurrence matrix.

But if the probability of each type's occurrence in a given unit depends only on that unit's distance from the occurrence midpoint for the type, then the probability of the joint occurrence of a given combination of types in a given unit will be just the product of the probabilities of each individual type's occurrence in that unit. This follows from the basic rule of probability calculus that the probability of the joint occurrence of two or more independent events can be found by multiplying all the probabilities of the occurrences of the events themselves. The most probable place for a given unit in the sequence, then, will be that place which maximizes the joint probability of occurrence for all the types which occur in the unit. This joint probability can be found by multiplying together the normal curve functions corresponding to each type which occurs in the unit (each function will have different parameters corresponding to the different predicted midpoints and different numbers of units in which each type occurs). The location corresponding to the maximum joint probability can then be found by differential calculus, by taking the derivative of the joint probability function, and solving for zero.

The result turns out to be very simple. To find the predicted occurrence point for some unit U, sum predicted midpoints divided by the square of the number of units in which the type occurs, for each type, and divide by the sum of the squared reciprocals of the numbers of units in which each type occurs. If L_U is the predicted location for unit U, m_i is the predicted midpoint for type i (obtained from the MDSCAL configuration), and g_i is the number of units in which type i occurs (that is, component g_{ii} of Kendall's G matrix), then

$$L_U = \frac{\Sigma_i \, m_i/g_i^2}{\Sigma_i \, 1/g_i^2} \tag{5}$$

where the summation is over all types that occur in unit U. Notice that if type A is the only type that occurs in unit U, then the predicted location for unit U is just the predicted midpoint for type A. If all the types that occur in unit

411

U occur in the same total number of other units, so that g_i is the same for all the types, then the predicted midpoint for unit U is the arithmetic mean of the predicted midpoints of all types that occur in unit U. In general, where the g_i's will be different, L_U is a kind of weighted mean.

Also, notice that the result does not depend on what values we assume for the constant of proportionality that relates the standard deviations of the 'probability of occurrence' functions to the numbers of units in which each type occurs; it only requires that we assume that the proportionality factor is the same for all types. That is, it turns out that it does not matter whether we assume that, relative to the ranges that would be observed if all occurrences of a type were to be consecutive, the probability of occurrence rises and declines gradually over a much longer time interval, or whether we assume that the probability peaks much more sharply over a relatively short interval. As long as we assume that for all types the probability curves are normal, and that for all types the proportionality factor relating the spread of the curve to the number of units in which the type occurs is the same, we do not need to make any specific assumption at all about what the proportionality factor is, in order to get specific and unique predicted locations for all the units. This means that one can make a distinctly weaker assumption about the details of culture change than one might expect, and still get a specific result for seriation.

However, if Equation 5 is used to compute the predicted occurrence point of a unit in which one relatively common type and one relatively scarce type occur, one finds that the predicted point is relatively close to the predicted midpoint of the scarcer type. It seems as if concentration or bunching of the occurrences of scarce types is given too much weight, at the expense of looseness or intermittence in occurrences of more common types.

A more intuitively satisfying prediction equation comes from simply summing the ratios of predicted midpoints to numbers of occurrences, and dividing by the summed reciprocals of numbers of occurrences, without squaring anything, thus,

$$L'_U = \frac{\Sigma_i \, m_i/g_i}{\Sigma_i \, 1/g_i} \tag{6}$$

Again, L'_U is just the arithmetic mean of the predicted midpoints of all types that occur in unit U, if all these types occur in the same number of units. If they do not, L'_U is a somewhat different weighted mean than L_U: a weighted mean that gives less emphasis to concentration for scarce types. An appealing feature of L'_U is that if types A and B are the only types in unit U, and if the predicted ranges of A and B just meet (so that, if all occurrences of both A and B are consecutive, A is predicted to end just before B starts, or vice versa), the predicted occurrence point for unit U is just at this meeting point – that is, midway between the last unit where A is predicted to occur and the immediately following first unit where B is predicted to occur. Whenever A and B overlap and are the only units occurring in U, the predicted occurrence point for U will be somewhere within the range of overlap, no matter how different the abundances of A and B are.

One could consider Equations 5 and 6 to be special cases of

$$L(k)_U = \frac{\Sigma_i \, m_i/g_i^{\,k}}{\Sigma_i \, \mathrm{I}/g_i^{\,k}} \tag{7}$$

where the parameter k happens to be 2 or 1. It would be of interest to experiment with other values for k. Another variation would be to make the joint probability function not only the product of the probability of occurrence of all the types that occur in a unit, but also the probability of non-occurrence of all the types that fail to occur in the unit, and then seek the location that would maximize *this* joint probability. But the mathematics of doing this seem considerably more difficult, and it may not be worthwhile.

Notice that Equation 7 and its special cases, 5 and 6, require only the predicted midpoints derived from MDSCAL, plus the number of units in which each type occurs. They do not depend at all on any particular starting sequence, nor on any trial assumptions about the best ordering of the occurrence matrix, nor on any iterative or successive approximations method. It is desirable that the predicted midpoints be scaled in terms of numbers of units, so that the predicted occurrence points will also be in terms of units. They will commonly be expressed in terms of fractional parts of a unit (as in the far right columns of Figs. 9.8, 9.10 and 9.15), but this causes no difficulties for *ranking* units in their predicted sequence. In fact, these values could be used to infer that some units are nearly contemporaneous, or at least nearly tied in terms of the seriation, while other consecutive units may be separated by much wider seriational gaps.

Equation 6 is so simple that it would not be too difficult to compute by hand for a moderate number of units, but since the object is to make life easier, I have written a short computer program which reads in the occurrence matrix row by row in any sequence, reads in the predicted midpoints derived from MDSCAL and the numbers of units in which each type occurs (obtained at the same time the S matrix is computed for MDSCAL input), uses Equation 6

413

to compute a predicted occurrence point for each unit, sorts the units according to this predicted order of occurrence, and prints this sorted sequence as a seriation of the occurrence matrix. Judged by the numbers of zeros interspersed in the occurrence ranges of types, the results have been not quite as good as the best results from fitting units by judgement to the skeleton plot derived from the same MDSCAL results, but they are nearly as good; the differences are because the computer is actually trying to satisfy a slightly different criterion, and the program takes almost no time. On a rather slow machine (IBM 1130) it took only a few seconds to seriate the same 129 units that took me more than a day to do by the skeleton plot technique.

Fig. 9.8 shows a randomized input sequence for the occurrence matrix of Fig. 9.4, plus the seriation produced by the computer program. It is identical to the postulated true sequence of Fig. 9.4, except that (1) for reasons already discussed, unit 1 is moved next to unit 4, and (2) units 5 and 6 are reversed. This second change is slight in terms of the total sequence, but highly significant. It is a clear violation of the concentration principle; a non-petrified sequence is preferred even though a petrified sequence is in fact possible. The model behind Equation 6 leads to a criterion that is somewhat different from the Petrie criterion. The Petrie model, as formalized by Kendall, requires only that each unit should preferably occur somewhere within the ranges of consecutive occurrences of all the types which occur in the unit. The model represented by Equation 6 puts emphasis on a unit's occurring relatively near the midpoints of the ranges of the types that occur in the unit, and finds a compromise value between the contradictory demands of the different midpoints that is weighted most heavily for scarcest types. This can lead to a preference for sequences that differ a little from the Petrie ideal. It is important to realize that seriations can be judged by criteria other than the concentration criterion; in what ways, and in what circumstances these other criteria may lead to seriations which are likely to be closer to true chronologies is a matter that needs more exploration.

For a second test of the technique, I invented another occurrence matrix, consisting of fifty units and ten types, for which the 'true' sequence (Fig. 9.9) is not a Petrie matrix, but contains some zeros (blanks) interspersed in the occurrence ranges of the types. Here the same steps were followed; a matrix of similarity coefficients was computed, and a two-dimensional MDSCAL configuration was obtained and inspected. It was again linear, with low stress (0·034). Distances of predicted midpoints were scaled from the long axis of the MDSCAL configuration, and plotted against the true *mean* points of type occurrences, derived from Fig. 9.9. The resulting agreement (Fig. 9.10) was

TYPES

A	B	C	D	E	F	G	H	I	J
				1		1	1	1	
	1								
				1	1				
1	1								
				1	1				
			1	1	1				
				1	1				
				1	1	1	1		
	1	1	1	1					
	1	1		1					
							1		1
						1	1	1	
	1								
							1	1	1
				1		1		1	
							1		1
1	1								
	1	1	1	1					
				1		1	1		
				1	1	1	1		
	1			1					
							1	1	1
							1		1
							1		1
							1		1

SERIATION RESULT

A	B	C	D	E	F	G	H	I	J	BEST FIT FOR OBSERVED COMBINATION	
							1		1	39.9	40
							1		1	39.9	
							1		1	39.9	
							1		1	39.9	
							1		1	39.9	
							1	1	1	36.9	
							1	1	1	36.9	35
						1	1	1		33.3	
				1		1	1	1		31.9	30
				1		1	1			29.9	
				1		1	1			29.9	
				1	1	1	1			27.7	
				1	1	1	1			27.7	25
				1	1					23.2	
				1	1					23.2	
				1	1					23.2	
			1	1	1					21.5	
	1	1	1	1						16.6	20
	1	1	1	1						16.6	
	1			1						15.4	
	1	1		1						14.3	15
	1									11.1	
	1									11.1	
1	1									3.8	5,10
1	1									3.8	

FIG. 9.8. Randomized rearrangement of the sequence of units (rows) in the occurrence matrix of Fig. 9.4, and result obtained from re-ordering the input sequence according to the predicted midpoints from Fig. 9.6, using Equation 6 and sorting units in order of predicted occurrence points.

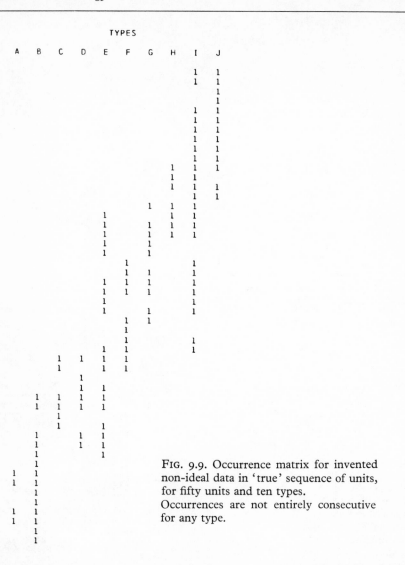

FIG. 9.9. Occurrence matrix for invented non-ideal data in 'true' sequence of units, for fifty units and ten types. Occurrences are not entirely consecutive for any type.

actually better than for the 'ideal' data of the first example. The same computer program as before was used to compute a predicted point of occurrence for each unit and to sort a randomized input matrix into this predicted sequence. The result (Fig. 9.11) is generally very similar to the 'true' sequence (Fig. 9.9) with two differences. First, all units which exhibit identical combinations of types are tied, and are listed consecutively (an inevitable consequence of any seriation technique). Second, by the Petrie criterion (as well as

416

by the criterion of Equation 6), the computer result is a distinct improvement over the 'true' sequence. That is, the occurrences of types are more nearly consecutive in Fig. 9.11 than in Fig. 9.9. The technique has been a little too successful.

Experiences like these should encourage a healthy scepticism about the detailed accuracy of any chronology based on a seriation, but they are hardly a reason for discrediting the method altogether. The sequences of Figs. 9.9 and 9.11 do not differ very much, and if one were presented with the jumble of Fig. 9.11 (top) it would be a major step toward the true chronology to

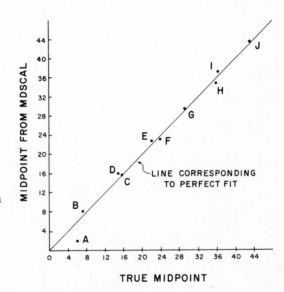

FIG. 9.10. Predicted occurrence midpoints, derived from MDSCAL results for the data of Fig. 9.9, plotted against true mean points derived directly from Fig. 9.9.

obtain the sequence of Fig. 9.11. Furthermore, if one were presented with Fig. 9.9 and not told that this in fact was the true sequence, there would be nothing in it to lead one to think it a more plausible or probable sequence than Fig. 9.11. In a situation of ignorance, it would be better to bet on Fig. 9.11. We are simply confronted with the fact that the betting odds favour the most probable sequence (assuming our probability model is a valid representation of culture change); it would not make sense to arbitrarily favour some less probable sequence; and yet we can be sure that in the real world it is not *always* the most probable event that occurs; so our most probable sequence is very apt to be untrue in some details.

Finally, how does the technique fare when confronted with some real data? I have tested it by applying it to an occurrence matrix representing fifteen

SERIATION RESULT

Fig. 9.11. Randomized rearrangement of the sequence of units (rows) in the occurrence matrix of Fig. 9.9, and result obtained from reordering the input sequence according to the predicted midpoints derived from MDSCAL, using Equation 6 and sorting units in order of predicted occurrence points.

pottery types in some 554 graves from the Hualfín valley of north-west Argentina. I am very much indebted to Dr Alberto Rex Gonzalez, who was responsible for gathering the data, doing the ceramic analyses and tabulations of materials in each grave, and keypunching of the data. I should add that since I have no expert knowledge of this material, and have not yet discussed

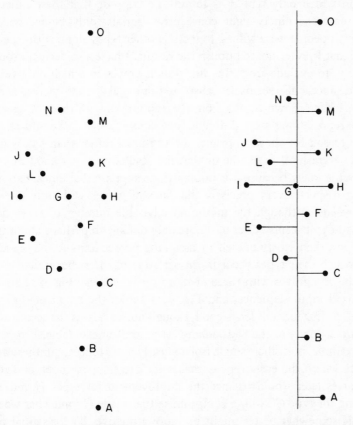

FIG. 9.12. MDSCAL configuration for data from the Hualfín Valley, Argentina, representing fifteen types and 554 units.

FIG. 9.13. Main axis and perpendiculars fitted to the configuration of Fig. 9.12, as a basis for scaling predicted occurrence midpoints.

the results in detail with Dr Gonzalez, my present results are *only* a test of the technique, and not a contribution to Andean prehistory (Dr Gonzalez and I plan to publish such a contribution elsewhere).[1]

The MDSCAL configuration for the fifteen Hualfín types is shown in Fig. 9.12. It is again quite linear, although the stress is rather high (about 0·30).

419

The line fitted to these points as a basis for scaling predicted midpoints is shown in Fig. 9.13. In the 554 graves 109 different type combinations occurred, resulting in 109 potentially seriatable intervals. The seriation derived from Equation 6 looks very good, but it includes a number of graves in which only one of the fifteen types occurs. For example, there are ninety-eight graves in which only type *F* is found. To suppose that these ninety-eight graves represent ninety-eight consecutive burials, only before which and after which people were willing to include other types along with *F*, is so unrealistic that I prefer not to publish the results. I have also decided, somewhat arbitrarily, to exclude from this illustration graves in which only two types occurred, since it also seems unrealistic to think that all these were consecutive. Instead, I have shown results from the 129 graves with three or more types present, representing sixty different type combinations. I should emphasize that the reason for showing results for 129 units rather than 554 is not that the latter were hard to handle or that the results were not good in a formal sense, but is solely because it is unrealistic to suppose that *any* seriation techniques can specify very precisely the dates of graves with only one or two types present. Although the minimum advisable number of types deserves further study, it seems better to seriate only units with perhaps about three or more types, than satisfy oneself by assigning poorer units to the broad intervals in which their types occur in the seriation of the richer units.

For the 129 graves with three or more types present, Fig. 9.14 shows the randomized input sequence, and Fig. 9.15 shows the result of seriation by Equation 6. In general it looks good, though not so tidy as the results with invented data. Many of the bad-looking cases seem unavoidable. Types *H* and *K*, for example, both show single isolated early occurrences, but these are both in graves where the early type *C* makes its latest appearances, and to place these graves later would balance the improvement for types *H* and *K* by a worsening for type *C*. Still, a compromise that made *C* somewhat worse and *H* and *K* somewhat better might be more attractive. The essential point is that, however we deal with it, we have a pair of graves here in which anomalous combinations of types occur. Perhaps some of the types have been misidentified or should be redefined, possibly a keypunch error is involved, or perhaps it is simply true that events which we think improbable nevertheless occurred.

At any rate, taking the input data as given, there is an anomaly here which no seriation technique could resolve very well, and which probably accounts in part for the fairly high stress of the MDSCAL solution (this high stress of course also suggests that, aside from using these data as a somewhat severe test

420

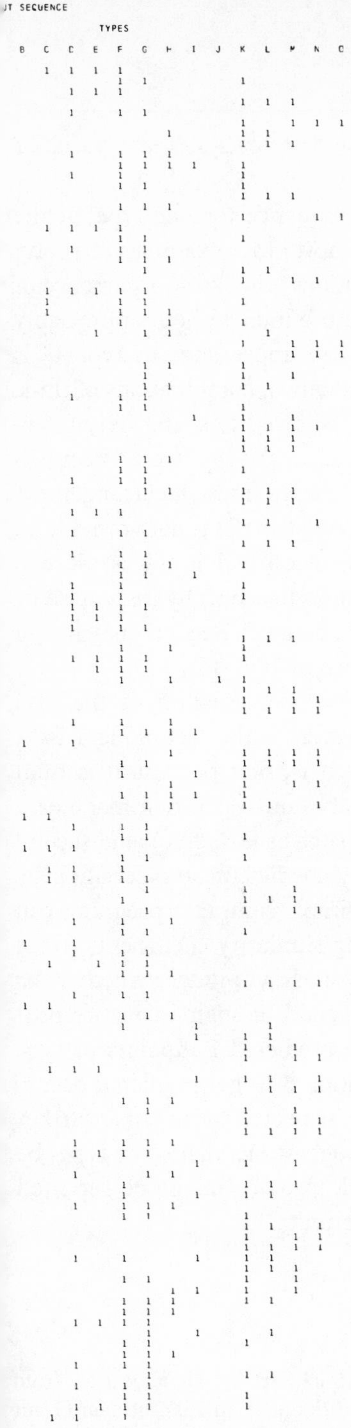

FIG. 9.14. Occurrence matrix model for e Hualfín data (129 graves with three or ore of the fifteen types present), in ran-m order of units (rows).

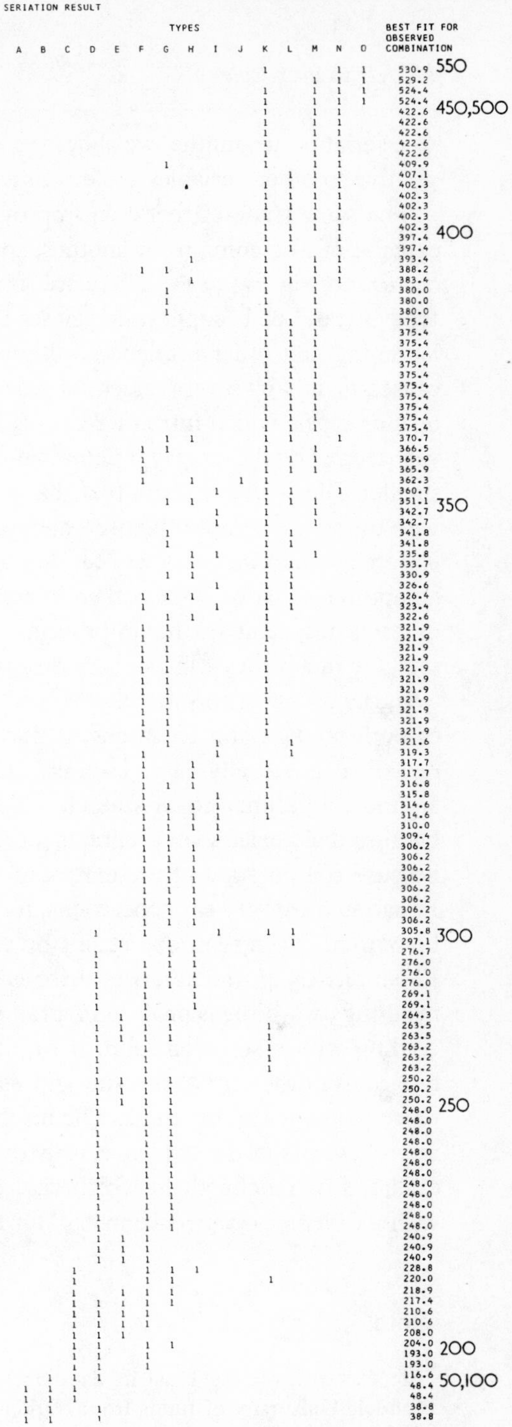

FIG. 9.15. Results obtained from reordering the sequence of Fig. 9.14, according to the predicted midpoints derived from Fig. 9.13, using Equation 6 and sorting units in order of predicted occurrence points.

of a seriation technique, we should examine the data for systematic variation relative to other variables besides time).

The same trade-off between improving the sequence for one type, at the expense of worsening it for another, applies to most other examples of spotty occurrences in Fig. 9.15. There are some exceptions; the latest occurrence of type *G* could be brought much closer to the main bunch without appreciably loosening any other sequences, although the bad appearance of type *G* is caused mainly by several blocks of graves with identical combinations of three or four types, which introduce ties. If Fig. 9.15 showed only the sixty intervals defined by the sixty type combinations that occur, the gaps would be much smaller. But I do not claim that this technique always finds the arrangement with the fewest zeros (or blanks) interspersed among the 1's. It does provide an extremely quick and easy way for deriving a sequence which is at least close to an optimal seriation. One is then in a good position to see if, by inspection or other means, some further improvement can be obtained. Readers may like to see how much they can improve on the sequence of Fig. 9.15.

In the course of this discussion of so many aspects of seriation, on the level of both method and technique, it may not seem as if the technique I have described is actually easy. I should stress that it is, first because it is built around multidimensional scaling, which is a laborious operation made easy because there exist good programs for doing it (such as MDSCAL), and second because computation of the matrix of similarity coefficients and seriation by Equation 6 are very easy operations, for which simple computer programs can be written. To repeat, one begins by computing similarity coefficients (from Equations 4*a*, 4*b* and 4*c*); uses these as input to MDSCAL; judges whether the resulting two-dimensional configuration looks good enough to justify proceeding with a seriation; and, if so, scales the predicted midpoints of type ranges from the MDSCAL result and uses Equation 6 to get predicted occurrence points for all the units. The result can be inspected for possible further improvements in the sequence, or perhaps for suggestions that some types be excluded or redefined, in which case the whole process might be repeated with a different occurrence matrix for the same units.

Notes

1 My work on the Hualfín data was supported in part by an allocation from Brandeis University of funds from National Science Foundation Institutional Grant GU2839, and in part by a grant from the Milton Fund of Harvard University. Gordon R. Willey provided valuable encouragement and assistance.

References

ASCHER, M. (1959) A mathematical rationale for graphical seriation. *American Antiquity*, **25** (2), 212–14.

ASCHER, M. and ASCHER, R. (1963) Chronological ordering by computer. *American Anthropologist*, **65** (5), 1045–52.

BORDAZ, V. VON H. and BORDAZ, J. (1970) A computer-assisted pattern recognition method of classification and seriation applied to archaeological materials. In GARDIN, J.-C. (ed.) *Archéologie et Calculateurs*, 229–44. Paris: Centre National de la Recherche Scientifique.

BRAINERD, G. W. (1951) The place of chronological ordering in archaeological analysis. *American Antiquity*, **26**, 301–13.

CLARKE, D. L. (1968) *Analytical Archaeology*. London: Methuen.

COWGILL, G. L. (1968) Review of Hole and Shaw's *Computer Analysis of Chronological Seriation. American Antiquity*, **33** (4), 517–19.

COWGILL, G. L. (1971) *Problems and Some Solutions in Seriating Large Data Sets.* Paper for Annual Meeting of the Society for American Archaeology, Norman, Oklahoma, May 1971.

DEMPSEY, P. and BAUMHOFF, M. (1963) The statistical use of artifact distributions to establish chronological sequence. *American Antiquity*, **28** (4), 496–509.

DETHLEFSEN, E. and DEETZ, J. (1966) Death's heads, cherubs and willow trees: experimental archaeology in colonial cemeteries. *American Antiquity*, **31** (4), 501–10.

DUNNELL, R. C. (1970) Seriation method and its evaluation. *American Antiquity*, **25** (3), 305–19.

FORD, J. A. (1962) *A Quantitative Method for Deriving Cultural Chronology.* Pan American Union Technical Manual No. 1. Washington D.C.: Organization of American States.

FULKERSON, D. R. and GROSS, O. A. (1965) Incidence matrices and interval graphs. *Pacific Journal of Mathematics*, **15** (3), 835–55.

GELFAND, A. E. (1971) Seriation methods for archaeological materials. *American Antiquity*, **36** (3), 263–74.

HOLE, F. and SHAW, M. (1967) Computer analysis of chronological seriation. *Rice University Studies*, **53** (3). Houston, Texas.

JOHNSON, L. JR (1968) *Item Seriation as an Aid for Elementary Scale and Cluster Analysis.* Museum of Natural History, University of Oregon, Bulletin No. 15.

KENDALL, D. G. (1963) A statistical approach to Flinders Petrie's sequence-dating. *Bull. Int. Statist. Inst.*, **40**, 657–80.

KENDALL, D. G. (1969) Some problems and methods in statistical archaeology. *World Archaeology*, **1** (1), 68–76.

KRUSKAL, J. B. (1964a) Multidimensional scaling by optimizing goodness of fit to a nonmetric hypothesis, I. *Psychometrika*, **29**, 1–27.

KRUSKAL, J. B. (1964b) Multidimensional scaling by optimizing goodness of fit to a nonmetric hypothesis, II. *Psychometrika*, **29** (2), 115–29.

KRUSKAL, J. B. and CARMONE, F. (1969) *How to use M-D-SCAL (Version 5M) and Other Useful Information.* MS., Bell Telephone Laboratories, Murray Hill, N.J.

KUZARA, R. S., MEAD, G. R. and DIXON, K. A. (1966) Seriation of anthropological data: a computer program for matrix ordering. *American Anthropologist*, **68**, 1442–55.

LIPE, W. D. (1964) Comments on Dempsey and Baumhoff's 'The statistical use of artifact distributions to establish chronological sequence'. *American Antiquity*, **30**, 103–4.

MEIGHAN, C. W. (1959) A new method for the seriation of archaeological collections. *American Antiquity*, **25**, 203–11.

RATTRAY, E. C. (1971) *A Seriation of Teotihuacan Ceramics*. Paper for the Annual Meeting of the Society for American Archaeology, Norman, Okla., May 1971.

RENFREW, C. and STERUD, G. (1969) Close-proximity analysis: a rapid method for the ordering of archaeological materials. *American Antiquity*, **34**, 265–77.

ROBINSON, W. S. (1951) A method for chronologically ordering archaeological deposits. *American Antiquity*, **16**, 293–301.

ROUSE, I. B. (1967) Seriation in archaeology. In RILEY, C. L. and TAYLOR, W. W. (eds.) *American Historical Anthropology*, 153–95. Carbondale, Ill.: Southern Illinois University Press.

ROWE, J. H. (1961) Stratigraphy and seriation. *American Antiquity*, **26** (3), 324–30.

SHEPARD, R. N. (1962) The analysis of proximities: multidimensional scaling with an unknown distance function. *Psychometrika*, **27** (2), 125–40, and (3), 219–46.

SOKAL, R. R. and SNEATH, P. H. A. (1963) *Principles of Numerical Taxonomy*. San Francisco: Freeman.

10
Computer models as tools for archaeological hypothesis formation

J. E. DORAN

S.R.C. Atlas Computer Laboratory, Didcot, Berkshire, England

Introduction

Although it is now more than a decade since digital computers were first used to process archaeological data, communication between archaeologists and computer scientists remains limited and intermittent. Given the great difference of academic training and *milieu* this is not surprising. It is understandable that computer scientists typically see archaeology as a remote and probably uninteresting field of application for their expertise, and that archaeologists typically expect nothing from computers but a tidal wave of unintelligible and ultimately valueless figures. However, what is understandable is not necessarily what is good. There is surely a real danger that potentially fertile interactions between archaeology and computer science will be missed or delayed, not because they have been considered and rejected as unpromising, but because there has never been a sufficient degree of communication between the two subjects for them to be considered at all.

There is therefore a need for rather broad attempts to relate archaeological problems to different aspects of computer science, both theoretical and practical. My discussion in this chapter is perhaps best seen in this light. I shall begin with some background remarks concerning the history and present state of computer science and computer archaeology. I shall then examine one of the most adventurous and potentially important areas of computer science research, that directed towards the automatic generation of hypotheses and theories, and try to see how the new concepts and techniques being explored there may come to be of service to archaeologists.

Computers and computer science

The first examples of digital computers, as we now know them, were built between twenty and thirty years ago. Extremely crude though they were by

425

present-day standards, they possessed certain crucial features. They were fully electronic. They could store numbers and perform the elementary arithmetic operations upon them at high speed. And they could be programmed – that is, they could be told the sequence of operations that made up a complex calculation, and then they could perform the calculation without further human intervention.

Since that time the power and the reliability of the machinery has been greatly increased. For example, both the speed at which a computation can be performed, and the quantity of information that the machine can store in its (direct access) memory have been increased by a factor of over a thousand in the latest models. These are, however, merely the 'top end' of a great range of computing machinery corresponding to the ramifications of demand and technological development. In addition, ancillary equipment of many kinds is now attached to computers in order to enlarge their capabilities. This includes for example, television cameras and C.R.T. displays, which make possible visual communication with the machine.

In spite of these developments the essential nature of a digital computer has not changed at the machinery level. There is a repertoire of extremely simple *machine instructions*, which the machine can obey sequentially under the control of an instruction list: a *program*. This is written out by the user and stored in the machine's memory alongside the 'data' that it is to manipulate. Only a minority of the machine instructions are directly concerned with arithmetic. Some specify purely logical operations. Many are concerned with the storage and retrieval of numbers or symbols, and others again with the tests and shifts of control which make it possible for a comparatively short program to specify an extremely long and complex computation.

Writing a program for a computer in order to make it perform some useful task is a fascinating but time-consuming business. The job to be done must be broken down into steps corresponding to the machine's primitive capabilities. The program must be precise and comprehensive, for the machinery will never 'understand' what the programmer means, nor 'guess' what he forgot to say.

A substantial part of computer science is ultimately concerned with making it easier for the computer user to write programs. A key development is the creation of artificially defined, relatively human-oriented programming languages such as ALGOL and FORTRAN. Such languages enable the programmer to specify what he wants done without going into quite the intricate detail necessary at the level of machine instructions. The machine can obey programs written in such languages because complex translator programs,

426

compilers, take the 'high-level' commands written by the programmer and convert them into sets of machine instructions. The compilers themselves are, of course, written at the machine instruction level.

A more recent development is the spread of multi-access and interactive computing. The key step here is that extremely complex 'systems' programs are written which, with the help of special machinery, make one large computer serve a wide range of users more or less simultaneously. The users program the machine and provide it with data for its computations by way of 'on-line' electric typewriters or *consoles*. A close analogy is the chess master who takes on twenty or thirty opponents at the same time. From the user's point of view, the benefit of this arrangement is that he has most of the capabilities of a large machine at his finger tips – a mode of computer usage that would be intolerably wasteful were the machine not able to serve someone else while one user dithers! In addition, it is often possible for a user to communicate with his program whilst the machine is obeying it. Such 'on-line' interaction makes computer usage much more flexible and convenient.

The effect of these and other developments – and I have only touched upon the most important – is to make it feasible to program a computer to perform a far wider range of tasks than was at first realized. In the early days computers were used to carry out calculations that had previously been done by hand. Typically these were calculations occurring in applied mathematics or statistics. For example, one of the earliest uses of a computer was to calculate artillery tables for the United States Army. Such calculations would normally be derived from some body of mathematical theory – for example, the theory of differential equations.

At a fairly early stage, however, it became apparent that computers could be programmed not only to perform calculations that had previously been done by hand or desk machine, but also calculations that were so tedious that they had never seriously been considered before, and for which there was no mathematical theory at all. An example is the growth of computer procedures for the construction of hierarchical classifications. Most of the programs written to construct such classifications by one method or another have had virtually no mathematical theory behind them. It is only recently that the mathematicians have really begun to come into the picture.

An even more important development is the realization that not only can computers be programmed to do things that are not in the standard mathematical and statistical repertoire, they can also be programmed to do things that have nothing to do with 'numbers' or 'arithmetic' or 'mathematics' at all. Thus we are coming to understand how to have a computer translate from Russian into English, or compose music, or tell us what it 'sees' through a television camera. Such programs are written in general 'information processing' languages, where the ability of the machine to do arithmetic is much less important than its ability to store and manipulate general information structures.

It follows that the potential scope for computer application is extremely wide. Even now we find that, in addition to governmental and commercial applications, there are very few academic or artistic fields that do not have some kind or other of computer work associated with them. While some of these applications are still of a very elementary kind and of no real importance, it seems unrealistic to expect them to remain so.

Computers and models

One of the more important uses of computers has been as an aid to scientific modelling. The general concept of a model is a subtle one and has aroused considerable philosophical and logical interest (see for example Byerly, 1969). Mathematical model building, often making use of computers, is rather more clear cut. Excellent general discussions are those of Kendall (1968) and Brennan (1968).

A limited view of modelling, which will nevertheless suffice for our purposes, is as follows. We are concerned with real-world entities which have a compound structure and which change with the passage of time. Examples are everywhere: a butterfly, the weather over Europe, China, current political opinion. Such entities we can call systems. Now suppose that there is a system which we can observe in a variety of ways, and the future course of which we wish to predict. Often we wish to go further and control the system, deflecting its course to our own advantage. One approach to these objectives is to set up a 'model' – that is, a system that we have ourselves created, which as far as possible mirrors those behavioural characteristics of the target system that we regard as important. We then answer our questions about the target system by studying or *experimenting* with the model. It is in this spirit that one constructs physical models of new aircraft, or mathematical models of the United Kingdom economy.

The mathematical model of the latter example would typically be formed of a set of mathematical equations expressing the ways in which a variety of economic variables influence one another and change with time. It might or might not have a stochastic element – that is, explicitly include a chance factor. The model might be capable of being 'solved', meaning that its behaviour can be worked out mathematically, or it might have to be used as a 'simulation', meaning that the model is set up in some particular way and then 'let loose' while we record its behaviour. For a simulation, the 'book-keeping' required is so complex and tedious that the use of a computer is usually essential. There are programming languages designed for such work. If the model can be solved mathematically, then a computer may or may not be required, depending upon the complexity of the solution process itself.

As the preceding remarks indicate, the usual practice is first to formulate a mathematical model of the target system, and then to write a computer program which solves or simulates the model. There are situations, however, where no mathematical model will suffice, but where a computer program can *itself* stand as a model. I shall call such models *program models*.

Important examples of program models are those formulated by experimental psychologists. Mathematical models can mimic the behaviour of animals and human beings only in very restricted contexts. A computer program, which is a much more flexible system than can be described by a set of mathematical equations, can do much more. The best known such psychological program model is the 'General Problem Solver' program of Newell and Simon (1963), which seeks to model human problem-solving behaviour.

We should pause a moment to consider the *explanatory* value of a model, in contrast to its predictive power. To the extent that a model captures everything of importance that is known about a target system, including the latter's behaviour, and is such that its own behaviour is intelligible, then it constitutes an explanation of the target system. Consider, for example, a simple demonstration model of a steam engine of the type found in museums. Mathematical models are rarely explanatory in this way – there are almost always aspects of the targets system which they omit as unimportant for the limited purpose of prediction but which must be included in any explanation. Interestingly enough, program models have sometimes been criticized as explanatory models on the grounds, not that they fail to mirror the target system, but that they are themselves too complex to be fully grasped.

Computers and intelligence

The foregoing implication that it is in principle quite possible to write a computer program to model human thought processes perhaps needs a little more discussion. The reader may feel that machines cannot think, or that the human brain or mind can never be modelled to any substantial degree.

The situation is as follows. At the level of philosophical debate the issue of 'thinking machines' has been one for ramified and inconclusive argument. However, a famous paper by Turing (1963) probably expresses the point of view of most interested computer scientists. In it Turing rejects one by one the variety of arguments put forward to deny the possibility of a thinking machine. In practice, very real progress has been made towards the goal of programming a computer to behave intelligently – uncertain and still distant though that goal is. Thus there are programs that play chess and draughts to a very respectable standard (to a higher standard than that of the programmer), solve conventional intelligence tests, 'learn' and 'plan ahead' in a variety of ways, and prove quite difficult mathematical theorems (Feigenbaum, 1969). In each case the program behaves in an 'intelligent' rather than 'machine-like' way. There seems no reason to doubt that progress will continue to be made, and that ultimately we shall possess both a theory of intelligent behaviour and the means to create a wide variety of intelligent machines. That this is not a fanciful view of the future is indicated by the very real governmental support being given to such research work both in the U.S.A. and in the U.S.S.R.

Computers and archaeology

Having looked very briefly at the history and current status of computers and computer science, we are now in a position to see in perspective the attempts that have been made to put computers to work in archaeology. I shall not, however, attempt a detailed survey of the development of computer archaeology over the last ten years. There is an excellent survey available (Cowgill, 1967), and conferences have brought together much of the more recent work (Gardin, 1970; Hodson, Kendall and Tautu, 1971). We should, however, note the main types of project that have been, and are being, conducted. They involve:

(*a*) The use of relatively standard techniques drawn from the statistical repertoire, such as regression analysis and factor analysis.

(*b*) The use of newly developed multivariate techniques such as cluster analysis and other forms of numerical taxonomy, and non-metric multidimensional scaling.

(*c*) The use of *ad hoc* techniques to sequence or 'seriate' archaeological data units, often with some idea of recovering chronology.

(*d*) The creation of computer-based archaeological data banks – including therein the formulation of standard archaeological codes.

This is by no means a clear-cut classification, and it is not difficult to find projects falling within more than one category. For example, there have been a number of attempts to combine automatic classification and seriation techniques.

The statistical projects of types (*a*) and (*b*) are ultimately directed at the provision of precise and objective methods for the discovery of significant patterns, or 'structure', in large bodies of archaeological data. The use of multivariate statistical methods in this way is akin to that common in the biological and social sciences. Seriation projects, type (*c*), involve problems more peculiarly archaeological, but even so it is not difficult to find analogous problems and solution procedures elsewhere.

Individual projects of these kinds have often been judged successful, and reasonably so, but the totality of such work is not itself very impressive. There is little feeling of coherent advance – rather a series of particular experiments arising out of particular needs or interests. It is only the most recent work that seems to be building upon the successes and failures of the past. Again, interest has often centred upon the evaluation of methods, with new archaeological insights being of secondary importance. In such cases success means using a new method merely to reach old conclusions. It is certainly true that 'nothing done so far has convinced the archaeological profession as a whole that there are any often encountered tasks or problems for which computers are to be used as a matter of course; that there are tasks for which it would show incompetence *not* to use a computer' (Cowgill, 1967, p. 331).

Projects of types (*a*), (*b*) and (*c*), although impossible without use of a computer, are of only limited interest to a computer scientist. The reason is simple – such projects use the machine in an elementary and almost 'old-fashioned' way. The more recent work directed towards the formation of computerized data banks (Chenhall, 1970) has a much more interesting potential. There are several reasons for this. Firstly, such data banks fit naturally into the world of multi-access and interactive computing. Secondly, they are likely to *absorb* work of a more routine statistical nature as they come to be directly supported by, or to have immediate access to, libraries of statistical programs. Finally, and most important, since data bank projects involve keeping on the machine a wide range of archaeological information, they encourage consideration of the machine's general information processing ability rather than merely its 'number-crunching' ability. This is, admittedly, a matter of potential rather than current practice. At the moment data bank projects are engrossed either with the difficult task of determining how best to code and handle the records of archaeological surveys or museum collections,

431

or with the laborious business of getting a particular body of data into machine readable form.

New concepts in archaeology

The use of mathematical, statistical and computer methods to aid the interpretation of archaeological data is, of course, but one part of the 'new' archaeology. There is no doubt that many archaeologists, observing the spread of new concepts and methods into subjects such as anthropology, geography and geology, have themselves begun to be critical of traditional procedures, and to look hopefully to a variety of more formally based disciplines and sciences. Part of the motivation is certainly a feeling that, without new tools, the archaeologist will be unable to make anything like full use of the steadily increasing quantity and diversity of excavation and other evidence becoming available to him.

The concept of a model is central to much current archaeological thinking, as this volume witnesses. Clarke (1968), in his encyclopaedic 'new frontier' work *Analytical Archaeology*, uses the model concept ubiquitously. In addition, he calls upon concepts drawn from a wide variety of subjects, ranging from those with virtually no formal structure, such as general systems theory and psychology, through those that are partially formalized such as linguistics, to branches of applied mathematics such as game theory and information theory. Prominent among many other examples of this search for new ideas and methods is the interest in information theory of some Russian archaeologists (Marshak, 1965; Kovalevskaja, 1970) and the linguistic models considered for use in archaeology by Hymes (1970) and others. Much effort has been expended in trying to understand or model the nature of archaeological procedure itself (for example Clarke, 1968, pp. 34–35; Fritz and Plog, 1970).

These examples are too few to capture the flavour of what sometimes seems akin to a rush to stake claims in a newly discovered and probably rich goldfield! It is easy to be critical, to point out that analogies can be intriguing without being helpful, and that translating an old problem into a new conceptual framework will not necessarily help with its solution (Doran, 1970a). A vigorous and often telling attack upon some of the weaknesses of the new archaeology is that of Bayard (1969). In particular he criticizes the tendency, as he sees it, to formulate theory without adequately founding it upon data: 'It is my belief that theory is developed through generalizations from the data, and it is not imposed upon them. . . . Archaeology . . . cannot achieve theoretical rigour through the triumph of the will' (Bayard, 1969, p. 380).

432

There is every reason to hope that what will ultimately emerge from the present ferment in archaeology is an agreed interpretative procedure with a set of powerful and rigorous tools at its disposal. But Bayard is surely right to stress that such a procedure can only be proved meaningful, rather than an involved flight of theoretical fancy, when it has been shown to be effective on a wide range of archaeological data. It is in a similarly sceptical spirit that the reader should approach the remainder of this chapter.

Archaeological hypothesis formation

Having looked briefly at the contemporary scene in both computer science and the 'new' archaeology, we must now turn to the main topic of this chapter, the process by which archaeologists move from a given body of evidence to a simple or compound hypothesis that explains that evidence. The manner in which archaeological theories and hypotheses are formed and tested has often been discussed in general terms, notably by Clarke (1968, pp. 641-7). I shall approach the topic from a computer science standpoint, in a particular context, and in some detail.

A brief look at terminology is necessary. Words such as 'hypothesis', 'theory', 'model', 'explanation', 'description' and 'law' have meanings that overlap and shift with context. Fortunately we can avoid most of the complications. I have already indicated the way in which I am using the word 'model'. I shall use 'hypothesis' with a conventional meaning, but always keeping in mind that a hypothesis is part of a reasoning process seeking to explain a body of evidence or observations. I shall use the term 'compound hypothesis' for a hypothesis with a variety of different strands to it. The actual form of a compound hypothesis might well be such that from a different viewpoint it would be called a 'theory' or a 'model'.

The archaeologist forms explanatory hypotheses at all stages of his work: when sorting out and interpreting the layers and features in a trench, when piecing together the rise and fall of a settlement and its relationship to the surrounding countryside, when tracing trade routes, when trying to establish the origins of some particular object such as the great *krater* of Vix. Probably no one would dispute that the mental faculties put to work in all these instances have much in common, nor would anyone assert that they are peculiar to archaeology. What *is* peculiar to archaeology is the frequency with which certain patterns of reasoning are called upon, and the wide range of information that may be brought to bear on any particular occasion. This latter can be

433

divided between three broad categories:

(*a*) Detailed evidence derived from the excavation, say, under consideration, including descriptions of artefacts, statements of association between artefacts, stratigraphical relationships, radiocarbon dates, bone counts and so on.

(*b*) Background archaeological knowledge – for example, the total of what has been learned from other relevant excavations, and such special knowledge as the time it takes for a ditch to silt or a coin to become very worn.

(*c*) General knowledge – for example, of such everyday matters as the uses to which human beings put cups, swords and buildings, and of the properties of fire.

The point I wish to stress here is that in all but the simplest situations archaeological hypotheses ultimately rest upon a great diversity of evidence whose complexity is comparable to that of the world around us. The implication is a simple one. Any aid to archaeological hypothesis formation that is incapable of handling a diversity of evidence will be effective only in a small and peripheral range of situations. This limitation seems to apply with some force to traditional mathematical and statistical methods. Such methods all work from one or more initial data matrices. This means in practice that the information of which they make use is only the 'tidy' part of that actually available – or alternatively the data are assumed to be what they are not in order to make them 'tidy'. Thus it may be assumed that a set of measurements all have equal significance even though it is obvious that they do not, or the hierarchical structure of an artefact may be ignored. Computer information processing, by contrast, can work from much more general data structures as the newer programming languages such as POP 2 and ALGOL 68 make explicit. It is this ability to handle general data structures that makes the computer so powerful a tool even beyond the point at which traditional mathematical and statistical procedures begin to falter.

Automatic hypothesis formation

Computer scientists and mathematical logicians have recently begun to investigate the precise mechanics of induction and hypothesis formation. Although it is too early for a great deal of progress to have been made, certain things are becoming clear. Firstly, any totally negative statement to the effect that there is a creative part of the mind that can never be understood or copied seems highly suspect. Meltzer (1970) has rejected such a view as evasive, and has shown how the application of very simple rules of abstraction and generalization can lead to the 'discovery' of advanced mathematical concepts. Secondly, it is important to distinguish between the range of alternative, or *candidate*, hypotheses of which a reasoner (human or machine) can conceive, and the process by which one particular candidate hypothesis is selected as the 'best' one. The range of candidate hypotheses available is a property of the reasoner, not of the problem. It is determined by the richness of the language or conceptual framework possessed by the reasoner. When the reasoner needs a hypothesis, he or it searches for a good one among the available candidates. Of course, only a few of the candidate hypotheses are ever 'in mind' simultaneously.

An important example of a computer program that generates explanatory hypotheses is that called HEURISTIC DENDRAL. It 'can formulate hypotheses from a given set of scientific data. The data consist of the mass spectrum and the empirical formula of an organic chemical compound. The hypotheses which are produced describe molecular structures which are plausible explanations of the data' (Buchanan, Sutherland and Feigenbaum, 1969, p. 209). Figure 10.1 is a flow chart of HEURISTIC DENDRAL. It is worth stressing that this program, within its domain of operation, can perform as well as graduate students and post-doctoral fellows. Some of the philosophical implications of this capability have been discussed in a paper by Churchman and Buchanan (1969).

A very substantial body of work in this general area is that of Amarel. Over a period of many years he has made a detailed study of the formal properties of problems and problem solving, including therein problems involving the generation of hypotheses and theories. In a recent paper he introduces as follows the facet of his work of most relevance here:

A theory in an empirical science emerges from a body of observed correspondences and has the function of an intellectual mechanism for explaining and predicting in the science. The theory evolves from a succession of hypotheses that are tested against experience, and it attains a degree of stability after it explains with reasonable consistency the given body of observations. The form of a hypothesis capable of emerging in a scientific culture depends on the language, the basic concepts, and the schemas that are available in the culture. (Amarel, 1971, p. 412)

435

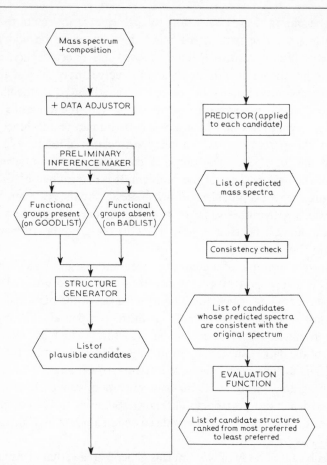

FIG. 10.1. Flow chart of the computer program HEURISTIC DENDRAL which generates explanatory hypotheses in organic chemistry. The program first uses the experimental data to generate plausible candidate hypotheses (molecular structure) and then
for each of these predicts the data that would have been obtained were it true. The
hypotheses are ranked by the agreement between the predicted data and the actual
data. There is a close correspondence with the processes by which archaeological
hypotheses are formed and tested (see Doran, 1972, flow chart from Buchanan,
Sutherland and Feigenbaum, 1969).

He argues convincingly that:

The main problem in the design of procedures for solving [hypothesis]
formation problems are:

(1) Selection of appropriate descriptions for the language in which
candidate solutions [hypotheses] are to be represented.

436

(2) Formulation of evaluation procedures for ordering candidate solutions according to their performance *vis-à-vis* the desired goal.

(3) Formulation of control strategies for directing intelligent searches in solution space [that is, the set of candidate hypotheses].

The problems of representation, evaluation and control are closely coupled; however, dominant among them is the problem of representation. (Amarel, 1971, p. 417; the words in brackets have been added)

These three problems of *representation*, *evaluation* and *search organization* have immediate significance for the archaeologist. The representation problem is that of selecting the conceptual or formal framework within which the hypothesis is to be expressed. What is needed is a mode of expression that is both general and such that it gives prominence to the key characteristics of a hypothesis rather than to details of minor importance. This problem is at the heart of the search for a 'new' archaeology. The evaluation problem is that of deciding how the adequacy of a hypothesis should be measured in practice. Clearly this problem will be easier to solve if a good solution has been found to the first. Finally, the search organization problem is, of course, that of deciding how best to organize the formation and rejection of candidate hypotheses so that the search rapidly 'homes in' on the best. Again, a good solution to the representation problem may be a crucial prerequisite of success.

It would be out of place to describe Amarel's detailed work here. It must suffice to say that he has studied these three general problems, their form and solution, in a range of specific task situations including the design of automatic program writing procedures.

The lessons to be learned from this brief look at work on automatic hypothesis formation are that it *is* possible to automate such reasoning processes, and that the foundations of a theory have been put down.

The La Tène cemetery at Münsingen-Rain

We have noted that the formation of explanatory hypotheses is fundamental to archaeology, and also that computer scientists are beginning to understand how to automate such reasoning processes. It is natural to ask what the practical implications of these two facts, put together, might be. At the present time this question can only be answered in barest outline. Nevertheless, let us try to see what automatic hypothesis formation might involve in the context of a particular archeological site, the La Tène cemetery at Münsingen-Rain.

437

This cemetery makes a convenient test case, partly because it is comparatively simple, and partly because much computer work is already associated with it.

The Münsingen cemetery is prominent among La Tène sites, and is important for our general understanding of that part of the European Iron Age (Hodson, 1964). Excavated in the early years of this century, it comprised some 200 graves, some rich and some barren, spread along a gravel terrace. The main information available for each grave is its location, orientation and depth; an estimate of the age and sex of the inhumation (available in many but not all cases); and descriptions of the grave goods associated with the burial – jewellery, weapons, etc. There is no vertical stratigraphy, but at a very early stage it became clear from the layout of the graves, and the distribution of chronologically significant artefact types, that there was a rough horizontal stratigraphy in the sense that the cemetery expanded from one end of the ridge to the other.

Data drawn from Münsingen have been used in a number of computer experiments (Doran, 1971). Interest has centred on the task of finding a computational procedure which, given only a statement of the artefact types present in each grave, will reconstruct the true chronological sequence in which the graves were created (Kendall, 1971). Of course, this true chronological sequence is unknown, so that the results of the various procedures tried have been measured against a best estimate of the true sequence obtained by a thorough conventional archaeological analysis (Hodson, 1968). Typically these comparisons have shown a very encouraging measure of agreement.

It is instructive to regard this task as an exercise in automatic hypothesis formation, with the range of candidate hypotheses being the choice of possible grave sequences. Amarel's concepts of representation, evaluation and search organization (see above) make immediate sense, though they have not always been distinguished in the actual work. Hypotheses have normally been regarded as permutations and handled accordingly. Evaluation of candidate hypotheses has been based upon the assumption that a particular type of artefact will probably occur only in relatively contemporaneous graves. The evaluation procedure has sometimes been made explicit, but not always.

Most attention has been given to the problem of how best to search through the candidate hypotheses – that is, the alternative grave sequences. The number of possible alternatives is extremely large, much too large for even the most powerful computer to consider all of them. In practice, all the search strategies used on this and similar problems, including some making use of multidimensional scaling, have concentrated on how best to move from one candidate hypothesis to a better one, and have given up when no small-scale

438

adjustment of the current hypothesis would yield an improvement. The effect has been to make the computation feasible, but to make it possible that the hypothesis ultimately chosen will be not quite the best available. For details, the reader should consult the papers cited.

Limited and somewhat artificial though it is, this Münsingen grave-sequencing work does serve as an initial illustration of what form automatic hypothesis formation can take in an archaeological context.

AN INITIAL MODEL FOR THE MÜNSINGEN CEMETERY

The task of recovering the true chronological sequence of the Münsingen graves is merely part of the wider problem of interpreting the cemetery as a whole, and of integrating it into the general picture that has been built up for the La Tène period. To have any chance of achieving these wider goals, one must obviously take into account not merely the types of the grave goods, but all the available evidence including, for example, the orientation of the graves, the nature of the burials where known, and external parallels for the grave goods. This means that one has crossed what Moberg (1971) has called the 'threshold of multitype-relations'. One is dealing with a variety of entities, with a variety of relationships between them.

Suppose now that we wish to learn how to automate the formation of archaeological hypotheses at this level of complexity. Then a promising initial strategy is to model both the human system that gave rise to the Münsingen cemetery as excavated, a settlement evolving over a period of hundreds of years, perhaps, *and* the archaeologist working back from the excavation evidence to that system. By applying the latter model to artificial data generated by the former we can begin our investigation with all the variables under experimental control. When we have achieved full understanding of these models and their interaction, then we can attempt to apply what we have learned to real archaeological data.

This is, of course, modelling with a vengeance. Is it possible that even program models can capture to a useful degree the essential features of the origins of a cemetery on the one hand, and of the reasoning of the archaeologists who study it on the other? I believe that they can. It would certainly be foolish to assume that they cannot – virtually the whole history of scientific modelling, and beyond that of mathematics itself, testifies to the ability of one system to express the essence of another far larger and far more intricate.

First let us consider the task of creating a 'cemetery' model which generates excavation data comparable to those obtained from the Münsingen cemetery. Ideally such a model would encompass all the important aspects of the human

439

systems of which such cemeteries are the product, touching as appropriate upon chronology, burial practice, social structure, technological competence, mode of subsistence and so on. To attempt a model of such generality is out of the question at the present time. Fortunately, the limited evidence available from the Münsingen excavation would in any case restrict us to much narrower conclusions. The following model, based on simple mathematical and statistical concepts, has enough complexity to be interesting and relevant, but not so much as to be unusable.

We envisage a small human population, together with the set of artefacts that they possess. Both the population and the artefact set change with the passage of time as they lose old members and gain new ones. A person is characterized by sex, age and social status, and an artefact by a hierarchy of measurements and features. When an artefact is created it is imperfectly derived from one of a set of artefact models (models within models!) which represent the artisan's 'concepts' or 'ideals', and which themselves evolve with the passage of time.

From time to time graves are formed. This means selecting a person, a set of artefacts from those in circulation, and the location and form of the grave itself. A partial list of partial descriptions of such graves, arbitrarily ordered, comprises an *excavation record* corresponding, for example, to that obtained from the Münsingen excavation.

As this model stands it is very vague. It can be made mathematically complete by specifying the missing details in precise but relatively simple mathematical terms. We could, for example, specify that the average number of graves to be formed in a time unit is three, with the number in any particular time unit being selected according to the Poisson distribution. Again we could specify that, when an artefact is generated from an artefact model, each of its dimensions is chosen with the mean value of the corresponding model dimension, but with a small error distributed according to the Gaussian distribution. The number of possible detailed specifications of this type is extremely large. The behaviour of the model (that is, the excavation record generated) will vary enormously as different choices are made. This will be in addition to the variation caused by the random variables necessarily involved.

A detailed specification of the model is too complex to be solved mathematically, and must be simulated as a program model. A simple version has, in.fact, been embodied in a computer program without great difficulty (Fig. 10.2). It is an interesting and important property of this simulation program that, although the main lines of the model are fixed by the user, it is left to the program itself to set the mathematical details by selecting at random from a wide range of alternatives. For example, the program, not the experimenter, selects the number of artefact models in use, the accuracy with which a new artefact mirrors the model from which it was derived, and the rate of turn-over of artefacts. And it is the program that selects the plan, or lack of it, according to which the cemetery is laid out. The effect of incorporating this additional choice capability in the simulation program is that it can be made to generate an excavation record based on a complex model many of whose properties are not known to the experimenter (although they can be later re-covered if need be).

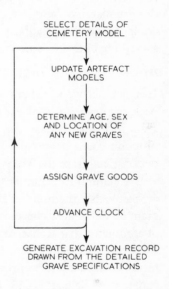

FIG. 10.2. Flow chart of a computer pro-gram which simulates the formation of cemeteries such as that of the La Tène period at Münsingen-Rain. The function of the program is to generate test data for experimental inference programs.

This simulation program is useful on three grounds. Firstly, it permits the overall behaviour of the cemetery model to be studied. Secondly, it can be used to generate artificial excavation records, with a known source, so pro-viding test data for hypothesis generating programs. Finally, it precisely *defines* a set of candidate hypotheses – the various detailed specifications of the model which it permits – for such cemeteries as that at Münsingen.

Before turning to the problem of how to construct the complementary model, that of the investigating archaeologist, some consideration should be given to this cemetery model's general archaeological adequacy. Could a description of the origins of the Münsingen cemetery, which takes into ac-count only the factors embodied in the model, be of any value? I believe that the answer is certainly 'yes', primarily because the model potentially allows us to consider, and to consider in a detailed mathematical way, the nature and evolution of the artefact models and their relationship to the social structure of the population. Some or all of the artefact models involved would, of course, correspond to already established La Tène types. More generally, there is no reason why the details of the model should not be specified having regard to general La Tène knowledge.

The prominent role of artefact models within the cemetery model will not appeal to all archaeologists. My own view is that artisans work within a cultural tradition, itself bounded by functional and technological constraints, and that to ignore this is a simplification likely to give more trouble than it avoids (for comparable views see, for example, Marshak, 1965; Rouse, 1970). The artefact models that appear in the cemetery model are an attempt to capture something of this tradition.

MODELLING THE ARCHAEOLOGIST

How should we set about writing a computer program capable of working back from an artificial excavation record generated by the simulation program just described, to the details of the model which it embodied? Such a program could potentially be applied not only to artificial data, but also to data derived from the Münsingen cemetery and similar cemeteries.

It is natural to begin by trying to imitate the procedures followed by the archaeologists themselves: that is, explicitly to try to construct a crude program model of an archaeologist. In practice this means that we note the kinds of arguments that archaeologists employ, and then try to put these together to form an effective program. In the particular context of the Münsingen cemetery, the most useful sources are Hodson's (1968) discussion of chronology, and that of Schaaff (1966) concerning burial practice. It is worth stressing that we are concerned with the nature of the arguments that these authors have used, rather than with the accuracy of their conclusions.

The most important questions a hypothesis generating program must try to answer are the following:

(*a*) What was the relative and absolute chronology of the graves, or of different parts of the cemetery?

(*b*) What rules or 'customs' were followed when the graves were positioned?

(*c*) What artefact models were current, and how did they change through the life of the cemetery?

(*d*) What systematic patterns were there in the association of grave goods with burials, and how did these vary with sex, age and date of burial?

These questions cannot be answered independently of one another. Thus the chronology we assign to the cemetery may well influence and in turn depend upon any decision about burial practices. Similarly the artefact models we identify will be bound up both with chronology and patterns of grave goods.

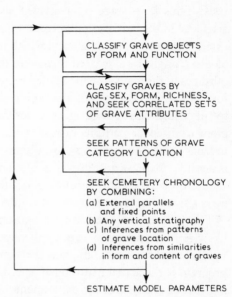

FIG. 10.3. Preliminary flow chart for a computer program able to interpret the cemetery excavation records generated by the simulation program of Fig. 10.2.

An analysis designed to answer these questions, as far as the available evidence will permit, might be divided into the following successive stages some of which might be omitted in particular circumstances (Fig. 10.3):

(i) Classify grave objects by function and form, taking into account any pre-existing classification.

(ii) Classify graves by age and sex of burial, and by form.

(iii) Seek sets of grave objects associated with particular classes of grave.

(iv) Use the result of (iii) to classify graves previously uncertain. ·

(v) Decide the basis upon which the cemetery has been laid out – at random, by family groups, etc.

(vi) Use any absolute dates, outside parallels, or vertical stratigraphy, together with the results of (v), to set up an outline chronology.

(vii) Use similarities in the form and contents of the graves to refine the chronology, within the framework of the grave classification.

(viii) Estimate parameter values (rates of change, etc.) as far as possible.

(ix) Put together the final compound hypothesis, with main alternatives.

443

There should be no great difficulty in having a computer program go through each of these stages. This is not, however, saying very much. The difficulty and interest lies in having the program reach 'sound' conclusions.

A problem that one can easily foresee is that the program would tend to become irretrievably committed to a mistaken view at an early stage in the analysis. Thus if in stage (i) it arrived at an unfortunate classification of the artefacts in the excavation record, then the whole analysis might well be utterly wrecked. This tendency, which is surely not unknown among archaeologists, might be alleviated by having the program repeat any stage or group of stages in the analysis which failed to produce useful or clear-cut answers. If, for example, no patterns of association were found in stage (iii) then stages (i) to (iii) could be repeated using different criteria. This should help the program to discover patterns of real significance, though there might also be a tendency for the program to 'discover' patterns not really there. More generally, there seems little doubt that to be most effective the program should cycle repeatedly through particular stages or sets of stages, so that the earlier stages can benefit from the results of the later.

The problem of premature commitment, in some shape or form, seems likely to be dominant as regards the analysis of excavation records generated by the simulation program, and the same may be true for an analysis by the program of the actual Münsingen data. How far the problem can be overcome in practice is a matter for experimentation. For cemeteries other than Münsingen and those very similar to it, another more fundamental problem is bound to appear. This is the problem of how to enable the program to cope with the diversity of kinds of evidence that may be relevant, and the very wide range of possibilities that exist in reality even within the limiting framework of the general cemetery model.

'On-line' collaboration between the program and an archaeologist would help with this latter problem. The archaeologist could compensate for the program's failings by directing it at points of potential error. Although it might seem that this would destroy any hope that the program would ever produce anything 'original', this is not the case. The originality of such a program would lie in its ability to combine unoriginal elements of hypotheses into a quite new compound whole. The intervention of the archaeologist or an experimenter at particular points in the formation process need not prevent a final outcome that he had not foreseen, although it might indeed make such an outcome that much less likely.

However, there is a point beyond which copying the archaeologist may cease to be profitable, even if reasonable solutions can be found to these pro-

444

blems. Pushed to its limit such a strategy seems likely to yield a hypothesis generating program, which, while inevitably failing to match the archaeologist in range of knowledge and insight, would retain all too many of his failings when it came to working with large quantities of diverse, detailed and conflicting evidence. Informative though such a program would certainly be, it is plausible that we can do better in the long run by following a different strategy. (Note: a simple program has now been written for Fig. 10.3.)

A theory of archaeological hypothesis formation?

An alternative but potentially much more difficult strategy to that of constructing a crude program model of the archaeologist is to make use of the ongoing work of Amarel and others to set up a solid *theory* of archaeological hypothesis formation, such that experimental computer programs can be written by reference to it. It is much too early to advance very far along these lines, but we can note one or two general points, and identify some of the more immediate problems.

A preliminary question concerns the extent to which, when developing such a theory, one can usefully draw upon the philosophy of the scientific method as it applies to archaeology. In a general way one can. But the philosophical issues themselves are not directly relevant, and methodological discussions tend to be too broad to be very useful. Certainly there is no question of merely putting into practice methods that have already been worked out in detail – and precise details are what we need to make real headway.

The central task is that of determining the formalism within which candidate hypotheses are to be expressed, and information conveyed to and stored in the machine. Amarel's work indicates that the way this formalism is structured can be crucial to success. *Ad hoc* models such as the cemetery model described earlier are too limited and inflexible for wide use. What is needed is a defined 'language' within which such models can be conveniently put together. On the other hand, we do want an archaeologically oriented formalism. To try to use the formalism of symbolic logic, say, seems bound to involve unneccessary and inefficient generality.

An important point is that the evidence available may well be only fragmentary, whether it comes from a simulation program or is real. Thus at Münsingen the sex of many of the burials is unknown, and some of the graves were lost by gravel digging. Hypotheses must obviously be formulated only to the level of detail that the evidence justifies. This suggests that we should

445

think of the set of candidate hypotheses as being not only laterally comprehensive, but also organized vertically from the simple to the complex. Consider, by way of analogy, the set of candidate hypotheses available to a doctor
when he diagnoses a patient. The more information the doctor has on the
patient's condition and symptoms, the more precise his diagnosis will be. And
whatever amount of information is available, the doctor will almost certainly
assign the patient to some diagnostic category, however tentative and vague.

How do we measure the success of candidate hypotheses in explaining the
data? This is Amarel's second problem. Obviously we require of a good hypothesis that it be consistent with the evidence. That is, we ask that, supposing the assertions of the hypothesis to have been true, we would expect to
have obtained the data that we have obtained. Further, we ask that the assertions of the hypothesis themselves be plausible, taking all that we know into
account. This suggests the statistical concept of Bayesian estimation, or the
rather simpler maximum likelihood estimation, a train of thought that fits in
well with the statistical nature of our cemetery model (compare Kendall,
1963, and Clarke, 1968, pp. 434–5). Unfortunately the standard procedures of
statistical estimation actually available are most unlikely to cope with problems of this complexity. At best it might be possible to relate heuristic
methods of evaluation to an ultimate criterion of this type.

There remains the fundamental problem of organizing the search for a good
hypothesis. The computer must be programmed to put together first simple
and then more complex candidate hypotheses, always concentrating on those
that look promising rather than those that are almost certainly bad. Where
appropriate it must construct hypotheses piecemeal, or put aside part of the
evidence for the time being, or keep a variety of alternatives in play simultaneously. In fact the organization of such searches has been, and is being,
much studied in computer science under the general label of 'heuristic
search'. The need for such searches arises in very many different contexts, and
not only has much experimental lore already been gathered, but elements of a
theory are beginning to appear (Sandewall, 1969; Nilsson, 1971). Thus on this
front the prospects are quite encouraging.

It is fairly easy to specify what might reasonably be called the 'inductive'
component of computer hypothesis formation. It is any part of the search
mechanism which, given data, selects by an exact process of generalization
one or more likely components of the final compound hypothesis. Thus if it
were the case that a particular set of artefacts occurred in all the Münsingen
graves definitely known to be female, and in no graves known to be male, then
it might well be reasonable to conclude that all graves with this set were

446

female. Or if it were known that some of a particular group of graves were early, then it might be reasonable to assume that they all were.

Within the general problem of search organization a particularly interesting question is the following. How far is it possible to split the process of creating a good compound hypothesis into a number of independent subprocesses whose results are combined only at a late stage? For example, an archaeologist might well hope to consider the chronological aspects of the Münsingen cemetery independently of its social aspects. The program model of an archaeologist sketched earlier goes part way towards such a 'factorization' of the argument.

There is no body of theory capable of answering this question. It is obvious enough that such a division of the argument is a great convenience, and it seems likely that up to a point no loss of final accuracy will result. But unless there is an adequate degree of communication between the subprocesses a measure of distortion or simple error may well creep in. This is certainly the case at Münsingen.

To sum up this section, although there exist many of the elements of a theory based approach to writing computer programs which construct archaeological hypotheses, the required synthesis is almost totally lacking. There are a number of interesting problems clearly visible, but as yet little in the way of solutions to them. Almost any sort of experimentation seems bound to clarify the issues involved.

Why not leave it to the archaeologists?

This discussion of the prospects for computer hypothesis formation in archaeology has been a largely speculative one, and the reader may feel that he wishes to reserve judgement until more substantial evidence is laid before him. Even if he is prepared to accept that the goal is realistic, he may still feel that it is a pointless one. In fact, if we leave aside the intrinsic interest of uncovering the mechanisms of hypothesis formation, then there are two kinds of benefit the archaeologist might hope to gain from research in this direction, one methodological and the other direct.

Firstly, it will force a clarification of just what is involved in archaeological hypothesis formation and, as noted earlier, the desire for better self-understanding is, rightly or wrongly, an important feature of current archaeological thought. Naturally one hopes that better understanding will lead to better practice. In particular, such clarification may help to remove some of the uncertainties now associated with the application to archaeological data of

447

methods of multivariate statistics such as cluster analysis and factor analysis. These general methods were not, of course, designed to fit the particular requirements of archaeological inference, and the objectivity and precision of the methods themselves is partially nullified by uncertainty as to the best way to apply them to the data – by uncertainty as to which method variant to use, and by uncertainty as to how to interpret the results once they are obtained. These problems might well be partially overcome if we could obtain a clearer understanding of the wider reasoning process within which such methods must be embedded (Doran, 1970b). This would, for example, enable an archaeologist to select for use a particular variant of cluster analysis, not just by reference to general mathematical criteria, important though these are, but also by reference to the immediate problem context.

The second reason for attempting to automate archaeological hypothesis formation is that such efforts may in the long run provide archaeologists with a program tool capable of making truly helpful proposals for the interpretation of complex evidence. Such proposals could be based on a more tediously precise study than the archaeologist can hope to perform. The natural context for such a tool is the large-scale, computer based, archaeological data bank. Important prerequisites are success in solving the problems associated with the design of efficient symbolic codes for the description of artefacts, and the availability to the archaeologist of a degree of interaction with the machine sufficient to enable him to make the program a natural and flexible extension of his own thought.

This last point needs some expansion. No hypothesis forming program is ever going to rival the archaeologist in width of knowledge and understanding. At most it will be able to throw up interesting and sometimes important suggestions within its limited sphere of competence. In this respect such a program would be similar to, but of course much more complex than, the statistical programs with which archaeologists are now growing familiar. As with the programs now in use, it would be essential that the archaeologist had a full understanding not only of the general mode of operation of the hypothesis forming program, but also of the route which it had followed to reach any particular set of conclusions. Nothing could be more hazardous than for the archaeologist to accept from the program a hypothesis, the arguments in favour of which he could not himself understand or agree with. Thus the program must certainly be 'transparent' in its mode of operation.

More generally, the archaeologist must be both prepared and able to involve himself in the program's reasoning; to monitor, to guide, to countermand, and to vary again and again as he judges fit. As stated earlier, this would by no means reduce the program to useless subservience. Such a cooperative approach is almost certainly the one that has most to offer. It has already had significant success in an admittedly substantially different field of endeavour – automatic theorem proving in mathematical logic (Allen and Luckham, 1969). It is understandable that archaeologists, already finding it difficult to assimilate relatively standard mathematical and statistical techniques into their subject, should be reluctant to concern themselves with research in computer science. But the effect of this reluctance could be an unnecessary period of uncertainty and wasted effort. Archaeology is an essentially non-numerical subject – how many archaeologists would disagree ? The surprising fact is that, in spite of its numerical origins and aura, the digital computer is also essentially non-numerical. This is why cooperation between archaeologist and computer scientist can be so rewarding to both.

References

ALLEN, J. R. and LUCKHAM, D. (1969) An interactive theorem-proving program. In MELTZER, B. and MICHIE, D. (eds.) *Machine Intelligence*, **5**, 321–36. Edinburgh: Edinburgh University Press.

AMAREL, S. (1971) Representation and modelling in problems of program formation. In MELTZER, B. and MICHIE, D. (eds.) *Machine Intelligence*, **6**, 411–66. Edinburgh: Edinburgh University Press.

BAYARD, D. T. (1969) Science, theory and reality in the 'new' archaeology. *American Antiquity*, **34**, 376–84.

BRENNAN, R. D. (1968) Simulation is wha-a-t ? Part II. In MCLEOD, J. (ed.) *Simulation*, 5–12. New York: McGraw-Hill.

BUCHANAN, B., SUTHERLAND, G. and FEIGENBAUM, E. A. (1969) HEURISTIC DENDRAL: a program for generating explanatory hypotheses in organic chemistry. In MELTZER, B. and MICHIE, D. (eds.) *Machine Intelligence*, **4**, 209–54. Edinburgh: Edinburgh University Press.

BYERLY, H. (1969) Model-structures and model-objects. *British Journal for the Philosophy of Science*, **20**, 135–44.

CHENHALL, R. G. (ed.) (1970) *Newsletter of Computer Archaeology*. Vol. 4 and other issues. Arizona State University.

CHURCHMAN, C. W. and BUCHANAN, B. (1969) On the design of inductive systems: some philosophical problems. *British Journal for the Philosophy of Science*, **20**, 311–25.

CLARKE, D. L. (1968) *Analytical Archaeology*. London: Methuen.

COWGILL, G. L. (1967) Computer applications in archaeology. *AFIPS Conference Proceedings: 1967 Fall Joint Computer Conference*, **31**, 331–7. Washington: Thomson Book Co.

DORAN, J. E. (1970a) Systems theory, computer simulations and archaeology. *World Archaeology*, **1**, 289–98.

449

DORAN, J. E. (1970b) Archaeological reasoning and machine reasoning. In GARDIN, J.-C. (ed.) *Archéologie et Calculateurs*, 57–69. Paris: Centre National de la Recherche Scientifique.

DORAN, J. E. (1971) Computer analysis of data from the La Tène cemetery at Münsingen-Rain. In HUDSON, F. R., KENDALL, D. G. and TAUTU, P. (eds.) *Proceedings of the Anglo-Romanian Conference on Mathematics in the Archaeological and Historical Sciences*. Edinburgh: Edinburgh University Press.

DORAN, J. E. (1972) Automatic generation and evaluation of explanatory hypotheses. *Proceedings of a Colloquium on Mathematical Methods in Archaeology, October 1971*. Centre d'Analyse Documentaire pour l'Archéologie. C.N.R.S. Marseilles.

FEIGENBAUM, E. A. (1969) Artificial intelligence: themes in the second decade. In MORRELL, A. J. H. (ed.) *Information Processing 68* (Proceedings of the IFIPS 68 Congress, Edinburgh), **2**, 1008–24. Amsterdam: North Holland.

FRITZ, J. M. and PLOG, F. T. (1970) The nature of archaeological explanation. *American Antiquity*, **35**, 405–12.

GARDIN, J.-C. (1970) *Archéologie et Calculateurs*. Paris: Centre National de la Recherche Scientifique.

HODSON, F. R. (1964) La Tène chronology. *Bulletin of the Institute of Archaeology*, **4**, 123–41.

HODSON, F. R. (1968) *The La Tène Cemetery at Münsingen-Rain*. Berlin: Stampfli.

HODSON, F. R., KENDALL, D. G. and TAUTU, P. (eds.) (1971) *Proceedings of the Anglo-Romanian Conference on Mathematics in the Archaeological and Historical Sciences*. Edinburgh: Edinburgh University Press.

HYMES, D. (1970) Linguistic models in archaeology. In GARDIN, J.-C. (ed.) *Archéologie et Calculateurs*, 91–120. Paris: Centre National de la Recherche Scientifique.

KENDALL, D. G. (1963) A statistical approach to Flinders Petrie's sequence-dating. *Bulletin of the I.S.I., 34th Session*, Ottawa, 657–80.

KENDALL, D. G. (1971) Seriation from abundance matrices. In HODSON, F. R., KENDALL, D. G. and TAUTU, P. (eds.) *Proceedings of the Anglo-Romanian Conference on Mathematics in the Archaeological and Historical Sciences*, 215–52. Edinburgh: Edinburgh University Press.

KENDALL, M. G. (1968) Model building and its problems. *Mathematical Model Building in Economics and Industry*, 1–14. London: Griffin.

KOVALEVSKAJA, V. B. (1970) Recherches sur les systèmes sémiologiques en archéologie par les méthodes de la théorie de l'information. In GARDIN, J.-C. (ed.) *Archéologie et Calculateurs*, 187–91. Paris: Centre National de la Recherche Scientifique.

MARSHAK, B. I. (1965). On the finding of criteria for similarity and difference between pottery assemblages. In KOLCHIN, B.A. (ed.) *Archaeology and the Natural Sciences*, 308–17. Moscow: Nauka (in Russian).

MELTZER, B. (1970) Generation of hypotheses and theories. *Nature*, **225**, 972.

MOBERG, C.-A. (1971) Archaeological context and mathematical methods. In HODSON, F. R., KENDALL, D. G. and TAUTU, P. (eds.) *Proceedings of the Anglo-Romanian Conference on Mathematics in the Archaeological and Historical Sciences*, 551–62. Edinburgh: Edinburgh University Press.

NEWELL, A. and SIMON, H. A. (1963) GPS: a program that simulates human thought. In FEIGENBAUM, E. A. and FELDMAN, J. (eds.) *Computers and Thought*, 279–93. New York: McGraw-Hill.

NILSSON, N. (1971) *Problem-Solving Methods in Artificial Intelligence*. New York: McGraw-Hill.

ROUSE, I. (1970) Classification for what? Comments on *Analytical Archaeology* by D. L. CLARKE, 1968. *Norwegian Archaeological Review*, **3**, 4–12.

SANDEWALL, E. (1969) Concepts and methods for heuristic search. In WALKER, D. E. and NORTON, L. M. (eds.) *Proceedings of the International Joint Conference on Artificial Intelligence 1969*, 199–218. New York: Association for Computing Machinery.

SCHAAF, U. (1966) Zur Belegung latènezeitlicher Friedhöfe der Schweiz. *Jahrbuch des Römisch-Germanischen Zentralmuseums Mainz*.

TURING, A. (1963) Can a machine think? In FEIGENBAUM, E. A. and FELDMAN, J. (eds.) *Computers and Thought*, 11–35. New York: McGraw-Hill.

11

Initial model formulation *in terra incognita*

C. F. W. HIGHAM

University of Otago, New Zealand

The theme of this paper is the role of the model in an area hitherto unknown archaeologically. This question is increasingly encountered as archaeological field work extends into new areas. Such archaeological blanks include large parts of Australia and south-east Asia, where, in contrast to the classic areas of research, such as western Europe, Mesoamerica or the Tigris-Euphrates valley, very few controlled excavations have been undertaken. Consequently, whereas the prehistorian working on American or European material can pose his theoretical formulations on the basis of reasonably adequate data, his colleague in the Antipodes necessarily constructs models on the basis of material scarcely out of the ground. Paradoxically, the structure of the initial, and highly tentative, models to be proposed is based on the characteristics of core-cultural variables, because these are the most amenable to qualitative and rapid laboratory diagnosis (Steward, 1955).

North and north-east Thailand is an area that has seen less excavation than at many single sites elsewhere. Most of the archaeological research remains unpublished, and basic data from recent excavations are still under study. There is little available artefactual material, relatively few radiocarbon dates (forty-five for the entire area) and hardly any basic comparative biological samples to allow a detailed analysis of relevant finds.

Consideration of the material obtained during the initial five year research programme poses the possibility that a complete revision of our concepts of south-east Asian prehistory will in due course be necessary. It is, perhaps, appropriate to compare at this critical juncture, the established interpretation of south-east Asian prehistory as a whole, and an alternative model that provides a considerably closer fit with data recently obtained from a relatively small circumscribed area. Views will differ on whether or not there is enough information yet from north and north-east Thailand to necessitate the rejection of the traditional model.

453

Before reviewing the few available fragments of material from north and north-east Thailand it is necessary to affirm the usefulness of the generalized cultural model discussed, with varying degrees of clarity, by numerous anthropologists. These stress the importance of the interaction between core-cultural variables, such as the economy, technology and social structure on the one hand, and the constraining environment on the other. The clear documentation of this balanced integration is the principal contribution of Star Carr (Clark, 1954); Childe (1956) has laid out its essentials with masterly brevity. It forms the basis of Steward's (1955) studies in cultural ecology, and, formalized within the framework of general systems theory, is a central feature of Clarke's (1968) recent major study in archaeological analysis. Its fundamental notion, that environmental as well as cultural data are pre-requisites for meaningful prehistoric research, has for long been an indispensable part of undergraduate prehistory courses. The type of model generated by initial research in a new area is, however, of a far more specific kind.

Research in south-east Asia prior to 1965

Although no research was undertaken in the northern and north-eastern provinces of Thailand before 1965, excavations in south-east Asian sites, particularly in Vietnam and Malaysia, have provided information employed by several synthesizers to characterize the situation in south-east Asia as a whole (Matthews, 1964; Clark, 1969).

These older texts refer to south-east Asia as a cultural backwater, which witnessed very little innovation before the historic period, when Chinese and Indian influence was instrumental in the development of the Funan and Khmer states. Those responsible for such syntheses are in no way culpable: they simply relied on the available evidence. Due to the virtual absence of careful, stratigraphical excavation before the mid 1960s and the lack of concern for biological data, a meaningful understanding of local prehistoric sequences was ruled out.

Colani's excavations in the late 1920s are reasonably characteristic of the period before 1965 (Colani, 1927). Unfortunately, she gave little attention to the cultural or natural stratigraphy of the many Vietnamese cave sites studied. Consequently, nothing is known of the nature of cultural deposits. They may have thick, homogeneous and rich deposits derived from regular occupation, or thin lenses representing temporary occupation. Colani was principally interested in items of material culture as evidence for migration

454

theories. Stone artefacts predominated, principally in the form of flaked river pebbles, but included items of bone and shell. The pottery fragments were thought by Colani to be of recent origin: indeed, at the time that she was working, there was no method of dating the cultural remains with the exception of using faunal evidence to define Pleistocene or post-Pleistocene occupation. The faunal species represented fell into the latter category.

Colani's research led to the definition of a previously unrecognized series of artefacts, which were grouped together as the 'Hoabinhian' culture. Excavations in Bac Son province by Mansuy resulted in the discovery of broadly similar material (Mansuy, 1924).

If one takes as characteristic of Hoabinhian sites, an unsophisticated stone-working technology and a hunting-gathering economy, then there can be little doubt that south-east Asia witnessed little of the cultural innovation characteristic of contemporary Mesoamerica or the Middle East. It should be remembered, however, that the recovery of bamboo, a major source of raw material in south-east Asia today, and the vegetable component of the prehistoric diet, would require techniques of excavation not practised in the early history of archaeological research into the Hoabinhian. Again, if the pottery dismissed by Colani as 'recent' were to be discovered in association with Hoabinhian occupation levels, reassessment of Hoabinhian technology would be necessary.

Available texts then refer to a continuation of the Hoabinhian Mesolithic culture and the introduction of agriculture, pottery and polished quadrangular-sectioned adzes by means of a migration from China (Sørensen and Hatting, 1967; Duff, 1970). This presumed sea-borne movement, often referred to as *Lungshanoid* after its putative centre of origin in the Chinese province of Shantung, brought Neolithic culture ready-made into south-east Asia during the early second millennium B.C. Strong evidence for such a culture infusion, according to Sørensen, comes from the early levels of Ban Kao in Kanchanaburi province, Thailand. This cemetery site yielded tripod-based ceramic vessels of presumed Lungshanoid affinities, together with C14 dates of 1360 ± 140 B.C. and 1770 ± 140 B.C.

Significantly, no bronze was recovered from burials at Ban Kao, and only fragments from the upper levels. Again, the available texts suggest that the first bronze casters in south-east Asia were centred in the Vietnamese province of Than Hoa, in particular the cemetery site of Dong Son. This proficient centre of bronze casting was active by the sixth century B.C., and intense Chinese influence has been observed not only in the form of the spearheads, drums and axes, but also in decorative motifs and nature of the

455

alloy. Clark (1969) has summarized the traditional view of bronze working in south-east Asia when he stated that the area did not experience 'a phase of technology fully comparable with the Bronze Age in certain parts of the Old World'.

This 'invasion' model is largely imprinted on the data without consideration of alternative possibilities. In its latest manifestation (Duff, 1970) it has been supported by an analysis of a single class of museum-bound, unprovenanced material, in conjunction with a blithe disregard for information that does not fit the author's preconceptions. Indeed, as Parker has stressed: 'Until 1960 our view of Thai prehistory rested almost entirely on chance finds, used to prop often ill-founded speculations about general patterns of development in south-east Asia as a whole. Detailed and precise scrutiny of particular areas was lacking, and in this situation serious prehistory was impossible' (Parker, 1968).

In the following review of recent research, which will precede the outline of an alternative model of cultural development in north and north-east Thailand, several factors will be taken as axiomatic. The most important is that the effective prehistoric research can only be undertaken when there is a constant interplay between the respective roles of field work, laboratory analysis and theory. There follows the dictum that such research can only be effective when a specific area is subjected to long-term study. These imply that the location of sites, definition of site types, assessment of changes in subsistence activities and characteristics of the environment are prerequisites to an understanding of the prehistoric cultural sequence.

North and north-east Thailand: archaeological evidence

The empirical nature of the present section is intended to redress the situation alluded to by Parker. Moreover, since most recent research remains unpublished, reference to the facts is necessary.

The area under review can be divided into three major environmental zones (Fig. 11.1). The first comprises the Khorat plateau, a flat, rolling plain drained by the Mun and Chi rivers; it is flanked in the east by the Mekong river, and in the west by the Petchabun mountains. The second zone, known as the North-west and Central Highlands, comprises a series of north-south running valley and upland systems. Alluvial deposits fill the valleys, with intervening hills made up variously of granite, sandstone and limestone. The Piedmont area between the Khorat Plateau and Central Highlands may be

FIG. 11.1. Northern and north-eastern Thailand: the area of the study with the sites mentioned in the text.

described as a third or intermediate zone, in that it comprises elements of the other two (United Nations, 1968).

These major areas may be subdivided into numerous small, localized resource zones. Research in the Piedmont zone has been concentrated in the Phu Wiang region, which is dominated by a large sandstone monadnock resembling an extinct volcanic crater (Fig. 11.2). Prehistoric sites have been located on the flat interior of the ring mountain and on the plain outside. As Bayard (1971) has shown, present inhabitants recognize at least seven distinct resource zones; of these, the margins of permanent streams and low-lying rice paddies on the favourable Roi Et sandy loams recur throughout the Khorat plateau.

Phu Wiang, however, has considerable local changes in altitude, and this increases the number of environmental zones when compared with the Khorat plateau. Thus, the area between the valley floor and the top of Phu Wiang mountain changes from a thin dry to a dense, triple-canopied monsoon forest. The present inhabitants use the lowland area for fishing and wet rice farming, the foothill forests for slash-and-burn or 'dry' rice agriculture, and the higher hill slopes for hunting wild game. Dry season hunting expeditions are common, with pig, deer, monkey and lizard the principal quarry.

While the flat nature of the Khorat plateau might give the impression of environmental uniformity, it is on closer inspection remarkably varied. This is clearly recognized by the modern rice farmer, for whom minor variations in soil type, changes in aspect and slope, and proximity to perennial watercourses, are of critical importance. The variations between small valleys and surrounding hill slopes in the Central Highlands are of basic importance in determining land use today, as presumably during the prehistoric past.

Most varieties of rice require a minimum of 1500 mm rainfall per annum to grow. Yet the Khorat plateau and Piedmont zones lie within the rain shadow of the Petchabun mountains. Moreover, rainfall is unpredictable. During the monsoon season (May to October), within which lies the crucial growing season for rice, rainfall is variable in extent. Of the 595 months for which records have been kept in Khon Kaen, 65·4% have had less than the average rainfall.

Not only is rainfall marginal for successful rice farming, but the soils of north-east Thailand are relatively infertile, sandy loams. While some soil types, such as the Khorat, are too permeable for rice farming, others such as the Roi Et series, are adequate.

As yet, no evidence for hunter-gatherer cultures has been found on the Khorat plateau or its Piedmont fringes. As Gorman (1971) has stressed in his

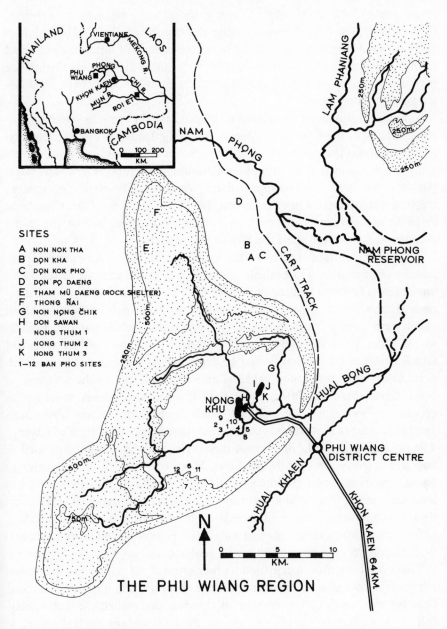

SITES

A NON NOK THA
B DON KHA
C DON KOK PHO
D DON PO DAENG
E THAM MÜ DAENG (ROCK SHELTER)
F THONG ÑAI
G NON NONG ČHIK
H DON SAWAN
I NONG THUM 1
J NONG THUM 2
K NONG THUM 3
1–12 BAN PHO SITES

THE PHU WIANG REGION

FIG. 11.2. The Phu Wiang area.

recent survey of the evidence, hunter-gatherer sites dated to 13 000–6000 B.C. – that is, the period encompassing the end of the Würm Glaciation in more extreme latitudes – tend to be restricted to upland limestone areas and former sea coasts. Due to considerable fluctuations in sea level during the period in question, many of the latter sites are assumed to have been destroyed by water action.

Although Gorman has discovered numerous cave sites yielding Hoabinhian-type material in the Central and North-west Highlands, he has restricted his own excavations to one small rock shelter, known as Spirit Cave. The deposits comprise five principal superimposed natural and cultural layers. The latest (Layer 1) has been dated to approximately 6000 B.C. The earliest occupation material has not yet been radiocarbon dated, but the fourth layer has been dated to approximately 10 000 B.C. This suggests strongly that the initial occupation falls within the Late Pleistocene period.

What of the cultural and biological remains recovered? All cultural levels contain characteristic Hoabinhian artefacts, and in his analysis of the stone implements, Gorman focused particular attention on the evidence for utilization. Microscopic wear patterns suggest that the flaked pebble tools and small flakes were used to manufacture tools from a perishable material, such as wood. Indeed, the absence of hunting artefacts in a site yielding abundant faunal evidence for hunting would be explained by this interesting proposition. About 7000 B.C. a new range of artefacts appeared in the sequence at Spirit Cave; these are pottery decorated with cord impressions, stone knives ground on both sides and polished quadrangular stone adzes. The stratigraphic context of these finds is undisputed: they lay on the surface of Layer 2. The pottery in the Hoa Binh caves themselves may have been dismissed as late and intrusive, but at Spirit Cave, however, these three categories of artefact pose important questions for the excavator. Were they the product of local innovation, of an ethnic intrusion into the area, of trade, or of diffusion from a technologically more advanced people? Choosing between these alternatives must await a review of remaining discoveries at Spirit Cave and excavations in other contemporary and earlier settlements.

There has been little speculation on the nature of the faunal spectrum from Hoabinhian cave sites. A considerable range of species is in question, including large bovines, small carnivores such as the civet cat, monkey, fish and shellfish. It is extremely hazardous, and of dubious anthropological value, to generalize about the economy of Hoabinhian-type sites. At the present early stage of investigations, more information can be gained from a detailed consideration of specific sites. Spirit Cave is a particularly appropriate example, because of the stratigraphical control of the excavations and the meticulous care taken during collection of the specimens.

The nature of the faunal remains was similar throughout the occupation of the cave. The primarily wooded environment that still characterizes the area is reflected in the presence of both sambar and barking deer, squirrel, monkey and pig bone. The one or two fragmentary bovine bones may come from either the gaur or the banteng, each of which now has a severely restricted range. Bat bones were remarkably unfragmented, due perhaps to their dying within the cave and incorporation in cultural deposits through natural rather than human agency. Fish bones and freshwater shellfish indicate exploitation of the nearby Khong Stream during both the dry and wet seasons.

Such remains indicate exploitation of the woodland and stream margins within the vicinity of the cave. This activity was extended to plant foods. Despite over forty years of research into Hoabinhian sites, it is an extraordinary fact that only at Spirit Cave have botanical remains been identified. The species identified include gourds, nuts, pepper and broad beans. Yen's (1971) study of the remains of peas and beans has led to the interesting possibility that they were cultivated rather than collected wild. Such suggestions are normally based on changes in size and shape between wild and domestic forms, which in turn are held to reflect deliberate selection of desirable strains. Until larger samples are collected and analysed, this question will remain hypothetical. If demonstrated, then the occupants of Spirit Cave and related sites will assume considerable theoretical importance as extremely early horticulturalists. If not, then the careful retention of fragmentary botanical remains will still have provided new insight into Late Pleistocene economic activities in south-east Asia.

Gorman's research at Spirit Cave is a particularly elegant example of the interaction between the role of theory and excavation technique. Had the links between economic, social and technological attributes not been realized, it is doubtful whether the importance of the biological data, however fragmentary and small, would have been realized. By collecting all recognizable relevant data, however, Gorman has contributed more to an understanding of the Hoabinhian than had he collected only artefactual material from a hundred sites. To have recovered a range of data from successive layers also provides evidence for temporal change. Spirit Cave was clearly a base, occupied during both dry and wet seasons, for what has been termed 'broad spectrum' hunting and gathering (Hole, Flannery and Neely, 1969). This term means that a wide range of resource zones were exploited when they were seasonally abundant, and the people in question were not reliant on any one dietary

461

item. Just the same pattern has been observed in the Tehuacan and Khorrama-bad Valleys (MacNeish, 1964; Hole, Flannery and Neely, 1969). Some of the food plants may have been selectively collected to the extent that they became morphologically distinct from the wild forms. Rather than see the widespread Hoabinhian sites as belonging to one, specific culture, Gorman has assigned them to a more generalized group, known as a technocomplex (Clarke, 1968). The latter concept implies a low frequency of shared artefact types between local groups, due in the main to a common adaptation to a similar environment. Any Technocomplex may comprise a considerable number of individual, regional cultures, each one having a high technological, social and economic homogeneity. Consequently, further research may well delineate coastal-riverine Hoabinhian cultures, and Hoabinhian cultures of the Thai, Malayan and Vietnamese highlands, each related in general terms but at the same time quite distinct.

There remains the problem of the appearance of three exotic artefact types at Spirit Cave on the surface of Layer 2: pottery, ground stone adzes and slate knives. While pottery by no means implies *per se* the presence of agri-culturally based societies, so many farmer cultures do use ceramics, and so many hunter-gatherer societies do not, that its presence archaeologically must always pose the possibility, at least, that agriculture was practised. This situation does have some basis in the realities of agricultural against non-agricultural life. Fired pottery vessels are particularly useful for storing and cooking cereals. Pottery vessels are often large, unwieldly and fragile. They are more likely to be valued in a permanently occupied village than in a temporary hunting camp. Naturally, there are exceptions to this statement. In Fiji, New Guinea and north-east Thailand to this day, pottery vessels are traded over wide distances from specialist manufacturing villages (Coutts, 1967; Calder, 1971), and it is reported that some Eskimo made use of pottery vessels. Nevertheless, the contemporaneity of pottery at Spirit Cave by 6000 B.C. and agriculture locally or within the general area needs to be carefully considered.

The rectangular, cross-sectioned polished stone adze is a particularly interesting and widespread artefact type and ethnographic studies indicate time and again the value of such implements for woodworking (Blackwood, 1950).

Since horticulture and agriculture in north and north-east Thailand would involve making inroads into woodland, the presence of polished, quadrangular adzes at Spirit Cave, like that of pottery, marks a technological and possibly also a basic economic innovation. Less is known of the use of bifacial slate

462

knives, although implements of similar form have been observed ethnographically as reaping tools in the Celebes and Java.

There is no direct evidence for agriculture at Spirit Cave: indeed, a small cave at the head of a steep-sided valley is an unlikely site for farming, and the faunal evidence indicates continuity in an established hunting pattern. It is necessary to seek evidence for early agriculture elsewhere in the study area.

In 1963, Solheim initiated a programme of archaeological research in north-east Thailand; of the twenty-one sites discovered particular emphasis was placed on the excavation of Non Nok Tha, a small, low mound some 400 m from the village of Ban Nadi. It was chosen for full-scale study because of the rich finds recovered during test excavations in 1964-5. The site was opened up under the direction of Parker and Bayard in 1966, and again for fifteen weeks in 1968 by Bayard (fig. 11.2).

Essentially, the part of Non Nok Tha excavated was intermittently used as both a burial ground and for occupation until the cultural deposit attained a depth of 1·5 m. As a result of the rigorous definition of material and cultural soil build-up and erosion, five soil types incorporating seventeen cultural levels have been recognized. Bayard (1971) has divided the sequence at Non Nok Tha into Early, Middle and Late periods: the Early period has three cultural levels, the Middle period eight, and the Late period six.

One of the particularly attractive features of excavating a prehistoric cemetery, apart from the obvious advantages of recovering palaeopathological data, is the common association of complete artefacts with human skeletal remains. Non Nok Tha is no exception. The superimposed inhumations were accompanied by a wide range of grave goods, including complete pottery vessels, stone adzes, bronze axes, bracelets and articulating limb bones of cattle, pigs, dog and deer.

Burial evidence indicates that at the time when the two earliest levels were formed, stone was the basic raw material in use for cutting implements. A copper socketed axe, however, was associated with a burial assigned to E.P. Level 3, and by M.P. Level 1 bronze was not only relatively common, but was cast at the site. Indeed, the double moulds for casting axes, as well as casting spillage and crucibles have been discovered. Bronze and stone continued as the basic raw materials used in tool manufacture until L.P. Level 2, by which time iron was also known. Iron appears to have been used first during the hiatus between the Middle and Late periods.

Technologically, the sequence at Non Nok Tha falls into a widely recognized pattern whereby stone was gradually replaced by bronze, and bronze by iron. This, naturally, reflects the inherent qualities of the materials themselves:

463

polished stone adzes are liable to fracture more easily than metal tools, bronze implements may be recast and their potentially thin cross section makes them efficient, and iron tools had the attributes of maintaining a keen edge, and of being relatively heavy. Weight and sharpness are two basic requirements for an efficient axe.

If gradual changes in pottery style within a common tradition are symptomatic of ethnic continuity, then the pottery at Non Nok Tha demonstrates that the technological developments that took place were accomplished in a stable cultural milieu. What of the economic activities of a society which could maintain a large mound as a focus of habitation and burial over an extended period which witnessed striking technological changes? The animal limb bones that accompanied human inhumations belonging from the earliest level to M.P. Level 6 are a particularly important source of information. It is probable, for example, that the higher, wooded resource zones of Phu Wiang were visited on hunting trips, thus accounting for the remains of the large sambar and the small barking deer; the pig remains may be from wild, domestic or feral animals. In view of their close numerical relationship with cattle bones in human burials, however, it is thought that they are more likely to come from domestic animals. More, however, can be said of the status of the Non Nok Tha cattle.

South-east Asia is particularly rich in indigenous bovine species. Theoretically, the limb bones from Non Nok Tha could derive from the wild gaur, its domesticated form (the mithan), the wild or domestic banteng, the kouprey, water buffalo, or a domesticated variety introduced from elsewhere. As a result of an analysis of the limb bones of the modern gaur and water buffalo, it is possible to remove these two species from consideration. The kouprey is restricted, if indeed any survive, to the remote forests of Cambodia. There is no large modern comparative sample in existence, and no means of discovering whether the Non Nok Tha specimens come from this species. Both the mithan and banteng are larger than the animals represented by the prehistoric bones. Indeed, the Non Nok Tha specimens are virtually indistinguishable from modern, female *Bos indicus* (zebu) from Thailand. From the earliest occupation level, therefore, the inhabitants of this site were acquainted with a type of bovine osteologically identical with the modern domestic Thai breed of zebu. That the overwhelming majority of limbs come from juvenile female animals suggests strongly that the animals were, indeed, domesticated (Higham and Leach, 1971).

Evidence for prehistoric agriculture may at first sight appear more difficult to obtain than that for stock rearing. This is not the case at Non Nok Tha.

On sectioning pottery sherds from the earliest level, Bayard recognized a temper made from rice chaff. Such temper became common from E.P. Level 3 onwards. Rice cultivation was clearly practised throughout the site's history.

In view of the close links between wet rice farming and the domestic water buffalo, it is particularly interesting to observe that there is no evidence for water buffalo at Non Nok Tha before L.P. Level 3. It is dangerous to argue on the basis of negative evidence, particularly in view of the highly selective nature of any data derived from burials. Quite simply, the early inhabitants of the site may have preferred to bury cattle rather than water buffalo limbs with their dead. At present, therefore, it is only reasonable to affirm that the earliest evidence for the presence of water buffalo at Non Nok Tha was recovered from a fourteenth century A.D. context. It may or may not be coincidental that this same level was also characterized by ironworking and the novel burial custom of cremation.

Hitherto, this resumé of the finds made at Non Nok Tha has carefully avoided reference to the site's chronology. Such is the pace of the development of scientific aids to archaeology that, even during the early 1950s, obtaining an estimate for the antiquity of the early levels of Non Nok Tha would have been impossible, but the advent of radiocarbon dating has removed this major obstacle to an understanding of the site's chronology. The establishment of a temporal framework is a precondition to a reasonable evaluation of cultural changes, but it cannot be stressed too strongly, however, that the technical difficulties involved in obtaining dates, quite apart from being certain beyond doubt of the stratigraphical context of samples from a burial site in which graves cross-cut each other, make interpretation of dates obtained a tricky exercise.

There are at present twenty-six C14 dates for Non Nok Tha, provided by five separate laboratories, and, after the exclusion of clearly erratic dates, there are two stratigraphically viable series. In neither case is there yet a C14 estimate for the earliest occupation level, but a sample from E.P. Level 3 of 3590 ± 320 B.C. is consistent with dates of 2390 B.C. for M.P. Level 3 and a further eight dates up to A.D. 130 for the end of the Middle occupation period. On the other hand, six dates calculated by the University of Florida also form an internally consistent, but much later sequence. This series appears to be erroneous in view of the fact that it dates Levels L.P.2 and L.P.4 into the future. This situation may well result from contamination of the samples between the field and the laboratory.

The choice between the long and short chronologies is not possible without comparing the dates in question with those obtained from other sites and, fortunately, three such comparative sites have been excavated: Ban Chiang, a Thai site containing inhumation graves and a distinctive pottery style not dissimilar to that from Non Nok Tha E.P. Level 3, has provided a thermoluminescence date of 4630 B.C.; the French archaeologist Saurin has obtained a date of 2120 ± 250 B.C. from the site of Han Gon in South Vietnam, which, like Non Nok Tha and Ban Chiang, contains bronze implements; and the New Zealand Institute of Nuclear Sciences has estimated an antiquity of 180 ± B.C. for a level at the site of Non Nong Chik, which closely resembles material from M.P. Level 8 at Non Nok Tha.

The dating of Ban Chiang, Han Gon and Non Nong Chik supports the long chronology for Non Nok Tha. If, until further evidence is available, the date of 3590 ± 320 B.C. for E.P. Level 3 at Non Nok Tha is accepted, then Levels 1 and 2 must be earlier still. It is not impossible that they go back into the sixth millennium B.C. If they did, then the presence of rice farmers in lowland north-east Thailand may account for the intrusive pottery, knives and polished stone adzes at Spirit Cave. Again, acceptance, for the moment at least, of the long chronology for Non Nok Tha would imply that cattle domestication, rice farming and bronze technology were all present earlier than in any other parts of south-east Asia or China examined archaeologically.

It is not the task of the prehistoric anthropologist to hunt aimlessly for early dates. Rather he should seek evidence for the entire prehistoric cultural sequence in his chosen area of study, and seek to explain it. The particular attention paid to Non Nok Tha reflects its long period of occupation, the extensive excavations undertaken there and the richness of the material recovered for intensive analysis. Like Spirit Cave, Non Nok Tha occupies a special place in the history of prehistoric studies in south-east Asia. The same will probably be said of the extraordinary concentration of sites discovered in 1969–70 in the Roi Et province of north-east Thailand (Higham and Parker, 1970).

Both Non Nong Chik and Non Nok Tha lie close to the mountain wall of Phu Wiang. Monsoon rains falling on the hillsides concentrate on the surrounding flatland and help obviate water shortages in an area where the rainfall is marginal for rice agriculture. The Roi Et province provides a striking contrast. Bayard has emphasized the environmental difference by ascribing the Phu Wiang sites to the 'Piedmont' area (Bayard, 1971). If present rainfall figures were similar during the period 6000 B.C. to A.D. 0, then the Roi Et region would have been extremely hazardous for dry rice farmers. On the other hand, with such technological innovations as iron tools for forest clearance and the water buffalo for ploughing wet paddy fields, it would have

466

become more amenable to settlement. Moreover, those occupying the area could have controlled a rich supply of three particularly valuable commodities: salt, iron ore and building stone.

Bo Phan Khan is a major source of salt. During the early part of the dry season, the occupants of five villages, which lie within about 1·5 km of the exposure of rock salt, move to temporary huts adjacent to the salt working. The start of the season is marked by the ritual slaughter of two white water buffalo and, in a Buddhist country where killing animals is anathema, such a rite hints at considerable antiquity for saltworking. Having concentrated brine in small enclosures on the flat bed of rock salt, they boil the liquid in metal trays until only salt is left; naturally, an alternative vessel would have been necessary if saltworking took place before large metal containers became generally available.

There is vigorous trade in the extracted salt at least as far north as the Laotian border, and probably further still, since, quite apart from its dietary significance, salt is important in the preservation of food. The saltworks lie in the centre of a wet rice region in which paddy fields concentrate on the better sandy loams, and the same families that produce salt also grow rice during the rainy season. The outcrops of consolidated laterite, a source of iron, and the finely bedded sandstone that overlies the rock salt, are two other raw materials of potential significance.

In initiating an archaeological reconnaissance of the area, three major problems requiring elucidation were posed. Clearly, one of these is the date of initial occupation of the Khorat plain by agricultural societies. If, as has been argued, wet rice and water buffalo were necessary prerequisites, some knowledge of the period when these agricultural techniques were developed would be obtained. Again, the date of a move into hitherto marginal areas, facilitated by improved agricultural techniques, might clarify the estimated antiquity of ironworking and buffalo domestication in the Phu Wiang area. Analysis of early plains material culture could indicate the direction from which the first settlers came.

A third question is the origin and development of the Chen-la state: the first Chinese record of Chen-la dates from the early seventh century A.D. and it is clear from Chinese records that Chen-la was a state of considerable political significance. It was in touch with China throughout the eighth century A.D. Briggs (1951) has suggested that Chen-la was situated in the southern part of the Khorat plateau. The archaeological documentation of Chen-la could provide evidence for or against trends towards complex culture in this part of north-east Thailand before the area was annexed by the Khmer in the ninth century, as well as demonstrate the existence of a people hitherto known of only in the vaguest terms through Chinese records.

The field work in Roi Et took the form of an intensive search for prehistoric sites in a limited area of *circa* 26 km². The area in question centred on the open salt deposits, and included a major concentration of villages, some land under rice cultivation, and the poor alluvial soils bordering a small stream known as the Lam Siao Noi (Fig. 11.3); it soon became apparent that the study area was intensively occupied during the prehistoric period. The salt deposits were ringed by a series of mounds, the sides of which contained quantities of pottery. The modern villages are situated on mounds, and the tracks and wells cut into them reveal a considerable depth of cultural material before natural soil is reached. Moreover, several large mounds at some distance from the salt deposits were of cultural origin, since fragments of pottery were found embedded in erosion gullies, or lying on the surface.

Small, so-called 'test' squares, 2 × 2 m in extent, were excavated in three mounds: Bo Phan Khan on the salt margins, Ban Tha Nen under the modern village of the same name, and Don Tha Pan, which is about 1·5 km from the salt deposits. The depth of cultural deposits in all three exceeded 5·5 m. Indeed, at Don Tha Pan and Bo Phan Khan, excavations terminated at the water-table although the natural substratum had not been reached.

The history of occupation of each site was quite distinct from the others. At Bo Phan Khan, the initial occupation period saw intensive salt extraction. The lowest layers contained thick-walled, coarse pottery, presumably used to contain brine, and a maze of intercutting pits and hearths. There followed a period during which the deposits, which were built up through soil creep from the surrounding hill, contained a thin scatter of cultural material. Finally, the site was occupied by the Khmer in exploiting and cutting the local red sandstone for building purposes. The Khmer level, which belongs at the outside limits to the period from 900 to 1400 A.D., was 5 m above the lowest salt-working deposits. While fine, thin-walled and painted ceramics from the basal levels of Bo Phan Khan are very similar to the pottery from Don Tha Pan, the coarser thick-walled type is rare at the latter site. The mound of Don Tha Pan covers approximately 12 ha. On the basis of one 2 × 2 m test square, it appears to have been built up by successive cultural layers and sterile, sand lenses. An analysis of the sand has indicated that it was deposited by water rather than wind action. Occasional wet season flooding by the Lam Siao Noi is the most plausible explanation for the number of clean, sandy levels. In contrast, the cultural horizons contain abundant pottery and fragments of charcoal, as well as pits and scraps of iron.

468

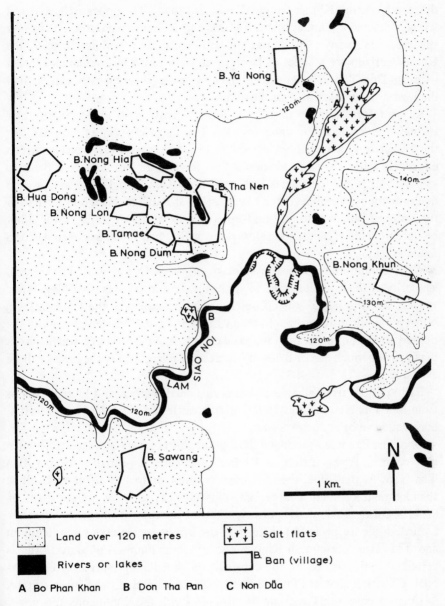

FIG. 11.3. The Roi Et area.

The excavation of the Ban Tha Nen village site was located near an eleventh-thirteenth century Khmer temple (Keakoorn, 1970). The upper archaeological levels contained a number of small bowls and Khmer stoneware. The former suggest ritual activity in association with the nearby temple. Beneath the Khmer horizon are a series of layers, similar in terms of artefactual content with the Don Tha Pan sequence, but these sea levels are clearly earlier than the lowest occupation at Don Tha Pan.

Any interpretation of these sites leans heavily upon evidence for their chronology. Radiocarbon dates for Don Tha Pan run from 25 ± 131 B.C. for the lowest level above the water-table, to A.D. 850 ± 80 for Level 5, which effectively dates the site's abandonment. Level 9 at Ban Tha Nen dates to 55 ± 83 B.C., which correlates well with early Don Tha Pan. There are no determinations available yet for Levels 13–17 at Ban Tha Nen, but in terms of the assumed rate of cultural build-up at the site a date of 500 B.C. would not be unreasonable. The earliest saltworking at Bo Phan Khan has been dated to A.D. 290 ± 81.

What should the archaeologist make of these C14 dates? The general similarity of the estimates from lower levels at all three sites is striking. They suggest that the region was occupied by the beginning of the Christian era, but not significantly earlier. Such an inference must be viewed against the limited amount of excavation undertaken in this area. Although further work may provide much earlier dates, it is necessary to argue only the basis of those available.

Early pottery from all sites contains rice chaff temper, and faunal remains from Ban Tha Nen include deer, domestic cattle and pig. The pig, like cattle, may well have been domesticated.

Don Tha Pan was abandoned during the ninth century A.D., at a time when new ceramic types, including Khmer stoneware, appeared at nearby Ban Tha Nen. At that time, the settlement covered an area of about 12 ha. The abandonment of such a large site, plus changes in such a basic item of material culture as domestic pottery, and the beginning of stoneworking in yet a third, argue for profound changes in the Roi Et region about a millennium ago. The actual presence of Khmer, either in large numbers or as overlords, is certainly demonstrated by the construction of a Khmer shrine at Ban Tha Nen. Phimai, which was for one brief reign the capital of the Khmer empire, is situated only 144 km from the Roi Et sites, and commands the upper reaches of the same river valley. Phimai was also linked by road with Angkor itself. The distribution of mound sites in north-east Thailand determined on the basis of an aerial survey is remarkable (Williams-Hunt, 1950). The Roi Et settlements form part of a closely grouped cluster of similar sites. Naturally, without widespread excavations, it is impossible to determine the range of dates for these sites. A hypothesis that could be tested through excavation is that they parallel the three excavated Roi Et sites temporally, and represent an economic adaptation to the dry Khorat plain known hitherto, through Chinese accounts, as the state of Chen-la.

The beginning of Khmer expansion into north-east Thailand represents the end of the local prehistoric period. Only a handful of sites have been excavated, of which only one, Non Nok Tha, has been the subject of a major programme of research. This situation, however, illustrates particularly well the procedure necessary during the initial stages of research in a new area. The first point is that prehistory is full of surprises, and the archaeologist, while seeking sites and excavating with all the skill and patience at his disposal, must expect to find the unexpected. Who would have imagined five years ago, that north-east Thailand would furnish evidence for the earliest known rice farming, and a sophisticated bronze technology which may well antedate anything of comparable expertise in China or India ?

Secondly, the establishment of a chronological framework against which to view cultural development is necessary. Granted that there are inconsistencies in the C14 dates from Non Nok Tha, the principal elements of the north and north-east Thai chronological framework are seen in Fig. 11.4. Even if excavations in north and north-east Thailand have been few, the analysis of finds that has already been undertaken makes it possible to frame a model for subsequent testing.

SYNTHESIS: AN INITIAL STADIAL MODEL

The model proposed to fit the available data is essentially stadial (Groube, 1967). It begins with a late Pleistocene hunting-gathering society belonging to a widespread south-east Asian Hoabinhian technocomplex. The people in question hunted the deer, pig, bovine and small game animals, collected shellfish and were reliant upon a variety of plants. Some of these, like the bean, may have been deliberately tended. Further research will clarify this point.

The broad-based hunting and collecting economy was compatible with small groups of people. Spirit Cave could not have accommodated more than an extended family. By the seventh millennium B.C. novel artefacts were present at Spirit Cave. The cord-marked pottery, polished adzes and bifacial knives taken together are strongly suggestive of an economic change. If the

471

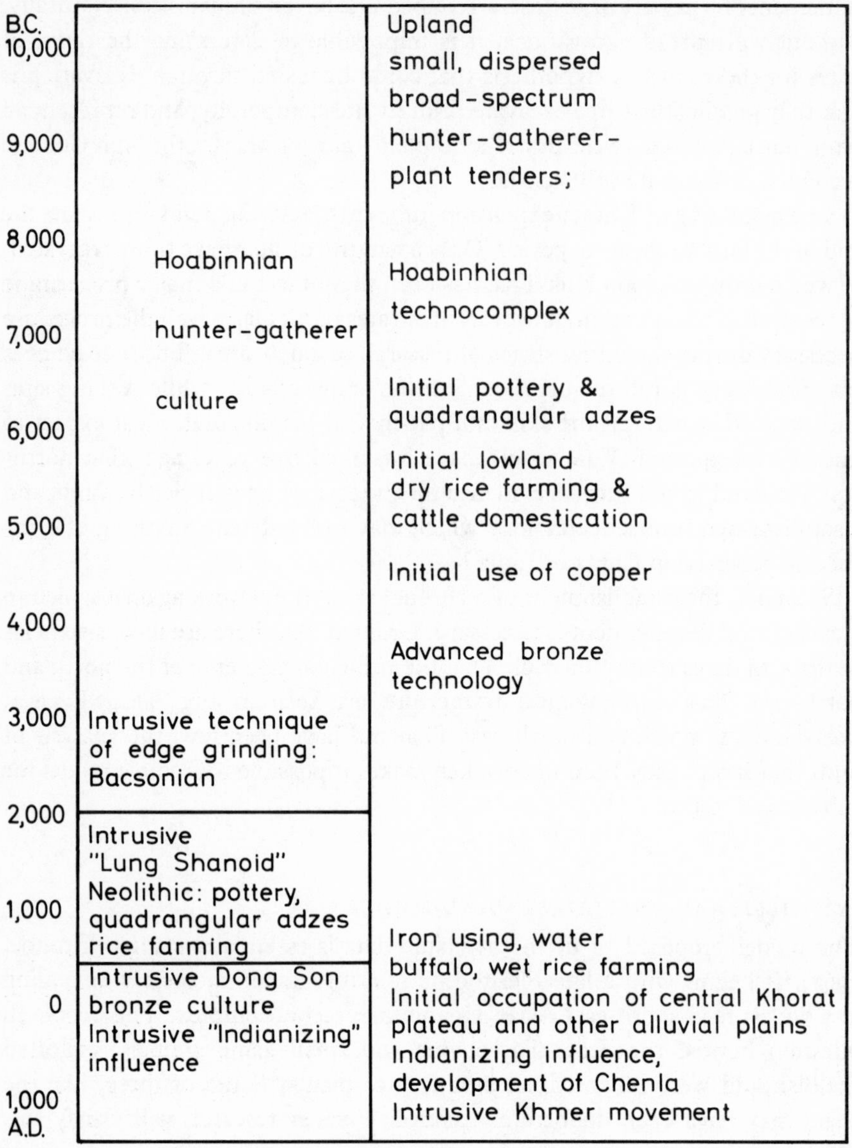

B.C. / A.D.	Model 1	Model 2
B.C. 10,000		Upland small, dispersed broad-spectrum hunter-gatherer-plant tenders;
9,000		
8,000	Hoabinhian	Hoabinhian technocomplex
7,000	hunter-gatherer	
6,000	culture	Initial pottery & quadrangular adzes
5,000		Initial lowland dry rice farming & cattle domestication
4,000		Initial use of copper
3,000	Intrusive technique of edge grinding: Bacsonian	Advanced bronze technology
2,000		
1,000	Intrusive "Lung Shanoid" Neolithic: pottery, quadrangular adzes rice farming	
0	Intrusive Dong Son bronze culture Intrusive "Indianizing" influence	Iron using, water buffalo, wet rice farming Initial occupation of central Khorat plateau and other alluvial plains Indianizing influence, development of Chenla
1,000 A.D.		Intrusive Khmer movement

FIG. 11.4. The basic structure of two alternative models for the prehistory of northern and north-eastern Thailand.

472

long chronology for Non Nok Tha is accepted, the change could well have involved early dry rice farming and cattle domestication in the Piedmont zone, where the Khorat plateau merges with the Petchabun range. Non Nok Tha and Non Nong Chik may well be two of a number of sites reflecting a major economic innovation, which led to relatively intensive utilization of soils suitable for dry rice farming. The continuity of settlement in the Phu Wiang area over at least five and perhaps as many as eight millennia saw further technological changes. Bronze implements cast in sophisticated double moulds were found in Early period burials (starting at between 3000 and 2500 B.C. in radiocarbon years), and iron tools were available by 300 to 600 A.D. The earliest evidence for the presence of water buffalo is the fourteenth century A.D.

The availability of iron and the tractive power of the water buffalo in northeast Thailand were of profound importance, since they opened up extensive but hitherto unoccupied tracts of the Khorat plateau by permitting wet rice farming. Settlement on the plateau was underway by the latter half of the first millennium B.C. Apart from rice farming, the early occupants of the Roi Et area exploited salt and iron deposits. By A.D. 850 at least, settlements of up to 12 ha were in existence. The southern portion of the plateau was then occupied by Khmer from Cambodia, whereas in western and northern districts, the indigenous culture continued to develop free of Khmer domination.

This model involves data relevant to technological, economic and, by inference, social factors. These three are by common consent basic cultural elements (Steward, 1955; Clarke, 1968). It is not fortuitous that the presence of rice chaff temper in occasional sherds from E.P. Level 1 at Non Nok Tha is, for the purposes of an initial model of cultural development, given precedence over the nuances of decorative style or pottery shape. Again, seed cases from Spirit Cave provide information as basic to the current model as the presence of quadrangular polished stone adzes. This situation reflects the recent development in the role of prehistory itself, from an interest in ethnic movement, origins and diffusion to a concern for all these, together with the documentation and explanation of regional patterns of cultural development. Although it is doubtful whether there is enough information available yet to permit the establishment of phases within the 12,000 year time span in question, certain basic trends have been identified. In due course these, and probably others yet to be isolated, will allow the proposition of such phases in a process analogous to those undertaken by MacNeish in the Tehuacan Valley, and by Hole, Flannery and Neely on the Deh Luran plain. At the moment

473

three major prehistoric eras or, in Groube's nomenclature, 'stadia', form the basis of the model (Groube, 1967):

(1) The era of hunting, gathering and plant tending ($-$6000 B.C.).
(2) The era of dry rice farming and cattle herding (? 6000–0).
(3) The era of iron using and wet rice agriculture (A.D. 0–900).

The hypothetical model proposed contrasts markedly with the alternative formulation of a series of migrations into south-east Asia, in that it has concentrated on the basic data from a specific area. No attempt has been made to identify whether or not the initial trend to agriculture was locally inspired or the result of some type of diffusion. Nor have the origins of the earliest known inhabitants of the Khorat plateau been identified. Speculation on the source of the pottery, knives and adzes at Spirit Cave has also been restricted.

There are several good reasons for this approach. In the first place, the long chronology at Non Nok Tha would place bronze technology, rice farming and bovine husbandry there among the earliest in the world. Without supporting evidence both locally and from south-east Asia as a whole, options on the origins of all three must be kept open. Moreover, the presence of agricultural societies in north-east Thailand without any hints of Lungshanoid 'influence' over a 6000–8000 year time span poses cultural ecological problems requiring intensive local research without an obsessive concern for origins. The same situation obtains for Spirit Cave. In terms of the local sequence, the importance of this site lies in its documentation of a long hunter-gatherer, possibly horticulturalist, tradition in the North-west Highlands. Tracing the origins of the intrusive, novel artefact types can only be done by excavating sites other than Spirit Cave, and this has yet to be done.

The unique ceramic styles of the Khorat plateau sites offer no clues for the location of the settlements of the people responsible for the initial intrusion onto the plateau. The lack of ceramic parallels with the material from Phu Wiang makes a westerly origin unlikely.

The cultural prerequisites to this settlement, in terms of technological-economic expertise, as well as the implication of this extension of settlement, can, however, still be profitably considered. The advantage of the present model is that several alternative hypotheses can be advanced to account for each successive critical period of technological and economic change. They include trait diffusion, intensified trade activity, immigration and local innovation, either singly or in combination. Although the testing of these hypotheses will in due course enlarge the scope and value of the present tentative stadial model, there is no question of embarking on such a procedure until more evidence is available.

At its simplest level, the present model reflects cultural trends in three major environmental zones, each integrated through radiocarbon chronology. It might well be seen by some as reflecting similar processes of innovation as have been documented in Mesoamerica and Iran, whereby successive hunter-gatherer, agricultural and urban societies have been recognized and their development explained. Those with an intimate knowledge of the material would pause before embarking on such cross-cultural comparisons. The model currently adopted is flexible, and further excavation will undoubtedly alter it. The degree and direction of alteration are at present unknown.

Acknowledgements

I acknowledge the advice of my colleagues at Otago, C. F. Gorman, D. T. Bayard and R. H. Parker, in preparing this paper. Khun Chin You-di and Khun Noom Yoonaid-hama made possible the research in Thailand, which was financed by the New Zealand University Grants Committee, the Wenner Gren Foundation and the National Science Foundation. W. G. Solheim II conceived the entire structure of the research pro-gramme which has made this article possible.

References

BAYARD, D. T. (1971) Excavations at Non Nok Tha, north-eastern Thailand, 1968: an interim report. *Asian Perspectives*, **13**, in press.

BLACKWOOD, B. (1950) *The Technology of a Modern Stone Age People in New Guinea*. Oxford University Occasional Papers on Technology No. 3.

BRIGGS, L. P. (1951) The ancient Khmer empire. *Transactions of the American Philosophical Society*, **41** (1).

CALDER, A. M. (1971) *An Ethno-archaeological Study of Pottery Distribution in Ban Koeng, Mahasarakam Province, Thailand*. Studies in Prehistoric Anthropology No. 4, Dunedin, New Zealand.

CHILDE, V. G. (1956) *Piecing Together the Past*. London: Routledge.

CLARK, J. G. D. (1954) *Excavations at Star Carr, an early Mesolithic Site at Seamer, near Scarborough, Yorkshire*. Cambridge: Cambridge University Press.

CLARK, J. G. D. (1969) *World Prehistory: A New Outline*. Cambridge.

CLARKE, D. L. (1968) *Analytical Archaeology*. London: Methuen.

COLANI, M. (1927) *L'Age de la Pierre dans la Province de Hoa-Binh, Tonkin*. Hanoi.

COUTTS, P. J. F. (1967) Pottery of eastern New Guinea and Papua. *Mankind*, **6** (10), 482–8.

DUFF, R. (1970) Stone adzes in South East Asia. *Canterbury Museum Bulletin* No. 3.

GORMAN, C. F. (1971) The Hoabinhian and after: subsistence patterns in S.E. Asia during the Late Pleistocene and Early Recent periods. *World Archaeology*, **2** (3), in press.

GROUBE, L. M. (1967) Models in prehistory: a consideration of the New Zealand evidence. *Archaeology and Physical Anthropology in Oceania*, 2, 3 (1), 1–27.

HIGHAM, C. F. W. and LEACH, B. F. (1971) An early center of bovine domestication in S.E. Asia. *Science*, 172 (3978), 54–6.

HIGHAM, C. F. W. and PARKER, R. H. (1970) *Prehistoric Investigations in N.E. Thailand, 1969–70: Preliminary Report*. Dunedin, New Zealand: Department of Anthropology, University of Otago.

HOLE, F., FLANNERY, K. V. and NEELY, J. A. (1969) *Prehistory and Human Ecology of the Deh Luran Plain*. Museum of Anthropology, University of Michigan, Memoir No. 1.

KEAKOORN, P. (1970) The Wat Phra That Phan Khan: Khmer ruins at the village of Bo Phan Khan. In HIGHAM, C. F. W. and PARKER, R. H. *Prehistoric Investigations in N.E. Thailand, 1969–70: Preliminary Report*. Dunedin, New Zealand: Department of Anthropology, University of Otago.

MACNEISH, R. S. (1964) Ancient Mesoamerican civilization. *Science*, 143, 531–7.

MANSUY, H. (1924) *Contribution a l'Étude de la Préhistoire de l'Indochine: Nouvelles de couvertes dan les Cavernes de Bac-Son (Tonkin)*. Memoires du Service Géologique de l'Indochine No. 4.

MATTHEWS, J. (1964) *The Hoabinhian in S.E. Asia and Elsewhere*. Ph.D. thesis, Australian National University, Canberra.

PALMER, B. (1971) Fijian pottery technologies: their relevance to certain problems of S.W. Pacific prehistory. *Pacific Anthropological Records*, in press.

PARKER, R. H. (1968) Review of Archaeological Excavations in Thailand by P. Sørensen and T. Hatting. *Journal of the Polynesian Society*, 77 (3), 307–13.

SOLHEIM, W. G., PARKER, R. H. and BAYARD, D. T. (1966) *Preliminary Report on Excavations at Ban Nadi, Ban Sao Loi and Phimai No. 1*. Hawaii: Department of Anthropology, University of Hawaii.

SØRENSEN, P. and HATTING, T. (1967) *Archaeological Excavations in Thailand, Vol. II: Ban Kao, Part I*. Copenhagen.

STEWARD, J. H. (1955) *Theory of Culture Change*. Urbana, Ill.: University of Illinois Press.

UNITED NATIONS (1968) *Atlas of Physical, Economic and Social Resources of the Lower Mekong Basin*. New York: United Nations.

WILLIAMS-HUNT, P. D. R. (1950) Irregular earthworks in eastern Siam: an air survey. *Antiquity*, 24 (93), 30–6.

YEN, D. E. (1971) The development of agriculture in Oceania. *Pacific Anthropological Records*, in press.

12
Socio-economic and demographic models for the Neolithic and Bronze Ages of Europe

A. G. SHERRATT
University of Cambridge, England

*A preliminary conception, indefinite but comprehensive, is needful as an intro-
duction to a definite conception. A complex idea is not communicable directly,
by giving one after another of its component parts their finished forms; since
if no outline pre-exists in the mind of the recipient these component parts will
not be rightly combined.*

HERBERT SPENCER

Introduction

Until recently there was at least a measure of general agreement among
European prehistorians on the aims of archaeology and the appropriate framework for its interpretation. The most explicit statements of these aims and
methods are to be found in the writings of V. G. Childe, in his series of syntheses of European prehistory from 1925 onwards, and in various later works
devoted specifically to methodology (Childe 1925, 1956). Childe's approach
was based on three related concepts: the 'stages of culture' classification of
Morgan and Engels, the key role of technology in relation to these, and a model
of technological change which assumed that innovation was a characteristic
of specific types of society. From this point of view, the progress of European
societies depended on their proximity to Near Eastern civilization through
the mediation of the 'secondary civilizations' of the Mediterranean, themselves
only made possible by the 'Urban Revolution' in the Orient. Thus the whole
process depended ultimately on one or two unique events – the achievement
of a regular surplus by irrigation agriculture in the alluvial valleys of the
Nile and the Tigris-Euphrates.

477

Both the theoretical basis of this, and the usefulness of these ideas in interpreting the evidence now available, have been questioned. In particular, on the theoretical side, it has become clear that more consideration must be given to factors which in the archaeological record are less obvious than technological change. The use of economic concepts such as 'surplus' cannot be separated from demographic questions, such as why this was not absorbed by population increase, or whether the productivity of Mesopotamian agriculture really was inherently greater than contemporary European systems. The role of technology must be assessed in the light of its relation to specific agricultural and economic systems, as it is only in relation to these that the significance of particular innovations can be judged.

Childe's interpretative framework grew directly from his own attempts to make sense of excavations and field work actively taking place when he wrote. Since his death in 1957 the amount of available information has greatly increased, and has highlighted the need for clarification of the principles and concepts used in evaluating and comparing it. Many of the earlier attempts at interpretation have now been made redundant by new evidence. For instance, many apparent gaps in the sequence of cultures have been closed by the discovery of 'transitional' phases. In consequence, the prominence given to invasion as an explanation of cultural change can be seen as in part due to an inadequate sample. The removal of this formerly dominant concept has clearly demonstrated the paucity of ideas employed by archaeologists in their interpretation of prehistory.

Similarly, techniques of absolute dating have demonstrated that important technological developments such as metallurgy or the use of wheeled vehicles did not reach Europe from the centres of Near Eastern civilization, but can be seen developing in non-urban contexts (Renfrew, 1969; Piggott, 1968). All these necessitate a much closer look at the processes of economic and social development within the 'barbarian' societies themselves, and suggest that contrasts with early urban societies may be more of degree than of kind.

It is clear then that the pioneer synthesis of Childe has been outgrown in many respects – hardly surprising as this basic framework had already provided a support for a quarter of a century's work, and the synthesis was first sketched out in a period when our knowledge was both quantitatively and qualitatively less than it is today. Now the framework must be expanded to take into account many new types of evidence. In particular, a much wider range of evidence of prehistoric economies is now becoming available from new recovery techniques and the systematic analysis of faunal and archaeo-

478

botanical evidence (Higgs, forthcoming). These require ideas and methods of analysis that have not up to now been developed by prehistorians – or indeed by any other discipline, since the study of relevant forms of change in subsistence economies is a primary aim neither of economic anthropology, which for the most part deals with relatively static, systems, nor of development economics, which deals with the impact of advanced economies on less developed ones. Useful guidance comes from economic history, particularly in suggesting the kinds of relationship existing between technological, demographic and social factors, but these studies concern types of society very different from those studied by the prehistorian.

Similar considerations apply to the stimulating ideas now current in the 'new geography' (Haggett, 1965), which emphasizes the potential of considering the spatial setting of economic and social processes, and provides elegant methods of investigating the logic of spatial patterns and the significance of the location of activities. The application of these ideas to the problems of prehistory has brought to light a hitherto neglected source of information about prehistoric economies.

Perhaps the most useful contribution of this movement for archaeology, however, is the model it provides for dealing with the abstraction of relevant aspects from a mass of data. One of the puzzling features of archaeology until recently was the contrast between the carefully compiled distribution maps, painstakingly accumulated dot by dot and then left unexamined as if this activity constituted an end in itself, and the casually drawn 'blanket' maps of (e.g.) 'Europe in Third Millennium', with their all-embracing cultural boundaries covering widely different kinds of territory, and often with inexplicably blank areas covering whole countries. The objection is not to the use of abstraction – which is after all basic to all cartography – but the gap between the highly particular and the highly general. It is in this aspect that the parallel of geography is most relevant, for the use of controlled and conscious abstraction of spatial patterns has been the basis of the recent revolution in geographical thinking.

The need for abstract models in archaeology is equally acute, and perhaps more so, as prehistorians have until now been constricted by their inability to describe and explain their data except in terms of known historical situations, visualizable in human terms – invaders, merchants, prospectors, royal dynasties, etc. But most of the societies studied by the prehistorian were fundamentally different even from the tribes described by Caesar. A historical scale and vocabulary are thus too limited to encompass the variety of situations encountered in prehistory: the events of the Neolithic and Bronze Ages cannot

479

necessarily be visualized in terms of any historical situation known to us. As a consequence of the hitherto limited set of ideas and terminology, little attempt has been made to describe objectively the various kinds of culture change encountered in prehistoric Europe. What is required is a frank recognition of the inadequacy of current language and concepts, and a systematic attempt to distinguish between different kinds of change. This involves the construction of a necessarily abstract series of models based upon the detailed examination of the culture history of specific areas. In this, the use of a specialized terminology – 'élite subculture', 'unit reorientation', 'centre/periphery diffusion', etc. – is an unavoidable consequence.

The difficulty of using historical situations to suggest hypotheses about the remote past can be to some extent alleviated by a closer attention to the findings of social anthropology, which deals with the properties of small-scale social organization, and thus might be expected on *a priori* grounds to be relevant to the study of Neolithic and Bronze Age communities. The fact that the societies known to ethnography exist for the most part in environments very different from that of Europe, however, requires that such hypotheses should be based on the general principles of social organization at various levels of complexity, rather than on simplistic parallels with particular tribes. Fortunately, the rapid development of social anthropology has produced useful generalizations of this kind that were not available in the early days of prehistoric archaeology, when 'ethnographic parallels' often produced diasastrous results.

While each of the disciplines mentioned above have techniques and concepts to offer, it still remains for the prehistorian to provide an answer to his own unique set of problems. But much of the necessary raw material must inevitably come from sources other than the evidence of his own researches – ideas of how population change occurs, or the necessary labour requirements for a particular crop, for example. The basic problem is how to integrate these types of information in the most useful way to illuminate the kinds of change evidenced in the prehistoric record. It is here that model building is an *essential* element of future progress in archaeology, because it makes explicit the character of the assumptions involved and thus allows a much greater flexibility of approach, especially by the technique of working from artificially simplified assumptions and gradually introducing the complexities of the real world. These abstract models have the additional advantage that they provide a way of comparing one situation with another in their general aspects, and thus offer the possibility of providing a common language and set of problems for archaeologists working in different periods and areas.

The systems approach

An appropriate way of thinking about the interaction of a variety of factors in a complex situation is provided by systems analysis. As Ashby comments (1956, p. 5), 'for two centuries it [science] has been exploring systems that are either intrinsically simple or that are capable of being analysed into simple components. . . . In the study of some systems, however, complexity could not be wholly evaded'. The scientific study of such complex systems – whether societies, organisms or sophisticated machines – depends on a set of ideas concerning control and regulation which have only been clarified in this century, largely by the progress of control engineering. These ideas are now being widely applied in fields such as ecology and economics, and are thus highly relevant to the kinds of situation discussed here.

The basic ideas of systems theory are essentially simple, and relate to the way in which the various elements of the situation effect each other. Where changes in one element cause corresponding changes in another, which act to return the first element to its initial value, the relationship is said to involve *negative feedback*, and results in an equilibrium position or relationship. For example: in a society where land is relatively scarce and there are property qualifications for marriage, a rise in population will cause the age of marriage to be deferred until an otherwise eligible partner has accumulated sufficient property. In this way, fertility will be lowered and the population will fall again. Where a system has many negative feedback links, its behaviour is *homeostatic*, and any disruption will be followed by a return to equlibrium.

Conversely, a change in one element may cause a change in another, which encourages a further change in the first element. This is *positive feedback*, and results in change at an ever increasing rate – unless checked by other, negative feedback, loops. An increase in population, for instance, may stimulate an advance in agricultural technique such as irrigation, which in turn, by increasing productivity, allows a further growth of population.

The analysis of complex systems is based upon the identification of the key variables in the situation, and the kinds of relationship existing between them. It is futile to attempt to find single 'causes' for changes in such networks: the whole set of variables must be taken into account. The relationships between these determine the way in which the system develops, and the way in which it reacts to changes in its environment.

Only certain aspects of the total natural and social environment are relevant to this analysis at a particular point in time, and moreover this 'effective environment' changes as the system itself develops. Environmental change consists both in short-term fluctuation and in long-term changes. The effect

481

of a change such as an increase in mean annual rainfall will depend on the economic basis of the society: if this is a small population confined to lowland areas, a rise in water-table may be critical for its way of life. If, on the other hand, it is mainly confined to the open uplands, the effect may be negligible unless it opens up new opportunities for the exploitation of lowland areas. What actually constitutes the 'effective environment' will thus be related to changes in the system itself. The development of a new metallurgical technique of ore extraction is an obvious example of this; but less obvious is the fact that, as a population grows and settlement spreads to new types of soil, a change in the effective environment of a society occurs even if factors such as rainfall remain constant.

Social systems represent highly complex arrangements which persist because of the ability of the different elements of the system to react to changes in individual elements or in the environmental input in such a way as to maintain the organization of the system as a whole. Because of this there exist restrictions on each of the component subsystems. Certain forms of exploitation, technology, social organization and size of population represent an optimum adjustment, both between themselves and with the environment. This is the form that minimizes the possibility of external disruption and internal breakdown, and in general is the one that requires minimum expenditure of energy for maximum return. The actual patterns of behaviour will represent a compromise between the various needs of the system to maintain itself with as little effort as possible in a given environment.

The idea of an optimum does not imply the most productive system of exploitation (or the maximum possible population, or the most efficient technology) but rather that the various elements will form consistent patterns and values, which are in balance with one another and allow the system to run smoothly. A particular set of balanced relationships between existing techniques of production and distribution and available resources serves to define a *state* of the system. Growth within the framework of a given state is possible as long as the relationship between key variables is preserved. Lotka's diagram (reproduced in Clarke, 1968, Fig. 108) of the constant ratios between the human, cattle, sheep and pig populations in the United States between 1871 and 1921 is an example of such a growth pattern preserving a key relationship (cf. allometric growth in organisms: D'Arcy Thompson, 1917). The more complex and efficient the regulation – based on the number and character of negative feedback loops – the faster such a system can expand while preserving the constant relationships between key variables.

The type of behaviour exhibited by the system, as it appears to an observer,

482

will depend on the period of time over which the system is studied, as in the short term a system may appear roughly in equilibrium, but in a longer term changes may be apparent. For a society to continue to exist as a coherent unit, an overall condition of homeostasis is necessary. However, this adjustment is rarely, if ever, complete, and in any case the environment of the system is also subject to change. The cumulative effect of small adjustments may thus lead to long-term changes in the system as a whole. If changes in any particular element are difficult to reverse (as with the growth of population or the degradation of the soil with over-use), the sequence of changes may produce an overall trend, conventionally known as the *trajectory* of the system.

The potential for growth within a given state, however, is inevitably limited, since not all the key variables are equally flexible. The response of population to the opening up of new resources is likely to be immediate and rapid, but the expansion of production to meet a rising population is more difficult, since only under certain circumstances is it possible to achieve this continuously over a long period of time. The phenomenon of diminishing returns to an increased scale of production with the same kind of exploitation (discussed in more detail below) makes it increasingly difficult to maintain the existing equilibrium.

When growth can no longer take place within the framework of a given state of a system, a number of outcomes is possible. The first is that mechanisms that inhibit further expansion come into play, and the system stabilizes at a certain point. The second is that an alteration in the methods of exploitation and related elements may take place, either by using new resources or by increased technological efficiency in exploiting those already used to produce a new stable pattern. This is possible only if the available resources are sufficiently elastic to respond to improvements in technique. If continuous growth by this means is possible, the system will pass through successive states, each representing a new balance both within itself (as a result of changes in scale) and with the new aspects of the environment (if it is expanding in a non-uniform landscape). If, however, one of the key variables expands beyond the ability of the others to adjust to it, the system will lose its equilibrium condition either temporarily or permanently, and population will probably fall, social organization disintegrate and sophisticated technologies go out of use.

There are thus three possible patterns of development: stabilization, disintegration, or progressive adaptation. In the course of prehistory, directional change is dependent on the existence of the third outcome. In a crude Darwinian model it is only the successful societies that matter. This may well be the only kind of model applicable to pre-Neolithic societies, because of the small sample of the surviving evidence. However, to deal adequately with the more abundant and wider range of evidence from later periods, all three possibilities must be taken into account – though, even so, the range of possible models must inevitably lack the sophistication of those made possible by historical evidence (see Wrigley, 1969).

In analysing the development of prehistoric societies, therefore, aspects such as technological progress cannot be abstracted and considered in isolation. Instead, the problem can only be clarified by examining the patterns of growth that result from the interaction of the various elements, and the constraints that slow down or prevent further development.

This conclusion is of major significance for archaeological model building, because it implies that realistic models of the development of prehistoric societies require a consideration of many features of these societies for which direct evidence is by no means obvious. This reinforces Binford's comments (1968, p. 17) on the nature of archaeological procedure: we must formulate hypotheses about the nature of prehistoric societies in order to be able to test them against the artefactual record. In order to formulate such hypotheses, however, we need a set of ideas about the ways in which our key variables interact with each other.

The following sections of this paper are an attempt to investigate the relationships between population levels, natural resources, technologies and patterns of exploitation, and social organization. Even a crude model of the way in which these adjust to each other and encourage or restrict further development would be an advance upon the inherently unsatisfactory device of examining in detail only those aspects of prehistoric societies for which evidence is easy to obtain.

Population

One of the most important aspects of prehistoric societies which has only recently been given systematic consideration is population. The potential for growth in human populations has been the subject of comment since Malthus, but the recognition of this as one of the most powerful factors in producing change in economic and social systems, although mentioned (e.g. Durkheim, 1933, pp. 260–2), has come about only with the crises produced by the spread of advanced medical techniques. As a result there is now a growing literature on demography and related problems, including a number of studies (e.g. Boserup, 1965) relating it to aspects such as technology and patterns of exploitation.

As a method of defining the principles at work, it is useful to take a series of artificially simple situation models and see what conclusions can be drawn from these. This approach underlies the classic work on population models, Sauvy's *General Theory of Population* (1969; see also Wrigley, 1969).

The first step is to investigate the kinds of equilibrium that would occur in a situation where resources cannot be expanded further. With an increase in population, but no compensating rise in productivity, natural checks will prevent a rise in population beyond a certain point. This is where the increased mortality rate due to lack of food, and the decreased fertility rate produced by undernourishment, together reduce the rate of growth to an insignificant level (see Fig. 12.1). Even animal populations, however, maintain a lower equilibrium than this, by lowering fertility before a drastic rise in

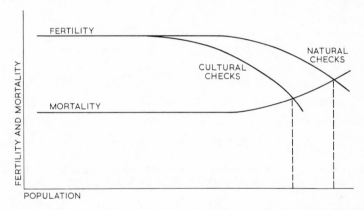

FIG. 12.1. Model for fertility and mortality levels with increasing density of population.

mortality occurs (Wynne-Edwards, 1962). In human societies a variety of methods of lowering fertility is available, including raising the marriage age, taboos on intercourse at certain times, (e.g. during lactation), abortion, exposure of infants or deliberate infanticide. As some of these are density-dependent, that is to say they come increasingly into effect as population rises above a certain point, there is another equilibrium position below that established by natural factors. This has to be defined by an economic analysis.

With a limited amount of land of variable quality and no possibility of improving techniques of exploitation, a rise in population from a small initial value will result first of all in a slightly increased amount of available food per person, by allowing the most productive labour-intensive techniques to be applied. Then, having passed this stage, the food available per person will begin to decline as the use of less productive land begins and the additional labour input does not increase productivity in proportion to the number of new workers. The point at which the maximum amount of food per person is available is the optimum, and mechanisms that reduce fertility will increasingly come into effect the more the population exceeds this (see Fig. 12.2). The situation thus possesses a ceiling, a limit beyond which further increase in

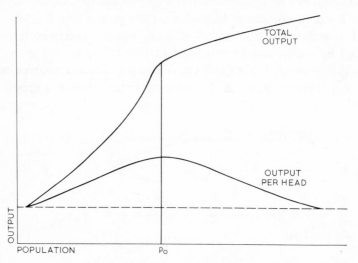

FIG. 12.2. Model for output with increasing density of population, with inelastic resources and a single pattern of exploitation (after Sauvy, 1969).

population could not be supported, and below this a suboptimal area of economic disincentive to growth. There is no intrinsic reason, of course, why food alone should be the limiting factor: in many cases it may well be shelter or fuel, or other essential raw materials. The same model still applies. Allowing for fluctuations in productivity (Fig. 1.15), this optimal figure could be as low as 20-30% of carrying capacity, calculated on purely ecological grounds. To prevent population rising far above this optimum *over a long period of time* it is probable that systematic infanticide would have to be practised (Birdsell, 1968, p. 236).

In order to understand the characteristics of human population growth, it is necessary to examine it from an evolutionary standpoint, and a number of relevant observations have recently been brought forward at the symposium on *Man the Hunter* (Lee and DeVore, 1968).

486

The slowness of the rise in global population during the Pleistocene (Deevey, 1960) indicates that, even with the possibilities offered by cultural adaptation, populations must have been stabilized for much of the time in the way discussed above. Thus the colonization of the ground niche in the Miocene produced a characteristically low pattern of population density: at least human population density for most of the Pleistocene was notably lower than that of most monkeys and apes, while human hunting groups are much smaller than those of the ground living apes. The colonization of this niche

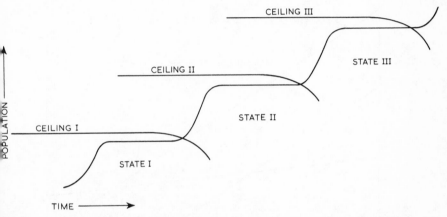

FIG. 12.3. Model of the reaction of population to a fluctuating environment in which changes in exploitation pattern occur under strong pressure produced by a lowering of the ceiling for a given pattern (system state). Only successful outcomes are shown.

was made possible by various kinds of 'cultural' behaviour, involving tool use, food preparation, greater mobility in use of resources, and probably family limitation through infanticide. This adaptation was characterized by its flexibility and lack of specialization and produced a low density with a high potential for further adaptation to new habitats. In terms of the use of available food, there seems to have been a tendency for only a fraction of the ecological potential to have been exploited, in comparison with the possibilities allowed by tool use, etc. The determinants of population density at a hunter-gatherer level seem to involve social factors such as kinship breeding taboos and large territories to reduce competition and prevent over-use of staple resources, thus producing population levels well below the carrying capacity. The use of small game such as mice and songbirds for food, for example, which could allow densities many times higher than those observed ethnographically, would thus probably have occurred only when the use of more attractive

487

resources would not have allowed population to reach this social optimum (see diagram, Fig. 12.4).

This formulation of the problem, consistent with the evidence both of physical and social anthropology, throws considerable doubt on the simplistic explanation of economic change by reference to inferred 'population pressure' at various points in the Pleistocene (Vita-Finzi and Higgs, 1970). Sahlins (in

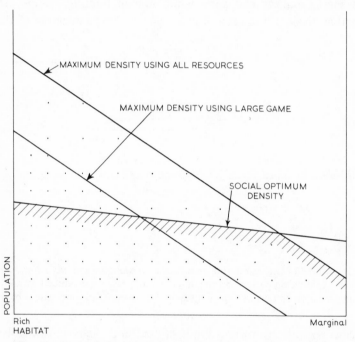

FIG. 12.4. Hypothesized relationship between population density, habitat and utilization of resources among hunter-gatherer groups.

Lee and DeVore, 1968) has emphasized the relatively low labour requirements of known hunter-gatherer groups. The slowness of population growth suggests that, rather than achieve a further increase in productivity entailing extensive modification of the existing way of life, most groups at this level would stabilize their populations well below carrying capacity for a given technology, and continue with a system of exploitation that gave a reliable supply of food for relatively little effort.

The culturally adaptive radiation of the human species in the Pleistocene was a natural consequence of its ecological strategy, the tendency for the population to stabilize at a low level and to bud off where possible. The spread into northern latitudes involved a greater reliance on the meat component of

488

diet, higher mobility, and a greater necessity for storage techniques. It is likely that the radical changes necessary to adapt to new environments came about at least in part as a result of the strong selective pressure produced by a *lowering* of the ceiling for the existing type of exploitation, with the advance of the glacial and periglacial zones into occupied temperate areas. In such a situation, only groups able to undergo radical changes in their way of life could survive, as described in a Darwinian model (Fig. 12.3).

In this way changes could occur despite the tendency to stabilize patterns of exploitation and population density, and from this model processes of change would be most likely to occur in environments subject to strong fluctuations. A model of this kind has been suggested by Huxley (1953), and is probably an appropriate framework for considering changes such as the Middle/Upper Palaeolithic transition in which biological and cultural aspects are closely interlinked.

This crude Darwinian model gives only a schematic explanation of the major shifts in exploitation patterns before the post-glacial. For the periods with which this paper is primarily concerned a closer analysis is required, taking into account the types of social and technological transformation involved in economic change. This involves a consideration of the resources used by particular groups, the way their exploitation fits together into an overall strategy, and their responsiveness to changes in these exploitation patterns. An additional element is the role of environmental factors in inducing change.

Resources and potential for growth

The above discussion suggested that economic expansion, far from being a characteristic of all societies, is a rather exceptional occurrence. Small scale economies appear to be characterized both by low levels of labour input and low population densities, even though human populations possess the ability to make use of a great range of food resources. The small fraction of these exploited at any one time makes the use of calculations based on 'carrying capacity' a dangerous procedure. The only alternative is a detailed reconstruction of prehistoric economies based upon evidence of food remains, technology and site locations.

The selection of resources used in subsistence economies has often been attributed to an arbitrary cultural choice. This reflects more the lack of attempts to apply economic models to such situations than a meaningful generalization. It is possible here to suggest only a few of the relevant factors, but the regularities in available data on prehistoric subsistence suggest that the constraints on choice are well defined and can be described in terms of a small number of basic principles.

A distinction was made in the preceding section between economies in areas where a wide range of choice is possible and those where most available resources must be utilized. While this has some analytic value in suggesting a generalized relationship between population levels and ecological factors, the examination of specific economic systems requires a full documentation of seasonal fluctuations and the geographical distribution of resources.

One of the most important factors to be taken into account is the fluctuation in the abundance of available resources. Not merely must population levels be adjusted to the season of greatest scarcity in the year but the economic strategy must minimize the effects of differences in yield from year to year. The effects of such fluctuations, however, can be cushioned by reliance on a combination of resources which assures the highest return under the most adverse conditions. This is particularly important in determining the balance between animal and plant foods, and accounts for the heavy emphasis on pastoralism in arid regions (Deschler, 1965).

Although animal resources are less productive than plant ones, being one step higher in the food chain, they possess the advantage of mobility, so that scattered flushes of vegetation in areas of variable rainfall, which are too erratic to be predicted and thus used for cereal growing, can be used to support moving herds. Even where the rainfall is more regular, but the area is still subject to droughts, the use of plant foods such as cereals still needs to be supplemented by a strong pastoral component, in case of crop failure. The types of social organization typical of such economies embody further security precautions, based on the circulation of animals on loan.

In less marginal areas, however, such considerations are not so important in determining economic strategies and population levels. In particular, there seem to be a number of stable patterns of small-scale exploitation. The lack of complex techniques for storage, for instance, or for intensive forms of cropping, places limits on the development of increasingly productive ways of utilizing many types of resources. Although shellfish may be conveniently gathered from beds exposed intertidally or in shallow water, any more intensive method would involve a 'leap' in technological capacity, including for instance the construction of large-scale dams, cages, etc. Similarly, the most productive method of exploiting an ungulate population is by a ranching technique, in which large numbers of animals are raised to a uniform age at which the gain in meat weight begins to be offset by the continuing cost of providing grazing

490

or fodder. In small-scale exploitation, however, this is impossible: what is required is a regular supply of daily food, which is best supplied by live animal products (blood, milk, etc.) if this is possible, or by occasional culling.

While an increase in yield is therefore possible, it is unlikely to be attempted by most groups practising small-scale economies. Only where there is a set of relatively simple transition possibilities, based upon a series of small modifications to an existing system, are changes likely to occur. Given the tendency of societies to 'fight to stay the same' (Schon, 1971, p. 32), by resisting innovations that would cause large-scale restructuring of established patterns, such possibilities are limited in occurrence, and are conceivable (*a*) only with resources with a high potential for expansion (elasticity), and (*b*) with resource systems including complementary resources which allow the problems created by the development of one element in the resource system to be overcome by the provision of – for example – a secure if low-yielding supply of food in case of the failure of the main element.

One of the most striking contrasts in patterns of growth is that between cereal-based economies, and those based on animal resources such as ungulates or shellfish. The root of the contrast lies in the relative elasticity of the resources. With an ungulate population, cropping above a certain percentage of the population will impair the ability of the herd to reproduce itself. The size of the total population can only be raised by drastic changes in the structure of the ecosystem. With cereals, on the other hand, by relatively small changes in the structure of the ecosystem – shifting plants with an annual habit into niches occupied by plants more successful in competition – the yield of useful products can be greatly increased. Moreover, there is a more or less direct relationship between labour input and return: clearance and sowing of small additional areas produces an immediate effect in terms of increased output. Similarly, even relatively minor advances in technology may have the effect of greatly increasing yield, both by allowing more efficient cultivation methods and by making possible the use of hitherto unused types of land.

The significance of the Neolithic Revolution lies in the almost continuous growth possible in cereal-based economies, and the increasing degree of interference with the ecosystem that it entails. The domestication of animals such as sheep provided a resource compatible with a sedentary pattern of exploitation in a system in which settlements needed to be located for access to cereal-growing soils, and provided not only additional protein but also security in case of crop failure. Patterns of animal exploitation were thus adjusted to complement an increased reliance on plant food. Despite the difficulties involved in actually identifying 'domesticated' animals (Higgs

491

and Jarman, 1969) the need for greater control over movement, breeding, etc., in this situation is clear, and the distinction between agricultural and 'hunter-gatherer' economies remains valid.

Patterns of growth in agricultural economies are thus closely related to the amounts and distributions of fertile land, which affect both the capacity for further expansion and the kinds of more intensive exploitation that can be developed. In areas of heavy leaching such as the tropics, the potential for growth with a pre-industrial technology is much smaller than in temperate areas, even though in almost every zone there are alluvial soils whose concentration of minerals and water retentive capacity makes them first class agricultural land. The capacity for further expansion thus depends ultimately on the availability of 'middle range' soils which allow expansion to continue when the first class ones are filled to capacity. A second factor is present in some areas where a diversity of different zones adjoin (or are connected by easy transport links) and the integration of zones of specialized production is possible through reciprocal redistribution and exchange networks.

One might therefore expect a fundamental difference in the demographic and cultural characteristics of cereal-based and non cereal-based economies. Demographic controls in the first group will not be as strict as those in the second, because of the ever present possibilities for expansion. This carries with it a need for constant technological innovation to overcome the difficulties of new effective environments, and also a much higher element of risk in that a sharp discontinuity in the landscape – a productive set of soils surrounded by a barren area, for instance – may interrupt the smooth pattern of growth. This pattern will be the most marked in areas such as Europe, where a wide range of fertile soils of glacial or post-glacial origin would allow a continuous expansion of the cereal growing area, even with a pre-industrial technology. In tropical areas, this potential is more limited, and agricultural systems in many areas have stabilized at levels of relatively low productivity, and in some cases seem to have reverted to hunter-gatherer systems (see Lathrap, 1968).

The phrase 'the colonization of Europe' has often been used by historians (e.g. Koebner, 1966) to describe the extension of settlement in the Middle Ages into hitherto uncultivated areas. Yet this marginal infilling is but the final phase of a continuous process with its beginning in the Early Neolithic. The demographic crises of the later Middle Ages reflect the increased difficulty with which the extension of the margin of cultivation could be carried out. In many documented instances, population was very close to the ceiling. As Postan and Titow (1959) noted for the estates of the bishopric of Winchester in the thirteenth century, poor harvests were directly reflected in mortality figures. Wrigley (1962) has suggested that the ceiling imposed by competing uses for available land caused a recession until the bottleneck was broken by technical innovation – in this case the development of machines based on coal and iron rather than wood. This was an essential element in a solution involving radical changes in settlement location, land tenure and more intensive systems of agrarian production, complemented by the growth of an imperialist colonial system based on the export of specialist manufactured products and the importation of food and raw materials.

This formulation of the problem suggests that similar, though smaller scale, phenomena might occur in areas of restricted land such as the Mediterranean peninsulae, and that this might be tested against the evidence for settlement expansion in earlier periods. This line is pursued below.

A further feature of continuous growth systems is their vulnerability in pre-industrial situations, when a ceiling of greater than usual difficulty is reached. When a system develops through states of increasing productivity, its momentum is maintained (through the absence of strong density-dependent regulators) until a simple solution is no longer possible, and temporary retrenchment becomes necessary. While this model therefore assumes a general trend towards population increase and intensification of production, it is also capable of dealing with situations where decline or collapse is evidenced. Complex economic systems with relatively fast rates of expansion are naturally vulnerable to this, though historians have usually preferred to attribute such phenomena to the invasions of barbarians.

Systems of land use

The economies of prehistoric Europe and the Near East thus belong to a class of economies characterized by the possibility of more or less continuous expansion. It might be expected from this that the economic, social and technological developments that characterize the post-Neolithic sequence could be explained in terms of this process of growth, and that the different patterns that characterize the Near East, the Mediterranean and inland Europe could be related to the geographical background – the distribution of soils, raw materials and transport routes. To follow the complications of this approach, some further discussion of the interrelationship between population, technology and economic strategy is required, in which ethnographic data are necessary to illustrate some of the requirements of different patterns of land use. It is at this level that the use of systems theory begins to have

493

practical advantages, as a way of handling the complex interrelationships between the various aspects of production.

An important set of information for the analysis of subsistence agriculture is the labour requirements of the various crops. As there is great variation in these, and as societies are generally unwilling to work harder than is necessary, certain resources possess clear advantages for populations of a given size. Thus it has already been noted that hunter-gatherer groups expend relatively little effort on subsistence in comparison with agriculturalists. The same contrast is true for the various stages of agricultural intensification.

An increase in output can be achieved by two means: either by an increase in the area of land utilized or by intensification – the more productive use of land already cropped. Both require changes in technology and both have implications for social organization, but intensification makes special demands on labour input. Expansion in a given system proceeds by a balance between the two processes related to the opportunities of an individual environment; but before introducing a spatial element into the model, some characteristics of the intensification process should be noted.

The most thorough discussion of this problem is by Boserup (1965). She points out that with a small population, the most economic agricultural system in terms of labour input is an extensive one, based on swidden (slash-and-burn) cultivation with a simple technology. Intensification is measured by the increased frequency of cropping of a given area, with a consequent shortening of fallow periods. This process has several implications. In the first place little preparation of the soil is necessary for long fallow systems, where cropping is for short periods only and it is not necessary to maintain fertility by manuring during this period, nor even worthwhile clearing tree stumps. In consequence, the use of the plough is unnecessary and the cultivated plot is abandoned when weeds begin to compete seriously with crops or when the nutrients released by burning off the forest are exhausted. For short fallow systems, however, both manuring and ploughing become necessary, as the land is cropped beyond the point at which initial fertility begins to decline, and fallowing is only long enough to allow the growth of grass, presenting problems in tillage. Further intensification, allowing even multicropping, depends on the introduction of techniques such as irrigation or terracing involving heavy capital investment.

In an extensive agricultural system, a relatively small labour input is sufficient to produce a good crop. As hoeing and weeding take a large amount of labour time, any increase in these is particularly important in this respect. It is these elements that become increasingly necessary with intensification.

In addition, yields are likely to fall somewhat even with manuring. With plough agriculture, considerations of scale are critical – draught animals must be fed and sufficient beasts are required for manuring to make cultivation profitable. In consequence of these, one of the corollaries of intensification is an actual fall in output per man hour. Since labour is in any case low in extensive systems, this is still a possibility, but intensification does imply longer working hours if output is to be increased. Intensification is thus not likely to be undertaken except in a situation where the population cannot be supported by existing systems of cultivation and until other possibilities have been exhausted – or would themselves involve a comparable increase in effort.

Boserup's scheme is artificial to the extent that it neglects local soil variation and presents only an economic analysis of the factors involved in intensification. In the analysis of the agricultural development of a specific area the range of available land types and their distribution must be an important element. The soils determine the degree to which intensification can proceed with a pre-industrial technology without causing permanent damage. Many tropical soils are easily overcropped, and in consequence the widespread occurrence of extensive systems can be seen in part as due to this. In other areas, however, extensive systems occur on land that would sustain a shorter fallow period: here land is simply abundant in relation to population and there is no need for a system involving higher labour input.

On the basis of African evidence, Allan (1965) has produced a sixfold land classification based on the ratio of crop time to fallow time. Although based on the use of the soils, for the long-settled agricultural areas there is a strong correlation between this and inherent fertility characteristics. An important distinction can be drawn, for example, between *permanent cultivation soils*, and others that require a longer fallow period. The latter range through *semi-permanent cultivation, recurrent cultivation, shifting cultivation, and partial cultivation* to wholly uncultivable soils, requiring progressively longer fallow periods. Although Boserup's model does not admit the existence of ceilings determined by soil type, it is clear that with a pre-industrial technology they must exist. Certainly the more fertile areas could formerly have been cultivated on an extensive system: but as population grew, intensification proceeded only as far as the nature of the soil allowed without artificial fertilizers.

With a small initial population, the richest soils will be settled first, especially permanent cultivation soils if they are available. The growth of population leads to the spread of settlement to poorer and more difficult soils, first on an extensive basis and then on to as intensive a system as the

495

soil will permit. As the good soils are filled up, a choice will open as to whether local intensification or extension of the margin of cultivation is more attractive. This depends on the character and availability of the remaining land – whether it is only slightly less fertile than that already cultivated, or much poorer – and thus on the relative cost-effectiveness of the two possibilities.

Many of the types of choice made by subsistence farmers in assessing the cost-effectiveness of various types of exploitation are conveniently expressed as programming models (e.g. linear programming, integer programming, etc.). These are techniques for finding the optimum allocation of labour on different resources with different degrees of productivity to give a maximum yield, and they make it possible to work out mathematically a solution found in practice only by trial and error. Its operation will be made clear by an example of linear programming taken from Joy (1967).

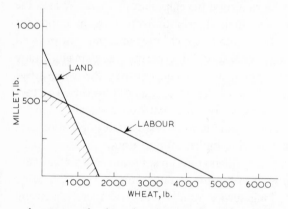

FIG. 12.5. Linear programming solution to the problem of finding the optimum allocation of land and labour in the situation described in the text (after Joy, 1967).

A community has the choice of two crops, wheat and millet, with different productivity and labour requirements. The former produces 800 lb per acre, the latter 400 lb per acre. Land available is limited; so is labour, since both crops ripen at the same time. Wheat takes eight days per acre to harvest; millet thirty-six days per acre. Two acres of land, and forty-eight days of harvest labour are available. Land and labour are thus the *constraints* on production. If all the land were used for millet, there would not be enough labour to harvest it: on the other hand, labour would be wasted if the whole area were sown with wheat. Maximum utilization can be achieved by sowing in the optimum proportions defined by the 'saddlepoint', the intersection of the two constraints in Fig. 12.5 (for further information see Vajda, 1960).

This simple example uses only two dimensions (two activities), but the method can be used to find optimum allocations of land, labour, etc., among any number of activities. Other considerations can be analysed by related methods. If crop productivity varies with the weather, the 'optimum' combination (in the sense used here) will be the one that ensures the highest yield in the most adverse conditions, rather than one with the highest yield if the weather were good. This is the principle used in Gould's analysis of crop combinations in Ghana (Gould, 1963; Clarke, 1968, p. 494).

The kinds of data needed for such analyses are to be found widely scattered in the literature of agricultural economics, human geography, zoology and related disciplines. For the labour requirements of different crops, Chisholm (1968) has summarized some of the available literature and quoted costs in man days per hectare for various Mediterranean countries. In the number of investigated instances there is a consistent pattern in labour requirements for different crops: vines, for instance, require roughly four times the labour needed for cereals. For animals, relevant facts include reproductive rates (very high for pig, low for deer, for example), and fodder requirements – both the type of feed and the amounts consumed by animals at various ages. The latter are particularly important in connection with the overwintering of numbers of animals that could not exist in a particular environment without human assistance. Arguments based on these facts, though not using programming techniques, have been used by Higham and Message (1969) and Jarman (1971) in analysing patterns of animal exploitation in Neolithic Europe, and, as more information becomes available on the types of crops and stock used in prehistory, the use of simple linear programming models and related techniques should be a valuable aid in evaluating the cost-effectiveness of various types of exploitation.

The interrelatedness of different aspects of production introduces constraints on the range of possibilities for expansion. A series of well-documented examples is provided by the farming systems of medieval Europe (see especially van Bath, 1963, pp. 9–18; Smith, 1967, pp. 191–256). In an intensive system of north European kind, where manure is utilized and the animals are overwintered largely on special crops and by products of cereal farming (stubble, chaff, etc.), the animal component has to be extended at the same time as the cereal element, and the balance between the two is closely defined. The network of rights over stubble grazing was therefore an important element in assuring maximum utilization of animal fodder. Figure 12.6 shows the connections between various parts of the system. By contrast, the Mediterreanean areas of Europe are characterized by a system where different elements could be developed independently; large areas of upland unsuitable for cereal growing encouraged the use of transhumance, while some lowland areas provided suitable places for fruit growing, often with small-scale

497

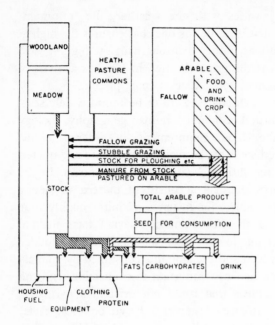

FIG. 12.6. Relationships between the two elements of a north European type of farming system, with two-course rotation and a seed/yield ratio of 6. Arable and pastoral aspects are closely linked (after Smith, 1967).

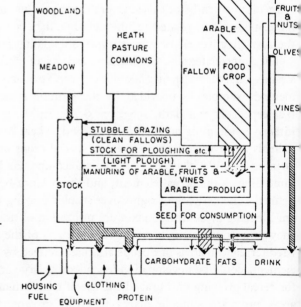

FIG. 12.7. Relationships between the elements of a 'Mediterranean' type of farming system, with assumptions as in Fig. 12.6. Note the greater independence of arable and pastoral aspects (after Smith, 1967).

irrigation (see Fig. 12.7). More specific models are needed for local contrasts: for instance, the wetter western areas of Britain possess similarities to the Mediterranean pattern in respect of transhumance, though hardly of fruit growing.

Bökönyi (1968) has noted the striking regularities in the relative percentages of different animals represented in sites of the various phases of the Neolithic, Copper and Bronze Ages in Hungary, each phase having a characteristic faunal assemblage. These regularities are the cumulative effect of a large series of individual choices in similar situations, following the principles outlined above. The effect of this is to produce a characteristic pattern of exploitation, with mutually adjusted aspects of land use, settlement location, and networks for the distribution of products.

For a given set of resources, and techniques for cropping them, there are optimum sizes and locations for settlement units. Regularities in settlement pattern represent the end result of decisions based on the need to minimize unproductive travelling time and the costs of bulk transport; thus locational decisions can be modelled in the same way as decisions on crop strategy. As transport technology, exploitation pattern or social organization changes, so the factors affecting site location will alter. Stable patterns of locational preference are thus valuable evidence for reconstructing these.

Individual site locations are chosen with a variety of factors in mind: on a large scale for distance from other sites and access to main areas of arable soil; on a smaller scale for access to water and building materials, freedom from flooding or for an easily defended position. If the site is in an area subject to flooding, the accumulation of a mound resulting from permanent settlement may be an advantage, as also for defence (Fig. 12.15). Where these considerations do not apply, villages may be liable to wander – as in many English villages of medieval origin where the church, once central, is now on the edge of the settlement. Occasional movement may also be desirable to avoid infestations, because of the exhaustion of 'kitchen gardens' or for purely ritual reasons. Stability of location is therefore largely dependent on the strength of the constraints.

The question of settlement relocation with extensive systems of agriculture is more complicated than has often been assumed. With a small population and abundant land, there is little necessity to remain in a single location, and where land is of poor quality, frequent shifts of settlement may be necessary. Nevertheless, data from central Brazil (Carneiro, 1960; see also Clarke, Chapter 1 of this volume) suggest that a shifting settlement pattern is not a necessary consequence of an extensive system of agriculture. Allan (1965) singles out three factors as critical: labour input (degree of intensification), soil capacity, and population agglomeration. Where villages are small, land within easy access of the village may be sufficient to allow a permanent occupation of a single site even when surrounding land is cultivated on a forest-fallow basis. However, if larger villages are necessary for defensive or other purposes, this area may be inadequate and periodic movement of the village may be essential. If in this situation there are also advantages in certain specific locations within the catchment area, a pattern of semi-permanent complementary sites may develop, in which two or more sites are occupied in rotation. Something of this kind seems to be behind the periodic abandonment of many Balkan tell sites, though a more definite answer would require estimates of population size, accessible arable and other land, etc., as in Carneiro's (1960) formula.

Within the framework of a single system of production growth proceeds through the replication of units of optimal size and location. Because of this, villages are characterized by roughly constant size of settlement and site catchment area (Clarke, Chapter 21 of this volume; Vita-Finzi and Higgs, 1970), and often by a characteristic zonation within this, from labour-intensive crops near the settlement to those requiring less attention further out (Chisholm, 1968). This process can proceed as long as there is land of a comparable kind open for colonization. When this is taken up, and the distribution of catchment areas rationalized through 'packing' – compression into a pattern giving maximum effective utilization – a change of state is necessary for further growth. If such a change is possible it usually involves readjustment of several elements, and may thus produce a new set of optimal locations and sizes with consequent alterations of settlement pattern in which some sites are abandoned and new ones are founded. An important change of this kind is one in which specialization in the functions carried out at different sites occurs, producing a hierarchy of sites consisting of units of different types. The specialized sites ('central places') thus have a different set of optimal sizes, and as the special functions they fulfil serve a number of lower order sites, these too have optimal 'catchment area' sizes for these particular services, which will be evident from the regularity in spacing (Figs 21.8, 23.1–23.10).

A model of growth in cereal-based economies

The potential for growth in a particular area and its pattern of development are determined in the first place by the range of soil types and their distribution. For the analysis of specific situations, therefore, a spatial model is essential, and data on archaeological site locations offer one of the easiest methods of testing predictions derived from these.

For a given technology and system of production various types of land are necessary, but the critical requirements are soils for growing cereals. In terms of cereal production the advantages of permanent cultivation soils are obvious, and the first stage of settlement will be to fill up the available areas of these by the spread of daughter settlements to situations comparable with those occupied by the initial settlements. The population involved in the founding of a new village is likely to be drawn from a number of existing villages (for emigration thresholds in different ecological zones see Hunter, 1966) as the population of villages at the core of original settlement would continue to grow

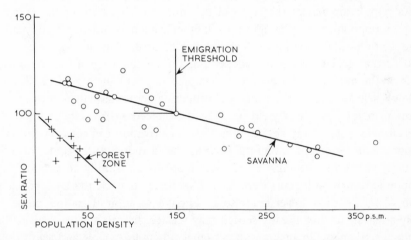

FIG. 12.8. Population and sex-ratio (males per 100 females) in two vegetational regions of Ghana, showing emigration of males above critical density (after Hunter, 1966). Each observation represents a local council area.

as well as those on the margin of settlement, even though the preferential emigration of males would cause temporary stabilization (see Fig. 12.8).Even if only for this reason, the unit of study must be a geographical region or micro-region, rather than an individual site.

Surrounding poorer quality land may be used for grazing and hunting in the relatively open landscapes typical, for example, of Balkan Europe: in a denser temperate forest landscape, away from upland areas, these possibilities may be more limited unless there is sandy heathland in the vicinity. If such extensive grazing areas are limited, a 'strategic' quantity of animals may require the intensive collection of leaf fodder at this stage. Where upland grazing areas are available, complementary temporary settlements in caves are likely to be used. For these areas deliberate clearing is probably unnecessary where sheep and goats are involved.

Where only high-grade soils are used, wheat rather than barley is likely to be the dominant cereal crop in a European situation. The growth of population within such an initial state may be expressed schematically, as in Fig. 12.9, although the actual course of the curve will of course be far from regular. The cultivated area increases as population grows, and production rises with it. Year to year fluctuations produce a temporary surplus in good years: this is the *normal surplus* of subsistence agriculture (Fig. 12.10; see Allan, 1965, also next section). There is little or no large-scale redistribution of food produce over any distance, since all the sites are growing similar crops.

As population passes the regional optimum for this state of the system, surplus population may emigrate to another region, if further high-quality land is still available. If not, stabilization or adjustment is necessary.

If further growth is possible (depending on the character of the remaining soils or the ability of those already occupied to stand further shortening of fallow), selection from the range of competing solutions will follow a least effort principle, in which yield per acre is balanced against labour input. If there remains land only slightly less fertile, cultivation can spread with only minor modifications of technique such as the introduction of some form of plough, either to maximize scarce soil moisture or simply to produce an economic return on labour. Cereals such as barley may be more appropriate than wheat for these lower grade soils. The colonization of an area immediately adjacent to that already settled may reduce the catchment areas of the original settlements in such a way as to make them less viable and lead to the abandonment of some earlier settlements: in this way the existing pattern may not simply be added to but structurally changed.

In areas where grazing is restricted to areas cleared of forest, the additional open areas produced by an extension of the cultivated area allow a complementary expansion of the stock element, and the development of a rotation system based on stubble grazing and manuring.

If the remaining land is of greatly inferior quality, it may not support an autonomous economy but may become dependent on the previously settled area. This usually involves a more intensive type of lowland cultivation and mechanisms for the intra-regional exchange of products. If the newly colonized area is immediately adjacent to the original area and small in size, a village/hamlet system may be sufficient to achieve this; otherwise a more centralized redistribution system becomes necessary. However, a system involving

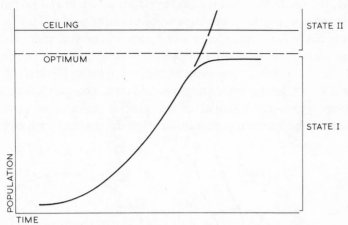

FIG. 12.9. Growth of population to a ceiling and transition to next state or stabilization at optimum for first state.

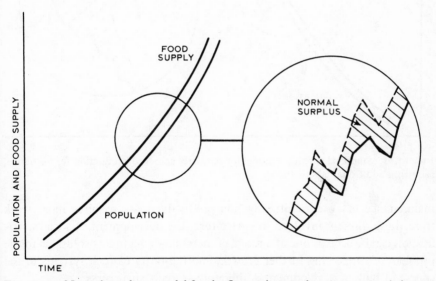

FIG. 12.10. Normal surplus – model for the fluctuating yearly excess over subsistence requirements.

exchange necessitates the production of a *standard surplus* (Fig. 12.11) by means of additional labour input.

Further growth in an area of *restricted* arable land involves inter-regional exchange of basic food products in bulk. A typical, and perhaps basic, form of this is an imperialist colonial system in which one region exports specialized manufactured products (often textiles) in return for grain and raw materials. Since the increase in grain production requires considerable additional labour input, it is likely that some element of coercion is needed to initiate an exchange system of this kind, even though the system may then be maintained by local élites – the main consumers of luxury products (Fig. 21.12).

The process of demographic and economic expansion thus has sociological implications which are essential to the general problem of growth, and particularly to the question of regulation of production and exchange. As the

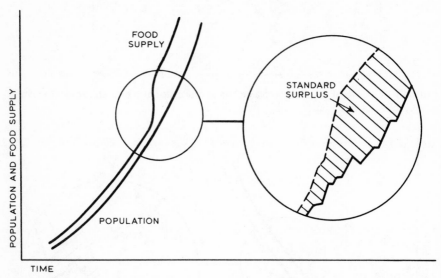

FIG. 12.11. Standard surplus – model for regularly achieved production for exchange, requiring additional labour input.

maintenance of an agriculturally non-productive class requires more work from those directly involved in agriculture, the development of social stratification can be seen as one of a range of increasingly high-cost solutions to the problem of supporting further growth, and the rarity of such systems in the course of human development is therefore scarcely surprising.

Social organization and economy

Having dealt with the interaction between the various aspects of the economy and produced a tentative dynamic model, some further comment is required on social organization.

504

Childe's scheme was based upon the nineteenth-century typology of Morgan, with more precise definition supplied by Childe himself. The difficulties of this system have become increasingly apparent as it has been applied to an ever wider range of material, especially from Africa and America. It has become clear that the correlation between the various features of the definition of civilization, for instance, is much looser than Childe imagined. These difficulties spring from the attempt to place societies on a single continuum with reference to a large number of features. This continuum is thus an average of a large number of possibilities based upon various types of criteria – the degree of social differentiation, the degree of nucleation of settlement and the specialization of individuals and areas, the density of population, the extent to which labour is channelled into the construction of public monuments, the degree of elaboration of public ritual, and so on. Clearly, there is a strong functional interrelationship between these various aspects: the existence of an administrative or aristocratic class is essential in many cases for regional specialization, and such societies frequently express the character of their social structure in monumental public architecture and keep track of the flow of goods by written records. However, monumental architecture or symbolic systems may arise from very different circumstances, and conversely societies with distinctive stratification may not involve these features. As a generalized statement of observed regularities therefore, the Morgan/Childe formulation is valid – as a working tool for the comparison of different societies in a wide range of environments and with a variety of *local* needs, it is frequently confusing.

More useful than an oversimplified typology is a scale. Much of modern social anthropology derives from Durkheim's (1893, translation 1933) observations on the significance of the increasing division of labour and its implications for the character of social institutions – law, government, morality, religion and ritual. These effects spring from the replacement of *mechanical solidarity* – the coexistence of a large number of similar units – by *organic solidarity* – the coexistence of a smaller number of dissimilar but complementary units each reciprocally dependent on the others.

The model put forward in the previous section suggested that regional economic specialization, and the administrative apparatus needed to regulate this, was a characteristic development in expanding systems faced with problems of feeding a growing population from purely local resources. If this is so, social stratification can be seen as one of a series of solutions of increasing cost to the system (in terms of labour expended on subsistence). 'Cross-cultural regularities' therefore result from the similar trend towards higher cost solu-

505

tions, and the way in which similar patterns of integration between the various aspects – economic, technological and social – tend to recur as they represent stable mutually adjusted patterns of high survival value.

While there is thus no single valid scheme of unilinear development, societies at different levels of organizational complexity will have very different characteristics, and it is useful to recognize this in a general system of classification. Rather than taking clusters of individual attributes, which may have no more than local significance – possession of writing, monumental architecture or irrigation, for example – it is more useful to use divisions on a scale of social integration – the degree to which the activities of individuals and groups are coordinated with others.

Durkheim's observations were carried further by Marcel Mauss, especially in his book *The Gift* (*Essai sur le Don*, 1923–4, translation 1954) which clarified the basic mechanisms of mechanical solidarity. The universal occurrence of gift exchange in small-scale societies – and indeed the exchange of marriage partners, which it partly mirrors – provide social links between groups of people who are not economically interdependent (Fig. 4.6). Such cycles of exchange, both within and between tribal groups, take place not primarily for economic reasons but as a basic mechanism of social integration. Useful commodities may circulate in this way, but such cycles would exist even if the goods circulated were of no more than symbolic value. It is this property that has led anthropologists to speak of the 'embeddedness' of the economy in primitive society. Dispersion of wealth within tribal units may also have ecological functions, in cushioning the effects of a poor harvest in a specific area.

Exchanges between tribal units are equally important on social grounds. Where there is no centralized authority with a mandate to conduct negotiations, a network of contacts between neighbouring groups is necessary to minimize the possibility of large-scale disruption of external relations. This is especially the case where both groups require access to certain resources such as seasonal grazing areas or fishing grounds. The classic study of such a system is Malinowski's (1922) work in the Trobriand Islands. Here the network of external contacts takes the form of ritualized exchanges of valued ornaments of *Spondylus* shell, which circulate around a ring of 'trading partners' from different tribal groups. Each partner is obliged to give the other assistance in affairs that concern his tribe.

Within a single society a variety of different exchange cycles may exist together independently, objects of one kind not being convertible into another as the various cycles perform different functions. Salisbury (1962) in New

Guinea distinguished three different cycles – subsistence, luxury and ceremonial. The first was the result of obligations to circulate foodstuffs, especially
perishables; the second had some element of self-interest, and served to maintain personal influence by a network of obligations, whereas the third was
important in the context of marriage alliance. While a rough scale of equivalence exists for each nexus, there was no standard of equivalence between
them: this had the effect of cushioning society as a whole from the personal
aggrandizement of ambitious individuals and ensuring that subsistence needs
were met for the group as a whole.

An important distinction was made by Karl Polanyi and his co-workers
(Polanyi, Arensburg and Pearson, 1957) between systems where such exchanges are purely reciprocal, and those where goods are collected to a centre
before being distributed. This he called the redistributive mode of transaction. Systems based on his latter principle are found in a variety of social
contexts, both primitive and advanced, and specialized market systems using
coined money appear to be a much later development than earlier writers
had supposed.

As a result of his studies of the economic systems of the ancient world,
Polanyi concluded that there was no evidence for a market system before
classical Athens, even in the complex economies of the Bronze Age states of
Mesopotamia, and that even Aristotle's description in the *Economics* referred
to a system very different from that analysed by Ricardo or Adam Smith –
for instance, in the influence on the price of the social standing of the persons
involved in a transaction. Thus even the use of coined money does not necessarily imply the full use of a market mechanism. Redistribution is linked to
political status because goods are collected to a centre, either institutional (as
in a palace economy) or through the more wealthy members of society, before
being distributed to consumers either as rations or as gifts to enhance prestige
and secure loyalty.

These mechanisms of distribution have to be seen in the context of the
system as a whole, and the way in which they relate to different types of
production and ecological circumstances. In any particular society all three
mechanisms may coexist, while one mechanism may be present in different
societies for a variety of reasons.

Centres of exchange become necessary either where the division of labour
produces too great a volume of specialized products to be distributed by a
purely reciprocal system, or where it is an advantage to even out inequalities in
production between different areas. The centres may either simply provide a
protected focus for redistribution, or in a specialized economy they may be

necessary to regulate the kinds and quantities of different goods. The former can be provided by the richer and more powerful individuals whose status may be achieved by their own manipulation; the latter requires on-going institutions with executive authority. In any event, the presence or absence of centres of power affects the whole of the social structure: where central institutions are lacking, other forms of social control are necessary.

DISTRIBUTION MECHANISMS AND POLITICAL ORGANIZATION

The existence of characteristic types of social phenomena at different levels of centralization is the basis of the series of stages defined by Service (1962), which provides perhaps the most useful scheme for use by prehistoric archaeologists, and one that has come increasingly into use among American writers on the subject (e.g. Sanders and Price, 1968; Hole and Flannery, 1967), and explicitly related by the cited authors to a demographic model of change.

It might be argued that a typology based upon generalization from existing societies known to ethnographers would be inapplicable to prehistoric societies, as the former represent more stable adaptations or marginal relicts. While it would be invalid to use them as 'survivals', the use of Service's scheme does not imply that specific solutions adopted by existing societies are paralleled by any society or group of societies in the prehistoric record; simply that different degrees of centralization have characteristic mechanisms of social integration, and that societies at similar levels have common needs which tend to be solved in similar ways. An important corollary of this is that historical analogies for prehistoric situations are particularly dangerous, being drawn from societies whose ability to coordinate the activities of their members is much more advanced than those usually studied by the prehistorian.

The categories defined by Service are *bands, tribes, chiefdoms* and *states*. Bands are characteristically found with low population densities and mobile economies, where groups are widely dispersed for most of the year and there is little need for more than a loose association of family units. Tribes are found with higher densities and more sedentary populations, where the units of settlement include more than a single family but where there is no need for centralized redistribution of products and reciprocal exchange fulfils both social and economic functions. Tribes also have special institutions such as age grade associations, secret societies or ritual groups which provide social cohesion at a local level.

Within the community, individuals may specialize as experts in some particular technique (wood or stone working, for instance), but this is in addition to subsistence activities, in the long periods of leisure typical for such societies.

508

The regulation of such production by a central authority is not necessary for the functioning of the economy. As the products of these activities are distributed by reciprocal exchange, the resulting patterns of distribution will be determined as much by social factors as by the 'rational' economic considerations of competitive commerce (see especially Clark, 1965; Bradley, 1971).

The word 'invasion' which is often used in archaeological literature to describe changes in territorial pattern is inappropriate to such contexts since:

usually the military posture is consistently held; that is, a state of war or near war between the neighbouring tribes is nearly perpetual. Ambush and hit and run raids are the tactics rather than all-out campaigns, which of course cannot be economically sustained by a tribal economy and its weak organization. True conquest, furthermore, would be self-defeating, for the productivity of a defeated tribe would not be great enough to sustain the conquerors. Limited objectives may include booty or driving out the enemy from a favoured zone, but territory is not easily taken and held in the absence of decisive engagements. Continual threat, sniping and terrorization which will discourage and harass the enemy is the typical form of action. In fact, headhunting, cannibalism and other forms of psychological warfare seem to be at their highest development in tribal society. At any rate, the bellicose state of intertribal relations tends to be unremitting and is thus a strong environmental inducement for a consistent unity of the various local kin groups or independent tribal segments. (Service, 1962, p. 115)

The distinction between tribes and chiefdoms is a loose one, and depends on the degree to which *centralized* (hence 'central place') redistribution is a feature of the economy. Reciprocal exchange continues to exist in more complex societies, though its economic significance is gradually reduced as more specialized mechanisms take over. The function of such mechanisms, however, can only be understood in relation to the ecology of food production and particularly the significance of the normal surplus.

The existence of a titular chief, who may perform a variety of functions, is not therefore the most important diagnostic. Indeed, in some societies a native title translated as 'chief' may imply no more than a purely consultative function (cf. Yaruro 'chiefs': see Leeds, 1969) and have no executive power. This is not a chiefdom in any significant sense; more important are those cases in which redistribution of produce serves to even out the surpluses and deficiencies within a social unit. This covers a diversity of phenomena from African beer parties to the north-west coast Indian *potlach* (Piddocke, 1969). These customs, in which the richer individuals acquire status and power by

509

giving away large quantities of goods, ensure a wide circulation of food and other produce. The surplus so distributed is the fluctuating normal surplus; where food storage is not practicable on any scale owing to the character of the staples and the nature of the climate, its distribution by chiefs has a valuable adaptive function, particularly where unpredictable shortages in localized areas are likely. A chiefdom system also facilitates distribution from those parts of the area it serves which concentrate on a limited range of specialized products, for instance where sheep or cattle raising predominates. It is therefore likely to be a feature of economies where a diversity of ecological zones are permanently occupied.

With increasing centralization the capture and control of territory becomes increasingly possible, and indeed there is a strong incentive for groups of individuals not well placed as landholders to move to seek new land. This does not lead to fission of the unit, as in non-centralized societies, but rather to a branching family structure with high-ranking lineages at the centre. The kinds of expansion often envisaged as of general occurrence in prehistory are thus in fact only likely to appear at this stage.

Systems with centres are able to handle a greater bulk of long distance trade in luxuries, and it becomes possible to ensure a constant supply of the highly specific raw materials necessary for an advanced metallurgical technology, for instance. The greater mobility of non-subsistence goods makes possible greater specialization in production, and craftsmen are typically attached to the redistributive centres (see Fig. 21.12).

A further step in the development of centralized control is represented by Service's final level, the state. This seems to be closely related to the degree in which long distance bulk exchange of products is critical to the functioning of the economy, and typically state organization begins at nodal points and extends along the routes of trade (cf. Morton-Williams, 1969). Historical geographers (e.g. Deutsch, 1953; East, 1968; Whittlesey, 1944) have elaborated models of the genesis of states, which are in fact applicable, with modification, to less centralized systems (see below). State systems exist to cope with large-scale flows of products; thus phenomena of this kind seem to be behind the growth of large oppida in southern Britain in the later pre-Roman Iron Age with the exports recorded by Strabo, a process of local development stimulated by, and progressively amalgamated into, the formal network of an expanding empire. This example illustrates the 'multiplier effect' (Hamilton, 1967), by which nodal areas propagate their organization outwards.

The internal organization of such units in a pre-market context requires large-scale public storage of staples (Polanyi *et al.*, 1957), reflected in the accounting systems and palace magazines of Bronze Age Mesopotamia or Greece. 'The authentic core of the Mycenaean economy was the palace household with its storage rooms and administration which listed goods and personnel, landownings and small cattle, assessed deliveries in wheat or barley, oil, olives, figs and a number of other staples, and handed out rations' (Polanyi, 1957; Dalton, 1968, p. 323). Even the complex functioning of the *karum* system of Assyrian trading colonies in Anatolia (e.g. Kültepe) was based on a trading commission, rather than a direct profit, and represented a form of administered, rather than market, trade.

With a state system expanding from a centre, 'invasion' phenomena are not merely possible but a basic mechanism of economic growth. Such extension of control may, however, concern only the administrative framework of the area colonized, and local social networks and cultural patterns may survive relatively unchanged.

ARCHAEOLOGICAL IMPLICATIONS OF INCREASING CENTRALIZATION

The previous section included some comments on the significance of social organization thresholds for the phenomena classed by archaeologists as 'invasions'. Another classic problem illuminated by consideration of its social basis is diffusion.

Social anthropologists since Malinowski have protested against a 'rags and patches' approach to culture which neglects the interrelatedness of different aspects of social systems. The discussion at the beginning of this paper emphasized the adjustment between different elements as a basic feature, and the last section attempted to show how social structure and ideology were related to patterns of economic life. Besides the closeness of adjustment between different subsystems, there is a special set of features of small-scale societies which inhibits diffusion: the low population densities, poor transport, lack of centralization and lack of role differentiation. All these features make exceedingly improbable reconstructions of – for instance – the spread of a 'megalithic religion' over a large area of western Europe from a limited area of origin.

A contrast is to be expected between acephalous societies and those with some degree of social differentiation, and between products manufactured and distributed on a local level and those involving sophisticated craftsmenship and implying a more complex social and economic network. For the latter, a *centre/periphery* diffusion model is appropriate (Schon, 1971, ch. 4); for the former, the distribution of specific styles relates to the primary social exchange networks involving reciprocity. In this case stylistic development is more likely to proceed in parallel, often over wide areas, rather than by 'waves' spreading over several cultures from a localized origin.

An exception to this may occur when several groups together reach a ceiling for a given type of exploitation, and a technological innovation such as the plough or cart which contributes to a solution of the problem may spread with amazing rapidity – so rapidly that its spread may appear instantaneous from the kinds of sample available to archaeologists.

With the development of social differentiation and centres of power, new phenomena emerge as it becomes possible for innovations to appeal to sectional interests and emerging élites in particular are likely to copy longer

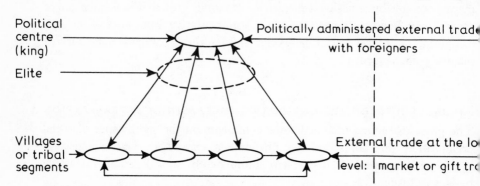

FIG. 12.12. Socio-economic transactions in the primitive economy within a centralized political authority system (from Dalton, 1969).

established élite subcultures elsewhere (e.g. Mycenaean/Cretan stylistic parallels) with whom they are in contact. Even more striking are the results of changes in the communication infrastructure of societies with a need to find external markets and sources of supply. With the growing disparity between 'advanced' and 'underdeveloped' countries, centre/periphery diffusion systems become increasingly common and the scale of their effects becomes increasingly wide. Even so, however, such effects are largely limited to the areas in which they have a direct economic interest, and large areas – even adjacent to the colonizing country – may remain relatively uninfluenced if they are outside this sphere of interest.

An archaeologically important problem in analysing the growth of economic organization is the recognition of 'centres', or *central places* in geographical terminology (see e.g. Garner, 1967; Harvey, 1967). The problem of central places cannot be separated from the study of the products they distribute. In societies where higher craftsmanship is limited to an élite, and village life is not greatly changed, the existence of centres may be difficult to demonstrate, at least with an archaeological sample, and clusters of rich burials may be the only clue. Indeed, specialized urban centres may not be present, but only the sites of regional fairs ('periodic central places'), often with religious overtones, although these should not be confused with medieval trade fairs and their specialized merchant class. These 'centres' may also serve a useful demographic function in periods of sparse and scattered settlement, and may exist for social reasons even before they have a significant economic role.

This pattern may be contrasted with a true urban system, in which the central places are also centres of population and have facilities for continuous storage, which is typical of state organization with bulk interregional exchange. The actual size of such 'cities', however, is a local problem, depending on the concentration of agricultural population. Where only a small agricultural community is resident, these may more aptly be described as palace or ceremonial centres. In Mesopotamia, by contrast, such centres seem often to have been surrounded by a zone empty of villages (Adams, 1970), implying that the land was worked by labour from the city, and the difference in size between central and non-central places is largely related to settlement nucleation and concentration of population for defence. In other environments, however, this may not be a rational pattern of population distribution. The true 'urban' functions of such sites are represented by the magazines, storage areas, administrative and religious 'core', and specialist manufacturing workshops.

The existence of a network of small 'market towns' is related to the degree to which the villages themselves consume specialist products, and such forms may be typical of a later phase either than fairs or urban centres as defined above. The contrast between regional fairs, increasingly under the protection of powerful local chieftains as their economic significance grows, and urban centres concerned with bulk interregional exchange, should be reflected in site locations. The former are often on large flat hilltops, accessible from a more or less radial catchment area. The latter are likely to be on interregional trade routes (and therefore in valleys rather than on isolated hilltops) typically at transhipment points where products are transferred from one mode of transport to another. The contrast between 'hill forts' and 'oppida' in later pre-Roman Iron Age Britain is a good illustration of this (Fig. 21.12).

European development in the Neolithic and Bronze Ages

Discussion has so far been on a highly theoretical level, and it remains to demonstrate the usefulness of the concepts formulated above to the sorts of problem studied by prehistorians. Over the last fifty years a great mass of data on archaeological distributions has been collected, some of it of outstanding quality and scholarship, (e.g. Mathiassen, Grinsell, French, Detev, to name but a few). Small-scale distribution maps were not greatly used by Childe, and it is this lack of contact with the pattern of prehistoric settlement 'on the ground', in a regional setting, that is the root of the inadequacy of much of his models today.

The study of archaeological distributions in these more detailed terms reveals the sequence of stages of exploitation in a given area, and reinforces the impression of a set of characteristic land utilization patterns for successive archaeological periods. To produce a convincing overall picture, a great deal of work is necessary in collecting and evaluating the data, since each area has its own characteristic pattern of development in relation to local resources. Before moving on to some examples, however, some consideration of purely methodological difficulties is required, for distribution maps of various kinds will have very different properties.

It is not necessarily possible to compare one kind of distribution map with another especially when maps of different periods may be constructed in terms of different features – settlement sites, burials, stray finds of various types, etc. What must be compared are the inferred systems of land use deduced from various kinds of map, in conjunction with the analysis of food remains from settlement sites.

This point is well illustrated by the case of Great Britain, as has recently been emphasized (Taylor, 1970; Ellison and Harriss, Chapter 24 of this volume). That large monumental burial structures tend to be situated on poorer quality land has often been pointed out (e.g. Overgaard, 1932), but the significance of this has seldom been taken into consideration in discussing the interpretation of distribution maps. The apparent concentration on exposed downland in Wiltshire, for example, is probably a truncated remnant, the least important area agriculturally, as the main grain growing areas (and the settlements connected with them) are likely to have been in the sheltered and more fertile areas which have been under cultivation ever since. Mathiassen's data on Jutland and Zealand (1948, 1957) show how detailed find-statistics can be used to gain a more accurate picture of actual settlement – a good example of the use of one dimension of evidence to control another.

This phenomenon of loss of settlement sites due to their position on permanently cultivated soils is a general one for much of Europe. For certain zones of South-east Europe, however, these difficulties are less acute: the phenomenon of tell building makes long-inhabited settlement sites much more easy to recognize (and harder to destroy). The reconstructed pattern of settlement for most prehistoric periods is thus more complete in areas of South-east Europe than further north and the possibility of using nearest neighbour statistics for given phases of occupation is thus greatly enhanced. However, even in this there is the complication, also discussed below, that the classic tell sites in Bulgaria were not occupied continuously and that settlement moved for shorter or longer periods during the time that any particular tell was in use. For this reason, many of the obvious formulae for analysing settlement lattices which assume contemporaneity of sites cannot be usefully applied in the current state of investigation and seem unlikely to become basic tools for analysis for many years to come, and then only in the most propitious circumstances.

This difficulty applies even to gross attempts at quantification, such as the total numbers of sites per period, since one may be comparing numbers of sites occupied only for ten to thirty years with sites with more continuous occupation. In fact, however, in many cases such statistics are revealing, for even granting the fact that earlier sites are likely to be over-represented, successive periods do show increasing numbers of known sites, if survey has been sufficiently detailed. Once again, the kind of survey data available may be critical: where settlements shift temporarily to defensive positions they may be missed by a non-intensive survey: comparison of the resulting curve with figures from more intensively searched areas can lead to mistaken conclusions concerning the relative degrees of population growth in the two areas (e.g. Renfrew, 1970).

The most striking fact, even when these are borne in mind, is the steady increase in many areas of the number of known sites from the Early Neolithic onwards, more rapid in some periods than others, and with occasional reversals of the trend, usually abrupt. This fact is not only interesting in itself, and indeed to be expected, but it is also of great importance for the interpretation of the development of European societies, for it suggests that the model elaborated above can usefully be applied to predict changes in agricultural practice, technology and social organization.

THE CHARACTER OF EARLY NEOLITHIC SETTLEMENT

The change to an economy based on planted cereals and pulses and the adjustment of complementary exploitation and settlement patterns, despite the slowness with which the various elements of this strategy were integrated, marks a significant transition to new patterns of demographic and economic growth for which Childe's description of a 'Neolithic Revolution' is not inappropriate. In Europe particularly, the introduction of new plant staples produced a sharply defined economic shift in areas of high agricultural potential, even though this had no immediate effect in areas where the exploitation of animal populations continued to be superior to primitive farming.

The restricted range of environments suitable for early farming systems has not been sufficiently emphasized in discussions of the spread of agriculture, and in particular the significance of soil fertility and moisture content in determining the pattern of occupation. Although the striking correlation between Neolithic settlement and loess soils in central Europe has been the subject of comment since Buttler, this phenomenon of close association with particular soil types is not limited to the Danube region but is a general feature of the initial agricultural colonization of Europe.

A characteristic of early cereal assemblages from Neolithic sites in the Near East is the presence of seeds of *Scirpus*, indicating a very moist immediate environment for cereal cultivation. This evidence is supported by the strong pattern of association between early village sites and permanent cultivation soils near springs, and especially near the backswamps of large lakes or the fringes of old lake basins (cf. Allan, 1970). This strongly suggests that an economic yield from cereal cultivation was generally possible only where a sufficient area of such soils was available, and that the recent geological history of the relevant areas should provide significant predictions about the kinds of area where early Neolithic sites are likely to be found.

Central Turkey and the areas of historic Macedonia and Thrace form an ancient crystalline massif against which later sedimentary rocks were intensively folded during the Tertiary mountain building phase, forming chains to the north and south of the original massif. The downfaulted areas of this were for a time occupied by arms of the sea, during which shallow water limestones were deposited in the Tertiary period. The inland basins were then cut off from the sea by further uplifting, and became freshwater lakes – or in some cases saltwater lakes in the case of internal drainage basins, e.g. Tuzgölü in central Anatolia. The levels of these lakes seem to have fluctuated considerably in the course of the Pleistocene, related to changes in temperature and humidity. In general the rise in temperature during interglacial phases would have increased evaporation (Butzer, 1970), and a postglacial recession of lake levels has been documented in Anatolia (Cohen and Erol, 1969; Cohen, 1970) and in the Dead Sea Rift (Vita-Finzi, 1969). Similar phenomena are likely to have occurred in the large flat basins of Thessaly and central Bulgaria, and in a multitude of small lakes in the Balkans and Anatolia.

The relationship between the areas of fine alluvium and backswamp soils produced by the Neothermal recession in lake levels, and the pattern of early settlement, has so far been intensively investigated only in Anatolia (Cohen, 1970; French, 1970). In the Konya plain, Neolithic settlement seems to be closely associated with backswamp soils, which, unlike the other soil types also associated with the receding lake such as marls, are not subject to strong seasonal desiccation. Although located for access to such backswamp soils, the settlements themselves are typically sited on the edges of alluvial fans which provide raised areas less liable to be flooded. The site of Çatal Hüyük, for example, occupies a highly favourable position on a spur where the fan seems to have broken through a sandspit representing an old shoreline, and the site has ready access to backswamp soils on three sides.

One piece of evidence which suggests that such areas were strongly preferred in spite of other disadvantages is the apparent incidence of malaria, for example at Çatal Hüyük and at Nea Nikomedia in a low-lying part of Greek Macedonia. Angel (1968) has suggested that the incidence of porotic hyperostosis in skeletal material from these two sites is associated with a form of anaemia conferring resistance to this disease. Certainly the tectonic basins of Macedonia occupied by the remnants of Pleistocene lakes were until recently highly malarial, as the French and British forces discovered in 1916–18 (see *Naval Intelligence Handbooks: Greece*, vol. 1, p. 272.).

Two basic reasons lie behind this pattern of land occupation. First, with low population densities, the model put forward in previous sections suggests that there would be a strong selection for permanent cultivation soils, and that excess population would move to other areas of similarly high-yielding soil before tackling poorer quality land or changing to a more intensive system of exploitation. Secondly, in dry Mediterranean climates frequent ploughing of land is necessary to prevent run-off and to encourage moisture absorption in order to produce an adequate crop on land where groundwater is not near to the surface (Clark, 1952, p. 100; Stevens, 1966, p. 93). It is most unlikely that the earliest agricultural communities in the Near East and south-east Europe used the plough, in view of Boserup's arguments summarized above. Instead, the initial stage of agricultural development seems to be characterized by a pattern of rapid spread with relatively low population densities, settlement systems being restricted to small areas of land of high agricultural potential, with specialized satellites.

This pattern of settlement has important implications for reconstructions of the types of social regulation and mechanisms for the distribution of goods, as well as being the unstable initial state of a system with great potential for change. To understand the character of contacts between regions, the patterning of cultural units, and the course of further development, a closer look at the details of the geographical background to south-east European prehistory is required.

THE GEOGRAPHICAL BASIS OF SETTLEMENT IN SOUTH-EAST EUROPE

While it is customary to describe the geographical background to archaeological cultures in broad terms, with an emphasis on climatic and vegetational regions, such distinctions are difficult to define in detail and are for many archaeological purposes irrelevant. More immediately useful are geomorphological divisions and their associated soil types. Thus, in the Balkans the original crystalline core is represented by the Rhodope massif (southern Bulgaria, eastern Yugoslavia and the north Aegean coast). One major chain of fold mountains is the Dinaric/Pindhos system forming the west coast of Yugoslavia and Greece, consisting for a large part of limestone and producing the typical karst landscape. A second chain forms the arc of the Carpathians and abuts onto the Rhodope massif in northern Bulgaria as the Balkan mountains (Stara Planina), dividing the Marica/Tundža basin of central Bulgaria from the lower Danube province: this chain is particularly significant for its metal ores. The Danube itself cuts through the chain at the Iron Gates (Fig. 12.13).

In the Miocene, both the lower and middle Danube areas enclosed by the Carpathian/Balkan chain, and also the downfaulted areas of the crystalline massif such as the Marica basin, the Morava and upper Vardar basins, and a multitude of smaller *poljes* (small rift valleys), were covered by the sea, and the extensive areas of Tertiary limestone which fringe these were laid down. By the Pleistocene, however, the lower and middle Danube basins had become dry land, and during glacial periods were extensively mantled by aeolian deposits such as loess and sand, through which the rivers now cut meandering and marshy courses with wide flood areas. Further south the marine phase was succeeded by a phase of freshwater lakes, some of which remain today (e.g. Lake Ohrid, Yugoslav Macedonia; Lake Volvi, Greek Macedonia; Lake Copais, Boeotia, etc.) As a result, many of the basins of this region are floored with old lake soils, the more fertile ones, like the backswamp soils of the Konya plain, being known by the Slav name of *smolnitsa* (Filipovski and Civíc, 1969). More localized patches of similar soil were produced in the areas around springs in the dissected Tertiary limestones.

This background is of importance in two ways. First, the contrasting character of the tectonic basins and intervening mountains results in a sharply demarcated series of settlement units, and to some extent determines the pattern of connections between them. Secondly the distribution of fertile soils is closely related to the availability of water, which in turn depends upon the nature of the underlying rock. This allows the isolation of a series of model landscape types, which are of great use in comparing the development of settlement in different areas (Fig. 12.15).

The features of greatest interest are the basins since settlement, at least in the Neolithic and Eneolithic periods, seems to have been heavily dependent on availability of water and well-watered soils. The major landscape model units may be summed up as follows:

(1) The larger sand and loess-covered basins in the north of the area, e.g. the middle and lower Danube (Fig. 12.15*a*). Here, well-watered areas are restricted to the major river courses, which tend to be meandering and produce broad marshy zones, contrasting with the drier areas in between, which had relatively little permanent settlement in Neolithic and Eneolithic times. Within these zones, there was strong selection for the small areas of drier soil as Nandris has demonstrated for the Körös culture in the Szeged region. The rivers frequently change course and the patterns of settlement are unstable.

(2) The larger basins in the southern parts of the area where lakes existed into the Pleistocene. Here, there are wide areas of well-watered soil, and settlement density was probably higher here than in any other situation. Once established, the settlement pattern showed great stability, and it is here that the classic tell pattern is found. Even where the valleys are broad, the sites present a relatively dense and even network (Fig. 12.15*b*).

(3) Small basins with limestone floors and relatively coarse alluvial material such as gravel with extensive alluvial fans on the fringes. This is the typical north Aegean form as represented for instance by the plain of Drama. Some of the smaller inland *poljes* are of this type, e.g. Ovče Polje. In this situation small areas of finer grained and well-watered alluvial soil assumed great importance, and the Neolithic and Eneolithic settlement pattern is closely related to these, villages being typically sited at the junction of the marshy alluvium and the drier limestone. These sites generally have a long life. In the plain of Drama and in the Struma valley, a greater area of fertile alluvium and old lake deposits exists as a result of the ponding-up of the larger rivers draining from the Rhodopes, whose exit to the sea is restricted by a localized limestone scarp. The minor rivers of local origin are intermittent, and do not produce fine grained alluvial soils. In the inland basins of this type such as Ovče Polje, the lack of areas of fine alluvial has greatly restricted settlement, and only one major Neolithic site is known from the *polje*, despite extensive searching, at Amzabegovo (personal communication from Dr D. L. Weide).

In Yugoslav Macedonia, the contrast between these 'dry' *poljes* and those with ancient lake soils (e.g. Pelagonia-Bitola basin) is very marked (Fig. 12.15*c*).

(4) Areas of dissected Tertiary limestone, e.g. Kragujevac region, Yugoslavia. These are not basins in themselves but are characteristically found on the fringes of freshwater lake areas, where they represent the older, marine phase of infilling. They thus typically form terraces, in a relatively young state of dissection. The landscape is composed of deeply incised valleys separated by high promontories and small plateaux. Fertile well-watered soils are widely distributed in narrow strips alongside the many streams, and in small patches by springs. This pattern allows a moderately high density of settlement, although the actual position of the villages is less important, since the landscape has a mosaic character and a wide range of soils is accessible from any single position. The settlement pattern of this area is more flexible, and the sites are less long lived (Fig. 12.15*d*).

(5) A further lowland unit must be mentioned, the north Aegean coastal plains. Here there is a marked contrast between the peninsulae that mark the lines of the old crystalline massif (e.g. Khalkidhiki) and the alluvial plains at the mouths of the rivers draining from the inland mountain areas. These were certainly accumulating in the period under consideration, a process best documented in the region of Thessalonika, where Pella, the regional centre in Hellenistic times, is now several miles inland.

In contrast to the basins are upland areas of various types, from the high acid parts of the crystalline massif such as the Rhodopes and Stara Planina with their coniferous woodland soils, to the more recent folded limestones, which occur largely in the west of the region and produce a karstic landscape over large areas of western Yugoslavia. These areas had a basically different economy from the lowland areas, with their mudbrick and timber villages and their close association with soils suitable for cereals. In areas of Mediterranean climate at least, the summer heat would necessitate the movement of flocks into higher areas, and with increasing population there would in any case be an increasing need to make use of such areas. Around each of the basins, therefore, one must imagine a zone of largely seasonal occupation, which probably became increasingly extensive. The map (Fig. 12.16) shows the seasonal movements recorded in historic times. It is probable that the long routes from Šar Planina to the Aegean coast reflect the presence of urban markets from classical times onwards, as a similar pattern has been demonstrated for Dubrovnik and its hinterland, which supplied sheep products to the Italian cities (Roglić, 1961). The smaller movements, however, probably took place in prehistory as they represent the most rational way of utilizing the various kinds of land seasonally available for grazing. Thus the distribution of cultural boundaries in the lower Danube demonstrates the way in which these cross-cut the ecological divisions to provide comparable mixed units.

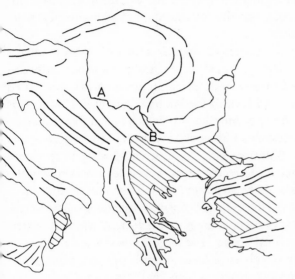

FIG. 12.13. Schematic map of structure of south-east Europe, showing crystalline massif and Tertiary fold trends. A and B represent the approximate positions of the two maps of Fig. 12.14.

In the older types of limestone caves are plentiful, and many of these, particularly on the north side of Stara Planina and in the Transylvanian Alps, were occupied in Neolithic and Bronze Age times, e.g. Baile Herculane, Romania, or Devetaskata Peshtera in north Bulgaria. These are likely to represent seasonal stopping points on transhumance routes, and should give useful information about these when examined from this point of view, since many are situated along river routes important in movements in historic times. The published information about these caves, however, has never been fully collated.

GEOGRAPHY AND SETTLEMENT PATTERN

No meaningful interpretation of cultural and social patterns in prehistory is possible without reference to this physical framework of settlement. The association of typical patterns of settlement with specific geomorphological areas makes it possible to construct a crude map of relative population

521

density for most parts of the area, based on these units. This, together with the links between basins, provides the physical basis for patterns of inter-regional integration (Fig. 12.17).

Comparisons of settlement density immediately confront the investigator with problems of sample bias. As both tell and non-tell settlements are known, it is possible that apparent regularities may be due to the association of the former with specific soil types, and the concentration of archaeological work on such deeply stratified sites.

A precondition for the accumulation of mounds is the use of mudbrick as a building material. The standard construction techniques in south-east Europe in the Neolithic and Bronze Ages, except in upland areas, were based on mud and timber, probably with earth used in roofing as well. However, as long-occupied sites are known (e.g. Amzabegovo) which do not form mounds, a further explanation is necessary. The association with old lake soils – it is significant that two large Bulgarian sites, Azmak and Ezero, have names implying a marshy environment in recent times – provides a reason why the accumulation of a mound should be an advantage, as a flood defence. Perhaps the major factor in the accumulation of large conspicuous mounds, however, is the length of the total period of occupation of the settlement, which is related to the landscape types described above. The largest mounds are in areas of type (2) where there are not merely large areas of fertile soil accessible from a single position (and the greatest danger of flooding), but also a lack of the defensible positions such as promontories which were increasingly used from the beginning of the Bronze Age onwards in areas where they were available.

A complicating factor is Georgiev's suggestion (1961) that the major tells of the Maritsa valley were not continuously occupied, but only in rotation or alternation. If this is so, then it emphasizes the advantage of existing mound sites as settlement locations, and points a contrast to areas such as type (4), where individual locations seem to have been advantageous only for relatively short periods. It also suggests that the cultural sequence in a given area is much more continuous than might appear from the succession at a single site, however deeply stratified.

Despite these complications, which require much more work before a full explanation is possible, a contrast does emerge between the kind of density possible for instance between basins floored with old lake soils with a water-table close to the surface and those covered with aeolian deposits, with their large dry areas between the river floodplains. The richness of the Neolithic and Eneolithic cultures of the Maritsa valley and Thessaly, for instance, reflects the large area of soils suitable for primary settlement in these large basins.

The connections between the main units of settlement are thus strongly influenced by the overall pattern of geological structure.

In the area of the crystalline massif, three major breaks running north–south provide links between units of the north Aegean coast and those inland. The most important of these links is the Vardar/Morava valley, with fertile soils along much of its length apart from the narrow stretches of gorge. This links the plain of Thessalonika with the middle Danube. A second and equally important length is the Struma valley, which links the Sofia basin with the Aegean coast to the east of Khalkidhiki. This has a similar character to the Vardar/Morava route. The Sofia basin occupies an extremely important position, with links eastward to the Maritsa/Tundža basin, westward to the Morava valley, and northward through the Isker gorge to the lower Danube basin. This last is one of the most important gaps in Stara Planina, which otherwise presents a formidable barrier. The third north–south route, the Nestos valley, has only a small area of fertile soil on its length, and does not cut through the Rhodopes, but has its source near the Rila block. Its importance was limited to its use as a transhumance route, and it is not a link between basins. This structure is reduced to schematic form in Fig. 12.17.

Available radiocarbon dates suggest that cereal-based economies and permanent villages show a spread from Anatolia to Greece, then to Bulgaria and Yugoslavia, and then into the lower and middle Danube. This movement took place during the seventh and sixth millennia, and by the mid-fifth millennium the further spread into central Europe had begun.

Three major phases of this process may be distinguished. The first is the occupation of the area to the south of the Danube, with its network of fertile basins separated by mountain passes. The second phase is the occupation of the loess-covered areas of the lower and middle Danube. Here settlement concentrated strongly in the floodplains of the rivers, and individual sites in these positions were short lived. Indeed the great number of these sites known from the Early Neolithic, with little depth of occupation (Nandris, personal communication) makes it possible that owing to seasonal flooding they were regularly abandoned for part of the year, when population moved with the sheep to upland sites. The third phase begins with the spread to the rolling loess-covered hills of Transdanubia. Here, occupation was possible by springs and along the network of small streams that this better-drained landscape provided.

The occupation of stream courses in the loess marks the transition to a new pattern of axial rather than frontal spread: from north-west Hungary the loess-floored river basins of the Danube and its tributaries, and then the

523

Rhine and the upper Oder provided similar environments linked by easy access along the rivers. The dates from Early Neolithic sites from Holland and north Germany, which on the present sample are statistically indistinguishable from comparable sites in Austria, Czechoslovakia and north Hun-

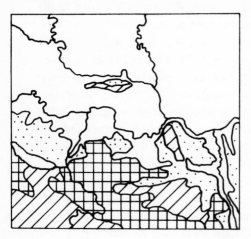
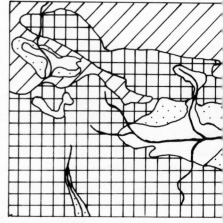

KEY

Ages of major deposits

☐ Quaternary

☐ Tertiary

▨ Mesozoic

▦ Palaeozoic

⋎ Major rivers

FIG. 12.14. Generalized geological features of two areas of Fig. 12.13, at approximately 1:2 500 000.

(*a*) Belgrade region showing the loess-covered Middle Danube Basin to the north, drained by the Danube, Sava and Tisza rivers and the Bosnian and Serbian uplands to the south, drained by the Drina. In the south-east the Morava valley represents an important southwards extension of Quaternary deposits and fringing Tertiary limestones.

(*b*) Sofia-Plovdiv region showing major faulted depressions in the crystalline massif with Tertiary limestones and Quaternary lake and fan deposits. To the north a broad zone of chalk extends towards the Lower Danube. The river Isker cuts northwards through the Balkan mountains from the Sofia basin in the west, the Plovdiv basin is drained eastwards by the river Maritsa, and the Nestos flows southwards from the crystalline uplands of the Rila block.

gary, indicate that a rapid spread took place along the major river axes, and suggest that the extension of settlement was governed by the need to maintain an optimal pattern of communication between earlier and later settlements, especially by river (cf. Bylund's (1960) study of the colonization of Lapland in the eighteenth and nineteenth centuries). If this were so, then the apparent halt to the extension of settlement beyond the loess area into the formerly glaciated zone of the north European plain could be related to a process of 'secondary infilling', by which the smaller and less well-connected loess-covered areas were occupied in preference to the colonization of more difficult or less productive soils.

Perhaps significant for the extension of settlement beyond the loess belt are the so called bored shafthole axes (Glob, 1951; Schwabedissen, 1967), which Glob has interpreted as primitive ploughshares because of the smallness of the shafthole and asymmetrical wear pattern. Examples have been found in association with early agricultural sites in the moraine areas of north Germany, and it is not unreasonable to see this as an indication of the kind of technological development associated with the colonization of a new range of soils as suggested by our model. As evidence for animal traction does not occur until a later phase (e.g. Higham and Message, 1969) it is likely that this was a simple device dragged by human traction.

GEOGRAPHY AND CULTURAL PATTERNS

This distribution of initial settlement, with permanent settlement sites concentrated in small pockets or along rivers, has important consequences for the pattern of social networks. The patterns of material culture can be used to reveal the changing ways in which these units were linked by social contacts at different periods.

The scattered nature of settlement and the lack of regional specialization in production evident from the consistency of locational preference, along with the absence of any evidence for social differentiation, implies that social organization at this stage was not based on centralized administration. Instead, uniformity within the units of ceramic style is likely to reflect the existence of socio-political units based on kinship, and the intensity of circulation of marriage partners and gift exchange within these.

South-east European archaeology in recent years has seen a proliferation of definitions of small units, usually called 'groups'. Such groups, corresponding to concentrations of population in favourable areas, form the *primary units* of social integration, with few impediments to communication between sites. In the Balkans, these are frequently tectonic units such as *poljes*, though larger basins such as the middle Danube tend to split up into a number of such units, related to the major rivers.

Although these groups may be marked by local peculiarities, more striking is the uniformity that characterizes a group of such primary units and marks the macro-unit defined by Childe as a *culture*. These are not simply reflections

525

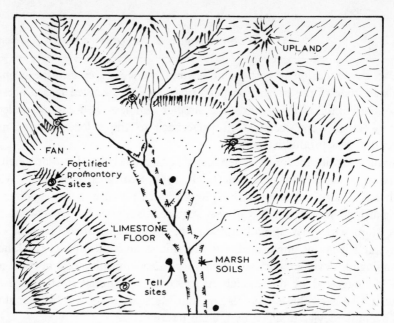

(*c*) Small rift valley with limestone floor, fan, and marshy flood area along the river. Filled circles represent Neolithic tell sites, double open circles are fortified Bronze Age promontory sites.

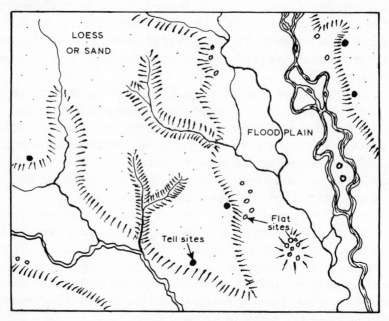

(*a*) Loess-covered basin with meandering river in wide floodplain. Open circles represent short-lived Neolithic sites, filled circles represent more continuously occupied Early Bronze Age sites.

FIG. 12.15. Landscape types and characteristic patterns of early settlement.

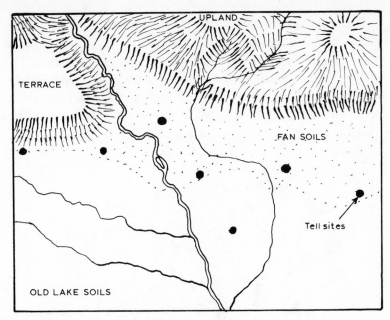

(*b*) Large basin with lake and fan deposits. Filled circles represent very long lived Neolithic and Bronze Age tell sites.

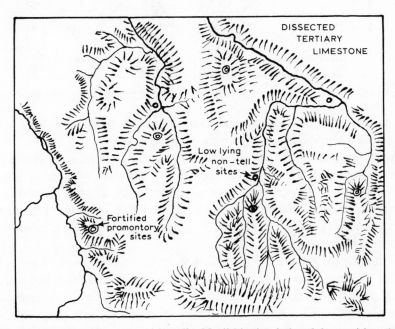

(*d*) Dissected limestone area with earlier Neolithic sites in low-lying positions (open circles) and later fortified hilltop and promontory sites (double open circles).
Fig. 12.15. Landscape types and characteristic patterns of early settlement.

of natural regions – indeed some cultures have extremely 'irrational' distributions from this point of view, straddling awkwardly over a number of tectonic basins. It seems likely that such units defined on 'folk styles' do correspond, however roughly to actual socio-political units based on kinship

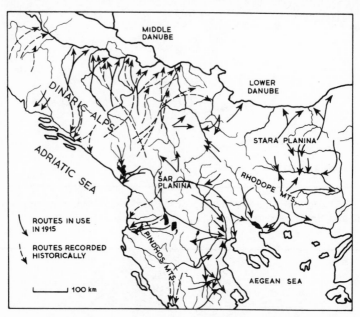

FIG. 12.16. South-east Europe showing routes used in transhumance in recent times.

ties (cf. Introduction to Fortes and Evans-Pritchard, 1940), or at least to the average of a series of such units over a period of time.

From the discussion of non-centralized or weakly centralized societies in a previous section, it is evident that the types of 'invasion' often envisaged by prehistorians are inappropriate for situations such as this. Nevertheless changes in cultural patterning do occur, and before a social interpretation is possible various phenomena previously lumped together as ethnic movements must be distinguished.

In the first place there is a phenomenon typical of large basins such as the middle Danube where cultures tend to have sharply defined boundaries, which persist, with fluctuations, for long periods of time. In this situation movements of such boundaries may occur, although only over relatively short distances, and usually to gain a small additional area of fertile land. Such a movement may be called *boundary readjustment*, and is usually a process of gradual progressive expansion.

528

Other types of cultural change are too rapid and large scale to be phenomena of the same kind, and typically affect complete primary units rather than having the character of a progressive movement. Useful here is the distinction used by human geographers concerned with the genesis of states (e.g. East, 1968) between 'core' and 'peripheral' areas. The primary units of a culture are not all of equal importance: some are in large fertile basins with a high density of settlement while others are in smaller basins or areas where settlement is more scattered. Similarly, some basins are well connected in several

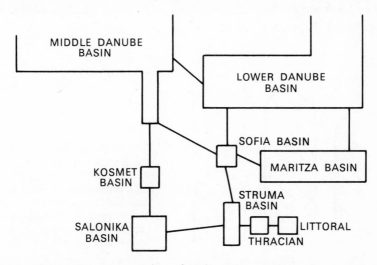

FIG. 12.17. Schematic representation of major concentrations of population (and linking routes) in south-east Europe in Neolithic times, from the Lower and Middle Danube basins in the north to the north Aegean coast in the south.

directions, while others may have only a few routes to other areas. Fertile well-connected areas, such as the Maritza valley or the Sofia basin, tend to have a more consistent and stable pattern of cultural development: conversely, areas less well connected and with lower densities, especially where they are adjacent to two or more core areas, tend to fluctuate between allegiance to different cores (Transylvania is a good example of this type). It is proposed to call this phenomenon *unit reorientation*.

An even larger-scale phenomenon may sometimes occur, where two formerly distinct cultures merge. This seems to happen in the Eneolithic where the cultures of the eastern lower Danube and the Maritza valley merge to form a single entity, the Gumelnitsa culture. It is unlikely that any kind of invasion was involved, and such a phenomenon may be termed *network linkage*.

These terms are not intended to form universal categories of cultural

529

change, merely to illustrate the kinds of distinction which must be made, especially in scale, in analysing the complexities of the prehistoric record. Indeed, if material culture reflects the patterning of social organization, the number of possible patterns must be almost infinitely large. The three types distinguished above are characteristic only of specific situations, especially societies with limited centralization and no administered interregional trade. Though these phenomena may persist even when, as in the Early Bronze Age, élites of limited executive power exist and higher-level distribution networks for luxury objects are superimposed on the patterns of folk style discussed here (Figs. 20.34, 21.12).

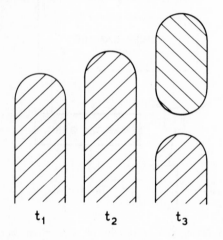

t_1 t_2 t_3

FIG. 12.18. Fission model for the genesis of a new culture during the colonization of a new area, assuming a critical size limit for the culture as a unit. Note 'flowback' in which new culture takes over peripheral area of original culture.

Between cultures, contact is often evidenced in the form of import sherds, and of objects from a distant source such as *Spondylus* ornaments. Where the élite distribution model (Fig. 12.12) does not apply, it is likely that such objects result from 'trading partner' exchanges, important in preserving relations between acephalous socio-political units. As Malinowski notes, 'not only objects of material culture, but also customs, songs, art motifs and general cultural influences travel along the Kula route' (1922, p. 92). This is important in maintaining the general similarities between members of a culture group (Clarke, 1968), and suggests that stylistic changes affecting wide areas are less likely to be the result of a centre/periphery diffusion system than of the continuous circulation of objects between related groups, resulting in parallel courses of development.

Culture groups do seem to relate closely to geographical regions, such as the 'north European plain' or the 'Atlantic province'. Cultures, on the other hand, seem to be functional units, giving advantages to individual communities in belonging to a defined group and thus having a limited effective size. This is significant in explaining the pattern of cultural fission found in the expanding network of primary colonization, where a 'flowback' pattern is often found (see Fig. 12.18; e.g. Körös/Bandkeramik situation in the south of the middle Danube). The lack of sharply defined units of the size of the culture in the central European loess region in the Early Neolithic (Linienbandkeramik) might well relate to a constantly changing framework of settlement during the 'filling up' of the loess area and the colonization of smaller patches less well connected to the main axes of expansion. In such a fluid situation, a sharply defined pattern of socio-political units need not necessarily emerge until some stability was reached (see Clarke, Chapter 1, random walk model).

INTERNAL EXPANSION: ENEOLITHIC AND BRONZE AGE

While there was still an adjacent expanding frontier allowing surplus population to emigrate, population levels in a given area would have remained low. In south-east Europe the association of settlement with marshy areas and the consequent prevalence of malaria would in any case have checked growth to some extent. However, over a long time the build-up of population continued, and resulted in changes in economy, settlement pattern and social structure.

As the frontier of external colonization moved northwards, the process of internal colonization began. It is likely that the first stages of this consisted in the occupation of the more isolated and restricted areas of permanent cultivation soil, such as those associated with springs and small streams in the dissected Tertiary limestones. This process has not been systematically investigated, but the number of late Vinča sites (late fourth millennium) in the dissected limestone terrace to the west of the Morava in Yugoslavia is suggestive in this respect. Within the major areas of old lake soil, occupation may have spread into the somewhat more marginal parts of the basin, either the drier areas or those well sited for access to surrounding uplands. In this way, the need for a major adjustment of pattern was deferred.

This pattern seems to have lasted until the third millennium and its climax is marked by the rich Eneolithic cultures of south-east Europe with their heavily decorated conservative pottery styles and ritual objects such as figurines giving an impression of a stable and well-ordered existence.

One aspect of technology that underwent considerable change during this phase is metallurgy, and the use of copper conventionally divides the earlier Neolithic from the later Eneolithic. Small amounts of copper used for ornaments are known from the early fourth millennium and may perhaps be related to a greater use of the upland areas where ores occur; but the extensive use of this metal for heavy objects and tools occurs only in the second half of this millennium. When Childe wrote, these early copper-using groups were assumed to be contemporary with the Early Dynastic period in Mesopotamia and knowledge of metallurgy was thought to have derived from there. The spread of metalworking was seen as a spur to economic development both by providing a more efficient technology and by stimulating trade in raw materials.

Recent research (summarized in Renfrew, 1969) has demonstrated that the beginnings of copper metallurgy in south-east Europe can be seen as an independent process, even if Europe itself was on the fringe of the area over which that process was operating, and that the inception of a European copper industry was not dependent on the introduction of techniques from outside. Nor can copperworking be seen as revolutionary in its economic effects. Although copper was used for axes and chisels, pure copper has few advantages over stone, and in any case the efficiency of forest-clearance was not a critical limiting factor in economic expansion. Indeed, it seems likely that most of the large copper objects were primarily of ritual or display value, much as the 'battle axes' further north.

The effect of the development of metalworking on distribution networks should not be overestimated. It has been suggested above that non-centralized societies are characterized by a great density of exchange, particularly within the socio-political unit. In the Eneolithic, large amounts of copper reached areas such as the centre of the middle Danube basin 200 km from suitable ore sources, but the concentration of metal finds is significantly within the boundaries of cultures which include metalliferous areas within their territories, such as Vinča and Bodrogkeresztur. Outside these territories, metal finds are noticeably rarer. In addition the specific artefact types show a strongly regional pattern. These facts suggest that specialized distribution networks were not involved, and that metal supplies were of no greater importance than other raw materials such as fine-grained stone, and not of vital strategic significance. Indeed, Childe's analysis could be inverted, and the specialized distribution networks capable of securing the highly specific raw materials needed for alloying could be seen as a result rather than a cause of social differentiation and administered trade. From this point of view the Bronze Age contrasts both with the Neolithic and the Eneolithic patterns.

A critical change in population density, distribution of settlement, technology and social organization seems to have occurred in many parts of Europe in the third millennium whether the groups involved are labelled 'Bronze Age', 'Copper Age' or 'Late Neolithic' according to regional terminologies.

While events in any particular region must be considered in the light of the progress of internal colonization in a specific local setting, many areas seem to have reached a significant threshold during this period.

Of particular significance is the point at which permanent settlement began to be extended beyond the range of soils typical of the initial settlement of the area. In the Konya plain third millennium settlements are found for the first time, in any number, on the drier terraces above the plain; doubling the number of sites known from the previous millennium. In the Balkans a shift in the preferred location of settlement occurs, typified by sites on defended promontories on the edge of the basins. In Czechoslovakia, similar hilltop settlements are found extending up the valleys from the covered Bohemian 'heartland'. In the north European plain, settlement extends onto the sandy heathlands previously avoided. These movements are not closely synchronous even within individual regions, but they represent critical points in a common process at work over the whole area.

Nor does the process manifest itself in the same way in different types of landscape, and to illustrate the diversity of patterns within a single region the set of landscape types distinguished in a previous section forms a useful basis. In the dissected limestone terrace area around Vratsa in north-west Bulgaria, with its small areas of *smolnitsa* accessible from a variety of situations, the increasing insecurity of the Eneolithic period is reflected in the move from riverside to flat promontory situations, and finally, in the late phases of the Salcutsa culture, to high hills with steep sides encircled by stone walls (information from Dr Bogdan Nikolov). In the broad flat-floored Maritsa basin, where population was too dense to be accommodated in defensible situations on the sides of the valley, settlements continue into the Bronze Age, perhaps with some measure of nucleation producing fewer, larger mounds, and here the important Early Bronze Age site of Ezero is defended by a large stone-built wall (information from Professor N. I. Merpert and Professor G. I. Georgiev). Both of these reflect the increased competition for land within the older settled areas. The Bronze Age in Bulgaria has been relatively little studied and there is as yet less evidence than from other regions of the occupation of other types of soil, though the drier areas surrounding the basins are densely dotted with tumuli which are presumed to be of later Bronze Age or Iron Age date.

In smaller basins such as the plain of Drama in north Greece a third pattern may be distinguished, in which tell settlements adjacent to marshy alluvial areas continue into the early part of the Bronze Age, when settlement shifts to fortified promontories round the edges of the plain. A number of factors is

533

likely to be at work here; the location of sites for access to upland sheep grazing, a truncation of the catchment areas of older-established sites by the proliferation of daughter settlements, the need to exploit the poorer fan soils for cereal growing (? barley), and the growing needs for defensible situations. The larger, flatter promontories are not occupied until later, suggesting that they required a larger resident population for adequate defence. The occupation of promontory sites is a typical feature of the Greek Middle Bronze Age onwards – e.g. Mycenae. This has persisted in the Mediterranean hill village pattern, especially typical of periods of insecurity, and lasting in north Greece down to the resettlement of Anatolian Greek-speakers in the lowland areas after 1921.

In floodplains of rivers in the loess areas of the middle Danube the Early Bronze Age is typified by permanently occupied settlements on the drier margins of the floodplain, forming tells probably both for flood protection and for defence. This pattern disappears in the Middle Bronze Age when occupation spreads to the drier areas between rivers and nucleated defended villages appear (e.g. Kovacs, 1969, fig. 5).

These diverse expressions of a similar underlying process in south-east Europe may be contrasted with the development of settlement in the north European plain where a similar framework of choice presented itself over a wide region. Most useful here is Mathiassen's careful study (1948) of the distribution of prehistoric finds in Jutland. The comparison of evidence from different classes of objects and monuments produces an interesting and highly significant pattern related to the three major facies of the Riss and Würm moraine landscape – hill sand, heath sand and clay. At the risk of oversimplification it is almost possible to see a reflection of Thomsen's 'Three Age System' in the successive occupation phases of these soil types: Neolithic settlement is concentrated largely on the more fertile hill sand; the late Neolithic Corded Ware period sees the occupation of the poorer heath sand areas, and this pattern persists until the occupation of clay areas in Iron Age times.

While the picture is complicated by the likelihood that settlements were placed on the edges of soil units in order to exploit two zones in a complementary way, the extension of finds and settlements into the heath sand areas in the Corded Ware period (second half of the third millennium) is supported by evidence from many other areas e.g. Sweden (Malmer, 1962) and Poland (Machnik, 1970). It is perhaps significant that the first evidence of animal traction (Higham and Message, 1969), the wheel (Van der Waals, 1964) and the plough (Glob, 1951) should appear at this period in these areas, suggesting that these were critical technological aspects of a system involving large-scale cultivation and manuring. It is likely that similar innovations accompanied the earlier extension of settlement in south-east Europe, and the change to barley as the characteristic Bronze Age cereal crop in sites away from the fertile lake basin soils shows how this affected crop strategies.

The process of agricultural expansion carried with it implications for social organization. One aspect of this was the competition for colonizable land distributed between the existing centres of population, reflected both in the selection of defensive locations and the development of effective metal weapons as opposed to small copper knives. Another was the occupation of a more diverse range of environments than the initial optimal ones, and the increased necessity for the redistribution of basic products. Even though some of the forested sandy soils taken into cultivation would originally have carried brown earths suitable for cereal cultivation, the agricultural use of these would rapidly encourage podsolization and reduce their value as arable. In this situation redistributive centres, even if only seasonal markets or fairs under the auspices or protection of a local chief, would take on increasing significance. The role of metal, increasingly a strategic raw material, would in these circumstances have been important in securing lowland cereal products, while the emergence of distributional centres and local chieftains made possible the exchange of specialized materials and objects between centres. In a similar way textiles – evidenced from the increased numbers and size of sheep in the Bronze Age of south-east Europe and from the appearance of heavy loom weights and fittings (the so called 'clay anchors') – would have been an important medium of exchange.

The emergence of a significant economic role for chieftainship is marked in the archaeological record by the conspicuous concentrations of wealth in graves and by monuments such as the very large tumuli of eastern Hungary (Kalicz, 1968) formerly believed to represent the intrusion of a steppe aristocracy. The power of such chieftains should not, however, be exaggerated and many of the more remote areas must have continued to be largely autonomous.

In one area of Europe, however, political development in the Bronze Age achieved a further degree of centralization. In peninsular Greece and Crete the areas of good quality arable land were limited in comparison with inland Europe or even with Thessaly. Close insight into the development of settlement in the south-western Peloponnese is given by the intensive survey data published by McDonald and Hope-Simpson for Messenia (1969). Settlement in the Neolithic, even in the coastal plains, was sparse and only in the Early Bronze Age are settlement sites established in locations suitable for cereal

535

growing, and even then only on the best soils. The area is thus marginal to the main population centres in the larger basins such as Thessaly. In the Middle Bronze Age, however, sites begin to appear in upland locations, almost certainly based on sheep rearing. By the Late Bronze Age (Mycenaean Period) a dense scatter of such sites is known, along with the palace at Pylos.

Killen's studies (1964) of the Knossos tablets have demonstrated that large numbers of male sheep were delivered annually to the palace, and he has explained this in terms of the importance of the wool industry to the Cretan palace economy. The settlement pattern in Messenia strongly suggests that the Pylos palace functioned in a similar way – much as the great Cistercian monasteries of Yorkshire – and indeed that this might be part of the reason for the whole palace system. The distribution of Mycenaean pottery in the Mediterranean and the parallel of later Greek colonization – for instance the interest in Sicily – would be consistent with an interpretation in terms of the colonial model elaborated above. In this case, the palaces would be regulating and redistributing centres for textile and other manufactured exports such as oil in return for imports of grain and metals.

The fate of this delicately balanced system is eloquently told in the distribution map of final Mycenaean (LH.III.C) sites. The map bears a striking resemblance to the Early Bronze Age one; the uplands have no settlements, and the palace is destroyed. Settlements are in defensible positions on the edges of the more fertile lowland areas. It is clear that the system would have been increasingly under pressure as population grew. A series of poor harvests causing unrest among the upland population and the sacking of the palaces would have destroyed the economic 'regulator' and caused the collapse of the whole system. The Dorian invasion, if it actually occurred, could have been as much a consequence as a cause.

Conclusion

The arguments set out in this paper are intended as much to indicate the range of evidence that must be considered in interpreting prehistoric cultural development as to advocate the use of specific models. Without an underlying framework of assumptions about the role of factors such as population growth there is no possibility of relating different aspects of prehistoric culture to each other and producing a convincing explanation for the contrasts in development between different areas. Only with this framework in mind can relevant models be selected for specific problems.

536

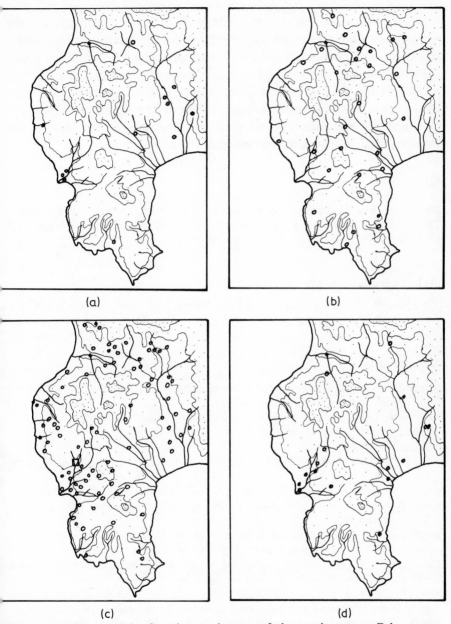

(a)   (b)

(c)   (d)

Fig. 12.19. The growth of settlement in part of the south-western Peloponnese (Messenia) during the Bronze Age. (a) Early Helladic, (b) Middle Helladic, (c) Late Helladic except L.H.IIIC, (d) L.H.IIIC (open circles) and Protogeometric (filled circles). Circles represent village settlements throughout, the square in (c) marking the palace of Pylos (after McDonald and Hope-Simpson, 1969).

537

It is inevitable in trying to look at old facts from a fresh perspective that the picture should appear incomplete. The diversity of information which from a *new* standpoint appears relevant to the study of prehistoric communities may also seem forbidding in its complexity and strangeness. But if archaeology is to provide a convincing account of the prehistoric past, archaeologists must pay heed to Voltaire's advice to the historians of his day: 'if all that you have to tell us is that one barbarian replaced another on the banks of the Oxus or the Jaxartes, what benefit have you conferred upon the public?'

Note

Revised versions of the paper circulated at the London Conference on Settlement Patterns and Urbanization are now published in a volume under the editorship of Dr P. Ucko, Professor G. W. Dimbleby and Dr R. Tringham (1972).

Acknowledgements

I am grateful to Dr D. L. Clarke and Robin Dennell for many conversations on the subjects covered in this paper.

References

ADAMS, R. M. (1970) *Patterns of Urbanization in Early Southern Mesopotamia*. Circulated seminar paper, London.

ALLAN, W. (1965) *The African Husbandman*. London: Oliver & Boyd.

ALLAN, W. (1970) *Ecology, Techniques and Settlement Patterns*. Circulated seminar paper, London.

ANGEL, L. (1968) Human remains at Karataş. *American Journal of Archaeology*, **72**, (3), 260–3.

ASHBY, W. R. (1956) *An Introduction to Cybernetics*. London: Chapman & Hall.

BATH, B. H. S. VAN (1963) *The Agrarian History of Western Europe, A.D. 500–1850*. London: Arnold.

BINFORD, L. R. (1968) Archeological perspectives. In BINFORD, S. R. and BINFORD, L. R. (eds.) *New Perspectives in Archeology*, 5–32. Chicago: Aldine.

BIRDSELL, J. B. (1968) Some predictions for the Pleistocene. In LEE, R. B. and DEVORE, I. (eds.) *Man The Hunter*, 229–40. Chicago: Aldine.

BÖKÖNYI, S. (1968) Die Geschichtliche Entwicklung der Tierhaltung in Mittel-und Osteuropa. *Agrártörténeti Szemle*, **10**, 1–4 (in Hungarian, with German summary).

BOSERUP, E. (1965) *The Conditions of Agricultural Growth*. London: Allen & Unwin.

BRADLEY, R. (1971) Trade competition and artefact distribution. *World Archaeology*, **2** (3), 347–51.

BROTHWELL, D. and HIGGS, E. S. (eds.) (1969) *Science in Archaeology*. 2nd ed. London: Thames & Hudson.

BUTZER, K. W. (1970) Physical conditions in eastern Europe, western Asia and Egypt before the period of agriculture. *Cambridge Ancient History*. 2nd ed. Cambridge: University Press.

BYLUND, E. (1960) Theoretical considerations regarding the distribution of settlement in inner north Sweden. *Geografisker Annaler*, **42**, 225–31.

CARNEIRO, R. L. (1960) Slash and burn agriculture: a closer look at its implications for settlement patterns. In WALLACE, A. F. C. (ed.) *Men and Cultures*. Philadelphia: University of Pennsylvania Press.

CHILDE, V. G. (1925) *The Dawn of European Civilization*. London: Routledge.

CHILDE, V. G. (1956) *Piecing Together the Past*. London: Routledge.

CHILDE, V. G. (1958) *The Prehistory of European Society*. London: Cassell.

CHISHOLM, M. (1968) *Rural Settlement and Land Use*. 2nd ed. London: Hutchison.

CHORLEY, R. J. and HAGGETT, P. (eds.) (1967) *Models in Geography*. London: Methuen.

CLARK, J. G. D. (1952) *Prehistoric Europe: The Economic Basis*. London: Methuen.

CLARK, J. G. D. (1965) Traffic in stone axe and adze blades. *Economic History Review*, 2nd ser. **18**, 1–28.

CLARKE, D. L. (1968) *Analytical Archaeology*. London: Methuen.

COHEN, J. (1970) The palaeoecology of south central Anatolia. *Anatolian Studies*, **20**, 119–37.

COHEN, J. and EROL, O. (1969) Aspects of the palaeogeography of central Anatolia. *Geographical Journal*, **135**, 399–98.

DALTON, G. (ed.) (1968) *Primitive, Archaic and Modern Economies: Essays of Karl Polanyi*. New York: Doubleday.

D'ARCY THOMPSON, W. (1917) *On Growth and Form*. Cambridge: Cambridge University Press.

DEEVEY, E. S. (1960) The human population. *Scientific American*, **203** (3), 194–204.

DESCHLER, W. (1965) Native cattle-keeping in west Africa. In LEEDS, A. and VAYDA, A. (eds.) *Man, Culture and Animals*. Washington: American Association for the Advancement of Science.

DEUTSCH, K. W. (1953) The growth of nations: some recurrent patterns of political and social integration. *World Politics*, **5**, 168–95.

DURKHEIM, E. (1933) *The Division of Labor in Society*. New York: Collier-Macmillan.

EAST, G. (1968) *The Geography Behind History*. London: Nelson.

FILIPOVSKI, J. and CIVIĆ, G. (1969) *The Soils of Jugoslavia*. Belgrade.

FIRTH, J. (ed.) (1967) *Themes in Economic Anthropology*. A.S.A. Monographs No. 6. London: Tavistock.

FORTES, M. and EVANS-PRITCHARD, E. E. (1940) *African Political Systems*. London: International African Institute.

FRENCH, D. (1970) Notes on site distribution in the Çumra area. *Anatolian Studies*, **20**, 139–48.

GARNER, B. (1967) Models of urban geography and settlement location. In CHORLEY, R. J. and HAGGETT, P. (eds.) *Models in Geography*, 303–60. London: Methuen.

GEORGIEV, G. I. (1961) Kulturgruppen der Jungstein- und der Kupferzeit in das Ebene von Thrazien. In BÖHM, J. and LAET, S. DE (eds.) *L'Europe à la Fin de l'Âge de la Pierre*. Prague.

539

GLOB, P. V. (1951) *Ard og plov i Nordens Oldtid.* Aarhus.

GOULD, P. R. (1963) Man against his environment: a game-theoretic framework. *Annals of the Association of American Geographers*, **53**, 290–7.

HAGGETT, P. (1965) *Locational Analysis in Human Geography.* London: Arnold.

HAMILTON, F. E. I. (1967) Models of industrial location. In CHORLEY, R. J. and HAGGETT, P. (eds.) *Models in Geography*, 361–424. London: Methuen.

HARVEY, D. (1967) Models of the evolution of spatial patterns in human geography. In CHORLEY, R. J. and HAGGETT, P. (eds.) *Models in Geography*, 549–608. London: Methuen.

HIGGS, E. S. (forthcoming) *Papers in Economic Prehistory.* Cambridge: Cambridge University Press.

HIGGS, E. S. and JARMAN, M. R. (1969) The origins of agriculture: a reconsideration. *Antiquity*, **43**, 31–41.

HIGHAM, C. and MESSAGE, M. (1969) An assessment of a prehistoric technique of bovine husbandry. In BROTHWELL, D. and HIGGS, E. S. (eds.) *Science in Archaeology*, 315–30. 2nd ed. London: Thames & Hudson.

HOLE, F. and FLANNERY, K. (1967) The prehistory of southwestern Iran: a preliminary report. *Proceedings of the Prehistoric Society*, **33**, 147–206.

HUNTER, J. M. (1966) Ascertaining population carrying capacity under traditional systems of agriculture. *Professional Geographer*, **18** (3).

HUXLEY, J. (1953) *Evolution in Action.* New York: Harper & Row.

JARMAN, M. R. (1971) Culture and economy in the north Italian Neolithic. *World Archaeology*, **2**, 255–65.

JOY, L. (1967) An economic homologue of Barth's presentation of economic spheres in Darfur. In FIRTH, J. (ed.) *Themes in Economic Anthropology*, 175–89. A.S.A. Monographs No. 6. London: Tavistock.

KALICZ, N. (1968) *Die Frühbronzezeit in Nordost Ungarn.* Budapest.

KILLEN, J. T. (1964) The wool industry of Crete in the Late Bronze Age. *Annual of the British School of Archaeology at Athens*, **59**, 1–15.

KOEBNER, L. (1966) The settlement and colonization of Europe. In POSTAN, M. M. (ed.) *Cambridge Economic History of Europe*, vol. I, 1–90.

KOVACS, T. (1969) A Szazhalombattai Bronzkori telep. *Archaeologiai Értesitö*, **96**, 161–9. Budapest.

LATHRAP, D. (1968) The 'hunting' economies of the tropical zone of South America. In LEE, R. B. and DEVORE, I. (eds.) *Man The Hunter*, 23–9. Chicago: Aldine.

LEE, R. B. and DEVORE, I. (eds.) (1968). *Man The Hunter*, Chicago: Aldine.

LEEDS, A. (1969) Ecological determinants of chieftainship among the Yaruro Indians of Venezuela. In VAYDA, A. P. (ed.) *Environment and Cultural Behaviour.* New York: Natural History Press.

LEEDS, A. and VAYDA, A. (eds.) (1965) *Man, Culture and Animals.* Washington.

MCDONALD, W. A. and HOPE-SIMPSON, R. (1969) Further explorations in the south-western Peloponnese. *American Journal of Archaeology*, **73**, 132.

MACHNIK, J. (1970) The corded ware culture. In WIŚLANŚKI, T. (ed.) *The Neolithic in Poland.* Polish Academy of Sciences.

MALINOWSKI, B. (1922) *Argonauts of the Western Pacific.* London: Routledge.

MALMER, M. P. (1962) Jungneolithische Studien. *Acta Archaeologica Lundensia* No. 2. Lund, Sweden: CWK Gleerups Förlag.

MATHIASSEN, T. (1948) Studier over Vestjyllands oldtidsbebyggelse. *Nationalmuseets Skrifter, Ark.-Hist. Ser.*, 2.

MATHIASSEN, T. (1957) Nordvestsjaellands oldtidsbebyggelse. *Nationalmuseets Skrifter, Ark.-Hist. Ser.*, 7.

MAUSS, M. (1954) *The Gift.* London: Cohen.

MORTON-WILLIAMS, P. (1969) The influence of habitat and trade on the policies of Oyo and Ashanti. In DOUGLAS, M. and KABERRY, P. M. (eds.) *Man in Africa,* 79–95. London: Methuen.

OVERGAARD, P. (1932) *Vestjyllands Oldtidsbebyggelse.* Copenhagen.

PIDDOCKE, S. (1969) The potlatch system of the southern Kwakiutle:a new perspective. In VAYDA, A. P. *Environment and Cultural Behaviour,* 130–58. New York: Natural History Press.

PIGGOTT, S. (1968) The earliest wheeled vehicles and the Caucasian evidence. *Proceedings of the Prehistoric Society,* **34,** 266–318.

POLANYI, K., ARENSBURG, C. M. and PEARSON, H. W. (1957) *Trade and Market in the Early Empires.* Glencoe, Ill.: Free Press.

POSTAN, M. M. and TITOW, J. Z. (1959) Heriots and prices on the Winchester manors. *Economic History Review,* 2nd ser. **11.**

RENFREW, A. C. (1969) The autonomy of the south-east European Copper Age. *Proceedings of the Prehistoric Society,* **35,** 12–47.

RENFREW, A. C. (1970) *Patterns of Population Growth in the Prehistoric Aegean.* Circulated seminar paper, London.

ROGLIĆ, J. (1961) The geographical setting of medieval Dubrovnik. In POUNDS, N. J. G. (ed.) *Geographical Essays on Southeast Europe.* Bloomington, University of Indiana Press.

SALISBURY, R. F. (1962) *From Stone to Steel: Economic Consequences of a Technological Change in New Guinea.* Cambridge: Cambridge University Press.

SANDERS, W. T. and PRICE, B. J. (1968) *Mesoamerica: The Evolution of a Civilization.* New York: Random House.

SAUVY, A. (1969) *The General Theory of Population.* London: Weidenfeld & Nicolson.

SCHON, D. (1971) *Beyond the Stable State.* London: Temple Smith.

SCHWABEDISSEN, H. (1967) Ein horizontierter Breitkeil aus Satrup. *Palaeohistoria,* **12,** 409–68.

SEEBERG, P. and KRISTENSEN, M. (1964) Mange striber paa kryds og tvaers. *Kuml,* 7–14.

SERVICE, E. R. (1962) *Primitive Social Organization: An Evolutionary Perspective.* New York: Random House.

SMITH, C. T. (1967) *An Historical Geography of Western Europe before 1800.* London: Longmans.

STEVENS, E. S. (1966) Agriculture and rural life in the later Roman Empire. In POSTAN, M. M. (ed.) *Cambridge Economic History of Europe,* vol. I, 92–119.

TAYLOR, C. (1970) *The Study of Settlement Patterns in pre-Saxon Britain.* Circulated seminar paper, London.

VAJDA, S. (1960) *Introduction to Linear Programming and the Theory of Games.* London: Methuen.

VAYDA, A. P. (ed.) (1969) *Environment and Cultural Behaviour.* New York: Natural History Press.

VITA-FINZI, C. (1969) Fluvial geology. In BROTHWELL, D. and HIGGS, E. S. (eds.) *Science in Archaeology.* 2nd ed. London: Thames & Hudson.

VITA-FINZI, C. and HIGGS, E. S. (1970) Prehistoric economy in the Mount Carmel area of Palestine: site catchment analysis. *Proceedings of the Prehistoric Society,* **36**, 1–37.

WAALS, J. D. VAN DER (1964) *Prehistoric Disk-Wheels in the Netherlands.* Groningen.

WHITTLESEY, D. (1944) *The Earth and the State.* New York.

WRIGLEY, E. A. (1962) The supply of raw materials in the Industrial Revolution. *Economic History Review,* 2nd ser. **15**, 1–16.

WRIGLEY, E. A. (1969) *Population and History.* London: Weidenfeld & Nicolson.

WYNNE-EDWARDS, V. C. (1962) *Animal Dispersion in Relation to Social Behaviour.* Edinburgh: Oliver and Boyd.

13

Ecosystem models and demographic hypotheses: predation and prehistory in North America

P. F. WILKINSON

University of Alaska, Musk Ox Project, U.S.A.

Despite the increasingly ecological orientation of contemporary prehistoric studies, ecological data continue to be used principally to provide 'scenery' for the cultural and technological 'drama' which is widely considered the province of archaeological investigations. Whilst this practice is legitimate and informative, I hope to demonstrate the value of ecological models for constructing directly testable hypotheses concerning the density and distribution of past human populations. Although I accept Willey and Phillips's (1958, p. 2) definition of the aim of archaeology as the search for regularities 'which are in a sense spaceless and timeless', I cannot accept their contention that archaeology 'concerns itself necessarily with the nature and position of unique events in space and time' (Willey and Phillips, 1958, p. 2). In important respects archaeological data do not record unique events, for they represent prehistoric man's participation in the trophic-dynamic system. Some details of this system will be discussed below, to demonstrate that man's position in the food chains through which energy is channelled resembles that of other predators, especially the social carnivores; to this degree a common denominator for the activities of diverse groups through space and time can be established, and in this sense the activities studied by archaeologists are not unique.

In the first part of this paper, I discuss certain concepts basic to my chosen approach, after which I review briefly the evidence for environmental fluctuations in North America at the time of man's arrival. On the basis of the data presented in these two sections I propose three hypotheses concerning the nature and success of man's colonization of North America and his role in the large-scale Late Pleistocene faunal extinctions. Finally, I attempt to test these

543

hypotheses against the available data to illustrate the feasibility of the procedure that I have adopted.

Part 1 Basic concepts

The trophic-dynamic model was formulated initially by Lindeman (1942) to facilitate study of the mechanisms by which energy is distributed throughout the biosphere. Within terrestrial ecosystems, four major levels of energy transfer can be recognized: the autotrophs or producers, capable of synthesizing energy from solar radiation or inorganic sources; the herbivores or primary consumers; and two levels of predators, known alternatively as secondary and tertiary consumers. In practice few ecosystems are as simple as this model suggests (Odum, 1966; Paine, 1969), and field studies of terrestrial ecosystems have been handicapped by the practical difficulties of handling and quantifying the many variables involved (Elton, 1966; Engelmann, 1969). Nonetheless, data from field and laboratory studies (Slobodkin, 1969) support the outlines of the model, which is generally accepted by ecologists (e.g. Engelmann, 1969; Slobodkin, 1962) and is considered adequate for the purposes of the present paper. Despite the absence of short-term 'steady states' in most ecosystems (Engelmann, 1969), the distribution of energy is limited by the laws of thermodynamics, so that the amount of available energy decreases at progressively higher trophic levels. This diminution of energy and the necessity for maintaining viable systems obviously impose behavioural constraints on the occupants of each trophic level and justify the assumption that comparisons between animals occupying similar positions in different ecosystems are not inherently unreliable, but are appropriate to the broad field of enquiry of the present paper.

The first task of the prehistorian must be to decide which trophic level the populations he is studying occupied. Washburn and DeVore (1961), for instance, used baboon troops as a model for the early African hominids, assuming, but not proving, that these hominids were primary consumers. If it can be shown that prehistoric man was predominantly a predator, wolves (Pilbeam, 1967; Woolpy and Ginsburg, 1967) or other carnivores (Eaton, 1969; Estes, 1967) might provide a more appropriate model. The hypothesis that the first colonists of North America practised economies based on predation has been implicitly tested in all syntheses of North American prehistory (e.g. Bryan, 1969; Mason, 1962; Willey, 1966) and may be accepted provisionally. Defining man as a predator does not imply that he relied exclusively on animal protein, and indeed one of the chief difficulties of quantifying the

544

role of individual organisms in ecosystems is the obvious fact that many organisms occupy two trophic levels simultaneously. Animals are classified as carnivorous, herbivorous or omnivorous principally on the basis of structural and anatomical characteristics; whilst such characteristics are well suited to erecting taxonomies, they do not always correspond exactly to the behaviour of every group or individual comprising the taxon, for the simple reason that animals tend to adopt the course of least resistance and do not always do that for which they are best adapted. For example, baboons (Washburn and De-Vore, 1961) and savannah chimpanzees (Ardrey, 1966), both predominantly herbivorous, occasionally eat meat and even hunt. Amongst the carnivores, coyotes (Errington, 1967), red foxes (Errington, 1967) and black bears in Alaska (Hatler, 1967) seasonally adopt almost exclusively vegetable diets. Hatler (1967) estimated that meat formed only 15% by volume of the diet of some black bears in autumn, even though immature game animals were readily available. Errington (1967, p. 12), a noted authority on predation, commented that 'omnivorous habits are indeed characteristic of many mammals that are labelled carnivorous.' Ethnographic studies reveal a similar pattern among modern hunter-gatherers, and of the twenty-four groups listed by Lee (1968, table 9, p. 46), only four rely on hunting (including fishing) more than on gathering.

The necessity of maintaining viable, integrated systems of energy transfer imposes particularly rigorous constraints on the size, density and distribution of animal populations. I have adopted Rappaport's (1963, pp. 157–8) definition of a population as 'an aggregate of organisms that belong to the same species, occupy a common habitat, and have in common certain distinctive means whereby they exploit one or more niches in one or more ecosystems.' The ultimate factor limiting populations is obviously the amount and accessibility of those resources indispensable to survival, but in general it appears that other, more direct mechanisms operate to stabilize animal populations below the level at which they threaten to overexploit their staple food resources (Lack, 1954; Wynne-Edwards, 1962). Predation, potentially an important mechanism of population regulation (Errington, 1956), appears commonly to be limited to levels easily sustained by prey populations: 'stability between prey and predator populations, as in other interspecific associations, seems to be the general rule, to be departed from only when the stabilizing mechanism is overtaxed' (Wynne-Edwards, 1962).

Cases of overkilling – that is, killing in excess of their apparent needs – have been reported for weasels (Errington, 1967) and for wolves (Kelsall, 1968) among others, but in some cases they are apparently aberrant, 'neurotic'

545

patterns of behaviour, and in the case of the wolf, overkilling seems in fact to be a form of winter food storage (Kelsall, 1968). Such situations are, however, unusual, and there is little evidence to support Volterra's (1931) thesis that predator populations tend to increase until they threaten their prey, followed by a decline until the equilibrium is re-established and the cycle begins once again. In the early 1950s a wolf control program was initiated in the Canadian Northwest Territories to stem a decline in the numbers of caribou which had begun some years earlier (Kelsall, 1968), although one contemporary estimate put caribou losses from wolf predation at only 5% of the population annually (Banfield, 1954). Despite the slaughter of many wolves, the caribou populations continued to decline with little change, suggesting that predation was a negligible factor in the observed decline. In the laboratory, Holling (1966) showed that mantids exposed to increasing numbers of house-flies soon reached a level of satiation, beyond which they did not needlessly exploit their prey. A similar pattern was observed among deer mice (*Peromyscus leucopus*) (Holling, 1965). When exposed to increasing amounts of a two-component diet, consisting of (to them) palatable sawflies and less attractive dog biscuits, the deer mice maintained a mixed diet and avoided overexploiting their preferred prey.

Among territorial species predation seems to be relatively unimportant in regulating population size. In the case of the muskrat, which maintains territories throughout the entire year, Errington (1967) was able to demonstrate that predation was largely restricted to those animals that failed to establish territories and were consequently superfluous to the requirements of group propagation and defence. Similar selective predation against the less important sectors of prey populations has been recorded among Dall sheep (Murie, 1944), moose (Allen and Mech, 1963), deer (Olson, 1938) and caribou (Tanner, 1968), for instance, although Schaller's (1967) study of tiger predation in the Kanha Park, India, showed clearly that mature and apparently healthy animals are taken by predators wherever possible. Population regulation through some form of territorial behaviour has been recorded for a variety of species, including Gould's manakin, titmice, great reed warblers (Wynne-Edwards, 1962), golden eagles, red grouse, chaffinches, song sparrows, dragonflies (Tanner, 1968) and rabbits (Mykytowycz, 1968). Other mechanisms, including the direct or indirect effects of cyclic fluctuations in sunspot activity (Chesemore, 1967; Errington, 1958; Lack, 1954; Pruitt, 1968; Wing, 1961), disease (Banfield, 1956; MacFadyen, 1963) and endocrine imbalance resulting from overcrowding (Tanner, 1968) may also be important. Chitty (1969) has suggested that under certain circumstances many animals may be capable of regulating their own numbers in equilibrium with their food resources without the assistance of any external mechanism. Territoriality is generally well developed among predators (Schaller, 1967; Scott, 1958) and is probably their chief means of population regulation. I must emphasize, however, that the above discussion is an oversimplification, and in any given instance the balance between populations and their resources is the result of a complex interaction of some of the factors discussed above and of others perhaps unrecognized. Although it is impossible to specify the nature and the relative importance of the factors operating to control given animal populations, the important point remains valid: that in general animal populations are in equilibrium with their resources. By virtue of their position within the trophic-dynamic structure, human populations are inevitably bound by the laws controlling the flow of energy, and their long-term survival (the concern of the prehistorian) demands that they do not overexploit their staple resources. Granted this assumption and given a knowledge of the energy budget of past ecosystems, it is possible for prehistorians to predict within limits the optimal size and distribution of past human populations of known technological efficiency. Birdsell (1958), for example, pointed out that the Australian hunter-gatherers whom he studied were in equilibrium with their resources, and Binford (1968) has considered some of the implications for prehistorians of the existence of such a balance. There is an implicit recognition of the relationship between human populations and the resources upon which they depend through the medium of their technologies in widely accepted statements to the effect that populations of hunter-gatherers are rarely likely to exceed a density of 1–2 per square mile (Lee and DeVore, 1968, p. 11).

The nature of the equilibrium between human populations and their resources depends largely on the technological efficiency of these populations, by which I mean the range and quantity of resources that they could exploit economically. In the present study, therefore, I consider artefacts from a technological rather than a cultural point of view (I realize that functional and cultural attributes form a single overlapping class of attributes and that the prehistorian possesses no infallible guide in distinguishing between the two). This is not to say that cultural and ecological interpretations in archaeology are in opposition, simply that they pose complementary questions and weight the available evidence in different ways. Estimates of technological efficiency must be based on assemblages rather than on individual artefacts, the function of which is rarely certain (see Clarke, 1968, pp. 665–70, for definitions). Recent demonstrations of task-specific sites in the Middle Palaeolithic of

Asia (Binford and Binford, 1966) and in North America (see Table 13.1), and of apparently function-specific areas within Upper Palaeolithic sites in Europe (Movius, 1966) demand that areas rather than single sites be studied, so that the artefacts from base camps, kill sites and other seasonal or temporary sites can be treated as single units from which reliable estimates of the technological efficiency of prehistoric human populations can be derived. I cannot accept Chang's (1967, 1968) thesis that settlements should form the basic units of archaeological investigations. Studies of the type I propose demand intensive investigation of small areas and a strict framework of absolute dates, but the work of the Tehuacan Project (MacNeish, 1961, 1962) and of Higgs in Epirus (Higgs and Vita-Finzi, 1966; Higgs *et al.*, 1967), for example, have demonstrated that both are often practicable and profitable. Estimating the efficiency of artefact assemblages relies both on the artefacts themselves and on the associated food debris. The total ecological background of the human populations in question must be known, so that the resources they exploited can be compared with the total spectrum of available resources and an estimate of efficiency can be derived, allowing wherever possible for cultural or preservational biases and for seasonal variations in the food supply. The recurrent absence of certain categories of artefacts (e.g. those associated broadly with fishing, woodworking or processing vegetable foods, for example) may be significant, provided that it can be demonstrated not to result from poor preservation or inadequate investigation. In some cases, the former presence of rarely preserved artefacts can be inferred from the types of faunal remains preserved (Meighan *et al.*, 1958). Although it is rarely possible to infer the precise function of individual artefacts from their morphology, I feel that it is possible to assign groups of artefacts to broad categories of activity; for example, hunting large terrestrial mammals, fishing, woodworking, or processing vegetable foods. Although the above approach to artefact analysis is admittedly generalized, I feel that it is sufficient for the purpose that I have in mind, and it has the additional advantage of being practicable given the large numbers of artefacts recovered under the increasingly refined conditions of modern excavation and the serious shortage of qualified personnel available to analyse them. Deevey (1968) highlighted the importance of distinguishing between the available resources and those actually used when he pointed out that a change in economic emphasis from deer to rodents in certain forest situations would permit up to 100-fold increases in human population.

Valuable light can be cast upon man's colonization of North America by studying recorded instances of the spread or introduction of exotic species into

TABLE I3.I. *Seasonal and/or task-specific sites in North America*

Site	State	Type of site	References
Dent	Colorado	Multiple mammoth kill	Sellards, 1952; Wormington, 1957
Lehner	Arizona	Multiple mammoth kill	Wedel, 1961; Wormington, 1957
Domebo	Oklahoma	Single mammoth kill	Leonhardy, 1966
Reagen	Vermont	Chipping site	Ritchie, 1953
Bull Brook	Massachusetts	Habitation site	Byers, 1959
Williamson	Virginia	Habitation site	McCary, 1951
Silver Springs	Florida	Habitation Site	Neill, 1958
Burnet Cave	New Mexico	Long, ? seasonal occupation	Hester, 1960
Shoop Site	Pennsylvania	Exotic chert suggests stone/group mobility	Witthoft, 1952
Folsom	New Mexico	Bison slaughter and skinning	Hester, 1967; Jelinek, 1957
Bonfire Shelter	Texas	Bison leap; visited seasonally	Dibble and Lorrain, 1968
Lindenmeier	Colorado	Kill site + habitation	Hester, 1967
Hell Gap	Wyoming	Seasonal camp + vegetable processing	Haynes, 1967
Wilson Butte	Idaho	Exotic chalcedony suggests stone/group mobility	Gruhn, 1961, 1965
Olsen-Chubbock	Colorado	Bison stampede	Wheat, 1967
Pine Spring	Wyoming	Altitude + fauna imply seasonal habitation	Sharrock, 1966
Frightful Cave	Coahuila	500 sandals suggest task-specific site	Jennings, 1964
Danger Cave	Utah	Chaff in level V suggests seasonal visits	Jennings, 1957, 1964
The Dalles	Oregon	Seasonal salmon fishing	Cressman, 1960
Lind Coulee	Washington	Riverine location implies seasonal occupation	Daugherty, 1956

new environments. A general pattern has emerged, characterized by· a rapid initial increase, commonly followed by a slight decline in numbers as a satisfactory equilibrium with predators, competitors, and staple resources is attained. Animals in which this pattern has been observed include the moth, *Cactoblastis cactorum* (Andrewartha, 1958), and the rabbit (Scott, 1958) in Australia, the dog and the rat in New Zealand (Sharp, 1956), the rat in Hawaii (Zimmermann, 1963), the muskrat and the fallow deer in parts of Europe (Lindemann, 1956), the raccoon in Siberia (Lindemann, 1956), and a variety of feral domesticates (McKnight, 1964). In the fossil record a similar pattern can be observed on a larger scale at the end of the Pliocene, when the reformation of the Panamanian land bridge permitted faunal migrations between North and South America. Many North American forms colonized the South so successfully that they displaced indigenous animals, which became extinct (Newell, 1962).

Whilst I must emphasize the provisional nature of certain of the hypotheses presented above, I feel that they are adequate to the purposes that I have in mind and that, given a knowledge of the environmental conditions in North America at the time of man's arrival, they are sufficiently precise to permit the construction of a model of this colonization which can be tested against the available archaeological data.

Part 2 The ecological background

The types of evidence relevant to reconstructing past ecosystems are as diverse as the relationships within modern ecosystems, and my discussion will be limited to those factors immediately affecting the size, density and distribution of human populations. Data to be presented below will suggest that man's arrival in North America can be dated to the period 25 000–20 000 B.P. For present purposes I am accepting a broad, tripartite division of the Final (Wisconsin) Glaciation (Fairbridge, 1961, p. 572; Flint and Brandtner, 1961, fig. 1, p. 458). An early cold period from c. 70 000–50 000 B.P. was followed by a warmer period lasting until c. 25 000 B.P., with perhaps one or more cooler intermissions. The glacial maximum followed, lasting until c. 16 000 B.P. Recent 016/018 analyses of samples from a 1400 m core from the Greenland icecap at Camp Century (Dansgaard *et al.*, 1969) have revealed a series of eleven rapid and violent temperature fluctuations between 15 000 and 10 000 B.P. Although the record is incomplete, there is some collaborative evidence for similar fluctuations in North America (Adam, 1967; Brush, 1967; Hafsten, 1961; Terasmae, 1967), and Heusser has suggested (1961, p. 642) that many climatic fluctuations are broadly synchronous on a global scale, although allowance must be made for the influence of local conditions upon their precise manifestations.

Haynes (1967, fig. 1) mapped the southward extension of the Wisconsin ice sheet in North America, the boundary running from near Vancouver Island south-east to the southern tip of the Great Lakes, and then gently north-east to the coast. Immediately south of the ice there are some loess deposits with evidence for local permafrost conditions (Wayne, 1967) and other periglacial phenomena (Black, 1964). Although these areas may have been treeless, there is no evidence for tundra climax biota (Wayne, 1967). Further south, periods of glacial advance were probably marked by increased rainfall (Hafsten, 1961; Shutler, 1961), and in mountainous areas the tree line may have been lowered (Wells and Berger, 1967). Whereas the advance of the ice sheets decreased the area available to large game animals, the associated eustatic lowering of sea level partly compensated for this. Remains of mammoth, mastodon, horse, tapir, sloth and musk ox have been recovered from the Atlantic shelf (Richards, 1959).

The Wisconsin fauna of North America comprised three basic elements: indigenous animals, including *Camelops* and *Megalonyx*, defined here as those animals established on the continent by the end of the Pliocene; Eurasian forms, which entered North America at various times throughout the Pleistocene when the Bering land bridge was exposed during periods of lowered sea level (see Table 13.2); South American immigrants, including *Pampatherium*, *Neochoerus*, *Boreostracon* and *Chlamytherium*. The indigenous Pliocene fauna was probably adapted to a variety of environmental conditions, with the possible exception of arctic and subarctic conditions. The route and time of the entry of the Eurasian immigrants suggests that they could tolerate arctic and subarctic conditions, although not all of them were strictly arctic forms. The South American forms, on the other hand, must have been adapted to warmer conditions. Most of them had a southerly distribution within North America and were probably not an important part of the North American faunal community. The large number of new arrivals from Eurasia, especially in the Illinoian and the Wisconsin glacials, and their apparent success in colonizing North America, imply very strongly that the indigenous fauna was incapable of utilizing fully the diversity of niches available, some of which may have come into prominence only with the onset of glacial conditions. There was a high proportion of predators among the immigrants, and they doubtless fulfilled an important role in maintaining the balance between the many primary consumers, for one of the effects of predation is that it often prevents naturally prolific animals from displacing less prolific forms (MacArthur, 1969, p. 135). It is obvious that there must have been a very delicate balance between the many species of the North American faunal community, a balance particularly susceptible to outside disturbance.

TABLE 13.2. *Faunal migrations from Eurasia to North America*

Date	Vangeneim (1967)	Hopkins & Péwé (1967)	Kurtén (1966)
Villa-franchian	?*Archidiskodon* ?*Ovibovinae*		*Euryboas* *Archidiskodon meridionalis* *Mammuthus trogontherii*
Kansan			*Ursus americanus* *Smilodon* *Homotherium*
Illinoian	*Mammuthus* *Bison* *Cervus*	*Castor* *Dicrostonyx torquatus* *Aenocyon* *Canis* *Vulpes* *Felis* *Mammut* *Mammuthus* *Cervalces* *Alces* *Rangifer* *Bison* (*Superbison*) *Bootherium* *Ovibos* *Ovis* *Ondatra zibethicus* *Equus*	*Bison* *Gulo* *Mustela erminea* *Canis* *Vulpes* *Cervus elaphus*
Wisconsin	*Saiga*		*Mustela lutreola* *Bison bison* *Ursus arctos* *Ursus maritimus* *Alopex lagopus* *Rangifer tarandus* *Ovibos moschatus* *Saiga tatarica*

The generally accepted picture of the faunal history of North America during the Wisconsin glacial suggests that North America was a rich reservoir of game animals and that their decline began relatively suddenly towards the end of this period, lasting into the early Holocene (Martin and Wright, 1967). I can find little evidence to support this hypothesis, and the data may be interpreted equally reasonably as suggesting that the process of extinction may have been under way as early as *c.* 25 000 B.P., roughly the date of man's arrival on the continent. The issue is complicated by the paucity of reliably dated faunal collections and by uncertainty as to how representative faunal collections are of the contemporary faunal communities. I agree with Guthrie (1968a), however, that it is reasonable to assume that there is in general a correlation between the representation of animals in palaeontological collections and their actual importance in the contemporaneous faunal communities. Two faunal collections are reliably dated to the Final (Sangamon) interglacial, at Good Creek (Dalquest, 1962) and at the Hill-Shuler site (Slaughter *et al.*, 1962) respectively, and both are rich and diverse in large mammals. Prior to the mid-Wisconsin interstadial(s) there are no reliably dated faunas, but within the interstadial complex the two sites of American Falls (Hopkins *et al.*, 1969) and Clear Creek (Martin, 1967; Slaughter and Ritchie, 1963) show fewer large mammals, although neither is actually impoverished. After this period, there is no evidence that the large-mammal community of North America was thriving, and indeed the earliest instance of extinction, that of *Boreostracon* (Slaughter and McClure, 1965), is dated to *c.* 23 000 B.P. The only faunal collection spanning the glacial maximum comes from Grosebeck Creek, Texas (Dalquest, 1965; Slaughter, 1967), and contains predominantly rodents and small mammals. The major period of faunal extinction appears to have occurred after the glacial maximum and will be considered below. The evidence is difficult to interpret confidently, and the apparent absence of large game animals may simply be the result of chance or may imply only that conditions suitable for their preservation did not exist. In Eurasia, on the other hand, where analogous glacial conditions may be assumed to have existed, there is abundant evidence for rich and diverse faunal communities at this period (Kurtén, 1968). Pending further evidence, it is possible to assume that the process of faunal impoverishment was under way perhaps as early as *c.* 20 000 B.P. Some of the possible causes of this impoverishment will be discussed below, but it is clear that large game animals form such an integral part of the trophic-dynamic structure that one may infer disruptions in some or all of the other components of this system from the reduction in the numbers and diversity of the large game species.

Combining the data presented in this section with the preceding discussion of the factors limiting the size, density and distribution of animal (including human) populations, I propose to offer three hypotheses concerning man's colonization of North America. These hypotheses are based on the following assumptions:

(*a*) That human populations tend in the long run to assume an equilibrium with their staple resources, such that they do not threaten the survival or regenerative capacity of these resources.

(*b*) That human populations tend also to adopt the 'course of least resistence' when faced with a choice of economic strategies.

(*c*) That human populations colonizing previously unoccupied areas will tend to follow the pattern observed for other colonizing species; namely, an initial rapid spread leading to the establishment of an equilibrium with respect to resources.

(*d*) That it is possible to estimate within an acceptable degree of accuracy the extractive efficiency of prehistoric technologies.

Granted these assumptions, I wish to offer for testing the following hypotheses:

(1) Given that the process of faunal impoverishment was already under way at approximately the time of Man's arrival in North America, Man's spread throughout North America is unlikely to have been rapid and dramatic. A rapid growth of human population is likely to have occurred only as the faunal community began to recover from the effects of the stimulus responsible for extinction.

(2) Since the areas traditionally thought to have been reservoirs of large game, notably the Southwest and parts of the Great Plains, are unlikely to have been as attractive as imagined, it is unlikely that they were given a high priority by colonizing groups; in other words, it is unlikely that economies based on hunting large game animals are appreciably older than those based on broad-spectrum exploitation in the areas often referred to as the Desert West.

(3) If it is true that the human predator tends not to overexploit his prey, it is unlikely that man played a critical role in the extinction of the large-game fauna of North America.

Testing these three hypotheses provides a means of testing the hypothesis fundamental to this paper: that analogies between animal species occupying similar levels in the same or different ecosystems are valid and useful, and that human populations are limited in important respects by the same factors that limit the populations of other animal species.

Part 3 The colonization of North America

In discussing the colonization of North America, I shall discuss only sites dated by the C14 method. In all tables I shall quote the C14 dates with three

TABLE 13.3. *Sites with evidence for man's presence in North America prior to 12 000 B.P.*

Site	State	Date	±3s	Reference
Lucy Site	New Mexico		> 12 000	Fitting, 1969
Sandia Cave	New Mexico	M-247, 349	> 20 000	Haynes, 1967; Hester, 1960
Wilson Butte Cave	Idaho	M-1409	14 500 ± 500	16 000 – 13 000	Gruhn, 1961, 1965
Santa Rosa Island	California	M-1132	25 000		Haynes, 1967
Scripp's Service Yard	California	W-142	21 500 ± 700	23 600 – 19 400	Haynes, 1967
Laguna	California	UCLA-1233B	17 150 ± 1 470	21 560 – 12 740	Haynes, 1967
American Falls	Idaho	W-358	> 32 000		Hopkins *et al.*, 1969
Lewisville	Texas	O-235, 248	> 37 000		Haynes, 1967
Scharbauer Site	Texas	L-304C	13 400 ± 1 200	17 000 – 9 800	Haynes, 1967
Driftwood Creek	Alaska	Shell 6713A	17 300 ± 800	19 700 – 14 900	Humphrey, 1966, 1969
Trail Creek Cave 9	Alaska	K-1210	15 750 ± 350	16 800 – 14 700	Tauber, 1968
Tlapacoya	Mexico	GXO-959	23 150 ± 950	26 000 – 20 300	Haynes, 1969
Taima Taima	Venezuela	IVIC	14 440 ± 435	15 745 – 13 135	Haynes, 1967

standard deviations on either side, treating them as ranges of dates within which events are likely to have occurred rather than finite, single dates.

Although it is generally accepted that man was present in North America by *c.* 12 000 B.P., there remains considerable controversy surrounding the date, and to a lesser extent the route, of his entry. In Table 13.3 I have listed the more important sites which provide C14-dated evidence for man's presence on the continent prior to this date. At some of these sites the evidence is suspect, and I am accepting as reliable only the following: Wilson Butte Cave, Laguna, Scharbauer, Driftwood Creek, Taima Taima and Tlapacoya. The combined evidence of these dates suggests to me that man may have entered North America perhaps as early as 25 000 B.P., if indeed not some time slightly before this. Whilst the route of man's entry remains unproven, entry via the area of the modern Bering Straits seems most probable, and I remain unimpressed with Greenman's (1963) arguments in favour of entry from Europe across the Wisconsin North Atlantic pack ice. Most commentators assume that man must have entered North America when the Bering land bridge was exposed (e.g. Bryan, 1969; Müller–Beck, 1967), but I can see no reason for assuming that this *must* have been the case, and I do not feel that it is possible to limit the likely dates of man's arrival to those periods when the bridge was exposed. Bryan (1969) has also argued that the junction of the Keewatin and Old Cordilleran ice sheets, which he dates to *c.* 25 000 B.P., would have created an insuperable barrier to human movements from Alaska to the south, but I agree with MacNeish (1969) that the spread of the ice sheets may have in fact favoured such movements by creating reservoirs of game in unglaciated, upland areas. Man's point of entry into North America may, of course, have been further south than is commonly assumed, and he may have moved from Alaska into British Columbia along a coastal route; in either case, many of the traces of his early activities must now be below sea level.

Although it is impossible to state the precise date of man's arrival in North America, the present evidence suggests very strongly that he was present some time before 20 000 B.P., yet it is some 10 000 years after this that there are significant traces of human activities, and these activities appear to coincide with the later stages of the megafaunal extinction rather than with its onset. Two explanations offer themselves immediately: either the human populations followed the common pattern of colonizing species and spread as rapidly as the contemporary environmental position permitted, but staple resources were in such short supply that his populations remained sparse of necessity. Alternatively, his technology may have been inadequate to exploit the available resources, so that human populations did not attain their potential. There is evidence to suggest that man was technologically quite capable of exploiting the large-game resources of North America, for the faunal collections of the early sites, although sparse, comprise large-game species, and the artefacts themselves testify to man's technological ability. In view of the data suggesting that the process of faunal impoverishment had commenced by the time of man's arrival in North America, it seems reasonable to attribute his slow spread to the paucity of resources rather than his inability to exploit the existing resources.

The earliest evidence of human occupation on a large scale postdates 12 000 B.P. Sites from this period are commonly divided into three major economic 'traditions', within which 'cultures' and 'complexes' have been described on the basis of the typology of the associated projectile points. In the present study I am adopting the economic traditions as defined by the food debris from the relevant sites rather than the projectile points, and I am making no inferences as regards the cultural affinities of their manufacturers. Tables 13.4–13.6 list some of the more important sites assigned to each of these groups and their C14 dates. The dates are summarized in Table 13.7.

The sites may be conveniently divided into three major economic groups: the Palaeo-Indian (Willey, 1966), or Big Game Hunting Tradition (Willey, 1966); the Desert Culture (Jennings, 1957, 1964); and the Old Cordilleran (Butler, 1961, 1965). Broadly, the Big Game Hunting Tradition may be divided into two subgroups: the Llano Complex, associated predominantly with the exploitation of animals now extinct, and the Plano Complex, based on hunting animals that survived the postglacial extinctions. Both the Desert Culture and the Old Cordilleran Tradition relied on a broad-spectrum diet, apparently with important seasonal shifts in economic emphasis. The geographic picture presented in Tables 13.4–13.6 is somewhat misleading, for sites of apparently considerable antiquity do exist in the eastern United States, but, with the exception of the Holcomb Site, Michigan (Cleland, 1965), they lack faunal remains and cannot therefore be included in the present discussion. I have omitted the important site of Marmes from the present discussion on account of the uncertainty surrounding its C14 dates (Fryxell *et al.*, 1968).

It has been traditional to derive the Folsom and Plano points from the Clovis on typological grounds, implying that the hunting of extant animals began only after the faunal extinctions were more or less complete, and that the hunting of these extant species represented an adaptation to changed environmental conditions rather than human choice in the face of available alternatives. It has also been assumed that the Desert Culture postdates the earlier Big Game Hunters, the implication being that the areas of the Desert

557

TABLE 13.4. *C14-dated Desert Culture sites*

Site		C14 date	(B.P.)	Range (±3s)	References
Fort Rock Cave	Oregon	C-428	9 053 ±350	10 103–8 003	Jennings, 1964
Frightful Cave	Coahuila	M-188	8 023 ±350	9 073–6 973	Jennings, 1964
		M-191	8 870 ±350	9 920–7 820	
		Tx-85	10 600 ±200	11 200–10 000	
Danger Cave	Utah	M-202	10 270 ±650	12 220–8 320	Jennings, 1957, 1964
		A-722A	9 030 ±350	10 080–7 980	
C. W. Harris Site	California	A-724	8 490 ±400	9 690–7 290	Haynes, 1967
		A-725	8 490 ±400	9 690–7 290	
Gypsum Cave	Nevada	C-221	10 455 ±340	11 475–9 435	Haynes, 1967
		LJ-452	11 690 ±250	12 440–10 940	
Lake Mohave	California	LJ-200	9 640 ±200	10 240–9 040	Meighan, 1965
Murray Springs	Arizona	A-69	8 250 ±200	8 850–7 650	Neuman, 1967
		A-805	11 230 ±340	12 250–10 210	
Fishbone Cave	Nevada	L-245	11 400 ±250	12 150–10 650	Haynes, 1967
		L-289KK	7 830 ±350	8 880–6 780	

TABLE 13.5. *C14-dated Old Cordilleran sites*

Site		C14 date	(B.P.)	Range (±3s)	References
Five-Mile Rapids	Oregon	Y-340	9 785 ± 220	10 455–9 125	Cressman, 1960
Lind Coulee	Washington	C-827	8 700 ± 400	9 900–7 500	Daugherty, 1956
Milliken	British Columbia	GSC-459	7 190 ± 150	7 640–6 740	Lowdon, et al., 1969
Drynoch Slide	British Columbia	GSC-530	7 530 ± 270	8 340–6 720	Lowdon, et al., 1969
Cougar Mountain Cave	Oregon	UCLA-112	8 510 ± 250	9 260–7 760	Davis, 1969
		Gak-1751	11 950 ± 350	13 000–10 900	
Wilson Butte Cave	Idaho	M-1410	15 000 ± 800	17 400–12 600	Gruhn, 1961, 1965
		M-1409	14 500 ± 500	16 000–13 000	
Yale, DjRi3	British Columbia	S-47	8 150 ± 300	9 050–7 250	Daugherty, 1958
		S-113	9 000 ± 150	9 450–8 550	
Ash Cave	Washington	UCLA-131	7 940 ± 150	8 390–7 490	Haynes, 1967
Palouse River	Washington	WSU-170	7 300 ± 180	7 840–6 760	Chatters, 1968
Weis Rockshelter	Idaho	TBN-319	7 340 ± 140	7 760–6 920	Chandler, et al., 1963

TABLE 13.6. C14-dated Big Game Hunting Tradition sites

Site		C14 date (B.P.)		Range (±3s)	References
Group A: Llano Complex sites, with faunas predominantly of mammoth and other extinct forms					
Naco	Arizona	A-9, 10	9 250±300	10 150–8 350	Hester, 1960; Krieger, 1964
Blackwater Draw 1	New Mexico	A-481	11 170±360	12 250–10 090	Haynes, 1967; Haynes & Agogino, 1966; Hester, 1967; Wedel, 1961
		A-490	11 040±500	12 540–9 540	
		A-491	11 630±400	12 830–10 430	
Dent	Colorado	I-622	11 200±500	12 700–9 700	Haynes, 1967
Lehner	Arizona	A-42	11 240±190	11 810–10 670	
		A-40b	10 900±450	12 250–9 550	Haynes, 1967
		A-375	10 940±100	11 240–10 640	
		K-554	11 170±140	11 590–10 750	
		M-811	11 290±500	12 790–9 790	
Domebo	Oklahoma	SI-172	11 220±500	12 720–9 720	Leonhardy, 1966
		SM-695	11 045±647	12 986–9 104	
Levi Shelter	Texas	O-1106	10 000±175	10 535–9 465	Hester, 1960, 1967; Alexander, 1963
Debert	Nova Scotia	P-966	10 557±121	10 920–10 194	
		P-974	10 824±119	11 181–10 467	Stuckenrath et al., 1966
		P-977	10 113±275	10 938–9 278	
Group B: Llano Complex sites, based on exploiting bison and other extinct forms					
Bonfire Shelter	Texas	Tx-153	10 230±160	10 710–9 750	Forbis, 1969; Haynes, 1967
Lindenmeier	Colorado	I-141	10 850±550	12 500–9 200	Haynes, 1967
Brewster	Wyoming	I-472	10 375±700	12 475–8 275	Haynes, 1967
Blackwater Draw 1	New Mexico	A-379, A-380	10 250±320	11 210–9 290	Haynes, 1967
		A-386	10 490±900	13 190–7 790	
MacHaffie	Montana	L-578A	8 100±300	9 000–7 200	Forbis, 1962; Haynes, 1967

Group C: Plano Complex sites, based on hunting predominantly extant large mammals

Hell Gap	Wyoming	A-499	10 000 ± 200	10 600–9 400	
		A-500	10 150 ± 300	11 050–9 250	
		A-501	8 600 ± 380	9 740–7 460	Haynes, 1967
		I-167	10 850 ± 550	12 500–9 200	
		I-245	8 600 ± 600	10 400–6 800	
Levi Shelter	Texas	O-1106	10 000 ± 175	10 535–9 465	Haynes, 1967: Alexander, 1963
		O-1129	9 300 ± 160	9 780–8 820	
Sisters Hill	Wyoming	I-221	9 650 ± 250	10 400–8 900	Haynes, 1967
Ray Long Site	S. Dakota	C-454	7 715 ± 740	9 935–5 495	Haynes, 1967; Hester, 1960
		C-604	7 073 ± 300	7 973–6 173	
		M-370	9 380 ± 500	10 880–7 880	
Plainview	Texas	A-504	10 600 ± 500	12 100–9 100	Haynes, 1967
		L-303	9 800 ± 500	11 300–8 300	
Graham Cave	Missouri	M-130	9 700 ± 500	11 200–8 200	Haynes, 1967; Willey, 1966
Red Smoke	Nebraska	C-824	9 153 ± 600	10 953–7 353	
			8 570 ± 300	9 470–7 670	

West were occupied by man from necessity rather than choice. The evidence I have presented supports neither of these assumptions, for the major economic traditions are apparently of similar antiquity, and the hunting of extant animals appears to be at least as old as the hunting of forms that became extinct.

TABLE 13.7. *Maximum age ranges of the major economic traditions*

Tradition	Complex	Point	Age range (B.P.)
Big Game Hunting	Llano	Clovis	13 000–8 000
		Folsom	13 000–7 000
	Plano	various	12 500–4 500
Desert		—	12 500–modern
Old Cordilleran		Cascade	?17 000–6 500

If one judges the success of an economic tradition on the basis of its longevity, the Llano Complex, based on hunting predominantly extinct forms, appears to have been the least successful of the early economies. At no time is there evidence to suggest that the Llano hunters were responsible for hunting their prey to extinction. From the outset, it seems that hunting presently extant animals and exploiting the wider spectrum of resources available in the Desert West and the Northwest coast and Rocky Mountains were at least as attractive a proposition as hunting the now-extinct fauna of the Southwest and parts of the Great Plains. The archaeological evidence, therefore, supports our hypothesis that the process of faunal impoverishment was well under way by 13 000 B.P., for man's spread and his chosen economic activities agree with the pattern hypothesized above (see p. 554, hypothesis 2). This same evidence also justifies our assumption that human populations tend to assume a state of equilibrium with respect to their staple resources, for there is no evidence to suggest that human densities in any areas exceeded those that could be supported by relatively impoverished faunas.

I wish now to test the third hypothesis proposed: that man is unlikely to have played an important role in the faunal extinctions. This hypothesis may be tested in two principal ways: either by showing that some other agency was responsible for the disappearance of the animals in question, or by demonstrating that the archaeological evidence for the density of human populations in the critical areas and for man's association with the animals that later became extinct is insufficient to support the hypothesis. The latter approach has been considered briefly in the preceding section, and the evidence suggests

562

that it is highly unlikely that man was the major agent in the extinctions. It is important to emphasize the overwhelming practical difficulties encountered by human groups attempting to annihilate, even on a local scale, thriving populations of large game animals. The Shinyanga game destruction experiment (Potts and Jackson, 1953) was a controlled experiment in such mass annihilation in order to control insect pests, but, despite the use of full-time professional hunters armed with rifles, it attained only limited success. Two unique features have been ascribed to the wave of extinction affecting the fauna of North America (Martin, 1967). Firstly, it is said to have affected selectively large game animals, those with a mature body weight of 50 kg or more; secondly, the extinct forms are said not to have been replaced by ecological equivalents. Whilst both points are strictly correct, I feel that they have commonly been misinterpreted, and they do not in my opinion justify the assumption that the wave of extinction in question must have had a unique cause. In the first instance, the loss of many genera and species must have been compensated for by an increase in the numbers and density (and perhaps by an increase in the ranges) of the surviving animals, and it is worthwhile recalling here the variety of animals present in North America prior to the extinctions; secondly, there has been no opportunity for recolonization since the extinctions occurred, and in many instances of geologically recorded extinctions with replacement, there may have been long intervals between the disappearance of the indigenous animals and their replacement by exotic ecological equivalents. I feel, therefore, that it is unjustified to describe the North American extinctions as 'extinction without replacement'. Secondly, I hope to demonstrate below that the processes responsible for the disappearance of many large animals affected many smaller animals, but that in the case of the latter the stimulus was sufficient only to cause distributional changes and perhaps extinction on a local scale.

One barrier to progress has been the use of genera in studies of the North American extinctions (see Martin and Wright, 1967), although they were chosen more from necessity than on account of their suitability: 'the generalized ecologic, chronologic and phylogenetic interpretations for discussing an extinct genus are likely to be speculative enough without entering a taxonomic level in which more than a dozen valid specific names may be available in a group that could not possibly have evolved into as many good biological species' (Martin, 1967, p. 76).

Extinction has been aptly described by Newell (1962, p. 603) as following 'a loss of adaptation'. It follows from this that the units adopted in studies of extinction should be the most practicable adaptive units of the animals in question; although the species and the genus may have a definable existence, they are not adaptive units (except perhaps in a very broad sense). Furthermore, although genera and species in different animals are identical units in terms of the criteria adopted for their definition, their adaptive significance appears to vary greatly from one animal to the next. Broadly, there appears to be a correlation between the size of an animal and the number of species and subspecies recognized for it (see Table 13.8). The same appears to hold true

TABLE 13.8. *Species and subspecies per genus for some members of the contemporary North American fauna* (from Hall and Kelson, 1959)

Genus	Spp.	Subspp.	Genus	Spp.	Subspp.
Didelphis	1	12	Dicrostonyz	3	10
Notiosorex	2	2	Erethizon	1	7
Parascalops	1	1	Microtus	24	129
Sorex	31	85	Lagurus	1	6
Blarina	2	17	Synaptomys	2	15
Cryptotis	1	5	Zapus	4	33
Dasypus	1	4	Canis	3	47
Ochotona	2	35	Vulpes	3	22
Lepus	11	51	Ursus	3	?
Sylvilagus	11	65	Bassariscus	2	19
Tamiasciurus	2	28	Procyon	9	31
Sciurus	12	79	Mustela	6	74
Glaucomys	2	32	Spilogale	4	22
Marmota	5	29	Gulo	1	4
Eutamias	30	72	Taxidea	1	5
Cynomys	5	4	Mephitis	2	18
Citellus	27	90	Urocyon	2	21
Geomys	7	35	Lutra	3	24
Thomomys	6	299	Martes	2	17
Perognathus	31	148	Felis	6	36
Dipodomys	24	113	Lynx	2	13
Castor	1	24	Tapirus	1	1
Sigmodon	13	43	Cervus	3	4
Reithrodontomys	31	67	Odocoileus	2	41
Baiomys	4	11	Alces	1	4
Peromyscus	92	209	Rangifer	1	14
Ondatra	2	16	Antilocapra	1	5
Onychomys	2	25	Bison	1	2
Oryzomys	20	56			
Neotoma	33	115			

for the number of genera, and Simpson (1945) listed 344 rodent genera, 114 carnivores, 6 perissodactyls, and only 2 proboscideans. Since it is increasingly apparent that populations are the basic adaptive units (see Ehrlich and Raven,

1969), it is clear that genera, species and subspecies of rodents are more likely to approximate to true adaptive units than the corresponding categories in larger mammals. It is also obvious that generic extinction is less likely to occur among rodent genera, for these appear to include a greater number of adaptive units than genera of large mammals. Since it is impossible to distinguish with certainty many species and subspecies of rodents osteologically (especially in the fossil record, where preservation conditions are frequently poor), a stimulus causing generic extinction among larger mammals may seem in the fossil record to have made little impact on rodents and small animals. I suggest that in such situations, an agency causing generic extinction among large mammals may have been sufficient to cause only local extinction or distributional changes in rodents and smaller animals. Evidence is accumulating in North America to suggest that this pattern did in fact characterize the late-glacial extinctions, so that in a sense they were not selective extinctions. The case for man as the agent of extinction has rested heavily on the fact that the species to which the extinction appeared to have been limited were those which would have been most attractive to hunters.

The causes of extinction in North America have recently received extensive review (Martin and Wright, 1967), and the agencies invoked have included man (Edwards, 1967; Jelinek, 1967; Martin, 1967), climatic change at the end of the Pleistocene (Guilday, 1967; Hester, 1967; Slaughter, 1967), an adaptive failure of the animals (Edwards, 1967), disease (Edwards, 1967), and fire-drives by man (Sauer, 1944). The date by which the extinctions were complete is equally the subject of discussion, and opinion favours variously 11 000 B.P. (Martin, 1967), 10 000 B.P. (Mehringer, 1967), 8000 B.P. (Hester, 1960; Lundelius, 1967; Martin and Wright, 1967) and 9000–7000 B.P. (Guthrie, 1968a, 1968b). I feel that too much attention has been paid to establishing the date by which the various animals had disappeared, for in my opinion the date at which the process of extinction *began* is more important. Even if exact terminal dates can be established (which seems unlikely), there is no reason to assume that this would materially assist the search for the cause or causes of the extinctions.

The Wisconsin faunal succession in North America was discussed briefly above, and I have already suggested that the process of faunal impoverishment may have begun as early as *c.* 23 000 B.P., if not earlier. Table 13.9 lists the final C14 dates associated with some animals and suggests very strongly that it is unrealistic to look for a single terminal date for the many extinctions. The mastodon, for instance, appears to have outlived *Boreostracon* by some 20 000 years. Two waves of extinction may be recognized from the presently avail-

565

able data, although their reality requires confirmation. The first wave involved a small number of animals, predominantly predators, which may have disappeared as early as *c.* 13 000 B.P. The predators included *Arctodus, Ursus optimus, Smilodon* and several canids and felids. *Holmesina*, a predominantly southern form, may have disappeared a little prior to this, but the

TABLE 13.9. *Terminal C14 dates associated with extinct animals*

Animal	Site	C14 date (B.P.)		References
Aenocyon	Gypsum Cave[a]	C-222	8 527 ± 250	Hester, 1960
Arctodus	Rancho La Brea	Y-354b	13 890 ± 280	Hester, 1967
Bison	Long Creek	post-	2 243	Forbis, 1962
Bootherium	Big Bone Lick	W-1358	10 600 ± 250	Levin *et al.*, 1965
Boreostracon	Sims Bayou		23 000	Slaughter and McClure, 1965
Breameryx	Blackwater Draw[a]	A-481	11 170 ± 360	Martin, 1967
Camelops	Gypsum Cave[a]	C-222	8 527 ± 250	Hester, 1967
Capromeryx	Kincaid	Tx-17	10 025 ± 185	Stipp *et al.*, 1962
Castoroides	Ben Franklin	SM-532	9 550 ± 375	Hester, 1967
Dasypus	Miller's Cave	A-326	7 200 ± 300	Lundelius, 1967
Equus	Gypsum Cave[a]	C-222	8 527 ± 250	Hester, 1967
Geochelone	Blackwater Draw[a]	A-386	10 490 ± 900	Martin, 1967
Holmesina	Ben Franklin		16 000	Hester, 1967
Mammut	Cromwell	M-138	5 300 ± 400	Hester, 1960
Mammuthus	Prillwitz	M-1400	8 260 ± 300	Crane and Griffin, 1965
Megalonyx	Evansville	W-418	9 400 ± 250	Hester, 1967
Mylodon	La Grande	SI-331	11 030 ± 800	Mielke and Long, 1969
Mylohyus	Lloyd Rock Hole	Y-727	11 300 ± 1 000	Martin, 1967
Nothrotherium	Aden Crater	Y-1163a	9 840 ± 160	Simons and Alexander, 1964
Platygonus	Sandusky County	M-1516	4 290 ± 150	Martin, 1967
Smilodon	Rancho La Brea	Y-354b	13 890 ± 280	Hester, 1967
Symbos	Pictograph Claim	W-223	9 700 ± 600	Hester, 1960
Tanupolama	Gypsum Cave[a]	C-222	8 527 ± 250	Hester, 1967
Tetrameryx	Ventana Cave[a]	A-203	11 300 ± 1 200	Martin, 1967

(*a*) Associated with traces of human activity.

survival of *Arctodus* until *c.* 11 500 B.P. at Burnet Cave (Hester, 1967) remains unconfirmed. It seems to me significant that the first group of animals to disappear should have consisted principally of predators, and it is interesting to note that *Arctodus* is thought (Martin and Guilday, 1967) to have been more carnivorous than the modern bears. The early disappearance of this group of predators seems to support my earlier inference that the process of extinction had begun well before the generally accepted end-Pleistocene date and is also consistent with the suggestion that human populations were sparse because of the low density of their staple game resources. The disappearance of the major game species seems to have been concentrated between 10 000 and 7000 B.P., although some forms, notably the bison and mastodon, survived appreciable intervals after this date; in both cases, their disappearance can be linked with confidence to changing environmental conditions. As I predicted above, there is evidence for distributional changes among rodents and smaller mammals contemporary with the disappearance of the large game. Such changes have been recorded for *Microtus gregalis, Citellus undulatus* and *Dicrostonyx torquatus* in Alaska (Guthrie, 1968a), and for *Sorex cinereus, Blarina brevicauda, Microtus pennsylvanicus, Pitymys pinetorum, P. quasiater, Microtus ochrogaster, Synaptomys cooperi, Mustela erminea* and *Peromyscus nasutus* in Texas (Lundelius, 1967).

There is no direct evidence that man was responsible for the observed extinctions, and in the case of the alterations in the distributions of the rodents, man seems an improbable agent. On the other hand, I have quoted evidence for an unprecedented series of rapid and violent climatic fluctuations beginning about 16 000 B.P. The fact that there is a temporal correlation between the climatic fluctuations and the faunal extinctions and changes in distribution is strongly suggestive of a cause-and-effect relationship between them, and a climatic agency is the only single agency likely to explain both the disappearance of some forms and the redistribution of others. If I am correct in assuming that the process of faunal impoverishment had begun in the mid-20 000s (also a time of climatic change), the North American fauna may have been in a precarious situation and particularly vulnerable to such external disturbances, and it is worthwhile recalling that the complex nature of the Wisconsin fauna of North America might have had a similar effect. In the present state of knowledge, it seems reasonable to accept the hypothesis presented in Part 2 that man was not an important agent in the extinction of the North American megafauna.

Discussion and conclusions

The explicit purpose of this paper was to develop the predictive role of ecological theory and data in archaeological studies by using the model of man as a

567

predator. The results seem to me to justify the use of ecological data to generate testable hypotheses of archaeological interest, for it proved possible in this case to generate and test three hypotheses that cast important light on man's colonization of North America.

Finally, it is interesting to note that the distribution of archaeological sites in North America prior to 8000 B.P. corresponds very closely to the present distribution of the wolf on that continent (Hall and Kelson, 1959, map 444, p. 849). Early man in North America was, as we have seen, a social carnivore limited by the natural scarcity of many of his staple resources. The modern wolf occupies an analogous position as a result of the spread of human populations and the destruction or diminution of many of the wolf's staple resources. The similarity, although inconclusive, remains nonetheless intriguing.

Acknowledgements

I am grateful to E. S. Higgs, John J. Teal, Jr, and M. R. Jarman, who commented on an earlier version of this paper.

My research was supported by the Institute of Northern Agricultural Research, which is financed principally by the W. K. Kellogg Foundation. I am indebted to the Trustees of both these organizations.

This is Institute of Northern Agricultural Research Publication 72/A/1.

References

ADAM, D. P. (1967) Late Pleistocene and Recent palynology in the central Sierra Nevada, California. In CUSHING, E. J. and WRIGHT, H. E., JR (eds.) *Quaternary Palaeoecology*, 275–302. New Haven, Conn.: Yale University Press.

ALEXANDER, H. L., JR (1963) The Levi site: a Palaeo-Indian campsite in central Texas. *American Antiquity*, **28** (4), 510–28.

ALLEN, D. and MECH, D. (1963) Wolves versus moose on Isle Royale. *National Geographical Magazine*, **123** (2), 200–19.

ANDREWARTHA, H. G. (1958) The use of conceptual models in population ecology. *Cold Spring Harbour Symposia on Quantitative Biology*, **22**, 219–36.

ARDREY, R. (1966) *The Territorial Imperative*. New York: Atheneum.

BANFIELD, A. W. F. (1954) Preliminary investigations of the barren-ground caribou. *Canadian Wildlife Service Wildlife Management Bulletin*, ser. 1, 10A and 10B.

BANFIELD, A. W. F. (1956) The caribou crisis. *Beaver*, Spring, 3–7.

BINFORD, L. R. (1968) Post-Pleistocene adaptations. In BINFORD, S. R. and BINFORD, L. R. (eds.) *New Perspectives in Archeology*, 313–41. Chicago: Aldine.

BINFORD, L. R. and BINFORD, S. R. (1966) A preliminary analysis of functional variability in the Mousterian of Levallois facies. *American Anthropologist*, **68** (2), 238–95.

BIRDSELL, J. B. (1958) Some population problems involving Pleistocene man. *Cold Spring Harbour Symposia on Quantitative Biology*, **22**, 47–69.

BLACK, R. F. (1964) Periglacial phenomena of Wisconsin, north-central United States. In DYLIK, J. (ed.) *Report of the Sixth International Congress on the Quaternary,* 21–8.

BRUSH, G. S. (1967) Pollen analysis of Late-Glacial and Postglacial sediments in Iowa. In CUSHING, E. J. and WRIGHT, H. E., JR (eds.) *Quaternary Palaeoecology,* 99–116. New Haven, Conn.: Yale University Press.

BRYAN, A. L. (1969) Early man in America and the Late Pleistocene chronology of western Canada and Alaska. *Current Anthropology,* **10** (4), 339–65.

BUTLER, B. R. (1961) *The Old Cordilleran Culture in the Pacific Northwest.* Occasional Papers of the Idaho State College Museum No. 5.

BUTLER, B. R. (1965) Perspectives on the prehistory of the lower Columbia river. *Tebiwa,* **8** (1), 1–16.

BYERS, D. S. (1959) The Eastern Archaic: some problems and hypotheses. *American Antiquity,* **24,** 233–56.

CHANDLER, J. B., KINNINGHAM, R. and MASSEY, D. S. (1963) Texas bio-nuclear radiocarbon measurements, I. *Radiocarbon,* **5,** 56–61.

CHANG, K. C. (1967) *Rethinking Archaeology.* New York: Random House.

CHANG, K. C. (1968) Toward a science of prehistoric society. In CHANG, K. C. (ed.) *Settlement Archaeology,* 1–9. Palo Alto, Calif.: National Press.

CHATTERS, R. M. (1968) Washington State University natural radiocarbon measurements. *Radiocarbon,* **10,** 479–98.

CHESEMORE, D. L. (1967) *Ecology of the Arctic Fox in Northern and Western Alaska.* M.Sc. thesis, University of Alaska.

CHITTY, D. (1969) Population processes in the vole and their relevance to general theory. In BOUGHEY, A. S. (ed.) *Contemporary Readings in Ecology,* 161–75. Englewood Cliffs, N.J.: Prentice-Hall.

CLARKE, D. L. (1968) *Analytical Archaeology.* London: Methuen.

CLELAND, C. E. (1965) Barren-ground caribou (*Rangifer arcticus*) from an early man site in southeastern Michigan. *American Antiquity,* **30,** 350–1.

CRANE, H. R. and GRIFFIN, J. B. (1965) University of Michigan radiocarbon dates X. *Radiocarbon,* **7,** 123–52.

CRESSMAN, L. S. (1960) Cultural sequences at the Dalles, Oregon. *Transactions of the American Philosophical Society,* n.s. **10** (50).

CUSHING, E. J. and WRIGHT, H. E., JR (eds.) (1967) *Quaternary Palaeoecology.* New Haven, Conn.: Yale University Press.

DALQUEST, W. W. (1962) The Good Creek Formation, Pleistocene of Texas, and its fauna. *Journal of Palaeontology,* **36** (3), 568–82.

DALQUEST, W. W. (1965) New Pleistocene formation and local fauna from Hardeman County, Texas. *Journal of Palaeontology,* **39,** 63–79.

DANSGAARD, W., JOHNSEN, S. J. and MØLLER, J. (1969) One thousand centuries of climatic record from Camp Century on the Greenland ice sheet. *Science,* **166,** 377–81.

DAUGHERTY, R. D. (1956) Archaeology of the Lind Coulee site, Washington. *Proceedings of the American Philosophical Society,* **100** (3), 223–78.

DAUGHERTY, R. D. (1958) Notes and news. *American Antiquity,* **23** (4).

DAVIS, W. A. (1969) Notes and news. *American Antiquity,* **34** (2), 217–18.

DEEVEY, E. S., JR (1968) Measuring resources and subsistence strategy. In LEE, R. B. and DEVORE, I. (eds.) *Man The Hunter*, 95–6. Chicago: Aldine.

DIBBLE, D. S. and LORRAIN, D. (1968) *Bonfire Shelter: a Stratified Bison Kill-Site, Val Verde County, Texas*. Miscellaneous Papers of the Texas Memorial Museum No. 1.

EATON, R. L. (1969) Cooperative hunting by cheetahs and jackals and a theory of the domestication of the dog. *Mammalia*, **33** (1), 87–92.

EDWARDS, W. E. (1967) The Late Pleistocene extinction and diminution in size of many mammalian species. In MARTIN, P. S. and WRIGHT, H. E., JR (eds.) *Pleistocene Extinctions*, 141–54. New Haven, Conn.: Yale University Press.

EHRLICH, P. R. and RAVEN, P. H. (1969) Differentiation of populations. *Science*, **165**, (3899), 1228–31.

ELTON, C. S. (1966) *The Pattern of Animal Communities*. London and New York: Barnes & Noble.

ENGELMANN, M. D. (1969) Energetics, terrestrial field studies and animal productivity. In BOUGHEY, A. S. (ed.) *Contemporary Readings in Ecology*, 336–73. Englewood Cliffs, N.J.: Prentice-Hall.

ERRINGTON, P. L. (1956) Factors limiting higher vertebrate populations. *Science*, **124**, 304–7.

ERRINGTON, P. L. (1958) Of population cycles and unknowns. *Cold Spring Harbour Symposia on Quantitative Biology*, **22**, 287–300.

ERRINGTON, P. L. (1967) *Of Predation and Life*. Ames, Iowa: Iowa State University Press.

ESTES, R. D. (1967) Predators and scavengers. *Natural History*, **76** (2), 20–9, and **76** (3).

FAIRBRIDGE, R. W. (1961) Convergence of evidence on climatic change and ice ages. *Annals of the New York Academy of Sciences*, **95** (1), 542–79.

FITTING, J. E. (1969) Comments on early man in America. *Current Anthropology*, **10** (4), 350–1.

FLINT, R. F. and BRANDTNER, F. (1961) Outline of climatic fluctuations since the last interglacial age. *Annals of the New York Academy of Sciences*, **95** (1), 457–60.

FORBIS, R. G. (1962) Comments on Palaeo-Indian in eastern North America. *Current Anthropology*, **3** (3), 252.

FORBIS, R. G. (1969) Review of Bonfire Shelter. *American Antiquity*, **34** (1), 90–1.

FOSBERG, F. R. (ed.) (1963) *Man's Place in the Island Ecosystem*. Honolulu: Bernice P. Bishop Museum Bulletin.

FRYXELL, R., BIELECKI, T., DAUGHERTY, R. D., GUSTAFSON, C. E., IRWIN, H. T. and KEEL, B. C. (1968) A human skeleton from sediments of mid-Pinedale age in southeastern Washington. *American Antiquity*, **33**, 511–15.

GREENMAN, E. F. (1963) The Upper Palaeolithic and the New World. *Current Anthropology*, **4** (1), 41–91.

GRUHN, R. (1961) *The Archaeology of Wilson Butte Cave, South-Central Idaho*. Occasional Papers of the Idaho State College Museum No. 6.

GRUHN, R. (1965) Two early radiocarbon dates from the lower levels of Wilson Butte Cave. *Tebiwa*, **8** (2), 57.

GUILDAY, J. E. (1967) Differential extinction during Late-Pleistocene and Recent times. In MARTIN, P. S. and WRIGHT, H. E., JR (eds.) *Pleistocene Extinctions*, 121–40. New Haven, Conn.: Yale University Press.

GUTHRIE, R. D. (1968a) Palaeoecology of the large mammal community in interior Alaska during the Late Pleistocene. *American Midland Naturalist*, **79**, 346–63.

GUTHRIE, R. D. (1968b) Palaeoecology of a Late Pleistocene small mammal community from interior Alaska. *Arctic*, **21** (4), 223–44.

HAFSTEN, U. (1961) Pleistocene development of vegetation and climate in the southern High Plains as evidenced by pollen analysis. In WENDORF, F., *Palaeoecology of the Llano Estacado*, 59–91. Reports of Fort Burgwin Research Centre No. 1.

HALL, E. R. and KELSON, K. R. (1959) *The Mammals of North America*. New York: Ronald.

HATLER, D. F. (1967) *Some Aspects in the Ecology of the Black Bear (Ursus americanus) in Interior Alaska*. M.Sc. thesis, University of Alaska.

HAYNES, C. V., JR (1967) Carbon 14 dates and early man in the New World. In MARTIN, P. S. and WRIGHT, H. E., JR (eds.) *Pleistocene Extinctions*, 267–86. New Haven, Conn.: Yale University Press.

HAYNES, C. V., JR (1969) Comments on early man in America. *Current Anthropology*, **10** (4), 353–4.

HAYNES, C. V., JR, and AGOGINO, G. (1966) Prehistoric springs and geochronology of the Clovis site, New Mexico. *American Antiquity*, **31** (6), 812–21.

HESTER, J. J. (1960) Pleistocene extinction and radiocarbon dating. *American Antiquity*, **26**, 58–77.

HESTER, J. J. (1967) The agency of man in animal extinctions. In MARTIN, P. S. and WRIGHT, H. E., JR (eds.) *Pleistocene Extinctions*, 169–92. New Haven, Conn.: Yale University Press.

HEUSSER, C. J. (1961) Some comparisons between climatic changes in northwestern North America and Patagonia. *Annals of the New York Academy of Sciences*, **95** (1) 642–57.

HIGGS, E. S. and VITA-FINZI, C. (1966) The climate, environment and industries of Stone Age Greece, Part II. *Proceedings of the Prehistoric Society*, **32**, 1–29.

HIGGS, E. S., VITA-FINZI, C., HARRIS, D. R. and FAGG, A. (1967) The climate, environment and industries of Stone Age Greece, Part III. *Proceedings of the Prehistoric Society*, **33**, 1–29.

HOLLING, C. S. (1965) *The Functional Responses of Predators to Prey Density and its Role in Mimicry and Population Regulation*. Memoirs of the Entomological Society of Canada No. 45.

HOLLING, C. S. (1966) *The Functional Response of Invertebrate Predators to Prey Density*. Memoirs of the Entomological Society of Canada No. 48.

HOPKINS, D. M. (ed.) (1967) *The Bering Land Bridge*. Stanford, Calif.: Stanford University Press.

HOPKINS, D. M. and PÉWÉ, T. L. (1967) Mammal remains of pre-Wisconsin age in Alaska. In HOPKINS, D. M. (ed.) *The Bering Land Bridge*, 266–70. Stanford, Calif.: Stanford University Press.

HOPKINS, M. L., BONNICHSEN, R. and FORTSCH, D. (1969) The stratigraphic position and faunal associates of *Bison (Gigantobison) latifrons* in southeastern Idaho: a progress report. *Tebiwa*, **12** (1), 1–7.

571

HUMPHREY, R. L. (1966) The prehistory of the Utukok river region, arctic Alaska: early fluted point tradition with Old World relationships. *Current Anthropology*, 7 (5), 586–8.

HUMPHREY, R. L. (1969) Comments on early man in America. *Current Anthropology*, 10 (4), 355–6.

JELINEK, A. J. (1957) Pleistocene faunas and early man. *Papers of the Michigan Academy of Science, Arts and Letters*, 42, 225–37.

JELINEK, A. J. (1967) Man's role in the extinction of Pleistocene faunas. In MARTIN, P. S. and WRIGHT, H. E., JR (eds.) *Pleistocene Extinctions*, 193–200. New Haven, Conn.: Yale University Press.

JENNINGS, J. D. (1957) *Danger Cave*. Anthropological Papers of the University of Utah No. 27.

JENNINGS, J. D. (1964) The Desert West. In JENNINGS, J. D. and NORBECK, E. (eds.) *Prehistoric Man in the New World*, 149–74. Chicago: University of Chicago Press.

JENNINGS, J. D. and NORBECK, E. (1964) *Prehistoric Man in the New World*. Chicago: University of Chicago Press.

KELSALL, J. P. (1968) *The Migratory Barren-Ground Caribou of Canada*. Canadian Wildlife Service Monograph No. 3.

KRIEGER, A. D. (1964) Early man in the New World. In JENNINGS, J. D. and NORBECK, E. (eds.) *Prehistoric Man in the New World*. Chicago: University of Chicago Press.

KURTÉN, B. (1966) Pleistocene mammals and the Bering bridge. *Commentationes Biologicae (Societas Scientiarum Fennica)*, 29 (8).

KURTÉN, B. (1968) *Pleistocene Mammals of Europe*. London: Weidenfeld & Nicolson.

LACK, D. (1954) *The Natural Regulation of Animal Numbers*. London: Oxford University Press.

LEE, R. B. (1968) What hunters do for a living, or how to make out on scarce resources. In LEE, R. B. and DEVORE, I. (eds.) *Man The Hunter*, 30–48. Chicago: Aldine.

LEE, R. B. and DEVORE, I. (eds.) (1968) *Man The Hunter*. Chicago: Aldine.

LEONHARDY, F. C. (1966) *Domebo: a Palaeo-Indian Mammoth Kill in the Prairie-Plains*. Contributions from the Museum of the Great Plains No. 1.

LEVIN, B., IVES, P. C., OMAN, C. L. and RUBIN, M. (1965) U.S. Geological Survey radiocarbon dates VIII. *Radiocarbon*, 7, 372–98.

LINDEMAN, R. L. (1942) The trophic-dynamic aspect of ecology. *Ecology*, 23, 399–418.

LINDEMANN, W. (1956) Transplantation of game in Europe and Asia. *Journal of Wildlife Management*, 20 (1), 68–70.

LOWDON, J. A., WILMETH, R. and BLAKE, W., JR (1969) Geological Survey of Canada radiocarbon dates VIII. *Radiocarbon*, 2 (1), 22–42.

LUNDELIUS, E. L., JR (1967) Late-Pleistocene and Holocene faunal history of central Texas. In MARTIN, P. S. and WRIGHT, H. E., JR (eds.) *Pleistocene Extinctions*, 287–319. New Haven, Conn.: Yale University Press.

MACARTHUR, R. H. (1969) Patterns of species diversity. In BOUGHEY, A. S. (ed.) *Contemporary Readings in Ecology*, 123–48. Englewood Cliffs, N.J.: Prentice-Hall.

MCCARY, B. C. (1951) A workshop site of early man in Dinwiddie county, Virginia. *American Antiquity*, 17 (1), 9–17.

MACFADYEN, A. (1963) *Animal Ecology: Aims and Methods*. 2nd ed. London: Pitman.

MCKNIGHT, T. (1964) *Feral Livestock in Anglo-America*. University of California Publications in Geography No. 16.

MACNEISH, R. S. (1961) *First Annual Report of the Tehuacan Archaeological–Botanical Project*. Andover, Mass.: Phillips Academy.

MACNEISH, R. S. (1962) *Second Annual Report of the Tehuacan Archaeological–Biological Project*. Andover, Mass.: Phillips Academy.

MACNEISH, R. S. (1969) Comments on early man in America. *Current Anthropology*, **10** (4), 357.

MARTIN, P. S. (1967) Prehistoric overkill. In MARTIN, P. S. and WRIGHT, H. E., JR (eds.) *Pleistocene Extinctions*, 75–120. New Haven, Conn.: Yale University Press.

MARTIN, P. S. and GUILDAY, J. E. (1967) A bestiary for Pleistocene biologists. In MARTIN, P. S. and WRIGHT, H. E., JR (eds.) *Pleistocene Extinctions*, 1–62. New Haven, Conn.: Yale University Press.

MARTIN, P. S. and WRIGHT, H. E., JR (eds.) (1967) *Pleistocene Extinctions*. New Haven, Conn.: Yale University Press.

MASON, R. J. (1962) The Palaeo-Indian tradition in eastern North America. *Current Anthropology*, **3** (3), 227–46.

MEHRINGER, P. J., JR (1967) The environment of extinction of the Late Pleistocene megafauna in the arid southwestern United States. In MARTIN, P. S. and WRIGHT, H. E., JR (eds.) *Pleistocene Extinctions*, 247–66. New Haven, Conn.: Yale University Press.

MEIGHAN, C. W. (1965) Pacific coast archaeology. In WRIGHT, H. E., JR, and FREY, D. G. (eds.) *The Quaternary of the United States*, 709–20. Princeton, N.J.: International Association on Quaternary Research, VIIth Congress.

MEIGHAN, C. W., PENDERGAST, D. M., SWARTZ, B. K. and WISSLER, M. D. (1958) Ecological interpretation in archaeology. *American Antiquity*, **24** (1), 1–23, and **23** (2), 131–50.

MIELKE, J. E. and LONG, A. (1969) Smithsonian Institute radiocarbon measurements V. *Radiocarbon*, **11** (1), 163–82.

MOVIUS, H. L., JR (1966) The hearths of the Upper Perigordian and Aurignacian horizons at the Abri Pataud, les Eyzies (Dordogne), and their possible significance. *American Anthropology*, **68** (2), 295–326.

MÜLLER-BECK, H. (1967) On migrations of hunters across the Bering land bridge in Upper Pleistocene. In HOPKINS, D. M. (ed.) *The Bering Land Bridge*, 373–408. Stanford, Calif.: Stanford University Press.

MURIE, A. (1944) *The Wolves of Mt McKinley*. U.S. National Park Service, Faunal Service No. 5.

MYKYTOWYCZ, R. (1968) Territorial marking by rabbits. *Scientific American*, **218** (5), 116–26.

NEILL, W. T. (1958) A stratified early site at Silver Springs, Florida. *Florida Anthropologist*, **11**, 33–52.

NEUMAN, R. W. (1967) Radiocarbon-dated archaeological remains on the northern and central Great Plains. *American Antiquity*, **32** (4), 471–86.

NEWELL, N. D. (1962) Palaeontological gaps and geochronology. *Journal of Palaeontology*, **36** (3), 592–610.

ODUM, E. P. (1966) *Ecology*. New York: Holt, Rinehart & Winston.

OLSON, S. (1938) A study in predatory relationships with particular reference to the wolf. *Scientific Monthly*, **46**, 323–36.

PAINE, R. T. (1969) Food web complexity and species diversity. In BOUGHEY, A. S. (ed.) *Contemporary Readings in Ecology*, 149–60. Englewood Cliffs, N.J.: Prentice-Hall.

PILBEAM, D. R. (1967) Man's earliest ancestors. *Science Journal*, **3** (2), 47–53.

POTTS, W. H. and JACKSON, C. H. N. (1953) The Shinyanga game destruction experiment. *Bulletin of Entomological Research*, **43**, 365–74.

PRUITT, W. R., JR (1968) Synchronous biomass fluctuations of some northern mammals. *Mammalia*, **32** (2), 179–91.

RAPPAPORT, R. A. (1963) Aspects of man's influence upon island ecosystems: alteration and control. In FOSBERG, F. R. (ed.) *Man's Place in the Island Ecosystem*, 155–74. Honolulu: Bernice P. Bishop Museum Bulletin.

RICHARDS, H. G. (1959) Pleistocene mammals dredged off the coast of New Jersey. *Bulletin of the Geological Society of America*, **70** (12), 1769.

RITCHIE, W. A. (1953) A probable Palaeo-Indian site in Vermont. *American Antiquity*, **18**, 249–58.

SAUER, C. D. (1944) A geographic sketch of early man in North America. *Geographical Review*, **34**, 529–73.

SCHALLER, G. B. (1967) *The Deer and the Tiger*. Chicago: University of Chicago Press.

SCOTT, J. P. (1958) *Animal Behaviour*. Chicago: University of Chicago Press.

SELLARDS, E. H. (1952) *Early Man in North America*. Austin, Texas: Texas Memorial Museum.

SHARP, A. (1956) *Ancient Voyagers in the Pacific*. Memoirs of the Polynesian Society No. 32.

SHARROCK, F. W. (1966) *Prehistoric Occupation Patterns in Southwest Wyoming and Cultural Relationships with the Great Basin and Plains Cultural Areas*. Publications of the University of Utah No. 77.

SHUTLER, R., JR (1961) Correlations of beach terraces with climatic cycles of pluvial Lake Lahontan, Nevada. *Annals of the New York Academy of Sciences*, **95** (1), 513–20.

SIMONS, E. L. and ALEXANDER, H. L., JR (1964) Age of the Shasta ground sloth from Aden Crater, New Mexico. *American Antiquity*, **29** (3), 390–1.

SIMPSON, G. G. (1945) *The Principles of Classification and a Classification of Mammals*. Bulletin of the American Museum of Natural History No. 85.

SLAUGHTER, B. H. (1967) Animal ranges as a clue to Late-Pleistocene extinction. In MARTIN, P. S. and WRIGHT, H. E., JR (eds.) *Pleistocene Extinctions*, 155–67. New Haven, Conn.: Yale University Press.

SLAUGHTER, B. H. and MCCLURE, W. L. (1965) The Sims Bayou local fauna: Pleistocene of Houston, Texas. *Texas Journal of Science*, **17** (4), 404–17.

SLAUGHTER, B. H. and RITCHIE, R. (1963) Pleistocene mammals of the Clear Creek local fauna, Denton County, Texas. *Journal of the Graduate Research Centre*, **31** (3), 117–31.

SLAUGHTER, B. H., CROOK, W. W., JR, HARRIS, R. K., ALLEN, D. C. and SEIFERT, M. (1962) *The Hill-Shuler Local Fauna of the Upper Trinity River, Dallas and Denton*

Counties, Texas. Reports of the Bureau of Economics and Geology at the University of Texas No. 48.

SLOBODKIN, B. L. (1962) Energy in animal ecology. In CRAGG, J. B. (ed.) *Advances in Ecological Research.* Vol. I. 69–101. London: Academic Press.

SLOBODKIN, B. L. (1969) Ecological energy relationships at the population level. In BOUGHEY, A. S. (ed.) *Contemporary Readings in Ecology.* 235–58. Englewood Cliffs, N.J.: Prentice-Hall.

STIPP, J. J., DAVIS, E. M., NOAKES, J. E. and HOOVER, T. E. (1962) University of Texas radiocarbon dates I. *Radiocarbon,* **4,** 43–50.

STUCKENRATH, R., JR, COE, W. R. and RALPH, E. K. (1966) University of Pennsylvania radiocarbon dates IX. *Radiocarbon,* **8,** 348–85.

TANNER, J. F. (1968) Effects of population density on growth rates of animal populations. In BOUGHEY, A. S. (ed.) *Contemporary Readings in Ecology.* 193–213. Englewood Cliffs, N.J.: Prentice-Hall.

TAUBER, H. (1968) Copenhagen radiocarbon dates IX. *Radiocarbon,* **10** (2), 295–327.

TERASMAE, J. (1967) Postglacial chronology and forest history in the northern Lake Huron and Lake Superior regions. In CUSHING, E. J. and WRIGHT, H. E., JR (eds.) *Quaternary Palaeoecology,* 45–58. New Haven, Conn.: Yale University Press.

VANGENEIM, E. A. (1967) The effect of the Bering land bridge on the Quaternary mammalian faunas of Siberia and North America. In HOPKINS, D. M. (ed.) *The Bering Land Bridge,* 281–7. Stanford, Calif.: Stanford University Press.

VOLTERRA, V. (1931) *Leçons sur la théorie mathématique de la lutte pour la vie.* Paris.

WASHBURN, S. L. (ed.) (1961) *Social Life of Early Man.* Chicago: Aldine.

WASHBURN, S. L. and DEVORE, I. (1961) Social behaviour of baboons and early man. In WASHBURN, S. L. (ed.) *Social Life of Early Man.* Chicago: Aldine.

WAYNE, W. J. (1967) Periglacial features and climatic gradient in Illinois, Indiana and western Ohio, east-central United States. In CUSHING, E. J. and WRIGHT, H. E., JR (eds.) *Quaternary Palaeoecology,* 393–414. New Haven, Conn.: Yale University Press.

WEDEL, W. R. (1961) *Prehistoric Man on the Great Plains.* Norman, Okla.: University of Oklahoma Press.

WELLS, P. V. and BERGER, R. (1967) Late Pleistocene history of coniferous woodland in the Mohave Desert. *Science,* **155** (3770), 1640–7.

WENDORF, F. (1961) *Palaeoecology of the Llano Estacado.* Reports of the Fort Burgwin Research Centre No. 1.

WHEAT, J. B. (1967) A Palaeo-Indian *Bison* kill. *Scientific American,* **216** (1), 44–52.

WILLEY, G. R. (1966) *An Introduction to North American Archaeology, Vol. I: North and Middle America.* Englewood Cliffs: Prentice-Hall.

WILLEY, G. R. and PHILLIPS, P. (1958) *Method and Theory in American Archaeology.* Chicago: University of Chicago Press.

WING, L. W. (1961) Latitudinal passage a principle of solar-terrestrial cycle behaviour. *Annals of the New York Academy of Sciences,* 95 (1), 381–417.

WITTHOFT, J. (1952) A Palaeo-Indian site in eastern Pennsylvania, an early hunting culture. *Proceedings of the American Philosophical Society,* **96** (4), 464–95.

WOOLPY, J. H. and GINSBURG, B. E. (1967) Wolf socialization: a study of temperament in a wild social species. *American Zoologist,* **7,** 357–63.

WORMINGTON, H. M. (1957) *Ancient Man in North America*. Denver Museum of Natural History and Population, Publication Series No. 4.

WRIGHT, H. E., JR, and FREY, D. G. (eds.) (1965) *The Quaternary of the United States*. Princeton, N.J.: International Association on Quaternary Research, VIIth Congress.

WYNNE-EDWARDS, V. C. (1962) *Animal Dispersion in Relation to Social Behaviour*. Edinburgh: Oliver & Boyd.

ZIMMERMAN, E. C. (1963) Nature of the land biota. In FOSBERG, F. R. (ed.) *Man's Place in the Island Ecosystem*, 57–64. Honolulu: Bernice P. Bishop Museum Bulletin.

14

Energy and ecology: thermodynamic models in archaeology

W. SHAWCROSS

University of Auckland, New Zealand

For the sake of persons of different types of mind scientific truth should be presented in different forms and should be regarded as equally scientific whether it appears in the robust form and vivid colouring of a physical illustration or in the tenuity and paleness of a symbolical expression.

JAMES CLERK MAXWELL (Thomson, 1931, p. 31)

The great French chemist Lavoisier identified the true nature of chemical combustion about the year 1780 (Partington, 1962, p. 426) and at the same time recognized that the chemical process of combustion of oxygen and fuel, releasing heat, was the same as respiration in an animal. The rate of combustion or respiration will alter in accordance with the activity of the organism. Lavoisier commented that 'Even the work of an artist or a plumber can now be expressed and measured in the same units as the work of a horse or an earthquake' (Kleiber, 1961, p. 310). A century later these predictions started to become realized in the work of the German scientist Rubner (McCance and Widdowson, 1960, p. 153), who established the calorific value of foods by measurement of living subjects and by the combustion of food in a bomb calorimeter, a device that enables the measurement of the heat released from total combustion of a food. The calorific value of food is now part of commonplace experience. The overfed of the world are continually being offered low calorie diets while others are anxiously attempting to balance the budgets between exponentially increasing populations and arithmetically increasing food production.

The interconvertibility of such diverse matters is made possible through the use of the standardized unit of energy, the kilocalorie (kcal), of nutritional study. The kilocalorie is 1000 times greater than the calorie of physics, which is defined as the amount of heat required to raise one g of water from $14.5°$ to $15.5°$ C (Kleiber, 1961, p. 115). But the recognition of this interconvertibility

577

goes back to the establishment by Mayer in 1843 of the definite rates of exchange of heat and work – that is, the *mechanical equivalent of heat*. This concept is the basis of the so-called law of conservation of energy, which was formulated as the first law of thermodynamics by Clausius (1850). It has been expressed as follows: 'Energy may be transformed from one form to another but is neither created nor destroyed' (Phillipson, 1966, p. 3).

The first law of thermodynamics is central to the whole of the following discussion. This means, in effect, that a mathematical relationship can be derived for the amount of food available, the number of people consuming it and the amount of work of which they are capable; which is what had been perceived by Lavoisier. Of course he did not imply that the quality of the different kinds of work he cited as examples could be expressed in a common unit, but he did imply that, whatever the form of the work, its magnitude could be expressed according to a common scale. The daily rate of metabolism of the reader, the writer, or a fattening pig, says nothing about the respective qualities of their work, yet it would be fallacious to deny the existence of significant relationships. Each individual organism is a consumer and transformer of food: the pig transforms a quantity of food not generally consumed by humans, some of which is stored as proteins and fats, which are then exploited by men through animal husbandry. Furthermore, it may be said that a proportion of such food, consumed by the writer, is used in the transformation of information which may or may not be consumed by the reader. This is a new level of energy transfer, which was hardly thought of by Lavoisier or his successors and is admittedly still not readily expressed or transformed into standard energy units, yet the relationship of energy and information has been recognized as a fundamental one in the relatively young science of cybernetics (Wiener, 1965, p. 11; Patten, 1959, p. 221).

There is one further illustration necessary to complete this condensed picture of the application of the first law of thermodynamics. This concerns the direction taken in the transformation of energy. The food of all animals is organic, and stems initially from plants. With a few exceptions, plants are capable of synthesizing their organic matter out of inorganic substances through the exploitation of light energy – that is, by photosynthesis. Expressed very briefly, plants can transform simple molecules of carbon dioxide and water, assisted by light energy, into more complex molecules of glucose and a surplus of oxygen as a by-product. This process is reversed when the plant is eaten as food and the glucose combusted. The complex molecule of glucose transforms back into simpler carbon dioxide and water, and the energy that bound it together is released. Furthermore, if a more roundabout transformation is achieved through fermentation of the glucose into alcohol, which is then combusted, the end product is still carbon dioxide and water and, most important, the same quantity of energy will have been released, divided between the two stages (Phillipson, 1966, p. 4). This not only illustrates the conservation and interchangeability of energy, but also that there is a perceptible gradient in these processes: an increasing amount of energy is accumulated in the formation of more complex molecules, and, vice versa, the reduction of complex molecules to simpler forms releases proportionately more energy.

This leads to the second law of thermodynamics, which was expressed concisely by Clausius as 'Die Energie der Welt ist constant. Die Entropie der Welt strebt einem Maximum Zu' (quoted by White, 1959, p. 33). Leslie White paraphrases the second law as 'the universe is breaking down structurally and running down dynamically; i.e. it is moving in the direction of lesser degrees of order and toward a more uniform distribution of energy. The logical conclusion of this trend is a uniform, random state, of chaos' (White, 1959, p. 33). The point about the illustration of the transformation of the glucose molecule now becomes apparent; the synthesis of a relatively complex molecule of glucose out of simpler molecules of carbon dioxide and water is characteristic only of something that has a far from general distribution throughout the universe, namely living matter. In other words, the evolution of life represents a very local counter-current of increasing complexity and concentration of energy, against the universal trend towards simplification and dispersal of energy.

This distinctive quality of living matter as running counter to the universal tendency towards entropy, moving in a direction of increasing order and concentration of energy, has suggested itself as a fundamental evolutionary process, first to some biologists and latterly to some social scientists. Towards the end of the nineteenth century the Austrian Ludwig Boltzman, and a little later Wilhelm Ostwald, were speculating on these evolutionary implications. In the early decades of the present century the notable mathematical biologist, Alfred Lotka, was describing organisms as 'energy catching systems' (White, 1959, p. 36; Lotka, 1956, p. 357), and suggesting that in organic evolution natural selection led to an increase in the total organic mass and an increasing rate of turnover of matter within the system (White, 1959, p. 37).

It is therefore not surprising that some of these ideas should appear in general surveys of human prehistory at about this time. G. G. MacCurdy in *Human Origins* (1933) suggested that 'the degree of *civilization* of any epoch, people, or group of peoples *is measured by ability to utilize energy for human advancement or needs*' (quoted by White, 1949, p. 356). However, it must be admitted that such an interesting scale seems never to have been applied in practice. The problem seems to be a general one in prehistory: the evidence of archaeology is often separated by a broad gulf from the ends to which the prehistorian wishes to put it, and the underlying objective of the present discussion is to investigate one such means by which prehistory and its evidence may be logically linked.

The most consistent and energetic application of the second law of thermodynamics to prehistory has undoubtedly been that of Leslie White, who published 'Energy and the evolution of culture' in 1943 and who subsequently expanded the concept in *The Science of Culture* (1949) and *The Evolution of Culture* (1959). White takes the biological concepts of (*a*) the organism as an energy accumulating system and (*b*) the evolutionary process as tending to select those organisms that take this process further, and transfers them to that impalpable phenomenon, culture. As will be apparent, his interest is evolutionary, an approach that conflicts with the cultural and social anthropology of many of his American and British colleagues. Thus, he employs a simple, four-stage evolutionary scheme, substantially derived from L. H. Morgan and E. B. Tylor. Culture is considered to have passed through successive stages, of which the earliest is characterized by a hunting and gathering economy. White pointed out that the human population would be drastically limited by the amount of energy that hunters can effectively win from their environment. The next stage commences in early postglacial times, in certain centres where the populations took the opportunity to increase their food supply through the invention of plant and animal husbandry and consequently became raised to an energy level significantly higher than all but perhaps a few most favoured hunter-gatherers. The increased potential for population growth was associated with the development of larger social units, culminating in the ancient empires. These large units would have taken the potentialities of the population size to its limit, beyond which point they would be too cumbersome and socially inefficient to hold together. It was not until a new source of energy, that hitherto lying untapped in the great reservoirs of fossil fuels (coal and oil), was exploited during the Industrial Revolution that a significant new stage could be recognized. Then, between the writing of his 1943 paper and *The Science of Culture*, White witnessed the beginnings of a fourth stage – that in which the ultimate reservoir of energy found in the structure of the atom has become accessible.

A prehistorian whose thinking runs parallel to that of White at times is the Australian Gordon Childe. The parallels are best seen in his highly influential and popular books, of which one of the first, *Man Makes Himself*, first published in 1936, introduced Childe's vivid analogy between the Industrial Revolution and what he termed the Neolithic Revolution. As with White, and for that matter Marx and Engels, Childe employed the framework of the nineteenth century social evolutionists, Morgan and Tylor: the whole Palaeolithic and its postglacial appendix was fitted to the hunter-gatherer stage, while the Neolithic became the food producing stage, heralding a Neolithic Revolution. In his postwar publications on the same theme Childe seems to have adopted some of White's cultural energetics argument, expressing these stages as representing increasing levels of energy exploitation, with a particularly significant increase in the cultivation of cereals which made readily available the large quantities of food fuel represented in the carbohydrates stored in grass seeds (Childe, 1963, p. 33).

The interpretation of cultural evolution in terms of energetics

In the earliest stages of cultural evolution, whether according to White and Childe or others, the ultimate source of energy is the sun, and the relatively low level of energy accumulation by hunters and gatherers results from the fact that they only have access to this source after it has passed through a succession of extravagant transformations – namely, photosynthesis in plants, then metabolism of plants by herbivorous animals – and only finally does man the carnivore, standing at the apex of the so-called 'Eltonian Pyramid' (Lindeman, 1942, p. 408; Macfadyen, 1963, p. 224; cf. Lee and DeVore, 1968, p. 11), have access to energy stored in the tissues of the herbivore. At first sight this might seem a contradiction of the evolutionary principle of accumulation of energy, and indeed also of the law of conservation of energy. However, the study of bioenergetics reveals that each stage of transformation is very inefficient and, without going too far into defining terms at this point, it is generally recognized that only about 10% of the energy available in the lower stage will be taken over by the higher stage, and indeed the proportion of available solar energy that is 'captured' by a plant is more in the order of 0·1%. Such a level of transmission may be expressed as a degree of *efficiency* and if, for the purposes of argument, an average of 10% is employed it will be apparent that Palaeolithic man would at best have access to 10% of 10% of 10% of available solar energy. Such a low level of energy transfer is not inconsistent with the law of conservation of energy: the energy is not destroyed, but is transmitted through a host of other biological circuits, including a high proportion of what are called in ecology *decomposing organisms*.

Other things being equal, the succeeding stage of these general schemes of cultural evolution, that centred on the control over plants and animals by domestication, is a most plausible step in terms of energetics. In effect, husbandry enables man to shorten the circuitous route by which he has access to solar energy. With cereal crops he is able to exploit plant-stored energy, particularly in the form of carbohydrates, cutting out the loss of efficiency previously incurred in eating food transformed by herbivores. In terms of efficiency, man will now have access to a maximum possible of 10% of 10% of solar energy. Living solely on (domesticated) plants he can cut out the 'middleman' herbivore, and accrue the profits to himself, just so long as he is ready to forgo an appetite for animal protein and fats. It must be admitted, however, that this is a simplification which should not be ascribed to the evolutionists. The Neolithic Revolution has always been considered to include animal domestication, which clearly does not offer such substantial gains in efficiency of energy transmission. Even so, some gains in efficiency may be surmised. Domestication, it is assumed, involves cutting out the ecological competitors of the domesticants,[1] while husbandry will ensure that varying proportions of the by-products of plant cultivation, not immediately available for human consumption, may be channelled through domesticants, thus shortening circuits and cutting out what amounts, in human terms, to wasteful circuiting through decomposers. Even a harsh critic will admit that this argument is impressively consistent. Given that the basic evidence for the origins of domestication is not in doubt, the advantages that become apparent through analysis in terms of energy make a highly satisfactory explanation of cultural evolution.

The third evolutionary stage, though lying outside the concern of prehistory, continues the logic of associating cultural evolution with increasing harnessing of energy. The new source of energy is in this case fuels derived from former plant matter, and consequently representing a stored fraction of former solar energy. These fuels are, volume for volume, highly concentrated sources of energy, but unlike living matter are not self-replenishing. Fossil fuels are either transformed into chemical energy, as in the form of smelting in a blast furnace, or into mechanical energy. That is, they do work either previously done by man and animals, and to a lesser extent by wind and falling water, or they are combusted to do totally new forms of work. For example, it was not until man had harnessed fossil fuels that it became possible to fly, more or less at will. The fourth, or atomic energy, stage of White's scheme is still a matter of speculation and has so far only supplemented trends developed in the fossil fuel stage. On the face of it, the vast potential of atomic energy seems a logical successor to earlier fuels, but at the present time two factors seem to stand in the way of its development. The first is that it does not seem to offer the significant financial economies anticipated of it, for its technology is extremely expensive; secondly, there are the increasing problems of environmental pollution. This was certainly a factor not accounted for in White's scheme and, without going into all of the aspects of pollution, it will only be noted here that the effect of harnessing increasing quantities of energy is to release such quantities of heat into the atmosphere and seas as to create a serious new hazard.

The various evolutionary schemes, commencing with those of Morgan and Tylor, up to those of Childe and White, have many points in common. In particular, there seems to be a general agreement over the nature and age of the first two stages, of hunting-gathering and food producing. These essentially economic stages are tied in with clusters of technological features, long recognized in archaeology, and are also associated with the hypothetical stages of social evolution. Childe, it may be observed in passing, is not primarily concerned to relate social evolution to the harnessing of energy. His stages are initiated by significant inventions (Childe, 1963, p. 166), but these may stem from many varied areas of human endeavour, such as tool technology, husbandry or writing. Only White consistently relates all of his successive social stages to inventions in the area of energy 'capture' (White, 1949, p. 368). He identified three factors present in cultural systems. First, the amount harnessed *per capita*, per year: second, the efficiency of the technology employed to harness the energy; third, the magnitude of the human need-serving goods and services so produced. With these factors he was able to extend MacCurdy's argument and say that, assuming habitat to be constant, the degree of cultural development is determined by the amount of harnessed energy and the efficiency of the technology. He further argues (White, 1949, p. 373) that the consequences of trapping increased quantities of energy will be an increase in population, larger political units, bigger cities, increased accumulation of wealth and the development of arts and sciences.

The basic nature of the population increase was recognized by Childe in his analogy between the Industrial and Neolithic Revolutions (Childe, 1956, p. 12). Subsequently, he collated a body of archaeological evidence, in the form of measured settlement areas, in his *Social Evolution* (1963). Site area is admittedly a fairly crude parameter by which to estimate population growth; its use requires implicit assumptions about the relationship between area and numbers. Since Childe's time the American anthropologist R. Naroll has prepared an estimate for such an index, giving a mean of 10 m^2 per person, derived from a sample of recent ethnographic peoples (Naroll, 1962, p. 588). This has been speculatively applied by the Binfords to the floor areas of Mousterian sites (Binford and Binford, 1966, p. 287). But it may be noted that there is a considerable apparent variation in requirements between societies and that extrapolation to societies for whom there are no close analogies introduces a further potential variation. Finally, it may be noted that a study of the Maori reveals a correlation between large area sites, containing tightly packed populations, induced by highly stressed political situations, and multiple, small, lower density sites developing the moment the social pressure is released (K. A. Shawcross, 1971). Thus, there is a risk in equating size of site with population, owing to the problems of archaeological sampling. Still, with due allowance for such factors, it remains a reasonable general hypothesis that gross population increase may be explained according to White's application of the second law of thermodynamics, with the corollary that it lies within the bounds of possibility for archaeology to test it objectively.

Discussion of inconsistencies in the thermodynamic approach

White's explanation of the mechanism of cultural evolution through the application of the thermodynamic theory was extended by others in the publication of *Evolution and Culture* (Sahlins and Service, 1960), where some particular issues, to be examined later, were raised, but subsequently the theme seems to have lapsed as a subject in anthropological discussion. It is worth searching for the causes of this apparent failure, before proceeding with the main theme of this paper.

In the first place, account must be taken of White's own explanation of barriers to his ideas. He observes that the majority of twentieth-century anthropologists, following Franz Boas, have been antagonistic to concepts of cultural evolution. This arises from the conviction that recent contemporary simple societies are not the fossil survivors of prehistoric stages. Such a view is logically stronger than the one it replaces and, of course, conforms with a moral attitude to the relationships between contemporary societies. However, it masks the fact that there is a generally shared intellectual attitude to their subject among anthropologists, who are usually concerned to observe and explain the operation of living societies, with minimal account of, or influence from, the time factor. This might appear to apply solely to cultural and social anthropologists, while prehistorians ought to be more amenable to evolutionary concepts. If they have not been so ready to explore White's ideas, and this is a speculation, it may be because of the close association of some schools of prehistory with anthropology, or the equally extreme isolation of others.

A second barrier to White's ideas lies in what is to some the individual and extreme manner in which he conceives of culture. It is certainly difficult to present a condensed yet fair account of so loaded a subject. However, it would seem to be not so much the continuum of that class of phenomena, including wisdom, beliefs, values, desires, misconceptions, capabilities, impulses and habits, which relates individuals to each other and to non-human phenomena (Tylor's definition is echoed here), that roughly accounts for what many anthropologists appear to mean, but somehow to be the sum of all of these, seen as taking on an entity all of its own.

In White's opinion, culture is to society what the psyche might be to the individual (White, 1949, p. 95). The view of culture as possessing an independent existence is hotly contested by other anthropologists: a reviewer remarked that it was 'a reduction to absurdity of the notion of a superorganic, superpsychic theory of culture' (Bidney, 1950, p. 519). The rationalization of such sharply conflicting views may lie in the personal attitudes and prejudices of individual anthropologists and prehistorians. If one's attitude is that the correct approach to a subject is through everyday, repeatable, generally acceptable experience, there may be something unsettling about following White's materialist arguments, only to find them hinging on what seems remarkably like a metaphysical concept. One may grow impatient with such a word as culture, which itself seems to take on an existence of its own, or one may, as others have, drop it entirely from one's vocabulary.[2] The not very original attitude throughout this discussion is that a word should be useful and not be allowed to become master. Culture can be convenient as an imprecise generalization, but it joins the ranks of those words over which blood is so futilely shed when its users claim for it a single, universal, unalterable meaning. After this diversion over the definition of culture it must be remarked that central though it is to White's whole thesis, it is not necessary to go the entire way with the definition to follow the operation of the thermodynamic argument. The critics seem to have been so carried away with the enormity of superorganic culture that they have largely failed to examine the thermodynamic mechanism.

It must be admitted that the fervour of some enthusiasts has led them to harm the use of energetics analysis through fatuous verbiage, as in statements such as 'thermodynamic superiority of Chinese culture', which belongs to what Professor Service has drily termed 'Mouthtalk'. The same author remarks, 'Whenever I hear hurrying footsteps behind me I fear some new graduate student wanting to tell me his wonderful idea for revolutionizing anthropology. Too often my apprehension is well founded and the revolution consists of a research project that would describe a culture in terms of the amount of energy harnessed or built into it' (Service, 1969, p. 69). While the article is primarily intended as an example of the way an explanatory concept becomes a vogue, ending up by seeking a body of evidence for its justification, it is peculiarly appropriate to this discussion, and deserves to be kept in mind.

Apart from the semantic difficulties in White's work, some more specific inconsistencies appear in the energy and evolution thesis. Every scheme whereby complex matters are observed in transformation through passage of time, which is subdivided into stages, must have an element of arbitrariness. If a simple event occurs, then it may be legitimately used to mark a boundary between two states of before and after. It is possible to have coincidences of loosely related or unrelated events, which may be used similarly though with increasing arbitrariness, to mark boundaries between states. However, when one examines what would now be advisedly termed 'culture', it must surely be seen to consist of a vast continuum of events. Here the imposition of stages must not only become extremely arbitrary, but also open to substantial error – a weakness that, of course, applies equally to all schemes of stages in pre-history. Arbitrariness is not necessarily wrong, it may ensure a most fruitful analysis of a phenomenon. But equally it may grossly distort. The nineteenth-century evolutionists had no well-founded idea of the time scale in which their ideas were intended to operate. Childe and White worked in a time scale that generously allowed man a 500 000 year span. There is now good evidence for Palaeolithic industries dated back to 2·5 million years, and there is no reason to suppose that they are the earliest. A scheme that in effect makes nothing significant happen for 2 490 000 years and squeezes all significant events into the latest 10 000 cannot be called illogical, but may be suspected of distortion. Did no significant invention in energy-capture take place in the Palaeolithic? An obvious example is the invention of fire (Oakley, 1956, p. 36). It would be possible to add more, but what needs to be clearly grasped is that such additional evidence would further substantiate White's general theory, though it might reveal the weakness of his particular analysis. Another example of the weakness of his particular analysis is his ignoring of wind power. Professor Cottrell points out that the Romans had developed large sailing ships operating at a good 100 hp/day, which completely altered the scale of trade (Cottrell, 1955, p. 49). But, again, the new evidence only strengthens White's general theory at the expense of his arbitrary stages.

On the other hand, there are inconsistencies which seem to lie closer to the core of the theory. In terms of energy alone, what distinguishes hunter-gatherers under optimal conditions from food producers under inferior conditions? The immediate answer to this would be that, given optimal conditions for both, the food producer will wrest a higher proportion of energy than the hunter-gatherer. But on reflection this may not be an entirely sound argument. There seems as yet to be no substantial evidence for the effectiveness of early 'food producing', once the circular argument that it gave rise to early village and urban communities is discounted. It is possible that hunter-gatherers were equally effective at energy capture and it must be admitted that the generally accepted view of the advanced Palaeolithic societies of the last glaciation strongly implies a level of effective energy capture far above any now observed among hunter-gatherers. At least there cannot have been any very substantial difference in energy levels between the Russian mammoth hunters and the earliest village farmers.

The weakness in the argument that relates cultural evolution to decreased inefficiency of energy capture – that is, a change from hunting-gathering to agriculture – makes too much of the polarized assumption of complete dependence of the former on animals and of the latter on plants. In terms of cutting out the herbivore food transformer, a food gatherer has just as direct access as a cultivator to plants. Indeed, recent ethnographic studies show how high the level of potential energy available to gatherers may be, as for example the !Kung Bushmen's use of mongongo nuts (Lee, 1968, p. 33). A comparable example of the importance of 'collected' food plants, in this case to a technically agricultural 'Neolithic' people, is that of bracken fern rhizomes to the prehistoric Maori of New Zealand, for whom there is a strong ethnographic case for the fern being a greater source of food than any of the cultivated crops (K. A. Shawcross, 1967).

Lastly, it has recently been suggested that the archaeological emphasis on a transition from hunting and gathering to domestication is an artificial distinction (Higgs and Jarman, 1969, p. 32). What is urged in replacement is a far more comprehensive scale of man/plant and man/animal relationships. Higgs and Jarman point out that evidence put forward to show a specialized association of man and particular organisms as proof of post-Palaeolithic domestication can be as likely found deep in the Palaeolithic, where, because of a strong prejudice, it is assumed that only hunting and gathering operated. The concept of the post-Palaeolithic invention of domestication is long established and deeply-rooted in prehistory and is difficult to divest from the mind, particularly when, at present, claims for yet earlier centres of origin are being eagerly put out in various parts of the world. However, if domestica-

587

tion is not an invention which separates two states – man living off un-domesticated organisms transformed to man living off domesticated ones – and if intensified levels of man/animal and man/plant associations go back to the Palaeolithic, then the Agricultural Revolution of Childe and White loses significance. If there was no revolution, then either there was no dramatic rise in population growth or the increase was the result of some other cause which has not yet been correctly identified.

In spite of these ominous-seeming weaknesses in White's theory, the essentials remain. The present dominance of technological 'high energy' civilization (a term coined by Cottrell, 1955, pp. 59, 92) cannot be doubted, whatever misgivings or reservations the individual may hold. The means by which this state has transformed out of preceding states during the past 2·5 million years and more, can best be explained in terms of evolution, rather than by, say, visitors from other planets or divine intervention. Likewise, there can be no doubting the difference in energy capture between the present era and 10 000 or 100 000 years ago. But by the same token, it is not so obvious that the men who hacked up elephant or hippopotamus carcasses with handaxes at Olduvai and Olorgesailie had a significantly higher capacity for such energy capture and conversion than hyenas or, supposing a higher proportion of plant food, bears.

These observations suggest two areas of explanation. The first concerns the theory of biological evolution and energy capture, which must be understood to operate at a much more general level, of order, class or even kingdom. This has a very curious implication; modern man, with his prodigious capacity to transform energy, might be said to be reclassifying himself in the biological world. The individual as such does not represent a significantly greater concentration of energy than many other animals, but he is part of a huge social organism which converts energy on an entirely different scale. The 'advantage' seems to lie not purely in terms of magnitude: the Egyptian pyramids, built entirely with biological energy conversion, are still massive by modern standards, but what mechanical energy conversion achieves advantageously is best seen in terms of increased velocity.

The second area of explanation concerns the operation of White's theory. Energy capture might well be a parameter of cultural evolution, in which, to express it metaphorically, localized spurts and fitful flickerings may be occasionally glimpsed in prehistory, but it surely cannot be thought of as in any way being a physical channel through which such evolution is directed – as for example, the genetic code. It is not clear that White has explained the *relationship between* energy capture and cultural evolution – rather, he has juxtaposed them in a suggestive manner. One might as well suppose that increased energy turnover is a subordinate or accidental consequence of evolution. Therefore, the problem that needs investigation is the hypothetical mechanism that links culture and energy conversion.

The application of the first law of thermodynamics in prehistory

There is a logical order in the sequence of the laws of thermodynamics: the second requires the operation of the first, and it is perhaps a weakness of the anthropologists' recognition of the applicability of the second law that relatively little attention has been paid to how the first works. The scholars' intuition grasps the possibilities of the second law and ignores the seeming pedestrianism of the first. Here there lies a danger, not only in attempting to run before one can walk, but in missing the opportunity to use an extremely effective means of analysis and integration.

The first law states that though energy may be transformed, it is never created nor destroyed. In life, as has already been seen, it passes between many forms; built up here, degraded there, and then taken up once more. Extending this physical image, it becomes apparent that the prehistoric archaeologist is frequently presented with fossil segments of this process. It would be no exaggeration to say that the majority of archaeological sites include the discarded debris of energy transformation by man, in the form of food wastes. Without exception, all sites are the product of such transformed energy, in the form of work. The humblest scatter of post-holes represents woodcutting, transport, and the labour of setting wood into the ground. Even handaxes, lying promiscuously scattered in an ancient river gravel, must originally have been transformed by force out of selected nodules of stone. In these two examples the scale of the work as a proportion of the capabilities of a man is infinitesimal. The manufacture of a handaxe would consume perhaps in the order of 10 kcal. In his turn, the individual human is an insignificant and minimal unit in prehistory, where cultures, traditions or technocomplexes (Clarke, 1968, p. 321) are generally considered to be the units. On the other hand, certain artefacts or structures obviously represent such a quantity of labour, many times that of an individual, that they become significant in the scale of these much larger units. The examples are everywhere, from the megalithic structures of western Europe, the monumental tombs of Egypt, the stepped pyramids of Mesomerica, to the earthen forts of New Zealand. These examples are all fairly easy to comprehend as work, for their construction was concentrated and coordinated to a single end, and that is how work is generally conceived. It is more difficult to see a complex structure of long growth, such as a tell or a Mississippian mound, as the product of work (they seem just to have 'grown'), yet they are equally the product of work: the whole mass and configuration of such structures is just as truly measurable in foot-pounds, however incidental or haphazard the construction process may have been.

The examples have all been of archaeological 'work', and they illustrate the effect of scale. Thus scale can cause unconscious compartmentalization. Handaxes belong to a wholly different class of phenomena from megaliths, and megaliths from tells, and tells from a Tasmanian lean-to. But if one chooses to view them all on yet another scale – that of mankind – instead of at the scale of archaeological cultures, then work expenditure becomes a factor common to all. Harking back to the energy and evolution theory, it is possible to see these artefacts as spaced along an evolutionary scale, at the lower end of which handaxes represent the expenditure of only a few kilocalories; whereas, for example, Abu Simbal must represent many millions. But, in order to do this, one must make a very sweeping assumption – that these artefacts are truly characteristic of their time and makers. However, to return to the theme of this introduction to the application of the first law of thermodynamics: the archaeologist recovers segments of the passage and transformation of energy, in a great many of which cases the evidence is represented by food debris. A living floor at Olduvai may have stone tools, manuports and animal bones mingled. Likewise a Tasmanian rock shelter may have scattered heaps of shells, plant matter and artefacts. According to ethnographic sources a Maori settlement ought to have a specialized area or midden for the disposal of food waste. One would expect a similar nicety in a Medieval village, yet the site of Upton, excavated by Hilton and Rahtz (Yealland and Higgs, 1966, p. 139), appears to include an indiscriminate scatter of over 1000 animal bones from the site of a single house.

In all of these, and countless other instances, there is a direct association between food consumption and the settlement. Furthermore, it is a reasonable first assumption (though open to modification) that the settlement and food waste belong to the same scale. The amount of food represented on a site bears a consistent relationship to the amount of food consumed. Until the relatively recent development of means of long distance transport of domestic rubbish (Wolman, 1956, p. 807) it may be taken as the archaeological rule that waste is tied to settlements. The differential survival of animal and plant remains, and the relative assiduity of archaeologists, are separate factors subservient to the first assumption.

In practice, archaeologists have rarely explored the implications of the food waste and settlement association as far as practicable. There are technical difficulties in transmitting the archaeological evidence to specialists in other disciplines, and in transforming their findings back into prehistory. An outstanding exception is Professor Grahame Clark's excavation of the Mesolithic site of Star Carr in northern England (Clark, 1954). The report has become a model of integration of typology, ethnography, stratigraphy, palynology, geology, radiocarbon dating and zoology, and has been so regularly chosen as an example in general surveys of archaeological method and theory during the past fifteen years that it is not necessary to repeat more than what is strictly appropriate to the present discussion.

First, it will be noted that Clark is explicit throughout his analysis. The assumptions and information on which a chain of argument is constructed are presented to the reader. There is no intuitive leap from observation of a number of bones to a statement on the size and permanence of the community: consequently, the report has a lasting scientific worth, because it is open to re-examination and reorganization in the light of new evidence and ideas. Instead, a six-stage train of argument is presented to show the relationship between the food waste, consisting almost entirely of mammal bones, and the Mesolithic community. The first stage arrives at an estimate of the numbers of individual beasts in each species represented among the bone waste. The second stage transforms the size of the kill into the amount of available dressed meat, using an average carcass weight. The third stage converts the weight of meat into kilocalories. The fourth stage draws in an estimate for the probable size of the human group occupying the settlement, by means of an ethnographic analogy. Fifthly, the probable daily consumption of kilocalories by such a group is calculated. In the sixth stage, the total of available kilocalories (Stage 3) is divided by the daily consumption of the group (Stage 5). A relationship has now been computed between the food debris and the prehistoric community, expressed as a period of duration for the settlement. It *could* be totally misleading: for example, if the reality were only known, it might be that a community of several hundred was permanently in occupation round the shores of Star Mere for the best part of a millennium, something admittedly unlikely according to the present state of knowledge on the Mesolithic. However, in the meantime, the present conclusions must stand as valid, if perhaps over precise, because they appear to account for most significant factors. One factor not adequately allowed for is that each stage of the argument is not really based on a single, fixed quantity. Human energy needs are variable and range between 2000 and 3000 kcal a day. The amount of meat

591

on a carcass varies among individuals, while the size of the analogous, ethnographic community is arbitrary. If allowance is made for the variables, the result will not be a fixed quantity, but a probable range, which has a greater chance of encompassing the true quantity.[3]

Star Carr is a uniquely innovative piece of thinking in British archaeology, but it is not without precedent elsewhere. For example, that remarkably fertile intellect, the American anthropologist Professor A. L. Kroeber, prepared an estimate of prehistoric Mexican population through division of estimated corn yields by a rate for individual corn consumption.[4] The presentation of explicit assumptions and argument from evidence was thus developing in the United States by the late 1930s, but the implications available when an argument is brought down to measurements in the fundamental units of energy was missed through short-cutting the full series of steps in the food chain analysis.

Kroeber's approach was taken up and extended by others in the United States. S. F. Cook and R. F. Heizer developed a comprehensive series of studies of the shell middens of California, in which particular emphasis was paid to the development of objective, quantitative techniques of analysis.[5] This work was directed towards population estimates, further extended by Ascher (1959) and Meighan (1959) and reviewed by Glasgow (1967). A somewhat similar approach, relating population, settlement duration and food debris, has also been applied in the Great Lakes area (Cleland, 1966). Specific calculations were made for the Schultz and Juntunen sites, at both of which it was possible to estimate the amount of meat killed, and thence calculate the number of man-days represented. Furthermore, the food debris from the Juntunen site included fish and mammal bones, from which it was possible to conclude that the fish were of substantially more importance to the community than the mammals, in the proportion of 40 million kcal to 7 million kcal (Cleland, 1966, p. 196). It is interesting to note that this comprehensive analysis, making considerable use of the potentialities of application of the first law of thermodynamics, shows the influence of Leslie White's thinking. Reference is made to Kaplan's 'law of cultural dominance' (Cleland, 1966, p. 39) which was stimulated by White's theories (Sahlins and Service, 1960, p. 69).

Example of the application of the first law of thermodynamics

The site of Galatea Bay (Terrell, 1967; Shawcross, 1967a) is typical of many round the coasts of New Zealand. It is late prehistoric and consists of a soil-capped layer of shells and other debris, in which numbers of small, contemporary ovens were set. It lies just above high water mark, on a low coastal platform at the mouth of a small stream, and is now being slowly eroded by the sea. Innumerable other such sites have been entirely destroyed by the same cause, or by building and roading, or survive only as some accidentally preserved peripheral part. In 1965 J. E. Terrell and W. Shawcross chose this site to investigate a hypothesis of L. M. Groube, whose careful re-examination of early documentary records on the Maori had revealed the temporary, seasonal nature of prehistoric settlement patterns – an aspect of Maori life that had been obscured by a century of European contact and cultural adaptation (Groube, 1964). It was thought that the site should represent a briefly occupied, summer fishing camp, of the kind implied in the early ethnographic accounts.

During the previous five years, developments had taken place in New Zealand in the technique of analysis of shell middens, principally following the course set in California. The species of shellfish were identified and quantified and chronological inferences drawn (Smart and Green, 1962). Refinements were proposed for sampling, a serious problem in a deposit that might weigh many tons and consist of perhaps millions of individuals from numerous different species. Experiments were also initiated in comparing archaeological shellfish with the living populations found in beds close to the sites (Ambrose, 1963, 1967; Davidson, 1964a, 1964b).

The deposits at Galatea Bay comprised not only shells of common bivalves inhabiting the adjacent shores, but bones of fish and mammals. The question that must first be asked of this diverse association of organisms is that of their relative importance. It is not possible to judge this by eye alone, for methods of excavation may emphasize different features. Because the shells constitute what is virtually a deposit in themselves they are sampled, whereas bones are collected entirely. As a result, the large numbers of fish bones appear dominant, though as surviving weight there would be little to choose between the relatively fewer mammal bones and the more numerous fish bones. It is no more helpful to try to visualize unaided the different organisms as food; shellfish are small fragments of flesh, whereas fish may depend on one's optimism as a fisherman. What is needed is to establish the relationships of the different foods within a single system of values; in fact, to express them in terms humanly common to all – namely, *food value* (Shawcross, 1970, p. 282). At its simplest, food value may be given as weight of meat, but different meats have different nutritional qualities, so it is preferable to convert the meats into a more fundamental scale of units of food energy: kilocalories. It is possible to transform all foods in these units, either directly from standard tables of the composition of foods (e.g. McCance and Widdowson, 1960), or by judicious use of analogies for foods not now encountered in medical or institutional diets. However, it must be emphasized that a scale based on units of food energy by no means necessarily corresponds to the values held by a prehistoric society; indeed, in the present instance it was concluded that shellfish were by far the most important food discovered on the site,[6] whereas there is ethnographic evidence that this food was almost entirely gathered by women, whose relatively lowly social status is inferred to have been carried over to the food they collected. Certainly, ethnographers during the past century have treated shellfishing so sketchily that without the archaeological evidence it might be supposed that inertidal gathering was nothing but a casual diversion on a prehistoric picnic.

Whatever the values operating in a prehistoric society, there are considerable advantages in using units of food energy for investigating prehistoric economy, and it is proposed that kilocalories serve as the unit for value measurement. A similar proposal has been made for energy units to replace money value in modern, market economics (Cottrell, 1955, p. 119). Clearly, a kilocalorie has a universality and a permanent, precisely defined value, which makes it superior to even the most stable of units of international currency. For the archaeologist the kilocalorie as a basis for value has the advantage that it may be objectively established for all foods, which are one of the universal Malinowskian 'needs' in all societies; and, according to the first law of thermodynamics, this value will be readily interchangeable and may be transformed by further calculations into corresponding units of work.

The results of the investigation of the relative values of the different foods represented at Galatea Bay are presented in Table 14.1. A visual presentation of the evidence was given in the original paper, which is reprinted elsewhere (Fagan, 1970, p. 157) and may be compared with the diagram prepared for a second site, to be discussed below.

Comparatively, at any stage, shellfish provide by far the major proportion of the diet at Galatea Bay, followed at a great distance by fish, of which one species, the snapper, is much the most important. Finally, mammal foods trail in as a poor third, hardly justifying any claims for the nutritional needs for cannibalism, except in their unique but restricted source of vitamin E, tocopherol. It is apparent, however, that when one examines the table vertically the vertebrate foods slightly increase their values as they are refined in successive stages from their archaeological occurrence, and thus they illustrate the biological evolutionary concept of energy concentration. Ethno-

594

graphically, these results lead to the recognition that the economics of the ancient Maori deserve to be completely re-examined. It becomes obvious that until the elements of the economy are put on a sound, quantitative basis, one is only observing the actions of a mechanism of no fixed magnitude, however beautiful, and indeed a mechanism whose proportions may not correspond at all closely to the reality, should it be discovered.

TABLE 14.1

	Shellfish	*Fish*	*Mammals*
Archaeological evidence	11 metric tonnes	1485 bones	59 bones
Expressed as meat	4224 kg	136 kg	15 kg
	96·5%	3·1%	0·3%
Expressed in kcal	2 752 116 ± 1 347 537	173 720 ± 87 473	54 900 ± 34 987
	92·3%	5·8%	1·8%
Total:			2 980 736 kcal

The results of the Galatea Bay analysis provide evidence from which a first step may be made towards establishing a concept of scale and magnitude for the prehistoric society (Shawcross, 1967a, p. 124). The sum of energy represented in Table 14.1 may be rounded off to 3 000 000 kcal, which may be divided by the quantity 2700 kcal, representing the consumption of a 'reference' man per day: this gives 1100 ± 600 man-days, which clearly covers a great range of possible interpretations, from the daily consumption of a single person for three years, to the consumption in one day of a modern New Zealand township, though there is no historical record of a Maori community ever approaching this size.[7] Following the Star Carr model, an ethnographic source was found for the size of the kind of community that might temporarily inhabit such a site. The specific example was taken from a group consisting of a man, two women, two adolescents, two children and an infant, observed by Captain Cook in 1773 at Dusky Bay. This locality is admittedly far distant from the present site, but there is a considerable body of later information from much closer at hand that this number was the commonplace minimal social unit, which would be found widely dispersed during the summer. The average daily consumption of such a group was calculated to be 17 400 kcal ± 35%, which gave a settlement duration of 172 ± 146 days. Unfortunately, this figure represents only the excavated part of the site and

595

further allowances must be made for the unexcavated, surviving area, and part eroded by the sea. With these allowances, and a crude estimate for cumulative error, a final figure of 692 ± 699 family-days was found for the site. When account is taken of the evidence for seasonality of occupation, lasting perhaps four months in a year, and the existence of at least two significant occupational strata, the 'reference' family would occupy the site for a maximum of seven years. If, as is possible, the community consisted of two or more such social groups, the duration reduces accordingly. But, however it is looked at, it is clear that a magnitude has been established for the population of such a settlement and its duration.

Magnitude is not solely established at the community level, for the community is but part of a larger population. There are several generally recognized levels in the social hierarchy to which such a community belongs, but the maximal unit that may be taken in the present case is the total prehistoric population, at one instant, of late prehistoric New Zealand. There can have been no significant breeding or contact with other populations outside this land area; it therefore represents an independent entity, within which breeding and cultural diffusion will have taken place, and which stands at the highest order of magnitude.

At first sight it might seem that midden analysis would be the appropriate tool for this task, as indeed it was intended to be when developed in California, but there are practical obstacles. It has been shown that a high level of error exists in even a well-excavated and carefully analysed site[8] and it is doubtful that, even were it possible to find the product of all contemporary, prehistoric sites, the result would be acceptable. The amount of labour expenditure required in such a project would certainly be out of all proportion to the value of the result obtained. There are more profound impediments to such an approach: as already stated, an unknown number of sites have entirely disappeared, so that one is sampling an unknown population. An equally basic difficulty, though not so obvious, lies in the need to establish true contemporaneity of sites. A midden may be the product of a season or less, or may have been continuously added to over the course of centuries. Clearly, entirely different results will arise in population estimates made from sites formed in either of these ways. To use an electrical metaphor, the sites are either formed in 'parallel' or in 'series', and the population 'voltage' will correspond accordingly. In addition to these theoretical problems, there arises with increasing seriousness the difficulty of accounting for foods not preserved on such sites. Thus it will be seen that the direct application of midden analysis to gross population estimation is an illusion; its value remains in establishing the magnitude of the settlement, and some other means must be found for estimating the larger unit.

It became evident, following the Galatea Bay investigations, that some alternative approach was necessary to the establishment of prehistoric populations. The original analysis had revealed the probability of the great importance of shellfish among animal foods in late prehistoric times and this suggested an experimental approach to the problem. The availability of resources is a limitation to the growth of a population. Crudely put, a population may be less, but cannot be more than the amount of available food which it exploits.[9] Expressed in the concept of energy, a population of energy transformers may not increase beyond the limit of the available energy, at any moment, which it is able to exploit: this is essentially the approach employed by Kroeber in estimating the prehistoric Mexican population. In ecological language this limit is called the *carrying capacity*, but it should be understood, as will be shown below, that the capacity is nowhere near the maximum potential.

A test of this idea was made in a study of the carrying capacity of a specific resource area, the Whangateau harbour, to support a theoretical human population (Shawcross, 1967b). The locality is an almost landlocked area of some 6·37 km² of soft shores, tidally connected with the Pacific Ocean, and therefore serving as a catchment for marine plankton and nutrients, as well as for matter washed in from the surrounding land. It should be added that there are extensive middens on the shores, particularly, close to the harbour mouth, though their full extent has not yet been recorded. Shellfish resources were chosen, because their prehistoric importance was now recognized and because they are relatively easy organisms to evaluate, having the merit, unlike some other foods of the ancient Maori, of surviving in a 'natural' state at the present time. Furthermore, there were already developed research techniques and facilities at the Auckland University Marine Research Station close to hand.

The technique of study was the systematic taking of small samples of the living shellfish populations in one arm of the harbour, from which the total population was estimated by proportion of area. A discussion of appropriate techniques of sampling would be out of place here (Shawcross, 1970, p. 284), though it needs to be stated that a subsequent study of the biological communities of the harbour indicates that the original estimate has exaggerated the population (Larcombe, 1968). The result of the original estimate gave a total capacity of 2 802 737 ± 10% kg of meat, say 500 000 man-days of food, present at one instant: this is the *stock* or *standing crop* (Macfadyen, 1963,

p. 158). It is equivalent to 4·4 tonnes of meat per hectare, 1·75 tons per acre, a very high meat productivity, or indeed cultivated food capacity by standards of modern husbandry. Statistics from New Zealand agricultural productivity give a ten-year average yield of 1·2 tons per acre of wheat, and 1·4 tons per acre of maize (N.Z. Dept. of Statistics, 1966, p. 412).[10] Because the shellfish are viewed as a resource open to human exploitation, the term *potential productivity* has been applied in preference to *stock* or *standing crop* in this estimate (Shawcross, 1970, p. 284).

It is an often surprising result of ecological population estimates to discover the immense numbers in which an organism exists; comparisons with estimates of shellfish in other harbours reveal that the present potential productivity is not wildly unrealistic. The commercial cockle fisheries of Llanrhydian Sands in South Wales yield an average crop fluctuating about 1250 tons annually and there is no reason to suppose that they are being exploited to their maximum (Hancock and Urquhart, 1966, p. 17). In New Zealand, a comparison may be made with a survey of the Ohiwa harbour 288 km south-east of Whangateau, and some 20 km² in area (Paul, 1966, p. 34), which is estimated to contain a stock of some 850 000 000 individual shellfish. If each animal is assumed to produce 1·5 g of meat, they would represent 1275 tonnes potential productivity of meat. There are several reasons for the apparent proportionate differences between the two harbours, but one factor in the highest figure for Whangateau is the account taken of shellfish in low densities, but large areas, outside the concentrated beds.

Clearly, as in the analysis of the midden, some kind of magnitude has been established for the potential productivity of an area of intertidal harbour; but equally, the figure in man-days is as meaningless from the viewpoint of a prehistoric population. The extremes, which might be expressed as the feeding of the population of Greater Auckland for a day, or of one man for twenty lifetimes, are clearly absurd, though somewhere between these there must lie an acceptable figure. But there is a further, biological difficulty which must be examined before the productivity may be used as a realistic assessment of population magnitude. This issue has already appeared much earlier in the discussion in the form of the 10% efficiency in successive energy transformations.

First, the problem may be examined from the extreme poles of possibility: with no human predation a shellfish population does not reproduce itself wildly out of control, but exists in a state of apparent equilibrium, or, if one prefers the expression, meta-stability. This is the balance achieved by a population between its frightening powers of reproduction and the factors of

598

mortality. These comprise senescence, disease, starvation, predation and disaster. The human shellfish gatherers merely operate shoulder to shoulder with other predators and, even under the pressure of commercial cockle fishing in South Wales, appear to do less damage than the dainty, long-legged oystercatcher bird (Hancock and Urquhart, 1965, p. 15). In short, the prey population accommodates its predators, and whether man has edged another predator from the feast or whether the prey's powers of reproduction have merely been extended remains debatable. The other pole is that at which the predator grows too demanding and withdraws so many reproductive adults from the population that it cannot replace its losses. There will be a point beyond which predation will have an irreversibly destructive effect upon a shellfish population, but this is not directly calculable from the mortality factors given above, because part of the shellfish reproductive cycle is passed in a microscopic, free-swimming spat stage not open to predation by the same organisms that prey off the adults. On the other hand, though a population may theoretically recuperate itself through survival of the spat, it runs the risk of its habitat being colonized in its absence by a competitor that is not subject to the same level of predation.

These issues have been discussed, because their existence must be recognized before any serious understanding can be achieved of the level at which the potential productivity may be exploited. In practice it is not possible to calculate the probable yield to man from the Whangateau shellfish beds on the basis of theoretical information only. For not only must the reproductive capacity of the prey be taken into account, but also factors affecting the effectiveness of the Maori gatherers. There is ethnographic evidence that one technique used – that of gathering under water – may have been productively advantageous (Hamilton, 1908, p. 12). Such techniques might usefully be tested by experiment, but none have yet been tried. Instead, the problem has had to be approached empirically from other lines of evidence. There is an extensive literature in ecology on laboratory experiments and field observations on the rates and effects of predation or cropping. Professor A. J. Nicholson carried out a long series of experiments on blowfly populations, isolated and cropped under laboratory conditions (Macfadyen, 1963, p. 144), where effects were observed of distinctive oscillations of population, comparable to those observed among some small wild mammals. An important original field study was that by R. L. Lindeman, who examined the ratios existing between successive levels of food resource and exploiter in a small isolated spring – a true ecosystem, not the vogue word it has become (Lindeman, 1942). Lindeman described these successive food/feeder stages as trophic levels, comparable to the stages of the Eltonian pyramid, and he recognized that only a fraction of the energy locked in the standing crop was successfully transferred to the next trophic level: the proportion of energy of the potential total so transferred may be thought of as a degree of *efficiency* (Macfadyen, 1963, p. 73). But efficiency is a comprehensive, quantifying concept which can be applied to any alteration between the output and input of anything being transformed. A number of different efficiencies relating to the transmission of food to feeder have been distinguished and classified by L. B. Slobodkin: among these the type of efficiency appropriate to this discussion is termed 'food chain efficiency' (Slobodkin, quoted by Macfadyen, 1963, p. 250). The same author states as a generalization that the efficiency of energy passage between levels will be of the order of 5–20% (Slobodkin, 1962, p. 99).

There is one specific example which is directly relevant to the present issue. The investigations of the Llanrhydian Sands cockle fisheries supply two vital pieces of information. Firstly, the measured cropping or efficiency operated at about 14%, well within Slobodkin's generalized range. Secondly, the production of each cockle-gatherer per tide ranged between 50 and 150 kg (Hancock and Urquhart, 1966, p. 21).

When the original analysis of the productivity of the Whangateau harbour was made, the problem of efficiency was recognized, but no way of measuring it seemed available, so that the result was unrealistically high. Subsequently, more information came to hand and the 14% efficiency of the Welsh shell fisheries was chosen. There are good grounds for applying this efficiency: the conditions under which the fisheries operate are approximately similar and both require hand labour. While no information is available on sea temperatures in South Wales, the average annual air temperature recorded at St Ann's Head, not far distant, is 9·4°C, compared with the Auckland average of 8·6°C (Fullard and Darby, 1967). The Welsh gatherers employ donkeys and carts for transport, a significant advantage over long distances compared with manhandling by the Maori. On the other hand, the Maori probably gathered under water, giving a greater advantage in this respect.

Applying 14% food chain efficiency to the original potential productivity gives a product of 67 134 kg of meat, equivalent to 32 224 000 kcal or 14 816 man-days at a consumption of 2175 kcal/day. Once more, these figures are no more than a measure of magnitude, but it is possible to manipulate this quantity to arrive at an estimate of the size of the social group which would gather some 67 tonnes of shellfish meat. To do this, the following assumptions must be made: (1) that shellfish-gathering was only seasonal, between late November and March – some 120 days; (2) that gathering would only be done during one tide a day; (3) that the average production per person per day of the Welsh cocklewives be taken as 105 kg; (4) that the proportions of the community are: active women = 1, men = 1, children = 1·5. These give the following equation:

$$P = W \times 3·5 \qquad \text{where } P = \text{population}$$
$$W = \frac{67\ 134}{120 \times 105} \qquad W = \text{active women}$$

The result, in round figures, is a seasonal population of 200 individuals.

DISCUSSION

Two hundred people, seasonally camped round Whangateau, is a plausible number, though perhaps on the high side if one takes a critical view of ethnographic accounts for other areas. It is also probable that this would have been an occasional population, not a regular, annual settlement over hundreds of years. At the same time, it is only fair to admit that the argument is dangerously circular: it rests on reducing a potential productivity to an acceptable level of efficiency and then saying: this quantity would have been produced in such a manner. However, the main purpose of the argument is to demonstrate the need for some concept of efficiency, for which the term *productive efficiency* has been coined (Shawcross, 1970, p. 285). Further thoughts on this suggest that it might be better expressed as *extractive efficiency*, indicating more clearly to whom the efficiency is important. Clearly it is immaterial to a dead cockle what becomes of its small store of energy, but the human predator may strive to increase his share by extractive efficiency.

The concept of efficiency proposed here should not be confused with increasing efficiency as it might be applied to the energy and evolution theory. Sahlins has pointed out that general progress is not to be equated with thermodynamic efficiency. He goes on to explain that 'an increase in efficiency may not be directed toward any advance whatsoever if the existing adaptation cannot accommodate it' (Sahlins and Service, 1960, p. 34). Extractive or food-chain efficiency does not suggest what will be done ultimately with the gains or losses, only that the immediate fate of the food is for a quantity to be metabolized.

The aim of this analysis of the possible relationship between a prehistoric population and intertidal resources is to establish a magnitude for the prehistoric population of the Maori. This may be very simply accomplished by measuring the total capacity of this resource, which is divided among 107 harbours with significant areas of intertidal flats, totalling some $2238 \pm 15\%$ km². By simple proportion, using the Whangateau evidence, it is estimated that the population associated with seasonal exploitation of shellfish would be 71 000 ± 13 000 persons (Shawcross, 1970, p. 287).[11] It is known that a proportion of Maori lived in the interior, exploiting freshwater or other resources, and these might total another 30 000, giving a round 100 000 for the total population. There is a substantial literature of estimates of Maori numbers at the time of European contact, ranging between 100 000 and 500 000, many of which refer to observations made by the earliest explorers. It seems incredible that these first opinions should be given such authoritative weight; the explorers landed at only a few points round the coast, never went inland, and were after all living at a time when the science of demography was at a most rudimentary level, and indeed when the populations of the great nations of Europe were only very roughly known. Comparable erroneous foundations of prehistoric estimates have been recognized in other parts of Polynesia (Schmitt, 1965, p. 57). The virtue of the present estimate is that it is quite independent of previous preconceptions, while its assumptions are explicit. It is not, however, an attempt at prehistoric demography, though population estimates are often loosely so termed. Demography is concerned with the structure as well as the quantity of population; it analyses the structure and explains its dynamics. What has been done in the present case is the estimation of population magnitude. The magnitude of late prehistoric Maori society may be expected to be of the order of 100 000 persons at an instant: it is within this scale that the amount of work of which such a population would be capable, may be seen to be done. The factor of prehistoric work will now be examined.

The investigation of the Galatea Bay site explored the inferences that might be drawn from a prehistoric midden of food debris. Aims and technique developed elsewhere were adapted to the local situation. It was evident that the research possibilities opened by this kind of work had not ended there and the first opportunity was taken to investigate an early site which might be usefully compared with this late one. But to understand what kind of issues are involved in comparing early and late sites in New Zealand it is necessary to give a brief account of some of the themes of its prehistory.

In the syntheses of New Zealand prehistory that have been made during the past decade considerable theoretical emphasis has been placed on settlement pattern and economy, which have been woven together into an interdependent structure. The more general view, derived from earlier prehistories and indirectly from Maori traditions, has been that the earliest phase of settlement was characterized by temporary camps, occupied briefly and then abandoned, associated with hunting and gathering. The popular name for the culture of this period is 'Moa-Hunter' and all the material evidence points to its being of eastern Polynesian origin. It has been variously stated that little or no agriculture was practised at first (Duff, 1956, p. 8), and that during the course of time the economy was altered by a local 'Agricultural Revolution' which, according to some, was the property of a new and superior migration, while others have contended that the revolution was internally inspired, either in technique or stimulated by climatic change. This new and supposedly more productive economic base gave rise to a markedly different settlement pattern, finally based on permanent, fortified villages, and bearing a rich and distinctive material culture termed 'Classic Maori' (Green, 1963, p. 38). Though cautiously expressed in terms of culture change, such a view seems to be essentially evolutionary, particularly because of the clear analogy to the Old World culture sequence, commencing with a Palaeolithic stage and concluding with a stage of permanent village communities subsisting on agriculture. This evolutionary sequence must have been greatly accelerated to have taken place within 1000 years in New Zealand, the most generally accepted time value based on radiocarbon dating and traditional genealogies (Shawcross, 1969, p.184). A closely related counter theory has been proposed by L. M. Groube, in which early settlements are seen to be large and just as permanent, or more, than later ones. It is argued that, as agriculture must have been part of the economy of the Oceanic ancestors of the Maori, there is no reason to suppose that it was largely abandoned during the earliest phases of settlement and only subsequently rediscovered (Groube, 1967, p. 15). The basis for this theory stems from a scrutiny of late prehistoric and early historic settlement patterns, which provided the impetus for the Galatea Bay study. The reason why such opposite theories could be applied to the same matter is due to the limited evidence for settlement and economy derived from early sites. The theories have, as a consequence, had to rest heavily on assertions of what the supporting evidence ought to be, rather than on interpretation of what there was.

The archaeological investigation of the early site of Mount Camel (see Fig. 14.1) is not yet fully analysed and published, and what follows is a preliminary account of findings relevant to the present discussion. A certain amount of description is thought necessary to enable the reader to assess the scale and application of the analyses.

The site lies at the foot of Mount Camel, commanding the mouth of the Houhora harbour, whose area is some 12 km². The prehistoric settlement was on a low platform, a few metres above high water mark, and about 1·5 ha in extent. A substantial part of the platform has been quarried away, leaving

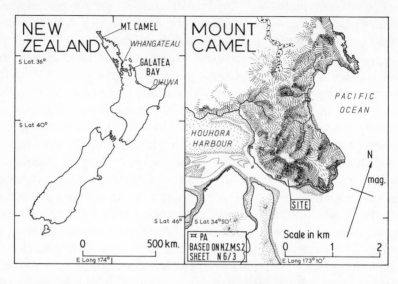

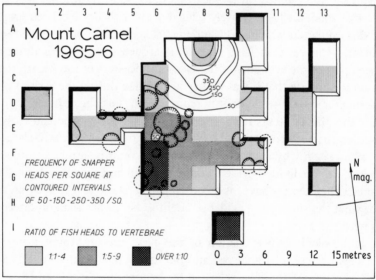

FIG. 14.1. The Mount Camel site, Houhora area, New Zealand.

two areas of 1500 and 3000 m² relatively undisturbed. There is evidence that the occupation formerly extended along the whole length of the platform, close to the foot of the mountain, but thinning towards the sea.

In all, some forty squares, controlled by a 3 m grid separated by half-metre baulks, amounting to 250 m² area were opened – that is, under 2% of the original maximum possible extent of the site.

STRATIGRAPHY

To the landward, the natural base of the site is a clay and rock colluvium from Mount Camel, grading seawards into rolled gravels which are the materials being quarried. Above the natural base there is a deposit of dune sand, abutting the foot of the mountain and increasing in thickness seawards. The occupation deposits lie on and within the sand and consist of a series of some twelve superimposed floors separated by sterile sand. The floors are capped to the landward by a lens of up to 30 cm thick of blackened sand containing oven stones. All of these deposits are truncated by a further layer of sand, stones and shells, containing some artefacts and associated with mounds and ridges on the present surface, identified as deposits formed during cultivation. This agricultural soil is capped by a modern soil, estimated to be about a century old. The stratigraphy thus suggests that the original occupation was on fresh sands with little plant cover and that the occupation was intermittent, with short abandonments during which thin skins of sterile sand were blown over the floors. The site was abandoned for an unknown length of time before being re-used for cultivation. A radiocarbon estimate for the earliest cultural deposits gives a date of A.D. 1154 ± 56, while the end of this occupation is dated at A.D. 1260 ± 44. The site is thus contemporary with a number of others stretching along the full coastal length of New Zealand.

THE NATURE OF THE SETTLEMENT

The plan of the main area of the excavation reveals a centre of high concentration of occupation debris (Fig. 14.1 (3)). There is a distinct floor area of about 100 m², close up against the foot of the mountain which protects the north. To the south-west some fourteen ovens are clustered and a further four lie due south. This area is surrounded by increasingly sterile deposits, and the excavated area may be reasonably interpreted as an isolated occupation segment of a larger community, now mostly obliterated, stretching along the coastal platform. The activities represented on the site include butchering, particularly apparent on the earliest occupation floor, fish scaling and preparation, cooking, fishhook manufacture and maintenance of fishing gear, and manufacture of bone and ivory ornaments. There is some hint that the other occupation floors, now destroyed, followed the same pattern, but with some emphasis on different artefacts, such as adzes and harpoons. Consequently, the economic analysis that follows may be treated as a statement about a distinct segment of a community.

ANALYSIS OF ECONOMIC EVIDENCE

Some 21 000 bones recovered from the site have so far been analysed, leaving a few hundred only of winged birds yet unstudied. The bones belong to seals, dolphins, fish (which are the most frequent), dogs and rats (see Fig. 14.3); no human bones were found. The dominant fish species was the snapper, *Chrysophrys auratus*, and from previous experience all three bones of the jaws and all vertebrae were studied. From this material it is possible to estimate minimum numbers of animals, according to the same procedure as described by T. E. White for mammals (White, 1953), and, because of the concentration of the site, such an estimate will be fairly close to the true number represented, not allowing for the unexcavated proportion. This is supported by the high level of agreement between 2325 left dentaries and 2332 right dentaries, suggesting that no very serious dispersal of material had taken place.

NUMBERS OF INDIVIDUALS

Fish

Snapper (*Chrysophrys auratus*)	2332
Trevally (*Caranx lutescens*)	100+
Kahawai (*Arripis trutta*)	50–80
Other fish	60

'Other fish' include barracouta, porae, eagle and stingrays, king fish, parrot fish, porcupine fish, rock cod, John Dory, hapuku, perch, red snapper and terakihi. The snapper is an eclectic carnivore, feeding on a wide range of animals including small fish, shellfish, echinoderms and carrion, and may be caught with baited hook or net. By contrast, the kahawai is a hunting carnivore, feeding only on small fish and rarely caught by any means other than a trolled lure.

The estimation of moa numbers is more difficult than for other vertebrate species owing to the bones being extensively broken to provide raw material for fishhook manufacture. The two species probably most frequently represented here are identified on the basis of comparative measurements with those established for these species in a pioneering taxonomic study by Sir

Gilbert Archey (1941). These are two of the smallest moa, measuring perhaps 1–1·5 m standing, not much taller than large breeds of turkeys, though substantially more massive, being ground dwellers and flightless.

Mammals

Seals (chiefly *Arctocephalus forsteri*)	43
Dolphins	8
Dogs	40
Rats	15

Birds

Moa (chiefly *Euryapteryx exilis* and *Euryapteryx curtus*)	50 ± 10

BUTCHERING TECHNIQUES

In reviewing the evidence for food debris from a site it is desirable to have some understanding of the parts of the animals found. The presence of a bone does not necessarily mean that the entire animal was ever present or consumed on the site. It may be evidence for industrial technology and not food consumption; thus earlier workers in New Zealand archaeology developed the criterion that a site could not be ascribed to 'moa-hunting' unless there were found industrially useless bones such as the skull, vertebrae, ribs and pelvis (Teviotdale, 1932, p. 99). This was thought necessary to overcome the criticism that moa bones found on sites might have been brought there for industrial purposes after being mined in a subfossil form elsewhere. At Mount Camel the industrially useful bones, particularly the humeri, are far the most common ones, but there are a few skulls, vertebrae, ribs and pelves, indicating that some fully articulated carcasses were brought to the site to be butchered. It would appear that most of the moa were slaughtered and butchered at some distance from the settlement, presumably also requiring overland transport, and that consequently only the meat-covered upper legs were thought worth bringing back. Virtually no tarso-metatarsi and phalanges have been found, and it may reasonably be concluded that the thighs combined the bulk of meat and industrially useful bone. The moa have been represented in the accompanying diagram (Fig. 14.3) as complete or trussed carcasses; this is because they make better visual images in this form than as dismembered legs.

On the other hand, a cursory examination of the mammals suggests that many of them were butchered and eaten on the site. A dolphin would require at least two men to shift any distance, though it might well have been stranded on the adjacent beach, as happened to two during the excavation. The majority of the seals are of the small species of native fur seal, and include some pups, but there are also larger species represented, capable of weighing several hundred kilogrammes. These must have been cut up on the kill site, but as useful meat would be present on all quarters and the jaws contained teeth prized as ornaments, it would seem that the entire animals must have been brought to the site dismembered.

It is possible that two different factors were operating over the fish, some being consumed entirely on the site and others apparently being divided, with their bodies being taken elsewhere. The proportions of the body parts of the fish may be expressed as a ratio of numbers of vertebrae to numbers of entire heads, represented by right and left dentaries (Fig. 14.1 (3)). Depending on the fish, there may be between twenty and forty vertebrae. On the main floor the ratio is less than one vertebra per head, while in the south-west corner, surrounding the ovens, the ratio rises to over ten per head – that is, approaching the proportions of a whole fish. This increase in vertebrae co-incides with the relatively greater abundance of fish other than snapper, and would therefore seem to suggest that these fish were consumed whole and disposed of on the site near the ovens, whereas the snapper were divided and their bodies taken elsewhere.

ANALYSIS OF THE SIZE OF FISH CAUGHT

Just as the butchering pattern is a guide towards the economic importance of the animals on a site, so it is important to know what the size range was of the individuals being caught. It could be quite misleading to assume that the catch is a random sample of a natural population, and it must be remembered that an adult may weigh several times more than a juvenile. A more general problem in archaeology is the determination of the constitution of a 'natural' population. Admirable though it is to use modern samples for comparative purposes, there remains the disturbing probability that even these natural poulations have also been modified by man (Higgs and Jarman, 1969, p. 35). The following brief discussion is confined to the structure of the archaeological fish population and examines its relationship to modern populations. Properly, the same procedures should be applied where possible to the other animals, though this has not been attempted. It will be seen that, although this analysis is primarily aimed at the limited question of the amount of food represented in a catch, it has other, much wider implications.

There is a generally held opinion in ecology that the population structure of a stock of animals that is being cropped adjusts to the level of cropping (Russell-Hunter, 1970, p. 195). An uncropped or virgin population of fish will be distinguishable from a severely over-cropped one; there will be a tendency for the former to include a large proportion of older, large fish which may be in poor condition (Russell-Hunter, 1970, p. 199). In the case of animals such as fish, their size increases with age; or, at least, within their natural life span there is not the same halt in growth following maturation as in man. Additionally, animals, such as many fish, reproduce seasonally and consequently form age classes, which are reflected as size classes. It is possible that such age classes appear in the two peaked size/frequency curves derived from the fossil populations at Galatea Bay and Mount Camel (Fig. 14.2). But this separation of size classes may become blurred if many samples are taken throughout the course of years. In the present cases the peaks may emphasize seasonal occupation of the sites. There is a further social factor that should be noted in connection with some fish populations: during their early years the fish will shoal in big groups but, at least in the case of the snapper, at some stage the larger, older fish separate and become solitary, occupying holes and prowling close to rocks. There will therefore be a significant economic difference between the catching of large solitary fish off rocks or smaller shoaling ones off beaches or in deep water.

While the question of size seems worth investigating (Akazawa and Watanabe, 1968), there are practical difficulties. The first is that of determining the size of the archaeological fish; the size of bones, such as jaws, will give a relative scale, but no absolute idea of size. This is achieved by experimentally establishing the ratio between bone size and body mass.[12] A second difficulty lies in the size measurements made by fisheries researchers, which are in body lengths. These require further conversions, either to transform jaw lengths into body lengths, or transform body lengths into live weights. The latter was chosen because the available data could be most readily used, but it introduces extra potential errors.

Two samples of modern snapper populations are available; the first, a very large one from the important fishery area of the Hauraki Gulf, in which the Galatea Bay site is located. This is a body of water in which the effects of over-fishing have been apparent for half a century. The second sample comes from off the Cavalli Islands, not far distant from Mount Camel, and is considered to be virtually a virgin population (Longhurst, 1958, p. 492).

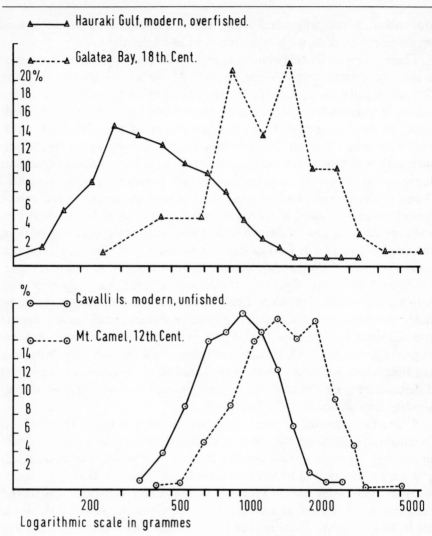

FIG. 14.2. Comparison between the weights of prehistoric and modern fish populations.

It is now possible to compare a modern, unexploited fish population with an archaeological fishery based on a presumably virgin population, and then to compare the early archaeological population from Mount Camel with the late one from Galatea Bay, and, finally, to compare that from Galatea Bay with a modern, overfished population from the Hauraki Gulf (Fig. 14.2).

The most frequent fish in the modern, unexploited fishery weigh about 1 kg, and only about 4% weigh 2 kg and over, whereas in the Mount Camel population the most frequent fish weigh between 1·5 and 2·0 kg and decline at a little over 3 kg, very few being over 3·5 kg. The Mount Camel population compares very closely with that from the site of Galatea Bay, though the most frequent classes at the latter are a little smaller, at just under 1·0 kg and over 1·5 kg respectively. These all contrast dramatically with the modern over-fished population from the Hauraki Gulf, in which the most frequent class is down to about 300 g and only about 15% weigh 1 kg and over. It would therefore look as if the occupants of Mount Camel were exploiting a virgin fishery, while possibly the effects of 600 years of Maori fishing may be represented in the most frequent classes falling to about 0·5 kg. However, for the purposes of the present discussion it is sufficient to note that the great bulk of the fish caught in prehistoric times weighed between 1 and 3 kg – that is, they would have been shoaling fish, and there can have been very few large, lone specimens of the kind that are caught off rocks. With these data it is possible to make a fair estimate of the weight of the prehistoric catch (Fig. 14.3).

It should be possible to carry out equivalent computations for all the other animal constituents of the Mount Camel midden. In practice, this cannot be directly followed, because there are not sufficient data for dolphins and seals, while the Maori dog and moa are extinct and can therefore only be reconstructed by analogy. The weights of dolphins have had to be determined from information given on comparably sized Japanese dolphins, with an average weight of 171 kg (Nishiwaki, 1966, p. 196). The sources on *Arctocephalus* weights are even more exiguous. Judith King gives the weights of three, averaging 110 kg (King, 1964, p. 35), while Gavin Maxwell states that they seldom exceed 136 kg (Maxwell, 1967, p. 43; Scheffer, 1958, pp. 8, 140). The meat weight of the dogs is taken from previous work and given as a round 5 kg per individual (Shawcross, 1967a, p. 122). The moa present again the most serious problem in estimation, because no living flightless birds have comparable body proportions and information is limited. However, it is reasonable to assume that all the major flightless birds are roughly comparable in having the bulk of muscles concentrated in the area of the pelvis and femur. The two species of moa on the site are found roughly in the proportions of 25% *E. exilis* (the larger) and 75% *E. curtus* (the smaller). Assuming, for the purposes of discussion, that the larger would have a live weight equivalent to an ostrich, for though shorter it is massive, and assuming the smaller is equivalent to a rhea, they will be assigned 90 and 20 kg live weights respectively (Hanzak, 1967, pp. 20, 21; Welty, 1964, p. 2).

It has previously been argued that meat weight is a more objective means of comparison between food animals represented on a site. This is shown, drawn to scale, in Fig. 14.3. To prepare this diagram, the weights of the animals are determined and then converted to available flesh weights, using a factor of 60% (Shawcross, 1967, p. 119). The volume measurement for the meat is based on the closeness of the specific gravity of all flesh to that of water. According to this analysis the most important constituent would be seals, followed by fish, then moa, dolphins, and finally dogs. It is possible that the seals and moa are somewhat exaggerated, but the general impression probably stands.

The Galatea Bay analysis stopped at the level of comparison in meat weights but the logical value system in which the foods should be compared is that of energy, as has been argued throughout this discussion. Meat weight can be readily converted into kilocalories by the use of tables, but these give results in the order of millions of kilocalories, which are not readily comprehensible; therefore, it seems worth applying a further concept. Professor L. G. Dudley Stamp has quite recently proposed the Standard Nutritional Unit (SNU) as a useful measure of food energy. It consists of 1 000 000 kcal/year, equivalent to the needs of one man for one year.[13] The SNU thus provides a shorthand guide to the population and duration issue which was discussed earlier in this chapter. The most striking result of these calculations is to raise greatly the importance of the two sea mammals; this is because of the high oil content of their meat. Correspondingly, the moa take a slight lead over the fish in terms of energy content, because fish have relatively low values. There is also a slight hint, from the observation of the resemblance of the depot fats in flightless birds to typical mammals, that moa meat would have a fairly high value (Hartman and Shortland, 1968, p. 232).

The question that arises from such calculations is what this food amounts to in human effort. The potential is incredibly high, equivalent to 1 million kW or 767 000 hp, which leads to the final level of analysis in the present discussion. These quantities of energy seem more appropriate to modern, industrial, fossil fuel powered society, though it should be noted that the energy would be dissipated within a second. However, the point is that prehistoric man is only capable of harnessing a fraction of this total. Throughout the food chain the efficiency of energy conversion is low and the human 'engine' is no exception as an inefficient converter. The work that may be done from the previously estimated supply of food may be calculated in the following two stages. Firstly, every individual must expend a considerable proportion of the food energy he has eaten in maintaining the functions of the body. This is the *basal metabolism*, for which an average figure for an adult is quoted as 1680

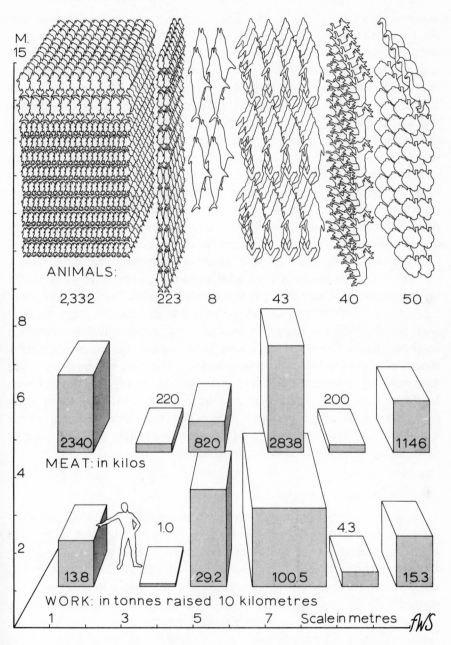

M.
15

ANIMALS:

2,332   223   8   43   40   50

8

6

220   200

2340   820   2838   1146

MEAT: in kilos

4

1.0

4.3

13.8   29.2   100.5   15.3

2

WORK: in tonnes raised 10 kilometres

1   3   5   7   Scale in metres   *fWS*

FIG. 14.3. The work value of the meat weight at Mount Camel.

kcal/day (Mottram, 1963, p. 37). This must presumably take into account such massive intermittent demands as reproduction, as well as body heat, metabolism and replacement. If an average adult consumption of 2700 kcal/day is assumed, this leaves 1020 kcal or 62% for work, but this cannot be directly applied, for it must be transformed at a rate of what Kleiber calls 'partial efficiency', at about 20% (Kleiber, 1961, p. 366), which leaves a modest 204 kcal/day, or 20% of 62% of the daily intake, for mechanical work.

It is now possible to transform the potential of available energy into estimates of work. Once more, this may be graphically represented in block diagrams, shown in the lowest row in Fig. 14.3. Work is generally thought of as unit weight raised a unit distance, the conventional form being in horsepower, equivalent to 550 foot-pounds per second. In the present instance the time element will be omitted and the work load expressed in the metric system as metre-kilogrammes (m kg) or tonnes raised to a height of 10 km. Furthermore, the diagram has been drawn to a scale in which the workloads, in tonnes, are represented as blocks of lead, with a specific gravity of 11·3. Thus, the lowermost row may be envisaged as a series of blocks, based on modules of 1 m^2 or 4 m^2 of floor area, each in proportion to amounts of energy available from metabolizing the respective food sources, and all raised to a common height of 10 km. The expression is admittedly fanciful, but underlying it is the statement of the first law of thermodynamics, that energy may be transformed from one form to another but is neither created nor destroyed. The work done by the ancient Maori inhabitants of Mount Camel must have taken many forms, such as hunting expeditions on foot, paddling canoes, digging, cutting wood, adzing dugouts, making tools, singing and dancing. All of these forms of work may be measured in metre-kilogrammes.

DISCUSSION AND CONCLUSION

How does the foregoing analysis apply to the problems of New Zealand's brief but enigmatic prehistory? Bearing in mind the high risk of error in generalizing about a settlement from a sample excavation, and of generalizing about a prehistoric society from one site, Mount Camel will be briefly assessed according to current archaeological thinking. Opinion has been markedly divided over the interpretation of early sites. On one hand they are seen as being populated by relatively smaller social groups than later, and subsisting by a robber economy which quickly decimated many of the animal resources. In consequence, the sites would be temporary and probably not reoccupied. On the other hand, there is the view that the earliest settlements would be likely to have retained much of the structure and economy of the already established eastern Polynesian pattern (which, it must be admitted, is not very well known). In this case, the early sites might be both larger and more permanent than subsequent ones, which would be part of a settlement pattern adapted to a strongly diversified, non-tropical environment. It would be possible to select fragments of evidence from Mount Camel to support either point of view: there seems no doubt that the exploitation of seals and moa was destructive and irreversible and that the site was not a permanent village. Equally, however, it is a far more extensive and longer lasting settlement than Galatea Bay or sites like it. Thus, the total energy value of the excavated proportion of the Mount Camel midden is 27·2 SNU, against 3·0 SNU from the excavated part of Galatea Bay (Shawcross, 1967a, p. 123).

Ideally, one should be able to translate these social concepts of settlement pattern into expressions of energy transfer, and a start may be made by introducing some control over magnitude in these arguments. The excavated part of Mount Camel has been described as a single segment of a multiple settlement, which, judging from the original total area, must have had four or five other comparable units. The question of duration of the occupation is important, and here the spacing of the radiocarbon dates by about a century should not be taken too literally; they only bracket the occupation. Instead, the stratigraphic evidence for a sequence of similar working floors, separated by thin, sterile sand lenses, suggests regular, cyclic occupations. Furthermore, there are hints of seasonality from some of the exploited resources, so that a reasonable inference may be made that the site represents a succession of consecutive, summer occupations over a relatively short span of perhaps twelve years. The total of animal food energy is 27·2 SNU, which may be rounded off to 30·0, to account for the unexcavated deposits and other losses. If the summer season is six months and if, for simplicity, it is assumed that all of the food is consumed on the site, this will give sixty man-years of occupation. Divide this sum by twelve years and the size of the social group occupying the excavated area is five individuals, no more than a nuclear family.[14] These estimates are very simple and take no qualifying circumstances into account, but the magnitude of the community that they suggest cannot be missed. There is only one qualification which will be mentioned here: shellfish-gathering is apparently insignificant in the occupation deposits and all of the foods represented are those that might be expected to be won by men. It seems unlikely that the women were idle, so it may be surmised that they were occupied in obtaining plant foods.[15] Even allowing for such un-

615

known factors, the size of the groups occupying the site segments need be no greater than extended families, and these would make the population of the entire site about fifty persons.

What now emerges is a scale of dimensions in which Mount Camel may be compared with Galatea Bay. The early site represents a coherent group of families moving about as a body through an otherwise humanly uninhabited landscape, probably following a seasonal pattern. The late site reflects a different pattern of behaviour, in which a related group of families, living as a unit during the winter, disperses into its constituent family parts during the summer. The reconstruction of the kind of social system to which Galatea Bay might belong is based on ethnographic sources, but it should not be supposed that this was the only pattern observed among the Maori. There are also recorded, from the early nineteenth century, examples of social groups that remained as a body throughout the year, in spite of moving between coast and interior. Yet other groups are recorded as permanently located in either the interior or on the coast (Shawcross, 1970, p. 287, derived from Shawcross, 1966), though it is not clear what the degree of permanence would be. Of these various forms the Mount Camel evidence seems to resemble most closely the groups that moved seasonally as a body. If this is so, there is little need to seek for a single, evolutionary process. Instead, the development of variants of this pattern can be seen as a likely outcome both of increasing population and the accompanying increase in complexity of rights of access to resources.

It is not easy to fit the archaeological evidence into any evolutionary argument that seeks to explain New Zealand as a local manifestation of cultural energy capture. On the face of it, at least, far more energy seems to have been concentrated on the earlier site than on the later. This should be a warning to any over-hasty efforts to test the energy and evolution theory. At the same time, it is a reasonable assumption that the population has increased between the times of the two sites and this can only mean that prehistoric man was increasing his share of free energy. But, having stated this, the evolution and energy theory appears to have no further application to the local sequence.

The form of this discussion has been frankly speculative, and its purpose has been to explore a few of the openings revealed by the kinds of measurements of archaeological evidence that thermodynamic models make possible. The application of thermodynamic concepts, particularly those derived from the first law, supply a unifying principle through which previously unrelated information may be drawn together and organized into an interpretable form, free from the need to make intuitive leaps between unconnected links of archaeological argument. This is not to deny the role of intuition or imagination in the subject: these qualities are vital for the development of thought, but their position should be at the initiating and interpreting ends and not somewhere in the middle, acting as some form of magical catalysts which convert archaeological evidence into prehistoric fact. It should be remarked that, so far from this kind of analysis leading the archaeologist away from his true subject of man, and losing him in the higher abstractions of the physical sciences, it must lead directly back to such issues as the nature of prehistoric society. At the present time these issues tend to be clouded by the absence of *quantity* and *magnitude*.

The objective of this study has therefore been to demonstrate how the fundamental phenomena, which are the concern of the laws of thermodynamics, may be recognized and applied, to what is at first glance the unpromising subject of archaeology. Certain abstract principles, notably value, potential productivity, magnitude, efficiency and work, are seen to operate as a consequence of this approach; and it would appear that archaeology might well benefit from the use of more such abstract concepts, in addition to its established cluster of terms cognate with stage, type and culture.

Notes

1. Curtis (1956, p. 734) discusses the analogous reduction by man of plant species and, interestingly, applies ideas derived from the second law of thermodynamics.

2. Kroeber (1952, p. 134) cites Chapple and Coon's *Principles of Anthropology*, from which the word 'culture' had apparently been expunged.

3. See Eisenhart (1968) for a discussion of concepts of error.

4. Kroeber (not consulted by the author), cited by Beals (1943, p. 487). Dr Richard Shutler (personal communication) has drawn attention to the pioneering work on population estimates from shell middens made by Professor E. W. Gifford in the San Francisco Bay area in the 1930s.

5. Cook (1946) and Cook and Heizer (1965); the list of relevant publications by these authors is much more extensive.

6. At the present time there is no means of directly evaluating the importance of foods that do not leave hard, indestructible remains on such a site.

7. The documentary evidence should not be confused with European speculations and Maori numerical imagination, both purporting to be 'historical'.

8. Coutts (1971) has recently examined the application of error estimates in the analysis of New Zealand middens.

9. Suttles (1968, p. 60) draws attention to the use by Bartholomew and Birdsell of 'Liebig's Law', which emphasizes the limiting effect on a population of the least available key resources.

10. This is an oversimplification of the issue; the husbandman is achieving sustained cropping.

11. Rhys Jones (personal communication), in comparing this analysis with the evidence of Tasmania, points out an inconsistency in assuming a basically hunter-gatherer economy for New Zealand, which is apparently supporting a much greater population than would be expected from such a base. He suggests that even limited food production may have a significant effect.

12. See Shawcross (1967a, p. 115): the original curve has been extended by many more measurements.

13. Stamp (cited by Lucas, 1968, p. 14) suggested the SNU, equivalent to 10^6 kcal in food as harvested. Its use is discussed among nutritional units appropriate to a human population scale.

14. It might be possible to apply Maori socio-political terms as in Firth (1959, p. 110) to these archaeologically identified groups, but it is felt preferable to confine speculation within the limits of the present evidence.

15. The idea of inferring the changing role of women in the economy has been developed by prehistorians working in Tasmania and New South Wales, notably R. Jones, E. Meehan and S. Bowdler.

Acknowledgements

The excavations in this discussion were carried out by members of the Auckland University Archaeological Society. The Mount Camel excavation was financed by a grant from the Auckland University South West Pacific Research Programme, and by a generous grant from the Auckland War Memorial Museum. Mr D. Witter analysed the mammal bones and Miss J. Fagan and Miss B. Knight analysed the fish bones. Thanks are also due to the Wagener family of Houhora, in particular the landowner, Mr W. J. Wagener, and Mrs Wagener.

References

AKAZAWA, T. and WATANABE, H. (1968) Restoration of body size of Jomon shell-mound fish (preliminary report). *Proceedings of the Eighth International Congress of Anthropological and Ethnological Sciences*, **3**, 193–7.

AMBROSE, W. (1963) Shell dump sampling. *New Zealand Archaeological Association Newsletter*, **6** (3), 155–9.

AMBROSE, W. (1967) Archaeology and shell middens. *Archaeology and Physical Anthropology in Oceania*, **2** (3), 169–87.

ARCHEY, G. (1941) *The Moa: A Study of the Dinorthiformes*. Bulletin of the Auckland Institute and Museum No. 1.

ASCHER, R. (1959) A prehistoric population estimate, using midden analysis and two population models. *Southwestern Journal of Anthropology*, **15**, 168–78.

BEALS, R. L. (1943) The population of northwest Mexico. *American Anthropologist*, n.s. **45**, 486–9.

BIDNEY, D. (1950) Review of *The Science of Culture* by L. A. White. *American Anthropologist*, n.s. **52** (4), 518–19.

BINFORD, L. R. and BINFORD, S. R. (1966) A preliminary analysis of functional variability in the Mousterian of Levallois facies. *American Anthropologist*, n.s. **68**, 2 (2), 238–95.

CHILDE, V. G. (1956) *Man Makes Himself*. 3rd ed. London: Watts.

CHILDE, V. G. (1963) *Social Evolution*. London: Fontana.

CLARK, J. G. D. (1954) *Excavations at Star Carr*. Cambridge: Cambridge University Press.

CLARKE, D. L. (1968) *Analytical Archaeology*. London: Methuen.

CLELAND, C. E. (1966) *The Prehistoric Animal Ecology and Ethnozoology of the Upper Great Lakes Region*. Anthropological Papers No. 29, Museum of Anthropology, University of Michigan, Ann Arbor.

COOK, S. F. (1946) A reconsideration of shell mounds, with respect to population and nutrition. *American Antiquity*, **12**, 51–3.

COOK, S. F. and HEIZER, R. F. (1965) *The Quantitative Approach to the Relation Between Population and Settlement Size*. Berkeley: University of California.

COTTRELL, F. (1955) *Energy and Society*. New York: McGraw-Hill.

COUTTS, P. J. F. (1971) Recent techniques of midden analysis and studies of modern shellfish populations in New Zealand. *Transactions of the Royal Society of New Zealand, General*, **2** (11), 143–56.

CURTIS, J. T. (1956). The modification of mid-latitude grasslands and forests by man. In THOMAS, W. L. (ed.) *Man's Role in Changing the Face of the Earth*. Chicago: University of Chicago Press.

DAVIDSON, J. M. (1964a) *The Physical Analysis of Refuse in New Zealand Archaeological Sites*. Unpublished M.A. thesis, University of Auckland.

DAVIDSON, J. M. (1964b) Concentrated shell middens. *New Zealand Archaeological Association Newsletter*, **7** (2), 70–8.

DUFF, R. (1956) *The Moa-Hunter Period of Maori Culture*. Wellington: Government Printer.

EISENHART, C. (1968) Expression of uncertainties of final results. *Science*, **160**, 1201–4.

FAGAN, B. M. (ed.) (1970) *Introductory Readings in Archaeology*. Boston, Mass.: Little Brown.

FIRTH, R. (1959) *Economics of the New Zealand Maori*. 2nd ed. Wellington: Government Printer.

FULLARD, H. and DARBY, H. C. (eds.) (1967) *The Library Atlas*. 9th ed. London: George Philip.

GLASSOW, M. A. (1967) Considerations in estimating prehistoric California coastal populations. *American Antiquity*, **32** (3), 354–9.

GREEN, R. C. (1963) *A Review of the Prehistoric Sequence of the Auckland Province*. Auckland: Auckland University Archaeological Society.

GROUBE, L. M. (1964) *Settlement Patterns in Prehistoric New Zealand*. Unpublished M.A. thesis, University of Auckland.

GROUBE, L. M. (1967) Models in prehistory: a consideration of the New Zealand evidence. *Archaeology and Physical Anthropology in Oceania*, **2** (1), 1–27.

HAMILTON, A. (1908) *Fishing and Sea Foods of the Ancient Maori*. Dominion Museum Bulletin No. 2.

HANCOCK, D. A. and URQUHART, A. E. (1965) The determination of natural mortality and its causes in an exploited population of cockles (*Cardium edule* L.). *Fishery Investigations*, ser. II, **24** (2). London: Ministry of Agriculture, Fisheries and Food.

HANCOCK, D. A. and URQUHART, A. E. (1966) The fishery for cockles (*Cardium edule* L.) in the Burry Inlet, South Wales. *Fishery Investigations*, ser. II, **25** (3).

619

HANZAK, J. (1967) *The Pictorial Encyclopaedia of Birds.* London: Paul Hamlyn.

HARTMAN, L. and SHORTLAND, F. B. (1968) Fatty acid composition of the depot of fats and liver lipids of the Takahe (*Notornis Mantelli*). *New Zealand Journal of Science*, **11**, 230–5.

HIGGS, E. S. and JARMAN, M. R. (1969) The origins of agriculture: a reconsideration. *Antiquity*, **43** (169), 31–41.

KING, J. E. (1964) *Seals of the World.* London: British Museum (Natural History).

KLEIBER, M. (1961) *The Fire of Life.* New York: Wiley.

KROEBER, A. L. (1952) *The Nature of Culture.* Chicago: University of Chicago Press.

LARCOMBE, M. F. (1968) *Distribution and Recognition of Intertidal Organisms in the Whangateau Harbour, and: A Classification for Sheltered Soft Shores.* Unpublished thesis for B.Sc.Hons., University of Auckland.

LEE, R. B. (1968) What hunters do for a living, or how to make out on scarce resources. In LEE, R. B. and DEVORE, I. (eds.) *Man the Hunter*, 30–48. Chicago: Aldine.

LEE, R. B. and DEVORE, I. (eds.) (1968) *Man the Hunter.* Chicago: Aldine.

LINDEMAN, R. L. (1942) The trophic-dynamic aspect of ecology. *Ecology*, **23** (4), 399–418.

LONGHURST, A. R. (1958) Racial differences in size and growth in the New Zealand snapper. *New Zealand Journal of Science*, **1** (4), 487–99.

LOTKA, A. J. (1956) *Elements of Mathematical Biology.* New York: Dover Publications.

LUCAS, J. W. (1968) The role of plant foods in solving the world food problem, I: energy requirements. *Plant Foods for Human Nutrition*, **1** (1), 13–21.

MCCANCE, R. A. and WIDDOWSON, E. M. (1960) *The Composition of Foods.* London: Medical Research Council.

MACFADYEN, A. (1963) *Animal Ecology.* 2nd ed. London: Pitman.

MAXWELL, G. (1967) *Seals of the World.* London: Constable.

MEIGHAN, C. W. (1959). The Little Harbor site, Catalina Island: an example of ecological interpretation in archaeology. *American Antiquity*, **24** (4), 383–405.

MOTTRAM, V. H. (1963) *Human Nutrition.* 2nd ed. London: Arnold.

NAROLL, R. (1962) Floor area and settlement population. *American Antiquity*, **27** (4), 587–9.

NEW ZEALAND DEPARTMENT OF STATISTICS (1966) *Official Yearbook 1966.* Wellington: Government Printer.

NISHIWAKI, M. (1966) A discussion of rarities among the smaller cetaceans caught in Japanese waters. In NORRIS, K. S. (ed.) *Whales, Dolphins and Porpoises.* Berkeley: University of California Press.

OAKLEY, K. P. (1956) Fire as a Palaeolithic tool and weapon. *Proceedings of the Prehistoric Society*, n.s. **21**, 36–48.

PARTINGTON, J. R. (1962) *A History of Chemistry.* Vol. 3. London: Macmillan.

PATTEN, B. C. (1959) An introduction to the cybernetics of the ecosystem: the trophic dynamic aspect. *Ecology*, **40** (2), 221–31.

PAUL, L. J. (1966) Observations on past and present distribution of mollusc beds in Ohiwa Harbour, Bay of Plenty. *New Zealand Journal of Science*, **9** (1), 30–40.

PHILLIPSON, J. (1966) *Ecological Energetics.* London: Arnold.

RUSSELL-HUNTER, W. D. (1970) *Aquatic Productivity.* New York: Collier–Macmillan.

SAHLINS, M. D. and SERVICE, E. R. (1960) *Evolution and Culture.* Ann Arbor: University of Michigan Press.

SCHEFFER, V. B. (1958) *Seals, Sea Lions and Walrusses.* Stanford: Stanford University Press.

SCHMITT, R. C. (1965) Garbled population estimates of central Polynesia. *Journal of the Polynesian Society,* **74** (1), 57–62.

SERVICE, E. R. (1969) Models for the methodology of mouthtalk. *Southwestern Journal of Anthropology,* **25** (1), 68–80.

SHAWCROSS, K. A. (1966) *Maoris of the Bay of Islands, 1769–1840: A Study in Changing Maori Attitudes Towards Europeans.* Unpublished M.A. thesis, University of Auckland.

SHAWCROSS, K. A. (1967) Fern-root, and the total scheme of eighteenth century Maori food production in agricultural areas. *Journal of the Polynesian Society,* **76** (3), 330–52.

SHAWCROSS, K. A. (1971) *The Influence of Politics on Northern Maori Settlement Patterns.* Paper read at the New Zealand Archaeological Association Conference, Auckland, May 1971.

SHAWCROSS, W. (1967a) An investigation of prehistoric diet and economy on a coastal site at Galatea Bay, New Zealand. *Proceedings of the Prehistoric Society,* **33**, 107–31.

SHAWCROSS, W. (1967b) An evaluation of the theoretical capacity of a New Zealand harbour to carry a human population. *Tane* (Journal of the Auckland University Field Club), **13**, 3–11.

SHAWCROSS, W. (1969) Archaeology with a short, isolated time-scale: New Zealand. *World Archaeology,* **1** (2), 184–99.

SHAWCROSS, W. (1970) Ethnographic economics and the study of population in prehistoric New Zealand: viewed through archaeology. *Mankind,* **7** (4), 279–91.

SLOBODKIN, B. L. (1962) Energy in animal ecology. In CRAGG, J. B. (ed.) *Advances in Ecological Research,* Vol. I, 69–101. London: Academic Press.

SMART, C. D. and GREEN, R. C. (1962) A stratified dune site at Tairua, Coromandel. *Dominion Museum Records in Ethnology,* **1** (7), 243–66.

SUTTLES, W. (1968) Coping with abundance: subsistence on the Northwest coast. In LEE, R. B. and DEVORE, I. (eds.) *Man the Hunter,* 56–68. Chicago: Aldine.

TERRELL, J. E. (1967) Galatea Bay – the excavation of a beach stream midden site on Ponui Island in the Hauraki Gulf, New Zealand. *Transactions of the Royal Society of New Zealand, General,* **2** (3), 31–70.

TEVIOTDALE, D. (1932) The material culture of the moa-hunters in Murihiku. *Journal of the Polynesian Society,* **41** (162), 81–120.

THOMSON, J. J. (1931) *James Clerk Maxwell.* Cambridge: Cambridge University Press.

WELTY, J. C. (1964) *The Life of Birds.* London: Constable.

WHITE, L. A. (1943) Energy and the evolution of culture. *American Anthropologist,* n.s. **45** (3), 335–56.

WHITE, L. A. (1949) *The Science of Culture.* New York: Grove Press.

WHITE, L. A. (1959) *The Evolution of Culture.* New York: McGraw-Hill.

WHITE, T. E. (1953) A method of calculating the dietary percentage of various food animals utilized by aboriginal peoples. *American Antiquity,* **18**, 396–8.

621

WIENER, N. (1965) *Cybernetics*. Cambridge, Mass.: M.I.T. Press.

WOLMAN, A. (1956) Disposal of man's wastes. In THOMAS, W. L. (ed.) *Man's Role in Changing the Face of the Earth*, 807–16. Chicago: University of Chicago Press.

YEALLAND, S. and HIGGS, E. S. (1966) The economy. In HILTON, R. H. and RAHTZ, P. A., Upton, Gloucestershire, 1959–1964. *Transactions of the Bristol and Gloucestershire Archaeological Society*, **85**, 139–43.

15

Ethno-historic and ecological settings for economic and social models of an Iron Age society: Valldalen, Norway

K. ODNER

University of Bergen, Norway

Introduction

The usage of the term 'model' in this essay can conveniently be subdivided into three groups: universal, analogous and predictive models.

On account of its fragmentary nature archaeological material can frequently be meaningfully interpreted in a variety of contexts. Pertinent to the phenomena one wants to explore there is a need to organize the information available in its widest possible context. *Universal models* can be looked upon as convenient tools for presenting in a structured and simplified form all the empirical data on the subject.

Surprisingly, many archaeologists use models with spatial and temporal limitations, when universal models would have been more relevant. For example, there is a tendency to explain prehistoric economic patterns on principles derived from our own economy, not taking into consideration that the economies in most primitive societies are structured differently (Dalton, 1961).

Under certain conditions *an analogous model*, which is derived from a study of a known society, can be very useful. If cultural continuity to the prehistoric society can be demonstrated, the elements in the model might be manipulated in order to give reasoned predictions about cultural conditions in the previous society. The underlying principle is that most cultures, even if they undergo changes due to adaptations, for a long time maintain a stable cultural core: 'When acted upon by external forces a culture will, if necessary, undergo specific changes only to the extent of and with the effect of *preserving* unchanged its fundamental structure and character' (Harding, 1960, p. 54).

623

Even if the universality of this statement is disputed, the concept can be conceived as a stepping stone from which problems of interpretation can be attacked. By way of illustration an analogous model might also be put into use when a certain problem needs to be tested in a real-world situation.

The models I have called *predictive* are interpretations based on reasoning by means of universal and analogous models, and upon conformity to archaeological and environmental reality. It is important to note that frequently not only one, but several or a range of interpretations might be given. Ideally the model(s) should be the framework of all possible interpretations.

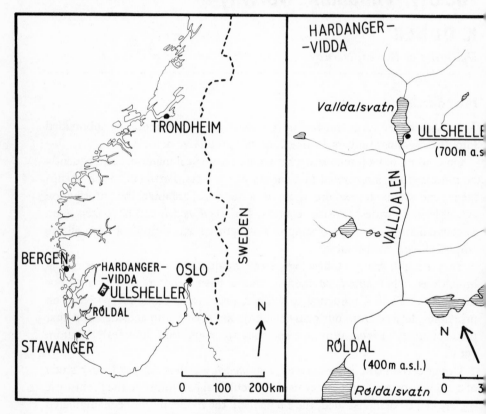

FIG. 15.1. The Ullshelleren site, Valldalen area, Norway.

Models are universally employed and shared by individuals within a culture in order to obtain a simplified picture of the essential characteristics of the culture. This important aspect of the nature of models is the justification for treating the Icelandic sagas in this essay as a source material on the old Icelandic society.

This study is based on specific archaeological material, namely the results of excavations in Ullshelleren rock shelter situated in Valldalen in the south-western mountain area of Norway (Fig. 15.1). The discussion will be centred around the problem of ecological reconstructions. What were the possibilities for survival for people in the Early Iron Age? I will discuss different alternatives:

(1) The group may exclusively have exploited local resources without any interference or aid from the outside. How could the resources be utilized in order to meet their need for calories?

(2) The group may have had exchange relations with other groups. Its survival would then have been dependent upon the efforts and cultural values of an undefined number of persons. In this case estimates of the calorie yield of resources will be irrelevant, but one can ask: What were the structural possibilities for people in Ullshelleren to participate in exchange relations?

The geographical background

Valldalen is a valley about 10 km long. It is situated about 700 m above sea level in a subalpine vegetation zone. The average temperature for January is $-6°$ to $-7°C$ and for July $+11°C$. The valley bottom is flat while the sides are steep. Areas of grass are found in the valley bottom. Vegetation on the valley sides consists mainly of a light birch forest, but there are possibilities for grazing, especially suitable for goats.

Higher country with glaciers and peaks up to 1700 m above sea level lies east and west of Valldalen. Towards the north the terrain is also considerably higher, and it gradually merges with Hardangervidda, an old mountain plain between 1100 and 1400 m above sea level. Reindeer, grouse and hare are the most important animal species in this country.

About 15 km to the south lies Röldal, a parish with 715 inhabitants. Agriculture is the most important occupation, especially livestock production. Röldal is the only place that has permanent settlement in this isolated mountain world.

The subsistence activities in Valldalen are likely to be conditioned by or related to the following three features: (1) *Grass in the valley bottom and on the slopes*. This yields good opportunities for summer grazing of cattle and for fodder collection. (2) *The birch forest*. This forms an important link in the yearly cycles of certain wild animals, particularly grouse and hare. When the snow during the winter covers the treeless surrounding areas, animals of these

625

species, which in the summer season inhabit a much wider area, migrate to Valldalen in order to feed on the birch trees. (3) *Easy accessibility to the huge flocks of reindeer in the surrounding high mountains.*

Excavation and pollen analysis

The total inhabitable area of Ullshelleren was 50 m², while the actually excavated area was somewhat less. The excavation, which had a maximum depth of 160 cm was carried out in artificial spits of varying depths. There is no reason to believe that reversal of layers has taken place.

According to the archaeological finds the spits above 20 cm from the surface belong mainly to a recent period. The spits between 20 and 100 cm seem exclusively to have been deposited between A.D. 300 and 700 (Late Roman Iron Age and the Migration Period). Two C14 dates produced the following results: 1700 ± 90 B.P. and 1610 ± 90 B.P. The ecological analysis will be based on the archaeological and faunal material from these spits only. The lowermost layers were mainly undatable and contained very few finds.

Animal bones in the layers between 20 and 100 cm were predominantly from five (six?) species: (1) domestic animals (cow, sheep and/or goat), (2) reindeer, (3) grouse, (4) hare. The quantity of bones was insufficient for statistical estimations of the diet.

In connection with the archaeological work pollen analysis was also carried out (Hafsten, 1965). In the profiles corresponding to Late Roman Iron Age/ Migration Period there was pollen from small nettle (*Urtica urens*) and small leafed plantain (*Plantago lanceolata*), and a substantial quantity of pollen from wild grass. These findings strongly indicate that the grazing of domestic animals had taken place, and also that human beings were present. Formerly many predators such as bear, wolf and wolverine inhabited this area, and the livestock were never left unattended.

The archaeological and faunal material, together with the results from the pollen analysis, indicate that the settlement was permanent. Almost all the bones from grouse belonged to adult birds. One must assume that most grouse catching took place in the season when the birds were fully grown – that is, the winter season. But pollen analysis confirms that animals and people must have inhabited Valldalen during the summer season as well. Eight to ten individuals were the maximum number Ullshelleren could possibly have had room for. Artefacts and/or activities, which can clearly be associated with women (spindle whorls, relief brooch) and men (arrow heads), indicate that the unit occupying Ullsheller may have been of the family type.

The archaeology of Valldalen: forms of exploitation of resources
Thorough archaeological explorations were carried out in Valldalen in connection with hydroelectric developments. In addition to Ullsheller the findings include one Middle Neolithic settlement, two rock carving sites from the Late Bronze Age, one house site, a quarry for mountain crystal from the Viking Period and forty-five abandoned house sites later than A.D. 1500. The archaeological picture tends to show that exploitation of resources in Valldalen must have been more intensive in the period after A.D. 1500 than in earlier periods.

It is commonly advocated in Scandinavian archaeology that models based on contemporary or recent peasant culture in the areas concerned are vital in order to understand prehistoric economic patterns. My objection to this is that these models are not universal. Used critically they are valuable, but they are inadequate as the sole instrument for the reconstruction of the past. I shall try to demonstrate this through an analysis of exploitation patterns in Valldalen after A.D. 1500.

The valley has been used for herding. For instance, in the spring merchants bought cattle in the fjord valleys in the western part of Norway, and they kept the animals grazing in Valldalen during the summer. In the autumn they drove them to the eastern part, and sold the animals for slaughter on the markets. This form of exploitation of the pastures in Valldalen was of great significance between A.D. 1740 and 1800.

A somewhat different form of exploitation took place between A.D. 1840 and 1964. For a fee the peasants in the fjord valleys rented out some of their domestic animals to people in Röldal who had grazing rights in Valldalen. This was of mutual benefit to the partners. In the coastal areas, where the cattle were kept in the open most of the winter, the pastures could be conserved. The peasants in Röldal, on the other hand, were able to convert an otherwise unexploited resource into capital (Blom, 1969).

Valldalen has also been utilized for permanent settlements. There is no evidence to prove unbroken settlement over a wide time span, but in distinct periods habitation has taken place, especially about 1660 and in the period between 1800 and 1938. The permanent settlement reached its largest size in the nineteenth century, and at least seven different places were then permanently inhabited in Valldalen.

The use of mountain pastures for transhumance ('sætring') was of course undertaken from farms in Röldal, but not to any great extent. It seems not to have commenced before about 1700. Of the animals grazing on the Valldalen pastures in the more recent periods only 7–8% of the goats and 20–30% of the

627

cattle belonged to farmers in Röldal. The most probable explanation of the fact that farmers in Röldal only exploited pastures in Valldalen to a small extent is that they had sizeable grazing areas closer to their homes. This seems to have been sufficient for a small population keeping as many animals as they were able to on fodder gathered around their home site. It was only when the population increased that the pastures in Valldalen had to be utilized: 250 persons lived in Röldal in 1660, a steady increase in the population took place in the following centuries, and in 1855 it had grown to 922 persons.

In order to explain conditions in the Early Iron Age, these modern exploitation patterns seem to be of comparatively limited value.

The first two patterns can be seen as a response to the industrialization which took place in the eighteenth and nineteenth centuries, involving a comparatively large non food producing population and a market economy, affecting the peasant's need for capital. An additional reason for rental of livestock was a general shortage of female working power, which made it more profitable to concentrate on larger production units. These two patterns must be considered as culturally specific, and irrelevant as models for the prehistoric situation.

The evidence of farms in Valldalen is highly interesting, since in the present Norwegian culture the climatic zone in which Valldalen is located is considered to be marginal to, or unsuitable for, permanent settlement. Grain or root crops will normally not ripen, and the people would have to rely on other activities, like animal husbandry or hunting, for a living.

Animal husbandry and hunting are the very activities upon which the models of exploitation of local resources during the Early Iron Age are based. The modern pattern might have been used as an analogous and manipulative model, had it not been for the fact that the peasants also relied on participation in the encroaching capitalistic society for a living. This makes it difficult to assess the importance of the local resources in a total setting.

The limited use of the Valldalen pastures for transhumance from Röldal highlights the importance of a proper analysis. Certainly, transhumance is what the Scandinavian archaeologist more or less automatically would think of in connection with a site like Ullsheller. As it is, I find it highly unlikely that transhumance can explain the archaeological features. Röldal was inhabited during the Early Iron Age, but the population was probably less than in 1660, since the area of settlement was extended during the Viking Period. In accordance with the arguments already given, the grazing opportunities around Röldal would then have been sufficient.

I shall now turn to the alternative approaches which I chose to use.

Alternative I

A family will be used as the basic unit for estimates of the efficiency of the working group, and as the consumption group. For quantification purposes we may assume that the family consists of two adults and three children. The yearly requirement of calories is estimated to be 4 356 000 calories (man 3300, woman 2800, each child 2000 calories per day).

As mentioned earlier, the bones from the layers belonging to the Late Roman Iron Age/Migration Period indicated that people had mainly exploited four resources: domestic animals, reindeer, grouse and hare. I will try to show *how* these resources could be utilized to meet the family's need for calories. Firstly, I will estimate the maximum return in calories from each of the four resources, and secondly, I intend to show how these resources could be used complementarily during one year.

ECOLOGICAL MODELS: GENERATION OF CHOICE AND CARRYING CAPACITY

Fig. 15.2 is an attempt to explicate the factors generating decisions when two or more resources might be exploited simultaneously. People are presented with a situation of choice of how to use their labour. The lower columns in the model represent quantitative and qualitative components of value of the crop, which in their turn are dependent on the variation of local resources and on people's ability to exploit these technically and organizationally. The latter variables are presented in the three upper columns, and each of the columns represents an exploitable resource.

When considering which resource to exploit, the average amount of expected energy capture will be significant. It is, however, also important that the resource contains an element of stability in utilization over an extended period. Stability can be achieved through skill and technology. One also has to take into consideration a reasonable margin of security. This is especially important in connection with resources with pronounced *fluctuations* (Fig. 1.15).

All social groups and individuals act according to patterns, which from a biophysical point of view may be unprofitable or totally irrational. The co-variations between cultural/psychological and techno/ecological factors produce these decisions.

The model, Fig. 15.3, has been developed from the above generative model. It may be looked upon as a static model, the purpose of which is to evaluate the maximum carrying capacity of each resource. Labour is considered, and psychological and cultural value considerations are irrelevant.

629

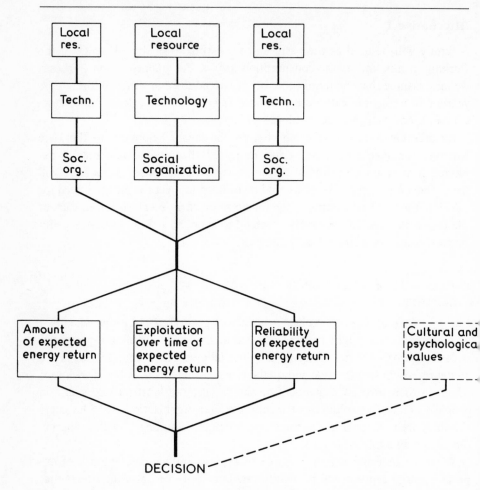

FIG. 15.2. Flow chart modelling decisions for the simultaneous exploitation of several resources.

MAXIMUM RETURN IN CALORIES FROM THE FOUR RESOURCES

Domestic animals (cow, sheep/goat)

The critical determinant of the number of domestic animals people could maintain in Valldalen (as in other Norwegian mountain valleys) was the amount of winter fodder available, and not the size of the summer pastures. Agricultural experiments in Valldalen show that the average yield of grass per 1000 m² unfertilized soil is 127 fodder units (F.U.). The climatic conditions in

630

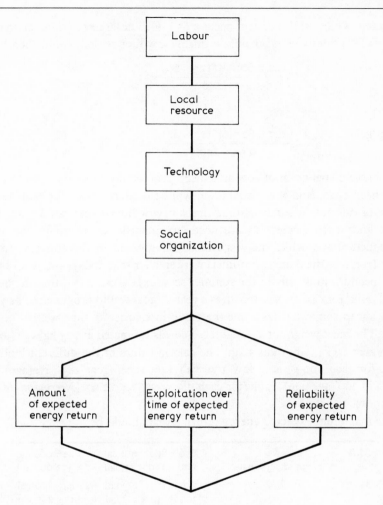

Fig. 15.3. Model of the capacity of a single resource.

Valldalen in the Early Iron Age should permit sixty days of fodder gathering annually. There is archaeological evidence that the equipment used for fodder gathering during the Early Iron Age was similar to that used in Norway 50 to 100 years ago. By using historical analogies, we may infer that a man should have been able to gather fodder from 1000 m² a day. The quantity of fodder could be increased by one third by collecting auxiliary fodder (twigs, moss, etc.) throughout the winter. The feeding of animals with winter fodder lasts about eight months annually. A cow needs 2·5 F.U. a day as a

631

minimum, while a sheep or goat needs 0·65 F.U. The largest number of domestic animals a family could maintain during a winter season would then be:

Cow:
$$\frac{(127 \times 60) + \frac{1}{3}(127 \times 60)}{2\cdot5 \times 240} = 16\cdot9 : 17$$

or

Sheep/goat:
$$\frac{(127 \times 60) + \frac{1}{3}(127 \times 60)}{0\cdot65 \times 240} = 65\cdot1 : 65$$

A probable distribution of cow and sheep/goat would be six cows and thirty-four sheep/goats, and this distribution will be used as a basis for estimates of return of calories. We may assume that a cow will have one calf a year. Two calves and seven lambs/kids are necessary in order to maintain the stock mentioned above, while the rest can be slaughtered in the autumn. In the Early Iron Age the domestic animals were smaller than today, and would probably produce milk only in the summer season. It is estimated that the quantity of milk from a cow was 800 litres a year. A goat would produce 160 l a year, and a sheep somewhat less, but the value in calories is supposed to be the same. The meat weight of a slaughtered cow is estimated at 125 kg, calf 30 kg, sheep/goat 10 kg, lamb/kid 5 kg. The calorie values of the different kinds of meat (for each 100 g) are: cow 179, calf 146, sheep/goat 283 (average) and lamb/kid 200 (average); milk (for each dl): cow 67, goat 62 (*Næringsmiddeltabell*, 1961).

The maximum expected energy return a year should be:

Milk:	6 cows	(670 × 800 × 6) cal	= 3 216 000 cal
	34 sheep/goats	(620 × 160 × 34) cal	= 3 372 000 cal
Meat:	2 cows	(1250 × 179 × 2) cal	= 447 500 cal
	4 calves	(300 × 146 × 4) cal	= 175 200 cal
	7 sheep/goats	(100 × 283 × 7) cal	= 198 100 val
	27 lambs/kids	(50 × 200 × 27) cal	= 270 000 cal
Total:			7 679 000 cal

The calculation would probably hold for a normal year. Throughout a succession of years, however, 'bad' years are bound to happen. The minimum yield for these years is estimated to be about half the amount of calories in a normal year (3 839 500 cal). A distribution of calories over time is possible by control of slaughter and coupling, and further by techniques of cheese making, churning and salting (of which there is archaeological evidence; Clark, 1952) and storage and drying.

Reindeer

In 1964 the reindeer stock on Hardangervidda and on the surrounding areas east and west of Valldalen (4800 km^2) numbered 25 000 animals. This is regarded as optimal for an efficient exploitation of the pastures. The number of animals in the Early Iron Age would normally hardly have been less. Wide fluctuations in animal populations in stable environments are unlikely to occur (Wrigley, 1967). I have argued elsewhere (Odner, 1969) that the observed recent fluctuations probably are due to the introduction of modern firearms. It would be too long to go into details here, but it might be mentioned that observations from Alaska tend to confirm this (Skoog, 1959).

The hunting equipment used was probably bow and arrow. In contrast to many other parts of the mountain area in southern Norway, very few animal trapping pits have been discovered. On the other hand, there are many finds of prehistoric iron arrows – supposedly lost while hunting. There were also many arrow heads of quartzite in the debris in Ullsheller.

If one takes into consideration the density of the reindeer and the hunting equipment used, it ought to have been possible for one man to hunt, kill, quarter and bring home (with a horse) two animals per day. The yield might have been augmented if two men were working together.

Throughout a year one would, however, expect a much lesser average. Allowing for days when hunting was unprofitable because of bad weather, the disadvantageous dispersal of animals, or just bad luck, I find that 180 animals a year is what an average hunter normally could hope for.

The average meat weight of reindeer is 35 kg. Each 100 g unspecified reindeer meat contains 124 cal. The maximum energy return of reindeer hunting should then be:

$$124 \text{ cal } (180 \times 350) = 7\ 812\ 000 \text{ cal}$$

Reindeer must be regarded as a comparatively reliable resource, since they are quite numerous. By the use of conservation techniques like salting and drying it should have been possible to utilize the meat over time in periods of shortage.

Grouse

Ecologically Valldalen is particularly good for grouse catching during the winter. Conversely, this is the only season when this activity could profitably have been pursued. Snow directs the grouse movements from the barren mountains to the valley, and it is also an element of the most efficient catching technique – snaring.

Snaring is a very old and widespread technique. There is evidence that

633

snares were used in Sweden during the Late Bronze Age (Clark, 1952, p. 39). We can infer that the people in Ullsheller knew this technique. Comparisons with catch results from the nineteenth and twentieth centuries show that 550 grouse is a good catch in a winter season. The meat weight of a grouse is about 250 g, and it contains 110 cal per 100 g. Yearly yield in calories should be:

$$110 \ cal \ (550 \times 2 \cdot 5) = 151 \ 250 \ cal$$

The possibility of exploiting this resource over time was somewhat reduced by its seasonal character, and the reliability of the expected energy return is low. Variations in basic living conditions, such as weather during the breeding season and relation to other animal species living in the same ecological milieu, produces variations ranging from bad to excellent in the quantity of grouse from year to year.

Hare

Almost all of what has already been said about the grouse applies to the hare. In some years the hare is plentiful, while in other years it is so scarce that one is tempted to believe that the species is dying out. Snaring seems to have been the most common technique during the winter season, and a catch of 100 hares a season seems to be reasonable estimate (by analogy). One hare weighs about 3·5 kg, and the meat weight is about 1·75 kg, containing 120 cal per 100 g. Yield in calories:

$$120 \ cal \ (100 \times 17 \cdot 5) = 210 \ 000 \ cal$$

Possibilities of exploiting the resource over time and reliability are the same as for the grouse.

COMPLEMENTARY EXPLOITATION OF THE RESOURCES THROUGHOUT THE YEAR

There are many ways in which a group can adapt itself to an ecological milieu. There is, however, a limit to organizational variation, mainly dependent on how plants and animals convert sun energy into common energy. This limit seems to be absolute, but social and other techniques make it relative. Given a certain technology some variations of organizational forms will cease to exist because of scarcity of bio-substances and uncertainty of energy return. Some ecological decisions will biophysically be more profitable than others. If ecology and technology are approximately the same in different areas, the way people get their necessities of life (how they socially organize their

634

	Summer	Autumn	Winter	Spring	Number of domestic animals
NJUNJES, Norrland, Sweden(a)	*Women:* domestic animals fodder gathering *Men:* fishing some fodder gathering	*Women:* domestic animals berrying *Men:* bird catching (capercailzie, black grouse)	*Women:* domestic animals *Men:* catching (esp. grouse and hare)	*Women:* domestic animals *Men:* fishing bird catching (capercailzie and black grouse)	circ. 4 cows 12–18 sheep
AMMARNÄS, Norrland, Sweden(b)	*Women:* domestic animals fodder gathering *Men:* fodder gathering	*Women:* domestic animals fodder gathering *Men:* fodder gathering bird catching (capercailzie and black grouse)	*Women:* domestic animals *Men:* grouse catching	*Women:* domestic animals *Men:* bird catching (capercailzie) fodder gathering (twigs, bark, etc.)	circ. 10 cows circ. 30 sheep 2–3 horses
BARDU, Troms, Norway(c)	*Women:* domestic animals herding *Men:* fodder gathering	*Women:* domestic animals *Men:* fodder gathering fishing bird catching (capercailzie and black grouse)	*Women:* domestic animals *Men:* home-driving of summer hay some fodder gathering grouse catching	*Women:* domestic animals *Men:* fodder gathering (auxiliary fodder)	circ. 7 cows circ. 14 sheep/ goat 1 horse (average on 9 farms, after bishop Krogh 1806)

(a) Campbell 1948.   (b) Campbell, 1948.   (c) Eggen 1950.

FIG. 15.4. The yearly cycle of work – three pioneer models.

activities) tends to be more similar the closer one gets to the minimum limit of biophysical profit (that is, survival). The condition is that people live in a situation of ecological isolation.

Such situations existed in Scandinavia during the period of pioneering. There are known examples from several places like Inner Norrland and from Målselv valley in Norway. There are no wild reindeer left in these areas, but apart from that the ecology is very similar to that in Valldalen. One has further to assume that the technology mastered by the inhabitants of Ullsheller must have been comparatively similar to that used by the pioneers. Three models of how resources were exploited are shown in Fig. 15.4. They indicate many organizational similarities, such as type, progress and allocation of work. To a certain extent these are environmentally determined, such as fodder gathering during the summer and grouse catching during the winter. Variations in decisions of ecological relevance, such as allocation of work, are also co-determinant of organizational forms: in Njunjes men can fish during the summer and leave most of the fodder gathering to women; or they can, as in Ammarnäs and Bardu, completely concentrate their activities around fodder gathering. In Ullsheller the men could possibly have used their labour either for fodder gathering or for reindeer hunting in the summer season. Two models have been constructed, representing these organizational solutions (Fig. 15.5).

		Summer/Autumn	*Winter*	*Spring*	*Number of dom. animals*
Model I	Women	domestic animals fodder gathering	dom. animals grouse and hare snaring	dom. animals	6 cows 34 sheep/ goats
	Men	fodder gathering	reindeer hunting	fodder gathering, (auxiliary fodder)	
Model II	Women	as in model I	as above	as above	2 cows 11 sheep/ goats 1 horse
	Men	reindeer hunting, some food gathering	reindeer hunting	reindeer hunting	

FIG. 15.5. Two alternative models for the Ullsheller annual cycle.

The total yield in calories according to model I

Animal husbandry	between	7 679 600	and	3 839 800 cal
Grouse catching	„	151 250	„	0 „
Hare catching	„	210 000	„	0 „
Reindeer hunting	„	3 255 000	„	? „
Total	„	11 295 850	„	3 839 800 + ? cal

and according to model II

Animal husbandry	between	2 559 867	and	1 279 933 cal
Grouse catching	„	151 250	„	0 „
Hare catching	„	210 000	„	0 „
Reindeer hunting	„	7 812 000	„	? „
Total	„	10 733 117	„	1 279 933 + ? cal

The minimum yield from reindeer hunting has been left open as I find it impossible to quantify. I do not, however, expect it to be less than half the yield in a normal year.

By comparing these figures to the yearly need of 4 356 000 cal, one can conclude that people normally had possibilities to invest time in less profitable activities without disturbing the ecological balance. It is not my intention to maintain that these two solutions are the only possible ones. They represent extreme points in a continuum.

Alternative II

Economy is considered to be structured arrangements for providing material goods and services. To assure constancy the economy must be embedded in social and economical institutions. These institutions give the scope and limitation for the transactions which can take place. From an archaeological point of view it implies that a study of the institutional matrix is just as important as a study of the artefact features.

The society to be investigated is that of western Norway between about A.D. 300 and 600–700. This is considered to be the territorial and chronological milieu of the people in Ullsheller. The time span corresponds broadly to the Migration Period of Scandinavian archaeology (the time usually allocated to the Migration Period is A.D. 400 to 600; the author shares the view with other

Scandinavian archaeologists that the period meaningfully could be extended both backwards and forwards in time).

I shall briefly mention some characteristic archaeological features of western Norway during the period in question:

(1) There seems to be an 'expansion' during the period. Among other things 'this expansion is characterized by a series of innovations such as "pail-shaped" pots, cruciform brooches, unusually many gold objects in the graves, and new types of bronze and glass vessels' (Herteig, 1955). At the same time a new grave type – the imposing stone cist – comes into being.

  In contrast to the new grave type with finds in the luxury class, the burial custom of the preceding period was egalitarian and 'poor'. The latter also persisted throughout the Migration Period.

(2) Coinciding with the above 'expansion' there is a sudden increase in habitation in rock shelters and caves along the entire length of the coast – often on very exposed locations. They cannot be considered as seasonal hunting camps on account of the faunal material, artefacts normally associated with female activities and human remains, ranging from new born babies to old women.

  With the coming of the Late Iron Age there is a marked decrease in habitation in caves and rock shelters.

(3) The majority of the many hilltop forts seem to have been constructed between the fifth and the seventh centuries, although few excavations have been carried out to prove this statement (Hagen, 1967, p. 147).

  Since warrior graves also abound we may infer a warlike attitude of the population and some form of social and military organization.

(4) A substantial number of bronze cauldrons and glass vessels, produced in the Rhine valley, found their way to western Norway during the Migration Period. Articles for daily use, however, were produced locally. This contrasts with conditions in the Late Iron Age, when whetstones, soapstone bowls and iron bars were widely distributed.

(5) Weapons and ornaments of gold, and silver and bronze objects – although of local design – show basic similarities to those in the entire west European Germanic area. This indicates a network of contacts on a large scale for the leaders of the society.

Few Scandinavian archaeologists today would probably quarrel with Asbjörn Herteig, who claims that the archaeological evidence shows internal development from the preceding period, indicating ethnic continuity (Herteig, 1955). The socio-economic relationships – if any – remain, however, to be explored. These, and the organizational consequences for the people in Ullsheller, will be considered in the remaining part of the article.

As no frontal attack on the problem of institutional patterns seemed feasible, a more indirect approach was applied – utilizing the Icelandic society in the Middle Ages as a model. It was based on information about the daily life of the Icelanders as it appears in the 'Family Sagas'.

At this point some clarification on the use of the Icelandic sagas as a source material may be welcome. The sagas were mostly written in the thirteenth century, but the events with which they are concerned are supposed to have taken place in the ninth and tenth centuries. It would have been unrealistic and partly irrelevant to argue that they contain the full historical truth. The institutions described, however, are probably comparatively accurate descriptions of those of the society as it existed when the sagas were written, or within memory of the population. A minimum of mental organizational models of their society must have been shared by the participants in the society, including the author(s) and the readers. A too distant deviation from these models is unlikely to have been tolerated.

We may infer that there is a cultural continuity between the pre-Viking society of western Norway and that of medieval Iceland. Traditions, archaeological finds, place names, etc., all agree that the Icelanders were predominantly made up of people who migrated from western Norway in the ninth and tenth centuries (Mageröy, 1965). The common reason given for their migrations was that they wanted to maintain their social structure as it was before king Harald Fair Hair became the sole ruler of Norway (about A.D. 900). In other words, *they underwent changes in order to preserve unchanged the fundamental structure and character of their society* (see p. 623). In the centuries following the first settlement the society was gradually modified. Still we may assume that the fundamental character was maintained until the submission under the Norwegian crown in 1262–4.

The assumed linear cultural development makes a model of the structuring of the economy on Iceland particularly relevant for predicting economic conditions in the earlier society. By changing the elements in the model (the social, economical and ideological institutions in which the economy was embedded) to fit conditions in western Norway during the Migration Period, a hypothesis on the economic arrangements may be formed.

The medieval Icelanders inhabited a country with a variety of resources. There were rich pastures, and fish, sea birds, seals and whales were also

639

abundant. Furthermore there were inexhaustible supplies of fuel in the form of driftwood and peat from the bogs. It might be added that the country was not too dissimilar to the country from where the people came.

A reasonable estimate of the Icelandic population is 60 000 (Foote and Wilson, 1970). Animal husbandry was probably the most important single occupation, but all the resources mentioned were exploited. Basically the country could provide for all the necessities of life.

The fundamental social unit was the farm. The people living on the farm must be considered as a corporate unit for management and defence purposes. These small entities were, however, vulnerable to attack, and commonly we find farms organized in larger units with variable political coherence.

The type of organization that gave the farmers the best protection was the semi-military organization headed by the titled chieftains – the *godar*. The *godar* were the political and judicial leaders of the society, but they had no central executive power. Their followers were called *thingmen*. Their chief obligation was to escort the *godi* to the annual judicial meetings, the *things*. The *things* settled disputes, but nobody had to abide by a court decision if he was sufficiently powerful to resist an attack. The structural distances between the groups had to be maintained by force if no agreement could be reached. The *thing* gatherings frequently degenerated into regular battles between opposing forces.

There were controls on the ambitions of the individual *godi*. Theoretically the farmers had the right to choose the *godi* they wanted to follow, but we may assume that this right was frequently illusory. The constitution provided that the number of *godar* should be forty-eight. This distribution of power controlled the ambitious reciprocally.

Solidarity within the nuclear family – and to a lesser degree within the extended family – was observed. Marriages were conceived as extensions of family solidarity, and amounted to alliances between the families involved. Solidarity could also be obtained through adoption and foster-brotherhood. As the leaders endeavoured to marry into other influential families, a widely dispersed network of family-based alliances in the upper class of society was developed. The alliances were, however, temporary arrangements. Conflicting loyalties and the geographical distances involved tended to destroy the alliances after a comparatively short time.

An aspect of the custom of intermarriage within the higher echelon of the society was that it gave opportunities for mobility to persons belonging to this class. A person could visit a kin relation and expect to be entertained. Fig. 15.6

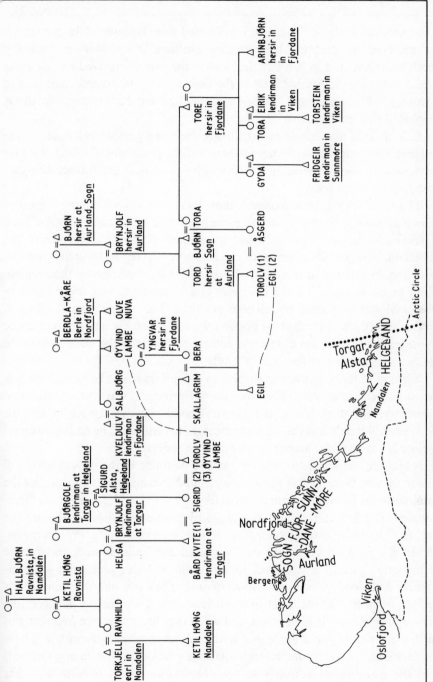

FIG. 15.6. Genealogy from Egil Skallagrimsson's Saga.

is a genealogy from Egil's saga. It is presented as an example of the geographical dispersal and distances between close kinsmen. It includes persons living both in Iceland and in Norway. In Norway they are distributed mainly along the coast, from the Arctic Circle to the Oslo Fjord. The central characters in the saga – Skallagrim and his brother, and Egil and his brother – intensely exploited the relationships.

It is obvious that family-based alliances between persons belonging to the inferior social classes would have a more limited geographical scope. We may assume that the opportunities for mobility decreased the further one descended the social scale.

The farm was the basic economic unit. Its growth as an economic organization was severely limited by its vulnerability to attack. To ensure 'peace' even a successful farmer commonly had to channel some of the surplus to the chieftain. The contributions to the chieftain were described by social customs, and may in relation to the *godar* also be viewed as justified by the religion. Both in the heathen and the Christian Old Icelandic society the position of the *godar* was sanctioned by religious practices. The central position of a *godi* in the society gave him the best possibilities to extract, but any person may be considered as a chieftain if he could enforce or persuade the other farmers to deliver surplus to him (pp. 843–7, 855).

A group of farms delivering surplus to a chieftain might be looked upon as an economic structure. The structuring principle was the institutional centricity, but there was also a personal bond between the leader and his followers. Not only had the chieftain the right to confiscate; he had also a moral obligation to provide succour in time of acute shortage.

A bias for reciprocal cooperation can also be found in the uneven nature of the resources. Some of the resources are available in quantities only during the summer – for instance, pastures, grass for winter fodder, eggs from sea birds, salmon. The full utilization is hampered by problems of how to allocate the labour. Distributional specialization is one way of solving the problems. When the produce from each unit is pooled and redistributed, an effective exploitation pattern is obtained. Other resources occur erratically – for instance, driftwood, whales or a shoal of seal. They can only be utilized if a person is present at the exact moment it occurs. There might, however, be long and lean periods in between, and when they occur they are frequently of such a magnitude that a single unit would not know what to do with it. These problems can be overcome through exchange relations within an organization, but the institutional reason that the organization could operate was that centricity in the group had been obtained (see pp. 508–10).

The theoretical considerations can be substantiated with an example:

Skallagrim was a great shipbuilder and there was no lack of driftwood west along the Myres (his first farm). He made a farmstead at Alptanes, and had there a second dwelling: he worked from there out-rowing and seal-fishing and egg-taking, seeing there was then enough of all those takings, and so too of driftwood to bring home with him. Then also were there great comings of whales ashore, and a man might shoot as he would. . . .

A third dwelling had he by the seaside westward of Myres. There were yet better sittings for drifts, and there he sowed the land and called the place Acres. Isles lay there out from the land where whales were found.

Skallagrim had men of his also up by the salmon rivers for fishing. Odd Live-Alone he set up by Gorge-water to mind the salmon fisheries there. . . . Sigmund was a man, whom Skallagrim set by Northwater. He dwelt there where it was called Sigmundstead. Afterwards he moved his homestead . . . to a readier place for salmon fisheries.

But when Skallagrim's livestock was much increased, then went the cattle all up on the fells in the summer. He found there was great odds in this, that those beasts became better and fatter, which went on the heaths, and this too that the sheep throve a-winters in the mountain dales, even though they could not be driven down. So now Skallagrim made a farm-stead up by the fells, and had a dwelling there: and there tended his sheep.

And now stood Skallagrim's estate on many feet. (from Egil Skallagrim's saga)

The chieftain's role as a central figure in the economic structure makes an analysis of his decisions on the allocation of the commodities collected, crucial for a deeper understanding of the economic life. We may infer that the cultural values of the chieftain were centred on prestige and the optimization of his position as a leader of the group and *vis-à-vis* other chieftains.

The products produced within the group were of two kinds. One was subsistence products which were not sold on the open market. These could be allocated back into the organization in order to create growth, or to create a military organization for defence or attack purposes. Institutionally they could also be used to acquire alliances with other chieftains through feasts of honour or acts of generosity.

Certain items – particularly cloth (vadmal) and furs – were easily market-able, either directly in western Europe or through middlemen coming to Iceland. The money obtained through this exchange could be used to buy luxuries or prestigious objects for gifts, or for personal consumption. It was also possible to buy farmland, although this conversion seems to have been restricted.

The institution of gift exchange needs further elaboration. One gave 'gifts' in order to obtain something politically: alliances, avoidance of attack, etc. Acceptance of a gift signified that the alliance was accepted, refusal or destruction that the alliance was undesirable. The objects were articles of prestige: gold rings, beautiful weapons and clothes, horses, etc. The institutional reason for the gift exchange, and also for the feasts of honour and the acts of generosity, was the segmentation of the country.

According to Weber, there are three pure types of legitimate authority: (1) legal authority, (2) traditional authority, (3) charismatic authority (Weber, 1947). On Iceland the legitimate authority of the chieftain was overwhelmingly of the second category. In the case of the *godar* there was an important element of legal authority. When the *thingmen* chose which *godar* to follow, there must have been an element of charisma.

The legitimate position of a chieftain rested on rules of inheritance. The chieftain and his organization had mutual interests in maintaining the structure. The governing principle of supply was difference in status. Maintenance of the structure was dependent on a regular flow of material resources to the chieftain. Competition for authority was also a competition for material resources.

The system of transactions was instrumental in maintaining stability in the society. The weak point was the monetary exchange, particularly sale of farmland, and it was at this point that entrepreneurial activities could set in. Money alone would have given access to a limited number of conversions. Using the egalitarian values of monetary exchange for buying farms, one obtained admission into a circuit where status was the governing principle. Men whose careers had been based on monetary transactions were sometimes – although grudgingly – admitted into the chiefly circles.

When fur and cloth were converted through monetary exchange into objects destined for gift exchange, it can, however, be looked upon as an adaption of opportunities offered by more advanced societies for preservation of the stability in their own society. On the whole price-forming markets must be considered as incompatible with traditional authority. This was clearly understood by Max Weber: 'An *oikos* maintained by the chief, where needs are met on a liturgical basis wholly or primarily in kind, in the form of contributions of goods and compulsory services. In this case, economic relationships tend to be strictly bound to tradition. The developments of markets are obstructed, the use of money is primarily oriented to consumption, and the development of capitalism is impossible' (Weber, 1947, p. 325).

From this point of view it is hardly surprising that the interior trade was poorly developed (Gjerseth, 1924). There were no market places. The only professional tradesmen seem to have been pedlars who brought around low priced merchandise. The lack of central executive power might have been a contributing factor to this. Acquisition 'by courage' was still practised.

We must disregard the merchants coming to Iceland as instruments for free market exchange. Cautiously the ships anchored in the river estuaries, and the trade was carried out from there. The trade was administered by the chieftains, who imposed set prices on the merchandise, and high-handedly expelled the merchants if they did not comply with the regulations. This type of trade was of an archaic character, institutionally reminiscent, on a small scale, of the 'ports of trade', for instance, on the west African coast under the kingdom of Dahomey (Polanyi, 1963).

Introduction of bureaucratic administration, where the ultimate source of authority was derived from a king, would change the role of market economy in the society because:

(1) It would have a levelling effect on the authority of the chieftains.
(2) A king would institutionally be in a position to guarantee security within his dominion.

During the Viking Period, western Europe, Norway included, entered into a process of bureaucratization. Concomitant with the change in the political milieu was the introduction of marketing institutions: a monetary system and merchant guilds. The towns were initially 'ports of trade', but later on true market places came into existence. The Icelanders evaded this development for some centuries, and the level of socio-cultural integration remained the same as before the exodus to Iceland.

We may now proceed with an evaluation of the institutions – economic and non-economic – that might have influenced the economy in the Migration Period in western Norway. A detailed argument on the socio-cultural setting will be published elsewhere, and only the results of the findings will be presented.

First there is a need to stress the similarity in environment to that of Iceland. The country exhibits a varied selection of ecological niches. Within a relatively small area there might be opportunities for farming, pasturing, fishing, hunting and collecting. The Valldalen technological equipment was not significantly different from that of the Icelanders.

The people lived on isolated farms or, as described, in caves or rock shelters. The size of the house(s) on the farm indicates that it could be the home of an extended family.

It is likely that chieftains existed. The archaeological evidence suggests considerable differences in statuses. Runic inscriptions on tombstones make references to chiefly titles, known from the later literary periods (*erilaR* = earl).

It is unlikely that there were *thing* gatherings of the size and importance comparable to the national *things* of Iceland. The earliest Norwegian west coast legal federation (*Gulathing*) was apparently created during the reign of Harald Fair Hair. We must consequently assume that there were less constitutional controls on the ambition of the chieftains.

Bilateral kinship systems are characteristic of all known Teutonic societies (Phillpotts, 1913). The linguistic data from runic inscriptions and place names show that the population of western Norway during the Migration Period was speaking a Teutonic language. It seems not unrealistic to believe that they had a bilateral kinship system. The interpretation is of course conjectural, but it is interesting to note how closely the archaeological source material is in agreement with a concept of bilaterality. One structural implication of a bilateral kinship system as it was practised according to the model (Fig. 15.6) was a wide and mutually adjusted geographical dispersal between high ranking kinsmen. In this milieu ideas idiomatically related to this social class would easily diffuse, which could explain the similarities of élite weapons and styles within the west European Germanic area.

Exploitation of many different kinds of resources might be considered as characteristic for societies of this level of social development and in this type of environment. The central issue is that competition for material resources is also a competition for authority. In principle the opportunities for a corporate group to obtain control over a larger amount of resources are limited to:

(1) Aggressive seizure from another group.
(2) More intense exploitation of resources already existing in their own area.

The two alternatives are interrelated. The more intensely and more completely the different kinds of resources are exploited, the stronger becomes the group. The stronger the group, the more effectively can it encroach upon the resources of other groups or defend its own resources (positive feedback).

Previously it has been demonstrated how a chieftain, through the strategic location of serfs, could obtain a high energy yield when many of the ecological niches that existed within his immediate territory were fully exploited. The exposed outer coastline is a potentially rich area. Nature provides homes in the form of rock shelters or caves. From these a variety of economic activities could be pursued: fishing, sealing, egg collecting, etc. The management difficulties for one family have already been commented upon, and also how these could be overcome through participation in a redistributive economic organization.

Therefore it would seem likely that there is a *functional interrelationship between the emergence of chieftains and the increase in the habitation in caves and rock shelters along the Norwegian coast.* It is further assumed that the undermining of the chiefly authority, which set in during the Viking Period through the interrelated introductions of bureaucracy and marketing institutions, would make a dependence on material resources less crucial and cause a contraction of habitation.

Under such circumstances we must expect emphasis on values oriented towards maintenance of the group. In the emerging Viking society this was partly achieved through religious group ceremonies where the chieftain performed the role of priest. We must also expect warlike attitudes. Alliances might provide temporary security, but basically the group had to defend its territory alone. One consequence might be the construction of hilltop forts as sanctuaries. Warlike attitudes and values oriented towards maintenance preconceive a tightly knit structure of the group.

This seems to be behind the organizations of the settlers when they arrived on Iceland around A.D. 900. They did not arrive as single familes or as clusters of families. They arrived in blocks – maybe comprising 400–500 persons – under the leadership of chieftains who claimed large tracts of land for themselves and their followers. Singlehandedly the chieftain administered the religious ceremonies and the legal proceedings. It was only afterwards, apparently after struggles, that the more comprehensive but also looser type of organization which we encounter in the sagas was obtained. (Larusson, 1930)

The assumed tightly knit nature of the economic structures would inhibit the transactions of a trader operating in a market situation. As I have previously explained, the egalitarian values of the transactions are incompatible with the principle of status-oriented delivery within a chiefly organization. The political segmentation of the country would create safety risks and difficulties in mobility.

The difficulties were augmented by ignorance of money as an instrument for comparative evaluation and indirect exchange. A. W. Broegger (1921) has shown that weighed gold – sometimes in the form of necklaces – might have been used as atonement for slayings, but it is not likely that gold or any other objects could have been used for the more varied purposes that money is supposed to have in a monetary economic system.

The scope for market exchange seems consequently to have been restricted. The economic, social and political institutions were all working against it. Under such circumstances the uncritical adoption of concepts derived from modern capitalistic economic theory are not justifiable when interpreting the archaeological material. Concepts like 'gold standard of coinage' (Holst, 1936), 'a North Sea block conditioned by the commercial-political situation' (Aaberg, 1953), 'a firmly constructed commercial organization' (Slomann, 1955), seem out of place.

The economic techniques applied by the Icelanders for the establishment of alliances – feasts, generosity and particularly gifts – may be considered as characteristic for societies on this level of social integration: 'We may then consider that the spirit of gift-exchange is characteristic of societies which have passed the phase of "total presentation" (between clan and clan, family and family), but have yet not reached the stage of pure individual contract, the money market, sale proper, fixed price and weighed and coined money' (Mauss, 1954). The techniques are well attested in the south Germanic societies during the period of the Great Migrations (Mauss, 1954, p. 59). The practices are also well known from old Norse society. This has for a long time been recognized by romanticists who nostalgically cite stanzas from Hávamál ('High one's speech', i.e. words of Odin) about the unselfish generosity of the Norsemen of bygone days. This view, commonly associated with ethnocentricity, could sensibly have been substituted with the less heroic view that the reciprocal generosity simply was a method to establish alliances for mutual aid, functionally not too far removed from the much despised bribery.

Whilst feasts and generosity usually would leave no tangible evidence, the chances are that the gifts would, especially as the old Norsemen were in the habit of being interred with their most precious objects.

This leads to another problem: How can we distinguish between objects received as gifts, and objects obtained through other types of transactions, also subgrouped under the term trade.

Most archaeologists would probably be in agreement with Polanyi, who defines trade as a relatively peaceful method to acquire goods from a distance (Polanyi, 1957). This definition can, however, be used in such a variety of contexts that the true nature of each transaction tends to get blurred. For instance, in the Icelandic model it would include the following types: (1) the impersonal monetary market exchange, (2) the trade administered by the chieftains, (3) the gift exchange.

By concentrating on kinds of goods found in an archaeological context, however, something might be said about the predominant form of transaction in the society. The theory is that the kinds will reflect the type of transaction, because this is conditioned by the level of economic integration. In a well-integrated market society the impersonal market will release a wide range of commodities to all walks of life. In chiefly societies prestige articles are the most likely goods to be exchanged. Commodities related to subsistence activities would normally not be exchanged except as occasional acts of generosity or through similar channels of conversion. It would be most unwise for a chieftain to budget the existence of his group on repetitive deliveries from bodies outside his jurisdiction.

The bronze cauldrons and the glass vessels that were imported to western Norway during the Migration Period can be considered as goods of prestige. Although the cauldrons were used as ossuaries, their primary function must have been as containers for drinks. In the old Germanic cultures – particularly in Scandinavia – drinking intoxicating beverages loomed heavily in the religious and social life (Foote and Wilson, 1970, p. 402). Odin himself lived on wine alone. It seems inevitable that the important functions of drinking should invoke an aura of prestige to the material items connected with it. We have literary evidence that the Roman legion commanders in Gaul used to give drinking vessels as gifts to neighbouring Germanic chieftains (Tacitus).

The kinds of goods therefore indicate that the transactions were of a prestigious nature, and circuits of gift exchange can probably be inferred. This underlines the assumption that chiefly structures dominated the economic life.

It will be recalled that articles for daily use (whetstones, soapstone bowls, iron bars) were widely distributed during the later Viking Period. This seems to conform with the concept that important institutional changes, facilitating market exchange, had taken place.

For a possible interpretation of Ullsheller as part of an economic organization, the similarities in habitation pattern to the rock shelters and caves along the coast seem to be important. These include: (1) habitation mainly during the Migration Period; (2) the habitation does not seem to reflect seasonal activities only; (3) the artefacts are related to both men's and women's activities.

If Ullsheller were part of an economic organization, it is reasonable to con-

649

sider it – like the habitation in caves and rock shelters along the coast – as a subsidiary element in a chiefly redistributive organization.
But does it necessarily have to be so ?

References

AABERG, N. (1953) *Den historiske relationen mellan Folkvandringstid och Vendeltid.* Kungl. vitterhets historie och antikvitets akademiens handlingar, del. 82, Stockholm.
BLOM, J. P. (1969) Ethnic and cultural differentiation. In BARTH, F. (ed.) *Ethnic Groups and Boundaries.* London: Allen & Unwin.
BROEGGER, A. (1921) Ertog og oere. *Videnskapsselskapets skrifter,* 2 (3).
CLARK, J. G. D. (1952) *Prehistoric Europe: The Economic Basis.* London: Methuen.
DALTON, G. (1961) Economic theory and primitive society. *American Anthropologist,* **63**, 1–25.
FOOTE, P. and WILSON, D. M. (1970) *The Viking Achievement.* London: Sidgwick.
GJERSETH, K. (1924) *History of Iceland.* New York: Macmillan.
HAFSTEN, U. (1965) Vegetational history and land occupation in Valldalen in the sub-Alpine region of central south Norway traced by pollen analysis and radiocarbon measurements. *Aarb. Univ. i Bergen.*
HAGEN, A. (1967) *Norway.* London: Thames & Hudson.
HARDING, T. G. (1960) Adaptation and stability. In SAHLINS, M. D. and SERVICE, E. R. (eds.) *Evolution and Culture.* Ann Arbor: University of Michigan Press.
HERTEIG, A. (1955) Is the expansion of the migration period in Rogaland caused by immigrants or is it an internal development ? *Viking,* XIX, 73–88.
HOLST, H. (1936) Norges mynter til slutten av 16. aarhundre. *Nordisk kultur,* **29**, 1–75.
LARUSSON, O. (1930) *Islands forfatning og lover i fristatstiden, Lov og ting,* Oslo: Universitetsforlaget Bergen.
MAGERÖY, H. (1965) Norsk-islandske problem. *Omstridde spoersmaal i Nordens historie,* III. Gjoevik.
MAUSS, M. (1954) *The Gift.* London: Cohen.
Naeringsmiddeltabell fra Statens ernaeringsraad, Landslaget for kosthold og helse (1961). Oslo.
ODNER, K. (1969) Ullshelleren i Valldalen, Röldal. *Aarbok for Universitetet i Bergen, Humanistisk serie* No. 1.
PHILLPOTTS, B. S. (1913) *Kindred and Clan in the Middle Ages and After.* Cambridge: Cambridge University Press.
POLANYI, K. (1957) The economy as instituted process. In POLANYI, K., ARENSBERG, C. M. and PEARSON, H. W. (eds.) *Trade and Market in the Early Empires.* Glencoe, Ill.: Free Press.
POLANYI, K. (1963) Ports of trade in the early societies. *Journal of Economic History,* **23** (1).
SKOOG, R. O. (1959–60) Caribou Management Investigations. *Alaska Department of Fish and Game Annual Report.*

SLOMANN, W. (1955) Folkevandringstiden i Norge. *Stavanger Museums aarshefte.*

WEBER, M. (1947) *The Theory of Social and Economic Organization.* London: Collier-Macmillan.

WRIGLEY, E. A. (1967) Demographic models and geography. In CHORLEY, R. J. and HAGGETT, P. (eds.) *Models in Geography.* London: Methuen.

16
Ethno-archaeological models and subsistence behaviour in Arnhem Land

C. SCHRIRE
State University of New York, Binghamton, U.S.A.

Introduction

Australian prehistorians rely heavily upon analogy to interpret archaeological data. They use a general model of hunter-gatherer behaviour and assume that these patterns have not changed substantially over the past 30 000 years (see Jones, 1968, pp. 201–11). Obviously, all written records of aboriginal behaviour are based on observations made after contact was established between the author and his subjects, and therefore they reflect to some extent aboriginal adaptation to this contact. When the archaeologist uses these data to construct a suitable model of hunter-gatherer behaviour to apply to a prehistoric situation, he automatically eliminates those elements that stem directly from contact and that he assumes are foreign to the traditional pattern. For instance, he may accept the integrity of certain hunting techniques whilst rejecting data about settlement patterns. In Ascher's terms, he uses the 'general comparative' analogy, rather than the 'direct historical' one, unless, of course, he is dealing with very recent post-contact aboriginal behaviour patterns (Ascher, 1961).

This chapter attempts to show how ethnographic sources can be used to construct analogue models of the pre- and post-contact aboriginal subsistence strategies. The question is particularly relevant to archaeologists, whose raw data usually allow them to infer subsistence behaviour more easily than any other aspect of social organization. Most of my comments are based on work done in Arnhem Land in central north Australia. The paper is divided into three sections: firstly a brief description of the area is given, secondly the pre- and post-contact aboriginal subsistence strategies are described, and finally the archaeological expression of these strategies is presented.

I Climate, topography and vegetation

The area under discussion is the coast, coastal plain, foothills and plateau complex of Arnhem Land, in the Northern Territory of Australia. It lies approximately between 11°–14°S latitude and 130°–137° E longitude (Fig. 16.1). The climate, geology, soils and plant ecology are explicitly described by Specht (1958a) but, for the purposes of this paper, the most relevant aspects of the local topography are as follows.

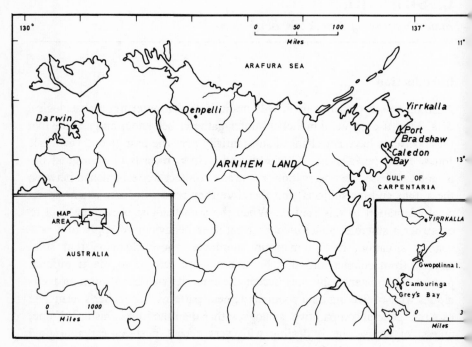

FIG. 16.1. Map of Arnhem Land, Northern Territory, showing the localities discussed.

The area is in the tropics and the climate is 'typically monsoonal with a well marked "wet" season alternating with a "dry" season' (Specht, 1958a, p. 333). The incidence of rainfall varies between about 86 and 153 cm per year and is relatively similar all over Arnhem Land, except for a marked increase on the coast of the Gulf of Carpentaria. The geology and soils of the area are complex and varied, but the basic pattern is a rocky plateau at the core of Arnhem Land, which is bounded by a fairly marked escarpment in

654

certain areas. Rivers originate in the high plateau and flow to the sea, cutting through the escarpment and across the rolling hills, coastal plain and dunes below.

The vegetation varies considerably in different parts of the area. The plateau supports a quartzitic and sandstone hills edaphic complex ranging from very sclerophyllous species in shallow cracks on extensive rock surfaces, to dense vegetational stands, which include monsoon forest species, in well-watered gorges and valleys. The rolling hills below the plateau support various types of tall, open forest, characterized by trees such as *Eucaluptus tectifica* or *E. tetradonta* (Specht, 1958a, pp. 367–8).

Progressing seawards from the plateau and hills, different vegetational complexes occur on the low-lying coastal plain. Areas subject to waterlogging for six to twelve months of the year support a freshwater stream, swamp and marsh edaphic complex in some places (Specht, 1958a, pp. 369–73) and a closely related estuarine plain edaphic complex on acid soils in others (Specht 1958a, pp. 373–83). The *E. tetradonta* forest extends down to the coast in places, but generally the coastal vegetation can be described as forming a mangrove forest edaphic complex in muddy tidal areas, and a coastal dune edaphic complex on well-drained sandy dunes and beaches (Specht, 1958a, pp. 375–80).

A simple diagrammatic representation of these zones is shown in Fig. 16.2. As noted earlier, the area is subject to marked seasonality, and seasonal fluctuations transform the vegetational zones, since the effective amount of precipitation dictates the density and nature of plant growth. For example, in the dry season the *E. tetradonta* forests are covered with brittle stubble, but once the wet season gets under way, they are carpeted with high, lush grass. Similarly, widespread dry flats supporting various tuberous plants occur on the edge of swamps and pools in the dry season, but disappear under water at the peak of the wet.

II Pre- and post-contact subsistence strategies

There seem to be three important factors in hunter-gatherer subsistence behaviour – the amount of work done in order to stay alive, the strategy employed to achieve a varied diet, and the settlement patterns adopted to maintain the level of subsistence success in the face of environmental variations. The extent to which these factors are affected by culture-contact is discussed below.

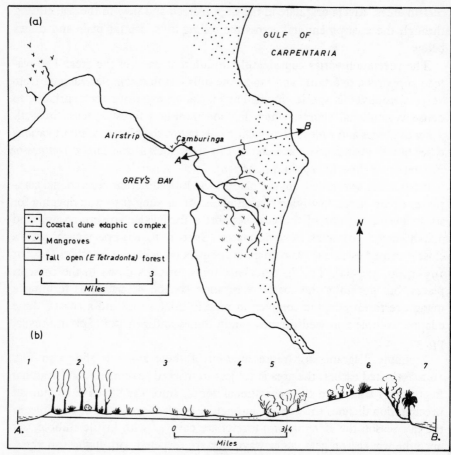

MAP 16.2. (*a*) Map showing position of the aboriginal 'bush camp' at Camburinga, Caledon Bay, in relation to the chief environmental zones. (*b*) Diagrammatic cross section at Caledon Bay, showing some of the habitats traversed by present-day forages in a typical day in the dry season. In the wet, zones 3, 4 and 5 become water-logged and impassable to foot traffic.

1 Bays and shores
2 *E. tetradonta* tall open forest
3 Sand flat and scrub
4 Sand flat
5 *Melaleuca* and *E. polycarpa* savannah woodland
6 Coastal sand dune
7 Shore of open sea

I INPUT-OUTPUT

Recent studies of hunter-gatherers have changed the popular concept of Man the Hunter living a precarious existence at starvation's door. Even though many modern hunter-gatherers live in somewhat unfavourable environments, such as the Kalahari Desert, they work relatively short hours to procure a balanced diet (Lee, 1969). One assumes, therefore, that prehistoric hunter-gatherers living in more congenial surroundings obtained satisfactory amounts of food even more easily (Lee and DeVore, 1968, p. 6).

The amount of time and effort expended on subsistence activities throughout the year by traditional Arnhem Land aboriginals is unknown. An attempt was made to discover 'the time factor in the aboriginal food quest' in 1948, when a study was made of two separate groups of foragers in the bush beyond mission stations (McCarthy and McArthur, 1960). The result is a meticulous and unique record of the daily round of a foraging group over a short period, but it does not constitute an entirely accurate view of pre-contact hunting and gathering, for two reasons. Firstly, it was impossible to assess the extent to which the foragers' familiarity with European food affected their output or their preference for certain bush foods. Secondly, the people who were studied were operating outside their home territory, and this might have affected the distance they were willing to venture from the base camp as well as the amounts of different foodstuffs they obtained.

Thus, the 1948 study presents a picture of the aboriginal input-output energy pattern in a post-contact context. The subjects of the study were bored with their late dry season diet of meat and fish (McCarthy and McArthur, 1960, p. 147) and grew anxious to return to the mission for flour and sugar. Here, under the 'hand-out' regime, they could obtain the maximum food for the minimum expenditure of energy.

2 STRATEGY TO ACHIEVE A VARIED DIET

Archaeological data and ethnographic sources both suggest that hunter-gatherers strive to achieve the maximum variation possible in the diet, rather than relying entirely upon a repetitive series of staple foods. Consequently they exploit as many microzones as possible (Coe and Flannery, 1964), with the hunting and foraging groups operating at right angles, as it were, to a series of parallel ecological zones (see Coles and Higgs, 1969, p. 69).

This strategy has been observed in Arnhem Land up to the present day (see Spencer, 1914, p. 32; Thomson, 1949, pp. 8–45; McCarthy and McArthur, 1960, p. 192; Worsley, 1961; White, 1969, 1970), since it is one of the few aspects of subsistence behaviour that is not necessarily affected by the presence of outsiders or European settlements in the area. However, it *is* affected by seasonal climatic changes. In the dry season, people are free to move about easily across the ecological zones, partly because the terrain is passable and also since water is generally available below, if not above, the surface of the ground. Movements are not severely restricted until the peak of the wet season (roughly February to mid-April), when the estuarine flood-plain and low-lying swamps are covered with several metres of water, and stretches of tangled reeds create severe hazards for foot traffic as well as for the simple aboriginal boats.

Water therefore acts as a barrier to men and beasts and both resort to a similar survival strategy – namely, withdrawal to better-drained ground. They retreat to high hills or sandy beaches that lie beyond the floodplain, and operate within these zones until the waters drain away. Consequently, a swing occurs in the operational axis of hunter-gatherers at the peak of the wet season, when they stop operating at right angles to certain ecological zones, and begin to move exclusively within a zone, along its parallel axis.

The climatic changes also dictate the diet of foragers in Arnhem Land. In the dry season, a wide variety of foodstuffs is available in different localities. Fish, shellfish and crabs are harvested from the sea, tidal creeks and inland pools. Fowl abound around swamps, and mammals and reptiles are pursued over land. Various edible plants are gathered in sufficient quantities to constitute staple foods, such as the tuberous spike rush (*Eleocharis dulcis*) in low-lying swamps and cycad nuts (*Cycas media*) in forested zones (Thomson, 1949, pp. 19–23; Specht, 1958b, pp. 482, 484).[1] At the peak of the wet season, however, many of these zones become inaccessible to men and other terrestrial fauna. As men and beasts retreat to better-drained ground, hunting becomes more popular. In addition, fruits and berries growing on well-drained tracts are harvested to replace the tubers and nuts of the dry season, and thus abundant plant foods with high carbohydrate values remain rare until the floodwaters recede at the end of the wet.

Since gross climatic changes occur irrespective of the occupants of the land, the basic model of seasonal responses to climatic changes can be applied to hunter-gatherers in both a pre- and post-contact context.

3 SETTLEMENT PATTERNS

The traditional view of pre-contact aboriginals is that they tend to be 'no-madic' in the dry season and 'sedentary' in the wet. Thomson, writing about the Wik-Monkan people of Cape York, whom he managed to observe before strong European influences were felt in the area, described the patterns as follows: 'Within the bounds of even a single clan territory a people may spend several months of the year as nomadic hunters, in pursuit of game, wild honey and small mammals, and exploiting the resources of vegetable foods of which a great number are known. A few months later the same people may be found established on the sea coast in camps that have all the appearance of permanence or at least of semi-permanence, having apparently abandoned their nomadic habits' (Thomson, 1939, p. 209).

In effect, he is making the point elaborated in the previous section, by describing the seasonal withdrawal to better-drained ground. Movements are affected by the over-abundance of water, though this alone need not create a greater degree of sedentism, since people, having reached well-drained hills or beaches, are still free to move around *within* this congenial zone. The chief factor that seems to have restricted movement was a lack of good, natural shelters, which forced the foragers to return to a permanent base camp of stout bark houses each night.

It would appear that an important consequence of aboriginal contact with foreigners is a marked change in the degree of nomadism practised. Hunters and gatherers all over the world tended to gravitate towards centres of contact – be they Australian mission stations, Arctic trading posts or Herero cattle stations (Lee, 1970, p. 7). There they set up camp, remaining in one place, with only occasional forays into the wilds.

This particular pattern can be observed today amongst aboriginals living in 'bush camps' in north-east Arnhem Land. These camps were deliberately constituted by aboriginals, many of whom spend most of their lives on mission stations and who, for various reasons, prefer not to live on the European operated station. Each camp is situated near a rough area of cleared ground which serves as an airstrip for small craft. An aeroplane operated by a missionary visits each camp roughly once every three weeks, and in this way the people living in the bush are able to obtain small amounts of European foodstuffs, medical aid and news. The airstrip therefore represents the effective centre of contact between the bush group and the rest of the world.

In 1968–9, I visited a small group of aboriginals living in such a camp at Caledon Bay (White, 1968, 1969). Their permanent camp at Camburinga, consisted of three or four bark houses on the shores of Grey's Bay about 1 km from the airstrip (Fig. 16.2). In the dry season they camped there, and also in the lee of temporary windbreaks on nearby beaches, but in the wet they remained at the permanent camp. In the dry season they foraged over a wide variety of zones lying along the axis of the peninsula but they tended to concentrate on the resources of the bay shore in the wet, when swampy tracts blocked off their passage across the peninsula. However, they seldom ventured more than 5·5 km from the airstrip, and whilst I was there they never camped more than 3 km (one hour's walking distance) away.

One might well wonder why their range was so limited, given that the regular plane visited the airstrip only once every three weeks. The answer is that the visiting schedule was not rigid: occasionally another craft landed, and once or twice a truck was driven to the camp from Yirrkalla Mission, some 64 km away. The people of Caledon Bay discussed these visits endlessly, and speculated on the possibility of others. Above all, they were determined to remain within reach of any possible sources of news and European food.

Thus the post-contact settlement pattern is closely related to a source of foreign influence, such as a small airstrip. The total pattern is even more sedentary than that found among pre-contact aboriginals during the wet season; whereas traditional people could shift their base camp within a well-drained zone, their more acculturated counterparts are forced to forage over a more limited area in close range of the only airstrip within 38 km. As a result, they rely heavily upon marine foods, which constitute a readily accessible source of protein throughout the year.

Given these data about foraging strategies, I can construct two contrasting models, for pre- and post-contact behaviour patterns of Arnhem Land aboriginals:

(a) Pre-contact hunter-gatherers work relatively short hours, operating across ecological zones to achieve a varied diet. Residence patterns, group size and diet are strongly dependent on seasonal changes and the most trying period is the peak of the wet season when movement and dietary variation are greatly restricted.

(b) Post-contact hunter-gatherers who live in the bush away from direct sources of contact (e.g. mission stations) resemble their pre-contact counterparts in most respects except for the fact that residence is more permanent so as to permit maximum interaction with foreigners. Thus their effective range is smaller, their diet less varied, and they tend to concentrate on a permanent food source, such as marine foods, throughout the year.

If these hypotheses are now translated into archaeological terms, pre-contact sites should contain evidence of the exploitation of a wide variety of local resources, often in one particular season of the year, whilst post-contact ones should reflect the exploitation of a more limited range of resources from the immediate vicinity, possibly throughout the year. Finally, one might expect to find exotic artefacts, obtained from the foreigners, in post-contact sites only.

III Archaeological evidence of subsistence patterns

I shall discuss the archaeological data from two areas in Arnhem Land, namely the Oenpelli area in the north-western part of the reserve (White, 1967, 1971; White and Peterson, 1969) and the Port Bradshaw area on the north-eastern coast (White, 1970).

The pre-contact adaptive pattern seems to have an antiquity of about 6000–7000 years in Arnhem Land. This date accords with the time that the postglacial sea attained its modern level and the land acquired its present ecological character (see Jennings, 1971, p. 10). In the Oenpelli area, a series of deposits dating from about 7000 B.P. until the present day was excavated on the coastal plain and in a valley in the adjoining plateau. A marked difference was observed in the dietary remains and associated implements in the two different zones. A number of possible explanations were suggested to account for the variations, and it was eventually concluded that they reflected seasonal changes in the diet and residence of the inhabitants (White and Peterson, 1969).

The conclusion did not stem directly from the archaeological data, but rather, it was based on the simple premise that terrestrial animals, ordinarily living on the coastal plain near Oenpelli, tend to retreat to high, well-drained country at the peak of the wet season when the plain is submerged. Thus, the presence of estuarine molluscs, crabs and water plants in plain shelters, suggests a dry season occupation, simply because these foodstuffs are inaccessible to foragers at the peak of the wet.

Evidence of pre-contact strategies also occurs in the Port Bradshaw area, where a recent excavation at a shelter called Borngolo, revealed an apparent succession of both strategies. Since the material is unpublished except for an interim report (White, 1970), I shall describe it in some detail here.

Borngolo is a shallow recess formed at the base of a consolidated dune, on the eastern shore of Port Bradshaw, about 1 km above the beach. From the brow of the dune, there is a clear view of Gwopolinna Island, lying about 5 km away in the middle of Port Bradshaw (Fig. 16.1). A famous Macassan site is situated here (McCarthy and Setzler, 1960, pp. 227–30) and, although it is undated, similar sites elsewhere on the coast of north-east Arnhem Land have suggested an antiquity of some 800 years (MacKnight, 1969). Historical and ethnographic sources record the visits of Macassan trepangers to this area in the wet season and the contact between the Indonesian visitors and indigenous aboriginals is discussed (Berndt and Berndt, 1954, 1964, pp. 424–5; Mulvaney, 1969, pp. 21–30). One might therefore draw some parallels between

661

the airstrip at Caledon Bay and the Macassan camp at Gwopolinna, by considering both as foci of contact between aboriginals and the outside world. Work in the area was begun, therefore, in the hope of discovering archaeological evidence of the post-contact exploitive strategies of aboriginals living near Gwopolinna which could be interpreted in the light of the data collected at Caledon Bay.

Borngolo shelter faces west and affords protection from sun, wind and rain. It might have been used throughout the year, but was probably used mainly in the wet season. The recess harbours a nasty pocket of humid air in the dry season, making it an unpleasant proposition for potential tenants who could be far more comfortable at that time camping out in the open, on a beach. Its attraction is considerably greater in the wet weather when it provides one of the few natural refuges in the area, to be used either as an overnight stop, or a permanent base for a small unsociable group, such as an elementary family. Finally, in addition to these features, the shelter is located on a peninsula between the open sea and a bay, and its occupants could therefore have easy access to a similar range of zones exploited by the aboriginals observed at Caledon Bay (see Fig. 16.2).

The deposit consisted of between 60 and 70 cm of debris resting on the uneven, sandy bedrock. Occupation remains occurred throughout, including food debris such as charred and broken animal bones, marine shells, eggshell and plant matter, as well as implements made of stone, shell and bone. No marked stratigraphic variations were observed in the field but subsequent analysis of the material suggested a broad two-part sequence. Thus an upper and lower level were distinguished, with the dividing line drawn in the middle of the deposit about 30 cm below the surface.

Three radiocarbon dates are available for the deposit. The base of the deposit is undated, but since it contains marine fauna it probably accumulated only after the sea reached its present level, 6000–7000 years ago (Jennings, 1971; White, 1971). The top of the lower level is dated to 4200 ± 160 B.P. (ANU – 399), the base of the upper level to 1220 ± 75 B.P. (ANU – 400), and the top to modern times (ANU – 401).

Both levels contained a wide variety of faunal debris, reflecting foraging in different habitats that occur within a 2 or 3 km radius of the shelter. These include the open sea (dugong, fish) and its shore (turtles, turtle eggs), the rocky shore of the bay (oysters, fish, crabs), mudflats (estuarine shellfish) and land (mammals, reptiles, echidnas and birds). Edible and non-edible plant remains, restricted by preservation to the uppermost levels, reflect similar foraging patterns on the sea shore (*Casuarina equisitifolia L.*), monsoon forests

(*Semecarpus australiensis* Engl.), savannah woodland, coastal dunes and sandy outwash plains (*Brachychiton paradoxum* Schott, *Terminalia* sp., *Pandanus* sp.) and eucalypt forests (*Melaleuca* sp., *Terminalia* sp.) (see Specht, 1958b). Finally, most of the associated implements are similar to those found in coterminous shell midden deposits on the plain near Oenpelli (White and Peterson, 1969) and include stone points, scrapers and hammers, bone points and shell scrapers.

On the basis of the data described so far, the Borngolo material is similar to that found in pre-contact sites. However, certain features suggest a change in the subsistence patterns of the occupants over time, and the most important of these is the distribution of fish and mammalian remains.

Fish and mammal bones occur throughout the deposit but the proportions vary considerably over time, as follows:

	Level			
	Upper		*Lower*	
	Fish	*Mammal*	*Fish*	*Mammal*
Weight (g)	1317·6	364·7	490·3	1789·6
Weight (% total)	78·25	21·75	21·55	78·45
Density (per m³)	515	142	219	799
Min. Nos. (per m³)	19·6	7	10·3	22·3

The variation holds true for each of the nine square metres sampled: fish bones tend to increase by weight over time whereas mammal bones decrease. The latter means that the effect is not due to selective preservation, but rather to differential deposition over time.

This statement is precisely true in the following sense: if H_0 denotes the statement 'Fish and mammal bones are deposited identically in time throughout the site', then the truth of H_0 would entail that, as a function of depth, the percentages of total bone weight removed for each of fish and mammal bones behave similarly. However, these two sample functions are significantly different at an extremely high significance level according to the Kolmogorov-Smirnov test shown in Appendix A.

Let us now consider two possible interpretations of these data.

CHANGES IN THE SEASONAL USE OF THE SITE OVER TIME

The situation observed might result from the earlier occupants using the site mainly in the dry season when they were free to forage widely and hunt

663

many mammals, as opposed to the later ones who generally used the shelter in the wet season, when widespread flooding restricted movements and forced them to rely more heavily than usual upon local, constant sources of food, i.e. fish.

No direct evidence is available to support or deny this hypothesis. The best indicators of seasonal occupation are edible plant remains, and unfortunately these are preserved in the uppermost levels only. Moreover, although these remains represent food eaten in the wet, the evidence does not exclude the possibility of dry season occupation too. More specifically, plants eaten in the wet season are mainly fruits and nuts, whose macroscopic remains preserve relatively well over time. In contrast to this, tubers and cycad nuts constitute the chief plant foods of the dry season, and their remains are unlikely ever to be preserved in a living site. Tubers are soft and decay easily, and the resilient cycad nut casing is invariably discarded in the forest, because the slightly toxic meat has to be leached in water for several days before it can be pulverized, baked and eaten (Specht, 1958b, p. 482; Worsley, 1961, pp. 164–165).

CHANGES IN THE INTENSITY OF SITE USE OVER TIME

Let us assume that both sets of occupants generally used the shelter in the wet season (see p. 662). Thus, the observed faunal change might result from the following situation. The earlier occupants used the shelter sporadically as a refuge from rain and cold, possibly as an overnight stop from the larger base camp. They cooked and ate food there which had been collected in the course of their moving over a fairly wide well-drained area. In contrast to this, the later occupants also used the site in the wet season, but in a more intensive manner, since they wanted to remain within the immediate area. They moved about less and were therefore forced to rely more heavily upon immediate sources of food, namely fish.

I tend to favour this hypothesis because the faunal change is associated with the following three elements that combine to suggest aboriginal-Macassan interaction during the accumulation of the upper level.

(i) *Exotic artefact*: A fragmentary chain of copper and faience, probably of south-east Asian origin, was found just below the surface of the deposit. Being of modern age, it simply documents Oriental influence in the area.

(ii) *Shell hooks*: J-shaped hooks made of pearl shell (*Melina ephippium* (Linne)) occurred in the upper level *only*. The collection of sixteen complete and seventeen unfinished specimens was apparently produced on the spot by aboriginal craftsmen. Prehistoric hooks have never before been excavated in Arnhem Land, and local aboriginals found them unfamiliar. However, similarly shaped bronze hooks occur on many Macassan sites (Mulvaney, 1969, plate 11b), including Gwopolinna Island (White, 1970). Thomson (1949, p. 86) records that aboriginals obtained metal hooks from Macassans, but a more relevant source (Campbell, 1834, p. 166) notes that Macassan fishermen used hooks made of pearl shell presumably when their supply of metal ones ran low. I suggest, therefore, that the sudden appearance of pearl hooks about 1000 years ago at Borngolo might reflect the influence of Macassan visitors upon local aboriginals. It is unlikely, however, that the use of these hooks was solely responsible for the increased numbers of fish bones deposited in the shelter, because line fishing in that area is certainly no more, and possibly even less, productive than the traditional spear fishing.

(iii) *Stone and bone tools*: Ethnographic sources suggest that stone-tipped spears were generally used in hunting, whilst bone-tipped ones tended to be employed in fishing and fowling (see White and Peterson, 1969, p. 60). One might therefore expect to find some correspondence between the incidence of different types of tools, and the faunal remains at Borngolo. This, however, is not the case: stone and bone tools are both more densely distributed in the lower level, as follows:

| | Level | | | | | |
| | Upper | | | Lower | | |
	No.	*%*	*Density (per m^3)*	*No.*	*%*	*Density (per m^3)*
Flaked stone tools	32	16·4	12·5	163	83·6	72·8
Bone tools	7	29·2	2·7	17	70·8	7·6
Total	39	17·8	15·2	180	82·2	80·4

The abrupt drop in the upper level is not associated with a sudden decline in the overall density of faunal debris. We may infer, therefore, that foraging continued to be practised throughout the time that the shelter was occupied, and thus the question arises as to what tools replaced the stone and bone ones of the lower level, in the later stages of occupation.

Shell hooks could have replaced the bone points in fishing, but there is no direct evidence of any such substitute for stone tools. If I am correct in inferring the presence of south-east Asian influence in the area some 1000 years ago, the decline in stone tools might have resulted from the introduction of iron, for use as spear tips and knives. Unfortunately, no iron was discovered in the upper level, but perhaps this is not conclusive, because it might have been a rare and valuable commodity that was seldom discarded and mislaid amongst the everyday household debris.

Taking all these data into consideration, I interpret the Borngolo sequence in terms of pre- and post-contact aboriginal subsistence behaviour. As an aside, one may well wonder why prehistoric aboriginals chose to maintain their relationships with outsiders such as Macassan trepangers. Historical sources indicate that the Macassans got the better part of the deal, receiving women, services and goods, such as tortoise shell, from the indigenes in exchange for the occasional iron or glass object. These facts probably tell only part of the story. Speculating freely, let us remember that the contact invariably occurred in the wet season when the foragers were short of tubers and cycad nuts: Macassan rice might well have been very attractive at this particular time. Finally, one should never underestimate the intrinsically repetitive nature of the life of a hunter-gatherer. Speaking as a former gatherer, the daily round is almost as boring as the life of a forager in the supermarket. Any interruption, any new face, any new gossip is welcome. For the prehistoric aboriginal living near Port Bradshaw, the sight of the Macassan fleet sailing into the Bay, must have lifted the Wet Season Blues considerably.

Conclusion

In considering the effects of foreign influence on the traditional social and economic life of aboriginal hunter-gatherers, most ethnographers tend to stress the importance of the introduced objects themselves. Thomson, for instance, suggested, that the goods (*gerri*) introduced into Arnhem Land by Indonesians, stimulated the development of the widespread ceremonial exchange cycles that he observed there. Talking of Eastern Arnhem Land, he said: 'although an extensive ceremonial exchange system undoubtedly existed long before visitors from the Celebes came to Arnhem Land, it is probable that the *gerri* introduced by these visitors did much to overcome the effects of the segmentary organisation and to infuse life and vitality into the ceremonial exchange cycle which developed on a large scale in this territory' (Thomson, 1949, pp. 5–6). Similarly, McCarthy and McArthur, studying aboriginal diet, concluded that: 'In the economic field, the main change brought about by contact with Europeans has been the introduction of modern substitutes for objects in daily use. The aborigines have metal tools and weapons; tins are used as containers; calico loincloths are worn...' (McCarthy and McArthur, 1960, p. 145).

Archaeologists might therefore be tempted to consider that exotic artefacts constitute the main indicators of culture-contact. In this paper, I have presented two models of aboriginal subsistence behaviour which suggest that, in Arnhem Land at least, certain foreign influences induced a marked change in the range, mobility and diet of the traditional foragers. Thus, interaction between indigenes and aliens may be inferred from an analysis of the dietary remains found in an aboriginal living site.

It may be argued that this constitutes a more reliable indicator of contact than the presence of exotic artefacts. Firstly, the nature and density of most faunal remains found at a camp site are not subject to the same type of distributional hazards that affect the presence of exotic objects: people often ignore gnawed bones, empty shells and husks, whilst cherishing a rare knife, axe or piece of jewellery. Secondly, the odd exotic artefact found in a site invariably tells little about the nature of the contact that existed, whereas a careful analysis of the dietary remains can provide evidence of the type of adaptation made by foragers, over a considerable period of time.

Appendix A

by W. L. Steiger, *Centre de Recherches, Mathématiques*

The following table shows how the weight of fish and mammal bones vary as a function of depth. Specifically, for three of the nine square metres dug, the total amount of bone material removed – as of each different depth – was computed for both fish and mammal bones. These were then expressed as percentages of the total weight of that type of bone, fish bone percentages appearing in column A, and mammal bone percentages in column B. Finally column C gives the differences between corresponding values of A and B, always taking the sign to be positive.

The maximum value in column C is 0·653 and occurs at a depth of 35 cm. If H_0 (the null hypothesis on p. 663) were true, columns A and B would look similar and a small value for the largest entry of C would be expected. However, assuming the truth of H_0, a value of 0·653 or larger could occur with a probability of less than 0·002 (Kraft and Van Eden, 1968, p. 318). Thus the Kolmogorov–Smirnov test is significant at the 99·8% level at which we are justified in rejecting H_0.

The Kolmogorov–Smirnov Test

Depth (m)	A % of Fish weight	B % of Mammal weight	C Difference
0·01	2·04	0·68	1·36
0·07	9·85	0·73	9·12
0·10	15·70	1·25	14·45
0·12	24·60	1·43	21·17
0·17	35·20	3·04	32·16
0·19	47·50	3·40	44·10
0·26	56·50	4·86	51·64
0·27	66·00	7·00	59·00
0·29	71·00	9·10	61·90
0·35	78·00	12·70	65·30
0·38	88·50	17·80	60·70
0·40	91·25	34·50	56·75
0·46	94·00	53·25	40·75
0·47	98·00	65·70	32·30
0·57	99·80	88·00	11·80
0·58	100·00	100·00	0·00

Notes

1. Worsley (1961, pp. 163–4) notes that cycad nuts (*burrawong*) were eaten on Groote Eylandt in the wet season. Since this disagrees with other sources I can only assume that he observed an atypical pattern.

Acknowledgements

I am grateful to the following people and institutions for their encouragement and assistance in the research described above: The Australian National University; The Australian Institute of Aboriginal Studies; Hawker-de Havilland, E.L.D.O., Gove; Dr W. L. Steiger, Centre de Recherches Mathématiques, Université de Montreal; Mr G. B. Morren, S.U.N.Y., Binghamton.

References

ASCHER, R. (1961) Analogy in archaeological interpretation. *Southwestern Journal of Anthropology*, **17**, 317–25.

BERNDT, R. and BERNDT, C. (1954) *Arnhem Land, Its History and Its People*. Melbourne: Cheshire.

BERNDT, R. and BERNDT, C. (1964) *The World of the First Australians*. Chicago: University of Chicago Press.

CAMPBELL, MAJOR (1834) Geographical memoir of Mellville Island and Port Essington, on the Cobourg peninsula, northern Australia, with some observations on the settlements which have been established on the north coast of New Holland. *Journal of the Royal Geographical Society*, 4, 129–81.

COE, M. D. and FLANNERY, K. V. (1964) Microenvironments and Mesoamerican prehistory. *Science*, 143 (3607), 650–4.

COLES, J. M. and HIGGS, E. S. (1969) *The Archaeology of Early Man.* London: Faber.

JENNINGS, J. (1971) Sea level changes and land links. In MULVANEY, D. J. and GOLSON, J. (eds.) *Man and Environment in Australia*, 1–13. Canberra: Australian National University Press.

JONES, R. (1968) The geographical background to the arrival of man in Australia and Tasmania. *Archaeology and Physical Anthropology in Oceania*, 3 (3), 186–215.

KRAFT, C. and EDEN, C. VAN (1968) *A Non-Parametric Introduction to Statistics.* New York: Macmillan.

LEE, R. B. (1969) !Kung bushman subsistence: an input-output analysis. *National Museums of Canada Bulletin*, 230, Anth. Ser. 86, 73–94.

LEE, R. B. (1970) *Work Effort, Group Structure and Land Use in Contemporary Hunter-Gatherers.* Paper prepared for the Research Seminar in Archaeology and related Subjects: Three-day Meeting on Settlement Pattern and Urbanization, Institute of Archaeology, University of London (mimeo).

LEE, R. B. and DEVORE, I. (eds.) (1968) *Man the Hunter.* Chicago: Aldine.

MACKNIGHT, C. C. (1969) *The Macassans.* Unpublished Ph.D. thesis, Australian National University.

MCARTHY, F. D. and MCARTHUR, M. (1960) The food quest and the time factor in aboriginal economic life. In MOUNTFORD, C. P. (ed.) *Records of the American-Australian Scientific Expedition to Arnhem Land*, 2, 145–94.

MCCARTHY, F. D. and SETZLER, F. M. (1960) The archaeology of Arnhem Land. In MOUNTFORD, C. P. (ed.) *Records of the American-Australian Scientific Expedition to Arnhem Land*, 2, 215–95.

MULVANEY, D. J. (1969) *The Prehistory of Australia.* London: Thames & Hudson.

SPECHT, R. L. (1958a) The climate, geology, soils and plant ecology of the northern portion of Arnhem Land. In SPECHT, R. L. and MOUNTFORD, C. P. (eds.) *Records of the American-Australian Scientific Expedition to Arnhem Land*, 3, 333–414.

SPECHT, R. L. (1958b) An introduction to the ethnobotany of Arnhem Land. In SPECHT, R. L. and MOUNTFORD, C. P. (eds.) *Records of the American-Australian Scientific Expedition to Arnhem Land*, 3, 479–503.

SPENCER, W. B. (1914) *Native Tribes of the Northern Territory of Australia.* London: Macmillan.

THOMSON, D. F. (1939) The seasonal factor in human culture, illustrated from the life of a contemporary nomadic group. *Proceedings of the Prehistoric Society*, n.s. 5, 209–21.

THOMSON, D. F. (1949) *Economic Structure and the Ceremonial Exchange Cycle in Arnhem Land.* Melbourne: Macmillan.

WHITE, C. (1967) *Plateau and Plain: Prehistoric Investigations in Arnhem Land, Northern Territory.* Unpublished Ph.D. thesis, Australian National University.

WHITE, C. (1968) *Report on Field Survey June–August 1968.* Australian Institute of Aboriginal Studies Doc. No. 68/738, 1–10 (mimeo).

WHITE, C. (1969) *Report on Field Trip to Caledon Bay, Northern Territory, December–January 1968–9.* Australian Institute of Aboriginal Studies Doc. No. 69/816, 1–8 (mimeo).

WHITE, C. (1970) *Report on Field Trip to Yirrkalla and Port Bradshaw, Northern Territory, August–September 1969.* Australian Institute of Aboriginal Studies Doc. No. 70/923, 1–9 (mimeo).

WHITE, C. (1971) Man and environment in north-west Arnhem Land. In MULVANEY, D. J. and GOLSON, J. (eds.) *Aboriginal Man and Environment in Australia,* 141–57. Canberra: Australian National University Press.

WHITE, C. and PETERSON, N. (1969) Ethnographic interpretations of the prehistory of western Arnhem Land. *Southwestern Journal of Anthropology,* **25**, 45–67.

WORSLEY, P. M. (1961) The utilization of food resources by an Australian aboriginal tribe. *Acta Ethnographica Academiae Scientiarum Hungaricae,* **10**, fasc. 1–2, 153–90.

17

A computer simulation model of Great Basin Shoshonean subsistence and settlement patterns[1]

D. H. THOMAS

American Museum of Natural History, New York, U.S.A.

Comprehensive models are built, if at all, by many hands over many decades.
JAMES DORAN (1970)

Introduction

As research progresses in science – any science – levels of inquiry tend to become increasingly complex, for sophisticated problems require equally sophisticated methods of analysis. One corollary of Parkinson's Law is that as research objectives become more complex, methodological advances will tend to fill the void. The physicist, for example, hardly needed a cyclotron until he became aware of the existence of the atom. In archaeology a similar relationship exists between research progress and analytical complexity. As long as cultural chronology was the focus of the archaeologist's attention, complex analytical methods were unnecessary. But as archaeologists began to take seriously their role as social scientists, the vagaries and nuances of sociocultural reconstruction required increasingly advanced techniques. Perhaps *Analytical Archaeology* by David Clarke (1968) stands as a benchmark in this regard. The 'new perspective' views culture as a 'point of overlap (or "articulation") between a vast number of *systems*, each of which encompasses both cultural and non-cultural phenomena – often more of the latter. . . . Cultural change comes about through minor variations in one or more systems, which grow, displace or reinforce others and reach equilibrium on a different plane' (Flannery 1967, p. 120; also see Judge, 1970, p. 41). It is hardly coincidental that the popularity of multivariate statistical techniques in archaeology arose with the emergence of the 'new' or 'systemic' archaeology.

The subsequent rise of the 'systems approach' to archaeology is likewise non-coincidental. Clarke (1968), Flannery (1968) and Judge, (1970), among others, have charted the way for archaeologists anxious to explore the potential of systems analysis with respect to archaeological problems. One aspect of the systems analytical approach involves the simulation of complex systems. By simulation I mean the dynamic representation achieved by building a model and moving it through time (McMillan and Gonzalez, 1968, p. 26).

Simulation is a problem solving technique, to be employed only when the systems under consideration defy analysis through more direct means. Overall systems complexity generally requires that these simulations be computer-assisted. As I view simulation, no rigid set of procedures should be followed, for the simulation develops as the research problem unfolds. No distinction is made here between the techniques of cybernetics, systems analysis and computer simulation. In discussion of the advantages and pitfalls of a single example of dynamic modelling (BASIN I), I hope to illustrate some general points regarding simulation studies. Since computer simulations have the disturbing side effect of becoming objects of study in themselves, the problem-oriented approach seems most appropriate at this point in their development.

The Reese River Ecological Project

The Reese River Ecological Project is a detailed archaeological investigation of a single valley in central Nevada. The Reese river valley is located in the centre of the state of Nevada, about 30 miles south of the town of Austin, Lander County. The criteria for selection and random sampling are discussed elsewhere (Thomas, 1969a). The sampling universe contains four primary biotic communities (see Fig. 17.1). The sagebrush-grass zone (A-zone) covers the flat valley floor, which ranges in elevation from about 5000 to 6000 feet above sea level. Sagebrush (*Artemesia tridentata*) is currently the dominant species, sometimes occurring in pure stands. The invasion of Mediterranean grasses and overgrazing of native varieties has, it seems, markedly changed this life zone from pre-contact times. The piñon-juniper belt (B-zone) flourishes between 6000 and 8000 feet above sea level in the Toiyabe mountains, to the east of Reese river. Above 8000 feet, an upper sagebrush-grass zone (C-zone) is apparent. A diminutive limber pine zone, shown in Fig. 17.1, is not considered in the model. To the west of Reese river, the rainshadow effect displaces these three zones approximately 1000 to 2000 feet upward in the Shoshone mountains. A fourth biotic community is the riparian life zone. Riverine vegetation of the flats differs little from the surrounding sagebrush-grass zone, but in the mountains this habitat is characterized by lush stands of cottonwood and birch trees. The riparian micro-environment is noted primarily because it possesses a distinctive economic potential (for more detailed discussion of the Reese river biotic communities, see Billings, 1951).

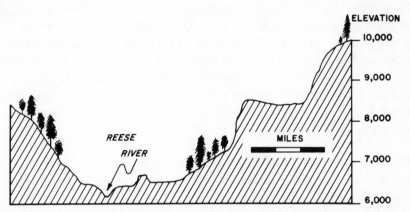

FIG. 17.1. Cross section of the Reese river valley, looking north. Shoshone mountains are on the left, Toiyabe mountains on the right. Vertical scale exaggerated.

THE SCIENTIFIC CYCLE

John Kemeny's (1959) discussion of the scientific method, or more precisely, the *scientific cycle*, provides the logical structure in which the Reese River Ecological Project is grounded (Fig. 17.2). One begins with facts, and

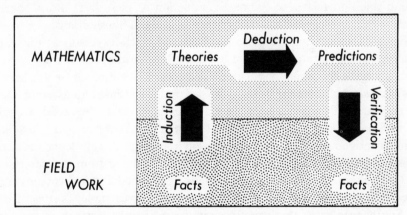

FIG. 17.2. Flow chart of the scientific cycle (after Kemeny, 1959, p. 86).

forms theories through the process of *induction*. Theories carry little information and can demand even less credibility. Theories can be judged neither by their attendant factors nor by the reputation of their author; rather, theories (or hypotheses) can be assessed only by their ability to predict phenomena.

The second process in the scientific cycle is the deduction of testable propositions from theories. These predictions must be verified with new facts. The phrase 'scientific cycle' emphasized Einstein's well-known dictum that science begins and ends with facts. Deduction and verification comprise the now-popular 'testing of hypotheses', a necessary step, for an unverified hypothesis has the epistemological status of a daydream. From a scientific point of view, it makes *no* difference who framed the hypothesis, for professional standing and experience are irrelevant to the truth value of a hypothesis. Untested theories cannot compete for serious attention in the arena of modern science (also see Binford, 1968).

THE SHOSHONEAN TECHNO-ECONOMIC SYSTEM

The theory under examination by the Reese River Ecological Project is Julian Steward's interpretation of Great Basin socio-economic patterns (esp. Steward, 1955). Initial facts are those that Steward himself collected in the 1930s and those of historic sources. These facts were induced by Steward into a consistent, articulate body of theory in *Basin-Plateau Aboriginal Sociopolitical Groups* (Steward, 1938).

There are actually two distinct issues involved here. The first is whether Steward could have misinterpreted the data at hand in 1930, an aspect that I do not question. I accept all of Steward's field work as unimpeachable. The second question relates to Steward's induction of these facts into a theory regarding the pre-contact situation of the Great Basin Shoshoneans.

Steward's inductions are quite involved and carefully reasoned; the main point is that the cultural ecology of the Great Basin had a socially fragmenting effect upon the aboriginal population. The constraints imposed by this harsh, *unpredictable* environment were such that traditional institutions other than the nuclear family were notably absent. The Shoshoneans depended, according to Steward (1970, p. 116), upon a *multiple subsistence pattern* which exploited contiguous but dissimilar micro-environments. A well-defined seasonal round permitted the Shoshoneans to extract a living from the deserts of the Great Basin. Steward's inductions thus form a model for interpretation of other primitive groups. Flannery (1966, 1968), for example, borrows from the Shoshonean case to interpret economic procurement systems of the prehistoric Tehuacan valley of Mexico. Similarly, Wilmsen (1970, p. 82) accepts the generalized Shoshonean example as suggestive of hunter-gatherer band organization of the Palaeo-Indians of North America. No criticism is implied here for the use of the Shoshonean model; the basis for analogy is a question not considered in this paper. The real question is to what degree does Steward's interpretation fit the actual prehistoric data of the Shoshoneans ?

Service (1962) and Owen (1964) have suggested that the pre-contact social organization of the Basin Shoshoneans may have been more complex than originally interpreted by Steward. Discussion of these issues, using archaeological data, is the ultimate objective, but the immediate problem at hand is a demographic one. The Shoshonean economic system was intimately associated with a distinctive settlement pattern. This economic orientation has been most concisely summarized in Steward (1938, pp. 19–20, 44–6), who termed the basic orientation 'gastric'. Ecological specifics varied from place to place, but the overall subsistence activities were constant for the central Great Basin. When I refer to Steward's model of Great Basin Shoshonean economic patterns, I refer to this overall subsistence orientation and seasonal round.

But the seasonal round depicted by Steward has never been directly observed. The pattern was reconstructed from 'memory culture', years after the actors and the resources had effectively disappeared. The ecological effects of white contact have already been discussed (Thomas, 1971a). It is sufficient to note here that the piñon trees were lumbered for fenceposts and firewood in the 1860s and that cattle overgrazed verdant stands of native grasses. Through these agents, the environment suffered irreversible changes. As an additional problem, the average birthdate of Steward's Shoshone informants was 1868 ± 2·6 years (data from Steward, 1941). These informants, therefore, actually had never experienced a pre-contact social or natural environment. The classic Shoshonean seasonal round is simply not a *fact*; it is a *theory*. Like all theories, credibility cannot be assessed until the logical consequences of that theory have been verified on independent data. The present discussion should not be construed as a challenge to Steward's theoretical model. The Reese River Ecological Project simply seeks to complete one cycle of the scientific process, a cycle that was initiated by Steward's ethnographic field work of the 1930s.

THE DESERT ARCHAIC LIFEWAY

Also of interest here is Jesse Jennings's (1957) use of Steward's theory as a model for the Desert Archaic (*née* Desert Culture) concept. According to Jennings, the Desert Archaic is a stable adaptation to a relatively stable environment, with no specific natural resource dominating the pattern. This generalized adaptation has existed in the Great Basin and other areas essentially unchanged, for some 10 000 years. The importance of Steward's theory as an analogy for the Desert Archaic is clear. If the Steward model does not fit the late prehistoric material, then the Desert Archaic concept would likewise require rethinking. The issue has relevance beyond the arid boundaries of the Great Basin, for the Desert Culture has itself served as an analogy for interpreting other prehistoric situations (e.g. Irwin-Williams, 1967; MacNeish, 1964). The Great Basin Shoshonean model and its Desert Archaic forerunner would rest much easier if Steward's inductions were verified in the archaeological record of the Shoshoneans.

The BASIN I simulation model

If we recognize the necessity of testing Steward's model, we are left with the uncomfortable position of having nothing to test. 'The key to verification of theories is that you can never verify them. What you verify are the logical consequences of the theory' (Kemeny, 1959, p. 96). The statement that the sun rises daily is a theory. But in order to test this theory, one cannot attempt to observe all sunrises on all mornings; this is an untestable proposition. The prediction that the sun will arise tomorrow morning is a logical consequence of the original theory. The prediction is operational in that it can be tested.

A similar situation exists with Steward's model (theory) of Shoshonean settlement patterns. The theory is an untested hypothesis and, as such, is scientifically objectionable. But one can never hope to verify Steward's model, since it is really a theory and theories can never be verified. The missing step is the *deduction* of the logical consequences of the theory. One needs to know the archaeological manifestations of such patterned behaviour. These consequences are specific to place and to time. If the late prehistoric Shoshoneans behaved in the fashion induced by Steward, how would the artefacts fall on the ground?

Predicting artefact frequencies is a highly complex problem. For one individual simultaneously to control all of the environmental and cultural parameters is most difficult, if not impossible. For this reason, the speed and efficiency of computers has been enlisted. A computer model has been constructed which takes Steward's inductive model and predicts attendant artefact frequencies. This simulation model is termed BASIN I, an acronym for Basic Algorithmic SImulation of Numic (Numic is the generalized linguistic designation for the Shoshonean-speakers). I present in this paper some basic elements of BASIN I as an illustration of computer simulation model building. Specific artefact frequencies and general implications of Steward's theory are beyond the scope of the present paper. The emphasis here is procedural, to describe how specific economic procurement subsystems can be simulated. Although substantive conclusions are not presented, all procedures described here are aimed at rather specific research objectives. See Thomas (1969a, 1970) for some preliminary results of the Reese River Ecological Project. This discussion is not intended to swell the bibliography of *tour de force* archaeology.

In terms of David Clarke's (1968) discussion of cultural systems, BASIN I seeks to determine the artefactual parameters of a *statistical equilibrium*. 'Systems are said to be in statistical equilibrium if the frequency of occurrence of the component populations continues to remain proportionally allocated according to certain probabilities, regardless of the vagaries of individual elements' (Clarke, 1968, p. 51). The concern is not to chart change over a cultural trajectory, but rather to establish the 'equilibrium basin' for the Great Basin Shoshonean techno-economic system. The simulation model does not employ time in the conventional sense. A 1000 year simulation run does not attempt to array systemic behaviour over 1000 continuous years. Rather, a computer run simulating 1000 years simply repeats artefactual deposition for the *same* year, 1000 times. The longer the run, the more accurate and stable are the estimates. For BASIN I, the target year is 1840, a period suitably before the first documented white contact of 1859. The assumption of environmental stability is valid, since the simulation treats the same year – 1840 – over *n* repeated trials.

SIMULATION MODEL BUILDING

BASIN I is a function-specific model, designed to simulate deposition of archaeological artefacts resulting from a posited ethnographic pattern. This Shoshonean settlement pattern is considered a system, a system being 'a set of objects together with relationships between the objects and between their attributes' (McMillan and Gonzalez, 1968, p. 1). In practice, a system boils down to simply those elements and relationships which the investigator wishes to study. A system has two properties: (1) its structure, (2) its behaviour. Both properties can serve as domains of study. Since BASIN I mimics artefact deposition, system behaviour – response to varied stimuli – is the ultimate objective. But before one can observe systemic behaviour, the structure of the system must be established. By systemic structure, I refer to the manner of arrangement of the elements of the system (Klïr and Valach, 1967). Elements are not rigidly defined, for they are simply the most convenient analytical building blocks. Elucidation of structure consists of: (1) defining elements suitable for analysis. (2) establishing inter-elemental relationships. Behaviour is subsequently studied by actuating the static structure into motion. The structure of a chess game, for example, consists of a grid, some carved statuettes, and an array of acceptable moves. These elements and their potential relationships remain only 'structure' until chess players input stimuli to the system; at this point, the system 'behaves'.

Construction of BASIN I follows these steps. It is first necessary to loosely delimit elements and their mutual relationships; the model is then activated into behaviour.

STRUCTURE OF BASIN I

Fig. 17.3 presents the structure of the Reese river Shoshonean subsistence pattern. Data were extracted directly from Steward (1938, esp. pp. 100–9). This flow chart has been explained in more detail in Thomas (1971b). Personal interpretations have been minimized, for my attempt has been to array Steward's model as faithfully as possible. Doubtless this attempt is not completely successful, because of the obtuse nature of the data. Nevertheless, misrepresentations of Steward's inductions constitute errors on my part.

The key to symbols is presented on Fig. 17.4. More or less standard flow-charting symbols have been employed. Conventions are primarily those of the FORTRAN IV computer language (e.g. Veldman, 1967). Such a diagram is standard prior to the actual programming of machine-readable statements, and allows the programmer to communicate to others the particular algorithm in use. White diamonds represent logical decision points, i.e. those in which a proposition can be answered 'yes' or 'no'. The upper diamond in Fig. 17.3, for example, is read 'Is piñon area good?'

Progression through the flow chart is determined by the truth value of these logical decisions. There are three 'activity box' types. 'Female activities' are denoted by a rectangle with excurvate sides, the parallelogram indicates 'male activities', and the rectangle represents both sexes. Inside each box is printed the activity, most of which involve distinctive tool kits. It is these assemblages that are observed in the archaeological record. For present purposes, the Tool Kit Units (TKUs) represent the 'elements' of this model. Activities are also coded by micro-environment; Fig. 17.4 indicates the types of coded shading employed. These life zones apply only to the upper Reese river valley. The activity in the upper right of Fig. 17.3, for example, is read as 'rabbit drive involving both sexes and taking place in the lower sagebrush-grass micro-environment'. The activity to the immediate left of this is read as 'piñon harvest involving only females and taking place in the piñon-juniper life zone'. The small oval represents the 'GO TO' statement in FORTRAN.

678

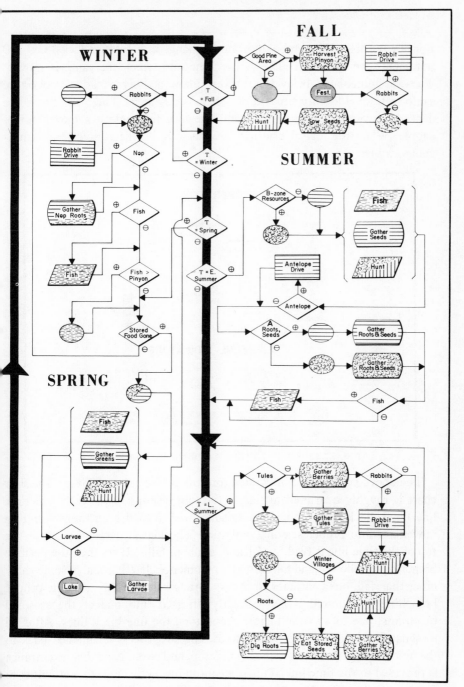

FIG. 17.3. System flow chart for Shoshonean economic cycle (data from Steward, 1938, esp. pp. 100–9).

For our purposes this symbol indicates a change in habitation locus. GO TO statements are likewise coded by life zone into which the camp is moved. The oval immediately below the 'harvest piñon' activity is read as 'move base camp to festival locality situated out of the study area'. The heavy black line denotes movement through time and the thin line indicates movement of people. When the logical priorities are unclear, brackets indicate an ambiguous sequence.

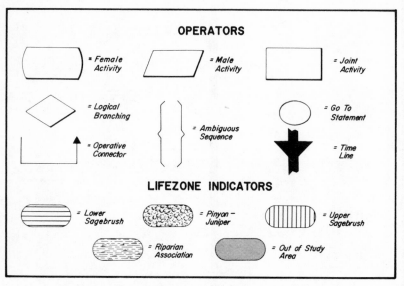

FIG. 17.4. Key to FORTRAN symbols used in Fig. 17.3.

The above symbols are integrated into the flow chart as follows. The flow chart is roughly quartered to signify the four seasons of the year. The time line flows clockwise through the seasons, with logical branchings shunting movement into proper seasonal activities. The logical decision point at the top of the time line is read 'is T [time] equal to fall?' If so, then the positive branching is followed and fall activities commence. If T is equal to some value other than fall, one continues clockwise through the seasons until the proper branching is followed. Once correctly diverted into one of the seasonal quadrants, one follows the logical connectors, the fine black lines. After all seasonal activities have been completed, and progress is channelled back to the time line, one proceeds to the next season, and so on. Note that no entrance is provided to the time line. This is a continuous cycle. Fig. 17.3 attempts to display a functioning system in statistical equilibrium. There is no speculation as to origin (see Collins, 1965).

Fall activities centre about the harvesting of piñon nuts. The piñon festival usually took place near Austin (Steward, 1938, p. 106), so groups temporarily left the study area. If local pine resources were satisfactory, groups returned to their regular winter villages. In the archaeological record, artefacts would be deposited primarily in the piñon harvesting areas and those zones connected with seed sowing and hunting. The harvesting, winter village and rabbit driving implements are in a clumped distribution, while hunting artefacts tend to be randomly distributed over piñon-juniper and upper sagebrush-grass zones.

Winter was a time when families remained in the piñon-oriented villages. Task groups left these ridge top sites only for ancillary trips to procure rabbits, roots and fish. If the fish resources proved more abundant than piñon crops, the winter village could be moved to the banks of the Reese river. Clumped artefacts tend to reflect sedentary activities. In this case, only the hunting implements would be expected to distribute in other than clumped fashion. Of particular interest is the final logical decision point in the winter quadrant – 'is stored food gone?' If so, then activities branch to the spring area of the flow chart, regardless of the season. Winter village activities could not continue once piñon stores were depleted. But if the stored foods were not exhausted in the winter, the village was not abandoned. In an exceptional piñon year, camp would not have to be broken at all. Occupants would simply have to remain in the village until the next winter. This is sedentary village living, a rather provocative thought given the conventional wisdom of Great Basin settlement patterns.

When caches were emptied, the families moved onto the flats in search of early ripening seed and root crops. The best area for this seems to be where snow melted first, near the river and streams. The ambiguous sequence brackets indicate that any course would be followed, depending upon the immediate availability of resources. Larvae were occasionally collected, out of the study area.

The summer activities were exceedingly varied, so the flow chart distinguishes early from late summer activities. Most of these activities seem to centre around the riparian and lower sagebrush-grass communities. A temporary summer camp was often established near the river, although Steward notes that '[the winter villages] were conveniently located, for the mountains behind them afforded pinenuts, roots and seeds, while the low and partly marshy valley floor provided seeds and roots, most of which grew within 4 to 5 miles of each camp' (Steward, 1938, p. 101). In terms of the archaeological record, it is crucial whether summer encampments were established along the

Reese river, and if so, how often. If these villages were commonplace, then habitation site artefacts such as drills, gravers, beads, house pits, and so on, would tend to be present. But if only temporary camps were erected by task groups, we would find only refuse from specialized activities. Steward admits the possibility of remaining in the piñon-juniper zone almost continuously. It would seem that in good piñon years, the winter village would be prolonged all year if possible. In other times, the riverside sites were probably occupied. The exact importance of riverside encampments is uncertain.

BEHAVIOUR OF BASIN I

According to Haggett and Chorley (1967, p. 23), the most fundamental feature of model building is the *selective* attitude toward information. Construction of Fig. 17.3 involved an eclectic appraisal of the Steward material. Some elements were selected because they involved artefact deposition, while other aspects were excluded. In this context, Clarke (1968, p. 75) ranked three types of variables or parameters: inessential, essential and key. *Inessential variables* are those 'not relevant to the study in hand and which consequently do not figure in the system as defined'. These variables constitute systemic *noise* and are excluded from Fig. 17.3. The owl-rodent predator cycle is an example of system noise. Although rodent and predator populations may fluctuate with respect to each other, these fluctuations are not relevant phenomena to the Shoshonean techno-economic system, as abstracted here. Negative feedback of increasing hunting pressure on large artiodactyl populations has likewise been excluded. A second sort of inessential variable is that which remains invariant in the system at hand (Clarke, 1968, p. 71). In isolating variables for behavioural simulation, those without relevant annual fluctuations are eliminated. The emphasis is upon statistical equilibrium, not dynamic equilibrium. BASIN I simulates the same year – 1840 – over and over again, and the only relevant fluctuation is on an annual basis. Resources with a relatively constant annual output are considered inessential variables in terms of system behaviour. They are simulated as constants. Activities such as this are: hunt (deer and mountain sheep), fish, gather berries, gather tules, and so on. BASIN I thus distinguishes two types of inessential variables:

(1) Noise – excluded from Fig. 17.3.
(2) Constants – included on Fig. 17.3, but simulated as invariant.

In terms of system behaviour, constant activities deposit artefacts on the ground, but such deposition is on a deterministic, rather than a stochastic basis.

682

Essential variables are 'those whose values or states change as part of the changing system' (Clarke, 1968, p. 75). In BASIN I, essential variables are activities whose occurrence is dependent upon annually fluctuating resources. Both constant and essential activities can deposit artefacts, but essential activities must be statistically modelled to simulate the annual fluctuations.

Clarke (1968, p. 75) defined *key variables* as 'those values or states not only changing as part of the changing system but which change in a correlated or non-random fashion'. BASIN I does not treat key variables at this point. Overall environmental factors, such as mean annual temperature, mean annual precipitation, seasonal distribution of rainfall, first frost, and so on, are key variables in this system. If future approximations in the BASIN series can satisfactorily control these key variables, then simulations of drought (altithermal?) conditions, for example, may be possible. Goal-directed systemic change (cultural trajectories) could perhaps also be studied if key variables could be integrated. Such possibilities are beyond the current capabilities of BASIN I.

Subsystems of BASIN I

TABLE 17.1

Resource	Resource type	Modelling type
Piñon nuts	Essential	Markov chain
Jack rabbits	Inessential	Constant
Hunt: deer and mountain sheep	Inessential	Constant
Nep roots (unidentified)	Inessential	Constant
Fish	Inessential	Constant
Greens	Inessential	Constant
Larvae	Inessential	Absent
Seeds: Indian ricegrass	Essential	Discrete Random Variable
Antelope	Essential	Discrete Random Variable
Roots	Inessential	Constant
Tules	Inessential	Constant
Berries	Inessential	Constant

Table 17.1 lists the relevant variables of BASIN I. All variables of Fig. 17.3 have been assigned to a variable category and also to a modelling procedure. Inessential-irrelevant effects have been excluded from the flow chart and from Table 17.1. Inessential-invariant variables are those that do not fluctuate from year to year. Quantities such as berry productivity, deer density, available tules, and so on, are considered constant, since these variables and their related TKUs occur annually. All TKUs for inessential invariant variables are deposited every simulated year of BASIN I.

683

Essential variables are those that fluctuate annually, but they are not necessarily the most important factors in the total dietary regimen. BASIN I variables classified as 'essential' are both random and uncorrelated. Two of these, piñon nuts and Indian ricegrass, are the most important food products of the system. The third essential variable, antelope driving, provides a minor portion of the overall diet.

A basic strategy of systems analysis is the reduction of complex processes into conceptual units more receptive to analysis. Many small, simple unit components are generally preferable to a few very complex units. BASIN I isolates resource procurement subsystems in much the manner described by Flannery (1968).

PIÑON NUT PROCUREMENT SUBSYSTEM

Nuts of the piñon pine (*Pinus monophylla*) were the staple food for the historic Western Shoshonean groups. Piñon caches, filled in the fall, could often last the village group throughout the entire year, but these native crops were notoriously erratic from one year to the next. 'Each tree yields but once in three or four years. In some years there is a good crop throughout the area, in some years virtually none. In other years, some localities yield nuts but others do not. When a good crop occurs, it is more abundant than the local population can harvest' (Steward, 1938, p. 27). When the local crop failed, families travelled to the nearest locality with a successful nut crop. Winter villages were located within a few hundred yards of the nut caches, because of the difficulty of transporting the bulky nuts.

Any worthwhile discussion of Shoshonean economic patterns must centre about the erratic piñon crop. Unfortunately, no study has been completed which adequately relates causal factors to *Pinus monophylla* annual fluctuations. Obviously some combination of growing season and monthly distribution of precipitation is involved, but the exact nature of these relations is unclear. The best data available are supplied by the United States Forest Service. From 1940 to 1947, the Southwest Forest and Range Experimental Station in Tucson advised local businesses of piñon crop densities so that they could plan for adequate harvesting crews. The species involved is *P. edulis*, rather than *P. monophylla*, but there seems to be little difference with respect to nut productivity (Little, 1938). Rangers were required to report the densities of pine nuts in their various districts, the average size of which is estimated at 37 200 acres (figure obtained by averaging all units reported in 1942). Crop success was measured in the original reports on a five-step ordinal scale from failure to bumper. These predictions have been combined into three categories and are compiled in Table 17.2. These data serve as input for formation of the simulation model. The Markov dependent case has been chosen as the proper simulation technique.

TABLE 17.2. *Piñon nut crops* (Pinus edulis) *in the South-west National Forests, 1940–7 (data from U.S. Forest Service)*

Year S	Year (S + 1)				
	Good	Fair	Failure	Total	%
Good	9	8	93	110	15
Fair	4	5	37	46	6
Failure	66	26	488	570	79
				726	100

The Markov dependent model

Markov models are quite popular in the literature of many sciences, especially geology and geography. But aside from Clarke's (1968) applications, Markov models have attracted little attention in archaeology. The reason for this is simple: archaeologists have only recently begun to phrase their research objectives in numerical terms. Markov chains will offer great assistance in a limited number of cases. For a system to be properly modelled as Markovian, the outcome of state S must be of value in predicting the state $(S + 1)$. All states before S are irrelevant in calculating transition probabilities. The Markov system is 'memoryless', for 'in a Markov dependent sequence, knowledge of the present makes the future independent of the past' (Clarke and Disney, 1970, p. 125).

In modelling the piñon nut production subsystem as a Markov process, nut production is treated as a random, or stochastic, variable. The crop is not an independent event; productivity depends upon the state of the previous trial, but no others. That is to say that the 1951 piñon crop in Austin, Nevada, relates in part to the quality of the 1950 crop. This relationship is probably due to the long maturation period of the piñon ovulates. Rainfall and other parameters must be favourable over at least two growing seasons for adequate pine cone yields. The data are too limited, but if one could establish that the 1951 crop likewise depended in part on the 1949 crop in that locality, the situation would be semi-Markovian, as described by Clarke (1968, pp. 64–7).

685

At this point, data suggest that strict Markovian procedures are adequate to handle piñon simulation.

The data matrix (Table 17.2) converts to the following probabilities:

$$
\begin{array}{ccc}
 & A & B & C \\
\end{array}
$$
$$
P = \begin{array}{c} A \\ B \\ C \end{array}
\begin{pmatrix}
0\cdot83 & 0\cdot05 & 0\cdot12 \\
0\cdot80 & 0\cdot11 & 0\cdot09 \\
0\cdot85 & 0\cdot07 & 0\cdot08
\end{pmatrix}
$$

where A is failure, B is a fair crop and C is a good crop. Markov matrices are read horizontally, by row. The transition probability from A to B, for example, is 0·05. The sum of the row probabilities must equal one. The P matrix is the probability distribution function of piñon nut crops in the American Southwest and, by extension, the Great Basin.

Monte Carlo simulation

The conversion from static probabilities to a simulated functioning subsystem is accomplished by the Monte Carlo technique. As the name implies, Monte Carlo simulation involves the selection of chance events, which input to the probability distribution function of a random variable. In this case, we wish to 'play' the above Markov chain with random numbers, assigned in the following fashion:

$$
IRN = \begin{array}{c} A \\ B \\ C \end{array}
\begin{pmatrix}
00\text{–}82 & 83\text{–}87 & 88\text{–}99 \\
00\text{–}79 & 80\text{–}90 & 91\text{–}99 \\
00\text{–}84 & 85\text{–}91 & 92\text{–}99
\end{pmatrix}
$$

As an example, if the system is in state B, and the random number 96 is selected, state B converts to state C. In terms of the piñon crop, this means that if year S had a fair (B) crop, the next year, $(S+1)$, would have a good (C) crop. All that remains is to devise a method to commence the run. Both the transition matrix (P) and the random number matrix (IRN) require an initial state for the system. This 'GO' state is selected from data on Table 17.2. The overall ratio of Failure: Fair: Good years is:

$$
\begin{array}{ccc}
A & B & C \\
79\% : 6\% : 15\%
\end{array}
$$

Converting this to random numbers:

$$
\begin{array}{ll}
\text{Failure } (A): & \begin{pmatrix} 00\text{–}78 \\ 79\text{–}84 \\ 85\text{–}99 \end{pmatrix} \\
\text{Fair } (B): & \\
\text{Good } (C): &
\end{array}
$$

The outcome of this trial determines the initial state of the system. Continuous random number generation maintains the system.

It remains to see how well the model simulates reality. Fig. 17.5 diagrams the graphic results of a 200 year trial simulation. The results indicate a 'good' crop every 7·7 years and an 'acceptable' (good or fair) crop every 5·4 years.

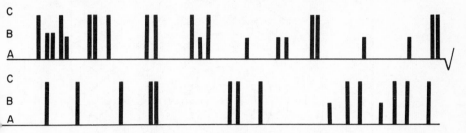

FIG. 17.5. 200 year simulation of piñon nut productivity.

This outcome agrees with Little (1941, p. 345): 'In a particular locality the interval between good [piñon nut] crops may vary from two to five years or sometimes more than ten years'. Fig. 17.5 likewise agrees with Steward's (1938, pp. 27–8) appraisal of the Great Basin piñon situation (see Fig. 1.15).

Contiguous areal simulation

The Markov method simulates a 'local' crop, one that is presumably associated with a given winter village. The minimal homogeneous units (ranger subdistricts) are 62 square miles (37 200 acres). This figure represents a pure forest stand, the area of prime interest to the Forest Service. But in the central Great Basin, topographic relief is so sharp that the piñon-juniper zone generally forms only a narrow belt on the mountain flanks (see Fig. 17.1). It becomes necessary to correct the Southwestern average to a figure more suitable to central Nevada conditions. From a Soil Conservation Service vegetational map of the region, I estimate the piñon acreage to cover about 30% of the total land surface. The correction factor changes the minimal piñon grove from 62 to 207 square miles. This figure spans all vegetational zones present in the Great Basin study area.

In order to further explore the implications of the Markov model, a *regional* piñon crop pattern has been simulated. If each minimal piñon grove unit can be considered independent, as the Southwestern data suggest, then how far must one be willing to travel to insure a successful piñon harvest year after year? Local groves and their associated winter villages were owned; it was presumably desirable to return to this home base when possible (Steward,

687

1938, p. 101). The practice of sowing wild seeds provided further impetus to stay as close as possible to one's winter village.

A two-dimensional representation is required to simulate contiguous areal units of known and fixed size. Both squares and rectangles seem to distort

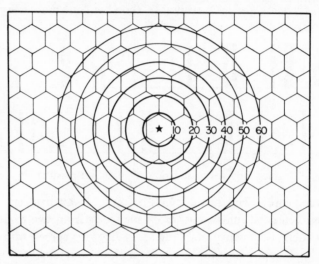

FIG. 17.6. Löschian model of homogeneous piñon groves in central Nevada. Star indicates winter village locus (G0) and concentric circles depict radius of foraging (R).

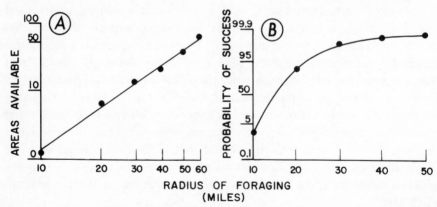

FIG. 17.7. Radius of foraging plotted against (A) logarithm of number of potential areas available and (B) probability of successful piñon harvest. (B) plotted on probability scale. Data from 100 year simulation run.

the natural areas. The *optimal-hexagonal* model (Lösch, 1954; Garner, 1967) seems most suitable because: (1) hexagons allow the greatest amount of packing of regular cells on a plane, (2) both total edge length and accessibility

688

(distance from centre to all faces) are minimized (Haggett, 1967, p. 649). The optimal-hexagon, or *Löschian* model results when a set of circles of equal radius are compressed. In the case of piñon areas, the size of each hexagon is 207 square miles, the minimal units of the data. By elementary geometry, the radius of each hexagon is computed as $r = 7 \cdot 7$ miles (Phillips and Fisher, 1896, consulted for the formulae). Fig. 17.6 presents the regional pattern of Löschian contiguous hexagons. A star indicates the winter village locus (GO), and the concentric circles indicate increasing radius of foraging (R). In Fig. 17.7A, the radius of foraging is plotted against the number of available hexagonal areas (A). A hexagon is considered available if 50% or more of its area lies inside the radius of foraging. When both variables are converted to logarithms by plotting on a log-log scale, the relationship appears to be approximately linear. This indicates that this is a power function, given by the generalized equation:

$$A = aR^b$$

where a and b are constants (see Allendoerfer and Oakley, 1955, p. 238). By simultaneously simulating piñon nut productivity in each of the available contiguous areas, a curve can be determined for probable success in piñon foraging. A 100 year simulation was run, considering each hexagon as independent. The results are plotted on Fig. 17.7B. The ordinate is the probability of finding either a good or fair piñon crop and the abscissa is the distance travelled from the winter village in miles (R). The simulation assumes that actors are aware of the states of all hexagons within the region. The assumption of a perfect communication system seems to hold for Australian hunter-gatherer groups (J. P. White, personal communication). Findings indicate that after about 30 miles, the increased probability of success tends to asymptote. This agrees remarkably well with Steward's information that Shoshoneans preferred to remain within about 20 miles of their winter village (1938, p. 232), but that they were willing to travel up to 40 or even 50 miles, when necessary, to secure a good piñon harvest (1938, p. 101). The possibility always exists that there are no successful areas in the entire system, but this remains an unlikely event.

Winter carrying capacity
The United States Forest Service data are based upon an annual yield of about 100 000 pounds of piñon nuts per township in a 'good' year (U.S. Forest Service, 1941, p. 40). A 'fair' year is considered to be about half of this total, or about 50 000 pounds per township. Since the average piñon-juniper

coverage is estimated at 30%, the piñon yield is corrected to 30 000 pounds per township in a good year, and 15 000 pounds in a fair year. The aboriginal population density of the Reese river valley has been estimated between 0·9 and 3·6 square miles per person (Steward, 1938, p. 49); the 1874 Powell and Ingalls estimate – 1·7 square miles per person – is used in subsequent calculations. Since a township is 36 square miles, the density figure is about twenty-one persons per township. Steward further estimated (1938, p. 27) that a family of four needed about 1200 pounds of piñon nuts to last one winter. This is the maximum amount that can be harvested in the limited time available, since cones are no longer suitable after they have fallen to the ground. At a *per capita* rate of 300 pounds, the twenty-one people per township require a minimum piñon harvest of 6300 pounds. In a good piñon year, one township could support approximately 100 people, or about five times the resident population. A fair year presumably could support fifty people during the winter. These figures are based upon piñon potential alone.

The Markov model projected over a Löschian landscape thus agrees with Steward's contention (1938, p. 27) that 'when a good crop occurs, it is far more abundant than the local population can harvest. . . . Persons lacking crops in their own country were welcomed, even invited, to harvest elsewhere.' The calculations also agree with Steward's statement that twenty to thirty families tended to camp within easy visiting distance of one another (1955, p. 105). At four individuals per family, these encampments numbered from 80 to 120 people. In a good piñon year, this number of people could be supported for an entire winter on only 36 square miles of land.

Serendipity and model building

Simulation studies are generally attempted as an aid to analytical research as models are constructed to simulate system behaviour. The output is then studied in relation to a rather carefully defined research problem, for most model building is highly goal-directed. The construction of models also has the fortunate side effect of presenting the investigator with unexpected results. Systems analysis *per se* often reveals significant insights; this condition is *serendipity*.

One such serendipitous discovery surfaced in the modelling of the piñon procurement subsystem. Steward repeatedly stressed the erratic character of Great Basin micro-environments. 'All of the plant and animal food had in common the extremely important characteristic that the place and quantity of their occurrence from year to year were unpredictable. . . . A locality might be very fertile one year and attract large numbers of families, but offer little food for several years thereafter' (Steward, 1955, p. 105; see also 1938, p. 233, and 1970, p. 118). According to Steward, it is the unpredictability rather than the harshness of the environment that accounts for the absence of traditional ties beyond the nuclear family level. Data gathered for the piñon procurement model, however, suggest otherwise. The United States Forest Service found that piñon nut crops can be predicted two full years before maturity (Little, 1938, 1939). The relative abundance of *ovulates* (female cones) can be estimated by macroscopic inspection, so that it is an easy matter to determine relative abundance of nuts for one and two years hence. Early frost and insects could diminish crop size, but the maximum crop can be readily estimated. This means that if the local crop is doomed, aboriginal foragers can discover this two years before the failure, and plan accordingly.

We will of course never know for certain whether the prehistoric Shoshoneans were aware of this predictive facility. Evidence on Northern Paiute native categories (Fowler and Leland, 1967) suggests that these Great Basin hunter-gatherers did have intimate knowledge of botanical phenomena, and it seems likely that pre-contact gatherers also would have observed the life cycle of piñon cones.

A powerful case could be made stressing the worth of predicting piñon crops in advance. Winter village groups could schedule their future locations. The winter village composition could be maintained, though the locus of habitation would change from time to time. Stable groups of 100 people could, it would seem, develop considerably more complex social interactions than relatively isolated family clusters. This option is unfeasible according to the Steward interpretation. I do not seriously present this 'predictable winter village locus hypothesis' as more plausible than Steward's classic model. I simply wish to emphasize that I became aware of the predictability of piñon crops, a botanical fact, as a discovery stemming from a systems analysis. This view exists as an alternative hypothesis *vis-à-vis* Steward's 'Brownian motion' approach. Neither alternative can demand one whit of scientific acclaim until properly tested and verified upon independent data.

A systems analytic approach, as used in BASIN I, can sharpen hypotheses to the point where they can be tested against the archaeological record. In such investigations, archaeologists are forced into more extensive and refined data collection. Simulation studies thus cannot be viewed as viable substitutes for field work, since such models tend to demand more comprehensive research designs than previously in use. Integrated research strategies are a necessary by-product of simulations experiments (Watt, 1968, p. 360).

691

INDIAN RICEGRASS PROCUREMENT SUBSYSTEM

Indian ricegrass (*Oryzopsis hymenoides*) produces seeds second only to those of piñon in dietary importance to the Reese river Shoshoneans (Steward, 1938, p. 104). Ricegrass grew primarily on the sagebrush flats (A-zone), although limited stands occurred in the piñon-juniper understorey. Generally harvested in June or July, ricegrass supplies had to last until the fall piñon harvest. During this period, ricegrass seeds were supplemented by roots, berries and other seed crops (esp. *Mentzelia* and *Sophia*). All of these resources, except ricegrass, produced an essentially constant crop and they are modelled as inessential-invariant variables. In years of complete piñon failure, stored seed crops, especially ricegrass, had to last the winter. This fail-safe factor was possible, of course, only in exceptionally abundant ricegrass years.

In modern times ricegrass has been an important herbage crop, generally used as food for domestic sheep. As a result, the United States Department of Agriculture has conducted extensive research on ricegrass productivity. Total ricegrass yield (herbage) is almost completely dependent upon rainfall over the fifteen month period prior to harvesting. The relationship is approximately linear, with $r = 0.89$ (data from Hutchings and Stewart, 1953, p. 28). Unfortunately, seed yield is not a direct function of total herbage. The causal factor in determining a good seed year seems to be quantity of rainfall in the spring and early summer. Data from Hutchings and Stewart (1953, table 8) indicate that localities with an April through June precipitation rate exceeding three inches will produce good seed yield. No quantitative estimate exists as to what constitutes a good seed year in terms of actual seed production.

For present purposes, ricegrass seed yield is considered as a dependent variable (Y) and April through June precipitation rate (X) is considered the independent variable. A successful seed year is determined by the relation:

$$\text{If } X \geq 3.00, \text{ then } Y = 1$$
$$\text{If } X < 3.00, \text{ then } Y = 0$$

where 1 is a good year and 0 denotes a poor seed year. If the rainfall pattern and quantity have not changed significantly from 1840, the target year, a rainfall density function can be determined. Furthermore, if this distribution is normally distributed, then the entire model can be simulated through use of normal (Gaussian) deviates. These random, yet normally distributed digits could serve as input to the proper regression equation. The April through June precipitation data from Austin, Nevada (1924–69), have been plotted in Fig. 17.8. The United States Weather Bureau station is about 30 miles from the study area. It is clear that the distribution of rainfall is too irregular and skewed to the right. The distribution is not normal and thus not amenable to Gaussian simulation. We must treat the simulation in a less elegant, yet more accurate fashion. Let X, April through June precipitation, be considered as a random variable. Although $F(X)$ is a continuous distribution, the con-

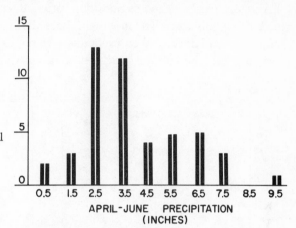

FIG. 17.8. Histogram of April through June rainfall in Austin, Lander County, Nevada, from 1924 to 1969 (data from U.S. Weather Bureau).

dition of the data allows us to operate only on the ordinal scale. X will be considered as a discrete random variable. Using the data from Fig. 17.8, the probability density function is determined to be:

$$Pr\,[X < 3\cdot00] = 18/46 = 0\cdot39$$
$$Pr\,[X \geq 3\cdot00] = 28/46 = 0\cdot61$$

The results are diagrammed on Fig. 17.9A. Simulation is accomplished by Monte Carlo means through assignment of the following random numbers:

$$IRN = \begin{matrix} 0 \\ 1 \end{matrix} \begin{pmatrix} 00,\,01,\,02,\,\ldots,\,37,\,38 \\ 39,\,40,\,41,\,\ldots,\,98,\,99 \end{pmatrix}$$

As with the piñon procurement subsystem, input to this relationship is supplied by a random number generator.

ANTELOPE PROCUREMENT SUBSYSTEM

Pronghorn antelope (*Antilocapra americana*) travelled in large herds which sometimes numbered in excess of 300. Since antelope tended to inhabit open sagebrush flats (A-zone), stalking by individual hunters was almost impossible. The Great Basin Shoshoneans procured antelope by means of large communal drives. A V-shaped sagebrush fence was constructed and a corral was located at the apex, where the long flanking arms met. Antelope were sys-

693

tematically scared ('charmed') into the corral, which was then sealed off. The herd was killed at leisure over the next few days. Steward (1938, p. 35) describes one such hunt in detail (see Heizer and Baumhoff (1962, pp. 214–16), Flannery (1966) and Thomas (1969b) for cultural and social implications of antelope drives).

Antelope herd size and composition varied, fluctuating randomly from year to year, not unlike deer and mountain sheep. Both deer and sheep were usually hunted by individuals, so entire herds were not radically affected by hunting pressure. But the cultural practices of decimating an antelope herd placed

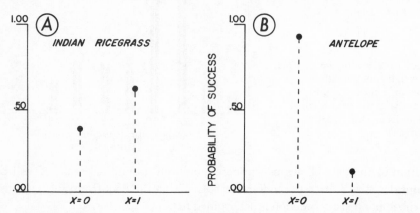

FIG. 17.9. Probability density function, $F(X)$, for successful procurement of (A) Indian ricegrass seeds and (B) pronghorn antelope.

severe stresses on pronghorn population numbers. Major Howard Egan (quoted in Steward, 1938, p. 35) commented that 'Indians told me that the last drive, before this one at this place, was nearly twelve years ago and the old man never expected to see another at this place, for it would take many years for the animals to increase in sufficient numbers to make it pay to drive.' It is the 'all or nothing' nature of the communal antelope drive that causes the severe annual fluctuation. This subsystem is thus regulated by cultural rather than natural mechanisms. Let us accept Egan's figure of twelve years as the best available estimate of drive frequency. Exogenous factors, such as immigration, disease, poor results in the initial hunt, and so on, add a stochastic element into this otherwise regular cycle. If o signifies no drive and 1 means a successful drive, the antelope procurement subsystem can be modelled as a discrete random variable. Procedure here is similar to simulation of the ricegrass procurement subsystem, although the regulatory mechanisms are quite different. The probability density function for antelope driving is:

694

$$Pr\ [X = 0] = 11/12 = 0\cdot92$$
$$Pr\ [X = 1] = 1/12 = 0\cdot08$$

In the long run, a successful drive will tend to occur every twelve years in a given valley. But the antelope procurement subsystem is subject to short-term random fluctuation. This model is represented on Fig. 17.9B. The states are mutually exclusive in that either an antelope drive occurs or it does not; there is no middle ground. The following random numbers are assigned:

$$IRN = \begin{matrix} 0 \\ 1 \end{matrix} \begin{pmatrix} 00,\ 01,\ 02,\ \ldots,\ 90,\ 91 \\ 92,\ 93,\ 94,\ \ldots,\ 98,\ 99 \end{pmatrix}$$

SUBSYSTEM SIMULATION

Although each essential variable has been assigned a theoretical probability distribution, the actual subsystem outputs are determined by random selection of two-digit numbers. To compare these predicted values with some

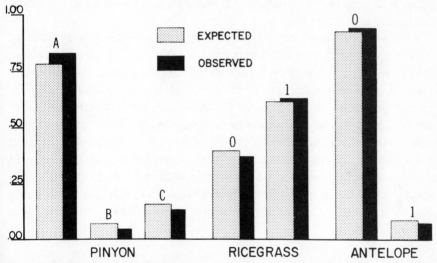

FIG. 17.10. Histogram comparing expected with observed frequencies for primary procurement systems of BASIN I. Observed frequencies were obtained from a 1000 year Monte Carlo simulation.

observed frequencies, a 1000 year simulation run was completed on each sub-system. These results, presented on Fig. 17.10, in no sense constitute a test of the modelling. The charts simply indicate how closely randomly generated input can be expected to conform to predicted results. The close correspondence between observed and expected values should surprise nobody familiar

695

with random procedures. The illustration is presented as an example to those archaeologists who still harbour a lingering mistrust of things random. The random condition is rigidly defined in statistics and in no sense should random be taken as synonymous with haphazard, casual, fortuitous or aimless.

INTRA-SYSTEM INTERACTIONS

BASIN I obviously ignores interactions between subsystems. In more advanced simulation models the interaction effect may be more significant than any of the main effects (Watt, 1968, p. 151). But BASIN I is not yet in such a complex form. The attempt here has been to simplify an intricate extractive system into component subsystems, so that artefactual deposition can be simulated. Piñon productivity, for example, has been modelled as a random process, although we know that the crop is ultimately dependent upon climatic factors. Rainfall and growing season are doubtless important parameters of ultimate piñon nut procurement; thus there must be some interaction between the piñon and ricegrass subsystems, since ricegrass was modelled as dependent exclusively upon precipitation.

At this point, we are constrained by the quality of the existing data, for the dependent relation of piñon nuts upon precipitation is manifestly unclear. It is known that piñon cones mature over a three-year period, so some combination of rainfall and length of growing season probably accounts for the annual fluctuation. But what is the key combination? Productivity of piñon has been modelled *as if* it were a random process. While future approximations can hopefully reduce this stochastic element, the *ceteris paribus* reasoning model building of this type must simply be accepted at the outset. This is not to say that models ought to be constructed willy-nilly from obviously fragmented data. The acid test for a simulation model of this sort is not how it was constructed, but rather whether it behaves in a fashion indicative of the activity it simulates.

ARTEFACT LEVEL PREDICTIONS

To this point, BASIN I has operated on the level of the tool kit unit, TKU. But to the archaeologist, the tool kit is an analytical unit, unobservable in the world of facts. The operational taxonomic unit (OTU) basic to archaeology must be the artefact. The transition from the tool kit level to the artefact level is a slippery one indeed. This aspect is discussed in more detail in Thomas (1971b), so it will suffice to here mention briefly the statistical models used in artefact prediction.

Typology

Recently, Longacre (1970) defined three dimensions of variation in archaeological artefacts: (1) stylistic, (2) technological, (3) functional. These sources of variation are in no sense independent, for they are interwoven into the fabric of all artefact typology. In statistical terms, the total variance in the system (the sum of squares) can be partitioned into components. Consider the analysis of variance model for a completely randomized three-factor design (Myers, 1966, ch. 3):

$$Y_{ijkm} = \mu + \alpha_j + \beta_k + \gamma_m + (\alpha\beta)_{jk} + (\alpha\gamma)_{jm} + (\beta\gamma)_{km} + (\alpha\beta\gamma)_{jkm} + \varepsilon_{ijkm}$$

This equation models artefact variability in terms of its constituent components. Y_{ijkm} is the specific measure of a single attribute to an artefact and μ is the mean of the parent population prior to the establishment of the treatments. The other sources of variation are:

$\alpha_j = \mu_j - \mu$, the main effect of treatment A_j, stylistics.

$\beta_k = \mu_k - \mu$, the main effect of treatment B_k, technology.

$\gamma_m = \mu_m - \mu$, the main effect of treatment C_m, function.

$(\alpha\beta)_{jk} = \mu_{jk} - \mu_j - \mu_k + \mu$, the interaction effect of A_j and B_k.

$(\alpha\gamma)_{jm} = \mu_{jm} - \mu_j - \mu_m + \mu$, the interaction effect of A_j and C_m.

$(\beta\gamma)_{km} = \mu_{km} - \mu_k - \mu_m + \mu$, the interaction effect of B_k and C_m.

$(\alpha\beta\gamma)_{jkm} = \mu_{jkm} - \mu_{jk} - \mu_{jm} - \mu_{km} + \mu_j + \mu_k + \mu_m - \mu$, the interaction effect of A_j, B_k and C_m.

$\varepsilon_{ijkm} = Y_{ijkm} - \mu_{jkm}$, the error component.

This model forces one to look beyond the main effects and consider the interactions. It may be, for example, that taken together, technological (B_k) and functional (C_m) criteria produce an interaction effect $(B\gamma)_{km}$, not altogether attributable to either treatment taken separately.

BASIN I is concerned primarily with functional variability, C_m. In real world terms, one must isolate *modes* (Rouse, 1960), measured as Y_{ijkm}, which best reflect functional variation. The C_m effect must be significant, but A_j, B_k and interaction effects must distribute by the null hypothesis. One of the best ways to isolate these functionally salient modes is through analysis of ethnographic artefacts. A paper by Gould, Koster and Sontz (1971) is of aid here. While working with documented Australian aboriginal material, the authors found a most significant correlation between the tool working edge and tool function. This finding was further validated in ethnographic artefacts from the New Guinea Highlands (White and Thomas, Chapter 7 of this volume). Gould, Koster and Sontz were able to demonstrate that different seeds and nuts require different motions of grinding, which is presumably detectable on the artefacts. What remains is to demonstrate statistically that the other treatment effects discussed here are not significant with respect to these modes.

BASIN I thus does not predict artefact types *per se*, but it predicts expected probabilities in terms of function-specific modes. The concept of the 'whole tool', i.e. phenetic affinity, is not relevant in this context. A butchering kit, for example, might be projected as a set of lithic items with edge angles between 12° and 36°. Other formal characteristics, such as shape, can simply interject noise into the problem of functional variability.

Artefact dispersal

The *Poisson distribution* can be most useful in treating artefact and feature dispersions in BASIN I. To exhibit a Poisson distribution, an array of items must have two properties (Sokal and Rohlf, 1969, pp. 83–95):

(1) The mean $(\overline{X})$ must be small relative to the maximum possible number of events per sampling unit.
(2) Occurrence of events must be independent of prior occurrences within the sampling unit.

Items in a Poisson distribution are thus 'rare and random events'. The Poisson distribution has been applied extensively in quantitative plant ecology, where data often take the form of density per sampling unit (Greig-Smith, 1964). Poisson techniques are also relevant to archaeological research designs which take the form of areal survey over large grid patterns (Binford, 1964; Thomas, 1969a). Curve-fitting programs (e.g. Ondrick and Griffiths, 1969) are readily available to determine whether data are distributed in Poisson fashion. Another relatively simple method for treating artefact and feature dispersal is illustrated in Fig. 17.11. The relationships of points in a regular grid system can be expressed as a *coefficient of dispersion* (Sokal and Rohlf, 1969, p. 88):

$$C.D. = s^2/\overline{X}$$

where s^2 is the sample variance and $\overline{X}$ is the sample mean. A value of *C.D.* much greater than 1 indicates a clumped sample and a value much less than 1 denotes repulsion between elements. In these cases, items are not statistically independent and therefore not distributed in a Poisson manner. The artefacts of a winter village should be in a clumped distribution, for they would not be expected to be randomly strewn across the landscape. An archaeological in-

698

stance of a dispersed distribution, however, does not come readily to mind. A value of *C.D.* roughly equal to 1 verifies a Poisson (random) distribution, if the $\bar{X}$ is small relative to the grid size. Projectile points lost while pursuing deer in the upper sagebrush-grass zone of the Reese river valley are expected to fall in a Poisson distribution (Fig. 17.11, upper example).

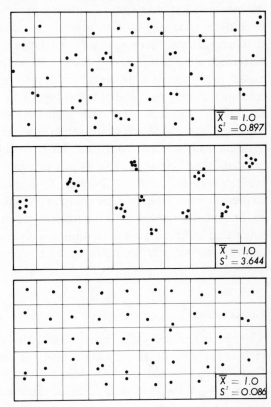

FIG. 17.11. Simulated point distributions within a grid system. Each example contains 48 points. Upper example: random distribution (C.D. = 0·90). Middle example: clumped distribution (C.D. = 3·64). Lower example: dispersed distribution (C.D. = 0·09).

Role of the computer in simulation

Since the general topic of this discussion is computer simulation models in archaeology, some mention of computing machinery is perhaps not untoward. Every calculation thus far performed for BASIN I could have been executed by manual means. Given unlimited personnel, in fact, *any* computer model could be simulated by pencil-and-paper means. The true role of the computer is a pragmatic one. The speed and storage capacity of modern computing machinery enables the investigator to undertake tasks which were previously impossible because of their complexity and tedious computations. With the computer standing ready, one is free to engage in 'fishing expeditions', whereby several computational methods are applied. This experimentation leads to more realistic simulation and often to serendipity. One is able to expand the model almost indefinitely, without fear of the calculations becoming overly cumbersome.

BASIN I is currently programmed in the FORTRAN IV computer language. All but the most elemental calculations presented here were performed on a Burroughs 5500 digital computer at the Computer Center, University of California, Davis. Since BASIN I is a relatively simple model, one could have performed all of these computations using simple desk equipment. But as the BASIN model increases in complexity, and begins to deal with key variables, computer processing becomes mandatory. The random number sequences, for example, were generated by machine, using the algorithm supplied by Golden (1965, pp. 210–12). At this early stage, however, random numbers could have been manually selected from a suitable table. The RAND Corporation (1955) has published one such table which presents a million random digits and 100 000 normal (Gaussian) deviates. By beginning with simulations directly tailored to a machine, in a programming language, one avoids the tedium of conversion from manual to automated means. At this point, manual and automated techniques are almost interchangeable. Perhaps this is one indication that we are only beginning to tap the potential of computer simulation models.

Conclusions

This discussion had called upon several kinds of models. The first one was really a theory – Julian Steward's theory of Shoshonean settlement patterns. Facts were examined and fitted into a plausible model, forming an *inductive model*. An infinite set of such plausible explanations, each an inductive model, can accompany each set of facts. All inductive models derived from the same set of facts have equal epistemological status, for there are no set rules for induction. The 'correct' model can be selected only by verification with independent data; the induction itself is not directly testable, since only the logical consequences of a theory can be verified. To facilitate charting these consequences, *deductive models* can be constructed. Unlike inductive models, deductive models observe a rigid set of rules – the rules of logic. It must be established at each step that components of the deductive model are true consequences of the original induction. BASIN I is a deductive model, constructed expressly to assist in the verification of Steward's inductive model. A third level of model building operates at the level of systemic variables. Subsystems have been modelled by *mathematical models* (Krumbein and Graybill, 1965, p. 15). Stochastic-mathematical models are utilized to simulate the major subsystem variables. Piñon productivity was modelled by Markov processes, ricegrass seed yield was considered as a discrete random variable, and so on. Deterministic-mathematical models were enlisted to simulate invariant resources such as roots and deer populations. When these models are integrated into a coherent research design, they input to each other to produce the desired simulation.

What of the future of such studies in archaeology? One safe prediction is that systems analytic procedures will become increasingly popular. Computers will see much more extensive service, due partly to the increased quality and availability of computing machinery. Equally important is the realization that quantitative techniques may be just the key to unlock some of the past's most carefully guarded secrets. It is for this reason that simulation studies will probably flourish.

Models operating in statistical equilibrium, such as BASIN I, seem to be a necessary initial step. From the lessons learned in simple simulation studies, we may become better able to chart complex cultural trajectories of dynamic equilibrium (Clarke, 1968, p. 51). As archaeologists approach such rates-of-change models, they must realize that their mathematical sophistication must likewise develop. Differential, difference and difference-differential equations, for example, are beyond the grasp of most contemporary archaeologists. As the level of model-complexity increases, archaeologists are likely to discover that the real world tends to be non-linear, rather than linear (Watt, 1966, p. 10). Models will tend to become increasingly quantified and mathematically oriented. Archaeologists will have to accept this ascent in stride – indeed even accommodate to it – if we are to continue to share a common body of literature. Sokal and Rohlf (1969, pp. viii–ix) have set out minimum statistical requirements for biology graduate students; those of archaeology pale by comparison. If graduate programmes cannot keep pace with current quantitative advances, archaeology faces a paradoxical future: the 'working archaeologists' may plod along, applying the techniques of the 1950s to the problems of tomorrow. In other laboratories, unseeing and unhearing, will be the 'mathematical archaeologists' (or whatever they may choose to call themselves), who continue to devise methodologies to solve questions which no one may be asking. Archaeological pluralism can be avoided only by emphasizing the interplay of the methodological and the substantive. Neither the atheoretical 'dirt archaeologist' nor the devotee of 'sterile methodological virtuosity' (Deetz, 1968, p. 48) commands a place in the archaeology of the future.

Notes

1. Contribution No. 6 of the Reese River Ecological Project.

Acknowledgements

I thank the following for sundry assistance along the way: M. A. Baumhoff, W. G. Davis, R. A. Gould, P. Grossbehk, T. C. Thomas, D. L. True, J. P. White and L. Williams. This paper was supported in part by funds from the National Science Foundation.

References

ALLENDOERFER, C. B. and OAKLEY, C. O. (1955) *Principles of Mathematics*. New York: McGraw-Hill.

BILLINGS, W. G. (1951) Vegetational zonation in the Great Basin of western North America. *Compt. Rend du Colleque sur les Bases écologiques de la Régénération de la Végétation des Zones Arides*, 101–22. Paris: Union of the International Society of Biology.

BINFORD, L. R. (1964) A consideration of archaeological research design. *American Antiquity*, 29 (4), 425–41.

BINFORD, L. R. (1968) Some comments on historical versus processual archaeology. *Southwestern Journal of Anthropology*, 24 (3), 267–75.

CLARKE, A. B. and DISNEY, R. L. (1970) *Probability and Random Processes for Engineers and Scientists*. New York: Wiley.

CLARKE, D. L. (1968) *Analytical Archaeology*. London: Methuen.

COLLINS, P. W. (1965) Functional analysis. In LEEDS, A. and VAYDA, A. P. (eds.) *Man, Culture and Animals*. Washington, D.C.: American Association for the Advancement of Science.

DEETZ, J. (1968) The inference of residence and descent rules from archaeological data. In BINFORD, S. R. and BINFORD, L. R. (eds.) *New Perspectives in Archaeology*, 41–8. Chicago: Aldine.

DORAN, J. (1970) Systems theory, computer simulations and archaeology. *World Archaeology*, 1 (3) 289–98.

FLANNERY, K. V. (1966) The postglacial 'readaptation' as viewed from Meso-america. *American Antiquity*, 31, (6), 800–5.

FLANNERY, K. V. (1967) Culture history v. cultural process: a debate in American archaeology. *Scientific American*, 217 (2), 119–21.

FLANNERY, K. V. (1968) Archaeological systems theory and early Mesoamerica. In MEGGERS, B. J. (ed.) *Anthropological Archaeology in the Americas*, 67–87. Washington, D.C.: Anthropological Society.

FOWLER, C. S. and LELAND, J. (1967). Some Northern Paiute native categories. *Ethnology*, 6 (4), 381–404.

GARNER, B. (1967) Models of urban geography and settlement location. In CHORLEY, R. J. and HAGGETT, P. (eds.) *Models in Geography*, 303–60. London: Methuen.

GOLDEN, J. T. (1965) *FORTRAN IV Programming and Computing*. Englewood Cliffs, N. J.: Prentice Hall.

GOULD, R. A., KOSTER, D. A. and SONTZ, A. L. (1971) The lithic assemblage of the Western Desert aborigines of Australia. *American Antiquity*, **36** (2), 149–69.

GREIG-SMITH, P. (1964) *Quantitative Plant Ecology*. London: Butterworth.

HAGGETT, P. (1967) Network models in geography. in CHORLEY, R. J. and HAGGETT, P. (eds.) *Models in Geography*, 609–68. London: Methuen.

HAGGETT, P. and CHORLEY, R. J. (1967) Models, paradigms and the new geography. In CHORLEY, R. J. and HAGGETT, P. (eds.) *Models in Geography*, 19–41. London: Methuen.

HEIZER, R. F. and BAUMHOFF, M. A. (1962) *Prehistoric Rock Art of Nevada and Eastern California*. Berkeley: University of California Press.

HUTCHINGS, S. S. and STEWART, G. (1953) *Increasing Forage Yields and Sheep Production on Intermountain Winter Ranges*. U. S. Department of Agriculture Circular No. 925.

IRWIN-WILLIAMS, C. (1967) Picosa: the elementary Southwestern culture. *American Antiquity*, **32** (4), 441–57.

JENNINGS, J. D. (1957) *Danger Cave*. University of Utah Anthropological Papers No. 27.

JUDGE, W. J. (1970) Systems analysis and the Folsom-Midland question. *Southwestern Journal of Anthropology*, **26** (1), 40–51.

KEMENY, J. G. (1959) *A Philosopher Looks at Science*. New York: Van Nostrand.

KLĬR, J. and VALACH, M. (1967) *Cybernetic Modelling*. New York: Van Nostrand.

KRUMBEIN, W. C. and GRAYBILL, F. A. (1965) *An Introduction to Statistical Models in Geology*. New York: McGraw-Hill.

LITTLE, E. L. (1938) *The Earliest Stages of Piñon Cones*. Southwestern Forest and Range Experimental Station (Tucson) Research Note No. 46.

LITTLE, E. L. (1939) *Suggestions for Estimating Piñon Nut Crops*. Southwestern Forest and Experimental Station (Tucson) Research Note No. 58.

LITTLE, E. L. (1941) Managing woodlands for piñon nuts. *Chronica Botanica*, **6** (15), 348–9.

LONGACRE, W. A. (1970) Current thinking in American archaeology. *Bulletins of the American Anthropological Association*, **3**, 2 (3), 126–38.

LÖSCH, A. (1954) *The Economics of Location*. New Haven, Conn: Yale University Press.

MCMILLAN, C. and GONZALEZ, R. F. (1968) *Systems Analysis: A Computer Approach to Decision Models*. Homewood, Ill., Irwin.

MACNEISH, R. S. (1964) Ancient Mesoamerican civilization. *Science*, **143** (3606), 531–7.

MYERS, J. L. (1966) *Fundamentals of Experimental Design*. Boston, Mass.: Allyn & Bacon.

ONDRICK, C. W. and GRIFFITHS, J. C. (1969) *FORTRAN IV Computer Program for Fitting Observed Count Data*. Computer Contribution No. 35, Kansas Geological Survey.

OWEN, R. C. (1964) The patrilocal band. *American Anthropologist*, **67**, 675–90.

PHILLIPS, A. W. and FISHER, I. (1896) *Plane Geometry*. New York.

RAND CORPORATION, THE (1955) *A Million Random Digits with 100 000 Normal Deviates*. Glencoe, Ill.: Free Press.

ROUSE, I. (1960) The classification of artifacts in archaeology. *American Antiquity*, **25** (3), 313–23.

SERVICE, E. R. (1962) *Primitive Social Organization*. New York: Random House.

SOKAL, R. R. and ROHLF, F. J. (1969) *Biometry*. San Francisco: Freeman.

STEWARD, J. H. (1938) *Basin-Plateau Aboriginal Sociopolitical Groups*. Bureau of American Ethnology Bulletin No. 120.

STEWARD, J. H. (1941) Culture element distributions, XIII: Nevada Shoshone. *University of California Anthropological Records*, **4** (2), 209–359.

STEWARD, J. H. (1955) *Theory of Culture Change*. Urbana, Ill.: University of Illinois Press.

STEWARD, J. H. (1970) The foundations of basin-plateau Shoshonean society. In SWANSON, E. (ed.) *Languages and Cultures of Western North America*. Caldwell, Idaho.

THOMAS, D. H. (1969a) Regional sampling in archaeology: a pilot Great Basin research design. *University of California Archaeological Survey Annual Report 1968–1969*, **11**, 87–100.

THOMAS, D. H. (1969b) Great Basin hunting patterns: a quantitative method for treating faunal remains. *American Antiquity*, **34** (4), 392–401.

THOMAS, D. H. (1970) Archaeology's operational imperative: Great Basin projectile points as a test case. *University of California Archaeological Survey Annual Report 1969–1970*, **12**, 27–60.

THOMAS, D. H. (1971a) Historic and prehistoric man-land relations in the Reese river valley, central Nevada. *Nevada Historical Quarterly*, **14** (4), 2–9.

THOMAS, D. H. (1971b) A cybernetic modelling of historic Shoshoni economic patterns. In AIKENS, C. M. (ed.) *Great Basin Anthropological Conference 1970: Selected Papers*, 119–34. Eugene, Oregon.

UNITED STATES FOREST SERVICE (1941) *Annual Report*. Tucson: Southwestern Forest and Range Experimental Station.

VELDMAN, D. (1967) *FORTRAN Programming for the Behavioural Sciences*. New York: Holt, Rinehart & Winston.

WATT, K. (1966) *Systems Analysis in Ecology*. New York: Academic Press.

WATT, K. (1968) *Ecology and Resource Management*. New York: McGraw-Hill.

WILMSEN, E. (1970) *Lithic Analysis and Cultural Inference: A Paleo-Indian Case*. Anthropological Papers of the University of Arizona No. 16.

18

A territorial model for archaeology: a behavioural and geographical approach

M. R. JARMAN

University of Cambridge, British Academy Project, England

The term 'model' has of late enjoyed a considerable vogue among archaeologists, and attention has been focused on the use of models by many publications, in particular those concerned with the application of mathematical analytical techniques to archaeology. The potential importance to the subject of a more conscious and controlled use of models cannot be doubted, but to date many archaeologists have changed their vocabulary rather than their mental attitudes, and little impact has been apparent in many areas of study. As Clarke (1968) said, 'it is in precisely those recent works in which the term is most courageously flourished that no actual model is ever erected, discussed, fitted against real data, or explicitly elaborated in any way'. This chapter arises from recent advances in field techniques for studying archaeological sites, which have been developed over a number of years by various members of the British Academy Major Research Project on the Early History of Agriculture. The data resulting from these techniques have important implications at both the methodological and the theoretical levels. Should the approach discussed here continue to prove useful and its implications be supported by future research, there seems every reason to hope that it may give rise to more complex and precise models for archaeological procedure and interpretation in the future.

The theory

Two recent publications provided between them an initial impetus for this research, and it is perhaps characteristic of archaeology at the present that neither of them was written by or for archaeologists, one indeed concerning a subject which many might think to be considerably outside the scope of proper archaeological interest. Chisholm's (1968) *Rural Settlement and Land*

705

Use and Lee's (1969) ' !Kung bushman subsistence: an input–output analysis' each brings into prominence a factor affecting modern human behaviour to so important a degree that its significance for studies of past human behaviour can hardly be in doubt. Certainly, recognition of this factor has been implicit in some archaeological work and has long been explicit in economic geography. The force and relevance of this factor for archaeology, however, can be greatly enhanced by its statement in formal terms, and when an effort is made to trace its logical implications for the subject as a whole.

In general terms the principle states that there is a close relationship between the ability of a human population to exploit a resource profitably and the expenditure of energy necessary for its exploitation. More specifically one may note that, as an expression of this principle, human populations are generally only able to exploit resources that exist within a certain distance of their occupation site, be this a camp, cave, village or town. The precise limits of the potential exploitation territory will of course vary greatly with the operation of a whole complex of factors, including technology, population pressure, and the prevailing economic system, but one may perceive behind the apparent variability occasioned by these factors the existence of a powerful limiting force which restricts the actual range of human behaviour to a relatively small area within the theoretical, possible range. Human populations, urban, rural, and non-agricultural, do not exploit their surroundings at random, and for any set of circumstances at a particular site there are norms that characterize the limits or thresholds beyond which exploitation of a resource is unprofitable and is unlikely to take place in the long run. There are unfortunately few data available on this subject especially for the smaller, less highly organized human groups. Yet we may note that the !Kung bushmen rarely exploit an area more than 9·5 km away from their campsite (Lee, 1969); that the Hadza women exploit vegetable food within one hour's walking distance of the camp, while the men will commonly abandon game not found within a day's tracking after being shot (Woodburn, 1968); and that 11 km is considered the approximate radius of the hunting territory among some Australian aborigines (Davidson, 1928). Similarly, Chisholm has demonstrated the drastic decrease in productivity as distance increases from the farm settlement in many modern agricultural societies. That the same relationship holds in urban situations is illustrated by the work of Dåhl (1957), for instance, who showed the high fall of movement with distance in a Swedish town. Furthermore it is evident that not only are urban dwellers accustomed to travel only within certain radii of their homes in the course of their day-to-day lives, but in a similar way towns serve definable rural 'catchment areas' which vary according to the commodity in question, the size of the town, local population, and so on. The concept of archaeological 'catchment analysis' has been discussed elsewhere (Vita-Finzi and Higgs, 1970; Jarman, Vita-Finzi and Higgs, in press).

As a logical outcome of these considerations it is possible to view archaeological sites as occupying positions within 'exploitation territories', and to attempt an analysis of the economic possibilities offered by the site location in relation to the available resources. It is of importance to clarify the meaning of the word territory in this context, the more so because of recent controversy as regards the implications of a territorial model in the studies of human behaviour. Recent popular studies by Lorenz (1963) and Ardrey (1967) have attempted to demonstrate the existence of important analogies between aspects of animal and human behaviour, among them the presence of a territorial 'force' or 'instinct', and published comment on their arguments has involved complex ramifications into such topics as aggression, the nature and reality of 'drives' or 'instincts', and the function and origin of social patterning in animal populations. So many different opinions have been expressed by writers of varying persuasions and disciplines that the issues involved are difficult to isolate and discuss logically. Crook's (1968) discussion is of some help here, and his emphasis on the variability and complexity of territorial and aggressive behaviour is a salutary warning against the dangers of facile generalization. The accepted ecological/ethological definition of the term territory requires that a location be defended: 'Individuals, pairs or family groups of vertebrates and the higher invertebrates commonly restrict their activities to a definite area, called the home range. If this area is actively defended it is called a *territory*' (Odum, 1959). Ardrey appears to accept this definition in his discussion of human behaviour, and it is partly his inability to demonstrate the existence of defended territories in early human populations that has exposed his views to so much criticism. It is to some extent unfortunate that so much emphasis has been laid on the defensive aspects of territorial behaviour, for it cannot be studied realistically as an isolated mechanism, its nature and even its existence being closely related to factors such as population pressure. As Crook says, 'Ecological and social conditions are thus important in determining whether a population does or does not exhibit territorial behaviour.' Similarly, Pitelka (1959) has argued that 'functionally territory is primarily an ecological phenomenon and not a behaviouristic one . . .'. Territory can thus be considered as a particular expression of a varied and widespread type of behaviour relating animal populations in an organized way to particular locations in the environment.

With this preamble we can return to a consideration of the archaeological *site exploitation territory*, which can be defined as an area around a site habitually exploited by a human group (Vita-Finzi and Higgs, 1970). It is vital to realize that this concept as used here contains no prejudgement as to whether or not maintenance of the territory involves active defence or aggression. As with other animal populations this will be affected by specific local conditions of demography and ecology, and certainly one could quote many examples of both defended and undefended human territories from the historical and anthropological literature. It could be argued that in view of the more specific meaning assigned to the word by ecologists it is merely confusing to use it in a different sense here. There are advantages in doing so, however. In common parlance the word 'territory' has a general meaning which is fully appropriate to its use as proposed here, and it provides a less cumbersome term than would an adaptation of the ecological 'home range' or 'core area' terms. A more important consideration is the necessity, as Higgs (1968) has pointed out, for archaeology to evolve its own framework of objectives, classifications and methods without allowing itself to be hampered and restricted by those of other disciplines. This is not a plea for an 'isolationist archaeology' but rather that archaeologists arrange their priorities so that they are able to make use of those features and techniques of other disciplines that are helpful to them, but that they do not allow classifications based on non-archaeological data (and erected for non-archaeological objectives) to deter them from different classifications and objectives. In the specific instance discussed here, it is evident that we are never likely to be able to tell whether or not most prehistoric human groups possessed defended territories in the ethological sense, but this is not sufficient reason to reject the use of the term 'territory' if this seems appropriate to our data and to our research objectives. The techniques and principles discussed here should be considered as an aspect of site catchment analysis (Jarman, Vita-Finzi and Higgs, in press).

Although it has received scant recognition in the archaeological literature, evidence is available which suggests that many human groups may in the past, as now, have relied to a large extent on a pattern of seasonal movement as a mechanism whereby they could optimize their exploitive relationship with the environment. Ethnological support for such a view is overwhelming, and in 1939 a paper was published in an archaeological journal entitled 'The seasonal factor in human culture' (Thomson, 1939). Writing for archaeologists, he was attempting to indicate some limitations of archaeological data, and he states of the Wik Monkan Australian aborigines that 'an onlooker, seeing these people at different seasons of the year, would
708

find them engaged in occupations so diverse, and with weapons and utensils differing so much in character, that if he were unaware of the seasonal influence on food supply, and consequently upon occupation, he would be led to conclude that they were different groups.' Archaeologists, however, seem in general to be all too 'unaware of the seasonal influence on food supply, and consequently upon occupation', and their data are of course a great deal more scanty and difficult to interpret than those available to Thomson's hypothetical contemporary onlooker. The archaeological culture hypothesis seems in many cases to have involved its proponents in an undue preference for the view that prehistoric sites were permanently occupied unless the reverse can be demonstrated. The possibility that a single human group might at different seasons and places be using a partially or wholly different tool kit has rarely been given much weight in considerations of prehistoric artefact assemblages; and the customary procedure, the erection of a taxonomic system based on similarity of assemblages, and the subsequent treating of these taxonomic clusters as cultures, or human groups, gives both an unnecessarily complex and an oversimplified view of the situation – too complex in that it invites the ever finer division of assemblage clusters into cultural units which may never have had reality from the point of view of the tool makers, and too simple in that it represents a vast over-interpretation of the data, with but a single basic model being considered for the overall interpretation. A step in the other direction has been taken by the recent work of Higgs *et al.* (1967) in north Greece, where a logical case was constructed for considering the two partly contemporaneous Palaeolithic sites of Asprochaliko and Kastritsa as being two elements within the 'exploitive strategy' of a single human group, in spite of the fact that some elements in the two assemblages were so different that one could, on another hypothesis, have construed them as representing two autonomous local cultures.

These considerations lead to a refinement of the concept of site exploitation territories, as the possibility must obviously be considered that two or more sites may form part of the total exploitation of a single group, thus expanding the territory of the human population far beyond that relating to a particular site. The resulting entity may be called the *annual territory* of a human group, that area habitually exploited in the course of a single year (Vita-Finzi and Higgs, 1970). The annual territory will contain one or more individual site territories which may be truly contiguous or linked only by a narrow corridor necessary for movement. This is in some ways similar to Jewell's (1966) 'lifetime range' concept for animal behaviour studies, attractive in that it has an absolute quality which is intellectually appealing. For our purposes, however, the more general indication of primary regular behaviour patterns is a more realistic goal than the all-inclusive analysis of total territorial behaviour, especially as archaeology is unlikely to supply data concerning exceptional or unpredictable movements.

It was said earlier that an important impulse for this work came from studies by Lee on the !Kung bushman, and by Chisholm on rural settlement. Both concern themselves with the factor of distance in questions of settlement and exploitation. 'Distance, then, is the central theme around which this book is written. . . . It is a factor which has its influence everywhere in the world in all location matters', says Chisholm. He goes on to suggest that one can perceive threshold distances beyond which subsistence agriculture is unlikely to be profitable, a circle of 1 km radius enclosing the area of greatest economic importance to a particular site, while exploitation is rarely important beyond a 5 km radius. Similarly Lee defined a 10 km limit as the maximum extent of normal !Kung exploitation from any site. Efforts made to apply this principle to field studies of archaeological sites have forced us to modify this concept, however, as it is evident that behind the factor of distance lies a more basic one, that of time/energy. This becomes apparent as soon as areas with rugged topography are considered; taking, for example, a site located on the intersection of a level plain and a precipitous mountain range, the limit of economic exploitation does not form a circular zone around the site, for more energy and time are required to exploit at a point, say, 2 km away on the mountainous side of the site than at a point the same distance away on the plain. In practical terms this means that site exploitation territories tend in many cases to be irregularly shaped, not circular; they are related ultimately to energy and efficiency, rather than to distance itself. For this reason technology may have a profound effect upon the size and shape of territories, increasingly sophisticated methods of transport, for instance, allowing greater catchment areas to be exploited economically. Figure 18.1 illustrates the disparity between chronological and topographical distance in Britain today. Railway electrification has brought London and Manchester equidistant from Birmingham in spite of the fact that in terms of topographic distance London is considerably further from Birmingham (*c.* 105 miles) than is Manchester (*c.* 75 miles). A useful approach here is that of Zipf (1965), who has proposed that in fact work distance is the factor that human populations attempt to minimize in all questions of site location and transportation. This forms part of a larger thesis in which Zipf claims that 'the entire behaviour of an individual is at all times motivated by the urge to minimize effort', that is, effort in the sense of probable average rate of work expenditure over time, collective behaviour being subject to the same principle. This hypothesis allows a much more sensitive analysis of individual site locations to be made, a necessity if local and often vital factors are to be related to the likely prehistoric exploitation of site territories. Here it is interesting to note that Zipf points out that 'there is an inherent economy of effort in repeatedly taking the same paths' in that the calculations of

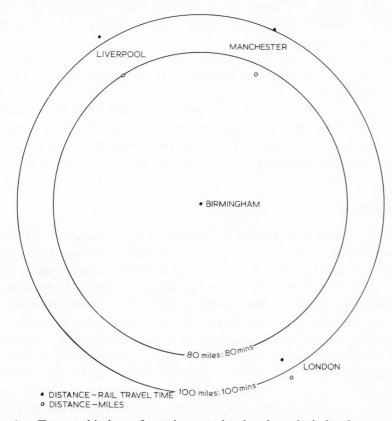

FIG. 18.1. Topographical transformation map showing chronological and topographic distance between Birmingham and three other cities.

efficiency that precede the choice between routes or courses of action are made once but are able to serve a large number of instances. Thus territorial behaviour inherently facilitates the creation of 'economies of repetitiveness', and the formation of such labour-saving habits and behaviour patterns is automatic. This suggestion is in accord with Southern's (1955) view that one of the primary functions of home range behaviour in owls is the formation of 'kinesthetic sense' whereby individuals can travel in and exploit their surroundings with the greatest efficiency and the least danger.

Thus in summary we may make the following assertions:

(1) That we are justified in suggesting that human populations behave territorially (in our sense) as do many other mammal species.

(2) That these territories, though variable, vary within definable limits which can be assessed and related to the major factors operating upon them.

(3) That the primary factor to be considered is the effect of increasing 'cost' or difficulty of exploitation as the effort and time expended in exploitation increases.

(4) That distance is a common variable through which this factor operates.

(5) That the study is worth undertaking in the hope that it may illuminate basic features of past human behaviour which are not susceptible to analysis by archaeological procedures commonly practised at present.

The method

In theory it might be possible to compute a hypothetical ideal territorial framework for an area, relating the total available resources to economic practices, technology, population, sociological pressures, and so on; and it is not impossible that this will be a worthwhile step towards the creation of a generalized model for settlement location when sufficient data from individual studies is available. It does not appear profitable to attempt such an analysis in the present state of knowledge, however. Our preliminary field experience has underlined the importance of detailed surveys of individual site locations, as it is frequently the individual and atypical features of the territory that seem likely to have been a primary reason for the precise location. Even the use of detailed maps will not give a satisfactory estimate of the important time/effort factor in delineating the exploitation territory, as this is often critically affected by minor features of topography.

The primary technique we have evolved in the mapping of exploitation territories involves the plotting of 'time contours' round the site, lines enclosing the area that can be comfortably reached from the site within a walk of ten minutes, one hour and two hours from the site. An approximate distance conversion can be made by the use of pedometers and maps, and our experience is that in easy walking conditions in flat or nearly flat terrain, the ten minute, one hour, and two hour limits correspond approximately to the 1 km,

5 km and 10 km limits noted by Chisholm and Lee. Different and more detailed contours can be plotted where they will be helpful. Of course a certain variability is inherent in individual walking pace, but this is unlikely to be of a sufficient degree to invalidate the method as a whole. The question must inevitably arise as to what constitutes an adequate sample of walked transects to map adequately the site territory. This must obviously be a question to be decided according to individual circumstances: not only will the archaeologist's resources be finite and limited, and his overall objectives variable, but sites themselves impose different responses; in a featureless plain a smaller number of transects will probably suffice, while the more varied and complex the topography, the more detailed the field analysis that is likely to be required. It seems that a minimum of four transects is a reasonable figure for most sites, but there will certainly be exceptions; sites on coastal promontories, for instance, may well be adequately described by fewer than four. Considerations of practicality must play a part, too. After all, the acquisition of Zipf's 'habits' and of Southern's 'kinesthetic sense' requires a considerable portion of the time and energy of the individuals concerned, and archaeologists can hardly spend several months or years living at each of the sites whose territories they wish to map.

The actual site territory inferred from this data will vary according to the supposed economy practised at the site. The indications of the work of Chisholm and Lee are that hunting or pastoralist economies may be expected to exploit a larger area from a single site than would be profitable for agriculture. Thus not only do the !Kung range regularly up to 10 km from their site, as opposed to the practical limit of about 5 km noted by Chisholm for agricultural societies, but in these latter Chisholm noted the common relegation of pastureland to the periphery of the territory, the more productive but more labour-expensive arable land forming a central core. Similarly Woodburn (1968) writes of Hadza women that they obtain the majority of the vegetable food 'within an hour's walk of the camp', while men are prepared to track game for up to a day's journey. These considerations will not provide precise territory sizes, of course, but allow approximate limits to be proposed for the successful operation of different economic systems. Thus we have taken as a starting point the prior assumption that Palaeolithic and Mesolithic sites are likely to be exploiting animal populations by hunting or loose herding, and that they will commonly range up to two hours from the site. Neolithic sites, on the other hand, have been assumed to be concerned primarily with arable agriculture, and thus confined to exploitation within an hour's walking distance. As will be seen below, the prior assumptions may on occasion have to be rejected, leading to reconsideration of some of our economic interpretations.

A further step can be taken by the assessment of the economic potential of the territory thus outlined. This process is subject to the uncertainties inherent in all archaeological data, but it is nevertheless possible to make useful generalizations that increase our understanding of site locations. We cannot date our material precisely enough to establish exact contemporaneity of sites or events, nor are our samples ever randomly deposited, preserved or recovered. It is possible, however, to set against these disadvantages a major advantage that such data have over more detailed and often more scrupulously collected information available to such disciplines as sociology, anthropology, and history. Many factors in the environmental situation are known to vary quite widely from year to year, or from decade to decade, sometimes with a relatively pronounced periodicity, sometimes apparently more haphazardly. Such factors include animal population numbers, climatic features and vegetation type. Viewing a mass of detailed information at a single point in time (or at what is effectively so, given the total time period of the process under consideration) it is often impossible to distinguish between the effects of minor short-term oscillations in the data and the possible occurrence of long-term trends, which may be linked to important and abiding processes. Both types of phenomena are of course worthy of study, as McBurney (1968) has demonstrated in his studies of flint artefacts, but while archaeology encounters considerable difficulty in its attempts to study effectively and to interpret the former, it is in a unique position to consider the latter. The lack of resolution inherent in most archaeological data forces us to adopt a broad view of prehistory, but the use of data from several sites over an extended time period allows the perception of long-term trends which might be obscured in more detailed analyses.

The assessment of economic potential can be approached in a number of ways which can act in some degree as checks upon each other. Modern land use and productivity give much basic information on the suitability of an area for particular types of exploitation. It must of course be borne in mind in assessing these data that changes may have taken place in both the type of land use and the productive capacity; marshes may be drained, erosion may denude hillsides, deposition may create fertile alluvial plains; overcropping may reduce fertility, improved strains may apparently raise it, and so on. However, geomorphological changes of any magnitude can often be assessed to a large extent; Vita-Finzi's (1969) studies of historical deposition in the Mediterranean area show for instance that in Greece the now highly productive Arta plain was not available for exploitation until comparatively recent times. Drainage of marsh and fen, too, can sometimes be inferred from the deposits, while historical records can prove an important source of supplementary evidence. For many areas there is considerable historical evidence of crop yields, and modern estimates of productivity by local farmers can be compared both with these figures and with official estimates of local productivity.

In consideration of the nature of the available evidence and the objective of this type of analysis, it is necessary to keep any classification of productivity or economic potential into categories at a simple and flexible level. Our own studies have indicated that three basic categories provide a useful framework: (1) arable/potentially arable, (2) rough grazing, (3) marsh, bare rock, etc. These of course can be subdivided where convenient, and different categories and definitions may be necessary in particular instances; for example, such a scheme does not incorporate a category suitable for coastal or marine resources. It has to be realized, too, that any such scheme is subjective, and that individual judgement must play a part in recognizing the different categories. For this reason an intermediate 'marginal arable' category may be found helpful; however, it is worth stressing again that the essence of the scheme is simplicity and that it seeks to distinguish broadly different land use potentials, not to draw firm dividing lines that would inevitably distort the reality, which does not in general provide such neat boundaries. Again, while it is certainly possible that under severe pressure a population might be forced to use as arable an area that might normally be classed as 'marginal arable', or even as 'rough grazing', it should be remembered that we are attempting to recognize long-term factors and processes, and that such marginal or temporary situations are not our primary concern unless they precipitate a lasting change in the total situation. Where it is appropriate the relative proportions of different classes of land potential can be calculated accurately, and a weighting factor introduced for distance, in order to assess more closely the probable contribution of each to the economy practised from the site. Vita-Finzi and Higgs (1970) illustrate the potential of this method.

The application of these methods of study provides data from which a description can be attempted of the overall integration of an area into an economic system. This is an important consideration which arises partly out of the hypothesis mentioned earlier that many archaeological sites may be more easily interpreted in the light of seasonal movement of human groups than by assuming sedentism in all cases except those where it is definitely disproved. In a situation where seasonal movement has taken place it will be

715

misleading to consider the single site territory in isolation, and an effort must be made to integrate it into a pattern of exploitation with one or more additional sites that are economically complementary. In fact, our ultimate concern is with annual exploitation territories, not with individual site territories. Higgs *et al.* (1967) have used this approach to analyse the Palaeolithic economy of Epirus, linking the resources offered by the sites of Asprochaliko and Kastritsa to produce an integrated picture of human economic behaviour in the region as a whole. Vita-Finzi and Higgs (1970) have treated Natufian sites in the Levant in the same way, and were as a consequence able to consider realistically the probable importance of cereals in the Natufian economy. It is evident that the economic system and the nature of its integration will be in a dynamic relationship, not a static one; this is especially obvious if modern industrial systems are compared with subsistence economies, and it seems that one of the main features of the former compared with the latter is a more sophisticated and complex network of intercommunications whereby an increasing number of resources can be integrated with increasing efficiency. The greater the number of different resources to be coordinated the less likely they are to be found within a short distance of each other, and consequently the larger will be the area that can be considered as an operating economic system. This leads to the consideration that technological changes may have a profound effect on the size and nature of both annual territories and economic systems; new resources may be brought within the exploitive range of the population, while formerly important resources may become of marginal interest or may cease to be exploited at all.

The results

There follows a brief description of the results of the application of these techniques to three sites in southern Italy. The sites have been chosen so as to illustrate a variety of chronological and topographical situations. Quite obviously they do not represent a complete survey of the sites or their time scale in the area, and although the archaeological significance of these results is discussed to some extent, the main intention has been to demonstrate the scope of such studies for archaeological research in general rather than to formulate particular hypotheses concerning individual sites.

GROTTA ROMANELLI, LATE UPPER PALAEOLITHIC (BLANC, 1928)

Romanelli is a coastal site on the east coast of the 'heel' of the Italian 'boot', about 20 km south of Otranto and 30 km north of Capo Santa Maria di Leuca. The cave is situated a few metres above modern sea level in steep limestone cliffs which rise to 50 m or so, giving way westwards to a rocky slope and then to undulating plateau country. To the north and south the coast remains steep and rocky, little or no shore intervening between the base of the cliffs and the sea, the cliffs in general continuing well below sea level, bringing relatively deep water (20–30 m) close to the coast. The territory exploitable from the site within two hours' travelling time is roughly kidney-shaped (Fig. 18.2), its boundaries being formed by the sea to the east and by a curved line at distances

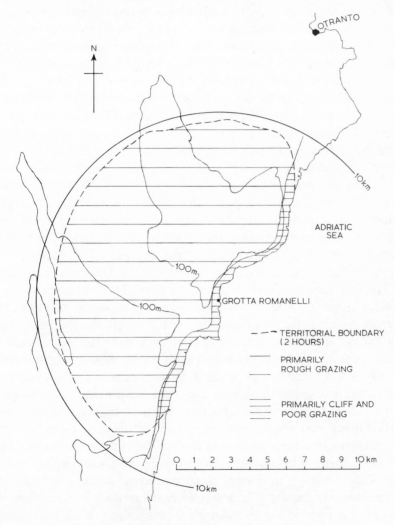

FIG. 18.2. Exploitation territory of Grotta Romanelli.

from 10 km to 6·5 km from the site to the north, west and south. The effect of topography on the shape of the territory is evident in the coastal zone, the relative difficulty of movement in the limestone boulder/maquis-scrub strip which follows the coast reducing the area accessible to exploitation from the cave.

The economic potential of this territory can best be considered in three zones: (1) the inland plateau, (2) the coastal strip, and (3) the sea. By far the larger proportion of the terrestrial part of the territory falls in Zone 1, an area of thin and stony red soils which often exposes areas of limestone bedrock. The modern exploitation pattern is heterogeneous, but with arable cultivation being only marginally successful and for the most part confined to favoured patches round modern villages, olives and rough grazing constitute the predominant modes of land use. In the Late Pleistocene the vegetation pattern was no doubt different from the recent one in response to different climatic and ecological factors, but this area seems likely to have been primarily rough grazing at this period. The scanty soil is a severe limitation on the modern productivity of the area, and recent work on erosion rates in Greece (Hutchinson, 1969) suggests that the limiting factors in the Upper Pleistocene may have been much as they are today, at least as far as soil cover and erosion are concerned. Indeed, the modern productive potential may be slightly greater than that of earlier periods, as extensive terracing and importing of soil have permitted the formation of small areas of soil suitable for grain and vegetable cultivation. Zone 2 forms less than 10% of the land area within the territorial limits, and its economic contribution was probably considerably lower than 10%. The zone comprises the limestone cliffs themselves (which must always have been of minimal productive capacity, although it is possible that they provided some protein in the form of sea birds or their eggs), and the steep slope linking the top of the cliffs with the edge of the plateau, an area containing much bare rock distributed in the thick maquis-scrub, providing a rather poor grazing. It is difficult to relate the sea, Zone 3, directly to Zones 1 and 2 in terms of economic potential without a method for conversion to common units between the resources available from the different areas. This is evidently a further step which must be pursued in the future, and Stamp's (1958) units for agricultural production may well be of some use in this problem, while estimates of the available biomass may help in other circumstances. It is possible, however, to attempt some assessment of the importance of marine resources at the site. The scanty evidence available suggests that the technology of the period was insufficiently sophisticated to allow the exploitation of marine vertebrates to any important degree. Doubtless fish were taken

718

occasionally or in particularly favourable circumstances, but nowhere is there evidence at a Palaeolithic site of their being in any way a staple resource. Some confirmation of this may be seen in the absence of important finds of fish bones in the cave. Shellfish on the other hand may well have formed an important part of the diet; not only were large numbers of shells found in the cave, but they can often be effectively exploited with a more simple tool kit than can fish or other marine vertebrates, boats, nets, hooks and lines all being superfluous. It seems probable that exploitation of marine resources was thus confined largely to the invertebrates of a narrow coastal strip, and here it is important to note that the coast during the Upper Palaeolithic occupation was likely to be similar to the modern one. Sea level was almost certainly below that of today, but the cliffs from Otranto to Capo Santa Maria di Leuca fall steeply below modern sea level to give deep water immediately off the shore, the depth immediately off Romanelli being about 15 m; in spite of the inadequacy of present knowledge of Pleistocene low sea levels, it does not seem probable that the sea level was depressed to a much greater degree than this during the Upper Palaeolithic occupation of Romanelli. The C14 dates for this (10 320 B.P. for the later stages) indicate that the cave was in occupation for the most part considerably later than the accepted period of maximum glaciation in the northern hemisphere, and indeed almost into the postglacial period, when sea levels must presumably have been approaching those of today. Therefore no substantial increase in terrestrial territory seems likely to have been occasioned by sea level fluctuations. The contribution of shellfish to the economy could thus have been considerable, and the very high productivity of coastal waters under favourable conditions suggests that it may indeed have been an important resource.

The exploitation territory of Romanelli can thus be viewed as being comprised of two main sections: an extensive area of rough grazing above the cave and a littoral marine component. The relative economic importance of the two sections is difficult to assess in the absence of information on the degree of marine exploitation, but there seems reason to suggest that efficient cropping may have been limited to the coastline itself and did not extend far out to sea. The small area between these two sections is unlikely at any time to have contributed to the economy to an important degree.

This is a factor of some interest when we consider the possible reasons for the site location. The terrestrial area accessible from the cave within ten to fifteen minutes is exclusively of low economic potential. The 1 km radius (which is the approximate distance covered from the site in this time) was found by Chisholm to be a critical threshold in land use in modern subsistence agricultural economies, and while precisely the same value is unlikely to have effect in other economies, the principle nevertheless applies that it is those resources most accessible to the site that are likely to be of paramount importance in affecting site location. It seems inherently unlikely that a site location would be determined primarily by the presence of a zone of low economic potential. A possible explanation would be that it was the existence of rich marine resources concentrated in a relatively small area along the coast that was a major factor affecting the site location. A further consideration must be taken into account, however: the proximity of a large area of potential grazing forming more than 90% of the terrestrial territory within the two hour radius. Judging by the importance of herbivorous animals in the cave, particularly *Cervus elaphus* and *Equus hydruntinus*, this grazing potential was indeed exploited to an important degree. However, the fact that the site is where it is, separated from the good grazing grounds by steep cliffs, stresses the influence of the marine resources. Had the herbivorous herds been of pre-eminent importance there is no reason why the site could not have been located in a position further inland, a strategy that would not only have made the herds more accessible, but would have nearly doubled the territory available for exploitation; for it is clear that the very fact of locating a site on a coast reduces drastically the land area which it is possible to exploit from it (except in possible special circumstances involving the exploitation of off-shore islands or of coastal lowlands in areas with a fjord topography). While it could be argued that the cave was a particularly convenient habitation, there is no doubt that the human population would have been able to provide adequate shelter elsewhere had it been advantageous to do so. The Palaeolithic mammoth and reindeer hunters of southern Russia evidently coped with a considerably harsher climate apparently inhabiting huts constructed of bones and skins, while recent examples of peoples exploiting climatically severe areas also indicate their ability to manage without fortuitously situated caves.

In reality, of course, both marine and terrestrial resources must have exerted important pressures upon the human population and their day-to-day life, in spite of the possibility that one factor may have been the crucial one as regards the site location. One further factor is worthy of comment in this context. Chisholm notes that among the many things affecting land use around occupation sites is an important influence exerted by the nature of the resources themselves; 'the disadvantages posed by distance in conducting various enterprises are very variable', and it is possible to assign values to different resources to show this relative disadvantage of distance, or cost to the community of exploiting different areas in different fashions. Thus, 'Arable land is usually more greedy of labour than grassland, requiring more cultivation and more transport of goods to and fro . . .' (Chisholm, 1968).

At Romanelli, a similar distinction may be seen between the two major resources of marine and terrestrial protein. The marine resources constitute a relatively high input/high return commodity, are difficult or expensive of labour to transport in large quantities, and, above all, are 'static'. The available molluscs would have been restricted to a relatively narrow zone of the littoral; if they were not to be overexploited and thus reduced in value as an available resource in the areas immediately adjacent to the site, then exploitation would have necessarily been extended north and south along the coast. A heavy expenditure of labour would be involved in any serious attempt to exploit a large catchment of sea coast. The animal herds are mobile, on the other hand, and require only a relatively small expenditure of manpower per unit of production; for whether herds are domesticated or wild they can often be successfully herded by small numbers of men, the more particularly if a close relationship arose between the human and animal populations (Higgs and Jarman, 1969) in which situation the animals would become to some degree accustomed to the proximity of humans. In this way the terrestrial resources could be exploited over a wide area while minimizing the cost of extracting and processing the economic surplus, animals being culled at a point near to the cave or at the point most advantageous for redistribution at that time. In such a situation it is probable that a 'least-cost location analysis' would favour a site as near as possible to the static (marine) resource rather than to the mobile (terrestrial) resource, even if the former did not necessarily outweigh the economic contribution of the latter.

MONTE AQUILONE, NEOLITHIC (Manfredini, 1968, 1969)

Monte Aquilone is a ditched settlement on the Tavoliere plain about 15 km south-west of Manfredonia and 20 km north-east of Foggia. Topographically speaking, the adjacent area is relatively undifferentiated, and the one hour territorial limit produces a nearly perfect circle (Fig. 18.3). Low limestone hills (up to 130 m) run across the territory approximately north-west to south-east. From the point of view of modern exploitation, the edge of the hills serves as a dividing line between two areas. The hills themselves are very poor in soil cover, carry sparse grassy scrub vegetation, and are presently used as rough grazing. The rest of the territory is occupied by arable exploitation of deeper soils, mainly wheat, but with some irrigated root crops. Thus the present exploitation of the area as a whole amounts to a mixed arable–livestock economy.

There seems no reason to believe that the exploitation during the Neolithic period was very different. The arable areas give relatively high yields today (in the order of 30 quintals per ha, a quintal being 100 kg), and these would have been most profitably exploited in this way in the past. It is possible that the

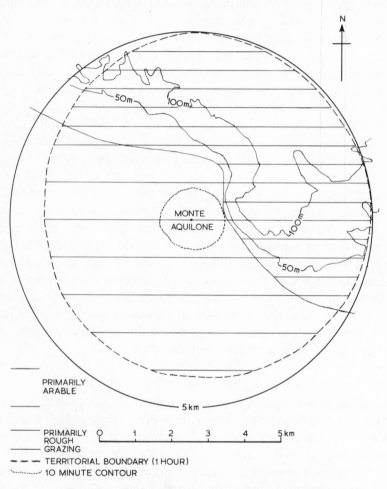

FIG. 18.3. Exploitation territory of Monte Aquilone.

heaviest soils may have been difficult to cultivate with the available Neolithic technology, but to a large extent the economic feasibility of many practices depends greatly on the available labour force as well as the technology. In addition, proximity to the limestone hills would have tended to produce a band of lighter soils along the foot of the hills which would have been more amenable. The hills would have produced an additional advantage in the form of seasonal run-off which would slightly mitigate the dry summers. The very heaviest soils, if indeed they were not cultivated, would provide the best summer grazing available within the territory. The limestone hills themselves can never have offered sufficient soil for profitable cultivation, and it seems likely that they were used as rough grazing in the past as today.

Figure 18.3 shows that 100% of the land accessible within ten minutes of the site is under high productivity arable exploitation today, and that slightly more than half the total exploitation territory also falls into this category. An area of the lighter, more easily worked soil at the base of the hills falls within the ten minute limit. This suggests that the primary factors influencing site location were the demands of an arable – presumably a cereal farming – economy. Recently cereals (both *Triticum* and *Hordeum*) and pulses (*Vicia* and *Lathyrus*) have been identified at the adjacent and comparable site of Passo di Corvo (Follieri, 1971), and it seems not unlikely that a fairly sophisticated form of rotation agriculture was already in progress.

GROTTA SANT' ANGELO, CASSANO ALLO IONIO, NEOLITHIC – BRONZE AGE (Tiné, 1964)

The Grotta Sant'Angelo is a small cave at the base of a steep limestone cliff about 0·5 km west of Cassano allo Ionio in Calabria. The site itself lies at about 300 m above sea level and the dominating topographical features of the area are the steep-sided gorge of the Torrente Garda below and the steep cliffs rising above the site.

Movement in any direction other than along the valley is difficult, as is indicated by the shape of the territory and the modern road system (Fig. 18.4). The restricting influence of the topography upon human exploitation is also clearly seen in the fact that the maximum distance walked from the site in one hour is only just greater than 4 km, as compared with the 5 km expected in flat country; the average distance accessible from the site being considerably less than 4 km.

The present-day exploitation is largely confined to olives, which occupy terraced fields on the less precipitous slopes of the valley. Small patches of arable (wheat) and market gardening (vegetables, confined to a narrow strip in parts of the valley floor) do occur, but are in insignificant proportions relative to the area as a whole. As much as 50% of the territory is not cultivated at all, the combination of steep slopes and thin or absent soil producing vegetation which varies from very thick acacia scrub and tall grasses near the river to thinner more open scrub where more rock is exposed. The ten minute

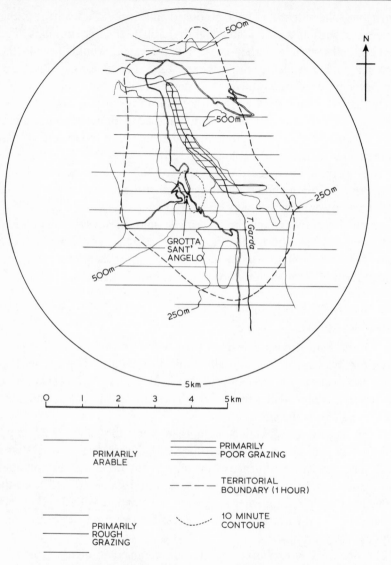

FIG. 18.4. Exploitation territory of Grotta Sant'Angelo.

contour encloses an area that is characteristic of the territory as a whole, with 40–50% marginal arable, growing olives, and 50–60% scrub grazing.

Thus the modern exploitation of the site territory is primarily olives and rough grazing, with some cereals on the fringes of the territory. There is no evidence that olive cultivation was practised or that olives were even available

724

in the area during the occupation of the site. Certainly their large-scale cultivation as a major form of land use seems unlikely, and it seems probable that we should think in terms of some other form of exploitation in those areas that are now under olives. The best of these areas could undoubtedly be used for cereals, but it does not seem likely that these were ever of importance in the area. Not only is grain cultivation only economic today in a few especially favourable patches, and with the expenditure of much effort in terracing and overcoming the difficulties imposed by the steep slopes, but even in those areas the yields are low, with 14 quintals per ha being considered a good yield for the area. It thus seems probable that this area would have been suitable for rough grazing in prehistoric times, as was the rest of the territory, and that pastoralism was the most likely primary form of exploitation from the site.

Discussion and integration

One of the advantages of site territorial analysis is that it offers a consistent framework for relating the resources and economic exploitation of a particular site with those of the surrounding area. This is of interest for a variety of reasons. For the later prehistoric periods in particular it is evident that many complex economic relationships grew up; trade was widespread and it seems likely that there was a degree of mobility in agricultural produce as well as in metals and luxuries. The analysis of site territories over broader areas will give information on the methods by which the whole resources can be utilized, and the ways in which the individual sites can best be integrated. This will give a clue to the function of sites within a larger framework of economic relations than is possible by consideration of individual sites alone. Another factor of great importance in the analysis of past human economic behaviour is the relationship of sites to seasonal resources and the question of the nature and length of their occupation. Again, territorial analysis can help in assessing the practicability of different economic strategies, and may be able to eliminate some apparent possibilities, ranking others in probable order of likelihood. The consideration of the sites discussed above in the light of these factors illuminates their probable role in the economic life of their occupants, and indicates lines of future enquiry which will expand our knowledge and test our assumptions and conclusions.

GROTTA ROMANELLI

It was concluded that at Romanelli, while to a large extent the economy depended upon herbivores, in particular *C. elaphus* and *E. hydruntinus*, the situation of the site itself strongly suggested that marine resources were also of importance, especially the mollusca *Patella* and *Trochus*, which occurred in large numbers in some levels. Further consideration of the site situation suggests that it is not suitable for year-round intensive exploitation of either herbivores or marine mollusca. The coastal location of the site cuts its exploitable terrestrial territory by about 50% immediately, and it is thus obviously at a disadvantage from this point of view relative to an inland location. On the other hand, the steepness of the coastal topography indicates that only a very narrow vertical band of cliff would be exploitable for mollusca without diving for submarine individuals. In any case shellfish productivity in many species tends to be highest near the surface of the water. If we assume that serious exploitation of mollusca was unlikely outside a band extending 1 m above and below mean sea level, then the productivity of the Romanelli stretch of coast cannot have been great, and certainly not of an order sufficient to support a human group on a yearly basis. The implication seems to be that, while the size of the site leaves no doubt as to its importance, it may have been a single element in a complex annual cycle rather than the representative of a self-supporting entity in itself. Figure 18.5 shows the position and site territories of some other sites in southern Apulia that have occupations archaeologically of comparable age with the upper levels of Romanelli, and it can be seen that they form part of a network which covers a considerable area of the peninsula. The presence of an avifauna believed to represent a cool or cold climate during the occupation at Romanelli suggests that it may have been primarily a winter occupation site. Coastal sites are indeed frequently favoured winter locations of Mediterranean pastoral economies, as the proximity to the sea can moderate the extremities of the inland winter; as a corollary the summer grazing grounds are frequently to be found inland. An area that was conspicuously unexploited by the sites shown in Fig. 18.5, according to our proposed model, was the central area, and it seems probable that future search may locate in this region complementary sites to Romanelli and the other coastal sites. The annual territory would thus consist of one or more coastal sites in conjunction with one or more inland sites.

MONTE AQUILONE

Territorial analysis at Monte Aquilone suggested that it was located with reference to the practice of cereal agriculture. On the other hand, over 40% of the area was rough grazing, unsuitable for arable exploitation, which seems likely to have been exploited by pastoralism. Here an apparent difficulty emerges in that today this area is so dry in summer that by the end of June it is of little use even as rough grazing. Assuming that the Neolithic climate was not sufficiently different to change this basic picture, it would be necessary to find some area to pasture animals from early summer until autumn if full use were to be made of the potential winter–spring grazing available in the exploitation territory. Figure 18.6 shows the relationship of Monte Aquilone

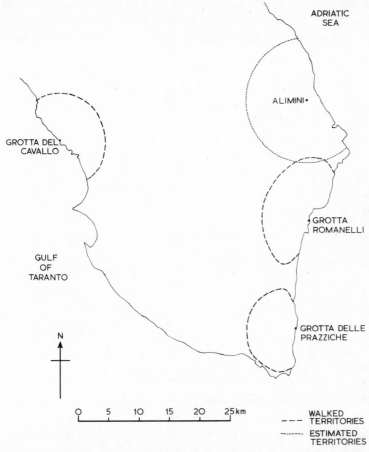

FIG. 18.5. Salento peninsula showing exploitation territories of some Romanellian sites.

to the Gargano hills to the north. These hills are today used as a summer grazing area for large flocks of sheep and goats which winter on the cereal stubble and rough grazing areas of the Tavoliere. These flocks travel to the Gargano in May, and return just in time to lamb in October. Figure 18.6 marks the location of a modern farm, which is used in winter by such a group

727

of transhumantic herders but is completely deserted during the summer. It will be noted that the farm is within the territorial boundary of Monte Aquilone.

How are we to interpret this composite picture of cereal husbandry, commonly assumed to be inevitably a sedentary occupation, together with pastoralism which can only have been run at a most marginal and inefficient level if it did not take account of the seasonal variation in available resources, as it does today ? The cereal husbandry, which we have inferred to have been

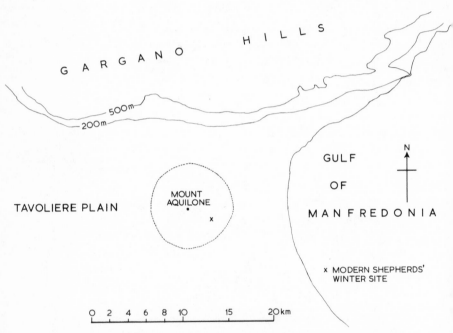

FIG. 18.6. Tavoliere and Gargano, showing position of Monte Aquilone.

of primary importance, would certainly have required occupation at the site during at least part of winter and in early summer; the grain harvest today is usually in June on the Tavoliere. Furthermore it seems reasonable to assume that the processing and storing of grain would involve a minimum of an additional few weeks' occupation. The animals, on the other hand, would have needed to be taken up to the hills in May, before the grain harvest had even got under way. Again, a mobile element in the economy seems to be indicated, but here the situation may have been rather more complex than that suggested at Romanelli. Both pastoralism and the early stages of the arable husbandry cycle lead to winter occupation of the lowlands, as at Monte Aquilone. In spring the two forms of economy diverge in their requirements, and the population seems likely to have split, with a number of winter lowland residents moving with the animals to the hills, leaving the remainder of the population to look after the cereal harvest. The movement need not of course have been very large in terms of distance travelled or numbers of people involved. One or two shepherds with a dog can control a considerable flock of sheep, and in early summer the maximum labour force is likely to be required in the lowlands for the harvest. Although we cannot be certain that this lowland population remained on the Tavoliere throughout the summer, this seems the logical time of year in which to process and store the cereal harvest; and in addition, if the suggested model is accurate, there would be little economic incentive for them to move, especially if a culling herd were left with them on the plain. Thus it seems probable that the lowland sites such as Monte Aquilone were permanently occupied by a majority of the local population, a minority of which left regularly for the hills during the summer. Whether this division took the form of individual members from lowland families taking family herds to the Gargano while the remainder stayed at the arable farm, or whether the two economies were in fact run separately by different groups of people, with the pastoralists utilizing winter grazing lands on the lowlands and moving as entire families to the hills in the summer, does not appear to be a question accessible to the available archaeological data, even by inference. Both situations occur today, and it seems doubtful whether the overall economic difference between the two modes of organization is perceptible or significant. If this suggested model for the overall past exploitation of the Tavoliere-Gargano region approximates the truth, we may expect that finds of comparable age to the Neolithic occupation of the Tavoliere will eventually be forthcoming from the Gargano, although here we should remember that the tool kits of pastoralists may be meagre in the extreme, and may indeed bear little apparent likeness to their arable counterparts even if they are in use by the same individual at different seasons (cf. Thomson, 1939).

GROTTA SANT'ANGELO

It was concluded at Grotta Sant'Angelo that the site must have been concerned primarily with pastoral exploitation. Considering the site more closely in relation to the surrounding area, however, it becomes apparent that this may be an oversimplification. The difficulties imposed by the terrain upon movement, and thus on exploitation of any kind, lead to a very small exploitation territory. Only about 25 km² are accessible within an hour's walk from Grotta Sant' Angelo, as opposed to *c.* 80 km² from Monte Aquilone. Even Romanelli, which loses half of its territory to the sea, contains a greater land area exploitable within an hour than does Grotta Sant'Angelo. It would certainly be a very bad choice of a site from which to pursue an arable economy; indeed it would be one of the worst positions in the immediate neighbourhood, for, as Fig. 18.4 shows, small areas of potentially arable land are available at the territorial limits and just beyond in several directions. The nearly vertical slopes along much of the river valley would even to some extent reduce the effectiveness of pastoral exploitation, and the extremely small area that is conveniently accessible from the site would severely limit its profitability in this respect. The conclusion would seem to be that the site is not a profitable one from which to exploit either an arable or a pastoral economy; the former would almost certainly be pursued from sites elsewhere in the vicinity; the latter, while feasible, would be unlikely to be economically successful.

The economic potential of the area as a whole suggests a hypothesis which may help to explain this situation. The coastal plains of Sibari to the south and east of the site are today an area of intensive arable exploitation. Like many comparable areas in the Mediterranean area they provide winter grazing grounds for flocks of sheep which spend the spring and summer elsewhere, in this case the Serra Dolcedorme mountains. The mountains cannot be used for winter grazing because of the regular 10–20 cm of snow. Figure 18.7 shows the relationship between Grotta Sant'Angelo and these two areas of seasonal grazing, and marks the modern road which forms the route of access between them for some of the modern flocks. As can be seen, the route passes directly below the site; especially favoured summer grazing is found in the wide valleys around Castrovillari, and they pass the site twice a year. It seems in no way improbable that in prehistory the site functioned as a transit site en route between summer and winter grazing areas, rather than as a site that was occupied for any considerable length of time in any one year. This would indeed seem to fit well with the nature of the site which contains material from a long period (Middle Neolithic to Bronze Age) but at no time seems to have been extensively occupied. The small size of the cave (maximum dimensions of the main chamber *c.* 20 × 10 m) and the shallow deposit (*c.* 1 m) indicate the scale of occupation involved. This certainly allows us to interpret the data supplied by territorial analysis in a more comprehensible way than does the hypothesis of permanent or even seasonal exploitation on an arable

730

or pastoral basis. It should be noted that this interpretation is at variance with the suggestions offered by Whitehouse (1968) that the site was one of a group of lowland 'mixed economy' sites.

Again, further field research should permit this hypothesis to be tested; the hypothesis indicates two areas in which complementary sites might be sought. If this is substantially correct, one would expect a site, probably a cave, in the Castrovillari region to represent the summer base, and another

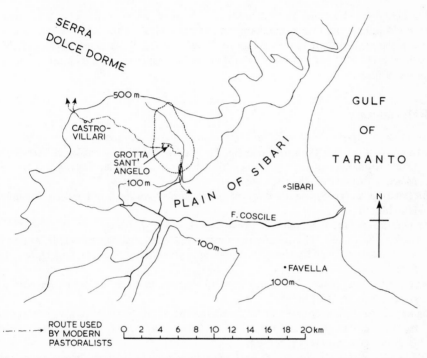

FIG. 18.7. Plains of Sibari and Serra Dolcedorme, showing position of Grotta Sant'Angelo and modern access route.

site on the coastal plain, perhaps in the Coscile valley, to provide the winter base. In all probability the lowland site would be an arable agricultural settlement broadly similar in economic terms to Monte Aquilone, and it seems likely that the site at Favella (Tiné, 1962) represents a site of this nature about 18 km to the south-east of Grotta Sant'Angelo (Fig. 18.7).

The degree to which this work has relied upon other disciplines for stimulus and ideas is self-evident. Equally, it is clear that much remains to be done in substantiating, elaborating and developing the model proposed here.

In particular the increasing body of data should permit a more sophisticated mathematical treatment of certain aspects than it has seemed profitable to attempt so far. No doubt many of the interpretations and estimates made here will quickly be superseded. This paper has offered a conceptual framework within which, it is hoped, such future developments may prove possible.

Acknowledgements

The field research leading to the delimiting of the exploitation territories of Romanelli, Monte Aquilone and Grotta Sant'Angelo, and the analysis of the patterns of land use, was accomplished with the assistance of G. W. Barker, R. W. Dennell and H. N. Jarman, each of whom was most helpful not only in collecting the data but also as a source of ideas.

References

ARDREY, R. (1967) *The Territorial Imperative*. London: Fontana.

BLANC, G. A. (1928) Grotta Romanelli, II: Dati ecologici epaletnologici. Atti della Prima Riunione dell'Istituto Italiano di Paleontologia Umana. *Archivo per l'Antropologia e l'Etnologia*, **58** (1–4), 365–411.

CHISHOLM, M. (1968) *Rural Settlement and Land Use: An Essay in Location*. London: Hutchinson.

CLARKE, D. L. (1968) *Analytical Archaeology*. London: Methuen.

CROOK, J. H. (1968). The nature and function of territorial aggression. In ASHLEY MONTAGUE, M. F. (ed.) *Man and Aggression*, 141–78. New York: Oxford University Press.

DAVIDSON, D. S. (1928) The family hunting territory in Australia. *American Anthropologist*, n.s. **30** (4), 614–31.

DÅHL, S. (1957) The contacts of Västerås with the rest of Sweden. In HAUNERBERG, D., HÄGERSTRAND, T. and ODEVING, B. (eds.) *Lund Studies in Geography, Series B, Human Geography*, **13**, 206–43.

FOLLIERI, M. (1971) *Researches on Prehistoric Agriculture*. Paper presented at the Third International Congress of the Museum of Agriculture, Budapest, 1971.

HIGGS, E. S. (1968) Archaeology – where now? *Mankind*, **6**, (12), 617–20.

HIGGS, E. S. and JARMAN, M. R. (1969) The origins of agriculture: a reconsideration. *Antiquity*, **43**, 31–41.

HIGGS, E. S., VITA-FINZI, C., HARRIS, D. R. and FAGG, A. E. (1967) The climate, environment and industries of stone age Greece: part III. *Proceedings of the Prehistoric Society*, n.s. **33**, 1–29.

HUTCHINSON, SIR J. (1969) Erosion and land use: the influence of agriculture on the Epirus region of Greece. *Agricultural History Review*, **17**, 85–90.

JARMAN, M. R., VITA-FINZI, C. and HIGGS, E. S. (in press) Site catchment analysis in archaeology. In UCKO, P. J., DIMBLEBY, G. W. and TRINGHAM, R. (eds.) *Settlement Patterns and Urbanisation*. London: Duckworth.

JEWELL, P. A. (1966) The concept of home range in mammals. In JEWELL, P. A. and LOIZOS, C. (eds.) Play, exploration and territory in mammals. *Symposia of the Zoological Society of London,* **18,** 85–109.

LEE, R. B. (1969) !Kung bushman subsistence: an input–output analysis. In VAYDA, A. P. (ed.) *Environment and Cultural Behaviour,* 47–79. New York: Natural History Press.

LORENZ, K. (1963) *On Aggression.* New York.

MCBURNEY, C. B. M. (1968) The cave of Ali Tappeh and the Epi-palaeolithic in north-east Iran. *Proceedings of the Prehistoric Society,* n.s. **34,** 385–413.

MANFREDINI, A. (1968) Villaggio trincerato a Monte Aquilone (Manfredonia). *Origini,* **2,** 65–101.

MANFREDINI, A. (1969) Notiziario: Monte Aquilone (Prov. di Foggia). *Rivista di Scienze Preistoriche,* **24,** 374–5.

ODUM, E. P. and ODUM, H. T. (1959) *Fundamentals of Ecology,* 2nd ed. Philadelphia: Saunders.

PITELKA, F. A. (1959) Numbers, breeding schedule, territoriality in pectoral sand-pipers of northern Alaska. *The Condor,* **61,** (4), 233–64.

SOUTHERN, H. N. (1955) Nocturnal animals. *Scientific American,* **193,** (4), 89–98.

STAMP, L. D. (1958) The measurement of land resources. *Geographical Review,* **48** (1), 1–15.

THOMSON, D. F. (1939) The seasonal factor in human culture. *Proceedings of the Prehistoric Society,* n.s. **5,** 209–21.

TINÉ, S. (1962) Successione delle culture preistoriche in Calabria alla luce dei recenti scavi in provincia di Cosenza. *Klearchos,* **4** (13–14), 38–48.

TINÉ, S. (1964) La Grotta di S. Angelo III a Cassano Ionio. *Atti e Memorie della Società Magna Grecia,* n.s. **5,** 11–55.

VITA-FINZI, C. (1969) *The Mediterranean Valleys.* Cambridge: Cambridge University Press.

VITA-FINZI, C. and HIGGS, E. S. (1970) Prehistoric economy in the Mount Carmel area of Palestine: site catchment analysis. *Proceedings of the Prehistoric Society,* n.s. **36,** 1–37.

WHITEHOUSE, R. D. (1968) Settlement and economy in southern Italy in the Neo-thermal period. *Proceedings of the Prehistoric Society,* n.s. **34,** 332–67.

WOODBURN, J. (1968) An introduction to Hadza ecology. In LEE, R. B. and DEVORE, I. (eds.) *Man The Hunter,* 49–55. Chicago: Aldine.

ZIPF, G. K. (1965) *Human Behavior and the Principle of Least Effort.* Facsimile of 1949 ed. New York: Harper & Row.

19

Set theory models: an approach to taxonomic and locational relationships

J. LITVAK KING and R. GARCÍA MOLL

The National University of Mexico, Mexico

The social sciences and the humanities have been generally slow in accepting and putting to profit some of the advances in technique that have been developed by other disciplines. This is increasingly true in recent years when radical changes in the natural sciences and mathematics have resulted in whole new fields of study which are unknown to most humanists and have increased the distance and lack of communication between both.

This is very much the case of the New Mathematics and, in particular, of set theory, an approach to analysis based on symbolic logic, which has revolutionized mathematics both in the classroom and in application. This system, although it is being taught in elementary schools throughout the world, is normally not known to the older generations and it is still seen by many as yet another device to make things more complicated and unintelligible.

Symbolic logic is not exactly new. Leibnitz in the seventeenth century laid down the principle of *logical calculation*, the formal use and operation of symbols in logical deduction, which served as the basis for the newer developments. Symbolic logic developed its proper language in the nineteenth century with the notation that was formulated by George Boole to handle sets. The application of Boole's system made the Aristotelian syllogism into just a special case of a variety of logical algebra. Boole's algebra was later modified and enlarged by other authors, among them de Morgan, Jevons, Peirce, Frege, Peano and finally Russell and Whitehead. Its propositions and notation are well known today and can be consulted in practically any standard textbook on mathematics.

The use of set theory for distribution studies is of more recent date. It can be traced to the first look that geographers, searching for new forms of analysis, took at its possibilities. Haggett and Chorley (1965, pp. 372-4) and Haggett (1965, pp. 243-5) stated a theoretical application of the technique for handling problems in area definition and as an aid to the description of regions and their components. Recognizing that a map is a special version of a Venn diagram, the standard form of graphication in set theory, they showed cases where criteria used for definition were either locational or non-locational or at least not wholly locational (Fig. 19.1).

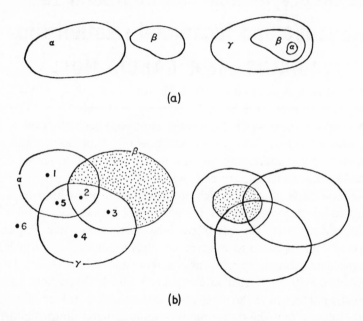

(a)

(b)

FIG. 19.1. Venn diagrams, as used by Haggett (1965, pp. 243–4) to describe: (*a*) the dialectic or hierarchic position of Bolivia as a part of the American hemisphere (the example is shown as α); (*b*) the United States (1), Colombia (2), Uganda (3), China (4), Chile (5) and the United Kingdom (6) as points in the intersections of the set of American countries (α), the set of tropical countries (β), and the set of underdeveloped countries (γ).

In the first case, Haggett described the situation as a simple problem in discrimination between two mutually exclusive groups, referred to as sets. The example, Bolivia, can be diagrammed to show that it is not a part of North America since it belongs to a set whose intersection with the set North America is nil, or as referred to in set theory, *the empty set*. In a different presentation of the same case a hierarchical, rather than a dialectical criterion was used to show that Bolivia (α) can be graphed so that it is a part – or a subset – of another set, South America (β), which, in its turn, is a subset of an even larger set, the American Hemisphere (γ) (Fig. 19.1, top).

Haggett's second case shows the effect of the multiplication of elements of judgement, both in complicating the problem and in giving a more complete solution. He states his example by defining a series of sets: *alpha* for the set of American countries, *beta* for tropical countries and *gamma* for the set of underdeveloped countries. It is assumed that the definition required for membership in these sets is clear (Fig. 19.1, bottom).

Diagramming the sets, it is found that Colombia, for instance, can be defined at a point located at the intersection of all three sets, being in America, in the tropical region and an underdeveloped country. Other cases are located in partial intersections – that is, in places where only two of the three sets overlap. Uganda, not being in America but being both in the tropics and an underdeveloped country, could be a case in point, as are China and Chile. Some others are members of one of the sets but are not located in intersecting situations: the United States, for example, being in America but neither in the tropics nor an underdeveloped country. Some countries, finally, can be represented at points outside the sets given, since they belong to none, like the United Kingdom; the intersection of a set whose member it would be with the sets given would be the empty set, represented in proper notation by the greek letter *phi* (ϕ).

Haggett and Chorley's postulation, although very important because of its influence on other authors, was not the first attempt in geography. Previous papers, which can be taken as antecedents, among them Kansky (1963), who is cited by Haggett and Chorley, had explored the explanation of geographical phenomena using Boolean algebra. In a paper on transport systems, Kansky used the technique not only to describe situations and define terms but also to state requisites for change and its consequences in his analysis, up to and including the deduction of trends. In that respect Kansky's work may be considered a very important step in the dynamic, rather than just a descriptive, use of Set Theory.

Other writers in geography have applied set theory for definition. Henshall (1967, pp. 433–5), writing on models for agricultural activity, describes several techniques for the definition of types of agriculture. In one of them she sets up a series of sets: set A for subsistence cultivation, both shifting and settled, Set B for commercial cultivation by either plantations and small farmers, and Set C for nomadic and settled herding. Of these sets, four possible intersection areas occur: R_1, described as the intersection of sets A and C (R_1 $A \cap C$); $R_2 = A \cap B$; $R_3 = B \cap C$ as partial intersections; and finally $R_4 = A \cap B \cap C$, which is a general intersection (Fig. 19.2). The intersection areas define types of tropical agriculture and can be, in their turn, subdivided by the application of other criteria that can be stated as sets, and thus produce

737

more definable intersection areas that correspond to different situations in reality.

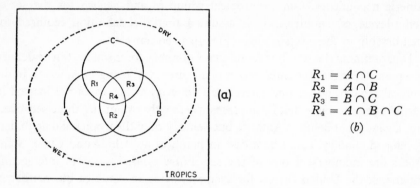

$$R_1 = A \cap C$$
$$R_2 = A \cap B$$
$$R_3 = B \cap C$$
$$R_4 = A \cap B \cap C$$

(b)

(c) *Tropical Agriculture*

Set Inter-section	Typical Environment	Sub-Division	Example
R_1	Savanna	Parallel	Southern British Guiana
		Dual	Brazilian sertão
		Symbiotic	Northern Nigeria – Hausa and Fulani
R_2	Humid tropics	Parallel	Amazon – Japanese and Indian
		Dual	New Guinea, Yucatan
		Symbiotic	West Indies
R_3	Irrigated or seasonally flooded	Parallel	Amazon varzea
		Dual	Gezira
		Symbiotic	Peru
R_4	Variable	—	East Africa – European, Masai and Kikuyu North-west Argentine – European, mestizo and Amerindian

FIG. 19.2. Henshall's (1967, pp. 434–5) representation of tropical agriculture as a series of sets of traits: (a) Venn diagram for sets A (subsistence cultivation), B (commercial cultivation) and C (herding); (b) notational explanation of the intersections resulting from the above; (c) types of tropical agriculture and their explanation as the intersections of sets.

Other works that have been important in the application of set theory have been those in linguistics, particularly those of Cooper (1964), Marcus (1966, 1967) and Solomon (1969), where they operate with language and language structure as sets and derive conclusions from very complete applications of Boolean algebra.

In archaeology, the use of set theory was first suggested by Clarke (1968, pp. 473–6) for the definition and description of a culture area. Clarke's preoccupation with polythetic definitions is well seen in the problem he presents; the solution he arrives at is a quite satisfactory approach to multi-dimensional, as opposed to unilinear, description of a case. Clarke sets up an imaginary area, which he calls Vennland (Fig. 19.3) and studies it by Set

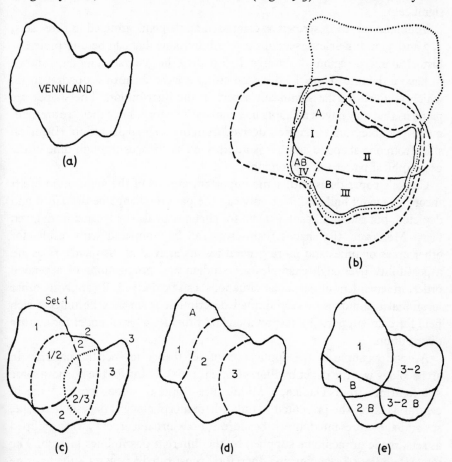

FIG. 19.3. Clarke's (1968, p. 475) diagrams for Vennland. A theoretical example of how set theory can assist in the definition of subregions and in explaining historical processes. (*a*) Vennland as an entity. (*b*) As an entity defined by a polythetic array of intersecting sets. (*c*) As an entity composed of intersecting sets in three principal components 1, 2, 3. (*d*) Lathe-form, a historical subdivision of Vennland in which boundaries reflect the descending hierarchy of sets 3, 2 and 1 and wherein distribution A was critical. (*e*) Quadrat-form, a historic subdivision of Vennland in which distribution B was critical and in which sets 1 and 3 were principal components.

739

Theory. Vennland can be defined by several ecological variables and the superposition on them of artefact distributions which can be taken as culture traits. These variables, represented as sets with members, have a location in the Vennland map and the sites in it have, therefore, characteristics that are components of sets. The resulting sets, diagrammed and formulated, show that they overlap (intersect) in some places and that these overlappings can be significant.

Vennland can be described as composed of elements grouped in three sets, 1, 2 and 3, and their intersections give subdivisions that can be interpreted as historical micro-regions of the area. By dividing the general region, it is shown to have a definite shape, in this case either a lathe form or a quadrat form, which is given by the significant aspect in the distribution. The shapes are patterns that may have a meaning in Vennland's history, since they are arrangements possible from the subsets derived from the original definition. Historical shift from one shape to another is interpreted as changes through time in the geographical pattern of the region.

Clarke's paper deals with some important aspects of the application of set theory to model building. Not only can the pattern change be described and depicted, but the significant element for change can also be located from given facts. Moreover, the shapes themselves can be compared with results for other areas or times and more general results arrived at. Sequence rules are a possibility if enough examples are studied and propositions of a general order, independent of particular situations, can be derived. By applying other locational techniques, a very limited description of an area becomes a rich field for data-supported interpretation and provides a basic model for culture distribution.

A good example of the application of set theory to specific materials in archaeology was the paper by Flores García (1968). Using for the purpose some 500 figurines from Tlatilco, a Middle Pre-classic (*c.* 1000–500 B.C.) site in central Mexico, she presented a study where morphological data such as type, sex and age represented, dress, headdress, body ornament, etc., were grouped as sets, made of members supplied by the different possibilities in each. The total attributes of each figurine, therefore, constituted a new set – the figurine itself – which was definable as the intersection of its attributes' sets. Each figurine had a position in the diagrams that could be formulated (Fig. 19.4) to describe it.

Since some of the characteristics in the sets coincided in another set while others were absent, the figurines themselves, previously defined only by one criterion, were now defined as either the intersection of several sets or as a set with the empty set, defined by several others, the polythetic aspect of the definition making the results more valuable. Indeed, the diagrams and the formulae could now be used to derive constants on the presence or absence of attributes, and to help in the identification of incomplete or formerly unclassified pieces by deriving their identity from the most likely sets to which they could belong (probability theory).

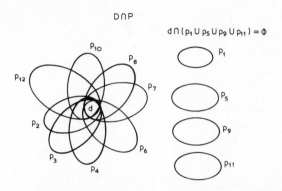

$$D \cap P$$

$$d \cap (p_1 \cup p_5 \cup p_9 \cup p_{11}) = \phi$$

FIG. 19.4. Some of Flores García's (1968, p. 19) diagrams and formulae describing the intersection of traits in Tlatilco figurines. Contents are: D (age represented: young adult) can be present when P_2 (necklace), P_3 (skirt), P_4 (short skirt), P_6 (nose plug), P_7 (ear plugs), P_8 (circle-shaped ear plugs), P_{10} (unclassified ear plugs) and P_{12} (naked body) are present, but absent when P_1 (body band), P_5 (breech clout), P_9 (ear plug with hanging ornament) or P_{11} (breast ornament) are present.

In fact, although Flores García's paper was conceived as a visual correlation to illustrate other work in the description of museum collections, its results were not only descriptive themselves but, as models, they provide a useful tool for analysis. It was later followed by another paper, by Velasco Mireles (1970), where pottery vessels from the same site were studied with success by the same means.

Litvak King and García Moll (1969) applied set theory model building for a somewhat different purpose. In studying a series of six sites in the La Villita region in the states of Michoacan and Guerrero in west Mexico, with a sequence of Classic to Postclassic dates (c. A.D. 300–900), their approach attempted not only area description and site definition, but also the examination of processes in each site for comparison between them, with a view to constructing a model for the entry and exit of elements in the culture they were working on.

Using vessel supports for the purpose of a simplified experiment, and having worked on their material with the usual statistical treatment, with few

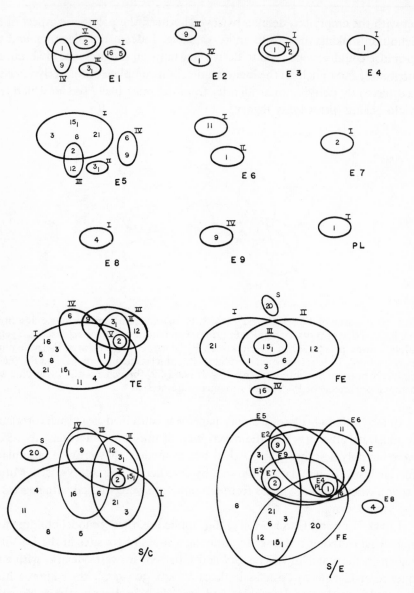

FIG. 19.5. Litvak King and García Moll's (1969, p. 46) diagrams for the distribution of vessel support types in a site in the La Villita region. Strata are represented as sets tagged by Roman numerals in their order from surface, marked S. Buildings are numbered by Arabic numerals prefixed by E and by PL, a plaza. TE is the total for building-located material. FE is the total for material found outside buildings. S/C is the total for the site, arranged by strata. S/E is the total for the site, arranged by buildings. Types are marked by Arabic numerals alone.

742

results, they decided to try set theory as a tool to build a model. Potsherds were classified into several morphological types, according to their shape and their situation in the excavation strata and buildings, whilst their intersection was stated to be a set whose members were the types obtained in sorting. Situations resulting from this approach could be diagrammed and formulated (Figs. 19.5 and 19.6).

Total per site	*Total per stratum*

$\text{V-1} = \{1, 2, 3, 3_1, 3_2, 4, 5, 6, 7, 8, 9, 11, 13, 14, 15_2, 17\}$

$\text{I} = \{1, 2, 3, 3_2, 4, 5, 6, 7, 8, 9, 10, 11, 12, 13, 14, 15_1, 15_2, 16, 17, 21\}$

$\text{V-3} = \{1, 2, 4, 8, 9\}$

$\text{II} = \{1, 2, 3, 4, 6, 8, 9, 10, 11, 12, 15_1\}$

$\text{V-6} = \{1, 2, 3, 3_2, 4, 6, 8, 9, 11, 12\}$

$\text{III} = \{1, 2, 3, 3_1, 4, 8, 9\}$

$\text{V-30} = \{1, 2, 3, 3_2, 4, 8, 9, 14, 15_1, 15_2\}$

$\text{IV} = \{1, 2, 3_2, 6, 8, 9, 16\}$

$\text{V-38} = \{1, 2, 3, 3_1, 4, 6, 8, 9, 10, 12, 21\}$

$\text{V} = \{1, 2, 3, 9, 10\}$ ∴

$\text{V-42} = \{1, 2, 3, 3_1, 4, 5, 6, 8, 9, 11, 12, 15_1, 16, 20, 21\}$

$\text{I} \supset \text{II}$

$\text{V-1} \supset \text{V-3}$

$\text{I} \supset \text{IV}$

$\text{V-1} \cap \text{V-6} = \{1, 2, 3, 3_2, 4, 6, 8, 9, 11\}$

$\text{I} \supset \text{IV}$

$\text{V-1} \cap \text{V-30} = \{1, 2, 3, 3_1, 3_2, 4, 8, 9, 14, 15_2\}$

$\text{I} \supset \text{V}$;

$\text{II} \cap \text{III} = \{1, 2, 3, 4, 8, 9\}$

$\text{V-1} \cap \text{V-38} = \{1, 2, 3, 3_1, 4, 6, 8, 9\}$

$\text{II} \cap \text{IV} = \{1, 2, 6, 8, 9\}$

$\text{V-1} \cap \text{V-42} = \{1, 2, 3, 3_1, 4, 5, 6, 8, 9\}$

$\text{II} \supset \text{V}$

$\text{V-3} \subseteq \text{V-6}$

$\text{III} \cap \text{IV} = \{1, 2, 9\}$

$\text{V-3} \subseteq \text{V-30}$

$\text{III} \cap \text{V} = \{1, 2, 3, 9\}$

$\text{V-3} \subseteq \text{V-38}$

$\text{IV} \cap \text{V} = \{1, 2, 9\}$ ∴

$\text{V-3} \subseteq \text{V-42}$

$\text{I} \cap \text{II} \cap \text{III} \cap \text{IV} \cap \text{V} = \{1, 2, 9\}.$

$\text{V-6} \cap \text{V-30} = \{1, 2, 3, 3_2, 4, 8, 9\}$

$\text{V-6} \cap \text{V-38} = \{1, 2, 3, 4, 6, 8, 9, 12\}$

$\text{V-6} \cap \text{V-42} = \{1, 2, 3, 4, 6, 8, 9, 11, 12\}$

$\text{V-30} \cap \text{V-38} = \{1, 2, 3, 4, 8, 9\}$

$\text{V-30} \cap \text{V-42} = \{1, 2, 3, 4, 8, 9, 15_1\}$

$\text{V-38} \cap \text{V-42} = \{1, 2, 3, 3_1, 4, 6, 8, 9, 12, 21\}$ ∴

$\text{V-1} \cap \text{V-3} \cap \text{V-6} \cap \text{V-30} \cap \text{V-38} \cap \text{V-42} = \{1, 2, 4, 8, 9\}$

(a) (b)

FIG. 19.6. Formulae describing general results for (a) site distribution of traits and (b) strata distribution of traits, in six sites in the la Villita region (Litvak King and García Moll, 1969, pp. 39–40). Individual site or strata statements are followed by analysis.

As examined, each set could show differences to other, contiguous sets – i.e. vertically, strata to the next strata, and horizontally, excavation square to excavation square. They also showed similarities, since the same types were contained in a number of situations. As a result each set could have different degrees of relation with the other sets used for comparison. Their intersections could be wide, when the elements present in both sets were a large part of the

743

contents of both, or narrow, when they were only a small proportion, or the empty set. This could be interpreted as taxonomic similarity between them and, given limits, could be of help in the characterization of phases and area components.

In the immediate problem, it was found that by looking at the resulting model vertically, by strata or by phase, each set represented a discrete time span and its intersection with other sets not only defined the phase but also meant variation in the content of a site, which could be explained as either small, minor changes in the culture content in different time positions or as large, revolutionary modifications of a given situation.

Some conclusions could be gathered from the above. When an element is present in several sets (strata or phases) it can be described as being a component of a tradition and, by consequence, a tradition could be formulated as the presence of elements in intersections in adjoining vertical (temporal) sets. The duration of a tradition would be derived from the number of sets that contain the elements, in proportion to the total number of sets contained in the sequence and thus could be measured by a fraction or percentage value. Another point of interest would be that each set (phase), containing a number of elements, shows a greater or lesser number of members than the adjoining set, and the change in size can be interpreted as an increase or a decrease in a constant culture trait, its stock or assortment.

By formulating the results and combining the two ideas expressed above in diagrams where the size of the sets is depicted proportionally, cases can be shown where a culture, in passing from one phase to another, either decreases or increases its stock as it acquires new elements and/or sheds some others. These diagrams can be pictured tridimensionally by assigning to each set a thickness of an agreed size, either equal, of a value comparable to the time that it lasted, or proportional to the number of pieces – as different from the number of elements in the sets – thus adding a frequential element in the graph. Some of the shapes obtained were considered to be basic in interpretation: one, for example (Figs. 19.7 and 19.8, V-3), shows the culture stock as more or less the same for two consecutive phases and then, in the last one, changing by a sudden growth. Tradition core is composed of type 9, which shows up throughout the sequence. The culture thus described does not lose elements but it does show a marked change at one time. In this case it was correlated with the sudden opening up of contacts with other regions and the resulting introduction of new types.

In another case (Figs. 19.7 and 19.8, V-6), the increase was gradual, probably as contact was made earlier but acting in the same general way. It is

744

interesting, though, to ponder the meaning of the differences in the two examples above. In the first one the change is sudden, in the second one slower. Moreover, while tradition is represented in the first case by one element, present in all phases, the second example shows that the introduction of the new elements 2, 4 and 12 increases the size of the set of elements that are present in several phases and thus affects the culture tradition by increasing its stock. The reverse – that is, the loss rather than the acquisition of elements – is also theoretically possible in other sequences.

Other shapes were also found to be present in cases that could perhaps be more common. A site, while acquiring new elements will also lose a few of the ones present in its stock up till then. Several possibilities in culture development can occur in those instances. The culture can be in the process of stock enlarging and the loss will be smaller than the gain, in which case the successive sets will be wider, although they will not completely cover the previous phase; or, inversely, they will be losing elements at a faster rate than they are acquiring them and the result will be a series of sets diminishing in size but not being totally covered by the previous phase. These processes can be shown to occur either by themselves or, as parts, in combination with other shapes described (Figs. 19.7 and 19.8, V-30, V-38, V-42, Fig. 19.9).

Other possibilities include the entry and successive loss of an element in adjoining sets, as is the case in Figs. 19.7 and 19.8, V-1. The formulae, the diagram and its tridimensional representation show this as an element belonging to a set but not to the next one, then reappearing in another, and, as such, as a partial intersection of non-successive phases.

The model building technique can be applied not only on a site by site basis but, once identification of phase has been done, to a general model for the area (Fig. 19.9) or for the description of focality within a region in a given phase (Fig. 19.10). Elements in tradition are represented in the same way and changes in set size should be given the same meaning as in the individual cases.

Some other possibilities can be explored as a result of the representation obtained in the model. The size of the intersections of adjoining sets, proportional to the size of the union of both sets, is a good measure of the amount of contact or difference between them in their stock. A large intersection is indicative of small change vertically or of close contact horizontally, while a small one can be interpreted as the reverse situation. In non-adjoining sets this ratio helps in giving a measure of their taxonomic similarity.

One of the more valuable aspects of set theory is its possibilities for classification. Results are a measure of the similarity or the difference between the subjects compared. They can be expressed by ratios where the upper member

745

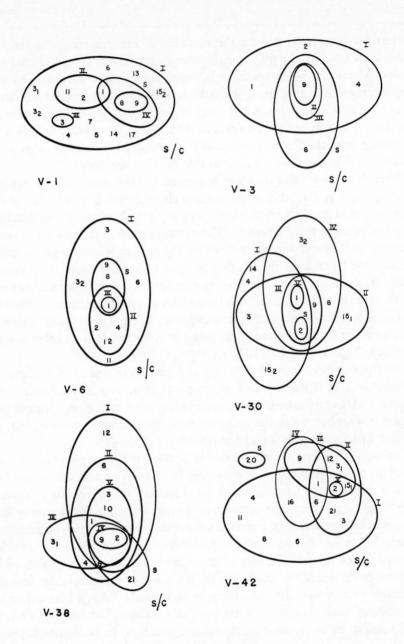

FIG. 19.7. Diagrams for S/C situations (total finds per site, by stratum) in six sites of the La Villita region (Litvak King and García Moll, 1969, pp. 41–6). Sites are identified by a number, prefixed by the letter V. The site shown in Fig. 19.5 (S/C) is V-42. Strata are tagged by Roman numerals, surfaces by the letter S.

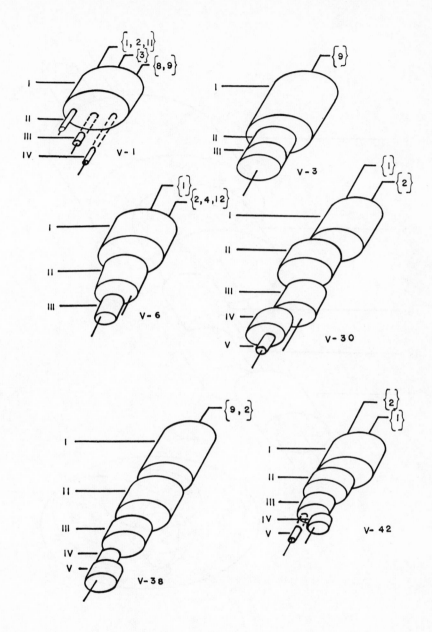

FIG. 19.8. Tridimensional models for S/C situations (total finds per site, by stratum in six sites in the La Villita region as shown in Litvak King and García Moll (1969, p. 48). Elements considered to be components of site traditions are in brackets, strata are stated in Roman numerals.

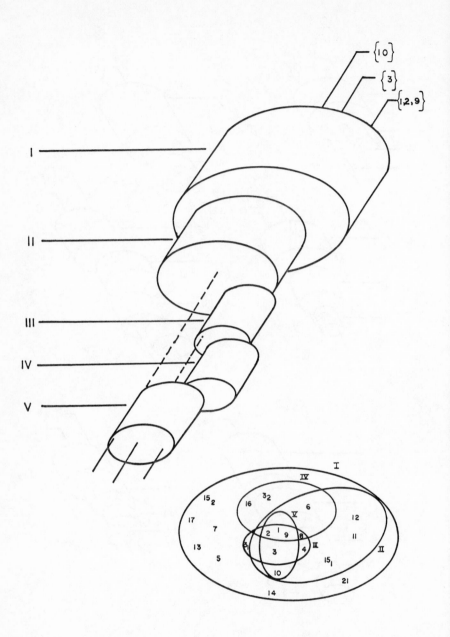

FIG. 19.9. Diagram and tridimensional representation of S/C results (total finds by stratum) for the six sites in the La Villita region (Litvak King and García Moll, 1969, pp. 47, 49). Elements are identified by Arabic numerals, phases by Roman numerals; elements in area tradition are in brackets.

is the number of elements present in the intersection while the lower presents the union of both sets. It can also, for more general uses, be represented from the number resulting from doing the division implied in the fraction. The limits are o and 1, when the sets are either totally different or equivalent. Differences in culture stock content between sets can then be expressed in the same way. Other uses include the idea that some, at least, of the elements introduced in a sequence are substitutes for some of the ones lost. Although

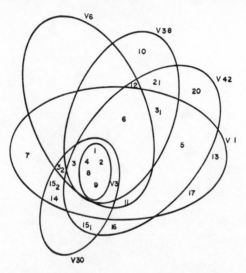

FIG. 19.10. Diagram for site results for the La Villita region (Litvak King and García Moll, 1969, p. 47). Sites are tagged by Arabic numerals prefixed by the letter V. Elements are unprefixed.

the technique proposed does not interpret the precise substitution, it does nicely point out the location of the problem.

Set theory model building has also been applied as an auxiliary technique, specially focused on solving specific problems. In that case, for archaeology, the fact that it is part of a group of tools and that it can be applied selectively speaks for its growing potential and methodological versatility within the discipline, since it does not necessarily depend on the universal application of one technique indiscriminately, whether it is the most efficient way of handling the problem, or even whether it will do the job at all.

Such was the case in another paper by Litvak King (1970, esp. pp. 190–1) where set theory was used to define a site whenever an identity problem between two or more adjacent subsites existed. Using, experimentally, the pottery from twenty-three sites in the Xochicalco valley, in the state of

749

Morelos in south central Mexico, in a sequence from Preclassic to Late Postclassic (*c.* 1000 B.C. to A.D. 1500), this study attempted to establish a model for contact between sites, since the problem, stemming from the co-existence of contemporary adjacent sites, had to be solved before a network model could be established.

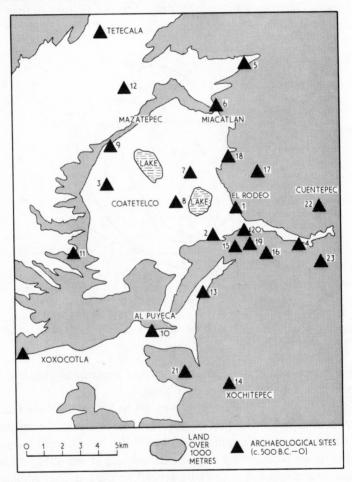

FIG. 19.11. Base map of protoclassic sites (*c.* 500–0 B.C.) in the Xochicalco valley. The relationships between the numbered sites are expressed in set theory terms in Fig. 19.12. (Litvak King, 1970, p. 41).

When materials were studied, it was found that they were arranged in a finite number of possibilities: either the materials in one site were a subset of those in the other, in which case it could be stated that the site observed was a

750

specialized aspect of a larger one, or else the subsites could show an inter-section in their contents that varied between large (almost total) or small (almost the empty set). Results were interpreted to signify that a large inter-section meant subordination of the site to a larger one. Small intersections were considered to be situations of independence with only the normal contacts between sites in the same area (Figs. 19.11 and 19.12).

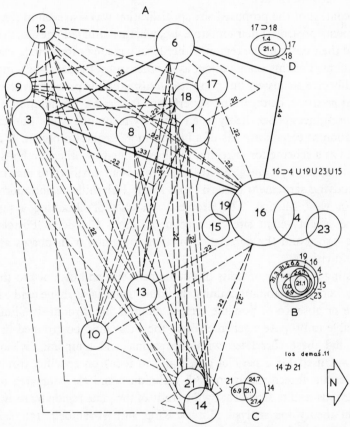

FIG. 19.12. Set theory used to define site identity in the Xochicalco valley (Litvak King, 1970, p. 223). Sites 4, 19, 23 and 15 are shown to be subsets of site 16 (B). Sites 14 and 21, although closely linked, are not parts of one site (C). Site 18 is a subset of site 17 (D). Types are identified by decimalized small numbers, sites by large numbers. The phase represented is the protoclassic, phase 2 (c. 500–0 B.C.).

The problem of appraising the size of the intersection was approached both by finding the ratio of its size *vis-à-vis* the size of the union of the sets, as in the La Villita example above, and also by the examination of the elements involved. If they were the ones normally present in the regional trade pattern, they were not regarded as significant and the sites were supposed to be independent settlements with normal, although very close, contacts. If they were, on the other hand, specific of the two sites or a small zone around them, limited in their distribution to the domain of the sites studied, then each was considered to be a satellite subsite of a larger unit and was so taken in building the final network model.

The context of the proposed site specialization was also seen in the light of the elements present. Their tentative use, whether ritual, domestic, industrial, etc., and their entry in the region, either locally made or imported, were taken into account. For this examination, as in other cases, the set theory model did not readily give an answer but permitted *focusing* on the problem with explicitness and *precision*, disregarding superfluous factors for the solution.

The usefulness of set theory as an auxiliary technique is not limited to the examination of certain aspects of a bigger, more general problem. It can also be useful as a scheme for checking results obtained by other methods. It was used in that way by Gonzalez Crespo (1970), as an auxiliary to matrix analysis in studying settlement pattern types in the Infiernillo region, north of La Villita in west Mexico. The problem was that of obtaining a taxonomy for some seventy-eight sites in a sequence from Classic to Postclassic (*c.* A.D. 600–1500) and the correlation of types obtained with phases and subregional divisions.

By listing a number of traits like settlement size and distance to the river, distance between habitation units, building materials, shape and size, the presence or absence of possible temple mounds, multiroom dwellings, etc., he was able to propose a scheme where the sites could be grouped in several classes, and these correlated with subregional and temporal divisions. Set theory was used for a parallel check and to focus on specific, troublesome spots. Results agreed nicely in both techniques and also, for area division, with previous results arrived at by the study of the same region by its figurines, using set theory for analysis (Litvak King and Mirambell, 1967). A more recent paper by Serra Puche (1971) also used both matrix analysis and set theory for a revision of existing typologies for Teotihuacan figurines in a sequence from Late Preclassic to Late Classic (*c.* 500 B.C. to A.D. 600).

Set theory model building techniques have been applied by García Moll (1972) in a different context, this time for the identification of settlement units in a cave, on material from Texcal Cave in the state of Puebla in central Mexico, with an occupation range from the Preceramic to the Postclassic (*c.* 4000 B.C. to A.D. 1500). The excavation grid was used as the basis, with each square defined as a set that had, as members, the types present in it. Results were mapped and areas of dispersion and concentration of types found. The resulting graphs showed sets with a larger stock and locational situations where type distributions centred. These were correlated with frequential mapping of each type and the use of the units determined. In this case, as in the one before it, set theory was used as an adjunct to statistical treatment of material, rather than as the main tactical technique. Its great disadvantage, the loss of information resulting from lack of quantitative data, was considered offset by the fact that several types could be mapped simultaneously by Venn diagramming without the difficulties involved in showing the distribution in quantity of a number of traits.

Although set theory model building in archaeology has by no means had a full trial, results obtained by the few applications and the variety of situations where it has been used can be considered to prove that its possibilities are ample. Even from the simplest point of view it provides the researcher with a clear, easy to understand way to describe materials and compare them with other data, found in different situations. If to this elementary use is added the mechanism of a fairly complete system of Boolean algebra (Fig. 19.6), the usefulness of the technique increases and it can be made into a powerful tool for analysis, especially when materials, either because of quantity or distribution, do not lend themselves to statistical handling.

It could be said that set theory models restore to archaeology a measure of the qualitative analysis that disappeared when highly subjective views were eliminated in favour of statistical ones. In the present case, the approach can be objective and, being polythetic by definition, it supplements the normal, frequential view without invalidating it.

Perhaps the most useful role for set theory in archaeology is that of an auxiliary technique. It does work quicker than other, more complicated analytic tools and has the added advantage of using unsophisticated mathematics for results that can be of a surprisingly deep penetration. Its results, in helping to open for the field the possibility of experimentation are also to be taken into account. Some precautions must be taken, though, when applying the proposed technique. While its possibility of error is no greater than that of other forms of analysis, the user should not forget that care should be taken in setting requirements for the work.

Type definition, for example, although it can be derived from set theory, can also be taken from existing typologies. In any case it should be rigid and discrete. Since the presence of an identified element in a given set is the backbone of the examination, the identity of the element itself should not be

753

modified in the work process. Also types, if they are to be used for special purposes, should not contain in their definitions traits that could affect results by autocorrelation. Thus, for example, no time-linked typology (that is one where the same type is given another identity because of a different time position) can be used for phase definition. A statigraphic or phase position is, of course, necessary, since it is stated to be a set, but the same type in different sets should be identified by the same nomenclature. If function is used, it should either be ascertained or left to be an *a posteriori* result rather than input.

Set theory is still in an experimental stage in archaeology. It should, therefore, be used only as a supplementary tool, or at least checked by the utilization of other techniques. Results obtained can then be compared and differences analysed to determine the appropriate application.

References

CLARKE, D. L. (1968) *Analytical Archaeology*. London: Methuen.

COOPER, W. S. (1964) *Set Theory and Syntactic Description*. Janua Linguarum, Series minor. The Hague: Mouton.

FLORES GARCÍA, L. (1968) *Diagramas, Preclásico Tlatilco Figurillas*. Antropología Matemática No. 6. Sección de Máquinas Electrónicas, Museo Nacional de Antropología, Instituto Nacional de Antropología e Historia, Mexico.

GARCÍA MOLL, R. (1972) *Estudio del Material de la Cueva de Texcal, Pueblo*. M.A. thesis, Escuela Nacional de Antropología e Historia, Mexico.

GONZÁLEZ CRESPO, N. (1970) *Patrones de asentamiento en el Balsas Medio: Un Ensayo Metólogico*. M.A. thesis, Escuela Nacional de Antropología e Historia, Mexico.

HAGGETT, P. (1965) *Locational Analysis in Human Geography*. London: Arnold.

HAGGETT, P. and CHORLEY, R. J. (1965) Frontier movements and the geographical tradition. In CHORLEY, R. J. and HAGGETT, P. (eds.) *Frontiers in Geographical Teaching*, 358–78. London: Methuen.

HENSHALL, J. D. (1967) Models of agricultural activity. In CHORLEY, R. J. and HAGGETT, P. (eds.) *Models in Geography*, 425–58. London: Methuen.

KANSKY, K. J. (1963) *Structure of Transport Networks: Relationships between Network Geometry and Regional Characteristics*. University of Chicago, Department of Geography, Research Papers No. 84.

LITVAK KING, J. (1970) *El Valle de Xochicalco: Formación y Análisis de un Modelo Estadístico para la Arquelogía Regional*. Doctoral thesis, Universidad Nacional Autónoma de México, Mexico.

LITVAK KING, J. and GARCÍA MOLL, R. (1969) *Aplicación de la Teoría de Conjuntos a la Formación de Modelos para el Desarrollo Cultural*. Antropología Matemática No. 9 Sección de Máquinas Electrónicas, Museo Nacional de Antropología, Instituto Nacional de Antropología e Historia, Mexico.

LITVAK KING, J. and MIRAMBELL, L. (1967) *Estudio Tipológico de las Figurillas de la Cuenca del Río Balsas.* Departamento de Prehistoria, Instituto Nacional de Antropología e Historia, Mexico (MS. report).

MARCUS, S. (1966) *Bibliography of Rumanian Works on Mathematical Linguistics.* Bucharest: Societatea de Stinte Matematice.

MARCUS, S. (1967) Mathematical aspects of linguistics. *International Social Sciences Journal,* **19**, (1), 52–63. Paris: UNESCO.

SERRA PUCHE, M. C. (1971) *Análisis Taxonómico de Figurillas Teotihuacanas.* M.A. thesis, Escuela Nacional de Antropología e Historia, Mexico.

SOLOMON, S.-Y. (1969) Lingvistica algebrica si teoria modelelor. *Studii Si Cerceteri de Matem,* **21** (7), 1107–34. Bucharest: Central de Calcul si Cibernetica Economica.

VELASCO MIRELES, M. (1970) *Vasijas de Tlatilco, Nomencladores.* Antropología Matemática No. 14. Sección de Máquinas Electrónicas, Museo Nacional de Antropología, Instituto Nacional de Antropología e Historia, Mexico.

20

Locational models and the site of Lubaantún: a Classic Maya centre

N. D. C. HAMMOND

University of Cambridge, Centre of Latin-American Studies, England

> . . . *the students should be warned that they are theories, and theories only, that their whole point and value is that they are not susceptible to proof; that what makes them amusing and interesting is the certitude that one can go on having a good quarrel about them, and the inner faith that when one is tired of them one can drop them without regret. Older men know this, but young men often do not.*
>
> HILAIRE BELLOC

The Classic Maya ceremonial centre of Lubaantún lies in the southern part of Belize (British Honduras) some 27 km from the Caribbean coast, in the low foothills that begin to rise from the coastal plain towards the Maya mountains to the north-west. The site was discovered at the beginning of this century and excavated in 1926–7 by the British Museum (Joyce, 1926; Joyce *et al.*, 1927). By 1970 the area in which it lay had become a backwater in Maya archaeology; for this reason, and because the previous work had shown Lubaantún to be a site with several idiosyncratic features, further investigations were carried out in that year. They included the mapping of the ceremonial centre and part of the surrounding area of settlement, excavation within the ceremonial centre to establish the cultural sequence, and ecological survey to determine the resources available within the site exploitation territory (Hammond 1970a, 1970b, 1971a, 1971b). The ceremonial centre, its surrounding settlement and other sites in the area were all found to date to the Late Classic period of the eighth and ninth centuries A.D., a discovery that raises important questions about Maya political and demographic history (Hammond, 1970a, p. 222); the purpose of this paper, however, is to examine how the spatial patterning of these relatively short-lived political entities is susceptible to analysis by the use of locational models.

The operational model for this study resembles a nest of Chinese boxes

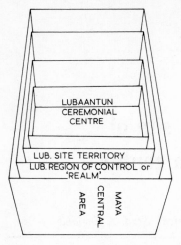

LUBAANTUN
CEREMONIAL
CENTRE

LUB. SITE TERRITORY
LUB. REGION OF CONTROL or
'REALM'

MAYA
CENTRAL
AREA

FIG. 20.1. The operational Chinese Box model.

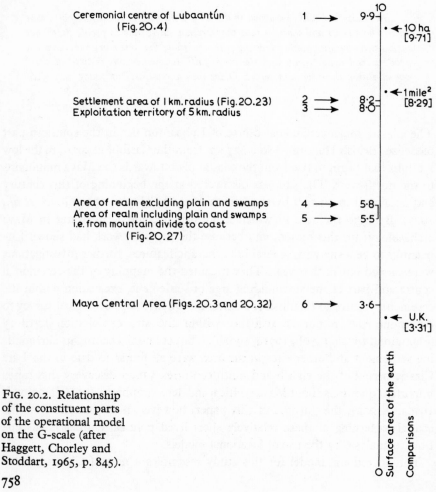

Ceremonial centre of Lubaantún
(Fig. 20.4)   1 ⟶   10
                                                         9·9
                                                         • ← 10 ha
                                                            [9·71]

Settlement area of 1 km. radius (Fig. 20.23)   2 ⟶   8·2   • ← 1 mile²
Exploitation territory of 5 km. radius   3 ⟶   8·0   [8·29]

Area of realm excluding plain and swamps   4 ⟶   5·8
Area of realm including plain and swamps   5 ⟶   5·5
i.e. from mountain divide to coast
(Fig. 20.27)

Maya Central Area (Figs. 20.3 and 20.32)   6 ⟶   3·6
                                                         • ← U.K.
                                                            [3·31]

Surface area of the earth

Comparisons

FIG. 20.2. Relationship
of the constituent parts
of the operational model
on the G-scale (after
Haggett, Chorley and
Stoddart, 1965, p. 845).

758

(Fig. 20.1). There are four such 'boxes', representing in outward progression the ceremonial centre, the settlement area and associated exploitation territory around it, the region of control or 'realm' of Lubaantún, and the Maya Central Area as defined by Thompson (1966, pp. 19–27). Even larger enclosing 'boxes' representing the Maya area as a whole and then Mesoamerica could be added; the largest of the four used, the Central Area, represents an area of about 132 000 km^2, that of the 'realm' between 1600 and 800 km^2, that of the site exploitation territory about 12 km^2 and that of the ceremonial centre about 0·06 km^2. The relationship between these areas is expressed on the G-scale (Fig. 20.2, derived from Haggett, Chorley and Stoddart, 1965, p. 845).

The ideal model of Fig. 20.1 may be distorted to fit the iconic model (map) of the area (Fig. 20.3) from which it is clear that the three inner 'boxes' are not centrally placed within the outer but lie within its lower right-hand or south-east quarter; neither are they orthogonal to it or to each other. The structure must be distorted still further to fit the true boundaries of the areas described at each level, which are influenced by topographic, linguistic and cultural factors; the extent of this distortion on the largest 'box' may be seen by comparing its edges with the actual boundaries of the Central Area marked on Fig. 20.3, after Thompson (1966, p. 18; 1970, pp. 6, 86).

Each 'box' represents an area of territory which is a fragment of that next enclosing it: the ceremonial centre is part of and related to the settlement and site exploitation territory, which is one of many such territories within the realm, while the realm has both direct contacts and indirect parallels with adjacent and distant realms. A comprehensive study would examine all territories at each level; this one is concerned only with the relationship of one site to its exploitation territory, one territory to its realm, and one realm to the rest of the Central Area. In the words of Apostel (1961, pp. 15–16), 'The mind needs to see the system in opposition and distinction to all others; therefore the separation of the system from others is made more complete than it is in reality. The system is viewed from a certain scale; details that are too microscopical or too global are of no interest to us. Therefore they are left out. The system is studied with a certain purpose in mind; everything that does not affect this purpose is eliminated.'

The innermost 'box' encloses the ceremonial centre of Lubaantún, located on a steep ridge 0·5 km north of the Rio Columbia; the iconic model of this is the contour plan made by Walton and Ah (1970), translated into a restored plan (Fig. 20.4) by Walton and Hammond using the conventions of Morley (1938–9, vol. V, pt 2) which have been adopted by subsequent workers. In this

759

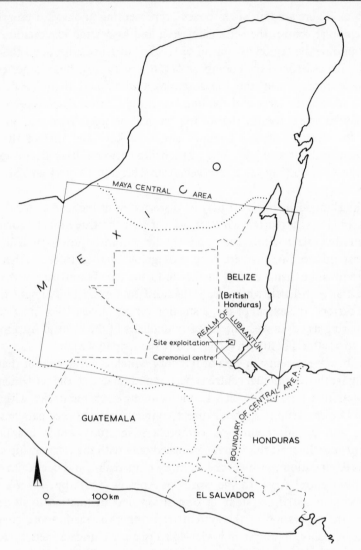

FIG. 20.3. The operational model fitted to a map of the Maya area.

convention the outer line delineating each structure represents the true basal area, while the inner rectangle and the diagonal lines linking it to the outer are approximate expressions of the height and top surface area; given that most Maya structures have stepped or sloping sides, a long diagonal and small inner rectangle are consistent with great height and the impression created by the convention is a reasonable one. In Fig. 20.4 construction units are num-

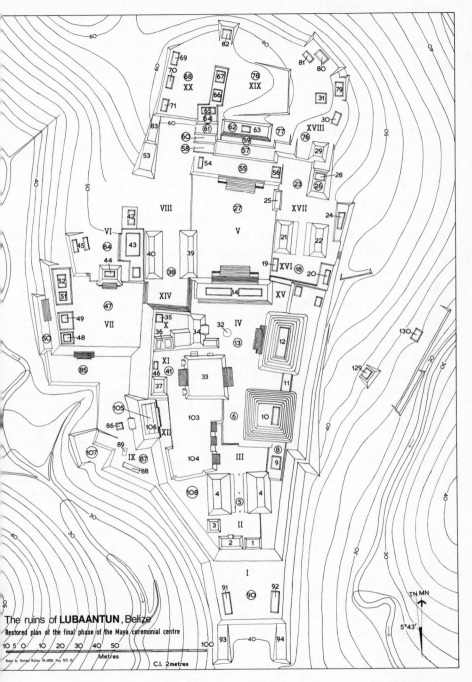

The ruins of **LUBAANTUN**, Belize

Restored plan of the final phase of the Maya ceremonial centre

10 5 0 10 20 30 40 50 100

Metres

Drawn by Michael Walton MA ARIBA May 1970 ©

C.I. 2 metres

FIG. 20.4. Restored plan of the final phase of the Lubaantún ceremonial centre, *c.* A.D. 850.

bered in Arabic, with Platform numbers circled and those of Structures not, while the open spaces of Plazas are numbered in Roman figures.

The construction of the site consists of a series of modifications of the pre-existing topography, and the investment of effort involved indicates that these modifications were purposeful and planned, and that the intermediate and final forms of the ceremonial centre were designed to serve specific functions. In my opinion the examination of this, which follows here, counters Bray's (1972) assertion that 'there is no pattern of . . . traffic routes and the location of buildings is determined more by local topography than by any attempt at town planning'.

The *construction units* that constitute the physical mass of the ceremonial centre may be divided into two classes, *Platforms* and *Structures*; *Platforms* are the massive units from which the artificial topography of the site is created, each consisting of a body of fill resting on the natural land surface and varying in depth over it so as to have a level and fairly horizontal top surface. On a sloping land surface the fill thins out at the uphill end, while on the downhill side(s) it is retained by high stone walls; a Platform occupying the top of a knoll would have walls on all sides, while one filling in a depression might have none. *Structures* are the constructions of varying dimensions and forms, mostly truncated-pyramidal and of stepped profile, which stand upon the Platforms and which are often called the 'buildings' of a ceremonial centre. At many sites they are surmounted by stone-walled superstructures, and are therefore known as 'substructures', but at Lubaantún all super-structures were of perishable materials and only these lower parts survive.

The variety of forms and dimensions among the Structures is clearly correlated with a variety of functions: on the basis of ethno-historic accounts and half a century of archaeological investigation, the high pyramidal Struc-tures are accepted as religious/ritual edifices, while small low ones, often grouped three or four around a patio, are known to have been residential and ancillary domestic structures. The Structures mapped at Lubaantún may therefore be categorized on a morphological basis; this categorization may be made by visual discrimination based on antecedent knowledge, or by using an explicit dimensions ratio such as those of basal area and height (Fig. 20.5). Here there is a definite cluster of Structures of 0·60–1·20 m height and 40–90 m² basal area, all of which would be classed by visual discrimination alone as being of residential/domestic function; another definite cluster is of Structures between 5·0 and 10·0 m height and 500–800 m² basal area, and the three examples in this group would be classed by observation as religious/ritual structures or 'temples'. A third cluster is apparent between these two, of

Structures ranging in height from 1·3 to 3·6 m and in basal area from 160 to 330 m². On the criterion of height alone the cluster falls into two groups, those of above and below 2·0 m height, a division supported by observation: those of below 2·0 m are in form large residential buildings, their increased height

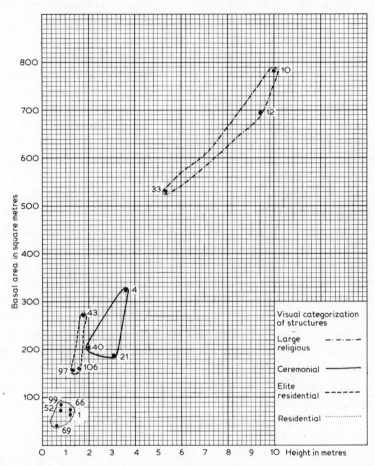

FIG. 20.5. Differentiation of structure functions by graphic means and visual discrimination.

and area due to the provision of a free-standing basal platform on which the Structure stands, while those of over 2·0 m are diverse non-residential and non-religious forms best called 'para-ritual' or 'ceremonial' Structures.

By observation and measurement it is therefore equally possible to isolate four categories of Structure at Lubaantún: religious/ritual, with basal area

500+ m² and height 5·0+ m; para-ritual/ceremonial of basal area 180–330 m² and height 2–4 m; residential/domestic of basal area up to 100 m² and height up to 1·20 m; and a subclass of what may be called 'élite residences' possessing a free-standing basal platform giving an area of 150–275 m² and a height of 1·30–1·90 m. The separation between residential, ceremonial and religious Structures is distinct, that between élite residences and ceremonial Structures understandably less so.

These categories of Structures have been obtained solely by considering their dimensions and morphology, but their relative locations reinforce the classification (Fig. 20.4); the three large religious Structures, 10, 12 and 33, are clustered around Plaza IV, while the ceremonial Structures are similarly clustered, to north and south of them around Plazas III and V. The élite residences are found adjacent to the ceremonial areas on the west and perhaps south, and beyond these and the ceremonial areas to north, west and south are the ordinary residential Structures.

It is clear that spatially, and, as the 1970 excavations showed, historically, the area of Plaza IV is the core of the site, where the main temples and the focus of ritual activity were situated. As such it might be considered analogous within the Lubaantún model to the Central Business District (C.B.D.) used in industrial urban geography, and the relationship of the ceremonial and residential areas of Lubaantún to the religious core can be described by a variant of the concentric zone model proposed by Burgess (1927), although Sjoberg (1960, p. 97) opposes its application to a pre-industrial situation. This applied to urban growth and its progressive radial expansion, but the form of Lubaantún in its final phase (the only one for which we have complete data) may be taken as a transect of such a model at a single point in time. In diagrammatic form (Fig. 20.6, after Haggett, 1965, fig. 6.15) a concentric zone model for Lubaantún has three zones, religious, ceremonial and residential, with the élite residences included in the latter. Comparison of the abstract model with the iconic shows that the former is an oversimplification of reality: ceremonial and residential Structures are clustered mainly to north and south of the core and more sparsely to the west, but are absent on the east. This contrast may be seen as a distortion of the ideal model by the micro-topography, which instead of being a plane surface consists of a sloping ridge between two ravines; the distortion may therefore be seen as a sectorial development under topographic constraint.

The description of ceremonial, religious or residential 'areas' suggests concentrations of Structures whose morphology indicates such functions, but the term 'area' also comprehends the open spaces of Plazas around which the

Structures are grouped. A Plaza as such is simply an open level space, at Lubaantún the top surface of a Platform, bounded on two or more sides by Structures or by the retaining walls of higher Platforms; it takes its character entirely from the functions of these Structures. Figure 20.7 is a spatial model of Lubaantún, each square representing a Plaza, numbered as in Fig. 20.4 and indicating the function ascribed to it, while Fig. 20.8 shows the relative sizes of Plazas. The incomplete concentric zone layout of the site is apparent, as is a general relationship between plaza size and religious/ceremonial function.

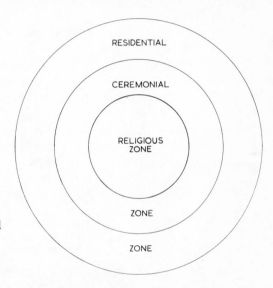

FIG. 20.6. Concentric zone model of the ceremonial centre of Lubaantún.

Variation in function might reasonably be expected to correlate with variation in the necessity and desirability of access to and traffic flow across the Plazas: a commonsense proposition would be that public areas would have easy access, religious areas would be easy or difficult of access depending on the nature of the cult, and residential areas would be comparatively secluded. This proposition and the accuracy of the attribution of functions to the sixteen Plazas within the ceremonial centre of Lubaantún (those shown on Fig. 20.4 with the exclusion of I, XIX and XX) may be tested by examining the connectivity of the pattern of Plazas shown in Fig. 20.7. In another case indices of *gross vertex connectivity* and *net vertex connectivity* were calculated for thirty-nine towns in medieval Muscovy by Pitts (1965), using graph-theoretic methods: the data on one-step connections were reduced to a connection matrix, which was then raised to the power of the graph's diameter d to give the number of d-step routes utilizable for each place and the number of *d*-step routes between pairs of places; a short-path matrix shows the number of edges traversed in the shortest path between pairs of places. This method could be used here, but with a network of only sixteen vertices and eighteen edges would come close to methodological overkill. Simpler methods can be used to establish the accessibility/isolation relationship of the sixteen Plazas.

The spatial model of Fig. 20.7 is converted to a network with the Plazas forming the vertices and the routes between them the edges on a planar graph

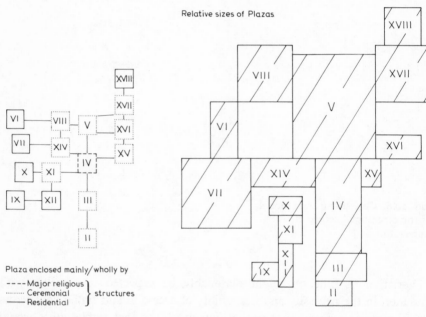

Plaza enclosed mainly/wholly by

- - - - Major religious ⎫
.... Ceremonial ⎬ structures
———— Residential ⎭

FIG. 20.7. Layout and functions of plazas in the ceremonial centre.

FIG. 20.8. Relative sizes of plazas in the ceremonial centre.

(Fig. 20.9); only the presence/absence of connection is noted, horizontal and vertical distance being ignored. The maximum number of steps on a direct route from any one vertex is the diameter of the graph, in this case six; the number obtained from each vertex is subtracted from the diameter to give an *index of centrality* of 2, 1 or 0, and contours may be drawn (Fig. 20.10), indicating that Plazas IV, V, XIV and XV are the most central and that Plazas II, VI, IX and XVIII are the most peripheral.

On the same graph the number of one-step connections from each vertex may be plotted to give an *index of accessibility*, and contours of accessibility drawn (Fig. 20.11); these indicate that Plazas IV and V are most accessible and Plazas II, VI, VII, IX, X and XVIII least accessible. Figures 20.11 and 20.10 may be combined to give an *index of central accessibility* (Fig. 20.12),

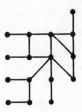

FIG. 20.9. Planar graph of connections between Plazas.

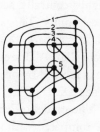

FIG. 20.10. Relative centrality of Plazas.

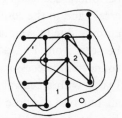

FIG. 20.11. Relative accessibility of Plazas.

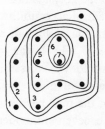

FIG. 20.12. Central accessibility of Plazas.

which shows that the most centrally accessible Plaza is IV, followed by V. A one-stage reduction in accessibility brings in Plaza XIV, and a further reduction of one stage in centrality includes Plazas VIII, XI, XV, XVI and XVII.

767

The most peripherally secluded Plazas are II, VI, IX and XVIII. If the *implied access* suggested by broad entries and small vertical distance between plazas is brought into consideration, then Plazas IV and V would have their positions reversed.

Figures 20.11 and 20.12 show that the most centrally accessible Plazas are eccentrically placed at the north end of the site, with those of the rank next below flanking them to east and west but those to the south being a further rank or ranks lower in their index of central accessibility. This eccentricity may be seen in Fig. 20.13, which shows three sections across Fig. 20.12: i and ii are west–east across Plazas VI-VIII-V-XVII and VII-XI-IV-XVI, while iii is north–south through Plazas V-IV-III-II. There is a trend towards peripheral seclusion both to the west, as the Plazas step down the slope to the creek, and to the south along the spine of the ridge, but that this trend is not entirely due to simple distance from the most centrally accessible Plazas may be seen from Fig. 20.14, where contours plotting the number of one-step connections necessary to reach Plazas IV and V show a contrasting pattern: Plazas with a central accessibility index as low as 3 are within one step, and all but one of those with an index of 1 are within two steps. Contrasting Fig. 20.14 with Fig. 20.12 it can be seen that immediately south of the highly centrally accessible Plaza IV is an area of unexpectedly low central accessibility. This seclusion is so marked as to appear intentional; its physical cause is apparent from Fig. 20.4, where the high retaining wall that runs south from Plaza VII around the south side of Plaza II and north again to Structure 12 is pierced by only one entry, the stair (not marked) from Plaza XII down to Plaza IX.

The model of central accessibility derived from the planar graph may now be compared with the concentric zone model based on structure morphology (Fig. 20.7). Those Plazas assigned a residential function have an average central accessibility index of 1·4, those of ceremonial function one of 3·85 and the Plaza of major religious function an index of 7, against an overall mean of 3·25. The initial commonsense proposition, that areas of public activity would be accessible and those of residence secluded, is confirmed. The range of index values for ceremonial Plazas, however, is from 1 to 6; five of the nine have values just above the mean and two others are well above it, i.e. seven are moderately to highly centrally accessible, but Plazas II and III with indices of 1 and 3 fall within the range of values for residential areas. Both are flanked by at least one residential Structure, but their most obvious function is to act as end zones for the ball court, Structure 4; with Structures 10 and 104 bounding Plaza III to north and west and Structure 2, a small religious structure, on the south side of Plaza II, the ceremonial character of both Plazas is clearly indicated. There is in fact a southward progression along the spine of the ridge from areas of high central accessibility to areas of high seclusion within the religious ceremonial core of the site; this may be seen even

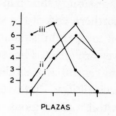

FIG. 20.13. Variation in central accessibility of Plazas with location.

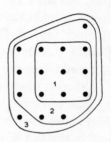

FIG. 20.14. Distance in one-step units from the most centrally accessible Plazas.

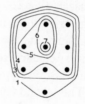

FIG. 20.15. Trend from high central accessibility to high seclusion within the religious-ceremonial core of the site.

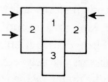

FIG. 20.16. Block diagram based on Fig. 20.15.

1. High
2. Moderate } central accessibility
3. Low
→ Exterior access

more clearly by excluding the residential Plazas from Fig. 20.12 to give Fig. 20.15, which may be reduced to the simple model of Fig. 20.16. The indication is that the sacred ball game *pok-ta-pok* was played in an area cut off from the rest of the site and accessible only via the main religious area.

The discussion so far has been concerned only with patterns of communication within the ceremonial centre, but Lubaantún also connected with the territory around for which it acted as a focus of religious, ceremonial and probably administrative and commercial interaction. From the pattern of accessibility shown in Fig. 20.11 we would expect exterior access to come at the northern end of the site; this is the case, with Plazas VIII and XVIII giving on to open hillside and Plaza VII having two stairways leading down to the western creek. The location of these connections, leading into areas of moderate central accessibility, emphasizes both the core nature of the high central accessibility Plazas and the seclusion of those of low central accessibility within the religious ceremonial area; it also shows, paradoxically, that areas such as Plazas VII and XVIII, which are peripherally secluded within the frame of reference of the ceremonial centre, also act as transit routes to the territory beyond. Peripherally secluded Plazas that do *not* have this double identity include VI, IX and XII, all the sites of élite residences; these are secluded relative to both internal and external route networks.

Although I have applied this method of analysing the structure of a pattern of areas of varying functions to only one site it should be applicable to other Maya sites and also to non-Maya ceremonial centres both in Mesoamerica and in the Old World – for instance, the palaces of Minoan Crete and Mycenaean Greece or those of Mesopotamia. All are in function and in many aspects of form instances of Sjoberg's (1960) 'pre-industrial city'. The fact that, in some aspects of form, centres such as Lubaantún diverge from Sjoberg's 'constructed type' is not necessarily an indication that their functions differ (Bray, 1970).

The second 'box' in the operational model is that enclosing the settlement area and site exploitation territory of Lubaantún. The ceremonial centre contains only a few residences, mainly on peripheral Plazas, but mapping a 1 km² area round it showed that there were many others in the vicinity. Their distribution is shown on Fig. 20.17, and is governed by a number of factors, largely environmental although selected for by human preference. The major factor is the local micro-topography; the almost level peneplain of the Toledo Beds has been dissected by stream erosion into a landscape of round-topped, steep-sided knolls and ridges. The ceremonial centre occupies one of the broadest and longest ridges, while most of the knolls have groups of residential and ancillary domestic Structures. The top of each knoll has been built up into a broad flat area by the construction of a rubble-filled Platform with stone retaining walls, on which stand the substructures of from three to ten buildings. The form and dimensions of these are similar to those

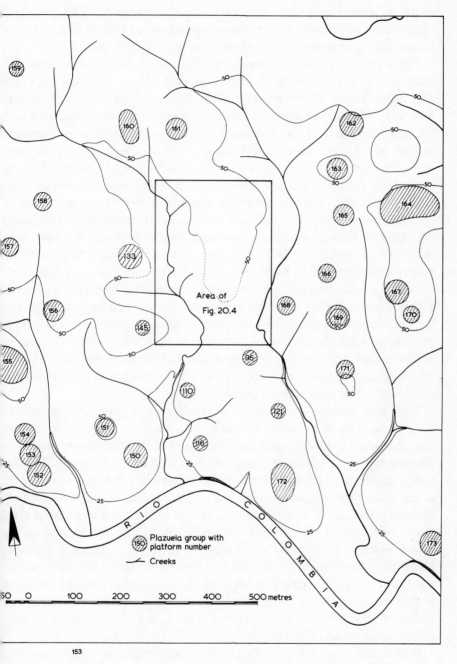

FIG. 20.17. Residential units in the sample area mapped around the ceremonial centre.

of the residential Structures within the ceremonial centre, with a basal area of less than 120 m^2 and a height of less than 1·2 m. A Platform with its superincumbent Structures is commonly known as a 'plazuela group'.

The tops of the knolls are among the few flattish areas in this landscape, and also have the advantages of ventilation, drainage and defensibility, which together overcome the disadvantage of having to go down to the creek or river for water. Within the sample area mapped every knoll was occupied for 0·75 km back from the river, and a visual check showed that this pattern continued at least to the west. Modern settlement in the area is subject to the same vertical constraints, but there is a contrast in the horizontal pattern, where the present low population density has resulted in a withdrawal to and a ribbon development along the Rio Columbia, the main water source and means of communication in the area. Although the settlement pattern seems adequately explained by these observed environmental factors they may not have been the only ones operational. As Trigger (1971, p. 330) remarks, 'The [settlement] pattern therefore is often a compromise among a number of conflicting tendencies. A simple example is the contradiction in some agricultural societies between the desire for dispersed homesteads in order to be near fields and for nucleated settlements for protection against enemies. It is not always possible to untangle the forces that have been at work, given the sort of archaeological data that are normally available.' The most that can be said is that other factors were clearly compatible with or insufficient to overcome the dictates of topography and environment.

With only a small area mapped in detail it is impossible to define the exact boundaries of the settlement area of Lubaantún, and even with more data it would be difficult since dispersed settlement often covers the whole distance between the local nucleations caused by ceremonial centres. For this reason an arbitrary radius of 1 km from the ceremonial centre has been adopted as the limit of the settlement associated with it; this figure might be justified, in that on the east it reaches near the margin of the low-lying coastal plain where both ancient and modern settlement diminish markedly, and on the west it reaches two thirds of the distance to the minor ceremonial centre of Uxbentún, which might be thought the focus of another but smaller settlement; but it is safer to treat it as arbitrary. The settlement area of Lubaantún is thus momentarily taken to cover a circular area around the ceremonial centre, of 1 km radius and 3·142 km^2 area, forming a fourth zone on the concentric zone model (Fig. 20.18).

Within this area each plazuela group could be taken as being a separate 'home base' with its own 'exploitation territory' (Vita-Finzi and Higgs, 1970, pp. 6–7), but the relationship between them would be impossible to elucidate without direct ethnographic observation because of the complex shifting mosaic of *milpa* plots (Reina, 1967, p. 2). One possible approach, however, is to analyse the internal structure of the settlement area as a spatial pattern, and then to treat the whole area as a 'complex home base' with a corresponding 'complex exploitation territory'. Vita-Finzi and Higgs's process of 'site catchment analysis' for the 'study of the relationships between technology and those natural resources lying within economic range of individual sites' may then be applied to the Lubaantún settlement as a whole, with estimates of maximum economic range derived from ethnographic observation of the land capability classes utilized for subsistence agriculture.

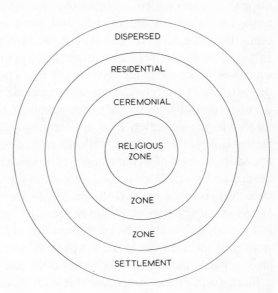

FIG. 20.18. Concentric zone model of Fig. 20.6 with settlement area added.

DISPERSED

RESIDENTIAL

CEREMONIAL

RELIGIOUS ZONE

ZONE

ZONE

SETTLEMENT

To analyse the internal structure or 'micro-articulation' (Chang, 1968, p. 7) of the settlement area it is necessary to assume that the pattern recorded in the sample mapped is consistent for the whole area, and also to assume, temporarily, the simultaneous and continuous occupation of all recorded residential groups throughout the 120–150 year history of Lubaantún.

As the map of the sampled area shows (Fig. 20.17) each plazuela group is surrounded by open land, sloping down from the knoll to the creeks or river or up to a higher knoll. The creeks form obvious natural boundaries to the land around each group, giving a shared water source, and a naive conclusion would be that the land within such boundaries was under the control of the inhabitants of that group. Equally it might be thought that all land nearer to that group than to any other would appertain to it, or indeed that boundaries established by both methods would prove largely coincidental. This theory may be examined by constructing a network of *Dirichlet regions* (Dirichlet, 1850), otherwise known as *Voronoi polygons* or *Thiessen polygons*, centred on the plazuela groups and indicating the territory nearest to each group (Fig. 20.19); from this it can be seen that, although the fit is not exact, many of the polygon boundaries do in fact follow the direction of the creek beds within a 50 m lateral range.

Complete polygons could be constructed for only 700 m north from the river, due to lack of data, and on the eastern and western margins of the mapped area incomplete polygons overlap into the unmapped territory; as a result only the area immediately east, west and south of the ceremonial centre could be divided. The sixteen resulting polygons range in area from 14 348 m^2 to 50 900 m^2, with a mean of 25 933 m^2, a median of 32 624 m^2 and a mode of 21 000 m^2 to the nearest 1000 m^2. There is, however, evidence that the two largest polygons, centred on plazuela groups 171 and 172, may be disproportionately so, on particular grounds: the area of Platform 172 includes a large piece of low-lying and frequently flooded territory, a feature not present in any other polygon, while the eastern end of the area around Platform 171 ends just short of an unmapped knoll, which might reasonably be expected to support a plazuela group and thus act as the centre of another polygon. If these two areas are omitted the mean falls to 22 908 m^2 and the median to 25 266 m^2; if the low-lying land is deducted from the Platform 172 polygon and the territory east of the creek from that of Platform 171 and the reduced areas then included the mean is 24 151 m^2 and the median 27 374 m^2. The mode remains the same in both cases at 21 000 m^2.

From these figures it appears that each plazuela group is surrounded by 23 000–24 000 m^2 of territory, including about 2500 m^2 occupied by the plazuela itself. The remaining 21 000 ± m^2 is all hill slope land suitable for *milpa* corn farming (Wright *et al.*, 1959), and the local six-year swidden cycle of one year's cropping and five years' regeneration under *wamil* (Wright, personal communication, 1970) would give 3500 m^2 annually for cultivation. This is only a ninth of the area needed annually by the present Kekchi and Mopan Maya inhabitants of the area (Wright *et al.*, 1959, p. 44) and only two thirds of the area used by the coastal Caribs for their high-yielding root crops. A Maya family without domestic pigs needs the produce of 1·2–1·6 ha annually (Thompson, 1930, p. 41); the recent increase to 3 ha is the result of pig raising as a cash crop (Wright *et al.*, 1959, pp. 127–8). The land available around each plazuela group is, at 0·35 ha, between a quarter and a fifth of that necessary, and clearly if all groups were simultaneously occupied they would have had to bring 75–80% of their food in from beyond the settlement area. Sufficient land would have been available if only 20–25% of the groups had been occupied at any one time.

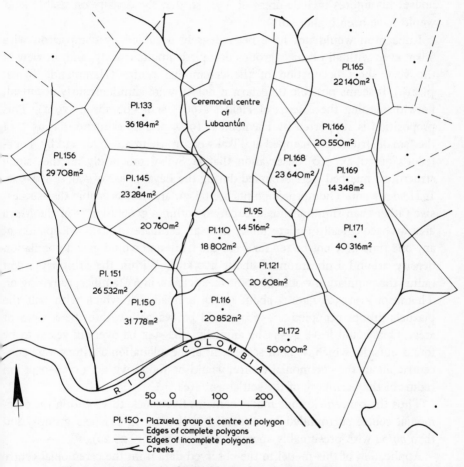

Pl.165
22140m²

Pl.133
36184m²

Ceremonial centre
of
Lubaantún

Pl.166
20550m²

Pl.156
29708m²

Pl.145
23284m²

Pl.168
23640m²

Pl.169
14348m²

Pl.95
14516m²

Pl.110
18802m²

Pl.171
40316m²

Pl.121
20608m²

Pl.151
26532m²

Pl.150
31778m²

Pl.116
20852m²

Pl.172
50900m²

COLOMBIA

RIO

50 0 100 200

Pl.150 • Plazuela group at centre of polygon
———— Edges of complete polygons
— — Edges of incomplete polygons
—<— Creeks

Fig. 20.19. Network of Dirichlet regions based on Fig. 20.17.

Without full excavation it is impossible to tell how many of the Structures in each plazuela group were residential and how many fulfilled other domestic functions, but on the basis of ethnographic observation of Maya settlement units a family size of ten seems a reasonable population for such a house cluster. If the distribution of plazuela groups mapped was constant then population density with all of them occupied simultaneously would have been about 413/km², and with 20–25% occupied density would be 83/km² to 104/km². Haviland (1970, p. 193) estimates the population density of central Tikal at 600–700/km² and that of peripheral Tikal at 100/km², on the basis of 84% of structures in plazuela groups being residential and 5·6 persons per house; his figures include areas of *bajo*, so that the density on usable land would have been higher still.

Lubaantún would not have been densely occupied by comparison with Tikal even with all plazuela groups occupied simultaneously, and, in view of the very short occupation of the ceremonial centre (Hammond, 1970a, p. 218), it seems possible that most if not all were simultaneously occupied, notwithstanding the *caveats* of Heider (1967) and Thompson (1971). This proposition is supported by Haviland's (1970, p. 192) estimate that 95% of the 'small structures' mapped at Tikal were in use in A.D. 770, and by Tourtellot's (1970, p. 410) observation that at Seibal practically all the 'small structures' mapped were occupied during the Bayal phase of A.D. *c.* 820–920. If Heider's and Thompson's points are taken, and it is arguable that successive rather than simultaneous occupation within a generation is in the Maya area archaeologically undetectable, then an estimate of 50% occupation at any one time may not be too far from the truth and would give a population density around Lubaantún of about 200/km². Within the arbitrary 1 km radius the population would be some 625 persons in 63 families, requiring on Thompson's (1930) figures about 94 ha annually, of which with half the plazuela groups occupied 40–50% would be available within the settlement area. This would leave 47–57 ha annually, 282–342 ha over six years, to be found outside, which, if both settlement and exploitation territory were concentric about the ceremonial centre, would be found within a 0·36–0·44 km radius of the periphery of the settlement area.

Thus the concentric zone model contains five zones, three within the ceremonial centre surrounded by dispersed settlement in plazuela groups, and then *milpa* with presumably sporadic settlement (Fig. 20.20).

Application of this model to the observed data from the ceremonial centre has shown how it is distorted by topographic and historical factors, and the two outer zones might be expected to exhibit a similar degree of distortion. The factors governing residence, then as now, were partly vertical and partly horizontal; at present the vertical constraints still operate while low population pressure enhances the effect of the horizontal. Modern settlement tends to occupy ancient sites, overcoming superstition (Hammond, field notes, 1970), for their vertical advantages, but largely restricted to a strip along the river. Higher population pressure during the Classic period enforced settlement away from the river, and proximity to the ceremonial centre may have been another competing factor, but within the mapped area a diminution in settlement density is noticeable as the creeks run out some 0·75 km north of the river.

We would therefore expect the settlement area, far from being concentric about the ceremonial centre, to be elongated along the river to the east and west, reaching 0·75 km away from it in the vicinity of the ceremonial centre

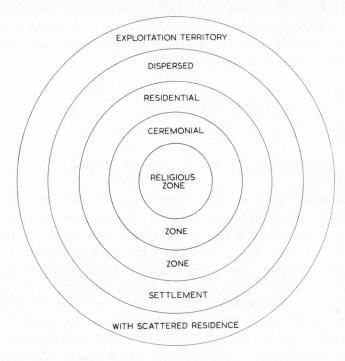

FIG. 20.20. Concentric zone model of Fig. 20.18 with exploitation territory added.

but with this distance diminishing as the pull of centre *v.* river decreases with distance. On the basis of observations made at other major Maya sites such as Piedras Negras, Yaxchilan and Altar de Sacrificios, it is unlikely that settlement continued across the river, although the counter-example of Pusilhà (Gruning, 1930, fig. 1) indicates that the field of settlement might be truncated rather than bounded by the river (e.g. Haggett, 1965, fig. 2·6-C). The inhabitants of a settlement area of 1 km radius, i.e. 3·142 km^2, would under these constraints more probably occupy a territory such as that depicted in

Fig. 20.21, with a maximum inland distance of 0·75 km and a length of 4–5 km. In the case of Lubaantún this would reach from the margin of the coastal plain at the downstream end to the great northward bend of the Rio Columbia west of Uxbentún, and would include that minor ceremonial centre. It is possible that Uxbentún was an independent settlement, since the figure for Lubaantún is an arbitrary one, and its presence within the Lubaantún settlement area on the figures used may indicate that they are too high. Possibly on the local level Lubaantún functioned as a settlement of only minor ceremonial centre size, although acting also as the seat of government for a large number of such populations; an analogy might be that of some of the English cathedral cities, which are *primus inter pares* on a religious/administrative basis among a number of towns of similar population.

FIG. 20.21. Postulated form of settlement area under environmental constraints.

Distortion of the site exploitation territory from the annular area of the model would be the result of several factors, including the probably non-annular form of the settlement area, the distribution of suitable soils, and the location of other settlements competing for them. With the settlement forming a long and relatively narrow east–west strip along the river the nearest agricultural land would be to north and south; the proximity of the coastal plain would limit its availability to the east. The distribution of soils in the area in terms of their suitability to *milpa* agriculture with a primitive technology has been usefully mapped by Wright (1970) from the basic data in Wright *et al.* (1959). Of his four classes labelled *A* to *D* in order of diminishing potential, *B* and (to a lesser extent) *C* are present in the area around Lubaantún, with a large area of class *D* to the north-west. The soils of classes *B* and *C* are those currently utilized by the local inhabitants. Fig. 20.22 shows the present extent of *milpa* and *wamil* in the area, taken from a 1970 air photograph, together with the locations of modern villages, with the positions of archaeological sites and the boundary of an annular exploitation territory for Lubaantún marked. The Kekchi villages of San Miguel and San Pedro Columbia and the Mopán village of San Antonio (off map) together exploit a broad band of territory running south-west to north-east, bounded to the south-east by the 25 m contour and the edge of the coastal plain, and to the north-west mainly by the 100 m contour and the interface of the Toledo Beds with the Cretaceous limestone (Wright *et al.*, 1959, fig. VII). The north-western margin of cultivated land may be determined by the administrative boundary of the Columbia Forest Reserve as much as by the geology. The preference for settlement and agriculture on the undulating Toledo Beds at elevations of 25–100 m, rising to 200 m towards the Guatemalan border, is however reflected in the distribution of both modern settlement and confirmed and reported archaeological sites in this part of the Toledo district (Hammond, in preparation).

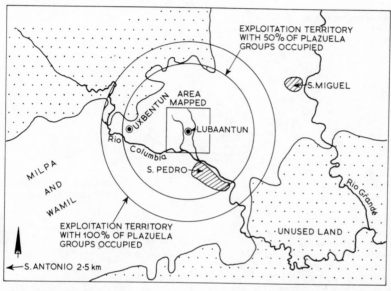

FIG. 20.22. Relationship of the concentric zone model to the present distribution of land used for *milpa* agriculture.

The ethnographic and archaeological information suggests that the exploitation territory of Lubaantún lay north and north-east and south and south-west of the settlement area. The nearest known competition to the south-west would have come from the settlement around the minor ceremonial centre at San Antonio, 7 km in air-line, well beyond the necessary radius of the exploitation territory. The strip-like form of the area presently utilized suggests constraints to the north-west and south-east; these may be identified as the Forest Reserve and/or the 100 m contour and/or the geological interface in the former direction and the low-lying coastal plain in the latter; all except the Reserve would have been operational in Classic times.

779

Figure 20.23 shows the concentric zone model distorted by these considerations of the probable form of the settlement area and exploitation territory: the complex home base contains part and is bordered to north-east and south-west by the remainder of its agricultural exploitation territory, which lies entirely within the micro-environmental zone of the low foothills on dissected Toledo Beds. The agricultural exploitation territory was complemented by a hunting-gathering territory from which meat, skins and forest plant products were obtained, the latter providing materials for shelter, domestic equipment,

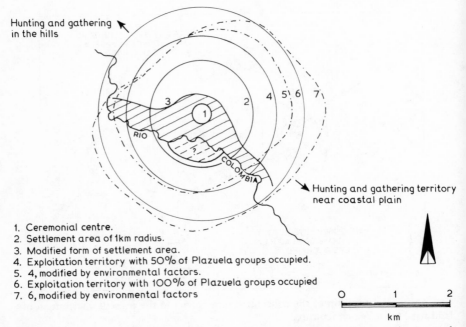

Hunting and gathering in the hills

Hunting and gathering territory near coastal plain

1. Ceremonial centre.
2. Settlement area of 1km radius.
3. Modified form of settlement area.
4. Exploitation territory with 50% of Plazuela groups occupied.
5. 4, modified by environmental factors.
6. Exploitation territory with 100% of Plazuela groups occupied
7. 6, modified by environmental factors

0   1   2
km

FIG. 20.23. The concentric zone model and distortions induced by environmental factors.

food and medicine. Each micro-environmental zone offered its own range of such resources, and Lubaantún, lying close to the junction of the foothills with the coastal plain, was in a position to exploit several such zones. Those present within a 5 km radius of the ceremonial centre included the low foothills under *milpa* and *wamil*, the higher limestone foothills to over 200 m elevation, the upper valleys of the Rio Columbia and Rio Grande running through both zones of foothills, the lower valleys of both rivers running across the coastal plain to their confluence, the plain itself and areas of swamp within it. The upper and lower valleys, the low foothills and the plain all meet in the vicinity of Lubaantún. Vita-Finzi and Higgs (1970, p. 5) point out 'the advantages of a contact situation for integrating economically complementary resources' which 'may be largely or wholly strategic', and emphasize that such contact situations should not be equated with ecotones, transitional areas where the overlap of two or more zones may result in unique qualities including higher productivity (Odum and Odum, 1968). Whether it lies in an ecotone or not, the fact that this location was selected as the site for a major ceremonial centre makes it 'atypical of the area in which it lies, and its abnormalities are as important to an archaeological study as its normalities' (Vita-Finzi and Higgs, 1970, p. 5). It is interesting to note that a straight line passing through all the micro-environmental zones listed above in the shortest possible distance runs almost at right angles to the axis of the agricultural exploitation territory, so that the hunting-gathering territory of Lubaantún would have been elongated north-west to south-east to exploit the maximum range of resources; the range of 5 km that comprehends these zones is only half the maximum distance to which !Kung bushmen will travel to hunt and gather, so it was probably economic to exploit all of them.

The site exploitation territory undoubtedly contained scattered settlement, which in Petén continues in most places between the more concentrated populations around the ceremonial centres, and this with the population of the settlement area estimated previously would give an average density for all the land within the margins of the settlement area and exploitation territory of 120–135/km²; with all plazuela groups in the area occupied simultaneously the population density would be almost double. Even the lower figure, the equivalent of 312–351/mile², is high compared with Cowgill's (1962) estimate that 100–200 persons/mile² of arable land could be sustained indefinitely by *milpa* agriculture. The exploitation territory may have been larger than has been calculated, or high calorie root crops may have formed a substantial part of the diet. Thompson (1930, pp. 184–7) noted the cultivation of *camote* (*Ipomoea batatas* (L) Lam.), *jicama* (*Bachyrrizus erosus* (L) Urban), *yuca* (*Manihot esculenta* Crantz) and *malanga/yaulia* (*Xanthosoma* spp.) in this area, and Wisdom (1940, p. 56) described the existence of special *yuca* plantations among the Chorti. The antiquity of the crops is indicated by Sahagun's (1963, XII, pp. 125–7) listing of all four as 'edible fruits which are within the earth', and Peter Martyr's (1612) mention that *camote* and *yuca*, and perhaps *jicama*, were grown by the Chol of the Golfo Dulce area in the sixteenth century. Bronson (1966, p. 262) points out also that their appearance in rituals in the Books of Chilam Balam suggests a pre-Columbian use. If these root crops were important then the exploitation territory of Lubaantún would possible have been smaller than calculated: where the Maya cuts 1·5 ha of *milpa* annually to feed his family, the coastal Carib cuts 0·5 ha and grows *yuca* and plantains. Another possible source of plant food in much of the Maya area was *ramon* (*brosimum alicastrum*), which is often found associated with ancient sites (Puleston, 1968), but in the area of Lubaantún it is scarce (Hood, 1970, field notes). Much of the land in the agricultural exploitation territory is within the 1 km range of home base that Chisholm (1968, p. 66) considers the limit for rewarding agriculture, although the modern Maya often farm 10 km or more from home, the likelihood of a temporary second home base being used at the *milpa* increasing with both *milpa* size and distance (Reina, 1967).

This distortion of the ideal concentric zone model has given a notion of the nature of the complex home base and site exploitation territory of Lubaantún which is more likely to err in the particular than the general; within the limits established by this process a detailed examination could be made of the distribution of land use capability classes and of micro-environmental zones to build up a fuller picture of the economy.

The third 'box' of the operational model (Fig. 20.1) is the 'region of control' or 'realm' of Lubaantún. This may be defined as 'the area within which Lubaantún was the sole member of the top rank of a hierarchy of sites', and is effectively the area within which Lubaantún was the main ceremonial, religious, administrative and probable commercial centre. The ranks of the site hierarchy have been defined by Bullard (1960, 1962) as the *household unit* corresponding to the plazuela group, the *cluster* or hamlet of 4–8 ha area, the *zone* averaging 1 km² associated with a *minor ceremonial centre*, and the *district* averaging 100 km² associated with a *major ceremonial centre*. Lubaantún is a major centre, albeit a small one, possessing two ball courts but lacking stelae. Sites in the south Toledo district such as Uxbentún, San Antonio and Seven Hills would be classed as minor ceremonial centres, while the nearest major centre is Pusilhà, 32 km south-west of Lubaantún on the Moho river.

I am not here concerned with the possible historical relationship between Pusilhà and Lubaantún (Hammond, 1970a, p. 222) except to note that their functions as centres of 'regions of control' may have been exercised either concurrently or successively, over adjacent or largely overlapping areas. It is the uncertainty of this relationship that makes it difficult to define the boundaries of the realm of Lubaantún; in this paper, for the sake of argument only, I prefer to regard them as concurrent centres of adjacent realms.

Bullard's estimate of the territory appertaining to a major centre as about 100 km² is based on his work in north-east Petén. Such an area concentric about Lubaantún would cover a circle of 5·7 km radius; Fig. 20.24 shows its relationship to the concentric zone model. Bullard's data showed the propinquity of major centres in Petén, but from the data available it would appear that in the marginal and late-settled region at the south end of the Maya

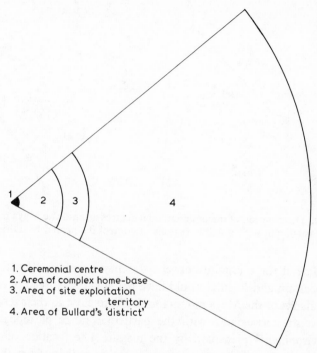

1. Ceremonial centre
2. Area of complex home-base
3. Area of site exploitation
                territory
4. Area of Bullard's 'district'

FIG. 20.24. A sector of the concentric zone model showing the relationship of the exploitation territory of Lubaantún to the 'district' controlled by a major ceremonial centre on Bullard's (1960, 1962) model.

mountains such centres were more sparsely distributed. Allowing for concurrent function of all the major centres known in the region, the distance of 32 km from Lubaantún to Pusilhà is matched by that from Lubaantún to Quebrada de Oro and from Pusilhà to Poptún, while Poptún is 24 km from Ixkun, and Ixkun is 34 km from Caracol. Poptún is also 50 km from Machaquilá, which is 40 km from Cancuen and 32 km from Seibal, all on the Pasión drainage. The average distance between the sites around the Maya mountains is 41 km, including distances across the main divide which all exceed 40 km;

distances between pairs of sites around the massif average 31 km (range 24–34 km) (Fig. 20.25). This regularity of spacing is paralleled by that of major centres along the Pasión-Usmacinta, where the range of air-line distances is 45–64 km with an average of 54 km. If the boundary between two regions of

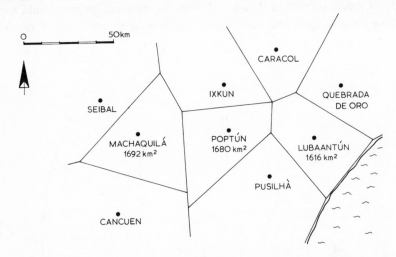

FIG. 20.25. Distribution of major ceremonial centres around the Maya mountains and in south-east Petén, with possible regions of control delineated by Dirichlet regions.

control came at the midpoint between the major centres, then the realms of both Lubaantún and Pusilhà would have had a lateral spread of about 32 km along the flanks of the Maya mountains, a figure close to the average distance between centres associated with the particular range of topographies and micro-environments presented by the massif. The location of each centre was on or near one of the major rivers draining radially from the massif, at an elevation between 50 m and 600 m. Of the six centres considered, Lubaantún on the Rio Grande, Pusilhà on the Moho, and Quebrada de Oro on the Bladen branch of Monkey river, all have direct access across the coastal plain to the Caribbean, while Poptún at the headwaters of the Rio Machaquilá is linked to the Pasión and Usmacinta, and Ixkun and Caracol on the Mopán and Chiquibul branches of the Belize river are on a route to north-east Petén, the Belize valley and the Caribbean (Fig. 20.26).

The realm of Lubaantún may thus be characterized as having within it at least part of the course of a major river, and in fact a circle of 32 km diameter centred on the site encloses almost the whole of the upper basin of the Rio Grande, as well as the Rio Blanco-Blue Creek tributary of the Moho. A circle of similar radius centred on Pusilhà comprehends the rest of the upper Moho basin together with much of that of the Temax, and one centred on Quebrada de Oro includes most of the Bladen and Trio basins as far downstream as the edge of the coastal plain. The same applies to Poptún, Ixkun and Caracol

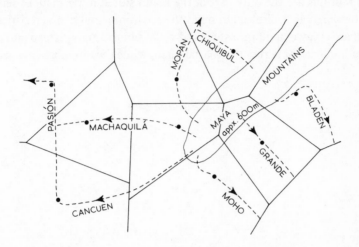

FIG. 20.26. The network of Fig. 20.25 with the Maya mountains and major rivers indicated.

– each has the upper basin of a major river within a circle of 31 km diameter centred on the ceremonial centre. The region of control of such a centre might be taken to be such a basin, the frontier with an adjacent region running along the watershed, especially where this is the main divide of the Maya mountains at over 1000 m elevation, and leaving only the downstream boundary to be established by other means. In the case of the realm of Lubaantún, the most obvious boundary is the Caribbean shore or the off-shore cays, and the maximum extent of the realm would have been from the crest of the Maya mountains to the sea, including the whole of the Rio Grande basin and the Rio Blanco-Blue Creek tributary of the Moho. The realm would have been some 32 km from north-east to south-west and 52 km from north-west to south-east (Fig. 20.27), an area of about 1600 km². This compares closely with the 1616 km² indicated by Fig. 20.25 and with the 1680 km² for Poptún and the 1692 km² for Machaquilá, the range for the three polygon areas being only 76 km².

The structure of this realm and the range of landforms and environments present within its boundaries may be seen in Figs. 20.28–20.29; each local environment – e.g. the limestone foothills – comprehends a range of subsidiary micro-environmental zones such as hilltops, slopes of varying aspect and soil cover, and valleys between the hills, each with distinct though sometimes overlapping resources available for exploitation.

The foothills are the only part of the realm suited to permanent settlement based on *milpa* agriculture, although the environmental characteristics of the foothill area may extend into sheltered valleys in the high plateau and into the river valley corridor across the coastal plain, while the off-shore cays are suited

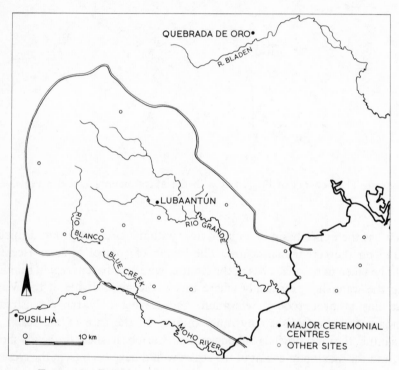

FIG. 20.27. Postulated boundaries of the realm of Lubaantún.

to a fishing economy. The present population of Kekchi and Mopan Maya live and farm almost entirely between the 25 m and 300 m contours, although archaeological sites are known up to 600 m elevation. Just over 400 km² of the realm lie between the 25 m and 300 m contours and a further 220 km² between 300 m and 600 m.

Although the population density in the vicinity of Lubaantún has been estimated at 120–135/km², that for the habitable areas of the realm as a whole

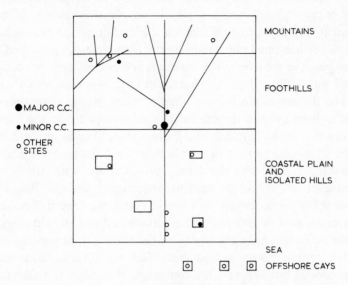

FIG. 20.28. Major landforms and site distribution within the realm of Lubaantún.

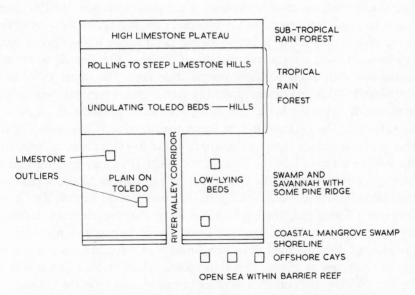

FIG. 20.29. Environmental zones within the realm of Lubaantún.

must have been much lower. It seems reasonable to accept Cowgill's (1962) estimates of 39–78/km², giving a population for the foothills of between 17 000 and 49 000 depending on whether the land up to 300 m or to 600 m is included. A further small population on the high plateau, on isolated hills in the coastal plain, in the river valley corridors and on the cays, say 1000, would give a total within the realm of Lubaantún of 18 000–50 000, with a median of 34 000. The density is much lower than at Tikal, where 10 000 people are estimated to have lived in the central 16 km² and 45 000 in the 'sustaining area' of 123 km² at the height of the Early Classic (Haviland, 1970, p. 193), but the possible total number of people ruled from the centre at Lubaantún is comparable not only with the Tikal figures but also with Adams's (1966, p. 69) estimate of 50 000 for ancient Sumerian cities and Bray's (1970) estimate of 5000–40 000 for the city states of Postclassic central Mexico, which had an average area of 200 km². The pattern at Lubaantún diverges from Bray's scheme in that only 2% to 6% of the realm's total population reside within the 'central ceremonial-governmental zone' rather than the 25% that he proposes, but supports his contention that there is a certain stable ceiling level of population which can be ruled in a state of this degree of social and administrative complexity.

The distribution of population and the location of natural routes together determined the network of communications within the realm (Fig. 20.30). Lubaantún itself lies close to the head of canoe navigation on the Rio Columbia, where the river enters the foothills and then passes into a region of limestone geology and karst drainage; at this point canoe traffic upriver had to continue on foot. Downstream the Rio Columbia–Rio Grande is navigable to the sea, with a few portages around large falls. The upper valley of the Rio Grande takes an ethnographically attested route up into the high plateau at the south end of the Maya mountains, from where the route descends on the far side to the Vaca plateau and the upper reaches of the Chiquibul. The river thus provides a route running the length of the Rio Grande basin, passing on the north-west over into the basin of the Belize river and eastern Petén and on the south-east out to the Caribbean. At right angles to this a land route runs along the low foothills, linking the river basins of the Bladen, Rio Grande, Moho and Temax and crossing the rivers where they are relatively narrow; the modern road from Stann Creek to Punta Gorda follows this route for some distance, as does the road from San Antonio to Aguacate and the foot trail which continues to Poité. This route passes close to both Lubaantún and Pusilhà. Within the foothills a network of minor trails links the villages.

Lubaantún thus lies at the point where the two major routes within the realm cross each other, having access along the flanks of the foothills to other realms centred in adjacent river basins, and also having a direct water route to the sea down the Rio Grande and a land route into and over the Maya mountains via the upper river valleys. The foothill zone in which Lubaantún is situated is the home of most of the present Maya population and contains sixteen of the twenty-four archaeological sites reported in the South Toledo district. The advantages of its location can be seen by comparing them with Cassels's (1971) set of factors suggested as governing settlement location

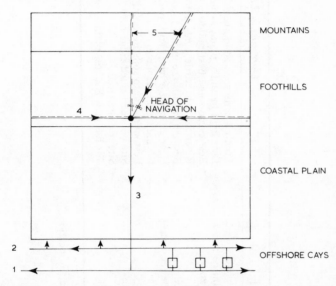

FIG. 20.30. Major routes within the realm of Lubaantún. 1, Long-distance canoe route up the coast of Yucatan. 2, Coastwise canoe route for local traffic. 3, Rio Grande canoe route. 4, Land route along flanks of foothills and margin of coastal plain. 5, Land routes along upper valleys of rivers.

(Fig. 20.31). Of the eleven factors proposed, nine are found to operate at Lubaantún. Five (1, 5, 8, 9, 11) operate on any elevated location within the foothill zone, another one (4) and two others (2, 3) operate within this zone near the river, Factor 2 and Factor 6 operate where the river crosses from the foothills into the plain, and Factor 3 operates by location on the cacao soils of the San Antonio valley. The large number of factors satisfied merely by location in the foothill zone explains the relative density of past and present settlement, while the satisfaction of additional factors indicates why Lubaantún is situated precisely where it is.

Factor [*after Cassels, 1971*]		Operating at Lubaantún
1. Proximity to resource zone with highest yield	*	Foothill zone with good maize/cacao soils
2. ” to greatest no. of different resource zones	*	Low/high foothills, plain, swamp, river valley
3. ” to certain high-yield resource zones	*	Best cacao soils; best building stone; river
4. ” to protein resource	*	River for fish, turtle, *juté*. Animals in *milpa*
5. ” to least moveable food resource	*	Best *milpa* soils are in low foothill zone
6. ” to trade routes [i.e. very mobile resources]	*	Near crossing of river and foothill routes
7. ” to industrial resource	–	No industrial resource
8. ” to agricultural soils	*	Best *milpa*/cacao soils in foothill zone
9. Location suited to defence	*	Site on steep-sided ridge between creeks
10. ” sheltered	–	Site not sheltered
11. ” with good view	*	Site has view E across plain to sea, across foothills, 10–35 km

FIG. 20.31. Possible factors governing settlement location.

The major internal lines of communication shown in Fig. 20.30 also acted as links beyond the realm of Lubaantún; in spite of its marginal location the realm was not cut off during the period when it flourished, but closely tied in to other parts of the Maya area. Communication was overland on foot or by canoe; the routes may be established from ethnographic and ethnohistoric documentation, and extrapolated back into the Classic period by considering the distribution of certain classes of archaeological material.

These indicate that two major route networks connected with the internal network of the realm of Lubaantún (Figs. 20.32–20.33), one a sea and river network along the Caribbean coast, the other an overland network along the flanks of the Maya mountains. A third network, crossing the Maya mountains into eastern Petén, was unimportant, although its existence is shown by the presence of stamped pottery at Actun Balam and Eduardo Quiroz Cave (Pendergast, 1969, fig. 9, j; 1971, fig. 11, o).

The long distance sea route from the Gulf of Mexico around Yucatán and south to the Ulua valley, the Bay Islands and lower Central America was fully operational when Columbus made his fourth voyage; the canoe he encountered near the Bay Islands (Las Casas, 1877, bk 2, ch. 20) was carrying ornamented cotton garments, copper goods and cacao among other merchandise. Thompson (1970, p. 127) suggests plausibly that the copper came from central Mexico and the textiles from Yucatán, and that the canoe had come round Yucatán from the Gulf of Mexico, picking up cacao as payment for goods along the coast of British Honduras, and was bound eventually for the Ulua or the entrepôts of the Gulf of Honduras. Cortés (MacNutt, 1908, p. 231) indicates that the men of the Gulf of Mexico knew the Caribbean coast at least as far south as Costa Rica, and indications that this contact existed in the Classic period include the glyph-inscribed disc in the San José Museum in Costa Rica (Stone, 1965, pp. 315–16, fig. 15) and the *tumbaga* pendant from an Early Classic tomb at Altun Ha in north British Honduras (Pendergast, 1970). Costa Rica may also be the source for some Maya jade; a characterization programme currently being carried out by J. R. Cann, C. K. Winter and N. D. C. Hammond may resolve this point.

The sea route connected at many points with the inland network of river routes and trails. Ascension Bay on the coast of Quintana Roo was the landfall for the overland trail to Chichén Itzá (Ciudad Real, 1873, 2, p. 408) and the Xiu towns at the foot of the Puuc hills were reached via Chetumal Bay, the Rio Hondo upstream to Ucum and then overland (Roys, 1943, p. 52). The Belize river around the north end of the Maya mountains gave access to northeast Petén, and the utilization of this route in the Classic is indicated by the

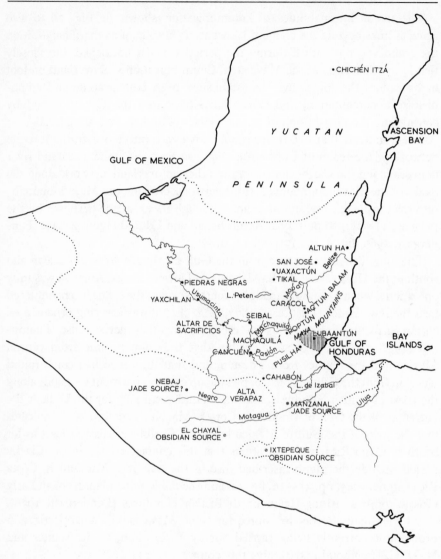

FIG. 20.32. The realm of Lubaantún in the Maya area.

fragments of Ulua marble vases from San José and Uaxactún and the lava *metates* from Tikal and Uaxactún (Thompson, 1970, p. 128). The lava came from highland Guatemala, and its relative abundance at Lubaantún bears out Thompson's suggestion that the goods were shipped down the Motagua and along the coast, although such *metates* are still brought overland to the Toledo

792

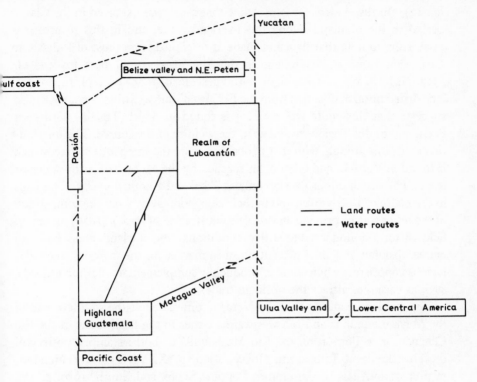

FIG. 20.33. External contacts of the realm of Lubaantún.

district from Cobán, and McBryde (1947, p. 73) notes that the load for a highland *cargador* is two *metates* and six *manos*.

Lubaantún is in fact close enough to the highlands for goods to be shipped either by sea or overland. An important ethnographic route, which survived until a few years ago, ran from the villages of South Toledo district south-west along the flanks of the Maya mountains to the upper Sarstoon valley, then climbed into the hills of the Alta Verapaz to Cajabón and Cobán. This route was functioning in the sixteenth and seventeenth centuries (Remesal, 1932, bk 11 ch. 18; Villagutierre, 1933, bk 9, ch. 2) when cacao was brought up from the lowlands and lowland Chol Maya attended the festival and market in Cajabón. Cacao was probably the main export of the realm of Lubaantún, since, although Millon (1955) does not mention it as a source area, large areas of the foothills are very well suited to it (Wright, 1970) and it is cultivated there today. Evidence for cultivation in the Classic period comes from a figurine of a musician with a cacao pod hung round his neck (Hammond, 1971b,

793

fig. 12). On the evidence it is probable that cacao was exported in the Classic period to the highlands along this overland route, and in this respect it is interesting to note that figurines made at or copied from those of Lubaantún have been found at Pusilhà and in the Alta Verapaz (compare Joyce *et al.*, 1927, pl. XIX, fig. 1, lower right, with Dieseldorff, 1926–33, I, pl. 10, no. 45). The distribution of obsidian from the El Chayal source (Stross *et al.*, 1968) also suggests that this route was used: it is found in South Toledo, north-east Petén and on the Pasión as well as in the vicinity of the source. The distribution contrasts strongly with that of obsidian from the Ixtepeque source, which is found in Yucatán and other areas reached by the Motagua-Caribbean coast route. The distributions overlap only at Tikal and Kaminaljuyú, and perhaps in the realm of Lubaantún, and in their elongation away from the competition of the other source provide an excellent illustration of Park's (1929) dictum of field distortion under competitive conditions: the lowland areas have no native obsidian and thus present an open market for the material; they also have a contrasting environment producing complementary desirable goods, such as cacao, to attract the obsidian trade.

The overland route to the Alta Verapaz bifurcated at the southern end of the Maya mountains and ran westwards, either to the headwaters of the Rio Cancuen or to Poptún on the Rio Machaquilá or both: stamped pottery of the kind made at Lubaantún (Joyce, 1926, p. XXVI, fig. 2; Hammond, in preparation) has been found at Poptún (Shook and Smith, 1950, p. 13), and the extension of the route down the Pasión to the Usumacinta is shown by its presence at Seibal (Sabloff, 1969, p. 242) and Altar de Sacrificios (Adams, 1971). Traffic in the other direction is indicated by the presence in late levels at Lubaantún of Fine Orange pottery made in the Pasión–Usumacinta basin.

The archaeological evidence indicates that the realm of Lubaantún had strong contacts with the highlands of Guatemala by both the Caribbean coast–Motagua valley route and by the overland route to the Alta Verapaz. The principal highland exports were obsidian, lava *manos* and *metates*, axes of volcanic rock, jade and quetzal feathers, together with other products not archaeologically attested at Lubaantún. The lowland realm of Lubaantún exported cacao, and other products that could have been shipped to the highlands include pitch pine for torches, lime for plaster, conch shell trumpets and other decorative shells, jaguar skins for chiefly raiment, tobacco, copal incense, vanilla, chile peppers, logwood, brazil wood and annatto dyes, bark cloth, palm products and iguanas for food (Thompson, 1970, ch. 5). Except for the *manos*, *metates* and axes, highland exports were, as Thompson points out, almost entirely of raw materials – obsidian cores, unworked jade, quetzal feathers, cinnabar and haematite. Imports from Yucatán to the Central Area also included raw materials – honey, wax and salt – as well as elaborately worked textiles, but none of these survive in an archaeological context. Lowland exports to the highlands included a much higher proportion of processed materials – fine painted pottery, worked flint and obsidian, bark cloth and pottery figurines – as well as cacao, tobacco and copal, all partly processed.

The list of goods exchanged includes items that are 'Useful' and those that are 'Functional' in Sabloff and Tourtellot's (1969) classification, the former including obsidian, axes, pitch pine, dyes and foodstuffs, and the latter including jade, incense, fine flint and obsidian work and fine pottery. Cacao falls into both categories, being Functional as a currency and Useful as a food, but the emphasis on its use is largely Functional. It seems from ethnohistoric evidence that the growing and distribution of cacao, the equivalent of possessing a private mint, would have been kept firmly under the control of the rulers, although Parsons and Price (1970, p. 28) argue for its use by all levels of Classic society, and it is arguable that other Functional products would be similarly treated. Such products were sumptuary goods whose use was concentrated at the upper end of the social scale, and the exchange of lowland and sumptuary products for those of the highlands presumably took place between the topmost ranks of society. The goods imported from the Ulua valley and from Yucatán were similarly luxury rather than subsistence products. In the latter, Lubaantún like other Maya realms was necessarily self-sufficient, with the produce of the *milpa*, the forest, the river and the sea to draw upon.

The exchange links between Lubaantún and other regions were used largely for the transfer of sumptuary goods between rulers and the symbiotic exchange between different environmental zones of their own particular desirable products. The sea route was of paramount importance, linking as it did the three contrasting zones of the arid Yucatán plateau, the tropical forests of the Central Area and the volcanic highlands via the Motagua valley; shorter distance exchange between the forest and highland zones was also facilitated by the overland route. The commercial model of Fig. 20.34 might be used equally to illustrate political and diplomatic contact, a situation similar to the Melanesian 'Kula ring'; as Harris (1968, pp. 562–7) points out, it is the combined exchange of Useful and Functional products that maintains the system, with the former being most widely redistributed within the receiving society in exchange for the goods collected and exported.

The evidence suggests that political-economic contact between Maya realms such as that of Lubaantún was firmly based on a system of redistributive exchange involving all levels of the ranked society and both reflecting and reinforcing its structure (Flannery, 1968; Sabloff and Tourtellot, 1969; Parsons and Price, 1971). A model of this system is shown in Fig. 20.33, and Fig. 20.34 indicates how the rank order of society might correlate with the site hierarchy, with all ranks present around a major centre, the top rank lacking at a minor centre, and only the lower ranks present in the dispersed hamlets. The ranks of society would have acted administratively and the site hierarchy locationally 'as mechanisms for the redistribution of goods' (Parsons and Price, 1970, p. 27), and such a construction of society would fit the dynastic

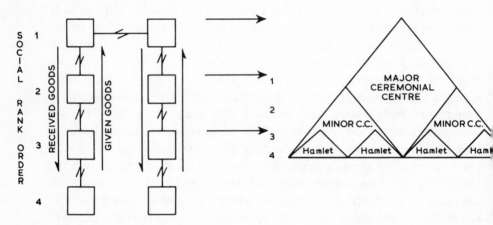

FIG. 20.34. A model for redistributive exchange and a possible correlation of social and site hierarchies.

model adduced by Proskouriakoff (1960) with the addition of a class of occupational specialists such as those listed by Adams (1970).

This description of the nature and function of the external contacts of the realm of Lubaantún shows how its local system of communications and trade ties in with the larger system operating within the Central Area, the fourth 'box' of the operational model, and between the Central Area and the Northern and Southern Areas.

The use of models in this paper has been descriptive rather than analytical, tentative rather than exhaustive; I have attempted to show how the imposition of an ideal abstract model on incomplete data, and its progressive distortion to fit what data there are, may indicate the nature of the systems of which only fragmentary evidence survives, and, more important, how this may give some understanding of the structure and function of a small, peripheral and short-lived Maya realm. As the Reverend Gilbert White of Selborne wrote to the Honourable Daines Barrington in 1778, 'without system the field of nature would be a pathless wilderness – but system should be subservient to, not the main object of, pursuit'.

References

ADAMS, R. E. W. (1970) Suggested classic period occupational specialisation in the southern Maya lowlands. *Papers of the Peabody Museum,* **61**, 487–502.

ADAMS, R. E. W. (1971) The ceramics of Altar de Sacrificios. *Papers of the Peabody Museum,* **63**.

ADAMS, R. M. (1966) *The Evolution of Urban Society: Early Mesopotamia and Prehispanic Mexico.* Chicago: Aldine.

APOSTEL, L. (1961) Towards the formal study of models in the non-formal sciences. In FREUDENTHAL, H. (ed.) *The Concept and the Role of the Model in Mathematics and Natural and Social Sciences,* 1–37. Dordrecht.

BRAY, W. M. (1972) *Land Use, Settlement Pattern and Politics in Prehispanic Middle America: A Review.* In UCKO, P., DIMBLEBY, G. W. and TRINGHAM, R. (eds.) *Settlement Patterns and Urbanisation.* London: Duckworth.

BRONSON, B. (1966) Roots and the subsistence of the ancient Maya. *Southwestern Journal of Anthropology,* **22**, 251–79.

BULLARD, W. R., JR (1960) Maya settlement pattern in northeastern Petén, Guatemala. *American Antiquity,* **25**, 355–72.

BULLARD, W. R., JR (1962) Settlement pattern and social structure in the southern Maya lowlands during the Classic period. *Actas y Memorias, XXXV Congreso Internacional de Americanistas, Mexico.*

BURGESS, E. W. (1927) The determination of gradients in the growth of the city. *American Sociological Society Publications,* **21**, 178–84.

CASSELS, R. J. S. (1971) *Locational Analysis of Prehistoric Settlement in an Island Area of the North Island, New Zealand.* Paper presented at the 28th International Congress of Orientalists, Canberra, January 1971.

CHANG, K. C. (1968) Toward a science of prehistoric society. In CHANG, K. C. (ed.) *Settlement Archaeology,* 1–9. Palo Alto, Calif.: National Press.

CHISHOLM, M. (1968) *Rural Settlement and Land Use.* 2nd ed. London: Hutchinson.

CIUDAD REAL, A. DE (1873) *Relacion breve y verdadora de algunas cosas . . . que sucedieron al Padre Fray Alonso Ponce en le Nueva España.* Madrid.

COWGILL, U. M. (1962) An agricultural study of the southern Maya lowlands. *American Anthropologist,* **64**, 273–86.

DIESELDORFF, E. P. (1926–33) *Kunst und Religion der Mayavölker im alten und heutigen Mittelamerika.* Berlin.

DIRICHLET, G. L. (1850) Über die Reduction der positiven quadratischen formen mit drei unbestimmten ganzen Zahlen. *Journal für die reine und angewandte Mathematik,* **40**, 209–27.

FLANNERY, K. V. (1968) The Olmec and the valley of Oaxaca: a model for interregional interaction in formative times. In BENSON, E. P. (ed.) *Dumbarton Oaks Conference on the Olmec*, 79–117. Washington, D.C.: Dumbarton Oaks.

GRUNING, E. L. (1930) Report on the British Museum Expedition to British Honduras, 1930. *Journal of the Royal Anthropological Institute*, **60**, 477–83.

HAGGETT, P. (1965) *Locational Analysis in Human Geography*. London: Arnold.

HAGGETT, P., CHORLEY, R. J. and STODDART, D. R. (1965) Scale standards in geographical research: a new measure of area magnitude. *Nature*, **205**, 844–7.

HAMMOND, N. (1970a) Excavations at Lubaantún, 1970. *Antiquity*, **44**, 216–23.

HAMMOND, N. (1970b) *Excavaciones en Lubaantún, Belice, en 1970*. Paper read at Congreso Internacional de Americanistas, Lima, August 1970 (proceedings forthcoming).

HAMMOND, N. (1971a) Lubaantún: a regional Maya capital. *Illustrated London News*, Archaeology 2353, 6 February 1971.

HAMMOND, N. (1971b) The arts and trade of Lubaantún. *Illustrated London News*, Archaeology 2354, 20 February 1971.

HAMMOND, N. (in preparation) *Lubaantún and the Archaeology of the South Toledo District, Belize (British Honduras)*. Ph.D. dissertation, University of Cambridge.

HARRIS, M. (1968) *The Rise of Anthropological Theory*. New York: Crowell.

HAVILAND, W. A. (1970) Tikal, Guatemala and Mesoamerican urbanism. *World Archaeology*, **2** (2), 186–98.

HEIDER, K. G. (1967) Archaeological assumptions and ethnographic facts: a cautionary tale from New Guinea. *Southwestern Journal of Anthropology*, **23**, 52–64.

JOYCE, T. A. (1926) Report on the investigations at Lubaantún, British Honduras, in 1926. *Journal of the Royal Anthropological Institute*, **56**, 207–30.

JOYCE, T. A. *et al.* (1927) Report on the British Museum Expedition to British Honduras, 1927. *Journal of the Royal Anthropological Institute*, **57**, 295–323.

LAS CASAS, B. DE (1877) *Historia de las Indias*. Mexico.

MCBRYDE, F. W. (1947) *Cultural and Historical Geography of Southwest Guatemala*. Smithsonian Institution Institute of Social Anthropology Publications No. 4.

MACNUTT, F. A. (1908) *Hernando Cortés: His Five Letters of Relation to the Emperor Charles V*. (ed. and trans.) London and New York.

MARTYR D'ANGHIERA, P. (1612) *De Novo Orbe. The History of the West Indies*. London.

MILLON, R. F. (1955) *When Money Grew on Trees*. Ph.D. dissertation, Columbia University. MS in Butler Library, ref. Burgess D378, 7CWO-M624.

MORLEY, S. G. (1938–9) *The Inscriptions of Petén*. Carnegie Institution of Washington, Publication No. 437.

ODUM, E. P. and ODUM, H. T. (1968) *Fundamentals of Ecology*. Philadelphia: Saunders.

PARK, R. E. (1929) Urbanization as measured by newspaper circulation. *American Journal of Sociology*, **35**, 60–79.

PARSONS, L. A. and PRICE, B. J. (1970) Mesoamerican trade and its role in the emergence of civilisation. In RITTEIZER, A. and GRAHAM, J. (eds.) *Observations on the Emergence of Civilization in Mesoamerica*. University of California Research Facility No. 11.

PENDERGAST, D. M. (1969) *The Prehistory of Actun Balam, British Honduras*. Royal Ontario Museum Art and Archaeology Occasional Paper No. 16.

PENDERGAST, D. M. (1970) Tumbaga object from the early Classic period, found at Altun Ma, British Honduras (Belize). *Science*, **168**, 116–18.

PENDERGAST, D. M. (1971) *Excavations at Eduardo Quiroz Cave, British Honduras (Belize)*. Royal Ontario Museum of Art and Archaeology, Occasional Papers No. 21.

PITTS, F. R. (1965) A graph theoretic approach to historical geography. *Professional Geographer*, **17**, (5), 15–20.

PROSKOURIAKOFF, T. (1960) Historical implications of a pattern of dates at Piedras Negras, Guatemala. *American Antiquity*, **25**, 454–75.

PULESTON, D. (1968) *Brosimum Alicastrum as a Subsistence Alternative for the Classic Maya of the Central Southern Lowlands*. M.A. dissertation, University of Pennsylvania.

REINA, R. (1967) Milpas and milperos: implications for prehistoric times. *American Anthropologist*, **69**, 1–20.

REMESAL, A. DE (1932) *Historia general de las Indias occidentales y particular de la gobernación de Chiapa y Guatemala*. Biblioteca Goathemala de la Sociedad de Geografía y Historia, vols. 4–5. Guatemala City.

ROYS, R. L. (1943) *The Indian Background of Colonial Yucatan*. Carnegie Institution of Washington Publication No. 548.

SABLOFF, J. A. (1969) *The Classic Ceramics of Seibal, Petén, Guatemala*. Ph.D. dissertation, Harvard University, No. HU90–9651.

SABLOFF, J. A. and TOURTELLOT, G., III (1969) *Systems of Exchange Among the Ancient Maya*. Paper read at the 68th Annual Meeting of the American Anthropological Association, New Orleans.

SAHAGÚN, B. DE (1963) *Florentine Codex: General History of the Things of New Spain*. Ed. and trans. by A. J. O. Anderson and C. E. Dibble. Monographs of the School of American Research (Santa Fé) No. 14.

SHOOK, E. M. and SMITH, R. E. (1950) Descubrimientos arqueologicos en Poptún. *Antropología e historia de Guatemala*, **2** (2), 3–15.

SJOBERG, G. (1960) *The Pre-Industrial City: Past and Present*, Glencoe, Ill.

STONE, D. (1965) Incised slate disks from the Atlantic watershed of Costa Rica. *American Antiquity*, **30**, 310–29.

STROSS, F. H., WEAVER, J. R., WYLD, G. E. A., HEIZER, R. F. and GRAHAM, J. A. (1968) Analysis of American obsidians by X-ray fluorescence and neutron activation analysis. *Contributions of the University of California Archaeological Research Facility*, No. 5, 59–80.

THOMPSON, J. E. S. (1930) Ethnology of the Maya of southern and central British Honduras. *Field Museum of Natural History Anthropological Series*, **17** (1).

THOMPSON, J. E. S. (1966) *The Rise and Fall of Maya Civilisation*. 2nd ed. Norman, Okla.: University of Oklahoma Press.

THOMPSON, J. E. S. (1970) *Maya History and Religion*. Norman, Okla.: University of Oklahoma Press.

THOMPSON, J. E. S. (1971) Estimates of Maya population: deranging factors. *American Antiquity*, **36** (2), 214–16.

TOURTELLOT, G., III (1970) The peripheries of Seibal. *Papers of the Peabody Museum,* **61**, 407–19.

TRIGGER, B. G. (1971) Archaeology and ecology. *World Archaeology,* **2** (3), 321–36.

VILLAGUTIERRE Y SOTO-MAYOR, J. DE (1933) *Historia de la conquista de la provincia de el Itza, reducción y progresos de la de el Lacandón.* Biblioteca Goathamala de la Sociedad de Geografía e Historia, vol. 9. Guatemala City.

VITA-FINZI, C. and HIGGS, E. S. (1970) Prehistoric economy in the Mount Carmel area of Palestine: site catchment analysis. *Proceedings of the Prehistoric Society,* **36**, 1–37.

WALTON, M. G. and AHl, B. (1970) *The Survey of Lubaantún.* MS and maps.

WHITE, G. (1789) *The Natural History of Selborne.* London.

WISDOM, C. (1940) *The Chorti Indians of Guatemala.* Chicago, Ill.: University of Chicago Press.

WRIGHT, A. C. S. (1970) *A Classification of the Soils of the South Toledo District, Belize (British Honduras) in Terms of their Utility to the Ancient Maya.* MS.

WRIGHT, A. C. S. et al. (1959) *Land in British Honduras.* Colonial Research Publication No. 24. London.

21

A provisional model of an Iron Age society and its settlement system

D. L. CLARKE

University of Cambridge, England

Archaeologists are everywhere devoting an increased effort to the location and excavation of settlement sites of all periods. In most cases, the location technology and the excavation methods employed are far in advance of those of the last century. However, in some respects the retrieval, analysis and interpretation of information from these settlement observations remain scarcely more developed today than the intuitive procedures employed by the best excavators of the nineteenth century.

There are many reasons for this state of affairs. Settlement sites preserve an embarrassing wealth of information, an abundance potentially multiplied by the many purposes and many new methods of analysis and classification that may now be applied to a site, its deposits, artefacts, features and context. It has been customary to accord a very uneven treatment to the different categories of information embedded within the observations recovered. Information about the particular numbers, kinds and positions of items is often effectively treated, but information about their mutual relationships and the strengths and covariation of those relationships in a variety of alternative classificatory dimensions is less often fully explored. Even just the spatial relationships between the artefacts, other artefacts, site features, other sites, landscape elements and environmental aspects present a formidable matrix of alternative individual categorizations and cross-combinations to be searched for information. These problems and their rich information content are, alas, artificially simplified and thus easily overcome by the archaeologist's tendency to fit the observations within a single preconceived interpretative model, derived without further discussion from some historical or ethnographic analogue. Whereas the least that these complex observations demand is the erection of a set of alternative models, explicitly justified and derived from many sources, embodying alternative reasonable assumptions and then the explicit testing between the alternatives or their consequences for predictive accuracy and goodness of fit, by using skilfully devised experiments in the field or upon the recorded observations. It may not always be possible for the archaeologist to substantiate various alternatives directly but it is usually the case that he can test between their differing consequences.

This particular study is the interim product of a long-term experimental exercise in information recovery from a selected settlement site of the kind so assiduously sought by the field archaeologist. The exercise is an attempt to meet the mass of observations from a selected site with a set of experimental models and the manipulative capacity of the computer. The model-using approach is essential in such a study if the site observations are to transcend the level of mere descriptive records, since these observations can only release fresh information in relation to some explicitly developed model or models. The computer is not essential but since the characteristic of this kind of problem is the superabundance of information hidden in the many possible dimensions of relationship and requiring very cumbersome data manipulation, then the role of this tool becomes self-evident.

The Iron Age settlement excavated at Glastonbury, Somerset, by Bulleid and Gray at the beginning of this century was selected for this exercise (Bulleid and Gray, 1911, 1917). The objective was simply to explore the old data in a variety of new ways. The question in mind was this – if a site as rich as Glastonbury was excavated in the 1970s, could we retrieve no more information today than was extracted by the excavators seventy years ago? We would inevitably recover a greater *quantity* of observations by virtue of our more advanced technical expertise, but much of this mass of data would be a redundant reiteration of information already registered. Can we not now extract more information from the data of the 1900s or have our analytical and interpretative procedures progressed no further than simply operating upon an increased volume of observations in the same old way?

The overall aims of the long-term experimental exercise are fourfold:

(i) To learn about the problems of information recovery from the kinds of site currently searched for but perhaps thankfully not yet found.

(ii) To produce a series of alternative models, based on differing assumptions, which might then be tested by further experiments.

(iii) To take *one* interim model towards the limits of its potential to expose the consequences of its chain of assumptions and thus to facilitate testing.

(iv) To explore as a provisional essay the kinds of information that might be recovered from the spatial relationships involving the site, its artefacts, structures and features as a system within a system or hierarchy of other sites, distributed in an interconnected network over a landscape distorted by distance into a contextual *Chinese Box*, receding from the site locus, its territory, its system catchment area to an englobing region of linked systems and beyond.

Several things must be very carefully emphasized about this exercise. It is merely an experimental exercise on the 'simplified' problem presented by the records and observations of an excavation conducted seventy years ago. No archaeological study can be any better than the reliability of the observations upon which it is based and the assumptions that frame the development of its analysis and interpretation. This study is no exception and the observations upon which it is based are patently limited in scope and accuracy. Nevertheless, the data can be understood as merely representing data of its type, so the exercise is not invalidated by the quality of the observations, although the potential of the results must be regarded as limited. The approach, therefore, is simply that of the classical exercise: let us take a as given, and assume b and c, then ... x, y and z follow. Now, at least, we can substitute alternatives for b and c and seek to test between the varying x, y, z by selected experiments.

The site: the post-depositional model and analyses

The Iron Age settlement at Glastonbury is set in the marshland of the Somerset Levels of south-western Britain, one and three-quarter miles north-west of Glastonbury Tor, between the Mendip and Polden hills, fourteen miles from the Bristol Channel (Figs. 21.7–21.9). This western peninsula region was the political territory of the loose confederation of sea-linked Celtic tribes known as the Dumnonii, where the Mendip hills formed a frontier zone facing the alien Durotriges and Dobunni to the east and the more comparable Silures to the north, on the Welsh coast. This tribal frontier was significantly selected by the Roman army for their military frontier based on the Fosse Way, established by A.D. 47–8 within a generation or so of the abandonment of the Glastonbury site.

The site itself was discovered in 1892, excavated between 1892 and 1907 and published in 1911 and 1917 (Bulleid and Gray). The excavation uncovered a settlement built on adjoining artificial mounds or crannogs of interlaced logs, brushwood, hurdles, peat, clay and rubble set on a raised bog and alluvium promontory at the intersection of a small river and the shore of an extensive rush fringed mere. An irregular embanked stockade surrounded the site, with one or possibly two gates providing land access in dry weather for carts, wagons, chariots and stock, whilst a causeway to the floodplain gave permanent access by boat from an ingenious deep water staithe in the river mouth. Within this perimeter lay an 'amorphous agglomeration' of ninety clay floors, hearths and timber structures – many of them frequently renewed in a shifting palimpsest as the timber footings rotted or worked loose and the underlying peat dried out, compacted and subsided under the weight and heat of the clay floors (Plate 21.1). The rubbish sealed in and around the floors and systematically dumped over the palisade for disposal by floods and scavengers produced some 9000 artefacts of wood, antler, clay, bone, stone, flint iron, bronze, lead, tin, glass, shale and amber, together with more than 12,000 bones of domestic and wild animals and many hundreds of domestic and wild plant remains. It is quite clear that these totals would have been substantially augmented by modern excavation techniques.

Any analysis and interpretation of an archaeological site must rest upon a post-depositional model which accounts for the structure of the site in its modern form (see Daniels, Chapter 5 of this volume, and Fig. 5.1). This vital category of model is all too frequently left unvoiced and often appears to imply that everything on the site lies where it was originally built, used or discarded such that the even continuation of this process over space and through time produces a stratified layercake, preserved in encapsulated form into the present day. Alternatively, if the site is very complex the excavator comfortingly adopts the model that it is a structureless rubbish dump or midden and promptly ceases to search for structure which would at least test the model. The demonstration that uneven accumulation has alternated with erosion and destruction, that much material was burned, removed, or lost beyond the site, whilst the remainder went through many life cycles and suffered a constant 'Brownian motion' of buffeting by daily human, animal and plant activity, inevitably leads to the customary archaeological cycle of interpretation and counter-interpretation. The original site structure and activity patterns can only be realistically recovered through the explicit use of a micro-geomorphological model covering the post-depositional period.

The post-depositional situation at Glastonbury is very complex in every respect. Preservation is excellent in the waterlogged and peaty deposits and has produced the hundreds of wooden artefacts but not a single sample of textiles or leather materials. In contrast, the preservation was quite different in the acid clay floors where timber, metal and alkaline materials have been severely eroded or demolished. Ash dumps and partially burned wooden, bone and antler artefacts underline the constant loss of combustible rubbish. Many other artefacts were gathered and dumped in land reclamation projects around the site margins and used for raising the house platforms. Old timbers were re-used, clay floors renewed up to ten times and hearths up to fourteen times at a single spot, leaving unrecorded the completely demolished timbers, floors and hearths. The palisade boundary was continuously extended on different occasions in the different sectors and the river jetty was smashed by unusually heavy winter floods and rebuilt twice. It seems that the daily activities on the site must have eroded and erased both deliberately and accidentally many of the traces of earlier activities and structures.

However, this still only accounts for the first post-depositional phase of scrambling. Eventually, the eastern riverside margin of the site flooded repeatedly, and the site was abandoned and became waterlogged, to be colonized by rushes and embedded in peat. The repeated flooding must have removed and altered many items and features. The inhabitants and their descendants must have salvaged and carried off much that remained useful – only the uneconomic, broken, too heavy or too deeply buried would be ignored. Then 2000 years of restless and relentless burrowing, rooting, subsiding and sliding activity by plants and animals brings us to the excavation. Although the site was almost completely excavated, the sampling characteristics of the excavation suggest that a significant quantity of small or microscopic items was missed. At Glastonbury 'time's arrow' left a continuous and destructive trace throughout its 2000 year trajectory (Ascher, 1968).

With a filter of this severity imposed upon the archaeological sampling 'window', what position may we legitimately take in the analyses that follow? It is at this point and many later nodes that a range of different assumptions may be made and different models employed in the analyses. However, we should note that the site as it survives is not without pattern; it is not amorphous. Definite house plans survive and in some cases part of their contents has been preserved *in situ* by rebuilding over the rubble of structures frequently destroyed by thatch fires. Almost every surviving quern stone may still be matched with fragments of its original opposing stone in the same geological material. It was even found to be possible to set up a series of simultaneous equation models predicting the expected relationship between numbers of querns, pots, spindle whorls, weaving combs, hut floors and food mass remains, based on the ranked survival capacity of each category and taking the settlement population and duration as common unspecified unknowns. The predicted proportional relationships were shown by statistical tests to deviate insignificantly from those implied by the observed sample. Reversing the situation and quantifying these proportions allowed various estimations of the population and duration to be made.

From these and other pieces of evidence it seems that the surviving material is a fragmentary, smudged and noisy sample of a series of activity patterns which changed with time over the lifetime of the settlement. That some traces of some patterns do survive in the debris from the site could be glimpsed by testing the null hypothesis view – that there is no significant difference between the relationships observed within the site and those that might be expected to arise from random agencies. It is these remaining patterns that the following analyses were designed to search for and prepare for testing.

First, however, we must summarize the position taken and assumptions made in the particular post-depositional model selected for further exploration in this essay (see aim (iii)).

(*a*) Many of the relationships observed within the site are indeed no stronger than might be expected from chance factors, but superimposed on this background 'noise' level are some patterned relationships well above that threshold – where the particular threshold setting may be discovered by suitable experiments.

(*b*) Whilst it is likely that discarded artefacts and rubbish have suffered a 'Brownian motion' of constant buffeting by animate and inanimate forces, nevertheless it is characteristic of Brownian motion in two dimensions that the buffeted particle will probably remain within a small radius of its point of deposition, given a long time span (Hersh and Griego, 1969). Even where these continuous random walk processes were overridden by directed human activity, such as gathering and dumping rubbish, we may hypothesize that inertial tendencies would in most cases ensure that the majority of the rubbish collected would probably have been produced by the dumping group itself and gathered by them from the immediate vicinity of their focus of operations. Even the rubbish dumped over the palisade would probably have derived very largely from the sector whose perimeter it formed and in the main from the huts nearest that stretch of the perimeter. It is assumed that there will have been exceptions to these probabilities but that they will not have been sufficiently regularly repeated either to reduce all traces of patterned relationships within the site to the 'noise' level or to introduce false patterns; these assumptions may be tested for in the analyses that follow (Fig. 1.6).

(*c*) Selective sampling and differential preservation have ensured that the available observations are a fragmentary and distorted selection of the observations that might have been recorded immediately after the abandonment of the site. However, the information loss is probably small because of the great repetitive redundancy with which most activities will have been recorded in their extensive artefact kits. This situation is greatly helped by the almost complete excavation of the settlement – further work would in part merely have recovered more spindle whorls, more undecorated sherds, more flints and so on. Fragmentary patterns of strong relationships may still be observed, well above the noise level, although others that must once have existed will have been destroyed or reduced to a level indistinguishable from that of chance relationships.

(*d*) The interpretation of structures on this and comparable complex sites was much confused in the past by a rather exclusive focus upon the clay floors. In this study structures are not simply defined by the clay floors but identified by fragmentary, composite 'signatures' recorded by distinct categories of articulated lines and repeated patterns of posts, together with their intersections and stratigraphic relationship with the clay floors, rubble patches and other features, punctuated by a characteristic debris pattern.

(*e*) It is assumed, on evidence already mentioned, that the site was occupied for many years. Any interpretation must therefore allow for the continuous but uneven and dynamic development of the site and its population, and consequently for an uneven rate of artefact production and deposition. For example, on demographic and preservation grounds, it is probable that the predominant proportion of the artefact sample and detectable activity patterns relate to the closing phases of the site.

The initial analyses of the Glastonbury data have been set up for examination against this framework of assumptions or post-depositional model, although it is hoped that the same data can in time be re-examined against alternative models for the site. These preliminary analyses fall into four groups of related experiments pursued in parallel, in order that fresh information gained from any stage of one group might be fed into an appropriate stage of the other analyses. The procedure thus resembles a developing lattice rather than a unilinear string or a set of separate parallel investigations.

The four groups of analyses include:

(1) Analyses of vertical spatial relationships
(2) Analyses of horizontal spatial relationships
(3) Analyses of structural relationships
(4) Analyses of artefact relationships.

(1) ANALYSES OF VERTICAL SPATIAL RELATIONSHIPS

This group of studies concentrated on the overlapping stratification of the

807

structures, clay floors and hearths and the artefacts that they contained, with the aim of unravelling the sequence of site development. The essential key to the development within and between the different settlement sectors is provided by more than seventy sets of recorded stratigraphic relationships between chains of neighbouring clay floors and structures. Fortunately, the sequence of structures within each sector can be broadly established from these relationships, although correlating the sequences of the different individual sectors derives in part from horizontal spatial adjustments observed during the site's development. The stratigraphic analyses provided the essential framework of the expansion of the settlement, and even in themselves already suggested certain structural and locational regularities which could be scrutinized against the evidence of the other analyses.

The information recovered suggests that the site ended as five interlinked settlement clusters on five crannogs stabilizing the margins of a centrally higher and drier enclosed area (Figs. 21.5, 21.6). These differentiated clusters were designated *sectors* of the site – the southern, central, eastern, north-western and north-eastern sectors – plus the separately categorized causeway and landing stage. The partially independent and successive development of these site sectors is apparent in the diverging lobed margins of the site perimeter, and is confirmed and documented in detail by the chain of floor stratigraphies, the artefact stratigraphies, artefact typology and marked trends in overall artefact densities. Since some ninety or more structures existed on the site a dynamic portrayal would theoretically require a sequence of not less than ninety successive 'frames'. However, in practice, the stratigraphic relationships allow no finer a resolution level than the clear representation of four crude 'phases' of this continuous site development (Figs. 21.2–21.5).

(2) ANALYSES OF HORIZONTAL SPATIAL RELATIONSHIPS

This group of analyses focused upon the non-random, mutually patterned relationships and spatially adjusted locations of the structures, clay floors, hearths and artefacts in order to attempt the recovery of the inherent rules of building followed by the inhabitants. The procedure commenced with the search for repeated locational relationships between structures on the site: a search to recover any locational regularities which deviated strongly from a simply random arrangement – the alleged 'amorphous agglomeration' of huts. By this means a building model was cumulatively assembled which it was hoped would gradually begin to converge with the conceptual planning model of the individual builders, suggesting something of the cultural and functional priorities and rules of construction they may have tacitly followed. This procedure employs in reverse the powerful general methods of modern architectural planning and micro-locational analysis. The contemporary discipline of architectural studies embraces a large and powerful array of relevant analytical procedures, dynamic models, computer graphics and simulation models for precisely such investigations in locational problems (March, Echenique *et al.*, 1971).

It is assumed that, although the settlement was developed on a piecemeal and individual basis, and not planned by a central authority, nevertheless each individual in the community would attempt to repeat a culturally accepted building format and similarly optimize the location of his structures within those common severe constraints to satisfy similar common functional, cultural and technological priorities. In this way even the most primitive human and animal settlements display a patently non-random development (Fraser, 1969).

Initially, the building model distinguishes three main elements: activities, building stocks, and the site building potential. The activities refer to those regularly repeated human activity patterns and combinations of activity patterns that make up the day-to-day, week by week, season by season routines for which the settlement is a principal arena – daily work tasks within and without the site, travelling to and from these tasks, and so forth. The building stock element refers to the built containers of these activities – cleared land, surfaced areas, floor space, transport routes, roads and paths. The site building potential derives from the parameters imposed by the amenity of a particular site to construction, in terms of cost, aspect, micro-climate and micro-environment, together with the ease of connectivity between activity patterns within the settlement and between the settlement and its context. The building model of a particular site then represents the detailed interaction between these various elements and the values given them by the particular set of inhabitants. But the important relationships emphasize the way in which the early activity patterns demand a certain built stock, which, once built, restricts the further development and location of activities and is itself initially restricted by the building potential of the selected site (Figs. 1.17, 21.2–21.5).

The study commences with an analysis of the stock on the site and the locational relationships between that building stock, including adapted spaces for floors, hardstanding, structures, etc., and channel spaces for transport and communication routes within the site, which must ultimately converge and link to routes running out of the site – an obvious but powerful constraint. The routes in most cases may be negatively defined as interlinking open spaces

809

without structures or barriers, and so access routes, through routes and linking routes could be distinguished, noting proximity to structural categories, exclusive linkage between structural categories and closure of groups of structures. These observations identified the main access routes (two gates and jetty), through routes (clay or rubble pathways and unbuilt dry spaces between structures), regularities in proximity patterns (distances between structural categories), repeatedly exclusive linkages (nearest neighbour structures directly linked to or facing one another) and deliberate closure patterns (superstructures so positioned as to prevent, according to width remaining, the passage between them of (*a*) pedestrians and animals and (*b*) carts and chariots).

The building model then considered the settlement development process at three levels: the choice of this locus as opposed to alternative local sites for the settlement, the layout chosen for this particular locus, and the deliberate allocation of different structural categories to selected relative positions within the site. A separate spatial analysis considered the relative locations of the activity patterns, artefacts and artefact categories in relation both to one another within and across the structural features, and to the overall settlement plan.

The model had to satisfy the very stringent requirement that any building 'rule' or constraint postulated from regularities in the relationships observed on the site for any one phase must be substantiated in every succeeding phase of the settlement and not merely satisfy the final arrangement. Thus, within the model, the input parameters of each building phase were specified from the output of the stratification studies and the successive solutions in terms of settlement layout were examined and judged against a series of variable criteria – increase in population, changes in social structure, etc. The results of this appraisal led either to the alteration of the interpretation proposed or to a modified estimate of the parameters. The building model therefore provided an invaluable interactive capacity which enables the experimenter to explore the different consequences of his different estimates, assumptions and hypotheses about the site (March, Echenique *et al.*, 1971).

The interim information already recovered by this group of analyses richly complemented that derived from the stratigraphies. It is apparent that the interlinked estuary, lakes and rivers running from the northern margin of the site will have provided rapid long-distance communications, capable of carrying heavy loads, to the foot of the Mendips three miles to the north and to more distant points. The more seasonal overland access routes appear to have approached the settlement from the south, running along the promontory parallel to the old river bed, from the direction of the Tor and the Poldens (Fig. 21.7). This directional linkage is shared by the contemporary settlement at Meare, three miles to the west, with trackways of many periods running back from these lake margin settlements towards the low hills behind. This linkage might be expected from a settlement pattern expanding onto freshly accessible, fertile alluvium and peat areas released by the periodically shrinking fen margin to the north.

The land route from the south probably forked around the southern sector of the settlement with an eastern branch hugging the riverside perimeter, serving the east gate and the landing stage, whilst a parallel track followed the western perimeter (Fig. 21.5). The stratigraphic evidence for these tracks suggests that they were simply broad lines of approach, patched with clay and tipped rubbish. Certainly, during the annual winter flooding of this low relief landscape the riverside branch would have frequently been unusable, which might explain the purpose of the alternative western fork. It may be noticed in passing that the presence of these two routes is strongly supported by the internal development of the built stock and its articulation with the internal transport network. Whilst there were repeated expansions of the settlement margins and palisades on the northern and north-eastern waterside perimeters, the western and south-eastern margins with admirable dry land were held comparatively rigid by virtue of these adjacent channel spaces. In addition, the internal routes approach the perimeter at these two points, which are marked at the juncture by probable guard huts.

In the final phase the settlement grouped around two open compounds, an *outer compound* entered from the hypothesized western gate, itself opening upon an *inner compound* surrounded by some of the oldest structures to survive into the last phase of the site (Figs. 21.2–21.5). The inner compound had once been surrounded by its own stockade, broached by routes to the landing stage and to the western approach track. There are also ample traces of elaborate internal stock fences and baffles, especially within the eastern sector and its gateway. The compounds clearly served many different purposes, but they could have provided the occasional capacity to corral more than 1200 Celtic sheep or some 300 head of Celtic cattle.

Within the site the analysis of the clusters of structures linked by pathways, by proximity and by facing doorways, and separated by access closure, produced many interesting and suggestive regularities. A repetitive linkage emerged between certain pairs of structures of the kind that may be noted on other 'Celtic' sites, but here there were at least two different categories of linked structures – pairs of interlinked substantial houses and smaller huts linked to subrectangular structures. Thus each sector of the settlement begins to resemble the varied replication of some kind of modular building unit based on these pairs of structures and their dependent work floors. At this stage the building model assumes a far greater significance in terms of the parallel analyses which had been devoted to structural features and artefact evidence for activity patterns.

(3) ANALYSES OF STRUCTURAL RELATIONSHIPS

This third group of analyses investigated the observations recording the attributes of the structures and features on the site with the aim of discovering different categories of structures and features and defining their characteristics. The main structural attributes and dimensions were reduced to a list of elements which were combined in various ways by the range of phenomena observed on the site, including size of structure, shape, total number and types of associated finds, substructure and flooring, frequency of floor renewal, hearth types, frequency of hearth renewal, pattern of marginal posts, pattern of internal posts, doorway features, porch features. Many structures combined only a few such elements, some combined all of them. The procedure was to search this matrix of combinations of structural elements in the hope of uncovering repeated structural categories with a distinctive polythetic 'signature' which might be identified even when some of the elements had been dismantled or destroyed, or had gone unrecorded.

These structural element analyses primarily scrutinized four sets of relationships. The first scheme examined the correlation matrix of the various states of the eleven multistate structural elements noted above, producing clusters of correlated structural elements which frequently recurred together – defining a number of different but recurrent construction categories within a continuum of relationships. The second and complementary scheme searched for groups of similar constructions by clustering the 100 or so structures on the site in order of their mutual affinity in terms of shared structural elements – arranging the observable structures in sets of similar construction. The numbered structures were also independently grouped in order of their mutual affinity in terms of the sets of artefact types that they contained. Finally, a study was set up to research the covariation of structural elements and artefact types across the 100 structures.

The structural studies so far completed suggest that the number of associated finds, the size of the structure, and the frequency of renewal, were especially critical if interdependent variables for this site. Two thresholds are seemingly important in this respect: structures with less than ten artefacts convey no evidence of residential use and structures with more than forty associated artefacts form a distinct and separate category. It is interesting to note that the causeway and jetty with an area twice or three times that of the other structures produced only twenty items lost or abandoned in its construction and use, thus falling below the 'lived in' threshold for this site. All the structures with more than forty artefacts stand out amongst the continuously renewed and intensively occupied set convergently identified by the locational analyses as substantial house pairs.

(4) ANALYSES OF ARTEFACT RELATIONSHIPS

Only the preliminary studies have been completed in this fourth group of analyses – the evaluation of the artefact information. Here the variety of different aims of the analyses require different classifications of the same data to be successively employed. However, these include a regression and trend analysis of the different artefact types one with another across the structures, represented as a network of contiguous cells. The artefact concentrations and residuals produced by this approach have already confirmed that the artefacts must be classified experimentally in a number of different ways, each designed for the different dimensions of clearly specified problems, otherwise much information on relationships is lost by the use of insensitive general purpose categorization (Clarke, 1970). The cross-occurrence of different artefact types on the floors of the structures has been set up and scrutinized for correlated clusters of artefact types categorized according to different special purpose classifications. These classifications include groupings defined by material, taxonomy, activity usage, male or female association, and rank-status association, including evidence from beyond the site itself. The information gathered from these studies on kinds and locations of activity patterns conducted within the site was fed back into the building model providing a fresh round of information output.

The detailed typological analysis of selected artefact types in terms of their intrinsic attributes also promises to be a most rewarding field, especially where the artefact is sufficiently abundant to occur frequently in space across the site and vertically in stratigraphies. A cluster analysis classification of the fibulae, bone combs and pottery elements may be expected to provide the basis for the detection of simultaneous spatial and temporal trends on the site, together with locational deviations. It may be noted here that any interpretation of such a pottery analysis must be made in the light of Peacock's important petrological work, which has identified the large-scale importation of fine ware from market sources to Glastonbury and Meare, where it was used alongside locally made utilitarian pottery (Peacock, 1969).

The site: assessment and a structural model

The combined information from the four groups of analyses integrates to define a distinct range of structures repeatedly reproduced on the site and repetitively clustered in such a way that each sector of the site resembles the varied replication of a single kind of modular unit (Fig. 21.1). This interim assessment rests on the many assumptions developed in the foregoing discussion and itself allows several different interpretations. However, in the interests of brevity the structural categories that have emerged will be listed and described briefly with an attached interpretative label deduced from the total associations of the structure – where these labels should be regarded merely as convenient handling devices.

Seven polythetic categories of construction may be distinguished in terms of their structural attributes, but these broad classes (I–VII) may then be internally subdivided by the intersection of their sets with differing sets of artefact association patterns and the structure's location relative to other structures. This produces thirteen different kinds of repeated built form on this site: major houses (Ia), minor houses (Ib), ancillary huts (IIa), workshop huts (IIb), courtyards (IIc), baking huts (IId), guard huts (IIe), annexe huts (IIf), work floors (III), clay patches (IV), granaries or storehouses (V), stables or byres (VI) and sties or kennels (VII). Since the development of the settlement is a dynamic continuum it must be recognized that structures may successively escalate or descend through these categories – starting as a major house, then becoming an open work floor and then a granary stance, and vice versa. Indeed, an immediate point of interest is the restricted and repeated direction in chains of succession of usages.

Ia: MAJOR HOUSE PAIRS (Plate 21.1, Nos. 4–5, 13–14, 29–35, 27–38, 42, 62–5, 74–76–70; the numbers are in Roman numerals on Plate 21.1)
There are fourteen major house structures, arranged for the most part in seven pairs (Fig. 21.1). These large circular houses are distinguished by the relatively substantial nature of their overall construction and by their lengthy occupation and successive renewal. They were built on individual substructures of interlaced timbers covered by successive clay floors and hearths; the walls were of wattle and daub and the roof was supported by a central post with peripheral subsidiaries. Three distinctive features are the doorways of

814

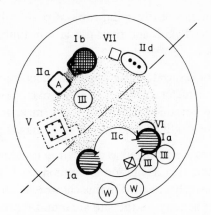

FIG. 21.1. The modular unit – the social and architectural building block of which the settlement is a multiple. The analyses of vertical and horizontal spatial relationships, structural attributes and artefact distributions convergently define a distinct range of structures (I–VII) repeatedly reproduced on the site. Each replication of the unit appears to be a particular transformation of an otherwise standardized set of relationships between each structural category and every other category. The basic division between the pair of major houses (Ia) and their satellites, and the minor house (Ib) and its ancillaries may be tentatively identified with a division between a major familial, multi-role and activity area on one hand and a minor, largely female and domestic area (see Fig. 21.6).

Below: the iconic symbols used to identify the structures in the schematic site models, Figs. 21.2–21.5.

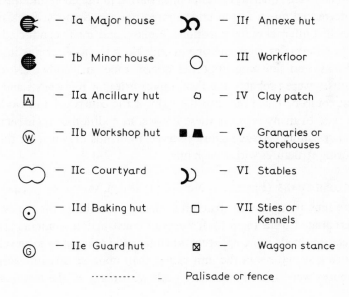

815

stone slabs, their porches of diverging rows of posts, which on occasion become an external fenced yard, and their use of split timber plank floorboards above the clay floors.

Average number of associated artefacts – 46 (max. 149 min. 12)
Average external diameter in feet – 30 (max. 34 min. 28)
Average number of stratified floors – 4–5 (max. 10 min. 3)
Average number of stratified hearths – 6–7 (max. 14 min. 3)

These major houses are arranged as one pair in each unit, set close together in one half of the unit area, facing on a common yard. Lean-to annexe huts and stables are exclusively attached to this category of structure. Facilities for almost every kind of activity on the site are found represented at these focal houses, including the bulk of the horse and chariot gear, together with most of the weaponry and finery. The abundant artefacts of all types suggest that the full range of male and female activities were either conducted here, or that their artefacts were stored here; in contrast, all other structures on the site contain a specialized selection from this repertoire. Thus, here, workshop activities are represented as but one element amongst many others – bronze smithing, carpentry and lathework, wool combing, spinning, weaving and embroidery.

The distinctive but not exclusive artefact associations are: furnace furniture, crucibles, iron and bronze tools and equipment, slingshot, needles, combs, small ovens, querns, human bones buried in the floor, and the highest ratio of decorated fine wares to undecorated pottery. Some, at least, of these structures had internal radial partitions (No. 65) and many conducted special productive enterprises, iron smelting in one (No. 71), shale turning in another (Nos. 62, 64) and finishing imported quern stones in another (Nos. 4, 5). These houses were probably the focal repositories for tool chests and equipment that could be taken out into the light of the courtyard and work floors for daily use. In many respects these houses, in addition to their social role, somewhat resemble cottage factories served by hands drawn from the many neighbouring structures within each unit.

Ib: MINOR HOUSES (Plate 21.1, Nos. 9, 11, 18, 49, 57, 70, 55, 30, 44)

There are nine minor house structures, closely resembling the major houses but differentiated from them by features of construction, contents and locations – features made more apparent when taken in relation to their values for neighbouring structures in the unit rather than upon an absolute scale. The minor houses were also substantially built with many of the features of the

816

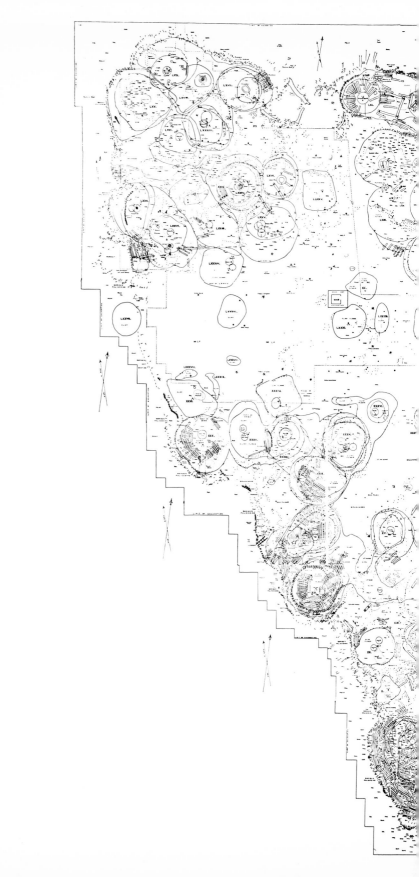

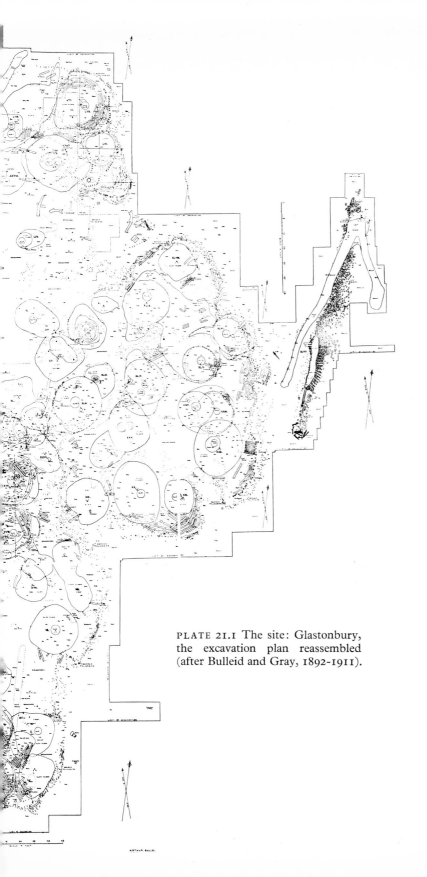

PLATE 21.1 The site: Glastonbury, the excavation plan reassembled (after Bulleid and Gray, 1892-1911).

major houses but on a smaller scale and lacking the funnel porch. Instead, these structures approach oval or pear-shaped outlines, a tendency in many cases caused by a transverse wind-baffle extension to the entrance – a feature found on stone huts elsewhere within the breezy Dumnonian territory (Fox, 1964, p. 91).

Average number of associated artefacts – 42 (max. 74 min. 12)
Average external diameter in feet   – 30 (max. 36 min. 24)
Average number of stratified floors   – 3–4 (max. 9 min. 2)
Average number of stratified hearths   – 4–5 (max. 10 min. 2)

A single minor house exists within each unit, set in the opposing half of the unit area to the major house pair, at more than twice the distance from that pair than each of its members is from the other (Fig. 21.1). These minor houses are linked by a short path to, or face directly on, an ancillary sub-rectangular hut (IIa). Activities are less extensive than in the major houses and all the male activities are missing – no furnaces, no slag, no crucibles, no weapons, no iron workshop tools; whereas the female activities remain – combing, spinning, querning, leather and fur working. Amber, glass and shale beads and bracelets are here positively associated with perforated teeth and boars' tusks, lead and tin spindle whorls, bronze tweezers and human bones buried in the floor – in some cases certainly female and in many cases very young children.

Other finds include iron hogback knives, sickles, a bone necklace and buttons, pigmy cosmetic pots perhaps for the red lead found elsewhere on the site, cereals in open dishes (No. 70), a wooden ladle (No. 9) and perhaps a dresser with its pottery (No. 44). There is a comparative abundance of pottery within this class of structure but the proportion of undecorated domestic ware is greater than in the major houses; six of the twelve perforated ceramic strainers from the site are from these minor houses, the remainder from associated work floors (III) and baking huts (IId). The presence of harness in several minor houses should perhaps be linked with their leatherworking equipment and seen as maintenance and production centres for mending, storing and making reins, leather harness and perhaps shoes and clothing from hides. The overwhelming proportion of female trinkets and gear suggests that these houses were not only foci of female activities but also the especial centres of female residence.

IIa: ANCILLARY HUTS (Plate 21.1, Nos. 83, 16, 25, 78, 12, 32, 48, 58, 17) There are nine ancillary huts on the site and possibly examples of one or two more (floor No. 34 and earliest phase No. 38). There is a single ancillary hut in each unit, immediately adjacent to the unit's minor house and granary, and usually linked thereto by a path or clay patch. The ancillary huts appear to be lightly built subrectangular structures made of hurdles and posts with one or two central roof posts and a hearth.

Average number of associated artefacts – 15 (max. 31 min. 3)
Average external dimensions in feet – 24 by 20 (max. 29)
Average number of stratified floors   – 2–3 (max. 4 min. 1)
Average number of stratified hearths – 2 (max. 4 min. 0)

The ancillary huts have no significant individual substructure, no floorboards, no porch and no doorway slabs. The number of artefacts found in these structures (average 15, minimum 3) runs at a level oscillating about the background noise threshold of scattered rubbish (around ten artefacts per structure). However, the association pattern is consistent and represents in all respects an impoverished version of the array found in the adjacent minor houses – no furnace or smithing equipment, no heavy-duty iron tools, no 'male' artefacts, but a sparse scatter of items from the 'female' complex: pottery, glass beads, shale trinkets, tin and lead spindle whorls, perforated tusks and teeth, some antler combs and a few immature human bones.

At least two of these huts failed to produce the characteristic black 'occupation layer', which marks the intensively occupied houses and possibly derives from a strewn rush floor covering. Flint scrapers, although sparsely represented on the site, were unusually abundant in these ancillary huts. The overall artefact pattern suggests displaced, dumped and abandoned equipment reinforced by the sporadic transference of activities from the linked minor houses. Taken with the structural lightness, the subrectangular form and the locational linkage with the female(?) minor houses, the artefact evidence might suggest that these huts served as milking parlours, foodstores and cowhouses for perhaps one or two milch cows, some milking ewes or goats and their offspring, kept on the site the year round.

IIb: WORKSHOP HUTS (Plate 21.1, Nos. 75, 45, 59, 23, 3, 61, 60, 44)
The eight detectable workshop huts are characteristically small, neat circular structures, mostly without any posts supporting the small roof span or cluttering the floorspace. There are one or two contemporary workshop huts in each unit, sited close to the major house pair and set in the same half of the unit area. Some of these workshops are the focus of groups of open work floors (III), presumably the centre of fine weather operations in the unobstructed daylight (floors 59–79, 45–46, 1–3, 73–75).

Average number of associated artefacts – 19 (max. 36 min. 9)
Average external diameter in feet   – 23 (max. 32 min. 21)
Average number of stratified floors   – 2–3 (max. 4 min. 2)
Average number of stratified hearths – 2–3 (max. 9 min. 0)

The workshop huts contrast strongly with the ancillary huts (IIa) in structure, location and the repeated presence of precisely the equipment pattern not found in those structures – crucibles, a stone mould for bronze bracelets (No. 44), iron heavy-duty tools, whetstones, flint flakes, antler, bone and shale production roughouts, waste and splinters, and an absence of floor burials, querns or any significant level of female artefacts. The associated iron tools include files, adzes, a billhook, saws, a gouge, nails, together with a bone bow-drill bow, sheet bronze waste and fragments of wooden lathe furniture (? X45, X51, X71). Many broken or unfinished lathe-turned products came from the vicinity of these huts: an unfinished wagon wheel hub, spokes, wheels, wooden tubs and barrel staves, and the by-products of shale work. The workshops represent selective and more intensive foci of the mending, maintenance and manufacturing activities and skills already noted in the major houses.

IIc: COURTYARDS (Plate 21.1, Nos. 33, 28, 73, 63–4, 40–41–26, 1–2, between 13–14)

Seven courtyards are represented by enclosed open spaces or irregular complexes of overlapping clay floors, crudely defining a rectangular area with no substructure, no substantial superstructure but a few scattered posts suggesting light roofing in parts.

Average number of associated artefacts – 23 (max. 35 min. 2)
Average dimensions in feet   – 40 by 20
Average number of stratified floors   – 2–3
Average number of stratified hearths – 2–3

One irregular courtyard area is attached to the major house pair of each of the seven units, either between or adjacent to the houses which may together face on the yard. The splayed porch of the major house is sometimes continued as a fence at one end of the courtyard, a feature found on other Celtic sites and in stone on Galatian oppida (Piggott, 1965, p. 224). Other hurdle fencing may open on and traverse the yard and a hearth is usually set assymetrically at one end of the floor. In some cases a separate rectangular area *c.* 10 by 6 feet is provided with a timber flooring, perhaps as a *wagon stance*. In one instance

819

the courtyard plan is developed into a formalized and almost architectural feature reminiscent of a rustic portico (courtyard No. 63–64, between house pair No. 62–65).

The average number of finds from these yards is equivalent to that of the workshop huts and it is clear from the range of artefacts that many productive and maintenance activities requiring ample space, heat and light were carried out on these partially covered yards, which probably doubled as threshing floors, unloading bays, loom stands, midden dumps and open workshop areas. However, male artefacts are dominant and there is a strong association with horse and wagon gear – harness, toggles, broken linchpins and antler goads. This would accord with the wagon stance platforms and strongly suggests that this is where the wagon and chariots might be accessibly stored under cover and the horses or oxen daily harnessed or unhitched from their gear. That these yards were the primary precinct of the many hunting and sheep dogs is suggested by a complete dog skeleton from one floor (No. 33) and many gnawed bones from others (e.g. No. 73).

IId: BAKING HUTS (Plate 21.1, Nos. 37, 51, 15, 6, 84, 80, 36)

The seven baking huts are arranged one with each unit, located slightly apart from other structures, perhaps on account of the fire risk, but adjacent to the granary and the small, rectangular, fenced sties or kennels (VII). The baking huts are therefore optimally sited for the daily routine of collecting grain, grinding, preparing and cooking food and dispensing the waste to the pigs. All the baking huts together with most of the granaries are set around the outer margins of the two main compounds (except No. 6). The structural characteristics of the baking huts include an irregular clay floor with a longitudinal array of hearths and ovens covered by a light roof carried on a pair of posts – no substructure, no floorboards, no stone threshold and no porch. Small ovens were also found in some of the major and minor houses and these doubtless served for small-scale daily cooking, whilst the bakehouse seems to have provided a large-scale communal facility for each unit, perhaps mainly concerned with the weekly routine of breadbaking in bulk; analogously focal bakehouses are common in European peasant villages of many periods and areas, including Neolithic examples (Vinča and Aichbuhl: see Clark, 1952, pp. 145–6).

Average number of associated artefacts – 14 (max. 37 min. 3)
Average external diameter in feet   – 22 (max. 25 min. 21)

Average number of stratified floors – 2–3 (max. 5 min. 1)
Average number of stratified hearths – 5 (max. 9 min. 1)

The artefact pattern is consistent with the use of these structures as centres of female activity. The large dumps of wood and bone ash around the floors contained a relatively large quantity of pottery, with the highest proportion of undecorated/decorated wares on the whole site, together with pottery strainers or sieves, glass beads, perforated tusks and teeth, shale trinkets, lead and tin spindle whorls, flint flakes, quern stones, bone needles, gouge pegs and the bones of many fur-bearing fenland mammals, especially beaver. Taken together, the information portrays the baking huts as local centres of female activity, taking grain and provisions from the granary, querning, preparing food, dressing and pegging out skins and furs to dry, gossiping pleasurably in the comfort of this warm and dry micro-environment on a very wet site. The clay ovens and floors acted as ceramic heat stores and radiators and were thus perhaps favourite foci to which to bring many minor tasks, both here and in comparable ethnographic situations.

IIe: GUARD HUTS (Plate 21.1, Nos. 21, 77)

Location and content are the chief features distinguishing the guard huts from the other classes of hut structure on the site. Hut No. 21 is on the immediate left flank of the eastern gate inturn so that the eastern branch of the perimeter track passes below the hut before swinging in through the seven feet wide gravelled gateway, with its smaller wicket gate, hung from pairs of six-inch thick posts. Hut No. 77 is on the immediate right of the probable position of the western gate and is again sited to overlook the western perimeter track before it turned to enter the main outer compound. It would be tempting to see a similar hut facing No. 77 and making a pair, but since the other gate has only a single guard hut and the arrangement is known elsewhere in Dumnonian territory, one should resist this symmetrical restoration.

Average number of associated artefacts – 9 (max. 16 min. 2)
Average external diameter in feet – 17 (max. 17 min. 17)
Average number of stratified floors – 2 (max. 3 min. 1)
Average number of stratified hearths – 1 (max. 1 min. 0)

The guard huts are small circular structures with finds below the 'residential' threshold and with evidence for only a very light superstructure. The finds from the vicinity are mainly discarded rubbish although a grain bowl is probably *in situ* (No. 21) and one may note the dice box and dice at the eastern gate, a favourite Celtic pastime well suited to guard duty. The location of the western gate itself is inferred not only from the associated guardhouse (No. 77) but from the unique tangential contact at this point between the perimeter, the outer compound and the western trackway, backed up by the litter of broken and discarded wheels, spokes and linchpins (X19, X43, X87). Antler harness toggles and a terret also suggest that the adjacent floors, Nos. 20 and 25, may have acted as hard-standing for unloading vehicles parked within the eastern gate and jetty way. Fragments of impaled skulls with sword cuts were found near both gates and elsewhere around the palisade in accordance with Celtic custom. Otherwise the guard huts are defined negatively – the absence of residential debris, querns, weaving gear, tools, beads or productive equipment.

IIf: ANNEXE HUTS (Plate 21.1, Nos. 43, 66)

This type of structure is frequently found on Celtic sites, often attached, as here, to a major house. The two annexe huts are lean-to constructions with a party wall shared with a major house but having a separate entrance. In the north-western sector annexe hut No. 66 is attached to major house No. 74, and in the central sector, annexe hut No. 43 is joined to major house No. 42; indeed, in many other ways the plan of the major half of the north-western unit resembles a deliberate reproduction of the terminal layout cumulatively developed in the corresponding area of the central unit based on house No. 42 (Fig. 21.5).

> Average number of associated artefacts – 8 (max. 12 min. 5)
> Average external diameter in feet – 19 (max. 21 min. 17)
> Average number of stratified floors – 1–2 (max. 2 min. 1)
> Average number of stratified hearths – 3 (max. 5 min. 1)

The annexe huts are simple, roughly circular structures with hearths but without any other special features. The evidence for the use of these annexes is circumstantial. The negligible level of the finds is below the residential threshold and includes no metal tools or weapons, little pottery and no beads or querns. To this negative artefact evidence we can add the locational and structural resemblance between these rather more substantial annexes and the similar class of smaller lean-to structures found against the other major houses on the site – the stables or byres (Class VI). Annexe hut No. 66 is directly linked with the probable stable No. 85 and contains horse bones buried in its floor, broken linchpins and an antler mallet. Annexe hut No. 43 has horse bones buried in its vicinity, also with linchpins, and, as has already been pointed out, the whole area between these structures and the eastern gate is fenced and stabilized in a manner suggesting service facilities related to traffic through the gate. Finally, these annexe huts may be directly compared with the closely similar stables or chariot sheds at Hod Hill and elsewhere (Richmond, 1968, figs. 10B, 13).

III: WORK FLOORS (Plate 21.1, Nos. 69, 7, 72, 20, 22, 46, 67, 53, 24, 56, 54, 68)

The twelve work floors are irregular areas stabilized with clay and timber, carrying small hearths and lacking any substantial substructure or super-structure. The absence of walling, doorways and substantial post patterns would imply that these floors were open to the sky or merely covered with lean-to roofs. The floors are peripherally distributed, often close to the pali-sade, with from one to four floors within each of the five wealthy units, clus-tered adjacent to the minor house or in the vicinity of the workshop huts.

Average number of associated artefacts – 19 (max. 40 min. 8)
Average external diameter in feet – 25 (max. 32 min. 15)
Average number of stratified floors – 2–3 (max. 5 min. 1)
Average number of stratified hearths – 2–3 (max. 5 min. 1)

The artefact association pattern indicates intensive activity on these floors, including both male and female artefact complexes – metalwork, spinning, querning, weaving and much antler and bone work, together with its debris and discards. These multipurpose work floors seem also to have served as convenient store caches or dumps for raw material, especially antler, and in general provided a setting for activities requiring heat, light and space.

IV: CLAY PATCHES (Plate 21.1, Nos. 52, 31, 88, 89, 34, 85, 81, 8, 19, 86, 90, 79, 10, 50, 72, 87, 39)

Seventeen irregular clay patches are scattered around the outer compound and west gate, where some at least are the eroded fragments of the earliest structures on the site attested by stratigraphy. Whilst some patches may be relics of earlier phases, others are merely small areas to provide dry approaches to granaries, stables or sties, which may also be paved with such a clay, rubble brushwood and rush-covered patch; yet others seem simply to patch potholes in access routes.

Average number of associated artefacts – 3 (max. 13 min. 0)
Average external diameter in feet – 17 (max. 27 min. 6)

Average number of stratified floors   – 1 (max. 3 min. 1)
Average number of stratified hearths   – zero

Few of these patches were renewed, none carried hearths, most of them were below the occupation threshold of around ten artefacts per floor and, together with the causeway, they provide a good example of the noise level underlying the whole pattern of associations – one or two sherds, flints, whorls, antler or bone fragments, only.

V: GRANARIES OR STOREHOUSES (Fig. 21.1)

There are traces of at least twenty-five granary or storehouse footings on the site – three or four per unit, of which it can be shown that only one per unit existed at any one time. The granary 'signature' was usefully stereotyped; in its most complete form an area uniquely devoid of artefacts, roughly ten by ten feet, with a scatter of cereals or legumes, is set with nine, six or four regularly spaced sugar-loaf piles driven through mortice holes in horizontal timber groundplates to spread the weight and prevent tilting. The whole complex is usually enclosed within a light fenced area eighteen feet square, with a 'stepped' perimeter and adjacent patches of clay hard-standing. Most of the granaries are square but some are trapezoidal as on some Durotrigian sites. The size of the granaries is strictly uniform with a single exception, ten feet by twelve feet, perhaps a communal or chiefly granary – significantly set at the focus of the somewhat elliptical outer compound (Plate 21.1 between patches Nos. 80–82).

The Glastonbury granary 'signature' interestingly resembles the features of a so-called Late Bronze Age 'ritual structure' recovered from a comparable bog site in the Netherlands at Bargeroosterveld, with similar sugar-loaf piles (Waterbolk and Van Zeist, 1961). It might be plausible to reinterpret that structure as a granary or storehouse and see it as yet another archaic Late Bronze Age element in the Dumnonian Iron Age.

It is possible to gain an impression of the granary structure on the basis of the dismantled granary timbers re-used in the substructure of floor No. 56 and the fragments, including the ladder, from the granary to house No. 29. They appear to have been rectangular frame platforms supporting a square superstructure of hurdles with an open vestibule, reached by ladder, the whole carried on the heads of the sugar-loaf piles perhaps with staddle tops, some three feet or more above the damp ground. The granaries were several times renewed in each sector, some after burning, and it is from these structures that the rectangular timber frame base plates were taken for re-use in the footings of other buildings (X33, X34, X96).

The granaries held barley, wheat and beans and their maximum individual capacity must have approached 500 cubic feet, or about 100 sacks weighing some 20 000 pounds when full, the equivalent of seventeen half-ton wagon journeys each. On a nine post granary the vertical load per post would thus be more than 2000 pounds, hence the need for the sugar-loaf pile and frame combination to spread the weight and prevent the posts being driven clean through the peat; even so, granary rebuilding was frequently made necessary by fires, rot and tilting.

VI: STABLES OR BYRES (Fig. 21.1)

One major house in every unit has either an attached annexe (IIf) or a lean-to smaller structure (VI) with the probable exception of the two units on the western side of the inner compound (Houses 13, 14, 29, 35). These lean-to stables(?) are represented by a lobed extension of the house perimeter, c. 6 by 16 feet, enclosed by an arc of hurdling; on this site, as on others, it is difficult to distinguish between stables and successive reconstructions of the house walls. The stables are tentatively identified by the repeated burial of butchered horse skeletons in and around them and an artefact level below the occupation threshold, suggesting the regular removal of manure and litter to a midden in the yard. The few artefacts associated with these areas include linchpins and cheekpieces from bits.

These stables would only accommodate some four head of horses or draught oxen, although the larger annexe huts might stable up to eight head so that the combined annexe plus stable complex of the north-western sector unit (Nos. 66, 85) has a potential capacity of some fifteen beasts. In winter, this head of stock would generate 4–15 kW of heat, the equivalent of 4–15 single-bar electric fires – a valuable by-product of stalling stock in or against the dwelling.

VII: STIES OR KENNELS (Fig. 21.1)

Some small rectangular stake enclosures, c. 6 by 5 feet, are found adjacent to the baking huts (IId), granaries (V) and ancillary huts (IIa). Pig bones, otherwise rare on the site, have been noted in the vicinity of these structures (No. 65), but they may at times equally have been used for dogs.

The combined information from all the analyses suggests that the Glastonbury settlement was built and enlarged in terms of the varied replication of a single kind of unit, regularly comprising the same set of different categories of structure (I–VII). Furthermore, these structures were systematically arranged in repeatedly similar relative locational patterns within all the units ever built on the site – presumably a near-optimal pattern adjusted to satisfy the common social, economic and cultural traditions of the inhabitants and the special conditions of the site. Presumably, this pattern had stabilized over long years of cultural development and living and building on similar sites.

On the basis of all the analyses it is possible to idealize the building model of the settlers, to consider its implications and the meaning of individual deviations from it, as well as testing it against comparable sites. For example, many of the puzzling features represented on dry sites by enigmatic complexes of pits, post-holes and irregular hollows are clearly preserved at Glastonbury in forms adapted to the wet environment. The conjectured 'amorphous agglomeration' of irregular structures emerges on this and other Celtic sites as a figment of our contemporary rectilinear controlling models. Instead, we now perceive an architectural universe based on rounded structures, laid out in arcs around courtyards and arranged in curvilinear sweeps around compounds, from which new development springs in a series of recurving convolutions significantly analogous to the aesthetic universe of the contemporary La Tène art.

The four peripheral bulges of the southern, eastern, north-eastern and north-western site sectors around the central area can now be seen to relate to the expansion of comparable building units within each sector, based upon four such units deployed around the inner compound. Each of these units allocates a limited number of defined structures to particular relative loci in fixed halves of their respective unit areas (Figs. 21.1–21.6). In one half of the unit area stands the pair of major houses (Ia), one of which will have attached stables (VI) and both of which share a courtyard area (IIc) and its wagon stance. In the immediate vicinity are one or two workshop huts (IIb) and open work floors (III). In the complementary half of the unit area a minor house (Ib) is linked to a subrectangular ancillary hut (byre? IIa) and nearby stands a baking hut (IId), pigsty (VII) and granary (V) (Fig. 21.1).

It follows that alternative interpretations of the Glastonbury settlement will hinge upon the alternative interpretations of the kind of social unit operating behind these building units. The internal evidence shows the units to be discrete organizations, theoretically self-supporting and self-servicing, each with its own housing, bakehouse, granary, stable, work floors and courtyard – apparently a stock, land and property owning modulus accustomed to burying some of their number in the floors of their houses. The three substantial dwellings in each unit – the two major houses and the minor house – do not simply duplicate facilities but complement one another; for example, the minor house seems to be associated with female residence and only one major house in each pair has the attached stable which serves the whole unit. The structural elements emphasize a degree of interdependent reciprocity within a social unit and not merely a repetition of independent elements in a group.

The size of this repeated social unit may be roughly gauged from the floor space of the main dwellings, the number of huts in the unit, and the capacity of the unit granary. The two major houses and the minor house together provide a maximum roofed area of about 200 m², which, according to the deterministic mathematical model of Cook and Heizer (1968) relating residential numbers and floor area, would give a theoretical maximum unit size of around twenty individuals. A parallel model derived from ethnographic data would suggest that on average two to three roofed structures of this size, or their equivalent, are required for each 'family' in a food producing society (Flannery, 1971). Finally, the maximum capacity of the unit granary of 500 cubic feet, allowing one third of the contents for seed, would support a maximum of some twenty-four people for one year. But if we allow for supplementary cereal fodder for several chariot ponies and draught oxen, together with a minimal surplus for trade and customary tribal dues, plus a safety margin – then a maximum of twenty individuals is again suggested for these units. Taken altogether the evidence points towards an inturned, internally networked, cooperative social unit averaging perhaps fifteen to twenty individuals including males, females, juveniles and adults, ancestrally linked to the unit houses, jointly owning and inheriting property; anthropologically such a unit would normally be a kin group based on an extended family or lineage system (Murdock, 1949).

The site: interpretation and a social model

A site occupation unit based on pairs of round houses with varying auxiliaries accords well with the abundant evidence on many other British and Irish Late Bronze Age and Iron Age sites. These settlements include units with 'great' houses up to fifty feet in diameter or the more modest thirty feet variety, and they embrace isolated single units and multiple complex units, enclosed and unenclosed settlements (Hamilton, 1968; Piggott, 1965, p. 237). However, it would be a sweeping mistake to assume that the units observed over this wide area of space and time are identical translations of a single social concept – although they may very well represent a family of related transforms

827

of such a concept. The test must come from the detailed consideration of the sizes, shapes, features, relative locations and artefact associations of all these structures. It would indeed be surprising if the variety of tribes and tribal groups throughout Britain's varied environment had not produced some equivalent variety in social and economic activities and ways of housing them and we may look forward to comparative research revealing them.

However, in passing we may note the remarkable parallels between the settlement unit of the twelfth century B.C. at Itford Hill, Sussex, the enclosed unit of the seventh century B.C. at Staple Howe, Yorkshire, and the units reiterated at Glastonbury (Piggott, 1965, p. 152, fig. 113). The Staple Howe and Itford Hill units have similar structural categories similarly disposed over comparable unit areas, which even include an entrance stock baffle like that glimpsed within the eastern gate of Glastonbury; indeed, if the Staple Howe complex is superimposed upon the north-eastern unit at Glastonbury an extremely close fit is obtained. Once again, the survival and continuity of late Bronze Age traditions is stressed in archaic, peripheral Dumnonian Glastonbury.

Within the region of the Dumnonii themselves direct parallels may be drawn with the four pairs of courtyard houses facing one another along the terrace at Chysauster or with the single unit settlement at Goldherring. Particularly striking in these later Cornish sites is the manner in which the structures represented by six or seven clustered floors at Glastonbury are precisely translated into a single nucleated stone structure with the same appurtenances – courtyard, wagon stance, stable, byre, pigsty, granary, roundhouse rooms. Perhaps even the room structure of the later Romano-Celtic farmhouses with a courtyard between two wings might represent a rectilinear transformation of the same kind of functional unit, or of its Halstatt predecessor (Fox, 1964, fig. 46; Piggott, 1965, figs. 83, 114).

In any event, the sequential development at Glastonbury can now be pursued in the further light shed by the artefact evidence and interpreted in terms of the social units tentatively linked with the repeated building modulus. Initially, the artefact evidence can be used to test and check the stratigraphic and locational evidence for the site development, to help estimate the length of occupation, and to provide a skeletal frame for a demographic and social sketch model of the community's development. This archaeologically derived model may then be briefly run against the biased but direct information on Celtic society as preserved from contemporary records.

The chain of stratigraphic relationships between the structures has provided a developmental basis which is confirmed by trend analysis studies of the artefacts – both in terms of density distributions and distributions of early and late forms within individual typologies. The overall quantitative trends in the most abundant artefacts found on the site – potsherds and sling shot – fall off dramatically over the north-west and north-east sectors. The trend maps depicting the ratios of early/late fibulae, early/late pottery, early/late comb types, early saddle querns/late rotary querns all reinforce this same pattern – where, it might be noted, the stratigraphies also allow an independent test of earliness or lateness. The same trend is brought out in the distribution of floors and hearths which had been many times renewed. Early cordoned and zoned sherds are heavily focused in the centre and southern sectors, whereas countersunk handle jars of the later Durotrigian model trend heavily to the north, significantly overriding the contrary overall potsherd trend. Clearly, the two units of the northern sectors represent a later expansion towards the lake margin, subsequent to the primary development of the central and southern sectors.

Indeed, it is the north-western lakeside sector that produces the very latest material on the site – some Romano–Durotrigian sherds left perhaps by fishermen or trappers sporadically reoccupying the lakeside debris of their ancestral home. The overall evidence from the artefact relationships thus heavily endorses the information from the stratigraphies, the locational development and minor points like the apparent reproduction of the final plan of the main central unit (House 42 and complex) in the initial plans of the north-western and north-eastern units.

The length of the occupation sequence at Glastonbury can only be approximately estimated at present by comparing an array of differently based estimates, ranked in order of dependability. The broad dating consensus has long been established for this site and the margin of error from the particular approaches remains virtually unchanged. If we take the most modern information on the typology of the fibulae, fine pottery and other key artefacts, and take the latest find stratified in the earliest floors, and the latest find stratified within the latest floors then an occupation span of about 100 years is suggested, within the period *c*. 150 ± 50 to 50 ± 50 B.C. This dating is crudely confirmed by pollen analysis, by the four to five feet of peat which accumulated during the occupation of the settlement, and by independent chains of assumptions involving the numbers of superimposed hearths and floors, the frequency of house and granary rebuilding, and the sample numbers of surviving fibulae, querns, spindle whorls, potsherds and food debris. Although this chronology could be refined by more detailed pollen analysis, radiocarbon, thermoluminescent and palaeomagnetic estimates, nevertheless the

829

most satisfactory chronology might still be recovered from this site by dendrochronology on timbers from carefully selected contexts in the different sectors. The advantage of this preliminary model building is that we can now pinpoint where such samples might best be taken to test the alternative chains of assumptions and interpretations.

With the crude parameters of the site established an interpretative sketch of its sequential development can now be made (Figs. 21.2–21.5).

Phase O: Some of the scattered floors clustered around the western gateway are amongst the earliest on the site, but no definite plan of this phase can be recovered – if, indeed, it ever had a separate existence. It is possible that it anticipated the form of the outer compound on a scale appropriate to the embryonic antecedent to the Phase I compound.

Phase I: 4 units, 12 houses, estimated population about 60 people. A roughly circular compound related to the 'banjo' class of Iron Age settlements (Bowen, 1969, p. 23). Two units on each side of the compound and traces of an encircling palisade. The units on the western side of the compound have special characteristics which will be discussed later; so too, does the especially elaborate compound around House 42, with its large annexe stable (?VI) and its direct access to the earliest jetty of lias, stone and timber (Fig. 21.2).

Phase II: 5 units, 15 houses, estimated population about 75 people. The inner compound expands on the landward and riverside perimeters, taking up the last 'dry' land. The southern sector unit is built. The whole of the area between the central sector and the jetty is remodelled and the eastern sector emerges. The sophisticated landing stage is built, the causeway rebuilt, several workshop huts are erected and the eastern gate and guardhouse complex constructed, all this as virtually an extension of the compound of House 42 (Fig. 21.3).

Phase III: 7 units, 21 houses, estimated population about 105 people. The northern area between the settlement and the lake margin is now reclaimed and occupied by the north-eastern and north-western sectors with their units. This is a spacious and planned development with a degree of architectural symmetry in which the major house pairs face one another and the older compound across the new outer compound with its western gate and guardhouse (Fig. 21.4).

Phase IV: 7 units, 15 houses, estimated population about 120 people. No new units are deployed and the site limits have virtually been achieved, although reclamation and rebuilding continues on the lakeside margin, taking

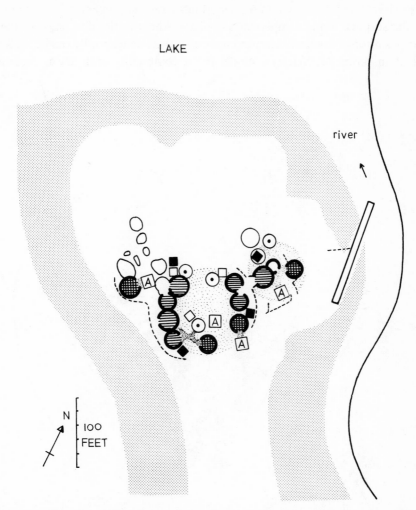

FIG. 21.2. The site – Phase I; 4 units, 12 houses, estimated population *c.* 60 individuals. This interpretative model and those that follow (Figs. 21.3–21.6) are 'best guess' interpretations of the combined output of all the analyses. These models are schematic and tentative (for iconic key, see Fig. 21.1).

the palisade to its final positions. The fifteen houses have accumulated some twelve auxiliary huts and workshops and these probaby shelter a population rather higher than that estimated, if we allow for a packing factor (Fig. 21.5).

There are too many unknowns to pursue a detailed demographic model for the Glastonbury population but the estimates suggest either a low population growth rate at *c*. 0·5% per annum or a higher rate accompanied by hiving off of the surplus. Some comparable populations grew little, if at all, over long periods of time, especially pastoral ones, and their demography can be understood in terms of Wrigley's model for a community with social customs

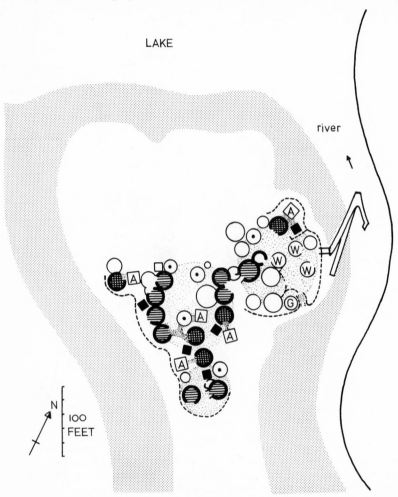

LAKE

river

N
100
FEET

FIG. 21.3. The site – Phase II: 5 units, 15 houses, estimated population *c*. 75 individuals. The expansion of the site probably under drier conditions, the rebuilding of the jetty.

affecting fertility (see polygyny), a significant infant mortality (marsh environment) and an adult mortality above average (see female deaths in childbirth and warfare casualties from this tribal boundary area) (Wrigley, 1969, model 2, pp. 18–22; Postan, 1966, p. 665). The crucial evidence of the community's cemetery is missing – a lacuna which may relate to the scarcity of suitable dry sites in the immediate vicinity. Perhaps the Glastonbury dead

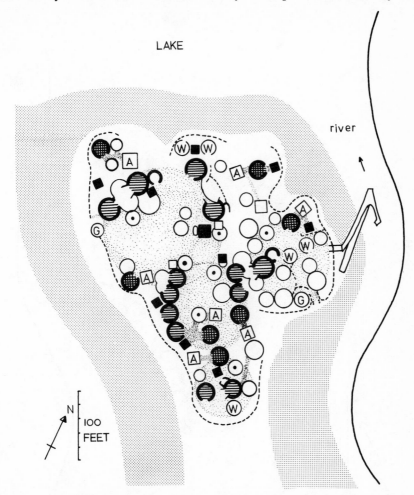

FIG. 21.4. The site – Phase III: 7 units, 21 houses, estimated population *c.* 105 individuals. Marginal reclamation continues on the unconstrained lake and river sides. The central inner compound is joined by a spacious outer compound.

were buried collectively with those of consanguineous fenland communities on a communal sacred 'island of the dead' – the traditional Avalon?

Any social model of the Glastonbury population must derive from the detailed analyses of the individual settlement units and their artefacts. A

833

first examination of the data gives a strong impression of the equality of the units involved. There is no uniquely large house in a focal location. The artefacts do not suggest a great range in the social status of the extended family

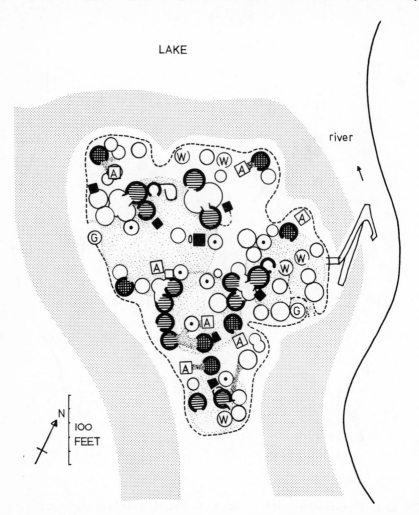

LAKE

river

N
100
FEET

FIG. 21.5. The site – Phase IV: 7 units, 15 houses, estimated population *c.* 105 plus, perhaps *c.* 120 or more with terminal packing within the limits of the site, now achieved in wetter conditions.

units nor do they support a great difference in their property and activities – indeed, rather the reverse. Each unit has its granary, its stable of draught animals, its chest of iron tools and its woollen industry and workshops.

Sampling problems apart, a polythetic picture prevails, a unit marginally richer in one respect is marginally poorer in another and vice versa. If there is a 'headman' then he would appear to have been a 'first amongst equals', in material terms at least.

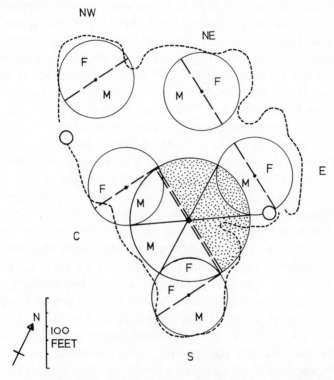

FIG. 21.6. The site – Phase IV: a tentative social model of the structural pattern of the site. The modular units deployed in each sector occupy closely comparable areas at relatively regularly spaced intervals. Each unit is shown divided, as the evidence suggests, into a major familial section (M) and a minor dependent sector (F). It is suggested that the mega-unit of the original inner compound area itself reproduces this same division at a higher level, with a major sector (shaded) and a minor dependent sector, each composed of several units.

A closer examination discloses deviations from this broadly accurate model. At a finer level of scrutiny the independent units of the north-western, north-eastern and southern sectors fit the prediction, but it begins to break down for the four older units arranged around the inner compound in the central and eastern sectors (Fig. 21.6). If there is a centre of wealth and status in the settlement then the evidence marginally favours the central sector in general and the complex around major House 42 in particular.

The central area of the settlement has produced traces of especial wealth – a hoard including a bronze mirror, tweezers, two dress pins and cosmetic galena, the only coin and currency bar (Z1, Z2), a bronze cup, another mirror fragment, a glass topped pin, amber beads, the mould for bracelets – all over and above the normal complement of bronze and iron tools, weapons, weapon mounts, bits and harness, beads and shale trinkets. The central area has three other unique features. House 42 contained more weaving combs than any other structure, and whereas the combs of the other units were apparently manufactured independently within each sector and differ accordingly, those from House 42 are drawn from every sector on the site – perhaps drawing female labour in the same way. The minor house of this unit (No. 49) contained the most comprehensive range of fine imported pottery found on the site. Finally, Houses 30 and 42 contained the most extensive variety of bronze fibulae of all periods, including heirlooms. If we add to these observations the central position of the sector, its early foundation and continuous rebuilding, its nodal relevance to the jetty and approach routes, then if there was a Glastonbury 'headman' his establishment might be speculatively identified with the inner compound in general and with the precinct of House 42 in particular.

Further analysis reveals an interesting contrast which heightens the preceding observations. The two units on the western margin of the inner compound (Nos. 29, 30, 35; 11, 13, 14) are negatively distinguished as against the site norms, whereas those on the eastern margin are positively emphasized (Nos. 18, 27, 38, 42, 43, 49). If the precinct around House 42 is marginally the 'richest' on the site, then the two complementary units on the western margin are demonstrably the 'poorest', notwithstanding the strongly advantageous sampling effect introduced by the latter's outstanding number of superimposed floors (rebuilt up to ten times). The structures of this 'poor quarter' are repeatedly reflected as significantly negative residuals when compared with the other units on the site in terms of spindle whorls, weaving combs, loom weights, querns, beads, shale trinkets and finger-rings. The many superimposed floors produced no evidence for the smithy that every other unit possessed, no heavy iron tools, no dependent workshop huts (IIb), no metal or antler harness or vehicle equipment of the many types abundantly scattered throughout the site, and no stables (VI). Yet in every other respect these two units, comprising some twelve structures and totalling fifty-four superimposed floors, faithfully reproduce the standard building unit features with their pairs of houses with floor burials, minor houses, ancillary hut, baking hut, granary and traces of male and female residence.

The evidence suggests that the two familial units of the western half of the

836

richest sector were the poorest on the site. They were comparable in every respect but two with the five other site units – they lacked independent means of production (iron tools, workshops, draught animals) and the wealth and status that went with that means (warrior equipment and female finery). Although they maintained the capacity to own and presumably to fill their private granaries they were somehow dependent. The labour surplus from the western half of the inner compound must have been invested to the benefit of inhabitants other than themselves – and here we may perhaps legitimately look across the compound to the *enceinte* of the 'primus inter pares', House 42, with its extra large annexe stable (43), the spare plough beam in the yard (X92), the workshops turning wagon parts (X59), and its levy of female weavers from all round the site (fifty-four textile frame pieces came from this sector alone, X65–66). This household seems to have exercised the capacity to export its products via the jetty it controlled, and thus to import the widest range of fine pottery and fibulae and barter for fine mirrors and currency in the Mendip markets.

The design of the inner compound itself lends some support to such an interpretation. The bilateral symmetry of the circle of houses is strongly reminiscent of the division between the minor house half and the major house half of each unit area, so scrupulously repeated in each of the seven units. Perhaps the relationship between the dependent, low status half of the compound and the rich, high status half might represent a structural analogue of the relationship between the minor, female half of each unit area and the major, familial half (Fig. 21.6). Certainly, the circular compound of structures itself appears as a modulus or mega-unit, found either independently, as here in Phase I (Fig. 21.2), or with penumbral units as in Phase IV (Fig. 21.5), enclosed or unenclosed, on British and Irish Late Bronze Age and Iron Age sites where they may embody differing versions of the kind of relationship inferred here.

If the individual characteristics of the extended family units and their artefacts are pursued to the limits of their reliability, some tentative information about the social relationships between the units on the site and with the outside world may be gleaned. Relationships between the units may be glimpsed, for example, from the idiosyncratic stylistic affinities between various household assemblages, and from the manner in which they deviate individually or in groups from the overall settlement trends. The differential selection of artefacts or designs exercised between a range of equally suitable alternatives marks out the products and imports of one unit from another – weaving combs with different motif preferences, glass beads of restricted types, imported raw materials, pottery, spindle whorls, and querns selectively acquired from different sources. Single element relationships of this kind are probably meaningless given the sampling problems but here we are dealing with a cumulatively reinforcing web of such relationships.

Some of these inter-unit and extra-unit relationships between artefacts are probably incidental to the circulation and interchange of women both in marriage and in the course of their economic activities. It is exceedingly unlikely, for instance, with the wealth of local material commonly used on the site for making spindle whorls (bone, antler, clay, pottery), that a single unattractive spindle whorl of Exmoor sandstone or Blackdown chalk was traded twenty miles to the site. It is altogether more probable that the occasional spindle whorl, weaving comb, beads and trinkets may have moved in a series, or in single, generational marriage moves. With other classes of artefact other social or economic mechanisms will be more appropriately invoked, including the whole network of customary tribal services. However, it is interesting to note the absence of the otherwise abundant finger-rings from the 'poor' half of the central compound in comparison with their universal distribution across all the other units. It may be tempting to interpret the rings as symbols of married and adult status exchanged only between individuals of a certain standing. Certainly, the strong pattern of idiosyncratic relationships discretely shared between the extended family units and their artefact characteristics, together with the restricted pattern of trivial exotics from beyond the settlement's territory, does suggest a degree of settlement inter-unit endogamy and extra-settlement exogamy. We are thus forcibly reminded that the site can only be meaningfully modelled against a network of related and different sites within an interrelated system.

The same class of evidence suggests that the different kindred units may also have maintained slightly different degrees of economic and social contact with different areas of the outside world, at this micro-level. The contrast that emerges with the appropriate classification is between the 'new' units in the north-west and north-eastern sectors on one hand and all of the remaining 'older' units on the other. The foreign exotics amongst the spindle whorls and imported pottery are here reinforced by a mass of circumstantial information.

Pottery and raw materials imported from the Mendip hills are common to all the units, but the southern unit combines an especial abundance of north Mendip pottery from the Dolebury area (Peacock Group 3) with fine ware from the south Mendip and Maesbury area (Peacock Groups 2, 4), as well as lias and sandstone whorls from the same localities, and maintaining the unique workshop turning out querns from blanks of Maesbury old red sandstone and andesite (Fig. 21.7). In contrast, the two northern sector units supported the workshop turning Dorset shale imported from the territory of the Durotriges in cylinders and discs. Furthermore, these northern units have produced a quite exclusive range of exotics – whorls of sandstone and chalk from south and west Somerset, the only exotic pottery from Cornwall (Group I) and the Exeter regions (Group 5), most of the countersunk handle 'Durotrigian' jars, and pyramidal loom weights and glass beads, also best paralleled at Hengistbury, a major Durotrigian oppidum and port.

This range of evidence suggests that the north-western and north-eastern units maintained especially strong connections with the trade routes extending to the southern seaways – the routes by which the settlement's tin and shale may have been imported – whereas the southern and central units preserved unusually strong ties with the Mendip range, a region with which the marsh villages were closely interdependent, and which was the main source of lead and iron (Figs. 21.7–21.8). Thus the exotic spindle whorls and female items would seem to indicate a measure of settlement exogamy perhaps related to the varied external connections of the individual kin units within the settlement. If this is taken with the evidence for the within-settlement exchange of women between the extended family units we have an impression of a settlement community of closely related exogamous lineages linked by bonds of settlement endogamy balanced with some settlement exogamy. This model is supported by the physical anthropology of the skeletal remains from the house floors, which imply 'one unmixed group of families', and is analogous to the social structure of comparable communities (Bulleid and Gray, 1917, p. 681; Murdock, 1949).

The consensus of information derived from the site and its artefacts therefore enables us to erect a very tentative social model for this fenland settlement. The social unit of the community appears to have been the patrilocal extended family, averaging some fifteen to twenty persons, embracing an older man, his wife or wives, his unmarried children, his married sons and their wives and children. This community will necessarily have contained extended family lineage units from several different agnatic clans who might thus intermarry within the settlement, creating community ties, The three lineage generations of each unit, including the nuclear families of father and sons, apparently lived in clusters of adjacent dwellings in which a female house served every pair of major familial houses. These cooperative kin groups were of broadly equal status, with the exception of the two 'dependent' units on the west side of the inner compound, and were potentially self-supporting and self-servicing – hence the existence of the single unit settlement type (Fig. 21.1). However, the evidence suggests that the community was not acephalous and that a 'headman' may have existed to focus community activities and coordinate the competing requirements of the family units. These units were in any event united by kinship linkages one with another within the settlement and also with clan kinsmen in neighbouring settlements, forming a consanguineous

FIG. 21.7. The territory – Box 1: analysis of imported and exported materials from the site suggests, by the distribution of their sources, a site exploitation territory of *c.* 10 miles radius. This exploitation territory has a radius appropriate to the sophisticated pack-horse, cart, wagon and boat transport at the disposal of the community; the territory will have been exploited by overlapping sites (e.g. Meare) and should not be confused with the exclusive agricultural territory of each site (see the 0·5 mile radius infield and 1·5 mile radius outfield suggested on the map).

The territory depicted is a segment of the fenland bowl running to the Mendip rim of limestone and sandstone hills, up to 1000 feet high. The site's exploitation territory runs from the major multivallate hill fort of Maesbury, from whose vicinity so many of the site's resources stem, to the Roman Fosse Way in the east, a later frontier which perhaps followed an earlier tribal boundary. Four smaller 'hill forts' within the area – Dundon Camp, Roundabout Camp, King's Castle Camp and Westbury Camp – may have been related within the Glastonbury and Meare settlement systems. For the wider setting of the territory see Figs. 21.8 and 21.9.

The details of the waterlogged areas on the map are speculative. The key to the resources exploited by the site community (below) indicates a particularly intensive relationship with the nearest sector of dry highlands between Westbury Camp and Maesbury (Maes is Celtic for upland field; Celtic fields are known from this area).

1 Clay sources for Peacock's Group 2 fine wares.
2 Oak forest source for heavy timber – dugout canoes, etc.
3 Probable main source for shed red deer antlers – the Old Red Sandstone ecology.
4 Quernstones of Old Red Sandstone.
5 Quernstones of Andesite lava.
6 Quernstones of Croscombe Lias.
7 Gannister clay for smelting crucibles.
8 Harptree chert for whetstones, etc.
9 Lower Limestone shales for hammers, whetstones, whorls, etc.
10 Fuller's earth from Maes Down.
11 Flint nodules from Dulcote gravels.
12 Flint nodules from Coxley gravels.
13 Alluvial clay sources for local coarse wares.
14 Upper Lias clay and rubble for floors, jetty, whorls, etc.
15 Draycott Triassic dolomitic conglomerate for hearthstones.
16 Closest area of upland limestone pastures and fields.
17 Lead ore sources.
18 Coloured lead ochre sources for paints, cosmetics, etc.
19 Iron ore sources, low quality, abundant limestone flux.
20 Chert from the Green Marls.
21 Estuarine and brackish water lake resources – shoals of shad, etc.
22 Freshwater fen resources – fowl, fish, fur-bearing predators.

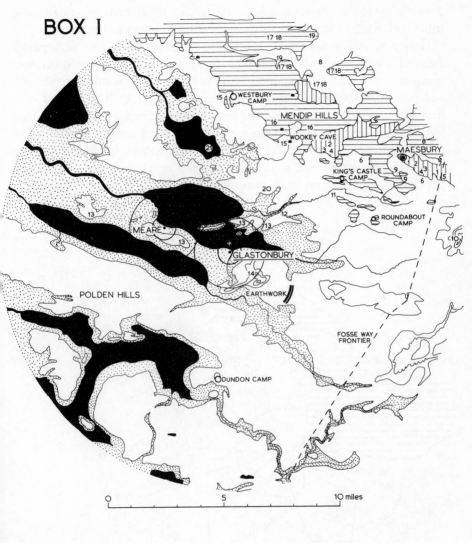

BOX I

17 18   19

19
17 18   8
17 18   17 18
15 ○ WESTBURY
        CAMP

MENDIP HILLS

16   16
WOOKEY CAVE
15   2
            3 4   8   MAESBURY

21   6   9
                    KING'S CASTLE 9 2 4 3 1
                        CAMP   9   6 1 5

20   11

13   12
MEARE •   13   13   ROUNDABOUT
            13   CAMP
    GLASTONBURY
                                                c10
            14

POLDEN HILLS   EARTHWORK

                                        FOSSE WAY
                                        FRONTIER

○ DUNDON CAMP

0   5   10 miles

Limestone, Uplands and Pasture	Fertile alluvium and Peat soils
Sandstone, Oak woodlands and Heather	Waterlogged peat, Fen and Reed swamp
Clay with some limestone, Woodlands	▬ Cave

841

network extending through agnatic clans and tribal sections, to regional tribes within the loose tribal confederation of the Dumnonii (Fig. 21.9).

However, this social model must be a dynamic one. The settlement's ancestral community included perhaps sixty people in four extended families, living around a circular compound with two 'dependent' families on one side and two 'independent' families on the other (Fig. 21.2). This early settlement became the constantly renewed nucleus of a community which expanded from four to seven extended family groups and from perhaps sixty to more than 120 people over some hundred years. It is perhaps significant that the settlement was abandoned at exactly the point at which it had generated a population surplus equal to its own initial size – sixty persons. Perhaps 120

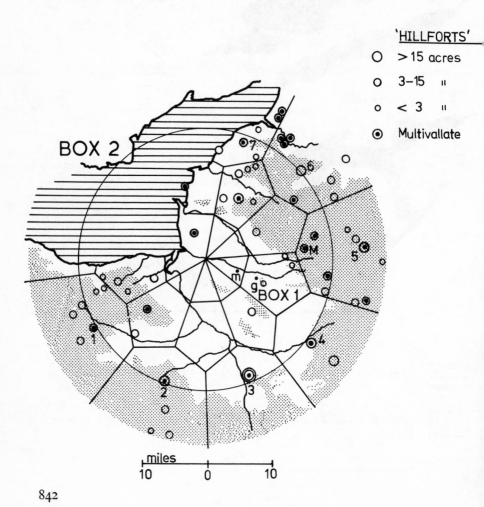

people represented a critical size at which the community could maintain itself no longer at this maximal density, and simultaneously represented the minimal size to generate two communities of viable size in this demanding environment, suggesting an almost cyclic pattern of settlement development through a hierarchy of categories (Phase I to Phase IV to two Phase I's . . . etc., 60 to 120 to 60 plus 60 . . .). If this dynamic model is acceptable it might prove possible to study the different hierarchy of site categories in different areas and establish their different critical thresholds in different environments. Certainly, it reminds us that settlement 'types' may only be phases in the life cycle of a community and not necessarily independent classificatory taxa, and this in turn uncovers the important criterion – that *certain* settlement forms may *not* be derived from or ancestral to certain other forms simply by growth transformation.

In conclusion, this tentative social model derived from the archaeological evidence may briefly be compared with the historical information on Celtic society preserved in the records of the classical authors and in the Irish vernacular tradition. There we learn that the Celtic tribal unit (*túath*) was usually ruled by a chieftain or king (*rí*) who was served by his client nobles, men of rank distinguished by the capacity to own, maintain and equip one or more chariots – the 'equites' of Caesar, the 'chariot' men (*eirr*) of the Irish epics.

FIG. 21.8. The area – Box 2: the Glastonbury territory (Box 1) is but one tessera of a mosaic of territories running from the encircling hills down into the undrained fenland basin. Contiguity, common resources and the drainage system converging on the Bristol Channel preform this area of *c.* 20 miles radius (Box 2) into a related settlement system.

The artificially regular tessellation suggested in this model is derived from a Thiessen polygon analysis of the major fortified site distribution; the relationship between this interpretative model and reality is envisaged as comparable to the relationship between reality and the model in Fig. 21.11. The analysis suggests a ring of large upland territories associated with central major earthworks:

1 Castle Hill	5 Tedbury
2 Castle Neroche	6 Maes Knoll Camp
3 Ham Hill	7 Cadbury Congresbury
4 Cadbury Castle	

This outer tier of territories dips to the fen edge and encloses a second tier of fenland/estuarine territories centred on isolated hills and island sanctuaries. Although the hill forts may not be exactly contemporary, they nevertheless are the man-hour insignia for considerable populations who both pre-existed and post-existed their construction.

  g = Glastonbury
  m = Meare
  M = Maesbury Camp, here seen as perhaps a lower order site of the Tedbury
     hierarchy.

843

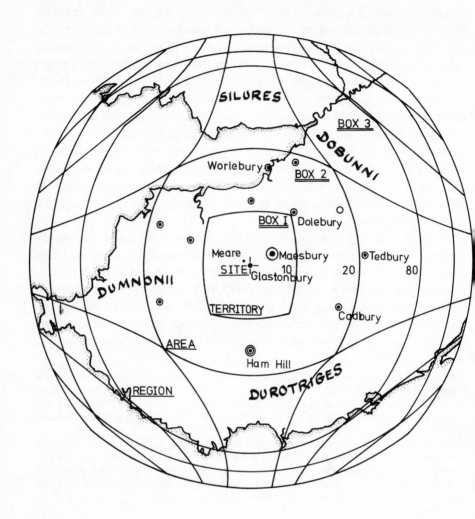

Fig. 21.9. The region – Box 3, a logarithmic transformation: the Dumnonian tribal region and the Chinese Box model of the Glastonbury site within its territory, area and regional systems (Boxes 1, 2, 3 – Figs. 21.7–21.9). A logarithmic transformation of distance is used to show that the significance of distant areas for Glastonbury falls away according to the volume of activity occurring between them; a prior correction allocates land transport and distance twice the value of the speedier sea transport. These transformations show the way in which sea transport united the Dumnonian region. The significance of regional and interregional trade is confirmed by the Cornish tin, fine pottery from Maesbury, Dolebury, Cornwall and Lyme Bay areas (Groups 1–6), Nailsea sand(?) glass, Forest of Dean high grade iron, Dorset shale and Scandinavian amber – all found on the Glastonbury site.

844

The noble grade were themselves supported by their client retinue of companions (*ceile*), warriors (*gaiscedach*) and charioteers. These were drawn from the non-noble freemen (*boaire*) who were cattle (*bo*) and property owning commoners, Caesar's 'plebs'; they were farmers, who might possess their own simple chariot and cart and carry arms, and whose skills included those of the craftsmen and smith. The druids, magicians and bards (*drui, fáith, bard*) served the spiritual needs of the noble grades from whom they were recruited, whilst below all came the unfree, propertyless men, without the status of arms: tenants, labourers, inferior craftsmen, indebted clients, slaves and handmaidens who laboured to the economic advantage of their masters (Jackson, 1964; Powell, 1959).

Of course, Celtic society varied through time and from tribe to tribe. Yet, everywhere, the web of Celtic kinship seems to have been cross-cut by broadly comparable grades, often elaborately distinguished by the almost heraldic significance of the subcultural artefact insignia appropriate to each status. The fabric of Celtic society appears to have derived its strength from kinship interwoven with allegiance. The Irish Laws confirm this and are much concerned with what property a man may be allowed to hold in keeping with his rank, carefully differentiating between the property of the ordinary freeman (*boaire febsa*) and a senior freeman who might be a local headman or magistrate (*boaire mruigfer*). We may appropriately compare their property, households and stock holdings with those of the Glastonbury units – and in particular compare their 'seven roofs' or 'houses' with the seven structures in each Glastonbury unit (I–VII) (Fig. 21.1).

Boaire febsa: Twice seven cumals of land; a house of twenty-seven feet with an outhouse of fifteen feet; a share in a mill [quern?], so that he grinds for his family and his companies of guests; a kiln [bakehouse?], a barn, a sheepfold, a calf fold, a pig sty. These are the *seven roofs* in respect of which every *boaire* is paid for injury. He has twelve cows, a half share in a plough . . . a steer is his customary due . . .

Boaire mruigfer: Land of three times seven cumals he has. He is *boaire* of adjudication, the senior *boaire* of his lineage, with all the artefacts of his house in their proper places; a cauldron with its spits and supports; a vat in which a boiling [of ale?] may be brewed; a cauldron for ordinary use, utensils including irons, trays, mugs, a trough, bath, tubs . . . knives for cutting rushes, ropes, an adze, an auger, a saw, shears, a trestle, an axe; tools for use in every season . . . a whetstone, mallets, a billhook, a hatchet, a spear for killing cattle; a fire always alive . . . a cask of milk and a cask of ale . . . he has three sacks always in his house . . . a sack of brewing barley, a sack of sea salt against the

845

cutting up of joints of his cattle, a sack of charcoal for the irons. *Seven houses he has*, a kiln, a barn, a mill – his share therein so that he grinds in it for others, a dwelling of twenty-seven feet, an outhouse of seventeen feet, a pig sty, a calf fold, a sheepfold. Twenty cows, two bulls, six oxen, twenty pigs, twenty sheep, four hundred hogs, two brood sows, a saddle horse with an enamelled bridle. Sixteen sacks [of seed] in the ground [stored?]. He has a bronze cauldron in which a hog fits. He owns pasture in which there are always sheep without [need to] change ground. He and his wife have four changes of dress. His wife is daughter of his equal in grade . . . three companions [*ceile*] are his retinue in the tribe [*túath*] . . . he protects his equal in grade . . . a cow is his tributary due.

In contrast, the tribal chieftain (*rí*) was entitled to a house of over thirty feet to sleep up to seventeen persons and encircled on occasion by a 'ditch of vassalage' (*drecht gialnai*) (*Crith Gablach*, Binchy, 1941; Hamilton, 1968, p. 72).

Now the finest artefacts from Glastonbury are of good quality but they are not abundant and they are never of the highest quality found elsewhere in this region – there is no enamelled harness comparable to the suite for a noble equipage of some seven chariots buried five miles away in the Polden hoard, no torques like those from Clevedon or Wraxall, no fine shield mounts, no coral, gold or silver like the material from Cadbury. There is no evidence in artefacts or house size of nobility; the Glastonbury craftsmen were skilled part-time operators making lower order goods and providing comparable services – they were village smiths not master craftsmen (Fig. 21.12).

There is, however, clear evidence at Glastonbury for the presence of independent wealth on a small scale and the possession of property, weapons, chariots, horses and stock, together with abundant evidence for skilled craftsmen in carpentry, lathework and elementary smithing. These attributes of the free man are precisely those redundantly repeated for all five of the independent lineages whom we might tentatively identify as the extended families of non-noble freemen (*boaire febsa*) and their dependents. The exceptions are the two 'dependent' units on the west side of the inner compound and the enclosure of the 'headman' on the east side. Perhaps here we might infer the presence of the senior man (*boaire mruigfer*) of the senior lineage served either by two unfree families or dependent clients.

Now, by chance, Caesar records as an interpolation in his narrative a fragmentary 'ethnology' of those parts of Britain best known to merchant adventurers before the Roman invasion – principally, the territories of the Dumnonii in the west and the Cantii in the east (Caesar, V. 1; Warner, 1960, pp. 94-5). In this 'ethnology' a brief description is given of the social organization of local Celtic communities, including the observation: 'women are held in common between groups of ten or twelve men, particularly between brothers or between fathers and sons; but the children born from these unions are considered to belong to the man to whom the woman was married first.'

This terse observation of the first century B.C. presents a condensed but intelligible record of an important complex of functionally interrelated Celtic social customs found together in many analogous societies – the patrilocal extended family, fraternal polygyny, and levirate (Murdock, 1949, pp. 23-41). Furthermore, the Celtic custom of fosterage, often historically viewed as a barbaric eccentricity, is a frequent element in the same recurrent set of customs (Murdock, 1949, p. 35). The classical authors and Irish evidence confirm that, although monogamous unions will have numerically prevailed, Celtic society was polygynous by rank and status, with a single principal wife (*cétmuinter*) in addition to others of subordinate rank (Powell, 1959, p. 84). All of these customs recur together where women have great economic importance and where the most efficient unit for economic cooperation is larger than the nuclear family. Certainly, the kindred units at Glastonbury seem to approach these conditions and one might dare to see the hypothesized units of fifteen to twenty men and women, in residential units such that each pair of familial houses holds in common a minor 'female' house, as a structural analogue of the social convention noted by Caesar (Filip, 1960, p. 94).

Economic and other factors predispose a society to move towards a limited set of viable family structures and residence patterns. The economic advantages of plural wives may be critical in circumstances where the numbers of an extended family must be maintained and where many hands are required for weaving, milking, shepherding, field work, light manufacturing and food production. The reproductive and working capacity of a single wife will often be too precarious, especially when she may be sterile or at best regularly incapacitated by pregnancy. These pressures towards an extended family form are redoubled wherever substantial time and cooperative effort have been locked up in the capital of animal herds, ditched, diked and manured fields, permanent structures or localized and interlocking resources such as fishing, fowling, trapping or grazing rights. Then property factors promote the development of extended family patterns and inheritance mechanisms of the levirate type (Murdock, 1949, pp. 36-40; Goody, 1969).

The type and size of family and tribal units may be modelled as a response surface varying with the mandatory or permissive constraints of the territorial area, within the range allowed by technology and the society's antecedent social pattern. The categories and sizes of site developed by the society in its settlement system or hierarchy, and even the numbers and structural organization of elements like the lineages, will be limited and controlled by the nature of the territory and its segmentation (Evans-Pritchard, 1940, p. 248). At Glastonbury, then, we have several patrilocal extended families of non-noble freemen farmers, united by kinship ties, and a system of allegiance through a headman, supported by a range of dependents or clients. We may suppose that the combined mechanisms of the patrilocal extended family, fraternal polygyny, levirate, clientship and fosterage may here have served to support and bind these cooperative kin groups within a most effective structural response to the uniquely burdensome group tasks required by their demanding but rewarding marshland home – clearing, ditching, diking, draining, building crannogs and tracks, droving, shepherding, manufacturing and exporting – a high risk but a high yield strategy.

The site: an economic model and its locational context

The preliminary analyses of the mass of information embedded within the site observations have enabled us to establish some crude parameters, to discuss social models for the Glastonbury community, and to compare both with indirect historical information. But no model for such a site can be complete without a consideration of the locally critical relationships between the community's ethology, economy and environment. Some attempt should be made to isolate the critical variables in the nexus of relationships between this community and its behaviour patterns and those of other communities, together with the mutual exploitation of their loci, territories, areas and regions. No site is, or was, an isolate and no site may be comprehended without a consideration of its possible or probable roles within a network of contemporary sites; whether or not those contemporary sites may still be identified is immaterial.

Once again, such a study logically leads to an array of alternative models to be tested against information from other sources. In the interests of brevity the most plausible and momentarily most powerful model will be outlined to show the significance that observations made beyond the site must have for interpretation within any site.

The area surrounding Glastonbury forms a geological bowl with a rim of limestone and sandstone hills barely five miles from the site (Fig. 21.7). The gravels at the feet of these hills merge into a succession of peats, clays and alluvium, which forms the fenland bottom, cleft only by the low spit of the Lias Polden hills running between the rivers Brue and Parrett. The limestone uplands carried open forest and rich pasture whilst the sandstone pockets supported acid soils with fine oak stands and patches of heather – an area rich in deer and pig herds. Below, the oak and ash woods of the sheltered gravels petered out amidst the many miles of shallow freshwater meres, reed swamps, sedge moors and fen carr, wooded with willow, alder, thorns, birch, dwarf oak and ash and interspersed by richly grassed herbaceous clearings in the summer drought. To the west, brackish waters came within five miles of the site and estuarine conditions within ten miles, each with their own rich and diverse ecology. Within the fen the occasional island offered hospitality in the maze of interlinked and sluggish waterways – so hostile to the newcomer, so rewarding to those with sufficient specialized knowledge of this rich but treacherous environment.

The 'Green Island' (*Ynys Glas*) at Glastonbury was just such a refuge: a small, verdant, conical peninsula of sand and clay defended on its landward eastern margin by an Iron Age earthwork, Ponter's Ball. Similar refuges and sacred sites presumably existed on comparable islands around the fenland bowl, serving the many focal purposes for the lowland communities around them that the more obvious hill forts similarly provided on the Mendip hills. The settlement at Glastonbury, like the broadly contemporary settlement at Meare, three miles to the west, was set amidst the fens close to the rich river silt and the alluvial flats exposed by the periodic contractions of the vast Meare pool. Probably every such island and peninsula supported several similar consanguineous communities scattered in a shifting but mutually adjusted distribution around their margins.

This sheltered, low-lying lakeside area occupied one of the warmest and driest climatic niches in the Dumnonian regions famed for their Atlantic warmth, wetness and mild winters. The location carried many other special advantages – the high quality alluvial and peat soils, the level surfaces, the availability of water, the year-through richness of fenland wildlife resources, the long-distance bulk-carrying and intercommunication permitted by boat, and the contiguity within a small radius of a great diversity of ecological habitats, ranging from estuarine marshes through freshwater fens to gravel terraces and geologically variegated hills (Figs. 21.7, 21.8).

However, this locality shared the many disadvantages and the basic paradox posed by most fenland sites. An excess of water is a handicap to farming – the stock become prone to foot rot, parasites and insect diseases, and the cooperative labour requirements of draining and diking are severe but essential if the

849

root systems of the crops are to be kept from waterlogging in the crucial weeks of the growing season. Furthermore, the severe annual flooding will have been disastrously exacerbated from time to time by concurrences of high tides, Atlantic gales and heavy rainfall in the hills, and from period to period climatic and sea level oscillations rendered most of this area temporarily uninhabitable.

If water and fen resources were abundant in the marshes there were other important staples that had to be imported – flint, stone, clay, metals and large timber. It is in this context that a marsh location close to the hills becomes an optimal solution on the Weberian model (Chorley and Haggett, 1967, pp. 362–417). Nevertheless, these advantages and disadvantages are almost trivial against the background of the fundamental paradox of this flat terrain – that in the course of every annual cycle two thirds of the little dry land available was inundated. The annually dependable dry land area, to which all permanent settlement was confined by the wet season, was less than one third of that richly grassed alluvium available during the summer drought; a dearth of land in winter, an unexploitable superabundance in summer. Thus the territory presented a high risk area for farmers, perhaps unacceptably high for small farming units below a critical labour level and outside a reciprocally supporting settlement network. But the territory also represented a potentially high yield terrain with easily worked rich soils and the rich wild resources.

In the periods before technology could attempt the drainage of the whole fenland basin this territorial paradox could be solved in only two ways:

(i) By adapting social organization and economy to the special conditions and resources of the fenland environment and accepting the flood constraint to semi-independent, small-scale, low density communities, with a low level of economic and political organization.

(ii) By adapting to the special conditions and resources but rejecting the flood constraint by establishing a system of territorial segmentation with the contiguous hill areas such that reciprocal, interdependent and symbiotic relationships would allow the ebb and flow of people and commodities to mutual advantage. This solution not only allows but demands community interdependence and reciprocal specialization over large areas, with larger scale, higher density society requiring a high level of economic and political organization.

In each solution the unique environment requires an adaptive response extending from social and political organization, through technology to

850

economic strategies with an emphasis on special crop, stock and wild resource management patterns. However, the second higher level solution requires some degree of sophistication and is simultaneously the more risky. We should certainly not make the mistake of ordering these two solutions in an evolutionary and chronological succession. Quite apart from the oscillating conditions of the fenland through time, it is evident that these two solutions are alternatives and communities of the first type might coexist amidst a society of the second category, although the more complex category of organization may only have been viable in 'dry' periods in the fenland – in Middle/Late Neolithic, Middle/Late Bronze Age, Middle/Late Iron Age and Later Roman periods. Thus, when similar conditions returned similar responses re-emerged with a slight technological advance; parallel conditions with similar sequences may also be observed for the East Anglian fenlands (Darby, 1940; Godwin and Dewar, 1963).

The information recovered from the site at Glastonbury and from the broadly contemporary sites of the surrounding territory points firmly to the existence of interdependent and reciprocally specialized communities of the second category, networking the fenland settlements to those of the surrounding hills and vice versa. It should be noted that this interdependence is not merely postulated on theoretical grounds, nor conjured from the hypothetically analogous Medieval transhumance patterns found both here and in East Anglia (Darby, 1940, fig. 13), but is demonstrated by the extensive range of items reciprocally exchanged between a limited area of the Mendips and the Glastonbury settlement (Fig. 21.7) and by the otherwise insupportable degree of idiosyncratic affinity between the artefact assemblages of the fenland and the Mendip slopes.

The material evidence points to an especially intensive volume of activity between the *locus* of the Glastonbury site and an exploitation *territory* of about ten miles radius – with an especial emphasis on the segment of Mendip between the large hill fort at Maesbury and the leadworkings at Charterhouse, above Cheddar Gorge (Fig. 21.7). There is evidence of a less intensive but pronounced volume of activity relating Glastonbury and this Mendip territory to a wider settlement *system catchment area*, some twenty miles radius from the site, itself apparently but one tessera within a mosaic of catchment areas running orthogonally across the resources from the Mendip rim to the fenland bowl (Fig. 21.8) (Clarke, 1968, p. 505). At a still more relaxed level similar evidence relates this site and the Somerset area network as a tribal sept within the eighty miles radius of a putative Dumnonian septarchy or tribal group (Fig. 21.9).

The Glastonbury site and its contents therefore relate to a series of successively wider networks or regional frames – from a local territory, through an incorporating area, to an englobing region. However, in activity terms land surface is far more complex than a homogeneous plane over which activity volume diminishes steadily with distance. The volume of activity focused on the Glastonbury site in reality falls away logarithmically in intensity over distance in a series of concentric but asymmetric frames, with an important major distortion – distance by sea appears to be less than half the impedance of distance overland, a distortion that in itself almost accounts for the existence of the Dumnonii as a regional unit (Fig. 21.9).

The successive frames may be arbitrarily named, crudely defined and subject to sampling problems, but they still seem to reflect zones of changing degrees of relationship with the site. The site exploitation territory maps an activity zone apparently related to the effective daily range of man, animal, canoe, cart and chariot load movements in and out of the site; it is interesting to note that the advanced technology and water transport give a larger site exploitation territory than elsewhere (see Jarman, Chapter 18 of this volume). The twenty miles radius area of the site system to which Glastonbury belongs represents the complex accumulation of the preceding factors for a large number of unknown sites interacting with ecological, economic, demographic and political elements within the network of adaptively located settlements of the Somerset bowl. Then, finally, the regional unit of the Dumnonii is represented by a tract of some eighty land miles radius but perhaps only ten sea hours sailing time, within which some six or seven area systems were interlinked by communication, reciprocity and common political, ethnic and linguistic constraints.

However, it is at the local territorial level that the most intensive connections demonstrate the interdependence of the Glastonbury fenlands and the Maesbury highlands. The exotic resources brought into the site from this territory include hundreds of tons of Upper Lias clay and rubble from the Tor, iron, lead and red lead ochre from Charterhouse, hearthstones from Draycott and flints from the Coxley gravels (Fig. 21.7). The immediate vicinity of Maesbury Camp, and its probable predecessor at Blacker's Hill, contributed Old Red Sandstone, Andesite and Croscombe Lias quern stone roughouts, doorsteps, hammerstones, whetstones, spindle whorls, fine pottery (Peacock's Group 2), special Gannister crucible clay from Oakhill, fuller's earth from Chewton and miscellaneous stones from the Lower Limestone shales, Dolomitic conglomerates and Harptree chert. The same Mendip slopes probably supplied the Glastonbury community with the many hundreds of feet of shed deer antler, the large oaks for canoes, but above all the potential of some twenty-five square miles of sheltered, well-drained winter browse and grazing at a season when the flooded fenland islands could measure their dry area in square feet. Conversely, when the summer droughts exposed acres of freshly grassed alluvium in the fens, the Mendip pastures would have been grazed to the ground and dried by the sun.

The archaeological evidence from this segment of the Mendips reciprocally supports the evidence from within the Glastonbury site. The Wookey Hole caverns, five miles away at the foot of the hills, have produced a wide range of artefacts, which are not only broadly contemporaneous but closely match the Glastonbury assemblage in a broad spectrum of structured idiosyncrasies which suggest that we are dealing with the material culture of communities from a common society. Many similar caves scattered along the limestone escarpment clearly show regular use at this period as seasonal base camps for transhumant shepherds and their flocks, as bivouacs for seasonal mining, smelting and smithing activities and in some cases as druid sanctuaries (Dobson, 1931, pp. 112–15). Wookey Hole alone produced many cubic feet of sheep and goat dung interspersed with fragments of milking pots, weaving combs and lathe fragments, and burials including one with an iron billhook, knife, dagger, latch-lifter and stalagmite ball closely comparable to those from Glastonbury.

Perhaps the most convincing evidence linking the Glastonbury settlement with the Maesbury fortified site is provided by the detailed concurrence between Peacock's petrological analyses of the Glastonbury and Mendip area pottery and the evidence from the petrology and taxonomy of the Glastonbury community's quernstones. Peacock has been able to show that fine pottery was being 'mass produced' in localities with suitable clays and suitable *in situ* demand and then marketed over wide areas (Peacock, 1959). Glastonbury, for example, was importing fine ware from north and south Mendip markets (Groups, 2, 3, 4) as well as acquiring the odd vessel from as far afield as Cornwall (Group 1) and Devon (Group 5), all within the Dumnonian region. Now Peacock has been able to trace the most likely source of the Glastonbury Group 2 wares to clays of the Sandstone deposits between Maesbury and Beacon Hill, near Shepton Mallet (Peacock, 1969, p. 46). These same deposits are the very source of the Glastonbury querns of Old Red Sandstone and Andesite which the settlement was importing in roughout form. Furthermore, the closest parallel to the peculiar Glastonbury quern type found outside the site itself comes from this source locality (Bulleid and Gray, 1911–17, pp. 610–11). It seems highly probable that the large-scale

853

quarrying and dressing of quernstones and the manufacture and kilning of fine pottery were connected with the location of the largest local hill fort at Maesbury, dominating as it does the central Mendip resources of timber, pasture, lead, coal, iron and a variety of stone resources. We may hypothesize, and subsequently test by excavation, that it was from this centre that Glaston-bury imported much of its raw materials and to which it exported its own pro-ducts. It was around this centre that the nearest hill pasture lay and it was perhaps to this centre that Glastonbury owed its political allegiance and thus its customary tribute.

It is only against this locational context that the internal site information on the economy of the Glastonbury community can now be intelligibly assembled. It is only against the context of the summer surplus of fine fen-land pasture and the Mendip surplus of dry winter grazing that we can under-stand both the choice of sheep as a fenland staple and the large numbers in which they were kept. Upon this in turn rests the community's textile in-dustry and the critical significance of the numbers of women who could be gathered and held together within polygynous extended families or the number of brothers who could be released for droving and shepherding for months in the year. Once again the information will bear several alternative chains of interpretations that must be tested, but at least the data on the settlement's domestic animals, crops and fenland resources now permit us to review the most likely pattern for their integrated management (Figs. 1.10–1.12).

Only a sample of the animal bones from the site have survived contempo-rary destruction by burning and dogs, only a sample of these were recovered and only a sample of this sample was analysed by species (Bulleid and Gray, 1911–17, p. 641). Precise calculations are therefore impossible and the range of estimates can only be accepted as indicating the rough scale of the activities. Nevertheless, arguments based on the estimated human population, sampling evidence and the relatively complete excavation suggest from the quantity of bones discovered and from the settlement span that the Glastonbury herds may have ranged from some 200–1000 sheep of Soay type, perhaps 20–30 small oxen and cows of Kerry type, 10–20 Celtic ponies and a few dozen pigs and dogs, expanding from the lower figure towards the higher figure over the 100 years of settlement expansion (Phases I–IV, Figs. 21.2–21.5). These figures receive a crude confirmation from estimates separately derived from the ex-panding stable, byre and sty facilities of the settlement and the developing capacity of the inner and outer compounds to corral when necessary up to some 1200 head of stock. This complement of livestock would be sufficient for the meat and milk needs of the estimated population with a sufficient surplus for safety, breeding, wastage, tribute and exchange purposes. Tacitus reminds us, for example, that the customary gift annually due to men of rank was an important economic mechanism at this time – 'it is the custom that each tribesman shall give the chieftain presents either of cattle or of part of his harvest. These free gifts are marks of respect, but they also supply the needs of those who receive them' (Postan, 1966, p. 273).

The main crops grown at Glastonbury were two-rowed and six-rowed barley, wheat and the small Celtic bean. Large quantities of threshed grain and beans were found around the granary stances and it is interesting to note that although beans and wheat often occurred together in the debris the barley usually appeared alone. This slight evidence might suggest the separate sowing of winter barley in the restricted dry area around the settlement and a main crop of wheat and beans sown in late spring over a wider expanse of fertile alluvial flats, river floodplain and burned-off peat and reed beds. These tactics resemble the Medieval practice in the Somerset levels and in this archaic form amount to a variety of infield-outfield system, which long survived in the peripheries of the Celtic fringe (Van Bath, 1963, pp. 58, 246, 263).

The infield, here defined by the winter floods, usually occupied less than one third of all the arable but was kept under continuous tillage by burning off, ashing and fertilizing annually with high phosphate and potash hearth debris (estimated site output *c.* 4000–7000 cubic feet per annum) plus manure and fouled sedge litter from the stables and byres (estimated site output *c.* 100 000–200 000 pounds per annum) and direct manure from grazing on the stubble fields after harvest. The alluvial and peat soils are also natural phosphate and nitrate reservoirs and, with the manuring and the nitrogen-fixative legumes, there should have been no difficulty in maintaining an infield permanently under the plough, without fallow.

On the outfield, cereals and legumes would be grown around a wider radius until the yields were no longer rewarding, after which the patches would be fallowed and used to fold stock. After this enrichment the land could again be sown annually for five years and then the cycle repeated. The 'waste' areas of sedge and reed flats beyond the outfield might be annually reclaimed by slashing and burning to provide land for short-term cultivation and by natural succession to rich pasture of sheep's fescue (*Festuca ovina*) and purple moor grass (*Molinia caerulea*). In this way three concentric zones of agrarian activity will probably have expanded and contracted around the settlement with the waxing and the waning of the fenland floods (Fig. 21.10).

Under these conditions yields would have been high but subject to severe annual fluctuations introduced by unusually wet years – a high return for

855

high risk and heavy capital investment. Certainly part of this investment in labour time, plant and capital must have taken the form of extensive ditching. The fenland soils cannot be exploited without the diking and draining that allow the crop roots the minimal period without waterlogging essential for their growth. We do not know which of the many simple forms of drained-field cultivation the Glastonbury community used, but the infield and much

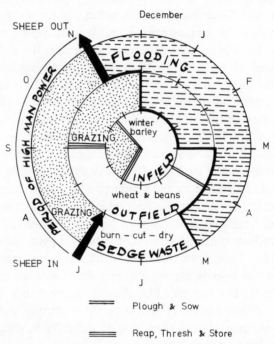

FIG. 21.10. A hypothetical economic cycle model for the Glastonbury settlement. The site is imagined at the centre of the diagram, in the middle of three zones of agrarian exploitation – the infield, outfield and sedge wastelands. The decisive factor in this strategy is the annual flooding of most of the outfield and sedge areas in winter and the superabundance of grazing in high summer. This inequality is defeated by moving large herds and flocks in and out of the area at key seasons. In actuality, the settlement's agrarian area occupied a semicircular radius forced by the lake margin to the north (see Fig. 21.7).

of the outfield areas must have possessed extensive systems of small open ditches. Aerial photography and extensive excavation would test this assertion and there is already some evidence that small, squarish, ditched fields may have been used in such contexts (Denevan, 1970; Bowen, 1969, plate 1.3; Norman and St Joseph, 1970, p. 67, figs. 38, 39). On this assumption the

856

Glastonbury cropland can hardly have required the digging and regular cleaning of less than fifteen miles of ditches – yet another activity in which the regular, cooperative and periodically intensive labour of kin groups will have been essential for the common good, firmly tying the community to the capital investment of its fields.

The Somerset tribes were no novices in wet farming, both the local and Celtic traditions inherited some 3000 years of successful agrarian experiment on lake margins, in marshes, on crannogs and islands. The perimeter of the Glastonbury site was, for example, ingeniously stabilized and repeatedly extended by a subtle reclamation technique in which pairs of converging banks dug in the drought were closed in a pincer and then levelled with dumped rubbish (Bulleid and Gray, plates XXIX, XXXIII). Banks and ditches dug with iron-shod oak spades were fundamental elements of Iron Age technology and it is significant that broken spade handles are amongst the more common artefacts found at Glastonbury, together with the sedge farmer's iron billhooks (Dobson, 1931, p. 118; Bulleid and Gray, 1911–17, pp. 319, 366).

The iron plough share (Z3) and the plough beam roughout (X92) from Glastonbury show that a light two oxen plough of the Donnerupland type was in use (Bowen, 1961, p. 8). If we accept the analogy between the Glastonbury residential units and establishments on the scale of the Irish freemen (*boaire febsa*) then we might expect one such plough and two draught oxen for each free unit – totalling perhaps two ploughs and four oxen in Phase I to five ploughs and ten oxen in Phase IV (Fig. 21.2–21.5). These draught oxen and the other settlement stock will have derived essential winter fodder from the bean plants during the crucial wet months, although both oxen and ponies will also have required a small supplementary ration from the cereal surplus.

Estimates of the cereal yield and area cultivated from the site can be very crudely approached from the separate evidence of the storage capacity of the granaries and from the minimum yield necessary to feed the population estimated from the site's structures. These lines of inference are in broad agreement with one another and with information from analogous sites in comparable circumstances. This evidence suggests that the ploughland in annual use would have risen over 100–200 acres (Phases I–IV), requiring a minimum total outfield area rising between 150–300 acres. Since the area north of the site was standing water the outfield area will have crudely extended over a half circle with a minimal radius of between half to one mile from the site. Beyond this outfield will have extended the zone of sedge farming and the extensive pasture confirmed by pollen analysis, and to these

857

minimal calculations must be added a substantial factor for inlying pockets of untillable terrain (Godwin, 1960; Godwin and Dewar, 1963).

All in all, it would be difficult to estimate the outer radius of ploughland, pasture and waste regularly exploited from the site at less than *c.* $1\frac{1}{2}$ miles. The significance of this figure becomes apparent when we note that the related site at Meare, three miles to the west, then emerges as a nearest neighbour site with a contiguous zone of activities on the same lake shore (Fig. 21.7). Taken further, the same chain of inference allows us to guess the most likely loci for other contemporary settlements in this area – and within its crude limits the model becomes predictive and testable.

No sketch model of the Glastonbury economy can legitimately ignore the vast resources offered to the settlement by the fenland itself – the shellfish, fish, water plants and rhizomes for food and fodder; hazel nuts, light timber and the finest smelting charcoal from the buckthorn and the carr, with willow for baskets and hurdles, reed and sedge for thatch, bedding and flooring, peat turf for fuel, fen mammals for fur, and wild fowl in superabundance. Fish, fur and fowl were the traditional fenland staples.

The lead net weights and bones confirm that fish were netted in the meres. A prolific variety of ducks, geese and swans were taken as eggs in the nest or on the wing with hunting dogs and slingshot from the margins of the site itself. The fur-bearing mammals – beaver, otter, fox and wild cat – were extensively taken and caches of their bones discarded from skinning were repeatedly found near the baking huts, where their pelts were perhaps dried and treated before stitching to the fine embroidered woollen cloaks. The seasonal fenland resources certainly contributed in no small measure to stabilizing the precarious agrarian regime of the settlement.

However, this static sketch model must be set into dynamic motion if the integrated management pattern for this complex of interdependent resources is to be simulated and ultimately quantified (see Thomas, Chapter 17 of this volume). The very complexity and seasonality of the many competing elements witnessed in the evidence imposes the limiting restrictions which make such an input-output study possible and an energy system model conceivable.

Waterlogging seasonally reduced the dry land area around the settlement by two thirds. Grazing was therefore virtually non-existent in the vicinity of the village for flocks of any size until the summer months, when there would have been a superabundance by late summer with the first flush of grass colonizing the alluvial flats and banks, purple moor grass dominating the burnt and cut sedge areas, the long stubble left after harvesting the entire infield and outfield with sickles, plus the extensive herbaceous browse of the waterside. In contrast, the better drained limestone and sandstone hillsides would have provided admirable overwinter and spring grazing but would have become too dry, overgrazed and nutritionally too poor to support very large flocks at the critical period when the ewes and lambs require their highest plane of nutrition in June and July (Large, 1970, fig. 1; Hurst, 1970).

Thus the fenland bowl provided its peak of surplus pasture of the very highest quality in exactly the months when the Mendip slopes would have been exhausted. The sheep were therefore most probably driven up to Mendip as the autumn became wetter and the outfield flooded, to return to the fenland settlements late the following summer as the maximum grazing became available and the crops safely harvested. In this way the sheep-carrying capacity of the upland-lowland system was far greater than could have been sustained by the individual component territories acting independently (Fig. 21.7).

Given this situation, the agrarian cycle of the community would have moved into operation as the spring floods receded, with the preparation, ploughing and sowing of the outfield (March–April) and any residual parts of the infield not already sown with winter barley the previous year (October–November) (Fig. 21.10). The community may have been short-handed at this time if many of the young men accompanied the flocks to the Mendip slopes, but once the spring sowing was completed the season would have been appropriate for egg collecting, fowling and fishing and it is at this time (May–June) that the big shoals of marine shad (*Clupea finta*) must have been netted as they came up to spawn in the brackish meres three miles distant (Fig. 21.7).

By June–July the winter sown infield crops might be harvested, threshed and carted to the granaries and later the sedge would be dry enough to cut for thatch and litter or ready for burning in preparation for pasture. With the maximum land area exposed for grazing the flocks could be driven down from Mendip with their three-month-old lambs now able to travel, just weaned and requiring the fresh nutritious pasture immediately available on the alluvial flats and the infield stubble. In July–August the fleece of the Soay sheep 'moults' and would be ready for pulling, perhaps using the antler 'weaving' combs and iron knives (Wild, 1970). This would be a busy time, with one harvest in, another to reap and up to 1000 sheep to fleece, but the community's full manpower would be available.

In August or September the main crop in the outfield would be ripe for harvesting, leaving yet more grazing to augment the freshly grassed sedge areas. When this harvest was in, there would remain a useful month or more of dry autumnal weather and full manpower when building and reconstruction tasks could be undertaken, land reclaimed by diking, ditches cleaned and extended and obligatory tribal works undertaken. This timing is confirmed by the discarded debris of lunches of hazel nuts left by the builders in the foundations of huts under construction at this fruitful season of nuts, hunting and wildfowling (Bulleid and Gray, 1911–17, pp. 70, 148).

By the close of October the rams would have served the ewes and the grazing around the village would have neared exhaustion, but the ewes would then have required a high plane of nutrition for the first four weeks after mating, if lambing was to be successful (Hurst, 1970). With the early November rains threatening to flood the fen pasture and close the trackways the shepherds would have gathered their flocks and left for the slow drive up onto the fresh Mendip pastures from nearby Shapwick, via the Sheppey valley, to Shepton and Maesbury (from Sheep-village, along Sheep-island valley to Sheep-town). Back in the fen it would be time to prepare, plough and sow the infield so recently manured by grazing stock and in general to prepare for the winter.

In the early winter the waterways and meres would have been restored to their fullest navigable extent by the rains and journeys by canoe were thus made the more effective. The presence within the settlement of sea shore pebbles, sea shells, cormorant and puffin bones suggests trips to the important saltings at the mouth of the river Brue to trade for 'a sack of seasalt against the [winter] cutting up of joints of his cattle' and perhaps for salted sea bird carcasses harvested from the famous Bristol Channel island sanctuaries. Winter itself will have brought the return of the thousands of migrant ducks, geese and swans flying back to their fenland refuge and the fur-bearing mammals will have been sleek in their new winter coats – the time for hunting fresh non-salted meat and trapping desirable pelts. For the women there still remained between 200–1000 pounds of wool to be combed, cleaned, washed dyed, spun and woven – enough for 40–200 fine blankets or cloaks fit for heroes, trimmed with fur, embroidered with the bronze needles on the special wooden frames found in the settlement (Bulleid and Gray, 1911–17, plate LV; compare *Objets et Mondes*, vol. VIII, No. 1, 1968, p. 56, fig. 12). Such Celtic woollen cloaks were a famed export from this area of Britain to the Roman empire and may have been the principal output of the Glastonbury community (Wild, 1970; Powell, 1959, p. 71).

This preliminary sketch of the economic model in its annual cycle immediately suggests that the annual movements of shepherds and flocks between the fenland settlements and the Mendip slopes may have provided the context and mechanism by means of which Mendip raw materials, antlers, querns, pots, lead and timber were collected and brought down to Glastonbury and the fenland products taken up to Wookey, Maesbury and the other caves and hill forts. Indeed, the extraction of local iron and lead deposits might also have been part of seasonal small-scale mining expeditions from the transhumant base camps. It is tempting to identify these winter base camps and stock corrals with the chain of smaller, univallate 'hill forts' distributed at intervals of a few miles along the escarpment, both here and elsewhere.

Such camps may presumably have been erected and held in common by consanguineous groups of lowland communities like Meare and Glastonbury and may either have been devoid of permanent habitation or held only a small resident group. These camps are ideally sited and constructed for the seasonal marshalling of the large united herds from the lowlands and as bases from which to graze these units in rotation on the adjacent sheltered valleys or on the more distant upland pastures commanded by convenient limestone caves. On the comparable escarpment around the East Anglian fenland, analogously sited camps are entirely lacking and there is some suggestion that the same problems there were solved by the exact converse of the Mendip solution – the major residential population of agrarian farmsteads and hamlets centred on the hills with a movement of stock down to seasonally occupied lowland camps amidst the fen pastures (Arbury Camp: Alexander and Trump, 1972).

All in all, an idealized model of the settlement pattern and area site system to which Glastonbury belonged can be assembled and, as with ideal gas models, although it may be unreal it provides a basis for prediction and thus for testing the degree of its reality or unreality. The landscape probably contained a mixed pattern of single extended family farmsteads comparable to the individual Glastonbury units and hamlets of cooperative clusters of such units – the former more abundant on Mendip and the latter the rule in the fenland. However, the status of the settlement in either category might be radically altered by the 'embedded' presence of noble establishments, with a great house (over 30 feet), attached clients and perhaps even a 'ditch of vassalage' (Kingsdown Camp, Somerset: Dobson, 1931, p. 202) (Fig. 21.12).

With the markedly uneven distribution of permanent and seasonal resources over the area and effective means of intercommunication, the settlements would inexorably tend to become reciprocally specialized and mutually supporting within an area network embracing segments of fen and the

861

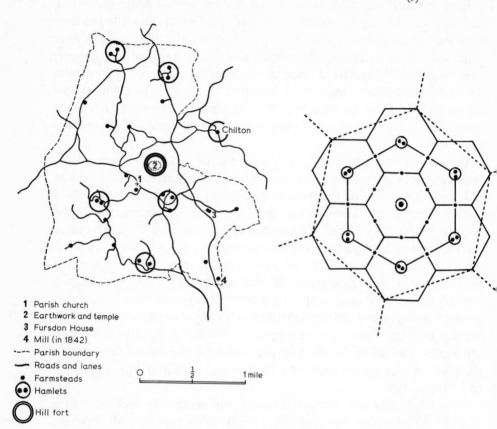

(a)   *(b)*

Chilton

1 Parish church
2 Earthwork and temple
3 Fursdon House
4 Mill (in 1842)
- - - Parish boundary
— Roads and lanes
• Farmsteads
(••) Hamlets
◯ Hill fort

O $\frac{1}{2}$ 1 mile

FIG. 21.11. The parish of Cadbury, Devon (after Hoskins, 1967). A Dumnonian multivallate hill fort of *c*. 3 acres, its territory and settlement hierarchy (*a*); an idealized model of the system (*b*).

(*a*) Special circumstances have probably preserved in this area a 'fossil' impression of a fully developed late Celtic settlement pattern – five multilineage hamlets, twelve single lineage farmsteads and a central hill fort with a Romano-Celtic shrine. The constraint of the massive boulder early field boundaries allowed minimal reorganization of the pattern, established before the eleventh century, in an area which remained Celtic and Celtic-speaking even after Saxon penetration in the eighth century (Hoskins, 1967, pp. 15–21).

(*b*) The model generalized from the Cadbury 'fossil' suggests a settlement pattern of *k* = 7 type, developed to a third order of settlement (farmsteads, hamlets, hill fort). Christaller showed that this type of 'administrative principle' system develops where firm central administrative control is important, such that all the dependent places owe allegiance to the central place (hill fort and cult centre) without divided loyalties. A Dumnonian network of this order is also supported by nearest-neighbour studies (Clarke, 1968, fig. 115).

Mendip slopes. A few 'centres' would be still further specialized, producing higher order complex manufactured goods and providing higher order services. These goods and services would in some cases be so costly or so restricted to rank that they must depend upon and serve a far wider population than that of the immediate area, distributing instead to a small portion of a larger market. Thus the individual areas themselves become mutually interlinked within a region for the supply of items such as fine mirrors, swords and pottery over and above the everyday requirements satisfied by each area's own internal network. Whether these market 'centres' can in all cases be simply and exclusively identified with the populations concentrated in or around the larger multivallate hill forts, like Maesbury, remains an arguable matter, open to test (Fig. 21.12).

Now, a rise in income, production and intensive employment in one group of economic activities in a site, territory, area or region stimulates the comparable expansion of other groups, through an increased demand from the former group for the goods and services of the latter (positive feedback). This process is expressed in economics as a Multiplier Model and it is already apparent that replicating processes of this kind lurk behind the 'spread' of many archaeological phenomena that are more usually 'explained' by diffusion, especially where the spread involves complexes of rather generalized elements (e.g. spread of redistribution economies, chieftainship, etc., in the European Early Bronze Age, or the spread of the Urnfield complex including settlement patterns with hill forts). The multiplier model may act between social segment and social segment as an internal economic multiplier within settlements, or as an external economic multiplier between adjacent or interlinked areas. In the Glastonbury area of the Dumnonian region multiplier analysis provides a valuable starting point for considering models of spatial variation and locational specialization in economic and settlement pattern (Chorley and Haggett, 1967, p. 275).

At the regional level there is ample evidence of reciprocity and specialization in adjacent areas of the Dumnonian system correlated with a growing volume of trade and the emergence of the settlement hierarchy required to manufacture, handle, redistribute and market the goods. Mendip lead and pottery products circulated against Cornish fine wares, silver, tin, copper and domestic products; high quality iron, gold, shale and glass were redistributed from external sources; perishable staples like dairy products, salt, corn, stock, wool and slaves moved overall (Fox, 1964, pp. 111–35). Although the primary production and manufacturing units were the settlements scattered throughout the region, the movement and organization of exports soon concentrated

863

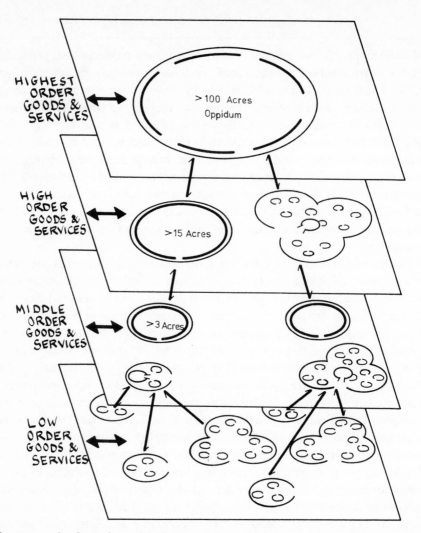

FIG. 21.12. A schematic model of a late, fully developed, Celtic settlement hierarchy suggesting the nature of its integration with the social hierarchy and grades on one hand and an economic hierarchy on the other. Evidence suggests that settlement patterns of the two lowest orders had widely developed during and because of socio-economic changes of the Early-Middle Bronze Age (see Sherratt, Chapter 12 of this volume). The 'high order' tier developed in the Late Bronze-Iron Age, as in the Glastonbury area. The Glastonbury area system did not fully develop a 'highest order' centre of the oppidum type, although Ham Hill may have latterly approached that status (Fig. 21.8, No. 3). The ditched-and-banked enclosures lumped together as 'hill forts' are seen as having different but overlapping functions; at the higher levels the settlements may be within or adjacent to these enclosures; for clarity only the latter case has been sketched. The model is generalized and speculative but presents a form which may be fully specified, tested and elaborated for particular areas by field work, excavation and aerial photography.

864

in certain centres optimally located with respect to a number of resources and at important links in transport routes, like the port of Mount Batten. As the export activity expanded the operation of the multiplier process will have stimulated the development of dispersed, locally oriented service industries feeding the system – pottery, textiles and metal industries, for example. The locational consequence of this development was the growing role of handling centres for collection and redistribution because of the economies of supply offered by their location, partly because of their strategic role as distribution centres, plus their growing importance as markets. These embryonic centres were thus increasingly able to attract a large proportion of the domestically oriented manufacturing and a large proportion of regional trade and service employment for the production of luxury goods. These centres would have grown comparatively rapidly with the growing aggrandizement of the chieftains who controlled the redistribution system and by population influx from the surrounding countryside – a context in which tribal allegiance, obligatory labour, fosterage and clientship will have been accelerating social mechanisms. The net result of the cumulative pattern of regional and locality specialization and interdependence was the transformation of a settlement system into a settlement hierarchy (Fig. 21.12).

The categorizing factors in the distinct settlement hierarchy of which Glastonbury was a lowly member include not merely absolute population size or ground area but also the order of services and products produced, their internal format, their distance from comparable sites, and the rank and status of the inhabitants. There emerges a progression from lower order settlements to those of higher order, where the lower order goods, services, skills and products would be repeated in the higher order sites but with the *addition* of distinctive, specialized activities which might act as classificatory indicators – enamel and glass workers, master craftsmen and armourers, coin and currency bar mints, workshops either producing élite goods or mass producing common goods, and marketing extra-regional materials like amber, coral, gold and shale. The higher order functions and products for high-status individuals required a greater population for their support and thus the range of the famous products of the Mendip school of La Tène master craftsmen included the entire Dumnonian peninsula (Fig. 21.9) (Fox, 1964, fig. 40, pp. 33–4).

As far as the evidence goes, Maesbury would fall into this category of higher order centre for the Glastonbury area, comparable to sites like Cadbury Castle and Ham Hill (Fig. 21.8). One can see that the later introduction of oppidum sites of an even higher order still, with yet richer services and

865

even greater political and economic range, is an indicator with considerable implications for the network and hierarchy supporting that order of site, with its almost international scale of operations.

To return to the particular segment of the Mendips to which the Glastonbury settlement relates, we might tentatively identify a settlement hierarchy with a broad base of a few noble and numerous non-noble first order family farm units scattered amidst second order hamlets of groups of such units, like Glastonbury and Meare. In the fens the emphasis may of necessity have been on the larger cooperative second order units, whereas on Mendip a more varied pattern may have prevailed amidst the abundant Celtic fields and upland pasture. If the earlier interpretation is accepted, the fenland communities independently or in conjunction with resident Mendip groups may have jointly maintained the small third order ditched base camps on sheltered spurs of the foothills. These simple hill forts would be the annual resort of the fenland drovers and may have served as territorial centres for the exchange of lower order goods, stock and women, as well as acting as unifying foci for the scattered communities that had cooperatively undertaken their construction.

These base camps, served by their own first and second order sites and satellite caves, were perhaps dependent upon the highest fourth order market centre at Maesbury, fifteen acres in extent, the multivallate 'citadel of the mining district' (Dobson, 1931, p. 202). Fenland sheep, stock, textiles, salt fish, fowl, furs and other products and services will have flowed as exchange and tribute through this network to Mendip, whence political protection and the first order products of the famous local school of master smiths, enamellers, weapon and mirror makers will have trickled back in return, where appropriate by rank, together with currency, ingots of imported and local raw materials, fine ware from the local kilns, and perhaps ponies, cattle, pigs and cereals when necessary (Fig. 21.12).

Conclusion

At this stage, the particular and merely interim conclusions of this study should be put on one side, bearing in mind the experimental nature of the exercise emphasized in the opening section of this chapter. Instead, it would be more appropriate to underline the critical role of the model-using approach in relation to studies of this kind. Settlement sites encapsulate a wealth of latent information involving both within-site and without-site relationships. This information remains latent and often unsuspected until the descriptive observations are selectively regrouped and scrutinized against an explicit model or a series of alternative models based on differing assumptions. Then experimental tests suggested by the predictive aspects of the different models may be used to discriminate between them as rival possibilities.

In this particular study the points at which branching series of alternative models might equally fit the range of variability of the data have been merely noted, in order that a chain of 'most plausible' interim models might here be pursued towards the limits of their potential. This provisional procedure usefully exposes the full consequence of the cumulative chain of assumptions for further testing, but it is in no way a substitute for the necessary testing between models.

It is important to note the many different kinds of model necessarily involved in a study of this kind, ranging from the post-depositional site model, through structural and building models, reconstruction models, social models, demographic models and economic models to locational and settlement hierarchy models. The models deployed here are but crude and elementary preliminaries but they suggest at once the ways in which they might be tested and the directions in which they must be refined. Thus the inferences based on the spatial trends are directly susceptible to statistical tests of significance and confidence. Field survey, limited excavation, dendrochronology, skeletal analysis and perhaps aerial photography may test the predictions about the location of comparable sites, the length of occupation, the site's social organization, and the claimed use of ditched field agriculture. The economic input-output sketch model is potentially quantifiable and might be used to simulate the system with a variable range of inputs and conditions to reveal the critical 'bottlenecks' in the economy. In these various ways a preliminary set of models and estimated parameters may serve to identify the target areas for the second and successive cycles of research within the project.

References

ALEXANDER, J. and TRUMP, D. (1972) Arbury Camp. *Proceedings of the Cambridge Antiquarian Society 1972.*

ASCHER, R. (1968) Time's arrow and the archaeology of a contemporary community. In CHANG, K. C. (ed.) *Settlement Archaeology.* Palo Alto, Calif.: National Press.

BATH, B. H. S. VAN (1963) *The Agrarian History of Western Europe A.D. 500–1850.* London: Arnold.

BINCHY, D. A. (1941) *Crith Gablach.* Dublin: Stationery Office.

BOWEN, H. C. (1961) *Ancient Fields.* London: British Association for the Advancement of Science.

BOWEN, H. C. (1969) The Celtic background. In RIVET, A. L. F. (ed.) *The Roman Villa in Britain*. London: Hutchinson.

BULLEID, A. H. and GRAY, H. ST G. (1911 and 1917) *The Glastonbury Lake Village*. Vols. I and II. Taunton: Glastonbury Antiquarian Society, Wessex Press.

CHORLEY, R. J. and HAGGETT, P. (eds.) (1967) *Models in Geography*. London: Methuen.

CLARK, J. G. D. (1952) *Prehistoric Europe: The Economic Basis*. London: Methuen.

CLARKE, D. L. (1968) *Analytical Archaeology*. London: Methuen.

CLARKE, D. L. (1970) Analytical archaeology: epilogue. *Norwegian Archaeological Review*, 3.

COOK, S. F. and HEIZER, R. F. (1968) Relationships among houses, settlements areas and population in aboriginal California. In CHANG, K. C. (ed.) *Settlement Archaeology*. Palo Alto, Calif.: National Press.

DARBY, H. C. (1940) *The Medieval Fenland*. Cambridge: Cambridge University Press.

DENEVEN, W. M. (1970) Aboriginal drained-field cultivation in the Americas. *Science*, 169 (3946), 647–54.

DOBSON, D. P. (1931) *Somerset*. London: Methuen.

EVANS-PRITCHARD, E. E. (1940) *The Nuer*. London: Oxford University Press.

EVERSON, J. A. and FITZGERALD, B. P. (1968) *Settlement Patterns*. Concepts in Geography Vol. I. London: Longmans.

FILIP, J. (1960) *Celtic Civilisation and its Heritage*. Prague: Czech Academy of Sciences.

FLANNERY, K. V. (1971) The origins of the village as a settlement type in Mesoamerica and the Near East: a comparative study. In UCKO, P., DIMBLEBY, G. W. and TRINGHAM, R. (eds.) *Settlement Patterns and Urbanisation*. London: Duckworth.

FOX, A. (1964) *South West England*. London: Thames & Hudson.

FRASER, D. (1969) *Village Planning in the Primitive World*. London: Studio Vista.

GODWIN, H. (1960) Prehistoric wooden trackways of the Somerset levels. *Proceedings of the Prehistoric Society*, 26, 1.

GODWIN, H. and DEWAR, H. S. L. (1963) Archaeological discoveries in the raised bogs of the Somerset levels. *Proceedings of the Prehistoric Society*, 29, 17.

GOODY, J. (1969) Inheritance, property and marriage in Africa and Eurasia. *Sociology*, 3, (1).

HAMILTON, J. R. C. (1968) *Excavations at Clickhimin, Shetland*. Ministry of Works Archaeological Report No. 6. Edinburgh: H.M.S.O.

HARVEY, D. (1969) *Explanation in Geography*. London: Arnold.

HERSH, R. and GRIEGO, R. J. (1969) Brownian motion and potential theory. *Scientific American*, 220 (3), 66–74.

HOSKINS, W. G. (1967) *Fieldwork in Local History*. London: Faber.

HURST, D. (1970) Feeding the lowland ewe. *Country Life*, 23 April.

JACKSON, K. H. (1964) *The Oldest Irish Tradition: A Window on the Iron Age*. Cambridge: Cambridge University Press.

LARGE, R. V. (1970) Getting the most out of your sheep. *New Scientist*, 9 July.

MARCH, L., ECHENIQUE, M. et al. (1971) Models of environment. *Architectural Design*, 41, 275–320.

MURDOCK, G. P. (1949) *Social Structure*. London: Collier-Macmillan.

NORMAN, E. R. and ST JOSEPH, J. K. S. (1970) *The Early Development of Irish Society: The Evidence of Aerial Photography*. Cambridge: Cambridge University Press.

PEACOCK, D. P. S. (1969) A contribution to the study of Glastonbury ware from south-western Britain. *The Antiquaries Journal*, **49** (1), 41.

PIGGOTT, S. (1965) *Ancient Europe from the Beginnings of Agriculture to Classical Antiquity*. Edinburgh: Edinburgh University Press.

POSTAN, M. M. (ed.) (1966) *The Cambridge Economic History of Europe: The Agrarian Life of the Middle Ages*. Vol. I. Cambridge: Cambridge University Press.

POWELL, T. G. E. (1959) *The Celts*. London: Thames & Hudson.

RICHMOND, I. A. (1968) *Hod Hill, Vol. 2: Excavations 1951–58*. London: Trustees of the British Museum.

WARNER, R. (1960) *War Commentaries of Caesar*. New York: New American Library.

WATERBOLK, H. T. and ZEIST, W. VAN (1961) A Bronze Age sanctuary in the raised bog at Bargeroosterveld. *Helinium*, **1**, 5–19.

WICKEN FEN (1964) (anon.) *Wicken Fen Guide*. London: National Trust.

WILD, J. P. (1970) *Textile Manufacture in the Northern Roman Provinces*. Cambridge: Cambridge University Press.

WRIGLEY, E. A. (1969) *Population and History*. London: Weidenfeld & Nicolson.

22

Locational models of Transvaal Iron Age settlements

R. J. MASON

University of Witwatersrand, South Africa

The role of models and analogies in prehistoric archaeology

The use of models and analogies plays an important part in the explanation of scientific data. No scientist can make effective use of a model or analogy unless he understands the hybrid nature of the model or analogy concept. The *Oxford English Dictionary* (*O.E.D.*) states that one of the meanings of analogy may be understood from the phrase 'A species or tribe in one region or at one period, which represents a different species or tribe elsewhere or at a different epoch', and develops a view that 'if things have some similar attributes they will have other similar attributes', (*O.E.D.* 3rd ed., revised 1967, London). The close relation between analogy and model in common language may be seen in the *O.E.D.* definition of 'model' as 'something that accurately resembles something else'. It is immediately clear that both the analogy and the model concept have a *crucial* role to play in the scientific explanation of phenomena in the prehistoric context. Prehistory deals with behavioural phenomena in an unwritten context, inferred from material traces of the behaviour. The prehistorian is forced to draw analogies and use models partly taken from his experience of the world today where he is able to apply direct measurement to phenomena in order to explain his reconstruction of the world of the past, which has mainly vanished.

D. Sapire (1971) notes: 'Models and analogies are often spoken of as if they were the same thing. Certainly they are intimately related, but they are not identical. Perhaps the central difference may be shown by stating that a model is essentially a thing, an analogy essentially a relation between two things, the analogues. Anything can become a model; it does so as soon as it is used to somehow represent another thing, or other things. In principle, an analogy can be set up between any two or more things'.

We may conclude by defining a model as something known, that is, close to our experience of the world, which is used to construct an explanation or hypothesis by drawing an analogy or making a comparison with something, say a prehistoric settlement, which is further from our experience of the world. For example, we take as a model the living Mangwato settlement of Serowe and use the more 'traditional' parts of that living settlement as a model to help us explain the dead Iron Age settlement of Kaditshwene, 380 km to the south and 150 years earlier in time, but associated with the same broadly defined Tswana group.

The Malete, a Tswana tribe with their capital of 11 000 people at Ramotswa in Botswana 96 km north of Kaditshwene, provide a model for analogy with the smaller Iron Age settlements in the western Transvaal. A recent analysis of Malete law of family relations, land and succession to property by Roberts, Campbell and Walker (1971) is essentially a statement of relationships between a community and its land, which probably recreates part of the behavioural network between some Iron Age settlements in the western Transvaal. The Malete analysis by Roberts, Campbell and Walker provides one of the many models necessary for the explanation of the Iron Age social landscape of the Transvaal.

History and ethnology are rich sources of models for explaining prehistoric data by drawing analogies. Andrew Smith's record of Moselikatse's scheme of satellite cattle posts used also as military observation points related to a central settlement provides a model for explaining settlement location in the terminal Iron Age world of the western Transvaal in the late 1820s and early 1830s (Kirby, 1940).

Observers have been obliged to use models and draw analogues to explain unwritten events for nearly 2500 years. In 431 B.C. the historian Thucydides drew analogies between Caria and Delos in terms of artefacts and burial methods, perhaps the earliest recorded use of analogy in prehistoric explanation. We may quote, 'This was proved during this present war, when Delos was officially purified by the Athenians and all the graves in the island were opened up. More than half of these graves were Carian, as could be seen from the type of weapons buried with the bodies and from the method of burial, which was the same as that still used in Caria' (Thucydides, 1954).

We may depict the logical process in scientific explanation applied to prehistory in the schematic diagram on the opposite page. The diagram sets out a formal scheme for the hypothetico-deductive-abductive system necessary for effective scientific thought in prehistoric archaeology. The system is a hybrid system and a thought-chain relevant to any problem may commence at any

DEDUCTION	Principles	← ABDUCTION	Models
↓	Theories		and
			analogies
↑	Hypothesis or	← ABDUCTION	from
INDUCTION	Explanation or model		living
	building		people
	↑		or
	Generalization	← ABDUCTION	ethnology
	↑		history
	Observations on the	← ABDUCTION	or
	ground at Prehistoric		historical
	Sites		documents

point in the system. I am indebted to my colleagues of the Philosophy Department at the University of the Witwatersrand, I. Thompson, who drew up the induction-deduction diagram, and D. Sapire, who defined analogy and model.

The hybrid nature of the analogy-model concept may be illustrated by comparing the *O.E.D.* definitions of model and analogy with definitions proposed by the logician R. Harré (1967). Harré, discussing mainly the physical sciences, distinguishes two kinds of model: the scale model or micromorph, an exact copy of something but of a reduced size, and the paramorph model, which represents parallels between quite different phenomena. Harré notes that there are rules for transforming information obtained in the paramorph or micromorph into information about the 'parent' or object of the investigation, but that these rules may be exceedingly complicated and require careful experimentation before they can be exactly settled.

Testing an analogy – a crucial problem in archaeological method

The testing of the validity or reliability of an analogy is an awkward problem in logic and perhaps the most important unsolved problem in archaeological method today. Presumably the reliability of an analogy or a model will be in proportion to the distance in time, space and behavioural relationships between the model and the object of the analogy or prehistoric observation we wish to explain by using the analogy.

Nicolas Peterson (1971) presents criteria for establishing 'the degree to which the conclusions reached by analogy are more or less probable'. The criteria are taken from Copi (1961) and are in six parts. Peterson's discussion is a brave attempt to present analogy in the prehistoric context but clearly the entire issue of the logic of analogy and models related to prehistory requires

873

the detailed study of a professional logician working in close collaboration with prehistorians.

Analogies, models and Transvaal Iron Age settlements

The explanation of the many thousands of prehistoric (that is, pre-1820, the earliest Transvaal written records) settlements in the Transvaal is one of the major responsibilities of African prehistorians today. The settlements are concentrated in the area that is the richest part of Africa today, having an annual gross product of approximately £1500 million, mainly from mining and industry. Modern education in Africa as a whole requires to know the precise historical relationship between the present-day Bantu-speaking population of the Transvaal and the immense wealth now pouring out of industry in the Transvaal. At least one of the keys to the solution of the historical problem lies in the study of relationships between the Bantu-speaking population today and the prehistoric settlements of the Transvaal. Such a study would answer questions such as 'Are the Bantu-speaking peoples of the Transvaal very recent arrivals or have they been resident in the Transvaal for a thousand or more years with a long record of mining, farming, metal production and village building technologically similar in some ways to those processes creating the wealth of the Transvaal today?'

The first steps in the study of prehistoric Transvaal Iron Age settlement have been made (Mason, 1968). Aerial photographs covering 124 105 km², 25°–27°S and 26°–31°E, revealed a total of 6237 settlements in five classes defined on the basis of plan form (Fig. 22.1).

The first analogy we may draw to explain the settlements is to note that all are variants of a simple basic African settlement form we observe over much of sub-Saharan Africa today occupied by Bantu-speaking people: the enclosure of a space by a roughly circular wall of stone or wooden poles to indicate a personal territory. The first model we may construct to explain the settlements is a distribution map locating the numbers of settlements in each of the five classes (Figs. 22.1, 22.2).

How are we to proceed to more complex explanations of Transvaal Iron Age settlement? The vast body of geographical location studies summarized by Chorley and Haggett (1967) provides a general store of models for explaining settlement as a whole. Unfortunately, the geographical studies are mainly concerned with location analysis for literate urban or rural societies. The distance in time, space and behavioural relationship is too great for us to directly relate location studies of modern societies to Transvaal Iron Age location studies. Then too, the literate context of the geographers' location studies provides a mass of quantitative data on such factors as population distribution, economic outputs, trading and political relationships, generally absent from the Transvaal Iron Age context. We do not even know how many of the 6237 Iron Age sites were contemporary with one another. The sites may, in fact, represent the end product of a thousand years, or more, of growth and decay, conquest and replacement of whole populations. Nevertheless, the Chorley and Haggett documents themselves provide a general model by suggesting to us the range of location factors we should search for in Iron Age settlement despite the technological gap between the modern and prehistoric contexts of settlement.

Classification of Transvaal Iron Age location models

There are hundreds of models to be found in libraries and on the African landscape, each contributing a part of the data for the body of hypotheses to explain Transvaal Iron Age settlement location. In the south-western Transvaal alone, one of the most densely settled Iron Age areas has today no less than nineteen Tswana reserves probably representing living reservoirs of people moved from the adjacent Iron Age sites. Air photos of some north Sotho settlements at Herwaarts, Pietersburg district, show modern African settlements directly overlapping prehistoric Iron Age settlements enabling immediate analogies to be drawn between the two (Mason, 1965), and Venda people may today be observed building Iron Age style stone walls (Mason, 1968).

Then we have a splendid set of written records from nineteenth-century missionaries, traders and explorers who recorded terminal Iron Age Bantu-speaking settlements in or near the Transvaal (e.g. Campbell, 1822; Smith, 1940; Moffat, 1841; Mackenzie, 1871; Broadbent, 1865; 1836; Broadbent-Hodgson letters, 1822–27). The study of both living people and the nineteenth-century historical records provides a wide range of models enabling us to explain the network of relationships that supported African settlements in or near the area of our Iron Age aerial photography survey. We cannot present a complete analysis here, but offer a classification of models to indicate the wide range of analogical processes accessible to the archaeologist for settlement analysis.

A GENERAL ECONOMIC MODEL FOR IRON AGE SETTLEMENT LOCATION

Study of living settlements relatable to our Iron Age settlements suggests that a network of political, social, economic and religious factors sustained the

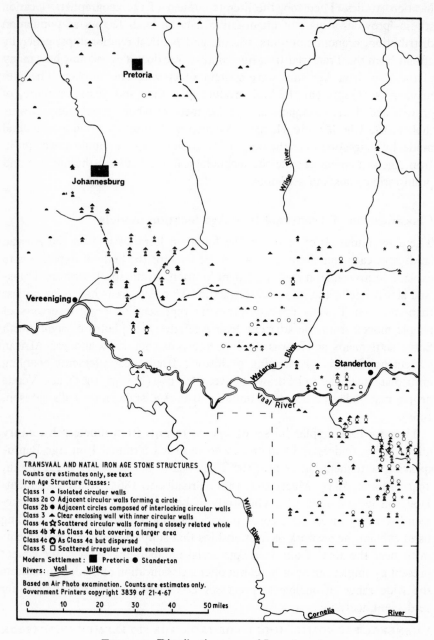

FIG. 22.1. Distribution map of Iron Age sites.

Iron Age settlements and determined their location. We know more about the economic factor than any other. The separate components of the Iron Age economic factor were: hunting wild game, collecting wild plants, herding domestic cattle, sheep and goats, cultivating millet, melons and other

CLASS 1

CLASS 2

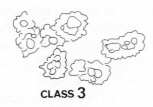

CLASS 3

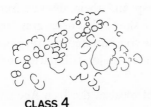

CLASS 4

FIG. 22.2. Plan views of Iron Age settlement classes.

plants, mining and smelting mineral ores, mining and processing salt, metalworking, woodworking, working of soft stone, working skins, weaving wild cotton, working ivory and shell, and the exchange of produced commodities either by trade or in war.

The economic basis of Iron Age economies in the Transvaal rested on at least these fourteen variables, probably many more. Historical evidence proves that different Iron Age settlements had different, though generally similar, economies. This is what we would expect, but it is our job as scientists to make a precise analysis of the variabilities. We now know that some Iron Age settlements such as Matluassi depended on food production and probably skin processing only, whereas other settlements such as Philabora supplemented their economies by metal production, and there may even have been others which were partly specialized in mining. Then, some parts of the Transvaal Iron Age economy in the Limpopo lowlands may have been affected by cattle diseases, and other parts may have been in areas whose climatic environments may not have been suitable for the domesticated plants produced in quantities in more favoured Iron Age settlements.

Regional variations in the fourteen components of Iron Age economy may be presented in a three-dimensional hardware model.

Starting from the lowest stratum of the model we represent the probably fairly uniform components of hunting wild game and collecting wild plants as common to all Iron Age settlements in terms of a base-board. The map placed on the base-board locates hypothetical areas of variation in output of any one of the non hunter-gatherer activities. The variations are shown in the form of painted shells, the height of the shell above the base-board indicating the output of that component in the region immediately below on the map, resembling a diagram of a Fourier transform.

A GENERAL ECOLOGICAL MODEL FOR IRON AGE SETTLEMENT LOCATION

The most striking feature of the Iron Age distribution map is the clustering of settlements in some parts of the map and their absence from other parts of the map. Study of the topography shows that open grassland is generally devoid of sites while the clustering is concentrated on hill slopes or hilltops in the neighbourhood of headwaters of major tributaries to the Vaal and Limpopo rivers.

The hill slope or hilltop location of most of the Iron Age sites leads us to draw the second analogy explaining their location. Detailed study of the ecology of the Melville Koppies Iron Age settlements in Johannesburg by plant, animal and insect ecologists (Mason, 1971) suggests that the Iron Age settlers chose Melville because it may have been a relatively more productive region than the open, lower relief grasslands north and south of Melville in terms of food and technological materials necessary for Iron Age life. We may explain hill slope location at other Iron Age sites by taking Melville as an ecological model. The greater relative productivity of hill slope regions may be one

878

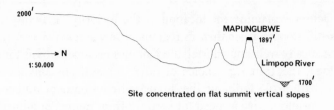

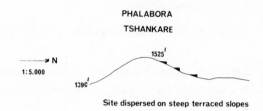

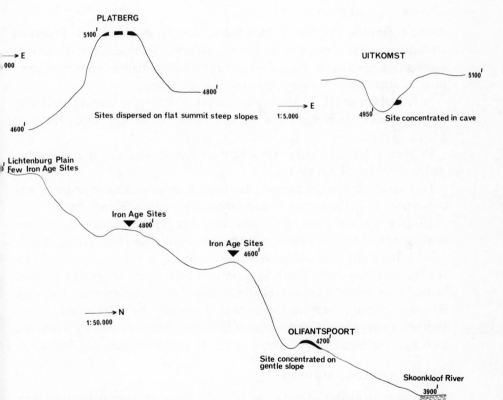

FIG. 22.3. Settlement profiles of Mapungubwe, Phalabora, Platberg, Uitkomst and Olifantspoort.

of the factors explaining the location of the majority of Transvaal Iron Age sites on hill slopes rather than in regions of lower relief. Here, the model of the scientifically well-known Melville Koppies provides a basis for explaining, by analogy, the Iron Age choice of other scientifically unknown hill slope localities within the limits of the Transvaal environment. Other factors for hill slope location, such as need for security from human or animal predators, were superimposed on ecological factors.

SOCIOLOGICAL MODELS FOR EXPLAINING TRANSVAAL IRON AGE SETTLEMENT

Malete law of land and succession to property defines a web of relationships between individuals controlling the use and arrangement of their settlements (Roberts, Campbell and Walker, 1971).

HISTORICAL MODELS

Andrew Smith's analysis of Moselikatse control over western Transvaal terminal Iron Age location of settlements radiating from central settlement at eGabeni, on the Marico river (Kirby, 1940). Smith's analysis is the most complete location model we have and is set out on p. 882.

S. Broadbent and T. L. Hodgson's analysis of Rolong settlement instability during terminal Iron Age tribal wars of 1820s (Broadbent, 1860; Hodgson letters, 1823–5).

D. Hunt's analysis of Iron Age – Pedi settlement instability during conflict within the tribe (Hunt, 1931).

D. Kuper's analysis of terminal Iron Age tribe defending settlements and possessions of salt resources in mid nineteenth century (Kuper, 1969).

J. Mackenzie's account of terminal Iron Age Tswana settlement location in relation to sizes and boundaries between tribal areas (Mackenzie, 1871).

W. J. Burchell's plan and section of Batlapin clay huts in wooden stockades at Lithakong, Kuruman, North Cape, in 1811 finds close analogy with location of clay huts in stone enclosures, Enclosures I–VI, Olifantspoort Iron Age Site, Rustenburg, Transvaal, excavated June–July 1971 (Burchell, 1822). Burchell's model assists explanation of locational processes within a Transvaal Iron Age settlement (see Clarke, Chapter 21 of this volume, and Fig. 1.17).

ARCHAEOLOGICAL MODELS

Archaeological models involve the use of known settlement location data inferred from the excavation of sites for explaining less well-known settlements.

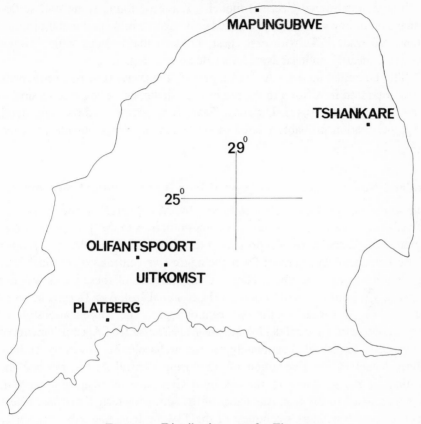

FIG. 22.4. Distribution map for Fig. 22.3.

The Mapungubwe model – sandstone hilltop settlements of the Limpopo valley. The model is Mapungubwe, which may represent many similar settlement location patterns in the Limpopo valley. The network of relationships includes trade with the east coast and the type of food economy represented at Mapungubwe. We do not yet know if the many thousands of Transvaal Iron Age settlements varied significantly in their food economies (Fig. 22.4). Marked social stratification inferred from gold ornaments in later part of Mapungubwe deposit suggests that settlement location may have been related to social class. No direct tribal analogy possible.

The Phalabora model – Isoloted lowveld koppie slope settlements such as Tshankare specialized in metal production, trade links with east coast. Direct tribal analogy possible with Phalabora tribe living in area today – have ancient rituals at Sealeng, traditional seat of tribal chief (Fig. 22.4).

The Kaditshwene (Zeerust) model – Large rambling stone wall settlements on hilltop and hill slope. Mixed economy, farming and metal production. No trade links with east coast. Direct tribal analogy with Tswana tribes in nearby homelands and also Botswana (Fig. 22.4).

The Uitkomst model – At least a part of Transvaal Iron Age settlement was organized in relation to the use of rock shelters as living sites or smelting sites (Mason, 1951). Uitkomst Cave demonstrates a three-stage Iron Age occupation probably related to settlement localities outside the cave (Fig. 22.4).

Andrew Smith model of Transvaal Iron Age settlement location

The early nineteenth-century conquest by Moselikatse of the Transvaal Tswana tribes introduced Nguni settlement practices to the Tswana Iron Age region. Moselikatse himself represents a terminal Iron Age military organizer whose behaviour was derived from the aggressive centralized terminal Iron Age Nguni tribes of northern Natal. The behaviour of these tribes was not necessarily related to the behaviour of the terminal Iron Age Tswana tribes of the western Transvaal, so that we cannot regard the Moselikatse style of settlement location as a model for the pre-Moselikatse Iron Age settlements of the western Transvaal. Fortunately for the archaeologist, however, Andrew Smith, leader of the Expedition for Exploring Central Africa, reached the terminal Iron Age tribes of the northern Cape late in 1834, and early in 1835 he crossed to the Iron Age tribes of the south-western Transvaal, where he observed Moselikatse's conquest of the Tswana Iron Age tribes especially in the Zeerust/Rustenburg area.

Smith's record of the centralized Moselikatse settlement system provides at least one model showing how the dispersal of tributary settlements was related to the military and political policies of a central Iron Age settlement. We quote from A. Smith's Diary (Kirby, 1940):

> (Moselikatse) has a son about fifteen or sixteen years of age; he lives at a kraal apart from his father (and) has charge of it, and all at that kraal are boys of about the same age as himself.
>
> Every year the entire community of boys is collected together and all about ten years of age are turned out and set apart to form a new post. They are told that they have charge of the cattle and are to defend them, though that is not really intended, the kraal being formed between some of the other posts. They are not required when of that age to go on commandoes, but when about sixteen they go out under the charge of an old man,

and when of this age they are said to fight equal to the grown up men. His posts are placed with considerable regularity. His own kraal is nearly in the centre of his country, and then his principal soldiers are placed round him in posts not very distant from each other and no one of them more than an hour's walk from his kraal. At these posts his best cattle and those for breeding are kept; outside of those again are placed posts about nine in number in each direction where he fears the approach of any enemies. Thus in the direction of Kuruman he has eight or nine posts, in the direction in which the Griquas can approach him eight or ten, in the direction of Sabiqua a like number, and in the direction in which Dingan's commando approaches also a number. Each of these divisions have the different kraals so placed that they are within sight of each other. Between each of those posts in the openings he has small Buchuana kraals, but these are within the outer circle so at these outposts the worst cattle are kept. Moselikatse will not eat of stolen cattle; he breeds cattle for his own use. Those taken in commandoes are employed for the people. The kraal where his own cattle are kept is in one of the most secure parts of the country and scarcely any of the people are permitted to go near it, lest by their traces an enemy should discover it. His son has also his own cattle for breeding.

Testing of Iron Age settlement location analogies

Following Copi's analogy criteria the first item for testing analogy is its relevance. The relevance of the model to the archaeological object or site of the analogy must be tested by finding artefacts similar to those associated with the model at the archaeological site, and also the distance in time and space between model and object of analogy cannot be too great. For example, it may be possible to achieve a vital reconstruction of the web of relationships that supported the Iron Age settlement of Kaditshwene by explaining the settlement in terms of a living Tswana settlement, provided the two can be linked by specific resemblances in a wide range of artefacts from pottery styles to architectural details. Of course, analogies could be further tested by discovering oral traditions current in the model settlement concerning the archaeological settlement.

The dispersal of cattle posts away from central settlements indicated by Andrew Smith's Moselikatse model could be archaeologically tested by finding settlements whose architecture indicates specialized cattle enclosure within the region of larger settlements whose architecture indicates more varied functions. We have an Iron Age settlement distribution of this very type at

Olifantspoort south of Rustenburg (Mason, 1962). There are strong contrasts between the grasslands of the Lichtenburg plain on the southern edge of the Olifantspoort area, the Bankenveld acacia hillocks of Olifantspoort itself and the bushveld of the plateau basin to the north of Olifantspoort. Iron Age settlements of complex layout lie on the slopes of the Bankenveld and were probably the central settlements to more simple Iron Age structures, probably cattle posts, a few kilometres to the south on the edge of the Lichtenburg plain gasslands. Excavations are now being made to test the relationship between the presumed satellite cattle posts and the central settlements.

Regional and reciprocal specialization between dispersed Iron Age settlements is suggested by the Matluassi Iron Age site whose artefact range and architecture suggests a cattle post. In 1823, T. L. Hodgson recorded the visit of a party of 'Bomanyana' from a settlement five days north of Matluassi, who had arrived with a load of manufactured metal objects they wished to trade with the Matluassi Rolong who did not produce metal but herded cattle and hunted wild animals. The Matluassi area on the southern edge of the Lichtenburg plain probably represented an Iron Age region specializing in animal products and exchanging these for metals processed in the Olifantspoort area on the northern edge of the Lichtenburg plain.

Further social and economic interdependence between these Iron Age settlement localities is indicated by S. Broadbent's account of the receipt of a beautiful young girl from one of the Iron Age settlements five days north of Matluassi by Sifonello, chief of the Matluassi Rolongs.

Conclusion

A very large-scale programme of careful excavation and isotope dating on an intensive regional basis is necessary to reveal the network of inter-site relationships we require for an adequate archaeological measurement of Iron Age settlement in the Transvaal. The thin catalogue of location models discussed in the present paper could be strengthened by field work among surviving tribes on the periphery of the Iron Age settlement areas and study of archival papers.

References

BROADBENT, S. (1865) *Narrative of the Introduction of Christianity Among the Bechuana Tribes.* London: Wesleyan Mission Society.

BURCHELL, W. J. (1822) *Travels in Interior of Southern Africa.* London: Longmans.

CAMPBELL, J. (1822) *Travels in South Africa.* London.

CHORLEY, R. J. and HAGGETT, P. (1967) *Models in Geography.* London: Methuen.

COPI, I. M. (1961) *Introduction to Logic*. New York: Macmillan.

HARRÉ, R. (1967) *An Introduction to the Logic of the Sciences*. London: Macmillan.

HODGSON, T. L. (1822–30 ?) *Letters to the Wesleyan Mission Society*. London: Methodist Mission Society.

HUNT, D. R. (1931) The Bapedi. *Bantu Studies*, 5 (4), 275–326.

KIRBY, P. (1940) *The Diary of Dr Andrew Smith 1834–36*. vol. 2. Cape Town: Van Riebeck Society.

KUPER, D. (1969) *The Eastern Transvaal Maatschappij, 1847–48*. Ph.D. thesis, University of Witwatersrand, Johannesburg.

MACKENZIE, J. (1871) *Ten Years North of the Orange River*. Edinburgh: Edmonston and Douglas.

MASON, R. J. (1951) Excavations of four caves near Johannesburg. *South African Archaeological Bulletin*, 6, (23), 71.

MASON, R. J. (1962) *Prehistory of the Transvaal*. Johannesburg: Witwatersrand University Press.

MASON, R. J. (1965) Origin of South African society. *South African Journal of Science*, 61 (7), 255–67.

MASON, R. J. (1968) South African Iron Age and present-day Venda architecture and pottery from the northern Transvaal, South Africa. *African Studies*, 27 (4), 181–3.

MASON, R. J. (1968) Transvaal and Natal Iron Age settlement revealed by aerial photography and excavation. *African Studies*, 27, (4) 167–80.

MASON, R. J. (1971) *The Archaeology and Human Ecology of Melville Koppies Nature Reserve, Johannesburg*. Occasional Papers of the Witwatersrand Department of Archaeology No. 6.

MOFFAT, R. (1841) *Missionary Labours and Scenes in South Africa*. London.

PETERSON, N. (1971) Open sites and the ethnographic approach to the archaeology of hunter-gatherers. In MULVANEY, D. J. and GOLSON, J. (eds.) *Aboriginal Man and Environment in Australia*. Canberra: Australian National University Press.

ROBERTS, S., CAMPBELL, A. C. and WALKER, J. M. (1971) *The Malete Law of Family Relations, Land and Succession to Property*. Gaborone: Government Printer.

SHAW, W. (1836) *Memoirs of Mrs Ann Hodgson*. London: Mason.

SMITH, A. (1940) *The Diary of Dr Andrew Smith 1834–6*. Vol. 2, No. 21. Capetown: Van Riebeck Society.

SMITH, E. W. (1957) *Great Lion of Bechuanaland*. London: Independent Press.

THUCYDIDES (1954) *The Peloponnesian War*. Harmondsworth: Penguin Books.

23

Locational models and the study of Romano-British settlement

I. R. HODDER

University of London, England

'All that is of importance in archaeology has been known since the beginning of this century. This applies not only to the methods and theory . . . but also to the results' (Neustupný, 1971, p. 35). This statement represents a rather extreme viewpoint, perhaps, but it does at least focus attention on the very real paucity of interpretative concepts in the subject. One means of widening the range of concepts is to 'make use of all the other knowledge that has been obtained up to now in all the other branches of social science' (Neustupný, 1971, p. 38). Models that have been developed and tested in other fields offer a systematic way of applying non-archaeological information to archaeological problems. By using them predictively, hypotheses may be suggested which might otherwise not have been considered by the archaeologist. One of the most important characteristics of models, indeed, is their predictive or suggestive value, and any promising model should have 'implications rich enough to suggest novel hypotheses and speculations in the primary field of investigation' (Black, 1962, pp. 232–3).

Yet if models are to be used, it is important to clearly define and separate the stages of procedure and to realize the limitations of each stage. In this way confusion and mistrust may to some extent be avoided. For example, a basic distinction is that between model and theory as procedural stages. 'Models . . . constitute a bridge between the observational and theoretical levels' (Haggett and Chorley, 1967, p. 24). They are simply aids to the construction of new theories concerning observed information, and more than one model may appear to fit the same data equally well. The predicted theories or hypotheses, on the other hand, must be testable by reference to known or knowable facts. If, due to the limitations of the data, it cannot ever be tested, then a hypothesis cannot be considered useful. Examination of a hypothesis may result in its retention, modification or rejection (Clarke, 1968, p. 643). A further result of the application of models is that a certain amount of 'feedback' may occur. For example, it may be found desirable to gather new types of information or to stress rather different problems. Another sort of feedback is that new information might be learned about the models themselves and possible modifications suggested.

In the following discussion an attempt is made, first, to argue that the predictive value of models may in certain cases be especially useful to the archaeologist; and this is illustrated by applying certain spatial models to the study of Romano-British settlement. A second aim is to illustrate the procedural stages from observed fact to applied model to testable hypothesis and to feedback information, again as part of a locational analysis of Romano-British settlement.

Procedure A[1]:

THE OBSERVED INFORMATION

The study summarized here is concerned with the walled towns of Roman Britain, as shown on the *Map of Roman Britain* (Ordnance Survey, 1956) but with the addition of more recent material. It is limited to the third and early fourth centuries A.D., and to the Romanized south-east of the province corresponding to the 'lowland zone' as defined by Fox (1943). In the first procedure, special attention is paid to the road system linking the major centres.

THE MODEL AND ITS APPLICABILITY

The first model to be applied is central place theory as developed by Christaller (1933). A fuller introductory account than that given here may be found in Berry (1967) and Haggett (1965).

Central place theory involves two important concepts (Morrill, 1970, p. 61):

(i) Even in simple agrarian societies, certain sections demand products or services that they do not provide for themselves. Service centres are necessary for the circulation and exchange of these products. For example, specialized goods may be distributed through local centres or markets to the dispersed population, in exchange for food and craft industrial products needed by the larger, more nucleated centres. Other services that may have to be distributed may be grouped under the headings of administration, military protection and religious control. Service centres can therefore be seen as a necessary part of the efficient organization of societies.

(ii) A second important factor is effort minimization. The effort in obtaining services of the type mentioned above is much reduced if the services are

888

agglomerated within one centre, which is located centrally within a roughly circular service or tributary area. Such a system is not only more efficient for the consumers whose maximum travelling distance is minimized by a circular trading area; but by being centrally located, the traders in the service centre can also be sure of the maximum possible trade. By being agglomerated within one centre the traders receive further benefits: 'a person coming to town for one purpose is likely, by the proximity of additional services, to use some of these services as well' (Morrill, 1970, p. 62). For certain activities or services, however, there is not sufficient demand to support their functioning at the level of the local market. These more specialist services are therefore provided by the larger centres spaced at greater intervals, again within roughly circular trade areas. Thus a hierarchy of service centres exists with the higher ranking centres containing a greater range of service functions. 'Central places are important . . . for the support of the economy. Since they exist to serve a local population, they are so located that a regular structure of markets is formed. Since the demand for goods varies, the spatial structure becomes a hierarchical one as well' (Morrill, 1970, p. 78).

Christaller's central place theory combines the above features of service provision and effort minimization with simple lattice packing theory, to suggest an idealized pattern of settlement. Assuming an isotropic or featureless plain with even population density, a triangular arrangement of centres, each surrounded by an hexagonal tributary area, has the most efficient geometric characteristics, as demonstrated by Haggett (1965, p. 49). Christaller also proposed that the hierarchy would be made up of levels or tiers recognizably distinct from each other. Within this horizontal and vertical framework a number of different patterns may exist. Most relevant to the present discussion is the $k=4$ transport principle in which, due to the importance of lines of communication within the economic landscape, centres are placed at the midpoints of the roads linking larger centres (Fig. 23.1*b*). They are thus dependent on two larger centres rather than three, as with the marketing principle (Fig. 23.1*a*).

Although Christaller's central place theory has been found to fit certain evidence fairly closely (Skinner, 1964), many modifications of the theory have been made to bring it more in line with the greater mass of empirical data derived from subsequent studies. Certain of these modifications will be considered later, but the first model to be applied to Romano-British settlement is the 'pure' transport principle of Christaller. Although 'searches for such patterns are naive' (Morrill, 1970, p. 72), it is the various characteristics of spatial behaviour that underlie the model that are really being considered. Certainly 'no one expects an ideal case to be found anywhere in the real world' (Berry and Pred, 1961, p. 6). In Roman Britain, however, there are reasons for expecting the model to fit rather more closely than in most recent and modern settlement distributions.

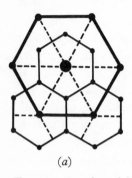 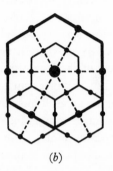

| (a) | (b) |

FIG. 23.1. Two patterns of spatial organization according to Christaller. (*a*) The $k = 3$ marketing principle. (*b*) The $k = 4$ transport principle.

For example, in many contemporary settlement patterns, factors such as the location of resources and of processing activities, or ease of movement provided by modern transport, have caused considerable distortion to any underlying regularities that might exist. In lowland Roman Britain in the third century A.D., on the other hand, the security supplied by Rome's empire allowed the peaceful existence and development of settlements with a simple 'traditional agrarian' economy. It might be expected that here, therefore, the level of distortion would be low enough to allow the recognition of the basic tenets of the model in its unmodified form. It is only in upland Britain that continuously troublesome tribes and a difficult terrain resulted in the imposition by Rome of an artificial pattern based on military and strategic considerations.

Another advantage in using the Roman British material is concerned with the definition of hierarchical levels. In modern examples a hierarchy can usually be identified (Garner, 1967, p. 325; Berry and Pred, 1961, p. 6). However, variation within each level tends to blur any clear-cut steps, which might otherwise have been visible, thereby approximating to a continuum (Vining, 1953). Thus 'in practice, more or less arbitrary divisions have to be made' (Haggett, 1965, p. 124). In Roman Britain, on the other hand, there is some basis for the objective definition of hierarchical levels. Highest in rank was the administrative, economic and social centre of the tribal area – the 'civitas capital'. These major walled centres can be clearly identified with the aid of literary and epigraphic evidence, and can be seen as distinct from a second level – the lesser walled towns. In reference to the walling of towns, 'it is becoming clear that every place of any political or commercial importance in Britain was so treated' (Rivet, 1964, p. 63). It seems reasonable to assume, therefore, that the presence of walls around centres that were not major centres (civitas capitals) may be used as a criterion for the definition of a second hierarchical level. The acreage enclosed by the walls may also be a useful criterion of rank (Pounds, 1969). The identification of these second level centres must rely wholly on the archaeological excavation of the town walls, and it is almost certainly the case that several have yet to be found, while the published evidence for others (Dorn and Worcester, for example) remains unsatisfactory. However, it seems unlikely that further identification will significantly alter the overall geographical pattern.

Evidence for unwalled centres is much less reliable. It is probable that a large number of these have yet to be identified, while many may not have survived at all. They have been divided on the *O.S. Map of Roman Britain* into 'other major settlements' and 'minor settlements', and, although this distinction is only subjective, it can be supported by the application of models (Procedure C). The unwalled settlements are at least 'distinct from the smaller native farms and hamlets' (Ordnance Survey, 1956, p. 10).

One type of site – the Roman colony – has not as yet been discussed because it is not in clear hierarchical relation to the above classes of site. The colonies consisted of settlements of Roman citizens – often veterans from the Roman legions – to which a certain amount of surrounding territory was allotted. Their identification is based on good literary and archaeological evidence, but it is difficult both to define precisely their relative hierarchical level, and to determine whether they acted as service centres in the same way as other walled towns.

Thus on the whole there are features of the Roman British material that make it especially favourable for the application of the unmodified Christaller model. It would be difficult, on the other hand, to apply rather more complex central place theories, such as that of Lösch (1954), because of the relatively simple and restricted nature of the evidence.

The applicability of the model was further investigated by examining the possibility of non-randomness in the distribution of walled towns. This was achieved by a nearest neighbour analysis. As outlined by Clark and Evans (1954), nearest neighbour analysis is a method of defining the spatial characteristics of a distribution of points, based on the distances from each point

891

to its nearest neighbour. The observed mean distance to nearest neighbour ($\bar{r}A$) is related to the mean distance to nearest neighbour expected in a random distribution of the same density ($\bar{r}E$), and the resulting value R is the nearest neighbour statistic ($R = \bar{r}A/\bar{r}E$). If $R = 0$ the distribution is fully agglomerated, if $R = 1$ it could have been produced by chance, and if $R = 2.1491$ it is perfectly uniform. In this study, the coastal and peripheral areas of lowland Britain were not included in the analysis, since 'the presence of a boundary beyond which measurements cannot be made will tend to make the value of $\bar{r}A$ greater than would be obtained if an infinite area were involved' (Clark and Evans, 1954, p. 450). The results of this analysis for Romano-British walled towns were as follows:[2]

A (area)	$= 367 \text{ cm}^{2\,2}$
N (number)	$= 25$
p (density $n - 1/A$)	$= 0.0653$
$\bar{r}A$	$= 2.644$ cm
$\bar{r}E$	$= 1.957$ cm
R	$= 1.351$
$\sigma_{\bar{r}}E$ (standard error of $\bar{r}E$)	$= 0.2046$
c (standard variate of the normal curve)	$= 3.352$

The chance of a greater difference between $\bar{r}A$ and $\bar{r}E$ is therefore 0.069%, using the Pearson type III distribution as suggested by Clark and Evans (1954, p. 448) for small samples. This result indicates that statistically it is highly probable that the relative spacing of walled towns in the area chosen for the analysis is not random, but suggests rather that some inter-site relationship does exist. Further, the R value shows that this relationship tends towards mutual repulsion and uniform spacing.

The identification of a non-random pattern to some extent justifies the application of locational models. If no distinction could be made by the nearest neighbour analysis between the observed and a random pattern, then it would be necessary to consider possible distorting factors such as incomplete site identification or site destruction before applying locational models, since these assume the observed pattern to be at least fairly representative of the original distribution.

APPLICATION OF THE MODEL

The spatial arrangement of walled towns, and in particular their relationship to the road system linking the major centres, has been idealized into the pattern reproduced in Fig. 23.2. The precise steps by which this was reached have been explained elsewhere (Hodder and Hassall, 1971), but the correspondence to the real distribution may be assessed visually by comparison with Fig. 23.3. The idealized pattern shows that the relationship between the major centres and the smaller walled towns corresponds broadly to the $k=4$ transport principle as envisaged by Christaller. Smaller centres lie midway between and are dependent on two rather than three larger centres as would be the case in a landscape corresponding to the marketing principle. That the $k=4$ pattern is found emphasizes the undoubted importance of well-maintained metalled roads in Roman Britain.

TABLE 23.1. *Key to sites in Figs. 23.2–23.10*

1	Buxton	15	Irchester	29	Dorchester (Oxon.)
2	Lincoln	16	Godmanchester	30	Silchester
3	Ancaster	17	Cambridge	31	London
4	Castle Hill	18	Great Chesterford	32	Rochester
5	Wroxeter	19	Braughing	33	Ilchester
6	Wall	20	Caerwent	34	Winchester
7	Leicester	21	Gloucester	35	Chichester
8	Great Casterton	22	Cirencester	36	Bitterne
9	Water Newton	23	Alchester	37	Dorchester (Dorset)
10	Kenchester	24	St Albans	38	White Walls
11	Droitwich	25	Colchester	39	Sandy Lane
12	Alcester	26	Gatcombe	40	Wanborough
13	Chesterton	27	Bath	41	Asthall
14	Towcester	28	Mildenhall		

PREDICTED HYPOTHESES AND THEIR EXAMINATION

The relative positions of the centres within the network allow a number of predictions that can be related to known evidence.

(i) Water Newton (9) is normally classed as a smaller walled town, yet its relative position in the pattern predicts that it should be considered more as a major centre. This is borne out by the archaeological evidence. In terms of the acreage enclosed within its walls (44 acres), Water Newton is the largest of the smaller walled towns, and is in fact larger than, or as large as, several of the civitas capitals (Caister St Edmunds, Brough of Humber and Caerwent). Also, 'that is was the centre of the flourishing pottery industry that goes by the name of "Castor" there can be no doubt' (Corder, 1956, p. 40). It is 'the obvious centre for the potters of the Nene valley' (Todd, 1970, p. 128).

Even more convincing evidence for the importance of Water Newton exists. It is known from literary sources that several of the smaller walled towns were at some time given the status of civitas capitals. A milestone with the mileage figure 'I' found at Water Newton has been suggested as indicating that this was a centre from which mileages in the surrounding area were measured.

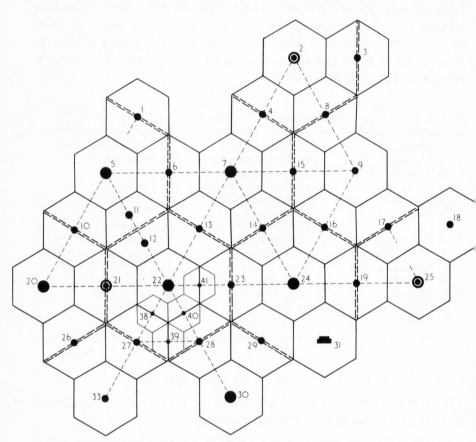

FIG. 23.2. The pattern of Romano-British settlement in diagrammatic form according to the transport principle of Christaller.

'This, coupled with the town's size and economic importance, suggests that here we have a likely candidate' for a 'civitas' centre equivalent in status to the major centres (Rivet, 1964, p. 135).

(ii) The position of Ilchester (33) in the pattern shown in Fig. 23.2 also predicts that it should be of greater importance than a smaller walled town.

It is thus of great interest that available epigraphic evidence indicates that Ilchester, too, seems to have been raised in status to the level of a major centre.

(iii) As already mentioned, the position of the colonies in the settlement hierarchy is not clear. This is emphasized in Fig. 23.2, in that although Lincoln (2) and Colchester (25) seem to be ranked similarly to the major centres, the

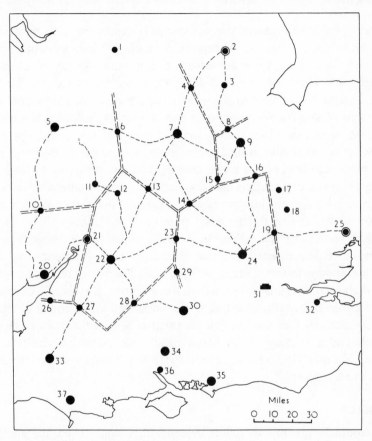

FIG. 23.3. The application of elements of Fig. 23.2 to the real distribution of Romano-British walled towns.

relative position of the colony at Gloucester (21) would suggest that it was of lesser status. Such a predicted difference in rank is supported by the known evidence for the size of the walled areas of these centres. Lincoln (97 acres) was well within the size range of the civitas capitals, while Colchester (108 acres), functioning as the tribal centre of the Trinovantes, had always been of considerable size. Gloucester (about 43 acres), however, was not much larger than some of the lesser walled towns such as Great Chesterford (37 acres). It seems likely that 'Glevum [Gloucester] was to a certain extent eclipsed by the growth of the neighbouring tribal centre of Cirencester' (Rivet, 1964, p. 139). It is notable that such an indistinct hierarchical position should occur with the only major type of settlement which was imposed on Britain by Rome.

Other predictions cannot be satisfactorily tested by known evidence, although in theory they are susceptible to testing. Three examples may be mentioned here. First, there is evidence to the south and east of Cirencester that the pattern can be extended down the hierarchy to include the 'other major settlements'. The prediction that the same is true in the rest of the study area must await further survey and excavation. Secondly, the apparent relevance of central place theory suggests that the reason for the greater prosperity of the smaller walled towns as opposed to other centres of settlement below the level of the major centres, was due primarily to their functioning as service centres. It is true that their initial positioning may sometimes have been related to the location of early forts to which settlement was attracted. Yet many fort sites did not develop into independent townships. It seems that their importance was rather more closely related to their relative position within the settlement lattice, so that ultimately 'their prosperity was due to normal economic factors' (Frere, 1967, p. 240). Further evidence, however, is needed about the origins and growth of these centres. Finally, the existence of a vertical hierarchy corresponding to the horizontal arrangement of sites has been established. This implies that the range of service functions to be found in each centre increases with hierarchical rank. Although there is some evidence for this (Hodder and Hassall, 1971), much more specific information needs to be collected.

FEEDBACK

(i) It would be possible to collect evidence that would allow the above hypotheses to be tested. In particular it is important to know more about the pattern of settlement below the level of the walled centres. Information could also be gained about changes through time, if comparisons with the Iron Age and post-Roman settlement distributions could be made. Truly prehistoric distribution patterns are of course much less susceptible to the application of specific locational models, but since a regular pattern of settlement has been established at one period in time, it may be possible to identify and compare earlier differences. This possibility must await further study, but at least

896

the application of the model has suggested lines along which such a problem might be considered.

(ii) Procedure A has also helped to provide information about the model itself. For example, it seems that in the absence of distorting factors in a simple agrarian society, the classical central place pattern may correspond quite closely to the observed distribution (see also Skinner, 1964). However, as shown in Figs. 23.2 and 23.3, the pattern cannot be successfully followed into coastal areas such as East Anglia. In fact there seems to be a central inland area where central place theory is relevant, contrasting with a periphery where the pattern is distorted. Christaller's central place theory was indeed only conceived as an inland model, and the areas where it has been studied, such as southern Germany (Christaller, 1933) and northern China (Skinner, 1964), do not include coastal areas. It is not immediately clear, however, how the model should be modified to include such areas.

Procedure B

THE OBSERVED INFORMATION

This consists of the same distribution of walled towns in inland lowland Britain. However, in this procedure the road pattern is not considered, emphasis being placed rather on the relative spatial location of the towns.

THE MODEL AND ITS APPLICABILITY

The model of central place location to be used in this procedure is a modification of the classical model already described. In Christaller's view a particular range of services is provided to tributary areas of constant size regardless of the hierarchical rank of the service centre. Thus in Fig. 23.1 the smaller hexagons around both the major and minor centres are of the same size. Kolb and Brunner (1946), on the other hand, have suggested that the size of the tributary area to which one range of goods is provided will vary with the size of the service centre (Fig. 23.4). 'The aggregate of all services provided by the higher centre attracts people from a greater distance and reduces the lower centres' areas even in those primary and secondary services in which they duplicate the higher centre' (Brush, 1953, p. 392). Thus 'the smaller centres are not likely to develop as close to large centres as they are to one another' (Brush, 1953, p. 393). As Morrill (1970, p. 69) has pointed out, this model corresponds rather better than does Christaller's to the empirical evidence. For example, the tributary areas around rural service centres in southwestern Wisconsin (Fig. 23.5) were identified by examining the direction of greatest traffic flow (Brush, 1953). This showed quite clearly both that larger

897

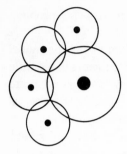

Fig. 23.4. An alternative pattern of spatial organization.

Fig. 23.5. Service areas of higher order and lower order settlement centres in south-western Wisconsin (after Brush and Bracey, 1955).

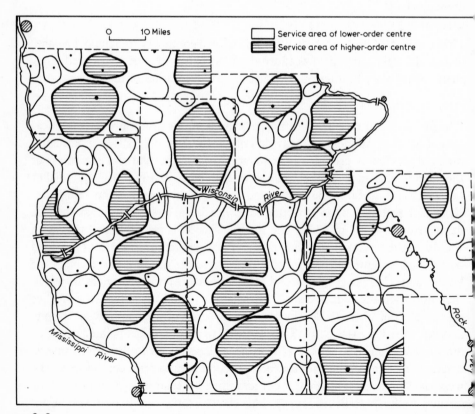

centres had larger service areas than smaller centres, and that the smaller centres were distributed around the larger centres in a pattern corresponding to the present model (Fig. 23.4). The blank areas in Fig. 23.5 were occupied by a lower level in the hierarchy. A similar pattern of settlements has been noted by Bracey (1956) in rural southern England (see Fig. 24.18).

The applicability of this model to Romano-British settlements was examined by constructing Thiessen polygons (Haggett, 1965, p. 247) around

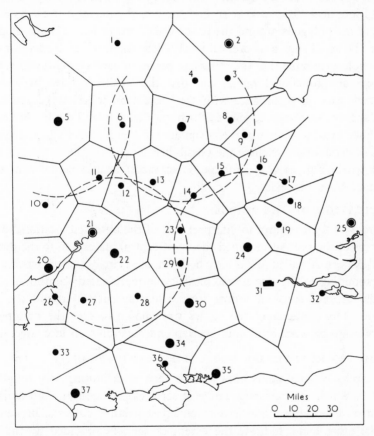

FIG. 23.6. Thiessen polygons constructed around the Romano-British walled centres.

the walled centres (Fig. 23.6). They are produced by drawing perpendiculars at the midpoints of lines joining adjacent centres. Given the observed distribution of sites, the polygons can be interpreteted as indicating the areas that might have been served by each centre. One of the assumptions made in

899

doing this, as noted above in the case of Christaller's central place theory, is that the power of each centre to attract people and business from the surrounding area is the same regardless of hierarchical rank. There are elements within the pattern that suggest that this is not the case. For example, the mean distance between the smaller walled towns (21·5 miles) is considerably less than that between the smaller walled towns and the major centres (32 miles). In effect, the smaller centres are simply clustering as far away from the larger centres as possible, as is emphasized in Fig. 23.6 by their relation to the broken arcs of identical radius drawn around some of the major centres. As a result most of the polygons around the lesser walled towns have a rather elongated shape. To avoid such a theoretically inefficient shape of service area, it seems reasonable to assume that the attractive power of each centre does vary with its rank and functional range, and that the smaller centres have smaller tributary areas in accordance with the present model. However, in certain cases at least, an elongated shape of tributary area around the smaller centres may have existed in view of the advantages of being near to the main arterial roads. This does not exclude the possibility of smaller tributary areas, since, as shown in Fig. 23.5, a combination of the elongated shape with smaller tributary areas may exist.

APPLICATION OF THE MODEL

Figure 23.7 is an attempt to interpret part of the observed locational pattern in terms of the present modified theory of central places. On to the distributional pattern of walled towns have been imposed circles of two constant sizes, corresponding to the two hierarchical levels represented (continuous lines). Broken arcs of constant radius were also constructed around the major centres. The diameter of the circles was chosen to give the best possible compromise between minimum overlap and maximum surface coverage.

PREDICTED HYPOTHESES AND THEIR EXAMINATION

The circles of continuous lines may be seen as delimiting very roughly the areas to which the particular range of services provided by both major and minor walled centres might have extended. The larger circles of broken lines, on the other hand, indicate the extent of services provided by the major centres only. However, what exactly these two ranges of services might have consisted of cannot be accurately gauged from known evidence. Theatres and amphitheatres are indeed largely confined to the major centres, and the broken circles may indicate the range of this social service. Tax collection, on the other hand, may have been centred on both the major centres and the lesser walled towns as indicated by the circles with continuous lines.

There is little evidence, however, that would allow the boundaries of tributary areas to be fixed empirically. Figure 23.8 shows the distribution of certain types of stamped tiles in the Gloucestershire and Wiltshire area. The distribution of these tiles, on which the names of the makers or the controlling authorities have been stamped, may be taken as an example of the service area around a given centre, and certainly there does appear to be some

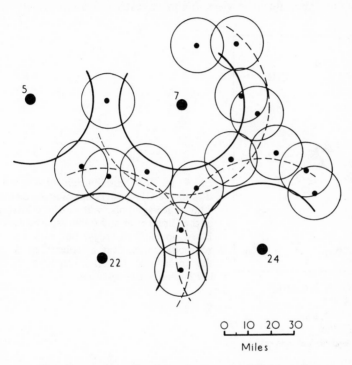

FIG. 23.7. Service areas predicted for the Romano-British walled centres.

tendency towards discrete groupings, indicating the extent of distribution of a comparatively local product. More specialized products and services, on the other hand, were provided by the major centres alone. An example of this type of distribution is given by D. J. Smith (1969). His examination of fourth-century mosaics in rich villas led to the conclusion that there is a 'tendency for certain subjects and themes to appear more or less localized' so that groups of related mosaics can be identified. 'Each group is characterized by features which are not found, or are found significantly less often or in a significantly different form, elsewhere' (D. J. Smith, 1969, p. 95). Smith suggests that this indicates 'schools' of mosaicists with their workshops at, for example, Cirencester (22)

901

and Dorchester (Dorset) (37). This is obviously a much more specialized service than the production of tiles, and as a result the distribution is much wider (Fig. 23.9), corresponding roughly to the extent of the tributary areas of the major centres as predicted in Fig. 23.7 (broken arcs). There is thus some empirical evidence that two distinct levels of trade provision existed: major centres providing specialist services to a wide area, and smaller centres providing less specialized services to a more restricted area.

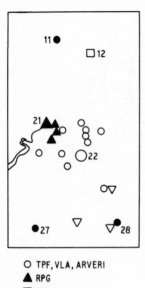

O TPF, VLA, ARVERI
▲ RPG
▽ IVC, DIGNI
□ TCD
● Other walled towns

FIG. 23.8. The distribution of stamped tiles in the Gloucestershire-Wiltshire area. The larger symbols indicate the positions of the Cirencester and Gloucester centres. Based on Clifford (1955) but with recent additional finds, over a wider area, from the annual reports on inscriptions from the *Journal of Roman Studies*.

FEEDBACK

Although the above evidence supports, in a general way, the predictions that have been made, Figs. 23.8 and 23.9 really serve to emphasize the present inadequacy of the data, since the samples, especially those of the stamped tiles, are too small to allow any definite conclusions to be drawn. It is only as more material becomes available that the predicted hypothesis about the size of tributary areas (Fig. 23.7) will be able to be fully tested. A further implication concerns the model itself. In Procedures A and B two models – which are in certain aspects contradictory – were applied to the same data with equally satisfactory results. This was possible because in each case different facets were emphasized. In Procedure A special attention was paid to the road pattern, and in Procedure B to the relative spacing of the towns. It is important, therefore, not to assume that only one model is 'right' for any one group of material. If the range of relevant models is left unexploited, then not only is there a limit to the potential amount of information that may be derived

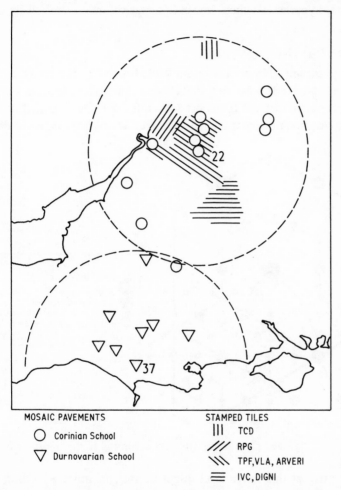

MOSAIC PAVEMENTS	STAMPED TILES
◯ Corinian School	||| TCD
▽ Durnovarian School	/// RPG
	\\\ TPF,VLA, ARVERI
	≡ IVC, DIGNI

FIG. 23.9. The distribution of certain types of mosaic pavements (D. J. Smith, 1969) and stamped tiles. The figure has been drawn to the same scale as Figs. 23.3, 23.6 and 23.7.

from the data, but the information that is obtained may be misleading. Whenever possible it is preferable to examine the applicability of a number of models to the same observed information (see p. 4).

Procedure C

The third example to be given here is much less satisfactory than in the above two cases, because both the observed information and the model itself are less acceptable. It is included in this study because it does allow the formulation of additional hypotheses which, however tentative, may be tested by further work.

THE OBSERVED INFORMATION

The average distance between adjacent walled towns in the study area is 26 miles. It was noted in Procedure A that there is some evidence to the south and east of Cirencester that the transport principle could be extended down the hierarchy to include the major unwalled centres. If this is the case, the distance

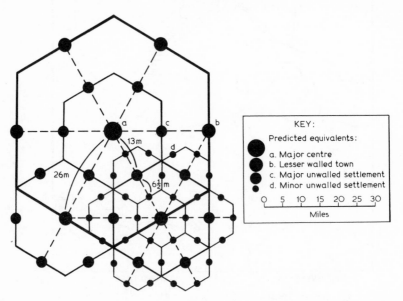

FIG. 23.10. The idealized pattern of settlement according to the transport principle.

between centres at this lower level might average 13 miles according to the geometric properties of the pattern (Fig. 23.10). This figure is only intended to give a very rough indication of the type of distance that might have been involved.

THE MODEL

The model in this case relates to commonsense considerations about the most efficient maximum distance that can be travelled to and from the local market.

In rural societies without mechanical means of transport, the maximum distance that is usually preferred is in the range of 2–4 miles. Above this distance, the effort involved in getting to market outweighs the advantages gained. But below 2–4 miles – that is about 6 miles between markets – the markets are so close together that the population cannot ensure enough trade for each market to continue. Thus there is a rough average figure of 6 miles which combines movement minimization with simple market economics to provide the most efficient distance between local markets (see Figs. 25.9–11).

There is considerable evidence for this figure. For example, a twelfth-century law forbade the setting up of markets within $6\frac{2}{3}$ miles of each other (Humbert de Romans). Also, in East Anglia, 'the *maximum* range of influence of the medieval market was about 6 miles. . . . The actual market area, however, rarely reached this limit' (Dickinson, 1932, p. 22). Dickinson in fact found that circles of four miles radius around each market gave the best compromise between circle overlap and land cover. Again, an important study by Brush and Bracey (1955) compared the distribution of centres in rural southern England – from Somerset to Oxfordshire and Hampshire – and in south-western Wisconsin. In spite of marked differences of population density and economic functions between the two areas, the distances between members of the hierarchical tiers were remarkably similar. Higher order centres were 21 miles apart, lower order centres 8–10 miles apart, and the smallest service centres 4–6 miles apart from each other and from centres of higher order. Brush and Bracey stressed that they were only considering the rural service functions of the centres, and suggested that the present pattern in the two areas is based largely on the situation prior to modern transport. 'During mediaeval times there were market towns in southern England, spaced at intervals of four to six miles, that served as rudimentary trade centres, accessible by cart roads from the rural villages within an hour's journey. . . . In the early nineteenth century, before the coming of railways and automotive vehicles, hamlets also developed in Wisconsin at intervals of five to six miles and served as rudimentary trade centres for the farmers living a journey-hour away by wagon roads' (Brush and Bracey, 1955, p. 568).

Further evidence for the spacing of markets has been provided by work in west Africa, where, as indeed may have been the case in Roman Britain, they tend to be periodic. For example, in the belt of Yorubaland in south-west Nigeria in which a regular pattern can be observed, 'the periodic markets are distributed fairly evenly at an average distance of 7·2 miles from each other' (Hodder, 1963, p. 103). A further study of markets in ten areas in west Africa showed that the average distance from a given market to the nearest adjacent market regardless of its day of meeting is 5·5 miles, with a range from 3·1 to 9·4 miles in the ten areas (R. H. T. Smith, 1969). These figures provided by Smith give the average minimum distance rather than the average distance to all adjacent markets that has been considered so far.

Thus there is much evidence that rural local markets are often separated by distances averaging approximately 6 miles, serving an area of 2–4 miles radius. No claim is made here for a universal 'law', since individual measurements may vary for a variety of local reasons. It is, however, possible to suggest a model that states that it is reasonable to assume that approximately these distances will lead to the most efficient and effort-minimizing arrangement of settlements in those rural societies in which other overriding factors, such as difficult terrain, or very low population density, are not at work.

APPLICATION OF THE MODEL

Resulting from the geometric properties of the transport principle pattern, the average distance between the hypothetical locations of the minor unwalled centres is $6\frac{1}{2}$ miles (Fig. 23.10).[3] The actual figure may have been rather less in view of the conclusions reached in Procedure B, but a general correspondence to the optimum distance between markets as predicted by the model is suggested. The empirical figures obtained by Brush and Bracey (1955) for the three lowest levels of service centres in south-western Wisconsin and southern Britain (21 miles, 6–8 miles, and 4–6 miles), are in approximate agreement with the distances between centres at the level of the lesser walled towns (26 miles), and the hypothetical distances at the level of the major unwalled settlements (13 miles), and the minor unwalled settlements ($6\frac{1}{2}$ miles).

PREDICTIONS

A tentative hypothesis might therefore be that the minor unwalled settlements do exist as a separate hierarchical level, as provisionally suggested on the *O.S. Map of Roman Britain*. This hypothesis is based on a commonsense realization that in simple agrarian societies a level of minor centres at approximately 6 mile intervals is necessary, and on the possibility that the minor unwalled settlements of Roman Britain might have been separated by a comparable distance. It is not, however, based on any good empirical evidence concerning their relative locations. There is no justifiable reason, for example, to assume that these minor centres corresponded to the same locational pattern as did the larger centres. Yet by making the hypothesis it is at least possible to collect evidence that would allow its retention, modification or rejection.

It has often been pointed out (Richmond, 1963, p. 91; Rivet, 1964, p. 72) that the spacing of Romano-British settlements along the major roads at least is related to the location of posting stations. Thus the observed average distance between these centres – for example along Watling Street (12 miles) – is taken as the result of the need to change horses at regular intervals. The fact that the 12-mile distance is a multiple of the predicted optimum distance between markets may be suggested as giving a further significance to this figure.

FEEDBACK

There is clearly a need for a much more careful examination of the predicted distinction between major and minor unwalled settlements, both horizontally by better field surveys, and vertically by examining the functional range of each settlement. Further, whether or not the distinction is corroborated by empirical evidence, information will be added to the model itself. Brush and Bracey (1955) have already shown that the basic distance to local market remains constant despite differences in population density, economy and methods of transport. By adding a greater time depth to the model, its applicability can be examined in a greater range of situations.

Summary

The Romano-British pattern of site distribution has been used as a basis for distinguishing procedural stages in the application of locational models. While eschewing any suggestion that such spatial models provide an entirely 'new' or alternative technique for the analysis of early sites, it has been shown that they do provide an additional tool for study and analysis by widening the range of hypotheses that may be formulated. In the present state of archaeological knowledge, however, it is possible to test only a few of the predicted hypotheses, and the need for further work along these lines is clearly indicated.

Notes

1 For greater detail, see Hodder and Hassall (1971).

2 Taken from the *O.S. Map of Roman Britain*, scale 1 : 1 000 000.

3 Similar results published by Hodder and Hassall (1971) are rather less satisfactory, being based on the distances along major roads, rather than on the average distance between sites, as in this study.

References

BERRY, B. J. L. (1967) *The Geography of Market Centers and Retail Distribution.* Englewood Cliffs, N.J.: Prentice-Hall.

BERRY, B. J. L. and PRED, A. (1961) *Central Place Studies.* Philadelphia: Regional Sciences Research Institute, Bibliography Series No. 1.

BLACK, M. (1962) *Models and Metaphors.* New York: Cornell University Press.

BRACEY, H. E. (1956) A rural component of centrality applied to six southern counties in the United Kingdom. *Economic Geography,* **32,** 39–50.

BRUSH, J. E. (1953) The hierarchy of central places in southwestern Wisconsin. *Geographical Review,* **43,** 380–402.

BRUSH, J. E. and BRACEY, H. E. (1955) Rural service centres in southwestern Wisconsin and southern England. *Geographical Review,* **45,** 559–69.

CHORLEY, R. J. and HAGGETT, P. (eds.) (1967) *Models in Geography.* London: Methuen.

CHRISTALLER, W. (1933) *Die zentralen Orte in Suddeutschland.* Jena.

CLARK, P. J. and EVANS, C. E. (1954) Distance to nearest neighbour as a measure of spatial relationships in populations. *Ecology,* **35** (4), 445.

CLARKE, D. L. (1968) *Analytical Archaeology.* London: Methuen.

CLIFFORD, E. M. (1955) Stamped tiles found in Gloucestershire. *Journal of Roman Studies,* **45,** 68–72.

CORDER, P. (1956) The reorganisation of the defences of Romano-British towns in the fourth century. *Archaeological Journal,* **62,** 20.

DICKINSON, R. E. (1932) The distribution and functions of the smaller urban settlements of East Anglia. *Geography,* **17,** 19–31.

FOX, SIR C. (1943) *The Personality of Britain.* New ed. Cardiff: National Museum of Wales.

FRERE, S. S. (1967) *Britannia: A History of Roman Britain.* London: Routledge.

GARNER, B. J. (1967) Models of urban geography and settlement location. In CHORLEY, R. J. and HAGGETT, P. (eds.) *Models in Geography,* 303–60. London: Methuen.

HAGGETT, P. (1965) *Locational Analysis in Human Geography.* London: Arnold.

HAGGETT, P. and CHORLEY, R. J. (1967) Models, paradigms and the new geography. In CHORLEY, R. J. and HAGGETT, P. (eds.) *Models in Geography,* 1–41. London: Methuen.

HODDER, B. W. (1963) *Markets in Yorubaland.* Ph.D. thesis, University of London.

HODDER, I. R. and HASSALL, M. (1971) The non-random spacing of Romano-British walled towns. *Man,* **6** (3), 391–407.

KOLB, J. H. and BRUNNER, E. DE S. (1946) *A Study of Rural Society.* Boston, Mass.: Houghton Mifflin.

LÖSCH, A. (1954) *The Economics of Location.* New Haven, Conn.: Yale University Press.

MORRILL, R. L. (1970) *The Spatial Organisation of Society.* Belmont, Calif.: Wadsworth.

NEUSTUPNÝ, E. (1971) Whither archaeology? *Antiquity,* **45** (177), 34–9.

ORDNANCE SURVEY (1956) *Map of Roman Britain.* 3rd ed. Chessington.

POUNDS, N. J. G. (1969) The urbanisation of the classical world. *Annals of the Association of American Geographers*, **59**, 135.

RICHMOND, I. A. (1963) *Roman Britain*. 2nd ed. London: Cape.

RIVET, A. L. F. (1964) *Town and Country in Roman Britain*. rev. ed. London: Hutchinson.

ROMANS, H. DE (1194–1277) Quoted in THOMAS, M. W. (1957) *Survey of English Economic History*, 64. London: Blackie.

SKINNER, G. W. (1964) Marketing and social structure in rural China. *Journal of Asian Studies*, **24**, 3.

SMITH, D. J. (1969) in RIVET, A. L. F. (ed.) *The Roman Villa in Britain*. London: Hutchinson.

SMITH, R. H. T. (1969) Market periodicity and locational patterns in west Africa. *Tenth International African Seminar*.

TODD, M. (1970) The small towns of Roman Britain. *Britannia*, **1**, 114.

VINING, R. (1953) Delimitation of economic areas: statistical conceptions in the study of the spatial structure of an economic system. *Journal of the American Statistical Association*, **18**, 44–64.

24

Settlement and land use in the prehistory and early history of southern England: a study based on locational models

A. ELLISON and J. HARRISS

University of Cambridge, England

Introduction

The demonstration of 'cultural continuity' is now a fashionable exercise dominating much current writing in British archaeology. But concentration on material culture in isolation has tended to obscure underlying economic and social trends, while at the same time changes in economic organization resulting from purely internal developments have also been ignored. In this paper we try to remedy this situation by analysing the developing pattern of land use in two regions of southern England during the period from about 1500 B.C. to A.D. 1000. The areas chosen for study are the county of Wiltshire and south-central Sussex (Fig. 24.1). The problems were investigated by the use of simple geographical models.

Our approach has partially been influenced by the results of recent research in historical geography. For a long time a considerable body of opinion concerning the origins of medieval field systems in this country relied heavily upon the work of H. L. Gray (1915). Gray classified English field systems on a regional basis for the first time, and explained their origins largely in terms of their supposed association with various groups of invaders entering the British Isles. It was a 'cultural' explanation of their origins. Latterly, however, work in the continental homelands of important invading groups has shown quite convincingly that the classic Three Field System of the Middle Ages did not in fact exist there until the thirteenth century, thus implying that the system developed in parallel in the two areas, and casting doubt on many of the assumptions that have customarily been made concerning the agricultural systems of the post-Roman period in England. Recent writers on this problem (Thirsk, 1964; Baker, 1963) have preferred to explain the evolution of field systems in terms of response to changing demographic and economic circumstances, and not in terms of particular ethnic or cultural origins. Our approach in this study has been to concentrate similarly on underlying factors of subsistence economy.

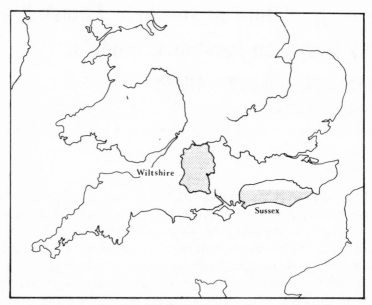

FIG. 24.1. Southern England, showing the areas studied.

In Part I of this study the experiment that we have carried out has been to plot known settlement sites of the Middle and Late Bronze Age, pre-Roman Iron Age, Roman Iron Age and post-Roman Iron Age on maps showing the distribution of land of different economic potential, and to examine the resources contained within the idealized 'catchment areas' of the sites. The evidence available for the reconstruction of settlement distributions consists in the pre-Saxon period of artefact assemblages, and in the Saxon period of place names. For the more detailed analyses of the post-Roman Iron Age settlement distributions in Part II of our study the evidence of burials has also been taken into account, though this has not been used in the earlier periods.

The comparison of maps compiled from such different sets of data is a dangerous procedure and it is the difficulty inherent in this that has led to so much confusion in comparisons of settlement distributions by archaeologists.

The factors affecting the survival of the evidence are different, and whereas the concentration of surviving prehistoric and many Roman sites on the higher Downland, complemented by the lowland distribution of most Saxon settlement sites, has been taken as evidence for a 'valleyward movement' (Fleure and Whitehouse, 1916; Wooldridge and Linton, 1933; Fox, 1932), the fresh evidence of recent years has led Taylor (1972) to observe that 'new material ... indicates that prehistoric and Romano-British people in Britain lived everywhere.' That is to say, in both upland and lowland situations. This subject is discussed in more detail below.

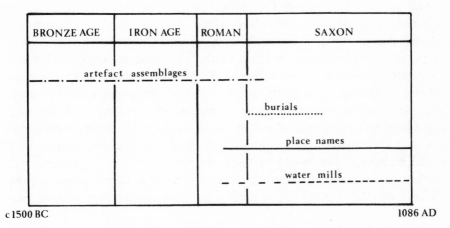

FIG. 24.2. The nature of the evidence used.

However, in the first part of this study we are concerned primarily with the locations of individual sites and with what can be inferred from them, rather than with the overall pattern of settlement. In this way the effects of the bias in the evidence towards upland sites in the pre-Saxon period and towards valley and vale sites in the Saxon phases will be minimized, although it must still be taken into account in interpreting our results. In the post-Roman period the evidence afforded by place names is so much more complete than the artefactual evidence of earlier periods that we feel justified in considering overall settlement patterns as well as the locations of individual sites, and we offer a more detailed study of patterns of settlement expansion in this period in the second part of the paper. Fig. 24.2 illustrates the kinds of evidence that we have used. But first we discuss in some detail the basic operational model that we have used throughout our study.

Part I

THEORY: THE BASIC MODEL

Some of the contemporary interest in theoretical approaches to prehistory derives its inspiration from modern geography, and in particular from Haggett's (1965) valuable synthesis *Locational Analysis in Human Geography*. Clarke refers extensively to the book in his *Analytical Archaeology* (1968), perhaps the most comprehensive attempt that has yet been made to produce a general theory for archaeology; and Renfrew (1969) has gone so far in his belief in the importance of Haggett's work for prehistory as to suggest that it could properly be re-entitled *Locational Analysis in Prehistoric Archaeology*. One of us has already referred elsewhere (Harriss, 1971) to the inherent danger in such sweeping suggestions for the application to prehistory of concepts and techniques worked out in another discipline, the more so when it is apparent that the concepts described in Haggett's book have been worked out almost entirely in the western, capitalist world. This is not to deny that experiment with techniques and ideas of other disciplines is important, for it has only been by dint of extensive experiment, much of it fruitless or even misleading, that 'modern geography' has emerged from the confusion of a belated numeracy. But before prehistorians venture out to experiment with rather sophisticated quantitative models borrowed from geography, we believe that it is worthwhile to explore the most fundamental ideas of locational analysis.

As we have said, most recent work in British archaeology, although showing considerable interest in the subject of 'continuity and change', has not been much concerned with land use or with the exploitation of resources, except in so far as certain assumptions are implicit in statements on settlement distributions. And yet the development of systems of land use is perhaps more fundamentally important than that of settlement distribution *per se*. It has been with the object of exploring this aspect of the problem that we have experimented with a simple locational model of von Thünen type.

The structure of Haggett's book alone hints at the most fundamental principles of locational analysis. The chapters are entitled: 'Movements', 'Networks', 'Nodes', 'Hierarchies' and 'Surfaces'; and the sequence indicates the underlying importance of movement in spatial organization. Settlements show a strong tendency to be located in such a way as to minimize movements, embodying what has been called 'the principle of Least Effort'. Further, the ordering of the chapters helps to make a point which we believe to be of vital importance for archaeologists: that 'settlement sites are not just points on the map, but may be seen rather as the "nodes" of areas of movement'. This is a possibility that seems to have been largely ignored by those who have used or who have attempted to interpret distribution maps. Where settlements in subsistence economies are concerned the movements that are most important are those from the settlement to the fields, rivers, woods and other resources on which the subsistence is based. Chisholm, in Chapter 6 of his book *Rural Settlement and Land Use* (1962), suggests that access to water, arable land, grazing land, fuel and building materials, each of which has a different relative 'pull', tends to determine the location of rural settlements in many parts of the world. Clearly there is a limit to the distance which it is economically worthwhile for members of a group to travel from a settlement to the places from which they derive their living, and that 'limit' effectively defines the area upon which the settlement must depend. It is this very simple, yet rather neglected idea that has suggested the concept of the 'site catchment area', a term coined by Vita-Finzi (1969) to describe the notion of dependence upon resources contained within a limited area about a settlement.

The definition of 'site catchment areas'
Vita-Finzi and Higgs and their collaborators (1970) have shown how 'catchment areas' may be defined by reference to Lee's work on the !Kung bushmen (1969) for groups that depend primarily upon hunting or collecting, and by reference to Chisholm's *Rural Settlement and Land Use* (1962) for agricultural communities. Chisholm has drawn together a large number of examples from a variety of regions, and from the past as well as the present, to show how rapidly intensity of land use decreases with distance from farm to village; and it seems that although 'it is easy to cite extreme cases where plots may be 10 or even 20 km distant from the farmstead' (p. 46), 'the average distance to the cultivated land is commonly of the order of 1 km or more and very commonly rises to 3 or 4 km' (p. 48), but rarely much more. As he says: 'A point which emerges . . . is the frequency with which the same *orders of magnitude* keep on recurring among peoples of widely different technical achievements and inhabiting areas with markedly different physical characteristics. Any distance up to about a kilometre from the dwelling is of such little moment for any but specialized systems of irrigation and garden farming that little adjustment is called for in either the pattern of settlement or of land use. Beyond about one kilometre the costs of movement become sufficiently great to warrant some kind of response; at a distance of 3–4 km the costs of cultivation necessitate a radical modification of the system of cultivation or settlement – for example by the establishment of subsidiary settlements –

though adjustments are apparent before this point is reached. If the distances involved are actually greater than this, then it is necessary to look for some very powerful constraining reason which prevents the establishment of farmsteads nearer the land' (Chisholm, 1962, p. 131).

One of the examples that he quotes, which is of particular relevance to the present study, is taken from the work of Beresford and St Joseph (1958) on 'The spacing of villages' and 'The bounds of villages' in Medieval England. They examined several areas of England and their results 'are consistent with the following proposition. In the process of crystallization into village units, the pattern which evolved and has survived is one that generally ensures a village having all its territory within a compass of 4 km' (Chisholm, 1962, p. 129).

Detached parcels of land belonging to distant parishes are documented in the medieval period, but such 'assarts' in wooded terrain as the 'denes' of the Kentish Weald are characteristic of a transitional phase in a process of colonization, and their existence does not invalidate the concept of a limited area from which the inhabitants of a particular settlement derived their subsistence.

The conclusions of Chisholm and of Beresford and St Joseph might have encouraged us to adopt a radius of 4 km in defining the 'catchment areas' of sites in southern England. However, we have taken a smaller area, that contained within a circle of 2 km radius, as our idealized or 'model' catchment area. As we have seen, all the land that was regularly utilized from one settlement is highly likely to have been within a circle of 4 km radius centred on the settlement, but the settlement is likely to have been located especially close to the most heavily worked land. A nearer limit, for which we have chosen the distance of 2 km, will include these most fully exploited areas. We have already referred to Chisholm's conclusion that the costs of movement become sufficiently great to warrant some kind of response even at a distance of 1 km from the site; and there is some evidence that our value of 2 km does correspond to the average radius of a typical compact medieval parish in southern England. It is further justified by some of the findings that we report in Part II of this paper.

The definition of 'site catchment areas' in this way yet leaves one important methodological problem unanswered. We have spoken of the 'ideal catchment area' as being circular, because a circle describes the most efficient shape for an area of movement. As Haggett explains (1965, pp. 48–50), the regular geometrical shape that most closely retains the advantages of the circle is the hexagon; and the packing of 'circular territories' into a uniform area would produce a regular hexagonal pattern of territories (see Haggett, 1965, fig. 2.10). But in the real world the form of catchment areas such as the estates of farms or villages may be very far from being circular, or hexagonal. A major cause of distortion is topography, and the Israeli experiment with the site catchment model (Vita-Finzi and Higgs, 1970) actually involved measuring access in terms of walking time, in order that distortions due to the rugged topography might be estimated. However, we have not felt that the nature of the topography of the areas of southern England with which we have been concerned is such as to make this kind of compensation essential for the uses to which our model has been put, although account has been taken of it in some cases. Possible distortions of the ideal form because of the localized occurrence of critical resources are likely to be much more significant, and they are given some theoretical discussion by Haggett (1965, pp. 94–5; see especially fig. 4.5, p. 95). Perhaps the most familiar example of the distorted territory known to English students, and certainly one that is especially relevant to our areas, is the characteristic long strip parish of the English Downland.

The parishes of England in fact represent an administrative formalization of the catchment areas of settlements, and are documented at least as far back as the ninth or tenth century A.D. (Addleshaw, 1954). There is some evidence indeed that this ecclesiastical organization reflected land divisions that already existed in the estate boundaries of early Saxon times or even of Roman establishments (Finberg, 1955; Bonney, 1966; Taylor, 1970a, pp. 71–2). Recognition of the fact that parish boundaries very often enclose areas with differing capacities is by no means new, and the distortion of the ideal catchment area into an elongated strip stretching up to the tops of the Downs from the valleys or scarp foot zones was noted by Topley as early as 1870, and has been discussed many times since, as for example by the Orwins for areas in Lincolnshire and Berkshire (Orwin and Orwin, 1954). In his study of the chalkland areas surrounding the Weald of Kent and Sussex Topley (1872) recognized that the strip form meant that each settlement had available to it an area of chalk upland used for pasture, areas of land on the slopes or in the scarp foot zone that were used for arable, and an area of low-lying heavy soil, which might have been forested or in some cases might have been used for meadowland.

The first documentary evidence for parish boundaries occurs in the ninth century, by which time the elongated strip parishes were definitely in existence. However, as we have previously mentioned, there is some evidence that might have suggested that the divisions could be projected back into the

917

very early Saxon period and possibly even into prehistory (see also Clarke, 1968, p. 506). But this seems a dangerous extrapolation, particularly in view of the hypothesis we set out in Part II, which suggests that the irregular village territories only evolved as a result of population increases, and perhaps because of the locational effects of the introduction of the water mill – both at a fairly late stage in the time span with which we are dealing (see also Fig. 24.2).

It is this argument, together with the fact that the results of locational analysis (as they are reported by Haggett) suggest that areas of movement will tend towards circularity, that has encouraged us to persevere with the circle as an idealized representation of reality, providing a simple model of a land use exploitation unit. And both for the sake of uniformity and to allow direct comparisons to be made the use of the model based on the ideal catchment area has here been extended into the early medieval period, even though the actual territories defined by parish boundaries may then have existed.

A classification of land resources
The concept of the 'site catchment area' is not concerned in the first place with the relationship of sites to one another, but with the location of settlements in relation to resources. Having defined 'ideal' or 'model' catchment areas, therefore, the next stage of the analysis is to make some assessment of the potential resources within them. For this purpose we might have used maps of actual land use and made 'corrections' for land usage related to the present economic situation, perhaps by reference to historical accounts such as T. Davis's survey of the agriculture of Wiltshire of 1794. But the Ordnance Survey *Map of Land Classification* of 1944 seemed particularly suitable for our purpose, using as it does 'a broad classification of land according to its general character and inherent quality for agricultural use'. The system is based on the fertility of the soil, on its drainage characteristics, on the relative ease or difficulty with which it is cultivated, and on such factors as slope. These are the characteristics that are reasonably taken into account in trying to assess resources in a historical context. The classification does not in fact relate to a specific set of economic circumstances, as does a map of actual land use, or indeed of land use in 1794, but rather to physical characteristics. In this way we have tried to avoid the pitfalls that would undoubtedly be involved in the attempt to evaluate the 'environmental perception' of Celts, Romans or Saxons.

The key to the 1944 Ordnance Survey map, which was drawn at a scale of 1:625 000 (or about 10 miles to 1 inch) states clearly that the map should not be scaled up, the point being, presumably, that all the boundaries that are shown are really approximations, for very rarely indeed can it be possible to draw a line on a map and say with confidence that the land on one side of it is 'fertile and easily worked' and that that on the other is 'poor and badly drained'. But we feel that this does not negate the value of the map as a framework especially when it is used in conjunction with one inch Ordnance Survey maps in areas of which the workers have personal field experience.

The scheme of classification used for the map involves ten categories of land use potential divided into three major groups. The first of these includes the four categories of 'Good Quality Land', each of which may be suffixed 'A' or 'G' to indicate greater relative suitability for arable or for grassland. Group II includes two categories of 'Medium Quality Land' on which 'productivity is limited by reason of the unfavourable operation of one or more factors – of soil or site, including shallowness or lightness of soil, defective water conditions, etc.' Again these categories are subdivided according to their greater potential for pasture or for cultivation. There remain four categories of 'Poor Quality Land' in Group III: poor quality heavy soils, or light soils, mountain land and areas of shingle, saltmarsh and similar terrain.

The categories of greatest importance in the areas of southern England that we have considered are as follows:

1A First class land with deep, fertile soil. Easily worked loams and silts. Suitable for intensive arable cultivation.

2A Good general purpose farmland. Well-drained soils of good depth and workable for much of the year.

3G First class land but with a high water-table or liable to flooding and so more suitable for grass than for arable cultivation.

4G Good but heavy land, usually on clay. Though the soils are often naturally fertile, they are heavy and cold and difficult to work when too wet or too dry. Thus the period of working is restricted and so is the range of crops.

5A Medium quality light land including land of several types, but soils are usually either shallow or light or both. An example of land of this type is 'Downland', large stretches of which have soils only a few inches deep. The disadvantage of this type of land is frequently the absence of surface water. (5A is 'barley-turnip-sheep land'; 5G is Downland; basic fescue pastures where unploughable.)

6AG Medium quality general purpose farmland, productive but by reason of soil slope or climate not first class. The suffix 'AG' refers to the fact that under present-day circumstances this class of land is used for crops and grass, especially under long leys in western England.

Inspection of the map for Wiltshire (Fig. 24.3) suggests that the distribution of these classes of land is closely dependent upon topography and on surface deposits. Thus the type 3G/4G is found exclusively in the river valleys, in the

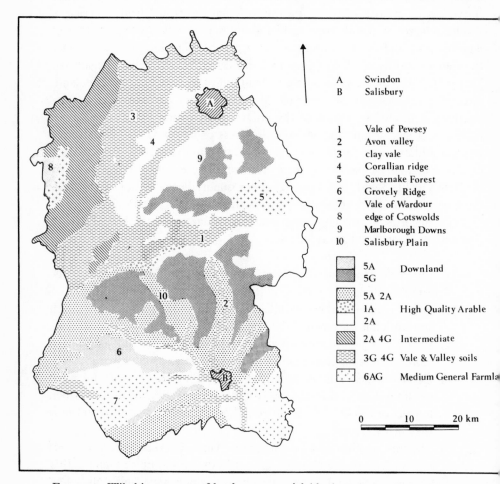

| A | Swindon |
| B | Salisbury |

1	Vale of Pewsey
2	Avon valley
3	clay vale
4	Corallian ridge
5	Savernake Forest
6	Grovely Ridge
7	Vale of Wardour
8	edge of Cotswolds
9	Marlborough Downs
10	Salisbury Plain

5A 5G	Downland
5A 2A 1A 2A	High Quality Arable
2A 4G	Intermediate
3G 4G	Vale & Valley soils
6AG	Medium General Farmla

0   10   20 km

FIG. 24.3. Wiltshire – zones of land use potential (the key also applies to Figs. 24.5, 24.15 and 24.22).

Vale of Pewsey and in the great clay vale that extends across the whole of mid-western Wiltshire; the important category 2A is found on the Corallian limestone ridge that cuts the clay vale, and in those areas of lower slopes of gentle relief. Sometimes 2A is replaced on the lower slopes of the Downs by the intermediate category 5A/2A, while the tops of the Downs are generally occupied by soils of the category 5G, except on the Grovely Ridge where the surface cover of clay-with-Flints gives rise to a deeper soil classified as 5A. This category is also found in the Cotswolds. Elsewhere areas of Clay-with-Flints are classified in the 6AG category, as in the area of Savernake Forest. The Vale of Wardour, much of which is also classified 6AG, is of varied lithology and topography, including outcrops of Greensand, Purbeck Beds and Portland Beds.

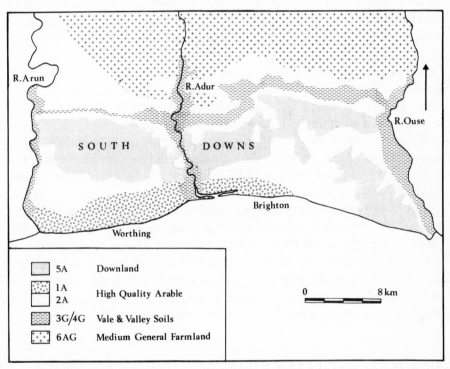

FIG. 24.4. South-central Sussex – zones of land use potential (the key also applies to Figs. 24.18, 24.20 and 24.25).

Such a close relationship between the distribution of land classes and topography is also apparent in south-central Sussex (Fig. 24.4). The type 3G/4G is found only in the valleys of the three rivers, Adur, Arun and Ouse, which cut through the South Downs, and on the band of Gault clay that outcrops to the north of the chalk escarpment between the Upper and Lower Greensand belts. The higher parts of the chalk are covered by soils of class 5, although here they are entirely of the type 5A, which are deeper than the 6G soils that are more widespread in Wiltshire. The lower stretches of the dip-slope of the South Downs, the slopes on either side of each of the main river valleys and the Upper and Lower Greensand belts are characterized by soils of the 2A category, while the Weald Clay at the extreme northern limit of this area supports 6AG soils. Here the subsoil is much less well drained than that of the Greensand or of the lower chalk slopes. The main difference between the areas of Wiltshire and of south central Sussex is that in the latter area there is a large tract of 1A land, occurring on the relatively wide coastal plain on a series of light superficial layers of Coombe Deposits (derived from the chalk) and Brickearth (light loams of aeolian origin, or resulting from shallow water sedimentation), which extend from the western edge of the chosen area to about the centre of Brighton.

The fact that such units or 'land systems' can be distinguished so effectively leads us to propose a slightly simplified classification for our present purpose. The category 3G/4G we will call 'Valley and Vale' soils, while 1A and 2A we will group together as 'High Quality Arable Land of the Lower Slopes' (HQA), into which category we will also place those areas in Wiltshire distinguished as 5A/2A. Areas of 5A and of 5G are taken together under the heading of 'Downland soils', and 6AG stands on its own as 'Medium Quality General Purpose Farmland'.

In many areas and for other periods the definition of resources must take into account changes in land use potential produced by geological and other agencies (Vita-Finzi and Higgs, 1970, p. 8). But at present our knowledge of the environmental history of southern England does not suggest that there has been the kind of change in land use potential through time such as is reasonable to suppose for the Levant, and the units that we have used seem likely to have been much the same throughout our period and up to the present.

RESULTS: THE COUNTY OF WILTSHIRE

Wiltshire seemed a most suitable area for the testing of our model, including as it does within its bounds a large block of Downland and a broad clay vale (see Fig. 24.3). It is also a county for which a modern and highly detailed archaeological gazetteer exists, that prepared by Grinsell for the *Victoria County History of Wiltshire* (Grinsell, 1957). This list summarizes the evidence as it was known in 1956, and we have referred to the annual reports published in the *Wiltshire Archaeological Magazine* for more recent information.

In covering so large an area we have not been able to examine the archaeological evidence for each site in so much detail as was possible in our study of south-central Sussex, and we have relied heavily on Grinsell's descriptions of the sites. Those sites that he defines as 'settlements' appear to be all those that have produced pottery and other artefact types, unless there is any chance that the pottery might have been sepulchral. Finds of hoards of metal objects or coins and finds of isolated artefacts are excluded. We have also not considered the pre-Roman Iron Age hill forts in our analyses, because the extent to which they may have been inhabited remains one of the outstanding problems in British prehistory. This means, however, that our conclusions on the settlement of this period are subject to revision, should it be demonstrated that hill forts have a primarily agricultural, rather than socio-political significance.

Middle and Late Bronze Age

A number of settlement sites with Middle and Late Bronze Age cultural affinities are known in south-central Sussex, but there is a dearth of evidence for them in Wiltshire. Of the twelve sites that were examined all except the settlement on Thorny Down at Winterbourne Gunner (Stone, 1951), have been described as enclosures possibly for cattle (see for example, Piggott, 1942). It remains to be seen whether or not this suggestion will prove to have been justified, for at the moment not enough excavation has been carried out inside these enclosures. It may be significant that when Pitt-Rivers excavated the interior of South Lodge Camp at Rushmore he noticed many patches of softer soil. It is possible that these may have been pits or the post-holes of internal structures (Ritchie, 1969).

However, for our present purpose we have treated all these sites as being possible 'settlements'. The catchment areas of all except two sites include at least 75% of Downland soils (5A/5G), with only small quantities of Higher Quality Arable soils (1A/2A) always distributed towards the edges of the catchments, suggesting that it was not much exploited. South Lodge Camp is situated in an area covered by uniformly intermediate soils of the 5A/2A variety, and only the catchment area of the Durrington 'egg enclosure' includes any Valley soil (3G/4G) at all. Although there were no Middle or Late Bronze Age sites in Wiltshire with large areas of Higher Quality Arable (1A/2A) in their catchments, such sites were found in Sussex.

Pre-Roman Iron Age

The catchment areas of fifty-two Iron Age sites were examined, and it was

923

found that the soils that were apparently of greatest significance were the 'Higher Quality Arable' (2A and 5A/2A) and 'Downland (5A and 5G) types. But the 'Valley and Vale' soils (3G/4G) also played an important role.

For fourteen of the sites significant areas of 'Valley and Vale' soils were found to be associated with 'Higher Quality Arable' soils (e.g. Little Woodbury); and in another eleven cases they were associated with the 5A/2A

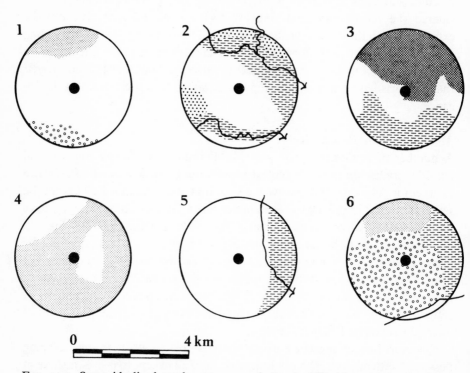

FIG. 24.5. Some idealized catchment areas of sites in Wiltshire and south-central Sussex. 1, West Blatchington, Sussex, Later Bronze Age. 2, Little Woodbury, Wiltshire, Iron Age. 3, All Cannings Cross, Wiltshire, Iron Age. 4, The Dykes, Sussex Romano-British native settlement. 5, Nuthills, Wiltshire, Roman villa. 6, Lancing, Sussex, Early Saxon. For key to land use categories, see Fig. 24.3.

category. Wherever soils of this intermediate category are present in the absence of any of the higher quality variant 2A, they occupy more than 50% of the total catchment area. The other class of importance is the 'Downland'. Around ten sites it is associated with 'Higher Quality Arable' (e.g. West Overton); and in a further nine cases it is associated both with 'Higher Quality Arable' and with an area of 'Valley and Vale soil' (e.g. All Cannings

924

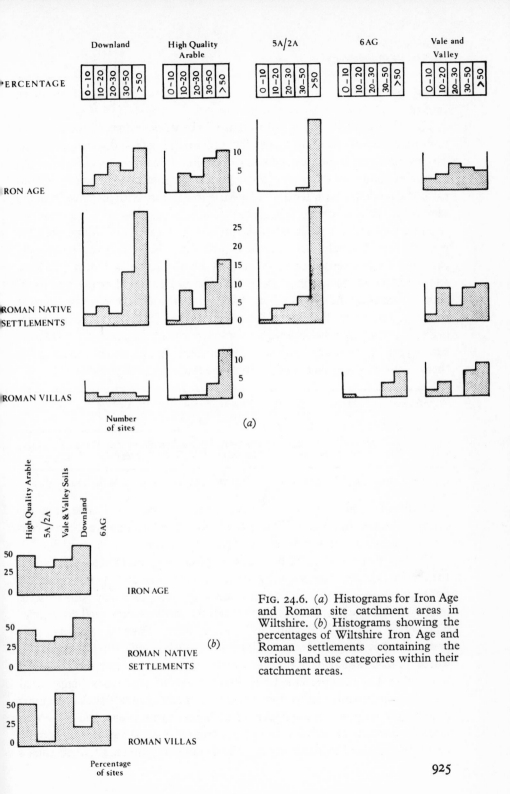

FIG. 24.6. (*a*) Histograms for Iron Age and Roman site catchment areas in Wiltshire. (*b*) Histograms showing the percentages of Wiltshire Iron Age and Roman settlements containing the various land use categories within their catchment areas.

Cross), the classic combination of the Downland parishes of southern England.

This picture of the likely utilization of the whole range of the available resources is borne out by more detailed examination of the distribution of the various land capability categories within individual catchment areas. As Chisholm points out (see p. 915 above) a fundamental principle of rural land use is the tendency for intensity of land use to decrease with distance from the settlement. In the light of this general tendency it seems very important to consider the land use potential of the immediate localities of all our sites, for it would seem unlikely that an area of 'Valley and Vale' soils was intensively exploited from a settlement 1.5 km away on the top of a Down. We have attempted to do this by examining the land use potential at the site itself, and by measuring the distance from that point to the nearest soils of a different category. The results for the pre-Roman Iron Age sites of Wiltshire are shown in Fig. 24.7. These results serve to emphasize the importance of the 'Downland' type, but they also illustrate the apparent significance of the so-called 'heavy soils' in the economy of the Iron Age settlements of Wiltshire.

Sites on:	HQA	5A/2A	Down	V & V	6AG
	10	13	16	2	2

Sites situated less than 0–5 km from HQA/Downland interface: 12
Sites situated less than 0–5 km from HQA/V & V interface: 12

FIG. 24.7. Locations of pre-Roman Iron Age sites of Wiltshire.

Of the sites not included in the two classes shown in the table, nine are centrally located in areas of 'Downland', but a further nine are located centrally in areas with intermediate soils of the 5A/2A type.

The fact that some of the sites we are considering are located right up on the Downs whereas others nearby are so situated as to give them easy access to 'High Quality Arable' soils (2A), and sometimes to Valley soils as well, might be seen as giving some further weight to ideas expressed by Applebaum (1954), and most recently by Bradley (1971). These writers have suggested the possible existence of a kind of 'outfield' and 'infield' system, in which animals would have been grazed for a part of the year on an upland 'outfield'.[1] The data presented here and our results for Sussex suggest that Iron Age settlements can be divided into two main groups – sites containing mainly 'Downland' soils (5A/5G) in their catchment areas, and sites with large proportions of arable soils (1A/2A and/or 3G/4G). Such a dichotomy could be explained in terms of an 'infield-outfield' system, although such a simple explanation of the data might obscure other factors affecting the choice of settlement sites. However, it has been demonstrated that the different sites within a small region, the area around the Vale of Pewsey, were dependent upon differing combinations of resources. In the Iron Age there were definitely both specialist 'Downland' sites and lower lying settlements, which taken as a whole provided access to a very wide range of resources.

It cannot be emphasized too strongly that these conclusions must be seen in the light of the fact that the fifty-two sites that we have examined do not represent a random sample of the Iron Age settlement of Wiltshire. There can be no doubt that Fowler's statement (in Thomas, 1966) – that they constitute a sample that is heavily biased towards the Downland – is correct. All the more noteworthy, then, in view of the assumptions that have been made by those who have based their analyses on studies of settlements as dots on distribution maps, that such a large number of the sites include substantial proportions of the 'heavy soils' within their catchment areas, and that an even larger number of them were located on soils of high quality.

Roman Iron Age

In this period the ranking of settlements into categories of differing size and function becomes more clearly apparent in the archaeological evidence, but even so the data as they exist at present are not such as to enable us to distinguish the different types of settlement on a map. We have concentrated on rural settlement, thus excluding analysis of the sites of Roman towns. The most useful division to make is the broad one between two groups conventionally labelled 'villas' and 'native settlements', recognizing that these are not well-defined categories (see Thomas, 1966).

Seventy-eight 'native settlements' were examined; and with these sites, just as with those of the pre-Roman Iron Age, we find catchment areas that include large proportions of the 'Higher Quality Arable' soils (2A), and large proportions of 'Valley and Vale' soils (3G/4G). The catchment areas of fifteen sites combine the two, and those of fourteen other sites combine them with areas of 'Downland' soils (5A/5G). The main difference is that an even greater proportion of the 'native settlements' than of the Iron Age sites have catchment areas that contain 50% or more of 'Downland' soils.

Our more detailed analysis of the distribution of resources within catchments strikingly confirms these conclusions (Fig. 24.8). The 'native settlements' of Roman Wiltshire were if anything more strongly oriented towards the 'Downland' soils than those of the pre-Roman Iron Age (see also Fig.

24.8), a situation which is clarified by examination of the catchment areas of thirty-three villas in the county. (Fig. 24.9).

Sites on:	HQA	5A/2A	Down	V & V	6AG
	13	12	27	7	6

Sites situated less than 0–5 km from HQA/Downland interface: 25
Sites situated less than 0–5 km from HQA/V & V interface: 11
Sites situated centrally in areas of Downland: 12
Sites situated centrally in areas of HQA: 5

FIG. 24.8. Locations of the 'native settlements' of Roman Wiltshire.

Again it is clear that both the 'Higher Quality Arable' soils (2A) and the 'Valley and Vale' soils (3G/4G) are important, and although for the first time the latter take a dominant position it should also be noted that a large number of the sites include more than 50% of 'Higher Quality Arable' soils within their catchment areas. The very slight importance of the 'Downland' soils may be seen as complementing the high place that they occupy in the catchment areas of the 'native settlements'. These conclusions are again amplified by more detailed analysis of the site catchment areas (Fig. 24.6). From these results it appears that access to 'Downland' soils was not of much importance for villa farmers, whereas it clearly was for those who farmed from 'native settlements'. Two-thirds of the villa sites of Wiltshire are oriented towards the 'High Quality Arable' soils and the 'Valley and Vale' soils, and most of the remainder include substantial proportions of 'Medium Quality' soils (6AG) within their catchment areas.

Sites on:	HQA	5A/2A	Down	V & V	6AG
	12	—	1	10	3

Sites situated less than 0–5 km from HQA/Downland interface: 1
Sites situated less than 0–5 from HQA/V & V interface: 9
Sites situated centrally in areas of Downland: 0
Sites situated centrally in areas of HQA: 6
Sites situated centrally in areas of 'Valley and Vale':   6

FIG. 24.9. Locations of the villas of Roman Wiltshire.

Although our site list for this period undoubtedly includes settlements that may have been occupied at different times, their numbers seem to suggest a fair concentration of settlement in some areas of Wiltshire. The apparent importance of both 'Higher Quality Arable' soils and of 'Downland' soils to many of the 'native settlements' might well suggest some 'packing' of the site catchment areas, such as we postulate in the second part of this paper for the later Saxon settlement. However, this is an argument which can be developed more precisely in connection with the Romano-British settlements of south-central Sussex.

The change towards more intensive exploitation in the Roman period is decidedly one of emphasis and there is no suggestion of any 'break' between the pre-Roman and the Roman Iron Ages.

It is important to point out here that economic development involved more than changes in the character and location of rural settlements. The emergence of 'central places' (urban and proto-urban centres), the consequent possibilities for regional specialization and the probability that we are no longer dealing entirely with subsistence agriculture must be borne in mind. Such factors are considered in more detail below.

Post-Roman Iron Age

In the case of south-central Sussex, it has been possible to discuss the earliest post-Roman sites, defined by place names in *-ingas*, with supplementary evidence from pagan Saxon burials. However, the settlement of the Wiltshire area was apparently rather later, to judge both from the fact that there is only one *-ingas* name in the county and from the evidence of the pagan Saxon burials. Of the sixteen cemeteries listed by Meaney (1964) and in subsequent reports in the *Wiltshire Archaeological Magazine* and *Medieval Archaeology*, six are located centrally in 'Downland' areas near to the peripheries of present-day parishes, and only four are located in valleys in positions similar to those of the medieval villages. The remainder are all located near to the 'interface' of 'Downland' and 'Valley and Vale' soils areas. This pattern does recall that of the Roman period, but the interpretation of cemeteries and isolated burials in terms of settlement patterns seems fraught with such difficulties that for our present purpose we have preferred to use for comparison the site locations of the fully developed Saxon settlement, marked by place names in *-tun*. We summarize our results and show them in comparison with those for the earlier periods in Fig. 24.10. Some further discussion of the significance of the burial sites in Wiltshire is given in Part II of this paper. Whereas earlier studies, following Crawford's conclusions (1924; and see Collingwood and Myres, 1936, p. 441; Hodgkin, 1935, p. 135), have all emphasized the apparent dichotomy between this pattern and those of the prehistoric and Roman periods, our approach suggests that it must be seen rather as the result of the intensification of them. As we have seen, even in the pre-Roman Iron Age in Wiltshire, a significant number of settlements had catchment areas that included the same range of resources as are included within many of the parish boundaries.

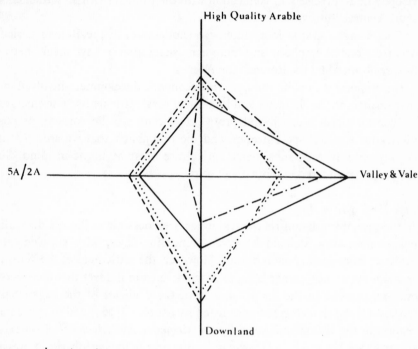

FIG. 24.10. Diagram illustrating the combination of land use types from the Iron Age to Saxon periods in Wiltshire (axes show the percentage of the total number of sites having some area of each category within their catchments).

RESULTS: SOUTH-CENTRAL SUSSEX

The area chosen for study (shown in Fig. 24.4, see p. 921) is bounded by the river Arun to the west, by the river Ouse to the east, by the coastline in the south, and by a line roughly joining the present-day villages of Pulbrough and Barcombe to the north. Geologically the area includes, from north to south, bands of Weald Clay, Lower Greensand, Gault Clay, Upper Greensand, Chalk and a zone of Brickearth and Coombe Rock – the whole

930

being cut by the three valleys of the Arun, Adur, and Ouse, all of which run roughly north to south to the coast.

There is no recent gazetteer of sites for Sussex, so that detailed distribution maps at the scale of 1:63360 were compiled using evidence gathered largely from Curwen's *The Archaeology of Sussex* (2nd Ed. 1954) and from the pages of the *Sussex Archaeological Collections* from 1848 onwards. The definition of sites as 'settlements' was on the basis outlined at the beginning of our section on Wiltshire.

Middle and Late Bronze Age

It is fortunate that there is so much more evidence of Middle and Late Bronze Age settlements in south-central Sussex than in Wiltshire.

It is now apparent that the class of pottery usually called 'Deverel-Rimbury' and dated entirely to the Middle Bronze Age in southern England can be divided stylistically and stratigraphically into two chronological phases, the later of which is Late Bronze Age in date (this topic is to be included in a Ph.D dissertation that is being prepared by one of us – A.E.). It is possible therefore to differentiate between Middle and Late Bronze Age sites in Sussex, but since they are so few in number we have grouped them together for the purposes of our present study to make comparison with later periods possible.

The sites belonging to the series of 'pastoral enclosures' recently recognized and discussed by Bradley (1971) that occur in our area have been included in this chronological category, even though some of them do continue in use into the Iron Age. Apart from the possible case of Highdown Hill, none of these enclosures has yielded evidence of interior structures to their excavators, so that their status as inhabited settlements is still in question. However, we have included them in our analysis since, presumably, some population group must have been nearby for at least part of the year. It is also possible that more extensive future excavations may reveal traces of human habitation.

The catchment areas of fourteen M/LBA sites were examined. 'Higher Quality Arable' soils (1A/2A) and 'Downland' soils were seen to be most important. In Wiltshire we found specialized Downland sites, while here we find specialized sites with high percentages of 1A/2A in their catchment areas, as well as settlements situated in the Downland. Only three sites however include any 'Valley and Vale' soils within their catchment areas, and in each case they are located at the extreme edge of the area (see Fig. 24.11).

Three important sites lie on the coastal plain, so that there are upland and lowland sites even at this early period. There are many other finds of Deverel-

931

Rimbury pottery from the coastal plain but in most cases it cannot be decided with certainty whether these finds represent domestic or sepulchral sites. Recent analysis of pollen sequences from valley peat deposits near Lewes demonstrates a marked increase in pollen of the weeds of cultivation at *c.* 1200 B.C. on the light fertile soils along the slopes of the Lower Ouse valley (Thorley, 1971). That the low-lying areas were utilized in some way during the later Bronze Age is also suggested by the distribution of hoards of bronze objects, which shows concentration on the coastal plain (Curwen, 1954, fig. 56).

Here, therefore, we have indications that a generalized 'infield-outfield' system, as we have outlined for Iron Age Wiltshire, was in operation at least from the later Bronze Age. However, it is also possible that the sites on the coastal plain may have been completely self-sufficient with easy access to first class arable land and a good water supply, and would not have needed to exploit nearby Downland soils at all. The more exposed areas of Downland would then have formed part of the catchment areas of settlements in the Downland valleys (Bradley, 1971).

Although we have not considered periods earlier than the Middle Bronze Age, because the evidence surviving from them is so much less plentiful, the Sussex material does suggest that a system involving the exploitation of both upland and lowland had already been established in the earlier periods. A very large number of the Middle and Late Bronze Age sites have also yielded Early Bronze Age or even Neolithic pottery in small quantities, suggesting that they were established in roughly the same areas as had been exploited in earlier times. The distribution of Bronze Age round barrows, many of which probably date from the Early Bronze Age provides further evidence in support of this hypothesis. Grinsell's map (1940, map III) shows them as clustering not only on the chalk uplands of the South Downs but also on the low-lying Lower Greensand outcrop. Barrows cannot be used as evidence of areas of settlement but this general distribution does suggest that both the chalk slopes and the light soils (2A) of the Lower Greensand were being exploited in the Early Bronze Age.

Pre-Roman Iron Age
The catchment areas of sixteen Iron Age sites were examined. The various types of palisaded and earthwork-defined Iron Age settlement enclosures which are so common in Wessex seem to be almost completely absent east of the river Meon in Hampshire (Perry, 1969, p. 39), so that the sites studied here

are mostly open sites comprising apparently unprotected groups of huts. The palisaded site at Muntham Court is the sole exception.

The catchment areas were found to contain combinations of 'Higher Quality Arable' soils (1A/2A) and 'Downland' soils (5A/5G), or 'Higher Quality Arable' alone, supplemented by 'Valley and Vale' soils (3G/4G) in a few cases. Eight sites have varying combinations of 'Higher Quality Arable' and 'Downland', while three sites have catchment areas including 100% of 'Higher Quality Arable'. Only three of the sites have areas of 'Valley and Vale' soils within their catchments, but in one of these cases the share of the valley soils exceeds 60%. The general picture recalls the pattern for the Middle and Late Bronze Age sites in Sussex, and that of the Wiltshire Iron Age. However, there does seem to have been a trend towards greater exploitation of the 'Higher Quality Arable' (Fig. 24.11).

Roman Iron Age
The sites were grouped in the same way as in our Wiltshire study, into the two categories of 'native settlements' and 'villas'. All the 'native settlements' have areas of 'Higher Quality Arable' soils (1A/2A) and 'Downland' soils (5A/5G) within their catchment areas; the average share of the arable soils being 37·5% and that of the Downland soils 82·5%. In addition four of the sites also have small areas of 'Valley and Vale' soils (3G/4G) (see Fig. 24.11).

As with the case of Wiltshire, this situation is clarified further by analysis of the villa sites. Most of the thirteen villa sites have catchment areas including high percentages of 'Higher Quality Arable' soils (1A/2A), and in five of them this is combined with moderate areas of 'Valley and Vale' soils (3G/4G). Another five of the sites also include zones of 'Downland' soils within their catchment areas, but they never exceed 25% of the total area. As in Wiltshire the slight importance of the 'Downland' complements its apparently greater significance for the 'native settlements'.

Although the map (Fig. 24.12) combines settlements of varying chronological span it can be used to demonstrate the great concentration of sites in a small area of Downland, suggesting that population densities were high. The fact that marginal 'Downland' soils were put under the plough, thus forming the 'Celtic field systems' (marked on the map), which have never been disturbed by subsequent ploughing, further substantiates the same general point. Field systems would have originally been present on the lower slopes and on the light lowland soils but they have since been removed by the plough. In Sussex we are fortunate in having some slight evidence of these in the form

933

of probable field boundary ditches at West Blatchington Hove, (Norris and Burstow, 1948; for Wiltshire see Fowler and Evans, 1967).

The spacing of the villas along the coastal plain was apparently extremely

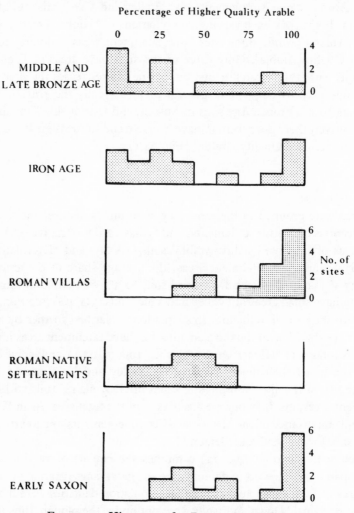

FIG. 24.11. Histograms for Bronze Age to Saxon
site catchment areas in south-central Sussex.

regular and recalls the pattern discussed by Branigan for the villas near Verulamium (Branigan, 1967).

The more detailed evidence that is available for south-central Sussex has

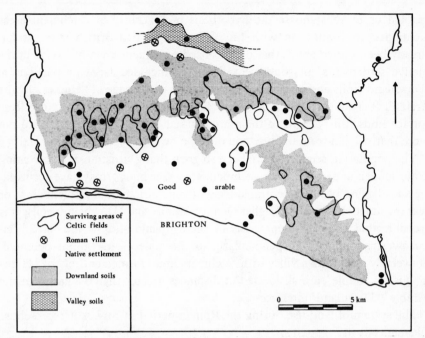

FIG. 24.12. The Romano-British settlement pattern of the Brighton district of Sussex.

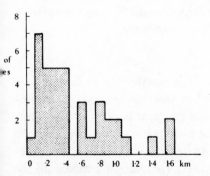

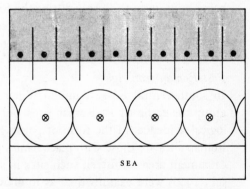

FiG. 24.13. Graph showing the distances native settlements in Fig. 24.12 from the ction of good all-purpose farmland and wnland soils.

FIG. 24.14. Model of Romano-British land use in the Brighton district. For key see Fig. 24.12. (Whether exploitation of villa and native settlements catchment areas were economically linked remains to be demonstrated conclusively.)

935

enabled us to substantiate the hypothesis of 'packing' of catchment areas mentioned in connection with the Wiltshire Roman-British sites. It has already been shown above that the idealized catchment areas of twelve of the 'native settlements' of south-central Sussex included large proportions of 'Downland' soils and a smaller but significant percentage of 'Higher Quality Arable'. It is not surprising then, that all the 'native settlements' known from surface finds (thirty-eight of them are marked on the map), are located not more than 1·6 km from the junction of these two land categories (Fig. 24.13).

The population seems to have been so great that a situation approximating to our models of packed linear catchment areas (see p. 958) may have occurred, the sites having been concentrated along a zone of maximum potential, at or near the junction between 'Higher Quality Arable' and 'Downland' soils. It is probable that the catchment areas of these upland sites would have been narrow strips aligned perpendicularly to the zone of maximum potential. Conversely, the Roman villas with catchment areas formed entirely by 'Higher Quality Arable', are all located at distances greater than 0·8 km from the 'Arable'/'Downland' interface.

The system of land use during the Roman period in Sussex is represented schematically in Fig. 24.14.

In general, then, as in Wiltshire, the Roman period is characterized by more intensive exploitation of both uplands and lower lying areas than in the earlier periods. In view of the arguments that we advance later in the paper, it is worthwhile to point out that there is no evidence that watermills were being built in south Sussex during the Roman period, but bearing in mind the importance of grain growing in the area, demonstrated by the extension of ploughed fields onto marginal land, it remains a possibility.

Post-Roman Iron Age

In south-central Sussex, unlike Wiltshire, it is worthwhile to discuss as a group the earliest post-Roman sites, defined by place names and by archaeological evidence, in the form of pagan Saxon graveyards. The earliest post-Roman sites are those with place names that include the suffix *-ingas*, and the catchment areas of fifteen such sites in south-central Sussex (listed in Dodgson, 1966) were examined so as to allow direct comparison between all the periods from the Middle Bronze Age to the earliest post-Roman Iron Age.

The most important classes of land were seen to be the 'Higher Quality Arable' soils (1A/2A) and, for the first time in Sussex, the 'Valley and Vale' soils (3G/4G). All the sites had some 'Higher Quality Arable' soils within their catchment areas, and in six cases the whole of the catchment was taken up by them. These six sites are those located on the fertile costal plain between the rivers Arun and Adur. The other nine sites had varying combinations of 'Higher Quality Arable' and 'Downland' soils, while in eight of these cases these two categories of land were combined with fairly low percentages of 'Valley and Vale' soils. These nine sites are all located in the scarp foot zone.

The main points to notice in comparison with earlier periods are the larger number of sites with catchment areas made up entirely by 'Higher Quality Arable' soils, and the complete lack of sites with no land of this category. However, that upland establishments possibly including none of the 'Higher Quality Arable' soils within their catchment areas were present in the later medieval period has now been demonstrated by field work. Twelve medieval sites were located and identified from inspection of earthworks and surface finds in the block of Downland between the river Arun and Findon alone, although none of them are datable to the period before the Norman Conquest (Curwen and Curwen, 1922; Holden, 1957, and personal communication).

PART I: SUMMARY

Earlier studies of the economy of southern England during our chosen period have concentrated upon the apparent dichotomy between pre- and post-Roman settlement in particular, and have used it as the basis for making judgements about the nature of 'Celtic' as opposed to Saxon agricultural systems. These views have been called into question by recent field work, which has suggested that 'prehistoric and Romano-British people in Britain lived everywhere'. The results of the application of our model confirm this conclusion, which is also in line with the whole tenor of present-day archaeological thinking, concerned as it is with issues of 'continuity' or 'change'. Equally our results may be seen as being validated by the more recent field evidence, but they may also enable us to develop further hypotheses concerned with the nature of the agricultural economy.

Our analysis suggests that most sites in all periods provided access to more than one class of land, and the evidence from Wiltshire, and for the Romano-British period in Sussex at least, shows that sites were often located close to the junction between two different land categories. Although our analysis quite clearly shows steadily increasing utilization of the better arable soils (1A/2A) throughout the period we have considered (Trend One), and increased utilization of the heavier soils towards the end of the period in particular (Trend Two), these now appear as the product of a continuous process of development probably involving demographic expansion as well as technical and social change. There were sites with very high percentages of

'Higher Quality Arable' soils even in the Middle Bronze Age in Sussex; but even more significant is our finding that there were apparently substantial numbers of sites throughout the later prehistoric period which had catchment areas including the same range of resources as those of the later Saxon villages, and in which the heavy soils were sufficiently close to the settlements themselves to suggest that they were essential in the economy. Further it seems highly likely that there were contemporary sites depending on different resources throughout the period, for we find evidence for specialist 'Downland' sites and for lower lying sites with access to a variety of resources in all periods. Nothing could be more misleading than a description of the 'Celtic' agricultural system which implies that settlements and fields were invariably situated in the Downland.

IMPLICATIONS FOR INTERPRETATION

By approaching the problem of rural economy simply from the preferred locations of rural settlements in different periods, we have seen that there is a continuous thread running through the Iron Age, Roman and Saxon evidence, suggesting increasing exploitation of heavier soils. This is the trend that earlier writers, following Fleure and Whitehouse (1916) somewhat confusingly called the 'valleyward movement'. Discussion of the problem has been complicated by attempts to attribute this to individual factors, usually technological or social.

In any case, the pattern is no longer as simple as it appeared at one time to be. As Taylor has observed for Dorset; 'The archaeological sites exist on the high land *only* because later people have not used this land intensively, and so it is in these areas that the remains have been well preserved. There is evidence that both the prehistoric and Romano-British peoples lived in the valleys and low-lying areas of Dorset, as well as, or even more than on the high ground' (Taylor, 1970, p. 25). The intensive field work associated with motorway building in south-west England (Fowler, 1971) shows the extent to which the available sample is biased by the circumstances of preservation and discovery.

However, in the light of the evidence presented above this so-called 'valleyward movement' can be seen as a further phase of internal colonization connected with the gradual growth in population: (see Sherratt, Chapter 12 of this volume). This gives perspective to the whole problem of rural economy and suggests 'continuity' at least in the broadest sense of the term. More detailed analysis requires further definition of such factors as techniques of cultivation, the existence of markets, and the social and political organization of the various periods.

Technology and patterns of land use

One factor that has perhaps been unduly stressed is that of changes in plough technology, particularly that which saw the introduction of the heavy plough with mouldboard and coulter. It must be borne in mind that simple plough forms continued in use even when more complex forms were in existence elsewhere, and indeed that simple ploughs held at an angle can be used to turn furrows.

The first evidence for the use of a plough in north-west Europe goes back to the Neolithic, and from then on there were gradual improvements in plough technology. The earliest known plough marks in Britain are the very deep ones uncovered at South Street, Wiltshire, beneath a Neolithic long barrow (Fowler and Evans, 1967). These are situated not on chalk at all, but on Coombe Deposits in a dry valley, and continental examples have been recorded both from light and heavy soils (Kjaerum, 1954). Evidence for the existence of a 'heavy plough' even in Belgic times (the later pre-Roman Iron Age) has now been questioned (Manning, 1964a), and it appears that although the mouldboard and coulter were used on some ploughs during the Roman period, the fully developed wheeled form may not have appeared until the time of the Danish invasions in the ninth century A.D. (see White, 1962). While there may be a general correlation, therefore, between the increased exploitation of heavy soils and improvements in plough technology, no single innovation seems likely to have exerted a critical effect.

Associated with the extension of the area under cultivation there developed specialized systems of production and exchange based on markets. This can be seen clearly in the Iron Age from the evidence of large non-village settlements (oppida) and from references in classical writers to exported products. The inclusion of England within the framework of Roman political organization would have accelerated this process and at the same time introduced new factors, both by the diffusion of new techniques and the introduction of wider scale effects such as fluctuations in 'international' trade (see Fig. 21.12).

The collapse of this system produced local readjustments involving some redistribution of population. A critical question here is the extent to which previous patterns of agricultural settlement continued in a new political situation, and their relationship to new settlement. Equally important are the patterns of settlement expansion in succeeding centuries. This is the subject of

939

Part II of this paper, in which the geographical approach that we have already used is extended and elaborated. Only when the pattern of change as reflected in the distribution of settlements is clarified can the effects of social and political changes be assessed.

A thorough attempt to explain observed changes must take into account factors not directly concerned with cultivation, but which might also have exercised a critical influence on village location. One development that has not so far been much discussed in connection with early medieval village locations is the introduction of the water mill.

The water mill

Until Roman times all grain was ground on querns, first of saddle and later of rotary type, in the homesteads of individual farmers (Curwen, 1937). Their use continued into the Roman period in Europe, and even into the eighteenth century in some areas (Bloch, 1966), but during the Roman period the use of the water mill gradually spread throughout Europe, following its invention in Mediterranean lands probably in the first century B.C. (Moritz, 1958, p. 131). They were certainly being constructed in Britain by the third century A.D., the best-known examples being those along Hadrian's Wall and the iron spindles interpreted as mill pivots from Great Chesterford and Silchester (Liversidge, 1968; Manning, 1964b). By Domesday times (A.D. 1086) the number recorded exceeds 5000 (Hodgen, 1939) and even this estimate may be too low (Lennard, 1959, p. 278). The sophistication of eleventh-century water mill technology is illustrated by the three vertical mills with their massive artificial ditch excavated at Old Windsor by Hope-Taylor (1958).

For the use of water mills a stream with an adequate rate of flow for most of the year is necessary. In the chalk regions these conditions are fulfilled only at the scarp foot zones and in the larger valleys. Considerable capital outlay would have been involved in building a mill. In order to reduce transport costs the main cereal growing areas are likely to have been concentrated in the near vicinity of the mills, where this was possible, in areas of lowland arable. The effect of this would be to produce 'packing' of site catchment areas, expressed in this case in parishes of elongated form, so that each settlement had access to its own critically important stretch of river or stream. In general we suggest that economic historians, geographers and archaeologists alike, have all neglected the significance of mills, particularly from the locational point of view, and it seems likely to be worthy of more detailed examination.

While developments in the early historic period are thus likely to be more complicated both in reconstruction and in interpretation, the more plentiful

940

evidence that is available allows the use of more elaborate models while retaining basic simplicity of approach.

Part II: Models of settlement expansion in the fifth and sixth centuries A.D.

METHOD

The main class of evidence to be used in this section is that of place names. The use of place name evidence requires caution (see especially A. H. Smith, 1956), but here we hold to the view expressed by C. T. Smith that 'Place names may give useful indication of the chronology of settlement and although it may frequently be impossible to pin down the origin of place names to absolute dates, the relative chronology of settlement as given by them may yield invaluable conclusions about the progress of settlement in an area in relation to its accessibility or its physical conditions' (C. T. Smith, 1967, p. 120).

The models of settlement expansion that we have constructed are based on the notion of an idealized circular catchment area with a radius of 2 km around each site. However, we develop it here in a somewhat different way from that of the first part of our paper. There we employed the catchment area model in a general way to suggest the possible range of potential land use available within an area of easy access from each site: the nature of the evidence was such as to make it impossible to do more than suggest possible relationships between sites. Using the evidence provided by place names, however, we believe that we can attempt to assess these relationships by using developments of our simple catchment area model, taking advantage of the much better sample of settlement site locations. As certain groups of place names can be arranged in relative chronological order, we have evidence for successive phases of settlement and so can study processes of development.

A concept that has not been much utilized in analysis of settlement distributions arises from our consideration of settlements as nodes of movement. This suggests that a dot representing a village implies not merely a community but an area of land, exploited by it and necessary to it for its subsistence. With a given technology and economic regime there would be an optimal size for the units of exploitation and one might expect to find some regularity in the size of the areas of land accessible from each village. This is the basis of the models developed in this section of the paper.

If the catchment areas are compact the distance between sites should be roughly constant. We have suggested that the catchment area of any individual site dependent upon subsistence agriculture will be defined by a radius of at least 2 km and probably more. If circles of 2 km radius are drawn around each site, the extent of the overlap between circles gives a rough measure of the degree to which this basic subsistence unit is distorted from the optimal circular or near circular pattern. It should be possible therefore, working from the evidence of successive phases of settlement as they are recorded in place names, to reconstruct the processes by which the site catchment areas reached the form in which they were formalized as parish boundaries. In this way it is hoped ultimately to define a series of characteristic processes and patterns of development which can usefully be abstracted in idealized model form, thus providing some theoretical understanding of the processes of settlement expansion in the period between the fifth and the eleventh centuries A.D.

It has long been observed that the main areas of early Saxon settlement (documented both by place names in -*ingas* and by burial sites) do not coincide with the main areas of late Roman settlement. When the Roman villas and -*ingas* place names are plotted with their idealized catchment areas on a map of the county of Sussex, it can be shown that the two distributions were significantly distinct. This suggests that the earliest Saxon sites were 'inserted' into the pre-existing Roman cultural landscape. This argument will be substantiated and its possible chronological and socio-economic implications considered in a future paper [A. E.].

The areas examined below include parts of Sussex and Wiltshire, and from the results some general models of settlement expansion have been constructed. The sources that we have used are the relevant volumes published by the English Place Name Society, and for more recent detailed information on the earliest Saxon place names, the papers by Dodgson (1966) and Gelling (1967). The Saxon burial sites were plotted using Meaney's *Gazetteer* (1964) .The distribution of the various types of land use potential is again derived from the Ordnance Survey *Map of Land Use Potential* (1944).

RESULTS

I The Chippenham – Calne area; Model I
The towns of Chippenham and of Calne are situated in the clay vale of Wiltshire immediately to the west of the area of Downland in which Marlborough is situated (see map, Fig. 24.15). Calne stands on the ridge of Corallian limestone which runs from north-east to south-west in the midst of the clay vale, and with which 'Higher Quality Arable' soils (1A/2A) are associated.

942

There is a further area of these soils lying immediately to the west of the Marl-borough Downs; and towards the Cotswolds, to the west of Chippenham, the heavy soils (4G) of the clay vale are replaced by a rather lighter variant described as 2A/4D.

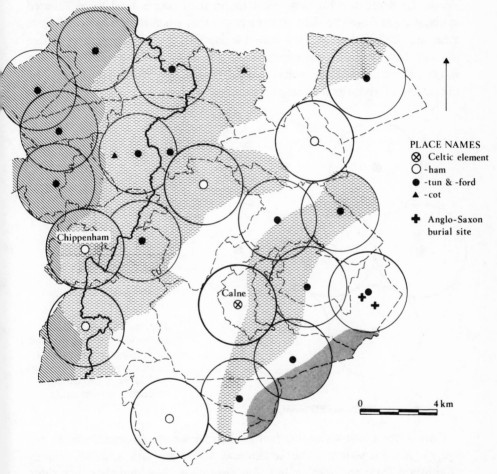

FIG. 24.15. The Chippenham area of Wiltshire. The broken lines are parish boundaries.

Although there are no -*ingas* place names in this region there is one derived from a British element (Calne), and there are five -*ham* names which can also be isolated as being relatively early. Brom*ham* and Tocken*ham* have catchment areas dominated by the 'Higher Quality Arable' soils of the Corallian limestone, and Calne is also situated on them, but includes an area of the heavier 'Valley and Vale' soil within its catchment area. The other three

943

places with *-ham* names are located on the heavier soils, but include some areas of 'Higher Quality Arable' or of 2A/4G in their catchments. These six sites are distributed regularly over the landscape.

The next phase of settlement is registered by place names in *-tun*, *-ford* and *-burgh*. Settlements with these elements in their names tend to be situated at about 4 km from the *-ham* settlements so that when their 2 km catchment areas are drawn, there is very little overlapping of the circles. From these observations we have constructed a simple model of settlement expansion shown in Fig. 24.16. The results of such a process are recorded in this area by the pattern of irregular but compact parishes.

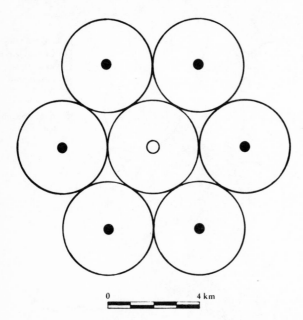

0   4 km

FIG. 24.16. Models of settlement expansion: Model I. (In diagrams of models open circles denote primary and filled circles denote secondary settlements.)

Only in the north-western corner of the map do the circles overlap to any very significant extent. The settlements there are still situated roughly equidistant from one another but they are rather closer together than those elsewhere in the area, resulting in a certain degree of 'packing' of their catchment areas. This process is reflected in the fact that the parishes are smaller than those to the south and east. The reason for such 'packing' in this limited area may be that the advantageous combination of the 2A and 4G types supported a higher population density than the heavier soils to the south and east.

There are only two known Anglo-Saxon burial sites in this particular area. Both are situated in the parish of Yatesbury, near to the site of the present village.

2 The Chichester area: Model II

The area around Chichester (see map, Fig. 24.17) includes a section of the coastal plain, the whole area of which is made up by 'Higher Quality Arable' soils (1A/2A) according to our simplified classification. However, we thought that for our more detailed experiments the division between 1A and 2A might prove to be significant, so we have shown it on the map.

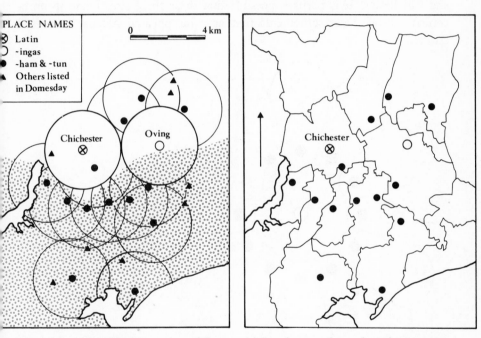

FIG. 24.17. The Chichester area of Sussex. (*a*) Land categories and catchment areas. (*b*) parish boundaries.

In this area the two earliest settlements on the place name evidence are Chichester, a name derived from Latin, and Oving which is an -*ingas* place name. These are both situated on soils of the 2A type but near to their boundary with the 1A soils. Place names with the suffixes -*ham* or -*tun* of the next phases of settlement are distributed around the two primary places, while the remainder of the settlements with place names that are recorded up to and in the Domesday Book (A.D. 1086) are situated further away from Chichester and Oving.

When catchment areas of 2 km radius are drawn an interesting pattern emerges. Firstly we notice that the *-ingas* settlement was established at a distance of exactly 4 km from Chichester, so that their idealized catchment areas touch but do not overlap; then we see that most of the *-ham* and *-tun* settlements were established just outside the perimeters of the two primary catchment areas. Only one of them occurs inside one of the catchments of the primary sites, while a few others were established further away, so that their catchment areas only overlap slightly with those of the *-ham* and *-tun* settlements situated near the perimeters of the catchment areas of Oving and Chichester. It is perhaps possible that these three sites relate to unrecorded coastal *-ingas* settlements that have disappeared because of coastal erosion.

0   4 km

FIG. 24.18. Models of settlement expansion: Model II.

The catchment areas of the *-ham* and *-tun* settlements overlap to a great extent. It is possible, then, that their real catchment areas were adjusted accordingly, and took the form of narrow strips radiating out from the boundaries of the two primary catchment areas. This process is idealized in Fig. 24.18.

The fact that eight of the secondary settlements lie to the south of Chichester and Oving on soils of the 1A variety, while only three of them are situated to the north on the 2A soils may be significant.

The next phase of settlement, which includes all the other sites mentioned up to A.D. 1086, apparently involved establishments near the bounds of the *-ham* and *-tun* catchment areas. Most of them are only farms or hamlets in the present day.

The process of settlement expansion illustrated by our Model II is further demonstrated by the form of the modern parishes (see Fig. 24.15). The *-ham* and *-tun* villages now have small and elongated parishes radiating from the two large subcircular parishes of Chichester and Oving.

There is only one possible pagan Saxon burial in this area, suggested by the finding of one decorated pot in Pagham Churchyard (Meaney, 1964, p. 253).

The main difference between the process of expansion described by Model I and that of Model II is that in the second situation there was apparently some factor requiring the secondary sites to be established as near as possible to the 'mother' settlements. It may be that there was a greater degree of economic interdependence than in the Model I situation, possibly involving the use of the primary settlement as a market and religious centre. In any event the primary settlement seems to have functioned as some kind of a 'central place'.

3 The Working area: Model IIIA

The country around Worthing (Fig. 24.19) includes broad zones of 'Higher Quality Arable' soils (1A and 2A) along the coastal plain and, in the north, the lower dipslope of the block of the South Downs between the rivers Arun and Adur. The latter area is covered by 'Downland' soils (5A/5G).

There is a particular concentration of *-ingas* place names here, and when 2 km catchment areas are drawn it can be seen that most of the sites have access to very large areas of the 'Higher Quality Arable' soils, and that there is hardly an area of these soils that is not included within the *-ingas* catchment areas. However, these circular catchment areas overlap to a considerable extent, and it is probable that the actual site territories were distorted from a very early period into a series of strips running from north to south, so that each one contained soils of 1A, 2A and 51/5G types. This is shown schematically in Fig. 24.23. The distortion of the catchment areas from the ideal circle ensured that each site had access to an equal share of the best arable land.

That such a process did take place is demonstrated in the pattern of strip parishes in the area, stretching northwards from the coast (see Fig. 24.19).

947

The two -*ingas* sites with the catchment areas that show the smallest amount of overlap (Peppering and Poling) are the only two settlements with near circular parishes.

The next phase of settlement is shown by the distribution of names in -*ham* and -*tun*, and other names recorded up to A.D. 1086. These show a tendency to cluster near the perimeters of the -*ingas* catchment areas, and in the east

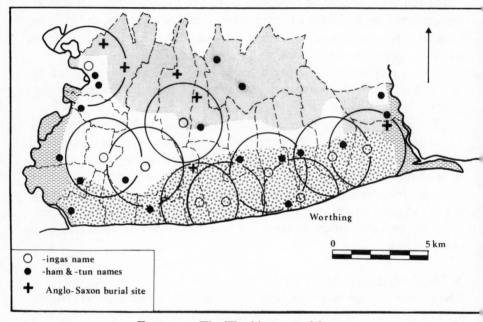

○ -ingas name
● -ham & -tun names
✛ Anglo-Saxon burial site

0   5 km

FIG. 24.19. The Worthing area of Sussex.

most of the names are those of hamlets in the -*ingas* parishes. Some colonization of the Downland is shown, however, by Clapham, Muntham and Findon.

In the west of the area, where the -*ingas* settlement did not take up all the 'Higher Quality Arable', the pattern conforms to our Model II, with -*ham* and -*tun* parishes radiating out from a compact -*ingas* parish (Poling). (Fig. 24.21). However, it appears that here, with limited space available for expansion, the primary catchment area became smaller to allow the development of later units with a viable area.

All the known Anglo-Saxon burial sites have been plotted on the map and it can readily be seen that they are located either near the present-day parish boundaries, or near to the perimeters of the -*ingas* catchment areas. We return to these observations below.

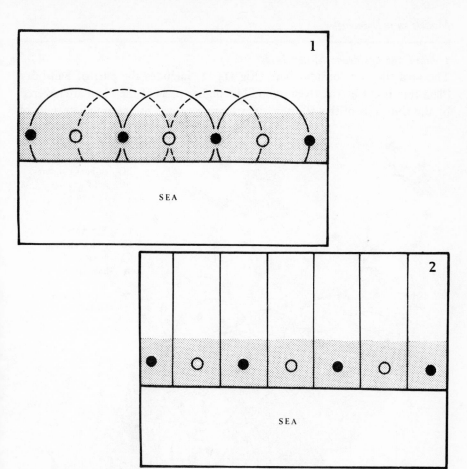

FIG. 24.20. Models of settlement expansion: Model IIIA (the circles are of 2 km radius).

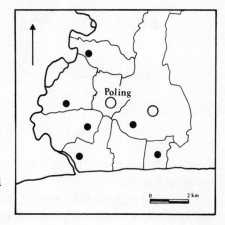

FIG. 24.21. Parish boundaries around Poling, Sussex.

949

4 The Cannings area: Model IIIB

The area that we consider here (Fig. 24.22) includes the part of Salisbury Plain that is cut by the river Avon. The higher parts of the Plain are covered by the thin soils of the 5G type, which are replaced by intermediate soils of

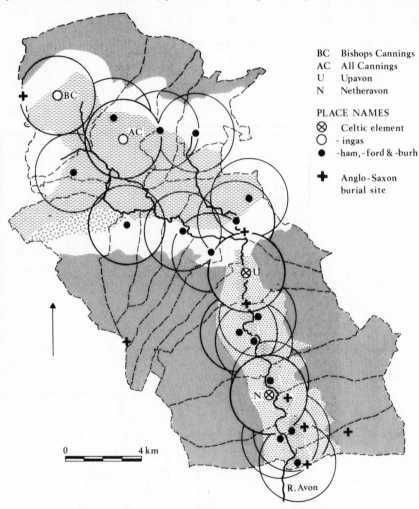

BC   Bishops Cannings
AC   All Cannings
U   Upavon
N   Netheravon

PLACE NAMES

⊗   Celtic element
◯   - ingas
●   -ham, -ford & -burh

✚   Anglo-Saxon burial site

FIG. 24.22. The Cannings area of Wiltshire.

the 5A/2A variety on the valley slopes. In the Avon valley itself there are heavy (4G) soils.

The northern part of the area is taken up by a section of the Vale of Pewsey, which shows a similar range of soil types. Here, however, the heavy 'Valley

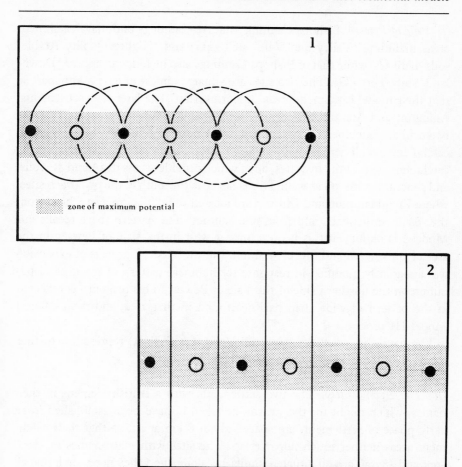

FIG. 24.23. Models of settlement expansion: Model IIIB.

and Vale' soils are more extensive, and instead of the rather thin 5A/2A soils on the lower slopes, we find arable soils of higher quality (2A).

The earliest sites, according to the place name evidence are two -*ingas* settlements, Bishops Cannings and All Cannings. There are also two settlements with a British place name element, Upavon and Netheravon, and we have taken these as being early settlements as well, though it may be that this incorporation of a Celtic river name occurred at a later period. The next phase of settlement is shown by the distribution of place names incorporating -*tun*, -*ford* and -*burgh* elements. Two processes of settlement expansion can be identified in this area.

(*i*) *Vale of Pewsey*. Bishops Cannings and All Cannings both have catchment areas including 'Valley and Vale' soils (4G) and 'Higher Quality Arable' soils (here 2A) while that of Bishops Cannings also includes an area of 'Downland' soils (here 5G). The two sites are situated almost exactly 4 km apart so that their model catchment areas do not overlap. The later -*tun* settlements, Allington and Stanton St Bernard, are located near the perimeters of the two primary catchment areas, and Alton lies near the boundary of the Stanton catchment area. There is consequently a large degree of overlap between the catchment areas of the five sites, all of which provide access to 2A and 4G soils, and generally some 5G as well. This is not so to the south of the two -*ingas* sites, where Etchilhampton and Chirton are located roughly 4 km away, both from the -*ingas* settlements, and from one another. The pattern there recalls our Model I situation, just as it does further west in the Vale of Pewsey in the area of Bulkington and Steeple Ashton. But the Model I process of expansion was apparently modified in response to the linear pattern of resource distribution on the northern side of the Vale of Pewsey. This response is reflected in the pattern of wide strip parishes found in that area, and is in effect a Model III process.

The names in -*stoc* (Beechingstoke) and -*cot* (Wilcot) represent a further phase of 'infilling' of gaps in the settlement pattern.

(*ii*) *The Avon Valley*. The two settlements with a British element in their names, which might for that reason be taken to have been established in an early phase of settlement, are spaced about 6 km apart, so that their catchment areas neither touch nor overlap. The sites with place names in -*ford*, -*tun* and -*burgh* are all situated similarly, along the valley floor, such that all have access to valley soils, the intermediate soils of the lower slopes and 'Downland' soils, within their catchment areas. The circles overlap to a considerable extent suggesting that the catchment areas were adjusted to form a series of narrow strips running at right angles to the river valley. This is the process we represent schematically in Fig. 24.23, which we consider to be a variant of our Model 3 situation. The process is again reflected in the pattern of narrow strip parishes in the area. However, it seems that in this region the process occurred at a relatively later stage than in the Worthing region described above.

The known Anglo-Saxon burial sites in the Cannings area are mostly situated either near village sites in the Avon valley, or near to the parish boundaries. Several of them are also located near the perimeters of our model circular catchment areas.

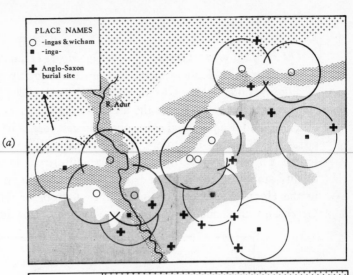

(a)

PLACE NAMES
○ -ingas & wicham
■ -inga-
✚ Anglo-Saxon burial site

R. Adur

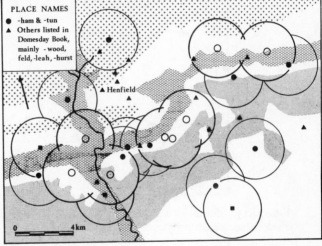

(b)

PLACE NAMES
● -ham & -tun
▲ Others listed in Domesday Book, mainly - wood, feld, -leah, -hurst

▲ Henfield

0   4 km

FIG. 24.24.
The Henfield area of Sussex.
(a) Early post-Roman settlements.
(b) Later post-Roman settlements.
(c) Parish boundaries. The figures inside circles represent the numbers of water mills recorded for particular manors in Domesday Book.

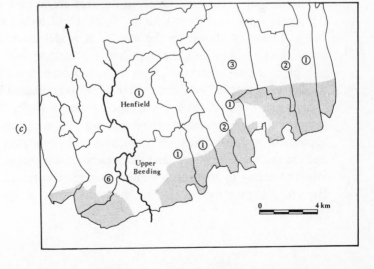

(c)

③   ② ①

① Henfield

①

②

① ①

⑥ Upper Beeding

0   4 km

5 The Henfield area: a further example of Model III, and an intermediate case
The area around Henfield includes a series of roughly parallel zones of soils of differing potential lying to the north and south of the South Downs, which run roughly east-west across the area (see map, Fig. 24.24). Where zones of different land use potential exist, one land category is likely to be particularly attractive to groups of settlers. This we will call the zone of maximum potential. For groups practising mixed agriculture the most useful soil is good quality arable, so the two bands of 'Higher Quality Arable' soils (here 2A) in the Henfield area, which follow the outcrops of the Upper and Lower Greensand, are shaded on the map as two zones of 'maximum potential'.

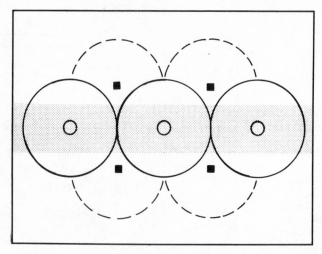

FIG. 24.25. Models of settlement expansion. Intermediate case (squares represent intermediate settlements).

The earliest Saxon settlements in the area are those with the suffix *-ingas* (Dodgson, 1966), and those with the element *wicham* in their names (Gelling, 1967). These are shown on the map with model catchment areas of 2 km radius, and it can be seen that together they include most of the total area of soils of 'maximum potential', with the exception of a large area in the centre which was not settled until much later, perhaps because of local circumstances of drainage. The next phase of settlement is shown by the distribution of place names with the intermediate element *-inga-*. Most of these settlements were apparently established near the perimeters of the catchment areas of the *-ingas* and the *wicham* settlements, and the process of settlement expansion that was involved seems to have been similar to that represented by our Model II. However, apparently because of the significance of the parallel zones of

954

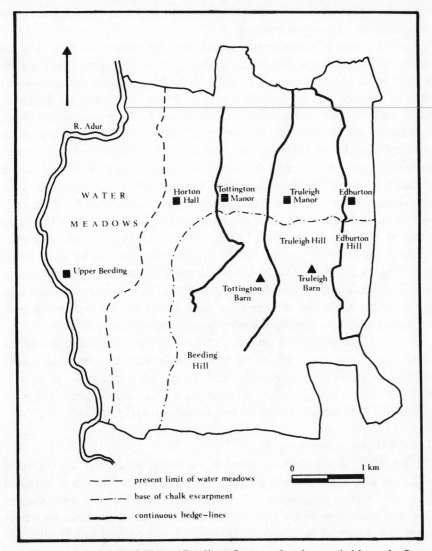

FIG. 24.26. The parish of Upper Beeding, Sussex, showing probably early Saxon boundaries marked by continuous hedge lines.

potential land use, the Model II process was modified and we have constructed a separate model shown in Fig. 24.25. It is a process that is rather intermediate between that of our Model II and those of our Model III situations, and it may well have been that of a transitional phase. This possibility is given support

955

by the facts that several of the *-inga-* places are no longer recorded as actual settlements by A.D. 1086 at least.

A third phase of settlement is represented by the distribution of place names in *-ham* and *-tun* (Fig. 24.24*b*). Most of these are situated on the zone of 'maximum potential' and seem to fill in the gaps between the early *-ingas* sites, so that the process that we observed in the Avon valley of Wiltshire, which we have shown schematically in our Model IIIB apparently took place, as is finally demonstrated by the pattern of narrow strip parishes aligned at right angles to the zone of 'maximum potential'. This pattern is shown up even more strikingly when internal divisions within individual parishes that almost certainly existed before the time of the Domesday Book (A.D. 1086) are taken into account as well. Such internal divisions can be established from charters, and on the ground in the form of almost continuous hedge lines that have survived to the present day. (Taylor, 1970). The large parish of Upper Beeding, not a 'strip parish', has five subdivisions defined by such hedge lines (Fig. 24.26). Each division almost certainly marks the catchment area of one of the settlements established up to 1086, and in four cases the chalk hills in the southern ends of the strips are named after the lowland settlements, suggesting again that each strip was exploited as one economic unit.

That this 'packing' of the catchment areas into the strip pattern during the *-inga- -ham -tun* phase (ended fairly arbitrarily here at 1086) was closely linked with growing usage of water mills in the scarp foot zone, as we suggested in a general way earlier, is borne out by the distribution of the mills recorded in the Domesday Book for the Henfield area (Fig. 24.24*c*).

The Anglo-Saxon burial sites

Bonney (1966) analysed the locations of the Saxon burials that are known in Wiltshire, and found that a significantly large number of them were situated on or very near to the present-day parish boundaries. He went on to suggest that these boundaries might well have existed as 'estate' boundaries very early in the Saxon period in Wiltshire. However, he recognized as well that this correlation of burial sites and parish boundaries does not occur in every county, and it is certainly not the case in south Sussex. Instead, as can be seen on the maps (Figs. 24.19 and 24.24), the burials in south Sussex are located either on or in the very close vicinity of the perimeters of the *model catchment areas* of sites with names in *-ingas* or *-inga-*. In Wiltshire it seems then that the Anglo-Saxon burials are those of settlements founded or occupied in the *-tun -ford -burgh* phase, and since this was the phase of the 'packing' process schematized in our Model IIIB, the boundaries of the villages may well have been the same as the parish boundaries formalized in the ninth century A.D. However, in south Sussex, where the burying of pagan Saxons seems likely to have preceded the 'packing phase', it is perhaps hardly surprising to find little correlation between burials and parish boundaries, and very interesting indeed to note that the burials do cluster near the edges of our idealized catchment areas for the earliest phase of the settlement.

PART II: SUMMARY

The various patterns of settlement expansion that we have identified in our two areas for the early medieval period are summarized in Fig. 24.27.

In relatively uniform areas the radial pattern of our Model I tends to appear, in which the actual area of each individual catchment depends to a great extent upon the quality of the soils that are available. Thus we suggested that the reason for the smaller area of the compact catchments in the northwestern part of our Chippenham–Calne area may well have been the rather greater tractability of the soils there.

The more daughter settlements that have to be accommodated, however, the more elongated their catchment areas will tend to be. A central position within the catchment area may place a settlement at an inconvenient distance from the nuclear or 'mother' settlement, and because of this the daughter villages may be sited eccentrically in relation to their catchment areas. This is the process that we identified in the Chichester area, and around Poling, and which we have represented in our Model II. There may indeed have been some additional factor in the Chichester case that produced the regularity in the siting of the daughter settlements at distances of just over 2 km. Bylund in his study of colonization in Lappland (Bylund, 1960; cited by Haggett, 1965, and by Clarke, 1968) confirmed a number of hypotheses regarding the colonists' wish to minimize the distance between their new settlement and (*a*) their parent settlement, (*b*) a church and (*c*) an available communication link. Perhaps Chichester had a central place function comparable with the possession of a church?

The introduction of a linear constraint produces the patterns of our Model III. This constraint may be a coastline, as in the case of the Worthing area and depicted in Model IIIA, or it may be a river valley, such as the Wiltshire Avon, or a geological outcrop, as in the Henfield area. The latter are depicted in our Model IIIB.

Also in the Henfield area, an intermediate phase or process is evidenced, though whether such a transitional phase is necessary in the 'packing' process is difficult to say. The secondary settlements in this intermediate case may be

957

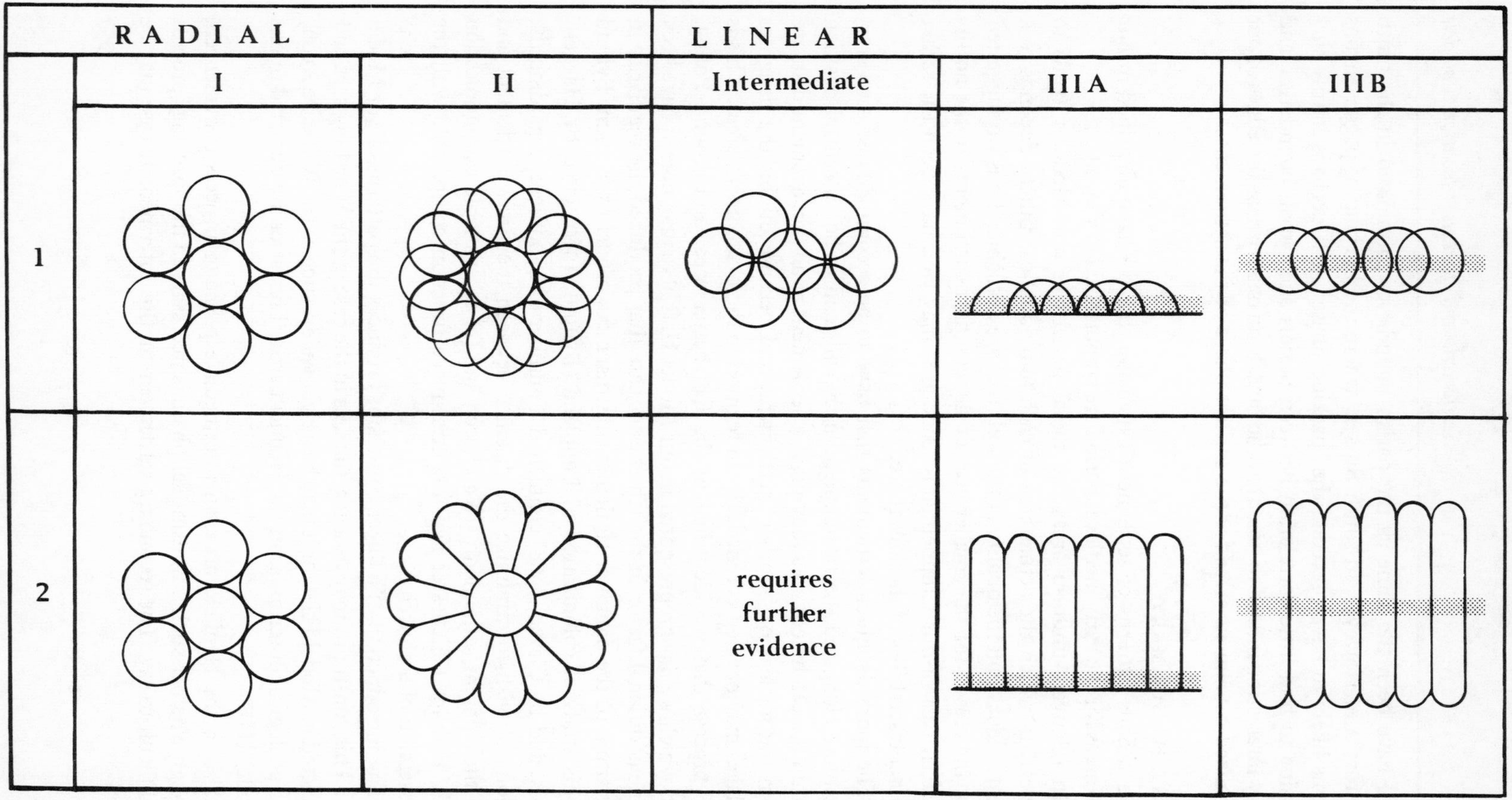

Fig. 24.27. Models of settlement expansion: summary diagram.

only seasonally occupied, or otherwise essentially dependent upon the primary settlements.

'Packing' seems to have taken place in the Worthing area in the earliest known period of Saxon settlement that can be distinguished on the basis of the place name evidence, while in the Henfield and the Avon Valley areas, as in the neighbourhood of Chichester, it took place in the later *-ham -tun* phase. In the Henfield area it took place from a base of extensive *-ingas* settlement.

It is dangerous, however, to go too far with reconstructions based on place name evidence alone, since this places so much emphasis on negative evidence, and the survival of place names is at present little understood. Wherever possible, therefore, it is well to supplement the place name evidence with that produced by archaeology, and we have tried to do this with the Saxon burials. The place name evidence for 'packing' of catchment areas can only be interpreted strictly as a *terminus ante quem*. For periods before this the archaeological evidence is of crucial importance for indicating the density of settlement. The results of the present analyses are sufficiently encouraging to suggest that further work along the same lines should be profitable.

Conclusion

The regularities that emerge from the use of the simple models we have employed and constructed in the course of the work described by this paper seem to justify the approach we have adopted. Taylor (1972) has suggested that 'The study of settlement patterns in pre-Saxon Britain, at least in the sense that historical geographers understand it, seems to this writer to be impossible either now or in the foreseeable future.' Clearly, the use of more complex techniques of analysis is dependent on progress in eliminating sample bias and, where it is possible, on the introduction of correction factors. Even from the data available at present, however, we hope to have shown that simple locational analysis can produce testable hypotheses of interest and general significance.

Notes

1 It must be emphasized that the system postulated by Applebaum and Bradley, and by the present writers, should not be confused with the 'infield-outfield' systems of economically marginal areas in Britain found throughout the medieval period and up to the present day in some areas.

Acknowledgements

The authors would like to express their gratitude to Mr Andrew Sherratt of Peterhouse, Cambridge for his help in the preparation of this paper; and to Mr Dafydd Kidd of Merton College, Oxford for his constructive criticism.

References

ADDLESHAW, G. W. O. (1954) *The Development of the Parochial System from Charlemagne (768–814) to Urban II (1089–99)*. St Anthony's Hall Publications (York) No. 6.

APPLEBAUM, S. (1954) The agriculture of the British Early Iron Age as exemplified at Figheldean Down, Wiltshire. *Proceedings of the Prehistoric Society*, **20**, 103–14.

BAKER, A. R. H. (1963) Howard Levi Gray and English field systems: an evaluation. *Agricultural History*, **39** (2), 86–91.

BERESFORD, M. W. and ST JOSEPH, J. K. (1958) *Medieval England: An Aerial Survey*. Cambridge.

BLOCH, M. (1966) *Land and Work in Medieval Europe: Selected Papers*. Trans. by J. E. Anderson. London: Routledge.

BONNEY, D. J. (1966) Pagan Saxon burials and boundaries in Wiltshire. *Wiltshire Archaeological Magazine*, **61**, 35–30.

BRADLEY, R. (1971). Stock raising and the origins of the hill fort on the South Downs. *Antiquaries Journal*, LI, 8–29.

BRANIGAN, K. (1967) Romano-British rural settlement in the western Chilterns. *Archaeological Journal*, **124**, 129–59.

BYLUND, E. (1960) Theoretical considerations regarding the distribution of settlement in inner north Sweden. *Geografiska Annaler*, **42**, 225–31.

CHISHOLM, M. (1962) *Rural Settlement and Land Use: An Essay in Location*. London: Hutchinson.

CLARKE, D. L. (1968) *Analytical Archaeology*. London: Methuen.

COLLINGWOOD, R. G. and MYRES, J. N. L. (1936) *Roman Britain and the English Settlement*. London: Oxford University Press.

CRAWFORD, O. G. S. (1924) *Air Survey and Archaeology*. London: H.M.S.O.

CURWEN, E. C. (1937) Querns. *Antiquity*, **11**, 133–51.

CURWEN, E. C. (1954) *The Archaeology of Sussex*. 2nd ed. London: Methuen.

CURWEN, E. and CURWEN, E. C. (1922) Notes on the archaeology of Burpham and the neighbouring Downs. *Sussex Archaeological Collections*, **63**, 1–53.

DODGSON, J. M. (1966) The significance of the distribution of the English place name in -ingas, -inga-, in south-east England. *Medieval Archaeology*, **10**, 1–29.

FINBERG, H. P. R. (1955) *Roman and Saxon Withington*. Occasional Papers of the Department of English Local History in the University of Leicester No. 8.

FLEURE, H. J. and WHITEHOUSE, W. E. (1916) The early distribution and valleyward movement of population in south Britain. *Archaeologia Cambrensis*, **16**, 100–40.

FOWLER, P. J. (1971) The M5 and M4 and archaeology. *Council for British Archaeology, Archaeological Review for 1970*, Grps XII–XIII, **5**, 5–10.

FOWLER, P. J. and EVANS, J. G. (1967) Plough marks, lynchets and early fields. *Antiquity*, **41**, 289–301.

FOX, SIR C. (1932) *The Personality of Britain*. Cardiff: National Museum of Wales.

GELLING, M. (1967) The English place names derived from the compound *wicham*. *Medieval Archaeology*, **11**, 87–104.

GRAY, H. L. (1915) *English Field Systems*. Harvard.

GRINSELL, L. V. (1940) Sussex barrows: supplementary paper. *Sussex Archaeological Collections*, **81**, 210–14.

GRINSELL, L. V. (1957) Archaeological gazetteer. In *Victoria History of the Counties of England: Wiltshire*, vol. I, pt. I. Folkestone: Dawsons of Pall Mall.

HAGGETT, P. (1965) *Locational Analysis in Human Geography*. London: Arnold.

HARRISS, J. C. (1971) Explanation in prehistory. *Proceedings of the Prehistoric Society*, **37** (I), 38–55.

HODGEN, M. T. (1939) Domesday water mills. *Antiquity*, **13**, 261–79.

HODGKIN, R. H. (1935) *A History of the Anglo-Saxons*. London: Oxford University Press.

HOLDEN, E. W. (1957) Section H of WILSON, D. M. and HURST, J. G. (eds.) Medieval Britain in 1956. *Medieval Archaeology*, **1**, 164–5.

HOPE-TAYLOR, B. K. (1958) Note. *Medieval Archaeology*, **2**, 184.

KJAERUM, P. (1954) Criss-cross furrows; plough marks under a Stone Age barrow in Jutland. *Kuml*, **28**.

LEE, R. B. (1969) !Kung bushman subsistence: an input-output analysis. In VAYDA, A. P. (ed.) *Environment and Cultural Behaviour*. New York.

LENNARD, R. (1959) *Rural England, 1086–1135*. London: Oxford University Press.

LIVERSIDGE, J. (1968) *Britain in the Roman Empire*. London: Routledge.

MANNING, W. H. (1964a) The plough in Roman Britain. *Journal of Roman Studies*, **54**, 54–65.

MANNING, W. H. (1964b) A mill pivot from Silchester. *Antiquaries Journal*, **44**, 38–40.

MEANEY, A. (1964) *A Gazetteer of Early Anglo-Saxon Burial Sites*. London: Allen & Unwin.

MORITZ, L. A. (1958) *Grain Mills and Flour in Classical Antiquity*. London: Oxford University Press.

NORRIS, N. E. S. and BURSTOW, G. P. (1948) A prehistoric and Romano-British site at West Blatchington, Hove. *Sussex Archaeological Collections*, **89**, 1–56.

ORWIN, C. S. and ORWIN, C. S. (1954) *The Open Fields*. 2nd ed. London: Oxford University Press.

ORDNANCE SURVEY (1944) *Map of Land Classification 1:625 000*. 2 sheets.

PIGGOTT, C. M. (1942) Five Late Bronze Age enclosures in north Wiltshire. *Proceedings of the Prehistoric Society*, **8**, 48–61.

PERRY, B. T. (1969) Iron Age enclosures and settlements on the Hampshire chalklands. *Archaeological Journal*, **126**, 29–43.

RENFREW, A. C. (1969) Review of *Locational Analysis in Human Geography* by P. Haggett, *Antiquity*, **43**, 74.

RITCHIE, A. (1969) *Settlements and Economy in Britain during the First Millennium B.C.* Unpublished PhD. dissertation, Edinburgh University.

SMITH, A. H. (1956) Place names and the English settlement. *Proceedings of the British Academy*, **42**, 67–88.

SMITH, C. T. (1967) *An Historical Geography of Western Europe Before 1800*. London: Longmans.

STONE, J. F. S. (1941) The Deverel-Rimbury settlement on Thorny Down, Winterbourne Gunner, southern Wiltshire. *Proceedings of the Prehistoric Society*, **7**, 114–33.

TAYLOR, C. C. (1970) *Dorset*. London: Hodder & Stoughton.

TAYLOR, C. C. (1972) 'The study of settlement patterns in pre-Saxon Britain'. In UCKO, P., DIMBLEBY, G. W. and TRINGHAM, R. (eds.) *Settlement Patterns and Urbanisation*, London: Duckworth.

THIRSK, J. (1964) The common fields. *Past and Present*, **29**, 3–25.

THOMAS, A. C. (ed.) (1966) *Rural Settlement in Roman Britain*. Council for British Archaeology Research Report No. 7.

THORLEY, A. J. (1971) Vegetational history in the Vale of the Brooks. In *Guide to the Sussex Excursions*, Institute of British Geographers Annual Conference, University of Sussex.

TOPLEY, W. (1872) On the relation of the parish boundaries of south-east England to great physical features. *Journal of the Anthropological Institute*, **3**, 32.

VITA-FINZI, C. (1969) Early man and environment. In COOKE, R. U. and JOHNSON, J. H. (eds.) *Trends in Geography*. Oxford: Pergamon Press.

VITA-FINZI, C. and HIGGS, E. S. *et al.* (1970) Prehistoric economy in the Mount Carmel area of Palestine: site catchment analysis. *Proceedings of the Prehistoric Society*, **36**, 1–37.

WHITE, L. (1962) *Medieval Technology and Social Change*. London: Oxford University Press.

WOOLRIDGE, S. W. and LINTON, D. L. (1933) The loam terrains of south-east England in their relation to its early history. *Antiquity*, **7**, 297–310.

25
Models in medieval studies

E. M. JOPE

The Queen's University of Belfast, Northern Ireland

Medieval archaeology as a systematic discipline is perhaps a little senior to prehistoric.[1] 'Gothic' as a taxonomic concept in the treatment of building design (rather than merely meaning 'barbaric') was in existence in Wren's time (Harvey, 1968, p. 67) and was fully established in the early nineteenth century (Piggott, 1959; Bialostocki, 1966) by the time Thomas Rickman in his *Attempt to Descriminate the Styles of English Architecture* (1819) systematized its development in a set of terms derived directly from the material itself and wholly descriptive: 'first pointed', 'decorated', 'perpendicular' (K. Clark, 1928, pp. 16 ff., 95 ff.). Here was a respectable taxonomic model, implying a whole set of propositions such as the crucial role of the pointed arch, to be tested against the observed data accruing from further research.

Some attempt at historical reality was brought into this model by the substitution of 'Early English' for 'first pointed'. But not until the present century, particularly the past few decades, has this subject been effectively humanized; men's names can be increasingly associated with the actual buildings and stylistic trends (e.g. Lethaby, 1906, 1925; Harvey, 1944, 1947, 1950, 1954; A. J. Taylor, 1950; Colvin *et al.*, 1963; Myres, 1967), which we can now see more exactly in their setting as part of an ever-changing medieval scene.

This progress from taxonomic analysis into historicity, and the cumulative data, the exactly analysed structural and stylistic expositions that have made it possible for individual buildings (or groups thereof), is really one of the great achievements of medieval studies, though rarely has it been expounded as such. Other branches of medieval archaeology have not been quite so forward in this kind of systematization, though we shall examine their progress.

In medieval studies generally, model building has long been a widespread and tacitly accepted procedure; remodelling or demolition has sometimes been more contentious (Round, 1898).[2] Historians have conceived their models of the medieval past as postulates or theoretical constructs out of their interpretation of available literary data, to be tried against new or reanalysed data and

963

so modified or rejected (Galbraith, 1961, pp. 12 ff., 28 ff.). Medieval archaeologists have inevitably drawn upon these models for their time frameworks and sociological, economic or other schemata, with consequent constraints from dynastic, regnal or other arbitrary divisions, such as the focal effect of particular chronicled events or important places (e.g. A.D. 1066). By proceeding thus archaeologists may not always fully exploit the information potential of their archaeological data. The danger is probably most serious just where there is most abundant written evidence. More and more models are, however, being built initially out of medieval primary archaeological data (Thompson, 1967), to be worked against historically based models. Progress in many aspects of medieval studies must now largely lie in the close and skilful interweaving of approaches, treated judiciously with the critical acumen appropriate to each.

It should be noted, of course, that some models in medieval studies have steadfastly maintained their acceptability over the years: the hypothesis, for instance, that certain settlements of Viking age (such as Hedeby, Birka and Kauspang) first rose to importance as trading centres in the ninth century seems clear from the coin evidence and has not been contradicted by other evidence, though their decline was not in each case for the same cause or at comparable times, and hence discussions have still continued on the latter (Sawyer, 1962, ch. 8). Yet a long-held stable model can be suddenly upset by one newly observed item (e.g. Herrnbrodt, 1958).

NATURE OF MEDIEVAL EVIDENCE

Archaeological and written data provide complementary evidence in medieval studies. Each type of data will reveal particular facets of the medieval real world, and can yield its own separate models thereof. When these are brought together they can yield more comprehensive and illuminating models than either alone. But most of the written data come to us through the eyes, tongues, ears and minds of medieval assessors and recorders, as well as a filtering through our own historians as interpreters. Even when such data had nominally a cold statistical purpose, as in the Domesday survey and closely related sources, human error or subterfuge, or special circumstances may sometimes have left their mark, which may condition the model (Jope, 1955; Lennard, 1959; Jope and Terrett, 1961; Galbraith, 1961).

Every medieval community, every nation, every generation, must be treated as a complex system with multiple internal network meshes of contacts of more specialized groups associated through work, trade, cultural activity, etc. (Jope, 1963), and itself must be seen as part of larger external networks. They must all therefore be treated in terms of suitably fluid and complex

PLATE 25.1 Hardware models—a scale model of Houchin's Farm, Feering, Essex. The house was built c. 1600. This model is now in the Science Museum, London.

models (cf. Doran, 1970); Smith (1964), for instance, shows a stage in making a model of one kind of timber construction – crucks – complex enough to be set in a pattern for the whole of medieval Europe. In medieval studies we have the advantage of great variety in kinds of evidence available; as well as the historical and the excavation evidence, we have very many buildings of all sorts, many standing to full height. Archaeological data judiciously used can moreover provide a degree of objectivity, although sampling distortion may operate in various ways, in mode of deposition, survival, chance discovery, or choice of site. We should be foolish indeed to neglect one kind of evidence and its models unduly in favour of another.

The multiple nature of medieval data also brings to the surface some matters of procedure and principle in model building. Arguing from the particular to the general is a process to some extent inherent in constructing models, and provided the elements of a hypothesis are clearly seen for what they are – aids to the constructive thought that is stimulated by rigorous testing – speculative model building is not so dangerous a practice as some would have us suppose (Brown, 1969a). Counsel for sense and restraint in medieval model building is, however, clearly valid. This greater range of interlocking evidence means that models built from medieval and post-medieval data can often provide an illuminating testing ground for prehistoric interpretations (Jope, 1963; Bradley, 1971).

Categories of models used in medieval studies

We may now consider the kinds of models used – or potentially useful – in medieval studies. We start with the simplest, the substantive hardware models, and progress towards the more abstract and notional. Some of our examples illustrate more than one category. There are other ways in which we could have grouped, which cut across the scheme here used: there are, for instance, *static models* (i.e. frozen) and *dynamic models* – that is, models that can readily feel the pulsating character of a community or other system; and we might equally have used the classification into iconic, analogue and symbolic models (Clarke, 1968, fig. 2) (see also Fig. 1.2 of this volume).

HARDWARE MODELS

These are often the bricks, the elements from which more general archaeological models are constructed. Any thinking archaeologist will use these – or working drawings of them – to reconstitute and present the original state of the site or building under investigation (Plate 25.1): a farm (Jope and Threlfall,

1958, pp. 118–19; Sprockhoff, 1937), a settlement (Winckelmann, 1954; West, 1969), timber constructions (Hewett, 1963, 1966; Fletcher and Spokes, 1964), houses (Pantin, 1957; Addyman, 1964, pp. 44 ff.; Barley, 1967; P. Smith, 1967), other domestic or civil structures (Herteig, 1959; Smith, 1965; Pantin, 1961, 1963b), earthwork and timber fortifications (Alcock, 1966, p. 186; Waterman, 1959; Herrnbrodt, 1958), a great church (Conant, 1959; Taylor, 1969), a potter's workshop (Hope-Taylor, 1956), a piece of furniture (Wilson, 1957), etc. But often the observed data do not present us directly with a simple entity; the site or building has usually been changed by successive users, and the structures must therefore be analysed in time, to yield a sequence of such substantive models (Figs. 25.1, 25.2; Herrnbrodt, 1958; Jope, 1961, p. 206; Taylor, 1969, p. 107, fig. 1). These are the basic data of archaeological model building; they provide analogies for the interpretation of other examples, and are the elements from which more general type models can be constructed, and such as can be related to historical models (Pevsner, 1962, p. 260, pl. 13a). Such time trajectories or developments may sometimes be more profitably traced forward from a given point rather than backwards from more recent times (Fletcher and Spokes, 1964) (Plate 21.1, Figs. 21.2–5).

There is also the kind of general model (but still usually practical rather than conceptual) that grows outwards from a single small item or unit, a datum, that provides vital evidence. The round vertical timbers of which the pointed stumps survive at the Husterknupp (Herrnbrodt, 1958), just high enough to reveal that they were squared off above ground level, show that an excavator's round post-holes need not necessarily preclude framed buildings of neatly squared timbers and exact joinery (Waterman, 1956, p. 82, fig. 7). Testing here is by the cumulative observing of corroborative examples, and the general model, though initially based on a small item of evidence, does stimulate research and sharpen observation for evidence otherwise liable to be overlooked.

We might take as another example of this type of 'cornerstone' or 'springer' model building, more far-reaching than the last in its historical implications, all the proto-historic constructions that can be grown outwards from the pivotal springer given by an increasingly exact attribution (and hence dating) of one crucial coin in the Sutton Hoo purse ('Dagobert' Grierson, 1952; Bruce-Mitford, 1969).

Even site plans, sections and pottery drawings, the standby of medieval archaeologists, are to be considered as selectively iconic models of complex real life phenomena. The customary multiplicity of pottery rim sections will not, however, get us very far, for such are only traits; each complete vessel is

966

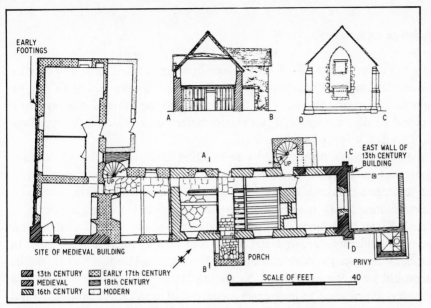

FIG. 25.1. House models – an iconic representation of the stages of growth of an Oxfordshire manor, Ascot Doilly, over *c.* 600 years. Models for buildings and structures should have a diachronic and dynamic capacity to simulate development and stages of growth (from Jope and Threlfall, 1959).

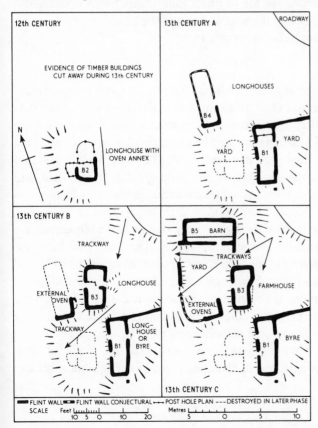

FIG. 25.2. Settlement models – a representation of the development from a twelfth century longhouse to a thirteenth century farm at Gomeldon, Wiltshire. Models for hamlets, villages and towns should also have the capacity to simulate successive responses to successive conditions (from Wilson and Hurst, 1966).

really to be seen as the datum unit in significant model-building, and only by adequate attempts to reconstitute complete vessel shapes and sizes can we begin to understand the place of the ceramics in the life and economy of a medieval family, a household, an establishment or a community (e.g. Jope and Threlfall, 1959, p. 257, fig. 16).

Analogue models have proved a stimulating extension of this substantive 'iconic' category. Thus the concept of the continental Teutonic settlement, with its large longhouses amongst the tiny *grubenhäuser* or working huts (e.g. Winckelmann, 1954), maintained the persistent search for larger houses in English Saxon settlement sites, which have now at last yielded evidence for houses of moderate size, first at Linford and now so fully at West Stow in Suffolk (West, 1969). More appropriate, however, to Hrodgar's great public hall would be the great halls at Yeavering (Hope-Taylor, 1957). It is also necessary, for instance, to have exact models of all the locational and structural details of Viking forts such as Trelleborg or Aggersborg before we can understand their full strategic role or their influence on fortified construction further afield, as in the British Isles. The same is true of, say, western European and Slav towns (Hensel, 1969) if we are to make valid comparisons between the rise of medieval urbanization to the west and east of the Elbe, between western Europe and eastern Europe (Barraclough, 1970).

TEMPORAL MODELS

Precise dating of items, or of their individual features, is a basic requirement of all archaeological studies. Only from the accumulation of such exact data can serviceable time trajectory diagrams be constructed, and from these more general time framework schemata can be assembled. Such iconic diagrams are in themselves largely factual presentations of data; but they provide a secure basis for the setting and extrapolation of less precisely determined data, and they can also serve as the models against which the ordering of analogous data can be tested (Figs. 21.3–21.6, 25.1, 25.2).

Annual increment methods of dating (i.e. tree ring or varve sequences) are therefore particularly valuable in medieval studies. Tree ring data have, for instance, set the development of medieval Novgorod on an exact chronological basis (Schove, 1964) and – of much more global significance – are providing for the exact annual increment calibration of radiocarbon dating. Here lie the primary data for constructing medieval time frame schemata and time trajectory models (Lavell, 1971, 7A–8B; Berger, 1970, fig. 24, p. 133).

Few time trajectory diagrams have been constructed for medieval data. Computer analysis of associations of changing types of stirrup, horse bit and arrowhead in tenth to fourteenth century Turkic graves has shown how a firm chronology of changing design can be extrapolated from a comparatively few coins (Fedorov-Davydov, 1965; Clarke, 1968). The major Saxon or Germanic cemeteries (Pirling, 1960; La Baume, 1967), or others such as at Birka (Arbman, 1943) should yield to similar treatment. At Junkersdorf (La Baume, 1967) or Birka the grave groups might be susceptible to treatment analogous to that for the Iron Age cemetery at Münsingen (Hodson, 1968), if not to full matrix analysis (Clarke, 1968; Kendall, 1969). But among Christianized peoples we have virtually no such assemblages of burial goods, and the requisite coherent body of artefacts is hard to assemble. Analogous analytical treatment, however, even full matrix or cluster analysis, should be possible for the vast quantities of medieval pottery excavated, such as is in some measure regularly practised by New World archaeologists. Simple time trajectory concepts lie hidden as postulates behind many pottery dating arguments extrapolated from one site to another (e.g. Fig. 25.8; Jope, 1958, p. 55, fig. 20), and such work really needs explicit full-scale quantitative analysis. For Europe generally we can so far go little beyond simple tabulations (Whitehouse, 1966, 1969; Hurst *et al.*, 1969) and even these are a considerable advance on the previous lack of ordered knowledge.

Time setting of excavated medieval layers, and hence of the reconstituted model of the whole site, depends so often in the last resort on the most abundant artefact – pottery. For this the dating depends in practice very much on a chain of reasoning through interpretation of architectural evidence and its relation ultimately with documentary evidence (Taylor, 1961b; Hurst, 1963).

Coinage, with its intricacies of die-linking, its progressively changing coin weights, and changing composition (Metcalf and Schweizer, 1971; Petersson, 1969) should be particularly susceptible to time trajectory studies, and indeed such work is gaining impetus. Particularly important for archaeologists would be probability studies of the time span of circulation of particular issues (Dolley, 1969). We should here draw attention to the unrepresentative sample of the original circulating currency that our preserved coins may present (Metcalf and Schweizer, 1971) and this model may be true of other artefacts in other situations.

Some quantitative time trajectory study of the introduction and spread of new ideas has been possible with a body of data from reasonably datable buildings (Figs. 25.3–25.5) (Jope, 1961). Such work could be profitably extended to making polythetic time trajectory diagrams (Fig. 25.6). Diagrams of this sort are largely factual presentations of observed data, but they do provide a predictive skeleton to contain less exactly determined data, and more

969

important, they give a model against which to see and test analogous data, and so to contribute a more general conceptual model, in this case for the dispersal of a new idea spatially, temporally and socially through a population. We are thus led on to our next category of models – for spatial distributions (Figs. 25.7–25.11).

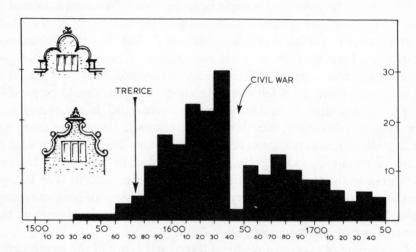

FIG. 25.3. Temporal models and buildings – a model of the rising popularity in Britain of shaped gables which were used on the continent from the 1490s onwards. Only datable examples are included, grouped by decades; the Cornish house at Trerice is thus shown in the forefront of this fashion in England (from Jope, 1961).

There is, however, another type of temporal model to be noted here, a model centred on a focal point in time. The whole study of events, life and culture in England during the second half of the eleventh century has been turned into such a model, with the historical date 1066 as its focal point. This is, however, in reality only a clumping perturbation of the more evenly flowing time trajectories proceeding in Europe, and the rest of the British Isles generally during the eleventh century, the models for which are discussed further below. We should also note, moreover, that the historically ascertainable model of the Norman conquest of England would be difficult to deduce from archaeological evidence alone; the latter would give a quite different account (Zarnecki, 1966).

SPATIAL DISTRIBUTION MODELS

Archaeologists have delighted in making distribution maps, without, however, always giving adequate attention to marshalling their spatial data and setting

970

them against a background of negative evidence (Fig. 25.8), or thinking what such spatial patterns might mean, especially if subjected to further analysis. Some of our spatial distributions blanket many features and need further analysis, just as we have already seen how a time trajectory diagram may on further analysis reveal a spatial substructure that will, for instance, illustrate how an innovation may be carried through a country and into various social levels (Fig. 25.3–4) (Jope, 1961, 1963; cf. Sauer, 1963, pp. 359f.). Other maps, such as can be constructed from the combination of archaeological and other evidence, provide composite models to show how it can come about that 'European Gothic' and various 'National Gothics' are valid stylistic concepts in building practice and design (Harvey, 1950, endpapers and pp. 23, 38, 51; Jope, 1961, 1963, p. 345; Taylor, 1961b, pp, 107, 111; Atkinson, 1948).

Similarly, many ceramic and other artefact distributions need analysing for substructure on temporal and other bases; with medieval ceramics this is at present a complex task (Le Patourel, 1968). Some distributions have been intended to reflect trading patterns (Fig. 25.8) (e.g. Dunning, 1959; Hurst *et al.*, 1969), but the complex chains and networks of circumstances under-lying them are still not sufficiently understood or indeed analysable. Finer imported ceramics were evidently often dispersed according to special circumstances such as the movements of a noble household (Hodges and Jope, 1956, p. 26), and some ceramic types were probably being produced at more than one centre, so that the data will need more refined trait analysis and remapping to reveal significant clusters (Fig. 25.8). Operative market centres also have to be considered (Figs. 25.9–11) (Hoskins and Jope, 1954, pp. 108–9; Hodges and Jope, 1956a, p. 26). Less refined vessels were being made by many rural communities for their own immediate use, and with these types the distributions must reflect the way in which trends spread through a population (cf. Sauer, 1963) as a complex network of social contacts, in which both rural and urban communities as well as specialist groups were interacting (Jope, 1963). We are barely on the threshold of formulating the problems, let alone the model, in such matters; but model-using procedure provides the key route to this new knowledge.

Other distributions provide inferential models for the bulk or long-distance transport facilities available, the distorted map surfaces being much more informative when documentary data are added to the archaeological data (Jope, 1956a, 1964, 1972); even mapping of the latter alone can summarize data into a model to show how extensively bulk transport by wagon might be employed in twelfth-century Britain, with rivers of only restricted use. The models thus constructed for building trade supplies illustrate one of Europe's earliest systematically organized large-scale industries in operation (Jones, 1952; Jope, 1964, pp. 92ff.). Some spatial distributions of particular materials, such as imported fine stone, were clearly dictated by special circumstances and needs (e.g. Waterman, 1959, 1970; Dunning and Jope, 1954), which are in

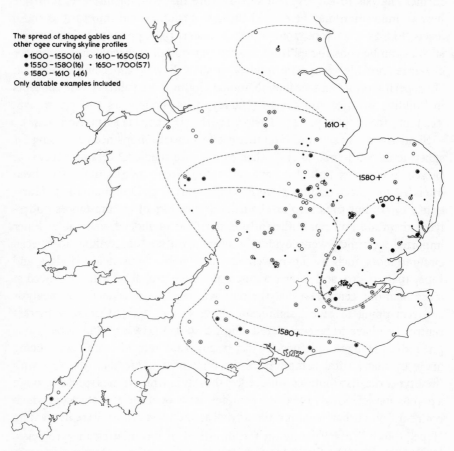

The spread of shaped gables and
other ogee curving skyline profiles
● 1500 - 1550 (6)   ○ 1610 - 1650 (50)
● 1550 - 1580 (16)   · 1650 - 1700 (57)
◉ 1580 - 1610 (46)
Only datable examples included

FIG. 25.4. Spatial models and buildings – a model of the penetration of an innovation, the shaped gable (see Fig. 25.3). Every temporal model has a spatial component and vice versa; compare the studies of Dethlefson and Deetz (1966) on the diffusion of dated tombstone styles in New England.

some degree included within some of the maps already noted. The extensive twelfth-century use of fine materials such as Purbeck or Tournai marble, or later on of alabaster, has never yet been adequately mapped.

The underlying conceptual significance of these spatial pattern models has

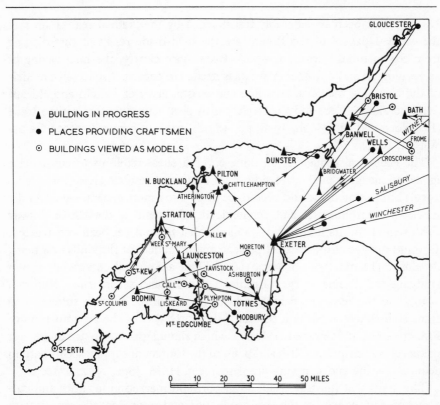

FIG. 25.5. Spatial models and buildings used as models – a map showing the extent to which fifteenth and sixteenth century craftsmen came from a distance to work on major structures and how distant structures served as patterns for new works. Existing structures usually serve as partial models for those under construction; under certain assumptions an analysis of affinity relationships may attempt to model such complex chains of derivation in structures ranging from megalithic tombs to hill forts, temples and cathedrals (from Jope, 1961).

been a persistent undercurrent in the discussion, emphasizing the value of constructing such models even when they may be at a very provisional stage.

ECOLOGICAL MODELS

This category needs a heading of its own, summarizing as it does how we present our evidence for the interaction of people or communities and their behaviour patterns with their changing environment, which is cultural as much as physical. The term 'human Palaeoecology' could justifiably be applied here.

Our models of changing rural life and economy and land use in north-east

973

Norfolk have been considerably transformed by the gradual realization that the water expanses of the Broads are the man-made result of turf digging from Saxon times (Lambert, 1960). Even more clearly, the interleaving of archaeological and documentary data is needed to construct successive models of the changing medieval coastline and coastal areas of Britain and Europe (e.g. the Zuider Zee) and their relation to port activity and maritime trade (Beresford and St Joseph, 1958, pp. 187 ff., 213f.; Sheppard, 1922; Carus-Wilson, 1963).

The ecological sequences on dune-covered sites enable us to construct a model of changing medieval land use for such now desolate areas (Dimbleby, 1959); but this model would need to be fitted into a more general model for the medieval environmental and economic development of the whole Solway Firth region and its hinterland – a model that has not yet been constructed. It would involve also the use of palaeoclimatic models, of the kinds now being developed (Lamb, 1966; Schove, 1964). These are of vital importance also in studying the decline of the Greenland and Iceland settlements (Nørlund, 1936), and the Icelandic fishing industry in which the English suffered also from Hanseatic competition (Carus-Wilson, 1933). But the accumulation of fishbone remains from medieval sites, which should give substance to the vast medieval consumption of fish and point to the sources of supply, seems hard to acquire (sieving and sampling problems) (e.g. H. M. Jope, 1952, p. 102).

The maps that illustrate trade, transport and marketing facilities and cultural contacts, as well as those of production and resources, all contribute to our construction of general overall human palaeoecological models.

A medieval community, rural, urban or institutional, was the focal point of a complex social and ecological system, and sets of ecological models are required if we are to understand them (Fig. 1.10). Some investigators have seen this (e.g. Biddle, 1962, pp. 71ff., 1970; Janssen, 1965; Kolchin, 1958), but it requires excavation on a very extensive scale with a fully programmed assembly of ancillary services to amass significant samples of the data reasonably free from selection and bias. To do this even for a small monastic house, a royal hunting lodge (Rahtz, 1968), or a moated seat of the gentry (Hurst, 1961) is a formidable project; but this must surely be the aim of medieval studies as much as for hunter-fisher-gatherers and primitive agriculturalists (Figs. 1.10–1.12).

HISTORICAL CONCEPTUAL MODELS

We have already noted how archaeologists have used the historians' models for constructing their time frameworks and for more specific dating purposes.

There are, however, other less pragmatic more generally conceptual matters for which archaeological data must be interwoven with and tested against the historical in model building, and vice versa. Our next examples deal with direct historical, economic, social or cultural concepts; in the following section we shall consider a few even more abstract concepts.

Every stage in the enquiry into medieval reality presents in effect a model to be tested and remodelled, leading cumulatively to a further stage in the synthesis. The processes of separate model building from archaeological and documentary or written data, and the problems of bringing the respective models together, are illustrated at the threshold of the effective written record in Britain, in work progressing on the Anglo-Saxon settlement, where convergence on generally acceptable conclusions seems still far off in some matters (Myres, 1969; Evison, 1965 and reviews); analogous difficulties also seem inherent in constructing models for the rise of Slav peoples (e.g. Graus, 1970; Perrott, 1965).

A model (Fig. 25.6) summarizing on a time framework the available information on the nature and designs of Saxon *burhs* leads to new thinking on the circumstances that brought them into being, and on the varied sources of design – native tradition and continental exemplars; it also brings into review the continental connections of Saxon rulers (Hassall and Hill, 1970; cf. von Uslar, 1964).

Exact data on the metal composition of silver pennies have been used to construct a working model of bullion movements under Henry I, and also to illuminate a little his personal character; an outflow of coinage taken as taxes from all over the country and spent by the king abroad, was compensated by an inflow from trade supplemented by newly mined English silver rich in gold, which, as the analytical data show, came to dominate the coin metal composition. This model and the data behind it can be used to test the contemporary model enshrined in the Anglo-Saxon chronicle complaints of debasement and forgery; the analytical data show in fact that the coinage was not significantly debased – failed harvests and the king's extravagance abroad were more probably the real culprits (Metcalf and Schweizer, 1971).

Numerous excavated medieval sites, especially villages, insistently prompt questions about the effects and causes of recessions in the fourteenth century: the failed harvests, the pandemics (especially of 1347–50, 1361–2 and 1349), which, however, also reduced the ravaging warfare that so many men enjoyed for social and political ends, for its excitement, its prospects of booty, and of wealth for those who supplied the armies. From that time on there have been innumerable economic recession models, though few general enough to

975

embrace all the causal and consequent factors. For a simple human system, a farm or even perhaps a hamlet, one set of factors might predominate (Fox, 1958); but a parish (Fig. 1.10), a town, even a small village (e.g. Biddle, 1962), was a much more complex polythetic system, and in tracing the ebb and flow of its fourteenth-century history we must be careful to treat it as such, especially when working with a small selected area.

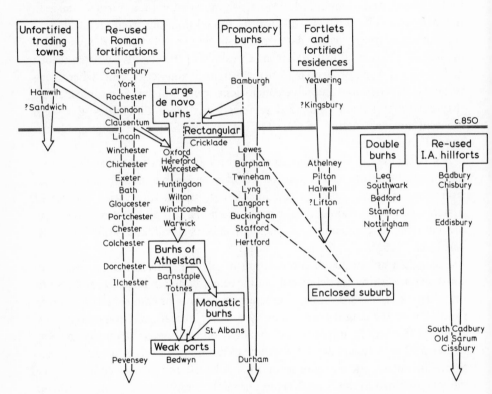

FIG. 25.6. Temporal models and settlements – a model of the different origins and developments of English Saxon 'towns' (*burhs*) *c.* 400–1000 (from Hassall and Hill, 1970).

Some factual data have been assembled into models to present the changes in specific matters such as building enterprises and their sensitivity to wars, famine and pestilences (e.g. Harvey, 1947, p. 160). The progress of the 1347–1350 pestilence can be traced across Europe and seen against estimates of fluctuating population through the fourteenth century (Langer, 1964). These models are all facets of the general model for Europe assembled from documentary sources, against which every detailed construct of fourteenth-century life produced by excavation must be fitted to give an ebb and flow of variance; with our general models it is as essential to assess the range of variance as to know the norms of the general parameters.

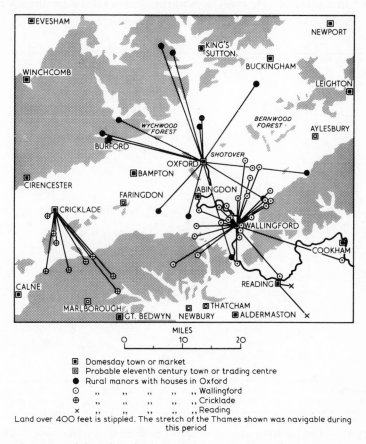

MILES
0   10   20

▣ Domesday town or market
▣ Probable eleventh century town or trading centre
● Rural manors with houses in Oxford
⊙ ,, ,, ,, ,, ,, Wallingford
⊕ ,, ,, ,, ,, ,, Cricklade
× ,, ,, ,, ,, ,, Reading
Land over 400 feet is stippled. The stretch of the Thames shown was navigable during this period

FIG. 25.7. Spatial models and settlements – towns and markets in the Oxford region of eleventh century England (Jope, 1954).

Norman institutions, military skill and cultural life have provided much scope for model building and demolition or reassembly (Brown, 1969a and reviews; Davison, 1969) based upon documentary and upon archaeological data, with increasingly informed interplay. The multiple concept of fortifications as communal enterprises, as castles or private residences in varying degree strongholds at the service (or disservice) of rulers or landowners, and marks therefore of a feudal society, is a sphere of model building hotly contested. Armitage (1912) firmly demonstrated that 'castles' that is, fortified residences with feudal connotation – were basically a Norman innovation in England; but this should not obscure the evidence from detailed structural analysis that some private residences in the British Isles were already convergently being given a measure of defensive character in pre-Norman times

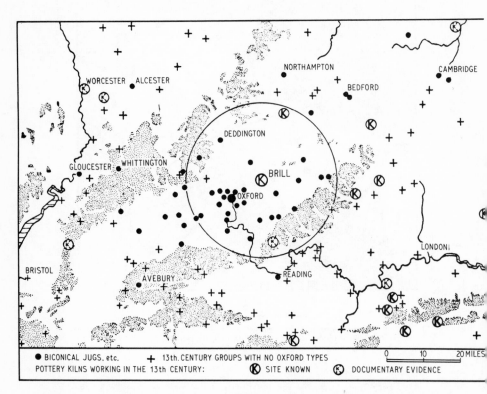

FIG. 25.8. Spatial models and settlements – the distinctive artefact as an indicator of market service areas. The distribution of later thirteenth century biconical jugs made at kilns in Brill, Bucks, near Oxford. Note the importance of plotting rival kiln sources and the distribution of negative evidence (thirteenth century find groups with no Brill types) (from Jope, 1963).

(Davison, 1967a, 1967b; Jope, 1966, pp. 116ff.), though, equally, this need not invest them with feudal significance. Here again it is the structurally analysed hardware models that provide the vital data to be worked in with the historical material, in order to assemble more realistic general models that can aid our understanding of a rising feudal society in England during the two or three

978

generations following 1066. The principle may be extended to Ireland and to parts of Europe. A newly proposed model arising out of this work on defensive structures (Davison, 1969), which softens the old concept of culture change following sharply upon invasion, has already drawn fire (Brown, 1969a). But it is well substantiated, particularly on the English side, by comparisons with the models built upon evidence from institutional (Lennard, 1959, pp. 1ff.) and military matters (Hollister, 1962), from technology in metalwork (Jope, 1956b) and ceramics (Hurst, 1963; Hurst *et al.*, 1969), and from contemporary cultural activities, architecture (Baldwin Brown, 1925; Conant, 1959, p. 285), sculpture (Zarnecki, 1966), manuscript illumination (Wormald, 1952), coinage (Dolley, 1969, pp. 20ff.; Rigold, 1965) and literature (Chambers, 1932).

Norman society cultivated knightly ways, part of its power stemming from a command of equine mounted combat, which depended to some extent upon the effective use of the stirrup. The model which sees the stirrup as the vital formative influence in shaping Western feudalism (White, 1962, ch. 1; Bloch, 1940, 1961) takes too little account of other factors, and is built on an inadequately critical use of some data (stirrups did not always beget feudalism), but it does illustrate how basically technological data can lead us directly into consideration of highly abstract conceptual models.

Technological models are another class that runs right through our present classification. They have immense but hardly yet realized potential in ordering the purpose of medieval archaeological thought into a structured system (Thompson, 1964), giving a new view of the role of medieval technology (for which much of the data is archaeological) and scientific thought in the rise of modern technological civilization (Jope, 1965).

ABSTRACT CONCEPTUAL MODELS

Some models constructed from archaeological data have already been seen to carry a more general conceptual significance. We now discuss others that penetrate even more deeply into the abstractions of the medieval *Weltanschaung*.

We might first examine the conceptual model in which the increasing later medieval prevalence of tall tower residences is seen as symbolic of rank and authority, their builders often little concerned with real defence or even safeguarding of possessions, but nostalgically conscious of being heirs to a tradition (never entirely broken) of the strong tower as the habitation proper to nobility, reflecting in its height and separateness the difference in station between the wealth and power of lordship and the relative dependence of followers and households (Taylor, 1958, p. 224; Jope, 1961). Here is a true conceptual model of hierarchical social relations in the later Middle Ages constructed out of archaeological data – a model to be tested against the climate of thought in medieval writings (see also the relative elevations of Maya house platforms, Fig. 20.5).

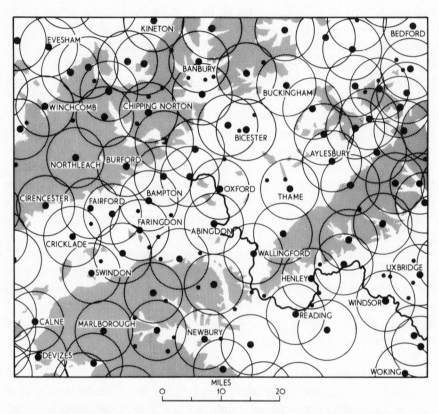

FIG. 25.9. Spatial models and settlements – towns and markets in the Oxford region of thirteenth and fourteenth century England. Markets flourishing throughout this period are shown as large spots ringed with circles of 5 miles radius. The smaller spots indicate markets of lesser importance. Land over 400 feet is stippled. The stretch of the Thames shown was navigable during this period (from Jope, 1954).

At an earlier time, in the eleventh and twelfth centuries, a tower seeming to rise from a mound might be thought to have a measure of deliberate show of rank and power about it; but we should remember, with the more precise data now available on mottes in relation to towers (Thompson, 1961, 1967a),

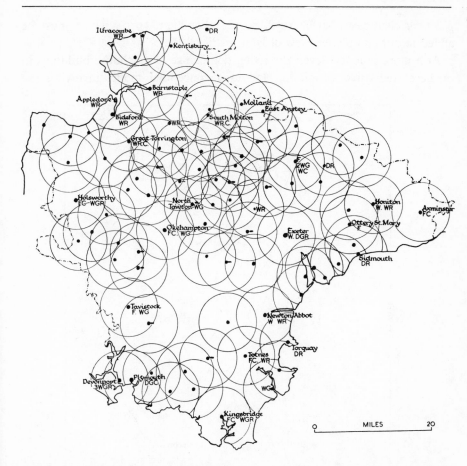

FIG. 25.10. Spatial models and settlement – towns and markets in the Devonshire region of post-medieval England. Each market is shown by a dot, surrounded by a circle of 5 miles radius. Only the heart of Dartmoor and a few small tracts elsewhere are more than 5 miles from a market and most farmers had a choice of several markets within that distance. All dots not otherwise marked indicate monthly livestock markets handling less than 10 000 head a year. A minus sign against the dot indicates a market held less frequently than monthly. Centres handling more than 10 000 animals a year are named, but only Exeter handles more than 60 000 (from Stamp, 1950).

Key for Figs. 25.10 and 25.11: D, daily; 2W, twice weekly; W, weekly; F, fortnightly; R, retail; G, general wholesale; C, corn.

the value of a mound piled against a tower in protecting its timber posts or stone footings against destruction by fire or sapping.

The parallel conceptual model of rising private magnificence in the later Middle Ages can be constructed from the courtyard houses and those of *palatium* character (Taylor 1958, p. 124; Faulkner, 1970), which must be added to our cumulative view of later medieval life.

At a more practical level, the rising dominance of gatehouse buildings in medieval defensive design has led to a conceptual model involving the

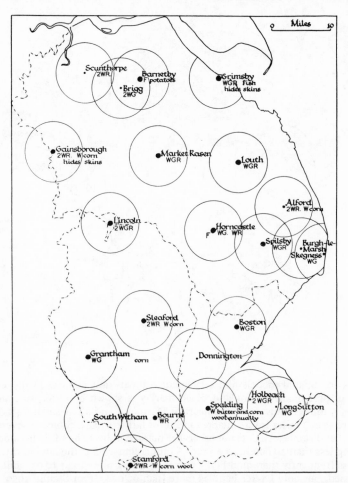

FIG. 25.11. Spatial models and settlements – towns and markets in the Lincolnshire region of post-medieval England. Each market is shown by a dot, surrounded by a circle of 5 miles radius. With the exception of Barnetby and Horncastle (fortnightly) and Lincoln and Stamford (twice weekly) all places marked have weekly stock markets but are concerned more with corn and the other products named. In contrast to such a west-country county as Devonshire, concerned largely with cattle which cannot be driven far to market and are expensive to transport, the markets of Lincolnshire are concerned more with other products and each serves a radius of far more than 5 miles (from Stamp, 1950). (For key see Fig. 25.10.)

changing relations between the lord and his armed forces, who came to be paid mercenaries rather than men tied by feudal obligations (Simpson, 1939, 1946).

Even at the humblest archaeological level we have seen how the most utilitarian pottery can provide the bulk data needed to construct models using all the resources of systems theory and computer analysis (Doran, 1970) to illuminate just those complex problems concerning the diffusion of ideas through a population, which deeply interest psycho-geographers today (Chorley and Haggett, 1967).

Today the very conceptual model 'Middle Ages' is itself being eroded at its fringes: at the earlier end by Late Antiquity, and at the later end from the New Humanism (note Crombie, 1961, pp. 103ff.; Bialostocki, 1966) and the rise of the new technology and scientific thought from the fourteenth century onwards.

Medieval people themselves had their own conceptual models, all manner of meaningful hardware devices, naive or abstruse and esoteric, by which they could visualize or grasp abstract elements of another more ephemeral world: the simple schematic model of the Trinity on a Norfolk font (Pevsner, 1962, p. 48), or the more vivid allegorical scenes in medieval paintings – the true iconic model of the medieval cosmology (Rickert, 1954, p. 156). Surely, not the least promise of the model-using approach in archaeology is the possibility that it offers for not simply constructing a model of the past but in the possibility of recovering the model that the past society itself espoused (see Clarke, Chapter 21 of this volume, and the recovery of the Celtic building model at a particular site).

PROCEDURAL MODELS

Every model constructed as a factual presentation of data of one kind, with added homogeneous extrapolations, can be set beside parallel models built from data derived from related spheres of activity within the same community. In this way a composite multithetic model is assembled, and the process can be multiplied to give a multidimensional synthesis for a whole people and an age, and we should be able even to test how far large global divisions such as western or eastern Europe really present coherent or unitary cultural patterns.

In making the primary models, a coherent body of data must be accumulated; this is often to be taken on a statistical basis, when it is necessary to know the limits of variance that can be tolerated for a datum to be accepted into the model construct. It is clear, moreover, that such analyses can be done only by employing the full resources of computer operation, and the whole array of analytical procedures and systems theory needed to operate them to full advantage (Clarke, 1968; Doran, 1970).

The use of models in medieval studies may thus be summarized as the formulation of propositions, as far as possible assembled out of observed coherent data, the testing of these against new or analogous data, the acceptance of what appears valid, and the rejection of anomalous material for recycling, and so on. This process may be summarized in a diagram (Fig. 1.2).

Sufficient has been said to show that model building, testing and remodelling has long been a procedure underlying all branches of medieval studies. Our present progress in understanding the medieval world is the fruit of such work. In medieval archaeology insufficient models have as yet been constructed primarily out of the archaeological data itself, but the process is clearly worth while, especially when testing and elaboration incorporate documentary and bio- or physical-ecological data; and the full resources of quantitative analysis must clearly be applied to such bulk data. It is through the interplay of model building from these multiple sources of information that the future of many branches of medieval studies must grow.

Notes

1 'Medieval' is here taken to include the broad sweep of European life from the time of Constantine in the A.D. 330s to the gradual dissemination of the new humanism in the fifteenth and sixteenth centuries.

2 Medieval archaeologists should perhaps be acquainted with this classic of informed and closely reasoned invective, which was not without some justification; no respectable journal would publish this review of an official publication, and J. H. Round therefore had to print it at his own expense, and for private circulation (120 copies in a limited edition).

References

It should be pointed out that in discerning model testing full attention should be given to serious critical reviews, some of which are accordingly noted here after the item cited. Many of the items noted have useful bibliographies.

ADDYMAN, P. V. (1964) A Dark-Age settlement at Maxey, Northants. *Medieval Archaeology*, **8**, 20–73.
ALCOCK, L. (1966) Castle Tower, Penmaen: a Norman ring-work in Glamorgan. *Antiquaries Journal*, **46**, 178–210.
ARBMAN, H. (1943) *Birka, I: Die Gräber*. Uppsala.
ARMITAGE, E. S. (1912) *The Early Norman Castles of the British Isles*. London.
ATKINSON, T. D. (1947) *Local Style in English Architecture*. London: Batsford.

BALDWIN BROWN, G. (1925) *The Arts in Early England, 2: Architecture.* 2nd rev. ed. London: Murray.

BARLEY, M. W. (1967) Rural housing in England. In THIRSK, J. (ed.) *The Agrarian History of England and Wales 1500–1640.* Cambridge: Cambridge University Press.

BARRACLOUGH, G. (1970) *Eastern and Western Europe in the Middle Ages.* London: Thames & Hudson.

BERGER, R. (ed.) (1970) *Scientific Methods in Medieval Archaeology.* Berkeley: University of California Press.

BERESFORD, M. W. and ST JOSEPH, J. K. S. (1958) *Medieval England: An Aerial Survey.* Cambridge: Cambridge University Press.

BIALOSTOCKI, J. (1966) Late Gothic: disagreements about the concept. *Journal of the British Archaeological Association,* **29** (3), 76–105.

BIDDLE, M. (1962) The deserted medieval village of Seacourt, Berkshire. *Oxoniensia,* **26–7,** 70–201.

BIDDLE, M. (1970) Excavations at Winchester. *Antiquaries Journal,* **20,** 277–326, with previous reports listed on p. 277.

BLOCH, M. (1961) *Feudal Society.* English trans. by L. A. Manyon. London: Routledge.

BRADLEY, R. (1971) Trade competition and artefact distribution. *World Archaeology,* **2,** 347–52.

BROWN, R. A. (1969a) *The Normans and the Norman Conquest.* London: Constable. Reviews in *Medieval Archaeology,* **13** (1969), 292–4; *Antiquaries Journal,* **50** (1970), 143–4.

BROWN, R. A. (1969b) An historian's approach to the origins of the castle in England. *Archaeological Journal,* **126,** 131–48 (and reply by B. K. Davison).

BRUCE-MITFORD, R. (1969) *The Sutton Hoo Ship Burial.* London: British Museum.

CARUS-WILSON, E. (1933) The Iceland trade. In POWER, E. and POSTAN, M. M. (eds.) *Studies in English Trade in the Fifteenth Century.* London: Routledge.

CARUS-WILSON, E. (1963) The medieval trade of the ports of the Wash. *Medieval Archaeology,* **6–7,** 182–201.

CHAMBERS, R. W. (1932) *On the Continuity of English Prose.* London: Early English Text Society.

CHORLEY, R. J. and HAGGETT, P. (1967) *Models in Geography.* London: Methuen.

CLARK, K. (1928) *The Gothic Revival.* London: Murray.

CLARKE, D. L. (1968) *Analytical Archaeology.* London: Methuen.

COLVIN, H. M., BROWN, R. A. and TAYLOR, A. J. (1963) *A History of the King's Works.* London: Ministry of Public Building and Works.

CONANT, K. J. (1959) *Carolingian and Romanesque Architecture: 800–1200.* Harmondsworth: Penguin Books.

CROMBIE, A. C. (1961) *Augustine to Galileo.* 2 vols. London: Heinemann.

DAVISON, B. K. (1967a) Three eleventh-century earthworks in England: their excavation and implications. *Chateau Gaillard,* **2,** 39–48.

DAVISON, B. K. (1967b) The origins of the castle in England: the Institute's research project. *Archaeological Journal,* **124,** 202–11.

DAVISON, B. K. (1969) Early earthwork castles: a new model. *Chateau Gaillard,* **3,** 37–47.

DETHLEFSON, E. and DEETZ, J. (1966) Death's heads, cherubs and willow trees: experimental archaeology in colonial cemeteries. *American Antiquity*, **31** (4), 502–10.

DOLLEY, R. H. M. (1969) British and Irish coins as dating evidence for the archaeologist. *World Archaeology*, **1**, 200–7.

DORAN, J. (1970) Systems theory, computer simulations and archaeology. *World Archaeology*, **1**, 289–98.

DUNNING, G. C. (1959) Anglo-Saxon pottery: a symposium. *Medieval Archaeology*, **3**, 50 ff., 59, 71 ff.

DUNNING, G. C. and JOPE, E. M. (1954) The use of blue slate for roofing in medieval England. *Antiquaries Journal*, **34**, 209–17.

EVISON, V. I. (1965) *The Fifth-Century Invasion South of the Thames*. London: Athlone Press. Reviews in *Antiquaries Journal*, **47** (1967), 299–301; *Medieval Archaeology*, **9** (1965), 221–3.

FAULKNER, P. A. (1970) Some medieval archiepiscopal palaces. *Archaeological Journal*, **127**, 130–46.

FEDOROV-DAVYDOV, G. A. (1965) On dating types of artefacts from burial assemblages. *Sovetskaia Archeologiia*, **3**, 58–65. English trans. in *Soviet Anthropology and Archaeology*, **5** (1966), 22–33.

FLETCHER, J. M. and SPOKES, P. S. (1964) The origin and development of crown-post roofs. *Medieval Archaeology*, **8**, 152–83.

FOX, A. (1958) A monastic homestead on Dean Moor, south Devon. *Medieval Archaeology*, **2**, 141–57.

GALBRAITH, V. H. (1961) *The Making of the Domesday Book*. London: Oxford University Press.

GRAUS, F. (1970) Slavs and Germans. In BARRACLOUGH, G. (ed.) *Eastern and Western Europe in the Middle Ages*. London: Thames & Hudson.

GRIERSON, P. (1952) The dating of the Sutton Hoo coins. *Antiquity*, **26**, 83 ff.

HARVEY, J. H. (1944) *Henry Yevele, c. 1320–1400: The Life of an English Architect*. London: Batsford.

HARVEY, J. H. (1947) *Gothic England*. London: Batsford.

HARVEY, J. H. (1950) *The Gothic World*. London: Batsford.

HARVEY, J. H. (1954) *English Medieval Architects: A Biographical Dictionary*. London: Batsford.

HARVEY, J. H. (1968) The origins of Gothic architecture: some further thoughts. *Antiquaries Journal*, **48**, 87–99.

HASSALL, J. M. and HILL, D. (1970) Pont de l'Arche: Frankish influence on the West Saxon *burh*. *Archaeological Journal*, **127**, 188–201.

HENSEL, W. (1969) Origins of western and eastern Slav towns. *World Archaeology*, **1**, 51–60.

HERRNBRODT, H. (1958) *Der Husterknupp*. Bonner Jahrbücher, Beihefte 6. Köln-Graz.

HERTEIG, A. E. (1959) The excavation of 'Bryggen', the old Hanseatic wharf in Bergen. *Medieval Archaeology*, **3**, 177–86.

HEWETT, C. A. (1963) Structural carpentry in medieval Essex. *Medieval Archaeology*, **6–7**, 240–71.

HEWETT, C. A. (1966) Jettying and floor-framing in Medieval Essex. *Medieval Archaeology*, **10**, 89–112.

HOLLISTER, C. W. (1962) *Anglo-Saxon Military Institutions on the Eve of the Norman Conquest*. London: Oxford University Press.

HOPE-TAYLOR, B. (1956) in SINGER, C. and HOLMYARD, E. J. (eds.) *History of Technology*, II. London: Oxford University Press.

HOPE-TAYLOR, B. (1957) Summary of excavations at Yeavering. *Medieval Archaeology*, **1**, 148–9.

HOSKINS, W. G. and JOPE, E. M. (1954) The medieval period. In MARTIN, A. F. and STEEL, R. W. (eds.) *The Oxford Region*. London: Oxford University Press.

HURST, J. G. (1963) White Castle and the dating of medieval pottery. *Medieval Archaeology*, **6–7**, 135–55.

HURST, J. G. et al. (1969) Red-painted and glazed pottery in western Europe from the 8th to the 12th century. *Medieval Archaeology*, **13**, 93–167.

JANSSEN, G. P. (1965) *Königshagen, eine archaeologisch-historischer Beitrag zur Siedlungsgeschichte des Sudwestlichen Harzvorlandes*. Hildesheim. Review in *Medieval Archaeology*, **10** (1966), 734–6.

JONES, G. P. (1952) Building in stone in medieval western Europe. In POSTAN, M. M. and RICH, E. E. (eds.) *Cambridge Economic History of Europe*, II. Cambridge: Cambridge University Press.

JOPE, E. M. (1955) Review of *Domesday Geography of Midland England* by H. C. Darby (1954). *Antiquaries Journal*, **35**, 109–11.

JOPE, E. M. (1956a) Ceramics. In SINGER, C. and HOLMYARD, E. J. (eds.) *History of Technology*, II. London: Oxford University Press.

JOPE, E. M. (1956b) The tinning of iron spurs: a continuous practice from the 10th to the 17th century. *Oxoniensia*, **21**, 35–42.

JOPE, E. M. (1958) The Clarendon Hotel, Oxford: the site. *Oxoniensia*, **23**, 1–83.

JOPE, E. M. (1961) Cornish houses 1400–1700. In JOPE, E. M. (ed.) *Studies in Building History*. London: Odhams.

JOPE, E. M. (1963) The regional cultures of medieval Britain. In FOSTER, I. L. and ALCOCK, L. (eds.) *Culture and Environment*. London: Routledge.

JOPE, E. M. (1964) The Saxon building stone industry in southern and Midland England. *Medieval Archaeology*, **8**, 91–118.

JOPE, E. M. (1965) Man's use of natural resources. *Adv. Science*, **22**, 455–64.

JOPE, E. M. (ed.) (1966) *The Archaeological Survey of County Down*. Belfast: H.M.S.O.

JOPE, E. M. (1972) Maps in DARBY, H. C., *Historical Geography of England and Wales*. 2nd ed. Cambridge: Cambridge University Press.

JOPE, E. M. and HODGES, H. W. M. (1956) The medieval pottery. In O'NEILL, H. E., Prestbury Moat: a manor house of the Bishops of Hereford in Gloucestershire. *Transactions of the Bristol Gloucestershire Archaeological Society*, **75**, 1–34.

JOPE, E. M. and TERRETT, I. M. (1962) Oxfordshire. In DARBY, H. C. and CAMPBELL, E. M. J. (eds.) *The Domesday Geography of South-East England*. Cambridge: Cambridge University Press.

JOPE, E. M. and THRELFALL, R. I. (1958) Excavation of a medieval settlement at Beer, north Taunton, Devon. *Medieval Archaeology*, **2**, 112–40.

JOPE, E. M. and THRELFALL, R. I. (1959) The twelfth-century castle at Ascot Doilly, Oxfordshire. *Antiquaries Journal*, **39**, 219–73.

JOPE, H. M. (1952) Faunal remains. In WATERMAN, D. M., Excavations at Greencastle, Co. Down. *Ulster Journal of Archaeology*.

KOLCHIN, B. A. (1958) *Work of the Novgorod Archaeological Expedition, I and II*. Moscow: Academy of Sciences of the U.S.S.R.

LAMB, H. H. (1966) *The Changing Climate*. London: Methuen.

LAMBERT, J. W. (1960) *The Making of the Broads*. London: Murray.

LANGER, W. L. (1964) The Black Death. *Scientific American*, **210**, 114–21.

LAVELL, C. (1971) Archaeological site index to radiocarbon dates for Great Britain and Ireland. *British Archaeological Abstracts Supplement*. Council for British Archaeology.

LENNARD, R. V. (1959) *Rural England, 1086–1135*. London: Oxford University Press.

LE PATOUREL, H. E. J. (1968) Documentary evidence and the medieval pottery industry. *Medieval Archaeology*, **12**, 101–26.

LETHABY, W. R. (1906) *Westminster Abbey and the King's Craftsmen*. London.

LETHABY, W. R. (1925) *Westminster Abbey Re-examined*. London.

METCALF, D. M. and SCHWEIZER, F. (1971) The metal content of the silver pennies of William II and Henry I (1087–1135). *Archaeometry*, **13**, 177–90.

MYRES, J. N. L. (1967) Recent discoveries in the Bodleian Library. *Archaeologia*, **101**, 151–68.

MYRES, J. N. L. (1969) *Anglo-Saxon Pottery and the Settlement of England*. London: Oxford University Press.

NØRLUND, P. (1936) *Viking Settlers in Greenland and their Descendants during Five Hundred Years*. Cambridge: Cambridge University Press.

NØRLUND, P. (1948) *Trelleborg*. Copenhagen.

PANTIN, W. A. (1957) Medieval priests' houses. *Medieval Archaeology*, **1**, 118–46.

PANTIN, W. A. (1961) Medieval inns. In JOPE, E. M. (ed.) *Studies in Building History*. London: Odhams.

PANTIN, W. A. (1963a) The merchants' houses and warehouses of King's Lynn. *Medieval Archaeology*, **6–7**, 173–81.

PANTIN, W. A. (1963b) Medieval English town-house plans. *Medieval Archaeology*, **6–7**, 202–39.

PERROTT, C. (1965) Great Moravia in the light of recent excavations. *Oxford Slavonic Papers*, **12**, 1–20.

PETERSSON, H. B. A. (1969) *Anglo-Saxon Currency*. Lund: Gleerups Berlingska Boktrycheriet.

PEVSNER, N. B. L. (1962) *The Buildings of England: N.E. Norfolk and Norwich*. Harmondsworth: Penguin Books.

PIGGOTT, S. (1959) *Approach to Archaeology*. London: Black.

POWER, E. and POSTAN, M. M. (eds.) (1933) *Studies in English Trade in the Fifteenth Century*. London: Routledge.

RAHTZ, P. A. (1963) The Saxon and medieval palaces at Cheddar, Somerset: an interim report. *Medieval Archaeology*, **6–7**, 67–108.

RAHTZ, P. A. (1968) *Excavations at King John's Hunting Lodge, Writtle, Essex, 1953–7*. London: Society for Medieval Archaeology.

RICKERT, M. (1954) *Painting in Britain: The Middle Ages.* Harmondsworth: Penguin Books.

RICKMAN, T. (1819) *An Attempt to Discriminate the Styles of English Architecture.* London.

RIGOLD, S. E. (1965) Review of *Anglo-Saxon Pennies* by R. H. M. Dolley. *Medieval Archaeology,* **9**, 231.

ROUND, J. H. (1898) *The Red Book of the Exchequer.* Printed for private circulation.

SAUER, C. D. (1963) *Land and Life.* Berkeley: University of California Press.

SAWYER, P. H. (1962) *The Age of the Vikings.* London: Arnold.

SCHOVE, D. J. (1964) Medieval dendrochronology in the U.S.S.R. *Medieval Archaeology,* **8**, 816–817.

SHEPPARD, T. (1922) The lost towns of the Humber. *Handbook to Hull,* 282–322.

SIMPSON, W. D. (1939) Castles of livery and maintenance. *Journal of the British Archaeological Association,* **4**, 39–54.

SIMPSON, W. D. (1946) Bastard feudalism and the later castles. *Antiquaries Journal,* **26**, 145–71.

SMITH, J. T. (1964) Cruck construction: a survey of the problems. *Medieval Archaeology,* **8**, 119–51.

SMITH, J. T. (1965) The structure of the timber kitchens at Weoley Castle, Birmingham. *Medieval Archaeology,* **9**, 82–93.

SMITH, P. (1967) Rural housing in Wales. In THIRSK, J. (ed.) *The Agrarian History of England and Wales.* Cambridge: Cambridge University Press.

SPROCKHOFF, E. (1937) Der Ringwall von Burg bei Altencelle. *Germania,* **21**, 118–23.

STAMP, L. D. (1950) *The Land of Britain: Its Use and Misuse.* 2nd ed. London: Longmans Green.

TAYLOR, A. J. (1950) Master James of St George. *English Historical Review,* **65**, 433–57.

TAYLOR, A. J. (1958) Military architecture. In POOLE, A. L. (ed.) *Medieval England.* London: Oxford University Press.

TAYLOR, A. J. (1961a) Castle-building in Wales in the later 13th century: the prelude to construction. In JOPE, E. M. (ed.) *Studies in Building History.* London: Odhams.

TAYLOR, A. J. (1961b) White Castle in the 13th century: a reconsideration. *Medieval Archaeology,* **5**, 169–75.

TAYLOR, H. M. (1969) The Anglo-Saxon cathedral church at Canterbury. *Archaeological Journal,* **126**, 101–30. See also discussions in *Archaeological Journal,* **127** (1970), 196–201, 202–10.

THOMPSON, M. W. (1961) Motte substructure. *Medieval Archaeology,* **5**, 304–5.

THOMPSON, M. W. (1964) Review of *Medieval Technology and Social Change* by L. White (1962). *Medieval Archaeology,* **8**, 314–15.

THOMPSON, M. W. (1965) Review of *Studien zu frühgeschichtlichen Befestigung zwischen Nordsee und Alpen* by R. Von Uslar (1964). *Medieval Archaeology,* **9**, 224–7.

THOMPSON, M. W. (1967) *Novgorod the Great.* London: Evelyn, Adams & Mackay.

USLAR, R. VON (1964) *Studien zu frühgeschichtlichen Befestigung zwischen Nordsee und Alpen.* Bonner Jahrbücher, Beihefte 11. Cologne.

WATERMAN, D. M. (1956) Excavations of a house and souterrain at White Port, Drumaroad, Co. Down. *Ulster Journal of Archaeology*, **19**, 73–86.

WATERMAN, D. M. (1959) Excavations at Lismahon, Co. Down. *Medieval Archaeology*, **3**, 139–76.

WATERMAN, D. M. (1970) Somerset shire and other foreign building stones in medieval Ireland. *Ulster Journal of Archaeology*, **33**, 63–75.

WEST, S. E. (1969) The Anglo-Saxon village of West Stow. *Medieval Archaeology*, **13**, 1–20.

WHITE, L. (1962) *Medieval Technology and Social Change*. London: Oxford University Press.

WHITEHOUSE, D. B. (1966) Medieval painted pottery in south and central Italy. *Medieval Archaeology*, **10**, 30–44.

WHITEHOUSE, D. B. (1969) Red painted and glazed pottery in western Europe: Italy. *Medieval Archaeology*, **13**, 143.

WILSON, D. M. (1957) An inlaid iron folding stool in the British Museum. *Medieval Archaeology*, **1**, 39–56.

WILSON, D. M. and HURST, D. G. (1966) Gomeldon, Wiltshire: Medieval Britain in 1965. *Medieval Archaeology*, **10**, 214–15.

WINCKELMANN, W. (1954) Ein westfälische siedlung des 8 Jahrunderts bei Warendorf. *Germania*, **32**, 189–213.

ZARNECKI, G. (1966) 1066 and architectural sculpture. *Proceedings of the British Academy*, **52**, 87–104.

26
Scientific inquiry and models of socio-cultural data patterning: an epilogue

R. P. CHANEY
University of Oregon, U.S.A.

Recently, there has been a flurry of articles concerning a scientific archaeology (Binford, 1962, 1968; Caldwell, 1966; Carneiro, 1970; Deetz, 1967; Fritz and Plog, 1970; Longacre, 1968). Much of this discussion is at odds with recent developments (1) in the history and logic of science, and (2) in anthropological cross-cultural studies.

Central to any discussion are the conceptual foundations of knowledge.

Introduction

REQUIRED: ACQUIRED

As far as recorded cultural history extends man's thinking, man has been born into existing explanatory systems. The salient characteristic of man is his explanatory systems which allow him to *perceive* (some degree and kind of) order in the 'buzzing blooming confusion' or differentiations in the 'un-differentiated aesthetic continuum' of physical phenomena and to *live* (some degree and kind of) order with potentially disorderly 'others'. Life for the majority of mankind has been one of the meaning already being assigned for them.

The history of man's ideas of himself and of the universe in which he finds himself can be viewed as one of the 'required explanations' for the majority of mankind. Man's view of his own explanatory systems as 'acquired explanations' has been a relative latecomer in the history of ideas and then only by some men for some areas of knowing. The full implications of explanatory systems (physical, biological and cultural) viewed as 'acquired' methods of explanation have yet to be discussed.

Written history brings to the present only some ideas of some men who have discussed the nature of man in the universe. These discussions characteristically have taken the form of stressing the problems or presenting explanatory systems that purportedly took care of the problems. Only a handful of men have been what one might refer to as 'inquisitively systematic'.

Anyone who critically surveys theoretical discussions in archaeology and anthropology is immediately struck by the multitude of variously interconnected and disconnected reading and quoting circles.[1] A distinguishing aspect of many of these discussions from the point of view of anyone familiar with the history of ideas is the extreme theoretical myopia of the discussions. Anthropologists and archaeologists have typically acted as if the 'problems' concerning explanation and knowing that have been discussed in the history of ideas were of no consequence to their own so-called 'explanations'. As a result, many of the debates viewed in retrospect have the flavour of the 'sighs of great (and not so great) men'. I stress 'sighs' because for the most part there have not been any agreed upon criteria to settle our conceptual differences.

The fundamental intertwined problems that 'theoretical anthropology' has faced are ones of conceptual analysis, criticism of criteria and revision of methods and ideas. Unfortunately, the 'rise of anthropological theory' has possessed more of the flavour of one attempting to 'prove' a principle or theory by merely contrasting one's own view with other views in terms of a 'yes' or 'no' according to whether the other views are conceptually similar to one's own, rather than the flavour of men attempting to learn through the coordination of concepts by postulation with observation and experience.

Any familiarity with the history of ideas or *debates* in the history of man's comments on the nature of the universe, man to man, or man in the universe, indicates that the *problem* is not just one of coming up with or developing a clever idea but rather one of also getting others to *see* or *experience* a discussion of 'an answer' or 'a problem' in the same way.

Scientific analysis may be conceptualized as an attempt by some men to go beyond the voices of mere 'authority' to explanatory systems that are coordinated with observation and experience in such a way as to be open to others for examination. The attempt has been one of creating a 'community of discussion' that extends in space-time to those who have come in contact with this way of knowing. Scientific analysis is able to transcend the 'local-focal' of the majority of mankind for the majority of discussions as a result of it not being mere words which are occasionally coordinated with observation and experience in ways that are never questioned. The essence of science in contrast to other ways of knowing is that it attempts to be self-corrective. That is, anything can be questioned if it is questioned in terms of how the existing man-made explanatory system is not coordinating with emerging (or existing) observation and experience.

Although *science* is often times viewed vaguely as some form of monolithic entity that merely changes in content, a detailed contextual analysis indicates that man's view of what he is actually doing in scientific analysis has developed over time. Anyone who examines the contextual details of theoretical discussions of the nature of scientific analysis can *not* but be struck by the incredible differences of opinion as to the relation of theoretical, conceptual statements to observation and experience.

Much of the staggering confusion in present debates as to the value of scientific analysis in social science can only be understood in terms of the majority of the discussants thinking that they understand scientific analysis after reading a few discussions of science.

The magnitude of the problem only becomes apparent if one wades into the confusion and forgets the usual bridge-table etiquette of not being too harsh to opponents and just euphorically floating along with implicit and explicit rule books. Further, as one examines various discussions it becomes obvious that the problem is not merely one of saying 'yes' or 'no' to entire books or statements, but rather to go through the contextual, fine detail and sort out the discussions.

The present discussion reviews some aspects of a central problem in comparative ethnology and archaeological interpretation: the meaning of joint occurrences of socio-cultural phenomena. Essentially this problem has been conceptualized as one of explicating the meaning of (seemingly) joint occurrences of socio-cultural phenomena in terms of the disjunctive historical-diffusional factors versus functional-dynamic factors. Further, the majority of cross-cultural researchers have been under the impression that one could directly infer functional-causal factors from socio-cultural data patterning. Much of the discussion has been in terms of one aspect of socio-cultural phenomena being related to another aspect, rather than in terms of what would the nature of the phenomena have to be for the data to pattern as they appear to be patterning.

Since all cross-cultural researchers (and others) are under the impression that they are scientific, an essential task is to review problems in scientific inquiry in addition to problems in contemporary discussions of the meaning of seemingly joint occurrences of socio-cultural phenomena.

As a lead-in to the next section on scientific inquiry, let us first glance at two recent anthropological texts: *Anthropological Research: The Structure*

993

of Inquiry (1970) by Pertti J. Pelto and *The Rise of Anthropological Theory* (1968) by Marvin Harris.

I PELTO AND THE STRUCTURE OF INQUIRY

On the whole, Pelto's (1970) discussion is well written and succinct. However, a major theoretical, conceptual problem emerges in the discussion of 'operationalism'. Pelto (1970, p. 47) correctly points out that 'a main requirement of the scientific method is that the procedures of the research should be clearly (and publicly) specified, so that other scientists can understand *how* particular results were produced and can replicate the research if they should wish to do so.' He then quotes from Nagel's *The Structure of Science* (1961):

> If . . . theory is to be used as an instrument of explanation and prediction, it must somehow be linked with observable materials. The indispensability of such linkages has been repeatedly stressed in recent literature, and a variety of labels have been coined for them: coordinating definitions, operational definitions, semantic rules, correspondence rules, epistemic correlations, and rules of interpretation (p. 93).

> The ways in which theoretical notions are related to observational procedures are often quite complex, and there appears to be no single scheme which adequately represents all of them (p. 94).

Pelto then immediately says that an:

> Examination of the pages of typical scientific reporting provides us with a fairly clear idea of what operationalism is all about. Descriptions of research in the pages of *Science*, for example, are full of information such as the following (all examples are from *Science*, 12 May, 1967):

> Calves were lightly anaesthetized with thiopental and then given a continuous intravenous infusion of succinyl choline (p. 827).

> A hyper-transfused-polycythemic (HP) state was induced by intraperitoneal injections of 0·5 ml of washed, packed, homologous red blood cells on 3 consecutive days and again on day 5 (p. 832).

> Five cocks received alcohol (9 ml/kg body weight, of 33% grain alcohol administered orally) and five cocks received an equal amount of water without alcohol 30 minutes before the initial exposure to newly hatched chicks (p. 836).

From the foregoing and a reading of the rest of his discussion one sees that Pelto is apparently thinking that 'operationalism' is synonymous with the other terms that Nagel refers to. Further, it is rather interesting that, whereas Nagel states that 'the ways in which theoretical notions are related to observational procedures are often quite complex, and there appears to be no single scheme which adequately represents all of them' (quoted by Pelto, 1970, p. 48), Pelto (1970, p. 48) thinks a look at 'the pages of typical scientific reporting provides us with a fairly clear idea of what operationalism is all about'. This clearly needs sorting out.

First, it is not at all clear that the logic of explaining and predicting will be the same in all fields. Hanson (1963, pp. 25–41) has stressed that Hempel's 'symmetry between explanation and prediction' fails when one examines a living, growing science as expressed in contemporary non-deterministic theories of microphysics.

Second, whereas Nagel hints of the complexity, Pelto implies that the various terms employed by various philosophers of science are coterminous. They are not. Further, description in the pages of 'Science' is typically the indispensable empirical correlations but *seldom* the presentation of discoveries of terse formulae. Thus, an examination of articles such as those cited by Pelto (1970, p. 49) will provide a rather distorted view of the history and logic of science.

'Operational definitions' refers to the indispensable explicit specifications of observational procedures, whereas a term such as Northrop's 'epistemic correlation' refers to the explicit specification of the type of patterning in the data that one would expect if one explanatory system is a better method of representation than another. Part of the confusion in Pelto's discussion is the lack of explicit understanding and discussion of the difference between formulating an explanatory system (and its influence on the course of future research) and merely doing science within an existing explanatory system or systems. Further, whereas physical science has built up a hierarchy of methods of representations, which has only been disturbed fundamentally by a handful of men such as Kepler, Galileo, Newton, Maxwell, Einstein, Planck, Bohr, Schrödinger and Heisenberg, the majority of individuals who have been scientists have merely worked within existing explanatory systems. 'The great unifications of Galileo, Kepler, Newton, Maxwell, Einstein, Bohr, Schrödinger and Heisenberg were pre-eminently discoveries of terse formulae from which explanations of diverse phenomena could be generated as a matter of course' (Hanson, 1958, p. 109). These new 'terse formulae' allowed man to conceptualize and view the world in different ways.

995

Each in its turn also provided obstacles for further reconceptualization within the same areas. Thomas S. Kuhn has recently provided a popular account of this in a book entitled *The Structure of Scientific Revolutions* (1962). Norwood Russell Hanson (1958) in a much more profound statement, *Patterns of Discovery*, has attempted to explicate the implication of this for a reconceptualization of the conceptual foundations of scientific analysis (this will be taken up again in the next section). Some further detective work reveals that Pelto, in his 'Epilogue', employs Kuhn's recent book in a rather curious way which is at odds with the entire point of Kuhn's argument. And, at this point, I would like to stress that the *plot* becomes incredibly complex and is plagued by our usual ways of phrasing the problem (which after memorization always seems to be free of staggering confusion). I wish to stress again that Pelto's discussion is singled out mainly because it is one of the 'better' discussions in the 'normal' way of discussing such matters.

Pelto (1970, p. 322) informs us that:

> T. S. Kuhn has recently examined in some detail this conservative and non-innovative side of established scientific activity (Kuhn, 1962). He notes that most scientists, social, physical and biological are not latter-year Franklins, Newtons, Darwins and Pasteurs. They are, rather, the patient and plodding followers of one or another established 'schools' of theory, concerned less with blazing new and hitherto unexplored scientific pathways than with converting established theoretical positions into yet another publishable example of paradigmatic progress.
>
> In general, I feel that social scientists, like their fellow workers in other research disciplines, can if necessary demonstrate the potential practical relevance of a very wide range of seemingly obscure information. The whole past and never-to-be-relived history of human culture is an area of study from which able investigators can produce practical evidence concerning basic patterns of human behaviour.
>
> Cross-cultural comparative studies have demonstrated the theoretical importance of descriptive data from the more exotic societies of mankind, and the resulting theoretical findings can have powerful application to the problems of our modern day.

A major point in Kuhn's discussion was the importance of the transition from the pre- to the post-paradigm stage in the development of a scientific field. 'A *paradigm* is what the members of a scientific community share, *and*, conversely a scientific community consists of men who share a paradigm' (Kuhn, 1970, p. 176). The above discussed attributes of the post-paradigm

996

stage are 'consequences of the acquisition of the sort of paradigm that identifies challenging puzzles, supplies clues to their solution, and guarantees that the truly clever practitioner will succeed' (Kuhn, 1970, p. 179). The 'patient and plodding followers' in the social sciences are operating in an entirely different conceptual world than their counter part in the physical sciences. A glance at the nature of discussion in the social sciences (as Kuhn pointed out) indicates that there is no agreed upon paradigm(s) in which research is taking place. Rather, in anthropological and archaeological discussions, for example, one encounters a number of variously interrelated reading and quoting circles expounding what are often conceptually distinct explanations. Kroeber and Kluckhohn (1952) attempted to survey the rather diverse uses and definitions of the concept 'culture'. Bidney (1953) attempted to make a conceptual analysis of the concepts and explanations existing in anthropology. Singer (1968) has recently re-emphasized the somewhat diverse theoretical orientations in his discussion on the concept of culture in the *International Encyclopaedia of the Social Sciences*. Anthropology faces the incredible task of establishing some form of agreed upon representation(s) for some areas of discussion as to the nature of man and the patterns and processes to be found in socio-cultural phenomena. Or another way to look at it is that we need to better understand what is in need of 'explanation'.

2 MARVIN HARRIS AND THEORETICAL ANTHROPOLOGY

Marvin Harris, in his book *The Rise of Anthropological Theory* (1968), gives the reader the impression that anthropology could make a step towards scientific rigour by starting out with his principle of 'techno-environmental and techno-economic determinism'. If anything, this type of approach is more reminiscent of the prose-laden theories of nature that were prevalent before Newton's 'mathematical philosophy': the theory of impetus, Cartesian vortex, Kepler's celestial 'spokes of force', etc. As Hanson (1963, p. 38) has pointed out, those latter theories all 'purported to make phenomena intelligible, by relating them to intuitively evident first principles'.

Any assertion must in principle be confirmable or disconfirmable if it is to be scientifically meaningful. A statement such as 'This principle holds that *similar* technologies applied to *similar* environments tend to produce *similar* arrangements of labour in production and distribution, and that these in turn call forth *similar* kinds of social groupings, which justify and coordinate their activities by means of *similar* systems of values and beliefs' (Harris, 1968, p. 4) is much too vague.

For Harris (1968, p. 4), 'To take a position concerning the direction of the causal arrow in socio-cultural systems does not oblige us to enter into a discussion of the ultimate nature of reality'. This would be like having a formula for the relationship between pressure, volume and temperature, but not having a method of representation that explicates the nature of the phenomena as a matter of course.

'A "science" that consisted of no more than a mere summary of the results of direct observation would not deserve the name' (Salmon, 1966, p. 5).

Kroeber is one of the few anthropologists who has tried to examine data other than the typical anthropological data with their focus on the so-called 'primitive peoples' of the world. In his *Configurations of Culture Growth* (1944), Kroeber attempted to see to what extent there are 'common features in the growth' of philology, sculpture, painting, drama, literature and music in civilizations and 'super systems' such as Egypt, Mesopotamia, India, Japan, Greece, Rome, Europe and China. Kroeber concluded his magnum opus: 'In reviewing the ground covered, I wish to say at the outset that I see no evidence of any true law in the phenomena dealt with; nothing cyclical, regularly repetitive, or necessary' (1944, p. 761).

From Harris's (1968, p. 330) deterministic, macro-event, physical model view, 'Despite the prodigious research effort expended upon this task, *Configurations* was a failure. Kroeber was able to discover no similarities whatsoever in the abstract growth curves of different civilizations. He discovered everywhere the mysterious "patterns" exemplified by sudden simultaneous bursts of creative energy in one or several of the aesthetic domains but the climaxes were sometimes multiple, sometimes singular, sometimes confined to one or two domains, elsewhere "across the board".'

Kroeber's monumental work is only a failure to someone who naively assumes that uniformities are the only interests of scientists. As Toulmin (1953, p. 153) has emphasized with reference to physical phenomena, '*Nor indeed is it necessarily uniformities and correlations which are specially interesting. Non-uniformities and non-correlations, independencies and disconnections are quite as important, for instance, in discrediting old wives' tales and quack remedies*' (italics mine). If a prominent philosopher of science can make the above statement with reference to physics where the essential task is to 'seek the form of given regularities' (Toulmin, 1953, p. 53), it behoves social scientists to realize that since the degree and nature of regularity in socio-cultural phenomena is still an open question, to state that no regularities have been found is just as important as to find regularities. If one does not know one way or the other, it is just as significant to implicate the extent of no regularities as to explicate the extent of regularities. This is no doubt painfully obvious to the majority of the anthropological and archaeological professions. Apparently it is not so obvious to a few theoreticians who seemingly are dashing madly into nineteenth-century science.

However, I wish to stress that this is a conceptual dash. Harris has no data of his own. Although Harris cites cross-cultural researchers when they appear to support him, he states *ad hoc* that they 'fail' when they do not support him. Thus we are informed that, 'Indeed, all of Murdock's contributions are suffused with painful paradox: While arguing persuasively for a nomothetic interpretation of the varieties of sex-regulating and kinship institutions, he has denied that whole socio-cultural systems also exhibit diachronic regularities and that long-range parallel and convergent evolution are significant features of culture change' (Harris, 1968, p. 611).

Harris (1968, pp. 377–8) has informed us also of the 'sterility of the concept of diffusion'.

> Although it is true, as Driver (1966) has shown, that geographical-historical propinquity is often a better predictor of traits than psycho-functional causality, under no circumstances can geographical-historical propinquity constitute a valid explanation of cultural differences and similarities. First of all, diffusion is admittedly incapable of accounting for the origin of a given trait, except by 'passing the buck' back through an infinite regression: $A \leftarrow B \leftarrow C. \ldots$

I would also like to point out the 'sterility' of the concept of techno-economic and techno-ecological determinism.

How can the principle account for the origin of a trait 'except by "passing the buck" back through an infinite regression: $A \leftarrow B \leftarrow C$'? What triggers the technology and economy to change? If the ecology remains the same, how can it act as a trigger? Where is the elusive trigger? Where is the variable?

Although Harris (1968, p. 621) is quite correct in stressing that 'additional logical-empirical operations are necessary before synchronic cross-cultural statistical comparisons can be made to contribute to the advance of knowledge', his methodological directive that 'we must process the data, question it, and code it, in relation to the expectations of our major premises. Then and only then can we accept a failure to stick to the wall as evidence against the major premise' (1968, p. 633) is at odds with contemporary philosophy of science. However, it is to be stressed that Harris is hardly alone in his misconception of the relationship of concepts to empirical data. Many philosophers fail to grasp the relationship, 'perhaps because they are inclined to regard physical theory

999

either as an inductive compound on the one hand, or as a kind of deductive system on the other' (Hanson, 1958, p. 88). The reasoning is from data to concepts, hypotheses and theories, not the reverse!

We need to go beyond mere histories of archaeological and anthropological theory and books such as Harris's, which 'is intended to prove a point' (1968, p. 5). If one starts out with a point to prove and selects all the statements with this in mind, he will indeed 'prove a point' for the uninitiated. And this is precisely the problem with Harris's book. His book is already being used in many courses on theoretical anthropology, and will no doubt shape to some extent a whole new generation of anthropologists if an explicit recognition is not made of its conceptual monorail. For example, no mention is made of Bidney's (1953) *Theoretical Anthropology* – no doubt because it comes in conflict with his basic thesis that the individual is of no consequence for macro-theory in his conceptual framework of techno-environmental and techno-economic determinism.[2]

Although one can hardly transfer the theoretical thinking of physics directly to theoretical discussions of the nature of culture, it behoves philosophers of culture to be aware of certain problems concerning conceptual organization and interpretation of data that have come steadily to the foreground in philosophy of science during this century.

On scientific inquiry

Science is a 'living process' which is busied mainly with conjectures which are either getting framed or getting tested. The dictionary defines science as systematized knowledge but science is a 'pursuit of living men' and 'the life of science is in the desire to learn' rather than 'the desire to prove the truth of definite opinion'.

Nothing is safe from change, not even the classification of the sciences themselves, which will have to be altered if it is to keep up with developments in scientific inquiry. What in science are called established truths are nothing more than 'propositions into which the economy of endeavour, prescribes that, for the time being, further inquiry shall cease. Science is radical in 'the eagerness to carry consequences to their extremes. Not the radicalism that is cocksure, however, but the *radicalism that tries experiments*'.

Peirce, quoted in Feibleman (1946, pp. 52–3)

Why is philosophy so complicated? It ought to be *entirely* simple. Philosophy unties the knots in our thinking that we have, in a senseless way, put there. To do this it must make movements as complicated as these knots are. Although the *result* of philosophy is simple its method cannot be, if it is to succeed. . . . The complexity of philosophy is not its subject matter, but our knotted understanding.

Wittgenstein

. . . the fact that it can be described by Newtonian Mechanics tells us nothing about the world; but *this* tells us something, namely, that the world can be described in that particular way in which as a matter of fact it is described.

Wittgenstein (1961, 6.342)

There is a sense, then, in which seeing is a 'theory-laden' undertaking. Observation of χ is shaped by prior knowledge of χ. Another influence on observation rests in the language or notation used to express what we know, and without which there would be little we could recognize as knowledge.

Hanson (1958, p. 19)

This retroductive procedure, this reasoning back from observations to formulae from which the observation statements and their explanations follow, is fundamental in modern physics. Yet it is least appreciated by philosophers, so often are they attentive to the (indispensable, but sometimes overestimated) empirical correlations of men like Boyle, Cavendish, Ampere, Coulomb, Faraday, Tyndall, Kelvin and Boys.

The great unifications of Galileo, Kepler, Newton, Maxwell, Einstein, Bohr, Schrödinger and Heisenberg were pre-eminently discoveries of terse formulae from which explanations of diverse phenomena could be generated as a matter of course; they were not discoveries of undetected regularities.

Hanson (1958, p. 109)

An incredible amount of confusion has emerged when social scientists have discussed the application of science to the study of socio-cultural phenomena. Much of the discussion has been based on the view that the essence of scientific methodology is invariant relationships and prediction. Thus, individuals who have attempted to emulate theoretical physics have supposed that the nature of the explication of socio-cultural phenomena would somehow take the form of explication of physical phenomena. Others, viewing socio-cultural phenomena as essentially different from physical phenomena, have stressed that to be scientific would somehow dehumanize the study of man and his works.

Common to much of the discussion by the 'scientists' and 'anti-scientists' in social science is a rather fuzzy view of the nature of science and the nature of knowledge.

At the present time in philosophy of science rather heated debate is raging with regard to the status of the logical symmetry between explanation and prediction. The hypothetico-deductive account of scientific practice which entails the 'symmetry' was given its classical exposition by Hempel and Oppenheim (1948). Hanson (1958, 1963) has argued that the symmetry thesis is the result of reflection on Newtonian mechanics treated as a finished system. From my present rather flimsy vantage ground, it appears that the argument is spinning also around the concepts of justification and discovery. The 'symmetry' group generally focuses its attention on justification and indicates we have little to say about discovery. Hanson in contrast is making a fine-detail, contextual analysis of 'discovery' and indicating that perception and discovery are intimately intertwined. The implication is that the concept of justification may have to be reviewed.

Much of the confusion in contemporary discussions of philosophy of science results from (1) thinking that there is one scientific method suitable for all stages of inquiry, and (2) treating as paradigms of scientific inquiry finished systems such as classical thermodynamics and planetary mechanics rather than the unsettled, dynamic research sciences like microphysics.

I F. S. C. NORTHROP

Northrop (1947) has drawn attention to 'the primacy of the problem and the attendant relativity of scientific methods' in his discussion of *The Logic of the Sciences and the Humanities*. He begins his discussion by pointing out that the most difficult aspect of any inquiry is its initiation. Where to start ? What to do ?

> There are many reasons for believing that perhaps more than anywhere else it is at the beginning of any investigation that the source of genius is to be found. For what characterizes a genius like Galilei, Lavoisier or Einstein is the economy of thought and effort by which he achieves his result. Each of these men found the key factor in the situation and went directly to the heart of the problem which had been baffling his predecessors. The methods which all three used at later stages of their investigation are well known. It was in finding the key difficulty and in knowing precisely at what points to direct the well-known methods that their genius consists. (pp. 1-2)

The problem as Northrop saw it was that although research physicists know how to conduct experiments after they know what experiments to perform, and theoretical physicists and pure mathematicians are able to carry out logical deductions and calculations after they know the postulates and assumptions to begin from, disagreement exists among authorities as to specific procedures at the very beginning of inquiry. In order to place his own conception of the primacy of the problem and the attendant relativity of scientific method in focus, he refers to the views of scientific method of Francis Bacon, René Descartes, Morris Cohen and Ernest Nagel, and John Dewey.

Francis Bacon

Francis Bacon saw the problem as one of going beyond Aristotle's method of syllogisms. As Bacon saw the problem, 'The cause and root of nearly all evils in the sciences is this – that while we falsely admire and extol the powers of the human mind we neglect to seek for its true helps' (Aphorism IX). And:

> The logic now in use serves rather to fix and give stability to the errors which have their foundations in commonly received notions than to help the search after truth. So it does more harm than good. (Aphorism XII)

> The syllogism consists of propositions, propositions of words, words are symbols of notions. Therefore if the notions themselves (which is the root of the matter) are confused and over-hastily abstracted from the facts, there can be no firmness in the superstructure. Our only hope therefore lies in a true induction. (Aphorism XIV)

Thus, Bacon saw at his time that man was hopelessly locked into existing explanatory systems that were treated as idols. Formal logic is viewed as fixing and giving stability to old errors.

René Descartes

Descartes in his *Discourse on Method* also tells of his discontent with existing explanatory procedures. Traditional natural science had broken down and 'humanistic' discussions were contradictory. Mathematics was one subject that stood out in terms of certainty. Reflection on the methods of mathematics led Descartes to stress the deductive method of formal logic. Since traditional knowledge except mathematics failed to stand up under examination, Descartes was led to the procedure of doubting everything that one can possibly doubt, and then deducing the remainder of one's knowledge from the indubitable minimum.

Morris Cohen and Ernest Nagel

Although Morris Cohen and his pupil Ernest Nagel appreciate both the empirical inductive method of Bacon and the deductive method of mathematical physics, they also found shortcomings in both which suggested another procedure. Thus they write 'it is an utterly superficial view . . . that the truth is to be found by "studying the facts". It is superficial because no inquiry can ever get under way unless *some difficulty is felt* in a practical or theoretical situation.' With respect to the theoretical intuition of supposedly self-evident postulates or axioms, they state (quoted by Northrop, 1947, pp. 10–11):

> Unfortunately, it is difficult to find a proposition for which at some time or other 'self-evidence' has not been claimed. Propositions regarded as indubitable by many, for example, that the earth is flat, have been shown to be false. It is well known that 'self-evidence' is often a function of current fashions and of early training. The fact, therefore, that we feel absolutely certain, or that a given proposition has not before been questioned, is no guarantee against its being proved false. Our intuitions must, then, be tested.

> We cannot take a single step forward in any inquiry unless we begin with a *suggested* explanation or solution of the difficulty which originated it. Such tentative explanations are suggested to us by something in the subject matter and by our previous knowledge. When they are formulated as propositions, they are called *hypotheses*.

> The function of a hypothesis is to *direct* our search for the order among facts. The suggestions formulated in the hypothesis *may* be solutions to the problem. *Whether* they are, is the task of the inquiry.

John Dewey

'Inquiry', writes John Dewey in his *Logic: The Theory of Inquiry*, 'is the controlled or directed transformation of an indeterminate situation into one that is so determinate in its constituent distinctions and relations as to convert the elements of the original situation into a unified whole'. 'The indeterminate situation,' he states, 'becomes problematical in the very process of being subjected to inquiry' (Northrop, 1947, p. 12).

Northrop stressed that 'this is a very important point. It means that for Dewey inquiry begins neither with the collecting of facts nor with either the projection of hypotheses or an act of thoroughgoing doubting followed by logical deduction from the remainder that is indubitable, but with the problematic situations' (1947, pp. 12–13).

Reflection on these diverse prescriptions for the initiation of inquiry led Northrop to stress that *scientific method is relative to the problem.* As a concrete example, Northrop presented Galilei analysis of why the motion of a projectile does not move the way Aristotelian physics says it should. Galilei analysis indicated that the problem was not in the projectile but rather in the Aristotelian concept of force as applied to any motion whatever.

The distinctive aspect of Northrop's analysis of the first stage is this stress that science progresses from problem to problem. Theories and explanatory systems run into trouble when they are extended from the evidence for which it is confirmed to all relevant evidence. Thus the solution of one problem generates other problems. The second stage or natural history stage of inquiry begins with immediately apprehended fact and ends with described fact. According to Northrop, immediately apprehended fact is free of concepts and theories whereas described fact is fact brought under concepts and takes the form of propositions. The third stage consists of hypotheses suggested by the relevant facts, which are then pursued to their logical consequences. The distinctive aspect of Northrop's analysis at this stage is his suggestion that, since the logical consequences of pursuing the hypothesis designates the theoretically defined experiments or operations necessary for an empirical test, the concept and theory determines the 'operation' more than the operation defines the concept and theory. Central to an understanding of this third stage is Northrop's distinction between concepts by postulation and concepts by inspection.

A concept by inspection is one the complete meaning of which is given by something immediately observable. (1947, p. 136)

A concept by postulation is one the meaning of which is proposed for it by the postulates of the deductive theory in which it occurs. (1947, p. 139)

The task of science as Northrop views it is the coordination of concepts by postulation with the concepts by inspection through what he calls 'epistemic correlations'. Epistemic correlations are not to be confused with statistical correlations. Statistical correlations always relate items in the same world of discourse – that is, either they relate factors designated by concepts of postulation to each other or they relate inspectable items denoted by concepts by inspection. Epistemic correlation refers to relating a postulated factor designated by a concept by postulation to an inspectable datum denoted by a concept by inspection. What I find interesting about Northrop's analysis at this point is his stress that although the elementary text books in logic indicate the formal logic fallacy of affirming the consequents, 'the mathematical physicist, as Einstein and others have emphasized ... does not verify his postulates directly but believes them to be tentatively true providing the theorems logically deduced from them are directly verified' (Northrop, 1947, p. 1908).

Northrop (1947, pp. 119–32) explicitly employs the term 'epistemic correlations' to distinguish his discussion of the relationship of the theoretically known, postulationally designated factors from the empirical factors of discussions in terms of operational definitions.

> Every scientific theory must have operational definitions for at least some of its concepts. These operationally defined meanings are joined to the theoretically designated meanings of the theory by means of epistemic correlations. Consequently, operational definitions are not the sole definitions of a deductively formulated scientific theory. Instead, they are merely correlates of quite different meanings existing throughout the entire deductively formulated theory which are designated by concepts by postulation. Failure to clearly distinguish purely empirically given meanings denoted by concepts by intuition from the theoretically proposed meanings designated by concepts by postulation has introduced an incalculable amount of confusion into the analysis of scientific method and scientific theory. (Northrop 1947, p. 125)

If 'operational definitions' defined in terms of the 'operations' at the data level (that is, descriptions of the experiment and/or how the observations were derived and manipulated) were enough, the 'operations' would define the concept. And one would expect the concepts to emerge from the data. However, a cursory view of the history of ideas indicates that rather diverse concepts have been employed often to discuss essentially the same data. In other words, the data do not speak for themselves. The laws of nature do not, as Ernst Mach has argued, 'contain nothing more than' the facts of observation for which they account. Rather, as Einstein has emphasized, 'we can only grasp' the subject matter of physics 'by speculative means' and 'our notions of this subject matter can never be final' – they are merely models.

> This entails that our scientific conclusions always involve a theoretical factor going beyond what the facts logically guarantee and this makes it absolutely essential in scientific inquiry that we make these theoretical factors *explicit* and carry on theoretical investigations as well as the accumulation of empirical data. (Northrop, 1947, p. 147)

Much of the confusion in so-called 'theoretical discussions' by social scientists is the result of their conceiving scientific method as being merely the experimental confirmation of theory. The mere experimental confirmation of theory leads to the fallacy of affirming the consequent. Thus, the methods of verification need to be supplemented by a theoretical investigation as to whether there is or is not other theoretical interpretations of the same data.

The implication of this contemporary view of philosophy of science is that 'in physics, as in travelling, the horizon shifts as we go along. With the development of new theories, new problems are thrown into prominence, ways are seen of fitting into physical theory things which before had hardly been regarded as matters requiring a place at all: the horizon accordingly expands' (Toulmin, 1953, p. 117).

2 NORWOOD RUSSELL HANSON

Norwood Russell Hanson (1958, 1963) has stressed that an overview of the history and logic of natural philosophy (physics) exposes men wrestling with conceptual aspects of physical problems. Much of the confusion as to the nature of the conceptual foundations of science results from treating as paradigms of scientific inquiry finished systems such as classical thermodynamics and planetary mechanics rather than the unsettled, dynamic research sciences such as microphysics. An appreciation of Hanson's discussion shifts our attention to how explanatory systems are 'built into our observations, and our appreciation of facts and data' (Hanson, 1958, p. 3). As one turns from theory-making and the testing of hypotheses to an examination of the nature of theory finding and discovery, one sees that scientific inquiry in an expanding discipline is better characterized as a discovery of new patterns of explanation – new controlling models.

Central to Hanson's discussion is his stress that theory not only influences interpretation, but rather observation itself; ' . . . seeing is a theory-laden undertaking' (Hanson, 1958, p. 19).

When language and notation are ignored in studies of observation, physics is represented as resting on sensation and low-grade experiment. It is described as repetitious, monotonous concatenation of spectacular sensations, and of school-laboratory experiments. But physical science is not just a systematic exposure of the senses to the world; it is also a way of thinking about the world, a way of forming conceptions. (Hanson, 1958, p. 30)

Physical theories provide patterns within which data appear intelligible. They constitute a 'conceptual Gestalt'. A theory is not pieced together from observed phenomena; it is rather what makes it possible to observe phenomena as being of a certain sort, and as related to other phenomena. Theories put phenomena into systems. They are built up 'in reverse' – retroductively. A theory is a cluster of conclusions in search of a premise. From the observed properties of phenomena the physicist reasons his way towards a keystone idea from which the properties are explicable as a matter of course. The physicist seeks not a set of possible objects, but a set of possible explanations. (Hanson, 1958, p. 90)

A profound implication of Hanson's work (1958, 1963) taken as a whole is that an *explanatory system* not only allows one to perceive phenomena in a meaningful way but is also an *obstacle* to further reconceptualization.

Further, this 'implication' may also apply to our conceptualization of the scientific process itself. Much of the discussion of the nature of scientific explanation takes the form of Hempel's 'symmetry between explanation and prediction'. I wish to stress that it is not at all clear that the logic of explaining and predicting will be the same in all fields. Hanson (1963, pp. 25–41) has stressed that Hempel's symmetry between explanation and prediction fails when one examines a living, growing science as expressed in contemporary non-deterministic theories of microphysics.[3]

Hanson (1963, p. 33), in his fine-detail analysis of *The Concept of the Positron*, has indicated that:

> There is an intimate connexion between Hempel's symmetry between explanation and prediction, and the logic of Newton's *Principia*. To have learned this from Hempel is to have learned something important ... about explanation and prediction, and about Newtonian science. But the professional historian need not regard himself as a Newtonian scientist; the quantum physicist necessarily cannot do so. There may be more to be said about the logic of explanation and prediction, as these concepts obtain in fields other than that one in which Hempel's analysis appears sound. Philosophers might still wish to know what is the logical structure of explanation and prediction as these function in living, growing sciences, and not only as they were employed for a brief period in a discipline which is by now little more than a computing device for rocket and missile engineers.

3 THOMAS S. KUHN

Thomas S. Kuhn (1962) has recently provided us with a popular account of the history of ideas in physics not as the mere accumulation of facts and theories but rather in terms of *The Structure of Scientific Revolutions*. Central to Kuhn's discussion is the distinction between (1) normal science where research scientists are working out the boundaries of some scientific explanatory system which he refers to as a paradigm, and (2) the recognition of anomaly in the existing explanatory system(s) by theoretical scientists and the search for a reconceptualization of the problem (which later becomes normal science). Important for our purposes is his stress on the relative scarcity of competing schools of thought in the developed sciences. In contrast, the most salient feature of archaeology, anthropology and the social sciences is the *multitude of essentially different paradigms* for the study of socio-cultural phenomena. Whereas, Kuhn is directing his attention to problems of paradigm shifts in time for the developed sciences, reflection on the nature of discussion of socio-cultural phenomena by social scientists indicates that we have the initial problem of sorting out various paradigms existing at the same time. David Bidney (1953) has been one of the few individuals in anthropology who has attempted to get at the conceptual basis and presuppositions of various 'theories'. Whereas the majority of anthropological theoreticians are concerned with justification, reflection on the existence of various explanatory systems for socio-cultural phenomena indicates that we should rather direct our attention to problems of 'discovery'. The term *discovery* is stressed because there is disagreement not only about the explanation but also about the criteria to settle our differences.

The majority of the existing discussions of the nature of socio-cultural phenomena are at the natural history stage of inquiry. That is, observable data are explained in terms of observable data. In order to go to the higher stage of inquiry one must learn to think deductively in terms of concepts by postulation. That is, what would the nature of the phenomena have to be for the data to be as they are?

The special feature of a critical and scientific education seems to be puzzle-solving as a goal. In the social sciences (even in research methods), in contrast, one is immediately struck by the lack of puzzlement. The following section will discuss some problems of explicating joint occurrences of socio-cultural phenomena in cross-cultural studies.

As the following section will indicate, when the method of verification in cross-cultural surveys is subjected to a theoretical investigation one finds that the observations and discussions are loaded with concepts and theories which are obstacles to further reconceptualization of the problem. These obstacles, however, are seen only in retrospect. We cannot so confidently describe the structuring of the present discussion by the ideas and concepts employed.

On cross-cultural surveys

The three main threads from the history of numerical classification in comparative anthropology that connect with the later discussion are the works of Harold E. Driver, George Peter Murdock and Raoul Naroll. In turn, the works of these men are intimately connected with early formulations of the problem of explicating the known co-occurrences of socio-cultural phenomena at various space-time coordinates of human experience.

Various discussions of the history of numerical classifications in comparative ethnology are to be found in Kluckhohn (1939), Köbben (1952), Driver (1953, 1962, 1965, 1970), Moore (1961), McEwen (1963), Naroll (1970a), and Naroll and Cohen (1970).

Many misuses of statistics in cross-cultural studies have been pointed out as being due to inaccurate measurement or classification of cases, inappropriate comparisons, technical errors, sampling methods and misinterpretation of correlation (Chaney, 1966a, 1966b, 1970; Chaney and Ruiz Revilla, 1969; Driver, 1961b; Driver and Chaney, 1970; Driver and Schuessler, 1967; Jorgensen, 1966; Köbben, 1952, 1967; McEwen, 1963; Murdock, 1957, 1966, 1967; Naroll, 1961, 1962, 1964a, 1964b; Naroll and D'Andrade, 1963; Sawyer and LeVine, 1966; Schapera, 1953; Whiting, 1961; Wilson, 1952).

The present study deals with only two of the above problems: sampling methods and interpretation of correlation. These problems will remain central in any discourse no matter what form reformulation of measurement and classification of cases may take in the future. For classic discussions of the problems of 'measurement' and classification of socio-cultural phenomena, see Kluckhohn (1953) and Goodenough (1956).

Anthropological statistical studies have tended to be either (1) studies that inferred historical, diffusional aspects from an examination of continuously distributed ethnic units, or (2) studies that inferred functional and/or causal aspects from an examination of societies, geographically sprinkled around the world.

(1) Boas's (1895) study of 214 elements (motifs, incidents and tale types) of North American Indian tales and myths among twelve ethnic units was the first statistical study of continuously distributed ethnic units. Driver (1970, pp. 620–1), in the only comprehensive account of statistical studies of continuous geographical distributions of socio-cultural phenomena, summarized Boas's principal conclusions of his 1894 and 1916 studies of folklore motifs:

> (1) Neighbouring peoples share more folklore inventory than distant
> peoples. The ethnic units in the continuous areas on the Northwest Coast

and Plateau share more with each other than with the Ponca, Micmac, interior Athapaskan group. Therefore very strong diffusions among neighbouring peoples have taken place. (2) Tribes speaking languages of the same family show significantly greater internal similarity with each other. Thus Boas distinguished the culture heritage migration explanation of resemblances from the diffusion one which must be postulated for elements spilling over language family fences. (3) Most resemblances do not arise independently from 'elementary ideas' shared by all peoples on the earth, but are determined by contacts of peoples. . . . (4) The elements (motifs) of a particular tale type or tale cycle tend to diffuse independently of each other as well as independently of the larger tale unit, which never diffuses as a whole. (5) The elements assembled in a tale type of a single society, however, are reinterpreted and integrated into each local literary style. (6) There is no way to tell which version of a tale type is prior historically and by this means to arrange them in a historical or evolutionary sequence. These and the earlier conclusions of 1894 gave rise to the theory of culture which Lowie (1920, p. 441) phrased as 'that planless hodge-podge, that thing of shreds and patches called civilization'. . . .

(2) In 1888 E. B. Tylor presented the first worldwide statistical analysis: 'On a method of investigating the development of institutions; applied to laws of marriage and descent'. Francis Galton (in Tylor, 1889) criticized Tylor's evolutionary interpretation of the 'adhesions' (or associations) in terms of the cases not being historically independent. 'It [would be] extremely desirable for the sake of those who wish to study the evidence for Dr Tylor's conclusions that full information should be given as to the degree in which the customs of the tribes and races which are compared are independent. It might be that some of the tribes had derived from a common source, so that they were duplicate copies of the same original' (Tylor, 1889, p. 270).

Tylor was unable to provide a satisfactory answer. Explicit techniques for solving this problem were not presented until the early 1960s (Naroll, 1961, 1964a; Naroll and D'Andrade, 1963).

Driver (1965, pp. 324–5) has succinctly summarized three statistical schools of thought:

The California and Yale schools
The California school, represented by A. L. Kroeber, his pupils and associates, used proximity coefficients first to determine geographical clusterings of ethnic units (tribes, tribelets, villages, bands, societies, and any other culture-bearing group of people) and second to reconstruct the history of

these ethnic units, of their total cultures, or of a restricted part of their cultures. In every case the universe of investigation was limited to an area of less than continental scope. In most of these studies the ethnic units were treated as variables and they were compared in terms of the amount of culture trait inventory shared. The conclusions arrived at were regarded as applying only to a restricted area of each study, and no attempt was made to establish universal generalizations about the culture of the entire human species. The California school stemmed from Boas.

The Yale school, represented by G. P. Murdock, J. W. M. Whiting, and their pupils and associates, aimed at establishing world-wide generalizations about all ethnic units from samples thought to be representative of the whole. These studies treat subject units (culture traits, elements, complexes, components, themes, patterns, and any other parts of total culture) as variables and compare them in terms of the number of ethnic units sharing the various combinations of subject units. The Yale school stemmed from Tylor, Sumner, and Keller.

The California method was largely empirical in that it was not bolstered by formal postulates, theorems, or propositions. However, it implicitly relied on the general principle that continuity of geographical distribution resulted from geographical factors, diffusion, migration, and other geographico-historical processes. It sometimes employed the age-area hypothesis, which assumes a perfect correlation between size of geographical area and age of the subject unit distributed over the area. The California method has been frequently labelled historical, but it was inferential undocumented history.

The Yale school, on the other hand, was largely postulational, in that considerable functional or psychological theory was formulated in advance, and only the data relevant to the theory collected. Murdock's *Social Structure* (1949) is the best known example of this method and Whiting's psychological studies (e.g. Whiting and Child, 1953) follow similar procedures. However, when Driver bluntly asked Murdock a few years ago if every theorem and proposition in his *Social Structure* was formulated in advance of the collecting of data and printed without alteration after the data was collected, Murdock gave a negative reply; the postulates were modified in the light of what the empirical data revealed. Therefore the dichotomy of postulational versus empirical (positive) method, so charming to some philosophers, does not fit the reality of actual research methods, in ethnology, and probably not in any other behavioural science. The Yale method has been labelled evolutionary because it interprets its correlations as causal sequences replicated over and over again among societies thought not to be connected historically. It has used tests of significance, especially chi-square, much more often than the California school.

The Kulturkreis influence on the California school

There was a third statistical school associated in the beginning with the Kulturkreis concept. Like the California school it was empirical rather than postulational and limited its comparisons to small, continuous areas. Jan Czekanowski (1911) intercorrelated, with Yale's Q coefficient, seventeen traits of material culture among forty-seven African tribes, and clustered the material into two geographical-historical units. His assumption was that all resemblances in this corpus of data were due to historical factors, such as migration or diffusion, but no distinction was made between genetic heritage and diffused elements (see p. 316 of this volume).

THE TYLOR–GALTON PROBLEM

There have been four approaches to deal with Galton's problem of statistical inference with socio-cultural phenomena.

(1) Murdock (1957, 1967; Murdock *et al.*, 1963; Murdock and White, 1969) has presented a number of worldwide judgemental samples in which he has attempted to control for obvious recent historical influences through structuring the universe of cultures.

(2) Driver (1966) has employed continuously distributed ethnic units in conjunction with an analysis of language family affiliation in order to separate out diffusion, culture-heritage migration and independent invention.

(3) Naroll (1961, 1964a) and Naroll and D'Andrade (1963) have attempted to work out explicit inductive techniques for dealing with the Tylor–Galton problem.

(4) Sawyer and LeVine (1966), Chaney (1966a, 1970), Jorgensen (1966), and Driver and Schuessler (1967) have employed geography as a variable (worldwide samples with regional breakdowns) in assessing the meaning of coefficients of association.

In contrast, the majority of cross-cultural researchers have assumed that they were controlling for the Tylor–Galton problem by selecting samples of societies geographically sprinkled around the world. Some recent writers have even suggested the advisability of using small samples (Benfer, 1968;

Rohner and Pelto, 1970). The general 'model' in the majority of cross-cultural studies has been to read off some form of functional and/or causal relationship from the worldwide coefficients of association. Chaney (1970) in reply to Rohner and Pelto (1970) indicated that the so-called Tylor–Galton problem might be better viewed in terms of regional differences in data patterning rather than in terms of historical relatedness inflating the magnitude of association as expressed by contingency tables.

Driver (1961a; Driver and Massey, 1957) has documented the problem of historical diffusional factors by mapping the presence and absence of single variables for nearly continuously distributed ethnic units of North America. Driver (1966) has recently emphasized that for North American Indian data historical-diffusional factors provide a better 'explanation' for the presence of kin avoidances than the association with functional and/or causal factors.

Raoul Naroll and Roy D'Andrade (Naroll, 1961, 1964a; Narroll and D'Andrade, 1963) are to be congratulated for their attempts to develop explicit inductive techniques for solving the Tylor–Galton problem. Nearly every cross-cultural researcher cites the above papers in his bibliography. And a few have even used the techniques. However, incredible as it may seem, no one had critically analysed the methods (see Naroll, 1970b, and Chaney, 1970).

Chaney, Morton and Moore (1972; Chaney, 1970) have recently critically analysed the 'Interval Sift Method' and the 'Matched Pair Method' (Naroll and D'Andrade, 1963) and indicated that the Naroll and D'Andrade solutions to the Tylor–Galton problem are better viewed as valuable *discussions* of the Tylor–Galton problem (cf. Driver and Chaney, 1970).

The problem occurs in that different researchers using samples of societies with varied geographical spreads and varied dichotomizations of the variables will often derive different so-called 'answers' as to the nature of the relationship between the variables! And the truly profound problems emerge in that man can always weave an 'explanation' no matter what kind of data patterns are exposed. For this latter reason, theoretical physicists such as Einstein tell us that one attempts to hold 'obviously' invalid conceptual organizations or explanatory systems in check by specifying a *unique* coordination between the concepts by postulation and any set of observations and/or experiences. Operationalism – that is, specified operations of deriving the observations and experiences – is not enough. Although some form of 'operational definition' of how the data that are being reflected upon were derived is mandatory in a scientific level of discourse, this is not enough. Recent discussions of the history of ideas have repeatedly indicated that man has assigned different meanings to the nature of physical phenomena and to the nature of his own socio-cultural life.[4] This overview indicates that all explanatory systems are methods of representation.

Areal differences

the significance of areal differences in worldwide correlations has been pointed out recently by a number of individuals (Chaney, 1966a, pp. 1468–9, 1966b, p. 1475; Driver, 1961b, p. 326; Driver and Schuessler, 1967, pp. 336–46; Jorgensen, 1966, pp. 161–9; Murdock, 1940, p. 369; Romney, in Hymes, 1965, p. 393; Sawyer and LeVine, 1966, pp. 719–27; Wilson, 1952, pp. 134–8). In general, the view is that truly functional relationships should hold up across geographical regions, whereas associations that are not functional are more influenced by historical, ecological and diffusional circumstances in the various continental regions (see Chaney and Ruiz Revilla, 1969, pp. 618–28).

Although sampling problems in general are common knowledge, the majority of cross-cultural researchers (with the exception of Driver, Murdock and Naroll) have attempted to control for the Tylor–Galton problem by selecting samples of societies geographically sprinkled around the world. Explicit attention was directed at the intertwined problems of sampling societies and regional data patterning in Chaney's (1966a) reanalysis of Spiro's (1965) discussion of 'A typology of social structure and the patterning of social institutions: a cross-cultural study' (see also Spiro, 1966). An examination of the eight possible configurations of descent-family-household in the six main geographical areas of the world indicated that there were significant differences from one continent to another in terms of the types of configurations and not just in terms of high or low correlation.

The intertwined problems of sampling 'ethnic units' and conceptually organizing the data was returned to in a discussion of 'Sampling methods and interpreting of correlation: a comparative analysis of seven cross-cultural samples' (Chaney and Ruiz Revilla, 1969).

In that paper, Murdock's sample of 412 culture clusters was assumed to be the most representative to date, and the other six samples were examined and evaluated in terms of it (Chaney and Ruiz Revilla, 1969, pp. 598–606). An analysis in terms of standard error of their difference established that the smaller non-random samples were referring to a universe of societies different from the base sample 412 societies. It was stressed that each of these three samples was differing from the base sample in different ways as a result of different biases in their selection; that is, different intercorrelated variables in each of the three samples were significantly different from those of the base sample.

In any interpretation of these results, it should be kept in mind that Pearson's C (and the Z values) when used with a three-by-three table as is encountered in the present analysis is not necessarily measuring a linear relationship but rather is measuring any systematic departure from independence or total unpredictability. Although a difference between coefficients reflects a true difference between samples, a similarity in coefficients does not necessarily mean that the two samples are giving the same results; that is, two samples may express the same degree of association between two variables, but the association in each sample may be due to different systematic departures from independence. Thus, if anything, the coefficient of association used in this analysis with a three-by-three table is underestimating the difference between the samples. This was substantiated by an analysis of the actual cell frequencies for the same intercorrelations in the different samples. Although different systematic departures from independence were not a problem in the larger samples when compared with the base sample, these did come into play occasionally among the three smaller samples. Among the three smaller samples the cell frequencies in the three rows and columns were sometimes found to be skewed in different ways from those found in the base sample even when the coefficients were similar in magnitude. As a result of different biases in the selection of the societies in the three small samples, different kinds of associations were sometimes found to be favoured. However, no systematic departures were found to exist for all three small samples; that is, each small sample did not necessarily differ from the base sample in the same way (this problem will be discussed further under areal differences). (Chaney and Ruiz Revilla, 1969, pp. 616–617)

In the discussion (Chaney and Ruiz Revilla, 1969, p. 624) of the significance of regional differences in terms of the standard error of the difference between the coefficients of association, it was stressed that

An examination of the three-by-three tables, upon which the coefficients are based, reveals that in nearly all the cases where there is a large range of difference in the coefficients for the regions, at least one of the areas yields a somewhat different type of relationship (not just a lack of association) than that found in the worldwide sample. In other words, regional circumstances often favour different associations of two variables. It cannot be overemphasized that the 'exceptions' for the majority of the intercorrelations are *not* randomly distributed among the six geographical regions of the world. Rather, there are clusterings of exceptions for the different intercorrelations

TABLE 26.1. *Cell frequencies for 3 × 3 tables of extra-local jurisdictional hierarchy and subsistence economy with a worldwide sample and six regional subsamples*

Cells	Category[a]	Regional subsamples						Worldwide
		Africa	Circum-Mediterranean	East Eurasia	Insular Pacific	North America	South America	
1	(1) o level (2) Gathering, fishing or hunting	5	0	12	12	133	23	185
2	(1) 1 level (2) Gathering, fishing or hunting	6	1	2	7	35	4	55
3	(1) 2, 3, 4 levels (2) Gathering, fishing or hunting	0	0	1	1	0	0	2
4	(1) o level (2) Pastoral	3	2	0	0	0	1	6
5	(1) 1 level (2) Pastoral	6	8	5	0	0	0	19
6	(1) 2, 3, 4 levels (2) Pastoral	4	10	6	0	0	0	20
7	(1) o level (2) Agriculture	52	8	16	57	25	46	204
8	(1) 1 level (2) Agriculture	90	14	21	32	17	8	182
9	(1) 2, 3, 4 levels (2) Agriculture	71	40	27	17	7	4	166
TOTALS		237	83	90	126	217	86	839
χ^2		5·93	4·93	23·02	1·68	31·17	2·21	149·68
Adjusted Pearson C		0·19	0·29	0·55	0·15	0·43	0·19	0·48

(a) Categories of: (1) Extra-local jurisdictional hierarchy; (2) Subsistence economy.

TABLE 26.2. *Cell frequencies for 3 × 3 tables of descen*

Cells	Category[a]	Afr
1	(1) Patrilineal: P	
	(2) Patrilocal or virilocal: P, V	17c
2	(1) Patrilineal: P	
	(2) Optional: B, D, N, O	6
3	(1) Patrilineal: P	
	(2) Matrilocal, avunculocal or uxorilocal: M, A, V, C	c
4	(1) Bilateral duolateral, quasi-lineages or ambilineal: B, D, Q, A	
	(2) Patrilocal or virilocal: P, V	19
5	(1) Bilateral, duolateral, quasi-lineages or ambilineal: B, D, Q, A	
	(2) Optional: B, D, N, O	4
6	(1) Bilateral, duolateral, quasi-lineages or ambilineal: B, D, Q, A	
	(2) Matrilocal, avunculocal, or uxorilocal: M, A, V, C	1
7	(1) Matrilineal: M	
	(2) Patrilocal or virilocal: P, V	6
8	(1) Matrilineal: M	
	(2) Optional: B, D, N, O	3
9	(1) Matrilineal: M	
	(2) Matrilocal, avunculocal or uxorilocal: M, A, V, C	28
TOTALS		237
χ^2		175
Adjusted Pearson C		0

(*a*) Categories of: (1) Descent; (2) Residence.

in the different geographical regions (for a somewhat different view of 'exceptions' see Köbben, 1967).

Reflection on the above discussed problems suggested that a computer program was needed that would present the data analysis in terms of the actual cell frequencies in addition to coefficients of association for both the worldwide relationship and regional subsamples in one continuous run. Further, under the influence of Driver's integration of mapped data with his interpretation of the meaning of joint occurrences of socio-cultural phenomena for North American Indian ethnic units (Driver and Massey, 1957; Driver, 1961a, 1966), a subprogram was incorporated which would plot *ence with a worldwide sample and six regional subsamples*

		Regional subsamples				
um- ter- an	*East Eurasia*	*Insular Pacific*	*North America*	*South America*	*Worldwide*	
7	66	41	35	14	383	
o	I	2	5	o	14	
o	o	o	o	I	I	
8	9	33	57	21	187	
I	4	14	30	16	79	
o	5	8	27	27	68	
3	I	6	3	I	20	
4	I	7	6	I	22	
o	6	15	25	7	81	
3	93	126	218	88	855	
9·86	57·95	48·80	68·01	24·83	390·36	
0·60	0·76	0·65	0·60	0·58	0·69	

the worldwide geographical distribution of configurations of socio-cultural phenomena.

The plotting of the geographical distribution of configurations of socio-cultural phenomena
The distinctive aspect of the present computer plotting is that it allows the presentation of the geographical distributions of *configurations* of socio-cultural phenomena. Any data (socio-cultural, linguistic, physical, archaeological, etc.) that can be localized in terms of latitude–longitude are able to be plotted with an Eckert IV map projection. The outline of the world is plotted from a digitized coastline tape from the United States Naval Office.

Although configuration of up to six variables may be presented, in the present illustration configurations of only two variables are being presented. The data for the present discussion are computed from a numerical version of IBM cards prepared by Herbert Barry from Murdock's 'Ethnographic Atlas' (1967) of coded data for 863 societies. The latitude-longitude as presented in the 'Ethnographic Atlas' is used as the plotting point for the coded configurations of socio-cultural phenomena.[5]

Tables 26.1 and 26.2 present the data from the computer printouts for the relationships (1) between Extra-local Jurisdictional Hierarchy and Subsistence Economy, and (2) between Descent and Residence. Each of these variables is scaled into three categories. Figures 26.1 and 26.2 present the geographical distribution of the nine configurations of the data for the societies represented in the nine cells for each of the six regions of Tables 26.1 and 26.2.

A possible significance of the present presentation of data for conceptualization of the relationship between joint occurrences of socio-cultural phenomena is best grasped if we compare it with a recent discussion by Murdock and White (1969). This paper is singled out because it represents both a continuation of Murdock to derive a more representative sample and a somewhat different attempt to deal with problems of sampling. In this paper, Murdock and White (1969, p. 330) stress that 'Methodologically, it is just as crucial to establish the actual concurrence of elements as to employ appropriate sampling and other statistical techniques to the analysis of their association.'

In their new 'Standard cross-cultural sample' of 186 societies, Murdock and White (1969, p. 330) have

> pinpointed every society in the standard sample to a specific date and a specific locality, typically the local community where the principal authority conducted his most intensive field research, and they have eliminated from the sample all societies for which the sources do not permit reasonably accurate pinpointing. It is often possible, of course, for coders to make fairly reliable inferences by extrapolation from data on neighbouring local groups with closely similar subcultures or from observations at somewhat earlier or later dates, but they should be instructed to use great caution in so doing and to specify their reasons. Focusing attention on a specific pinpointed date and locality should, it is believed, substantially enhance the accuracy of cross-cultural research.

The discussion departs from previous presentations of samples by Murdock in that it employs a modification of the Linked Pair Method to segregate that portion of the correlation attributable to historical influences from that due to functional parallelism (Murdock and White, 1969, p. 348). A distinctive aspect of their technique (Successive Pairs test) is, in their own words, 'In developing this modification of the Linked Pair Method, we have employed an index of similarity between pairs instead of using Naroll's technique of calculating the correlation between pairs on a single attribute' (Murdock and White, 1969, p. 349).

It is to be emphasized, however, that they have not shown the power of the Linked Pair Method with their modification; rather, they have employed the technique and assumed that the method solves the Tylor–Galton problem.

Some problems emerge if we compare the conceptualization derived from their data analysis with that derived from an examination of the geographical distribution of configurations of socio-cultural phenomena.

Murdock and White (1969, p. 351) tell us that by,

> using a modification of the Internal Sift Method on a sample of 53 societies in which the correlation between the presence of agriculture among neighbouring societies is phi $= -0.05$, we have calculated a phi of 0.32 ($p < 0.01$) for the relation between agriculture and supra-community sovereignty. The true functional correlation between the two variables probably lies between 0.32 and 0.36 still statistically significant after a reduction from the original correlation by about 30%, the portion of the correlation due to historical influences in the sample.

Although the combination of a structured universe of societies and an explicit inductive technique to deal with the Tylor–Galton problem is a big step forward, the discussion of the results in terms of a worldwide coefficient of association masks the degree and kinds of regional data patterning. Table 26.1 presents the cell frequencies of a 3×3 comparison of the variables of jurisdictional hierarchy beyond the local community and subsistence type with Murdock's sample of 863 societies. Figure 26.1 presents the geographical distribution of the nine different configurations coded numerically 1 through 9.

An examination of the regional difference in data patterning underscores the value of using a large sample of societies that are historically interconnected. Thus, whereas the use of a modification of the Linked Pair Method with worldwide coefficients of association yields data patterns that might lead one to conceptualize a 'true functional correlation' of 0.32–0.36 as merely a weak or strong relationship, an examination of the actual cell frequencies in a regional comparison approach yields data patterns that lend

FIG. 26.1. Extra-local jurisdictional hier

themselves to a conceptualization which deals with the nature of regional differences.

Further, reflection on Table 26.2 and Fig. 26.2 which present a relationship between residence and descent, indicates that whereas one might postulate a rather strong association for these variables in terms of the worldwide (or regional) coefficients of association, an examination of the actual cell frequencies exposes somewhat different associations between the attributes of these variables in the six main geographical regions of the world.

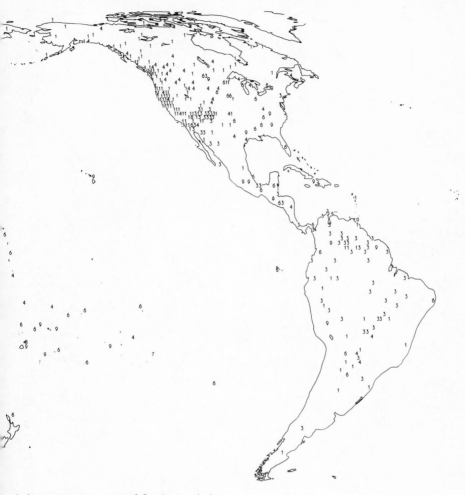

subsistence types, mapped for 839 societies.

In the present analysis the coefficient of contingency is being employed to summarize the data.[6] The coefficient is not being used to establish (or discover) functional or causal relationships. One misuses statistics such as chi-square when one thinks that it can yield direct information relating to functional or causal explanation with socio-cultural data (see Chaney and Ruiz Revilla, 1969, p. 630). The intertwined tasks of the cross-cultural researcher are to help find the degree of regularity in socio-cultural phenomena and to explicate the nature of the regularity.[7]

FIG. 26.2. Residence and de

It has been suggested recently that the 'weight of evidence' from cross-cultural comparison 'indicates that an interpretation of socio-cultural phenomena in terms of realms of order and different degrees of invariant relationship and contingency works better than an interpretation in terms of the disjunctive functional-causal factors versus historical-diffusional factors' (Chaney and Ruiz Revilla, 1969, p. 625).

Socio-cultural phenomena, the process of: a *potentially* creative imagination expanding against different degrees of psychosociocultural invariant

s, mapped for 855 societies.

relationship and historical-ecological contingency. (Chaney and Ruiz Revilla, 1969, p. 628)

Although there are many modes of cultural integration, the view expressed here is that from a temporal perspective the unity of *a* culture consists to a large extent in its continuity. Habituation and conditioning have been essential characteristics of *a* culture. The *meaning* is assigned by man. Further, this view appreciates, the possible integrative functions of cultural ideals. (Chaney and Ruiz Revilla, 1969, p. 630)

1025

Epilogue

The intertwined problems of selection and conceptual organization are at the nexus of man's awareness of the texture of knowledge.

A statement on the nature of man is only as representative as it is able to elucidate the nature of man in the continuum of human existence.

Actualized human nature varies with the degree of man's awareness of the texture of his own knowledge.

Meta-anthropology: The findings of archaeology and anthropology on the intertwined problems of meanings that man has assigned and the degree of epistemic integration of these with the actions of man need to be analysed and coordinated with the findings from other disciplines that are focusing on various areas of the continuum of human existence (see Bidney, 1953, pp. 156–182).

Notes

1. See D. J. Price (1965, pp. 510–15) for a discussion of 'Networks of scientific papers'.

2. Bidney (1953, p. 177) has succinctly stated a fundamental question as to the nature of man:

> In the development of modern cultural anthropology one may discern two major 'themes'. On the one hand, there is the theme derived from the naturalistic, positivistic, evolutionary tradition of the nineteenth century that cultural reality represents an autonomous, superorganic, superpsychic level of reality subject to its own laws and stages of evolution. On the other hand, there is the recurring theme, which dates back to the humanistic tradition of Greek philosophy, the Renaissance, and the rationalism of the eighteenth-century philosophers, that human culture is the product of human discovery and creativity and is subject to human regulation.

3. R. B. Angel (1967) has argued that the reaction to the 'symmetry' discussion by Hanson, Scriven *et al.* is a retrograde movement in the philosophy of science. The basic policy of writers like this is that we can only be rational and objective if there is a logical symmetry between explanation and prediction. Otherwise, we will be staggering in irrationalism. This is not at all clear. There is the possibility of meanings being viewed as tentative methods of representation. There are 'problems' in the data *and* the conceptual organization and these are intimately intertwined.

Michael Scriven (1965) has stressed 'An essential unpredictability in human behaviour'. Reflection on this problem of predicting human behaviour has shifted his attention to a 'pattern' model of explanation which 'allows for retrospectively applicable patterns as well as for those which can be grasped in advance of their completion' (Scriven, 1968, p. 88). See also Scriven's (1956) discussion on 'A possible distinction between traditional scientific disciplines and the study of human behaviour'. For some views of the controversy over the adequacy of covering law explanation for historical actions see Leach (1968) and Goldstein (1969). A. R. Hall (1954) has indicated the conflict between authority and investigation in the scientific revolution of 1500 to 1800 during which a higher level of discourse emerged.

4. The explanatory paradox: although 'explanation', and 'meaning' are at the focus of man's uniqueness and provide the 'lenses' through which man mediates with himself, others and the physical world, these explanatory systems once inculcated serve as obstacles to further reconceptualization.

5. The original subprogramme for the map projection was written by Clyde P. Patton, Professor of Geography, University of Oregon. The specifics of the present computer program were written by Mike Franek, computer consultant at the Computer Center, University of Oregon. The implications of the plotting of configurations were first presented in a paper, 'On the intertwined problems of data patterning and conceptual organization', presented at the 69th annual meeting of the American Anthropological Association, San Diego.

6. It is stressed that other scalings of these variables might express somewhat different regional data patterning.

7. It is stressed that scaling studies of cross-cultural data (Bowden, 1969a; Carneiro and Tobias, 1963; Freeman and Winch, 1957; Schwartz and Miller, 1964; Young and Young, 1962) are subject to the same limitations as correlational analyses without regional breakdowns and representative samples (see Chaney and Ruiz Revilla, 1969). Further, the results of the multivariant analysis of fifty-five societies by Bowden (1969b), which yielded a three-dimensional socio-cultural evolution model, are subject to the same criticism. Although the above researchers are in a somewhat different 'quoting circle' from individuals who have discussed the Tylor–Galton problem and the influence of areal differences on the interpretation of worldwide correlation coefficients, the same problems permeate their results. One is reminded of Michael Scriven's (1964, pp. 173–4) comment that, 'Mathematical economics is a nice example of a subject which has been carried away by the idea that if you can make something mathematical, you are making it precise, and it brings out very nicely the way in which the crucial point is not whether you can produce a precise law governing an ideal case but how precisely you can relate the ideal case to actual cases'.

References

ANGEL, R. B. (1967) Discussion: explanation and prediction: a plea for reason. *Journal of Philosophy of Science*, **34**, 276–82.

BACON, FRANCIS (1889) *Novum Organum, Aphorisms Concerning the Interpretations of Man*, edited by Thomas Fowler, Oxford: Clarendon Press.

BENFER, R. A. (1968) The desirability of small samples for anthropological inference. *American Anthropologist*, **70**, 949–51.

BIDNEY, D. (1953) *Theoretical Anthropology*. New York: Columbia University Press.

BINFORD, L. R. (1962) Archaeology as anthropology. *American Antiquity*, **28**, 217–25.

BINFORD, L. R. (1968) Archaeological perspectives. In BINFORD, S. R. and BINFORD, L. R. (eds.) *New Perspectives in Archeology*. Chicago: Aldine.

BOAS, F. (1895) *Indianishe Sagen von der Nord-Pacifischen Küste Amerikas*. Berlin: Asher.

BOAS, F. (1916) Tsimshian mythology. *Bureau of American Ethnology Annual Report*, **31**, 27–1037.

BOWDEN, E. (1969a) An index of sociocultural development applicable to precivilized societies. *American Anthropologist*, **71**, 454–61.

BOWDEN, E. (1969b) A dimensional model of multilinear sociocultural evolution. *American Anthropologist*, **71**, 864–70.

CALDWELL, J. R. (1966) The new American archaeology. In CALDWELL, J. R. (ed.) *New Roads to Yesterday*. New York: Basic Books.

CARNEIRO, R. L. (1970) A quantitative law in anthropology. *American Antiquity*, **35**, 492–4.

CARNEIRO, R. L. and TOBIAS, S. L. (1963) The application of scale analysis to cultural evolution. *Transactions of the New York Academy of Science*, ser. II, **26**, 196–207.

CHANEY, R. P. (1966a) Typology and patterning: Spiro's sample re-examined. *American Anthropologist*, **68**, 1456–70.

CHANEY, R. P. (1966b) A reply to Spiro, or on the misplaced banderillas. *American Anthropologist*, **68**, 1474–6.

CHANEY, R. P. (1970) Conceptual contention: a reply. *American Anthropologist*, **72**, 1456–61.

CHANEY, R. P. and RUIZ REVILLA, R. (1969) Sampling methods and interpretation of correlation: a comparative analysis of seven cross-cultural samples. *American Anthropologist*, **71**, 597–633.

CHANEY, R. P., MORTON, K. and MOORE, T. (1972) On the entangled problems of selection and conceptual organization. *American Anthropologist*, **74**, 221–30.

COHEN, M. R. and NAGEL, E. (1934) *An Introduction to Logic and Scientific Method*. New York: Harcourt, Brace and World.

CZEKANOWSKI, J. (1911) Objektive Kriterien in der Ethnologie. *Korrespondenzblatt der Deutschen Gesellschaft für Anthropologie und Urgeschichte*, **42**, 71–5.

DEETZ, J. (1967) *Invitation to Archaeology*. New York: Natural History Press.

DESCARTES, R. (1649) *Discourse on Method. Metaphysical Meditations*. Facsimile of 1649 ed. Folkestone: Dawsons of Pall Mall.

DEWEY, J. (1938) *Logic: The Theory of Inquiry*. New York: Henry Holt.

DRIVER, H. E. (1953) Statistics in anthropology. *American Anthropologist*, **55**, 42–59.

DRIVER, H. E. (1961a) *Indians of North America*. Chicago: University of Chicago Press.

DRIVER, H. E. (1961b) Introduction to statistics for comparative resarch. In MOORE, F. W. (ed.) *Readings in Cross-Cultural Methodology*. New Haven: Human Relations Area Files.

DRIVER, H. E. (1962) *The Contribution of A. L. Kroeber to Culture Area Theory and Practice*. International Journal of American Linguistics Memoir 18.

DRIVER, H. E. (1965) Survey of numerical classification in anthropology. In HYMES, D. (ed.) *The Use of Computers in Anthropology*. The Hague: Mouton.

DRIVER, H. E. (1966) Geographical-historical versus psycho-functional explanations of kin avoidances. *Current Anthropology*, **7**, 131–82.

DRIVER, H. E. (1970) Statistical studies of continuous geographical distributions. In NAROLL, R. and COHEN, R. (eds.) *A Handbook of Method in Cultural Anthropology*. New York: Natural History Press.

DRIVER, H. E. and CHANEY, R. P. (1970) Cross-cultural sampling and Galton's problem. In NAROLL, R. and COHEN, R. (eds.) *A Handbook of Method in Cultural Anthropology*. New York: Natural History Press.

DRIVER, H. E. and MASSEY, W. C. (1957) Comparative studies of North American Indians. *Transactions of the American Philosophical Society*, **47**, 165–456.

DRIVER, H. E. and SCHEUSSLER, K. F. (1967) Correlational analysis of Murdock's 1957 ethnographic sample. *American Anthropologist*, **69**, 332–52.

FEIBLEMAN, J. K. (1946) *An Introduction to the Philosophy of Charles S. Peirce*. Cambridge, Mass.: M.I.T. Press.

FREEMAN, L. C. and WINCH, R. F. (1957) Societal complexity: an empirical test of a typology of societies. *American Journal of Sociology*, **62**, 461–6.

FRITZ, J. M. and PLOG, F. T. (1970) The nature of archaeological explanation. *American Antiquity*, **35**, 405–12.

GOLDSTEIN, L. J. (1969) Theory in history. *Boston Studies in the Philosophy of Science*, Vol. IV. Dordrecht: Reidel.

GOODENOUGH, W. H. (1956) Residence rules. *Southwestern Journal of Anthropology*, **12**, 22–37.

HALL, A. R. (1954) *The Scientific Revolution 1500–1800* (2nd ed. 1962). London: Longmans, Green.

HANSON, N. R. (1958) *Patterns of Discovery*. Cambridge: Cambridge University Press.

HANSON, N. R. (1963) *The Concept of the Positron*. Cambridge: Cambridge University Press.

HARRIS, M. (1968) *The Rise of Anthropological Theory:* New York: Crowell.

HEMPEL, C. G. and OPPENHEIM, P. (1948) Studies in the logic of explanation. *Journal of Philosophy of Science*, **15**, 135–75.

HYMES, D. (ed.) (1965) *The Use of Computers in Anthropology*. The Hague: Mouton.

JORGENSEN, J. G. (1966) Geographical clusterings and functional explanations of in-law avoidances: an analysis of comparative method. *Current Anthropology*, **7**, 161–9.

KLUCKHOHN, C. (1939) On certain recent applications of association coefficients to ethnological data. *American Anthropologist*, **41**, 345–77.

KLUCKHOHN, C. (1953) Universal categories of culture. In KROEBER, A. L. (ed.) *Anthropology Today*. Chicago: University of Chicago Press.

KÖBBEN, A. J. F. (1952) New ways of presenting an old idea: the statistical method in social anthropology. *Journal of the Royal Anthropological Institute*, **82**, 129–46.

KÖBBEN, A. J. F. (1967) Why exceptions? The logic of cross-cultural analysis. *Current Anthropology*, **8**, 3–34.

KROEBER, A. L. (1944) *Configurations of Culture Growth*. Berkeley: University of California Press.

KROEBER, A. L. and KLUCKHOHN, C. (1952) *Culture: A Critical Review of Concepts and Definitions*. Papers of the Peabody Museum of American Archaeology and Ethnology, 47.

KUHN, T. S. (1962) *The Structure of Scientific Revolutions*. Chicago: University of Chicago Press.

KUHN, T. S. (1970) *The Structure of Scientific Revolutions*. 2nd ed. Chicago: University of Chicago Press.

LEACH, J. L. (1968) The logic of the situation. *Journal of Philosophy of Science*, **35**, 258–73.

LONGACRE, W. A. (1968) Some aspects of prehistoric society in east-central Arizona. In BINFORD, S. R. and BINFORD, L. R. (eds.) *New Perspectives in Archaeology*. Chicago: Aldine.

LOWIE, R. (1920) *Primitive Society*. New York: Liveright.

MCEWEN, W. T. (1963) Forms and problems of validation in social anthropology. *Current Anthropology*, **4**, 155–69.

MOORE, F. W. (ed.) (1961) *Readings in Cross-Cultural Methodology*. New Haven: Human Relations Area Files.

MURDOCK, G. P. (1940) The cross-cultural study. *American Sociological Review*, **5**, 361–70.

MURDOCK, G. P. (1949) *Social Structure*. New York: Macmillan.

MURDOCK, G. P. (1957) World ethnographic sample. *American Anthropologist*, **59**, 664–87.

MURDOCK, G. P. (1966) Cross-cultural sampling. *Ethnology*, 97–114.

MURDOCK, G. P. (1967) Ethnographic atlas: a summary. *Ethnology*, **5**, 109-236.

MURDOCK, G. P. et al. (1963b) Ethnographic atlas. *Ethnology*, 2, 249-68.

MURDOCK, G. P. and WHITE, D. R. (1969) Standard cross-cultural sample. *Ethnology*, **8**, 329-69.

NAGEL, E. (1961) *The Structure of Science*. New York: Harcourt, Brace and World.

NAROLL, R. (1961) Two solutions to Galton's problem. *Journal of Philosophy of Science*, **28**, 16–39.

NAROLL, R. (1962) *Data Quality Control*. Glencoe: Free Press.

NAROLL, R. (1964a) A fifth solution to Galton's problem. *American Anthropologist*, **66**, 863–7.

NAROLL, R. (1964b) On ethnic unit classification. *Current Anthropology*, **5**, 283–312.

NAROLL, R. (1970a) What have we learned from cross-cultural surveys? *American Anthropologist*, **72**, 1227–88.

NAROLL, R. (1970b) Sampling methods: Chaney and Ruiz Revilla, Comment 1. *American Anthropologist*, **72**, 1451–3.

NAROLL, R. and COHEN, R. (eds.) (1970) *A Handbook of Method in Cultural Anthropology*. New York: Natural History Press.

NAROLL, R. and D'ANDRADE, R. G. (1963) Two further solutions to Galton's problem. *American Anthropologist*, **63**, 1053–67.

NORTHROP, F. S. C. (1947) *The Logic of the Sciences and the Humanities*. New York: Macmillan.

PELTO, P. J. (1970) *Anthropological Research: The Structure of Inquiry*. New York and London: Harper & Row.

PRICE, D. J. (1965) Networks of scientific papers. *Science*, **160**, 510–15.

ROHNER, R. P. and PELTO, P. J. (1970) Sampling methods: Chaney and Ruiz Revilla, Comment 2. *American Anthropologist*, **72**, 1453–6.

SALMON, W. C. (1966) *The Foundations of Scientific Inference*. Pittsburgh: University of Pittsburgh Press.

SAWYER, J. and LEVINE, R. A. (1966) Cultural dimensions: a factor analysis of the world ethnographic sample. *American Anthropologist*, **68**, 708–31.

SCHAPERA, I. (1953) Some comments on comparative method in social anthropology. *American Anthropologist*, **55**, 353–66.

SCHWARTZ, R. D. and MILLER, J. C. (1964) Legal evolution and societal complexity. *American Journal of Sociology*, **70**, 159–69.

SCRIVEN, M. (1956) A possible distinction between traditional scientific disciplines and the study of human behavior. In FEIGL, H. and SCRIVEN, M. (eds.) *The Foundations of Science and the Concepts of Psychology and Psychoanalysis*. Minnesota Studies in the Philosophy of Science, vol. I. Minneapolis: University of Minnesota Press.

SCRIVEN, M. (1964) Views of human nature. In WANN, T. W. (ed.) *Behaviorism and Phenomenology*. Chicago: University of Chicago Press.

SCRIVEN, M. (1965) An essential unpredictability in human behavior. In WOLMAN, B. B. and NAGEL, E. (eds.) *Scientific Psychology*. New York: Basic Books.

SCRIVEN, M. (1968) The philosophy of science. *The International Encyclopaedia of the Social Sciences*. Vol. 14. New York: Macmillan.

SINGER, M. (1968) The concept of culture. *The International Encyclopaedia of the Social Sciences*. Vol. 3. New York: Macmillan.

SPIRO, M. E. (1965) A typology of social structure and the patterning of social institutions: a cross-cultural study. *American Anthropologist*, **67**, 1097-119.

SPIRO, M. E. (1966) A reply to Chaney, or it all depends on whose ox is being gored. *American Anthropologist*, **68**, 1471-4.

TOULMIN, S. (1953) *The Philosophy of Science*. New York: Harper & Row.

TYLOR, E. B. (1889) On a method of investigating the development of institutions applied to the laws of marriage and descent. *Journal of the Royal Anthropological Institute*, **18**, 245–72.

WHITING, J. W. M. (1961) The cross-cultural method. In MOORE, F. W. (ed.) *Readings in Cross-Cultural Methodology*. New Haven: Human Relations Area Files.

WHITING, J. W. M. and CHILD, I. L. (1953) *Child Training and Personality*. New Haven: Yale University Press.

WILSON, T. R. (1952) Randomness of the distribution of social organization forms: a note on Murdock's Social Structure. *American Anthropologist*, **54**, 134–8.

WITTGENSTEIN, L. (1961) *Tractatus*. Trans. D. F. Pears and B. F. McGuiness. London: Routledge. (German ed. in *Annalen der Naturphilosophie*, 1921).

YOUNG, F. W. and YOUNG, R. C. (1962) The sequence and direction of community growth: a cross-cultural generalization. *Rural Sociology*, **27**, 372–86.

Index

Stella I. Clarke

This is an index of authors, ideas, topics and key archaeological sites. It is hoped that the index will serve to bring together the many models and elements common to the different contributions.

Book titles cited in full in the text are entered in the index in italics. Page references to literature cited in the reference sections are given in italics, thus: *448*.

Aaberg, N., 648, *650*
'Abka, Sudan, 206
Acheulean, 20, 28, 119, 122, 123, 125, 126, 128, 129, 130, 131, 135, 136, 137, 138, 139, 142, 143, 144, 145, 149, 151, 156, 157, 168, 171, 188, 189, 190–1, 194
Achinstein, P., 309, *376*
Actun Balam, 791
Adam, D. P., 550, *568*
Adams, R. E. W., 794, 796, *797*
Adams, R. M., 61, 62, 67, 79, *103*, 234, *270*, 513, *538*, 788, *797*
'Adaptive hierarchical clustering schemes', 372
Addleshaw, G. W. O., 917, *960*
Addyman, P. V., 966, *984*
Adesina Oja, Nigeria, 13, 206
Aggersborg, 968
Agogino, G., 560, *571*
agriculture, 458, 462–3, 471, 473, 474, 490–504, 515–18, 534–5, 603, 625, 628–632, 692–3, 722–3, 726–30, 738, 774, 778–82, 849–51, 854–61, 939–40
Ah, B., 759, *800*
Aibura, 281
Aichbuhl, 820
Akazawa, T., 609, *618*
Alcock, L., 966, *984*
Alexander, H. L., 560, 561, 566, *568*, *574*
Alexander, J., 201, *228*, 861, *867*
ALGOL, 426, 434
algorithm models, 35

All Cannings, 924, 951, 952
Allan, W., 495, 499, 502, 516, *538*
Allen, D., 546, *568*
Allen, D. C., *see* Slaughter, B. H. *et al.*
Allen, H., *see* Bowler, J. M. *et al.*
Allen, J. R., *449*
Allen, W. L., 46, *57*
Allendoerfer, C. B., 689, *702*
Allington, 952
Alta Verapaz, 794
Altar de Sacrificios, 777, 794
Alton, 952
Altun Ha, 791
Aluni, 285, 287, 288, 289, 290, 291, 296, 298, 299, 300–3
Amarel, S., 435, 437, 438, 445, 446, *449*
Ambrose, W., 593, *618*
American Anthropologist, 240
American Falls, 553
Ampere, A. M., 1001
Amzabegovo, 519, 522
analysis: artefact relationships, 807, 813–814; horizontal spatial, 807–12; nearest neighbour, 810, 858, 862, 891–2; structural relationships, 807, 812–13; vertical spatial, 807–8
Analytical Archaeology, 192, 432, 671, 914
analytical procedures, 218–24
Anasazi–Hohokam tradition, 362
ancillary huts, 814–15, 817–18
Andrewartha, H. G., 550, *568*

Angel, L., 517, *538*
Angel, R. B., 1026, *1027*
Ankermann, B., 316
annexe huts, 814–15, 822–3
Anthropological Research: The Structure of Inquiry, 993
Antiquity, 129
Apostel, L., 759, *797*
Applebaum, S., 926, 959, *960*
Arbman, H., 969, *984*
Arbury Camp, Cambridge, 861
Archaeological Epistemology: Two Views, 101
Archaeological Perspectives, 194
'Archaeological systematics and the study of culture process', 254
Archaeology of Sussex, 931
Archey, G., 607, *618*
Ardrey, R., 545, *568*, 707, *732*
areal differences, 1015–19
Arensberg, C. M., *see* Polanyi, K. *et al.*
Arikara, 41
Aristotle, 507, 735, 1003, 1005
Armitage, E. S., 977, *984*
Arnhem Land, 653–67
Arta Plain, 715
artefact dispersal, 698–9
artefact information, 175–6, 177
artefact level predictions, 696–700
Ascher, M., 321, 322, *376*, 381, 386, *423*
Ascher, R., 13, *57*, 64, *103*, 275, 276, *306*, 321, 322, *376*, 381, *423*, 592, *618*, 653, 668, 805, *867*
Ascot Doilly, manor house at, 967
Ashby, R., 250
Ashby, W. R., 481, *538*
Asprochaliko, 709, 716
associational patterning, 145–51, 155, 156
Atkinson, R. J. C., 77
Atkinson, T. D., 971, *984*
Attempt to Discriminate the Styles of English Architecture, 963
Aurignacian, 327, 344, 346, 347, 348, 351, 352, 354, 355, 357, 359, 361, 362, 363, 364
Azmak, 522

Bac Son, 455
Bacon, F., 54, 64, 233, 1003, 1004, *1027*
Badegoule, 344, 347, 352, 354

Baile Herculane, 521
Baker, A. R. H., 912, *960*
Baker, L. L., *see* Simmons, R. T. *et al.*
baking huts, 814–15, 820–1
Bakka, E., 235, *270*
Baldwin Brown, G., 979, *985*
Ball, G. H., 371, *376*
Balout, L., 123
Ban Chiang, 466
Ban Kao, Thailand, 455
Ban Tha Nen, 468–71
Banfield, A. W. F., 546, *568*
Bantu, 874, 875
Bargeroosterveld, Netherlands, 824
Barley, M. W., 966, *985*
Barraclough, G., 968, *985*
Barrett, S. A., 316, *376*
Barrington, D., *797*
Bartholomew, G. A., 617
basic pairs, 335–9
BASIN I simulation model, 672, 676–84, 691, 696–700
Basin-Plateau Aboriginal Sociopolitical Groups, 674
Batari, 281
Bath, B. H. S. Van, 497, *538*, 855, *867*
Batlapin, 880
Baumhoff, M. A., 318, *377*, 381, *423*, 694, *703*
Bayard, D. T., 432–3, *449*, 458, 463, 465, 466, *475*, *476*
Bayesian estimation, 446
Beach, E. F., 1, *57*
Beacon Hill, 853
Beals, R. L., 617, *618*
Beechingstoke, 952
behaviour: animal, 157, 172–5, 544–7, 707; human, 707; territorial, 707, 711–712
Belous, R. E., 318, *376*
Benfer, R. A., 1013, *1027*
Benjamin, A. C., 232, *270*
Beresford, M. W., 916, *960*, 974, *985*
Berger, R., 551, *575*, 968, *985*
Berlin, B., 298, *306*
Berndt, C., 661, *668*
Berndt, R., 661, *668*
Berry, B. J. L., 888, 890, *908*
Bialostocki, J., 963, 983, *985*
bias, 72, 74, 96, 205, 252
Biddle, M., 974, 976, *985*

Bidney, D., 585, *618*, 997, 1000, 1009, 1026, *1027*
Bielecki, T., *see* Fryxell, R. *et al.*
Billings, W. G., 673, *702*
Binchy, D. A., 846, *867*
Binford, L. R., 30, 32, 33, 41, *57*, 61, 62, 67, 68, 69, 74, 75, 76, 77, 82, 84, 89, 94, 95, 102, *103*, *104*, 123, 133, *163*, 168, 172, 177, 178, 186, 193, 194, *195*, 254, 261, 267, 268, 270, 304, *306*, 484, *538*, 547, 548, *568*, 584, *618*, 674, 698, *702*, 991, *1027*, *1028*
Binford, S. R., 33, *57*, 62, 76, 89, *104*, 133, *163*, 177, 178, 193, *195*, 548, *568*, 584, *618*
Birabon, J. N., 19, *57*
Birdsell, J. B., 486, *538*, 547, *568*, 617
Birka, 964, 969
Bishops Cannings, 951, 952
Black, M., 65, *104*, 887, *908*
Black, R. F., 551, *569*
black box systems, 31, 35
Blacker's Hill, 852
Blackwood, B., 462, *475*
Blake, W., *see* Lowdon, J. A. *et al.*
Blanc, G. A., 716, *732*
Bloch, M., 940, *960*, 979, *985*
Blom, J. P., 627, *650*
Bo Phan Khan, 467–71
boaire febsa, 845, 846, 857
boaire mruigfer, 845, 846
Boas, F., 102, 315, *376*, 584, 1010, 1011, 1012, *1028*
Bodrogkeresztur, 432
Bohr, N. H. D., 995, 1001
Bökönyi, S., 499, *538*
Boltzman, L., 579
Bomanyana, 884
Bonham-Carter, G. F., 335, *376*
Bonney, D. J., 917, 956, *960*
Bonnischsen, R., *see* Hopkins, M. L. *et al.*
Boole, G., 735
Boolean algebra, 737, 738, 753
Bordaz, J., 381, 410, *423*
Bordaz, V. von H., 381, 410, *423*
Bordes, F. H., 119, 120, 125, 126, 127, 131, 142, *163*, 168, 177, 178, *195*, 346, 361, 362, *376*
Borngolo, 661–6
Boserup, E., 485, 494, 495, 517, *538*
Boucher de Perthes, J., 111, 169

Bourgon, M., 125, *163*
Bowden, E., 1027, *1028*
Bowdler, S., 618
Bowen, H. C., 830, 856, 857, *867*, *868*
Bowler, J. M. *et al.*, 279, *306*
Bowler-Kelly, A., 126, *163*
Boyce, A. J., 293, *306*, 334, *376*
Boyle, R., 1001
Bracey, H. E., 898, 899, 905, 906, 907, 908
Bradley, R., 509, *538*, 926, 931, 932, 959, 960, 965, *985*
Brain, C. T., 174, *196*
Brainerd, G. W., 317, 331, 350, 362, *377*, 388, 391, 395, *423*
Braithwaite, R. B., 63, 103, *104*
Brandtner, F., 550, *570*
Branigan, K., 934, *960*
Bray, W. M., 762, 770, 788, 797
Breedlove, D. E., 298, *306*
Brennan, R. D., 428, *449*
Breternitz, D. A., 237, *270*
Breuil, H., 125, *163*, 177, *195*
Brew, J. O., 235, 236, 244, 245, 246, 251, 261, *270*
Briggs, L. P., 467, *475*
Brill, 978
Broadbent, S., 875, 880, *884*
Broegger, A., 648, *650*
Broken Hill, 129, 135, 139, 145, 146, 147, 150, 152, 193
Bromham, 943
Bronson, B., 781, 797
bronze technology, 455–6, 463, 466, 471, 473
Brookfield, H. C., 277, *306*
Brothwell, D., *538*
Brough on Humber, 893
Brown, R. A., 965, 977, 979, *985*; *see also* Colvin, H. M. *et al.*
Brownian motion, 22, 691, 804, 806; *see also* random walk
Bruce-Mitford, R., 966, *985*
Brunner, E. de S., 897, *908*
Brush, G. S., 550, *569*
Brush, J. E., 897, 898, 905, 906, 907, *908*
Bryan, A. L., 544, 556, *569*
Buchanan, B., 435, 436, *449*
Buchuana, 883
building models, 808–12, 972–3
Bulkington, 952

Bullard, W. R., 782, 783, *797*
Bulleid, A. H., 802, 803, 839, 853, 854, 857, 860, *868*
Bulmer, R. N. H., 277, 279, 287, *306*
Bulmer, S., 279, 281, 283, *306*
Burchell, W. J., 880, *884*
Burgess, E. W., 764, *797*
Burkitt, M. C., 171, *195*
Burnet Cave, 549, 566
Burroughs Advanced Statistical Inquiry System (BASIS), 290
Burstow, G. P., 934, *961*
butchery, 141–2, 184, 363–4, 607–8
Butler, B. R., 557, *569*
Butser Hill Experimental Farm, Hampshire, 13
Buttler, W., 516
Butzer, K. W., 184, *196*, 516, *539*
Byerly, H., 428, *449*
Byers, D. S., 242, *270*, 549, *569*
Bylund, E., 524, *539*, 957, *960*
byres, 814–15, 825

Cadbury, 846, 862
Cadbury Castle, 843, 865
Cadbury Congresbury, 843
Caerwent, 893
Caesar, Julius, 479, 843, 845, 846, 847
Caistor St Edmund, 893
Calder, A. M., 462, *475*
Caldwell, J. R., 991, *1028*
California School, 1011–13; Kulturkreis influence on, 1013
Calne area, 942–5, 957
Camburinga, 659
Campbell, Major, 665, *669*
Campbell, A., 635
Campbell, A. C., 872, 880, *885*
Campbell, B. G., 173, *195*
Campbell, J., 875, *884*
Cancuen, 783
Cann, J. R., 791
Cannings area, 950–2
Cantii, 846
Caracol, 783, 784, 785
Carmichael, J. W., 375, *377*
Carmone, F., 396, *423*
Carneiro, R. L., 19, *58*, 499, 500, *539*, 991, 1027, *1028*
Carter, P. L., 51, *58*

Cartesian vortex, 997
Carus-Wilson, E., 974, *985*
Cassels, R. J. S., 789, 790, *797*
Castanet, 344, 352, 354
Castle Hill, 843
Castle Neroche, 843
Çatal Hüyük, 28, 517
catchment area analysis, 500, 502, 706–8, 773, 851, 915–59
Cavendish, H., 1001
Celtic society, 843–7
central business district, 764
central place theory, 50–2, 509–10, 512–513, 888–9, 891, 896–900
centralization, 511–13
cereal-based economies, a model of growth in, 500–4
Cerralbo, Marquis de, 171, *195*
Chamberlain, T. C., 83, 95, *104*
Chambers, R. W., 979, *985*
Chandler, J. B. *et al.*, 559, *569*
Chaney, R. P., 1010, 1013, 1014, 1015, 1016, 1023, 1024, 1025, 1027, *1028*, *1029*
Chang, K. C., 7, *58*, 62, 64, 73, 102, *104*, 548, *569*, 773, *797*
Chapple, E. D., 617
Charterhouse, lead workings at, 851, 852
Chartkoff, J. L., 89, *104*
Chatters, R. M., 559, *569*
Chelles-Acheul complex, 122, 128
Chenhall, R. G., 431, *449*
Chen-la state, 467–8, 471
Chesemore, D. L., 546, *569*
Chewton, 852
Chichester area, 945–7, 957, 959
Child, I. L., 1012, *1031*
Childe, V. G., 172, *195*, 454, *475*, 477, 478, 505, 514, 515, 525, 532, *539*, 580, 581, 583, 586, 588, *618*, *619*
Chinese box models, 49, 757–9, 803, 844
Chippenham area, 942–5, 957
Chirton, 952
Chisholm, M., 497, 500, *539*, 705, 706, 710, 713, 719, 720, 721, *732*, 782, *797*, 915, 916, 926, *960*
Chitty, D., 546, *569*
Chorley, R. J., 9, 11, 30, 31, 42, *58*, 193, *195*, *539*, 682, *703*, 735, 737, *754*, 758, 759, *798*, 860, 863, *868*, 874, 875, *884*, 887, *908*, 983, *985*

Christaller, W., 862, 888, 889, 890, 893, 894, 897, 900, *908*
Christaller models, 17, 891, 987
Churchman, C. W., 435, *449*
Chysauster, 828
Cirencester, 896, 901, 902, 904
Ciudad Real, A. de, 791, *797*
Civíc, G., 518, *539*
civitas capitals, 891, 893–6
Clactonian, 28, 125, 128, 131, 142, 151, 171
Clapham, 948
Clark, J. D., 128, 129, 130, 131, 135, 137, 138, 139, 141, 142, 143, 157, *163, 164,* 171, 172, 177, 184, 193, *195*
Clark, J. G. D., 172, *196,* 231, *270,* 280, *306,* 454, 456, *475,* 509, 517, *539,* 591, *619,* 632, 634, *650,* 820, *868*
Clark, K., 963, *985*
Clark, P. J., 891, 892, *908*
Clarke, A. B., 685, *702*
Clarke, D. L., 2, 7, 8, 19, 20, 24, 28, 29, 30, 31, 33, 36, 37, 41, 43, 44, 45, 51, 55, *58,* 113, 114, 118, *164,* 167, 176, 185, 192, 194, *196,* 231, 243, 250, 251, 265, 266, *270,* 317, *377,* 382, *423,* 432, 433, 446, *449,* 454, 462, 473, *475,* 482, 497, 499, 500, 530, 531, *539,* 547, *569,* 589, *619,* 671, 672, 677, 682, 685, 701, *702,* 705, *732,* 739, 740, *754,* 813, 851, 862, *868,* 880, 887, *908,* 914, 918, 957, *960,* 965, 969, 983, 984, *985*
class, definition of, 232–3
classification, 231–68
classification schemes, some examples of, 237–48
clay patches, 814–15, 823–4
clay tobacco pipes, 18–19
Clear Creek, 553
Cleland, C. E., 557, *569,* 592, *619*
Clevedon torque, 846
Clifford, E. M., 902, *908*
CLUSTAN program, 372
cluster search, 331–3, 350–2
clustering models, 310–75
Coe, M. D., 7, *58,* 657, *669*
Coe, W. R., *see* Stuckenrath, R. *et al.*
Cohen, J., 516, 517, *539*
Cohen, M. R., 77, *104,* 109, *164,* 1003, 1004, *1028*
Cohen, R., 1010, *1030*

Colani, M., 454, 455, *475*
Colchester, 895
Cole, G. H., 135, 139, 143, *164,* 172, *197;* *see also* Howell, F. C. *et al.*
Cole, J. P., 49, *58*
Cole, S., 128, *164*
Coles, J. M., 13, *58,* 657, *669*
Collingwood, R. G., 929, *960*
Collins, D., 113, 126, 127, 142, 162, *164,* 171, 177, 178, 188, *196,* 362, *377*
Collins, P. W., 680, *702*
Colton, H. S., 236, 237, 243, *270, 271*
Colvin, H. M. *et al.,* 963, *985*
combinatorics, 34, 37
commonalities, 140
Commont, V., 171, *196*
computer archaeology, 425, 430–49
computer programs, 426, 429, 435, 440–5
computer science, 425–8
computers; 425–49; role in simulation, 699–700
Conant, K. J., 966, 979, *985*
concentric zone models, 764–5, 772–3, 776–7, 779–80, 783–3
Concept of the Positron, The, 1008
Configurations of Culture Growth, 998
contiguous areal simulation, 687–9
control mechanisms, combining of, 211–13
controlling models, 5–10
Cook, Captain J., 595
Cook, S. F., 19, *58,* 592, 617, *619,* 827, *868*
Cook, S. W., *see* Sellitz, C. *et al.*
Coombs, C. H., 68, 87, 103, *104*
Coon, C. S., 617
Cooper, W. S., 738, *754*
Copernicus, N., 6
Copi, I. M., 873, 883, *885*
Corder, P., 893, *908*
Cottrell, F., 586, 588, 594, *619*
courtyards, 814–15, 819–20
Coutts, P. J. F., 462, *475,* 617, *619*
covariant patterning, 151, 155–7
Cowgill, G. L., 264, 265, 381, 386, *423,* 430, 431, *449*
Cowgill, U. M., 781, 788, *797*
Craig, B., 306
Crane, H. R., 566, *569*
Crawford, O. G. S., 929, *960*
Craytor, W. B., 314, 317, 320, 321, 323, 325, 330, 375, *377*

Craytor's PRORAM SERIATE, 320, 321, 322, 323, 330, 347, 375
Creighton, J. E., 62, 69, *104*
Cressman, L. S., 549, 559, *569*
Crith Gablach, 846
Crombie, A. C., 983, *985*
Cronin, C., 99, *104*
Crook, J. H., 174, *196*, 707, *732*
Crook, K. A. W., 279, *308*
Crook, W. W., *see* Slaughter, B. H. *et al.*
cross-cultural surveys, 1010–25
Culbert, P. T., 239, *270*
cultural evolution, 581–4
cultural patterns, 525–31
culture, 115, 116–19, 123, 126, 127, 159, 162, 525, 528–31, 584–6
Curry, L., 28, *58*
Curtis, J. T., 617, *619*
Curwen, E., *960*
Curwen, E. C., 931, 932, 937, 940, *960*
Cushing, E. J., *569*
Czekanowski, J., 316, 333, 366, *377*, 1013, *1028*

Dåhl, S., 706, *732*
Dalquest, W. W., 553, *569*
Dalton, G., 511, *539*, 623, *650*
D'Andrade, R. G., 1010, 1011, 1013, 1014, *1030*
Daniel, G. E., 169, 194, *196*
Daniels, S. G. H., 13, 26, 34, 218, 219, 220, 221, 227, *228*, 804
Dansgaard, W. *et al.*, 550, *569*
Danubian, 20, 22
Darby, H. C., 600, *619*, 851, *868*
D'Arcy Thompson, W., 482, *539*
Darwin, Sir C., 86, 169, *196*, 996
Darwinian model, 483, 489
data, 86–9, 94–9; collection of, 70–3, 74; ethnographic, 275–7, 304
Daugherty, R. D., 549, 559, *569*; *see also* Fryxell, R. *et al.*
David, N., 275, *306*
Davidson, D. S., 706, *732*
Davidson, J. M., 593, *619*
Davis, E. M., *see* Stipp, J. J. *et al.*
Davis, J. C., 293, *308*
Davis, T., 918
Davis, W. A., 559, *569*
Davison, B. K., 977, 978, 979, *985*

deductive approach, 62, 63, 68–101, 700
Deetz, J., 7, 23, 44, *58*, 64, 74, 76, 89, 99, *104*, 115, 116, 118, *164*, 186, *196*, 234, 243, 269, 270, 277, *306*, 381, *423*, 701, 702, 972, *986*, 991, *1028*
Deevey, E. S., 487, *539*, 548, *570*
Deh Luran Plain, 318, 473
Dempsey, P., 318, *377*, 381, *423*
dendrograms, 334–42, 352–5, 371, 375
Denevan, W. M., 856, *868*
Descartes, R., 1003, *1028*
Deschler, W., 490, *539*
Dethlefson, E., 381, *423*, 972, *986*
Deutsch, K. W., 510, *539*
Deutsch, M., *see* Sellitz, C. *et al.*
Devetaskata Peshtera, 521
DeVore, I., 172, 173, *196*, *197*, 276, *307*, 486, 488, *540*, 544, 545, 547, *572*, 575, 581, *620*, 657, *669*
Dewar, H. S. L., 851, 858, *868*
Dewey, J., 1003, 1004, *1028*
Dibble, D. S., 549, *570*
Dickinson, R. E., 905, *908*
Dieseldorff, E. P., 794, *797*
digital computers, first examples of, 425–6
Dimbleby, G. W., 7, *59*, 60, 206, 228, 538, 974
Dingan, 883
Directing of Archaeological Excavations, The, 201
Dirichlet, G. L., 774, *797*
Dirichlet regions, 774, 775, 784
Discourse on Method, 1003
Disney, R. L., 685, *702*
distribution mechanisms, 508–11
Dixon, K. A., 318, *377*; *see also* Kuzara, R. S. *et al.*
Dixon, R. B., 316, *377*
Dobson, D. P., 853, 857, 861, 866, *868*
Dobunni, 803
Dodgson, J. M., 936, 942, 954, *960*
Dolebury, 838, 844
Dolley, R. H. M., 969, 979, *986*
Dolní Vestoniče, 214
domestication: of animals, 464, 466–7, 470, 491–2, 497, 582, 587–8, of plants, 461, 582, 587–8
Don Tha Pan, 468–71
Dong Son, 455
Donnerupland type plough, 857

Doran, J. E., 28, 31, 35, *58*, 374, *377*, 432, 438, 448, *449*, *450*, *702*, 965, 983, 984, *986*; *see also* Hodson, F. R. *et al.*
Dorchester, Dorset, 902
Dorn, 891
Draycott, 852
Driftwood Creek, 555, 556
Driver, H. E., 316, 318, 319, 366, 367, *377*, 999, 1010, 1011, 1012, 1013, 1014, 1015, 1018, *1028*, *1029*
Duff, R., 455, 456, *475*, 603, *619*
Dumnonii, 803, 817, 821, 824, 828, 842, 844, 846, 849, 851–2, 853, 862, 863, 865
Duna, 278, 279, 284, 285, 286, 288, 289, 294, 298, 306
Dundon Camp, 840
Dunnell, R. C., 231, 248, 251, *270*, 381, 382, 384, 388, *423*
Dunning, G. C., 971, 972, *986*
Durkheim, E., 484, 505, 506, *539*
Durotriges, 803, 824, 829, 839
Durrington, 923
Dykes, The, 924

East, G., 510, 529, *539*
Eaton, R. L., 544, *570*
Echenique, M., 7, 47, 49, 50, *58*, *60*, 809, 810, *868*
Economics, 507
ecosystems, 550–4, 599
Eden, C. van, 668, *669*
Eduardo Quiroz Cave, 791
Edwards, W. E., 565, *570*
Egan, H., 694
Eggen, F., 635
Ehrlich, P. R., 564, *570*
Einstein, A., 674, 995, 1001, 1002, 1006, 1014
Eisenhart, C., 617, *619*
El Chayal, 794
Elliot-Smith, G., 173, *196*
Ellison, A., 514
Elton, C. S., 544, *570*
'Eltonian pyramid', 581, 600
energetics, 47, 581–4
'Energy and the evolution of culture', 580
Engelmann, M. D., 544, *570*
Engels, F., 477, 581

Epirus, 548, 716
ergodic theory, 24, 28, 29
Ericson, J. E., 264, *270*
Erol, O., 516, *539*
Errington, P. L., 545, 546, *570*
error, 204–5; gross, 205
error-producing factors, control of, 209–213
Estes, R. D., 544, *570*
Etchilhampton, 952
Ethnographic Atlas, 1020
Evans, C. E., 891, 892, *908*
Evans, J., 169, *196*
Evans, J. G., 934, 939, *961*
Evans-Pritchard, E. E., 528, *539*, 848, *868*
Everson, J. A., *868*
Evison, V. I., 975, *986*
Evolution and Culture, 584
Evolution of Culture, The, 580
evolution, theory of, 169
explanation, 2, 115–19
explication, 111–15
exploitation territories, 706–16, 759, 772, 779–83, 840, 851–2
exploration, 110–11
Ezero, 533

factor analysis, 292, 293
factor scores, 151–5
Fagan, B. M., 227, *228*, 594, *619*
Fagg, A. E., *see* Higgs, E. S. *et al.*
Fairbridge, R. W., 550, *570*
Faraday, M., 1001
Faulkner, P. A., 982, *986*
fauna, 328–44, 347, 551–3, 562–7
Favella, 731
Fedorov-Davydov, G. A., 969, *986*
feedback, 173, 481, 646, 863, 888, 896–7, 902–3, 907
Feibleman, J. K., 1000, *1029*
Feigenbaum, E. A., 430, 435, 436, *449*, *450*
Ferrassie, La, 344, 346, 352, 354
Filip, J., 847, *868*
Filipovski, J., 518, *539*
Finberg, H. P. R., 917, *960*
Finden, 948
Firth, J., *539*
Firth, R., 618, *619*

Fisher, I., 689, *704*
Fisher, R. A., 210, *228*, 325, 335
fishing, 593–602, 606, 608–11, 664–5, 718–21, 726, 858, 859
Fitting, J. E., 555, *570*
Fitzgerald, B. P., *868*
Flanders, R. E., 318, *377*
Flannery, K. V., 6, 7, 30, *58*, 62, 75, *104*, 461, 462, 473, *476*, 508, *540*, 657, *669*, 671, 672, 674, 684, 694, *702*, 796, 798, 827, *868*
Fletcher, J. M., 966, *986*
Fleure, H. J., 913, 938, *960*
Flint, R. F., 550, *570*
Flores García, L., 740, 741, *754*
Follieri, M., 723, *732*
Font Robert, 344, 351, 354
Foote, P., 640, 649, *650*
Forbis, R. G., 560, 566, *570*
Ford, J. A., 74, *104*, 117, 121, *164*, 234, 235, 236, 242, 244, 246, 261, *270*, *271*, 312, *377*, 382, 384, 388, *423*
Fortes, M., 528, *539*
FORTRAN, 293, 369, 375, 426, 678, 680, 700
Fortsch, D., *see* Hopkins, M. L. *et al.*
Fosberg, F. R., *570*
Foster, G. M., 276, *306*
Fourier transform, 878
Fourneau-du-Diable, Le, 344, 351, 352, 354
Fowler, C. S., 691, *702*
Fowler, P. J., 927, 934, 938, 939, *960*, *961*
Fox, A., 817, 828, 863, 865, *868*, 976, *986*
Fox, Sir C., 172, *196*, 888, *908*, *961*
Fox, R., 174, *196*
Franklin, B., 996
Fraser, D., 809, *868*
Freeman, J. D., 24, *58*
Freeman, L. C., 1027, *1029*
Freeman, L. G., 184, *196*
French, D., 514, 517, *539*
Frere, J., 111, 169, 194, *196*
Frere, S. S., 896, *908*
Frey, D. G., *576*
Fritz, J. M., 62, 64, 65, 66, 68, 72, 79, 82, 84, 89, 101, 102, *104*, 233, *271*, 432, *450*, 991, *1029*
Fryxell, R. *et al.*, 557, *570*
Fulani, 275
Fulkerson, D. R., 392, *423*
Fullard, H., 600, *619*

Gajduskek, O. C., *see* Simmons, R. T. *et al.*
Galatea Bay site, 592–5, 602–3, 609–16
Galbraith, V. H., 964, *986*
Galileo, 6, 53, 54, 995, 1001, 1002, 1005
Galton, F., 1011, 1013
games theory, 37
García Moll, R., 741, 742, 743, 746–9, 752, *754*
Gardin, J.-C., 7, 35, *58*, 430, *450*
Garland, L. H., 219, *228*
Garner, B. J., 512, *539*, 688, *703*, 890, *908*
Gartlan, J. S., 174, *196*
Garvin, P. L., 29, *59*
Gaudry, A., 169, *196*
Gaussian distribution, 440, 692, 693, 700
Gearing, F., 132, *164*
Geertz, C., 160, *164*
Gelfand, A., 381, 387, 392, *423*
Gelling, M., 942, 954, *961*
General Problem Solver program, 429
General Theory of Population, 485
George, F. H., 35, *59*
Georgiev, G. I., 522, 533, *539*
Gifford, E. W., 617
Gifford, J. C., 234, 238, 239, 242, 244, *271*, *273*
Gift, The, 506
gift exchange, 644, 648, 666–7, 795–6, 855, 866
Ginsburg, B. E., 544, *575*
Gjerseth, K., 645, *650*
Glassow, M. A., 101, 592, *619*
Glastonbury, 802–66
Glevum, *see* Gloucester
Glob, P. V., 525, 534, *540*
Gloucester, 895, 896, 902
Glover, I. C., 33, *59*
Godwin, H., 851, 858, *868*
Golden, J. T., 700, *703*
Goldherring, 828
Goldstein, L. J., 1027, *1029*
Gomeldon, 13th century farm at, 967
Gonzalez, A. R., 419
Gonzalez, R. F., 672, 677, *703*
González Crespo, N., 752, *754*
Goodall, J. M., 160, 174, *196*
Good Creek site, 553
Goodenough, W. H., 1010, *1029*
Goody, J. R., 847, *868*

Gorman, C. F., 283, *306*, 458, 460, 461, 462, *475*
Gould, P. R., 37, *59*, 497, *540*
Gould, R. A., 176, 185, *196*, 275, 276, *306*, 697, *703*
Graham, J. A., *see* Stross, F. H. *et al.*
granaries, 814–15, 824–5
Graus, F., 975, *986*
Gray, H. L., 911, *961*
Gray, H. St G., 802, 803, 839, 853, 854, 857, 860, *868*
Graybill, F. A., 701, *703*
Graydon, J. J., *see* Simmons, R. T. *et al.*
Great Chesterford, 896, 940
Green, R. C., 593, 603, *619, 621*
'Green Island' (*Ynys Glas*), 849
Greenman, E. F., 556, *570*
Greig-Smith, P., 698, *703*
Griego, R. J., 806, *868*
Grierson, P., 966, *986*
Griffin, J. B., 566, *569*
Griffiths, J. C., 698, *703*
Grinsell, L. V., 514, 922, 923, 932, *961*
Griquas, 883
Grosebeck Creek, Texas, 553
Gross, O. A., 392, *423*
Grotta Romanelli, 716–21, 725–6, 727
Grotta Sant'Angelo, 723–5, 729–31
Groube, L. M., 471, 474, 476, 593, 603, *619*
Gruhn, R., 549, 555, 559, *570*
Gruning, E. L., 777, *798*
guard huts, 814–15, 821–2
Guilday, J. E., 565, 567, *570, 573*
Gumelnitsa culture, 529
Gustafson, C. E., *see* Fryxell, R. *et al.*
Guthrie, R. D., 553, 565, 567, *571*

Hadrian's Wall, 940
Hadza, 706, 713
Hafsten, U., 550, 551, *571*, 626, *650*
Hagen, A., 638, *650*
Haggett, P. H., 3, 9, 11, 24, 30, 31, 42, *58, 59*, 193, 195, 233, *271*, 293, *307*, 479, *540*, 682, 689, *703*, 735, 736, 737, *754*, 758, 759, 764, 777, *798*, 860, 863, *868*, 874, 875, *884*, 887, 888, 889, 890, 899, *908*, 914, 916, 917, 918, 957, *961*, 983, *985*
Hall, A. R., 1027, *1029*

Hall, E. R., 564, 568, *571*
Hallowell, A. I., 160, *164*
Halsbury, Earl of, 18, *59*
Ham Hill, 843, 864, 865
Hamilton, A., 599, *619*
Hamilton, F. E. I., 510, *540*
Hamilton, J. R. C., 827, 846, *868*
Hammond, N. D. C., 757, 759, 776, 779, 782, 791, 793, 794, *798*
Han Gon, S. Vietnam, 466
Hancock, D. A., 598, 599, 600, *619*
Hanson, N. R., 62, 68, 69, 72, 88, 102, 103, *105*, 252, *271*, 995, 996, 997, 1000, 1001, 1002, 1007–8, 1026, *1029*
Hanzak, J., 611, *620*
Harding, T. G., 623, *650*
Hareke, 285, 287, 289, 290, 291, 296, 298, 299, 300, 302
Hargrave, L. L., 236, 237, 243, *270, 271*
Harman, H. H., 141, *164*, 292, *307*
Harré, R., 873, *885*
Harris, D. R., *see* Higgs, E. S. *et al.*
Harris, M., 67, 72, 74, 101, 102, *105*, 232, 233, *271*, 277, 304, 305, *307*, 795, *798*, 994, 997–1000, *1029*
Harris, R. K., *see* Slaughter, B. H. *et al.*
Harriss, J. C., 514, 914, *961*
Hartman, L., 612, *620*
Harvey, D., 1, 2, 3, 9, 11, 15, 17, 20, 28, 29, 49, 50, *59*, 109, 115, *164*, 512, *540*, 868
Harvey, J. H., 963, 971, 975, *986*
Hassall, J. M., 975, 976, *986*
Hassall, M., 893, 896, 907, *908*
Hatler, D. F., 545, *571*
Hatting, T., 455, *476*
Haviland, W. A., 776, 788, *798*
Hawkes, C., 64, 67, *105*, 234, *271*
Haynes, C. V., 141, *164*, 184, *195*, 549, 550, 555, 558, 559, 560, 561, *571*
Hedeby, 964
Heider, K. G., *306*, *307*, 776, *798*
Heizer, R. F., 19, *58*, 69, 70, 71, 72, 73, 74, 76, 77, 78, 89, 97, 100, 101, 102, *105*, 169, *196*, 234, 241, 243, 244, 248, 249, 252, *271*, 592, 617, *619*, 694, *703*, 827, *868*; *see also* Stross, F. H. *et al.*
Hempel, C. G., 63, 66, 69, 70, 72, 80, 82, 83, 84, 85, 89, 95, 98, 103, *105*, 255, *271*, 995, 1002, 1008, *1029*
Henfield area, 953–6, 957, 959

Hengistbury, 839
Henry I, 975
Hensel, W., 968, *986*
Henshall, J. D., 737, 738, *754*
Herrnbrodt, H., 964, 966, *986*
Hersh, R., 806, *868*
Herteig, A. E., 638, 639, *650*, 966, *986*
Hesse, M. B., 2, 4, *59*
Hester, J. J., 549, 560, 561, 565, 566, *571*
HEURISTIC DENDRAL, 35, 435, 436
heuristic models, 35
Heusser, C. J., 550, *571*
Hewett, C. A., 966, *986*, *987*
Hiatt, B., 276, *307*
Higgs, E. S., 7, *59*, 479, 488, 491, 500, *538*, *540*, *542*, 548, *571*, 587, 590, 608, 620, 622, 657, 669, 707, 708, 709, 715, 716, 721, *732*, *733*, 772, 773, 781, *800*, 915, 917, 922, *962*
Higgs, E. S. *et al.*, 548, *571*, 709, 716, *732*
High Lodge, 172
Higham, C. F. W., 7, *59*, 464, 466, *476*, 497, 525, 534, *540*
Highdown Hill, 931
Hill, D., 975, 976, *986*
Hill, J. N., 7, 41, *59*, 68, 69, 73, 76, 77, 81, 82, 89, 95, 97, 98, 99, 100, 102, *105*, 234, 252, 255, 256, 257, 258, 265, *271*, *272*
Hill Shuler site, 553
Hilton, R. H., 590
historical factors, 202
Hoabinhian complex, 283, 455, 460–2, 471
Hod Hill, 823
Hodder, B. W., 905, *908*
Hodder, I. R., 893, 896, 907, *908*
Hodgen, M. T., 940, *961*
Hodges, H. W. M., 971, *987*
Hodgkin, R. H., 929, *961*
Hodgson, T. L., 875, 880, 884, *885*
Hodson, F. R., 7, *59*, 367, 371, 374, 375, *377*, 430, 438, 442, *450*, 969
Hodson, F. R. *et al.*, 367, 374, 375, *377*
Holcomb site, Michigan, 557
Holden, E. W., 937, *961*
Hole, F., 69, 70, 71, 72, 73, 74, 76, 77, 78, 89, 97, 100, 101, 102, *105*, 206, *228*, 234, 241, 243, 244, 248, 249, 252, *271*, 318, 319, 321, 323, 348, 365, 366, *377*, 381, 386, 396, 398, *423*, 461, 462, 473, *476*, 508, *540*

Holling, C. S., 546, *571*
Hollister, C. W., 979, *987*
Holst, H., 648, *650*
Hood, J., 782
Hoover, T. E., *see* Stipp, J. J. *et al.*
Hope Fountain, 28, 128–30, 148, 151
Hope-Simpson, R., 535, 537, *540*
Hope-Taylor, B. K., 940, *961*, 966, 968, 987
Hopi-Tewa, 275
Hopkins, D. M., 552, *571*
Hopkins, M. L. *et al.*, 553, 555, *571*
Hoskins, W. G., 862, *868*, 971, *987*
Howell, F. C., 130, 131, 135, 139, 143, 157, *164*, 171, 172, 184, *196*, 197
Howell, F. C. *et al.*, 172, *197*
Hrodgar, 968
Hualfín valley, Argentina, 419–22
Human Origins, 579
Hume, D., 64, 65, 233
Humphrey, R. L., 555, *572*
Hunt, D. R., 880, *885*
Hunter, J. M., 501, *540*
hunter-gatherers, 38–9, 276, 280, 459–61, 471, 474, 487–8, 492, 494, 545, 547, 580, 581, 587, 602, 618, 653, 655–60, 666, 674, 689, 691, 780–1
hunting, 557, 562, 628, 633–4, 665, 693–5, 858, 860
Hurst, D., 859, 860, *868*
Hurst, D. G., 967, *990*
Hurst, J. G., 969, 971, 974, 979, *987*
Husterknupp, 966
Hutchings, S. S., 692, *703*
Hutchinson, Sir J., 718, *732*
Huxley, J., *540*
Hymes, D., 432, *450*, 1015, *1029*
hypotheses, 3, 13–14, 41–2, 63, 65, 69, 79–86, 88, 94–101, 103, 252, 253, 255, 257, 433–49, 474, 484, 543, 553–4, 730–1, 887, 893, 900–2, 906, 1004, 1005; necessity for, 63, 72, 79–86, 252
hypothesis formation, 64, 433–7, 445–9
hypothesis testing, 89–92, 674, 896
hypothetico-deductive method, 63, 64, 69–101, 872–3, 1002; objections to, 94–101

Iban, 24
Igbo Ikwu, Nigeria, 206

Ilchester, 894, 895
index: of accessibility, 767; of central accessibility, 767, 768; of centrality, 766
Indianische Sagen von der Nord-Pacifischen Küste Amerikas, 315
inductive approach, 62, 63, 64, 65, 66, 67, 68, 70, 86, 446, 673–4, 676, 700
Industrial Revolution, 580–1, 583
infield–outfield system, 840, 855–6, 926, 932, 959
Infiernillo region, Mexico, 752
information recovery, 802
information theory, 209
Ingalls, G. W., 690
internal expansion, 531–6
internal sift method, 1021
International Encyclopedia of the Social Sciences, 997
intra-system interactions, 696
Introduction to Prehistoric Archaeology, An, 102
Irwin, H. T., *see* Fryxell, R. *et al.*
Irwin-Williams, C., 676, *703*
Isaac, G. Ll., 20, *59*, 130, 131, 135, *165*, 168, 172, 174, 176, 178, 181, 182, 184, 186, 188, 189, 192, *197*, 304, *307*
Isimila, 130, 135, 137, 143, 145, 146, 147, 150, 151, 152, 153, 154, 171, 179, 188
item classification by clustering, 315–17
item manipulation, 321–4
item ordering and computerization, problems of, 318–24
item seriation, 330–1, 340, 347–50, 372–4; chronology, 317–18; definition, 310–14
Itford Hill, Sussex, 828
Ives, P. C., *see* Levin, B. *et al.*
Iwo Eleru, Nigeria, 207, 208, 224
Ixkun, 783, 784, 785
Ixtepeque, 794

Jaccard, P., 406
Jackson, C. H. N., 563, *574*
Jackson, K. H., 845, *868*
Jahoda, M., *see* Sellitz, C. *et al.*
Janssen, G. P., 974, *987*
Jarman, M. R., 37, 492, 497, *540*, 587, 608, *620*, 707, 708, 721, *732*, 852
Jelinek, A. J., 549, 565, *572*

Jennings, J. D., 549, 557, 558, *572*, 661, 662, *669*, *703*
Jevons, W. S., 735
Jewell, P. A., 14, *59*, 206, *228*, 709, *733*
Johnsen, S. J., *see* Dansgaard, W. *et al.*
Johnson, F., 242, *270*
Johnson, L., 314, 320, 321, 323, 375, *377*, *378*, 381, *423*
Jolly, C., 174, *197*
Jones, G. P., 972, *987*
Jones, N., 128, *165*
Jones, R., 618, 653, *669*; *see also* Bowler, J. M. *et al.*
Jope, E. M., 964, 965, 966, 967, 968, 969, 970, 971, 972, 973, 977, 978, 979, 980, *986*, *987*, *988*
Jope, H. M., 974, *988*
Jorgenson, J. G., 1010, 1013, 1015, *1029*
Journal of Roman Studies, 902
Journal of Anthropological Institute, 316
Joy, L., 496, *540*
Joyce, E. B., 283, *307*
Joyce, T. A., 757, 794, *798*
Joyce, T. A. *et al.*, 757, 794, *798*
Judge, W. J., 671, 672, *703*
Junkersdorf, 969
Juntunen site, 592

Kaditshwene, 872, 882, 883
Kafiavana, 281
Kalambo Falls, Tanzania, 130, 135, 137, 138, 143, 146, 147, 149, 150, 151, 152, 153, 154, 171, 179
Kalicz, N., 535, *540*
Kaminaljuyú, 794
Kansky, K. J., 737, *754*
Kaplan, A., 72, 73, 86, 99, *105*, 253, 271, 592
Karanovo, 522
Karandusi, 135, 139, 146, 147, 150, 152
Kastritsa, 709, 716
Kaupang, 964
Keakoorn, P., 470, *476*
Keel, B. C., *see* Fryxell, R. *et al.*
Keller, A. G., 1012
Kelsall, J. P., 545, 546, *572*
Kelson, K. R., 564, 568, *571*
Kelvin, W. T., 1001
Kemeny, J. G., 673, 676, *703*

Kemp, W. R., 33, *59*
Kendall, D. G., 381, 387, 388, 389, 392, 394, 395, 296, 397, 398, 399, 404, 410, 411, 414, *423*, 430, 438, 446, *450*, 969
Kendall, M. G., 428, *450*
kennels, 814–15, 825
Kepler, J., 995, 997, 1001
Khon Kaen, 458
Khorat plateau, 456, 458, 467, 471, 473, 474
Khorramabad valley, 318, 462
Kidder, A. V., 237, 241, *271*
Killen, J. T., 536, *540*
kinesthetic sense, 712, 713
King, C. A. M., 49, *58*
King, J. E., 611, *620*
King, L. J., 293, *307*
King's Castle Camp, 840
Kingsdown Camp, Somerset, 861
Kinningham, R., *see* Chandler, J. B. *et al.*
kinship, bilateral, 646
Kiowa, 281
Kirby, P., 872, 880, 882, *885*
Kjaerum, P., 939, *961*
Kleiber, M., 577, 614, *620*
Klein, R. G., 214, *229*
Kleindienst, M. R., 130, 131, 135, 136, 137, 139, 140, 143, 145, 150, 151, *164*, *165*, 172, 177, 184, *197*; *see also* Howell, F. C. *et al.*
Klima, B., 214, *229*
Klimek, S., 366, *378*
Klir, J., 677, *703*
Kluckhohn, C., 242, *271*, 997, 1010, *1029*
Kneberg, M., 316, *378*
Köbben, A. J. F., 1010, 1018, *1029*
Kóčka, W., 316, *378*
Koebner, L., 492, *540*
Kolb, J. H., 897, *908*
Kolchin, B. A., 974, *988*
Kolchina, B. A., 7, 55, *59*
Kolmogorov–Smirnov tests, 207, 663, 668
Konya plain, 533
Körös culture, 24, 25, 26, 28, 519, 531
Koslowski, L., 125, *163*
Koster, D. A., 697, *703*
Kovacs, T., 534, *540*
Kovalevskaja, V. B., 432, *450*
Kraft, C., 668, *669*
Kretzoi, M., 172, *197*

Krieger, A. D., 115, *165*, 233, 238, 241, 242, 244, 245, 269, *271*, 560, *572*
Kristensen, M., *541*
Kroeber, A. L., 316, 333, 366, 367, *377*, *378*, 592, 597, 617, *620*, 997, 998, 1011, *1029*
Krumbein, W. C., 701, *703*
Kruskal, J. B., 311, 367, 368, 369, 374, *378*, 396, *423*
Kruskal's scaling procedure, 368–9, 374
Kuhn, T. S., 5, 7, 8, 10, 43, *59*, 61, 62, 64, 72, 73, 101, *105*, 109, 110, *165*, 193, *197*, 276, *307*, 996, 997, 1008–9, *1030*
' !Kung bushman subsistence', 706
!Kung bushmen, 587, 706, 710, 713, 781, 915
Kuper, D., 880, *885*
Kurtén, B., 552, 553, *572*
Kuzara, R. S. *et al.*, 314, 319, 321, 322, 323, 324, 366, *378*, 381, 383, *423*
Kuzara's criterion, 324

La Venta, Tabasco state, Mexico, 318
La Villita region, Mexico, 741, 742, 743, 746–9, 751
Labattut, 344, 351, 354
Lack, D., 545, 546, *572*
Laguna, 555, 556
Lamb, H. H., 974, *988*
Lambert, J. W., 974, *988*
Lancaster, J. B., 174, *197*, *198*
Lancing, 924
land resources, classification of, 918–22
land use systems, 493–500
Langer, W. L., 975, *988*
Langness, L. L., 283, *307*
Laplace, G., 362, 363, *378*
Larcombe, M. F., 597, *620*
Large, R. V., 859, *868*
Lartet, 344, 352, 354
Larusson, O., 647, *650*
Las Casas, B. de, 791, *798*
Latamne, 172
Lathrap, D., 492, *540*
Laugerie-Haute, 344, 346, 352, 354
Lavell, C., 968, *988*
Lavoisier, A. L., 577, 578, 1002
Lazarsfeld, P. F., 82, *105*
Le Patourel, H. E. J., 971, *988*
Leach, B. F., 464, *476*

Leach, J. L., 1027, *1030*
Leakey, L. S. B., 121, 123, 128, 135, *165*, 171, 177, 194, *197*
Leakey, M. D., 122, 123, 135, *165*, 171, 184, 188, *197*
Leblanc, S. A., 258, 262, *273*
Lee, R. B., 142, *165*, 173, *197*, 276, *307*, 486, 488, *540*, 545, 547, *572*, 581, 587, *620*, 657, 659, *669*, 706, 710, 713, *733*, 915, *961*
Leeds, A., 509, *540*
Leibnitz, G. W., 735
Lejre, Denmark, 'prehistoric' farmstead at, 13
Leland, J., 691, *702*
Lennard, R. V., 940, *961*, 964, 979, *988*
Leonhardy, F. C., 549, 560, *572*
Lepervanche, M. de, 282, *307*
Lethaby, W. R., 963, *988*
Levallois, 125, 126, 127, 188
Levin, B. *et al.*, 566, *572*
Levine, M. H., 41, *59*
Levine, R. A., 1010, 1013, 1015, *1031*
Lewis, B. N., 35, *59*
Lewis, T. M. N., 316, *378*
Liebig's law, 617
Lincoln, 895
Lindeman, R. L., 544, *572*, 581, 599, *620*
Lindemann, W., 550, *572*
linear programme models, 37
Linford, 968
Linguistic families of California, 316
linked pair method, 1020, 1021
Linton, D. L., 913, *962*
Lipe, W. D., 326, *378*, 388, *423*
Lithakong, 880
Little, E. L., 684, 687, 691, *703*
Little Woodbury, 924
Litvak King, J., 741, 742, 743, 746–9, 750, 751, 752, 754, 755
Liversidge, J., 940, *961*
location of excavation, 214–15
Locational Analysis in Human Geography, 914
Lochard, 135, 139, 146, 147, 150, 152, 153, 154
Logic of the Sciences and the Humanities, The, 1002
Long, A., 566, *573*

Longacre, W. A., 7, 23, 41, *59*, 76, 82, 89, 98, 99, *105*, 255, 256, *272*, 697, *703*, 991, *1030*
Longhurst, A. R., 609, *620*
Lorenz, K., 707, *733*
Lorrain, D., 549, *570*
Lösch, A., 688, *703*, 891, *908*
Löschian models, 688, 689, 690
Lotka, A. J., 482, 579, *620*
Lowdon, J. A. *et al.*, 559, *572*
Lowie, R., 1011, *1030*
Lowther, G. R., 174, *198*
Lubaantún, 757–97
Lubbock, J., 169, *197*
Lucas, J. W., 618, *620*
Luckham, D., *449*
Lumley, H. de, 172, 184, *197*
Lundelius, E. L., 565, 566, 567, *572*
Lyell, C., 169, *197*

McArthur, M., 657, 667, *669*
MacArthur, R. H., 551, *572*
McBryde, F. W., 793, *798*
McBurney, C. B. M., 171, 194, *198*, 714, *733*
McCammon, R. B., 371, *378*
McCance, R. A., 577, 594, *620*
McCarthy, F. D., 657, 661, 667, *669*
McCary, B. C., 549, *572*
McClure, W. L., 553, 566, *574*
MacCurdy, G. G., 579, 583
McDonald, W. A., 535, 537, *540*
McEwen, W. T., 1010, *1030*
MacFadyen, A., 546, *572*, 581, 597, 599, 600, *620*
McGregor, J. C., 237, 241, *272*
Mach, E., 1006
Machaquila, 783, 785
Machnik, J., 534, *540*
Mackenzie, J., 875, 880, *885*
McKern, W. C., 241, *272*
MacKnight, C. C., 661, *669*
McKnight, T., 550, *573*
McMillan, C., 672, 677, *703*
MacNeish, R. S., 7, *59*, 60, 269, 462, 473, *476*, 556, *573*, 676, *703*
MacNutt, F. A., 791, *798*
McPherron, A., 7, *60*
MacWhite, E., 67, 73, *105*, 234, *272*
Maes Knoll Camp, 843

Maesbury, 838, 840, 843, 844, 851, 852, 853, 854, 860, 861, 863, 865, 866
Magdalenian, 346, 347, 362
Mageröy, H., 639, *650*
Mai-Asaro watershed, 277
major houses, 814–16
Malete, 872, 880
Malinowski, B., 506, 511, 530, *540*, 594
Malmer, M. P., 534, *541*
Malthus, T. R., 484
Manfredini, A., 721, *733*
Mangwato, 872
Man Makes Himself, 580
Manning, W. H., 939, 940, *961*
Mansuy, H., 455, *476*
Man The Hunter, 173, 486
Maori, 584, 587, 590, 593, 595, 597, 599, 600, 601, 602, 603, 611, 614, 616, 617, 618
Mapungubwe, 879, 881
Maramba quarries, Rhodesia, 128
March, L., 7, 47, *60*, 809, 810, *868*
Marcus, S., 738, *755*
markets, 814, 865, 904–6, 939, 980–2
Markov process models, 20, 24, 28, 685–7, 690, 701
Marmes, 557
Marshak, B. I., 432, 442, *450*
Martin, P. S., 256, *272*, 552, 553, 563, 565, 566, 567, *573*
Martyr D'Anghiera, P., 781, *798*
Mason, R. J., 544, *573*, 874, 875, 878, 882, 884, *885*
Massey, D. S., *see* Chandler, J. B. *et al.*
Massey, W. C., 318, 319, *377*, 1014, 1018, *1029*
Mathiassen, T., 514, 534, *541*
Matluassi, 878, 884
Matson, R. G., 367, 371, *379*
Matthews, J., *378*, 454, *476*
Mauss, M., 506, *541*, 648, *650*
Maxwell, A. E., 215, *229*
Maxwell, G., 611, *620*
Maxwell, J. C., 995, 1001
Maya, 757–97
Mayer-Oakes, W. J., 70, *105*
MDSCAL technique, 367, 369–71, 396–422
Mead, G. R., *see* Kuzara, R. S. *et al.*
Meaney, A., 929, 942, 947, *961*
Meare, 811, 814, 840, 843, 849, 858, 861, 866

Mech, D., 546, *568*
Medieval Archaeology, 929
Meggers, B. J., 7, *60*
Meggitt, M. J., 259, *272*, 280, *307*
Mehringer, P. J., 565, *573*
Meighan, C. W., 386, *423*, 558, *573*, 592, 618, *620*
Meighan, C. W. *et al.*, 548, *573*
Mellaart, J., 28, *60*
Mellars, P., 168, 178, *198*, 284, *307*
Meltzer, B., 435, *450*
Melville Koppies, 878, 880
Merpert, N. I., 533
Message, M., 497, 525, 534, *540*
Messenia, 535, 536, 537
metallurgy, 531–2
Metcalf, D. M., 969, 975, *988*
Method and Theory in American Archaeology, 240
Michener, C. D., 334, *379*
Mielke, J. E., 566, *573*
Mill, J. S., 64, 233
Miller, J. C., 1027, *1031*
Miller, J. G., 75, 76, *105*
Millon, R. F., 793, *798*
minor houses, 814–15, 816–17
Mirambell, L., 752, *755*
Moberg, C.-A., 439, *450*
model building, 3, 690–1, 745, 749, 752, 753, 963, 965, 966–8, 975, 977–8
models:
  abstract conceptual, 979–83
  accuracy of, 4
  'activity variant', 177, 178
  additive, 173
  alternative, 801, 802, 848, 867
  analogue, 623–4, 653, 871–5, 883, 968
  application of, 892–3, 900, 906
  archaeological, 880–2
  architectural, 48
  artefact, 440–2
  artificial theoretical, 15–42
  categories used in medieval studies, 965–84
  commercial, 795–6
  comprehensiveness of, 4
  definition of, 1–2, 194, 871–2
  demographic, 831–4
  deterministic, 18, 19
  ecological, 629, 878–80, 973–4
  economic, 848–66, 875–8

efficiency of, 4
Garin–Lowry activity location, 48
general concept of, 428
hardware, 13–15, 878, 965–8
historical, 880
historical conceptual, 974–9
historic-ethnographic, 40–2
iconic, 759, 966–7
interim, 802, 867
locational, 757–95, 808–12, 826, 854, 871–84, 887–907, 911–59
mathematical, 34, 42, 428–9, 701
micro-geomorphological, 804
multiplier, 863–5
'phylogenetic', 177, 178
post-depositional, 803–14
predictive, 624
predictiveness of, 4
procedural, 983–4
research design, 201–29
settlement hierarchy, 861–5
social, 827–48
sociological, 880
spatial, 500–4, 970–3, 977–8, 980–2
stadial, 471–5
statistical, 18, 19
stochastic, 19, 20, 23–4, 28, 178, 186
structural, 814–27
system, 15, 29–40
temporal, 968–70, 976
territorial, 705–32
traditional, 177, 233–6
universal, 623–4
Weberian, 850
modes, 247, 249, 251, 265, 269, 386, 697
Moffat, R., 875, 885
Møller, J., see Dansgaard, W. et al.
Molodova I, 214
Monte Aquilone, 721–3, 726–9, 733
Monte Carlo technique, 20, 24, 26, 686–7, 693, 695
Montelian principle, 45
Moore, F. W., 1010, 1030
Moore, T., 1014, 1028
Morgan, L. H., 580, 581, 583
Moritz, L. A., 940, 961
Morley, S. G., 759, 798
Morrill, R. L., 888, 889, 897, 908
Morris, D., 172, 174, 198
Mortelmans, G., 194, 198
Mortillet, G. de, 169, 198

Morton, K., 1014, 1028
Morton-Williams, P., 510, 541
Moselikatse, 872, 880, 882–3
Mottram, V. H., 614, 620
Mount Batten, 865
Mount Camel, 603–16
Mousterian, 28, 119–20, 125, 131, 156, 157, 171, 284, 361, 584
Movius, H. L., 162, 165, 283, 284, 307, 548, 573
Müller-Beck, H., 556, 573
multidimensional scaling, 367–71, 372, 374, 375, 383–4, 387, 396–422
multivariate analysis, 192, 383, 384, 671
Mulvaney, D. J., 283, 307, 661, 665, 669
Münsingen-Rain, La Tène cemetery at, 437–47, 969
Muntham, 933, 948
Murdock, G. P., 41, 241, 272, 827, 839, 847, 869, 999, 1010, 1012, 1013, 1015, 1020, 1021, 1030
Murie, A., 546, 573
Mycenae, 534
Myers, J. L., 697, 703
Myers, O. H., 206, 229
Mykytowycz, R., 546, 573
Myres, J. N. L., 929, 960, 963, 975, 988

Nagel, E., 9, 10, 60, 62, 69, 72, 77, 79, 83, 104, 105, 106, 994, 995, 1003, 1004, 1028, 1030
Nandris, J. G., 25, 519, 523
Naroll, R., 583, 584, 620, 1010, 1011, 1013, 1014, 1015, 1021, 1030
Naval Intelligence Handbooks: Greece, 517
Nea Nikomedia, 517
Neely, J. A., 461, 462, 473, 476
Neill, W. T., 549, 573
Nenquin, J., 194, 198
'Neolithic Revolution', 515, 581, 582, 583
Netheravon, 951
Neuman, R. W., 558, 573
Neustupný, E., 175, 198, 887, 908
'New Archaeology', the, 53, 54–5, 56–7, 62, 75, 102, 432, 433, 671
Newcomb, R. M., 30, 31, 32, 60
Newell, 429, 450
Newell, N. D., 550, 563, 573
New System, The, 54

Newton, Sir I., 6, 995, 996, 997, 1001, 1002, 1008
New Zealand Dept of Statistics Official Yearbook, 598, *620*
Nguni, 882
Nicholson, A. J., 599
Nikolov, B., 533
Nile valley, 187
Nilsson, N., 446, *450*
Niobe, 281
Nishiwaki, M., 611, *620*
Noakes, J. E. *see* Stipp, J. J. *et al.*
Næringsmiddeltabell, 632
Non Nok Tha, 463–6, 471, 473, 474
Non Nong Chik, 466, 473
Norbeck, E., *572*
Nørlund, P., 974, *988*
'normal science', 61, 64, 73, 87, 1009
Norman, E. R., 856, *869*
Norris, N. E. S., 934, *961*
North America, colonization of, 554–67
Northrop, F. S. C., 995, 1002–7, *1030*
Novgorod, 968
Nsongezi, 139, 146, 147, 149, 150, 151, 152, 153, 154
Numerical Taxonomy, 114
Nuthills, 924

Oakley, C. O., 689, *702*
Oakley, K. P., 122, *165*, 586, *620*
'Objective Kriterien in der Ethnologie', 316
Objets et Mondes, 860
occupation sites, 171
occurrence matrices, 388–422
Odner, K., 633, *650*
Odum, E. P., 75, *106*, 544, *573*, 707, *733*, 781, *798*
Odum, H. T., 75, *106*, 707, *733*, 781, *798*
Oenpelli, 661, 663
Olduvai Gorge, 28, 121–2, 151, 168, 171, 173, 179, 184, 188, 588, 590
Old Windsor, 940
Olifantspoort, 878, 879, 880, 884
Oliver, W. D., 233, *272*
Olorgesailie, Kenya, 128, 129, 130, 135, 136, 145, 146, 147, 150, 152, 153, 154, 168, 171, 179, 180, 181, 182–3, 184, 188, 189, 190–1, 194, 588
Olson, S., 546, *574*

Oman, C. L., *see* Levin, B. *et al.*
Ondrick, C. W., 698, *703*
operational models, 5, 10–42
operational taxonomic unit, 696
Oppenheim, P., 1002, *1029*
optimal-hexagonal models, 688–9
Orangia I, 214
ordering criteria, 318–21
Ordnance Survey Map of Land Classification, 918, 942, *961*
Ordnance Survey Map of Roman Britain, 888, 891, 906, 907, *908*
Orwin, C. S., 917, *961*
Ostwald, W., 579
Overgaard, P., 514, *541*
Overton Down, Wiltshire, experimental earthwork at, 14, 206
Oving, 945–7
Owen, R. C., 186, *198*, 675, *704*
Oxford English Dictionary, 871, 873

Paine, R. T., 544, *574*
Palmer, B., *476*
Pan-African Congress on Prehistory (1947), 171, 194
Pantin, W. A., 966, *988*
Papua–New Guinea, Central Highlands region, 277–8
paradigms, 6–10, 43–53, 61–2, 101, 110, 111, 115, 125, 189, 193, 996–7, 1009; anthropological, 7, 43, 45–6; ecological, 7, 43, 46–7; geographical, 7, 43, 47–52; morphological, 6, 43–5
Park, R. E., 794, *798*
Parker, R. H., 456, 463, 466, *476*
Parsons, L. A., 239, *272*, 795, 796, *798*
Partington, J. R., 577, *620*
Passo di Corvo, 723
Pasteur, L., 996
Pataud, Abri, 346
Patten, B. C., 578, *620*
Patterns of Discovery, 996
Paul, L. J., 598, *620*
Peacock, D. P. S., 813, 814, 838, 840, 852, 853, *869*
Pearson, H. W., *see* Polanyi, K. *et al.*
Pearson, K., 325, 406, 892, 1016
Pech de la Boissière, 344, 352, 354
Pecos Conference, 237
Pelto, P. J., 994–7, 1014, *1030*, *1031*

Pendergast, D. M., 791, *799*; *see also* Meighan, C. W. *et al.*
Peppering, 948
Perigordian, 327, 344, 346, 347, 348, 351, 352, 354, 355, 357, 361, 362, 363, 376
Perrott, C., 975, *988*
Perry, B. T., 932, *961*
Petén, 781, 783, 784, 788, 791, 794
Peterson, N., 276, *307*, 661, 663, 665, *670*, 873, *885*
Petersson, H. B. A., 969, *988*
Petrie, F., 316
Petrie matrix, 389, 392, 393, 394, 399, 400, 405, 414, 416
Pevsner, N. B. L., 966, 983, *988*
Péwé, T. L., 552, *571*
Peyrony, D., 119, *165*, 344, 347
Pfeiffer, J. E., 173, *198*
Phalabora, 879, 881
Phillips, A. W., 689, *704*
Phillips, P., 64, 67, 73, *107*, 234, 238, 240, 258, 260, 267, *272*, *273*, 543, *575*
Phillipson, D. W., 227, *229*
Phillipson, J., 578, 579, *620*
Phillpotts, B. S., 646, *650*
Phu Wiang region, 458, 459, 464, 466, 467, 473, 474
Piddocke, S., 509, *541*
Piedras Negras, 777
Piggott, C. M., 923, *961*
Piggott, S., 167, *198*, 478, *541*, 819, 827, 828, *869*, 963, *988*
Pilbeam, D. R., 544, *574*
Piltdown hoax, 173
Pitelka, F. A., 707, *733*
Pitt-Rivers, J. A., 201, *229*, 923
Pitts, F. R., 765, *799*
place names, 941–59
Planck, M., 995
planned information loss, 225
platforms, 762, 774
Platt, J. R., 83, 86, 96, 103, *106*
plazas, 764–70
Plog, F. T., 82, 89, 101, *104*, *106*, 263, 432, *450*, 991, *1029*
Point St George, California, 276
Poisson distribution, 440, 698–9
Polanyi, K., 511, 645, 648–9, *650*
Polanyi, K. *et al.*, 507, 510, *541*
Polden hoard, 846
Poling, 948, 949, 957

political organization, 508–11
pollen analysis, 626
Ponter's Ball, Iron Age earthwork, 849
POP, 434
Popper, K. R., 103, *106*, 111, 161, 162, 163, *165*
Poptún, 783, 784, 785, 794
population, 484–9, 501–3
Port Bradshaw, 661, 666
positivist approach to typology, examples of, 255–60
Posnansky, M., 135, *165*, 184, *198*
Postan, M. M., 492, *541*, 833, 855, *869*, *988*
post-depositional factors, 202, 205–9
Potts, W. H., 563, *574*
Pounds, N. J. G., 891, *909*
Powell, J. W., 690
Powell, T. G. E., 845, 847, 860, *869*
Power, E., *988*
Pradel, L., 361, *378*
Pred, A., 890, *908*
Price, B. J., 508, *541*, 795, 796, *798*
Price, D. J., 1026, *1031*
principal components analysis, 291, 292, 293, 294
Principia, 1008
Principles of Anthropology, 617
problems, importance of, 77–9
procedural rigour, 209
procurement subsystems, 692–5
program models, 429, 439, 442–5, 496
PROGRAM SERIATE (Craytor's), 320, 321, 322, 323, 330, 347, 375
Proskouriakoff, T., 796, *799*
Pruitt, W. R., 546, *574*
Psychometrika, 371
publishing procedures, 224–5
Puleston, D., 782, *799*
Pusilhà, 777, 782, 783, 784, 785, 788, 794
Putnam, H., 103, *106*
Pylos, 536, 537

Q-technique, 334, 342, 361, 366
quality control, 210–11, 212
Quebrada de Oro, 783, 784, 785
queueing theory, 24, 28

R-technique, 342–4, 355–60, 361, 366

Rahtz, P. A., 590, 974, *988*
Ralph, E. K., *see* Stuckenrath, R. *et al.*
Rand Corporation, the, 700, *704*
random noise, 204–5
random selection, 695–6
random walk, 20–4, 178, 184, 186, 194, 691, 804, 806
randomization, 209–10
Rapoport, A., 10, *60*
Rappaport, R. A., 34, *60*, 276, *308*, 545, *574*
Rattray, E. C., 386, *424*
Raven, P. H., 298, *306*, 564, *570*
Read, K. E., 277, *307*
recovery procedures, 215–18
Redman, C. L., 258, 262, *273*
redundancy, use of, 209
Reed, C. A., 46, *60*
Reese River Ecological Project, 672–6
Reina, R., 773, 782, *799*
Remesal, A. de, 793, *799*
Renfrew, A. C., 167, *198*, 381, *424*, 478, 515, 532, *541*, 914, *961*
research factors, 202
resources and potential for growth, 489–493
Reynolds, V., 174, *198*
Ricardo, D., 507
Richards, H. G., 551, *574*
Richardson, J. B., 46, *57*
Richmond, I. A., 823, *869*, 907, *909*
Rickert, M., 983, *989*
Rickman, T., 963, *989*
Rigold, S. E., 979, *989*
Rise of Anthropological Theory, The, 994, 997
Ritchie, A., 923, *961*
Ritchie, R., 553, *574*
Ritchie, W. A., 269, 549, *574*
Rivet, A. L. F., 891, 894, 896, 907, *909*
Roberts, F. H. H., 237, *272*
Roberts, S., 872, 880, *885*
Robinson, W. S., 313, 317, 318, 319, 326, 330, 350, 362, *378*, 388, 391, 392, 395, 396, 397, 398, *424*
Robinson index of agreement, 313, 317, 326, 327, 330, 332, 333, 335, 336, 339, 340, 341, 342, 347, 349, 350, 351, 352, 353, 355, 361, 363, 370
Roe, D. A., 188, 190–1, *198*
Roglić, J., 520, *541*

Rohlf, F. J., 371, 372, *378*, 698, 701, 704
Rohner, R. P., 1014, *1031*
Röldal, 625, 627–8
Rolong, 880, 884
Romans, H. de, 905, *909*
Roque Saint-Christophe, La, 344, 351, 354
Round, J. H., 963, 984, *989*
Roundabout Camp, 840
Rouse, I. B., 64, 65, 67, 70, 73, 74, 77, 99, 102, *106*, 231, 234, 235, 236, 241, 242, 243, 244, 246, 247, 248, 249, 265, 269, *272*, 381, 383, 384, *424*, 442, *451*, 697, 704
Roys, R. L., 791, *799*
Rubin, M., *see* Levin, B. *et al.*
Rudner, R. S., 69, *106*
Ruiz Revilla, R., 1010, 1015, 1016, 1023, 1024, 1025, 1027, *1028*
Rural Settlement and Land Use, 705–6, 915
Russell, B., 735
Russell-Hunter, W. D., 609, *620*
Ruxton, B. P., 279, *308*

Sabloff, J. A., 62, *106*, 231, 239, 241, 242, 244, 269, *272*, 794, 795, 796, *799*, *800*
Sackett, J. R., 127, *165*, 168, 170, 176, 189, *198*, 233, *272*, 288, *307*, 376, *378*
Sahagún, B. de, 781, *799*
Sahlins, M. D., 488, 584, 592, 601, *621*
St Joseph, J. K. S., 856, *869*, 916, 960, 974, *985*
Salcutsa culture, 533
Salisbury, R. F., 506, *541*
Salmon, W. C., 998, *1031*
salt working, 467, 468, 470
Sampson, C. G., 214, *229*
San Antonio, 779, 782, 788
San José, 792
Sanday, P. R., 277, *307*
Sanders, W. T., 508, *541*
Sandewall, E., 446, *451*
Sangoan, 129, 143, 144, 151, 154
Santa Monica mountains, California, 89, 103
Sapire, D., 871, 873
Sauer, C. D., 565, *574*, 971, *989*
Sauvy, A., 485, 486, *541*
Sawyer, J., 1010, 1013, 1015, *1031*

Sawyer, P. H., 964, *989*
scaling models, 310–75
Schaaf, U., 442, *451*
Schaller, G. B., 174, *198*, 546, 547, *574*
Schapera, I., 1010, *1031*
Scharbauer site, 555, 556
Scheffer, V. B., 611, *621*
Schmitt, R. C., 602, *621*
Schon, D., 491, 511, *541*
Schove, D. J., 968, 974, *989*
Schuessler, K. F., 1010, 1013, 1015, *1029*
Schultz site, 592
Schwabedissen, H., 525, *541*
Schwartz, R. D., 1027, *1031*
Schweizer, F., 969, 975, *988*
Science, 994
Science of Culture, The, 580
Scientific American, 317
scientific cycle, the, 673–4
scientific inquiry, 1000–9
Scott, J. P., 547, 550, *574*
Scriven, M., 1026, 1027, *1031*
Seale, H., 292, 293, *307*
Sealeng, 881
Sears, W. H., 61, *106*, 238, *272*
'seasonal factor in human culture', 708
seasonal movement, 715
Seeberg, P., *541*
Seibal, 776, 783, 794
Seifert, M., *see* Slaughter, B. H. *et al.*
Sellards, E. H., 549, *574*
Sellitz, C. *et al.*, 71, 79, 86, 88, 89, 95, 98, *106*
serendipity, 690–1, 700
seriation, 310–75, 376, 381–422; as a formal technique, 381–3; brief history of, 315–18
Serowe, 872
Serra Puche, M. C., 752, *755*
Service, E. R., 240, 258, 260, 267, *273*, 508, 509, 510, *541*, 584, 585, 586, 592, 601, *621*, 675, *704*
set theory models, 735–54
settlement patterns, 521–4, 658–60, 772, 789–90
Setzler, F. M., 61, *106*, 661, *669*
Seven Hills, 782
Shapwick, 860
Sharp, A., 550, *574*
Sharrock, F. W., 549, *574*

Shaw, M., 206, *228*, 318, 319, 321, 323, 348, 365, 366, *377*, 381, 386, 396, 398, *423*
Shaw, T., 206, 207, 224, *229*
Shaw, W., *885*
Shawcross, K. A., 584, 587, *621*
Shawcross, W., 283, *307*, 592, 593, 595, 597, 598, 600, 602, 603, 611, 612, 615, 616, 618, *621*
Shepard, R. N., 311, 367, *378*, 396, *424*
Sheppard, T., 974, *989*
Shepton, 860
Shera, Y. A., 7, 55, *59*
Sherratt, A. G., 864, 938
Shook, E. M., 794, *799*
Shortland, F. B., 612, *620*
Shoshonean, 674–84, 692–4, 700
Shotwell, J. A., 327, 328, 329, 330, 331, 333, 334, 335, 340, 341, 342, *378*
Shutler, R., 551, *574*, 617
Sifonello, 884
Silchester, 940
Silures, 803
similarity scores, 324–6, 335, 336, 347, 351
Simmons, R. T. *et al.*, 280, *307*
Simon, H. A., 429, *450*
Simons, E. L., 566, *574*
Simpson, G. G., 564, *574*
Simpson, W. D., 983, *989*
simulation, 672, 676–701; role of the computer in, 699–700
simulation model building, 677–8
Singer, M., 997, *1031*
site location, 712, 714, 719–20, 725
Sjoberg, G., 764, 770, *799*
Skallagrimsson's Saga, 641, 642–3
Skinner, G. W., 889, 897, *909*
Skoog, R. O., 633, *650*
Slaughter, B. H., 533, 565, 566, *574*
Slaughter, B. H. *et al.*, 553, *574*
Slobodkin, B. L., 544, *575*, 600, *621*
Slomann, W., 648, *651*
Smart, C. D., 593, *621*
Smith, Adam, 507
Smith, Andrew, 872, 875, 880, 882, 883, *885*
Smith, A. H., 941, *962*
Smith, C. T., 497, 498, *541*, 941, *962*
Smith, D. J., 901, 903, *909*
Smith, E. W., *885*

Smith, J. T., 965, 966, *989*
Smith, M. A., 65, *106*
Smith, P., 966, *989*
Smith, P. E. L., 187, *198*, 327, 345, 346, 362, *378*
Smith, R. E., 231, 238, 239, 241, 242, 244, 269, *272, 273*, 794, *799*
Smith, R. H. T., 906, *909*
Smith, W., 243, *273*
Snaketown, Arizona, 318
Sneath, P. H. A., 113, *165*, 288, 293, *308*, 317, 325, 334, 335, 336, 375, *377, 379*, 406, *424*; see also Hodson, F. R. *et al.*
Social Evolution, 583
social organization and economy, 504–8
Social Structure, 1012
Sokal, R. R., 113, *165*, 288, 293, *308*, 317, 325, 334, 335, 336, *379*, 406, *424*, 698, 701, *704*
Solheim, W. G., 463, *476*
Sollas, W. J., 169, *198*
Solomon, S.-Y., 738, *755*
Solutrean, 327, 344, 346, 347, 348, 351, 352, 354, 355, 359, 362, 363, 364, 376
Sonneville Bordes, D. de, 168, *195*, 241, *273*, 327, 345, 346, 361, 362, 365, *379*
Sontz, A. L., 697, *703*
Sørensen, P., 455, *476*
sorting procedures, 218–24
Sotho, 875
South Lodge Camp, 923
South Street, 939
Southern, R. N., 711, *733*
Spaulding, A. C., 112, *165*, 233, 235, 246, 253, 256, 258, 261, 262, 263, 264, 266, 267, 269, *273*
Specht, R. L., 654, 655, 658, 663, 664, *669*
Spencer, W. B., 657, *669*
Spirit Cave, 283, 460–3, 466, 471, 473, 474
Spiro, M. E., 1015, *1031*
Spokes, P. S., 966, *986*
Sprockhoff, E., 966, *989*
stables, 814–15, 825
Stamp, L. D., 612, 618, 718, *733*, 981, 982, *989*
standard nutritional units, 612–15, 618
Stanislawski, M. B., 275, *308*
Stanton St Bernard, 952
Staple Howe, Yorkshire, 828

Star Carr, 454, 591, 592, 595
Steeple Ashton, 952
Steiger, W. L., 667–8
Stekelis, M., 172, *198*
Stephenson, W., 312, *379*
Sterud, G., 381, *424*
Stevens, E. S., 517, *541*
Steward, J. H., 61, *106*, 234, 235, 244, 246, *273*, 453, 454, 473, *476*, 674, 675, 676, 678, 679, 681, 682, 684, 687, 689, 690, 691, 692, 694, 700, *704*
Stewart, G., 692, *703*
Stickel, E. G., 264, *270*
sties, 814–15, 825
Stipp, J. J. *et al.*, 566, *575*
Stoddart, D. R., 758, 759, *798*
Stone, D., 791, *799*
Stone, E. H., 13, *60*
Stone, J. F. S., 923, *962*
Stonehenge, 13
storehouses, 814–15, 824–5
Strabo, 510
Strathern, M., 279, 286, 294, 305, *308*
Stross, F. H. *et al.*, 794, *799*
structure of inquiry, 994–7
Structure of Science, The, 994
Structure of Scientific Revolutions, The, 61, 996, 1009
structures, 762–5
Stuckenrath, R. *et al.*, 560, *575*
Study of Archaeology, A, 61, 71
subsistence patterns: archaeological evidence of, 661–6; multiple, 674
subsystem simulation, 695–6
successive pairs test, 1021
Sumner, W. G., 1012
Sussex Archaeological Collections, 931
Sutherland, G., 435, 436, *449*
Suttles, W., 617, *621*
Sutton Hoo, 966
Swartz, B. K., 64, 67, 70, 78, *106*, 234, 236, 250, *273*; see also Meighan, C. W. *et al.*
symbolic logic, 735
Systematic Zoology, *371*
systems theory, 62, 75–6, 103, 481–4, 671, 672, 677, 691

Tacitus, 649, 855
Taima Taima, 555, 556

Tallgren, A. M., 61, *106*
Tanner, J. F., 546, *575*
Tauber, H., 555, *575*
Tautu, P., 430, *450*
Taylor, A. J., 963, 969, 971, 980, 982, *989*; *see also* Colvin, H. M. *et al.*
Taylor, C. C., 49, 60, 514, *541*, 917, 938, 956, 959, *962*
Taylor, H. M., 966, *989*
Taylor, W. W., 61, 62, 64, 67, 70, 71, 74, 77, 101–2, 103, *106*, 234, 265, *273*
technocomplexes, 462, 589
Tedbury, 843
Tehuacan valley, 462, 473, 548, 674
Terasmae, J., 550, *575*
Terra Amata, 172, 184
Terrell, J. E., 592, 593, *621*
Terrett, I. M., 964, *987*
territories, 797–16; annual, 709, 726; exploitation, 706–16, 759, 772, 779–83, 840, 851–2; village, 918
Tester, P., 126, *165*
Teviotdale, D., 607, *621*
Theoretical Anthropology, 1000
theoretical anthropology, 997–1000
theory, influence of, 73–7
Theory of Data, 87
thermodynamic approach, inconsistencies in, 584–9
thermodynamics, laws of, 578–9, 580, 584, 589–601, 614
Thiessen polygons, 775, 843, 899
thinking machines, 430
Thirsk, J., 912, *962*
Thomas, A. C., 927, *962*
Thomas, D. H., 30, 37, 305, 672, 675, 677, 678, 694, 696, 697, 698, *704*, 858
Thompson, I., 873
Thompson, J. E. S., 759, 774, 776, 781, 791, 792, 794, 799
Thompson, M. W., 964, 979, 980, *989*
Thompson, R. H., 64, 65, 98, 102, *106*, 234, *273*
Thomsen, C. J., 534
Thomson, D. F., 185, *198*, 657, 658, 659, 665, 666, 667, *669*, 708, 709, 729, *733*
Thomson, J. J., *621*
Thorley, A. J., 932, *962*
Thorne, A. G., *see* Bowler, J. M. *et al.*
Thorney Down, 923

Thousand Oaks, California, 90
three age system, 534
three field system, 911
Threlfall, R. I., 965, 967, 968, *987*, *988*
threshold system, 218
Thucydides, 872, *885*
Tiger, L., 172, *198*
Tikal, 776, 788, 794
Tiné, S., 723, 731, *733*
Titow, J. Z., 492, *541*
Tlapacoya, 555, 556
Tlatilco, Mexico, 740, 741
Tobias, S. L., 1027, *1028*
Tobler, W. R., 31, 35, 49, *60*
Tockenham, 943
Todd, M., 893, *909*
tool kit units, 678, 683, 696
Tools of Neanderthal Man, The, 194
Topley, W., 917, *962*
Torgerson, W. S., 367, *379*
Torralba, 168, 172, 184
Torralba-Ambrona, 168, 172, 184
Toulmin, S., 998, 1007, *1031*
Tourtellot, G., 776, 795, 796, *800*
trade, 645, 648, 791–6, 860, 863–5, 889
Transvaal, 871–84
Trelleborg, 968
Trerice, Cornish house at, 970
Trigger, B. G., 7, 9, *60*, 125, *165*, 167, *198*, 772, *800*
Tringham, R., 7, *60*, 538
Trinovantes, 895
Troike, R. C., 318, *379*
True, D. L., 367, 371, *379*
Trump, D., 861, *867*
Tshankare, 881
Tswana, 872, 875, 880, 882, 883
Tugby, D. J., 317, *379*
Turing, A., 430, *451*
Two New Sciences, 54
Tyler, M. J., 277, *306*
Tylor, E. B., 580, 581, 583, 585, 1011, 1012, *1031*
Tylor-Galton problem, 1013–15, 1021, 1027
Tyndall, J., 1001
type, definition of, 232–3, 269
types, 238, 239, 242, 386–7
typological debate, the, 231, 254
typology, 697–8

Uaxactún, 792
'Ubeidiya, 172
Ucko, P., 7, 60, 538
Uitkomst, 879, 882
Ullsheller, 625–8, 633–7, 649
United Nations, 458, 476
United States Forest Service, 684, 685, 689, 691, 704
Upavon, 951
Upper Beeding, 955–6
Upton, 590
Urquhart, A. E., 598, 599, 600, 619
Uslar, R. von, 975, 989
Uxbentún, 772, 778, 782

Vajda, S., 37, 60, 496, 542
Valach, M., 677, 703
Valldalen, 625–37
Vangeneim, E. A., 552, 575
variability: distributional, 112–16; organizational, 112, 113–16
variables, 135–45, 292, 293, 683, 692–3; essential, 682, 683, 684; inessential, 682, 692; key, 682, 683, 700
Vayda, A. P., 276, 308, 540, 542
Velasco Mireles, M., 741, 755
Veldman, D., 678, 704
Venda, 875
Venn diagrams, 736, 738, 753
Vennland, 739–40
Vértes, L., 172, 197
Vertesszöllös, 172
vertex connectivity, 765
Verulamium, 934
Victoria County History of Wiltshire, 922
Villagutierre y Soto-Major, J. de, 793, 800
Vinča, 531, 532, 820
Vining, R., 890, 909
Vita-Finzi, C., 488, 500, 516, 542, 548, 571, 707, 708, 709, 714, 715, 716, 732, 733, 772, 773, 781, 800, 915, 917, 922, 962; see also Higgs, E. S. et al.
Volterra, V., 546, 575
Von Thünen locational model, 914
Voronoi polygons, 774

Waals, J. D. Van der, 534, 542
Waechter, J., 126, 166
Wahlstedt, W. J., 293, 308

Walker, I. C., 19, 60
Walker, J. M., 872, 880, 885
Wallace, A. R., 169, 198
Wallace, W. J., 90, 106
walled towns, 891–6
Wallrath, 239, 273
Walton, M. G., 759, 800
Warner, R., 846, 869
Warren, S. H., 177, 198
Washburn, S. L., 172, 174, 196, 198, 544, 545, 575
Wasley, W., 238, 239, 242, 244, 273
Watanabe, H., 609, 618
water mills, 940–1, 953, 956
Water Newton, 893, 894
Waterbolk, H. T., 824, 869
Waterman, D. M., 966, 972, 989, 990
Watling Street, 907
Watson, J. B., 277, 308
Watson, P. J., 258, 262, 273
Watt, K., 691, 696, 701, 704
Wayne, W. J., 551, 575
Weaver, J. R., see Stross, F. H. et al.
Weber, M., 644, 645, 651
Wedel, W. R., 549, 560, 575
Weide, D. L., 519
Wells, P. V., 551, 575
Welty, J. C., 611, 621
Wendorf, F., 187, 199, 284, 308, 575
Wenninger, G., 371, 378
West, S. E., 966, 968, 990
West Blatchington, 924, 934
West Stow, 968
Westbury Camp, 840
Wetherhill, G. B., 227, 229
Whallon, R., 7, 60, 77, 89, 91, 99, 107, 231, 244, 248, 250, 261, 269, 273
Wheat, J. B., 238, 239, 242, 244, 273, 549, 575
Wheeler, R. M., 201, 229
White, C., 657, 659, 661, 662, 663, 665, 669, 670
White, D. R., 1013, 1020, 1021, 1030
White, G., 797, 800
White, J. P., 277, 278, 279, 281, 282, 285, 305, 308, 689, 697
White, L., 939, 962, 979, 990
White, L. A., 159, 160, 166, 579, 580, 581, 582, 583, 584, 585, 586, 588, 592, 621
White, T. E., 606, 621

Whitehead, A. N., 236, 735
Whitehouse, D. B., 969, *990*
Whitehouse, R. D., 731, *733*
Whitehouse, W. E., 913, 938, *960*
Whiting, J. W. M., 1010, 1012, *1031*
Whittlesey, D., 510, *542*
Wicken Fen Guide, 869
Widdowson, E. M., 577, 594, *620*
Wiener, N., 578, *622*
Wik-Monkan people, 658, 708
Wilcot, 952
Wild, J. P., 859, 860, *869*
Willey, G. R., 62, 64, 67, 73, *106*, *107*, 234, 236, 238, 240, 241, 244, 247, 258, 260, 267, *271*, *272*, *273*, 543, 544, 557, 561, *575*
Williams, F. E., 306, *308*
Williams-Hunt, P. D. R., 470, *476*
Wilmeth, R., *see* Lowdon, J. A. *et al.*
Wilmsen, E., 674, *704*
Wilson, D. M., 640, 649, *650*, 966, 967, *990*
Wilson, E. B., 80, 86, 95, 99, *107*
Wilson, T. R., 1010, 1015, *1031*
Wilson Butte Cave, 549, 555, 556, 559
Wiltshire Archaeological Magazine, 922, 929
Winch, R. F., 1027, *1029*
Winckelmann, W., 966, 968, *990*
Wineburg, S., 49, *60*
Wing, L. W., 546, *575*
Wisconsin, 897, 898, 905, 906
Wisdom, C., 781, *800*
Wishart, D., 372, *379*
Wissler, M. D., *see* Meighan, C. W. *et al.*
Wittgenstein, L., 1001, *1031*
Witthoft, J., 549, *575*
Wolman, A., 590, *622*
Woodburn, J., 706, 713, *733*
Wookey Hole caverns, 853, 861
Wooldridge, S. W., 913, *962*
Woolfenden, P. J., 35, *59*
Woolpy, J. H., 544, *575*

Worcester, 891
workfloors, 814–15, 823
workshop huts, 814–15, 818–19
Wormington, H. M., 549, *576*
Worsley, P. M., 657, 664, 668, *670*
Worthing area, 947–9, 957, 959
Worthington-Smith, G., 171, *199*
Wraxall torque, 846
Wren, Sir C., 963
Wright, A. C. S., 774, 778, 793, *800*
Wright, A. C. S. *et al.*, 774, 778, 779, *800*
Wright, H. E., 552, 563, 565, *576*
Wrigley, E. A., 484, 485, 493, *542*, 633, *651*, 832, *869*
writing procedures, 224–5
Wurm, S. A., 277, 280, *308*
Wyld, G. E. A., *see* Stross, F. H. *et al.*
Wynne-Edwards, V. C., 485, *542*, 545, 546, *576*

Xochicalco valley, Mexico, 749, 750, 751

Yale school, 1011–13
Yamane, T., 215, *229*
Yaxchilan, 777
Yealland, S., 590, *622*
Yeavering, 968
Yen, D. E., 461, *476*
Yerushalmy, J., 219, *229*
Yorubaland, Nigeria, 905
Young, F. W., 1027, *1031*
Young, R. C., 1027, *1031*
Yule process models, 21

Zarnecki, G., 979, *990*
Zeist, W. van, 824, *869*
Zigas, V., *see* Simmons, R. T. *et al.*
Zimmerman, E. C., 550, *576*
Zipf, G. K., 49, 710, 711, 713, *733*